DRAMA
CRITICISM

Guide to Gale Literary Criticism Series

For criticism on	Consult these Gale series
Authors now living or who died after December 31, 1999	*CONTEMPORARY LITERARY CRITICISM (CLC)*
Authors who died between 1900 and 1999	*TWENTIETH-CENTURY LITERARY CRITICISM (TCLC)*
Authors who died between 1800 and 1899	*NINETEENTH-CENTURY LITERATURE CRITICISM (NCLC)*
Authors who died between 1400 and 1799	*LITERATURE CRITICISM FROM 1400 TO 1800 (LC)* *SHAKESPEAREAN CRITICISM (SC)*
Authors who died before 1400	*CLASSICAL AND MEDIEVAL LITERATURE CRITICISM (CMLC)*
Authors of books for children and young adults	*CHILDREN'S LITERATURE REVIEW (CLR)*
Dramatists	*DRAMA CRITICISM (DC)*
Poets	*POETRY CRITICISM (PC)*
Short story writers	*SHORT STORY CRITICISM (SSC)*
Literary topics and movements	*HARLEM RENAISSANCE: A GALE CRITICAL COMPANION (HR)* *THE BEAT GENERATION: A GALE CRITICAL COMPANION (BG)* *FEMINISM IN LITERATURE: A GALE CRITICAL COMPANION (FL)* *GOTHIC LITERATURE: A GALE CRITICAL COMPANION (GL)*
Asian American writers of the last two hundred years	*ASIAN AMERICAN LITERATURE (AAL)*
Black writers of the past two hundred years	*BLACK LITERATURE CRITICISM (BLC)* *BLACK LITERATURE CRITICISM SUPPLEMENT (BLCS)* *BLACK LITERATURE CRITICISM: CLASSIC AND EMERGING AUTHORS SINCE 1950 (BLC-2)*
Hispanic writers of the late nineteenth and twentieth centuries	*HISPANIC LITERATURE CRITICISM (HLC)* *HISPANIC LITERATURE CRITICISM SUPPLEMENT (HLCS)*
Native North American writers and orators of the eighteenth, nineteenth, and twentieth centuries	*NATIVE NORTH AMERICAN LITERATURE (NNAL)*
Major authors from the Renaissance to the present	*WORLD LITERATURE CRITICISM, 1500 TO THE PRESENT (WLC)* *WORLD LITERATURE CRITICISM SUPPLEMENT (WLCS)*

ISSN 1056-4349

Criticism of the Most Significant and Widely Studied Dramatic Works from All the World's Literatures

VOLUME 50

Lawrence J. Trudeau
Editor

GALE
CENGAGE Learning

Detroit • New York • San Francisco • New Haven, Conn • Waterville, Maine • London

Drama Criticism, Vol. 50

Layman Poupard Publishing, LLC

Editorial Directors: Richard Layman,
 Dennis Poupard

Editorial Production Manager: Janet Hill

Permissions Manager: Kourtnay King

Quality Assurance Manager:
 Katherine Macedon

Production Technology Manager:
 Natalie Fulkerson

Content Conversion, Data Coding,
 Composition: Apex CoVantage, LLC

Advisors to LPP:
 Ward W. Briggs
 James Hardin
 Joel Myerson

Volume Advisors:
Andrea R. Stevens, University of Illinois at
 Urbana-Champaign (for "Richard Brome")
Douglas O'Keefe, Jacksonville State University
 (for "David Garrick")
Stephanie Byttebier, Boston University
 (for "Tony Kushner")

For product information and technology assistance, contact us at
Gale Customer Support, 1-800-877-4253.
For permission to use material from this text or product,
submit all requests online at **www.cengage.com/permissions.**
Further permissions questions can be emailed to
permissionrequest@cengage.com

Gale
27500 Drake Rd.
Farmington Hills, MI, 48331-3535

LIBRARY OF CONGRESS CATALOG CARD NUMBER 76-46132

ISBN-13: 978-1-4144-8521-8

ISSN 1056-4349

Printed in Mexico
1 2 3 4 5 6 7 18 17 16 15 14

Contents

Preface vii

Acknowledgments xi

Advisory Board xiii

Preface

*D*rama Criticism (*DC*) is principally intended for beginning students of literature and theater as well as the average playgoer. The series is therefore designed to introduce readers to the most frequently studied playwrights of all time periods and nationalities and to present discerning commentary on dramatic works of enduring interest. Furthermore, *DC* seeks to acquaint the reader with the uses and functions of criticism itself. Selected from a diverse body of commentary, the essays in *DC* offer insights into the authors and their works but do not require that the reader possess a wide background in literary studies. Where appropriate, reviews of important productions of the plays discussed are also included to give students a heightened awareness of drama as a dynamic art form, one that many claim is fully realized only in performance.

DC was created in response to suggestions by the staffs of high school, college, and public libraries. These librarians observed a need for a series that assembles critical commentary on the world's most renowned dramatists in the same manner as Gale's *Short Story Criticism* (*SSC*) and *Poetry Criticism* (*PC*), which present material on writers of short fiction and poetry. Although playwrights are covered in such Gale literary criticism series as *Contemporary Literary Criticism* (*CLC*), *Twentieth-Century Literary Criticism* (*TCLC*), *Nineteenth-Century Literature Criticism* (*NCLC*), *Literature Criticism from 1400 to 1800* (*LC*), and *Classical and Medieval Literature Criticism* (*CMLC*), *DC* directs more concentrated attention on individual dramatists than is possible in the broader, survey-oriented entries in these Gale series. Commentary on the works of William Shakespeare may be found in *Shakespearean Criticism* (*SC*).

Scope of the Series

By collecting and organizing commentary on dramatists, *DC* assists students in their efforts to gain insight into literature, achieve better understanding of the texts, and formulate ideas for papers and assignments. A variety of interpretations and assessments is offered, allowing students to pursue their own interests and promoting awareness that literature is dynamic and responsive to many different opinions.

Approximately three to five entries are included in each volume, and each entry presents a historical survey of the critical response to a playwright's work, an individual play, or a literary topic pertinent to the study of drama. The length of an entry is intended to reflect the amount of critical attention the author has received from critics writing in English and from critics whose work has been translated into English. Every attempt has been made to identify and include the most significant essays on each author's work. In order to provide these important critical pieces, the editors sometimes reprint essays that have appeared elsewhere in Gale's literary criticism series. Such duplication, however, never exceeds twenty percent of a *DC* volume.

Organization of the Book

A *DC* entry consists of the following elements:

- The **Author Heading** cites the name under which the playwright most commonly wrote, followed by birth and death dates. Uncertain birth or death dates are indicated by question marks. If the author wrote consistently under a pseudonym, the pseudonym will be listed in the author heading and the author's actual name given in parentheses on the first line of the biographical and critical information. Also located here are any name variations under which a playwright wrote, including transliterated forms for authors whose native languages use nonroman alphabets.

- The **Introduction** contains background information that introduces the reader to the author and the critical debates surrounding his or her work.

- The list of **Principal Works** is ordered chronologically by date of first publication and lists the most important works by the author. The first section comprises dramatic works or works by the author about dramatic theory. The second section gives information on other major works by the author. In the case of authors who do not write in English, an English translation of the title is provided as an aid to the reader; the translation is a published translated title or a free translation provided by the compiler of the entry. In the case of such authors whose works have been translated into English, the **Principal English Translations** focuses primarily on twentieth-century translations, selecting those works most commonly considered the best by critics.

- Essays offering **overviews of the dramatist's entire literary career** give the student broad perspectives on the writer's artistic development, themes, and concerns that recur in several of his or her works, the author's place in literary history, and other wide-ranging topics.

- **Criticism** of individual plays offers the reader in-depth discussions of a select number of the author's most important works. In some cases, the criticism is divided into two sections, each arranged chronologically. When a significant performance of a play can be identified (typically, the premier of a twentieth-century work), the first section of criticism will feature **production reviews** of this staging. Most entries include sections devoted to **critical commentary** that assesses the literary merit of the selected plays. When necessary, essays are carefully excerpted to focus on the work under consideration; usually, however, essays and reviews are reprinted in their entirety. The critic's name and the date of composition or publication of the critical work are given at the beginning of each piece of criticism. Unsigned criticism is preceded by the title of the source in which it appeared. All plays and works of dramatic theory by the author featured in the entry are printed in boldface type. Footnotes are reprinted at the end of each essay or excerpt. In the case of excerpted criticism, only those footnotes that pertain to the excerpted texts are included. Criticism in topic entries is arranged chronologically under a variety of subheadings to facilitate the study of different aspects of the topic.

- Critical essays are prefaced by brief **Annotations** describing each piece.

- A complete **Bibliographical Citation** of the original essay or book precedes each piece of criticism. Citations conform to recommendations set forth in the Modern Language Association of America's *MLA Handbook for Writers of Research Papers,* 7th ed. (2009).

- An annotated bibliography of **Further Reading** appears at the end of each entry and suggests resources for additional study. In some cases, significant essays for which the editors could not obtain reprint rights are included here. Boxed material following the further reading list provides references to other biographical and critical sources on the author in series published by Gale.

Cumulative Indexes

A **Cumulative Author Index** lists all of the authors that appear in a wide variety of reference sources published by Gale, including *DC*. A complete list of these sources is found facing the first page of the Author Index. The index also includes birth and death dates and cross references between pseudonyms and actual names.

A **Cumulative Topic Index** lists the literary themes and topics treated in *DC* as well as in *Classical and Medieval Literature Criticism, Literature Criticism from 1400 to 1800, Nineteenth-Century Literature Criticism, Twentieth-Century Literary Criticism, Contemporary Literary Criticism, Poetry Criticism, Short Story Criticism,* and *Children's Literature Review.*

A **Cumulative Nationality Index** lists all authors featured in *DC* by nationality, followed by the number of the *DC* volume in which their entry appears.

A **Cumulative Title Index** lists in alphabetical order the individual plays and works of dramatic theory discussed in the criticism contained in *DC*. Each title is followed by the author's last name and corresponding volume and page numbers where commentary on the work is located. English translations of titles published in other languages and variations of titles are cross-referenced to the title under which a work was originally published so that all references to discussion of a work are combined in one listing.

Citing *Drama Criticism*

When citing criticism reprinted in the Literary Criticism Series, students should provide complete bibliographic information so that the cited essay can be located in the original print or electronic source. Students who quote directly from reprinted criticism may use any accepted bibliographic format, such as Modern Language Association (MLA) style or University of Chicago Press style. Both the MLA and the University of Chicago formats are acceptable and recognized as being the current standards for citations. It is important, however, to choose one format for all citations; do not mix the two formats within a list of citations.

The examples below follow recommendations for preparing a works cited list set forth in the Modern Language Association of America's *MLA Handbook for Writers of Research Papers,* 7th ed. (New York: MLA, 2009); the first example pertains to material drawn from periodicals, the second to material reprinted from books:

Barker, Roberta. "The Circle Game: Gender, Time, and 'Revolution' in Tom Stoppard's *The Coast of Utopia.*" *Modern Drama* 48.4 (2005): 706-25. Rpt. in *Drama Criticism.* Ed. Thomas J. Schoenberg and Lawrence J. Trudeau. Vol. 30. Detroit: Gale, 2008. 356-66. Print.

Rocha, Mark William. "Black Madness in August Wilson's 'Down the Line' Cycle." *Madness in Drama.* Ed. James Redmond. Cambridge: Cambridge UP, 1993. 191-201. Rpt. in *Drama Criticism.* Ed. Thomas J. Schoenberg and Lawrence J. Trudeau. Vol. 31. Detroit: Gale, 2008. 229-35. Print.

The examples below follow recommendations for preparing a bibliography set forth in *The Chicago Manual of Style,* 16th ed. (Chicago: The University of Chicago Press, 2010); the first example pertains to material drawn from periodicals, the second to material reprinted from books:

Barker, Roberta. "The Circle Game: Gender, Time, and 'Revolution' in Tom Stoppard's *The Coast of Utopia.*" *Modern Drama* 48, no. 4 (Winter 2005): 706-25. Reprinted in *Drama Criticism,* Vol. 30, edited by Thomas J. Schoenberg and Lawrence J. Trudeau, 356-66. Detroit: Gale, 2008.

Rocha, Mark William. "Black Madness in August Wilson's 'Down the Line' Cycle." In *Madness in Drama,* edited by James Redmond, 191-201. Cambridge: Cambridge University Press, 1993. Reprinted in *Drama Criticism,* Vol. 31, edited by Thomas J. Schoenberg and Lawrence J. Trudeau, 229-35. Detroit: Gale, 2008.

Suggestions are Welcome

Readers who wish to suggest new features, topics, or authors to appear in future volumes, or who have other suggestions or comments are cordially invited to call, write, or fax the Product Manager:

Product Manager, Literary Criticism Series
Gale
Cengage Learning
27500 Drake Road
Farmington Hills, MI 48331-3535
1-800-347-4253 (GALE)
Fax: 248-699-8884

Acknowledgments

The editors wish to thank the copyright holders of the excerpted criticism included in this volume and the permissions managers of many book and magazine publishing companies for assisting us in securing reproduction rights. Following is a list of the copyright holders who have granted us permission to reproduce material in this volume of *DC*. Every effort has been made to trace copyright, but if omissions have been made, please let us know.

COPYRIGHTED MATERIAL IN *DC*, VOLUME 50, WAS REPRODUCED FROM THE FOLLOWING PERIODICALS:

American Drama, v. 4.1, 1994. Copyright © 1994 American Drama Institute. Reproduced by permission of the publisher. —*Anglophonia,* v. 3, 1998. Copyright © 1998 Presses Universitaires du Mirail. Reproduced by permission of *Anglophonia.* —*BOMB,* v. 43, 1993. Copyright © 1993 *BOMB*. Reproduced by permission of the publisher.—*British Magazine,* v. 4, 1749. Public domain.—*Comparative Drama,* v. 45.2, 2011. Copyright © 2011 *Comparative Drama.* Reproduced by permission of the publisher.—*Contemporary Literature,* v. 50.3, 2009. Copyright © 2009 the Board of Regents of the University of Wisconsin System. Reproduced by permission of University of Wisconsin Press.—*Drama Review,* v. 56.1, 2012. Copyright © 2012 MIT Press. Reproduced by permission of the publisher.—*Early Theatre,* v. 10.2, 2007. Copyright © 2007 *Early Theatre.* Both reproduced by permission of the publisher.—*Forum for Modern Language Studies,* v. 47.1, 2010. Copyright © 2010 James Corby. Reproduced by permission of Oxford University Press.—*Journal of Men's Studies,* v. 5.1, 1996. Copyright © 1996 Men's Studies Press. Reproduced by permission of the publisher.—*Modern Language Notes,* v. 36.2, 1921; v. 36.3, 1921; v. 72.4, 1957. All public domain.—*Modern Philology,* v. 13.5, 1915. Public domain.—*More Books,* v. 22.8, 1947. Public domain.—*Notes and Queries,* v. 36.3, 1989. Copyright © 1989 Robert C. Evans; v. 53.1, 2006. Copyright © 2006 Brett D. Hirsch. Both reproduced by permission of Oxford University Press.—*PMLA: Publications of the Modern Language Association of America,* v. 49.3, 1934; v. 74.3, 1959. Both public domain.—*Restoration and 18th Century Theatre Research,* v. 6.2, 1967; v. 11.2, 1972; v. 19.1, 2004; v. 19.2, 2004; v. 23.1, 2008. Copyright © 1967, 1972, 2004, 2008 University of Denver. All reproduced by permission of *Restoration and 18th Century Theatre Research.*—*Review of English Studies,* ns v. 29.114, 1978; ns v. 58.236, 2007. Copyright © 1978, 2007 Oxford University Press. Both reproduced by permission of the publisher. —*Shofar,* v. 25.4, 2007. Copyright © 2007 Purdue University Press. Reproduced by permission of the publisher.—*Tennessee Studies in Literature,* v. 19, 1974. Copyright © 1974 University of Tennessee Press. Reproduced by permission of the publisher.—*Theatre Notebook,* v. 55.3, 2001. Copyright © 2001 the Society for Theatre Research. Reproduced by permission of the publisher.

COPYRIGHTED MATERIAL IN *DC*, VOLUME 50, WAS REPRODUCED FROM THE FOLLOWING BOOKS:

Anonymous. From **Lethe** *Rehears'd; or, A Critical Discussion of the Beauties and Blemishes of That Performance.* Roberts, 1749. Public domain.—Birkett, Audrey. From *"Divining Thoughts": Future Directions in Shakespeare Studies.* Ed. Pete Orford et al. Cambridge Scholars, 2007. Copyright © 2007 Pete Orford with Michael P. Jones, Lizz Ketterer, Joshua McEvilia, and contributors. Reproduced by permission of Cambridge Scholars Publishing.—Brooks, Douglas A. From *The Book of the Play: Playwrights, Stationers, and Readers in Early Modern England.* Ed. Marta Straznicky. University Massachusetts Press, 2006. Copyright © 2006 University of Massachusetts Press. Reproduced by permission of the publisher. —Cibber, Theophilus. From *Theophilus Cibber, to David Garrick, Esq; with Dissertations on Theatrical Subjects.* Reeves and Phipps, 1759. Public domain.—Davidson, Jenny. From *Shakespeare and the Eighteenth Century.* Ed. Peter Sabor and Paul Yachnin. Ashgate, 2008. Copyright © 2008 Peter Sabor and Paul Yachnin. Reproduced by permission of Ashgate Publishing, Ltd.—Efstathiou-Lavabre, Athina. From *Representing France and the French in Early Modern English Drama.* Ed. Jean-Christophe Mayer. University of Delaware Press, 2008. Copyright © 2008 Rosemont Publishing and Printing Corporation. Reproduced by permission of Associated University Presses, Inc.—Frantzen, Allen J. From *Before the Closet: Same-Sex Love from* **Beowulf** *to* **Angels in America.** University of Chicago Press, 1998. Copyright © 1998 University of Chicago. Reproduced by permission of University of Chicago Press.—Holland, Peter. From *Players, Playwrights, Playhouses: Investigating Performance, 1660-1800.* Ed. Michael Cordner and Holland. Palgrave Macmillan, 2007. Copyright © 2007 Peter Holland. Reproduced by permission of Palgrave Macmillan, Ltd.—Myhill, Nova. From *Imagining the Audience in Early Modern Drama, 1558-1642.* Ed. Jennifer A. Low and Myhill. Palgrave Macmillan, 2011. Copyright © 2011 Jennifer A. Low and

Advisory Board

The members of the Advisory Board—reference librarians from public and academic library systems—represent a cross-section of our customer base and offer a variety of informed perspectives on both the presentation and content of our literature products. Advisory board members assess and define such quality issues as the relevance, currency, and usefulness of the author coverage, critical content, and literary topics included in our series; evaluate the layout, presentation, and general quality of our printed volumes; provide feedback on the criteria used for selecting authors and topics covered in our series; provide suggestions for potential enhancements to our series; identify any gaps in our coverage of authors or literary topics, recommending authors or topics for inclusion; analyze the appropriateness of our content and presentation for various user audiences, such as high school students, undergraduates, graduate students, librarians, and educators; and offer feedback on any proposed changes/enhancements to our series. We wish to thank the following advisors for their advice throughout the year.

Barbara M. Bibel
Librarian
Oakland Public Library
Oakland, California

Dr. Toby Burrows
Principal Librarian
The Scholars' Centre
University of Western Australia Library
Nedlands, Western Australia

Celia C. Daniel
Associate Reference Librarian
Howard University Libraries
Washington, D.C.

David M. Durant
Reference Librarian
Joyner Library
East Carolina University
Greenville, North Carolina

Nancy T. Guidry
Librarian
Bakersfield Community College
Bakersfield, California

Heather Martin
Arts & Humanities Librarian
University of Alabama at Birmingham, Sterne Library
Birmingham, Alabama

Susan Mikula
Librarian
Indiana Free Library
Indiana, Pennsylvania

Thomas Nixon
Humanities Reference Librarian
University of North Carolina at Chapel Hill, Davis
  Library
Chapel Hill, North Carolina

Mark Schumacher
Jackson Library
University of North Carolina at Greensboro
Greensboro, North Carolina

Gwen Scott-Miller
Assistant Director
Sno-Isle Regional Library System
Marysville, Washington

Richard Brome
c. 1590-c. 1652

English playwright.

INTRODUCTION

Brome was a fixture of the London theatrical establishment during the 1630s and among the most popular playwrights of the Caroline period (1625-49) in English literature. He is best known for a succession of "city comedies" that depict various facets of London life and politics in the seventeenth century, such as the gradual expansion of the suburbs and the influx of immigrants and other foreign visitors. In his treatment of these subjects, Brome has often been compared to his onetime employer, the English playwright Ben Jonson. Both authors favored convoluted plots and large casts, and neither was likely to pass up the opportunity to satirize his detractors. During Brome's lifetime, *The Weeding of the Covent Garden* (1632) was his most celebrated work, although modern critics generally regarded his later plays, especially *The Antipodes* (1638) and *A Jovial Crew* (1641), as superior. Considered in aggregate, Brome's comedies address mounting political tensions during the reign of Charles I, documenting the unenviable position of the playwright in a culture increasingly hostile to public entertainment.

More generally, Brome's plays have been used as a source of information on Caroline England, containing commentary on such diverse topics as the real estate market and women's cosmetics. His plays continue to figure prominently in studies of early modern English drama, illustrating the evolution of the genre in the decades leading up to the English Civil Wars (1642-51). Brome's well-documented career has also provided scholars with information about the everyday realities of life as a seventeenth-century playwright. With the exceptions of a high-profile revival of *The Antipodes* in 2000 and an earlier Royal Shakespeare Company production of *A Jovial Crew* in 1992, Brome's work is rarely performed today. This may change, however, owing to the 2010 launch of the *Richard Brome Online* project, which makes Brome's collected works easily accessible to scholars and theater practitioners for the first time.

BIOGRAPHICAL INFORMATION

Few details of Brome's early life survive. He is thought to have been born around 1590, though there are no baptismal records or other concrete evidence to support this attribution. Before embarking on his career as a playwright, he worked as an assistant for Jonson, who mentioned Brome in this capacity in his 1614 comedy *Bartholomew Fair.* Their relationship was apparently one of mutual respect, and Jonson contributed a laudatory dedication to the 1632 printed edition of Brome's *The Northern Lass* (1629), while Brome's stylistic debt to Jonson is evident in nearly all of his surviving works. Although little is known about Brome's private life, his professional relationships are well documented. He wrote for several important London theater companies, including the King's Men and the Red Bull troupe, during the late 1620s and early 1630s, attaining some popularity with *The Northern Lass* and rising to prominence with the King's Revels production of *The Sparagus Garden* at the Salisbury Court Theatre in 1635. Following this success, Brome was hired as a house playwright with the King's Revels playing company. The arrangement was intended to last for three years, but an inconsistent salary soon led Brome to seek additional work with rival theaters. This sparked an ongoing legal battle between the playwright and his various employers that lasted until an outbreak of bubonic plague in 1636 closed down the city's theaters entirely.

The playhouses reopened more than a year later, and while the King's Revels had by then disbanded, Brome soon found work with Queen Henrietta's Men, another Salisbury Court troupe. In spite of his prolific output, Brome is believed to have struggled financially. The dedication to *A Jovial Crew* identifies the author as one of the "harmless beggars" whose lives are the subject of the play. Brome's poverty was almost certainly exacerbated by the outbreak of the English Civil Wars. The Puritan faction, who were opposed to theatergoing as a matter of policy, seized control of the city of London in 1642 and closed its theaters. They would not reopen during Brome's lifetime. On the basis of a posthumous dedication by the English poet Alexander Brome (no relation), Brome is generally believed to have died in late 1652 or early 1653. However, Robert C. Evans (1989) provided evidence that the playwright was admitted in 1650 to an almshouse, or poorhouse, in the Smithfield area of London. He reports that the register of that institution gives Brome's date of death as 24 September 1652.

MAJOR DRAMATIC WORKS

Highly regarded in their time, Brome's plays are virtually unknown today outside of academic scholarship, where his comedies are generally regarded as historically significant works of uneven craftsmanship. Brome established his characteristic style in *The Novella,* an early play first performed in 1632. In the play, the young Venetian nobleman

Fabritio schemes to avoid an arranged marriage to the wealthy Flavia so that the two will be free to elope with lovers of their own choosing. The unwilling couple must avoid the wrath of their parents through disguise, deceit, and cross-dressing—one of Brome's favorite dramatic devices. Brome's later comedies draw on similarly complicated plots of trickery and romance, but nearly all of them are set in London. *The Weeding of the Covent Garden* satirizes the development of the city's Covent Garden district, which was hastily built as a prospective home for wealthy Londoners. Brome's play shows the fruitless efforts of ambitious builders and promoters to preserve the neighborhood's image by "weeding" it of prostitutes, outlaws, and upwardly mobile commoners. The forces of law and order are represented by the buffoonish constable Cockbrain, who claims to be a descendant of Justice Adam Overdo (a judge from Jonson's *Bartholomew Fair*) but who is even more naively self-righteous than his ancestor. Cockbrain's major adversaries are the "Brothers of the Blade," a gang of cowardly ruffians who are eventually rounded up and expelled from the neighborhood.

Brome's first big success, *The Sparagus Garden*, contains a similar mixture of well-worn comedic tropes and contemporary social commentary. Its story of forbidden love and feigned pregnancy unfolds against the backdrop of the asparagus gardens once located in the Lambeth district of London, a popular meeting place for couples wishing to make use of the vegetable's supposed aphrodisiacal properties. In modern scholarship, *The Antipodes* and *A Jovial Crew* have received special praise for their literary merit. In the former, a bookish and travel-obsessed young man named Peregrine is "cured" of his disinterest in sex through an elaborate dramatic ruse that convinces him he has been transported to a faraway land. *A Jovial Crew,* which likewise makes use of the play-within-the-play motif, presents the misadventures of two well-born young women who chafe at the restrictions of their genteel lifestyle and decide to embark on a life of vagabondage. Posthumous collections of Brome's plays appeared in 1653 and 1659 and were followed in the twentieth century by a succession of individual critical editions. Brome's collected works are available via *Richard Brome Online,* a scholarly electronic edition.

CRITICAL RECEPTION

Brome's works are most valuable to modern critics for capturing the spirit of his times. *The Weeding of the Covent Garden* and *The Sparagus Garden* have been characterized as reactions to the rapid changes that took place in the London landscape as early modern capitalists and celebrity architects transformed formerly communal lands into homes and pleasure grounds for the wealthy. Mimi Yiu (2007) interpreted *The Weeding of the Covent Garden* as an uneasy reflection on the "alien" architectural style employed in these fashionable districts, which were envisioned by their builders as zones that excluded common tradespeople. For Denys Van Renen (2011), Brome's plays are somewhat more explicit in their social commentary in that they charge London's new neighborhoods with displaying the mismanagement and lawlessness characteristic of Britain's overseas colonies. Other critics have commented on how Brome's works capture the anxieties and mixed allegiances of theater practitioners in the years leading up to the English Civil Wars. Julie Sanders (2002; see Further Reading) discussed how *A Jovial Crew* deftly illustrates this double bind in its portrayal of a troupe of beggar-actors who are economically disenfranchised by the policies of an "over-demanding absolutist monarch." Likewise, Michel Bitot (1995; see Further Reading) commented on the play's depiction of Britain's increasingly powerful Puritans, whose disapproval of public entertainment was a direct threat to London's theater groups.

Brome's works have also been consulted to clarify various aspects of the professional workings of Caroline theater. Tiffany Stern (2001) looked to Brome's plays to understand the duties of the prompter, or "book-holder," in Shakespearean theater, while Eleanor Collins (2007) used Brome's agreement with the King's Revels to explore early modern contracts between playwrights and theater companies. Audrey Birkett (2007) saw *The Antipodes* as a reflection of "the lack of control that was fundamental to the commercial theatrical community" in Brome's day. According to Birkett, the play's overbearing poets try unsuccessfully to set themselves up as petty tyrants who dictate the exact terms under which their works will be produced. Some scholars have discussed Brome's use of various devices typical of Caroline drama in his comedies, including an attempt by the playwright to establish authority over the audience with a view toward placating potential critics. Nova Myhill (2011) argued that Brome used "inductions," or introductory scenes, to directly address spectators, instilling an element of "self-consciousness" in his sophisticated and judgmental viewers. Brome's plays also display a shrewd awareness of contemporary Londoners' prejudices and stereotypes. Athina Efstathiou-Lavabre (2008) pointed out that while Brome saw little truth in the English depiction of the "false Frenchman," he repeatedly used the supposed deceitfulness of the French as a plot device.

Brome is generally numbered among the "Sons of Ben," a group of Jacobean and Caroline authors who shared Jonson's preference for satirical comedies with urban settings and labyrinthine plots. Elizabeth Cook (1947) gave an overview of other Jonsonian traits that Brome seems to have inherited, not all of them positive. She claimed, for example, that Brome sometimes "pushed" otherwise tragicomic plays "within the borders of comedy by the addition of a 'humorous' character or a 'humorous' by-plot." Cook also argued that English playwright John Fletcher influenced Brome's efforts at tragicomedy, although she called the clearest example of such inspiration, *The Love-Sick Court* (1639), a "dull play, lacking all the ethereal hyperbole that carries heroic contests of love and friendship into a favorable climate." Other critics have found more to appreciate in Brome's interpretation of earlier playwrights' characteristic styles. John W. Crowther (1962; see Further Reading) found an example of such reappropriation in *A Jovial Crew,* which he described as both a romantic comedy in the tradition of William Shakespeare and as a comedy of humors in the spirit of Jonson. For Crowther, this eclectic approach successfully distinguished Brome from his predecessors, allowing him to draw on popular playwriting strategies of the past while catering to the tastes of a new generation of London theatergoers.

Michael J. Hartwell

PRINCIPAL WORKS

Plays

The Northern Lass. Blackfriars Theatre, London. 1629. Pub. as *The Northern Lasse.* London: Vavasour, 1632.

The City Wit. Salisbury Court Theatre, London. c. 1630.

The Queen's Exchange. Blackfriars Theatre, London. c. 1631. Pub. as *The Queenes Exchange: A Comedy.* London: Brome, 1657.

The Novella. Blackfriars Theatre, London. 1632.

The Weeding of the Covent Garden. Blackfriars Theatre, London. 1632.

The Late Lancashire Witches. With Thomas Heywood. Globe Theatre, London. 1634. London: Fisher, 1634.

The Queen and Concubine. Salisbury Court Theatre, London. 1635.

The Sparagus Garden. Salisbury Court Theatre, London. 1635. Pub. as *The Sparagus Garden: A Comedie.* London: Constable, 1640.

The New Academy. Salisbury Court Theatre, London. c. 1635.

The English Moor. Salisbury Court Theatre, London. 1637. Pub. as *The English Moore; or, The Mock-Mariage.* Ed. Sara Jayne Steen. Columbia: U of Missouri P, 1983.

The Antipodes. Salisbury Court Theatre, London. 1638. Pub. as *The Antipodes: A Comedie.* London: Constable, 1640.

The Damoiselle. Salisbury Court Theatre, London. 1638.

The Love-Sick Court. Salisbury Court Theatre, London. 1639.

A Mad Couple Well Match'd. Cockpit Theatre, London. 1639.

The Court Beggar. Cockpit Theatre, London. 1640.

A Jovial Crew. Cockpit Theatre, London. 1641. Pub. as *A Joviall Crew; or, The Merry Beggars.* London: E. D. and N. E., 1652.

*Five New Playes. London: Moseley, Marriot, and Dring, 1653.

†Five New Playes. London: Crook and Brome, 1659.

The Dramatic Works of Richard Brome. 3 vols. London: Pearson, 1873.

The Antipodes. Ed. Ann Haaker. Lincoln: U of Nebraska P, 1966.

A Jovial Crew. Ed. Haaker. Lincoln: U of Nebraska P, 1968.

A Critical Old-Spelling Edition of Richard Brome's A Mad Couple Well Match'd. Ed. Steen H. Spove. New York: Garland, 1979.

An Edition of The Late Lancashire Witches. With Heywood. Ed. Laird H. Barber. New York: Garland, 1979.

A Critical Edition of Brome's A Northern Lasse. Ed. Harvey Fried. New York: Garland, 1980.

A Critical Edition of Richard Brome's The Weeding of Covent Garden and The Sparagus Garden. Ed. Donald S. McClure. New York: Garland, 1980.

The Witches of Lancashire. Ed. Gabriel Egan. New York: Routledge, 2003.

‡Richard Brome Online. Ed. Richard Cave. Royal Holloway, U of London, 2010.

*Includes *The Madd Couple Well Matcht, The Novella, The Court Begger, The City Witt,* and *The Damoiselle.*

†Includes *The English Moor; or, The Mock-Marriage; The Love-Sick Court; or, The Ambitious Politique; Covent Garden Weeded; The New Academy; or, The New Exchange;* and *The Queen and Concubine.*

‡Contains Brome's collected works.

CRITICISM

Robert Grant Martin (essay date 1915)

SOURCE: Martin, Robert Grant. "Is *The Late Lancashire Witches* a Revision?" *Modern Philology* 13.5 (1915): 253-65. Print.

[In the following essay, Martin considers the evidence for the claim that The Late Lancashire Witches *(1634), a melodramatic collaboration between Brome and Thomas Heywood, is a reworking of earlier material by Heywood rather than a wholly new play. Martin finds little support for this view and concludes that the play was composed in the summer of 1634.]*

An article by Professor C. E. Andrews in *Modern Language Notes* of June, 1913,[1] brings up for renewed consideration the question of the authorship, and incidentally the date, of Heywood and Brome's play, **The Late Lancashire Witches.** In *A History of Witchcraft in England from 1558 to 1718*[2] Professor Wallace Notestein has taken issue with historians of the drama as to the history of this play. It is well known that it was put upon the stage in 1634 to take advantage of the excitement caused in London by the bringing to the city of certain women from Lancashire who had been tried for witchcraft in 1633, and that a considerable portion of the play is based upon the depositions of witnesses and defendants in the case. In chapter vii of his scholarly and extremely interesting book Notestein gives the history of the affair. He had, in the preceding chapter, given an account of another Lancashire witchcraft delusion taking place in 1612, as a result of which eleven persons had been condemned to death. Of this trial we possess a contemporary account, *The Wonderfull Discoverie of Witches in the Countie of Lancaster,* by Thomas Potts.[3] The later disturbance was directly connected with the earlier, both occurring in the Forest of Pendle. Early in 1633 charges of witchcraft were brought against a group of women who were tried at the Lancaster assizes, the principal witness against them being an eleven-year-old boy, Edmund Robinson. Of the accused a large number were found guilty. The judges apparently suspected a miscarriage of justice, for they reported the case to the Privy Council. Dr. Bridgman, Bishop of Chester, was deputed to investigate the case, and as a result of his work four of the women were, in June, 1634, sent up to London for examination by the king's surgeons and a committee of midwives. The boy Edmund Robinson and his father were likewise summoned to London, and presently confessed that the witchcraft charge was an imposture pure and simple. Notestein goes on to say:

> Before final judgment had been given on the Lancashire women Thomas Heywood and Richard Brome, well-known dramatists, had written a play on the subject which was at once published and "acted at the Globe on the Bankside by His Majesty's Actors." By some it has been supposed that this play was an older play founded on the Lancashire affair of 1612 and warmed over in 1634; but the main incidents and the characters of the play are so fully copied from the depositions of the young Robinson and from the charges preferred against Mary Spencer, Frances Dickonson, and Margaret Johnson that a layman would at once pronounce it a play written entirely to order from the affair of 1634.[4]

For the theory that the present play is a reworking by Brome, or by Heywood and Brome, of an earlier play by Heywood, Fleay is responsible. His opinion may be summarized as follows. The story of Mrs. Generous, I, i; II, ii, v; III, ii; IV, ii, iv, v; V, ii, iii, iv, v (part), is Heywood's, "considerably accommodated by Brome," and "is founded on *The Witches of Lancaster* by T. Potts, 1613." Brome contributes the Seely story, I, ii; III, i, iii; IV, iii; V, i, v (part). The witch scenes, II, i, iii*a*, iv; IV, i, are Heywood's, with alterations by Brome. In brief, then, this is an old play of Heywood's, from which a very considerable portion was excised and replaced by Brome's story of the troubles of the Seely family, while the rest was subjected to revision by Brome.

This opinion is echoed by Ward in his *English Dramatic Literature*[5] and in his chapter on Heywood in the *Cambridge History of English Literature,* where he says:

> **The Late Lancashire Witches** was printed in 1634 as the joint work of Thomas Heywood and Richard Brome. But the story of the play was based, in part, upon an account, published in 1613, of the doings of certain Lancashire women, of whom twelve had suffered death as witches in the previous year; and it is possible that Heywood was the author of a play much earlier than that put upon the stage in 1634.[6]

Schelling does not mention the theory of an older play, finds the source in "the notorious trials for witchcraft of 1633," adds that "the composition of the play must have followed so close on the events that its influence in forestalling the judgment of the courts which tried these unfortunate creatures can scarcely be considered as negligible,"[7] and then misdates the play 1633. Andrews brings forward additional evidence for the revision theory, but takes from Brome a large portion of the play which has heretofore been credited to him. That Notestein is right in his assumption that **The Late Lancashire Witches** was an entirely new play, the product of the joint authorship, of Heywood and Brome, written in 1634, it is the purpose of this paper to show.

Deferring for the present any discussion of authorship, let us consider the question of source. Is there any use of material older than 1633 which would give ground for assuming that we have a 1634 revision of an older play? The account of the play in the *Biographical Chronicle of the English Drama*[8] presents some sound reasoning by Fleay, but is marred by an unusual number of Fleavian errors, inconsistencies, and contradictions. Fleay, followed by Ward, asserts that the story of Mrs. Generous is founded upon Potts's account of the 1612 affair. So far from being accurate is this statement that there can be found but two points of similarity between the play and Potts's narrative. (*a*) In each case a woman of good birth and social standing is found guilty of witchcraft; otherwise Mrs. Generous has no points of resemblance to unfortunate Alice Nutter. (*b*) In IV, ii, after Mrs. Generous has confessed that she has made a contract with the devil, occur these lines:

GEN.:

> Resolve me, how farre doth that contract stretch?

MRS.:

> What interest in this Soule, my selfe coo'd claime
> I freely gave him, but his part that made it
> I still reserve, not being mine to give.

GEN.:

> O cunning Divell, foolish woman know
> Where he can clayme but the least little part,
> He will usurpe the whole; th'art a lost woman.[9]

In the examination of James Device, one of the accused in the trial of 1612, he deposed that there appeared to him

> a thing like a browne Dogge, who asked this Examinate to giue him his Soule, and he should be reuenged of any whom hee would: whereunto this Examinate answered, that his Soule was not his to giue, but was his Sauiour Iesus Christ's, but as much as was in him this Examinate to giue, he was contented he should haue it.[10]

Again in his confession:

> that the said Spirit did appeare vnto him after sundrie times, in the likenesse of a Dogge, and at euery time most earnestly perswaded him to giue him his Soule absolutely: who answered as before, that he would giue him his owne part and no further. And hee saith, that at the last time that the said Spirit was with him, which was the Tuesday next before his apprehension; when as hee could not preuaile with him to haue his Soule absolutely granted vnto him, as aforesaid; the said Spirit departed from him, then giuing a most fearefull crie and yell, etc.[11]

The verbal likeness is not so close as to be striking, and the parallel loses most of its force when we remember that the belief voiced by James Device was common at the time, and may be found in various contemporary treatises on witchcraft.[12] For the delusion that the play is "founded on" Potts, Crossley, the editor of Potts's narrative, may be inadvertently responsible. In his notes he says: "Alice Nutter was doubtless the original of the story of which Heywood availed himself ... which is frequently noticed by the writers of the 17th century—that the wife of a Lancashire gentleman had been detected in practising witchcraft and unlawful acts, and condemned and executed."[13] Now note that Crossley does not state that Heywood used Potts, but only a story frequently referred to, one version of which may be found in Potts's account. The plain fact is, of course, that so much of the play as can be traced to any recognizable source is not based upon Potts's narrative at all, but upon the depositions, etc., quoted by Crossley in his introduction. The characters of the play who were taken from real life are the witches Moll Spencer, Mawd (Hargrave), Meg or Peg (Johnson), Gill (Dickison), and the boy, evidently the young rascal Edmund Robinson, who caused all the trouble. The incidents borrowed are those of the boy and the greyhounds (II, iii, iv), the boy's ride through the air with Goody Dickison (II, iv), the milk pail which obeys Moll's summons[14] (II, vi), the witches' feast (IV, i), the boy's story of his fight with a devil (V, i), Peg's confession (V, v). In these incidents the authors, as has been noted by all critics, kept very close to the terms of the depositions.

There is, then, nothing in the source material which would suggest a date earlier than 1633. Fleay[15] brought forward as a bit of external evidence confirming the existence of an early play a reference in Field's *A Woman Is a Weathercock,* 1612, to Lawrence of Lancashire.[16] Now Lawrence, according to Fleay's own theory, is one of Brome's characters, appears only in those scenes of the play ascribed to Brome, and must therefore belong to the 1634 revision; how, then, can Field have been referring to a character who made his first entrance upon the stage twenty-two years after Field's play was written? As a matter of fact, the name seems to have been proverbially applied to a man of vigorous physique, "Lusty Lawrence" being the more common variant.[17] It may be found in Beaumont and Fletcher's *The Captain* (IV, iii):

> Lusty Lawrence,
> See what a gentlewoman you have saluted;

and its origin is thus explained by Dyce: "This expression occurs again in *Woman's Prize,* I, iii, and is found in other early dramas. It is explained by the following passage of a rare tract: 'This late *Lusty Lawrence,* that Lancashire Lad, who had 17 bastards in one year, if we believe his Ballad, &c.' *A Brown Dozen of Drunkards,* &c, 1648, sig. C."[18] Thus the use of the name by Field in 1612, instead of glancing at an old play of Heywood's, looks the other way: to the probability that Brome chose the name of a rather well-known local hero in order to give more point to the vulgar situation of which Parnell complains so bitterly.

The play was entered in the Stationer's Register October 28, 1634, and was brought to its present form in the summer of that year. In the prologue there is a reference to the arrival for examination in London of the women charged with witchcraft:

> The Project unto many here well knowne;
> Those Witches the fat Iaylor brought to Towne.

From the *Calendar of State Papers*[19] we learn that they were brought to town some time between June 15, when the Bishop of Chester sent on the results of his examination of Margaret Johnson, Mary Spencer, and Frances Dickonson, and June 29, when the Privy Council passed an order for midwives to "inspect and search the bodies of those women lately brought up by the Sheriff of Co. Lancaster" (the fat jailer); from the same order we learn that the women were lodged at the Ship Tavern in Greenwich. There are two or three pieces of corroborative internal evidence. Fleay noted the allusion to Prynne's punishment. Whetstone says to Bantam, "if thou, Bantam, dost not heare of this with both thine eares, if thou hast them still, and not lost them by scribbling. . . ."[20] Prynne was sentenced on February 17, 1634, to lose his ears and be pilloried, and the sentence was carried into effect on May 7 and 10.

There are two references to a recent issue of farthing coins, which apparently was making some stir in London: "no longer agoe than last holiday evening he gam'd away eight double ring'd tokens on a rubbers at bowles. ..." (I, ii);[21] "from the last Farthings with the double rings, to the late Coy'ned peeces which they say are all counterfeit" (II, iv).[22] Legal farthings of copper were first coined in 1613, and the lead farthing tokens up to that time issued by merchants and tradesmen were declared illegal. The authorities had great difficulty in getting the new coins into circulation and protecting them from counterfeiting. We find frequent references to the matter in the state papers during the remainder of the reign of James and that of Charles I.[23] Finally to defeat the counterfeiters a new coinage was issued.

> In 1634, at a time when Lord Maltravers had a share in the patent, the patentees were allowed to decry all the old farthings, and a new farthing of better make was introduced, distinguishable by an inner beaded circle, the so-called double-rings.[24]
>
> So serious had the counterfeiting of the farthing tokens become, that the patentees were allowed to introduce a token slightly different in design. The general design continued in accordance with the terms of the original patent, but all the details were altered, and as a mark to distinguish the new issue, a second beaded circle was placed on the obverse and reverse, whence the farthings were known as "double rings."[25]

There is, finally, one other passage which seems to carry on its face evidence of having been written in the summer of 1634. This is in the speech of Generous in IV, ii, a scene surely from the hand of Heywood. Generous is speaking of his wife, whom he is beginning to suspect of some criminal practice, though the idea of witchcraft has not yet occurred to him.

> The Gentile fashion sometimes we observe
> To sunder beds; but most in these hot monthes
> Iune, Iuly, August. ...

The specific mention of present time seems to me to possess some corroborative value; at any rate, I set it down for what it may be worth. To sum up, common-sense would point to a date of composition in July or August, while the excitement over the near presence of the supposed witches would be at its height, and all the time indications that we have are in agreement with that inference.

In proof of the revision theory Andrews in his article presents three pieces of internal evidence: "the obvious interpolation of an episode, and an omission of one or two incidents that we are led to expect, and a mention in two places of names of witches or spirits inconsistent with the names in the rest of the play."

The episode which Andrews considers to be interpolated is that of the boy and the greyhounds on pp. 196-97, 199-201. The boy comes upon a brace of greyhounds, which he

takes to have strayed from their owner, to whom he decides to restore them in hope of reward. On the way the dogs start a hare, but refuse to give chase. The boy, angered by their apparent laziness, beats them, whereupon one of the dogs turns into Goody Dickison and the other into a boy. Mrs. Dickison changes the second boy into a horse, catches the first boy up in her arms, and they ride off on the horse. Andrews asserts that this episode has no connection with any of the threads of interest. On the contrary, ample preparation has been made for it. In the first scene of Act II (pp. 187-89) the witches are gathered to discuss what new deviltry they will play in order to throw their neighbors into confusion. They refer to the hunting party that is in progress, and Meg proposes to change herself into a hare to lead the dogs astray, while Gill says:

> I and my puckling will a brace
> Of Greyhounds be, fit for the race;
> And linger where we may be tane
> Up for the course in the by-lane.

The boy's experience is the obvious sequel of these plans; the dogs are Gill and her Puckling, and the hare is Meg. The boy next appears at the witches' feast, IV, i (pp. 220-21), whither he has been carried by Gill, and whence he escapes, to appear again in the final scene to give his evidence against the witches. The episode then, far from being interpolated, has a very definite connection with what precedes and what follows, and its dramatic purpose is plain—to show the witches in action. The part played by the boy Edmund Robinson in the actual Lancashire delusion was well known in London, he had been brought up to London for examination, and to omit him from the play would have been well-nigh impossible.

Andrews' second point, the omission of one or two incidents which we might expect, has some basis. It is true that the connection between the mortgage transaction (p. 178) and the incident of the receipt (p. 210) is not clear, and the business of the mortgage is dropped rather unceremoniously after the last reference to it (p. 182). It is to be noted, however, that the mortgage affair has served its dramatic purpose of bringing Generous and Arthur together, and thus furnishing a bond of connection between the plots. The reason for Arthur's appeal to Generous is the refusal of Arthur's uncle Seely to assist him with a loan, and the refusal, in turn, is occasioned by the confusion wrought by the witches in the Seely household. Such a knitting-together of plots is considerably closer than is the case in several others of Heywood's plays, e.g., *Woman Killed with Kindness* and *English Traveller*. Moreover, the granting of the loan has characterized Generous, and Robin's presentation of the receipt proves to Generous that Robin has actually been in London, as he alleges. The failure to connect the two incidents more clearly and to refer again to the mortgage does not necessarily point to revision. It should be remembered that the play was composed, probably in some haste, to take advantage of a passing excitement, and any failure on the part of the authors to bring to a logical conclusion all the minor interests of the play may be laid more readily to haste of composition than to a supposed revision. This is particularly true since we have to deal with Thomas Heywood and Richard Brome, both of whom were somewhat rough-and-ready workmen, not distinguished for the careful finish of their plays.[26]

For the other so-called revision Andrews points to the abrupt ending of II, iv (p. 199), where a betting scene terminates "without the interference of witchcraft which we are led to expect." The scene ends with a reference to a hare which has just been started. At the opening of the next scene the boy enters with the greyhounds, crying, "A Hare, a Hare, halloe, halloe!" and beats the dogs for not giving chase, whereupon the dogs are transformed into Gill and a boy. This, surely, is a display of the expected witchcraft, although the hunters are not present to witness the transformation. The betting scene, however, like the mortgage episode, has served its dramatic purpose. The main interest of the scene is not in the betting, but in the foolish behavior of Whetstone, and when he makes his exit we are interested more in his threatened revenge for the baiting to which he has been subjected than in the comparative speed of the brown dog and the pied. The failure to provide a logical termination for the betting episode may again, I think, be laid to hasty composition, especially since the following scene does provide a display of witchcraft which accounts for the hare mentioned at the end of scene iv.

Andrews' third evidence of revision is the one suggested by Fleay, that in two instances there seems to be a confusion in the naming of the witches. Thus, at the end of Act IV, Mrs. Generous, calling a convocation of witches at the mill, says:

> Call *Meg,* and *Doll, Tib, Nab,* and *Jug,*
> Let none appear without her Pug,

while Moll, Nab, Jug, and Peg are named in V, ii (p. 244). There is a tendency toward looseness in the names of the witches, anyway; thus Mrs. Johnson is called Meg or Peg indiscriminately (cf. p. 189, and V, v, where she is called Peg throughout). In IV, v, Mrs. Generous says: "Summon the Sisterhood together"; that is, she is giving directions for a general convocation. May not the sisterhood have comprised more than the four who are brought upon the stage, as it did in real life? Fleay thinks that before alteration V, ii, must have been Doll, Nab, Jug, and Tib. Why must we discard Moll and Peg, whom we know, because we have Nab and Jug whom we do not know? Fleay and Andrews want the names to be perfectly consistent; I think that they are loosely and carelessly used, and that the inconsistency is evidence only of haste of composition.

Having thus accounted for the evidence presented in behalf of the revision theory, let us consider the respective shares of Heywood and Brome. Andrews argues against collabo-

ration in revision (and hence, inferentially, in actual composition) because "Heywood was writing for the Queen's Company in 1633 and the *Lancashire Witches* [*The Late Lancashire Witches*] was brought out by the King's Men, the company for which Brome was writing in 1633 and 1634." Supposing for the moment that Heywood was writing for the Queen's Men at the time *The Late Lancashire Witches* was produced—has it been proved that a playwright in the employ of one company never did any work for another company? In fact, Andrews refutes his own argument when he states that Brome was connected in 1634 with both the King's Men and the Red Bull Company, and that while he was under contract to the King's Revels Company at Salisbury Court he had written a play or two for the Cockpit.[27] Such general argument, however, is in this case not necessary to meet Andrews' objection. *The Late Lancashire Witches* was written in 1634, not in 1633, and Fleay on the basis of our play infers that at some time between the date of *Love's Mistress,* produced at court by the Queen's Men in 1633 and *The Late Lancashire Witches* Heywood transferred his services to the King's Men. Andrews cites the 1634 title-page of *Maidenhead Well Lost,* date of composition being probably 1633, but what would he say of the 1636 title-page of *Challenge for Beauty,* a play performed in 1635 by the King's Men, which, therefore, supports Fleay's theory?

Andrews accepts Fleay's assignment of the main plot—the Generous story—to Heywood. The first of his reasons, that the story is based upon the 1612 trial, is untenable. The second, that the general handling of the story, particularly in the treatment of the erring wife by her husband, is in Heywood's manner, is sufficient. The hunting scenes, also, may be compared with the first scene of *Woman Killed with Kindness.*

The attribution to Brome of the Seely story Andrews rejects because he can find no good reason for the assignment. Yet Andrews, when he accepts the Generous story as Heywood's because of its likeness to the Frankford story of *Woman Killed with Kindness,* has used precisely the kind of reasoning that Fleay did when he gave the Seely story to Brome because of its general resemblance to the inverted situation in *Antipodes.* Why the distinction?

That part of the story of the Seely household which concerns the servants Lawrence and Parnell is given by Andrews to Heywood because, as he says, "it is so involved with all the different interests that I have mentioned that I cannot see any possibility of a separate authorship for it." Truly, the best reason for assigning the Lawrence-Parnell story to the same hand that wrote the Seely story is that the former is an integral and essential part of the latter. But the hand is Brome's, not Heywood's. The mere fact that certain characters of the main plot, Heywood's, e.g., Bantam, Shakstone, Whetstone, are present at the Parnell-Lawrence wedding is very slender evidence upon which to assign the wedding scenes to Heywood. The union of the two plots through Moll Spencer, who gives Lawrence a bewitched cod-piece point while she is carrying on an intrigue with Robin, is not so ingeniously close that it must point to a single authorship for both plots; it is just the sort of connection that might readily be arranged by two collaborators. The argument that Lawrence belongs to Heywood because of an allusion in Field's play of 1612 has already been disposed of. Finally Andrews refuses to accept Fleay's attribution of the Lawrence-Parnell scenes to Brome on the basis of the dialect, which Fleay compared with that in Brome's **Northern Lass.** Andrews asserts that the dialect of **The Late Lancashire Witches** differs from that of **Northern Lass,** and points out that Heywood also used a northern dialect in *Edward IV,* without, however, clinching his point by proving that the dialect usages of **The Late Lancashire Witches** and *Edward IV* are identical. To base any argument on dialect forms and spellings that have been subjected to the tender mercies of printers of playbook quartos seems a rather risky business. But since Andrews has introduced argument of this sort I have acted upon the suggestion made by him in a note, and have made comparison of the words listed by Eckhardt in his *Die Dialekt- und Ausländertypen des älteren Englischen Dramas*[28] with the following results:

Forms[29] found in all three plays—*E.IV,* **L.L.W.**
    [**The Late Lancashire Witches**], **N.L.**
    [**The Northern Lass**] 4
Forms found in all three plays—*E.IV* and
    L.L.W., not in **N.L.** 6
Forms found in all three plays—*E.IV* and
    N.L., not in **L.L.W.** 6
Forms found in all three plays—**L.L.W.**
    and **N.L.,** not in *E.IV* 18

Now such a table proves nothing, beyond the fact that both Heywood and Brome were acquainted with north country dialects and used them freely on occasion, but if any inference were to be drawn as to authorship it looks as though Andrews' remark that "Fleay's argument is useless" were something of a boomerang.[30] As positive evidence of Brome's authorship of the Lawrence-Parnell scenes it may be noted that Parnell's "Whaw, whaw, whaw, whaw!" (p. 186) is also used by Randal in *A Jovial Crew,*[31] and that the inelegant expression "piss and paddle in't" (p. 185) is found in the same play.[32]

Andrews would restrict Brome's part in the play to those scenes which are based directly on the depositions in the 1633 trial, some "nine pages in all, out of a play of eighty-nine."[33] Most of this material Fleay assigns to Heywood. It seems to me impossible to ascribe the witch scenes to either author with any degree of confidence. But for the broad general division of the play into main plot and subplot, the first to Heywood, the second to Brome, I should agree with Fleay, dissenting from Fleay's opinion that the main plot shows "accommodation" by Brome. In short, I regard the play as a straight piece of collaboration by the two men, done in the summer of 1634.[34]

Notes

1. Reprinted in Andrews, "Richard Brome: A Study of His Life and Works," *Yale Studies in English,* XLVI (1913), 48-53.

2. Prize Essay of the American Historical Association, 1909. Published by the Association, Washington, 1911.

3. Ed. by James Crossley in *Chetham Soc. Publ.,* VI (1845).

4. Pp. 158-59.

5. Ed. of 1899, II, 575.

6. VI, 118.

7. *Elizabethan Drama,* I, 363.

8. I, 301-3.

9. *L.L.W.,* p. 227.

10. Crossley, *op. cit.,* sig. H3 verso.

11. Crossley, *op. cit.,* sig. K.

12. E.g., Reginald Scot, *Discovery of Witchcraft,* Book III, chap. x.

13. *Op. cit.,* pp. 35-36.

14. This incident does not appear in the depositions quoted by Crossley. Its origin may be found in the report of the examination of Mary Spencer by Dr. Bridgman, as given in the *Calendar of State Papers* (Dom. Ser., 1634-35, June 15, 1634): "Cunliffe accused her [Mary Spencer] to call a collock, or peal [pail], which came running to her of its own accord. . . . When she was a young girl and went to the well for water, she used to tumble or trundle the collock, or peal, down the hill, and she would run along after it to overtake it, and did overhye it sometimes, and then might call it to come to her, but utterly denies that she could ever make it come to her by any witchcraft."

15. *Biog. Chron.,* I, 185.

16. Hazlitt, *Dodsley,* XI, 85.

17. Cf. *L.L.W.,* p. 231, and Hazlitt, *English Proverbs.*

18. Dyce's Beaumont and Fletcher, III, 295. Besides being used in the four plays mentioned—*L.L.W., A Woman Is a Weathercock, The Captain, Woman's Prize*—the expression occurs in the fifth satire of

Marston's *Pygmalion and Satires* (Bullen's ed., III, 289), and Bullen in a footnote refers to a ballad on the subject; this ballad, according to Hazlitt (*op. cit.*), was licensed in 1594. I have run across the phrase in Burton's *Anatomy of Melancholy,* but am unable to supply the exact reference.

19. Dom. Ser., 1634-35.

20. *L.L.W.,* p. 198.

21. *Ibid.,* p. 182.

22. *Ibid.,* p. 197.

23. Cf. Thomas Snelling, *A View of the Copper Coin and Coinage of England,* 1766; R. Ruding, *Annals of the Coinage of Great Britain,* 3d ed., 1840; H. Montagu, *The Copper Tin and Bronze Coinage of England from Elizabeth to Victoria,* 2d ed., 1893.

24. *British Numismatic Journal,* 1906, First ser., III, 190.

25. *Ibid.,* p. 200. Illustrations of the "double rings" are given in Plate I, Nos. 29, 30, 31, opp. p. 191. The royal proclamation, authorizing the new issue, was dated February 23, 1634 (Patent Rolls, 11 Chas. I, Part V, No. 30).

26. Ward holds haste of composition responsible to some degree for the bad structure of the play: "The process of composition was evidently too hurried to allow of more being attempted than a succession of scenes half realistic, half grotesque, etc." (*Engl. Dram. Litt.,* II, 578).

27. *Richard Brome,* p. 14.

28. Bang, *Materialien,* XXVII, 81-83, 86-91.

29. I have confined this list to words actually used in more than one of the three plays, including variant spellings such as *deaft, deft* = pretty, *sic, sick, sike* = such.

30. Cf. also Andrews' comment on Brome's use of dialect in *N.L.* and elsewhere: "The *Lancashire Witches* [contains] considerable fairly accurate Lancashire" (*Richard Brome,* p. 66, note). This certainly seems to imply that Brome wrote the scenes in which the Lancashire dialect is employed.

31. Brome, *Works,* III, 439.

32. *Ibid.,* III, 374.

33. From this list are omitted two episodes that should be in it: Moll's calling of the pail (p. 202), and Peg's confession (pp. 258-59).

34. As an example of Fleay's curious processes of reasoning it may be worth while to place side by side three of his statements regarding date and authorship.

(1) "Heywood's part is founded on *The Witches of Lancashire* by T. Potts, 1613." (2) "The story of Mrs. Generous ... is Heywood's, but considerably accommodated by Brome." I.e., the story of Mrs. Generous is the part founded on Potts. If so, it must have been written early and formed part of the early play. (3) "The turning Robin into a horse (and therefore the Mrs. Generous story) dates 1634." The parenthesis is Fleay's. How may this be reconciled with the previous statements? According to Fleay, moreover, Brome's part, consisting of the Seely story, must have been written to take the place of some other scenes in Heywood's early play, and dates, of course, 1634. This leaves only the witch scenes for the early play. But the witches are all 1633 people, and their deeds are based on the 1633 depositions. By the application of Fleay's own reasoning all of the early play disappears, and we have an altogether new one.

Since completing this article I have discovered that the views expressed in it are in agreement with those of Professor Ph. Aronstein of Berlin, in his article entitled "Thomas Heywood," in *Anglia,* June, 1913.

Alwin Thaler (essay date 1921)

SOURCE: Thaler, Alwin. "Was Richard Brome an Actor?" *Modern Language Notes* 36.2 (1921): 88-91. Print.

[*In the following essay, Thaler examines a "strangely neglected" royal warrant that mentions Brome as "an actor of some prominence." Thaler speculates that Brome, like many other English playwrights, may have begun his career as an actor, suggesting that Jonson's reference to him as a "servant" should be understood in this sense.*]

Of the early career of the author of **The Antipodes** and **A Jovial Crew** comparatively little is known. Andrews, whose study[1] of Brome is the most complete that has yet appeared, thinks the playwright was born about 1590. But few facts have come down to us concerning Brome's activities between that date and 1635, when, according to the contract discovered by Professor Wallace,[2] he agreed to deliver to the King's Revels Company at the Salisbury Court—and to this company only—three plays annually for a period of three years, at a salary of 15s. weekly, and with the understanding that he should not print any of his plays without the consent of the company. All that has hitherto been known concerning Brome's history before 1635 has been inferred from the commendatory verses prefixed to his plays, from references or allusions in the plays themselves, or from his relations with Ben Jonson. The latter's striking reference to "his man, Master Brome, behind the arras," in the Induction to *Bartholomew Fair* (1614), and his prefatory verses to Brome's **Northern Lass** (printed 1632):

> I had you for a servant once, Dick Brome,
> And you performed a servant's faithful parts ...

have been interpreted in various ways. Some have thought that Brome was simply Ben's menial servant, and account for the coarseness in his dramas by the assumption that he "describes life from the groom's point of view."[3] Professor Baker,[4] on the other hand, concludes that he acted as a sort of amanuensis to Jonson, while Fleay[5] speaks of him simply as Ben's "apprentice," without saying anything as to the nature of the apprenticeship. Andrews,[6] finally, thinks that "Brome probably began his relations with Jonson as a witty young serving-man who interested his master to such an extent that he undertook his education, as he had already that of the young Nathaniel Field." The reference to Field is significant here, since a strangely neglected bit of evidence would seem to indicate that Brome, like Field, was an actor before he became a playwright, and that, like Field, he may have been indebted to Jonson in both capacities.

This evidence appears in the form of a royal warrant under date of June 30, 1628, reprinted without comment by Mrs. Stopes in the *Shakespeare Jahrbuch* for 1910.[7] The warrant is one of a miscellaneous list of orders for payment of court performances, allowances for actors' liveries, and the like. It reads as follows:

> Warrant to swear the Queen of Bohemia's players[8]
> groomes of his Majesties chamber without fee,
> viz. Joseph Moore, Alexander Foster, Robert Gylman
> *Richard Brome,* John Lillie, William Rogers,
> George Lillie, Abel Swinnerton, George Gibbes,
> Oliver Howes; June 30, 1628.[9]

The chances are strongly in favor of the conclusion that the Richard Brome thus mentioned as an actor of some prominence[10] in the Lady Elizabeth's Company in 1628, was the playwright. If so, Fleay's conjecture[11] that Brome's "apprenticeship" to Jonson extended over the seven years 1623 to 1629, will have to be modified; incidentally some new light may be thrown upon the nature of that apprenticeship. "Bengemen Johnson, *player,* borrowed money from Henslowe in 1597 and 1598, and he may have had a share in the Admiral's Men for a time."[12] I see no reason, then, why at some later date Ben Jonson, actor-playwright, might not have taken on a theatrical apprentice, who would perhaps serve him as amanuensis, but also get a chance to act. Augustine Phillips, Shakspere's colleague in the King's Men, had just such an apprentice. In his will[13] Phillips left 30s. to "my servaunte Christopher Beeston," who later become an actor-sharer and business manager of the Cockpit company. John Heminges, business manager of Shakspere's company, also had his theatrical apprentice, Alexander Cooke,[14] who later became an actor-sharer in his "master's" company. Similarly, Brome may have been "made free o' th' Trade" of acting (as well as of playwriting) by Jonson. The apprentices of Jones and Downton ("Jones' boy" and "Downton's boy") of the Admiral's Men are known to have acted in the plays of that

company given in 1599 and 1699.[15] And so I think it not unlikely that Jonson put "his man, Master Brome, behind the arras" in *Bartholomew Fair* because Master Brome was acting a small part in that play. It would have been a good-natured bit of advertising for the young actor, in keeping with the mention, later in the play, of Field, "your best actor," who played a part in the piece.[16] Perhaps Jonson, when he recalled how Brome had "performed a servant's faithful *parts,*" had in mind the acting as well as the other services of his former apprentice.

When *Bartholomew Fair* was produced in 1614 Brome must have been somewhere between twenty and twenty-five years old; it was the time when he was undergoing his training for his later activities as an actor-sharer and playwright. In 1623 he collaborated in a play which is not extant; in 1629 his first independently written play was produced. It is impossible to say whether Brome continued long as an actor after 1628, but I think the evidence to which I have called attention indicates that he was one of "the quality" before that date. "I love the quality of playing," says Letoy in *The Antipodes*;[17] and I believe he is voicing Brome's sentiments towards his old profession. Indeed this play and many others of Brome are full of allusions which support the conclusion that Brome, like Shakspere, Jonson, Heywood, Rowley, Field, Armin, and a host of other Elizabethan playwrights, passed his apprenticeship upon the stage, and that it was in this sense that Jonson called him his "servant."

Notes

1. C. E. Andrews, *Richard Brome: A Study of His Life and Works,* Yale Studies in English, XLVI, 1913.

2. See his "Shakspere and the Blackfriars," *Century Magazine,* Sept., 1910, and Andrews, p. 13.

3. Compare *Cambridge History of English Literature,* VI, 225.

4. See Gayley's *Representative English Comedies,* III, 417.

5. See note 11.

6. P. 4.

7. See C. C. Stopes, "Shakespeare's Fellows and Followers," *Shakespeare Jahrbuch,* XLVI, 94; printed from Warrant Book V, 93, 1628-1634, p. 26.

8. The Lady Elizabeth's Men.

9. Murray (*Elizabethan Dramatic Companies,* I, 259) did not know of the existence of this warrant. In his sketch of the history of the Lady Elizabeth's Men between 1625 and June, 1629, he gives but one partial list of actors. This list (based on an incomplete document recorded in the *Calendar of State Papers, Domestic,* 1628-9) is dated December 9, 1628, and names but four actors: "Joseph Moore, Alexander

Foster, Robert Gylman, Joseph Townsend, with the rest of their company."

10. Only the more prominent actors, not the "hirelings," are listed among those who received royal liveries or other court grants. The Richard Brome here mentioned must have been an actor-sharer.

11. *Drama,* I, 37; compare *Camb. Hist. of Eng. Lit.,* VI, 224.

12. See *Henslowe's Diary,* ed. Greg, I, 47, 200; II, 289. Jonson's acting at Paris Garden is referred to in Dekker's *Satiromastix.*

13. See J. P. Collier's *Actors,* p. xxxi.

14. "I do intreate my Master Heminges" (he writes in his will) to look out for the interests of his orphans. See Malone-Boswell, *Shakspeare,* III, 482.

15. *Henslowe Papers,* ed. Greg, p. 154.

16. See *Bartholomew Fair,* Act V, Sc. 3, and Fleay, *Drama,* I, 172. Similar bits of advertising of the actors appear in many Elizabethan plays. See, for example, the Induction to *The Malcontent,* and Greene's *Tu Quoque.*

17. See Act I, Scenes 5 and 6; Act II, Scenes 1 and 2, etc.

Elizabeth Cook (essay date 1947)

SOURCE: Cook, Elizabeth. "The Plays of Richard Brome." *More Books* 22.8 (1947): 285-301. Print.

[*In the following essay, Cook provides an overview of Brome's life, which is poorly documented, and his works, for which much better records exist. Cook compares Brome's works to those of his influential predecessor Jonson on several points, including his style and settings, his generally weak characterizations, and the moral purpose of his comedies and tragicomedies.*]

I

The dramatic historians of the seventeenth century recorded that Richard Brome was poor and that he was Ben Jonson's servant; nothing more was said about his life. A few episodes in his later career have been discovered recently, but even the dates of his birth and death are unknown and his character is hidden from conjecture. His plays are all that he has left.

Most of the dramatists who made their living by the theatre did not care about perpetuating their fame, and the players tried to stop them from publishing their work in prosperous years. As it is, five of Brome's plays are lost, and the plays which have survived appeared sporadically when the theatres were in difficulties or during the long silence of the Commonwealth. The most popular of his early plays, *The*

Northern Lasse, was printed in 1632 during a visitation of the plague. *The Sparagus Garden* and *The Antipodes* came out in 1640, not long before the theatres were closed by order of Parliament. Twelve years later Brome published *A Joviall Crew*; a quarto like the previous first editions, but much more handsomely printed in larger type. He died before the end of 1653, for in the course of that year Alexander Brome edited and published a posthumous volume, *Five New Playes,* in octavo, which includes *A Mad Couple Well Match'd, The Novella, The Court Begger, The City Wit,* and *The Damoiselle.* Opposite the general title-page he inserted a crudely engraved portrait of the author which scarcely illuminates his account of him. In 1657 another namesake, the stationer Henry Brome—again no relation to the dramatist—published *The Queen's Exchange* in quarto with a small double-column text, and promised another collected volume if this play sold well. He brought out the second *Five New Playes* in octavo in 1659, containing *The English Moor, The Love-sick Court, The Covent-Garden Weeded, The New Academy,* and *The Queen and Concubine.*

These books are rare and it is unusual to find a complete set. The Barton Collection of the Boston Public Library, which possesses a magnificent series of early playbooks, has copies of all the first editions of Brome except for *The Northern Lasse,* and it has a copy of the second edition of this play published in 1663. The volumes are in very fine condition.

The information on the title-pages of these first editions is the only real evidence about the dates of Brome's plays. (The statement that *The Court Begger* was "Acted at the Cock-pit, by his Majesties Servants, Anno 1632" has been proved to be false, but the mistake occurred through mechanical transcription of the previous title-page in the 1653 volume.) They give fairly reliable dates of performance for *The Antipodes, A Joviall Crew,* and *The Novella. The Covent-Garden Weeded* must have been written at about the same time as Thomas Nabbes's play of 1632, because his prologue shows that there were charges of plagiarism current, and he says that he discovered the idea. But the conjectural dates of the other plays create a problem which is too complicated to be discussed adequately here, especially since Brome wrote for more than one company at first. *The Court Begger* and *A Mad Couple Well Match'd* are known to have belonged to Beeston's Boys and were presumably acted during Brome's term at the Cockpit from 1639 to 1642. *The English Moor* belonged to the new Queen Henrietta's Company and must have been acted after 1637, when they moved into the Salisbury Court. *The Queen and Concubine* is evidently a Revels play and must be prior to 1637. It seems possible that *The Love-sick Court* is the play licensed as *The Brothers* on 4 November 1626 and wrongly ascribed to Shirley.[1]

In 1873, during the heyday of antiquarian devotion to the minor dramatists of the seventeenth century, R. H. Shepherd edited Brome's plays for the series of Pearson reprints in London, following the text of the first editions in punctuation and orthography, except for some slight variants which may mean that he used a different issue. References are given here to his edition for the sake of convenience. After this revival two American scholars dealt with Brome's work—H. F. Allen in *A Study of the Comedies of Richard Brome,* 1912; and C. E. Andrews in *Richard Brome: A Study of His Life and Works,* 1913, which traced his dramatic career and assigned his un-Jonsonian passages to the influence of other Jacobean dramatists. Of course Swinburne's essay, published in 1919 in his *Contemporaries of Shakespeare,* interprets the plays much more enjoyably, and in a perceptive paragraph at the end he noticed the modernity of Brome's style.

It is more inviting to follow this path now, especially since an interest in the archetypes of Restoration comedy is abroad; and, because Brome is not a highly individual writer, it is easier to see how he deflected Jonson's comedy of humors into a more "refined" comedy of manners, and conversely how he brought the realism of Jonson and Dekker into the new tragicomedy. But his plays are not mere specimens of the period: his theatrical workmanship is unusually good, and at his best he writes with grace and competence.

Brome stayed on as servant to Ben Jonson long after he had served his apprenticeship. He was never quite free of the *Tribe of Ben*; he was too poor and too plebeian to associate with the wits who paid homage to the Laureate's dramatic theories and embroidered upon them the flourished patterns of Caroline classicism. More than one gentleman revived Jonson's irritated pun on Brome's "sweepings" from his table, ten years after *The New Inn* quarrel was over and Jonson had emended the unkind line. There is nothing to show that Brome enjoyed any distinguished literary connections besides the friendship of his namesake Alexander. "The English Maecenas," the Duke of Newcastle, might condescend to a hack playwright and fish for a compliment without implying familiarity on either side.

Brome spent his years of service at the Globe and the Blackfriars, where Jonson pointed at him crouching behind the arras, in the Induction to *Bartholomew Fair.* His first independent ventures were plays written for the Red Bull and for the Revels Company, and he continued to work for the King's Men. In 1635 he signed a contract with the Salisbury Court, one of the three private theatres, which was by no means a rival of the Blackfriars or the Cockpit, to which he moved in 1639. Thomas Randolph, who was chosen and favored as Jonson's successor, had tried out the position at the Salisbury Court during hard times; and, finding the company unrewarding and intractable, he fled back to Cambridge to take up his fellowship at Trinity as soon as the plague abated there. Brome had to remain at the Salisbury Court. Here he wrote plays on the model of Jonson's because they came readiest to hand, and

his literary obedience was still menial. He learned the craft not from Jonson's principles but from his practice; and his own practice changed to accommodate the taste of his audience and the exigencies of his stage. His work reflects the dramatic age fairly, since he had to mix old and new wine without a connoisseur's scruples; and it is unusually open to examination because he did not need, like a courtier or scholar, to pretend that his plays were the sport of idle moments and an unlabored brain. Like Jonson, he was not ashamed to show the marks of his file, and his acquaintance ranged from high to low in life and language. It was no disparagement to either poet, Alexander Brome reminded the scornful Reader:

> It seems (what ere we think) *Ben* thought it diminution for no man to attend upon his Muse. And were not already the Antients too much trod on, we could name famous wits who served far meaner Masters than *Ben Johnson.* For, none vers'd in Letters but know the wise *Aesop* was born and bred a wretched slave ... and (which for our purpose is most of all) our Authors own *Master* handled the *Trowel* before he grew acquainted with *Seianus* or *Cataline.*[2]

Brome always protested that he was conscientiously upholding the old Jonsonian drama against the absurd refinements of the new stage. Many commendatory verses confirmed his own declaration:

> *Opinion,* which our *Author* cannot court,
> (For the deare daintinesse of it) has, of late,
> From the old way of *Playes* possest a Sort
>   Only to run to those, that carry state
> In Scene magnificent and language high ...
> ... But it is knowne (peace to their Memories)
>   The *Poets* late sublimed from our Age,
> Who best could understand, and best devise
>   Workes, that must ever live upon the *Stage,*
> Did well approve, and lead this humble way,
>   Which we are bound to travaile in tonight ...[3]

He writes as though he were on his guard against the sneers of the courtly clique where each had written his "brace of plays." He has a grudge against their gilt-edged folios, lavish scenes, and impossible fables of platonic love. He is too impatient in his censure of the dilettante romancer; and there is some animus in his denunciation of bad acting and "fibulating" with the bandstring in the University plays. Brome knew London better than Sicily, but he was ready to try an unprepared hand at romantic tragicomedy. Even in his London comedies the stock figures are dressed so differently from Jonson's that the fashion shows that Brome was not observing his master's critical precepts.

Of course the flavor of Brome's comedy is produced in part by infiltration from the other Jacobean dramatists; however humble a plagiarist he may have been, the proportions of the mixture would be his own. But he acquired something from the romanticism of his own nobler contemporaries, and his wit begins to ape the good-breeding and good-sense of a new day. His comedy is external, and it is sometimes sterile and sometimes naive; it wavers between a dying imagery and a growing descriptiveness. The agreeable plays of the decade before the Civil War are slight, and the weakness and vulgarity of decadence are certainly apparent in many of them; but they are also written in a mode which survives and is established at the Restoration. In comedy it holds the stage for a while; in its counterpart, hardly to be called tragedy, it passes into the novel.

II

The core of discussion upon Caroline comedy has naturally been Jonson's picture of Humors. Not that Jonson was the inventor of a doctrine or an exile from the wider Elizabethan world; but he took apart one of the frames in which the Elizabethan saw men and women and turned it into a methodical dramatic structure. Whether the neoclassicism or the English ancestry of his technique has been turned uppermost, his critics have agreed that the personification of a dominant idea is his manner of characterization, and the interplay of conflicting ideas is the groundwork of his plotting. In the Induction to *Every Man Out of His Humour* he gives his warning to all the poetasters who might turn his outward conventions into an easy *gradus ad Parnassum.* Evidently he expected theft, and he was justified:

> ... *Johnson* is decryed by some who fleece
> His *Works,* as much as hc did *Rome* or *Greece*:
> They judge it lawfull Prize, doing no more
> To him, than he to those that dy'd before ...
> ... These East-and-West Translators, not like Ben.
> Do but enrich Themselves, He other men.[4]

At first sight Brome seems to flock with the other magpies. His plays are often pushed arbitrarily within the borders of comedy by the addition of a "humorous" character or a "humorous" by-plot, and his comic figures are scarecrows made out of a physical habit and a conversational tag. There is an ample population of shadows, like the hearty squires in *A Joviall Crew* and the touchy justices who acknowledge their descent from Jonson's Adam Overdoe. Certainly some of these whimsical persons are allowed to control the intrigue: Lady Strangelove, the contrary widow of *The Court Begger,* happens to reverse the ordinary dramatic motivation, but neither she nor any of the others are the embodiments of human desires. None the less they do catch a trick of speech and behavior which is true to the passages of average existence; they are accurate as the figures of domestic tragedy were never meant to be accurate. Brome is beginning to work on a situation from its setting and social tone. His shop scene in *A Mad Couple Well Match'd* opens with a parade of small talk which is not there to particularize a poetic impression of wealth and wit—Jonson would have made it contrapuntal between the citizen's clumsiness and the lady's flippancy. Here the detail is to insinuate Saleware's worldly wisdom and Lady Thrivewell's nonchalance, so that their conversation is exactly what might be expected at such a place and time. The same reaction is invited by Lady Strangelove's open-

eyed jeers upon her young mercenary suitors. She is not the Lady Fortune of a morality play; she speaks in a cynical phrase which makes it likely that she would fall in love with the Court Puritan and marry the converted rake.

Brome's characters are not often so recognizable; they may be inconsistent like Erasmus and Sir Stephen Whimblie in *The New Academy,* who vacillate between sense, scheming, and affection; more often they are quite empty. On the other hand these persons do speak and act recognizably according to circumstances and their own breeding, and a good part of the pleasure sought in a comedy of manners is a pleasure of recognition. Brome was aware that he did not portray Humors as the past generation saw them; he uses the word in senses which show that its meaning is shifting to express a momentary whim or an individual style:

> I would their extream qualities could meet each other at half-way, and so mingle their superfluities of humour unto a mean betwixt 'hem ... What dirty dogged humour was I in when I got him troe?

> I will not lose
> An haires breadth o' my humour ... [*of baby-talk*]

> This is one of his un-to-be-examin'd hastie Humours, one of his starts ...[5]

Brome's plotting has been complicated and sophisticated to accommodate the *dramatis personae.* The intrigue indeed seems to determine the comedy; but it is usually made upon a stock model, and both the development of the story and the behavior of the persons reflect a modern mood. They produce the effect as independently as Inigo's scaffolding and Vitruvian ornaments made up a "Scene." Most of Brome's material is lifted straight off an earlier stage. He presents time after time the gulling of a country bumpkin, the academy of roarers, January and May, averted incest and such well-tried devices of Jonson and Fletcher. But he is not often content with one of them singly; and the component parts of his plot tend to fall into a design akin to the structure of our present detective novel. The wedding-night takes the place now held by the murder—it may happen at the beginning, as it does in *The English Moor* or at the end as in *The Northern Lasse*—and to and from this scene lead all the relationships of persons in various sub-plots, all the errors of mistaken children, disguised fathers, and masquerading strumpets, until the parson ties and unties the knots. *Epicoene* provides an obvious "source" for the wedding-mystery, but the nature of Jonson's plot is entirely different, because it grows from the unnatural selfishness of Morose and the normal world's revenge upon him. The "Labyrinth" of Brome's *The Sparagus Garden* affords an exercise in the discovery of "true proportion." It is a maze composed of various walks of life which are all rather crooked and rather quaint, filled with figures propelled to meet, cross, and interchange partners; and the interest of the performance lies in the neat execution of the steps and the disposition of the final *tableau.*

Brome's friends defended the moral purpose of his plays, but his comedy is not meant to cure excesses. He could not have seen an image of universal folly in the fripperies of *Bartholomew Fair,* nor aroused the echo of "vanity of vanities" that rings through that play. He presents a society made up like a jig-saw puzzle, so that nearly all the parts are irregular, and he may elicit laughter or sentiment as he fits them together; both responses are tempered by his clever indifference.

The author's weakest play is *The Novella.* It is 'prentice-work in every sense; and he chose an unsuitable fable. But his mistakes show the compulsion of the rising drama. An Italian scene and a simple elopement are the essentials of this play, and these are characteristically Elizabethan. They are not improved by Brome's elaboration of a doubly crossed marriage, a spurned lady disguised as a strumpet, a substituted bedfellow, and the other set moves of his comic game. His one attempt at a poetic surrender to the theme of gold, which in its beauty and viciousness was an Elizabethan obsession, is decidedly prosaic. This Italy is no more the glittering rank palace of a Machiavel grown legendary; Venice is a curious place that the latest traveller described. Dress, balconies, gondolas, all receive the attention which an observer of style would give to foreign peculiarities. In his *Trappolin* Sir Aston Cockain filled two play-book pages with a versified guide to his European tour. Italy had been spoiled for the hero and the villain, and romancers escaped to Greece and the "Persian scene."

Brome turned the same inquisitive eye upon England and London. His remarks upon the architectural novelties are too long to be concealed stage-directions. Beyond illustrating the temper of London life, his allusions betray an interest in local color for its own sake. His two "original" characters, the "country-thing" Constance and the re-claimed vagabond Springlove, are nostalgic studies in rustic custom. Indeed Brome's collection of rusticities is the only excuse for *A Joviall Crew,* which was made into an opera in the next century and continued to satisfy an appetite for antiquarian folklore. The studiously picturesque scenes written in gypsy cant are scarcely related to the slight framing plot in which young ladies of the country try out the joys of a roving life with their lovers in Shakesperian fashion, and admit that Touchstone was right about Arden. Middleton's *Spanish Gypsy* has been accepted as the "source" of Brome's play, but there is no born gypsy in it. The exiled courtiers who are thus disguised feel the necessities and the beauties of their state much more romantically than Brome's heroines remember their night in the straw; so do the vagabonds of Fletcher's *Beggars Bush,* another "source." Perhaps it is no accident that *A Joviall Crew* is reminiscent of *As You Like It,* instead of the gypsy plays of Middleton and Fletcher.

III

While Brome among the humbler Sons of Ben was diverting Jonsonian comedy into fresh channels, he was ready to adapt the tragicomedy of "neat Fletcher" cultivated by his aristocratic rivals. The two masters are not far apart, for the slippery versification and thin conceits in Fletcher's plays were affected by the courtier's verse which he wrote on the model of Jonson's, who confessed that "next to himself he (Fletcher) could make a masque." Brome however inherited not one lyric grace, and *The Love-sick Court* is a dull play, lacking all the ethereal hyperbole that carries heroic contests of love and friendship into a favorable climate. The sub-plot of gentlemen's gentlemen belongs to the higher London world which he knew better. In the midst of a movement to refine the stage, Brome tried to write graceful poetry and he speaks as awkwardly as the would-be gentlemen in his own plays. In *The Love-sick Court* there is at least a geometrical story which Beaumont might have approved; but *The Queen's Exchange* and *The Queen and Concubine* belong to the later school of Fletcher, where theatrical intrigue is obscured in a series of wonders and discoveries. Brome is happier even in the "sugry" scene of the latter play in Queen Eulalia's village-school than in a soliloquy upon the delights of pastoral solitude. *The Queen's Exchange* is patched up from late Shakespearian themes which have lost their enchantment; and where a courtly amateur would have given his time to the conflict of love and duty, Brome is distracted by buried treasure in the cellar and *amours* in the butler's pantry.

By inclination a dramatist of the *minutiae* and the temper of daily life, he found at the end of his career, not long before the closing of the theatres, that romance and refinement had banished "merry jigges":

> We wish you, then, would change that expectation,
> Since Joviall Mirth is now grown out of fashion.
> Or much not to expect: For, now it chances,
> (Our Comick Writer finding that *Romances*
> Of Lovers, through much travell and distresse,
> Till it be thought, no Power can redresse
> Th' afflicted Wanderers, though stout Chevalry
> Lend all his aid for their delivery;
> Till, lastly, some impossibility
> Concludes all strife, and makes a Comedie)
> Finding (he saies) such Stories bear the sway,
> Near as he could, he has compos'd a *Play,*
> Of *Fortune-tellers, Damsels,* and their Squires ...[6]

The play thus introduced is refined in Brome's own way, and it affords the earliest example of the word "genteel" in its present sense. Whereas Brome fails to create romantic illusions just as he failed to recreate Dekker's pathos, in his comedy he can reach the level of aristocratic conversation. In *A Joviall Crew* he catches the accent of the country gentry as successfully as Shirley set down the gossip of fashionable London:

Vincent:

> ... Shall we project a journey for you? your Father has trusted you, and will think you safe in our company; and we would fain be abroad upon som progress with you. Shall we make a fling to *London,* and see how the Spring appears there in the *Spring-Garden*; and in *Hidepark,* to

see the Races, Horse and Foot; to hear the *Jockies* crack; and see the *Adamites* run naked afore the Ladies?

RACHEL:

We have seen all already there, as well as they, last year.

HILLIARD:

But there ha' been new *Playes* since.

RACHEL:

No: no: we are not for *London* . . .

VINCENT:

. . . Will you up to the hill top of sports, then, and Merriments, *Dovors Olimpicks* or the *Cotswold Games.*

MERIEL:

No, that would be too publique for our Recreation. We would have it more within our selves.[7]

The banter of the ladies with their lovers sustains the light "anti-romantic" drift of the whole escapade. Brome had raised his witty women above the monotony of City talk before, especially in *The Court Begger* of a year or so earlier. Lady Strangelove's dialogue with her suitors and their back-chat with Philomel in the lobby are thoroughly urbane. (Brome tends to enter great houses through servant's quarters.) Millamant's voice is audible in the early thirties behind the mask of Widow Fitchow:

> . . . let me studie my remembrance for after Marriage. *Imprimis.* To have the whole sway of the house, and all domestical affairs, as of accounts of household charges, placing and displacing of all servants in general; To have free liberty, to go on all my visits; and though my Knights occasions be never so urgent, and mine of no moment, yet to take from him the command of his Coach. . . .[8]

There are more glimpses of genteel nonchalance in *A Mad Couple Well Match'd,* rough contemporary with *The Court Begger.* The two suitors in this play are equally remarkable for polish and inconsiderateness. Jonson's Truewit and Alamode in *Epicoene* were the first of a succession of young men-about-town to have more distinguished manners than First and Second Gentlemen, but they dealt in harmlessly poetical compliments. The portrait of an attractive rake is an innovation, and it is interesting to compare it with the much more unflattering picture which Brome painted seven years earlier in *The Covent-Garden Weeded.*

IV

The population of Caroline drama is changing. In Brome's world a gentleman's wit is worth more than a poet's and the value of good sense is rising fast. A sensible woman rarely appeared on the Jacobean stage with the exception of Shakespeare's Beatrice and her kind. The sober good sense with which Brome endowed Mrs. Fitchow is characteristic of the Caroline woman; and the study stands in relief against his skit upon the ridiculous stage widow in

The City Wit. Mrs. Fitchow is matched by his benevolent and endearingly eccentric Lafoy and his sensible fathers and country squires. The subject of enforced marriage takes a new turn through the contrast between these liberal parents and the old disciplinarians. It is no longer a source of individual ruin or an opportunity for showing how to tame a shrew; the lovers are not star-crossed and only a miserly father would interfere with their choice. A tribe of pampered idiots proposed as eligible husbands render the misers even more disagreeable. Of course, the outwitting of the old by the young is a Plautine staple, and the University dramatists must have refreshed the London stage from its springs in Rome. When various Jonsonian drinking academies turn into covert brothels in *The Sparagus Garden* and *The New Academy,* Brome's transformation may be ascribed to the same influence.

Brome's contribution of wit, sense, and refinement was made in prose or in an unobtrusive colloquial verse. He twinkles in a constellation of lesser dramatists who prepare for the Restoration stars. The novelty of his technique is important, because apart from their style some of his plays seem closer to Elizabethan court comedy than to the serious caricature of Jonson or the serious hyperbole of Fletcher. In *A Joviall Crew* he pricks bubbles as lightly as Shakespeare; there is no comedy so clear between Shakespeare and the younger disciples of Jonson. The whole chasm between poetry and prose divides the new comedy from the old, but in both the essence of a play is its style and shape. It is not governed by the passions which dominate the Jacobean stage, and which finally break the mould of Jonsonian comedy and of tragedy. The style is new and the incidents are Jonsonian, but there is an Elizabethan touch even to comedies like *The Court Begger* and *A Mad Couple Well Match'd.* It can be felt distinctly in *The Antipodes,* where Brome has invented a lunar world; only his regions are below the earth, and they mirror not man's intellect and senses but the absurdities of his outward habits. Bypassing the whipping satire of the Jacobeans, Brome's inversion of the classical myth seems to carry him back to the Elizabethans and the ancients. Craftsmanship and sophistication go to make the last scenes, where one lunacy invades another and the theatrical illusion vanishes like a last bubble.

The Antipodes is also a throwback to Tudor design. The sequence of sketches is patterned upon the entrances of characters in an interlude; the persons are mouthpieces of topical fads and fancies. The play-within-a-play allowed the Elizabethans to relate their characters to the outer world, because it simplified the main action by reflecting it in miniature. The infatuation of the "audience" and the foolery of the "actors" in *The Antipodes* produce a parallel development of "matter" and "mirth"; a movement which belongs to the form of the morality, and often appears in Brome's last plays. In *The Court Begger* Mendicant is outwitted like an orthodox Plautine legacy hunter, but his downfall is presented as the fate of a sinner, and his progress is diversified by the antics of apes and fools, who are stripped of their vanities in turn.

The return of the interlude is sponsored by Jonson's last plays, where his systematization of character has run its course and come round to simplicity again. His favorite "son," Thomas Randolph, took up his allegorical method and found that it mixed easily with the conventions of the Latin Show in which he was trained. In *The Muses Looking-Glass* he wrote a moral play-within-a-play that is constructed much like **The Antipodes.** In both plays the substance of an interlude is presented in the style of natural conversation, more conspicuous in Brome's because his verse is more unstressed and prosaic. But the revival of Tudor techniques in this period spreads beyond the imitations of Jonson's "dotages." Brome repeatedly introduces a masque to epitomise the social implications of his London comedies, and John Ford uses dance and dumbshow to crystallize the mood which is the meaning of his tragedy. Since the writing of light comedy had lapsed for more than two decades, some likenesses in the construction of Elizabethan and Caroline plays are inevitable; both are characterized by the pervasive style indispensable to comedy.

The real tragedy of the Caroline stage is made out of the same matter; it springs from an attitude and a situation, instead of passion and will. The imagery of Ford throws out ideas instead of enlarging or defining them; the poet's grip begins to loosen in Webster, last of the Jacobeans, who instils a single note into all his emotions. Their metaphor is a corollary of the neat colloquial wit practised by Jonson's followers.

V

Touching moral intention, there has been more recent argument about Brome. It has turned upon his observation of poetic justice, or rather his violation of it, in *A Mad Couple Well Match'd.* There is really a confusion of two standards in his time, precipitated by the Puritan attacks upon any exhibition of vice. The early Tudor plays were so purely imaginative, or so didactic, that the first neoclassicists could profess that poetry showed virtue and vice in brighter colors besides distributing rewards and punishments justly. The growing tragedy was on the contrary expressive, not instructive; and so were the deeper scenes of Jonsonian comedy. Jonson accordingly adopted the medicinal theory of satire, which claimed to purge vice by making it ridiculous: a theory that could be used to justify the grossest exhibition as the most moral. This position was undermined by the courtier-dramatists as doggedly as by their Puritan enemies. They wanted to expunge barbarities, and display an exalted virtue triumphant. The doctrine of poetic justice was equally open to abuse; it allowed an opportunist like James Shirley to invent scenes of exquisite pruriency and reveal in the last act that they were meant as a trial of pure virtue.

Brome was an uncritical writer and his plays fall between two stools. Inasmuch as he frequented the City more than the Court, his tavern and brothel scenes bear the Jonsonian moral stamp and usually end in the discomfiture of the customers. On the other hand, in the romances, and even in a London play like **The English Moor,** he is intent upon achieving the reward of virtue and the ruin of villainy. Sometimes these conclusions are awkwardly mixed, and the machinations that tested the heroine's virtue are dissipated into absurdity. Valentine in **A Mad Couple Well Match'd** is a rake whom Brome could neither punish nor cheat, because he had to save him for his *dénouement.* Brome was apparently associated with the aristocratic school in moral questions; Alexander Brome refers to the cleanness of his page in opposition to the obscenities of an earlier age:

> *I love thee* for thy *neat* and *harmlesse wit,*
> Thy *Mirth* that does so *cleane* and *closely hit* …[9]

Another compliment that occurs in innumerable commendatory verses praises the author's clarity; and Alexander Brome duly paid it:

> No stradling Tetrasyllables are brought
> To fill up room, and little spell, or nought.
> No Bumbast Raptures, and no lines immense,
> That's call'd (by th' curtesie of *England*) sence.
> But all's so plaine, that one may see, he made it
> T' inform the understanding, not invade it.[10]

The renewal of comic writing may well be encouraged by such grumbling dissatisfaction with turgid verse. The lyricists were tired of inarticulate Donnish conceits, and the playwrights found the tragedies which retained them primitive and preposterous. The clowning was silly and the rant was vulgar. Even Brome, the maker of "merry jigges," deplored the bad old days in 1638:

> … in the dayes of *Tarlton* and *Kempe*
> Before the stage was purg'd from barbarisme,
> And brought to the perfection it now shines with.
> Then fooles and jesters spent their wits, because
> The Poets were wise enough to save their own
> For profitabler uses …[11]

One spring of that casual indifference which is the breath of a comedy of manners rises from the parody of tragic seriousness. It is faintly perceptible in the Jacobean tragedies; the flippancies which Chapman interspersed among political issues cast a skeptical pettiness over great actions. Skepticism grows into the political themes of Beaumont and Fletcher and into the tragicomedies of Shirley. The manoeuvres of first ministers and favorites and the miry smartness of servants alternate with dialogue rarefied above all apparent meaning. The pastoral illusion destroys itself. When nobility is banished into Arcadia, the first touch of cynical realism makes Arcadia itself vanish. These plays are fundamentally divided, and they do really provide comic relief. Brome already felt the artificialities of disillusion: his songs have the usual operatic burden,

The frantique mirth
And false Delights of frolique earth.[12]

Ford was alone in seeing tragedy within the death of tragedy. To all the rest of Brome's immediate contemporaries it was a source of amusement. Randolph mimicked poetic bombast and Puritan outlandishness in the same breath, and Field made his tragic poet a Ninny who filled his emptiness with "Newington conceits"; as he said, he had been "vexed with vile plays" himself a great while. The garret poet enters the Caroline stage alongside the antiquary; both are cranks who live outside the world of affairs, and cultivate one recondite faculty at the expense of sociability. Brome's pompous Bounce and his lachrymose Sir Stephen Whimblie are near ancestors of the Augustan hack and virtuoso. In his simulated tragic raptures there is a dash of the next age's flair for mock-heroic.

Some of the Caroline poets were quite aware of the trends of the times. Brome was Jonson's servant in nothing more truly than in incorporating ghosts of the past and wraiths of the future into his *dramatis personae*. The comedy of manners is more securely grounded by the labors of Brome and Nabbes and Shirley than it would have been if the Killigrews and Carliles had written unrivalled. Between them, the two dramatic clans began to draw the fine taste and accuracy which were always admired in Jonson's comedy out of the image and into the remark; out of poetry into prose.

Notes

1. The plays of certain date are: *A Fault in Friendship,* 1623 (lost); *The Love-sick Maid,* 1628 (lost); *The Novella,* 1632; *The Sparagus Garden,* 1635; *The Antipodes,* 1638; *A Joviall Crew,* 1641.

   Approximate dates can be given for: *The Love-sick Court,* c. 1626; *The Northern Lasse,* before 1632; *The Covent-Garden Weeded,* c. 1632; *The Late Lancashire Witches* (revision of Heywood's play), before 1634; *The Queen's Exchange,* before 1635; *The Life and Death of Sir Martin Skink* and *The Apprentices Prise* (lost revisions of Heywood), before 1635. *The Queen and Concubine,* 1629-1637; *The English Moor,* 1637-1639; *The Court Begger* and *A Mad Couple Well Match'd,* 1639-1642.

   No dates are known for: *The Damoiselle, The New Academy,* and *The City Wit*; or for *Wit in a Madness, Christianetta,* and *The Jewish Gentleman* (lost plays). They were not protected for the King's Men in 1641 or for Beeston's Boys in 1639, and are probably the missing Salisbury Court and Cockpit plays for 1635-1639; possibly they are earlier plays for the Blackfriars or the Red Bull.

2. II, A5r.

3. III, (230).

4. William Cartwright, *Comedies,* 1651, 4*3r (cancellans).

5. II, 29 (*The Covent-Garden Weeded*); 22 (*The New Academy*); 21 (*The Queen and Concubine*).

6. III, (351).

7. II, 372-73.

8. III, 14.

9. III, (349).

10. I, vii.

11. III, 260.

12. II, 1 v. (*The Queen and Concubine*).

Robert C. Evans (essay date 1989)

SOURCE: Evans, Robert C. "Richard Brome's Death." *Notes and Queries* 36.3 (1989): 351. Print.

[*In the following essay, Evans presents evidence of Brome's admission to the Charterhouse, a London home for impoverished gentlemen. In addition to giving a precise date of death for Brome (24 September 1652), Charterhouse records confirm that the author was in dire financial straits during the last years of his life.*]

The date of Richard Brome's death, like that of his birth, has long been a matter of conjecture. Apparently he was alive at some point during 1652, since the dedication to his play *A Jovial Crew,* published that year, implies as much. Similarly, a statement by Alexander Brome published in 1653 implies that by that year, Richard Brome had died. These data led Brome's latest biographer, Catherine M. Shaw, to conclude that the playwright's death must have occurred 'in late 1652 or early 1653.'[1] Evidence lately found among the records of the Charterhouse provides an exact date for Brome's death and also tells us something about his circumstances in his final period.

Charterhouse, a charitable 'hospital' endowed by the wealthy money-lender Thomas Sutton, was designed to provide housing for poor gentlemen as well as lodging and schooling for needy boys. Established in 1611, by mid-century the institution had developed a widespread reputation as one of the most sterling examples of English Protestant philanthropy.[2] Brome's admission to the Charterhouse provides independent confirmation of what always has been widely assumed—that his final years were financially impoverished.[3] Yet his admission also indicates something about the esteem in which he was held, since applicants for admission to the Charterhouse required letters of recommendation from prominent people, and since not all applicants were accepted. Brome must not only have seemed to need charity but also to have seemed worthy of it.

An entry in the early register of Charterhouse (on fo. 30^r) reads as follows:[4]

> Richard Brome
>
> entr at o$^{[ur]}$ Lady day
>
> 1650. dyed on fryday
>
> the 24 of September
>
> 1652

Lady Day, 25 March, is mentioned in many other records from the register, along with various other festival days; this fact seems to suggest that the dates of entry listed were conventional or approximate. However, the date of Brome's death is helpfully exact and specific; this datum seems finally to end any uncertainty about the circumstances in which he spent his last days and about the date on which he died.

Notes

1. Catherine M. Shaw, *Richard Brome* (Boston, 1980), 17.

2. On Sutton see, for instance, Gerald S. Davies, *Charterhouse in London: Monastery, Mansion, Hospital, School* (London, 1921).

3. See, for instance, R. J. Kaufmann, *Richard Brome: Caroline Playwright* (New York and London, 1961), 33.

4. Most of the Charterhouse records now have been transferred to the Greater London Record Office, where a reproduction of the register exists on microfilm reel X76/1.

Tiffany Stern (essay date 2001)

SOURCE: Stern, Tiffany. "Behind the Arras: The Prompter's Place in the Shakespearean Theatre." *Theatre Notebook* 55.3 (2001): 110-18. Print.

[*In the following essay, Stern argues that in the early modern playhouse, the prompter—the person who assisted actors with forgotten lines—typically stood offstage in the tiring-house, or dressing room, of the theater. Stern supports this contention with descriptions of the prompter's role and position in works by Brome and several other roughly contemporary playwrights.*]

It has long been an open question as to where the prompter sat—or, indeed, stood—in the early modern theatre. From his position, was he visible to the audience? Could he watch *and* hear the play? And could he be seen *and* heard by the actors? The new Globe ('Shakespeare's Globe') has, of course, run up against this problem, and the answer its researchers originally reached was that the prompter sat backstage in the tiring-room: from there, it was argued, he could direct actors' entrances and exits and also, when necessary, give his prompts. Almost immediately, however, the notion started to cause difficulties. The main problem was that a prompter situated behind the new Globe's heavy oak *frons scenae* could not see or hear the actors perform; similarly actors on stage could neither see nor, again, hear the prompter. The conclusion the new Globe ultimately reached, therefore, is that the early modern prompter did not really control events on stage; specifically, that he did not, in fact, 'prompt' (as the actors would not have heard him). Despite the fact that this leaves the prompter with very few jobs to do in the theatre (even indicating the correct doors of entrance would be difficult without hearing what is happening on stage), the idea has taken on, and has been articulated in a number of books and articles as a new Globe discovery.[1] Indeed, partly as a result of this, the term 'prompter' itself is now generally eschewed in favour of 'book-holder' or 'book-keeper,' which have no obvious 'prompting' connotations.

Yet a brief look at Renaissance plays shows a marked preference for the word 'prompter' over any other. This is clear in the works of Shakespeare, who never used 'book-holder' or 'book-keeper' at all, but did write of outdated prologues 'faintly spoke / After the Prompter' (*Romeo and Juliet*, perf. Theatre, 1594-6), and cues that do not need prompting ('Were it my Cue to fight, I should haue knowne it / Without a Prompter' (*Othello*, TLN 301, perf. Globe, 1603-04)).[2] Moreover, glossaries from the period both use the word 'prompter,' and, unsurprisingly, describe his main function as 'prompting': 'a prompter': explains Thomas Thomas in his 1587 *Dictionarium* is 'he that telleth the players their parte.'[3] True, this same functionary seems sometimes to have been known as book-holder or book-keeper, names that at first glance imply more of a concern with caring for the theatre's full playtext, the 'book,' than helping out actors who are stuck. But what was the purpose of 'holding' a book during performance, in view of the fact that practical business, like entrances, exits and props, seem to have been covered by a different document (the 'plat' or 'plot' of the play which hung backstage)?[4] In fact it is perfectly clear that the prompter 'held the book' in order to prompt from it: when Thomas Rogers, for instance, conjectures a metaphorical theatre in which to place contemporary political characters, he suggests 'lame brooke' [Henry or his brother George Brooke] should 'hould the booke, and sit him still / to prompte, if any mist or acted ill.'[5] In fact, so connected were holding the book and prompting that the verb 'to hold the book' was sometimes itself used to mean 'to prompt.' Thus Will Summers in Nashe's *Summer's Last Will* [perf. Whitgift's household? 1592] asks the prompter to 'holde the booke well,' as a way of ensuring that 'we be not *non plus* in the latter end of the play.'[6] It is no surprise, then, that the titles 'book-holder,' 'book-keeper' and 'prompter' were, like the activities they represented, interchangeable: John Higgins in his *Nomenclator* describes 'He that telleth the players their part when they are out and have forgotten' as 'the prompter or booke-holder';[7] Florio in his *Worlde of Wordes* defines 'Burriasso' as 'a prompter, or one that keepes the book for plaiers.'[8]

Despite the modern tendency to favour the terms 'book-holder' and 'book-keeper' over 'prompter,' the early play-house accepted all three, but had a clear preference for 'prompter.' My rough count of plays performed before 1660 that refer to the functionary, shows five opting for 'book-holder' (three of which are by Jonson),[9] two, 'book-keeper' (the term also used by Henry Herbert, Master of the Revels),[10] and ten, 'prompter.'[11]

This paper sets out to show that the person whom, for ease of reference, and because of the subject of this article, I will call the 'prompter,' was indeed situated in the tiring-room. That fact is mentioned in passing by Braithwait, when he compares the world to a theatre in which 'Man must needes be an Actor. The Booke-holder stands in the Tyring-house; but the Action must be presented on the Stage.'[12] But I will extend the argument to suggest that the prompter was situated specifically behind the curtain that separated tiring-room and stage; from here his commands and prompts *could* easily be heard: and from here he was also able, when necessary, to peep out to see the action.

Firstly, it is clear that in early modern theatres what was said backstage could be heard on the stage and vice versa: plays of the time harp metatheatrically on the to-and-fro between both places. One prologue begs for silence because 'I heare the players prest, in presence foorth to come': the prologue on stage, hears someone off stage, telling the actors to enter.[13] That that someone was the prompter is suggested by Brome's ***Antipodes,*** in which a voice emanates from 'within' urging 'Dismisse the Court,' to which Letoy responds, 'Dismisse the court, cannot you heare the prompter?.'[14] The reverse was also the case: people situated behind the *frons scenae* could hear what was happening on the other side, as is illustrated by the simple fact that the actors' notice of entrance was a verbal 'cue' or 'watchword' from the stage (consisting of the last one, two or three words to be spoken before they were due to emerge). On hearing the entrance cue, actors needed to go out onto the stage immediately. So Shakespeare in *A Midsummer Night's Dream* [perf. Theatre, 1596], has Bottom/Pyramus give out his line 'Curst be thy stones for thus deceiuing mee,' followed by the explanation, '*Deceiuing me* / is Thisbies cue; she is to enter, and I am to spy / Her through the wall' (TLN 1983-6); while George Wilkins, perhaps co-writer, with Shakespeare, of *Pericles,* describes in his prose narrative *Pericles Prince of Tyre,* the moment when the Pander told Marina 'that the Lorde Lysimachus was come, and as if the word Come had beene his kew, he entred the Chamber.'[15] Butler in his 1633 *English Grammar* defines a 'Q' as 'a note of entrance for actors ... showing when to enter and speak';

and many plays casually refer to the use of entrance cues: 'She's perfect, & will come out vpon her qu, I warrant you'; 'step aside, and come when thy que is'; 'she hath entred the Dutches iust at her que'; and so forth.[16] Surviving 'play-books' (playhouse texts marked up for theatrical use) sometimes show the names of actors added into the margins a few lines in advance of their actual entrance, which confirms that there was good audibility between front- and back-stage—for the prompter (or perhaps, as in later theatres, a call-boy) needed to hear when that specific moment had been reached in performance in order to ready the players in the tiring-house for entrance. These players, then, presumably stood by a portal listening for the cue itself. In other words, people back-stage and people on stage relied on hearing each other.

But how could they hear each other through heavy wooden doors? One obvious answer is that the doors were kept open through the performance, and were covered over by much lighter hangings. Dictionaries and glossaries would seem to promote this hypothesis. Thomas in his *Dictionarium* defines 'cortina' as 'the couered place in a stage, whence the players come out'; and numerous other texts suggest the regular use of curtained areas that gave straight from the tiring-house to the stage, the famous references to clowns peeping between curtains (Tarlton sticking his head 'The Tire-house doore and Tapistrie betweene,' Reed 'peeping through the Curtain') being the most obvious.[17] Hangings through which a hidden actor could 'peep' are used to embellish the story of various plays—as when Volpone '*peepes from behinde a trauerse,*' or Cromwell enters in *King Charles I,* '*having been seen to peep through the hangings, during the Colloquie*'; or '*Fresco peepes fearefully forth from behinde the Arras.*'[18] Playhouse curtains were also used for more furtive practical purposes. Players, for instance, are described as sneaking a look through them to find out how many people had come to watch the performance: would this be a good house or not? Davenant, writing in the 1640s about the theatres of the past, mentions how the 'halfe dress'd Player' would stare 'Through th' hangings' in order 'to see how th' house did fill.'[19] References from various plays of the period suggest that there was a curtained area for concealing a player, through which the hidden actor could hear everything: 'I would you ... had beene behind the Arras but to haue heard her'; 'wee'le stand behind the Arras & heare all.'[20] Whether entrance doors, discovery spaces, or both are being used in this fashion, it certainly seems to have been normal to have at least some curtained access between tiring-house and stage.

Shakespeare, who wrote specifically for the Globe Theatre, certainly used hangings regularly. He had Polonius convey himself 'Behinde the Arras ... To heare the Process' in *Hamlet* (TLN 2302-4); Falstaff decides to 'ensconce mee behinde the Arras' in *The Merry Wives* (TLN 1430); while the executioners in *King John* are told to go 'hence, and watch' from a position 'Within the Arras' (TLN 1575, 1572). Of course, many of these references are part of the 'fiction' of the story—but they are backed up by a host of stage-directions confirming the regular use of hangings in the Globe and elsewhere. Dessen and Thomson quote fifteen plays in which stage directions directly refer to characters behind the arras, nine in which they are behind the hangings, five in which they go behind the curtains, and two in which they hide behind traverses.[21] To these I would add a reference from the 'plot' of *Alcazar,* a Rose Theatre play: 't>o them <1>lying behind the Curt<a>ines 3 Furies.'[22] Doubtless a 'curtain rail' could have been fixed up on stage if a moveable arras were necessary—but, significantly, characters behind curtains do not always have to enter back out on to the stage in order to effect their exits. Going through curtains often amounts to going off stage—a further indication that at least one covered space opened directly onto the back-stage area. And as for characters who re-enter—re-entries illustrate the total audibility which the curtain provided, for from behind there performers have no problem picking up on their entrance cue.

The difficulty with becoming any more precise than this, is that the configuration of the *frons* and the placement of the curtains in the early modern playhouse are still matters of dispute. Not all theatres necessarily had a central discovery space—the Swan, for instance, does not have one in the notorious Van Buchell/De Witt drawing.[23] But as Tim Fitzpatrick and Wendy Millyard suggest in a fascinating reinterpretation of the evidence, the tiring-house wall in 'round theatres' may have been curved to follow the cants of the polygonal structure of the building. If that were the case, then the *frons* would have contained a hollow space in its middle that could be curtained off and turned into a central discovery space.[24] Alternatively the two doorways alone may have constituted the space in question: their wooden doors could have been pinned back for performance, with curtains hung across the gap and drawn back to reveal discoveries.[25] Dessen and Thomson show that on a surprising number of occasions the knocking sound for a door was made from 'within,' and the temporary absence of a real door could explain why. It is also possible that every portal was curtained: in literature of the time entrances are frequently described as happening *through* hangings.

Here I am simply concerned to demonstrate that hangings were regularly used, that they were used for listening through and peeping out of, and that at least some of them led straight to the tiring-house. For this argument has direct bearing on the position of the prompter who needed to be somewhere where he could hear what was being said by the actors (in order to prompt), to see, selectively, what was happening on stage (in order to control stage-business), and yet to be hidden from public view. And when we turn to the anonymous *Lady Alimony* (published in 1659, but thought to be a revision of a Caroline play) we find a suggestion that he did indeed stand behind a curtain. For in that play, a playwright and a book-holder hold a scene-setting conversation. Both, it emerges, have names relevant to their profession. The playwright is called Timon because of his 'rich *Timonick* Fancy,' while the '*Booke-holder* to my Revels for decads [*sic*] of years' is named 'Siparius,' curtain.[26]

The precise definition of 'siparium' is given by Thomas Thomas in his 1587 *Dictionarium*: 'a courtaine or veile drawne when the players come vpon the stage'—the siparium is a curtained place of entrance.[27] But in *Lady Alimony,* the space covered by the hanging is more precisely identified. Timon asks Siparius the question designed to explain the latter's title: 'Be your Stage-curtains artificially drawn, and so covertly shrouded, as the squint-ey'd Groundling may not peep in to your discovery?'[28] The curtains in question cover a 'discovery space': in this play at any rate, prompter, curtains and discovery-space are all linked together.

A curtained space also, on occasion, held another person who was concerned to hear and watch the play without being seen by the audience: the playwright (or play-reviser). On the first performance of a new play, poets were generally in attendance but 'hidden.' They were anxious to discover whether their text had been 'damned' (or, as they hoped, greeted with a 'plaudite'), and to find out what changes, if any, the audience wished them to make.[29] This is how the author's position is described. In Beaumont and Fletchers' *The Woman-Hater,* the trembling poet 'towardes the latter end of [his] new play' stands 'peeping betwixt curtains,' so scared of failure that he mistakes the opening of bottled ale for a hiss [perf. Paul's, 1606]. Similarly in Shirley's *The Duke's Mistress,* the poet is 'listning behind the arras / To heare what will become on's Play' [perf. Cockpit, 1636]; while in **The English Moore** Brome is keen no one should accuse him of skulking 'behind the hangings' as though he were afraid of receiving 'a hard censure' [perf. Salisbury Court, 1637] (he had, however, on 13 October 1614, hovered with Jonson—whose servant he was—'behind the Arras' to watch how the 'new sufficient Play' of *Bartholomew Fair* was received).[30] When Glapthorne in *Ladies Privilege* describes the playwright as standing 'pensive in the / Tyring-house to heare / Your Censures of his Play' [perf. Cockpit, 1637-40], he indicates both that the poet's place is 'in the tiring-house,' and that he *can* hear what is happening on stage from there.[31] Moreover, from his first-performance hidey-hole, the author tends also to take on tasks otherwise more usual to the prompter: prompting, and helping with entrances and exits. In Shirley's *The Cardinal* the actor Pollard starts his epilogue by claiming that he has just been 'thrust on stage' by the author himself

> I am coming to you, Gentlemen, the Poet
> Has help'd me thus far on my way, but I'l
> Be even with him . . .[32]

There will have been a limited number of curtained spaces free for backstage functionaries: the one occupied by the poet is, I hesitantly suggest, the same as that occupied by the prompter.

Precisely which aperture the prompter occupied depends on what we take to be the configuration of the theatre in question. He could hide behind either the right or left curtained entrance door or in the middle 'discovery space.' If the central enclosure was as it is in the present new Globe, then the constant use which prompter and author had for it would explain why set-piece 'discoveries' are not very often required there by Globe plays—an observation made some years ago by Bernard Beckerman.[33] If on the other hand, all the portals were curtained, he could move around backstage from one to another as appropriate.

Having curtained entrances in 'Shakespeare's Globe' would also be useful for a number of other reasons. It would improve audibility between back and front stage, and give actors quieter and less time-consuming entrances. All of this, on one level, Shakespeare's Globe recognises. Its doors are, these days, covered with hangings for some productions, and new possibilities for the arrangement of the *frons* are being examined: in a recent workshop, curtains of different weight and texture were placed over the various openings, and actors were asked to use them to explore entrances, concealments and funny business.[34] That won't, of course, deal with the the fact that beautifully constructed new Globe, with its carefully crafted solid wooden frame, is simply too well built to allow the free-flow of sound between tiring-house and stage that probably naturally occurred in the actual Globe—a playhouse assembled out of the pared-down left-overs from an earlier theatre. But it will, perhaps, encourage new thinking, and possibly lead to actual discoveries, not just about the coverings themselves, but also about associated questions, like the real position and role of the prompter.

Notes

1. See, for instance, Scott McMillin and Sally-Beth Mac-Lean, *The Queen's Men and Their Plays*, Cambridge, 1998, 116; Andrew Gurr, 'Maximal and Minimal Texts: Shakespeare V. The Globe,' *Shakespeare Survey*, LII, 1999, 68-87. See also Gurr's 'Stage Doors at the Globe,' *Theatre Notebook*, LIII, 1999, 8-18, for the alternative suggestion that cues cannot be heard backstage because of the nature of the doors—a point I enlarge on.

2. William Shakespeare, *Romeo and Juliet*, 1597, Cla; *Othello* in William Shakespeare, *The First Folio*, facs. ed. Charlton Hinman, New York, 1968—all subsequent Shakespearean references will be to this edition. Dates and place of first performance are taken from Alfred Harbage and S. Schoenbaum, *Annals of English Drama: 975-1700*, London, 1964.

3. Thomas Thomas, *Dictionarium Linguae Latinae et Anglicanae*, 1587, definition of 'monitor.'

4. See W. W. Greg, *Dramatic Documents*, I, 1-171.

5. From Folger MS X.d.241 fols 1v-3, attrib. Thomas Rogers, quoted in *The Poems of Sir Walter Raleigh: A Historical Edition* ed. Michael Rudick, Tempe, Arizona, 1999, 184.

6. Thomas Nashe, *The Works of Thomas Nashe,* ed. R. B. McKerrow, 2nd edn., rev. F. P. Wilson, 5 vols., Oxford, 1958, III, 290. See also *Maid in the Mill* in Francis Beaumont and John Fletcher, *The Dramatic Works,* ed. Fredson Bowers, 9 vols., Cambridge, 1966-94, IX, 601 [perf. Globe/2nd Blackfriars, 1623]: 'they are out of their parts sure, It may be 'tis the Book-holders fault: Ile go see'; and *Lady Alimony,* 1659, A3a [perf. Rhodes' Company at Cockpit?, 1559]: 'Be sure, that you hold not your Book at too much distance: the Actors, poor Lapwings, are but pen-feathred: and once out, out for ever.'

7. John Higgins, *The Nomenclature, or Remembrancer of Adrianus Junius, Physician,* 1585, 501.

8. John Florio, *Worlde of Wordes,* 1598. The two are paired and equated again by Taylor the water-poet, who used to know 'one *Thomas Vincent* that was a Book-keeper or prompter at the Globe play-house': see John Taylor, *Works,* 3 vols., 1630, III, 70. John Downes, writing in 1708, described himself as 'Book-keeper and Prompter' to Davenant's men in his *Roscius Anglicanus,* ed. Judith Milhous and Robert D. Hume, London, 1987, 2.

9. For Fletcher's *Maid in the Mill,* see note 6. In Jonson's *Cynthia's Revels* [perf. Paul's, 1600-01] the poet does not, claim the boys, 'stampe at the booke-holder'—see Benjamin Jonson, *The Works,* ed. C. H. Herford and P. and E. Simpson, 11 vols., Oxford, 1925-52, IV, 40. 'Book-holder' is also a character in Jonson's *The Staple of News* [perf. Globe/2nd Blackfriars, 1626], and *Bartholomew's Fair* [perf. Whitefriars/Hope, 1614], as well as the anonymous *Lady Alimony.* See also John Crouch's prose and verse diatribe *Man in the Moon,* 1649, 221, in which 'Hugh Peters,' chaplain to Cromwell, is described as having been 'a *Book-holder* at the *Bull-play-house.*'

10. 'Book-keeper' is referred to in *Everie Woman in Her Humor,* 1609, F3a [perf. Whitefriar's 1599-1608?]: 'He would ... stampe and stare ... like a play-house book-keeper, when the actors misse their entrance'; and Thomas Kyd's *The Spanish Tragedy,* 1592, K3a [perf. Cross Keys Inn, 1585-89?]: 'brother, you shall be the booke-keeper. This is the argument of that they shew.'

11. 'Prompter' occurs in *Othello* and *Romeo,* as quoted. He is also a character in *Thorny Abbey,* 1662 [thought to be a redaction of a sixteenth-century play], and is spoken of in the anonymous *Timon,* Oxford, 1980, 22 [perf. Cambridge? Inner Temple? c. 1581-90]: 'Be gone from me, I neede noe prompter . . . I remember . . .'; Richard Brome, *The Antipodes* in *The Dramatic Works,* ed. R. H. Shepherd, 3 vols., 1873, III, 292 [perf. Salisbury Court, 1636-38]: 'Dismisse the court, cannot you heare the prompter?'; Thomas Goffe, *Careless Shepherdess,* 1656, 7-8 [perf. Cockpit? 1638]: spoken when an actor is 'out': 'Pox take the Prompter'; John Ford, *The Broken Heart,* 1633, C1b-C2a [perf. Globe/2nd Blackfriars, c. 1630-33]: 'I . . . but repeat a lesson Oft conn'd without a prompter'; William Hawkins, *Apollo shroving,* 1627, 58 [perf. Hadleigh school, 1626]: '. . . goe on. I am to say your Monkey will recouer. Master Prompter doe your part'; L. S. [Lewis Sharpe], *The Noble Stranger,* 1640, E3b [perf. Salisbury Court, 1638-40]: 'because she shall / Not say I speak without book this learned / Littleton shall be my prompter'; James Shirley, *Hide Park,* 1637, F2a [perf. Cockpit, 1632]: '[Have] you no prompter to insinuate / The first word of your studied Oration.' Other plays also use 'prompter'; this is only a list of texts in which specific reference to a theatrical prompter is clear. See also 'The Character of an Excellent Actor' who is described in Sir Thomas Overbury's 1615 *Characters,* as someone whose voice ''tis not lower than the prompter, nor louder than the foil and target,' ed. W. J. Taylor, Oxford, 1936, 77. The idea, widely quoted, that the word 'prompter' did not come into use until after the Restoration may also be the sideways result of an attempt to rename what has wrongly been called the 'prompt-book' the 'book': in the process theatre historians have managed also to rename the prompter the 'book-keeper,' which makes logical sense but is not borne out by the facts.

12. Richard Braithwait, *A Survey of History,* 1638, 217.

13. Nathaniel Woodes, *The Conflict of Conscience,* 1581, A2b [offered for acting, 1570-81?].

14. Brome, *Antipodes* in *Dramatic Works,* III, 292.

15. George Wilkins, *Pericles Prince of Tyre,* 1608, 59.

16. Charles Butler, *English Grammar,* 1633; Thomas Dekker, *Northwood Ho* in *Dramatic Works,* ed. Fredson Bowers, 4 vols., Cambridge, 1953-61, II, 466 [perf. Paul's, 1605]; Thomas May, *The Heire,* 1622, B4b [perf College? this ed. Red Bull, 1620]; John Day, *Ile of Guls,* 1606, D1a [perf. 2nd Blackfriars, 1606].

17. Henry Peacham, 'To Sir Ninian Ouzell' in *Thalia's Banquet,* 1620, C8a; T. Goffe, *Careless Shepherdess,* 5.

18. Jonson, *Volpone* in *Works,* V, 113 [perf. Globe, 1605-6]; *The Famous Tragedie of King Charles I,* 1649, 33 [perf. closet, 1641]; Cyril Tourneur, *Atheist's Tragedy* (1611), F1a [perf. Globe/2nd Blackfriars? 1607-11].

19. William Davenant, *The Unfortunate Lovers,* 1643, A3a [perf. Globe/2nd Blackfriars 1638].

20. George Chapman, *The Widow's Tears* in *The Plays of George Chapman: The Comedies,* ed. Allan Holaday et al., Urbana, Chicago, London, 1970, 516 [perf. 2nd Blackfriars, 1604-5]; Beaumont and Fletcher, *The Noble Gentleman* in *Dramatic Works,* III, 167 [perf. Globe/2nd Blackfriar's, 1625].

21. Alan C. Dessen and Leslie Thomson, *A Dictionary of Stage Directions in English Drama 1580-1642,* Cambridge, 1999, 12, 110, 62, 235.

22. *The Plot of Alcazar* in W. W. Greg, *Two Elizabethan Stage Abridgements,* Oxford, 1922, 28.

23. Reproduced in R. A. Foakes, *Illustrations of the English Stage 1580-1642,* London, 1985, 52-3. Gurr in 'Stage Doors,' discusses the possibility that the Swan did, in fact, have a central aperture that was either covered by hangings, or edited out by De Witt in his attempt to show how like the London playhouse was to a Roman theatre.

24. Tim Fitzpatrick and Wendy Millyard, 'Hangings, Doors and Galleries: Conflicting Evidence or Problematic Assumptions,' *Theatre Notebook,* LIV, 2000, 2-23. Their argument does not address the nature of the discovery space in square theatres, or on travelling stages.

25. A suggestion made by Richard Hosley in 'The Discovery-Space in Shakespeare's Globe,' *Shakespeare Survey,* XII, 1959, 35-46, who also discusses two alternatives: there may have been a curtained booth set against the tiring-house façade on the inside; or hangings may have been fitted along the length of the outside of the *frons scenae.* Any would make sense in conjunction with the arguments I have offered. For the suggestion that doors in the Globe theatre could be fastened both back into the tiring-house and forward against the *frons,* see Gabriel Egan, 'Geometrical Hinges and the *Frons Scenae* of the Globe,' *Theatre Notebook,* LII, 1998, 62-4.

26. *Lady Alimony,* A3a.

27. Thomas Thomas, *Dictionarium Linguae Latinae et Anglicanae,* 1587. Florio concurs in *Worlde of Wordes,* describing what he calls 'Sipario,' as 'a curtaine or vaile drawne when the players come vpon the stage.' Presumably the word is rendered in the masculine form in *Lady Alimony,* because the prompter is himself a man.

28. *Lady Alimony,* A3a.

29. See Tiffany Stern, *Rehearsal from Shakespeare to Sheridan,* Oxford, 2000, 113-20.

30. Beaumont and Fletcher *The Woman-Hater,* in *Dramatic Works,* I, 175; James Shirley, *The Duke's Mistress,* 1638, K4b; Brome, *The English Moore,* in *Dramatic Works,* II, 86; Jonson, *Bartholomew Fair,* in *Works,* VI, 13, 15.

31. Henry Glapthorne, *Ladies Privilege,* 1640, J2b. The poet is also described as being in the tyring house in Abraham Cowley, *Love's Riddle,* 1638, G4a [unacted, 1633-36]; and *Wily Beguiled,* 1606, A2b [perf. Paul's, 1601-2].

32. James Shirley, *The Cardinal,* 1652, F3b [perf. Globe/2nd Blackfriars, 1641]. Epilogues and Prologues were spoken only on the first day of performance. See Stern, *Rehearsal from Shakespeare to Sheridan,* 116.

33. See Bernard Beckerman in *Shakespeare at the Globe 1599-1609,* New York, 1962, 87. His observation that the space was used more for concealment than revelation adds to the suggestion that, for most of the performance, there were hidden people occupying that area.

34. See David Carnegie, 'Curtains and Comedy: Explorations of the Uses of Stage Hangings for Comedy at Shakespeare's Globe,' *Globe Research Bulletin Number 11,* December 1999, found on http://www.rdg.ac.uk/globe/research/1999/rb11-1299.htm. [accessed 27 August 2000].

Douglas A. Brooks (essay date 2004)

SOURCE: Brooks, Douglas A. "Inky Kin: Reading in the Age of Gutenberg Paternity." *The Book of the Play: Playwrights, Stationers, and Readers in Early Modern England.* Ed. Marta Straznicky. Amherst: U of Massachusetts P, 2006. 203-28. Print.

[*In the following essay, originally presented at a colloquium in 2004, Brooks interprets* The Antipodes *as evidence of a change in early modern attitudes toward the relationship between print and performance. Brooks contends that whereas earlier works of literature associate printing technology with virility and procreation,* The Antipodes *portrays written texts as enervating and emasculating.*]

> A madman is not only a man who thinks he is a rooster, but also a man who thinks he is directly a man—that is to say, this material body he feels directly as his own.
>
> Slavoj Žižek, *The Plague of Fantasies*

Given the focus in this part of the book on the intersections between dramas—many of which were written to be viewed in performance, not read[1]—and the early modern publishing industry, I want to concentrate in this chapter on a play that we might agree is rather readerly: Richard Brome's ***The Antipodes.***[2]

NEEDING SPECTACLES

The plot of Brome's play is centered largely on a character named Peregrine whose pathological obsession with reading travel narratives began, as his long-worrying father (Joyless) makes clear, when he was just a child:

JOYLESS:

> In tender years he always lov'd to read
> Reports of travels and of voyages.
> And when young boys like him would tire themselves
> With sports and pastimes and restore their spirits
> Again by meat and sleep, he would whole days
> And nights (sometimes by stealth) be on such books
> As might convey his fancy all round the world.

(1.1.31-37)

Now that Peregrine is a grown man "Of five and twenty" years his single-minded passion for reading threatens to undermine the dynastic future of the family name, for he has shown no conjugal interest in Martha, the wife he married "divers years since." Peregrine, to borrow a coinage of Jeffrey Masten's, prefers textual intercourse.[3] In fact, so profound is his marital negligence that Martha is naïvely compelled to interrogate another woman about the mysteries of procreation:

MARTHA:

> Pray tell me, for I think Nobody hears us,
> How came you by your babes? I cannot think
> Your husband got them you.
> . . . .
> For were I now to die, I cannot guess
> What a man does in child-getting. I remember
> A wanton maid once lay with me, and kiss'd
> And clipp'd and clapp'd me strangely, and then wish'd
> That I had been a man to have got her with child.
> What must I then ha' done, or, good now, tell me,
> What has your husband done to you?

(1.1.245-47, 251-57)

Certainly this passage has a homoerotic subtext which, in a different critical context, would be worth exploring; but my immediate interest in Martha's lack of schooling in the facts of life is somewhat superficial. Peregrine's bookish interests apparently interfere with his conjugal duties. Indeed, given the nature of Joyless's concern and the seriousness of Martha's reproductive dilemma, it could be argued that here, near the end of act 1, scene 1, reading has disrupted the relationship between a father and son, and threatens to prevent the son from ever becoming a father.

Reading and husbanding, *The Antipodes* suggests, appear to be incompatible activities—an incompatibility first intimated (in English at least) in the prologue to the *Wife of Bath's Tale* and currently evidenced by the correlation in many societies between low literacy rates and high birthrates. All is not lost, though, for in its proto-psychoanalytic wisdom, *The Antipodes* offers up a play-within-the-play as the remedy for Peregrine's reading disorder. This dramatic strategy will enable Peregrine to exorcise Mandeville's ghost on stage and to reenact his marriage to Martha as a courtly ceremony in which a royal heir is at stake in their coupling. Freud attended a production of an earlier London drama that featured a play-within-the-play and found Oedipus; Peregrine goes to a production of *The Antipodes* and finds Martha: the potency of a book's impact on his impotence is significantly dissipated once the curative power of performance is brought to bear on the specific circumstances of his malady: drama as Viagra. If only Hamlet had been less well read . . .[4]

In *The Antipodes,* then, Brome would seem to be pitting ink against kin, book against play, reading against playing, the closet against the stage—and for Peregrine, hanging in the balance of this conflict is his future as a husband and potential father. By act 4, spectators/readers of the play who might side with reading in this contest are poised to win, because Peregrine's peculiar madness appears to be contagious and spreading. Inevitably conflating us with Peregrine, a stage direction near the beginning of the act signals—to the play's audience and the play-within-the-play's audience—the following literary event:

> *Enter an* OLD WOMAN, *reading* [*a handbill*];
> *to her young* MAID [*with a book*].

(4.1.5-6)

This stage direction, this textual dumbshow-in-a-glance that silently disembodies a bit of acting and translates it onto the printed page for a future reading audience, constitutes something like a microcosm of the entire play inasmuch as it suggests the confrontation between watching a play and reading a text. (The bracketed insertions made by the play's editors further clarify the nature of the confrontation, inasmuch as they specify two very different types of texts: the former, indicating a printed handbill used by theaters to advertise plays, belongs to the world of the stage; the latter, indicating a book, belongs to the world of the page.) The Doctor, the most knowledgeable member of the-play-within-the-play's audience, indicates that something important is happening at this point when he tells Peregrine, "Stand close, sir, and observe" (4.1.7). Indeed, the moment the old woman begins to speak, one of the play's central concerns becomes legible:

> What though
> My sight be gone beyond the reach of spectacles
> In any print but this, and though I cannot—
> No, no, I cannot—read your meditations,

> [*strikes down* MAID's *book*]
> Yet I can see the royal game play'd over and over,
> And tell which dog does best, without my spectacles.
> And though I could not, yet I love the noise;
> The noise revives me, and the Bear-garden scent
> Refresheth much my smelling.

(4.1.17-23)

An old woman who can barely see to read anything smaller than the large—presumably, black-letter—type of printed handbills luxuriates in the fleshy entertainments that often preceded the performance of a play, while a maid who has presumably not yet luxuriated in the flesh prefers a book.[5]

The opposition that structures this scene, as we might expect by now, is stage versus page, the comparative quietude of reading versus the smell and noise of dying bears at the playhouses. Once upon a time, of course, the distinction between books and dying animals was less clear. After the invention of the codex a century or so before the Christian era, this new technology served for nearly 1,500 years as the main point of convergence between flesh and book. Indeed, it must have been very difficult to ignore the embodiment of the word when using a parchment codex: the difference in color between the flesh side and the hair side of any given page served as a constant reminder that one was handling the skin of a dead animal.[6] For Peregrine and the play's audience, however, reading and theater also meet in the two meanings of the word "spectacles" (staged entertainments and lenses for correcting imperfect vision); and it is hard not to think of the rusted outlines of eyeglasses that have been preserved on a few pages of some 1623 Shakespeare folios—the book that contributed so much to seventeenth-century efforts to translate Shakespeare's plays from the stage to the page.[7]

Subsequently, another character in the play-within-the-play offers a different version of the juxtaposition implied by the old woman's reference to spectacles:

GENTLEMAN:

> Nay, prithee, be not angry.
> [*arranges cloak on* SERVINGMAN's *arm*]
> Thus; and now
> Be sure you bear't at no such distance but
> As't may be known appendix to this book.

(4.1.44-47)

Books prevent Martha from bearing children, and an old woman prefers dying bears to books. Here, in something like an acting tutorial that begins with the Gentleman instructing his servingman to "Publish it, sirrah. Oh, presumptuous slave, / Display it on one arm!" (4.1.42-43), bearing a cloak is linked to a textual apparatus (appendix) that is also a body part. Furthermore, in the quoted passage I think we can glimpse what is perhaps an erudite allusion to a key moment in the New Testament when books, cloaks, and flesh share a page. Remarkably, the only Greek writer of the first century AD to mention the parchment codex is Paul in 2 Timothy 4:13: "The cloak that I left at Troas with Carpus, when thou comest, bring with thee, and the books, but especially the parchments [*membranas*]."[8] Paul's choice of words here to refer to the recent invention, the Latinate *membranas* phonetically transcribed into Greek,[9] begins to suggest why shortly after its introduction the parchment codex generated a number of rhetorical, metaphorical, and conceptual convergences between the body and the book.[10]

As the play written for the sake of curing Peregrine of his compulsive reading habits proceeds, references to various forms of reading and reading materials abound. Nevertheless, since reading is what ails him, it is only fitting that in the end, the theater carries the day. Both the play-within-the-play and the play that houses it conclude with a kind of mini-masque in which Dischord and its faction run amok for a few moments before the approach of Harmony and its followers abruptly ends their brief, chaotic reign. Accordingly, the frame play ends with an epilogue that brings the doctor and his patient back on stage to tout one other Viagric element of the theater that will presumably ensure that Peregrine finds his way back to Martha's bed after three years of marital celibacy—the audience:

DOCTOR:

> Whether my cure be perfect yet or no
> It lies not in my doctorship to know.
> Your approbation may more raise the man
> Than all the College of Physicians can,
> And more health from your fair hands may be won
> Than by the strokings of the seventh son.

PEREGRINE:

> And from our travels in th'Antipodes
> We are not yet arriv'd from off the seas;
> But on the waves of desp'rate fears we roam
> Until your gentler hands do waft us home.

Nearly twenty-five years earlier another adventurer whose love of books and excessive reading got him into trouble similarly appealed to an audience to help him return home:

> Let me not,
> Since I have my Dukedom got,
> And pardon'd the deceiuer, dwell
> In this bare Island, by your Spell,
> But release me from my bands
> With the helpe of your good hands.[11]

In an early study of the shifting relations between the stage and the page in the early modern period, Doris Fenton argues that a rupture of sorts occurred in 1616 which bifurcated the first era of the professional theater in England (1576 to 1642) into two distinct phases. Focusing on the presence of direct audience addresses in dramatic texts, Fenton notes that approximately two-thirds of the extant drama written before 1616 featured such addresses. After 1616 the use of such addresses by play-wrights declined

steeply, a change Fenton attributes to an evolving textual self-consciousness in the early modern English theater industry.[12] Thus, while these two direct theatrical addresses are thematically very similar, in light of Fenton's analysis we might expect them to be somehow different. In fact, there is one significant difference between the two plays' epilogues that is entirely consistent with Fenton's findings. In the earlier (pre-1616) play, when Prospero addresses the theater audience he gets the last word; in the latter, Peregrine's address to the audience is not the final direct address of the play. Rather, in the dramatic text that has come down to us, someone else addresses a very different kind of audience, and, in doing so, somewhat undermines the primary argument of the play that has just come to an end. As Peregrine heads off stage to give his poor wife her first— long overdue—lesson in the facts of life, the author of the play that dramatizes their bizarre story steps forward on the page to give readers the facts of the book:

> Courteous Reader,
>
> You shall find in this book more than was presented upon the stage, and left out of the presentation for superfluous length (as some of the players pretended). I thought good all should be inserted according to the allowed original, and as it was at first intended for the Cockpit stage, in the right of my most deserving friend Mr William Beston, unto whom it properly appertained. And so I leave it to thy perusal as it was generally applauded and well acted at Salisbury Court.
>
> Farewell,
> Ri. Brome

Published for the first time in 1640, some two years after it was initially performed, the quarto text of **The Antipodes** ends with the name of its author signing (in print!) an address he has written for his prospective readers. And there's the rub: immediately after the theater has apparently succeeded in persuading Peregrine to give up his travel books, Brome tries to persuade future readers of Peregrine's plight to purchase a book about traveling by claiming it is superior to the version that was presented on stage. Players left things out of the "presentation" because they decided it was of a "superfluous length"; the occasion of publication has enabled the author to reassert his control over the play and restore it "according to the allowed original." Thus, a play about the perils of reading for paternity and the curative powers of the theater will be reinvigorated for readers not long after its life on stage has come to an end. I will have more to say with regard to what **The Antipodes** may be reporting to us about drama and reading as the first era of the professional theater in England is about to be eclipsed. For now, however, I want briefly to sketch out a historical context for understanding Brome's reader address, as well as the printed play's other paratexts.

THE PLACE OF THE PAGE

Adrian Johns has observed that "when early modern readers determined a book not to be worthy of credit, they could do so on a number of grounds. It was in the attribution of 'piracy,' however, that the issues of credibility and print particularly converged."[13] Focusing more specifically on issues of drama publication, I have argued elsewhere that the construction of individual authorship within the largely collaborative conditions of the early modern theater frequently necessitated the production of an oppositional relation between the stage and the page, and that one precedent for this effort can be found in strategies used by printers to distinguish between their texts and those of a competitor.[14] As early as 1590, Richard Jones, the printer of a quarto edition of Marlowe's two *Tamburlaine the Great* plays, had introduced a comparably oppositional structure in his note "To the Gentlemen Readers: and others that take pleasure in reading Histories"—though the opposition was no longer between himself and another printer he was accusing of piracy. Rather, a new opposition had emerged that is still viable fifty years later when Brome signs off on the publication of his playscript. Hoping that his printed edition of the plays "wil be now no lesse acceptable vnto you to read after your serious affaires and studies, then they haue bene (lately) delightful for many of you to see, when the same were shewed in London vpon stages," Jones proceeds to describe how publication has enabled him to take a few authorial liberties with a work he didn't write:

> I haue (purposely) omitted and left out some fond and friuolous Iestures, digressing (and in my poore opinion) far vnmeet for the matter, which I thought, might seeme more tedious vnto the wise, than any way els to be regarded, though (happly) they haue bene of some vaine co[n]ceited fondlings greatly gaped at, what times they were shewed vpon the stage in their graced deformities.[15]

Both Jones and Brome claim that the published play is to be distinguished from the play that was previously performed, though they approach the distinction very differently: Jones takes things out, Brome puts things back.

In general, early addresses "To the Reader" reveal that printers and readers, if not yet authors, valued authentic and reader-friendly texts. That all of these early addresses preoccupied with textual matters were written by printers[16] and directed at readers seems only logical. And yet, the fact that playwrights eventually took over the self-consciously important textual space of the reader address indicates that the space could be appropriated[17]—an appropriation that points to a significant transition in the history of the relation between the early modern stage and page. Jonson, as has often been remarked, substantially reinforced the oppositional relation between the theater and the text in the preface to *Sejanus* by differentiating between "this Booke" and the play "which was acted on the publike Stage." Quite aware, like Jones, of the transformative power of publication, Jonson did not disguise his preference for print.

No surprise then that Jonson was one of the first English playwrights to commandeer the space of the address previously occupied by printers in the note "To the Reader"

included almost as an afterthought to the 1602 quarto edition of *Poetaster or The Arraignment*:

> Here (Reader) in place of the Epilogue, was meant to thee an Apology from the Author, with his reasons for the publishing of this booke: but (since he is no lesse restrain'd, then thou depriv'd of it, by Authoritie) hee praies thee to thinke charitably of what thou hast read, till thou maist heare him speake what hee hath written.[18]

Is this the printer speaking on behalf of Jonson, as the location of the address after the main text would suggest, or is this Jonson speaking on his own behalf in the third person within a discursive textual space previously reserved for printers? Either way the address captures and frames a threshold moment in Jonson's career as it constitutes the first time his authorship will be linked to the purposeful publication of a play.

What I hope this brief digression on the space of the dramatic author's address suggests is that in 1640 Brome's address to the "courteous reader," appearing at the end of the book, is something of an anomaly. Indeed, its colonization of the space usually reserved at this point in the history of printed dramatic texts for the transcription of a theatrical epilogue makes the text's privileging of its current reader over its prior spectator, the printed play over the performed play, all the more obvious. If, following Fenton, we credit this privileging of the book over the theater to an increasing text-consciousness, the symptoms of which—according to her analysis—can be clearly recognized after 1616, then perhaps the published text of *The Antipodes* offers up another clue or so about the drama and its readers.

For at least a century, the publication of Jonson's folio *Workes* in 1616 has been viewed by scholars of Renaissance drama as constituting a profound shift in the complex relation between playhouse and printing house in England.[19] During the past few decades, the 1616 folio has figured prominently in studies of early modern authorship, often being treated as a singular achievement of emergent authorial awareness—especially with regard to the meaning of print.[20] Summing up the current scholarly consensus on the Jonson folio, Elizabeth Hanson observes, "In many recent accounts of his career, Jonson's location of his authorship in the printed book heralds the proprietary author, who is linked through implication and theoretical filiation to possessive individualism, modern subjectivity, and bourgeois culture."[21] By 1640, when Brome's play was first published, the author who had done so much to transform acting scripts into reading texts had been dead for three years.[22] And yet, in the printed text of *The Antipodes* (written a year before Jonson's death), in the space so frequently reserved for the author's address to the reader, the following opening lines of a commendatory verse appear instead:

> To censuring Critics on the approved Comedy,
> **The Antipodes**
> Jonson's Alive! The world admiring stands,

And to declare his welcome there, shake hands,
Apollo's pensioners may wipe their eyes
And stifle their abortive elegies;
Taylor his goose quill may abjure again,
And to make paper dear, scribbling refrain;
For sure there's cause of neither.

Thus, a play whose title, at least for readers familiar with Mandeville's writings, promises travel to exotic lands begins with that most anti-theatricalist and bookish of playwrights, then refers to another rather bookish writer—John Taylor, who, like Peregrine, was also obsessed with a set of travel narratives—and even offers up a partial list of the tools of the writer's trade. Only in the last line of this verse, some fifteen lines later—after we have been told to "praise each line / Of his *Volpone, Sejanus,* and *Catiline*"—do we learn that Jonson is dead, but still "sojourns in his Brome's *Antipodes.*" In a subsequent commendatory verse, the next and last page of textual apparatus before the "Dramatis Personae," the writer actually seems to have come down with the same illness that threatens the well-being of the play's hero. Addressed this time "To the Author on his Comedy, / *The Antipodes,*" rather than to the play's "censuring Critics," the verse begins:

Steer'd by the hand of Fate o'er swelling seas,
Methought I landed on th'Antipodes,
Where I was straight a stranger; for 'tis thus:
Their feet do tread against the tread of us.
My scull mistook; thy book, being in my hand,
Hurried my soul to th'Antipodean strand,
Where I did feast my fancy and mine eyes
With such variety of rarities.

What performance, one wonders, might cure this poor reader of his affliction? Like Peregrine, he seems to suffer from an ailment that—with a nod to Edward Said—we might call the "textliness of the world." Nor, for that matter, do the writers of these verses indicate that they have seen a performance of the play, or even that the play was ever performed. Indeed, for both writers, *The Antipodes* is always already a book to be read, and the only reference to its stage life—"generally applauded and well-acted at Salisbury Court"—appears, strangely enough, as the last line of the book, that is, the last line of Brome's address "to the reader."

When, however, we move just beyond the printed text of Brome's play to the broader historical conditions under which it appeared, then it becomes obvious that the plot's privileging of performance over reading, its faith in the curative powers of the theater, specifically the capacity to bring a life-affirming conjugal harmony to lives threatened by discord, is either something of a last hurrah or a fantasy of one. First, there is the fact that when Brome was writing the play, the theaters were closed by an outbreak of the plague, and remained closed from May 1636 to October 1637. It is a little hard to consider the play's promotion of a theatrical remedy without also recalling that it was written during a time when the theater represented a particularly dangerous site for the spread of contagion. Then, no more than four years after the play was performed in 1638 and two years after it was published, the performance of plays in London's theaters would for all practical purposes be banned for the next two decades. Having gotten his cure while the getting was still good, Peregrine couldn't have had better timing. For the theater, however, time was about to run out.

Moreover, the play's narrative privileging of the theater over the book comes, paradoxically enough, at a time when printed dramatic texts were poised to eclipse performed play scripts in prominence. One clue to the changing status of printed drama as the closing of the theaters forced plays back into the closet can be gleaned from the status of dramatic authorship at that moment. If, as seems clear from a number of recent studies,[23] dramatic texts were more likely to be authorized when they made their way from the playhouse to the printing house, and by extension into the hands of readers, then it stands to reason that what was good for the early modern publishing industry may also have been good for authors and their readers. An examination of Stationers' Register entries for dramatic texts bears this out. Only during the last full decade of the professional stage (1631-40), when the publication of dramatic texts soars, does the number of attributed entries (ninety-one) surpass the number of anonymous entries (sixty-two). Such an abrupt increase in the recording of authors' names by the Stationers' Company suggests two important concomitant developments with regard to the relationship between the theater and the book that the printed text of Brome's play dramatizes: not only had the authorship of dramatic texts become an important factor in the regulation of their publication, but also the locus of a play's authority had shifted from the collaborative conditions of the theater to the individualized agency of the author—an agency that was much better suited to the marketing practices of the book trade. And the newly heightened status of the dramatic author would only be enhanced during the next two decades when the closing of the theaters in 1642 temporarily foreclosed future links between a given play and a given playing company and/or playhouse. In short, the time was very right for Brome to place an author's address to the readers of *The Antipodes* after the two epilogues directed at an audience that was about to be rendered obsolete. Indeed, that the play ends with an account of its passage from the playhouse to the printing house by instructing us first about what audiences must do to make the play's elixir of love fully function, then about what the author had to do to make the play suitable for readers, seems remarkably prescient.

I turn now from what the published text of *The Antipodes* and its paratexts say about the relation between stage and page to the complex links between books, reproduction, and paternity—links that, as I noted earlier, Brome's play suggestively thematizes.

AFTER DEATH DO US PART

At an important early moment in his *Mechanick Exercises, or the Doctrine of Handy-Works Applied to the Art of Printing,* published in London in 1683, Joseph Moxon offers a detailed description of "the office of the Master Printer." While informing the reader that "a Master Printer provides a fount (or fund) of letter of all bodies," Moxon suddenly expresses an uncharacteristic bit of uncertainty in the following note: "It is not clear whether our word 'body' or its French and German equivalents (corps, Kegel) first attached themselves to the dimension of the type or to the part of the mold which determines it."[24] The history of writing technologies has always been deeply engaged with the body, from the time of the earliest invention when clay served as both the material base of cuneiform and the matter out of which the Sumerian gods fashioned the first humans in the earliest extant creation narratives, to the January 2004 issue of *Wired*—a magazine devoted to the computer industry—which features as its "exclusive" womb-red cover story "The Making of a Human Clone: 7 Days Inside a Maverick Embryo Lab."[25] And, of course, the early modern printer relied on a matrix (a womb) to produce type, each of which—Moxon's illustrations of type make clear—is a little human. As Margreta de Grazia observes, "Type-founders and printers have always regarded the single moveable type character as a human being standing erect, each type having a body, a face, beard, neck, shoulder, back, belly, and feet."[26] The fact that all of these erect beings have beards suggests that typefounders' wombs carried only sons to term.

Whereas manuscript culture largely relied on a primal scene of sorts in which the scribe's pen had its way with the virginal page, each printed book was a collection of memories of inked bodies no longer present: an originary absence that, grammatologically speaking, underwrote a graphic presence and thus made the early modern book a kind of mausoleum or monument. The early modern London book trade was a deadly business, one that traded in bodies and orphaned texts. Some acknowledgment of the macabre, embodied nature of print is articulated in the elegiac pronouncements of John Heminge and Henry Condell in their address "To the great variety readers" of the 1623 Shakespeare folio. Lamenting "that the Author himselfe had [not] liv'd to have set forth, and overseen his owne writings," Heminge and Condell offer their readers Shakespeare's remains "cur'd, and perfect of their limbes."[27]

More than a decade before his death would be transformed into the occasion of his material birth as an author, Shakespeare briefly alluded to some of the conceptual systems that made such a transformation possible, and he did so in the context of an orphaned character named, appropriately enough, Posthumous. A British war hero in the conflict with Rome who has been mistakenly imprisoned by British forces, Posthumous falls asleep and dreams one of the strangest bits of stage business in Shakespeare's canon. In the dream, his family, beginning with the dead father he never knew, assembles around him, bemoans his suffering, then appeals to Jupiter to "take off his miseries" (*Cymbeline,* TLN 3120). That relief, when promptly doled out by Jupiter, comes oddly enough in the form of a tablet given to the apparitional family with the instructions that they lay it "vpon his breast" (TLN 3145). Although we may pass over the subtle connection here between the resurrection of the dead and the miraculous appearance of a text, Posthumous himself compels us to look more closely. Upon waking up from a dream peopled by the father who died while he was in the womb, the mother from whom he was untimely ripped, and Lucina, the goddess of childbirth, Posthumous asserts, "Sleepe, thou hast been a Grandsire, and begot / A Father to me" (TLN 3160-61). Upon discovering the tablet a few lines later, he remarks, "A book? O rare one, / Be not, as is our fangled world, a Garment / Nobler then that it covers" (TLN 3170-72).

Given that the play in which Posthumous sleeps and wakes is set in Roman Britain at the time of Christ's birth, then the book that so delights him must be a rare one indeed, a very recent technological innovation known as the parchment codex, which, as I noted earlier, was referred to by Paul as "membranas." And yet, his fear that the noble cover of the book passed on to him from beyond the grave belies its less than noble contents suggests that Posthumous has been compelled to ventriloquize a characteristically Shakespearean anachronism. Evidence from extant codices and paintings of their earliest users indicates that the noble cover was a later fashion development in the history of scribal publication. Thus, I suspect that Shakespeare had books produced and sold by London stationers in mind when he wrote those lines.

I rely on this suspicion to shift attention briefly from Posthumous's concern with noble covers to the paratexts of a self-avowed crude book that would have been very much at home on Peregrine's bookshelf next to his copy of *Mandeville's Travels.* The book I have in mind is the 1611 edition of *Coryats Crudities.*[28] It is not difficult to see in the *Crudities* an act of "possessive authorship" that Joseph Loewenstein attributes in its purest form to Jonson. Rather, we need only to juxtapose the title page of the 1611 *Crudities* with the title page of the 1616 *Workes* to sense that Jonson must have figured out something about authorial self-promotion in print from this earlier publishing venture. Furthermore, William Stansby, who printed the 1611 *Crudities,* would subsequently be called upon to print the 1616 Jonson folio.

What interests me most about the 1611 edition of the *Crudities* here, however, is what appears on its second title page, a page that, I want to suggest, played an extraordinarily important role in generating Thomas Coryate's authorial persona. To begin with, the second page is the first to indicate the details of the text's production: "London: Printed by W. S. Anno Domini 1611." Then there are the opening lines of the page, which inform readers that this is not an edition of a text by a single author but rather a volume that gathers related texts by more than one author. In much the same way that Jonson, Shakespeare, and Beaumont and Fletcher will be author-ized through the publication of collections (even multiauthor collections in the case of both the Shakespeare folio and the Beaumont and Fletcher folio), Coryate makes his grand authorial debut within a hodgepodge of travel narratives. But what is particularly striking about this collection is how the contents of the volume are narrated: "THREE CRVDE VEINES ARE PRESENTED IN This BOOKE following (besides the fore-said CRVDITIES) no lesse flowing in the body of the BOOKE, then the CRVDITIES *themselues, two of* Rhetoricke and one of POESIE." Decades before William Harvey theorized the circulation of the blood, this book seems almost to be alive, the veins of its body flowing with what we might call Coryate crude. If Coryate's authorial persona becomes so readily available for appropriation by future writers,[29] this availability can be traced in part to the fact that Coryate is initially exposed to the world via a complex set of transfusions from other narratives and writers, one of whom, we shall see momentarily, appears to come from his father.

Referring to the emergence of the early modern author function, Robert Weimann observes that "the ties between product and producer had by this stage become so close and personal that the process of appropriation was often sanctioned by metaphors of procreation. . . . [T]he political economy of the product (the text in the marketplace, the book as a unit of exchange-value) could be almost obliterated in the biological metaphor of procreation, which suggested the process of 'bringing forth one's own.'"[30] One such obliteration seems to be under way in the political economy of bringing forth the *Crudities* to market. No doubt the bizarre and outrageous authorial persona Coryate crafted for himself contributed significantly to the longevity of a posthumous career that produced several travel narratives under his name during the next two centuries; but I also suspect that the proto-biologist effort of this publishing venture to link him to other travel writers contributed a great deal to Coryate's eventual transformation into a kind of Mandeville figure, an empty authorial signifier that comes to signify almost anything associated with the particular literary genre of the travel narrative. Accordingly, I think we need to hold William Stansby equally responsible for the construction of Coryate's authorship, as his proto-Jonsonian fingerprints can be spotted all over the 1611 edition of the *Crudities*.

In this context, what seems most remarkable about the second title page I've been dwelling on is the description of the fourth and last book included in the edition: "Then in the Posterne of them looke, and thou shalt find the *Posthume Poems of the Authors Father,* coming as neere Kinsmen to the worke, being next of blood to the booke, and yonger brothers to the Author himselfe." The father

referred to here is George Coryate, of whose work no extant text remains except that which is included in the *Crudities*. As with Shakespeare's Posthumous, the resurrection of a dead father is implicated in the appearance of a book, and just in case we miss the reproductive point—the links between ink and kin—Jonson amplifies it in the dedicatory acrostic he writes for the 1611 edition of the *Crudities*:

> C ome forth thou bonnie bouncing booke then, daughter
> O f *Tom of Odcombe* that *odde* Ioviall Author,
> R ather his sonne I should have cal'd thee, Why?
> Y es thou wert borne out of his travelling thigh
> A s well as from his braines, and claimest thereby
> T o be his *Bacchus* as his *Pallas*: bee
> E uer his thighes *Male* then, and his braines *Shee*.

(A3r)

Coryate's father writes a book that is "next of blood to the booke" his son writes, and the son gives birth to a daughter—and/or perhaps a son—that is a "bouncing" book. Having spent ten sonnets extolling the physical beauty of a certain young man and instructing him to procreate so that said beauty will not be lost, Shakespeare concludes the next sonnet by advising him, "Thou shouldst print more, not let that copy die."[31] As Ann and John O. Thompson have shown, Shakespeare frequently relied on words and phrases pertaining to the early modern publishing industry throughout his career when it came to matters of biological reproduction;[32] and Richard Wilson observes that in the later plays, especially the romances, Shakespeare turned increasingly to "the proprietorial rights and productive relations" of the London book trade to express his character's concerns about procreation, the legitimacy of sons, and patriarchal authority.[33]

The frequency of conceptual and/or lexical conflations of parenting and printing—and there are dozens of them—in Shakespeare's work suggests just how readily metaphors of textual reproduction could be appropriated for the discourse of human reproduction. In the case of the acrostic Jonson devises to represent Coryate's act of literary production, however, the metaphorical cross-fertilization goes in the opposite direction. For Shakespeare, who wrote almost nothing about authorship or publication, books and print provided a ready set of terms with which to represent the facts of life. By contrast, for Jonson, who wrote often and in depth about authorship and publication, the facts of life provided him with a ready set of terms with which to characterize the material being in the world of his (and other authors') works. Jonson does, of course, write of children, but textual reproduction metaphors are conspicuous in their absence. Even in epigram 45 ("On My First Son"), which meditates on fatherhood and loss, Jonson famously calls the dead son "his best piece of poetry," but makes no mention of the poem-child's textuality. Or, to return to the opposition that structures *The Antipodes,* a playwright closely affiliated with the stage sees children in terms of print; a playwright closely affiliated with the page sees print in terms of children.

I can't prove it, but I am tempted to speculate that Stansby wrote the material on the second title page of the *Crudities*. After all, as the printer/publisher, Stansby was taking a substantial risk in underwriting the costs of producing a text by a writer who was about to make his authorial debut in print. Therefore, Stansby had the greatest interest in devising a successful approach to marketing the book, and he might rightly have viewed the bundling of several travel narratives into one volume as constituting both a good way of lending a new entry into the travel writing business some much-needed credibility and a smart bit of value-added retailing. And while I'm feeling tempted to speculate, I also want to suggest that Jonson was responding to Stansby's description of the relation between the *Crudities* and Coryate's father's book as he set out to depict the nature of the son's authorial accomplishment. By 1611, Jonson—who may already have started to think about publishing a collection of his own—has learned much from Stansby's approach to marketing books and their authors. Thus, he may well be following Stansby's lead as he writes an acrostic based on the author's name in order to describe the authorship of a text that will soon be inexorably linked to that name.

As for what Stansby's approach is, I think it can best be characterized—to borrow from the rhetoric of the publishing venture itself—as crude commodity fetishism. In the first volume of *Capital,* Marx famously intimates that there is a significant relation between "the whole mystery of commodities, all of the magic and necromancy that surrounds the products of labour on the basis of commodity production," and the rather ghoulish logic of the fetish, in which objects associated with the dead come to be imbued with magical powers not inherent in the objects themselves.[34] And so at this early stage in the capitalist game when the workings of commodity production have not yet been completely hidden, printed books—lifeless bodies with no inherent powers of their own—often appear in the world accompanied by acknowledgments of the dead ancestors that imbue them with their peculiar magic, or as oedipal textual children poised to take the places of the fathers who bring them into the world with the help of midwives/stationers. And if authorship, the form of fetishism that so successfully facilitates the commodification of printed books, is so often represented within proto-biologistic narratives of reproduction, it is partly because such narratives of fathers and children, of blood and kinsmen, constitute the epistemological foundations of ancestor worship and life after death. In this sense, posthumous authorship, the veneration of objects attributed to an author after his or her death, is the most transparent form of the commodity fetishism that emerged from the early modern publishing industry. When Posthumous awakes, he naïvely observes, "Sleepe, thou hast been a Grandsire, and begot / A Father to me." In fact, it is the book placed on his chest that awakens him and triggers the recollection of a visit from the dead. Such book-driven visitations were a commonplace in the London book trade.

EX UTERO OR THE MATRIX UNLOADED

Margreta de Grazia observes that "in the English Renaissance, comparisons of mechanical and sexual reproduction, imprints and children seem to multiply. ... The textual imprint as child recurs in preliminaries to early modern books, putting into play the semantics shared by biological and textual reproduction."[35] One of the earliest extant examples of the semantic intercourse between biological and textual reproduction can be found in the letter Gargantua writes to his son Pantagruel in Rabelais's first published work (1533).[36] In this brief—and uncharacteristically serious—episode, a father writes his "most dear son" that of all God's embellishments of "human nature," the greatest is "the one by which we can, in this mortal state, acquire a kind of immortality and, in the course of this transitory life, perpetuate our name and seed: which we do by lineage sprung from us in lawful marriage."[37] Next, having confided that "I might seem to have desired nothing but to leave you, after my death, as a mirror representing the person of me your father," Gargantua makes this rather odd assertion: "The elegant and accurate art of printing, which is now in use, was invented in my time, by divine inspiration."[38] Two different methods of God-given reproduction are brought together courtesy of a father, a son, and a mirror, suggesting that the fundamental conceptual link between the two methods is the promise (or perhaps fantasy) of producing identical copies. It is worth noting that Gargantua's missive follows a chapter devoted to cataloguing "the fine Books in the Library of Saint Victor's."[39]

As many of the examples I have examined here suggest, the conceptual, semantic, and metaphorical ties that bind printing and parenting become significantly strengthened as the burgeoning early modern publishing industry comes into its own. In this light, *The Antipodes* stands out as something of an anomaly. Certainly the published drama's paratexts work hard to market the book of the play sub rosa, according to "the whole mystery of commodities," resurrecting the dead—printed drama's earliest and most vocal proponent, Ben Jonson—in the first of its two commendatory verses and privileging the printed play over the performed play in Brome's concluding address to the reader. But there is no biology lurking here. No texts-as-babies cry out to be taken home with a prospective buyer; no author apologizes here for the premature birth of a text untimely exposed to the world by a greedy printer. In fact, the play itself makes the disjunction of books and babies, of reading and reproducing, one of its principal themes, even as it privileges the power of the stage over the power of the page. How might we account for these innovations?

I want to conclude by answering this question from the perspectives of both sexual and textual reproduction, the two sides of the same metaphorical coin that constitutes the main interpretive investment of this essay. In the case of sexual reproduction, I would argue that Brome's play is responding to an important moment in the history of patriarchal culture when the reign of Gutenberg paternity, nearly two hundred years on the throne, has finally consolidated its authority. If, as Friedrich A. Kittler observes, the paternal contribution to reproduction was once chiefly articulated in terms of "an omnipresent metaphor [that] equated women with the white sheet of nature or virginity onto which a very male stylus could then inscribe the glory of its authorship,"[40] it is also true that the invention of the printing press provided stiff competition for the primal scribal scene in terms of the proto-biological effort to understand and put into words those reproductive functions that remained largely invisible and unknowable till the nineteenth century. And although scribal publication continued to be a vibrant medium well into the eighteenth century, the early modern father—compelled to await the certitude of scientific evidence that blood "types" and DNA testing would someday offer him—had pretty much completed the conceptual, semantic, and metaphorical transition from scribal technology to print technology by the middle of the seventeenth century. As such, the Gutenberg Father, armed with upgraded technological notions of paternity, may well have had a vested interest in covering his epistemological tracks. Not to do so, in some sense, would have called attention to the fundamental absence at the core of paternity and paternal authority, as well as many of the cultural structures relied on to maintain them in their privileged position. Thus, although Brome's play intimates links between fathers and books, literacy and legitimacy, ink and kin—links that are concisely expressed in Shakespeare's sonnets, in plays such as *Cymbeline* and *The Winter's Tale,* and in the paratexts of books such as the *Crudities*—it nevertheless thematizes their disjunction and mutual exclusion by making them the before and after of Peregrine's rather Jonsonian/humoral malady. We've come a long way in the century that separates **The Antipodes** from the letter Gargantua writes to Pantagruel.

In the case of textual reproduction, I would argue that the various embodiments that enabled the fetishistic commodification of printed books in the emergent book trade have been deployed so often by the time **The Antipodes** is published that they have lost a bit of their marketing magic. In short, as Peregrine might have guessed, by 1640 these two interrelated discursive systems—these *mentalités,* Foucault might have called them—have traveled far and wide and are in need of a respite.

Notes

1. Lukas Erne has, of course, notoriously called into question this assertion, especially in the context of Shakespeare, who, he argues, produced reading texts for publication that had to be shortened subse-

quently for performance. See his *Shakespeare as Literary Dramatist* (Cambridge: Cambridge University Press, 2003).

2. Richard Brome, *The Antipodes: A Comedie* (London: J. Okes, for Francis Constable, 1640). I will be using the Globe Quarto edition, ed. David Scott Kastan and Richard Proudfoot (New York: Theater Arts Books/ Routledge, 2000), cited parenthetically in the text.

3. Jeffrey Masten, *Textual Intercourse: Collaboration, Authorship, and Sexualities in Renaissance Drama* (Cambridge: Cambridge University Press, 1997).

4. On Hamlet's reading habits, see Eve Rachele Sanders's astute analysis in *Gender and Literacy on Stage in Early Modern England* (Cambridge: Cambridge University Press, 1998), 57-88.

5. On early modern rhetorical conflations of book and flesh, see Gordon Williams, *Shakespeare, Sex, and the Print Revolution* (London: Athlone Press, 1996), 46-55.

6. See Colin H. Roberts and T. C. Skeat, *The Birth of the Codex* (London: Oxford University Press, 1983), 19-22.

7. Peter W. M. Blayney includes some of these images in *The First Folio of Shakespeare* (Washington, D.C.: Folger Library Publications, 1991).

8. Quoted in Roberts and Skeat, *Birth,* 22.

9. Roberts and Skeat argue that Paul's use of the word *membranas* refers to the word (*membraneae*) used in contemporary Rome for parchment notebooks (ibid., 22).

10. On the history of these convergences, see my introduction to *Printing and Parenting in Early Modern England,* ed. Douglas A. Brooks (Aldershot: Ashgate, 2005), 1-23; and my essay "Bodies That Mattered: Technology, Embodiment, and Secretarial Mediation," in *Literary Secretaries/Secretarial Culture,* ed. Leah Price and Pam Thurschwell (Aldershot: Ashgate, 2005), 129-51. See also the essays in Dolores Warwick Frese and Katherine O'Brien O'Keefe, eds., *The Body and the Book* (Notre Dame: University of Notre Dame Press, 1997).

11. William Shakespeare, *The Tempest* (1623), cited from *The Norton Facsimile of the First Folio of Shakespeare,* prepared by Charlton Hinman, 2nd ed., with a new introduction by Peter W. M. Blayney (New York: Norton, 1996), TLN 2326-30. Quotations from Shakespeare are cited parenthetically by through line numbers (TLN) from this edition.

12. Doris Fenton, *The Extra-dramatic Moment in Elizabethan Plays before 1616* (Folcroft, Pa.: Folcroft Press, 1970), 8.

13. Adrian Johns, *The Nature of the Book: Print and Knowledge in the Making* (Chicago: University of Chicago Press, 1998), 32.

14. Douglas A. Brooks, *From Playhouse to Printing House: Drama and Authorship in Early Modern England* (Cambridge: Cambridge University Press, 2000).

15. Christopher Marlowe, *Tamburlaine the Great* (London: Richard Jhones, 1590), A2.

16. I am using the word "printer" here somewhat loosely to denote the printer and/or publisher of a given text. The distinction between printer and publisher was not yet firm in the early modern book trade.

17. On the "prehistory" of prefatorial addresses, see Gérard Genette, *Paratexts: Thresholds of Interpretation,* trans. Jane E. Lewin (Cambridge: Cambridge University Press, 1997), 163-70.

18. Ben Jonson, *Poetaster or The Arraignment* (London: [R. Bradock] for M. L[ownes], 1602), NIV.

19. G. E. Bentley, for example, remarks of Jonson's *Workes* that "probably no other publication before the Restoration did so much to raise the contemporary existence of the generally belittled form of plays" (*The Profession of Dramatist in Shakespeare's Time, 1590-1642* [Princeton: Princeton University Press, 1971], 55-56). More recently, significant research by Alan B. Farmer and Zachary Lesser has given us a much richer and more historically accurate portrait of this shift. See their "Vile Arts: The Marketing of English Printed Drama, 1512-1660," *Research Opportunities in Renaissance Drama* 39 (2000): 77-166. See also Lesser's astute essay "Walter Burre's *The Knight of the Burning Pestle," English Literary Renaissance* 34 (1999): 335-61.

20. See, for example, Joseph Loewenstein, *Jonson and Possessive Authorship* (Cambridge: Cambridge University Press, 2002); Richard C. Newton, "Jonson and the (Re-)Invention of the Book," in *Classic and Cavalier: Essays on Jonson and the Sons of Ben,* ed. Claude J. Summers and Ted-Larry Pebworth (Pittsburgh: University of Pittsburgh Press, 1982), 31-58.

21. Elizabeth Hanson, *Discovering the Subject in Renaissance England* (Cambridge: Cambridge University Press, 1998), 120.

22. Brome had strong ties to Jonson. He was first employed as a servant in Jonson's household in 1614, later becoming a protégé and friend.

23. See, for example, David Scott Kastan, "Plays into Print: Shakespeare to His Earliest Readers," in *Books and Readers in Early Modern England: Material Studies,* ed. Jennifer Andersen and Elizabeth Sauer (Philadelphia: University of Pennsylvania Press, 2002), 23-41. For an overview of the impact of printing on authorship, see Wendy Wall, "Authorship and the Material Conditions of Writing," in *The Cambridge Companion to English Literature, 1500-1600,* ed. Arthur F. Kinney (Cambridge: Cambridge University Press, 2000), 64-89.

24. Joseph Moxon, *Mechanick Exercises, or the Doctrine of Handy-Works Applied to the Art of Printing (1683-84),* facsimile, ed. Herbert Davis and Harry Carter (New York: Dover Publications, 1958), 19.

25. For a discussion of these engagements, see Brooks, "Bodies That Mattered."

26. Margreta de Grazia, "Imprints: Shakespeare, Gutenberg, and Descartes," in *Alternative Shakespeares,* vol. 2, ed. Terence Hawkes (New York: Routledge, 1996), 74.

27. *Mr. William Shakespeares comedies, histories, & tragedies* (London: Isaac Jaggard and Ed. Blount [at the charges of W. Jaggard, Ed. Blount, J. Smithweeke, and W. Aspley], 1623), A3r.

28. *Coryats Crudities Hastily gobled vp in five Moneths trauells in France, Sauoy, Italy, Rhetia co[m]monly called the Grisons country, Heluetia aliàs Switzerland, some parts of high Germany, and the Netherlands; Newly digested in the hungry aire of Odcombe in the County of Somerset, & now dispersed to the nourishment of the trauelling Members of this Kingdome* (London: W[illiam] S[tansby] for the author, 1611).

29. The appropriation of Coryate's authorial persona can be said to commence as early as 1612, when John Taylor—who appears in the commendatory verse of *The Antipodes* that proclaims "Jonson's alive!"—addresses the first poem of his first collection of poems, *The Sculler,* "To Tom Coriat." A year later, Taylor published another book, *Laugh and Be Fat: or A commentary upon the Odcombyan Banket,* which parodies the *Crudities.* The following year (1613) Taylor produced two more books about Coryate's travels: *Odcombs Complaint* and *The Eighth Wonder of the World.* Coryate returns as one of several world travelers in Taylor's *The Praise of Hemp-seed* (1623), and some of Coryate's notes and letters are published

in Samuel Purchas's *Hakluytus Posthumous* in 1625. A subsequent text, *Another Traveller! Or Cursory Remarks and Critical Observations made upon a Journey through Part of the Netherlands In the Latter End of the Year 1766,* is ascribed to Coryate Junior. For a detailed study of Coryate's authorial afterlives in print, see M. G. Aune, "Thomas Coryate for the Ages: Constructing Authorship and Celebrity" (unpublished conference paper).

30. Robert Weimann, *Authority and Representation in Early Modern Discourse,* ed. David Hillman (Baltimore: Johns Hopkins University Press, 1996), 180.

31. Sonnet II, in *Shakespeare's Sonnets,* ed. Katherine Duncan-Jones (Walton-on-Thames: Thomas Nelson, 1997), 133.

32. Ann Thompson and John O. Thompson, "Meaning, 'Seeing,' and Printing," in Brooks, *Printing and Parenting,* 50-77.

33. Richard Wilson, *Will Power: Essays on Shakespearean Authority* (Detroit: Wayne State University Press, 1993), 165.

34. Karl Marx, *Capital: A Critique of Political Economy,* vol. 1, trans. Ben Fowkes (New York: Vintage Books, 1977), 169. For a lucid analysis of the role of fetishism in Marx's thought, see William Pietz, "Fetishism and Materialism: The Limits of Theory in Marx," in *Fetishism as Cultural Discourse,* ed. Emily Apter and William Pietz (Ithaca: Cornell University Press, 1993), 119-51.

35. De Grazia, "Imprints," 74.

36. Marshall McLuhan points to the broader significance of the letter for understanding print culture: "Anybody who looks at the Gutenberg question at all, runs very soon into Gargantua's Letter to Pantagruel. Rabelais, long before Cervantes, produced an authentic myth or prefiguration of the whole complex of print technology. ... [P]antagruelion [is] the symbol and image of printing from moveable type" (*The Gutenberg Galaxy* [Toronto: University of Toronto Press, 1962], 179-80).

37. François Rabelais, *Gargantua and Pantagruel,* trans. J. M. Cohen (New York: Penguin, 1955), 193.

38. Ibid., 194.

39. Ibid., 186-89.

40. Friedrich A. Kittler, *Gramophone, Film, Typewriter,* trans. Geoffrey Winthrop-Young and Michael White (Stanford: Stanford University Press, 1999), 186.

Brett D. Hirsch (essay date 2006)

SOURCE: Hirsch, Brett D. "Werewolves and Severed Hands: Webster's *The Duchess of Malfi* and Heywood and Brome's *The Witches of Lancashire.*" *Notes and Queries* 53.1 (2006): 92-4. Print.

[*In the following essay, Hirsch identifies a possible precedent for Brome's use of a severed hand in* The Late Lancashire Witches. *Hirsch notes that the same motif occurs in a tale from* Discours des sorciers *(1590), a work by the French judge Henri Boguet.*]

In his popular treatise on witches and witchcraft, *Discours des Sorciers* (Lyon, 1590), the judge Henri Boguet reports the following case of lycanthropy:

> Here it will be relevant to recount what happened in the year 1588 in a village about two leagues from Apchon in the highlands of Auvergne. One evening a gentleman, standing at the window of his château, saw a huntsman whom he knew passing by, and asked him to bring him some of his bag on his return. As the huntsman went his way along a valley, he was attacked by a large wolf and discharged his arquebus at it without hurting it. He was therefore compelled to grapple with the wolf, and caught it by the ears; but at length, growing weary, he let go of the wolf, drew back and took his big hunting knife, and with it cut off one of the wolf's paws, which he put in his pouch after the wolf had run away. He then returned to the gentleman's château, in sight of which he had fought the wolf. The gentleman asked him to give him part of his bag; and the huntsman, wishing to do so and intending to take the paw from his pouch, drew from it a hand wearing a gold ring on one of the fingers, which the gentleman recognised as belonging to his wife. This caused him to entertain an evil suspicion of her; and going into the kitchen, he found his wife nursing her arm in her apron, which he took away, and found that her hand had been cut off, Thereupon the gentleman seized hold of her; but immediately, and as soon as she had been confronted with her hand, she confessed that it was no other than she who, in the form of a wolf, had attacked the hunter; and she was afterwards burned at Ryon.[1]

Albert H. Tricomi has recently argued that Boguet's narrative 'is a pertinent source' for *The Duchess of Malfi,*[2] in relation to the dead man's hand episode during Act IV of Webster's play:

FERDINAND:

> I come to seal my peace with you: here's a hand
>   *[Gives her a dead man's hand.]*
> To which you have vow'd much love; the ring upon't
> You gave.

DUCHESS:

> I affectionately kiss it.

FERDINAND:

> Pray do: and bury the print of it in your heart:
> I will leave this ring with you for a love-token;

And the hand, as sure as the ring; and do not doubt
But you shall have the heart too; when you need a friend
Send it to him that ow'd it; you shall see
Whether he can aid you.

DUCHESS:

You are very cold.
I fear you are not well after your travel:—
Hah! lights!—O, horrible!

FERDINAND:

Let her have lights enough.
[*Exit.*]

DUCHESS:

What witchcraft doth he practise that he hath left
A dead man's hand here?

(IV.i.43-55)[3]

While Webster's play and Boguet's narrative share the common elements of a werewolf and a severed hand with a wedding ring, the suggestion that Boguet is the ultimate source for this episode in *The Duchess* is not convincing. There is no evidence that Webster read in French, and Boguet's treatise—popular as it was on the Continent—was only available in the French original.[4] Moreover, Boguet's tale is barely analogous to the play: the hand in question in *The Duchess* is not severed from the lycanthropic character Ferdinand—whose hands remain intact throughout the play—but rather it is intended to be mistaken by the Duchess as belonging to her husband Antonio. Whereas the audience knows that her husband in still alive, the Duchess is momentarily shocked by the possibility that the severed hand *does* belong to her husband. However, as soon as the lights return she recognizes that the hand is not Antonio's, but instead 'a dead man's hand' (IV.i.55). We never learn the actual origin of the severed hand in Webster's play, whereas the origin of the severed hand in Boguet's tale is unequivocally clear. Even in the unlikely event that Boguet was the source for this scene, Webster is only faithful to Boguet's narrative insofar as he retains the three separate elements of a severed hand, a werewolf, and a wedding ring. What is noticeably lacking in Webster's version is the precise link between the three found in Boguet. In light of these doubts, Gunnar Boklund's earlier assertion that Simon Goulart's *Admirable and Memorable Histories* (London, 1607) is Webster's ultimate source for the references to lycanthropy in *The Duchess* is confirmed, since Goulart's account is clearly identifiable in Webster's play and it was readily available in English translation.[5]

Although it seems that Boguet's narrative is not a source for Webster's play, it reappears in a clearly identifiable form in Thomas Heywood and Richard Brome's **The Witches of Lancashire** (London, 1634).[6] During the night, a Soldier has been 'nipp'd, and pull'd, and pinch'd' by 'a company of hell-cats' (V.iii.74-5), but managed to injure one of the offending animals in the melee:

SOLDIER:

Yet I have kept my face whole thanks to my scimitar,
My trusty bilbo, but for which I vow,
I had been torn to pieces. But I think
I met with some of them. One, I am sure,
I have sent limping hence.

(V.iii.77-81)

When the Soldier retires to the local inn, he reports his attack to the owner and another local, Generous and Arthur, who request to see the Soldier's bloodied sword—or any evidence to support his tale of supernatural swashbuckling—but instead find a severed hand:

SOLDIER:

What's here? Is't possible cats should have hands
And rings upon their fingers?

ARTHUR:

Most prodigious!

GENEROUS:

Reach me that hand.

SOLDIER:

There's that of three I can best spare.
                    [*He gives the hand to* GENEROUS.]

GENEROUS:

[*Aside*] Amazement upon wonder, can this be?
I needs must know't by most infallible marks.
Is this the hand once plighted by holy vows?
And this the ring that bound them? Doth this last age
Afford what former never durst believe?
Oh, how have I offended those high powers
That my great incredulity should merit
A punishment so grievous, and to happen
Under mine own roof, mine own bed, my bosom?

ARTHUR:

Know you the hand sir?

GENEROUS:

Yes, and too well can read it.

(V.iii.93-106)

Generous, like the château owner in Boguet's tale, recognizes the ring immediately and concludes that the hand belongs to his wife, who, as of the night of the Soldier's attack, has mysteriously taken ill. Taking the severed hand, Generous confronts his wife with the damning evidence:

GENEROUS:

In company there's comfort. Prithee, wife,
Lend me thy hand, and let me feel thy pulse.

Perhaps some fever—by their beating I
May guess at thy disease.

MRS GENEROUS:

My hand, 'tis there.
                  [GENEROUS *feels her pulse.*]

GENEROUS:

A dangerous sickness and, I fear't, death.
'Tis odds you will not'scape it. Take that back
And let me prove the t'other if perhaps
I there can find more comfort.

MRS GENEROUS:

I pray excuse me.

GENEROUS:

I must not be denied. Sick folks are peevish
And must be o'errul'd, and so shall you.

MRS GENEROUS:

Alas, I have not strength to lift it up.

GENEROUS:

If not thy hand, wife, show me but thy wrist,
        [*He shows her the hand found at the mill.*]
And see how this will match it. Here's a testate
That cannot be outfac'd.

MRS GENEROUS:

I am undone.

                                          (V.iv.43-56)

Whilst the other supernatural episodes that appear in the play are culled directly from the evidence given at the 1633-4 trial at Lancashire—many of which, such as the reported metamorphoses of a witch and a boy into greyhounds and a horse, are in fact a child's recollection and reinterpretation of the stories coming out of the earlier Lancashire witch trials of 1612—any references to a severed hand are noticeably absent from the trial transcripts. Therefore, Heywood and Brome must have found their source for this episode elsewhere; and, in light of the obvious similarities present in both texts, it would seem highly likely that Boguet's narrative—or a version of it—was this source.

Critics usually credit Heywood for writing the witchcraft scenes in **The Witches** [**The Late Lancashire Witches**]—leaving the domestic comedy to Brome—since Heywood was fascinated by witchcraft and was familiar with the literature of many Continental demonologists, including Jean Bodin and Johannes Weyer, whom he quotes at length in his Γυναικειον, *or Nine Bookes of Various History Concerninge Women* (London, 1624). It is possible that Brome wrote the severed hand episode; however, like Webster, neither Heywood nor Brome appear to have read in French,[7] but, as Martin has shown, both have relied on translations of their sources. This presents the same

problem for assigning Boguet as a direct source for **The Witches** as for *The Duchess,* since Boguet's tale is unique and no earlier source for the tale has been proposed,[8] and it was only available in the French original. Assuming that no earlier version of the tale can be found, and that Boguet is the origin of the severed hand motif, we are left with three possible sources of transmission: first, that either Heywood or Brome *did* in fact read French and had access to French demonological works including Boguet's *Discours des Sorciers,* but in most other cases opted for Latin translations instead; second, that there was a Latin translation of Boguet's *Discours des Sorciers,* in manuscript form or otherwise, which has been subsequently lost; or third, that Heywood or Brome came to knowledge of the severed hand tale via word of mouth.

Notes

1. Henri Boguet, *Discours des Sorciers* (Lyon, 1590); translated into English as *An Examen of Witches,* trans. E. Allen Ashwin, ed. Montague Summers (London, 1929), 140-1.

2. Albert H. Tricomi, 'The Severed Hand in Webster's *Duchess of Malfi,' Studies in English Literature,* xliv (2004), 347-58, 356.

3. All references are from *The Duchess of Malfi,* ed. John Russell Brown (London, 1964).

4. Tricomi recognizes the 'defect in designating Boguet as a source is that despite Webster's strong attraction to Continental sources, he usually resorted to them in translation' (351).

5. Gunnar Boklund, *The Duchess of Malfi: Sources, Themes, Characters* (Cambridge, 1962), 32.

6. Although published under the title *The Late Witches of Lancashire,* it is clear from the running heads of the 1634 edition as well as contemporary accounts that the play was performed as *The Witches of Lancashire*: Herbert Berry, 'The Globe bewitched and *El Hombre Fiel,' Medieval and Renaissance Drama in England,* i (1984), 211-30. All references to the play are from *The Witches of Lancashire,* ed. Gabriel Egan (London, 2002).

7. Critics doubt whether Heywood had any command of the French language: W. Bang, *Pleasant Dialogues and Dramma's Von Tho. Heywood,* Materialien Zur Kunde Des Älteren Englischen Dramas, vol. III (Louvain, 1903), 339; and R. G. Martin, 'A Critical Study of Thomas Heywood's *Gunaikeoin,' Studies in Philology,* xx (1923), 160-83, 175. However, Arthur C. Clark believes that Heywood translated and used songs taken from other languages, including French: 'Thomas Heywood's *The Rape of Lucrece* [Review],' *Review of English Studies,* n.s iii, 11 (1952), 285-9.

8. The folklore surrounding this tale, at least in England, seems to have been generated by the play itself: John Roby, *Popular Traditions of Lancashire,* 3rd edn, III (London, 1843), 218-53. Rauchbauer suggests that the Generous incident is 'another example of the dramatist's use of an international migratory tale motif': 'The Subplot of Thomas Heywood's *The Captives*: Some Facts and Speculations,' *Etudes Anglaises,* xxx, 3 (1977), 345. However, it appears that neither Rauchbauer nor Roby were familiar with Boguet's treatise.

Eleanor Collins (essay date 2007)

SOURCE: Collins, Eleanor. "Richard Brome's Contract and the Relationship of Dramatist to Company in the Early Modern Period." *Early Theatre* 10.2 (2007): 116-28. Print.

[*In the following essay, Collins argues that Brome's 1635 contract with the King's Revels theater company, which is often interpreted as "exemplary of the conditions of the 1630s dramatist," actually fails to reflect the practices of the time. Collins notes that several contemporary playwrights, including Jonson, entered into formal agreements with theater managers but continued to cultivate new business relationships on the side.*]

In 1635, Richard Brome made a career decision that was to have significant consequences for the understanding of early-modern theatre history. He agreed to the contract drafted on the 20 July made with the King's Revels company, then under the leadership of Richard Gunnell, which bound his services as a playwright exclusively to the Salisbury Court theatre. Brome's contract has been interpreted as symptomatic of changing modes of theatrical production and regulation into the Caroline period, and as exemplary of the condition of the 1630s dramatist, bound under contractual agreement to impresarial management.[1] Andrew Gurr describes the impresario system, as exemplified by Philip Henslowe, Christopher Beeston, and Gunnell (and, later, Richard Heton) as 'an autocratic form of rule imposed on a profession which had grown into being by means of a long tradition of collaborative and democratic practices.'[2] This kind of management is placed in opposition to the 'collective responsibility' of the King's Men,[3] and has contributed to the perception of the decline of drama and its quality into the 1630s, in which theatrical managers become 'entrepreneurs rather than players, individualists in commerce, not stars in the teamwork of performance,' ruthlessly binding playwrights to their whims.[4]

This model has become an accepted fact of Caroline drama. The interpretation of Brome's contract has become fundamental to the way in which we consider these dramatists and the autonomy that they had within the professional theatrical market. The distinctions between whether a dramatist sold a play to a company, was commissioned by that company or contractually bound to it are crucial to the personal and professional relations that we construct, and the characters and motivations of the history that we tell: they affect the whole landscape of early modern stage history. How far Brome's contract is treated as representative of routine theatre practice impacts not only upon the ways in which individual dramatists are thought to have worked and negotiated within the theatrical marketplace, but also those in which managers and companies operated, and the means by which they accumulated competitive repertories. This paper aims to reassess the nature and implications of Brome's contract, in the context of the history of theatrical contracts and the production rates and patterns of his contemporaries. It takes issue with G. E. Bentley's statement that 'the primary significance' of the Brome contract documents lies within 'their revelation of actual customary relations between a playwright and an acting company,' and attempts to show that the current model for understanding the commitments and obligations of the early modern playwright requires careful reassessment.[5]

To the best of our knowledge, Brome's contract itself no longer survives. We know of it only because Brome violated its terms, prompting a Requests Proceedings Bill of Complaint filed on 12 February 1640 by the company then renting the Salisbury Court, Queen Henrietta's Men. In these documents, Richard Heton—Gunnell's successor as manager of the theatre—and the actors, claimed that Brome had agreed 'for the terme of three years ... with his best Art and Industrye [to] write everye yeare three plays and deliver them to the company of players there acting for the time being.'[6] Furthermore, they added that Brome had assented that he would not provide 'any play or any part of a play to any other players or play house.' In return, Brome would receive a regular payment of fifteen shillings a week, and an extra day's profit for every new play. By 1638 however, Brome had failed to deliver four of his nine promised plays. He had also sold 'one of the playes which he made ... in the said time unto Christopher Beeston gent and William Beeston' at the Cockpit.[7] Despite this breach, Heton renewed the contract in 1638. The revised contract specified that Brome's salary would rise to twenty shillings a week, but demanded the same production rate of three plays annually, for an extended term of seven years. In addition, Brome was required to produce the plays owed to the company from the prior agreement. Once more, Brome failed to do so. By the end of the year, he was in arrears by one new play. The Heton complaint records that by this time, Brome had 'wholly applie[d] himself unto the said Beeston and the Companie of players Acting at the playhouse of the Phoenix [or Cockpit] in Drury Lane.'[8] As a further complication, Brome argued in his answer to the Requests that he *had* composed a new play for Heton around September of 1639, and another before Easter, but that both had been refused by the company.

The story told by the court proceedings reveals a narrative of tension and antagonism. Yet the cause of this disruption to professional dealings—the contract itself—is figured in criticism as an essential component of company management, regulating and assuring consistent dramatic output.[9] An overview of contractual precedents will provide some framework against which to situate the nature of the Brome contract, and determine the validity of its application to the practices of other playwrights. There exists only one other known formal contract to bind a playwright in similar manner to an employer, made between Lawrence and John Dutton, Thomas Goffe, and Rowland Broughton.[10] Again, this contract is documented only as a consequence of its dishonouring—a lawsuit of 26 January 1572/3 records that Broughton failed (perhaps unsurprisingly) to deliver the *eighteen plays* that he had promised at periodic deadlines throughout the space of one year. Such measured demands, although an extreme case, had proved an unsuccessful mode of theatrical production sixty years prior to Brome's agreement.

Roslyn Knutson has also drawn attention to two contracts documented in Henslowe's papers. The first, made on 28 February 1598, is an agreement between Henslowe (on behalf of the Admiral's Men) and Henry Porter. Henslowe had lent Porter forty shillings 'in earnest of' a play, but had agreed with Porter that 'for the Resayte of the money he gave me his faythfulle promysse that I shold have alle the boockes wch he writte him sellfe or wth any other.'[11] This agreement establishes Henslowe's rights to exclusive ownership of all of Porter's plays—even those produced collaboratively—but does not specify an expected rate of production, which—according to our understanding of the later 1630s company management—is a crucial component of Brome's undertaking. Furthermore, this 'contract' appears to be situated within a face-to-face (or oral) era of theatrical production: a 'faythfull promysse' is all that is required, and the lack of formalisation suggests that this kind of assurance was sufficient both for the manager and the playwright. There is one further entry in Henslowe's papers that might suggest the contractual commitment of Henry Chettle to Henslowe. On 25 March 1602, Henslowe lent Thomas Downton and Edward Alleyn three pounds to secure Henry Chettle's services 'to writte for them the some of' an unspecified number of plays.[12] The entry appears to be unfinished, and fails to specify the terms of the arrangement. This ambiguity aside, the arrangement with Chettle resembles more of a standard play commission, common to the way that Henslowe solicited plays for the Admiral's Men during this time, than the kind of contractual terms that Brome was subject to. This evidence suggests that although dramatists often made agreements with managers concerning the destination and ownership of the plays that they produced, formalized contracts in the sense that are suggested by the Brome court depositions were deemed neither necessary implementation nor standard theatrical practice.

Contracts between players and their managers were far more common. After Richard Jones, Thomas Downton,

Robert Shaw, and William Bird left the Admiral's Men in 1597 to play for Pembroke's Men at Langley's Swan, the ensuing scandal over *The Isle of Dogs* necessitated their prompt return to Henslowe at the Rose, who consequently enforced bonds from all company members.[13] Langley had similarly imposed bonds and sureties upon five of Pembroke's Men at their opening, of 100*l* per actor ensuring their employment for twelve months.[14] These bonds appear to have set a formulaic precedent for future company procedure, as Gunnell also arranged a contractual agreement with his players in 1624 who obliged 'themselves to the said Mr Gunnell to stay and play there' at his theatre.[15]

The economic exigencies of owning permanent playhouses, as theatre historians now recognize, resulted in the requirement of managers such as Henslowe and Gunnell to formalize relations between players in order to regulate income. As K. E. McLuskie and Rebecca Rogers observe, 'fixed London venues increased the stakes: theatrical activity became a bigger, more commercial enterprise, and in turn became a more capital-driven, contract-governed venture.'[16] It is important to note the conditions under which contractual bindings arose, however. In the cases of Henslowe, who had recently experienced the autonomous caprice of his players, and Langley, at the outset of a new theatrical investment, these were times of stress. Gunnell enforced his bonds to the Palsgrave's Men during perpetual financial struggle following the burning of the Fortune playhouse. Knutson has suggested of the Henslowe/Porter arrangement that it may have anticipated the imminent move of the Chamberlain's Men to the nearby Maid Lane.[17] The evidence suggests that contracts constituted insurance policies during periods of disruption and uncertainty, and are not to be classified as generally representative. Furthermore, while systems of bonds and contracts amongst players continued to hold currency over the decades, Henslowe's 1597 bonds suggest that it was neither a customary nor an appropriate means of managing relations with playwrights: Thomas Heywood was contracted to the company in the specific capacity of a player, agreeing 'not to playe any where public about London' besides the Rose, and while Jonson returned from prison to Henslowe and wrote five plays for the company in five years, there survives no evidence of a formal agreement. E. K. Chambers has suggested that Jonson may have invested in a share, in a voluntary expression of allegiance to the company, but evidence is lacking, and Jonson does not appear to have followed the economic logic of shareholding as his concurrent commitment to the Queen's Revels and Chamberlain's Men reveals.[18]

The notion that playwrights felt themselves free to form their own allegiances and locate buyers for plays, *despite* 'cementing' relations with managers in the form of either a promise or pre-payment, is also evidenced by Robert Daborne's behaviour while working for Henslowe. Henslowe had commissioned *The Arraignment of London* from him, but Daborne's suggestions that he might sell it on to the

King's Men suggests that the cement that held dramatists to companies was nothing like as strong as Brome's contract might imply.[19] The apparent negotiability of commitments prior to the emergence of the 1640 court depositions might explain the notable discrepancies between the expectations of the Salisbury Court management and Brome himself, who claimed that he had harboured misgivings about the stringent requirements that Gunnell's contract made of him, and had been 'unwilling to undertake ... more than he could well perform.'[20] As Ann Haaker notes however, Brome had been assured by the Salisbury Court players that the annual stipulation of three plays was no more than a guarantee of dedication, and that given his loyalty and hard-work for the company, he need not produce more plays than he 'could or should be able well and conveniently to do and perform.'[21] Heton's demands for the plays owed in arrears, and the testimony of the court documents, contradict this liberal interpretation. Brome had argued, furthermore, against the normalcy of halting weekly payments during plague time, unless specified between the company and dramatist. The interpretative gap between what the contract explicitly stated and what it failed to articulate struggles over definitions of standard theatrical practice, and reveals the fundamental discontinuity in the theatrical ideologies that Brome and Heton attempt to naturalize in competition.

The patterns of production identifiable in the work of contemporary playwrights are a further consideration in the assessment of the typicality of Brome's contractual binding. An analysis of professional attachments reveals that contractual obligation such as defined in the Brome-Heton documents is an inappropriate description of common methods of production, which doesn't always apply. John Fletcher's dramatic production does not resemble *exclusive* contractual behaviour until after Shakespeare's death, after which he may have taken on a share in the company that would effectively ensure his loyalty. While from 1610 the King's Men performed an average of one of his plays a year, from 1607 to 1615, Fletcher also produced at least seven plays performed by the Children of the Queen's Revels and Lady Elizabeth's Men.[22] During the years 1597 to 1602, Ben Jonson was writing for the Lord Admiral's Men, the Lord Chamberlain's, and the Queen's Revels, followed by the composition of *Bartholomew Fair* for Lady Elizabeth's Men at the Hope. There follows a period of sustained but erratic work for the King's Men, culminating in *A Tale of a Tub* for Queen Henrietta's.

Jonson's tendency to work periodically for a set of established employers while branching into new relationships and securing relatively short-term associations with a variety of companies is also evident in the professional strategies of both Dekker and Heywood. Dekker's career exhibits the most variance, in his commitment to nine theatrical companies. Gurr observes that some dramatists of the period 'shopped around with their services,'[23] but Dekker's activities are placed into perspective by the recognition that strong elements of continuity exist among many of these troupes, which constituted various components and stages of the Henslowe enterprize: the Admiral's Men, Worcester's, and the Prince's Men. Yet interspersed among these associations are three plays that were performed by the Children of St. Paul's.[24] These dual commitments were succeeded by three plays for the Queen Anne's/Red Bull Revels company, followed by two for Prince Charles' Men, and one for Lady Elizabeth's (all of which played at the Cockpit between 1617-1625). Similar patterns of association are also present in Heywood's commitments. After a relatively long-term attachment to the Henslowe companies as a player and (secondarily) a playwright, following the 1597 bonds, Heywood turned his attention to the Beeston companies, followed by a brief but concentrated spell with the King's Men. Similarly, Ford transferred company allegiances frequently while maintaining a network of companies the employment of which he might return to. Most interestingly, Ford appears to have written for Queen Henrietta's Men and the King's Men intermittently, interspersing his ten-year association with the Cockpit with a six year interval productive of (at least) three Blackfriars plays.

These production patterns and rates reveal that dramatists, driven by opportunism and commercialism, appear to have established relationships and networks with a number of companies, which they could maintain simultaneously and might revisit. They reveal no evidence of contractual obligation as stringent as Brome's. The playwright to whom the tenets of Brome's contract is most frequently applied is James Shirley, in the interpretation of his steady production of plays for the Cockpit. Gurr describes Shirley as the Cockpit's 'resident writer,'[25] and Bentley states that 'he was associated with the company as no other playwright was.'[26] Bentley perceives a pattern of an average two plays a year for the company, suggestive to him of contractual conditions identical in essence, though less demanding, to those of Brome. While the vagaries of dating plays will always provide obstacles to interpretation, Shirley's activities are unusually clearly recorded in Herbert's office-book, and suggest that the annual quantity of plays produced by Shirley rose significantly from 1631 until 1635. The intervention of plague might explain these variations, which in turn implies—rather than a regulated yearly quota, as defined by Heton—the intervention of circumstantial factors such as supply and demand.[27] These factors might also be affected by what other playwrights were doing at the time: it may not be coincidental that in the years prior to 1631, when Shirley was at his least active for Queen Henrietta's Men and producing an average of one play every eighteen months, Heywood and Brome were immersed in their most active engagement with the company.

In the midst of his activity for Queen Henrietta's Men, Shirley composed *The Changes* performed by the King's Revels at Salisbury Court—a case, frequently neglected by theatre historians, which has significant consequences for the interpretation of his association with the Cockpit. If Shirley had been formally contracted to the company, this play would dishonour such an agreement in a manner identical to Brome's apparent transgression. We hear of no legal action or discontent over Shirley's 'infidelity,' however, and in the context of the patterns of production of his contemporaries, Shirley's deviance from a permanent commitment to only one company is far more representative of playwriting customs than the requirements of Heton. It is also the way in which Brome seems accustomed to working. Before 1635, Brome had worked for Prince Charles' Men at the Red Bull—an arrangement in which, as Brome states in the depositions, he was 'very well intertayned and truly paied without murmering or wranglinge.'[28] The Prince's Men not only keep Brome's services on good terms, but also appear to have accepted his involvement in projects that were extraneous (and potentially opposed) to their own interests, for in 1634 Brome wrote **The Late Lancashire Witches** with Heywood for the King's Men.[29]

The condition of exclusive loyalty to a company rarely held, then. It is more helpful to consider the nature of the theatrical market, even as established as it was by the 1630s, as governed by the variable factors of plague time, repertory strategy, and playwright availability, than as a regulated and stable enterprise. The essential concern of the contract-holding manager remained not only the provision of new plays as assets for his company, but also the maintenance of an established core of repertory, composed of a significant proportion of revivals in the Caroline period. This meant that while the production of new plays was still a primary concern of managers, the commodity provided by the playwright and that provided by the player differed in value more than ever; a state of affairs reflected in the contractual binding of players. Dramatists were required to stock the playhouses with which they chose to associate themselves as and when new plays were needed—and this level of commitment was dependent not only on factors such as plague closure, but also upon the relations and commissions struck by the company with other dramatists. Furthermore, there were mutual benefits for playwrights and companies to work regularly together, beyond the ownership of shares and contractual bindings: the identification of a company that required a dramatists' services indefinitely or periodically was also a situation that might be manipulated through his provision of repertory and establishment of particular kinds of fare. As Joseph Loewenstein suggests, internal company relations 'maintained the loose linkages of company, performance style, distinctive performers and dramaturgic idiom that gave the theatrical 'market' its coherence.'[30] The influence that playwrights had over the creation of expectations in company repertory and fare, perpetuating and shaping traditions and market niches for commercial exploitation, constituted an essential part of this market. Other advantages of committing to a company were more practical—a working knowledge of a specific playhouse's performance

conditions, for example, or familiarity with readily available property and costume holdings. Shirley's association with Beeston's Cockpit, and Fletcher and Massinger's with the King's Men, may have been prompted by no more than such considerations: we need not infer the contract from what looks at first to be 'contractual' behaviour.

The extent to which Brome's contract was unusually strict, and to which he understood it as negotiable, also indicates the reformulation of managerial priorities into the 1630s—or at least those of Heton. Beeston and Gunnell had both emerged from backgrounds of playing and (presumably) had some appreciation of the conditions entailed by the everyday operation of theatrical companies. Henslowe had gradually developed these familiar expectations and procedures over his life-long career; yet Heton's position as a manager is unique, as he possessed no expertise in theatrical enterprises. The unforgiving conditions of his contract, misunderstandings generated in its discursive formalisation, contradictory conceptions of playhouse practice, energetic demands for legal compensation, and repeated misplacement of emphasis upon Brome's word (his orally delivered promise) may demonstrate professional inexperience and naivety rather than shrewd autocracy. Matthew Steggle has drawn attention to the immediate historical context of the contract's breaking, which involved the movement of two players—George Stutville and Edward Gibbs—from Salisbury Court to join the new Cockpit company of Beeston's Boys—which may have been assisted by intervention on the part of Sir Henry Herbert, Master of the Revels. Steggle observes that 'Brome was not the only theatre worker whose loyalties at this time were being transferred from the King's Revels to Beeston,' prompting Heton's concern and subsequent court action.[31] Martin Butler has recently taken up this argument in an analysis of impresarial models of management, and also argues that Heton's 'distinctive' managerialism was 'reactive' rather than preordained: 'an attitude that crystallised haphazardly in response to changing circumstances,' which included not only Brome's infidelity, but ongoing antagonism with the Cockpit playhouse.[32]

Heton was moving, at the same time, to formalize relations and tighten his governance through written conditions across the entire company: maintaining contractual relations with Brome was just part of this process. He argued in the collection of documents now held in the British Library and known as 'Heton's Papers,' that written conditions 'would be the occasion to avoyd many differences and disturbances that happen both between the Company and housekeepers, amongst the Company themselves, and many generall discontents.' One of these discontents appears to be the unreliability of his players: Heton complains that 'for their owne benefite companies of Actors have removed from their residence, and dispersed themselves into severall places, soe that noe certaine place of abode is knowne where they may be found.'[33] Steggle has pointed out that the circumstances surrounding Brome's contract suggest that 'stage-writers were regarded as only one element of the theatrical machine, rather than being in a unique class by themselves.'³⁴ These are certainly the terms in which Heton regarded Brome, as a supplier of plays that required regulating in terms comparable to the players of the company. But as the evidence suggests, dramatists appear to have exerted a degree of autonomy over the professional relations that they struck: this model was not paradigmatic. The necessity that Heton felt for formal contracts and the inadequacy of the spoken promise—for Heton and, as it emerged, for Brome in a court of law following his liberal interpretation of the required quantity of plays—highlights the vulnerability of the 'impresarial' manager in this specific instance: Gunnell and Heton needed Brome's plays, and Brome was quick to recognise this in his observation that the Salisbury Court company was 'in the Infancie of theire setting upp.'³⁵

The extent of Brome's own dependency upon Heton and the conditions of the contract has also recently been confirmed. Owing to new documents discovered by Eleanor Lowe in the course of research undertaken for the *Complete Works of Richard Brome* project, it is possible to consider specific motivations that may have prompted Brome to subscribe to Heton's demands, despite their stringency. Lowe has identified Brome's signature in a series of rent books belonging to the archives of the Charterhouse Hospital, which record payments made to pensioners resident at the Charterhouse.³⁶ This affirmation of Brome's poverty at the end of his life adds further nuance to his professional activities prior to this. Heton's contract pre-empted any opportunity for Brome to raise extra funds from the publication of his plays: it categorizes even the textual afterlife of his drama as company property, explicitly specifying that Brome 'should not suffer any playe made or to bee made or Composed by him for yoʳ subiects or theire successors in the said Companye in Salsbury Courte to bee printed … without the License from the said Companye.'³⁷ On the other hand, contracted work meant that he was paid regularly, regardless of the amount of plays that he actually produced: in theory, he had a fixed weekly salary, rather than living from the unpredictable profits made from his drama and returns from any shares that he may have held. These special and specific conditions that held, both for Brome and Heton, serve to contextualise the contract and its attempted enforcement, in ways that undermine is application as paradigmatic.

The resituation of Brome's contract that is offered here reveals the fundamentally vexed and particular conditions of its nature. The breaking of Brome's contract, rather than our knowledge of its existence, constitutes the 'primary significance' of these documents, and reveals far more of the characteristic relations between dramatist and company than the conditions of the contract are able to reveal. This paper reveals the importance of contextualization as a critical approach, and the extent to which our narratives of early modern theatre history—particularly those of the

1630s—are grounded upon generalizations that require careful reworking and examination, with implications for the status and autonomy of the renaissance dramatist, the role of the impresarial manager, and the ways in which repertories were acquired in the established and competitive environment of the Caroline theatre.

Notes

1. See, for instance, G. E. Bentley. *The Jacobean and Caroline Stage,* 7 vols. (Oxford, 1956) 5: 1068: 'the regularity of his composition for plays for the Cockpit suggests that he may have had a contract with Christopher Beeston similar to that of Richard Brome.'

2. Andrew Gurr, *The Shakespearian Playing Companies* (Oxford, 1996) 9.

3. Ibid., 8.

4. Ibid., 16.

5. Bentley, *The Jacobean and Caroline Stage,* 3: 53

6. For a full transcript of the depositions and a discussion, see Ann Haaker, 'The Plague, The Theatre, and the Poet,' *Renaissance Drama* n.s.1 (1968): 283-306, esp. 297.

7. Ibid., 298.

8. Ibid., 299-300.

9. At various points, G. E. Bentley has speculated about contractual relations for Fletcher, Massinger, and Shirley Bentley. Bentley states of the King's Men that 'It seems likely that they entered into some sort of contract with Fletcher' (3: 308). Of Massinger, Bentley indicates that his plays written for the Cockpit 'show that Massinger was evidently not bound by contract to the King's company in the last years of Fletcher's life … [I]t is possible that a better dating of the plays might show a complete break with the King's company and an attachment to Beeston's troupes for two or three years … [A]fter Fletcher's death in August 1625 Massinger became the regular dramatist for the King's Men' (4: 754-5). Bentley also writes that 'Evidently Shirley was under contract to the company or the manager of the Phoenix, as Richard Brome is known to be at Salisbury Court' (1: 227).

10. Mark R. Benbow, 'Dutton and Goffe versus Broughton: A disputed contract for plays in the 1570s,' *REED Newsletter* (1981) 3-9.

11. R. A. Foakes (ed.), *Henslowe's Diary,* 2nd ed. (Cambridge, 2002), 105.

12. Ibid., 199.

13. Ibid., 238-41.

14. E. K. Chambers, *The Elizabethan Stage,* 4 vols. (Oxford, 1923) 2: 131.

15. Bentley, *The Jacobean and Caroline Stage,* 6: 158.

16. K. E. McLuskie, and Rebecca Rogers, 'Who Invested in Early Modern Theatre?,' *Research Opportunities in Medieval and Renaissance Drama* 41 (2002), 38.

17. Roslyn Knutson, *Playing Companies and Commerce in Shakespeare's Time* (Cambridge, 2001), 55.

18. Jonson's *Every Man in His Humour* and *Every Man Out of His Humour* were performed by the Chamberlain's Men in 1598 and 1599; from *c.* 1597 to 1609 Jonson wrote for the Children of the Queen's Revels at the Blackfriars, contributing five plays between 1600 and 1609 (*The Case Is Altered, Cynthia's Revels, The Poetaster, Eastward Ho!* (with Chapman and Marston) and *Epicoene*). From 1603 he was concurrently writing for the King's (previously Chamberlain's Men), before selling *Bartholomew Fair* to Lady Elizabeth's Men, who were playing at this time at Henslowe's Hope Theatre.

19. Knutson, *Playing Companies and Commerce,* 55.

20. Haaker, 'The Plague, The Theatre, and the Poet,' 301.

21. Ibid., 302

22. In 1613, the Children of the Queen's Revels merged with the Lady Elizabeth's Men, who appear to have inherited some of their plays. Fletcher wrote *The Knight of the Burning Pestle* and *The Scornful Lady* for the Children of the Revels with Francis Beaumont, and (alone) *Cupid's Revenge*. After 1613, it appears that he wrote *The Honest Man's Fortune* and, with Beaumont, *Wit Without Money,* for Lady Elizabeth's Men. *Monsieur Thomas* and *The Nightwalker* were written for either the Queen's Revels company or Lady Elizabeth's.

23. Andrew Gurr, *The Shakespearean Stage, 1576-1642* 3rd ed. (Cambridge, 1995) 20.

24. These were *Satiromastix,* performed jointly by the Children of St. Paul's and the Lord Chamberlain's Men and published in 1602, and *Westward Ho!* and *Northward Ho!* (1604-5).

25. Gurr, *Playing Companies,* 419.

26. Bentley, *The Jacobean and Caroline Stage,* 1: 227

27. As Leeds Barroll examines in *Politics, Plague and Shakespeare's Theater: The Stuart Years* (Ithaca, 1991), and Haaker emphasises in 'The Plague, The Theatre, and the Poet,' 287-9.

28. Haaker, 'The Plague, The Theatre, and the Poet,' 301.

29. Interestingly, Heywood was distracted by this play from his work for the Cockpit in the same way that Brome was from the Red Bull; their collaboration on *The Late Lancashire Witches* constitutes a break from their usual working pattern at this time that again

highlights the peculiarity of its provenance—see Herbert Berry, 'The Globe Bewitched and El Hombre Fiel,' *Medieval and Renaissance Drama in England* 1 (1984): 211-230; Heather Hirschfeld, 'Collaborating Across Generations: Thomas Heywood, Richard Brome, and the Production of *The Late Lancashire Witches,*' and lately Kathleen E. McLuskie, 'Politics and Aesthetic Pleasure in 1630s Theater' in Adam Zucker and Alan B. Farmer (eds), *Localizing Caroline Drama: Politics and Economics of the Early Modern Stage* (New York, 2006), 43-68. At the same time, it illuminates the entrepreneurship of professional dramatists, and the fact that they were at liberty to make the most of opportunities as they arose.

30. Joseph Loewenstein, *Ben Jonson and Possessive Authorship* (Cambridge, 2002) 55.

31. Matthew Steggle, *Richard Brome, Place and Politics on the Caroline Stage* (Manchester, 2004) 107.

32. Martin Butler, 'Exeunt Fighting: Poets, Players, and Impresarios at The Caroline Hall Theaters,' in Zucker and Farmer, *Localizing Caroline Drama,* 97-128.

33. For Richard Heton's Papers, see Bentley, *The Jacobean and Caroline Stage,* 2: 684-7 and Peter Cunningham, *Shakespeare Society's Papers,* 4 vols. (London, 1844-9), 4: 95-100.

34. Steggle, *Richard Brome,* 107.

35. Haaker, 'The Plague, The Theatre, and the Poet,' 301.

36. Eleanor Lowe, 'Confirmation of Richard Brome's Final Years in Charterhouse Hospital,' *Notes & Queries,* 54:4 (December 2007).

37. Haaker, 'The Plague, The Theatre, and the Poet,' 298.

Mimi Yiu (essay date 2007)

SOURCE: Yiu, Mimi. "Facing Places in Richard Brome's *The Weeding of Covent Garden.*" *Early Theatre* 10.2 (2007): 149-58. Print.

[*In the following essay, Yiu interprets* The Weeding of the Covent Garden *as a meditation on "the consequences of marrying an alien architectural form" to a traditional one. Yiu argues that Brome dramatizes these consequences in the "unweeded sexuality" of the play's female characters, who represent a combination of idleness and luxury.*]

Much like its namesake square, Richard Brome's play ***The Weeding of Covent Garden*** deliberately essays into speculative territory, undertaking an imaginative exercise in urban planning on a very public stage. Although Brome's title suggests that Covent Garden was a site not only familiar to audiences, but indeed so long-established and overgrown as to require weeding, this area of London was actually a massive construction project just starting to take shape in 1632-3, when the play itself was likely plotted and performed.[1] With a design commissioned from Inigo Jones, then at the height of his fame as Surveyor of the King's Works, the fourth Earl of Bedford set out to transform a largely undeveloped patch of land, used as pasturage since the times of Henry VIII, into an architecturally innovative and coherent neighbourhood of roughly twenty acres. Anchoring this planned community would be an elegant residential square modelled after an Italian piazza, a public space heralding a style and function yet unseen in London's urban fabric. Workers had broken ground on the square's west flank with the construction of St. Paul's Church, likely begun in 1631, although the landmark rowhouses along the north and east sides belong to a later period of building spanning 1633-4 to 1637.[2] Thus faced with an embryonic site undergoing a rapid metamorphosis, a more cautious playwright might have deferred writing about Covent Garden until clearer outlines emerged from the muck of construction, awaiting especially the completion of Bedford's showpiece piazza. Yet by firmly planting his feet on the unfinished ground of 1632-3, by founding his play on a contingent site yet to signify securely in the public imagination, Brome raises cogent questions about the kinds of social script soon to play out in this space of potentiality, a space structurally marked by a destabilizing foreignness. What are the consequences of marrying an alien architectural form to a local *habitus*? For Brome, it seems, such anxieties of spatial miscegenation can be figured by a conflicting notion of the feminine—understood doubly as the gendered body of architecture and as the unweeded sexuality of women within the new Covent Garden.

Bounded by St. Martin's Lane to the west, Drury Lane to the east, Long Acre to the north, and the Strand on the south, Covent Garden stands at the heart of an expanding seventeenth-century London, occupying an area adjacent to the grand residences pushing ever westwards down the Strand. Situating his own impressive house at the southern end of Jones's square, Bedford undertakes a considerable personal and financial investment in his decision to develop Covent Garden, negotiating delicately around James I's ban on new construction in London while paying thousands of pounds for licences and fines. As part of his overarching vision to erect a home neighbourhood virtually *ex nihilo,* a socially and geographically exclusive community lacking even an access road to the Strand, Bedford partners with Inigo Jones to demonstrate cultural sophistication and difference in tangible form.[3] No architect could be more suited to Bedford's sensibility than Inigo Jones, the intellectual disciple of Palladio and a court favourite; importing Italian design features yet unseen in England, Jones uses Covent Garden as an urban crucible for his neoclassical architectural principles, designing a community remarkable for its adherence to a single aesthetic. Although Jones's original drawings have been lost,[4] late seventeenth-century depictions of the central square reveal rows of uniform brick houses, set over wide vaulted

walkways intended as a covered promenade for high society: interestingly, it is these portico houses and not the square itself that Londoners called the 'Piazza,' a shift in semantics indicating the novelty and foreignness of such architectural elements.[5] Indeed, while the cosmopolitan Jones clearly knows his way around an Italian 'piazza,'[6] the execution of his design would fall to those whose neoclassical credentials were less than stellar, to a cadre of speculators who leased plots of land from Bedford and built for commercial profit. In an effort to enforce aesthetic conformity, Bedford not only stipulated in his leases an extremely detailed set of instructions for builders to follow, but also built a model range of three houses to serve as a visible reminder of the expected results.

This schism between speculative construction and architectural integrity surfaces in Brome's character Rooksbill, a builder introduced in the play's first scene. As he and Cockbrayne, a Justice of the Peace, await a potential tenant in Covent Garden, the topic of discussion turns quickly from the aesthetics of Bedford's development to the promise of cold hard cash:

COCK.:

> Your money never
> shone so on your Counting-boards, as in those Structures.

ROOK.:

> I have pil'd up a Leash of thousand pounds
> in walls and windows there.

COCK.:

> It will all come again with large encrease.
> And better is your money thus let out on red and
> white, then upon black and white, I say.

> (pp. 1-2)[7]

In this moment of masculine bonding, Cockbrayne praises his friend's shrewd investment and cultivation of wealth in choosing to build, envisioning gold as somehow structurally embedded in the shining houses before him. Indeed, in banking on a 'large encrease' from the 'red and white' of brick and stone, Rooksbill not only deploys architectural components ('walls and windows') as sites of hoarding, but also transforms the building itself into a womb generating ever more money, a weeded and constructed garden that dutifully provides a monetary harvest. Such a masculinist logic of production proves no different from the 'black and white' of mercantile banking; instead of trafficking in bills of exchange that convert foreign currency at a profit, instead of riskily letting out money to foreigners and travellers, Rooksbill sows exoticism into the home and hearth of central London, gambling that buyers will embrace a foreign aesthetic as representing cultural and financial capital.

While *Weeding* [*The Weeding of the Covent Garden*] seems to endorse such a means of reaping commercial gains through a domestication of the alien, a more feminine exploitation of the same values proves not to be so easily assimilated into London. Indeed, a gendered imbalance in the registers of Italian culture emerges towards the end of this opening scene, after Cockbrayne and Rooksbill have duly met with the country gentleman, Crosswill, who wishes to occupy one of the new houses in Covent Garden. Just as Cockbrayne is in the midst of allaying Crosewill's doubts about the modest appearance of Rooksbill, advising that 'we have able Builders here, that will not carry least shew of their buildings on their backs' (p. 8), a spectacu-larly showy personage enters the stage as if in direct coun-terpoint to these words; 'habited like a Curtizan of Venice' (ibid, s.d.), this flamboyant woman catches the enraptured eye of Gabriel, Crossewill's son, as she emerges from the upper storey of a house and stands 'upon a Bellconie [bal-cony]' (ibid). Largely unseen in her aerie until Gabriel points out 'that painted idolatrous image yonder' (pp. 8-9), this Venetian courtesan provokes an uproar not only because of her un-English, unchaste, unweeded sexuality on display, but also—oddly—because of her spatial loca-tion. Indeed, when the men below finally look up, their astonished reaction pertains more to the balcony than the woman herself:

COCK.:

> O heresie! It is some lady, or Gentlewoman standing upon her Bellconey.

BOLT.:

> Her Bellconey? Where is it? I can spy from her foot to her face, yet I can see no Bellconey she has.

COCK.:

> What a Knave's this: That's the Bellconey she stands on, that which jets out so on the forepart of the house; every house here has one of 'hem.

BOLT.:

> Tis very good; I like the jetting out of the forepart very well; it is a gallant fashion indeed.

(p. 9)

Such lexical confusion might well be understandable, since balconies constituted one of the Italian innovations first introduced in London at Covent Garden; thus, not only for Crosswill's servant Bolt but even members of Brome's audience, the term would hold less meaning than *piazza*.[8] Beyond injecting a teaching moment into the ac-tion, however, Brome clearly intends a bawdy pun on 'Bellconey' as a female body part, a mysterious and for-eign erogenous zone that Bolt vainly tries to pinpoint through visual examination. While 'coney' is a common slang term for female genitalia, as used elsewhere in the play, Brome's 'bellconey' seems curiously unanchored: it is both something the courtesan stands on and a 'jetting out of the forepart,' a reference suggestive of the legendary bared breasts of Venetian courtesans. Unlike Rooksbill's

discreet concealment of his income source by not showing his buildings on his back, this shockingly public woman not only displays her assets on the forepart, at least by implication, but her body seems to merge indistinguish-ably with the new architecture, calling into question what kinds of commerce, what kinds of transactions, the new Covent Garden actually demands.[9]

By juxtaposing the sale of Rooksbill's house against the sale of a woman's body, Brome implicates Bedford's urban development in selling out the homeland to a suspect for-eignness, focalizing a perceived clash between high Italian architecture and low Italian morals through a consideration of the feminine body. In this obliteration of difference between domestic architecture and its traditionally female occupants, the container and the contained, Jones's fancy buildings shoulder some responsibility for destroying the boundaries that keep a woman chastely continent and a garden weeded, for thrusting out the 'bellconey' as a pub-lic commercial stage. Such a persistent outward impulse, threatening the structural integrity that protects a valued interiority, infects even a naïve enthusiast like Cockbrayne as he surveys Covent Garden:

COCK.:

> Marry Sir! This is something like!
> These appear like Buildings!
> Here's Architecture exprest indeed! It is a most sightly scituation, and fit for Gentry and Nobility.

(p. 1)

Privileging the visual above any other mode of apprehen-sion, Cockbrayne absurdly lauds the buildings before him because they 'appear like Buildings,' just as he correlates the site's fitness for certain social classes merely by observ-ing its 'sightly scituation.' Indeed, content with 'something like' rather than the thing itself, Cockbrayne confidently assesses architecture from a purely external perspective: the façades constitute 'Architecture exprest' not only by artic-ulating classical principles of proportion and harmony, but also by pressing spatial meaning outwards onto an aesthet-icized exterior.

Such a strong evaluative emphasis on the visible surface almost inevitably leads to anxieties about a feminization of architecture, a sense that essential function has been sacri-ficed at the altar of 'painted idolatry'; ironically, Inigo Jones himself believed that the clean, orderly lines of neo-classical architecture constituted a 'masculine and unaf-fected' way of building.[10] In the gendered universe of Brome's play, however, the contamination of unweeded decoration in elements like balconies cannot be detached from a concomitant degradation of femininity into artifice and vulgarity, a femininity that desires to provoke a purely visual and visceral response. In the prologue to *Covent Garden* (1632), a play that seems to offer a satirical rebut-tal to Brome, Thomas Nabbes trumpets the difference ap-parent in his own superior work by homing in on precisely this inability of his rival's to separate spatial and bodily deviance:

> Do not expect th'abuses of a Place
> Nor th'ills sprung from a strumpet's painted face
> To be exprest.[11]

In this mocking dismissal of Brome, the end rhymes of 'Place' and 'face' neatly encapsulate the problematic coupling that **Weeding** tries desperately to resolve, the conflation of strumpet and building that implicitly turns Rooksbill and Cockbrayne into panders. That is, Rooksbill's meretricious houses function as commodities of exchange, as architectural bodies for hire, by triggering a homosocial exchange involving a builder, a justice who acts as go-between, and that archetypal gull, the country gentleman seeking to settle in the city. Since purchasing one of these gussied-up homes perpetually threatens to detour into purchasing a prostitute, Rooksbill, when angered by Crossewill's perversity during the property transaction, aptly retorts: 'I had rather all my Rents were Bawdy houses' (p. 6).

The painted face of these new Italian houses, then, sullies the vision of gold that irrepressibly radiates from within, the promise of natural increase from wealth solidly leashed up in red and white.[12] Indeed, in contrast to the Petrarchan conceit of intermingled roses and cream, these feminized architectural faces have been spackled over with paint and powder, cosmetics intended to distract attention from the buildings' inherent lack of rootedness in the English soil. Just as the Venetian courtesan, who has just joined the bawdy house that morning, essays speculatively into a realm of female liberation from native norms of sexuality and labour, indeed voicing a passionate manifesto in favour of a more Italian outlook on gender, the Covent Garden development that enables her escape from these conventions similarly constitutes an experiment in an imported 'progressive' sociality that literally builds upon a traditional English pasturage. The fates of these feminized bodies seem inextricably conjoined, the status of their fertility and productiveness a beacon for how an increasingly cosmopolitan London, a worldly city increasingly penetrated by foreignness, can successfully integrate such alien commerce and culture into its very centre. After all, as Cockbrayne's son Anthony asserts, the courtesan who challenges gender rules should be understood not as one of the punks who crop up later in the play, but rather as an innovative gardener, 'a She-Gallant that had travelled *France* and *Italy* [who would] Plant some of her forraign collections, the fruits of her travels, in this Garden here, to try how they would grow or thrive on English earth' (p. 11). In this description of a brave new woman whose trajectory sounds alarmingly close to that of Inigo Jones's career, Brome questions whether the planting of exotic ideas and values, no matter how highly prized by in some arenas, ultimately proves to be as sterile and unsatisfying as a whore's artificially beautified body. Such an

anxiety about the construction of these multiple feminine figures, designed by a human rather than divine architect, ultimately resolves with a trick that lifts the veneer of foreignness to expose a thoroughly native core. Thus, the courtesan on the balcony, despite voicing a defiant manifesto advocating a more Venetian notion of liberated female sexuality and labour, ultimately turns out to be Crossewill's runaway niece, Dorcas, a wronged country girl who has remained chaste all along and simply wants a good English husband; casting aside her foreign identity like an ill-fitting, ill-proportioned façade, this putative Venetian *puta* returns to the fold as an unblemished English rose, her wild ways weeded before her bloom has been irretrievably blighted.

Despite this rather convenient and conservative legerdemain that substitutes one façade for another, Brome's text itself seems unable to eliminate the spectre of femininity that perverts its very structure, its dramatic lineaments. That is, by drawing on the name-brand appeal of Covent Garden, by musing extensively on the meaning of this yet unfinished place, **Weeding** expresses a feminine preoccupation with the dichotomy of place/face that hinders the cultivation of its masculinely well-tended plot, its linear development as a five-act drama. Indeed, Brome's seeming inability to wrench his eyes away from the minutiae of a place, especially evident in its opening scene, has prompted Theodore Miles to categorize the play as belonging to a set of Caroline works that exhibit 'place-realism,' a generic characteristic marked by 'a photographic realism which seems to have been introduced for its intrinsic appeal, rather than for its effectiveness as setting.'[13] That is, Brome yokes his work to Covent Garden for the sake of greater commercial cachet and audience titillation rather than any literary concern, awkwardly and needlessly injecting passages discussing actual places to the detriment of artistic cohesion. Echoing Miles's sentiments, R. J. Kaufman's study of Brome deplores the 'misguided emphasis' of place-realistic works that 'in attaching themselves to over-specified settings, devote too much of their space to descriptive exercises, to exploring evanescent outcroppings of eccentricity, and to minor reformatory suggestions.'[14] As an unassimilated outcropping ruining the play's proportioned body, as a passing fad foreign to Brome's corpus more generally,[15] place-realism proves to be an obstacle to fulfilling the proper dramatic trajectory, stopping the temporal flow of events for an irrelevant and inconsequential excursus on space.

Minor, deviant, over-specific, photographic, intrinsically appealing, structurally counterproductive—such terms oddly resonate with Laura Mulvey's analysis of the glamour close-up in Hollywood cinema. In her classic 'Visual Pleasure and Narrative Cinema,' Mulvey contends that these lingering, soft-focus close-ups of the female body, offered up as an object of desire, serve to arrest and divert the otherwise straightforwardly masculine action that propels the plot.[16] Just as the camera glorifies bodily surfaces by encouraging the eye to roam over every aesthetically enhanced, magnified detail of a specific part, place-realism likewise indulges in a minute exploration of a glamourized and staged terrain, fetishizing sites with passages (truly *loci*) of descriptive extravagance that rove intimately over every contour: in this sense, place-realism might better be called place-hyperrealism for its valorization of a heightened representation, an unattainable potentiality, over any experiences outside the theatrical world. Indeed, beyond a structural feminization that such passages introduce into a concise and masculine text,[17] the subjects chosen by place-realist playwrights tend to be locales problematically associated with femininity; in the case of Covent Garden, whose name derives from a convent vegetable garden that supposedly once occupied the site, the play's unweeded passages of place-realism conflates a feminized close-up of a problematic *hortus non conclusus,* eminently pleasurable in its luxurious and inherently useless self-absorption, with a more conflicted, scopophilic gaze at the feminine sexuality and feminine architecture on display all around the square itself.

Indeed, by treating Covent Garden as an imported *topos,* physically and discursively, the play arrests the forward motion of construction in the square itself to interject a external note of literary reflection, an aesthetic time-out that moves the attention of Londoners from a real space to the possibilities of a performed, conditional, feminized one. Here, as elsewhere, theatre marries itself to the construction of a new reality.

Notes

1. Dates for the play's composition and first performance have not been established conclusively, although scholars seem to agree on 1632-3 due mainly to internal historical evidence. But if we accept that Thomas Nabbes' *Covent Garden,* first performed in 1632, constitutes a hastily written response to Brome, then an early date seems reasonable. Matthew Steggle's 'Brome, Covent Garden, and 1641' discusses the implications for dating in light of the play's 1641 revival '[s]ome ten years since'; see *Renaissance Forum* 5 (2001)': <http://www.hull.ac.uk/renforum/v5no2/steggle.htm> (accessed 17 September 2007).

2. *Survey of London: The Parish of St. Paul Covent Garden,* vol. 36, F. H. W. Sheppard (gen. ed.) (London, 1970), 5, 30. Dianne Duggan's recent discovery of documentation indicates that, in 1629, the local parish authorities of St Martin's in the Fields had issued Bedford a warrant for a licence to build; see ' "London the Ring, Covent Garden the Jewell of the Ring": New Light on Covent Garden,' *Architectural History* 43 (2000), 140-61. Yet not until 1631 did Bedford obtain a licence to build from the Crown, which had bestowed the property on the first Earl of Bedford in 1552. In return for £2000, Bedford received a warrant in January of 1631, followed by the licence itself in February; Bedford's household accounts show building activity commencing not long afterwards. The first recorded lease of a rowhouse dates from November 1634.

3. Duggan, ' "London the Ring, Covent Garden the Jewell of the Ring," ' elucidates new links between Jones and Bedford, particularly the choice of a royal favourite as architect as a possible condition of obtaining building licences; see esp. 143-5.

4. Duggan tentatively identifies a schedule of measurements as being labelled in Jones's handwriting 'Covent Garden 1629,' 144-5; this list of measurements, however, does not correspond with the ultimate shape of Covent Garden.

5. Cf. the usage of 'piazza' to designate covered colonnades at markets such as Leadenhall. See Kathryn A. Morrison's *English Shops and Shopping: An Architectural History* (New Haven and London, 2003), 16.

6. Jones's design is indebted to the late sixteenth-century piazza at Livorno, which in turn influenced both the Place Royale and the Place Dauphine in Paris, built by Claude de Chastillon during the first decade of the seventeenth century. Jones likely visited both cities during his trips abroad with Lord Arundel. See *Survey of London,* 64-5.

7. Richard Brome, *Five New Plays* (London: 1659). All play quotations are cited parenthetically, and come from this 1659 edition, with line breaks reproduced as in the original.

8. Though, of course, balconies were commonly a part of English stage sets, themselves inspired by Italian architecture. Adam Zucker notes how both Brome and Nabbes 'drew upon the technology of their stages (the Cockpit for Nabbes and probably the Blackfriars for Brome) to reproduce the architecture of the Covent Garden piazza'; see 'Laborless London: Comic Form and the Space of the Town in Caroline Covent Garden,' *The Journal for Early Modern Cultural Studies* 5 (2005), 102. Reciprocally, Zucker astutely observes that these same balconies in Covent Garden likely conjured theatrical associations in the minds of passersby.

9. Cf. Zucker's analysis of the balconies in both Brome and Nabbes' respective Covent Gardens as eroticized sites of feminine display, 102-6.

10. From Jones's notebooks at Chatsworth.

11. Thomas Nabbes, *Covent-Garden a pleasant comedie* (London: 1639), Prologue.

12. 'Leash' here thus signifies not only 'a set of three,' as editors usually gloss the term, but also the more common sense of 'restraint.'

13. Theodore Miles, 'Place-realism in a Group of Caroline Plays,' *The Review of English Studies* 18 (1942), 431.

14. R. J. Kaufmann, *Richard Brome: Caroline Playwright* (New York and London, 1961), 15-6.

15. Miles, 'Place-realism,' lists only six plays written between 1631 and 1635 as demonstrating place-realism. Brome's two contributions to this sub-genre are *Weeding* and *Sparagus Garden.*

16. Laura Mulvey, 'Visual Pleasure and Narrative Cinema,' *Screen* 16 (1975): 6-18.

17. We might also think here of Roland Barthes' *The Pleasure of the Text,* in which a writerly text defies the masculine logic of progression to embrace a more feminine *jouissance.* It seems to me that the pleasure of such place-centred passages goes beyond what Miles, 'Place-realism,' calls 'the pleasure of recognition,' 436.

Audrey Birkett (essay date 2007)

SOURCE: Birkett, Audrey. "Actors, Audiences and Authors: The Competition for Control in Brome's *The Antipodes.*" *"Divining Thoughts": Future Directions in Shakespeare Studies.* Ed. Pete Orford et al. Newcastle: Cambridge Scholars, 2007. 53-68. Print.

[*In the following essay, Birkett analyzes* The Antipodes *as a testament to "the lack of control that was fundamental to the commercial theatrical community in the late Caroline era." For Birkett, this theme is evident in Brome's mockery of poets who attempt to exercise total authority over their works without making any concessions to the actors.*]

Throughout the 1630s the commercial theatre was increasingly mired in economic, social, and political crises. The professional theatre was under strain toward the end of the Caroline era as opposition increased both from within the dramatic community and from different factions in the wider society. The competition for audience favour amongst the different commercial theatres led to somewhat hostile relations and derogatory slander between the playhouses. The citizen theatres like the Red Bull received the harshest treatment, whilst playwrights writing for the prestigious Blackfriars decried all other theatres as being too crude and vulgar for respectable patrons.[1] Not only did professional playwrights face opposition from their professional peers, but they also had to defend themselves against the slights of the amateur courtier poets who were writing for the commercial stage. The Caroline audiences seemed to desire the plays that more closely resembled those staged at court that the amateur writers were producing rather than those comedies that were more in the vein of the Elizabethan and Jacobean plays that had been staged at the public theatres.[2] The pressure on the professional playwrights was further compounded by sanitation concerns. Plague closures threatened to put an end to the public theatrical institution at the same time the Puritan faction was mounting opposition toward the ribaldry they associated with the London playhouses. Publication was also becoming an attractive option for playwrights who had not relinquished the rights to their plays after selling them to companies to be staged. Within this context, as I will show, Richard Brome's **The Antipodes** directly addresses all of these threats in turn. Brome criticises one playing company, whilst praising another. He turns the scrutiny of the Puritans and the courtiers back on themselves. He diminishes the threats posed by the plague and encourages the audiences to return to the theatres. He also portrays those in the courtly circle as foolish and insincere. In a play that's based on opposites and reversals, Brome highlights and stresses the threats to the real-life London theatrical society by demonstrating what the alternatives may be.

When Brome originally wrote **The Antipodes** he intended it not for the players of Salisbury Court, but for The King and Queen's Young Company performing at William Beeston's Cockpit. There had been contractual disputes between Brome and Salisbury Court leading up to Brome's writing of the play. He was obliged to write three plays a year for the company and could not publish any of the plays that he had written for them of his own accord.[3] However, when the theatres closed in 1636, Salisbury Court suspended Brome's wages forcing him to seek an alternative income at the Cockpit. The play was never staged at Beeston's theatre, however but was instead bought back by Salisbury Court and staged in 1638 after the theatres had reopened. Brome seemed dissatisfied with the performance and thus initiated the printing of the play in 1640, thereby again breaking the terms of his contract with Salisbury Court. Brome's post-script in the published version suggests that his original play was altered slightly for the 1638 performance to fit time constraints and possibly to avoid the controversy Brome had inserted into the drama against Salisbury Court.[4] Brome seems to have found fault with the staging and made amends to what was removed, calling attention to the fact that his words had been tampered with by the theatrical company. The 1640 printed version seems to have been written and re-edited by Brome himself and firmly declares that he holds the authority over the play. Through the different versions, the author, the actors, and the theatre manager leave a distinct mark on the play which brings into question who holds final authority over a play. Brome asserted his ownership when he gave it to Beeston for performance at the Cockpit. However, Beeston then demonstrated his authority over the play by getting it printed.[5] The vigorous reclaiming of the play from Beeston's Cockpit by Salisbury

Court suggests the theatrical company was eager to establish firm control over the play and thus over Brome himself who was legally contracted to the theatre. Finally, the publication of the play, complete with post-scripts and amendments, restored the power of authority back to Brome.

Widely considered a playwright for the stage and a defender of the commercial theatre, Brome adopted, at times, a slightly detached attitude toward both the stage and the wider institution of the commercial theatre in *The Antipodes.* The very insistence on writing it for the Cockpit, a stage with which he was not affiliated and defying the contractual obligations he was under, detracts from the idea that Brome had cultivated throughout his career, the belief the stage came first, even above the playwright. He had spent a career criticising the courtier poets who tended to write for the most select of theatres and yet when writing *The Antipodes,* Brome decidedly set it to be staged in a theatre that was foreign to him. His further decision to publish the play also contradicts the reputation he had established as a writer for the stage. Only three of his plays were printed during his lifetime, despite the fact that more were entered into the Stationers' Register prior to the publication of *The Antipodes.*[6] Despite his feigned aversion to publication, those plays that went to press in his lifetime seem to have been initiated by the dramatist himself, and, even more surprising, conformed to the expectations of publication, including fawning commendations from peers and sycophantic dedications to gentlemen patrons. However, only *The Antipodes* and *The Sparagus Garden* were printed in 1640 and the fact that several of the others never reached the printer shows hesitancy toward publication. Brome did initiate the printing of several more plays in 1640 after his chief rival William Davenant took control over the Cockpit when Beeston was suspended for allowing controversial plays to appear on his stage. It would appear as though the move was simply a reaction to the courtier writers' threat against the commercial theatre and not a desire on Brome's part to see his name in print.[7] Yet the 1640 publication of *The Antipodes* is a reassertion of authorial rights and a bold proclamation of authority against the commercial theatre.

The Antipodes is about the therapeutic nature of the theatre and its ability to restore the natural order. The primary focus is on Peregrine, a young man who has gone mad from reading too many travel narratives and thus has lost touch with reality. To combat his son's illness, the gentleman Joyless hires a doctor to cure Peregrine's delusions. The doctor arranges an elaborate play whereby Peregrine can act out his dreams of travelling and thus purge the fantastic desire. It is at the Lord Letoy's private theatre that the spectacle is staged and Peregrine travels to the Antipodes—a world that mirrors his own. By showing Peregrine the opposite of what he's accustomed to, the doctor creates an environment that is both remarkably similar and exceptionally alien to the patient, thereby demonstrating the benefits of the real society he has been alienated from. Through the staging of the farce, Peregrine's senses are restored and at the same time Joyless's marital problems with his young, beautiful wife, Diana, are mended, and long-lost families are reconciled. The play ends with a return to the normal, "real" world where all are restored to their natural places and natural states, but it is only thanks to Letoy's fictional "The Antipodes" that such a restoration occurs. Brome champions the commercial theatre as a place of therapy and escape, allowing the pressures from the "real" world to be alleviated. Brome treated the theatre as a place for catharsis and therapy and through comedy he could combat "melancholy, his age's pervasive disease."[8] Nevertheless, just as Peregrine, Joyless, and Diana must return to their everyday lives, so too are the curative effects of the theatre temporary as a return to normality is what is expected and inevitable.

The parallels between the plot of the play and its staging (both intended and probable) could not have been lost on Brome who was, by 1636, one of the premier professional playwrights. Although he maintained a prominent position in the professional theatre, writing *The Antipodes* for an alternative commercial stage mirrors the outline of the play as the characters seemingly travel to a place that is very like their home, but different, and at times more accommodating and agreeable. David Stevens contends that the private commercial theatres were very similar which allowed plays to be interchangeable amongst the different stages.[9] With the similarities between the different, upscale commercial theatres being so prevalent, it became a question of what company was situated in a particular theatre, and to Brome, what manager was in charge. Beeston was a widely respected and revered theatre manager and moreover, he and Brome seemed to have a personal, friendly relationship.[10] The more amenable conditions at the Cockpit suggested Brome could have exercised more creative control over the production.

Brome's growing anger and disillusionment toward the professional theatre, and more specifically toward Salisbury Court, is seen through what he included in the ancillary material of the published version. The dedication to William Seymour, the Earl of Hertford displays a need, on Brome's behalf, for publication.

> If the publicke view of the world entertain it with no lesse welcome, then that private one of the Stage already has given it, I shall be glad the World owes you the Thankes: if it meet with too severe Construction, I hope your Protection. What hazards soever it shall justle with, my desires are it may pleasure your Lordship in the perusal, which is the only ambition he is conscious of, who is My Lord, Your Honour's humble devoted: Richard Brome.[11]

Brome's terming of the stage as "private" and his belief in the "publicke" domain of the printed book runs contrary to the previous notions he had issued in plays and prologues.[12] The stage had always been the place for a play and it was important that anyone and everyone had access to drama in performance. Furthermore, the price of books and the relatively low level of literacy meant that only certain (often higher class) patrons could purchase and consume printed play texts.[13] Because the play had been staged at Salisbury Court, Brome could be criticising the exclusivity of the theatre as being too "private" for what he had written. However, the Cockpit was not an open, public theatre inviting all and sundry, but rather it enjoyed a very privileged clientele.[14] His dedication to the "Earle of Hertford, &c" further suggests that Brome was opening the play up to a wider audience than it had previously been available to, and that the audience is mixed and varied as is the "&c." His primary dedicatee, however, is Hertford, a well respected and well connected gentleman.[15] His further declaration that he hopes the play receives Hertford's "Protection" suggests a boastful assertion that it is above his dedicatee's reproach, a contrast to the attitude Brome has adopted in the past where he begged audiences for a kind reception. This assertion makes Brome sound more like the courtier dramatists that he opposed, especially when he declares his "only ambition" is to please Hertford and not to entertain the audience, which had previously been his primary aim. He finally declares himself Hertford's "humble" devotee, which again conflicted with Brome's past declarations of subservience to the commercial theatre audiences. The dedication gave authority to Hertford over the play, in the process taking it away from the theatre where it had previously been known. Brome's giving it to Hertford is also an attempt to re-establish his own authority over *The Antipodes.* It is now his to give away rather than the possession of the "private" audiences whom had already "given it" their judgement.

The post-script that Brome added to the published version of *The Antipodes* does little to clarify Brome's attitude toward the professional theatre or demarcate the ultimate authority over the play. Whereas he seems to have given ownership to Hertford in the dedication, Brome gives possession to Beeston in the epilogue.

> You shal find in this Booke more then was presented upon the *Stage,* and left out of the *Presentation,* for superfluous length (as some of the *Players* pretended) I thoght good al should be inserted according to the allowed *Original*; and as it was, at first, intended for the *Cock-pit Stage,* I the right of my most deserving Friend Mr. *William Beeston,* unto whom it properly appertained.[16]

Brome gives authority to Beeston "unto whom [the play] properly appertained." However, as it is now in printed form and not a staged presentation, the ownership seems questionable with Brome, the literary audience, and Beeston all able to claim ownership and authority over it. Brome stresses the "Booke" is now the most important item as it contains all that he had intended for the stage. As such, it would be the reader who exerted complete control over the literature. At the same time, Brome clearly states that it is Beeston who is the controlling agent as he is the one that the play was intended for from the start. Nevertheless,

Brome's switching of authority suggests that it is he who is the ultimate controller over the play and dictator of its fate. The one group that he does not allocate any form of authority to, however, is the players. He begrudges their attempts to assert authority over the play. All of this is further complicated by the manner in which the epilogue is printed. Assuming that Brome did exert control over the publication, the decision to highlight the words "Stage," "Presentation," "Players," "Original," "Cock-pit Stage," and "William Beeston" suggest close ties and a determined affiliation with the performance as opposed to the published book.[17]

Although *The Antipodes* does ultimately praise the therapeutic power of the theatre, it also exposes the complications that arise from the competition for control between the actors, the writers, the authors, and the audiences. The owner of the small, private theatre, Letoy, controls the overall action and direction of the play-within-the-play from afar, as well as influences the response of Joyless, his captive audience. Letoy is also the author of the play and thus exerts even more influence and control over the play. In fact, the only thing he does not do is act, yet he still tries to keep a tight reign on how the action proceeds. He states that he "must looke to all," implying that every single aspect of the play is his to determine and control.[18] However, the insertion of Peregrine into the play as an unknowing actor alters the circumstances to the point that the original plot is dramatically changed and Letoy's power is diminished as the actors react to the participant. Although the outcome remains the same, Peregrine's cure, the direction in which it is realised is largely determined by Peregrine himself in his interactions with the acting Antipodeans. Whilst Letoy plays the role of both author and manager, it is the actors who ultimately drive the play as they react to Peregrine's whims and fancies. The whole play is staged for the benefit of the Joylesses who have facilitated the entire staging to have their son's health restored. Although Joyless's wishes are not always followed, his reactions, and those of his wife, determine the action and remain the driving force behind Brome's narration.

Letoy exerts his authority over the play by exerting his authority over the actors that he employs. As he owns his own private theatre, he keeps a private troupe that is on-hand at all times solely for his amusement:

> Stage-plays, and Masques, are nightly my pastimes,
> And all within my selfe. My owne men are
> My Musique, and my Actors. I keepe not
> A man or boy but is of quality:
> The worst can sing or play his part o'th' Violls,
> And act his part too in a Comedy,
> For which I lay my bravery on their backs;
> And where another Lord undoes his followers,
> I maintaine mine like Lords. And there's my bravery.[19]

Letoy claims that the actors belong to him and that they are, in fact, his "followers." His conceit highlights the abilities of the players, but more importantly shows the greatness of Letoy himself. "His" men are the best, there-fore, "his" theatre is the best. His insistence that his actors are of the highest "quality" speaks to the high levels of competition amongst the theatres and the boastfulness of managers in attracting audiences with the promise of the best players. Letoy claims that he writes "all the playes my selfe" and even though he is responsible for what is staged, the confession that his "bravery" comes from the manner in which he keeps his players suggests that he realises they are the most important faction in playing. Despite Letoy's admittance of the importance of the players, he is still anxious to maintain strict control over the direction of the play. He is very dictatorial about what should be staged and how it is to be acted:

> Trouble not you your head with my conceite,
> But minde your part. Let me not see you act now,
> In your Scholasticke way, you brought to towne wi' yee.[20]

Letoy's advice to his actors sounds very much like Hamlet's advice to the travelling players who have come to Elsinore. He even suggests that his own troupe is lately come from the country and as such, do not fully understand how a play should be acted in "towne." His reference to "Scholasticke" acting methods suggests the actors could have come from a university troupe and they are therefore unaware of what is expected on the London stages. His directions to "trouble not you your head with [his] conceite" shows the tenuous balance of power that exists between himself and his actors. He tells the actors to disregard his "conceite," but then dictates to them how they should act, saying he will have it no other way in "his house." The play in his house makes him the ultimate authority to the point of deciding if and when a play is to be staged.

In a later exchange with the actors, Letoy concedes some of the authority he has previously claimed by giving the actors license to interpret what he has written for themselves:

> Take license to your owne selfe, to adde unto
> Your parts, your owne free fancey; and sometimes
> To alter, or diminish what the writer
> With care and skill compose'd: and when you are
> To speake to your coactors in the Scene,
> You hold interloqutions with the Audients.[21]

In this speech to his actors, Letoy bestows on them the power to alter what is scripted as they see fit, trusting their abilities and their discretion. He is sure to remind them of the importance of his own careful and skilful wording, but he admits that the power to convey the messages ultimately rests with the actors. Furthermore, his final command to acknowledge the "Audients" demonstrates the power that the viewers have and that ultimately the play is designed to be viewed. Therefore the spectator holds as much power as the actors and the interaction between the two is what drives the play and makes it successful, not the script. Letoy constantly grapples for control with his actors, yet he betrays his own belief in the importance of the players and the audience over the writer:

> Ile none of these, absurdities in my house.
> But words and action married so together,
> That shall strike harmony in the eares and eyes
> Of the severest, if judicious Criticks.[22]

Letoy himself seems to be the most "judicious Critick" of all and as he influences the reception of the plays to the small, intimate audiences he hosts, he controls to a degree how the play is viewed.

Letoy does all he can to control any and all aspect of the play and not just the actors, but the audience reception as well. As he is situated alongside the viewers, he is able to manipulate their responses to his ends:

> And for my Actors, they shall speake, or not speake
> As much, or more, or lesse, and when I please,
> It is my way of pleasure, and ile use it.
> So sit: They enter.[23]

The control the audience exerted over the play is very limited in both the actual *The Antipodes* and the fictional one. Letoy's order to the audience is "sit" and thereby respect the entrance of the actors, whom now command more attention and respect then the audience. The authority of Joyless and Diana is subject entirely to Letoy's will as he holds nearly complete influence over how the couple react to what's being staged for their benefit, manipulating them and their responses. Joyless several times expresses a desire to leave the theatre and Letoy's house. However, he is again and again denied and ends up something of a prisoner in Letoy's house in the final act. Byplay warns him to "take your dungeon Sir" suggesting that Letoy is not of his own free will, but also establishes his subservient role to the actors as well as Letoy.[24] In fact, it is through the play that he is cured of his jealousy and therefore he is being manipulated and not acting of his own free will at all. All of this is designed, by Letoy, to reveal that Diana is his daughter and that Joyless has no cause for jealousy. Diana and Joyless are being manipulated from the very beginning of the play as they are invited under false pretences to the performance.

> Letoy: know sir, that I sent for him, and for you,
> Instructing your friend *Blaze* my instrument,
> To draw you to my Doctor with your sonne,
> Your wife I knew must follow, what my end
> Was in't shall quickely be discover'd to you[25]

Letoy's "The Antipodes" ends up being the design of Letoy himself and not the result of the Joyless's desire to cure their son. Although they believed this was why they were coming to Letoy's theatre, his ends are what brought them rather than their own needs. Even when he confesses that the audience did not act of their own free will, he still dictates the terms by which his motives will be discovered.

It is when Letoy exerts his role as the writer of the play that the most conflicted view of the playwright is seen. Letoy presses his status as the owner of the theatre (and subsequently the owner of the actors) and is more forceful in exerting that role than he is the role of the author. In fact, both Letoy and the actors are quick to denounce "the poet" and the privileged position held by the writers.

> For I am none of those Poeticke furies,
> That threats the Actors life, in a whole play,
> That adds a sillable, or takes away.[26]

He wishes the performance to be spontaneous and reactionary to the whims of the audience and the actors themselves. Although Letoy is proud that he is the author of the play, he will not refer to himself as a poet. Rather, he views poets as "furies" intent on destruction rather than on creation. He associates poetry with drama as he declares that the "poetic furies" threaten the actors. The decidedly anti-poet slant that is portrayed in "The Antipodes" is likely a reflection of Brome's disdain toward the amateur courtly playwrights who termed themselves poets and who opposed the commercial theatre. In "The Antipodes," Letoy claims "all their Poets are Puritanes," which would seem to reconcile the two enemies who are normally so at odds with one another. However, as both the courtier dramatists and the Puritans were strong opponents of the professional stage with each faction wanting to eradicate the commercial theatre, the comparison makes the two extremes seem very much alike.

The critique of "poets" continues as Letoy scripts them to be professional and austere, characteristics Brome seems to have completely disassociated with the "poets" living and working during his own time. The poets in "The Antipodes" are industrious and professional, as opposed to their lazy, real-life counterparts:

POET.:

> Yes, of all
> My severall wares, according to the rates
> Delivered unto my debitor,

DIA.:

> Wares does he say?

LET.:

> Yes, Poetry is good ware
> In the Antipodes, though there be some ill payers,
> As well as here; but Law there rights the Poets.[27]

The poets are professionals in the Antipodes, selling their "wares" for financial gains rather than reputation and acclaim as they do in the real London. Furthermore, the fact that the law protects these poets criticises the tendency to slight the professional writers in his real London. Brome's troubles with the Salisbury Court played a part in developing this critical attitude toward the slights at the professional dramatic community. He viewed himself as unprotected from the injustices that he found within the professional community and begrudged the protection that his non-professional, courtly counterparts enjoyed. It was this mentality that led Brome to write the play for Beeston.

His own theatre's refusal to pay his wages during the closures suggested that the playwright was considered to be of lesser import than the actors or the managers and therefore it was unnecessary to pay him when no plays could be staged and new plays were not needed.

The sobriety exemplified by the Antipodean poets also runs contrary to the characterisations of the men who deemed themselves poets that Brome had created in so many of his other plays.[28] Letoy claims they "Are slow of tongue, but nimble with the pen," again implying that the reverse is true in the real London, that the real-life poets are boastful of their substandard work.[29] The poet is seen negotiating with a lawyer and in their final discussion, the poet tries to force money on the lawyer for his council. "The counsaile and the comfort you have given / Me, requires a double fee."[30] The notion of a poet paying for anything, including council is portrayed as outrageous and completely alien. There seemed to be a prevalent belief that the courtier poets did not pay for anything and in fact, ran into large debts that they then relied on their aristocratic allies to protect them from.[31] In the vision painted of the poets, both Brome and Letoy demonstrate them to be completely contrary and opposite to their real-life counterparts and whereas they are allies to professionalism in the upside down world, they are enemies in the real-life London.

While Letoy distances himself from the title of poet, suggesting that the writer is the least authoritative agent in dramatic production, the actors become more powerful as they gain more and more control over what occurs on stage. Peregrine's participation in the play means they have to act and react according to his behaviour:

LET.:

> I see th'event already, by the ayme
> The Doctor takes, proceed you with your play,
> And let him see it in what state he pleases.[32]

Peregrine's unknowing part as an actor gives his fellow thespians control over the production as he is the central concern of the fictitious play. Despite Letoy's scripting and supposed advanced knowledge of how Peregrine will react to the events and circumstances around him, the actors cannot follow exactly what is put down for them as they are working with an active and participatory audience:

LET.:

> Hoyday! The rest will all be lost, we now give over
> The play, and doe all by *Extempore,*
> For your sonnes good, to sooth him into's wits.
> If you'l marre all, yon may. Come nearer cocks-combe,
> Ha you forgotten (puppy) my instructions
> Touching his subjects, and his marriage?[33]

Allowing the players to act extempore means that Letoy now holds no power over what is to happen next. He tries to maintain control by speaking harshly to Byplay in an attempt to solidify his authority. Byplay takes control of the situation when he is asked by Peregrine what is happening, effectively stripping any control away that Letoy may still have held:

PER.:

What voyce was that?

BYP.:

A voyce out of the clouds, that doth applaud
Your highnesse welcome to your subjects loves.

LET.:

So, now ho's in. Sit still, I must goe downe
And set out things in order.[34]

Byplay's terming Letoy merely "a voyce out of the clouds, that doth applaud" makes him a spectator and not the controlling agent of the play. Letoy must go down to the stage and become a participating actor if he wants to regain the authority he once held over the production. As "The Antipodes" continues and the actors work extemporaneously, Letoy loses more and more control. It is only in the manipulation of the audience watching, Joyless and Diana, that he is still able to wield any influence. The actors now possess all the authority on the stage and are the only ones that can bring about the desired effect on Peregrine by interacting with him. Letoy gives over the play to the actors entirely from the balcony where he is viewing the play along with his audience, the Joylesses. Although he desires to maintain control, he realises that his must "give over" in order for the play to continue on and its effect to be realised. Brome himself gave over both the original version and the published one to outside agents. He intended *The Antipodes* to go to Beeston, giving it over to him with the belief that it would be staged at the Cockpit rather than at Salisbury Court. However, by giving over the play, Brome, like the fictional Letoy, lost the ability to control the direction of his play. When he did reclaim control over the play, with print in 1640, the controlling party was impossible to define with the playwright, the dedicatee, the manager, and the literary audience all being able to claim authority, despite the admittance that it was intended for the stage, and therefore any and all involved in the staging of the play.

The result of the play-within-the-play is to restore social order and provide a happy outcome. What the control and authority over the action gives is plain to see, and as it is Letoy who exerts the most effort in controlling the play, it is his wishes and desires that are fulfilled at the end, but with benefit to all. The entire play of *The Antipodes,* however, proved to be much more divisive than its fictional byplay counterpart, not only in terms of the conflicts that it references, but also in terms of the way Brome portrays his affiliations as a professional writer. Throughout his career, Brome had carefully developed a reputation as a staunch defender of the professional, public theatre. He was an outspoken opponent against the amateur courtier dramatists whom he felt threatened the traditions and inclusiveness of the commercial theatre. Yet in *The Antipodes* he conveys a muddled and often negative view of the professional theatre. The lack of cohesion and the growing opposition that centred on Brome demonstrated in the theatrical community of the 1630s seems to have left him with a bitter taste in his mouth. Whilst he never demonstrated a possessive attitude toward his plays, the events surrounding the performance and publication of *The Antipodes,* as well as the matter contained within each highlight the lack of control that was fundamental to the commercial theatrical community in the late Caroline era.

Notes

1. See Gurr, *The Shakespearean Stage,* pp. 201-203. Gurr discusses the hostility that is displayed by various playwrights of the Caroline era who use the theatrical affiliation to criticise their peers.

2. See Neill, "'Wits Most Accomplished Senate': The Audience of Caroline Private Theatres," pp. 341-360 and Gurr, *The Shakespearean Stage,* pp. 199-215.

3. See Steggle, *Richard Brome: Place and Politics on the Caroline Stage,* pp. 105-118. The contract clause was reinforced by the addendum that he could not initiate the publication of any of the plays that he wrote for the Salisbury Court, regardless of whether or not they were staged.

4. Brome, *The Antipodes,* 1.1.1-9.

5. Steggle, *Richard Brome,* p. 118. Brome's contract with Salisbury Court stipulated that he could not print the plays that he wrote for the company without consent from them. Brome's falling out with the company led him to join Beeston's company at the Cockpit in 1639, a year before *The Antipodes* was printed. It is unlikely that the company at Salisbury Court would initiate the printing of the play with the changes and additions that are included in the published version and which effectively blame and chastise the company for ruining Brome's original intentions. It makes sense that Brome himself initiated the printing, thereby breaking the terms of his original contract, in order to restore his original message and stress his intent.

6. See Steggle, *Richard Brome,* pp. 156-157. On 4 August 1640, Brome entered six plays into the Stationers' Register for publication. Those being *Chistianetta, The Jewish Gentleman, A New Academy* or *Exchange, The Love Sick Court, The Covent Garden Weeded,* and *The English Moore.* The plays were never printed, however, and subsequently, two of these plays have been lost. The remainder of Brome's plays, including four of the six he initiated the printing of in 1640 would not be published until after his death in 1652.

7. See Freehafer, "Brome, Suckling, and Davenant's Theatre Project of 1639," pp. 367-383. It seems as though Davenant stopped Brome's plays from being printed at the Cockpit and thus Brome again had to look to alternate methods to get his plays out into the public sphere, this time being publication. Brome's initiating the printing of six plays seems to have been a reaction to Davenant's placement at the Cockpit, rather than his desire to further his name and reputation through print.

8. Nania, "Richard Brome" in *Dictionary of Literary Biography*, p. 27.

9. Stevens, "The Staging of Plays at the Salisbury Court Theatre, 1630-1642," pp. 522-523.

10. Eades Bentley, *The Jacobean and Caroline Stage*, Vol. VI, "Theatres," pp. 71-72. Bentley contends that "Beeston as a manager, producer, and coach at the Phoenix must have been a significant influence in the drama of late Caroline London."

11. Brome, "To the Right Honourable William Earle of Hertford, &c" in *The Antipodes*.

12. Brome, *The Sparagus Garden*, prologue and Brome, *The Antipodes*, prologue. *The Sparagus Garden*, which was printed in the same year as *The Antipodes*, displays much more antagonism toward publication. In the prologue, Brome contends "It sayes the *Sparagus Garden*; if you looke / To feast on that, the Title spoiles the Booke." Even the prologue to *The Antipodes* itself decries publication as the primary means of transmission for a play when he says that "Workes, that must ever live upon the Stage."

13. Cressy, *Literacy and the Social Order: Reading and Writing in Tudor and Stuart England*, specifically pp. 121-122. Cressy maps out the levels of literacy across social borders and, not surprisingly, it is the higher classes that have a much higher level of learning than the lower orders.

14. Eades Bentley, *The Jacobean and Caroline Stage*, V, p. 6.

15. See Smith, "William Seymour, first marquess of Hertford and Second Duke of Somerset" and Brome, *The Northern Lasse* and *The Sparagus Garden*.

16. Brome, *The Antipodes*, epilogue.

17. Jonathan Okes printed *The Antipodes* and *The Sparagus Garden* for Brome. Okes had a hand in printing many plays from some of the most prominent playwrights including Shakespeare and Jonson. As Jonson was known to have been very strict with his control over the publication of his "Workes" it is likely that Okes was not opposed to giving creative control to the authors.

18. Brome, *The Antipodes*, II.ii.11.

19. Brome, *The Antipodes*, I.v.62-70.

20. Brome, *The Antipodes*, II.ii.15-17.

21. Brome, *The Antipodes*, II.ii.42-47.

22. Brome, *The Antipodes*, II.ii.68-70.

23. Brome, *The Antipodes*, III.i.16-19.

24. Brome, *The Antipodes*, V.i.5.

25. Brome, *The Antipodes*, V.vi.9-13.

26. Brome, *The Antipodes*, II.i.23-25.

27. Brome, *The Antipodes*, III.ii.14-20.

28. Brome, *The Damoiselle, The City Wit*, and *The Love-Sick Court*. Brome was adamant that he was not a poet in *The Love-Sick Court* when he stressed in the prologue that "A little wit, lesse learning, no Poetry / This Play-maker dares boast: Tis his modesty." In *The Damoiselle*, he again emphasised that "he won't be calld / Author, or Poet."

29. Brome, *The Antipodes*, III.ii.94.

30. Brome, *The Antipodes*, III.ii.95-96.

31. See Edmond, *Rare Sir William Davenant*, p. 27. Brome's chief rival, William Davenant, had been embroiled in a lawsuit with a tailor over the non-payment of fees, a case that was dismissed due to Davenant's courtly connections. The backlash created by this denoted fury over peer protection amongst the cavalier playwrights and poets.

32. Brome, *The Antipodes*, III.v.41-43.

33. Brome, *The Antipodes*, IV.ix.146-151.

34. Brome, *The Antipodes*, IV.ix.153-157.

Works Cited

Boas, Frederick S. *An Introduction to Stuart Drama*. Oxford: Oxford University Press, 1946.

Brome, Richard. *The Antipodes*. London: John Okes, 1640.

———. *The Northern Lasse*. London: August Matthes, 1632.

Cressy, David. *Literacy and the Social Order: Reading and Writing in Tudor and Stuart England*. Cambridge: Cambridge University Press, 1980.

Eades Bentley, Gerald. *The Jacobean and Caroline Stage*. Oxford: Clarendon Press, 1968.

Edmond, Mary. *Rare Sir William Davenant*. Manchester: Manchester University Press, 1987.

Freehafer, John. "Brome, Suckling, and Davenant's Theatre Project of 1639." *Texas Studies in Literature and Language: A Journal of the Humanities,* 10 (1968) 367-83.

Gurr, Andrew. *The Shakespearean Stage 1574-1642.* Cambridge: Cambridge University Press, 1992.

Nania, John S. "Richard Brome." In *Dictionary of Literary Biography,* Vol. 58, ed. by Fredson Bowers. Detroit.

Neill, Michael " 'Wits Most Accomplished Senate': The Audience of Caroline Private Theatres." *Studies in English Literature, 1500-1900* Vol. 18, No. 2 (1978), 341-60.

Smith, David L. "William Seymour, first marquess of Hertford and Second Duke of Somerset." In *Oxford Dictionary of National Biography.* Oxford: Oxford University Press, 2004.

Steggle, Matthew. *Richard Brome: Place and Politics on the Caroline Stage.* Manchester: Manchester University Press, 2004.

Stevens, David. "The Staging of Plays at the Salisbury Court Theatre, 1630-1642." *Theatre Journal,* Vol. 31, 4 (1979), 511-25.

Athina Efstathiou-Lavabre (essay date 2008)

SOURCE: Efstathiou-Lavabre, Athina. " 'False Frenchmen' in Richard Brome's Plays." *Representing France and the French in Early Modern English Drama.* Ed. Jean-Christophe Mayer. Newark: U of Delaware P, 2008. 207-22. Print.

[*In the following essay, Efstathiou-Lavabre discusses Brome's complex relationship to the French stereotypes commonly embraced in early modern England. Although Brome was wary of such reductive attitudes, she suggests, he nevertheless used the supposed licentiousness and dishonesty of Frenchmen as plot devices in his comedies.*]

In his recent monograph, *Richard Brome: Place and Politics on the Caroline Stage,* Matthew Steggle regards the dramatist "as an important early inheritor of Shakespeare ... a cleverer and more cerebral author than has generally been recognized."[1] For Brome, representing foreigners in his plays did not constitute an innovative dramaturgical trait, but was a theatrical modus operandi that had been in force for several years. As A. J. Hoenselaars's seminal study has shown, the plays of Brome's predecessors provide striking examples of this practice.[2] However, when compared with the dramatists of his own generation, it was Brome who "presented more foreigners in an English setting than any of his contemporaries."[3] Yet he also represented foreigners outside of England. A short extract from *The Novella,* a 1632 comedy set in Venice, both refers to and represents numerous foreigners in the same play. In act 2, scene 2, Paulo, "By-named *Burgio,*" lists the representatives of at least eight nations that have come to woo the Novella (Victoria disguised as a "Curtezan"), hoping to purchase her virginity:

PAOLO.:

> Here lies the no lesse politick then stout
> *Italian* force, and there your sprightly *French;*
> Here the brave *Spaniard,* there the *German* bold;
> Here the *Polonian,* and *Sclavonian* there;
> *Persian* and *Grecian*—

(2.2.; p. 130)[4]

In this moment of the play where clichéd descriptions of foreigners flourish, Brome's work is synonymous with imitation as opposed to innovation. This quasi pan-European stereotyping through which other national characteristics are underlined was also developed in Robert Burton's *The Anatomy of Melancholy* (1621). In *Democritus Junior to the Reader,* Burton writes:

> *Turkes* deride us, wee them, *Italians, Frenchmen,* accounting them lightheaded fellowes; the *French* scoffe againe at *Italians,* and at their severall customes; *Greeks* have condemned all the World but themselves of *Barbarisme,* the World as much vilifies them now; we account *Germans* heavy, dull fellowes, explode many of their fashions; they as contemptibly thinke of us; *Spaniards* laugh at all, and all againe at them. So are we Fooles & ridiculous, absurd in our Actions, Carriages, Dyet, Apparell, Customes, and Consultations; we scoffe and point one at another, when as in conclusion all are fooles. ...[5]

In the Brome canon, if the representation of foreigners in general is significantly exploited, there is, nonetheless, one country and one language (albeit imperfect for the most part when spoken) for which and one foreigner for whom the playwright had a penchant: France, the French language, and the French. From a purely quantitative angle, the French nation, its manners and its people, amount to the majority of foreign references and representations in the dramatist's works. *The New Academy, or The New Exchange* (1635) and *The Damoiselle, or The New Ordinary* (1638), which can be regarded as a diptych in that both comedies set up locations that are said to specialize in the instruction of French carriage, exemplify Brome's two most French-related plays. However, while references to France and French fashions are made, along with the representation of French nationals, none of Brome's plays is actually ever set in the country "beyond sea," referred to elsewhere by means of the adverbs "abroad," "over," or "there." Unlike his predecessors who staged their works in the realm of England's age-old foe, Richard Brome's choice city is London,[6] echoing Jonson's prologue to *The Alchemist.*[7] How can this be explained?

Drawing on critical works that have brought the Caroline period, the playwright, and his plays back to center stage, my essay will begin with a short sociohistorical contextualization of Caroline London as a means of explaining the incentive for Brome to continue to represent France and French fashions and to stage French characters well into the 1630s. I will then use examples from various Brome plays with a view to showing what characters voice about France and the French and what the dramatist's intentions may have been. My final section will focus on *The Damoiselle.* In this comedy, the supposed French nationality of the eponymous personage becomes an expedient strategy through which Brome not only capitalizes on the subject of selling sex, but also maintains disguise and role-playing as staples of his dramaturgy.[8]

MATCHIL:

> ... so leave my house.
> There's *French* enough in town, that may befriend you.
> To pack you o're to *Paris* ...

(2:1.1, p. 10)

In the opening scene of Brome's *The New Academy,* Matchil, an Englishman, holds Lafoy, a Frenchman, responsible for the presumed death of his son. Having exchanged children with his friend "these dozen years" (1.1, p. 1), he draws his French foster daughter's attention to the fact that there are "enough" of her compatriots in London who can escort her to her hometown. For all the unreliability that a character's words can have, two things need to be underlined. First, recourse to the word "town" reflects the "topographical shift"[9] of Brome's comedies to the western parts of the capital, and, second, as in the playwright's fictional London, French nationals were indeed present in the English metropolis when the play was "written under the Salisbury Court contract."[10] The representative par excellence was Henriette-Marie de France, daughter of Henri IV and sister of Louis XIII.

When Henrietta Maria set foot on English soil in 1625, she had not sailed across the Channel unaccompanied, bringing retinue, priests, and musicians with her.[11] Her arrival in England and subsequent influence on Charles's court have drawn considerable attention from numerous critics and theater historians.[12] Consequently, only a few of the theatrical events or personal aesthetic exploits with which Henrietta's name is associated will be referred to here. Henrietta Maria's predilection for spectacle and her incentive to advance her model of mores and of theater were entrenched in her motherland's own theatrical pursuits.[13] Through her, court entertainments became attached to portraying *préciosité,* NeoPlatonism, and the pastoral, all of which were brought to fruition by the queen herself.[14] For example, in 1626 she acted in Racan's *Arténice,* and in 1633 she performed in Walter Montague's *The Shepherd's Paradise,* a pastoral play from which the name of William Prynne cannot be dissociated, for in his thousand-page *Histrio Mastix, the Players Scourge, or, Actors Tragoedie* (1633), the oft-quoted phrase, "Women-actors, notorious whores" was seen as a denunciation of Henrietta's thespian conduct.

Not only did Henrietta Maria enact fictions literally,[15] but as Sophie Tomlison puts it, she also played the part of "theatrical patron."[16] In 1629, Sir Henry Herbert's records reveal that a French acting company performed respectively at the Blackfriars, at the Red Bull, and at the Fortune,[17] a theatrical occasion repeated in 1635 when under the auspices of the royal couple, a French company of players performed at "the house of Drury-lane, where the queenes players usually playe."[18] Even though important figures of the French literary and theatrical milieu had sojourned in England before 1625,[19] the unprecedented French influence on court theater and court masque was stimulated first and foremost by Henrietta Maria who also became the first queen of England to grace London's theaters with her presence. Given that Charles I's queen of French origin displayed such a fervent interest in theater and performance in general, it was not surprising that Brome's theater would draw on an obvious French presence in Caroline London and from the queen's influence over matters relating to performance. For instance, in *The Damoiselle,* the first images of Brome's French character are as follows:

OLIVER:

> Is she French borne?

VALENTINE:

> Yes, she was born and bred there: And can speak
> English but brokenly. But, for French behaviour,
> Shees a most compleat *Damoiselle,* and able
> To give instructions to our Courtliest Dames.

OLIVER:

> Shee must be seen.

(1:2.1, p. 398)[20]

As will be examined later, the "demoiselle" to whom Valentine refers in this moment of the play will result in a case of *deceptio visus.* Thanks to a superb coup de théâtre in the closing act of the comedy, Brome's Frenchwoman (fittingly called Frances) will be discovered as an Englishman in disguise. Putting this piece of information aside for the moment, Frances's origins inevitably recall those of Henrietta Maria. Like Brome's supposed demoiselle, Henrietta was born and bred in France and initially spoke English but brokenly. In his study on Charles I, Charles Carlton refers to Henrietta Maria's interpreter Toby Mathew, as well as "her ignorance of English history [and] initial awkwardness with the English tongue."[21] The queen's lack of English was used as a justification of her acting, for by performing in plays she could also practice and perfect her husband's tongue. Moreover, Henrietta was known for having given "instructions" to her ladies on various occasions as she did when *Florimène* was performed in 1635, an "anonymous lost pastoral" for which "she has [also] been suggested as author."[22] If Brome's allegedly French demoiselle is not a representation of Henrietta Maria, in a highly informative article which focuses on gender, female performance, boy actors, and "the performative nature of sexual difference," Alison Findlay makes a case for connecting Brome's French character to female performance at court. Findlay writes: "The name 'Frank' and his/her French education link female agency and its relation to performance to the figure of Henrietta Maria."[23]

The French influence that held sway at court was also felt beyond Whitehall. For example, in *The Weeding of the Covent-Garden, or The Middlesex-Justice of Peace* (1632-33), Brome made use of the world immediately outside the theater to create the fictional one on stage via the representation of "the Paris Tavern."[24] Thanks to Matthew Steggle's valuable research on the play, which is based on archival records, it transpires that this place really existed. In terms of its location and the people with which it was closely connected, our appreciation of the French tavern can now be reassessed as it was run by a Frenchman and situated in a "part of London that had controversial French links."[25] For Brome, staying local was thus fairly effortless. The Paris Tavern bears testimony to "the strong French presence" in Covent Garden that Brome brought into play in his comedy.[26] Moreover, by embedding a fraction of real London in his portrayal of the city, the playwright also gave his convoluted plots a pinch of verisimilitude, without seeking to create a theater of illusionism. This practice of drawing upon the names of real places was also exploited by French playwrights in the 1630s. Brome's contemporary Pierre Corneille whose tragicomedy *Le Cid* was translated by Joseph Rutter in 1638 and was performed in and out of court, also wrote comedies with telling titles: *La Place royale*[27] (1634) and *La Comédie des Tuileries* (1635). As Veronique Sternberg explains in "An aesthetics of reflection," "the feeling of familiarity between the world of the stage and that of the audience can arise from a community of spaces";[28] the latter corresponds to English "place-realism" comedies, a term coined by Theodore Miles in 1942[29] and entirely reevaluated by Steggle in 2004.[30]

Returning to the opening quotation in this section, when Matchil continues his antagonistic remarks to Gabriella, "But let your black bag guard you, 'tis a fashion / Begun amongst us here by your own Nation" (1.1, p. 16),[31] the reference to this novel item of clothing of French origin points out "a contemporary fashion, imported from France" and in so doing allows Brome to use French fashions in real London when creating his fictional characters and their imaginary world.[32] Given the various forms of French influence in force, to reword Shakespeare's Prologue in *Henry V,* Brome does not have to work his spectators' imagination by having them cross the Channel. In the wake of Ben Jonson's or Thomas Dekker's city comedies, if Brome's fictional Caroline London can on occasion "be recognizable as a version of the one just outside the playhouse door,"[33] how do references to France and things French and representations of the French emerge? Is there a given context?

MATCHIL:

> My childe is lost by treacherous neglect
> In that false Frenchman . . .
> (Hang his French friendship) over my dear childe,

(1.1, p. 8)

In *The New Academy,* Matchil's harsh description of Lafoy reveals a recurring image of the Frenchman in Renaissance texts, that of a betrayer. The "faithless" character was still staged in Brome's time. Hoenselaars traces this trait along with "flattery, guile and effeminacy" as far back as "the thirteenth century; in the political and satirical songs of this period."[34] Nevertheless, not all of Brome's plays that refer to the French, more often than not by means of their manners and fashions, can lay claim to the same dubious legacy, the image of the French "churlish perfidious Guardian" (1.1, p. 9), or as Matchil states elsewhere, the "hollow Frenchman" (5.1, p. 89), a stereotype that Brome introduces early on in the play all the better to break it instead of backing it, in the final act.[35]

In comedies where France and the French are peripheral to how the dramatic action unfolds, recourse to the adjective "French" is used for different purposes. For example, in *The Sparagus Garden* (1635), Striker's inventive reference to "the French fly-flap" (3:1.4, p. 127) exposes his harsh humor. While the latter is intensified by use of a fricative (the character "strikes at" his servant Friswood through speech), the adjective French becomes a substitute for slighting remarks. In the same play, Brome has Moneylacks, *"a needy Knight, that lives by shifts,"* utter another idiosyncratic turn of phrase via the "new French Bumtrick" (4.9, p. 194). If Donald S. McClure stresses that "Moneylacks coins the term to appeal to the fashionable love for French courtesies[36]—but gives it a contemptuous, crude name,"[37] Brome also has another agenda in mind, best expressed in "The Prologue to the Play":

> the *Subject* is so low,
> That to expect high Language, or much Cost,
> Were a sure way, now, to make all be lost.
> Pray looke for none: He'le promise such hereafter,
> To take your graver judgments, now *your laughter*
> *Is all he aymes to move.*[38]

While evoking both Brome's customary, self-proclaimed though debatable modesty, and the "embellished language" to which Aristotle[39] refers or "high and excellent Tragedy" as Sidney[40] puts it, it is the "low" or "common" language of comedy for which the dramatist makes a case here. Thalia is Brome's beloved muse.

In other comedies, the country of choice for those characters who journey from their birthplace is France. However, whether their departure for this country is actually *true,* as in *The English Moor or The Mock Marriage* (1637) where Meanwell and Rashley "past over into *France* . . . to fight, like fashion followers" (2:5.1, p. 72), or what will prove a fabricated departure as in *The Sparagus Garden*[41] and in *The Damoiselle,* where Samuel and Frank respectively are said to be in France—given the geographical proximity between the two nations—the choice of country remains credible. Certain characters also consider France as representing a means of establishing their social status following marriage. In *The Northern Lasse* (1629) Widgine declares, "I mean to marry first, as other young Heirs do. ... 'Twill be brave going into *France* then" (3:1.2, p. 5), and in *The New Academy* Nehemiah's French fantasy is in line with that of his forerunner: "For I mean when I am married / to travel into *France*" (4.1, p. 72). If France thus continues to represent a plausible nation in which to be, Brome's treatment of the English would-be traveler is, however, satirical. Another example of satire can be found in *The English Moore.* When Buzzard explains that his forebears "are all gentlemen [who] came in with the Conqueror"[42] (3.2, p. 43), the character whose master "turn'd him away" banks on gaining the esteem of the city gallants: "Our name (as the French has it) is *Beau-desert*; which signifies—Friends, what does it signifie?" (3.2, p. 43). If Vincent has no qualms in replying, "It signifies that you deserv'd fairly at your masters hands" (3.2, p. 43), the actual signification of *Beau-desert* is not given. Instead, Vincent fools about with the semantics of Buzzard's name whose remarks about his own lineage recalls Sir Amorous La Foole's in Jonson's *Epicoene*.[43] In this moment of the play, Brome keeps Jonson's satiric thrust alive.

In *The New Academy* and *The Damoiselle* where references to France and the French and representations of the French abound, for the most part Englishmen and Englishwomen fantasize about receiving instruction in the manners of that nation at large, thus securing social ascent for themselves. As Ira Clark puts it, "The scramble for status is featured in Brome's frequent satire of academies for the aspiring."[44] These places of French instruction have a magnetic-like effect on both genders. However, given that going abroad to seek the newest fashions is not in view, the New Academy and the New Ordinary, which are merely ersatz of France, provide the ideal solution since they are situated in the English capital city. In *The New Academy,* Nehemiah expresses his desire to go to the academy in a striking lapsus linguae, conveying Brome's own attachment to the genre of comedy and frequent expression of self-conscious theatricality: "Pray let us go to th'Acomedy, / what dee call it?" (4.1, p. 72). In *The Damoiselle,* when voicing her aspiration to go to the New Ordinary, Magdalen Bumpsey, who is infatuated with French fashions to the extent that her husband scoffs at her "fine French Frippery" (3.2, p. 426) and diagnoses her as being "Infected with the Fashions; Fashion-sick!" (3.2, p. 427), commits her own striking slip of the tongue: "I long to see this French young school-mistress. / The *Damasin* do you call her?" (3.2, p. 433). To borrow Wat's expression, which is not only indicative of his initial prejudice toward the French demoiselle, but also allows

Brome to resort to paronomasia, Magdalen longs to become "Frenchified" (3.1, p. 416). The Englishwoman's "French disease" is not, however, of the venereal type. Magdalen's sickness is linked to fashion and manners, of which one of the symptoms is her nonsensical speech.

These locations, which ostensibly specialize in French deportment, are sought after for the qualities they market. While the New Academy offers "the rarest musick and dancing" instruction in "the finest Complements, and other courtly qualities" (3.1, p. 50), the New Ordinary offers "The teaching of Court-carriage and behaviour" (3.2, p. 427). It appears, though, that for some characters, attending a French institution corresponds to something entirely different:

Erasmus:

> It is but private lodgings kept by
> Both men and women, as I am inform'd, after the French manner.
> That professe Musick, Dancing, Fashion, Complement.

Valentine:

> And no drabbing?

Erasmus:

> A little perhaps in private.

(*The New Academy,* 3.1, p. 55)

Even though the verb "to drab" signifies "Associate with prostitutes, whore" (*OED*), in Valentine's eyes, for whom, as Steggle notes, "Sex ... is an act of barter," the New Academy suggests the fulfillment of a fantasy of the sexual sort.[45] Set up by the dishonest Strigood, Matchil's half-brother, as a money-making venture—even though the former fails "to sell [Joyce and Gabriella's] Maidenheads"[46] (4.2, p. 73)—the academy is a budding brothel in disguise, a location whose "professors" have undergone "Metamorphosis" (3.2, p. 61) (that is, Strigood, alias Lightfoot; Joyce, alias Jane; Gabriella, alias Frances; and Cash is "disguiz'd in bravery").[47] The first visitors are not who they seem to be either: Galliard is Young Lafoy, and Papillion is Young Matchil, who feigns his French identity, allowing Brome to play on the very notion of representation.[48] In effect, representing France and the French can not be dissociated from role-playing, a technique that is emblematic of Brome's work and aesthetics in general. However, perhaps the most stimulating example of a false French national is that of Frances in *The Damoiselle.*

* * *

Sir Humphrey Dryground, a "decayed Knight," disguises himself as the father of a French demoiselle and founds the New Ordinary.[49] He has Frank Brookeall, who is supposed to be in France, cross-dress as the demoiselle Frances whose virginity is up for bid. Dryground's ploy involves raising as much money as possible and handing it over to

Frank for a "Charitable use" (5.1, p. 461), the latter's father having been "undone" by Vermine, a usurer. Among the multiple issues that this comedy addresses,[50] identity and gender prove to be focal points, as Frances is really a "man in women's clothing,"[51] a discovery that is made in the final act of the play, "*Discover Franc*" (5.1, p. 464). As we have already seen, while the French demoiselle fascinates the "fashion-sick," she also stimulates sexual fantasy in characters who pigeonhole her person and origins, false though they are in this case. The prospect of having "easy" sexual relations with a Frenchwoman is also at the fore of fantasizing about the Other in this play.[52]

In act 3, scene 1, even though Wat, who will be disguised as Dryground's (Osbright's) servant, "thinks / He understands it all" (p. 415), he is neither au fait with Frances's *true* identity, nor fully aware of Dryground's "businesse." During the seduction scene that opens the act, Wat attempts to induce Frances "to Lewdnesse before Marriage" (3.1, p. 414).[53] It is not, however, the prospect of sex with a woman that is ultimately at stake, but the threat of homosexual sex. As Jean E. Howard has argued, cross-dressing is "a staple of comic tradition with a long dramatic lineage" which did not necessarily give grist to the mill of antitheatricalists.[54] Even so, the homoerotic implications of the exchange between Wat and Frances would have been recognized by Brome's audience; the latter knew that the actor playing Frances was a boy.

Following this failed attempt to take the virginity of Frances, Dryground and Wat's exchange of words spells out the extent to which Londoners were prepared to partake in gaming to fulfill their sexual fantasies, for if the promise of sex in *The New Academy* is reduced to "bartering" or "exchange,"[55] in *The Damoiselle* it takes on the status of gaming:

DRYGROUND:

She shall be rifled for.

WAT.:

How! Rifled Sir?

DRYGROUND:

Yes, rifled *Wat*; the most at three fair throws,
With three fair Dice, must win and wear her, *Wat*.

(3.1, p. 418)

In this moment of the play, Dryground's words evoke Valentine's in the previous act.[56] The loaded verb *rifle* originates from the French verb *rafler* meaning either to "play at dice; gamble (*for* a stake) or to dispose of by dicing or raffling; gambling away." (*OED*); this is precisely how the demoiselle's virginity is to be won. Moreover, the modal segment "must win and wear her" emphasizes that the prospect of having sex is ultimately bought and made use of like a commodity, a "depersonalizing language"

which, as Steggle puts it in his analysis of *The New Academy,* "commodifies sexual relations."[57] However, in *The Damoiselle,* gambling for potential foreign sex may facilitate an increase in the stakes. When Wat informs Ambrose about the sorts of men who "Are to be of the Riflers" (3.1, p. 424), the last group who have registered are "Merchant Venturers that bid for the / Forreine Commodity, as faire, as any" (3.1, p. 425). Stressing here the way in which sex is saleable by having Frank not only dress himself in women's clothing (a first level of disguise), but also usurp the identity of a French demoiselle (a second level of disguise), Dryground will be able to draw a huge crowd, "A full hundred" (3.1, p. 419), as he himself boasts. As Hoenselaars puts it: "to Londoners, anything labeled 'French' is guaranteed success."[58]

When the first "riflers" arrive at the New Ordinary, the characters' perception of person and place is diametrically opposed:

OLIVER:

Did not I tell thee 'twas a Bawdy-house?

AMBROSE:

I cannot think so yet: there is some other
Trick in it; the Maid you see is very modest . . .

OLIVER:

Come, shee's a Jugling whore I warrant thee,
For all her Fee-fees, and her Laisse-moys.
Pox of her counterfeit Gibbrish Ile make her speak
In plainer English, ere I ha' done with her.

(3.1, pp. 420-21)

If Oliver's hostile discourse is a sign of his prejudice (Ambrose is more temperate in his judgment) when he addresses Frances, the Englishman voices an age-old stereotype of the French once again:

OLIVER:

Thou art a handsome Hyppocrite:
And this Cunning becomes thee well.

(3.1, p. 423)

Etymologically, the actor playing the "crossbreed" character is the *hupocritēs* par excellence, proving to be the perfect actor.

In sum, "the commodity" in *The Damoiselle* is a euphemism for female prostitution and the New Ordinary a substitute for a "Bawdy-house" (3.1, p. 420) that cannot, however, be advertised in the English capital city in these precise terms. "*Prostituere*" signifies "expose publicly, offer for sale," just like the "sale of [Frances's] Virginity" (3.1, p. 424). This suggestion is best expressed by the demoiselle when she defends her honor in faultless English, declaring that had she "a Father . . . To prostitute (her) spotlesse Vergine honour / To Lust for Salary, (she) would as sure prevent it" (3.1, p. 425). By the end of act 3, Frances's defense will have had the virtue of challenging Oliver's initial bias: "And I have found (I thinke) a vertue, that / Might save a City" (3.1, p. 426). As for Brome, Findlay has argued that the dramatist "satirizes the commodification of women ... Marriage and prostitution appear disturbingly similar in a commercialized culture in which men determine the dowries or 'prices' of all the female characters."[59]

Through the presence of the French demoiselle in the New Ordinary, which advertises instruction in French manners of the civil sort, it appears that "lewdnesse" is perhaps one of the most sustained and blatant labels surrounding the Frenchwoman. This unfounded opinion is so forceful at times that when Magdalen Bumpsey's fantasy about seeing the French demoiselle and being instructed by her is finally fulfilled, Brome provides Magdalen, like her precursors, with a highly original turn of phrase. Whereas the French "school-mistress" (5.1, p. 456) is about to instruct her English novices in "French Carriage"[60] (5.1, p. 453), and more specifically in "the Art of dressing, setting forth Head, Face, Neck, Breast" (5.1, p. 455-56), in what represents a volte-face regarding Magdalen's fantasy about French fashions, she proudly stresses that she is "Free from French Flea-bits" (5.1, p. 456).[61] Does the use of the hyponym here suggest the French disease? Whatever that may be, instruction is cut short. By act 5, Wat, who is on the way to complete "conversion," interrupts the pupils by exposing the ordinary for what he believes it really is, "a Bawdy-house" (5.1, p. 458). Horror-struck, the fashion-sick Magdalen, who by this stage of the play has had one too many glasses of wine and who will soon be in "a Mawdlin fit" (5.1, p. 459), goes on to voice perhaps one of the most revealing passages in the play about the alleged lewdness of the female that is at the foundation of her French fantasy:

MAGDALEN:

O deare! and is it so? What are we then? Is this your boun fashion? Is this the carriage of the Body, that you would teach us? What, to bee Whores? We could learn that at home, and there were need, without your teaching.

(5.1, p. 458)

* * *

On the face of it, certain Brome plays may therefore seem to spread similar stereotypes to those of the playwright's predecessors, be they linked to the Frenchman's alleged "falseness" or the Frenchwoman's "lewdnesse." However, in accordance with Montaigne's assertion that "there is no permanent existence in our being or in that of objects,"[62] one can say that Brome's fictional representations of France and the French in London are "flowing and rolling ceaselessly ... ever shifting and changing," just like the dramatist's characters for whom disguise and role-playing

are second nature.[63] Far from representing a homogeneous discourse, descriptions of France and the French thus serve different purposes and change according to the dramatic situation and the character's point of view. As for Brome, it would be wrong to regard him as being "xenophobic and patriotic."[64] Rather than endorsing the supposed veracity of the representation or stereotype under consideration, the dramatist mocks and satirizes the English characters' use of stereotypes, along with the fervor linked to adopting French fashions in the English capital.[65] As Ira Clark has argued, "Not atypical of the era, Brome is a subversive traditionalist whose plays, reflecting and satirizing human folly, damn no one."[66] But is there no more to Brome than a satirist or "subversive traditionalist"? Representing France and the French also allows the playwright to provide a sympathetic and surgical diagnosis of "sickness," as in Magdalen Bumpsey's case, or excesses of all his characters, French or otherwise. In so doing, Brome is equally a "doctor" as Alexander Brome[67] had said of him, further developed in *Five New Playes* (1659) by Thomas Stanley:[68]

When he strook *vice,* he let the *person* go,
Wounded not *men* but *manners;* ...
But as the *Surgeon* at once *hides* and *cures,*
And bindeth up the *limb* which most indures
The *sore* and *pain:* so he with gentle hand
Did heal the *wound,* and yet conceal the *man.*[69]

Notes

1. Matthew Steggle, *Richard Brome: Place and Politics on the Caroline Stage* (Manchester, UK: Manchester University Press, 2004), 4.

2. Hoenselaars, *Images of Englishmen.*

3. Ibid., 186.

4. Brome, *The Novella,* in *The Dramatic Works of Richard Brome Containing Fifteen Comedies in Three Volumes,* ed. John Pearson (London, 1873), vol. 1. Subsequent references to Brome's plays are to act, scene, and page number from this edition.

5. Robert Burton, *The Anatomy of Melancholy,* ed. Thomas C. Faulkner, Nicolas K. Kiessling, and Rhonda L. Blair, 6 vols. (Oxford: Clarendon Press, 1989), 1:56-57.

6. When referring to France and when representing French characters, James Shirley, Thomas Nabbes, and William Cavendish also set the scene of their plays in London. See Hoenselaars, "Foreigners in England, 1625-1642," in his *Images of Englishmen,* 196-99 and 205-15.

7. "Our *Scene* is *London,* 'cause we would make known, / No country's mirth is better than our own" (5-6). Ben Jonson, *The Alchemist,* ed. F. H. Mares (Manchester, UK: Manchester University Press, 1997), 10.

8. For the importance of role-playing in the works of Brome and his contemporaries see Ira Clark, *Professional Playwrights: Massinger, Ford, Shirley, and Brome* (Lexington: Kentucky University Press, 1992). See also Jackson I. Cope, *The Theatre and the Dream: From Metaphor to Form in Renaissance Drama* (Baltimore: Johns Hopkins University Press, 1973).

9. See Julie Sanders, "City and Town," in her *Caroline Drama: The Plays of Massinger, Ford, Shirley, and Brome* (London: Northcote House, 1999), 44 and 43-55. For a political reading of the "rise of the town," see Martin Butler, "City comedies: courtiers and gentlemen," in his *Theatre and Crisis 1632-1642* (Cambridge: Cambridge University Press, 1984), 142 and 141-80.

10. See Steggle, *Richard Brome,* 70.

11. See Jean Jacquot, "La Reine Henriette-Marie et l'influence française dans les spectacles à la cour de Charles Ier," *Cahiers de l'Association Internationale des Études Françaises* 9 (June 1957): 128-60.

12. For example, see Butler, "Court Drama: The queen's circle 1632-37. Platonic politics," in his *Theatre and Crisis,* 25-54; Sophie Tomlinson, "She That Plays the King: Henrietta Maria and the Threat of the Actress in Caroline Culture," in *The Politics of Tragicomedy: Shakespeare and After,* ed. Gordon McMullan and Jonathan Hope (London: Routledge, 1992), 189-207; and Julie Sanders, "Gender and Performance," in her *Caroline Drama,* 43-55.

13. On matters of religious influence and devotion relating to Henrietta, see Erica Veevers, *Images of Love and Religion: Queen Henrietta Maria and Court Entertainments* (Cambridge: Cambridge University Press, 1989), passim.

14. See ibid.

15. Clare McManus has recently made a convincing case for situating the advent of the female court actress in the person of Queen Anna. See Clare McManus, *Women on the Renaissance Stage* (Manchester, UK: Manchester University Press, 2002).

16. Tomlinson, "She That Plays the King," 190. See also previous works cited.

17. See N. W. Bawcutt, ed., *The Control and Censorship of Caroline Drama: The Records of Sir Henry Herbert, Master of Revels, 1623-73* (Oxford: Clarendon Press, 1996), 169.

18. Ibid., 191. The actors were also given permission to perform at a riding academy managed by a Frenchman. See Ralph James Kaufmann, "*The New Academy,*" in

his *Richard Brome, Caroline Playwright* (New York: Columbia University Press, 1961), 53-57.

19. See Claire-Eliane Engel, "Connaissait-on le théâtre anglais en France, au XVIIe siècle?," *XVIIè siècle. Problèmes de politique étrangère sous Louis XIV* (1st-2nd trimesters, 1960): 1-15.

20. Jane's description of the demoiselle echoes that of Valentine. See Brome, *The Damoiselle,* 3.2, p. 427.

21. Charles Carlton, *The Personal Monarch,* 2nd ed. (London: Routledge, 1995), 65.

22. See Nancy Cotton, "Women Playwrights in England," in *Readings in Renaissance Women's Drama: Criticism, History and Performance 1594-1998,* ed. S. P. Cerasano and Marion Wynne-Davies (London: Routledge, 1998), 38.

23. Alison Findlay, "Gendering the Stage," in *A Companion to Renaissance Drama,* ed. Arthur F. Kinney (Oxford: Blackwell, 2002), 409 and 409-12. For the entire article, see 399-415.

24. For the difficulty of providing an exact date for the play, see Steggle, *Richard Brome,* 43.

25. Ibid., 51. For the full account of Steggle's findings, see "Place-realism in *The Weeding of Covent Garden,*" in ibid., 46-53.

26. Ibid., 49.

27. Present-day Place des Vosges.

28. My translation. Véronique Sternberg, *La poétique de la comédie* (Paris: Sedes, 1996), 114.

29. Theodore Miles, "Place-realism in a group of Caroline plays," *Review of English Studies* 18 (1942): 428-40.

30. See Steggle, *Richard Brome,* passim.

31. For reference to the "black bag," see *The Damoiselle,* 3.2, p. 429.

32. Steggle, *Richard Brome,* 95.

33. Anne Barton, "London Comedy and the Ethos of the City," *London Journal* 4, no. 2 (1978): 160. See pp. 158-80 for the entire article.

34. Hoenselaars, *Images of Englishmen,* 16.

35. Matchil's "rash and unadvis'd" (5.1, p. 90) labeling of Lafoy will be invalidated. The Frenchman proves to be "an honest and a temperate man" (5.1, p. 90).

36. Cf. Doctor Hughball's reference to the "French cringe" in *The Antipodes* (3:1.6, p. 249).

37. *A Critical Edition of Richard Brome's "The Weeding of Covent Garden" and "The Sparagus Garden,"* ed.

Donald S. McClure (New York: Garland, 1980), 413 n.23.

38. My emphasis.

39. Aristotle, *Poetics,* trans. James Hutton (New York: Norton, 1982), 50.

40. Sir Philip Sidney, *An Apology for Poetry (or The Defence of Poesy),* ed. Geoffrey Shepherd, revised by R. W. Maslen, 3rd ed. (Manchester, UK: Manchester University Press, 2002), 98.

41. Before Samuel embarks for French shores, Touchwood's advice, albeit abridged and altered in content, is reminiscent of Shakespeare's *Hamlet.* If part of Polonius's counsel draws Laertes' attention to "habit" (1.3, pp. 70-74), it is the sole subject of Touchwood's advice to his son. See *The Sparagus Garden* (2.4, p. 147).

42. Cf. The origins of Letoy's "pedigree" in *The Antipodes* (3:1.5, p. 243).

43. Richard Brome, *The English Moore or, The Mock-Mariage,* ed. Sara Jayne Steen (Columbia: Missouri University Press, 1983), 7.

44. Clark, *Professional Playwrights,* 165.

45. Steggle, *Richard Brome,* 93.

46. Following his daughter's disappearance, Matchil accuses Strigood of having "sold her then into some Bawdihouse" (2.2, p. 40).

47. Like his English counterpart, when the Frenchman Galliard arrives at the academy, he also fantasizes about the possibility of sexual relations. See *The New Academy* (3.2, pp. 63-64).

48. *The Novella* is Brome's first play which stages a Venetian, Horatio, who disguises himself as a Frenchman. See 3.1, pp. 135-39.

49. For reasons of space, a detailed synopsis of *The Damoiselle* cannot be provided here.

50. For example, see Butler, "Brome's estates satires," in his *Theatre and Crisis,* 210-14, and Steggle, "*The Damoiselle* and the Temple Walks," in his *Richard Brome,* 130-36.

51. See Laura Levine, *Men in Women's Clothing: Antitheatricality and Effeminization, 1579-1642* (Cambridge: Cambridge University Press, 1994).

52. When Frances exchanges words with Oliver, whereas she is more at "ease" (*aise*) in French, he clearly refers to her supposed easiness: "Easie! Yes yes, I thinke you would be easie / To one that knew but how to manage you, / For all the boast of your Virginity" (3.1, p. 423).

53. See *The Damoiselle* (3.1, pp. 414-15).

54. Jean E. Howard, "Crossdressing, The Theatre, and Gender Struggle in Early Modern England," *Shakespeare Quarterly* 39, no. 4 (Winter, 1988): 429. For the entire article, see pp. 418-40.

55. See Steggle, "*The New Academy* and the New Exchange," in his *Richard Brome,* 90-100.

56. "This very night / There will be some great Rifling for some Jewell, / Or other rare Commodity they say. / I cannot nam't" (2.1, p. 398).

57. Steggle, *Richard Brome,* 93.

58. Hoenselaars, *Images of Englishmen,* 193.

59. Alison Findlay, "Playing the 'Scene Self': Jane Cavendish and Elizabeth Brackley's *The Concealed Fancies,*" in *Enacting Gender on the English Renaissance Stage,* ed. Viviana Comensoli and Anne Russell (Urbana: Illinois University Press, 1999), 173 n. 10; and Findlay, "Gendering the Stage," in Kinney, *Companion to Renaissance Drama,* 407, 409.

60. Regarding the supposed French promiscuity inherent in this scene, see Hoenselaars, *Images of Englishmen,* 193-96.

61. Cf. "French Fleas" in *A Jovial Crew: or The Merry Beggars* (3:3.1, p. 401).

62. Michel de Montaigne, "An apology for Raymond Sebond," in *The Complete Essays,* trans. M. A. Screech (London: Penguin, 1993), 680. The broader context of this quotation relates to Montaigne's writing on judgment and the senses.

63. Ibid.

64. Hoenselaars, *Images of Englishmen,* 186.

65. Ibid., 214-15.

66. Clark, *Professional Playwrights,* 161.

67. "To Master Richard Brome, upon his Comedie, called, *A Joviall Crew: or, The merry Beggars* [printed in 1652]," in Pearson, *The Dramatic Works of Richard Brome,* vol. 3. Alexander Brome was not a relative, but a friend of Richard Brome. He wrote commendatory poems to the 1653 and 1659 editions of Brome's plays.

68. See Steggle, *Richard Brome,* 183.

69. Brome, *Five New Playes* (1659), in Pearson, *The Dramatic Works of Richard Brome,* vol. 2.

Selected Bibliography

EARLY TEXT AND EDITION

Brome, Richard. *The English Moore or, The Mock-Mariage.* Edited by Sara Jayne Steen. Columbia: Missouri University Press, 1983.

CRITICAL AND HISTORICAL SCHOLARSHIP

Hoenselaars, A. J. *Images of Englishmen and Foreigners in the Drama of Shakespeare and His Contemporaries.* Rutherford, NJ: Fairleigh Dickinson University Press, 1992.

Denys Van Renen (essay date 2011)

SOURCE: Van Renen, Denys. "A 'Birthright into a New World': Representing the Town on Brome's Stage." *Comparative Drama* 45.2 (2011): 35-63. Print.

[*In the following essay, Van Renen analyzes* The Weeding of the Covent Garden *and* The Sparagus Garden *as critiques of the rapid development of the London suburbs under Charles I. Van Renen argues that Brome characterized these new neighborhoods as sites of danger and disorder similar to Britain's overseas colonies.*]

England in the 1630s witnessed increasing hostilities between Puritans and Royalists as different religious and political groups competed to shape the way the English conceptualized the newly constructed town locales. During this period, sites such as Covent Garden, Asparagus Garden in Lambeth across from Whitehall, and the New Exchange in the Strand at Westminster, among others, emerged as contested spaces among the court, the city, and the country.[1] Most critics characterize the dramatist Richard Brome as siding with the town gentry and depicting these upscale districts in his plays as oppositional hotbeds to Charles's increasingly autocratic rule. While R. J. Kaufmann, Julie Sanders, Martin Butler, and, more recently, Matthew Steggle and Adam Zucker emphasize the setting in Brome's plays, they largely overlook the way these suburban developments were imagined as colonial ventures.[2] This essay examines how the establishment of the town, as represented in Brome's plays, is framed by European models of both internal colonialism and New World expansion.[3] Although my essay treats mainly Carolinian drama, I also discuss Ben Jonson's plays, in order to contextualize the ways in which Brome brings together two seemingly different functions of Jacobean drama: to familiarize recent arrivals to London to their fast-changing milieu and to marginalize an English underclass that cannot assimilate into the competitive marketplace of these new urban spaces. Teasing out the tensions of these two representational models, Brome identifies how elite speculators and the state collude as they attempted to increase profit margins and solidify their control of these expanding districts. By dramatizing how developers incorporate foreign architecture, install foreign workers in the town, and construct the town as an overseas territory, Brome lays bare an urban topography that upends traditional social relationships grounded in land ownership among the underclass, "middling sort," and aristocracy.[4]

In the first section of the essay, I analyze Ben Jonson's *The Entertainment at Britain's Burse* (1609), which registers the bewilderment of Londoners who have trouble comprehending the transformation of the western suburbs, as formerly remote green spaces became integrated into a global network of commerce. In this masque, which was performed before James I at the inaugural ceremony of the New Exchange in the Strand at Westminster, Jonson depicts this high-end shopping center as an initial foray into the town by developers who intended to displace the area's inhabitants. The New Exchange, one of the main developments of the West End, along with Hyde Park, Tottenham Court, and Covent Garden, specializes in luxury consumer items from the Far East—products from a region of the world that testified to Dutch trading supremacy. As I will demonstrate, because the Netherlands permeates the way the English conceive of the town, these sites come to be characterized as extensions of Dutch commercial activities, alienating the English from their homeland.[5]

I then consider the construction of London's suburbs as a New World plantation that must "weed" undesirable elements in order to form a community fit for the nobility in Brome's topographical comedy, or "place-realism" play, *The Weeding of Covent Garden* (1633). Alternately called a "forest" and a "lawless" precinct inhabited by "Amazonian trulls" and "tribe[s]" of men and women,[6] Covent Garden contains an underclass thriving on the disorder inherent in this new suburb. Primarily, developers of the suburbs introduced foreign architecture to draw the city's elite to the area to maximize profits; in his study of this play, Zucker points out that the "building of the Covent Garden piazza signaled the consolidation of the city's first neighborhood based on wealth."[7] As contemporary pamphlets demonstrate, this gentrification was disguised as a colonial venture an inducement to nonlocals to settle in the area, but only if they strictly conform to the builders' image of the development as an exclusive setting designed for a new merchant elite. Yet, Brome depicts residents as treating the area as a temporary stage set, subverting and supplanting the developers' scheme to control who can occupy the suburbs.

Finally, I turn to *The Sparagus Garden* (1635), a play that offers the Netherlands' delicate nation-building project as an ambivalent model for England's colonialist ambitions. On the one hand, the Netherlands' embattled status—its precarious natural and political boundaries and low-lying lands threatened by the sea as well as by France and Spain, powerful Roman Catholic powers—differs markedly from conceptions of England as this "fortress built by Nature for herself / Against infection and the hand of war."[8] On the other hand, the Netherlands' practice of claiming new land from the sea and turning it into viable production units offers a lucrative model to apply to schemes in England for fen drainage. From 1570 to 1640, Holland added 40 percent to its stock of arable land, and investors in land reclamation became some of the richest men in the

Netherlands, although most of the country's elite made their money in overseas trade.[9] When the English aristocracy in the 1630s intensified development in fen areas long abandoned to the peasantry, it hastily colonized these sites by employing Dutch-style land reclamation projects and then introducing buildings that catered to an economic elite.[10] Brome reveals how these projects contribute to growing social unrest because they treat the fens as an undomesticated wilderness and drastically alter England's environment, forcing the former inhabitants to move to less fertile land. Moreover, these large-scale projects ruin local livelihoods and "settle" the countryside with foreign workers. Brome, therefore, suggests that the English developers appropriate the worst aspects of the Dutch economic "miracle," amassing land for short-term profit and threatening traditional English values that prioritize land for the way it orders society and constitutes individual and social identity.[11]

I

Jonson's *Entertainment at Britain's Burse* stages the ways in which London's immersion in global trade provides a pretext to modernize the city as a commercial entrepôt. In the guise of condescendingly ridiculing the provinciality of suburban Londoners who cannot imagine the worldly schemes of their betters, the doorman for the bourse gently chides town planners for ignoring more pressing needs, including "an Arsenall for decayed Citizens" and "a store howse for westminster, of Corne here aboue, and wood and Seacole belowe; to praeoccupy the nexte greate froste."[12] The Key Keeper's rhetoric satirically implies that developers should have addressed the exigencies of a wide set of English society. Before inventorying these possibilities, the Key Keeper articulates the confusion of the West Enders: "And before the shops were vp, the perplexityes, that they were in, for what it shoulde be" (ll. 36-37). The syntax of the sentence actually enacts the confusion and excitement that the innovative architecture incites.

Even King James needs a guide to navigate these new surroundings. The host comments, "I thinke you scarse knowe, where you are now nor by my troth can I tell you, more then that you may seeme to be vppon some lande discouery of a newe region heere, to which I am your compasse" (ll. 9-12). Prior to his role as a not-so-informative guide, the Key Keeper worked as an innkeeper and a bartender; in that capacity, he "coulde entertayne my guestes in my veluet cap, and my red Taffata doublett; and I coulde aunsuer theyr questions, and expounde theyr riddles" (ll. 24-27). Clearly mindful of the way that the proper display of newly arrived commercial products, in this case fashionable clothing, stands in for his knowledge of the fast-changing local topography,[13] the Key Keeper foregrounds his "taffeta doublet" and "veluet cap" as semiotic indicators of his mental map of the city: velvet was first manufactured around 1580 in London and silk-tuftaffeta began in 1590, and both were trades predominantly practiced by Dutch and

French immigrants.[14] Luxury items from the Far East, however, disorient both the vender and the aristocratic consumer. As David Baker points out, this project "brings alien climes into contiguity with London streets and, by so doing, gives rise to problems of knowing that no one, not even the king, could hope to escape."[15] Yet, the "Hollanders fleete" mediates the contact between the English and the Far East.[16] As the master of the shop informs the king, the Dutch have overtaken other European powers in their trade with the East Indies and therefore regulate the commerce from this region: a "Hangings of the Ilande of Coqin . . . and thousand such subtitlyes, which you thinke to will haue cheape now at the next returne of the Hollanders fleete from the Indyes" (ll. 173-76).[17] Unable to domesticate the manufacturing of wares from China and India, as with velvet and silk-tuftaffeta, the English buy products imported from the Dutch. English demand for these luxury goods from the Far East expands the suburbs and creates the New Exchange but does little to assimilate foreign workers and the wares they produce into the fabric of the city. Therefore, Londoners' mental map of their surroundings becomes less familiar and is mediated by Dutch commercial networks. Whereas Jacobean drama "provided a representational space in which different urban subjectivities and communities could project themselves, as in a cartographic mirror,"[18] Jonson demonstrates that that "cartographic mirror" is increasingly one that reflects the Netherlands' sense of the world.

II

In *The Weeding of Covent Garden,* Brome depicts Covent Garden as a place where the young sons of the gentry cavort with masterless men and prostitutes at the same time their fathers try to domesticate it to maximize their profits. Cockbrain asks that the builder of a new row of brick residences, Rooksbill, leave him the work of "weeding them [the lewdest blades] out" of this west bank site (1.1.sp10). This justice of the peace for St. Martin's in the Fields—the larger district from which Covent Garden was later carved out just north of Whitehall—compares the gentrification of the suburb to the gradual process of improving the quality of the settlers in newly formed colonies. He asks, "What new plantation was ever peopled with the better sort at first?" (1.1.sp10). References to tobacco (1.2.sp154) underscore the play's ambivalent stance toward the urbanization of the countryside. Depictions of the Americas as inhospitable and dangerous, the last refuge of English society's execrable elements, dominated the popular imagination throughout the seventeenth century, but as recent critics have shown, by the late 1620s, with economic conditions in the colonies improving, English playwrights and audience members alike began to envision the New World as a respectable destination.[19]

A reprisal of Ben Jonson's character Justice Adam Overdo in *Bartholomew Fair* (1614), Cockbrain disguises himself to observe the criminal or vulgar offenses committed by those who take advantage of the lawlessness of the new suburb:

> These are a parcel of those venomous weeds,
> That rankly pester this fair garden plot,
> Whose boisterous growth is such, that I must use
> More policy than strength to reach their root.

(3.1.sp495)

For Cockbrain, "policy" operates as a stand-in for the social control that the pristine town—Covent Garden itself—is supposed to induce. As Rachel Ramsey asserts in her analysis of seventeenth-century London, "changes in the physical environment are portrayed as compelling changes in social behaviors and patters."[20] Cockbrain tries to imagine Covent Garden as a "fair garden plot" to meet the social demand by those of Rooksbill's class—entrepreneurs and builders who try to capitalize on the changing topography in order to ascend the social ladder—that these "lands" be treated as though they were equal to aristocratic estates. At the same time, he also depicts the town as overrun with a rank "parcel of those venomous weeds," necessitating government intervention, when the rising gentry's own mismanagement of the development foments this social disorder. Crosswill, a member of the country gentry who sells his estate to move into the town, reveals Rooksbill's social climbing. As Rooksbill has created new property through fen drainage, he must sanitize the land by offering it on the marriage market to Crosswill; in exchange for social status, Rooksbill provides Crosswill with a foothold in the town. Yet, Crosswill cannot hide his disgust at Rooksbill's proposal to marry off his daughter, Lucy, to his eldest son, Gabriel: "What a mechanic slave is this, to think a son of mine ... a fit mate to mingle blood with his Moorditch breed. True, his estate is great ... but of all fowl I love not moorhens" (2.2.sp339). Rooksbill has accumulated his capital by fen drainage, a particularly fraught project in 1630s London. First drained in 1527 and "laid out in pleasant walks in the reign of James I,"[21] Moorfields is representative of the hasty gentrification of the suburbs. Despite its developers' pretentions, Moorfields continued to attract thieves and prostitutes, prompting one commentator to maintain that the area is "impossible to reform."[22] Because Crosswill eventually agrees to marry his youngest son to Rooksbill's daughter, Brome seems to suggest that the town papers over disputes between old money/land and new money/land and establishes a venue that subsumes religious and social divisions. Yet, in this exchange, Crosswill trades a country estate and the authority it underwrites for reclaimed marshland fraught with negative associations, including claims to the land by peasants who occupied the area before its gentrification.

Much of the new construction in the London suburbs involved fen drainage schemes, including those proposed by the Dutch engineer Cornelius Vermuyden. These "projectors" included men who often proposed underhanded, impractical schemes to realize a quick profit and who are satirized in numerous plays of the period, starting with Ben Jonson's *The Devil Is an Ass* (1616), through Brome's ***Weeding of Covent Garden*** and ***Sparagus Garden,*** to his ***The Court Beggar*** (1640). They proposed to drain marshland to create viable land for agriculture or urban growth at the expense of local livelihoods, which were threatened by these large-scale developments. Andrew McRae states that these projects "epitomiz[e] the exploitation of a preexistent rural order by the acquisitive ethos of the city."[23] Yet King Charles himself encouraged such drainage schemes to augment England's arable land, "despite numerous outbreaks of unrest, sabotage, and even fatal violence during the 1630s."[24] He tried to assuage this unrest by addressing egregious mismanagement of the fens, including dismissing the unpopular Bedford from overseeing the Great Level of the South Fens.[25] Yet Charles, eager to emulate the Dutch and add revenue to his depressed coffers, spurred these projects onward, partly by convincing himself of their "public good."[26] H. C., calling attention to the perceived similarities between fenlands and the Netherlands, wrote in 1629 that fen drainage could yield "a goodly Garden of a Kingdome; yea, a little Kingdome it selfe: as much and as good ground ... as the States of the Low-Countreys enioy in the Netherlands."[27] Charles allowed visions of Dutch success to delude him into ignoring how these projects antagonized an already angry populace.

Brome also caricatures propaganda written on behalf of courtiers and others who made claims to the outlying fens in order to take advantage of Charles's assault on the English countryside in his desperate attempts to raise money. These fens were extremely valuable to their inhabitants; Keith Lindley explains that villagers "enjoyed common of pasture, without stint, for all kinds of livestock ... and it was the availability of commons that had attracted 'multitudes of people' to settle there."[28] Therefore, schemes to "reduc[e] the area of pasture were bound to be intensely unpopular and provoke resistance."[29] In a "True and Natural Description of the Great Level of the Fenns," a project also called the "Bedford Level" for its principal financier and architect, Francis Russell, Earl of Bedford, the anonymous poet writes, "could we joyn / To England's blessings, Holland's industry / We all the World in wealth should far outvie."[30] In an attempt, though, to graft "Holland's industry" onto a country that was conceived of by its people as a geographical entity apart from Europe, these projectors and their apologists shatter a traditional, if imaginary, English sense of national identity. Because locals objected to the seizure of common land by private enterprises, these projectors imported Dutch and French workmen who eventually settled in the area.[31] The poet, however, argues that the Great Level project will render superfluous overseas commercial enterprises, save Englishmen from having to emigrate to the New World, and, above all, realize fantastic profits:

Courageous Merchants, who, confronting fates,
Trust Seas and Pyrates with your whole Estates,
Part in this Bank, methinks were far more sure;
And ye, whom hopes of sudden Wealth allure,
Or wants into Virginia, force to fly,
Ev'n spare your pains; here's Florida hard by

(80)

The fantastic profits, including metaphorical "heaps of Gold, and Indian Ore," that the poet promises read like an advertisement for a colonial venture:

Would you repair your fortunes, would you make,
To this most fruitful land your selves betake
Where first your Money doubles, in a trice,
And then by new Progression, multiplies

(81)

Eliding the actual threat to the trades of local inhabitants, the poet advertises the project as an opportunity for potential colonists who can find Virginia and Florida right outside London. He implies that fen drainage will convert a rootless underclass into propertied farmers, downplaying how developers engrossed the best common land that had provided livelihoods for rural commoners.

The poet also addresses the long-held concerns that the fens breed illness and death, and he assures his readers that the drainage projects will purify the air:

When all dire Vapours ... are turn'd to Air,
Pure as the Upper Region
. . . .

When *Agues, Scurveys, Coughs, Consumptions, Wind,*
All crude distempers here their Cure shall find.

(75)

And, because the early moderns imagined an "interlocked physicality" between the land and the people,[32] the project to improve the environment at the Great Level promises to alter the makeup of the inhabitants:

When with the change of Elements, suddenly
There shall a change of Men and Manners be;
. . . .

When for sordid Clowns,
And savage *Scythians,* There Succeeds a Race
Worthy the Bliss and Genius of the place.

(75-76)

The poem also promises to reward settlers to the reclaimed fens whose only other option is emigration to the New World, transforming internal immigrants into proper English citizens.

The prospect of creating an England to match or exceed the climate of Virginia or Florida and to offer the economic opportunities of an untapped land not only obviates the impetus for emigration but also addresses early seventeenth-century representations of the lower class as "savage *Scythians.*" Depicting these country inhabitants as "Souls of Sedge," the poet promises "New hands shall learn to Work, forget to Steal, / New legs shall go to Church, new knees shall kneel" (75-76). As Mark Netzloff explains, "laws in early modern England constructed a racialized class among laborers who refuse to adapt to the regime of workhouses ... consequently designating these groups for forced transportation to the colonies."[33] In an affected display of forestalling this forced overseas colonization, the poet promotes this area as an empty space available for new plantations, but only under the condition that fen dwellers strictly comport themselves according to a new and proper mode of respectable existence. After developers undertake this project, they will create a "new land" in which the current inhabitants cannot exist: if they fail to adhere to the law and observe their religious and social duties, then they are not fit to remain in the area; if, however, they agree to abandon their traditional pursuits and support these large-scale projects, the poem and similar propaganda will have succeeded in promoting the colonizing and civilizing of the fens.

Fittingly, Brome first came to public attention in Ben Jonson's *Bartholomew Fair.* In the same breath, this play introduces Brome and employs the space of Smithfield to imagine the Atlantic world: "But for the whole play, will you ha' the truth on't?—I am looking, lest the poet hear me, or his man, Master Brome, behind the arras—it is like to be a very scurvy one. ... When't comes to the Fair once, you were e'en as good go to Virginia for anything there is of Smithfield."[34] A young apprentice when the play was performed, Brome internalizes the way his mentor imagines the outlying areas of London as a site to stage the increasing fragmentation of English society. Jonson's comedy dramatizes how the English at home as well as the "savages" abroad are in need of a civilizing force, one absent from the fair's chaotic world. Brome, however, seems to have objected to the way the aristocracy develops sophisticated ways to conflate the most troublesome elements of English society with individuals who choose not to or cannot compete in a society that envisions itself as part of globalized network of commerce.[35] If the land is perceived as not realizing its profit potential, developers exoticize broader sectors of English society, delegitimizing their right to occupy the land.

When Wasp characterizes Jonson's fairgoers as a "kind o' civil savages that will part with their children for rattles, pipes, and knives" (3.4.30-32), he presents the English underclass as naive dupes, with no comprehension of how to navigate the flood of commercial items available for consumption—and, by extension, a rapidly expanding world. Rebecca Ann Bach suggests that the individuals represented in the play—masterless men, the Irish, English economic criminals, and so on—"elude proper domination and beg (in the imaginations of their dominators) for civilization" by "an explorer to settle [them] in the proper English mode."[36] Jonson (in the second performance of the play) appeals to the king to address the ills he presents to him, namely, the way the Puritans seem to control the city.[37] He safely sets the disorder of the play at Smithfield, a site traditionally identified with religious dissension; indeed, it was the site for the execution of Jack Straw, the leader of the 1381 Peasants' Revolt, dramatized in a 1593/94 play, *The Life and Death of Iacke Straw, A notable Rebell in England: Who was kild in Smithfield by the Lord Maior of London.* Jonson can, therefore, safely stage religious and political divisions in Smithfield without burdening other city or town landmarks with fraught associations.

In his version, Brome suggests how the liminal site of Covent Garden triggers social disorder. While critics such as Butler argue that in "Brome's account of Crosswill's despotism over his children" he offers a "protest to Charles about the contradictions inherent in arbitrary rule,"[38] Michael Leslie, in the introduction to his recently edited version of the play, moderates this strand of criticism. Noting the play's 1632 or 1633 composition date (Parliament had sat as recently as 1629) and claiming that "for many subjects . . . there was much that was admirable about a mode of ruling that produced the quiet and prosperity of the early 1630s," Leslie refocuses our attention on "the ambiguous territory of Covent Garden and the divide between that and the traditional social organizations" of the city and the country.[39] Just as his children defy his interdictions, Crosswill flouts royal authority by moving to the town; Mihil says his father "never was fully bent on't [moving to the town] until the Proclamation of restraint spurred him up" (2.1.sp212). Crosswill's arrival in Covent Garden challenges Charles's Royal Proclamation of 1632 to keep landholders on their country estates, establishing the town as a site that not only comes to embody the clash between royal and aristocratic power but also plays a central role in conceptualizing the ways in which topography (dis)orders social relationships. Paradoxically, Crosswill refuses to submit to Charles's decree, suggesting his unwillingness to permit his physical environment to define him, but also seemingly moves to the voguish town to mitigate Gabriel's radical Puritanism, relying on the town to refashion his wayward son.[40] In fact, he encounters a site in which all recent arrivals draw on the contested meanings of the town to further their own agendas.

As these developments have successfully displaced the peasantry who worked and lived on the land, recent settlers respond to the way the speculators portray the town as a "plantation," exploiting the chaos of the suburbs to garner their share of the profits. Dorcas, Crosswill's niece who was seduced in the country by Nicholas, Rooksbill's son, proposes to act the part of Venetian courtesan in order to glamorize a brothel run by Madge and Francesca. Her venture satirizes the schemes of town developers, who imitate foreign architecture to cater to an economic elite, even as they create a physical environment in which the

rest of English society is effectively dislocated. In 1631, Charles allowed Francis Russell, Earl of Bedford, to develop Covent Garden. As with his fen drainage works which "Shall Parallel the Streights of Magellane,"[41] this project was imagined as a daring overseas expedition to open up new worlds to English colonists. Invoking the Age of Discovery, enthusiasts for town developments envisioned these ventures as a colonial project to establish new trading ports. Bedford "had started a large development . . . based around an enormous Italian-style open square 420 by 613 feet . . . [with buildings] which required construction from brick or stone, a uniform frontage . . . and the first balconies in Britain."[42] In keeping with the original Italianate design, Dorcas appears "upon a balcony . . . habited like a courtesan of Venice," subverting the original grand designs of Bedford (1.1.sp69).[43] She supposedly "travelled [to] France and Italy, and . . . [intends to] plant some of her foreign collections, the fruits of her travels, in this garden here, to try how they would grow or thrive on English earth" (1.1.sp101, 103). Her "brave rebellion" against the "stricter laws" of England recalls the popular lore of tracts that commemorate successful prostitutes: a woman warrior who defies an authoritarian state, Dorcas attempts to establish a thriving business outside city jurisdiction. She hopes that her foreign "fashion . . . [m]ay persuade justice to allow our games" (1.1.sp82). Because she participates in the state's attempt to exoticize Covent Garden, she effectively forces "Justice" to permit an otherwise illegal activity, testing the limits of its authority. These women entrepreneurs co-opt and Anglicize the state's attempt to remake the city. When it turns out that Madge, "old Countess of Codpiecerow," and Francesca "travelled 'cross the seas from the Bankside hither" (1.2.sp132), Nicholas and the rest of the "Brother[s] of the Blade and the Battoon" ally themselves with the "Sisters of the Scabbard" (1.1.sp83, 1.2.sp167). Arriving from the notorious southern suburbs, these bawds answer the call of tracts that beckon potential colonists by promoting the suburbs as unsullied lands like Virginia and Florida, which offer lucrative economic opportunities. Yet, the physical environment of the town has not reformed the deviant behavior of London's underclass. Underneath the veneer of cultural sophistication lies a "party purple, or rather parboiled bawd" (1.2.sp130). Brome suggests that the English can see through the schemes of their betters; like the exotic costumes of these prostitutes, the Italian architecture is merely a facade by powerful entrepreneurs to capitalize and exploit these suburbs.

Dorcas's appearance on a balcony singing to attract customers is one of several performative acts by Covent Garden residents that parody the way in which Jacobean theater familiarized Londoners with this new suburb. Gazing up at the balcony, Clotpoll and Nicholas call her a "device" and a "show." Yet, the cadre of roving masterless men and dissatisfied sons shatters this fantasy. Nicholas, Rooksbill's son, is correct when he first posits, but then rejects, his theory that the brothel was started by "the mountebank's wife that was here; and now come to play some merry new tricks by herself" (1.1.sp92). This mountebank or "antifounder" of Covent Garden, a sort of underworld Earl of Bedford, "brought the first resort into this new plantation [and] drew such flocks of idle people ... that the players ... cursed him abominably" (1.1.sp93, sp95). An earlier iteration of Dorcas, Madge, and Francesca, the mountebank operates as a one-man theatrical troupe who draws crowds to this suburb. Brome implies that new illegal enterprises will simply replace ones that are suppressed by the authorities or exposed as clumsily disguised, quotidian criminal schemes.

In these instances, Brome reveals the ways in which these enterprises strive to capture the imagination of Covent Garden's inhabitants by appropriating the function of the theater, usually the venue, as Jean Howard puts it, by which "people of the period ... made sense of this fast-changing urban milieu" (2). In earlier Jacobean versions of the place-realism comedy, Henry Turner argues, plays set in the city "reproduc[ed] in miniature ... specific identifiable elements in the streets around them, correlating a concept of citizenship ... with physical placement in a realistic urban topography."[44] Playwrights performed this civil function because, as Mimi Yiu reminds us, "At the center of a flourishing economy sparked by new trade routes and colonial ambitions, metropolitan London underwent a seismic reorganization of its topography, anchoring a widespread program of spatial restructuring that historians have called the Great Rebuilding."[45] Rather than domesticating this wilderness-turned-colonial outpost, these initial settlers establish the community as forever in strife. As Clotpoll puts it, the mountebank "sowed so much seed of knavery and cozenage here, that 'tis feared 'twill never out" (1.1.sp93). The threat of colonial or mercantile chaos resides in the very heart of the town and in the very scheme to modernize and expand the city.

Brome's metatheatrical commentary on the ineffectiveness of the stage to shape people's perceptions of Covent Garden forces us to question the concluding lines spoken by Crosswill. Crosswill, a more authoritative figure, replacing the absurd Cockbrain, issues the edict: "Go now, while ye are well, and be seen no more in this precinct." To which summons the prostitutes, rabble-rousers, and confidence men respond, "Never, and 't please your worships, never" (5.3.sp1247). Crosswill then reiterates Cockbrain's opening sentiments as he operates as a mouthpiece to convey the state's intention to establish an upscale, urban precinct:

> 'Twas built for no such vermin. Hence, away,
> And may the place be purged so every day
> 'Til no unworthy member be found,
> To pester or to vilify this ground;
> That as it was intended, it may be
> A scene for virtue and nobility.

> (5.3.sp1248)

Supposed to be the setting for aristocratic pleasure seekers, Covent Garden instead seems already tainted with the stigma of its less illustrious inhabitants. While the opening and concluding passages may indicate a tripartite agreement among the state, Puritan city power, and (former) country landholders to develop Covent Garden, we hardly need the too tidy assurances of the undesirable elements to notice the cracks in this uneasy alliance.[46]

Instead, masterless men, a dissatisfied and adrift younger generation, and an emboldened merchant class lay claim to the new suburb. Mihil complains that in this quarter tradesmen have encroached on the prerogatives of gentlemen: owners of shops "are removed into the new plantation here, where, they say, are a tribe of infidel tradesmen, that have made a law within yourselves to put no trust in gentlemen" (2.1.sp230). Nicholas states quite explicitly and forcefully that they intend to defend against any incursion of state power. He vehemently assures his comrades that he will violently thwart any attempt by the state to encroach upon what he views as his territory: "I would but see the carcass of authority prance in our quarter, and we not cut his legs off" (5.3.sp1123). Rooksbill, at least, takes these threats very seriously when he walks into Paris Tavern, the site of the play's climatic confrontation: "My wicked, caitiff, reprobate son is here too. Pray let me flee. I am but a dead man else" (5.3.sp1170). Brome draws attention to how Rooksbill's aggressive social climbing initiates a breakdown in familial as well as civic order. While Jacobean playwrights portray heirs as openly desiring their fathers' deaths—usually for comic effect—Brome describes a town society that witnesses open warfare between father and son. If Rooksbill can create an estate by land reclamation that ignores former tenants' rights, circumventing traditional channels to obtain the social status that land confers in English society, Nicholas can just as callously hasten patrilineal succession to gain control of his inheritance.

Gabriel's restoration from a Puritan to his former "manly carriage," characterized by "Stout and brave action" (4.2. sp851), also sets into motion his superimposition of a military scene on the Paris Tavern in Covent Garden. This scene, which finally dramatizes the overt generational conflict of the play, outwardly seems to defuse the tension between the different factions but, more deeply, secures the town as the prevailing prototype for a new topography embodying a state of ongoing war and thus invalidates any pretense of a social contract between a ruler and the body politic. This pivotal scene, in which the roving gang forces him to drink and then wakes him up by blaring military alarms, prompts Gabriel to map out an imaginary battle formation in the tavern. He resolutely assures the onlookers:

> I know how to have my ordnance artillery for discharging missiles planted here, my cavalry mounted here, my battery-discoverer on such a point, my trenches cut thus, my mine carried thus, my gabions raised thus. Here my parapet, there my pallisado o'th' top of that. The enemy made saultable six hundred paces there. And I draw out

my musketeers to flank 'em in their trenches here, while
my pikes and targeteers advance to the breach there.

(5.3.sp1157)

Steggle describes this scene as demonstrating how the
stage molds the perception of space in the new city suburbs: "On Brome's stage, and by extension in the empty
new urban spaces of west London, geography is not an
objective given but something that can be imposed by
force of will and is dependent upon the agreement of
others."[47] While Steggle rightly calls attention to the way
the force of imagination constructs the town, he seems to
misconstrue the larger implications of this scene. Fabricat-
ing a military crisis, Nicholas and the others lead Gabriel
to institute what might be termed "a state of exception."[48]
Finally bringing to a head the violent intimations and calls
to "cut" the legs from under the authorities, Gabriel gives
the signal to attack when Crosswill and Rooksbill arrive:
"An ambuscado of the enemy. Alarm! Lieutenant, charge
in with your shot! Now, gentlemen, for the honour of
Covent Garden, make a stand with your pikes; in to the
short sword; well fought, take prisoners" (5.3.sp1165).
Believing representatives of a hostile enemy are attacking
Covent Garden's inhabitants, Gabriel establishes an internal warzone, defeating the overbearing authority figure
and the Puritan builder who try to impose an urban topography designed only for the wealthy. Like Charles and his
fen drainage schemes, the planners of Covent Garden imported foreigners to work on and benefit from the projects
at the expense of the English. The Paris Tavern, the site
Gabriel recaptures, represents what William Prynne desig-
nated as a growing territorial footprint by foreign powers:
Queen Henrietta Maria's French servants, " 'who doe suck
the marrow of our estate,' had secretly obtained a number
of properties in the area," including Paris Tavern.[49]
Spurred to take up arms under supposedly false premises,
he lays claim to the ground as English territory.

Although Gabriel's assault is provoked by Nicholas's "military blare" intended to awaken him from his Puritan dol-
drums, he responds to a real threat to English society. While
Crosswill tries to "purge" undesirables from the town, the
play underscores that the "true" natives are the bawdy
house owners and the itinerant mountebank. When Gabriel
becomes "Captain" of the "Blade and the Battoon" with
Nicholas as his lieutenant, Brome suggests the real-world
implications of Gabriel's resistance to the upper-class incursion in Covent Garden. In an understatement, Clotpoll
remarks, "This goes beyond the Blade and the Baton," to
suggest the wider political and social ramifications for this
scene.[50] Brome represents Charles and Henrietta's internal
colonization as affecting all aspects of traditional English
life, including, of course, the way that the nation mis-
manages its urbanization. In this way, the Crown makes
it impossible for playwrights to constitute a cohesive social
imaginary. While the previous generation of playwrights
domesticated their audience by familiarizing them with an

urban topography that signified the growing importance of
the city, Brome shows how developments that prioritize
profits at the expense of local livelihoods have frittered
away any chance of a shared social imaginary. Gabriel's
imagery also gives new meaning to the deterritorialization
suggested by references to Covent Garden as a "forest" or a
"lawless" precinct inhabited by "Amazonian trulls" and
"tribe[s]" of men and women. His mock military incursion
seems a natural outgrowth of the way Covent Garden is
portrayed.

Populated by various New World types, in an urban topography controlled by French courtiers, Brome's stage lays
bare the type of city the Crown institutes. When Crosswill
banishes this underclass represented as New World indi-
genes, the town is imagined as a space where the inhabitants of the fens and suburbs have only marginalized roles
in society and no recourse to the law whatsoever. The most
trenchant critic of the way the state imagines space to
consolidate its rule by creating conditions in which it
can revoke its citizens' rights, Giorgio Agamben, describes
this set of circumstances by revising how we have mistakenly understood the state of nature and its relationship
to civil society. Agamben explains how Carl Schmitt "as-
similates" the "*ius publicum Europaeum*"—the juridical
region that "corresponded to the New World, which was
identified with the state of nature"—or "zone 'beyond the
line' to the state of exception, which 'bases itself in an
obviously analogous fashion on the idea of delimited,
free and empty space' understood as a 'temporary and spatial sphere in which every law is suspended.'" He then
argues that "the Hobbesian mythologeme of the state of
nature ... is not a real epoch chronologically prior to the
foundation of the City but a principle internal to the City,
which appears at the moment the City is considered *tan-
quam dissoluta,* 'as if it were dissolved.'" In this respect,
the state of nature and the state of exception "are nothing
but two sides of a single topological process in which what
was presupposed as external (the state of nature) now reappears ... in the inside (as state of exception)."[51] Portraying the newly built precincts as temporarily lawless zones,
Brome demonstrates how different political entities conceive of space free from the traditional, if superficial, social
relations that mask the actual conditions within the City—
an environment designed to declare at any time a state of
(lawless) nature in which the sovereign can declare martial
law. Brome, however, suggests that the state has miscalcu-
lated its ability to control the populace, and even questions
the Crown's prerogative to declare a state of exception that
would allow it to treat its subjects as though they were New
World "savages."

III

Starting as early as Thomas Dekker's *Shoemaker's Holiday* (1599) in which Lacy, a nobleman, disguises himself as a Dutch worker to act as a go-between for Simon
Eyre and a Dutch merchant importing luxury items from

"Candy," or Crete, the Dutch are both scorned and admired on the stage and in popular literature for their commercial reach and skill. Indeed, Nicholas Goodman's pamphlet *Hollands Leaguer; or, An Historical Discourse of the Life and Actions of Dona Britanica Hollandia, the Arch Mistress of the wicked women of Eutopia* (1632) portrays the expansion of the city as a project that cannot be interwoven into an English national narrative. Questioning traditional interpretations of the pamphlet as a parable of the Anglican Church's decay into Papism, Jean Howard suggests that *Hollands Leaguer* instead celebrates a bawdy house madam named Elizabeth Holland as a "heroic embodiment of the entrepreneurial spirit."[52] Pointing out that Holland "may write *Annales,* and *Comentaries* to teach *Rome, Venice, Florence,* and the *Turks Seralia,*"[53] Howard suggests that "*Britannica Hollandia* had Englished the trade [and] indicates the perverse national pride she embodies."[54] Holland's brothel certainly captured the popular imagination;[55] both of Brome's place-realism plays feature bawds who take up residence in the town, embodying in different ways the commercial spirit that the town encourages. I would like to supplement Howard's account by focusing on Goodman's exploration of how the Dutch influenced the way the English conceive of urban expansion and commercial practices. Goodman portrays the entrepreneurial activities of the west suburbs as leading to the welter of confused and confusing identities typified by popular accounts of the Netherlands.

Initially named *Britanica Hollandia,* "by reason of some neere allyances betwixt them and the *Neatherlands*" (56), the allegorical figure is identified as Dona Britanica in the city; but when she opens up her brothel across the Thames, Goodman, without an explanatory note, renames her Dona Hollandia (76). In the city, the "buildings [that] are so linkt one to another" represent a tight, unified community. Outside of the city, specifically across the Thames, which Goodman describes as a territory across the ocean, "she betakes herself to the Sea, and makes a discovery vpon the water," a wilderness outside the borders of the state and a coherent community. She eventually chooses a place fit for her purpose: "[S]hee made for that coast, where shee found such aboundance of Naturall and Arteficiall intrenchments, that ever the house seemed to be in itself a little City" (75). The playhouses that attract a "Concourse of Strangers" on the Bankside produce ready customers who serve as a heterogeneous collection of citizens of her little state (76). The "Taxes" they pay allow her to augment her defenses, increase her workforce, and to purchase "sundry retainers" and sophisticated fashions (78, 79). In this little kingdom, she makes up her own "Lawes and Ordinances" (78). Her growing wealth, the topography of her island kingdom, and the suggestion that her riches contribute to her transformation from a "mayd in the time of her innocence" (56) to the chief magistrate of a flourishing realm strongly suggest an identification with the Dutch Republic. Goodman's pamphlet thus criticizes the Netherlands as

an upstart Protestant state that has been corrupted by its overriding commercial motives.

Later in the seventeenth century, in "The Character of Holland," Andrew Marvell scorns the Dutch for cynically permitting religious freedom; the financial prowess of the state depends on its willingness to subordinate religious principles to crass moneymaking:

> Hence Amsterdam, Turk-Christian-Pagan-Jew,
> Staple of sects and mint of schism grew;
> That bank of conscience, where not one so strange
> Opinion but finds credit, and exchange.[56]

Marvell underscores the ease with which various immigrants embrace financial markets which, in his view, foster a dangerous transculturation; Dutch society produces individuals who do not make up a cosmopolitan state but instead are so adaptable that they have no distinct attributes whatsoever. Economic indices like "exchange" and "credit" have been so thoroughly internalized that the people have no stable sense of national or religious selfhood. The Netherlands thus represents, for Goodman, Marvell, and many of their contemporaries, a problematic world in which individuals cannot count on a common social imaginary to face external threats. Instead of Anglicizing the trade, bawdy houses embody the way profit motives corrupt the sanctity of the state.

In ***The Sparagus Garden,*** Brome stages this internal colonization of the west part of London as a profitable and violent enterprise, drawing on the ways in which the English represent the Netherlands. The plot, in which three friends, Gilbert, Walter, and Samuel, endeavor to overcome their guardians' tightfistedness and efforts to dictate who they can marry, seems a conventional one. While Samuel succeeds in marrying Annabel and Walter gains his inheritance from his stingy uncle, access to the gardens and what they represent in the 1630s eludes the otherwise triumphant younger generation. While ***The Weeding of Covent Garden*** suggests that just as the ground must undergo a gradual process from supposedly degraded to pure land, the quality of the individuals who frequent the island must improve over time, the purveyors of Sparagus Garden attempt to draw and encourage wealthy city merchants who visit the "island" to transgress against social strictures. A "rich old merchant" with a "poor young gentleman's wife in the yellow bedchamber" and "the knight with the broken Citizens wife . . . in the blue bedchamber" frequent the garden, indicating how Sparagus Garden serves as a brothel and a sanctuary for those who prevail in the increasingly nasty economic warfare.[57] Martha relegates the three friends, Walter, Samuel, and Gilbert, to the gardens rather than allowing them a room because they have no women with them, assuming that they are not likely to lavish delicacies on each other. Walter reasons, "'Tis enough for them to weed their garden, not their guests" (3.1.sp466). Although their fathers were "worthy and well reputed members of the city while they lived"

(1.1.sp13), the younger generation has only limited access to the garden because their attempts to consolidate their fathers' wealth and marry to patch up interfamily feuds do not recommend them to the gardeners who capitalize on pleasure-seeking Londoners.

In other accounts of the garden, such as James Shirley's *Hyde Park* (1632), playwrights portray it as the stylized resort for West London gentry; Mistress Caroline stipulates that even if she is to be married, she must remain free to visit these urban pleasure gardens: "I'll not be / Bound from Spring-garden, and the 'Sparagus."[58] Brome, however, shows the underside of these suburban projects. This Dutch enterprise is represented in the play by a gardener of unspecified origins and his Dutch wife, whose commercial instincts extend solely to efforts to maximize their profits. She informs her husband, "'tis not your dirty 'Sparagus . . . your tulips . . . can bring you in five hundred pound a year if my helping hand, and brain too, were not in the business" (3.1.sp413). Her "business" largely consists of procuring rooms at the garden for merchants' affairs with other citizens' wives and overcharging these customers—"all to mall as they do in the Netherlands"—for the "dirty 'Sparagus" and wine (3.1.sp428). Her profit depends on the repeat business of these merchants and she fears that "great courtiers and ladies" will by "their coming . . . keep out some of our more constant, and more profitable customers" (3.1.sp422, sp423), the city merchants of some money and dubious morals. Lacking the clearly delineated districts within the City that supposedly separate upper-class and commercial districts, the Sparagus Garden discourages both upwardly mobile cits and aristocratic patrons in favor of a middling sort who maximize the profit potential of these "two Acres."

Brome overdetermines the gardens as a Netherlands-like territory and the two caretakers as Dutch overlords. One character refers to the host and hostess of Sparagus Garden as "prince and princess of the province of Asparagus," while another greets Martha and her husband as "lord and lady of the new plantation here" (3.1.sp441, sp440). Yet the gardener and his wife, Martha, do not own the land but merely cultivate it: "and two or three years toil more, while our trade is in request and fashion will make us purchasers. I had once a hope to have bought this manor of marshland, for the resemblance it has to the Low Country soil you came from—to ha'made you a Bankside lady" (3.1.sp414). This explicit identification of the gardens with "the Low Countr[ies]" mobilizes anti-Dutch sentiment as a satiric device. Aspiring to the position of a "Bankside Lady," or a potent bawdy house owner, like Elizabeth Holland, Martha seeks to evade state strictures as she and her husband plot to become "purchasers" of an estate. As profits tail off for the gardener and his wife, though, they become increasingly selective in their clientele and aggressive in the way they pursue profits.

Samuel, a young heir to his father's wealth, describes Sparagus Garden as "[t]he island of two acres here more profitable than twice two thousand in the fens till the drainers have done there" (3.1.sp442). A small prototype of the type of land that will be available when larger inland fen drainage projects are completed, the "island of two acres" grows specialized cash crops—"this precious plant asparagus . . . [imported from] Burgundy, Allemagne, Italy, and Languedoc" (3.1.sp475)—and operates under its own rules. When Martha's servant bullies a visitor accompanied by a Mistress Hollyhock ("the precise draper's wife") to pay the inflated price that Martha demands, the gentleman replies that taverns which charge exorbitant rates should compromise to avoid being shut down. His thinly veiled threat that "the Countess of Copthall is coming to be her neighbor again" (3.1.sp642) suggests he may inform the authorities about Martha's procuring prostitutes for her guests. The servant derisively replies, "My mistress scorns your words, sir" (3.1.sp643), underscoring that the garden is not subject to the authorities' jurisdiction.

Brome portrays the Sparagus Garden as a contested site where the scheming commercial class is pitted against members of the upper class who are trying to lay claim to the area. A courtier encourages the ladies to dance by suggesting that the nobility's indisputable ownership of land stems from their exclusive power to purify and rejuvenate it: "You shall fresh vigour add unto the spring, / And double the increase, sweetness and beauty / Of every plant and flower throughout the garden" (3.1.sp556). Yet by commercializing and therefore undermining the very ideological framework that authorizes the aristocracy's rule, the courtier exposes the ideological fissures in this belief. The ladies tease the courtier by sarcastically remarking,

> If I thought so my Lord, we would not doe
> Such precious work for nothing; we would be
> Much better huswifes, and compound for shares
> O'th' gardeners profit.

> (3.1.sp557)

Treating the Sparagus Garden as a joint-stock enterprise that promises exponential growth, the lady casts Martha's operation as a second front of the Dutch West India Company, an enterprise catering to wealthy traders, while at the same time, cutting out the English aristocracy from their lucrative profits.

The ladies treat the grounds simply as what it is—a pleasure garden—and finally agree to dance but "[n]ot to improve the garden." Their graceful dancing at least represents a more worthy occupation than the activities that normally take place within the confines of the garden: "You have done nobly, ladies, and much honoured / This piece of earth here." Rather feebly, the courtier states, "May the example of our harmless mirth / And civil recreation purge this place / Of all foul purposes" (3.1.sp563, sp565). Seeing Moneylacks and his cronies, the practical lady replies, "But wishes weed no gardens; hither come / Some wicked ones" (3.1.sp566). While these courtiers discern that these troublemakers challenge their efforts to lay claim to and civilize the newly developed land, they exaggerate the peril that the "wicked ones" pose. After all, Moneylacks is an object of ridicule to everyone else in the play. This rhetoric, like the seemingly overwrought threats to murder authority in Brome's *Weeding of Covent Garden,* demands closer scrutiny. While the court imagines it can wait for an opportunity to exert its influence and eventually assume control over the suburbs, Brome suggests the land is already being appropriated for other uses. The courtier says, "We seek not to abridge their privilege; / Nor can their ill hurt us. We are safe" (3.1.sp567). Despite his reassurances, the ladies decide to return to their lodgings in Whitehall, leaving Sparagus garden to Moneylacks' devices. The exaggerated menace of physical violence—something the state has dealt with and can conceptualize—masks an economic threat that is not immediately present in Moneylacks; instead he raises the Dutch specter of economic hegemony, closing off domestic "markets" to the aristocracy.

Worse yet, Martha uses the English as middlemen to maximize her profits, suggesting the way the Dutch control English domestic markets. In his role as the "Fly of *The New Inn* there" (1.1.sp89), Moneylacks drives potential customers to Sparagus Garden. He packages the asparagus as possessing the power to transform rural yeomen into nobles. In an attempt to fleece Hoyden, a recent arrival from the country, of his four hundred pounds, he explains that to make him into a gentleman, "your blood shall be taken out by degrees, and your veins replenished with pure blood" (2.1.sp289). To do that, he must consume asparagus, which "shall set ... your blood as high as any gentleman's lineally descended from the loins of King Cadwallader" (2.1.sp297). Ironically, Hoyden literally consumes his inheritance, expunging his only social status, to strengthen his claim to an illusory class identity. Exposing the troubling disruptions to conceptions of English identity that commerce has introduced, Moneylacks promotes the social status of consuming this foreign plant by explaining how it was imported from "Burgundy, Allemagne, Italy, and Languedoc." Thus, Moneylacks reifies pure Briton blood unalloyed with past invaders into another object for consumption. The cultural geography that defines Britain is available for consumption in the town, and Brome suggests that this space fosters exchanges not only of goods and services but of social identities.

Moneylacks insists that the asparagus must only be eaten at the garden: "Where would you have it [the asparagus]? Here in our own house? Fie! The virtue of it is mortified if it pass the threshold from the ground it grows on. No, you must thither to the garden of delight" (2.1.sp217). He satirizes the aristocratic worldview that values the land over the goods produced on it. The real value of land can be measured, Brome implies, by how much profit it can generate for entrepreneurs. This enterprising commercial class exploits these newly created lands, while the characters identified with the court belatedly and futilely attempt to consecrate the land. Indeed, the court and the gentry seem to be outmaneuvered, unable to compete with an ever-adaptable commercial class. For Brome, these new town sites offer fresh venues to reinterpret traditional conceptions of the land. While the town blurs the already hazy distinctions among English merchants, developers, and the aristocracy, the efforts of these stakeholders to augment their socioeconomic position are undercut by entrenched inhabitants who refuse to cede easily their real and symbolic power in the town and by foreign powers who have already claimed these sites as part of a global commercial network.[59]

IV

Brome's *A Jovial Crew* (1641) dramatizes how the chaos inherent in the town has now spread across the country.[60] Oldrents, the patriarch in the play, unreasonably fears that his family's fortunes will decline, and his melancholy forces his children out of his house. The younger generation leaves the domestic safety of their father's estate to seek their "birthright into a new world."[61] Their "birthright" is defined not by the rewards they reap from land ownership but by the freedom to roam the countryside; the promise of patrilineal claims to the land no longer affords social protection or ensures political authority.[62] The play, which was staged on 2 September 1642, the day the London theaters were shut down by order of Parliament, attacks the "love and honour" drama of William Davenant, Sir John Suckling, and Thomas Killigrew, but suggests that the right kind of drama could serve as the means to prevent England from descending into civil war.[63] One of the commendatory letters of the play, written by the dramatist and city poet John Tatham, criticizes the audience for rejecting traditional if old-fashioned plays for "a faction ... in town":

> Ingrateful Negro-kind, dart you your rage
> Against the beams that warm'd you, and the stage!
> This malice shows it is unhallowed heat
> That boils your raw brains, and your temples beat.[64]

Alluding to climatic explanations of racial identity, Tatham contrasts the alien productions that have racialized the English to the native "beams," or plays by Shakespeare, Jonson, and Beaumont and Fletcher, that formed the English. Tatham assures them, "th[is] well-wrought piece" (*A Jovial Crew*) may "Draw th' curtain of th[e] errors" of the "Adulterate pieces" that have been foisted on English theatergoers. The conceit of the acceptance of debased coin by the masses in their demand for "love and honour" drama captures the sense that the London audience, striving to adhere to the French fashions introduced into London by Henrietta Maria and aped by courtiers, have allowed a foreign standard of value to replace their native one. Tatham compares the audience to "Indians, who their native wealth despise, / And dote on stranger's trash and trumperies." The "unhallowed heat" that Whitehall has introduced into England has altered the racial makeup of its citizens. While constructing the English as a heterogeneous population has enabled, as we have seen, internal colonial ventures in England, these projects have undermined the welfare of the state—a condition that the stage, Tatham implies even as he praises Brome, is now powerless to rectify.

Notes

1. See Martin Butler, *Theatre and Crisis, 1632-1642* (Cambridge: Cambridge University Press, 1984), esp. chap. 7; in the 1630s, Butler reminds us, "The traditional configuration of court, city and country now had a fourth term, the town" (141).

2. See Butler, *Theatre and Crisis*; Julie Sanders, *Caroline Drama: The Plays of Massinger, Ford, Shirley, and Brome* (Plymouth: Northcote House, 1999); R. J. Kaufmann, *Richard Brome: Caroline Playwright* (New York: Columbia University Press, 1961); Matthew Steggle, *Richard Brome: Place and Politics on the Caroline Stage* (Manchester: Manchester University Press, 2004); and Adam Zucker, "Laborless London: Comic Form and the Space of the Town in Caroline Covent Garden," *Journal for Early Modern Cultural Studies* 5, no. 2 (2005): 94-119.

3. In *England's Internal Colonies: Class, Capital, and the Literature of Early Modern English Colonialism* (New York: Palgrave Macmillan, 2003), Mark Netzloff provides a historical overview of the term *internal colonialism* (6-8). He "emphasize[s] the domestic foundations of early modern colonial discourse and practices" (6).

4. See Brian Walsh, "Performing Historicity in Dekker's *The Shoemaker's Holiday*," *SEL* 46, no. 2 (2006): 343n2, for a detailed explanation of the term *middling sort,* a rough approximation of our term *middle class.*

5. As Joyce Oldham Appleby explains in *Economic Thought and Ideology in Seventeenth-Century England* (Princeton, N.J.: Princeton University Press, 1978), the "sustained demonstration of this Dutch commercial prowess acted more forcefully upon the English imagination than any other economic development of the seventeenth century" (73). See ibid., chap. 4., "The Dutch as a Source of Evidence," 73-98.

6. Richard Brome, *The Weeding of Covent Garden; or, The Middlesex Justice of Peace: A Facetious Comedy,* Modern Text, ed. Michael Leslie, *Richard Brome Online,* accessed May 2011, http://www.hrionline.ac.uk/brome, 3.2.speech695, 4.1.speech792, 4.1.speech709, and 4.2speech887. Subsequent references to this play are from this edition and are cited parenthetically by act, scene, and speech number (abbreviated "sp"). This newly published online scholarly edition of all of Brome's plays includes dramatic stage readings of many passages, revealing interpretative nuances that are discussed in some detail in the critical introductions.

7. Zucker, 95.

8. William Shakespeare, *Richard II,* ed. Stanley Wells (New York: Penguin, 1981), 2.1.43-44.

9. Benjamin Schmidt, *Innocence Abroad: The Dutch Imagination and the New World, 1570-1670* (Cambridge: Cambridge University Press, 2001), 140; Jonathan Israel, *The Dutch Republic: Its Rise, Greatness, and Fall* (Oxford: Oxford University Press, 1995), 346-48.

10. As Robert Brenner points out in *Merchants and Revolution: Commercial Change, Political Conflict, and London's Overseas Traders, 1550-1663* (London: Verso, 2003), the "newer trades had as their raison d'être . . . to be built up in commercial struggle against the Dutch" (599). Although the landed class in England sought to create permanent settlements abroad, an increasingly powerful up-and-coming merchant class were "hostile to any expenditures not immediately productive of profit and were constantly urging their agents to spend as little as possible on fortification or buildings of any sort" (171). I argue that this profit motive affects their domestic settlements as well as colonial fortifications abroad.

11. In *Richard Brome: Place and Politics,* Steggle notes the many references to Holland in *The Sparagus Garden*; he concentrates on Brome's comparison of "this two-acre project to a miniature fen-drainage" (76), arguing that "fen drainage raised difficult questions of land-ownership, authority, and 'legitimate title' to lands that did not previously exist" (77).

12. Ben Jonson, *The Entertainment at Britain's Burse: Re-Presenting Ben Jonson,* ed. Martin Butler (New York: St. Martin's Press, 1999), ll. 51, 45-47.

13. See Arjun Appadurai's introduction to *The Social Life of Things: Commodities in Cultural Perspective* (Cambridge: Cambridge University Press, 1986), 3-63.

14. Eric Kerridge, *Textile Manufactures in Early Modern England* (Manchester: Manchester University Press, 1985), 126-27.

15. David J. Baker, *On Demand: Writing for the Market in Early Modern England* (Stanford: Stanford University Press, 2010), 101.

16. See Israel, 318-27.

17. Jonson immediately tries to lessen the anxieties over the reach of Dutch overseas trade by assuring the

king that "my factors from Iygourne [a trading port in Greece] haue aduertised that Warde the man of warre, for that is nowe the honorable name for a pyrate; hath taken theyr greatest Hulke [.] ... [I]t is thought they will come whom [home] verye mvch dissolued" (ll. 176-81). Ward, though, represents another threat to the king; as Daniel Vitkus points out: Ward "exemplified the success and autonomy that may be achieved through an unruly masculine virtue that is willing and able to defy the rules laid down by the Christian authorities." See Daniel J. Vitkus, ed., *Three Turk Plays from Early Modern England: "Selimus," "A Christian Turned Turk" and "The Renegado"* (New York: Columbia University Press, 2000), 26.

18. Henry Turner, *The English Renaissance Stage: Geometry, Poetics, and the Practical Spatial Arts, 1580-1630* (New York: Oxford University Press, 2006), 195.

19. See Rebecca Ann Bach, *Colonial Transformations: The Cultural Production of the New Atlantic World, 1580-1640* (New York: Palgrave Macmillan, 2000), 120, 144.

20. See Rachel Ramsey, "The Language of Urbanization in John Stow's *Survey of London*," *Philological Quarterly* 85, nos. 3-4 (2006): 247-70 (255). She draws attention to the way urbanization shapes what she terms the "social topography" of London: "[E]xamples of indiscriminate building narratively precede accounts of social and economic change, so ... the material topography appears to dictate the social topography" (254-55). I concentrate on the "shock" Londoners register as they try to make sense of their new surroundings. See Greg Dening, *Islands and Beaches: Discourses on a Silent Land Marquesas, 1774-1880* (Honolulu: University Press of Hawaii, 1980), 94.

21. See Walter Thornbury, *Old and New London: A Narrative of Its History, Its People, and Its Places,* 2 vols. (London: Cassell, Petter, Galpin, 1881), 2:196.

22. Quoted in Thornbury, 2:196.

23. Andrew McRae, *God Speed the Plough: The Representation of Agrarian England, 1500-1660* (Cambridge: Cambridge University Press, 1996), 105.

24. Steggle, *Richard Brome: Place and Politics,* 76-77. See also Julie Sanders's discussion of this issue in her introduction to *The Sparagus Garden, Richard Brome Online,* para. 18 (see n. 57, below).

25. Bedford became a lightning rod for fen drainage opponents prompting Charles's intervention; see Kevin Sharpe, *The Personal Rule of Charles I* (New Haven, Conn.: Yale University Press, 1995), 255.

26. Ibid., 252-54.

27. H. C., *A Discourse Concerning the Drayning of Fennes and Surrounded Grounds in the Six Countreys of Norfolke* (London, 1629), A₄.

28. Keith Lindley, *Fenland Riots and the English Revolution* (London: Ashgate, 1982), 8.

29. Ibid., 9.

30. "A True and Natural Description of the Great Level of the Fenns," in *The History or Narrative of the Great Level of the Fenns, called Bedford Level* (London, 1685), 69-81 (78).

31. Lindley, 19.

32. Susan Scott Parrish, "Rummaging/In and Out of Holds," *American Literary History* 22 (2010): 289-301 (297).

33. Netzloff, 4.

34. Ben Jonson, *Bartholomew Fair,* ed. G. R. Hibbard (New York: Norton, 1977), pr. 7, ll. 6-11.

35. The play describes the Puritans and an economic underclass as equal scourges to the state. When the play was presented at court, the prologue welcomed James I by alluding to the ongoing hostilities between Puritans and the Crown: "Your Majesty is welcome to a Fair; / Such place, such men, such language, and such ware, / You must expect; with these, the zealous noise / Of your land's Faction, scandalized at toys, / As babies, hobby-horses, puppet-plays" (pr. 1-5).

36. Bach, *Colonial Transformations,* 124, 120.

37. Jonson's *The New Inne,* as Bach explains, was supposed to serve as a rejoinder to *Bartholomew Fair*'s unruly state: "As a later development of Smithfield, *The New Inne* is a domesticated colonial space" (135).

38. Butler, *Theatre and Crisis,* 156.

39. Michael Leslie, introduction to *The Weeding of Covent Garden, Richard Brome Online,* para. 48 and 51.

40. Crosswill claims that James's and Charles's insistence on the continuation of traditional country sports and pastimes—practices Puritans denounced—forced Gabriel into the town: "And he has done nothing but hanged the head, as you see now, ever since holiday sports were cried up in the country. And but for that, and to talk with some of the silenced pastors about it, I should not have drawn him up" (1.1.sp40). He was only induced to accompany his father because, in the teeming metropolis, he could commiserate with small pockets of his radical brethren.

41. "A True and Natural Description," 74.

42. Steggle, 47. See J. Newman, "Inigo Jones and the Politics of Architecture," *Culture and Politics in Early Stuart England* (Stanford: Stanford University Press, 1993), ed. Kevin Sharpe and Peter Lake, 229-56, for a discussion of Inigo Jones's involvement as the King's Surveyor in Covent Garden's uniform architecture. Zucker states, "in the planning of the piazza, Bedford sought the assistance of Inigo Jones . . . the driving force behind the Stuart aesthetic of urban uniformity" (99). Discussing the Earl of Bedford's connections between fen drainage schemes and the development of Covent Garden, Sanders, in her introduction to *The Sparagus Garden,* notes: "much of the profits he made from the lucrative fen drainage schemes was ploughed back into the very material and tangible product of building the area of London known as Covent Garden" (para. 18).

43. This is akin to Zucker's formulation that "the erotic tension occasioned by the threshold space of the balcony structures a scene of disorderly sexuality that directly threatens the social tenor of the neighborhood by invoking the labor of prostitutes" (106).

44. Howard and Turner articulate an oft-repeated sentiment about early Jacobean seventeenth-century drama. Butler states: "Plays by Brome, Shirley, and Davenant offered the audience images of themselves in parks, squares, taverns, and gaming houses, supplying standards against which forms and codes of behavior could be established" (*Theatre and Crisis,* 110-11).

45. Mimi Yiu, "Sounding the Space between Men: Choric and Choral Cities in Ben Jonson's *Epicoene; or, The Silent Woman,*" *PMLA* (Jan. 2007): 72-78 (73).

46. Zucker takes Crosswill's injunction at face value: "a conventional story of young lovers effects an imaginary space on stage temporally purged of dis-ease, labor, and disorder. The Covent Garden neighborhood reproduced in comic form is finally 'fitt . . . for gentlemen of ability'" (108).

47. Steggle, *Richard Brome: Place and Politics,* 52.

48. For Carl Schmitt, sovereignty constitutes a transcendent figure by which a ruler can declare a state of emergency, suspending all laws, in such circumstances as civil war or other conditions that threaten to topple the state: "Sovereign is he who decides on the exception."

49. Steggle, 48.

50. As Victoria Kahn explains, a highly charged and unstable political authority prompted unrest throughout the early seventeenth century, "From James I's early political treatises through the parliamentary pamphleteers of the 1640s, reasoning about the exceptional case (or, in the rhetoric of the period, reason of state) was a burning political issue" ("Hamlet or Hecuba: Carl Schmitt's Decision," *Representations* 83 [2003]: 67-96 [70]).

51. Giorgio Agamben, *Homo Sacer: Sovereign Power and Bare Life,* trans. Daniel Heller-Roazen (Stanford: Stanford University Press, 1998), 36-37, 105, 37.

52. Jean Howard, *Theater of a City: The Places of London Comedy, 1598-1642* (Philadelphia: University of Pennsylvania Press, 2007), 158.

53. Nicholas Goodman, *Hollands Leaguer: A Critical Edition,* ed. Dean Stanton Barnard Jr. (The Hague: Mouton, 1970), 80; hereafter cited in the text by page number from this edition.

54. Howard, 160.

55. As Steggle puts it, the site's "perceived sexual and pseudo-military unruliness clearly touched a raw nerve in Caroline culture" ("*The Knave in Grain* Puts Holland's Leaguer on Stage," *Notes & Queries* 51 [Dec. 2004]: 355-56 [356]).

56. Andrew Marvell, "The Character of Holland," *The Poems of Andrew Marvel,* ed. Nigel Smith (Harlow, UK: Pearson Education, 2007), 246-56, ll. 71-74.

57. Richard Brome, *The Sparagus Garden,* Modern Text, ed. Julie Sanders, *Richard Brome Online,* 3.1. speech416, 3.1.speech418. Subsequent references to this play are from this edition and are cited parenthetically by act, scene, and speech number (abbreviated "sp"). As Sanders points out, we need not think of these gardens as the only such site in London, but possibly one of several, "competing with one another for business" (introduction, para. 23).

58. *The Dramatic Works and Poems of James Shirley,* 2 vols. (London: Murray, 1833), 2.4 (this edition has no line numbers).

59. William Harbert writes in his *A Prophesie of Cadwallader* (London, 1604): "Cesar was twice repulst ere he could see This litle world from all the world remote" (H$_4$).

60. Butler writes: "Brome asks insistently what the 'country' is. . . . *A Jovial Crew* is a truly national play written at a turning point in the history of the English stage and the English nation" *Theatre and Crisis* (275).

61. Richard Brome, *A Jovial Crew,* Modern Text, ed. Richard Cave et al., *Richard Brome Online,* 3.1. speech364.

62. When Patrico, the patriarch of the beggars, divulges his true identity as "grandson to that unhappy Wrought-on / Whom your grandfather craftily wrought / Of his estate" to Oldrents, Brome suggests

how tenuous the claims of even supposedly respectable landholders have to their estates. These cracks in English society are raised only to be too easily resolved. Patrico continues, "I do not charge / You with the least offence in this" (5.1.sp1034), implying that the continuation of a system—even a corrupt one—that orders society trumps his personal entitlement to the estate (in addition, we learn his nephew is Oldrents's beloved steward and newly discovered son, Springlove, restoring part of the estate to his heirs). Patrilineal succession, then, is still the way the characters in the play understand their world. As Randall, Oldrents's servant, proudly states earlier in the play, the estate "has been my master's and his ancestors' in that name above these three hundred years, as our house chronicle doth notify, and not yet to be let" (4.1.sp610).

63. See Martin Butler's entry for Brome in the *ODNB*.

64. Richard Brome, *A Jovial Crew*, Quarto Text, ed. Richard Cave et al., *Richard Brome Online*, A_4V; subsequent citations of Tatham's letter refer to this page in the front matter of the Quarto text.

Nova Myhill (essay date 2011)

SOURCE: Myhill, Nova. "Taking the Stage: Spectators as Spectacle in the Caroline Private Theaters." *Imagining the Audience in Early Modern Drama, 1558-1642*. Ed. Jennifer A. Low and Myhill. New York: Palgrave Macmillan, 2011. 37-54. Print.

[*In the following essay, Myhill considers three inductions (introductory scenes) to Caroline English comedies, including Brome's prologue to a revival of Thomas Goffe's* The Careless Shepherdess *(1638), in terms of their characterization of the audience. Noting the many reasons why an early seventeenth-century playgoer might attend the theater, Myhill shows how Brome's induction opened these different types of spectators "to criticism, or at least self-consciousness."*]

Ben Jonson's *The Magnetic Lady* (1633) begins with two gentleman playgoers, Probee and Damplay, entering the Blackfriars stage in search of "the poet o' the day" (Induction 13) to "entreat an excellent play from you" (49).[1] The two gentlemen are seated on the stage throughout the play, presumably among the playgoers who have paid for stools on the stage. At first glance, the Induction and between-act sections of *The Magnetic Lady* would seem to function as a simple didactic model, an explicit attempt, like Jonson's other prologues and inductions, to encourage certain behaviors in his audience and discourage others: the two gentlemen comment, and the playhouse boy who serves as Jonson's mouthpiece approves the sentiments of Probee and discredits those of Damplay. In what follows, however, I wish to suggest that inductions such as Jonson's are

ultimately less concerned with either enforcing or catering to a particular mode of spectatorship within the private theater audiences than with acknowledging the variety of available methods of watching, "provid[ing] the spectator with a sharpened perception of his [or her] own processes as a spectator,"[2] and ultimately refocusing the attention of the members of the audience onto the play rather than onto each other.

In "'Wits Most Accomplish'd Senate': The Audience of the Caroline Private Theaters," which remains the most useful study of the Caroline audience, Michael Neill argues that the Caroline private theater is frequented by and caters to a "highly sophisticated audience" that conceives of itself as "a court of taste ... a closed group of *cognoscenti* who came to the playhouse not merely to be entertained but to appreciate and judge the offerings of the poet's fancy."[3] The essay suggests a single, idealized model of spectatorship, which all members of the audience, regardless of their education and social status, wish to present themselves as embodying, thus becoming corporate members of the "court of taste" ultimately defined by "the aristocrats who ... exercised an influence out of all proportion to their actual numbers."[4] This model is reinforced by "the dedications, prefaces, prologues, and epilogues ... [that] are the record of the [playwrights'] relationship with this audience of discerning patrons and intimates";[5] Neill presents this relationship, in practice, as one of appeasement on the part of the playwrights in the face of "a hypercritical audience—[an attempt] to woo them into acquiescence."[6] The audience attends the theater for the purpose of judging plays, and authority in the playhouse lies exclusively with the audience.

But the inductions I discuss here, Jonson's Inductions to *The Magnetic Lady* and *The Staple of News* (1626) and Richard Brome's **Praeludium** written for the 1638 revival of Thomas Goffe's *The Careless Shepherdess*,[7] suggest two important corollaries to this model: this self-conscious audience functioned as spectacle as well as spectators and, as a result, the plays make judgments about their spectators as thoroughly and visibly as the audience judges the plays. The theater offered not only the chance to develop the "essential accomplishment" of "the appreciation and judgment of works of dramatic art"[8] but also, as importantly, the chance to publicly display one's possession of this accomplishment. As Neill observes, "[T]he profession of critical connoisseurship was open to any gentleman who could buy admission to the private playhouses";[9] Brome's Induction to *The Careless Shepherdess* suggests that the stage offers not only a place for gentlemen to show their membership in this "profession" but also a chance to display their clothes and for their social inferiors to "occupy a place near you: there are / None that be worthy of my company / In any room beneath the twelve penny."[10] In dramatizing members of the audience sharing the physical space of the stage with the actors—the gallants on stools who make up a prominent part of the stage spectacle, at times actively competing with the players for both space and attention—Jonson and Brome's staging of spectatorship reclaims the stage for the players and suggests that the experience of playgoing is as subject to judgment as the plays themselves. Like the actual audience of the private theater, the audience members represented in these inductions come to the theater for a variety of reasons, including interest in costumes, topical application, stylistic judgment, and self-display. Jonson and Brome's interest in the variety of methods of spectatorship opens all of them to criticism, or at least self-consciousness.

While evidence certainly suggests that the Caroline private theaters served a much more socially homogenous clientele than their Elizabethan predecessors, the representations of this audience emphasize, to a much greater extent than representations of Elizabethan audiences, the diversity of tastes and viewing practices both between members of different social groups and within members of the same group. Probee and Damplay, for instance, are socially and economically united, speaking on behalf of "the better and braver sort of your people! Plush and velvet outsides!" (31-32), who are willing to pay eighteen pence or two shillings for seats in Blackfriars, not "your sinful sixpenny mechanics" (30). Probee and Damplay are represented as typical members of that segment of the Blackfriars audience. In most important ways, they are identical to one another—the significant difference is only how they watch a play. This divergence in their viewing practices might be important in how we imagine the relation between the Caroline audience and the actors and playwrights, particularly since Probee and Damplay's social uniformity presents a challenge to Neill's claim that "such distinctions [in viewing practices] tended to be largely fictitious and designed to flatter the aristocrats."[11]

Neill's analysis does not distinguish between literary and theatrical prefatory materials; a crucial feature of his argument indeed depends on understanding the literary qualities of Caroline drama as the central feature admired by the audience of connoisseurs whose tastes shaped the drama. The most interesting aspects of the inductions, and to a lesser extent the prologues and epilogues, however, are precisely their theatrical features, through which the audience and the play explicitly occupy the same space and are visible in the same ways. In their recent work on Elizabethan prologues, Douglas Bruster and Robert Weimann emphasize the liminal qualities of the prologue—both as a piece of writing and as a figure on the stage—"alternately deferential and commanding," recognizing both the audience's power over the play (including the power to simply silence it by refusing to stop talking) and the play's power over the audience, to take it to another world.[12] This sense of liminality is even more pronounced in inductions than in prologues and epilogues; if the prologue and epilogue function as a "threshold, a liminal space between the actual and the potential that characterized the 'playing holidays'

of dramatic fiction in the early modern playhouse," they do so for the space of about thirty lines, with the body of a single actor.[13] The induction extends over much more time and, importantly, space.

In her discussion of "critical inductions," those with a specific focus on theatrical production and reception, Thelma Greenfield notes that by 1604 such inductions are considerably more common in plays performed at private theaters than in plays performed at public theaters. She attributes this to Harbage's suggestion that "the Globe theater audience was less in need of a lesson in good manners than the more elegant patrons of the private theaters."[14] It seems to me that the greater frequency of inductions that include representations of the audience in private theaters than public is more significantly a product of the physical than the social configuration of the audience. Only in the private theaters do members of the theater audience physically share the space of the stage with the performers, competing for space and the attention of the rest of the audience. While the presence of spectators on the stages of the private theaters, particularly the Blackfriars, was a well-established theatrical convention, it was also the subject of regular satire and other forms of complaint from some of the playwrights, particularly Jonson, who seems never to have accepted the situation and whose anxieties about reception are amply visible in his inductions, prologues, and printed prefatory matter.[15] I would like to view these anxieties as reasonable rather than hyperbolic here and consider the stage sitters as a potentially serious alternative focus for the theater audience.

Theater historians have in general been at pains to minimize the potential disruption from these spectators, consistently making the smallest possible estimate of their numbers that the evidence will allow. This reading of the evidence seems to stem from a visceral distaste for an audience that might authentically compete with the play for the rest of the audience's attention: "[W]hether or not the space available for acting is sufficient, one winces at the thought of drama huddled in such an extensive frame of spectators in all postures."[16] Precisely because of this uneasy sense that any large number of stage sitters might fatally compromise the production, it seems worth taking Jonson's complaints, which routinely mention physical contact between actors and stage sitters, seriously for a moment.[17] The prologue to *The Devil is an Ass* (1616) is almost entirely concerned with the physical constraints the stage sitters—the "grandees"—impose on the actors. Jonson asks the audience not to force them to "act / In compass of a cheese-trencher"[18] and specifically complains about the physical contact "when you will thrust and spurn, And knock us on the elbows" (11-12) and the assumption that the audience controls the stage space "and bid [the actors], turn; / As if, when we had spoke, we must be gone, / Or till we speak, must all run in, to one, / Like the young adders to the old one's mouth!" (12-15). The prologue complains that the audience wants not live actors but "Muscovy glass," translucent images, "that you might look our scenes through as they pass" (17-18). The substance of the audience threatens that the play "through want of room ... must miscarry" (23), as the stage affords room for only one set of bodily presences. In the *Gull's Horn Book* (1609), Dekker similarly observes that should the gallant seated on the stage "rise with a skreud and discontented face ... and draw what troop you can from the stage after you: the *Mimicks* are beholden to you, for allowing them elbow room."[19]

Recently, Tiffany Stern has imagined the spectacle of the stage sitters in considerable detail, considering how this "living decoration" of "colored silks, satins, and feathers" provided both a backdrop for the plays and serious competition for the attention of the playgoers.[20] In this context, inductions that represent stage sitters, as in *The Staple of News, The Magnetic Lady,* and *The Careless Shepherdess,* represent not the audience's intrusion into the stage space but the actors' intrusion into the space of the audience, if the stage itself can be said to be demarcated into actor space and audience space. The inductions themselves suggest that this division is physically impossible; if the liminal stage space is to be divided, then this must happen based on newly drawn boundaries not in space but in behavior.

At this point, I would like to return to Probee and Damplay in their position as precise representations of the gentleman playgoers who command the stage of the Blackfriars. The fundamental difference between these gentleman playgoers is their sense of what their payment buys; Damplay sees himself as having bought the right to do whatever he wishes in the theater, certain that the play is there for him, not he for the play, while Probee defines his experience in the terms the playwright provides for judging the play: "[O]ur parts that are the spectators, or should hear a comedy, are to await the process and events of things, as the poet presents them, not as we would corruptly fashion them" (4 Chor. 10-13). Probee thus claims that the search for personal satire is "an unjust way of hearing and beholding plays," while Damplay is certain that nothing can be "out of purpose at a play[.] I see no reason if I come here and give my eighteen pence or two shillings for my seat but I should take it out in censure on the stage" (2 Chor. 59-62). Probee and Damplay may have paid the same amount of money, but they have not paid for the same experience.

When Probee urges him to "mark the play" (3 Chor. 18), Damplay makes explicit his sense of his relation to the play: "I care not for marking the play: I'll damn it, talk, and do that I come for. I will not have gentlemen lose their privilege, not I myself my prerogative, for ne'er an overgrown or superannuated poet of 'em all. He shall not give me law; I will censure, and be witty, and take my tobacco, and enjoy my Magna Carta of reprehension, as my predecessors have done before me" (3 Chor 19-25).

Damplay's legalistic language of privilege, prerogative, and precedent emphasizes the power dynamic between the play and its audience, which depends on both parties allowing the other certain rights. When the Boy objects to his determination to read the play as personal satire in the second-act chorus, Damplay protests that "this were a strange empire, or rather a tyranny, you would entitle your poet to over gentlemen, that they should come to hear and see plays and say nothing for their money" (2 Chor. 53-56). The "tyranny" that Damplay objects to is the silencing of the audience; his understanding of his "rights" as a playgoer includes the right to be heard as well as seen, and to offer an interpretation that differs from that of "your poet." The fear of tyranny and insistence on the gentlemen's "Magna Carta of reprehension" emphasizes the audience's rights as subjects to the play. The play is imagined as the sovereign, but Damplay's status as a gentleman and his payment for his place in the theater protects him from the arbitrary and absolute power he sees the Boy demanding for the playwright.

While Probee is certainly presented in a more favorable light than Damplay, they are both equally exaggerated figures; Probee's willingness to subordinate his judgment to the play is no more or less plausible than Damplay's refusal to do so, and Probee's utter rejection of "the solemn vice of interpretation" or application (2 Chor. 34) is clearly inconsistent with both the mode of spectatorship practiced by many of the private theater audience and the interests of Jonson's satire, however it may accord with the rhetoric of Jonson's other prologues and epilogues. The central difference between Probee and Damplay is that Damplay is focused on his rights (what the Boy cannot prevent him from doing), while Probee is focused on his responsibilities (what he should be doing himself): "We come here to behold the plays and censure them, as they are made, and fitted for us" (4 Chor. 14-15). Probee, like the Boy, sees the play as a whole, and his main objection to looking for personal satire is that doing so "deforms the figure of many a fair scene by drawing it awry" (2 Chor. 34-35). Damplay's experience of the play is visceral and immediate: a series of moments that he cannot connect, a hunger for activity and conclusion. But despite this fundamental difference in their habits of viewing and interpretation, the gentlemen share the assumption that the play cannot change them; both Damplay's insistence that he need not "mark the play" and Probee's definition of their "parts as spectators" imply that the play, not they, is subject to judgment, and if the Boy proposes Damplay as a negative model, he is able to do so because he shares the space of the actors and speaks; Probee is in some important sense invisible by contrast.

Damplay, while not an entirely desirable spectator, is not an impossible, naïve, or inexperienced one. He still remembers Jonson's complaint that "you make a libel of a comedy" from "a prologue long since" (2 Chor. 28-30), although remembering the words is apparently an entirely different thing than applying them to himself, and he never interrupts the play or fails to understand exactly what his situation is. If he presses his rights as a gentleman "even to license and absurdity," he is free to do so. The Boy gives up Damplay as a hopeless case but hopes that he will serve as a negative example that will reform other playgoers: "[B]e yourself still, without a second. Few here are of your opinion today, I hope; tomorrow I am sure there will be none when they have ruminated this" (2 Chor. 79-82). Damplay's ways of watching are made ridiculous, both by presenting them on stage at all and by Probee consistently siding with the Boy when the latter puts Damplay down, but they are significantly contractual in nature, as is the Boy's formulation of the theater as a shop where, like the playgoers envisioned in the prologue to *Bartholomew Fair,* every person may censure in proportion to, but not beyond, his or her payment (2 Chor. 63-65).[21]

It seems worth noting that in almost all early modern plays in which characters watch a theatrical performance, "the audience plays its part badly and misinterprets the play."[22] Despite the flattering gesture of the prologue's address to "gentles," the early modern stage presents an audience that accords with the antitheatrical image of the playhouse as a gathering place of the foolish or wicked, in pursuit of mindless pleasure, anxious to corrupt or be corrupted, and impervious to the beneficial effects of the stage that its defenders insisted were available to those who would only watch the play in the correct frame of mind. Compared to the represented audiences of Elizabethan plays, who routinely lack "the most basic form of theatrical competence—the ability to recognize the play as such,"[23] Damplay has considerably more potential. The audiences represented in Caroline drama present a much more varied and sophisticated set of problems—"competence" has come to be defined in increasingly specialized and complex ways. This is particularly noticeable in the way that audiences are represented as having significantly different experiences of the play because of the ways in which they watch.

As Neill suggests, these representations are frequently satirical, and it is certainly possible that "such distinctions tended to be largely fictitious,"[24] but if we divorce the variety of interpretive practices from the vexed question of satire and social class, several things are apparent that suggest some limitations of Neill's reading of the "taste" of the Caroline playgoer as uniform. First, many behaviors represented on the stage or attested to in prologues were certainly not confined to these types of dubious evidence. The claim that there existed an audience who preferred the drama of twenty or thirty years past is amply verified by the records of repertories of the 1630s, and the King's Men's seasonal move from the Blackfriars to the Globe shifted not only repertory but also audience members between public and private playhouses. The frequent, if less systematic, transfer of plays and companies between the

Cockpit and the Red Bull under Christopher Beeston's management suggests that the King's Men were not entirely anomalous in their use of multiple playhouses.[25]

Similarly, an interpretive practice consistently inveighed against was that of "application," or "interpretation"—that is, matching the characters on stage to public persons in Caroline London as Damplay does in the second interval. This in no way suggests that such a practice did not exist, and the mention of it, particularly in the self-protective gesture of satirical playwrights such as Jonson, encouraged rather than diminished its practice. The conventions for attending the private theaters (rather than the public amphitheaters) are far more likely to be brought on the Caroline stage than the old joke of audience members who have never seen a play and cannot recognize the distinction between fact and fiction.

Theatrum Redivium, Richard Baker's response to William Prynne's massive antitheatrical tract *Histriomastix* (1633), argues for the public benefit offered by the stage: "[I]t is a general delight, general to sex, to age, to quality . . . it is a sociable delight, many do at once enjoy it, and all equally."[26] But the representations of contemporary theater audiences—in prologues, epilogues, interscenes, and in the plays themselves—strongly emphasize the segmentations to be found in this "general" audience. "The ladies" are frequently differentiated as a type of audience member, as are citizens, country gentry, Inns of Court men, and courtiers, all of whom are assumed to have their own reasons for coming to the play. If Probee embodies a fantasy of the Caroline audience entertained by playwrights of the period, there is equally a recognition that any production will inevitably play to responses that vary based on the playgoer's interpretive practices.

And the audience is potentially even more segmented by viewing practices than by social class. While Brome's Induction to *The Careless Shepherdess* presents one member each of the court, the Inns of Court, the country gentry, and the London citizenry, Jonson's inductions to both *The Staple of News* and *The Magnetic Lady* present multiple members of the same playgoing class—the gossips and the court gentlemen—watching the plays in significantly different ways that reflect their individual interests and previous theatrical experience rather than their shared social class. In what follows, I am not so much interested in either the qualities of the ideal audience envisioned by Jonson in a figure like Probee or the satirical butts of jokes like Thrift, the citizen from *The Careless Shepherdess,* who certainly does function as a means of flattering the taste of the courtly playgoers as Neill suggests. Instead, I am interested in the variety of ways of watching plays available in Caroline London and what this might suggest about the flexibility of the relationship between spectators and spectacles, the possibility of judgment going both ways, and the mutual shaping power of plays and their viewers.

COURTIERS, CITIZENS, AND GHOSTS: THE
AUDIENCES OF *THE CARELESS SHEPHERDESS*

Richard Brome's **Praeludium** to the 1638 revival of Thomas Goffe's *The Careless Shepherdess* at Salisbury Court
provides a particularly interesting representation of the private theater audience in terms of both social class and
viewing practices. The induction addresses the increasingly
vexed question of why one would attend the private theater,
or, to put it another way, what a shilling buys for each of the
spectators represented in the Induction.

Set in the Salisbury Court theater itself, the scene consists
of conversation among four playgoers and Bolt, the door-
keeper. The "actors" in the scene represent varied approaches to the theater: the courtier, the Inns of Court
man, the country gentleman, and the citizen. Entering separately, they find seats on the stage. While Spark, the Inns
of Court man, and Spruce, the courtier, are previously acquainted, the stage provides an occasion for Thrift, the
citizen, and Landlord, the country gentleman, to become
part of a social circle defined by money and physical space.
The last to enter is Landlord, who proclaims it "my ambition / To occupy a place near you" (3); cost no longer
functions to differentiate classes. Landlord can buy a
"place" near the cash-strapped Spark and Spruce, and
Thrift's haggling that begins the play insists that the play
is itself a commodity. Ultimately, however, the commodity
is not the play but rather the "company" that Landlord and
Thrift can easily buy their way into. Landlord's interest in
the play is utterly secondary to his interest in the "place" his
shilling buys him among courtiers and Inns of Court men.

As the correlation of place with social status taken for
granted by Damplay and Probee breaks down, Spruce
and Spark become increasingly anxious to differentiate
themselves from Thrift and Landlord. When Landlord proclaims that "I have found fault with very good Sermons /
In my daies, and now I desire that we / May passe our sentences upon this Play" (3) and Thrift eagerly takes up the
metaphor, wishing that he "had my Gown" (3), Spruce and
Spark both vehemently deny Landlord and Thrift's competence to "censure poetry," which is "the Prerogative of
the wits in Town" (3). But this censure is not what Probee
envisions; Spark is pleased with his choice to "spend [his]
money at the play / [rather] Then at the Ordinary" because
he has found Spruce, and "if the play should prove dull /
Your company will satisfy my ears" (3).

After a long discussion of poetry and dramatic construction, in which Spruce and Spark demonstrate their familiarity (and Thrift and Landlord's lack of familiarity) with a
very specific set of literary standards based in text rather
than performance, Spark asks Landlord, "cause you will be
prodigious," to tell him "what part you think essential for a
play? / And what in your opinion is styled wit[?]" (4).
Landlord defines the pleasure of the play as visual rather
than verbal; his desire for "a Fool in every Act" is based not
on the language that such a character would produce but
rather on his desire "to see what faces the Rogue will
make" (4). Thrift, seconding this desire, shares Landlord's
pleasure in physical activity—he "would rather see him
leap, laugh, or cry / Than hear the gravest speech in all the
play." But Thrift also attends to language, albeit in a very
different sense than Spruce or Spark: "His part has all the
wit / For none speaks carps or Quibbles besides he" (5).

Spark and Spruce's ridicule is predictable but interesting.
Spark sees both Landlord and Thrift as "ghosts"—those
with the same tastes as their forefathers, "whose dull intellect did nothing understand / But fools and fighting" (5).
The pleasures of the contemporary theater have evolved,
insists Spark, so that that audience is moved "to admire,
not to laugh"; puns went out of style with trunk hose, "And
since the wits grew sharp, the swords are sheathed" (5).
Here, as in the Induction to *The Magnetic Lady,* the Elizabethan theater (there expressed as Damplay's appeal to
precedent—his rights to do "as my predecessors have
done before me") is marked as conducive to a style of
interpretation ill-suited to the new drama of the Caroline
private theater. But while Jonson suggests that Damplay's
tastes might be reformed in the rest of the audience if not in
Damplay himself, Brome's **Praeludium** suggests these
tastes are class-based and might instead be redirected to
another venue; Thrift, true to his name, determines to take
back his money, "for now I have considered that it is too
much," and go instead to the much cheaper Red Bull or
Fortune, "and there see a play for two pence / And a jig to
boot" (8).

Dismayed at the promise of a comedy with no fool, no
wordplay, and no swordplay, Landlord determines to
leave: "[T]he Comedy / Will be as tedious to me as a sermon, / And I do fear that I shall fall asleep / And give my
twelve pence to be melancholy" (5). Spark promises him
other forms of "mirth," and Landlord consents to remain, if
only "that I may view the Ladies and they me" (5-6); the
spectacle of the audience is ultimately more compelling
than the play. Ultimately, however, none of the participants
in the **Praeludium** remain on the stage: Spruce and Spark
determine to watch the play from "some private room" (8)
lest their presence should intimidate a third actor into forgetting his lines, though Landlord suspects it is less concern
for the actors than fear that "some Creditor should spy
them" that leads them to "take sanctuary amongst / The
Ladies" in the boxes, where he will join them, concealed
by "a Ladies head / Or . . . a lattice window," which interrupts both their vision and their visibility (8).

Despite the Induction's interest in the range of possible
responses to the play, all of these responses are ultimately
banished from the stage to either the boxes or other theaters altogether. The Induction ends with the onstage spectators leaving the "open stage" to the Prologue, but the
Prologue is himself "an actor plac't in the Pit" (8) who
takes over from the second actor; he is a plant who

comes from the offstage audience to begin the play by speaking for the absent author. While Spark, Spruce, Landlord, and Thrift all proclaim their right to judge the play, all the varieties of this model of audience as judge are utterly rejected by the structure of the prologue itself.

The prologue, that thing that will actually allow the play to begin, is interrupted by a combination of incompetence from the actors and the onstage audience; the first actor to attempt to deliver the prologue stops after one line: "Must I always a hearer only be?" (7). When the onstage audience laughs at him and the prompter fails to rescue him with the next line, the actor playing the Prologue exits, cursing the prompter, and is succeeded by a second actor, who manages to add the second line: "Mayn't a Spectator write a Comedy?" before losing his place and being laughed off the stage by the "actor plac'd in the Pit." He too departs, challenging "him that laughs [to] speak the Prologue for me" (8). At this point, the actor speaks his only lines from the pit, promising to "do the Author justice" (8) in the absence of a script. The opening conceit of the prologue is that of the spectator as author, the hearer gaining voice; this is emphasized by being three times repeated and by its finally being delivered by an actor playing a member of the portion of the audience ordinarily confined to the pit. The implication here is that the self-conscious wits who occupy the stage, far from serving as models of superior judgment, ultimately serve as distractions from the play, incapable of providing substantial and informed criticism. The play itself, not the self-conscious display of wit no less absurd in Spark and Spruce than in Landlord and Thrift, becomes the model of judicious criticism, and, significantly, the pit, rather than the "open stage," becomes the site from which the spectator's comedy originates.

The prologue itself is a preemptive defense of the play from the inappropriate assumptions of the audience members in the pit; the actor mocks the poor judgment of those he heard in the Pit say,

> There n'ere was poorer language in a Play;
> And told his Neighbour, he did fear the vile
> Composure would go neer to spoil his stile.
> Another damn'd the Scene with full-mouth'd oaths,
> Because it was not dress'd in better cloaths;
> And rather wish'd each Actor might be mute,
> Then he should loose the sight of a fine suit.
>
> (9)

The prologue cites this as judgment appropriate to "the Antipodes," claiming that "what they do raise / To prejudice, is here the chiefest praise" (9): the play's merits lie in its suiting its language and costume to its pastoral genre rather than its place on the stage. In the same way that the Induction offers a variety of methods of viewing, all of which are ultimately rejected for their usurpation of the place of the play and the privileging of the audience over

the author, the prologue demands that the audience bring a more discriminating taste to the play, one that is shaped by the terms of the play rather than its location. In this context, the academic judgment of Spark and Spruce is more of an infringement of the prerogative of the author than are the plot- and actor-centered views of Thrift and Landlord. The fantasy here is not a fantasy of an audience drawn from the court and the Inns of Court; it is the fantasy of the stage occupied by the play alone, spectators tidily dispersed to the boxes and pit, "hearers only," while the play occupies both their attention and that of the rest of the theater audience.

"COME TO SEE AND TO BE SEEN": WOMEN OF FASHION AT *THE STAPLE OF NEWS*

If the Prologue of *The Careless Shepherdess* can begin the play only after multiple audiences are silenced and removed from sight, his counterpart in Jonson's *The Staple of News* has no such luck. Jonson's four Gossips, like Probee and Damplay, occupy the stage for the duration of the play and dominate the intermeans between acts as well as the Induction. If the Gossips, with their love of costume, desire for news, and interest in topical application, are marginalized as a satire of the audience Jonson dreads, they equally serve to emphasize the centrality of the audience to the playhouse experience and offer a range of more or less desirable viewing habits that are, significantly, all focused on the play and its performance. The true object of Jonson's scorn is the real audience of Blackfriars, who watch each other, not his fictional creations who watch the play.[27]

Six words into his speech, the Prologue to *The Staple of News* is interrupted by "four gentlewomen ladylike attired," the most theatrically experienced of whom, Mirth, demands that he cease his function as "gentleman usher to the play" and become their usher instead and "help us to some stools here," which they will occupy for the duration of the play.[28] Mirth insists on the propriety of the Gossips taking their place in explicitly social terms. In response to the Prologue's apparent surprise that she and her companions want to sit "O' the stage" (7), Mirth identifies herself and her companions as "persons of quality . . . and women of fashion . . . come to see and to be seen" (8-10). The stage direction "ladylike attired" supports Mirth's claim here; as satirical portraits of the Blackfriars audience emphasize, dressing for the theater was a crucial aspect of playgoing, especially for those who purchased the relatively small number of seats particularly designed to be seen as the actors were seen.

The Prologue objects to Mirth's desire for seats on stage in terms that echo Gosson's "To the Gentlewomen Citizens of London," which warns, "you can forbid no man, that vieweth you, to note you and that noteth you to judge you."[29] "What will the noblemen think, or the grave wits here, to see you seated on the bench thus?" (15-17), he asks. Mirth confidently counters this attempt to present the Gossips as mere spectacle—they have come to see, as well as to be seen, and to "arraign both them and their poets" (22). If the Gossips are to be judged, in Mirth's formulation, then so are the male audience members who share the stage, the plays, and the poet himself—a fantasy literalized in Mirth's discussion of her sight of Jonson in the tiring-house "rolling himself up and down like a tun" (63).

While Mirth, Tattle, Expectation, and Censure are allegorical rather than literal figures—Mirth identifies herself as the daughter of Christmas and Spirit of Shrovetide—Mirth insists on their likeness to the other stage sitters, both in class and motive and because "they had mothers, as we had, and those mothers had gossips (if their children were christened) as we are, and such as had a longing to see plays, and sit upon them, as we do, and arraign both them, and their poets" (18-22). The Gossips are fellow humans, and fellow Christians, and thus fellow judges. While the Prologue mocks this judgment, entreating Expectation to "expect no more than you understand" (32), he also recognizes that he is powerless to prevent its influence; Expectation "can expect enough . . . and teach others to do the like" (33-35). He also underestimates their scope of judgment; while he expects "Curiosity, my Lady Censure" (39) to care only for "whose clothes are the best penned (whatever the part may be)" (40-41), she cares too for "which amorous prince makes love in drink, or does overact prodigiously in beaten satin" (45-46). Censure, that is, judges not only the costumes (though these, of both the actors and the audience, are certainly her main concern) but also the actors' ability and technique.

Mirth, Tattle, Censure, and Expectation place themselves on the stage among the gentleman audience members, who apparently share the Gossips' desire "to see, and to be seen" (9). The Induction's explicit focus on the likeness between the Gossips and the parts of the audience the Prologue defines as normative—"the Noblemen . . . or the grave wits here"—is supported by the probable staging of their entrance. While the note in Parr's edition of *Staple* suggests that the Gossips, like Nell and her prentice Rafe in Beaumont's *The Knight of the Burning Pestle* (ca. 1607), enter from the auditorium, Jonson's stage direction, "Enter Prologue. After him Gossip Mirth, Gossip Tattle, Gossip Expectation, and Gossip Censure, four gentlewomen, ladylike attired" (1 s.d.), suggests that the Gossips follow the Prologue onto the stage from the tiring-house (where Mirth has "see[n] the actors dressed" [63]),[30] from which patrons seated on stools would also have entered. While the entrance of Beaumont's Nell from the audience immediately marks her entrance as a violation of the decorum of space, the case with the Gossips is more ambiguous. Nell is, after all, the wife of a citizen; she is emphatically not part of the audience the Blackfriars envisioned for itself in terms of both gender and, significantly, class.[31] Her entrance to the stage, like her husband's, is founded on ignorance of the theatrical and the social conventions of the Blackfriars. But Mirth, if not one of Jonson's judging spectators, is nonetheless exceptionally aware of what to expect in the theater, capable of making distinctions between "the old way" of representing vices with their wooden daggers, and the present practice: "[N]ow they are attired like men and women o' the time" (2 Int. 13-16). If Jonson hopes for a more discriminating audience, he does not expect one, and the stage itself, a male preserve, becomes open to women not as a means of staging incursion, as Nell's entrance in *The Knight of the Burning Pestle* does, but as a means of suggesting the extent to which the gallants on the stage resemble the "ridiculous gossips that tattle between the acts."[32]

In a play obsessed with true and false judgments, the purchase of status, and the right and wrong uses of wit and wealth, the Gossips literally stage the competition over the play's meaning (and the audience's attention) between Jonson and his actors on the one hand and the audience and their preconceptions on the other. At stake is the function of the theater—social or pedagogical. While Jonson deprives the Gossips of the last word in the play, the note "To the Readers," which complains that the play (particularly the Staple scenes) has been so misinterpreted "as if the souls of most of the spectators had lived in the eyes and eares of these ridiculous Gossips that tattle betweene the *Acts*" (5-6), suggests that Jonson, to no one's surprise, was finally unable to control the play's outcome on the stage. The Gossips, Jonson's representations of the theater audience, are the only part of that audience over which he can exercise complete control.

While the Prologue questions Expectation's understanding and mocks what he presumes to be Censure's fascination with the relation between costume and action, he also recognizes Expectation's power to make other audience members see as she does, and Censure seems quite as interested in the actors' readiness (or drunkenness) in their parts as in their costumes. The Gossips are abundantly qualified to make certain types of judgment, particularly Mirth, who despite her shortcomings seems far closer to the audience Jonson might envision than "most of the spectators" (To the Readers, 4-5), who apparently do watch as the Gossips do and "censure by contagion."[33]

The practice Jonson explicitly condemns in his address to the reader is that of application, an interpretive practice that Mirth at least explicitly speaks against. The most theatrically experienced (and up to date) of the spectators, Mirth exposes the variety of viewing practices in play and trains her less astute cohort how to watch as surely as Probee does; she rejects Censure's claim that Pecunia is a satire of the Spanish infanta and provides an interpretive lens that corrects Tattle's understanding of allegorical drama as it was practiced in the previous century. Jonson may disavow the "ridiculous gossips" to the reader, but Mirth actually functions as an internal gauge that raises issues of interpretation for the viewer as Jonson does for the reader. It is through Mirth that the author Jonson is constantly rendered visible as the creator of the *Staple*; and if the Gossips are always fully aware that they are watching a play, then this is not to their discredit.

When the Prologue is finally allowed to resume his speech seventy lines after Mirth interrupts it, he expresses the poet's grave doubts about whether the audience at large will pay appropriate attention to the play when there are so many other distractions—all of them to be found among the audience itself. Wishing that his audience "had come to hear, not see, a play," the poet

> prayes you'll not preiudge his Play for ill,
> Because you marke it not, and sit not still;
> But haue a longing to salute, or talke
> With such a female, and from her to walke
> With your discourse, to what is done, and where,
> How, and by whom, in all the towne; but here.

> (Prologue 7-12)

The sense of the competition between the play and the audience for the attention of the rest of the audience is acute—the anxiety that the playhouse is only a gathering place to exchange gossip about "what is done, and where, / How, and by whom, in all the towne; but here." Despite his apparent contempt for the judgment of the Gossips, the inattentive audience the Prologue here envisions is male, distracted from the play by the prospect of "talk with such a female." The fantasy of an audience that sits quietly in their seats and listens to the actors competes with the fantasy of the constantly shifting, never silent audience incapable of benefiting from the play. Even as the Gossips watch the play in the expectation of "new and fresh" news (Ind. 25), the Prologue voices the anxiety that the audience will be sharing news that falls quite outside the play:

> Alas! what is it to his Scene, to know
> How many Coaches in *Hide-parke* did show
> Last spring, what fare to day at *Medleyes* was,
> If *Dunstan,* or the *Phoenix* best wine has?
> They are things—But yet, the Stage might stand as wel,
> If it did neither heare these things, nor tell.

> (Prologue 13-18)

Although the play mocks the pretensions of Cymbal and his desire to develop a monopoly on news analogous to the monopoly the stationer's company has on printing[34]—the news to "be examined, and then registered, / And so be issued under the seal of the office, / As Staple News, no other to be current" (1.1.34-36)—it also hopes for an audience that will come to the Blackfriars to be entertained by the play rather than each other. Paradoxically, Jonson's introduction of the Gossips among the stage sitters serves to shift the focus from the audience to the play rather than the other way around.

The Gossips drive the act breaks with their constant conversation, and it seems worth considering how audible they are to the rest of the audience during the intermeans. The Blackfriars audience is, as Jonson frequently laments, extremely prone to taking advantage of the intermeans to stand, stretch, chat with their neighbors, and possibly change seats. None of this is going to change if the Gossips keep talking. But Mirth leads the discussion toward judgment, and if this is a judgment that Jonson is not anxious that the rest of his audience share, it is at least a discussion centered on the play, not "how many coaches in *Hide-parke* did show last spring."

Regardless of how the Caroline audience was composed, or how it may now be imagined, the prologues, epilogues, and representations of audiences in the 1630s consistently present not one audience but multiple ones. In some cases, one type of audience member is clearly encouraged over the others—as in the case of Probee's vastly more astute comments than Damplay's—but there is never any pretense that other types of audience do not exist or can consistently be retrained. If Probee embodies a fantasy of the Caroline audience entertained by playwrights of the period, there is equally a recognition that any production will inevitably play to varied responses and that all of these responses might be understood in terms of judgment that might or might not coincide with that of the playwright.

The presentation of versions of the onstage audience in the private theaters only incidentally stages model behaviors to imitate or avoid; more significantly, it suggests the closely intertwined relation between play and audience and the threat that this poses to the play itself. The reversibility of the positions of spectator and spectacle focuses attention on the centrality of the position of the author—one that is marginalized in the assumption that the spectators alone control the meaning of the play and that the theater serves more as a place to display one's clothing and "wit" than a showplace for the play itself. The onstage audience staged in these Inductions ultimately expands the frame of the play to include the entire theater, placing the theater audience on display in the terms of the playwright rather than the reverse.

Notes

1. Ben Jonson, *The Magnetic Lady,* in *Ben Jonson,* ed. C. H. Herford, Percy Simpson, and Evelyn Simpson, vol. 6 (Oxford: Oxford University Press, 1954). Citations refer to act, scene, and line numbers and appear parenthetically in the text.

2. Thelma N. Greenfield, *The Induction in Elizabethan Drama* (Eugene: University of Oregon Books, 1969), 67-95.

3. Michael Neill, "'Wits Most Accomplish'd Senate': The Audience of the Caroline Private Theaters," *Studies in English Literature 1500-1900* 18 (1978):

341, 344. Neill's description of this group for whom "theater-going ceased to be a mere matter of occasional entertainment" (345-46), becoming instead a daily event that allowed one to develop and demonstrate one's connoisseurship of dramatic literature contrasts interestingly with Paul Menzer's discussion of the "everyday audience" in this collection (29-33); while Neill sees this habituation as ultimately granting authority to the audience at the expense of the playwrights, Menzer sees it as demonstrating the institutional success of the playhouses.

4. Neill, "Caroline Private Theaters," 342.

5. Ibid., 344, 346.

6. Ibid., 347.

7. For the case for Brome's authorship of the Induction, see Matthew Steggle, *Richard Brome: Place and Politics on the Caroline Stage* (Manchester, UK: Manchester University Press, 2004), 121.

8. Neill, "Caroline Private Theaters," 346.

9. Ibid., 345.

10. Richard Brome, Praeludium to *The Careles Shepherdess,* by Thomas Goffe (London, 1638), 3. Subsequent page citations appear parenthetically.

11. Neill, "Caroline Private Theaters," 342.

12. Douglas Bruster and Robert Weimann, *Prologues to Shakespeare's Theatre: Performance and Liminality in Early Modern Drama* (New York: Routledge, 2004), 33.

13. Bruster and Weimann, *Shakespeare's Theatre,* 37.

14. Greenfield, *Elizabethan Drama,* 87.

15. Peter Happé usefully compiles Jonson's comments on and staging of his audience in "Jonson's On-Stage Audiences," *Ben Jonson Journal* 10 (2003): 23-41.

16. Herbert Berry, "The Stage and Boxes at Blackfriars," *Studies in Philology* 63 (1966): 174. Andrew Gurr, while interested in the remarkable obtrusiveness of the gallants seated on stage, restricts their number to "as many as ten." *Playgoing in Shakespeare's London* (Cambridge: Cambridge University Press, 2004), 157.

17. Emma Rhatigan's discussion in Chapter 8 of the inability of the performers in the Gray's Inn Revels of 1594 to complete the performance because the number of spectators on stage left no room for the actors is another forceful reminder of this potential competition.

18. Ben Jonson, *The Devil is an Ass,* in *Ben Jonson,* ed. C. H. Herford, Percy Simpson, and Evelyn Simpson, vol. 6 (Oxford: Oxford University Press, 1954),

Induction, 3, 7-8. Subsequent citations appear parenthetically.

19. Reprinted in E. K. Chambers, *The Elizabethan Stage* (Oxford: Clarendon Press, 1923), 4:368-69.

20. Tiffany Stern, "Taking Part: Actors and Audience on the Stage at Blackfriars," in *Inside Shakespeare: Essays on the Blackfriars Stage,* ed. Paul Menzer (Selinsgrove, PA: Susquehanna University Press, 2006), 42.

21. Ben Jonson, *Bartholomew Fair,* ed. E. A. Horsman (Manchester, UK: Manchester University Press, 1960), Induction, 86-97.

22. Alvin Kernan, "Shakespearean Comedy and Its Courtly Audience," in *Comedy from Shakespeare to Sheridan,* ed. A. R. Braunmuller and J. C. Bulman (London: Associated University Presses, 1986), 93.

23. Keir Elam, *The Semiotics of Theatre and Drama* (London: Methuen, 1980), 87.

24. Neill, "Caroline Private Theaters," 342.

25. Gurr, *Playgoing,* 183-90. See also Mark Bayer's "The Curious Case of the Two Audiences: Thomas Dekker's *Match Me in London,*" Chapter 3 in this volume, especially 57-61.

26. Richard Baker, *Theatrum Redivivum* (London, 1662), 138.

27. Jonson's blanket condemnation of the gossips in his note "To the Readers" has led most critics to adopt uniformly unfavorable interpretations of the women and, perhaps more significantly, to discuss them as a single unit rather than as representing diverse habits of viewing. Despite Happé's claim that Jonson "induces us to see them so adversely that we are more or less bound to disagree with everything they say" ("Jonson's On-Stage Audiences," 30). Julie Sanders "challenge[s] a purely antifeminist reading of the *Staple* gossips characterization," noting that "in terms of the knowledge of theater repertoire (and some of its political resonances and applications) these women are astute theatergoers." "'Twill Fit the Players Yet': Women and Theatre in Jonson's Late Plays," in *Ben Jonson and Theatre: Performance, Practice, and Theory,* ed. Richard Cave, Elizabeth Schafer, and Brian Woolland (London: Routledge, 1999), 186.

28. Ben Jonson, *The Staple of News,* ed. Anthony Parr (New York: St. Martin's Press, 1988), Induction 1 s.d., 5-6. Subsequent citations refer to act, scene, and line numbers and appear parenthetically.

29. Stephen Gosson, *The Schoole of Abuse,* ed. Edward Arber (London: Alex Murray and Son, 1869), F2.

30. Parr, *Staple of News,* 64n2.

31. Laurie E. Osborne, "Female Audience and Female Authority in *The Knight of the Burning Pestle,*" *Exemplaria* 3 (Fall 1991): 495-98.

32. Jonson, *The Staple of News.* This comment appears in the address "To the Readers," curiously located between the end of the second intermean and the beginning of act 3 (line 6).

33. *Bartholomew Fair,* Induction, 99.

34. Anthony Parr, introduction to *The Staple of News,* by Ben Jonson (New York: St. Martin's Press, 1988), 22-31.

FURTHER READING

Bibliographies

Haaker, Ann. "Richard Brome." *The Later Jacobean and Caroline Dramatists: A Survey and Bibliography of Recent Studies in English Renaissance Drama.* Ed. Terence P. Logan and Denzell S. Smith. Lincoln: U of Nebraska P, 1978. 172-91. Print.

> Reviews twentieth-century research up to 1978 on Brome's life and works.

Lidman, Mark J. "Richard Brome." *Studies in Jacobean Drama, 1973-1984: An Annotated Bibliography.* New York: Garland, 1986. 249-54. Print.

> Updates Haaker's bibliography (see above), covering English-language studies of Brome through 1984.

Biography

Steggle, Matthew. *Richard Brome: Place and Politics on the Caroline Stage.* Manchester: Manchester UP, 2004. Print.

> Incorporates original archival research in a detailed discussion of Brome's life and works. Steggle discusses all of Brome's surviving plays and concludes with an evaluation of his stagecraft.

Criticism

Bitot, Michel. "'Alteration in a Commonwealth': Disturbing Voices in Caroline Drama." *Cahiers Élisabéthains* 47 (1995): 79-86. Print.

> Explicates the political message of *A Jovial Crew,* which Brome wrote just prior to the start of the English Civil Wars. Bitot contends that Brome's pastoral comedy dramatizes the need for national reconciliation and shows that the theater can play an important role in fostering unity.

Cave, Richard Allen. "The Playwriting Sons of Ben: Nathan Field and Richard Brome." *Jonsonians: Living Traditions.* Ed. Brian Woolland. Aldershot: Ashgate, 2003. 69-91. Print.

> Summarizes the nature and extent of Jonson's influence on Brome and Field, another popular Caroline playwright. Cave argues that Brome's "city comedies," besides containing several specific allusions to the senior playwright's works, are Jonsonian in their overall style and tenor.

Clark, Ira. "Brome's Comedy of Types and Inversions." *Professional Playwrights: Massinger, Ford, Shirley, and Brome.* Lexington: UP of Kentucky, 1992. 155-96. Print.

> Offers one of the first revisionist accounts of the literary merits of Brome's works. Clark argues that greater attention should be paid to the achievements of Caroline dramatists such as Brome, who have often been overlooked in comparison to Elizabethan and Jacobean playwrights like Shakespeare and Jonson.

Crowther, John W. "The Literary History of Richard Brome's *A Joviall Crew.*" *Studies in English Renaissance Literature.* Ed. Waldo F. McNeir. Baton Rouge: Louisiana State UP, 1962. 132-48. Print.

> Analyzes *A Jovial Crew* as a fusion of two historically disparate modes of English comedy: the romantic comedy characteristic of the late Elizabethan age (1558-1603) and the more realistic, satirical comedy of the Jacobean period (1603-25).

Gaby, Rosemary. "Of Vagabonds and Commonwealths: *Beggars' Bush, A Jovial Crew,* and *The Sisters.*" *Studies in English Literature, 1500-1900* 34.2 (1994): 401-24. Print.

> Examines Brome's representation of the figure of the rogue, or vagabond, in his play *A Jovial Crew.* Gaby argues that Brome's placement of the rogue within a rural rather than an urban landscape constitutes a more benign view of social "deviancy."

Hirschfeld, Heather Anne. "Collaborating across Generations: Thomas Heywood, Richard Brome, and the Production of *The Late Lancashire Witches.*" *Journal of Medieval and Early Modern Studies* 30.2 (2000): 339-74. Print.

> Discusses Brome's partnership with Heywood in the composition of *The Late Lancashire Witches,* a melodrama depicting a witchcraft trial. More broadly, Hirschfeld explores the collaborative nature of early modern authorship.

Karim-Cooper, Farah. "'This Alters Not Thy Beauty': Face-Paint, Gender and Race in Richard Brome's *The English Moor.*" *Early Theatre* 10.2 (2007): 140-49. Print.

> Analyzes the use of blackface in *The English Moor* (1637), characterizing it as a work concerned primarily with the "transforming power" of cosmetics and only secondarily with race. Karim-Cooper cites a range of early modern texts that associate makeup with deception and promiscuity.

Lowe, Eleanor. "Offstage and Onstage Drama: New Approaches to Richard Brome." *Early Theatre* 10.2 (2007): 109-16. Print.

Briefly describes the current state of Brome studies and explains the playwright's significance to the history of English theater. Lowe then provides synopses of several contemporary essays on various aspects of Brome's work.

McInnis, David. "Therapeutic Travel in Richard Brome's *The Antipodes*." *Studies in English Literature, 1500-1900* 52.2 (2012): 447-69. Print.

Analyzes *The Antipodes* and its representation of travel in a psychological rather than physical sense. McInnis argues that the play's primary concern is "the pleasures and risks of vicarious travel" and compares this theme to the modern concept of "armchair travel."

Munro, Lucy. "Richard Brome and *The Book of Bulls*: Situating *The New Academy, or The New Exchange*." *Ben Jonson Journal* 13 (2006): 125-38. Print.

Aims to narrow the range of dates during which *The New Academy* (1635) is supposed to have been composed and first performed. The work's allusions to a 1636 joke book called *The Book of Bulls* are instrumental in Munro's determination that the play was completed in early 1636.

Ryner, Bradley D. "Commodity Fetishism in Richard Brome's *A Mad Couple Well Matched* and Its Sources." *Early Modern Literary Studies* 13.3 (2008): 1-26. Print.

Identifies a narrative tradition termed the "'lover's gift regained' story" as the source of Brome's *A Mad Couple Well Match'd* (1639). Ryner examines Brome's reworking of this narrative, demonstrating the lack of distinction between financial and sexual transactions in "a desire-driven consumer culture."

Sanders, Julie. "City and Town." *Caroline Drama: The Plays of Massinger, Ford, Shirley, and Brome*. Plymouth: Northcote, 1999. 43-55. Print.

Assesses Brome alongside several of his contemporaries, illuminating the playwrights' focus on issues of community and hierarchy in the decades preceding the English Civil Wars.

———. "Beggars' Commonwealths and the Pre-Civil War Stage: Suckling's *The Goblins*, Brome's *A Jovial Crew*, and Shirley's *The Sisters*." *Modern Language Review* 97.1 (2002): 1-14. Print.

Reflects on the depiction of beggars in a trio of mid-seventeenth-century English plays, including *A Jovial Crew*. Sanders interprets the play as a product of its time, suggesting that the existence of a "'beggar's commonwealth" was the result of misrule by the "over-demanding absolutist monarch" Charles I.

Stevens, Andrea. "Mastering Masques of Blackness: Jonson's *Masque of Blackness*, the Windsor Text of *The Gypsies Metamorphosed*, and Brome's *The English Moor*." *English Literary Renaissance* 39.2 (2009): 396-426. Print.

Discusses Brome's blackface disguise comedy *The English Moor* as a parodic revision of two of Jonson's court masques, both of which also feature blackface performance.

Zucker, Adam. "Laborless London: Comic Form and the Space of the Town in Caroline Covent Garden." *Journal for Early Modern Cultural Studies* 5.2 (2005): 94-119. Print.

Notes contemporary reactions to the "attempt to craft and conserve London's first elite neighborhood" at Covent Garden in the early seventeenth century. Zucker credits Brome's *Weeding of the Covent Garden* with providing a satirical glimpse of the initial optimism that attended building projects in that area.

Additional information on Brome's life and works is contained in the following sources published by Gale: *British Writers Supplement,* **Vol. 10;** *Dictionary of Literary Biography,* **Vol. 58;** *Literature Criticism from 1400 to 1800,* **Vol. 61; and** *Literature Resource Center.*

David Garrick
1717-1779

English playwright, poet, actor, and theater manager.

INTRODUCTION

Garrick is an icon of eighteenth-century theater. The foremost actor of his age, he was also a prolific playwright and the manager of London's Theatre Royal in Drury Lane for nearly thirty years. In all three capacities, he reformed and professionalized the English stage, negotiating a careful balance between the conventional and the innovative that both catered to and transformed the tastes of the theatergoing public—and brought them to Drury Lane in unprecedented numbers. Garrick is primarily remembered for the influence he asserted on the repertory and techniques of the English stage as an actor and theater manager. In his own day, however, Garrick was also recognized as an accomplished dramatist. He was perhaps best known among his contemporaries as the rescuer of William Shakespeare from oblivion through his highly successful adaptations.

BIOGRAPHICAL INFORMATION

Garrick was born on 19 February 1717 in Hereford, England, where his father, Patrick, an army officer, was temporarily stationed. The family made their permanent home in Lichfield, and it was there that Garrick received his education. He then engaged in a brief course of study under the tutelage of Samuel Johnson at his short-lived school in nearby Edial. After the school's closing in January 1737, Garrick served for a time as a salesman for his uncle's wine business, but he soon turned to acting and playwriting to capitalize on the theatrical connections he made with the help of Johnson.

Garrick's first play, the comic satire *Lethe,* was staged in 1740 by Henry Giffard's company at Drury Lane. By 1741, Giffard had reopened his theater at Goodman's Fields after managing to evade the Licensing Act of 1737, which created a monopoly of two London theaters—Drury Lane and Covent Garden—and instituted strict censorship guidelines. It was at Goodman's Fields on 19 October 1741 that Garrick made his London debut as an actor, playing the title role in Colley Cibber's adaptation of Shakespeare's *Richard III.* Garrick's successful performance rejected the usual declamatory style of bombast, mugging, and rhetorical gesturing. He instead delivered a more natural portrayal that approximated everyday speech and mannerisms and individualized the villain-hero. Elizabeth P. Stein (1938) reported that the regular patrons of Drury Lane and Covent Garden went "horn-mad" for Garrick and caused tremendous traffic congestion in the streets as they deserted their theaters and flocked to Goodman's Fields to witness Garrick in the play.

During the next several years, Garrick enjoyed repeated success in roles such as Chamont in Thomas Otway's *The Orphan* (1680), Abel Drugger in Ben Jonson's *The Alchemist* (1610), and the title roles of his own adaptions of *King Lear* (1756), *Hamlet* (1772), and *Macbeth* (1744). Garrick capitalized on physical traits previously considered impediments, using his slight build, short stature, and thin, melodious voice to reduce the larger-than-life qualities of the heroes he played. He was able to inhabit a wide range of characters—comic as well as tragic—through subtle changes in facial expression and body language that humanized each of the roles he assumed. Garrick rose rapidly to the top of his profession and, by 1747, had earned enough money to buy a half-share in the management of Drury Lane with James Lacy. Over the next twenty-nine years, Garrick revitalized the theater, bringing discipline to rehearsals and performances; adopting new techniques for lighting, costumes, and scene design; and overseeing renovations to the interior that changed the seating arrangements to accommodate the growing crowds. He appeared onstage more than two thousand times and took on ninety-six different roles. At the same time, Garrick selected and produced the entire repertory and wrote nearly fifty plays of his own; he also created more than one hundred works of poetry, mostly in the form of prologues and epilogues to the evening's entertainment.

Garrick used his position of influence to indulge his obsession with Shakespeare, which was most elaborately manifested in his plans for a "Shakespeare Jubilee" to be held at the playwright's birthplace, Stratford-upon-Avon, in September 1769. The three-day festival was to include feasts, balls, poetry readings, fireworks, and performances of several of the plays. The first day went well, but torrential rains spoiled the rest of the festivities, which ended up being a financial disaster for Drury Lane and substantial fodder for Garrick's enemies in the theater. Singular in his genius for crafting his own public image, Garrick wrote a play, *The Jubilee* (1769), that incorporated the canceled pageant of Shakespeare characters and answered critics of "Garrick's Folly" with witty repartee.

Garrick made his last stage appearance on 10 June 1776 and officially retired as manager of Drury Lane the following December, selling off his shares to playwright Richard

Brinsley Sheridan for the sum of thirty-five thousand pounds. Garrick died on 20 January 1779; he was survived by his wife of thirty years, the former dancer Eva Maria Violetti. His funeral was an impressive affair staged by Sheridan and attended by local and visiting nobility, leading actors, and many members of The Club, Garrick's elite literary and intellectual circle. Crowds lined the streets to watch the procession move from Garrick's home on Adelphi Terrace to Westminster Abbey, where he was interred in Poets' Corner at the foot of the monument to Shakespeare.

MAJOR DRAMATIC WORKS

Garrick composed forty-nine dramatic works: twenty-two original plays and twenty-seven adaptations. Twelve of his adaptations are versions of Shakespeare, and the rest are mainly updates of popular Restoration and Jacobean fare. All but three of his original plays are short works intended to accompany the main drama, and most of these function as afterpieces; among them are *Lethe, Miss in Her Teens* (1747), *Lilliput* (1756), *The Male Coquette* (1757), *The Jubilee,* and *Bon Ton* (1775). Licensing and financial considerations of the time dictated that a full-length drama had to belong to the standard repertoire or be an alteration to an old play. Innovation was reserved for the smaller elements of the bill, such as preludes, interludes, and afterpieces. Garrick made a specialty of social satire in his short works, but he also displayed a talent for farce, burlesque, pantomime, comic opera, and musical spectacle. Some of Garrick's afterpieces were popular enough to be staged over several consecutive seasons; the most notable of these is the rehearsal play *A Peep behind the Curtain* (1767), which ran for eight years without a break. In their introduction to their seven-volume *Plays of David Garrick* (1980), Harry William Pedicord and Frederick Louis Bergmann noted, "As a manager Garrick had to fill the latter part of each evening, and the demand for variety far outstripped the material available. Thus management dictated the form and increasing artistry Garrick demonstrates in the genre. . . . Garrick turned to the afterpiece almost through necessity and produced more successful ones than any of his contemporaries."

Afterpieces have long since disappeared from the stage, and Garrick's original plays are mostly forgotten by all but scholars of the theater. The exception is the five-act comedy *The Clandestine Marriage* (1766), jointly written by Garrick and George Colman the Elder and staged for ten consecutive seasons at Drury Lane. The story concerns romantic intrigues and misunderstandings between two households, one headed by the wealthy merchant Mr. Sterling and the other by Lord Ogleby, the descendant of an ancient family fallen on hard times. Mr. Sterling's niece Elizabeth is engaged to Ogleby's nephew Sir John Melvil, but Melvil and Ogleby are both in love with Fanny, Elizabeth's sister, who is secretly married to Mr. Lovewell, an impoverished cousin. Much of the comedy turns on Mr. Sterling's gauche pretensions to gentility and Fanny and Lovewell's efforts to fend off her admirers. *The Clandestine Marriage* formed part of the stock theatrical repertoire for decades. It was revived to great acclaim in a 1995 London production featuring Nigel Hawthorne, who went on to star in the 1999 BBC film version.

Garrick's adaptations of Shakespeare's plays formed part of the grand effort in the eighteenth century to establish Shakespeare as the supreme bard of the nation, thus rescuing him from the hands of his earlier corrupters. By modern standards, Garrick modified Shakespeare intensively. His usual method was to add and delete as necessary in order to highlight the aspects of the stories that would most appeal to a public that demanded the sentimental and affective in tragedy as well as comedy. Among Garrick's most famous changes are his removal of the entire gravedigger scene from *Hamlet* and his addition to the death scene of his *Romeo and Juliet* (1748) of a poignant, seventy-five-line dialog between the two lovers.

CRITICAL RECEPTION

Garrick dominated the stage of his day. Considered second only to Sheridan and Oliver Goldsmith as a dramatist, Garrick also enjoyed unrivaled success as an actor. He parlayed his international celebrity as the high priest of Shakespeare into flattering publicity for Drury Lane, which he transformed into one of the most lucrative and well-attended theaters in all of Europe. His contemporary celebrity was powerfully popularized in a multitude of theatrical portraits painted by such luminaries as Sir Joshua Reynolds, Thomas Gainsborough, and William Hogarth. Still, Garrick's position as manager of Drury Lane placed him at the center of theatrical debates, and he was a frequent target of satiric attacks by disgruntled actors and playwrights whose work he had rejected. Often accused of sacrificing his artistic integrity for the sake of profit and the adulation of the upper classes, Garrick was pilloried, as John Pruitt (2008) noted, "as an emblem of the unethical entrepreneur, shifting from object on stage to subject of topical satires blatantly epitomizing and embodying gross economic inequality and social jealousies dissociated from bourgeois merit, diligence, and industry." Chief among Garrick's opponents was Theophilus Cibber (1759), son of former Drury Lane manager Colley Cibber, who turned his resentment at Garrick's meteoric rise into a stinging assault on his acting and management style.

Vanessa Cunningham (2008; see Further Reading) observed, "In the centuries since Garrick's death, two accounts, over-simple but persistent, of his relationship with Shakespeare have predominated. The first hails Garrick as the great restorer to the stage of plays not seen in their original forms since Shakespeare's day; the second, paradoxically, condemns him for choosing to stage travesties when he could have presented what Shakespeare actually wrote." The first view was fostered by Garrick biographer and fellow Drury Lane member Thomas Davies (1780; see Further Reading), who recalled that Garrick "was determined to restore [Shakespeare] to his genuine splendour and native simplicity, unencumbered with the unnatural additions, and gaudy trappings, thrown upon him by some writers who lived in the reign of Charles the Second." Davies exempted from this praise Garrick's alterations to *Hamlet,* which he considered unnecessarily cutthroat. George Winchester Stone, Jr., (1934) summed up the general opinion when he quoted James Boaden, who wrote in his preface to *The Private Correspondence of David Garrick,* an 1831-32 collection of Garrick's letters, "If there be any one act of his management which we should wish to blot out from these pages it is his *rash violation of the whole scheme of Shakspeare's Hamlet.*" By the early nineteenth century, when the type of alteration that involved rewriting Shakespeare went out of fashion, so too did Garrick. The efforts of Stone, beginning with his discovery of Garrick's edited copy of *Hamlet* in the 1930s, went a long way toward creating a textual basis for the study of Garrick's relationship to Shakespeare and helped soften his reputation as a mutilator of the plays. Although there is some consensus that Garrick sought to retain as much of the original language as possible while still producing scripts that would be commercially viable, he has been only a marginal figure in modern Shakespearean textual studies. He has been more often admired for introducing a generation of theatergoers to the plays in a popular format. For better or worse, Garrick has also been credited with launching the "Shakespeare industry" with his jubilee, which received extensive critical commentary from Dane Farnsworth Smith and M. L. Lawhon (1979), among others.

Garrick's modern reputation principally rests on his revolutionary achievements as an acting phenomenon and theater manager. Yet several scholars have advocated for greater recognition of his talents as a dramatist. Pedicord and Bergmann made a persuasive appeal: "We tend to dismiss his plays because we do not really know them and because they represent only what appears to be a minor facet of his genius when compared to his acting and managerial careers. But the fact remains that David Garrick's place in the drama of his century is paramount because he was a solid link between his own age and that of the greater personages of the past."

Janet Mullane

PRINCIPAL WORKS

Plays

Lethe; or, Æsop in the Shades. Theatre Royal in Drury Lane, London. 15 Apr. 1740. London: Cooke, 1745.

The Lying Valet. New Theatre, Goodman's Fields, London. 30 Nov. 1741. London: Vaillant, 1742.

Macbeth. Adapt. from *Macbeth,* by William Shakespeare. Theatre Royal in Drury Lane, London. 7 Jan. 1744. London: Bell, 1774.

The Provok'd Wife. Adapt. from *The Provok'd Wife,* by John Vanbrugh. Theatre Royal in Drury Lane, London. 16 Nov. 1744. London: Brindley, 1761.

Miss in Her Teens; or, The Medley of Lovers. Theatre Royal in Covent Garden, London. 17 Jan. 1747. London: Tonson and Draper, 1747.

Romeo and Juliet. Adapt. from *Romeo and Juliet,* by Shakespeare. Theatre Royal in Drury Lane, London. 29 Nov. 1748. London: Tonson and Draper, 1750.

Every Man in His Humour. Adapt. from *Every Man in His Humour,* by Ben Jonson. Theatre Royal in Drury Lane, London. 29 Nov. 1751. London: Tonson and Draper, 1752.

Catharine and Petruchio. Adapt. from *The Taming of the Shrew,* by Shakespeare. Theatre Royal in Drury Lane, London. 18 Mar. 1754. London: Tonson and Draper, 1756.

The Chances. Adapt. from *The Chances,* by John Fletcher. Theatre Royal in Drury Lane, London. 7 Nov. 1754. London: Becket, 1773.

The Fairies. Adapt. from *A Midsummer Night's Dream,* by Shakespeare. Theatre Royal in Drury Lane, London. 3 Feb. 1755. London: Tonson and Draper, 1755. (Libretto)

Florizel and Perdita. Adapt. from *The Winter's Tale,* by Shakespeare. Theatre Royal in Drury Lane, London. 21 Jan. 1756. London: Tonson, 1758.

The Tempest, an Opera. Adapt. from *The Tempest,* by Shakespeare. Theatre Royal in Drury Lane, London. 11 Feb. 1756. London: Tonson, 1756.

King Lear. Adapt. from *King Lear,* by Shakespeare. Theatre Royal in Drury Lane, London. 28 Oct. 1756. London: Bell and Etherington, 1773. Rev. ed. *King Lear, a Tragedy: Altered from Shakespeare by David Garrick, Esq. Marked from the Variations in the Manager's Book; at the Theatre Royal in Drury Lane.* London: Bathurst et al., 1786.

Lilliput. Theatre Royal in Drury Lane, London. 3 Dec. 1756. London: Vaillant, 1757.

The Male Coquette; or, Seventeen Hundred Fifty-Seven. Theatre Royal in Drury Lane, London. 24 Mar. 1757. Pub. as *The Male-Coquette; or, Seventeen Hundred Fifty-Seven.* London: Vaillant, 1757.

Isabella; or, The Fatal Marriage. Adapt. from *The Fatal Marriage,* by Thomas Southerne. Theatre Royal in Drury Lane, London. 2 Dec. 1757. London: Tonson, 1757.

The Gamesters. Adapt. from *The Gamester,* by James Shirley. Theatre Royal in Drury Lane, London. 22 Dec. 1757. London: Tonson, 1758.

The Guardian. Theatre Royal in Drury Lane, London. 3 Feb. 1759. London: Newberry, 1759.

Harlequin's Invasion; or, A Christmas Gambol. Theatre Royal in Drury Lane, London. 31 Dec. 1759.

The Enchanter; or, Love and Magic. Theatre Royal in Drury Lane, London. 13 Dec. 1760. London: Tonson, 1760. (Libretto)

Cymbeline. Adapt. from *Cymbeline,* by Shakespeare. Theatre Royal in Drury Lane, London. 28 Nov. 1761. London: Tonson, 1762.

The Farmer's Return from London. Theatre Royal in Drury Lane, London. 20 Mar. 1762. London: Tonson, 1762.

A Midsummer Night's Dream. Written by Shakespeare: With Alterations and Additions, and Several New Songs. As It Is Performed at the Theatre Royal in Drury Lane. Theatre Royal, Drury Lane, London. 1763. London: Tonson, 1763.

The Clandestine Marriage. With George Colman the Elder. Theatre Royal in Drury Lane, London. 20 Feb. 1766. London: Becket and De Hondt, 1766.

The Country Girl. Adapt. from *The Country Wife,* by William Wycherley. Theatre Royal in Drury Lane, London. 25 Oct. 1766. London: Becket and De Hondt, 1767.

Neck or Nothing. Theatre Royal in Drury Lane, London. 18 Nov. 1766. London: Becket, 1766.

Cymon. Theatre Royal in Drury Lane, London. 2 Jan. 1767. London: Becket and De Hondt, 1767.

Linco's Travels. Theatre Royal in Drury Lane, London. 6 Apr. 1767.

A Peep behind the Curtain; or, The New Rehearsal. Theatre Royal in Drury Lane, London. 23 Oct. 1767. London: Becket and De Hondt, 1769.

The Jubilee. Theatre Royal in Drury Lane, London. 14 Oct. 1769. New York: Rudge, 1926.

Songs, Choruses &c. Which Are Introduced in the New Entertainment of the Jubilee. Theatre Royal in Drury Lane, London. 1769. London: Becket and De Hondt, 1769.

The Institution of the Garter; or, Arthur's Roundtable Restored. Theatre Royal in Drury Lane, London. 28 Oct. 1771.

The Irish Widow. Theatre Royal in Drury Lane, London. 23 Oct. 1772. London: Becket, 1772.

Hamlet, Prince of Denmark: A Tragedy. As It Is Now Acted at the Theatre Royal in Drury Lane, and Covent-Garden. Theatre Royal in Drury Lane, London. 18 Dec. 1772. Carbondale: Southern Illinois UP, 1980.

A Christmas Tale. Theatre Royal in Drury Lane, London. 27 Dec. 1773. London: Becket, 1774.

The Meeting of the Company. Theatre Royal in Drury Lane, London. 17 Sept. 1774.

Bon Ton; or, High Life above Stairs. Theatre Royal in Drury Lane, London. 18 Mar. 1775. London: Becket, 1775.

The Theatrical Candidates. Theatre Royal in Drury Lane, London. 23 Sept. 1775.

May Day; or, The Little Gipsy. Music by Thomas Arne. Theatre Royal in Drury Lane, London. 28 Oct. 1775. London: Becket, 1775. (Libretto)

Zara. Adapt. from *Zara,* by Aaron Hill, and *Zaïre,* by Voltaire. Theatre Royal in Drury Lane, London. 23 Jan. 1766. London: Bell, 1776.

A Bundle of Prologues. Theatre Royal in Drury Lane, London. 28 Apr. 1777.

The Dramatic Works of David Garrick, Esq. 3 vols. London: Millar, 1798.

Three Plays by David Garrick. Ed. Elizabeth P. Stein. New York: Rudge, 1926.

The Plays of David Garrick. Ed. Harry William Pedicord and Frederick Louis Bergmann. 7 vols. Carbondale: Southern Illinois UP, 1980.

The Plays of David Garrick. Ed. Gerald M. Berkowitz. 4 vols. New York: Garland, 1981.

Other Major Works

Mr. Garrick's Answer to Mr. Macklin's Case. London, 1743. (Nonfiction)

An Essay on Acting, in Which Will Be Consider'd the Mimical Behavior of a Certain Fashionable Faulty Actor, and the Laudableness of Such Unmannerly as Well as Inhumane Proceedings. To Which Will Be Added a Short Criticism on His Acting Macbeth. London: Bickerton, 1744. (Essay)

An Ode on the Death of Mr. Pelham. London, 1754. (Poetry)

The Fribbleriad. London: Coots, 1761. (Poetry)

The Sick Monkey: A Fable. London: Fletcher, 1765. (Fable)

An Ode upon Dedicating a Building, and Erecting a Statue, to Shakespeare, at Stratford upon Avon. By D. G. London: Becket and De Hondt, 1769. (Poetry)

The Poetical Works of David Garrick, Esq. Ed. George Kearsley. 2 vols. London: Kearsley, 1785. (Poetry)

The Private Correspondence of David Garrick, with the Most Celebrated Persons of His Time. Ed. James Boaden. 2 vols. London: Colburn and Bentley, 1831-32. (Letters)

The Diary of David Garrick, Being a Record of His Memorable Trip to Paris in 1751, Now First Printed from the Original Ms. Ed. Ryliss Clair Alexander. New York: Oxford UP, 1928. (Diary)

The Journal of David Garrick, Describing His Visit to France and Italy in 1763, Now First Printed from the Original Manuscript in the Folger Shakespeare Library. Ed. George Winchester Stone, Jr. New York: MLA, 1939. (Diary)

The Letters of David Garrick. Ed. David M. Little, George M. Kahrl, and Phoebe de K. Wilson. 3 vols. Cambridge: Belknap P of Harvard UP, 1963. (Letters)

CRITICISM

R. B. (letter date 1749)

SOURCE: R. B. "Remarks on the New Entertainment, Called *Lethe.* In a Letter to the Author, from a Gentleman of the *Temple.*" *British Magazine* 4 (1749): 22-8. Print.

[*In the following letter, the writer, identified as R. B., offers a mostly negative account of a performance of* Lethe. *The writer delights in the fact that Garrick's shills in the audience, described by the writer as "friends of the house," betrayed him early in the performance. The writer goes on to snidely observe that Garrick was not short on self-esteem, since he took it upon himself to assume the jobs of manager, author, and actor of three roles.*]

Temple, Jan 18.

SIR,

By my dating my letter from this place, and the subject of it being remarks on a dramatick performance, you will naturally expect a great deal of severity in my censures: But tho' I am proud to live among the wits and criticks of this age, I would fain be of an honest service to the world in setting them right, as to their general opinion of our particular love of the ill-natured part of the criticks character; and shew them that is possible for a templer to be an impartial observer.

I went with two gentlemen, Sir, to the first performance of this piece, both as impartial as myself; all of us wishing very well to the house, and to the diversions of the town, and much more desiring the satisfaction of an agreeable entertainment, than the noise of a riot.

We were very sensible that we were to see a Farce which had been three times damn'd already, that was originally written by a French author, and was very bad in the original, and that had been already mended for the worse, (as the wits phrase it,) in three successive translations. These were considerations that might have prejudiced us against the thing; but as we considered it now in a new light, the denison of the sovereign lady of the theatre, and brought on by a manager, whom even his worst enemies will allow to be at least sufficiently careful of his own interest, and not a little solicitous about his reputation; and who had not only brought it on as his own work, but was to appear in it as an actor, in three different characters; we were willing to believe that he must have either some remains of judgment, or some friends; and were very sensible that if he had the smallest grain of the former, or but one single sample of the latter, with a degree of more sense than an ideot, he would never in so pompous a manner usher in what was not worthy the acceptance of the town.

There is an old fashion'd maxim in Cato, '*tis not in mortals to command success. But we'll do more, Sempranius we'll deserve it.* But this is out of fashion now, and our hero has found a way to modernize it, as he has done Dancour by contradicting it: He has prudently established a counter maxim in his own breast, and seem to have parody'd the old one in this manner, *It is not in us to deserve success; but we'll do more by far, we will command it.* This he had excellently put in practice in the present affair; for tho' we were soon sensible by the course of the farce, that it never would be in his power to deserve success, we were informed before it began that he had found the means of certainly commanding it.

In the upper box where we were posted, there were behind us three people, who by their figure did not seem to have paid five shillings apiece for their places; and one of whom I soon recollected to be a servant to my very good friend Mr. Brittle, the Glass-man in the Strand: Upon expostulating with him, as to the manner in which he and I had got into the same place; the fellow ingenuously confessed to me, that the manager had once bought a drinking glass of his matter, that was to be broke in the Beggar's Opera; that he had sent him word he should be glass merchant to the theatre for the future, with large promises of making it a considerable advantage to him; and that he would let three of his servants see the Play and the new Farce that night for nothing: The fellow added, that he had been about an hour before introduced to the gentleman, who had given him money for three full-pots of beer, for himself and his friends, and had ordered them to be placed in the back seat of that box, where they might make a great noise, and be seen by no body; and that all they had to do was to clap their hands together as hard as they could every time any body went out; and every time any one spoke louder than ordinary on the stage.

The simple fellow's confession let us a little into the artifices to which the conductors of publick diversions are reduced, when they act upon wrong principles. It was natural to imagine that an uncontroulable applause was secured from hence; and that the audience could have no share in the determining the fate of the piece: but this was nothing to what we soon after heard from the next box; three other persons had been admitted there on the same footing with our back friends, and soon informed us and the rest of the neighbouring company of their office and employment. These we found were a set of understrappers of the play house, the friends and acquaintance of some of the lower actors, people who dangle after them at rehearsals, and live in hopes of some time arriving to the honour of acting a bailiff, or a highwayman themselves: These had seen the farce rehearsed, knew all the strokes that the author admired in it, and had their cues of entrances, exits, and words by heart, at which they were to give their applause.

Mischief when too high charg'd, often returns upon the heads of the people who contrive it; and so it happened here; for these people, elevated beyond their usual bounds, by hot-pot and all powerful gin, grew noisy before their time, betrayed their own secrets, and their friends, and calling to their brother heroes in other parts of the house, explained to us that there was not a corner where some of these people were not planted, to answer one anothers clapping; and finally confessed that they saw sixty *orders* by one hand, which carrying in one hundred and twenty people, would be a match alone for the templars, or the devil was in it.

With all this provocation we yet resolved to be silent, and hear the whole fairly out. The Play concluded, the audience grew impatient, and the Farce began: On the drawing up of the curtain we saw two figures enter, the one something like the punch in F—'s puppet shew, but too clumsy; and the other we supposed by his dress and appearance, to be some brewers servant, who in a quarrel with some body, had picked up a baker's peel by way of weapon; but we were soon misinformed of this error by these good natured personages, telling us who they were; and found that the one was Charon, and the other the Ghost of Æsop. You will not be severe upon us for confessing, Sir, that we did not know these people at sight, when you consider that tho' people have seen the Farce a fortnight, they do not know

the Ghost yet, but are amazed at our friend in the Haymarket's advertising such a lot in his auction, and cannot recollect that there is any Ghost in Lethe.

I don't know whether the author will attribute this to the stupidity of himself or his audience; but I am sure it will serve very well for our justification, since there is no doubt but he was much more like the Ghost of Æsop, than the other to Charon.

These remarkable persons open the Farce, by telling us that Pluto had granted a boon to Proserpine in favour to mortals; which was so contrived, that not one of them should ever be the better for it; and that they were coming to drink the waters of oblivion, for things for which Æsop would never give them. Mercury after this sings Æsop a song, which is the summons to the mortals on the other side the Styx; and as soon as that is over, away they come as fast as if they had heard it.

Every man now applies himself to Æsop, and confesses his follies and vices; for not one of which Æsop will give them the waters. The ladies are full as free in their confessions, and to full as much purpose; and when Æsop has sent them together into a shady grove, and stood pimp for them a sufficient time, he calls them all out and sends them back about their business.

Thus ends the Farce! all we are able to make out by the confessions of the several parties, is, that a poet is a beggar, a Frenchman a cheat, an Englishman who has travell'd an ass, a drunkard a brute, and a fine lady a whore: This new doctrine is delivered to us in the very words in which we have read it in fifty different books before, from the immortal Addison to Joseph Andrews; and the true moral of the Farce seems to be that all people are fools who want to get rid of their misfortunes.

During the acting of the Farce the audience seemed much dissatisfied, but they would have been thoroughly kept under by the clapping and vociferations of the *friends of the house,* had not our neighbours in the next box turned tail upon their employer: These were of the number of the choice spirits of the age, and had much more joy in an uproar than in the best tragedy of Shakespear. Their drink had thoroughly banished reason, and given a double violence to their passions by that time the Farce began; and having been let into the defects of the piece, by the same means that were used to let them into its beauties; and having heard it degraded, even below what it deserved, by their friends of the company, who were not thought worthy to act in it, they had both means and inclination sufficient for the overthrow of a much better piece. These they exerted to the utmost, none were so noisy, none so inexorable; as they knew the bad characters before hand, they put people in mind of their resentment, by issuing them before they spoke; and then bellowing out *off! off! off!* at the end of every line they uttered.

These people gave the signals of damnation, and the audience found they were in the secret, and knew the merits of the cause before-hand, and consequently at length unanimously joined with them. The Farce was sufficiently condemned before a third part of it was over on all parts, except by some staunch friends in the pit, who opposed loud applauses to all the vociferations, by which the rest doom'd it; and claped so long, and claped so loud, that they would certainly have saved it to perfection, had not a subtle friend of ours found out that these peoples heads were as hard as their hands, and driven them all off to the other party by a new stratagem; this was leading on a clap in the wrong place.

This facetious gentleman, who had hissed in the beginning of the entertainment, now never heard a bad thing but he claped heartily; this found his hands very sufficient employment, and the friendly party finding him as they thought, a convert to the merit of the performance, never failed to second him with a doubly loud volley.

This new species of raillery was highly entertaining to the audience, and would have very thoroughly compleated the damning as it is called of any piece the author of which had but the common chance to stand: but the author and manager being here one person, there is no room to doubt of their sticking by one another; and the result of such a combination was, that the manager determined to stand by the author to the utmost, and to compel the town to like the Farce whether they would or no, till he had the advantages of benefits, &c. &c. &c, from it.

The piece has certainly some pleasing things in it; there is in the Frenchman's part a very home satire upon that great vice of the English, their encouragement of foreigners, out it had been better had it been either more new, more just, or more delicate; the sot's meeting his wife is an unexpected and pleasing incident, but looses something of its merit, when we remember the Sir John Brute of Vanbrugh, who stumbles upon his lady in the Vaux hall scene not wholly unlike this. The characters of the fine ladies seem to want that delicacy also of which the whole piece is so very barren; and the rest of the characters are so easily traced up to their originals in the common plays of the last age, and appear such bad copies on the comparison, that it is no wonder all the artifice and address used by the author-manager could not bring about an approbation of it.

The audience are certainly highly to be commended, not to let this sort of common place raillery pass upon them for new, even tho' displayed with more than common address before them: With all their disapprobation, I cannot but think however, that it will be prudent to suffer this piece to be occasionally played hereafter, as the rest of our Farces are so few in number, and in general so bad, that we are tired with the quick repetition of them; and as I think we never saw so many of the superior personages of the theatre exhibited in a Farce before. This seems a very good hint to the town towards an amendment of this latter part of their theatrical diversions, and it will not appear unreasonable to the generality of the audience, that the worse the Farce is, the better actors should be engaged in it. On this plan the Devil to Pay may stand about as it does, but the Mock Doctor should have one more good actor in it. The Intriguing Chamber Maid should not escape without two additional hands of consequence; and Miss in her Teens should not be endured without Mr. Garrick, Mr. Barry, Mrs. Pritchard, and Mrs. Cibber.

If we are obliged to Mr. G— for shewing us so many of his good actors in this Farce, how much more so are we for the three-fold manner of his bringing his self before us. This Gentleman having so great an opinion of his own writing, and so mean a one of his players performing, that he chose to represent three characters in it himself. The length of face this hero assumed, on being hissed in the first portion of his triple capacity, might have been measured by a scale of inches, but the conflict of passions within, which were so much the more violent, by how much it was the more impossible to give them vent, would have required a masterly hand in painting to have expressed them. Pride and shame, insolence and dejection, anger and fear, never appeared so strangely blended in any countenance before, nor were passions ever so well *marked* in playing as here, by the player reduced to real life. The town will not be displeased at this little mortification to this great man; as punishments have always good effects on the mind, and a little humility will not render his character at all less amiable.

Far be it from any man of common understanding, to censure a person in one capacity for his defects in another, or to think him the worse actor for being a very bad author; on the contrary, we ought to quarrel with the world for shewing such a dearth of wit in general; that printers are forced to write their own books, and players act their own farces; and while tho' we shake our heads at Clarissa, we make allowances for the thickness of that of the unnatural parent, let us not refuse a like acknowledgment by way of palliation for the stupidities of Lethe; and, while the publick advertisements tell us of a surgeon's apprentice, not only translating, but as he modestly expresses it, *improving* the great Duverney on the ear; and pompously introduce to us the Christian Magazine, written by a physician, and corrected by the printer; let it not appear a singular crime in such an age of absurdities, that an English actor should translate the farce of a celebrated French author, and endeavour to improve it by alterations.

It would be unjust to the actor, whatever we may think of the author, not to allow that he played the Frenchman better than any man perhaps ever played it on an English theatre: His censure of his real self in the assumed character of the poet, when he makes that ragged writer complain of him for endeavouring to bring down the writings of other authors to his own, and his impatience of merit in another, where he supposes he has some himself; tho' but a borrowed thought, is not without its merit: An old saying well applied, is allowed by the criticks to be as good as a new one; and unless the original author of this, spoke it prophetically of the present adopter of it, it certainly never was so well applied before.

If there was some merit in this heroic personages thus taking shame upon himself on his own confession; there was yet more in an occasional witticism thrown in during the acting. When the shade of Æsop advises the poet to give Lethe in large draughts to his audience, the present audience gave the usual signal of their disapprobation in a loud hiss; and the poet, with a conscious blush replied, *you see Sir, Lethe will not go down with the audience.* Many of the people present went away on this, much pleased with the author's modesty and submission; but what must be their resentment to see the name of it the next day in the bills? and to find that tho' the author gave it up, the manager would thrust it down their throats, and compel them to swallow it whether they liked it or no, nay, tho' he knew they did not like it,

I am, Sir, yours, &c.

R. B.

Anonymous (essay date 1749)

SOURCE: Anonymous. Lethe *Rehears'd; or, A Critical Discussion of the Beauties and Blemishes of That Performance.* London: Roberts, 1749. 1-52. Print.

[*In the following essay, the author creates an imaginary conversation among five followers of the theater. The members of the group debate whether Garrick wrote character or caricature and question the sense and propriety of using dramatic satire to construct a moral. The criticisms of Mr. Snipsnap, one of the participants, motivate the others to praise Garrick's acting abilities and the educational value of his plays.*]

INTERLOCUTORS

MEN

SIR FRANCIS FRIENDLY, *a very worthy, sensible, and learned Gentleman.*
DR. HEARTFREE, *a very candid and judicious Person, who has a great Opinion of Mr. Garrick.*
MR. SNIPSNAP, *a vociferous modern Critick.*

WOMEN

LADY FRIENDLY, *a good-natur'd Woman, with a very sound Understanding.*
MELISSA, *her Niece, inclined to be a very fine Lady.*

[*A Back Parlour in Russel-street, Covent-Garden*:
SIR FRANCIS FRIENDLY, DR. HEARTFREE, *AND* MR. SNIPSNAP]

SIR FRANCIS FRIENDLY:

Gentlemen, I am very glad to see you.—You were at the Play last Night.—I carried my Wife and my Niece thither.—We are strangely divided in our Opinions, about the new Entertainment.—You'll oblige me much, by giving me yours.

DR. HEARTFREE:

Why really, Sir *Francis,* I shall give you mine very freely. I think, if honest *David* could, as a Poet, have contrived to get a large Quantity of the Waters o *Lethe* behind the Scenes, he had best have brought it out; and as a Manager, prevailed upon the *Audience* to have drank each a Cup of it to prevent future Prejudices.—There was a Time when I admired him. But, with me, I must confess, the *Poet* has done the Business both of the *Player* and of the *Patentee.*

SIR FRAN. FRIENDLY:

Your Sentiments, *Doctor,* upon the Point in Question.

DR. HEARTFREE:

Just the Reverse of my Friend here. I always liked the Man, because I thought he had Merit, and now I am so much pleased with him as an *Author,* that I am sure he will for the future, give me double Pleasure as an *Actor.* His Piece seems to be a Copy of one of *Lucian's* Dialogues; and as from the Action it moves us more, methinks it ought not to charm us less. Instruction, is the Business of the Stage, and therefore in minding that he minds his own Business, and at the same Time puts us on minding ours.

MR. SNIPSNAP:

Ha! ha! ha! The first Time that ever I knew Business and the Play-House brought together; why now I thought we went there to forget Business, and to Church to hear Sermons? Then, for *Lucian,* I'll be hanged if he knows any more of him than I do. Walsh's *Hospital for Fools,* and Sir John Vanbrugh's *Æsop,* furnished the Materials, Dodsley's *Toy-Shop* was the Original, and this but a Copy. For my Part, I looked upon a *Dramatick Satire,* to be in Effect a *Libel* upon the *Stage*—The Inspector would have interposed, if the Author's Abuse had not fallen upon the *Nation.*

SIR F. FRIENDLY:

Indeed, Mr. *Snipsnap,* you are too hard upon poor *David.* Let him have come by it how he would, the Fable appears to me very easy and natural. I dare say, there is not a fine Gentleman in the Kingdom, who at the Age of Forty, would not drink a Gallon of the Waters of *Lethe* to forget, rather than a Bottle of *Champagne* to the Remembrance of his past Life; the Thought therefore was natural enough.

MR. SNIPSNAP:

Not in Respect to the Ladies sure, for I never knew an old Woman in my Life, that did not delight in thinking of, and repeating the Follies of her Youth. The Widow *Evergreen,* over the Way, would not be deprived of the Retrospect of her Amours, upon any Consideration under Heaven, but that of repeating them.—Nor am I quite certain, Sir

Francis, that you are perfectly right, as to the Men; there is our old Acquaintance *George Goatish* is never weary of talking of what he has been past acting these thirty Years.

Dr. HEARTFREE:

Then he has the more need of the Waters, Mr. *Snipsnap*; and as for Mrs. *Evergreen,* if we had but a Jar of them, I would prevail upon Sir *Francis,* to do what he never did, lay his Commands upon his Lady to engage her to drink Tea here this Afternoon.

SIR F. FRIENDLY:

Pray, Gentlemen, come a little to Particulars; what think you of *the Poet*?

MR. SNIPSNAP:

Why, his is a *damned* Character upon the very Face of it.

DR. HEARTFREE:

True, Mr. *Snipsnap*; but it is not a *dead* Character for all that.—There are some *Criticks* too now living, that it would prove a great Comfort to the World, if a Bottle of this Water could be as easily provided for them as a Bottle of *Pyrmont.*—It is but a *Fable,* and that's the Misfortune.—What an Advantage would it be to themselves, or at least to Society, if some troublesome People could be but taught *to forget!*

MR. SNIPSNAP:

Lord, Sir! you are in love with this Fellow to Madness. Now to me his *Poet* is his *own* Character, and I think every new Farce he writes, is a Proof that the last is not the *worst* that could be written: His **Lying Valet** was poor, his **Miss in her Teens** Trash, his **Lethe** fetched from *Hell,* and I wish *it* and *him* both at the *Devil.* Why, Sir, you talk of Society; this Fellow's an Enemy to Society, he makes us all a Jest to one another.

SIR F. FRIENDLY:

There, Mr. *Snipsnap,* you have hit it, that's poor *David's* Crime; he has a Knack of showing People as *they are,* and they can't bear it. Queen *Bess,* when she grew old, would not suffer a Looking-Glass in her Palace; but in the present Age People can't endure *Mirrors* while they are young. But consider, dear Mr. *Snipsnap,* it is the *Monster* makes the *Reflection,* why then would you break the *Glass*?

DOCTOR HEARTFREE:

Look ye, Mr. *Snipsnap,* this same *Poet* is a pert, prating, pretending Poet? such a one as you may meet in the *Mall* every Day; he mistakes the wild Flights of a troubled Imagination for fine Strokes of Wit, an impudent Abuse of high Characters for exalted Satire, and would fain hide his own Vices by exposing those of other People.—Do you think *David* was in the Wrong to drag this Fellow out of his Obscurity, and expose him upon the *Stage*?—There cannot be a more laudable Diversin than hunting such Vermin.

SIR F. FRIENDLY:

Well, but what say you to the *Old Man*?—That is certainly a real Character; old Mr. *Skinflint* that died but t'other Day seems to have sat for it, he who employed his Thoughts in deceiving his Friends *as long* as he *lived,* and cheated his *Brother* upon his *Death-bed.*

MR. SNIPSNAP:

Why really that Character is not much amiss. I was thinking that an honest Friend of mine in *Westminster* had sat for it; but now I think of it, he *never* had a *Friend* to *deceive*; and as for his *Family,* cheating them, perhaps, would have been no *Injustice.*—But by the Way, is there not a little Confusion in it?—The old Fellow does not well know what he would be at.—He does not *remember* what he would *forget.*—Sometimes 'tis that he must die, and anon how he came by his Money.

DOCTOR HEARTFREE:

And can there be any thing more natural? When a Man feels a thousand Stings in his Conscience, and his Body is crazy into the Bargain; is Incoherence a Blunder or a Beauty? Put the Case to Sir *William Lutestring,* which of his Actions he would *forget,* and nothing would puzzle him more, unless it was to find *one* he could consent to *remember.*

SIR F. FRIENDLY:

Hold, Gentlemen, you begin to be outrageous.—I find Satire is catching.—Let us proceed to the next Character.

MR. SNIPSNAP:

What, *the fine Gentleman!*—Why I look upon that to be sheer Abuse.—Egad I don't know but a great Part of the Audience had a Right to beat him for it.—Shall a little saucy impertinent Fellow, who lives by the Waste of our Time, presume to ridicule us for the Use we make of it?—'S death, I wish it was a Fashion to go to a City Lecture, I am sure I'd make one, and enable the *Non Cons* to feast while the *Players* starve.—That would raise a Rebellion in his own Theatrical Dominions.

DR. HEARTFREE:

But, my good Friend, is not your Anger raised from a very *different* Cause than *that* which you assign?

MR. SNIPSNAP:

How so, dear Doctor?

DOCTOR HEARTFREE:

Why *David* would not let you *waste* your *Time.*—He would needs make you *improve* it.—A sad Offence indeed.—And then for the *Lecture,* how could you bear *that,* when you could not bear *his*?—If, indeed, you could find such another Friar *Bungay* as preached a late COURT *Sermon* it might do.—Such a Preacher would regale all the dull *Debauchees* in Town, and leave the *Stage* to entertain Persons of Taste and Virtue.

SIR F. FRIENDLY:

Upon my Word I was of Opinion, that this Character was a little outrageous.—But my Niece *Melissa* convinced me of the contrary; she told me she was sure it was drawn for my Ld *Strut*; and the very Moment that she mentioned him, I was satisfied the Character was not out of Nature. Lady *Friendly* reckoned up two or three more; and when my Recollection was once awakened, I must confess I grew in Pain for the Author, lest some of this numerous Fraternity should get him into their Clutches, and exhibit a second Time the *Scene* at the *Lebeck*'s Head.

MR. SNIPSNAP:

So then you think it extremely reasonable that the Manners of People of Quality should be ridiculed, their Foibles exposed, and every thing they do censured, by every little Fellow that takes himself to be a Wit.—At this Rate, Sir, what does Birth, Title, Rank, Place, or Seat in either House signify?

DOCTOR HEARTFREE:

Nothing, Sir, if a Man possesses them without Desert.— Such a worthless Fellow *libels* his *Species* and the *Constitution,* and is therefore very justly below the Notice of the Laws, and delivered up to the Contempt of Mankind.— This, Sir, is a *Writ* of *Reprisal* that *Virtue* issues against *Fortune.*

MR. SNIPSNAP:

And so your beloved Author dwindles into a *Catchpole.*

SIR F. FRIENDLY:

An *Officer* of *Justice,* if you please, who by a proper Authority seizes such as would impose upon the Vulgar for *fine Gentlemen,* and thereby bring into Discredit a Character they never had. But what say you to the next Scene?

[*Enter* LADY FRIENDLY *and* MELISSA.]

MELISSA:

Good-morrow, *Uncle*; your Servant *Doctor*; Mr. *Snipsnap* your Servant.—Perhaps we interrupt, you were somewhat loud.—*Politicks,* I suppose, or *Philosophy.* O no! upon that Subject People are seldom so much in earnest.

LADY FRIENDLY:

Shall we withdraw Sir *Francis*?

SIR F. FRIENDLY:

By no Means, my Dear; we were talking of the *Entertainment* last Night, and were got as far as the Scene of Mrs. *Tatoo* and her *Husband.*

MELISSA:

Upon my Word the only tolerable Part of the Thing. Mrs. *Tatoo* is a Girl of Spirit, and talks very naturally. But instead of a *Drum,* methinks the Author might have afforded the Man a *Pair* of *Colours.* A giddy Wench, his Helpmate,

to be sure, but has some very agreeable Flights,—and then *Matrimony* is so well described.

LADY FRIENDLY:

True Niece,—such *Matrimony.*—Then methinks you are a little too squeamish about the *Drum,* it's not so long ago that a *Lady* of *Quality* and Fortune threw herself away upon a *Valet de Chambre,* and shewed herself afterwards a very Mrs. *Tatoo* in *Fickleness* as well as *Fondness.*—But alas! good Sense and Purity of Manners are the Effects of a strict Education, and that is now out of Fashion. Girls are left to themselves almost from the Time they go alone, and in consequence of that, are but bigger Girls all their Lives.

MR. SNIPSNAP:

With Submission to your Ladyship, methinks the *Sex* never made a brighter Figure than they do at present. Heretofore it was *all Constraint,* now we see them as they are, and admire them for being what they seem.—Foils and Candle Light are requisite to give Lustre to false Stones, but Brilliants need none of these Contrivances to add to their Beauty.

LADY FRIENDLY:

Very true, Mr. *Snipsnap*; but even Diamonds receive that Brightness for which they are admired from being polished, which I have been told is a Work of Difficulty, and are besides capable of great Improvements from their Setting.—Your Simile is indeed very pretty and pleasant, but, as you see, not absolutely just.—Even Pebbles, when they fall into the Hands of great Artists, discover such Beauties, as render them little inferior in Brightness and in Value to precious Stones.

DR. HEARTFREE:

Spoken like a Woman of Sense, and one who sets a true Value upon her Sex.—Mrs. *Tatoo* is a downright female Savage.—A rough Diamond that sparkles through its flinty Coat, and discovers just so much of its native Lustre, as makes us regret the Want of those Advantages that might have been bestowed upon it.

MELISSA:

For my Share I hate Art. The wildest Prospects give the greatest Pleasure. When People have once learned to disguise their Tempers, we never know what they are till it is too late. That she married the Man was a Proof she liked him; and the Obligation she conferred upon him ought to render him indulgent to her Failings. We are none of us perfect; and methinks there is a laudable Sincerity in not pretending to it. Mr. *Tatoo* gives himself Airs that by no Means become him; but as they are natural and copied from the Life, they shew us what ingrateful Creatures Men are, when Female Frailty has given them Power.

SIR F. FRIENDLY:

Bless me, Niece, how you talk!—Can you expect that such Boarding-School Elopements can end otherwise than in Misery?—Are Girls to think of marrying as soon as they have parted with their Babies?—Is there any thing in Nature that can shock a well-meaning Mind more than such impertinent Behaviour?—Don't those forward Girls first shame their Families by imprudent Marriages, next shame their Husbands by their Imprudencies after Marriage, and thereby double the Shame of such as have the Misfortune to be related to them?—How hapless in this Age is the Lot of Parents!

MR. SNIPSNAP:

Dear Sir *Francis,* you begin to be too serious.—Women, as well as Men, have different Inclinations; and believe me, with all the Education in the World, Madam *Tatoo* would still have had her Follies, tho' perhaps her Follies might have been of a different Kind.—Besides, with all their Follies there is something so bewitching in the Sex, that—

LADY F.:

You can't help being diverted with them for a little while.— When weary with one set of Follies you seek Relief from another, and fancy you are making a Compliment to the Ladies, when you tell us in plain *English*, Nature meant them for your Amusement.—A very noble Purpose truly! and the Women must have very elevated Ideas that can pique themselves upon diverting one Coxcomb after another, and in practising such ridiculous Sallies of Humour as may render them the Subject of Laughter to those who stand in the very same Light to their own Sex, and are only tolerable at such Seasons as Time itself is a Burthen.—But Women whom Nature has not neglected, and whose Talent; have been improved, scorn such Praises.

MELISSA:

Oh the Blessings of a regular Education! First the Hornbook, then the Sampler, next the *French* Spelling-book, then Scrawling, then Dancing, then the Spinnet, and so on from one thing to another, till we have learned twenty Accomplishments, which are all knocked on the Head by the Prudish Maxim, *that it is a Crime to use them.* To what End all the Plagues of Learning, if after we have run through them; it's indecent to read a Novel, its scandalous to write a *Billetdoux*, past bearing to go to a Ball with a Friend; and downright Impudence not to tell a Man one likes, that we can't bear him?

DR. HEARTFREE:

Indeed, Madam, the Picture you have drawn is not at all pleasing; but if you will be pleased to consider, that Giddiness is the readiest Road to Care; that unseasonable Mirth certainly ends in Sorrow; that liking at first Sight is no happy Omen for living together without Quarrels; and that, after all, it is better to take Advice in our Youth, than to collect it from Experience, which is very truly said to be the Mistress of Fools, because Fools only stand in need of her Lectures; you will find your Reasoning will lead to no just Conclusion.

SIR F. FRIENDLY:

Pray, Niece, what do you think of Mrs. *Tatoo*'s Description of a fine Lady?

MELISSA:

Pretty enough, and not quite wide of the Thing.—She speaks what many only think.

SIR F. FRIENDLY:

Very well, and do you imagine a fine Lady, at least such a fine Lady, can be amiable in any Eyes but her own?

MELISSA:

Perhaps she may'nt desire it.—But to be sure, Uncle, she will be told she is.

SIR F. FRIENDLY:

Aye, dear Niece, but for what End, and how long?—That she may be deceived, and not discover it, till she is undone.—Then comes a Time of being serious in spite of her Teeth.—What has she to do then, Niece?

MELISSA:

Why, she may be a fine Lady still, if she had but Sense enough to preserve her Fortune.—She may be tired with their Approbation who cease to approve her,—and find others.

LADY F.:

What! if she has lost her Reputation?—No, *Melissa,* take my Word for it, Hoydens that begin the World madly lead a short Life in Misery, and are sure to die wretched. There is not in Nature so idle and so fantastic a Being as a fine Lady. Her Charms attract many Flatterers, but no Admirers; she may confer Favours, but never Obligations; those of her own Stamp will be the first to expose her; such as are wiser must necessarily laugh at her, and only a few great and beneficent Minds may condescend to pity her, and to wish that her Follies may end in forcing her upon so much Recollection as may serve to make her pity and despise herself.—Such is the Beginning, Progress, and End of a fine Lady, who without a Metaphor, by that Time she arrives at the Noon of Life, would think a Cup of *Lethe* the finest Liquor in the World, provided after she had drank herself, she could recommend it to her Friends.—For Oblivion is certainly preferable to Infamy.

MR. SNIPSNAP:

I am quite tired with moralizing, let us go on. The *French* Marquis is a Character equally new and natural, except that it is to be found in most of *Shadwell*'s and *Sedley*'s Plays, and that very few *English* Gentlemen are capable of mistaking a Barber for a Man of Quality.

DR. HEARTFREE:

Your Remark would be perfectly decisive, if in spite of so many Cautions as we have received, we did not see such Mistakes made every Day.—Every Body knows, that want of Civility to Strangers, is want of Decency, and what can proceed from nothing but want of Sense. But there is a wide Difference between good Breeding and Affection; that Respect which is due to a Stranger, and the Caresses that ought to be reserved for the best and dearest of our Friends. Besides, are we ever the better for it? Has not one of the most illustrious Wits of *France* distinguished us by the glorious Title of *the Nation of Dupes*? and did not a little trifling Writer t'other Day, raise a Reputation amongst the great Vulgar over all *Europe,* by representing us in a Manner as remote from

Truth, as from the Gratitude which ought to have been paid to those Persons of Distinction who had loaded them with Kindnesses?—After such Instances as these, ought we not to be cautious? Nay, if this Caution went even to Coldness, who would Foreigners have to thank for it but themselves?—What say you, Mr. *Snipsnap,* am I not in the right? and is not the Author in the right too?

MR. SNIPSNAP:

Undoubtedly! Grant every *Fact* that you have advanced, and every *Argument* you raise, and all you say is certainly right.—Just so it is with your admired Author, he assumes a *Character,* behaves ridiculously in *that* Character; and then thinks the *World* must conclude the Character *ridiculous.*—But suppose the World should not be inclined to *admit* either *his* Conclusion or *yours,* what then?

SIR F. FRIENDLY:

Dear Mr. *Snipsnap,* instead of new stating, you have shifted the Question. If the Doctor's Facts are Facts, and if the Character *David* has drawn is natural, their Conclusions are just; and it is a hundred to one the World thinks so, unless their Prejudices are very strong indeed, and even that will abate nothing of the Strength of the Doctor's Argument, or the Justice of *David's* Ridicule.—Opinions very often vary, but Things hardly ever change their Natures.

MELISSA:

But, dear Uncle, supposing the Men at Liberty to do what they will, is it necessary that we Women should hate all *Outlandish* Creatures?—Must we run away at the Sight of a *Foreigner,* as Country-Wenches do from *Soldiers?*—Or if a *French* Marquis is inclined to *speak* to one, must we call him *Names* in return for his Civility?—I was taught better than this, Uncle, even at the *Boarding-School.*

SIR F. FRIENDLY:

By no Means, Niece.—You ought to be *civil* to a *Stranger,* because he is a *Stranger.*—But, methinks, there the Obligation ceases.—*Complaisance* may be sometimes as a great a Fault as *Ill-breeding.* If a Foreigner has *Merit,* he will shew it, and *Respect* is due to *Merit* wherever it is found.—But to Grimace, Impertinence, Fiddling, Contempt of your own Nation, crying up the Manners of his Country, and making *French* Sense the Standard of Rectitude and Politeness,—there is nothing due but *Pity* decently expressed.—besides a *Stranger* owes it to himself, to have proper Recommendations, without these he cannot expect Admittance into good Company, for if he should, his *Valet de Chambre* dressed in his cast Cloaths, has as good a Title to it as he.

MELISSA:

Oh law! If this Doctrine should prevail *abroad,* what a fine Time our *travelling* Gentry would have of it?

DR. HEARTFREE:

I should be very well content, Madam, if that was the Rule.—Treat Foreigners as they treat you, be but as much inclined to see *their* Faults, as they are to see *ours,* and it will justify all that I have advanced.—You have read

French Authors, and you know how we are treated. You see what an Opinion they have of our Temper, our Understandings, and our Manners.—The *English* say they are gloomy, buried in Speculations, and incapable of Sprightliness or Gaiety.

MELISSA:

And you would have us *despise* and *maltreat* them, in order to shew—that we *are* just what they *take* us to be.—Is it not so Sir?—
[*Curtesies.*]

SIR F. FRIENDLY:

No, sweet *Niece,* nothing like it, we only argue against adopting *their* Manners, that they may like *ours.*—There is no reason in the Thing.—Manners are the joint Effects of Climate, Education, and Constitution.—These are all natural to every Nation, and it is fit and just they should be so, and therefore to attempt wearing the Manners of *one* Country in another, is unnatural and Affectation. We see and know the bad Effects of this, we suffer by it, and therefore we ought to avoid it. *French* Influence in more serious Matters, arises from our regard to *French* Taste in Trifles; there is no more Reason that we should follow their *Whims,* than that we should be directed by their *Politicks.*—Both are to be shunn'd, if we know our own Interests.

LADY F.:

But seriously, Sir *Francis,* do you think that Complaisance for *French* Modes, can ever prove a step to Slavery?—Methinks that is pushing the Matter too far.—I may like the *Dress* of a Nation very well, without falling in Love with their *Principles,* and change my *Gown* and *Petticoat*—without fear of *changing* my *Religion.*

DR. HEARTFREE:

Very true, Madam. Your Ladyship judges rightly.—But permit me to enquire why the *French* Taste is to give Law to ours?—Is it because they are *more* [...]? Why then perhaps their Notions ought to govern us in other Things.—Let us Speak the Truth plainly.—Is not the Power of *French* Taste derived from a secret Sense of *Superiority?* And ought we not to search thoroughly, how well this is founded! Dress and Modes are *Trifles* in themselves, but Dress and Modes govern the unthinking Part of a Nation, and how *great* a *Part* that is I need not tell you, Madam.—One thing I will take the Liberty of saying; when the *House* of *Austria* was as great as the *House* of *Bourbon* is now, *Spain* gave the *Mode,* our Slash-Sleeves and Close-Doublets, and the Ruffs and Fardingals of your Ladyship's *Grandmother,* came from thence.—Thus you see *Modes* are not quite such insignificant things.—Flags are but painted Silk or Linen, yet where they are display'd, we know who commands within.

MELISSA:

O law! now we are running into *Politicks.*—I can't bear *Politicks* indeed Uncle.

MR. SNIPSNAP:

Nor I neither, Miss.—Proceed we then to Mrs. *Riot.*—That, Doctor, is a wonderous fine Character.—So natural—so just—and so free from Exception.

DR. HEARTFREE:

Truly I think so—It's a Character drawn from Life, and that makes it so much disliked.—Ridicule misapplied is never felt.

MELISSA:

But pray, Doctor, wherein does it differ from Mrs. *Tattoo.*

DR. HEARTFREE:

Mrs. *Tattoo* is, in my Judgment Madam, a *fine Lady* in her *leading-Strings*; whereas Mrs. *Riot* is a fine Lady *full grown*; the former *would* be she cannot tell *what,* the latter is the very *thing* she *would* be and could not *tell.* Mrs. *Tattoo* is just running wild. Mrs. *Riot* is come to Maturity in Madness. The one fills us with fear of what she may come *to,* and the other is the Picture of *that* of which we are *afraid*—A Woman of Fashion equally *distracted* in her *Notions* and *corrupted* in her *Manners.*

LADY F.:

You are satisfied, *Niece,* as to the *Difference* of the *Characters.*

MELISSA:

I am satisfied that the Author's a Brute, and makes very bad returns to the Ladies for the Obligations he lies under to them.—Who brought him into Credit? Who made him what he is?—Was it not our running to *Goodman's-Fields*—Crowding the House at *Drury-Lane,* following him to *Covent-Garden,* and crowding even that great House too for his *Benefits*?—But Men will be insolent and ingrateful.

LADY F.:

Very well, *Niece.* But this Man either had *Merit,* or he had none.—If he had *Merit,* he owes what he *is* to *himself.*—If he had *none,* he owed the *Reputation* of it to the *Caprice* of the *Ladies.*—If so, he has Merit *now,* for he has exposed their *Caprices.*

DR. HEARTFREE:

Excellent, Madam, excellent!—The *Logician* in the *Schools* does not argue closer. I see your *Niece* is convinced, her *Looks* speak it.

MELISSA:

That is more than my *Tongue* shall.—In my Judgment Mrs. *Riot*'s is not a Character but a *Caracatura.*—In short it is all Outrage, Insolence, and Distortion, a scandalous Reflection on the innocent Liberties of Women in a *superior Sphere,* who enjoy their *Freedom* and take such Liberties as keep the *Cares* of *Life* at a Distance—If Women are naturally superstitious or melancholy, let 'em fly to *Nunneries,* or, which will do full as well, mope themselves up in some antiquated *Country-House* surrounded with a *Meat* and covered from the bleak Winds by a *Rookery.*—Silence and Solitude may have Charms, and let those who like enjoy them.—I confess I'm not of the Number.

LADY F.:

Nay, *Niece,* now you are angry, and angry People are always in the wrong.—If I were a fine Lady, now I should

either laugh at you or leave you; but as I never aspired to that Character, so I will tell you my Sentiments, with the same Freedom you have given us yours.—If in this World there can be any thing called Happiness; Health, Fame, and Fortune must make the principal Ingredients.—Now my Dear, a fine Lady can never enjoy these long.—Late Hours, a continual Flutter of Spirits, and an unceasing Succession of Passions, is incompatible with the first; then Losses at Play, and habitual hearing of double Entendres, and certain unguarded Seasons, may through her frailty deprive her of the second, or, which is almost as bad, draw a general Scandal, which Malice will mistake for Truth.—Want of Oeconomy, multiplied Whims, unforeseen Expences, the Arts of Flatterers, and a hundred other Incidents, will bring down the last, let it be ever so great.—See her then in her last Stage, plunged in the Vapours, vexed with Affronts, and besieged with Duns, what think you then of *a fine Lady*?—Is she the proper Object of Compassion or Contempt?

SIR F. FRIENDLY:

Aye, *Niece,* what think you then of a *Cup* of *Lethe* for her?—Would it not be preferable to Imperial Tea or Citron Water?—You hate the Country: but you have been in the Country; and I have observed, that you asked the Name of every Town through which you passed, and how far we had to go. Why not make the same Enquiries in the *Road* of *Life*?—Why travel without considering the Journey's End?—Balls, Masquerades, and Assemblies, are, I grant you, very agreeable *Inns*; but if the Passage through them leads to a *lonely Cottage,* or an *Alms-house,* methinks this must damp the Pleasure.

MELISSA:

I grant it, Uncle; but we were talking of People above these Apprehensions.

SIR F. FRIENDLY:

My dear *Niece,* who are those?—Extravagance in low and high Life is the same.—There is no Fortune that can bear it; if it could, it would not be Extravagance.—Do but recollect the Lords and the Ladies too, that you have known undone.—Call to Mind the Shortness of the Space, and then reflect whether the momentary Happiness of two or three Winters, granting it to be Happiness, can atone for whole Years in Misery?—Consider, that Mrs. *Riot* talks with the Fit upon her; it is the Language of that Madness that leads to this Misery, and leads to it inevitably.—Natural Madness is not a surer Road to *Bedlam,* than this preposterous Passion for Pleasure is to *Penury* and *Penitence.*—Or, which is worse, to *Drinking* or *Distraction.*

MR. SNIPSNAP:

Don't look so grave, Miss, a fine Lady has a thousand Charms, these Charms will have a thousand Admirers, out of these she may make Choice of one able to maintain her in the Possession of all she desires. It is the Duty of a Husband to comply with the Temper of his Wife; a fine Lady may always command Obedience; and in Consequence of that every thing else.

LADY F.:

All which amounts to no more than this, That if a fine Lady does not while single undo herself, she may all in good Time undo her Husband, and through his Fondness make him a Sacrifice to her Folly. Is not that a hopeful Character?—What comfortable Speculation will the former Part of such a Life furnish, in the Silence and Solitude that must conclude it? and how excellently will a few Years of Profusion steel the Heart against all the Anguish and Distress that is to attend the Sequel!—The Remembrance of past Luxury, will make People wondrous easy in a narrow Fortune!

MELISSA:

Well! all I am able to collect, either from the humorous Entertainment, or from the moral Remarks upon it, amounts to no more than this; that the Sight of Pleasure is not more engaging than the Pursuit of it is dangerous.—To live out of the World is to be buried alive, and to live in the World it seems is a very difficult thing.—For my Part, I take the Decision of such Points to be too difficult for an unexperienced Female Mind; and therefore, tho' I have taken the Liberty of speaking my Thoughts of the fine Lady upon the Stage, yet before I undertake to act the fine Lady in Life, I promise you, I shall take the Advice of my Friends.—But by the Way, there is one Thing I cannot forgive the Author; he makes his fine Lady trip in her Expressions; and tho' we might not expect a fine Lady to speak Sense, yet sure, as an *English* Lady, she might have been allowed to talk *English.*—That Point, I believe, even the Doctor will decide in my Favour.—Mrs. *Riot'*s keeping high Company could not prejudice her Language, tho' it might her Morals.

DR. HEARTFREE:

There is so much *good Sense* in your last Declaration, that I would readily *grant* you any thing; but perhaps a little Explanation will make this needless.—You must consider, young Lady, that the Character of Mrs. *Riot* previously supposes *want* of *Education.*—At least this is a Compliment the Author very judiciously pays to the *better bred* Part of the *Sex.*—He would give us to understand, that those sort of Flights enter only empty Heads, take Possession of unfurnished Minds, and are the pure Effects of want of true good Sense happily cultivated.

MR. SNIPSNAP:

Now the duce take you and your Explanations.—You will have this Author a fine Gentleman, a Wit, a Scholar, and the Lord knows what.—He is ever in the right, let him act ever so absurdly; and with the Help of such friendly Excuses, his very Insults become Compliments; and what he meant for downright Abuse, you construe into decent Exhortation.—Instead of Physick, methinks Law should have been your Profession, and the very worst Cause in the World would have prospered in your Hands.—No Client of yours would have been guilty.

SIR F. FRIENDLY:

In truth, Mr. *Snipsnap,* you have given us a Cast of a very different kind of Oratory; for your very Civility is Abuse, and your Panegyrick Satire concealed.—I do not mean upon my Friend here, but upon poor *David.*—You won't allow him the Benefit of his own Thoughts, the Praise due to the obvious Meaning of his Words, or the common Privilege of being understood in the most favour-

able Sense.—It is happy for Mankind you were not bred to the Law, for a *Critick* without *Candour,* would in another Station be a *Judge* without *Mercy.*—Every Man had been a *Criminal* that came before you.

MELISSA:

Let us get to the End of it however; there is but a Scene or two more.—What say you to the Scene of Mr. *Riot*? Is there not something very *coarse* in his Character; and somewhat very *low* in that of his Companion?—Come, Doctor, there is a new Topick for your Eloquence.—Set me right in this Particular, and you shall be the *Director* of my *Taste,* and the Preceptor of my Studies.

MR. SNIPSNAP:

Thank you, dear *Miss,* you are come in seasonably to my Relief; and have fixed upon a Subject that will puzzle this Man of Logic and Learning.—You may rub your Brows, Doctor, but you are fairly caught; nor will all your Wisdom and Wit furnish you with so much as a handsome Excuse for your Favourite's Folly. Come, come, confess that his small Genius deserted him, that he had got to the utmost Extent of his Abilities, and was forced to wrap up his brighter Scenes in this filthy Sheet of brown Paper.—The Actor stumbled in his *Exit,* that's all.

DR. HEARTFREE:

Sir *Francis* I find thought right.—You are not only a Judge without Mercy, but without Patience; the Indictment no sooner read than you pronounce Judgment, and are for hanging a Man without hearing, for fear he should prove himself innocent.

MELISSA:

But, *dear Doctor,* come to the Point, it is within five Minutes of Eleven, and my Aunt and I are going to see Mr. *What d'ye call em'*s Paintings.—Give me therefore, in few Words, a good Account of this Thing, or give it up.—What say you?

DR. HEARTFREE:

Why really, Madam, the *Scene* gives a good Account of itself.—Mr. *Riot'*s Drunkenness, is an Appendix to his Wife's *Foibles.*—You must conceive him a fond Husband till undone by his Consort's Vanity, and then drinking to drown his own Cares, and, if possible, the Remembrance of her Faults. In this Situation where should you expect to find him, but in low Company; and after applying to so vile a Remedy, what could you expect better than this wild Discourse?—As for poor *Snip* the *Taylor,* he is introduced for a Fool, talks like a Fool, and tells the Tale of a Fool; that he suspects his Wife, and has not the Courage to tell her his Suspicions.—It is indeed a Scene of *low Life,* but very well introduced, to shew the Malignancy of *Corruption,* and what an unaccountable *Contagion* there is in *Depravity* of *Manners.*—Had Mrs. *Riot* been a prudent Woman, her Husband had been *sober,* and no more a Companion for Mr. *Snip* the *Taylor* than for his own *Footman.*

MELISSA:

This does not thoroughly satisfy me, indeed, Doctor.—Mrs. *Riot* may be possessed with a Kind of Madness; the

Passion of appearing a *fine Lady* may be little less in every Woman affected with it. But what has this to do with Mr. *Riot*'s Drunkenness?—Or, at least, what has it to do with his being the Companion of his *Taylor*?—Because the giddy-brain'd Mrs. *Riot* will keep high Company, does it follow that her Husband must *besot* himself with *low*?

MR. SNIPSNAP:

Excellent, Madam! Excellent! the Logick of the Schools to your Reasoning is Nonsense.—Now, my learned Doctor, for your refined Criticism to prove to us, that because Madam *Riot* will *game* with none but *Dutchesses*; therefore, by necessary Consequence—her Spouse will *drink* with none but *Taylors*.—Demonstrate that, thou dear Admirer of *Bays* the younger.

DR. HEARTFREE:

As a Man need never be ashamed to be *set right* by a Lady, so the good Sense of a Lady will always defend a Man from the Imputation of Incivility who sets *her* right, with that Submission that is always due to Beauty and to Authority.—Give me leave then to say.

MR. SNIPSNAP:

[*Aside.*]
Now the Devil take his Compliment,—any kind of Argument will do his Business.—His good Breeding has half convinced her already.

DR. HEARTFREE:

You will observe, Madam, that my Friend here,
[*pointing to* SNIPSNAP]
puts me upon proving too much, there is nothing of *necessary Consequence* in the Case; the Point is, Whether the Poet's Contrivance be *probable* or not?—The Temper of Husbands in general, are the *sweet,* the *firm,* and the *sullen.* Now, Mr. *Riot*'s seems to be the first of these; his Tenderness for his Wife made him give Way to her Foibles, 'till they had gained the Dominion over her; then Remonstrances coming too late, he had endeavoured, since he could not *reclaim* his Spouse, to *console* himself.—He had Recourse to the *Lethe* of Mortals, *strong Liquors.*—*Snip*'s was the same Case, he had met with the like Misfortune, and was inclined to the like Remedy.— Drunkenness, Madam, is an universal Leveller; for the Bottle, the Bed, and the Grave, bury all Distinctions.— For my Part therefore, I see nothing either absurd or unnatural in this *Scene*; and as for the Conversation, such as are proper Judges, which by the Way I take none of this Company to be,—allow that it is quite in Character; and that the same thing may be heard about *two* in the Morning at *Twenty* Coffee-houses in this Neighbourhood; and upon their Report in this Matter, (tho' in nothing else) I consent to rely.

LADY F.:

I must confess I was at first of my Niece's Opinion; but I am now convinced the Author has Reason on his Side; and from what the Doctor has been saying, I am confirmed in what I have long thought, that Domestick Misfortunes as often arise through Female Mismanagement, as from want of Virtue or Honesty in the other Sex.—Not that I believe Men are without Faults.

SIR F. FRIENDLY:

Far from it, Madam,—Experience shews us,—*that Women have more* Foibles, *and Men more* Vices.—

DR. HEARTFREE:

That is an excellent *Maxim,* Sir *Francis*; and give me leave to add, that the *Manners* of an Age are influenced chiefly by the *Ladies.* If they are virtuous and wise, the Men must be so; for they will naturally desire to be agreeable to the fair Sex.—When Children, we derive our Principles from our Mothers; when in the Flower of our Age we either court the Esteem, or gratify the Humours of the Fair Ones with whom we converse; and when we enter into Family Engagements, we are prudent or profuse as the Temper of our Wives direct.—Thus, like absolute Monarchs, we have only the *Title* to Dominion, and are really the *Slaves* of those the World fancies we *command.*

MELISSA:

Very *gallant* Morality truly!—I shall think of it, Doctor,— and whenever I have a Propensity to be a *fine Lady,* shall be checked by the Thoughts of making either a *Brute* or a *Sot* of my *Husband.*—An excellent *Memento* without Question! Adieu Routs, Drums, and Card Assemblies.

MR. SNIPSNAP:

Admirable!—The Ladies, I see, are to be flattered *into* as well as *out* of their Senses. I remember a *Spanish* Proverb, *With the Fair and the Fierce a smooth Tongue is the best Weapon.*

MELISSA:

The Coach is at the Door, Aunt.—Good Morrow, Uncle. Gentlemen your Servant.

LADY F.:

We shall be back by two, Sir *Francis.*—Gentlemen, Good Morrow.
[*Exeunt Ladies.*]

SIR F. FRIENDLY:

Well, now the Ladies are gone, I have an Objection or two to propose, Doctor.—You must know, tho' I am very well satisfied with all that you advanced, and am persuaded that the Ladies will see *Lethe* the next Time with greater Pleasure, and with abundantly more Profit; yet give me leave to ask, Whether this is a proper *Stage* Entertainment; and in what Light we ought to consider these *Dramatick Satires*?

MR. SNIPSNAP:

Aye, Dr. *Heartfree,* let us hear that. Tragedies, Comedies, Operas, Tragi-Comedies, Pastorals, Masques, and Farces, with and without Musick, I have heard of.—But for these *Dramatick Satires,* whence came they? Did we borrow them from the *Greeks* or the *Romans,* from the *Italians,* the *French,* or the *Dutch,* Doctor?

DR. HEARTFREE:

Suppose they were our *own* Manufacture, would they be the *worse* for that?—But if we may guess from the

Sentences that have been preserved to us by *Publius Syrus,* it appears that the *Romans* had something of the same kind. Be that however as it will, *Dramatick Satires* deserve to be approved and improved too, because they are a useful Kind of Writing.—When the witty Mr. *Congreve* apologized for his own Writings, in answer to Mr. *Collier's* Objections, the strongest thing he was able to say in Defence of modern Comedy, was, that, generally speaking, it closed with a moral Reflection in Verse, that that left a just and useful Impression upon the Mind.—Now if there be any Weight in this Argument, as I confess I think there is a great deal, then surely the *Dramatick Satire* is the best contrived Entertainment that can be; for let the Play have been what it will, the *Audience* are sure to leave the *House* with something in their Heads *worth remembering.*

Sir F. Friendly:

Why, I must own, that it is preferable to *Pantomimes* and *Dances,* which however they might please, could not possibly turn to the *Profit* of any but the *Performers.*—This certainly justifies your Friend as a *Manager,* because it plainly shews, that he meant the *publick Good* should go along with his *own.*—As to his extraordinary *Abilities* as an *Actor,* the several Parts he plays in this Piece are sufficient Testimonies.

Mr. Snipsnap:

And of his *Vanity* too methinks.—Pray allow me that, *Doctor*; for a Man to play *three* top Parts in the same *Farce,* and that *Farce* his *own,*—is, in my shallow Judgment, a little *extraordinary,* and not a little *fantastical.*—Under favour, Doctor, it was reserved for this Object of your Approbation.

Dr. Heartfree:

It may be so, Sir.—But since you will have it *fantastical,* I am glad you allow it to be *extraordinary.*—Find me *one* that can play these *three* Parts as well, and I shall allow it to be *ridiculous.*—'Till then, it is a Proof that he will spare *no Pains* to *please.*—In this, I think, you and I agree.

Mr. Snipsnap:

Agree! dear Doctor, yes; like the *Poles,* we agree to be as far asunder as possible.—You admire, and I despise his *Parts.*—As for his *Pains,* let him write like an *Ass,* and toil like a *Horse,* and that to the Day of Doom, he shall never *please* me.—You see how well we agree.

Sir F. Friendly:

I have another Objection still, Doctor.—The Whole of this Performance is to me little more than *taking off.*—That's an Objection that does not lie against the *Toyshop.*

Mr. Snipsnap:

That was in my Head too.—Why, when all comes to all, *Doctor,* this same *Dramatick Satire* is a downright *Auction.*—A sort of *Drury-Lane* Pyracy upon the *Vagaries* of the *Hay-market.*

Dr. Heartfree:

With Submission, Gentlemen, there never was an Objection more groundless.—Taking off *Persons* is a *Reflection,* but exposing vicious *Characters* is truly *Dramatick.*—I admire the *Toyshop,* as much as you do, Sir *Francis*; it is a very moral and a very instructive Entertainment.—But I remember there was *an Objection* to that too.

Sir F. Friendly:

Pray, Sir, what was the Objection?

Dr. Heartfree:

That it was *too serious,*—which I think does not at all affect *this.*—It has all the Life and Spirit of a *Farce,* and at the same Time the good Sense and Merit of a Satire; In short, it has that kind of Salt, that enhances the Merit of *Horace.*—The Author *makes his desperate Passes when he smiles.*

Mr. Snipsnap:

This is past all bearing. *Horace* and little *David* upon a level.—Well, I thank you for that, Doctor.—If I can't ruin his Credit with you, I have at least the Satisfaction of knowing,—hat I can ruin yours with *all Mankind.*—*Quintus Horatius Flaccus,* after all Doctor *Bentley's* pains about him, no better a Writer than Squire *David* of *Drury-Lane*!—Farewel to Criticism.

Sir F. Friendly:

But, my Friend, you exaggerate.—The *Doctor* did not say, that they were *equal,* or even that they were *alike*; he only said, that his Favourite *David* resembled *Horace.*—And tho' no doubt he meant this as a Commendation, yet I dare say, he did not dream of a *Parallel.*

Dr. Heartfree:

Not in the least, Sir *Francis.*—I have as little of the Flatterer about me as my Friend here.—I begin to think that we have no Chance for Reformation now but from the Stage; and therefore I am pleased with every thing that tends that way.—*Exhortation* has quite lost it. *Force*; but, thanks to Providence, *Ridicule* preserves its *Sting.*

Sir F. Friendly:

I have one thing more to offer, which, I must confess, stuck with me from the first Scene to the last, and I very much doubt, whether you will be able to remove it.—It is this, I cannot see why the Author has made Choice of *Æsop,* to entertain Mortals on the other Side of *Styx.*—In this too, I am the less satisfied, because we have *Mercury* at the Opening of the Piece; who seems to have been the proper Person to have entertained such Visitants.—The Ancients, if I remember right, recommended themselves when dying to *his* Care, because it was understood, that he conducted *Souls* to the Places of their respective Abode.

Dr. Heartfree:

Very true, Sir *Francis*; and therefore it seems to me, that he would not have been the *proper* Person upon this Occasion.—These were not *Shades* to be conducted to their respective *Dwellings,* but *living* Persons, who by the Favour of *Proserpine* (an unusual Favour I must confess) were permitted to *pass* and *repass Styx,* upon a particular Occasion.—This, if I am not mistaken, is an allowable Distinction.

MR. SNIPSNAP:

By your leave, Doctor, you have not answered, but evaded the Objection.—Why not *Mercury*? is one thing, but why *Æsop*? is another.—So you chose the easiest.—Very judicious, upon my Word.

DR. HEARTFREE:

If you had given me Time, I had come to the other.—It was reasonable upon such an Occasion, that the Orator should be a Person *generally known,* and *generally esteemed* by Mankind. If they were not acquainted with him upon first Sight, they would have been *at a Loss*; and if they knew him, without having a *Confidence* in him, the Knowlege would not have answered the *Writer*'s Purpose.—Now in both Respects, I cannot recollect any fitter Person than *Æsop*; his Shape hindered any mistake; for what Man ever had a Form so distinguished? His Character was the most inviting, humane, beneficent, and remarkable for Easiness of Access.—Taking all these Qualities together, Sir *Francis,* the Author seems to be not very much in the Wrong.

MR. SNIPSNAP:

No, Sir, in the Wrong! This Author never is in the Wrong with you, nor any other Man in the Right. You compared him just now to *Horace*; have not you another fine Writer in your Eye, in order to burlesque him by a Comparison?—No celebrated *Greek* or *Roman* to Sacrifice?

DR. HEARTFREE:

No indeed Sir. I only speak my Mind as you do.—And supposing you in the Right, as to my Prepossession in his Favour, your Prejudice is altogether as inexcusable.

SIR F. FRIENDLY:

Well, I give up this Objection, on the score of the Reasons you have assigned. I have somewhat else to say, but it's of no great Importance,—and therefore let it pass.—

DR. HEARTFREE:

Nay, Sir *Francis,* that's unkind. I shall believe that you side with my Friend here, and look upon me as a partial Judge, instead of a disinterested Critick.—I protest to you, Gentlemen,—

MR. SNIPSNAP:

Have a Care, Sir! If you mean to gain Credit, you must say more.—Will you make *Oath* Sir?

SIR F. FRIENDLY:

Well, Doctor, what I was going to say was—the Songs do not charm me,—the *second* Stanza in the first, is not *over decent*; there is not much *point* in the second; and as for the *third,* I don't well see the Meaning of it.—Besides, *Æsop*'s concluding Reflection directly contradicts it.

DR. HEARTFREE:

Now, Mr. *Snipsnap,* you and I are Friends; I give up all the Songs in a Lump, for the very Reasons that Sir *Francis* has

assigned.—I could have wished the Entertainment had either been without them, or that they had been *better,* for the sake of the Audience.—But I suppose they were necessary to the *Form* of the Entertainment, and to that *Matter* is too often sacrificed.—Now
[*turning to* SNIPSNAP]
am I not impartial?—And that too, even in your Opinion?

MR. SNIPSNAP:

I can't tell.—An Artifice perhaps,—in order to sanctify all you said before. But, to deal ingenuously with you, I laugh'd at the *first,* and was less displeased with the other *two,* than with any thing else.—So that you see, Doctor, you and I continue to *differ,* to the *End* of the *Chapter.*

SIR F. FRIENDLY:

But you have answered the Objection, much better than the Doctor could have done, if he had endeavoured it.—You have convinced me, there might be *some,* whom the Songs did not *displease.*—This shews it less an Absurdity than I imagined.

DR. HEARTFREE:

But does not *excuse* it, Sir *Francis,* the *first* more especially. There can be nothing right, that extorts a Blush.—*Congreve*'s Wit, and *Vanbrugh*'s Humour, cannot attone for *that,*—nor the *Custom* of the *Age,*—nor any Plea a *Poet* can invent.

MR. SNIPSNAP:

Why to you, Gentlemen, of *nice Morals,* it may be so.—But to us who go to the *Play-house,*m merely to be *diverted,* and to *kill* Time, we can easily pardon such Errors.—For my Part, to deal ingenuously with you, the *Devil to Pay,* or the *Virgin Unmask'd,* are to me worth all the *Dramatick Satires* in the World.—I laugh for an Hour, and think no more about them.

SIR F. FRIENDLY:

This being your *Humour,* I am thoroughly convinced, that you dispute without Acrimony, and contradict without ill nature.—Your Malice to the *Author* is only momentary; and before you get to *White*'s, you will have forgot your *Dispute* with the *Doctor.*

MR. SNIPSNAP:

Highly probable indeed, Sir *Francis.*—And yet some Things have passed worth remembring.—I love Contradiction, it affords us *Exercise* while we sit still, and turns Conversation into a Game at *Tennis.*—But my Friend,
[*turning to* DOCTOR HEARTFREE]
answer me one Question seriously, and I shall be so much obliged to you, that I will remember that Answer, if not as long as I *live,* at least as long as I *can.*—Which, let me tell you, is an extraordinary Promise from me.

DR. HEARTFREE:

[*bowing*]
Mighty well Sir.—And pray what is this very serious Question?

MR. SNIPSNAP:

Why, Sir, I would be glad to know, how a sensible Man, as you are, can expect to be believed, when you say, you expect a *Reformation* from the *Stage*?—Contend so very warmly for the good Sense and Morality of a little paltry *Entertainment*?—And seem to expect Lessons only of *Wisdom* and *Virtue* in a *Play-house*?—These, dear Sir, are to me Things *incomprehensible*; and all I beg to know is,—Whether you have not been as much in *Jest,* as your humble Servant?

SIR F. FRIENDLY:

Remember, Doctor, you are to answer him, not only seriously, but sincerely.

DR. HEARTFREE:

I will, Sir *Francis.*—I can assure you, Sir,
[*turning to* SNIPSNAP]
that I have spoke the very Sentiments of my Heart. I think Virtue, Beneficence and publick Spirit, the *Principles* upon which the *Happiness* of *Mankind* must be established, whether considered as Individuals or as Members of Society.—For the Propagation of these *Principles,* we must depend upon the *Pulpit,* the *Stage,* and the *Press.*—In this light, *theatrical* Entertainments are of the greatest Consequence. Every body knows, that the great End of *Tragedy* is to cleanse and purify the Passions, to shew us how they contribute to great and glorious Actions, when conducted by right Principles, and become the Source of Crimes and Miseries, when they assume the Place of Principles, and Men only seek to gratify them at any Rate.—Hence *Poetical* Justice often becomes *essential* to a *Good Play.*—The Design of *Comedy* again, is to correct the *Follies* of Mankind, by shewing that a Departure from Truth and Rectitude, whether from Whim, from Humour, or from Constitution, is often *dangerous,* and always *ridiculous.* Hence the Obligation of the *comic* Poet to treat the *Manners* of Mankind as they are, and not to introduce Characters improper or fictitious.—The View of *Dramatick Satires* is to expose *Vice* authorized by *Custom*; and in this they differ both from *Tragedies* and *Comedies*; for they do not ascend so high as the former, nor are they calculated merely to chastise the Foibles that are the proper Subject of the latter.—In short, each of these Kinds of Theatrical Instruction combats a separate Adversary.—*Tragedy* shews the Blackness of *Vice, Comedy* exposes the Consequences of *Folly,* and *Dramatic Satires* are calculated to repress the *Tyranny* of *Fashion.*—You see, Sir, the Motives of my *Zeal*; and I leave you to judge, whether they have not some Foundation.

MR. SNIPSNAP:

As you have *stated* them, Sir,—I must allow that your *Motives* are very well founded.—But you will give me leave still to think, that the Number is not great of such as frequent the *Theatre* upon these Principles.—I dare say, if any Question was proposed between you and I in that House, how little Weight soever my Arguments have had here, I should be able to carry it there by a *vast Majority.*

SIR F. FRIENDLY:

That may possibly be, Sir; but as People do not always find what they seek, so it sometimes falls out that they find

what they never sought; therefore with what *Intention* soever a Man comes to these *Entertainments,* Care should be taken, that what he meets with be *wholesome.*

MR. SNIPSNAP:

All this is very true, Sir *Francis.*—That ought to be the *Manager*'s Care.—But then the young *Wrongheads* of our Time will have a *Care* of their own.—For if the Manager's Provisions are not *palatable,* as well as *wholesome,* they will turn up their Noses and not *care* to *eat* them.—In which Case *he* and his *Myrmidons* must *starve* literally, while theirs is only a metaphorical *Abstinence.*

DR. HEARTFREE:

Notwithstanding I have insisted so much upon the *useful,* it was ever far from my Intention to exclude the *pleasant.* I know very well, that *preaching* is not the Business of the *Theatre,* nor *moralizing* directly.—Something of *this* there must be, but the *less* of it the *better.*—Instruction of this kind is to be convey'd imperceptibly, and ought to arise rather from the *good Sense* of the *Audience,* than from the *direct* Application of the *Author* through the Mouth of the *Actor.*—Nor is this so difficult as may be imagined; *Truth* like *Light* reveals itself without any Assistance, and if Characters are *well marked,* they will *strike* the Mind *right,* and the *Moral* will be convey'd in the *Representation.*—I readily grant you, that the *Multitude* frequent the *Play-house* with a View of being *pleased* rather than *reformed*; neither does any Inconvenience arise from hence, but quite the contrary.—If the Performance be good in its kind, it will leave an *Impression*; and those who were *pleased* with the *Representation,* must, whether they will or not, be *instructed* by the *Remembrance.*

SIR F. FRIENDLY:

Very true, *Doctor.*—This shews of what Consequence it is to support a *right Taste.*—For if the *Few* will but exert themselves in defending *good Plays* and condemning *bad,* the *Many* will follow their *Examples,* without considering the *Reason.*—And thus the Dignity and Usefulness of the *Stage* will be preserved, even by the *Suffrage* of those who have very little Conception of its *Honour* or its *Utility.*

MR. SNIPSNAP:

Very plausible truly.—Then you are of Opinion the *Men* of *Pleasure* are *Dupes* to the *Men* of *Sense*; now that I never thought in my Life;—and I'll lay you *fifty* Guineas to *five,* that put it to the Trial, we carry the *gallant* Comedy against the *grave,* in spite of all the Power of the *Criticks.*

DR. HEARTFREE:

There you are quite mistaken, Friend.—*Men* of *Pleasure* will as little approve of *bad* Plays as *Men* of *Sense.*—The only Difference lies here; *Men* of *Sense* know why they are *pleased,* and *Men* of *Pleasure,* provided they are pleased, enquire *no farther.*

SIR F. FRIENDLY:

That is precisely the Case, Mr. *Snipsnap.*—In what passes upon the great *Stage* of the *World* we are all *Actors,* and a

Man naturally *resents* the questioning his *Behaviour.* But upon the *Stage* at *Drury-Lane,* we consider others as *Actors,* and ourselves only as *Spectators*; and tho' the Tables are very often turned, and the *Players* in Reality act *our* Parts, yet from the Persuasion of being disinterested, we decide as if we were really so, and approve that *Ridicule,* which, for the *present,* does *not* hurt us.

MR. SNIPSNAP:

Upon the whole, I believe there is a great deal of *Truth,* Gentlemen, in what you say.—For now I think of it, I have read abundance of *loose* Plays that are *never* acted.— Some of *Shadwell's* and *Durfey's* no-body would bear; and I begin to suspect the Reason is, that their *Pleasantry* is unaccompanied with *Meaning.* So that *Taste* it seems supplies the Place of *Principle,* and to avoid being *stupid* one must preserve a *Regard* for *Morals.*

DR. HEARTFREE:

Your Conclusion, Sir, is very natural and very just.—The Mind of Man is so contrived, that independent of the *Biass* of his *Passions, Truth* and *Rectitude* will always please.— This was very early discovered, upon this Foundation stands the *Merit* of the *Ancients.*—This gave *Excellence* to their Works, which have stood the *Test* of *Ages.*—Had it been otherwise, they had been long decried;—whereas we are sensible, that in all succeeding Ages, in *Proportion* to the *Extent* of *Knowledge,* and *Nicety* of *Judgment,* they have been more or less *esteemed.*

SIR F. FRIENDLY:

Give me leave also to observe, that upon the *first* Cultivation of *Arts* in every Nation, Authors have, generally speaking, worked upon their *own* Stock, and have exhibited Pieces fuller of *Imperfections* than of *Beauties*—But by Degrees, as Experience discovered wherein *Excellence* consisted, all have recurred either to the *Ancients* themselves, or to the very *Rules* by which they were guided.— This manifestly shews, that *Right* and *Wrong, Deformity* and *Beauty, Excellence* and *Imperfection,* depend not upon the *Opinion* of Men, but upon the *Qualities* of *Things.*—Otherwise this could never have happened in all polite Nations.—Rest satisfied therefore, Mr. *Snipsnap,* that *Taste* is no trifling Thing, and that while we retain it, in spite of the *Corruption* of the *Age,* Knaves will be abhorred, and Fools appear ridiculous.

MR. SNIPSNAP:

Upon the *Stage,* Sir *Francis,* I believe they may.

SIR F. FRIENDLY:

And while on the *Stage,* every *where* else.—In other Places a thousand Circumstances may concur to oblige Men to *conceal,* or even to *dissemble* their Sentiments.— But, Sir, every Man has a *Stage* in his *Breast,* and tho' he does not laugh out, yet he laughs heartily within, at *Knaves* and *Fools* of every Species.

DR. HEARTFREE:

It gives me very great Satisfaction, that setting out so *wide* of each other at first, my Friend and I should come in

together at the Close.—I shall have the better Opinion for the future of the Lovers of *Contradiction,* and shall not apprehend it a *Sign* either of *ill Nature* or *Obstinacy.*— Disputes without Animosities on either side, end in finding the *Truth,* which is what both Parties seek, tho' in a different way.

MR. SNIPSNAP:

That has been always my Sentiment; and I freely own, that I am never better pleased than when I meet with a Man of Parts and Knowledge who is *tenacious* of his *Opinions.* For then, by *thwarting* him a little I put him upon his *Mettle,* and get out of him in *half* an *Hour* more than I could have acquir'd myself in *half a Year.* But let us see how the Day goes, [*looks upon his Watch*] I vow almost *Twelve.* Two Hours have run away in our talking over this *Entertainment.* Sure we might have spent our Time better.

SIR F. FRIENDLY:

Very possibly we might.—But I think it is at least an even Chance, that we might have spent it worse. I must own I never think Time *thrown away* in Conversation upon any *useful* Subject, when it is treated with *Life* and *Spirit,* and at the same Time with *good Sense* and *good Manners.* What say you, *Doctor,* I flatter myself you will concur in my Opinion?

DR. HEARTFREE:

Most sincerely.—I join likewise with my Friend here, and am firmly persuaded, that if most of the *common Topicks* of *Discourse* were handled with the same innocent Freedom and honest Intention that has been shewn upon this Occasion, they would be *better understood.* And after all, what concerns us *more* than to gain a thorough Insight into *Human Nature?*—The common *Chit Chat* at the *Coffeehouse* of the Weather, the News, the little *private Scandal* of the *Town,* and such like, is a real Waste of *Time* and of *Words.*

MR. SNIPSNAP:

As a Proof of which give me leave to observe, that it makes *no Impression* upon the Memory.—I have often remarked, that upon being asked at Dinner what I have *heard* in the Morning, I have often been at a Loss to *recollect* any thing of the Matter; and when with some Trouble this has been *effected,* I have found it of so little Consequence that I was *ashamed* to *repeat* it; whereas many Things I have heard this Morning will stick with me *a long Time,* and furnish a rational Amusement when I take a solitary *Walk* in the *Park.*

SIR F. FRIENDLY:

The Doctor and I are much obliged to you.—But now you talk of Walking, Mr. *Snipsnap,* I should be glad to take a *Turn* with you; and if you are not otherwise engaged, Gentlemen, you would do me a particular Favour, if you would return hither and take a *Family Dinner.*—What say you, the Ladies will be back by Two?

MR. SNIPSNAP:

I am entirely at your Service, Sir *Francis,* and think the Obligation wholly on my Side.—I hope, *Doctor,* we shall have your Company.—Tho' I am afraid we shan't *dispute* again in haste.

DR. HEARTFREE:

I have a little Business to dispatch, which will hinder my attending you to the *Park,* but you may depend upon me at *Two,* or a Quarter after.—As to *Disputes,* my good Friend, you and I can hardly avoid them.—We are naturally warm, and tho' we should resolve to keep clear of them as much as possible, our Tempers would not suffer the *Agreement* to be of any *long Duration.*

MR. SNIPSNAP:

Nay, if that is your Resolution—*Contradiction* is the Word—and *Wrangling* will ensue.

DR. HEARTFREE:

Adieu, *Gentlemen,* till Dinner.

SIR F. FRIENDLY and MR. SNIPSNAP:

Adieu, dear *Doctor,* adieu.

[*Exeunt omnes.*]

Theophilus Cibber (essay date 1756)

SOURCE: Cibber, Theophilus. *Theophilus Cibber, to David Garrick, Esq; with Dissertations on Theatrical Subjects.* London: Reeves and Phipps, 1759. 1-76. Print.

[*In the following excerpt, originally presented in 1756, the English actor and playwright Theophilus Cibber is highly critical of Garrick's management of Drury Lane. Cibber accuses Garrick of cronyism and greed and complains that he "mangles, mutilates, and emasculates" Shakespeare's plays. Cibber's attack is at least partially motivated by the opposition of Drury Lane and Covent Garden theaters to his founding a new theater company to compete with Garrick's.*]

Wit, Good-sense, and Politeness, were always thought necessary to support the Character and Dignity of the Stage, and that the Management of it ought to be instructed to Persons justly qualified to judge of all Performances fit to be introduc'd there: That Works of Genius might meet with proper Encouragement—and Dullness, and Immorality, be effectually excluded.

Has this been the constant Conduct of the present grand Director? I am about to speak but of one now.—That one will afford ample Theme enough.

Let us then view the Acting-Manager of *Drury-Lane:*—In the Year 1747,—He open'd that Theatre with an excellent Prologue:—The Conclusion of which gave the Town to hope—'twould be their Fault if, from that Time, any Farcical Absurdity of Pantomime, or Fooleries from *France,* were again intruded on 'em.

'Twas the Town who were (from that auspicious Night of his Theatrical Inauguration)

To bid the Reign commence
Of rescu'd Nature, and reviving Sense;
To chace the Charms of Sound, and Pomp of Shew,
For useful Mirth, and salutary Woe;
Bid *Scenic* Virtue form the rising Age,
And Truth diffuse her Radiance from the Stage.

But has he kept his Word during his successful Reign? Has the Stage been preserv'd in its proper Purity, Decency, and Dignity? Have no good new Plays been refus'd or neglected? Have none, but the most moral, and elegant, of the old ones been reviv'd? Have we not had a greater Number of those unmeaning Fopperies, miscall'd Entertainments, than ever was known to disgrace the Stage in so few Years? Has not every Year produc'd one of those patchwork Pantomimes? These Masquing Mummeries, replete with Ribaldry, Buffoonery, and Nonsense;—but void of Invention, Connection, Humour, or Instruction? These *Arabian* Kickshaws,—or *Chinese* Festivals,—These,—call 'em what you please—As any one silly Name may suit 'em all alike—These Mockeries of Sense—These larger Kind of Puppet Shews—These idle Amusements for Children, and Holiday Fools;—as ridiculously gaudy as the glittering Pageantry of a Pastry-Cook's Shop on a *Twelfth-night!*—Cou'd he plead Necessity, for this Introduction of Theatrical Abuse, this Infamy of the Stage!—This War upon Wit, in Behalf of Levity and Ignorance?—No—he wanted no Encouragement to establish the Theatre, on a reputable Foundation, without these Auxiliaries;—his Theatre was constantly crowded, his Performances applauded; nor did the Spectators grudge paying the rais'd Prices, for a Play alone:—If he fear'd this Taste for good Sense wou'd not last,—'twas at least worth a little longer Trial.

But Avarice is ever in haste to encrease its Store.—It never stays to consider what is most Laudable, when what may prove most Profitable is the Question.

Our Politic Man of Power therefore, wou'd not lose this Opportunity (of being in full Possession of the Favour of the Town) to introduce these Motley Mummeries, while he had it in his Power to make every Thing go down, that he judg'd for his Ease or Profit. In Consequence whereof, what large Rewards have been given to the Compiler of these Interludes, stol'n from the stale Night-Scenes of *Sadler's-Wells,* and *Bartholomew-Fair?* Such Rewards as wou'd have satisfied some Authors of Merit for as many good Plays.

More Money is annually squander'd on one of these foolish Farces—than, judiciously laid out, wou'd decorate three or four Tragedies, or Comedies,—in the bringing forward of which the Time, (lost on the other) might be more eligibly employ'd.

Has this little Giant Queller, who step'd forth in his Prologue, and promis'd the Town, to drive exotic Monsters from the Stage—has he kept his Word? On the contrary, has he not commission'd

> Great *Harlequin* to lay the Ghost of Wit?
>
> Exulting Folly Hails the Joyful Day,
>
> And Pantomime, and Song, Confirms her Sway.

'Tis True, he has given us some New Plays; and, we have been constantly told, that each succeeding one was to be more excellent than the former: So pregnant of Promises were our Stage Puffers,—the Ecchoes of their little Monarch,—to have given them Credit, one must have imagin'd, all former Poets, Men of little Genius, compared to the all-be-praised Writers for the present Stage: But, unluckily for the Moderns, and happily for the Reputation of the old Writers, the Productions of both are Printed.—Cou'd the Pen, or Pencil, describe, or delineate the Graces, and Excellencies, of some former Actors;—we shou'd not be pester'd with impertinent Comparisons, or a preposterous Preference, of any living Actor to a *Booth,* or a *Betterton*; as we have been with a Profusion of Praise equally bestow'd on a *Barbarossa,* and the noble Productions of *Otway,* and *Shakespear*:—Yet 'till *Barbarossa* was Printed,—what a Parade of pompous Praise was lavish'd on it?

Unless a Play comes strongly recommended from some high Interest, how difficult is it to get it read?—And how much more difficult it is, even then, to have it Acted, is well known to Several, who have gone through the ridiculous Ceremony: And to many more, who scorn'd the Attendance required by these Stage Dictators; to gain Admittance to them is frequently more difficult, than to come at a Prime Minister.

How drole to see the Mockeries of State—when one of these petty Princes is surrounded by his little Theatrical Dependants, watching the Motion of his Eye,—all joyous if he deigns to smile,—as downcast if his Looks are grave or fullen; but if the pleasant Prince condescends to joke,—like Sir *Paul Pliant,* they are prepar'd to laugh incontinently:—They stand like *Antony*'s Kings,—"who, when he said the Word—wou'd all start forth like School-boys to a Muss."—Thus is the little Pride of a Manager puff'd up, by the servile Adulation of his Theatrical Dependants;—who, poor unhappy Objects of Pity, never consider their abject State; Use has made their Fetters easy to 'em: Yet, how natural is it to demand, as on the Entrance of the Blacks in *Oroonoko*—"Are all these Wretches Slaves?—All, all Slaves;—they, and their Posterity, all Slaves!"—

From hence, this mock Prince presumes to expect such Solicitation, as Gentlemen, every Way his Superiors, cannot stoop to.—Then what avails the Merit of a Play, while such Monopolisers can prevent its Appearance?—What

Man of Spirit will undergo the ungenteel Treatment he is like to meet with from falacious Triflers?—Thus many a Piece is lost to the Town, that perhaps had given Credit to the Stage.

I will venture to affirm, there is now in being some dramatic Pieces (of which I have been favour'd with a Perusal) no ways inferior (I shall not say too much, if I add of superior Merit) to most that a partial Patentee, in his Wantoness of Power, has thrust upon the Town; and by his Stage Politicks, has supported for an unusual Number of Nights: Such is the Power of our Stage Dictators—who may cry out, *Drawcansir* like,

> All this I do, because I dare,

The common Put-off to an Author, when the Patentee is not inclin'd to serve him, is "The Thing is pretty,—to be sure there's Merit in it,—But it wants Alteration;—yet; if it was alter'd, they have not Time:—Their Hands are full,—The Business of their Season is wholly plan'd,—They have not a Night to spare."—And such paltry Put-byes as no one believes, not even themselves who say 'em. Not to dwell on the indifferent Plays they have acted, or some of more Merit that may have been refused by 'em,—let us enquire a little what mighty Business has so employed their Time, that not a few Nights can be found to give an Author fair Play;—the present Season[1] is now above half over, and what has been done?—Why, the Town has been entertained with a frequent Repetition of their old Plays, and stale Farces;—and one Farce, entitled the *Fair Quaker of Deal,* has been palm'd upon the Town as a reviv'd Comedy, and exhibited a greater Number of Nights, than formerly better Plays, much better acted, were ever known to reign:—As *Bartholomew Fair* has been some Years suppress'd, the politic Manager contriv'd to introduce Drolls on the Stage, at the Theatre Royal in *Drury-Lane.*—'Twas usual with the Masters of Droll Booths to get some Genius of a lower Class, to supply 'em with Scenes, detach'd from our Plays,—altered and adapted to the Taste of the holiday Audiences they were commonly perform'd to:—This Hint the Manager has taken—and of this gallimaufry Kind was the Pastoral (as he call'd it) exhibited at *Drury*'s Theatre.—

The *Winter's Tale,* of *Shakespear,* tho' one of his most irregular Pieces, abounds with beautiful Strokes, and touching Circumstances;—the very Title (*A Winter's Tale*) seems fix'd on by the Author, as an Apology for, and a bespeaking of, a loose Plan, regardless of Rule, as to Time or Place:—The Story affected his Mind, and afforded a large Field for his lively Imagination to wander in:—And here—the Poet:

> Fancy's sweetest Child,
> Warbles his native Wood-Notes wild.

In the Alteration, many of the most interesting Circumstances, the most affecting Passages, and the finest Strokes in writing, which mark the Characters most strongly, and are most likely to move the Heart, are entirely omitted, such as the Jealousy of *Leontes*, the Trial of *Hermione*, &c. What remains is so unconnected,—is such a Mixture of piecemeal, motley Patchwork, that *The Winter's Tale*, of *Shakespear*, thus lop'd, hack'd, and dock'd, appears without Head or Tail.—In order to curtail it to three Acts, the Story of the three first Acts of the original Play (and which contain some of the noblest Parts) are crowded into a dull Narrative; in the Delivery of which, the Performer makes no happy Figure:—So at the Beginning of the third Act, the principal Parts of the Story, which in the Alteration we might have expected to have seen represented, were given in two long-winded Relations, by two unskill'd Performers,—whose Manner, made 'em appear—"As tedious—as a twice told Tale, vexing the dull Ear of a drowsy Man."—And this hasty Hash, or Hotchpotch, is call'd altering *Shakespear*.—Whenever *Shakespear* is to be cut up—let's hope, some more delicate Hand, and judicious Head, will be concern'd in the Direction.

Let's carve him, like a Dish fit for the Gods!

Not hew him, like a Carcass fit for Hounds.

I have heard of an Actor, who humourously told one of his Brother Comedians, that, whenever he had a Part, where the Redundancy of the Author run into too great a Length in the Scenes,—he had recourse to a whimsical Expedient for the shortning of 'em: He had the whole Part wrote out, and then, gave it his Cat to play with:—What Puss claw'd off, the Actor left out; yet he generally found enough remain'd to satisfy the Audience.

In this frolicksome Manner, seems Master *Davy* to have laid his wanton Claws on *Shakespear*'s *Winter's Tale*.—Or, perhaps, he follow'd the Actor's Example, and left the Laceration of it to his Cat.—Sure, he was not so avaritiously unreasonable, to demand of his Brother Manager, the Profits of the Third, Sixth and Ninth Nights, for the Benefit of his Cat.

However, his Houses were crowded; for what he designs to give must be receiv'd.—It is *Hobson*'s Choice with the Town.—These monopolising Venders of Wit, like Fellows that sell Wine in a Jail, consult not the Health, or Pleasure of their Customers:—But, as it adds to their Profit, force a Sale of their Balderdash, and then demand the Price of the best Wines;—No Matter, whether or no it pleases the Palates of the Purchasers.—They must have that or nothing.—Were *Shakespear*'s Ghost to rise, wou'd he not frown Indignation, on this pilfering Pedlar in Poetry,—who thus shamefully mangles, mutilates, and emasculates his Plays? *The Midsummer's Night's Dream* has been minc'd and fricaseed into an indigested and unconnected Thing, call'd, **The Fairies**:—*The Winter's Tale,* mammoc'd into a Droll; *The Taming of the Shrew,* made a Farce of;—and, *The Tempest,* castrated into an Opera.—Oh! what an agreeable Lullaby

might it have prov'd to our Beaus and Belles, to have heard *Caliban, Sycorax,* and one of the Devils trilling of Trios. And how prettily might the North-Wind (like the Tyrant *Barbarossa*) be introduc'd with soft Musick!—To crown all—as the *Chinese* Festival prov'd the Devil of a Dance; how cleverly might it have been introduc'd, in the *Tempest* new-vamp'd, as a Dance of frolicksome Devils?—Rouse *Britons,* rouse, for shame! and vindicate the Cause of Sense, thus sacrific'd to Mummery! Think you see *Shakespear's Injur'd Shade,* with Patriot-Anguish, sighing over your implicit Belief, and Passive Obedience; your Non-Resistance to this Profanation of his Memory:—He grieves, to see your tame Submission to this merciless *Procrustes* of the Stage, who wantonly, as cruelly, massacres his dear Remains.—Are you not ready to cry out.—

Ye Gods! what Havock does this Scribbler make, among *Shakespear*'s Works!

Yet this fly Prince would insinuate, all this ill Usage of the Bard is owing forsooth to his Love of him.—Much such a mock Proof of his tender Regard, as *The Cobler's Drubbing his Wife.*—

In the two last Bellman-like nonsensical Lines, of his absurd Prologue to the *Winter's Tale,*—he tells you,—

That 'tis his Joy, his Wish, his only Plan,

To lose no Drop of that immortal Man!

Why truly, in the aforemention'd Pieces, he does bottle him up with a Vengeance!—he throws away all the spirited Part of him, all that bears the highest Flavour;—then, to some of the Dregs, adds a little flat Stuff of his own, and modestly palms it on his Customers—as Wines of the first Growth; a pleasant Beverage to offer Gentlemen, by way of *Bonne Bouche*:—Did every tricking Vintner brew so scandalously? But thus it will be, 'till his Play-House-Puffers are thoroughly enquired into;—and that it is publickly made known, both who and what they are; a Number of which, to the Amount of some Hundreds, are made free of the House,—or sent occasionally in with Orders, by one of his Agents; who, from thence, in Mockery, is not improperly call'd, the Orderly Serjeant.—From hence, the great Applause that always is lavishly bestow'd on every Thing, that is brought on that Stage:—But when these Place-Men, as they may be literally call'd, are pointed out,—as little Regard will be paid to the Claps of these Mercenaries,—as to the bawling Hirelings in *Smithfield*—who are appointed to roar out, Gentlemen, this is the only Booth in the Fair,—*The Wonder of the World* is here, Gentlemen.

So strongly had Fashion prevail'd, in Behalf of this lucky Son of Fortune,—that it became a Kind of Treason, among some People, even to hint a Possibility of his being in an Error: Such was the Infallibility of this Patentee, that if you heard any Tale of the Theatre, it reminded you of the *Tale of a Tub*,—where Lord *Peter*, having the sole Possession of the Will of his Father, paid no Regard to the Remonstrances of his Brethren;—his Power was not to be disputed,—he became exceeding rich:—But he kept his Brain so long, and so violently, on the Rack, that at last it shook of itself, and began to turn round for a little Ease:—In short, what with Pride, Projects, and Knavery, poor *Peter* was grown distracted, and conceived the strongest Imaginations in the World: In the Height of his Fits (as it is usual with those who run mad out of Pride) he would call himself Almighty, and sometimes Monarch of the Universe: Elate with Power, and puffed up with Pride, *Peter* determined to thrust down Peoples Throats the coarsest Bread; and, with an insolent *Ipse Dixit,* insisted on its having all the Qualities of every other Food.

But *Peter*'s Pride, and Power, were at last pull'd down;—and a Pontiff-like Patentee may be shaken:—Then may "he strut and fret his Hour on the Stage."

"Then look aghast, when unforeseen Reproof comes pouring in on him from Box and Pit." Or in a Fit of disappointed Pride, start, and cry,—"Shall I, who to my kneeling Players cou'd say, Rise a Theatric King,—shall I fall down at the proud Publick's Foot,—and cry, Have Mercy on me?"

Silence the Clamour of these Mercenaries,—ye generous Sons of *Britain!*—Exert your Power; laugh the Herd to Scorn, who condescend to be thus meanly purchas'd: No longer endure this insolent Innovation, on the Works of your dear Countryman (your Nation's Glory) by the unmerciful Hand of this mongrel Pigmy of *Parnassus*: "*The insulted Bard complains that ye are slow, and* Shakespear's *Ghost walks unreveng'd amongst us.*" Resent the Injuries offer'd to this Poet. 'Tis expected from ye, Gentlemen, in Vindication of your Taste;—as in a political, and patriot Sense, 'tis your Duty to resist any audacious Attempt on your Liberties, or the Insolence of a *French* Invasion on your Country:—No Wonder *Shakespear*'s Name is insulted by Foreigners, while he is tamely suffer'd to be thus maltreated at Home.

Note

1. This Dissertation was first deliver'd towards the End of January, 1756.

Joseph M. Beatty, Jr. (essay date 1921)

SOURCE: Beatty, Joseph M., Jr. "Garrick, Colman, and *The Clandestine Marriage.*" *Modern Language Notes* 36.3 (1921): 129-41. Print.

[*In the following essay, Beatty seeks to determine the separate contributions of Garrick and Colman the Elder to the writing of* The Clandestine Marriage. *Basing his investigation on extant correspondence and play notes the two men exchanged, Beatty concludes that Colman the Elder was responsible for the major characters and most of the details of acts 1 through 4, while Garrick was the sole author of act 5.*]

With the exception of the plays of Goldsmith and Sheridan, **The Clandestine Marriage** was probably the best English comedy of the second half of the eighteenth century. Its authors were George Colman, the elder, and David Garrick, respectively one of the most widely known dramatists of his generation and one of the greatest actors that England has produced. The part each had in the writing of the play was in dispute even during their lives, and has remained in dispute until the present. It is my purpose to examine the evidence both internal and external that has any bearing upon the indebtedness of the play to each of its two authors, and to state the conclusions that can be drawn from such an examination.

Since much of the discussion will pre-suppose familiarity with the details of this now slightly known play, it will be advisable to give a brief account of the plot:

> Fanny Sterling, the daughter of a rich city-merchant, has been clandestinely married to Lovewell, a worthy but impecunious kinsman of an amorous nobleman, Lord Ogleby. Sir John Melvil, a nephew of Lord Ogleby, and the lord himself accompanied by Canton, a Swiss valet, and Brush, another servant, arrive at the Sterling house to complete arrangements for Sir John's marriage with Miss Sterling, Fanny's elder sister. Unfortunately, Sir John, upon seeing Fanny, falls in love with her, and is discovered by the elder sister on his knees before her. The sister is naturally very indignant. Because of parental objection to Lovewell, it seems unwise to announce the marriage, even though Fanny is with child. Fanny and Lovewell decide that in order to warn Sir John, she should explain the whole affair to Lord Ogleby. While she is telling Lord Ogleby the story, however, she is interrupted at a point which makes it seem to the lord that she is really in love with him. The denouement comes when Lovewell is discovered in Fanny's room. The whole situation is cleared satisfactorily for Fanny and her husband. Other characters are Mrs. Heidelberg, the vulgar widowed sister of Sterling, a chambermaid, several lawyers, and Betty, Fanny's maid and confidante.

The play was first produced at the Theatre-Royal in Drury Lane on February 20, 1766 ([Genest, J.,] *Some Account of the English Stage, from the Restoration in 1660 to 1830.* In ten volumes. Bath, 1832. vol. v, pp. 92-3). It was later printed as by George Colman and David Garrick, with the motto on the title-page,

> Huc adhibe vultus, et in unâ parce duobus:
> Vivat, et ejusdem simus uterque parens!

It was reviewed in *The Critical Review,* vol. XXI, pp. 221-225.

The author of the article on **The Clandestine Marriage** in *Biographia Dramatica* makes certain remarkable statements about the respective parts of Colman and Garrick in the play. He says, "We have usually heard that Garrick's share of this piece was Lord Ogleby and the courtly family; and Colman's, Sterling and the city family. But the following was related to us by a gentleman who declared that it was from the mouth of Mr. Colman himself; 'Garrick composed two acts, which he sent to me, desiring me to *put them together,* or do what I would with them. I did put them together, for I put them into the fire, and wrote the play myself'" (*Biographia Dramatica; or a Companion to the Playhouse* ... Originally compiled, to the year 1764, by David Erskine Baker, Continued thence to 1782, by Isaac Reed, F. A. S. And brought down to the End of November 1811 ... by Stephen Jones. In 3 volumes. London, 1812. vol. II, p. 106). In the discussion of *False Concord,* a farce by the Rev. James Towneley, acted at Covent Garden, March 20, 1764, and not printed, it is noted that "It is worthy of remark, that in this farce were three characters (Lord Lavender, Mr. Sudley an enriched soap-boiler, and a pert valet) which were afterwards transplanted, with the dialogue of some scenes, nearly *verbatim,* into **The Clandestine Marriage** (brought out two years afterwards), under the names of Lord Ogleby, Mr. Sterling, and Brush" (*ib.* p. 218). This alleged fact was disclosed by "Mr. Roberdeau in his *Fugitive Verse and Prose,* 1801; Mr. R. having married a daughter of the late Mr. Towneley" (*ib.*).

When George Colman, the younger, in 1820, published in London *Posthumous Letters from Various Celebrated Men; Addressed to Francis Colman, and George Colman, the Elder,* he did not allow such statements as these to pass unchallenged. In the *Addenda* to his volume he printed a defence of his father which included in his father's handwriting a document submitted to David Garrick apparently before the play was begun. In this document, Colman suggests numerous details concerning both characters and plot.

In his discussion of the characters, Colman first of all suggests that the Earl of Oldsap—to be played by Garrick—should be an old Lord who thinks every woman in love with him. Because of this belief he ogles at every woman he meets. Colman completes his remarks about the earl with this significant statement: "But this notion you are more fully possest of than I" (*Posthumous Letters,* p. 334). He then mentions as the other characters, Lord Sapplin, son of the Lord; Traffick, a rich city merchant, anxious to be thought "generous and genteel, wch serves more effectually to expose his Bourgeoise manners"; Lovewell "privately married to Miss Bride—warm, and sensible" [it will be noted that Colman sometimes substitutes for the names of the characters the names of the actors who were to play the parts, J. M. B.]; "Mrs. Clive, Kennedy, or Bradshaw—Sister to Traffick—and something of the same char-

acter in Petticoats—only that he is rough & hearty in his manner, & she affects to be delicate & refined. Her dialect is particularly vulgar, aiming at the same time to be fine, not by murdering words in the slip-slop way, but by a mean twang in the pronunciation, as *Qualaty—famaly,* &c": "Miss Pope—eldest daughter to Traffick, a keen smart girl, full of spirit, sense, wit, humour, mischief, & malice": "Miss Bride—youngest daughter to Traffick,—a sensible girl, of a soft & amiable temper, not without proper spirit."

Turning from the characters, Colman proceeds to make a rough draught of the general scheme of the play: "A Treaty of Marriage is supposed to be set on foot between the Court and City Family, in wch it is intended that Lord Sapplin, Garrick's Son, shall be married to Miss Pope, eldest daughter to Traffick; It happens, however, that the young Lord has contracted a violent affection for Miss Bride, who is *before the beginning* of this play clandestinely married to Lovewell. The efforts made by Lord Sapplin to bring about his match with Miss Bride, instead of Miss Pope—the perplexities arising therefrom to the young Couple, Lovewell and Miss Bride—the growing jealousy, & malicious artifices of Miss Pope—& then naturally involving the old Earl (Garrick) in circumstances tending to shew his character—together with the part wch Traffick & his Sister may naturally take in this affair—to make up the Story of the Play."

Colman comments upon the fact that he is simply making a sketch of his plan, that his purpose is "merely to enable you to think in the same train with me: & that you may be still better acquainted with *the stuff of my thoughts,* I have here subjoined some loose hints of Acts, Scenes, manner of conducting the Story, of shewing the characters to advantage, &c" (*ib.* p. 336). He suggests that perhaps the plot might be still further "pleasantly embarrassed by introducing a character (a *good* one) openly intended to be married to Miss Bride." The result of this plan he believes would be to make the situation of Lovewell and Miss Bride more difficult and would direct Miss Pope's jealousy to the wrong object.

In quoting Colman's hints for the Acts and Scenes, I shall italicize the details that were incorporated in the finished play. In Act I *he wishes to let the audience know* (1) *of the marriage* and (2) *of Lord Sapplin's attachment to Bride instead of to his intended wife* [inserted in Act II]. He suggests that this will best be done and Lovewell will be raised somewhat above the others *if the latter is made a relative, perhaps nephew of the earl. Because of this relationship the young lord will the more naturally make him his confidant.* Furthermore, *the old earl could be shown dressing* [inserted in Act II], "& he might speak of himself—hold his son cheap as a man of gallantry—talk of what *he* c^d do *with the women—that even now all the family are more in love with him,* &c, &c—*a short lawyer scene (à la Hogarth*) with some *family-strokes on mortgages, set-tlements &c might perhaps be introduced* [inserted in Act III]. *If the City Family are at all produced in this Act, they may be supposed in expectation of the arrival of the Lords—Preparations making on all hands—Traffick talk-ing of his venison, turbot, pine-apples, &c. His sister on tenterhooks to receive persons of famaly & Miss Pope's Elevation & Pride ab^t her noble match, & contempt of her sister—&c*" (*ib*. p. 338).

For Act II, Colman suggests that *the Lords should have arrived between Acts I and II,* and that in Act II, Scene I, Oldsap be shown with the women. *A humorous scene might be produced by having Traffick show his garden and remark upon the modern improvements in it.* Colman says, "You will not find many materials for this in y^r own garden at Hampton; but you may among y^r neighbors." *Lord Sapplin might find a chance to make a declaration to Miss Bride—she will speak of the indelicacy of his transferring his attentions to her, and will not encourage him. Miss Pope is to be aroused to jealousy by some inci-dent and will then become incensed against both Lord Sapplin and her sister.*

At the beginning of his remarks upon Act III, Colman says, "N. B. Though I mark the acts thus, I by no means w^d suggest to you that I have here planned out anything like the form of the business of the Play" (*ib*. p. 339). He suggests that *Lovewell and Miss Bride shall decide that since Lord Oldsap apparently has taken a kindly interest in her, she should tell him of Lord Sapplin's attentions and also of her marriage. While she is telling the first part, she becomes embarrassed, and leaving without a full confes-sion, leads him to think when she says her affections are elsewhere, that she is in love with him. Miss Pope may complain to him of Lord Sapplin and Miss Bride, but in that case Lord Oldsap will deny this and say he can tell her where Miss Bride's affections are placed.* Colman believes that if the character intended to be married to Miss Bride were now introduced, he might be used as a tool by Miss Pope if she should tell him of the wrong that was being planned against her, and should ask him to counteract the plot. *Miss Bride and Lovewell agree that Lovewell shall now tell Lord Oldsap of the marriage, but before he can get fully under way, Lord Oldsap confesses his love for Miss Bride. Lord Oldsap is to break the whole matter to the family, by speaking to Traffic's sister,* who first thinks he is making love to her. When she finds she is mistaken, she treats him with contempt.

Colman ends his paper by remarking, "Of the Denouement I have not as yet even conceived those imperfect ideas I have got of some other parts. Think of the whole, & think in my train, if it appears worth while, & when you have thrown y^r thoughts on paper, as I have done mine, we will lay our heads together, Brother Bayes."

The younger Colman believed that it was after a consulta-tion with Garrick that his father wrote the latter part of the following Loose Hints of Act V:

> Scene of Sterling, Ogleby, lawyers &c on filling up blanks, & settling all the clauses of the settlement—disputes arise, & Sterling agst both matches, declaring that he will not marry his family into a Chancery suit—in the midst of their disputes enter Miss Sterling laughing immoderately, & brings in Betty trembling, who, being *interrogated* dis-covers the whole of the Clandestine Marriage.

> V.

> Lovewell, & Fanny, & Betty in Fanny's apartment—Betty may tell them that Mrs Lettice has been pumping her—Lovewell tells Fanny that finding the misconstruction of Ld. O., he was just on the point of explanation when Sir John appeared—but that he will certainly break it the next morning to Sir John—& this night shall conclude her anxi-eties on the clandestine marriage—(sc. 2). Another apart-ment, Miss Sterling & Mrs H. in their night-cloaths [sic]—to them Lettice, who tells them she has been on the watch, & saw a man go into Miss Fanny's room—They immedi-ately conclude it to be Sir John—& Miss Sterling resolves to expose her sister & Sir John—the family alarmed—various night figures—Betty brought in trembling, who discovers the whole affair—then Lovewell & at length Fanny, who being pardoned, Sir John's match breaks off, & the piece concludes by Sterling & Ogleby both joining in good hu-mour about Fanny & Lovewell.

> (*ib*. pp. 343-4)

From even a most casual comparison of the completed play with the notes sent by Colman to Garrick, it is evident that whichever author wrote the first three acts, Colman was responsible for the early part of the plot in almost every respect. In Act I, Fanny and Betty let the audience into the secret at once. Lovewell is made a kinsman of Lord Ogleby. The Sterling family is preparing to receive the distin-guished guests. Sterling, as prearranged, discusses the food for his dinner: "But, pray, sister Heidelberg, let the turtle be drest to-morrow, and some venison; and let the gardener cut some pine-apples, and get out some ice. I'll answer for wine, I warrant you: I'll give them such a glass of Champagne as they never drank in their lives; no, not at a duke's table" (*The Dramatick* [sic] *Works of George Colman.* In four volumes, London, 1777. Vol. I, p. 179).

The characters of Mrs. Heidelberg, Miss Sterling, and Lord Ogleby as elaborated in Act I and the following acts are simply amplifications of Colman's notes. When Mrs. Heidelberg speaks to the housekeeper, Mrs. Trusty, about the anticipated arrival of the guests, she says, "Oh, here, Trusty; do you know that people of qualaty are ex-pected this evening?" (*ib*. p. 175). Or, again, she says to Fanny, "Go, child! you know the qualaty will be here by and by; go, and make yourself a little more fit to be seen [*exit Fanny*]. She is gone away in tears; absolutely crying, I vow and pertest. This ridicalous love! We must put a stop to it. It makes a perfect nataral of the girl" (*ib.* p. 177). Miss Sterling, thinking of her marriage with Sir John, makes her sister exceedingly uncomfortable: "My heart goes pit-a-pat at the very idea of being introduced at court: gilt chariot! pye-balled horses! laced liveries! and then the whispers buzzing round the circle! Who is she? 'Lady Melvil, Ma'am!' Lady Melvil! my ears tingle at the sound … if Mr Lovewell and you come together, as I doubt not you will, you will live very comfortably, I dare say … perhaps I may meet you in the summer with some other citizens at Tunbridge. For my part, I shall always entertain a proper regard for my relations: You shan't want my countenance, I assure you" (*ib.* pp. 174-5). Miss Sterling's characterization of Ogleby is even more strikingly like Colman's notes: "He is full of attention to the ladies, and smiles, and grins, and leers, and ogles, and fills every wrinkle in his old wizen face with comical expressions of tenderness. I think he would make an admirable sweetheart" (*ib.* pp. 178-9).

The only suggestions not utilized in this act are those of having a lawyer-scene and of showing the old earl dressing. It is interesting, however, that the former is used in Act III and the latter in Act II. The arrival of the lord's servant at the end of Act I prepares for the arrival of the guests between acts as suggested by Colman.

At the beginning of Act II the original plan was modified by the introduction of a servant-scene in Lord Ogleby's ante-chamber, followed by the appearance of the lord himself. The plan is further modified by Sir John's telling Lovewell that upon visiting his room early in the morning he had found it empty. This scene, as anticipatory to Act V was in all probability suggested by Garrick. After the garden-scene, Sir John admits to Lovewell his love for Fanny, and failing to induce Lovewell to convey a letter to her from him, was in the act of declaring his love to Fanny herself when Miss Sterling discovered him. This scene gave the occasion that Colman desired to arouse Miss Sterling to jealousy.

The lawyer-scene suggested for Act I was inserted in Act III. Mrs. Heidelberg was made a more prominent figure by emphasizing the power she wielded in the family by reason of her money. The relations between Mrs. Heidelberg and the others in the group take up most of this act.

The suggestions made by Colman for Act III, in regard to the complications among Fanny, Lovewell, and Lord Ogleby were followed finally in Act IV, and carried out to the letter. The matter is further complicated by the request that Lord Ogleby makes to Sterling for his daughter's hand.

It is noteworthy that the first suggestions for Act V were not used, except in part for Act IV, and that the last sugges-

tions were followed in the main. The order of disclosure was altered somewhat, however. Betty came out of Fanny's room first, but did not confess. She was followed by Fanny and finally by Lovewell.

From a survey of the internal evidence it is apparent, therefore, that Colman was responsible for the basic characterization of most of the chief *dramatis personae*, including Lord Ogleby, and also for the most important details of the first four acts. For more specific information we must turn to external evidence.

George Colman, the younger, suggests the method which his father and Garrick followed in their collaboration: "The probable process was, that they consulted, first, as to the general plan, and, secondly, as to the conduct of the incidents and scenes; then wrote *separately* and then compared and modified, *together,* what each had composed" (*Posthumous Letters,* p. 333). He states, furthermore, that his father had told him Garrick did not write all of Lord Ogleby, that, for instance, Colman wrote the whole of Lord Ogleby's first scene. This evidence is important, as coming from Colman's son, but his last statement, as we shall see later, is controverted by one of his father's own letters.

The elder Colman's letters from Garrick give considerable information in regard to the progress of the play and the methods of collaboration. *The Clandestine Marriage* was apparently well under way as early as 1763, for in December of that year Garrick wrote from Naples to Colman, "I have not yet written a word of the fourth or fifth acts of **'The Clandestine Marriage,'** but I am thinking much about it" (Peake, R. B., *Memoirs of the Colman Family, including their Correspondence with the most distinguished Personages of their time.* In two volumes. London, 1841, vol. I, p. 93). This reference would place the date of Colman's notes at least three months before the first production of *False Concord* on March 20, 1764, and should dispose of the charge of plagiarism as far as the conception of Lord Ogleby is concerned. It is also significant that Garrick was abroad at the time of the first production of *False Concord.* He wrote to Colman from Rome, April 11, 1764, a very intimate letter in which he said about *The Clandestine Marriage,* "Speed your plough, my dear friend; have you thought of **'The Clandestine Marriage'**? I am at it" (*ib.* p. 102). Since Garrick continued abroad during 1764, it is improbable that his part of the play could have been plagiarized. Furthermore, it is probable that had any great part of it been filched from another work, the borrowing would have been exposed at once instead of a half-century later. In a letter from Paris, dated November 10, 1764, Garrick says, "Did you receive my letter about our Comedy? I shall begin, the first moment I find my comic ideas return to me, to divert myself with scribbling; say something to me upon that subject. I have considered our three acts, and with some little alterations they will do; I will ensure them" (*ib.* p. 126).

If we may judge from these letters and from the length of time that elapsed between the inception and completion of the play, it would seem probable that neither author was burningly enthusiastic about his task. By September 24, 1765, however, the work was nearing an end. On that date, Doctor Hoadly, in a letter to Garrick, says, "I am pleased to hear that Mr. Colman's Comedy, two acts of which you shewed me at Hampton some years ago, is in such forwardness, as I found, by his talk at his own house last winter that he had not worked any farther upon it; I did not let him know I had seen any part of it, or was privy to the scheme, which surely is a good one. God bless you both" (*ib.* pp. 156-7).

From the beginning, it would seem that Colman expected Garrick to play the part of Lord Ogleby. For some reason, however, when the play was completed, the great actor refused to undertake the part. Thomas Davies, Garrick's friend and biographer, attributed his change of mind to his advanced age and his frequent attacks of the gout and stone (Davies, T., *Memoirs of the Life of David Garrick, Esq. . . .* a new Edition in two volumes. London, 1808, vol. II, p. 102). Tate Wilkinson, the actor, said that Garrick wrote the part of Lord Ogleby before he went to Italy. When he returned, he decided not to play that part, both because of his health and also because, "if he himself should play Lord Ogleby, it would lead into applications from authors to request his performing in their pieces; to prevent which, he had come to a determination not to study any new character whatever, and desired Mr. King would do the part" (Wilkinson, T., *Memoirs of his Own Life.* In four volumes, York, 1790, vol. III, p. 254). At first King would not take the rôle, but he was at last persuaded. When he recited part of a scene to Garrick in a tremulous voice, "Garrick was all astonished, and thundered out, 'By G—d, King, if you can but sustain that fictitious manner and voice throughout, it will be one of the greatest performances that ever adorned a British theatre'" (*ib.* p. 255). Peake, the biographer of the Colmans, says that Garrick was unwilling to study a new part, and hints that it may have been because of a resemblance between Lord Ogleby and Lord Chalkstone in Garrick's own play, **Lethe.** He suspects that a meddler carried to Garrick some remarks made by Colman upon his collaborator as a manager (Peake, *op. cit.* vol. 1, p. 157).

Whatever was the cause of Garrick's refusal to play the part of Lord Ogleby, his failure to fulfill Colman's expectations brought about a break between the two friends. On November 9, 1765, James Clutterbuck, writing to Garrick, says,

> Colman and you are men of most quick sensations, and are apt sometimes to catch at words instead of things, and those very words may probably receive great alterations by the medium through which they pass. I know you love one another, and a third person might call up such explanations as would satisfy ye both; I myself should not

doubt being able to do it were we assembled together. He had communicated his griefs (but no acrimony, I assure you) before your letters came and I commiserate his disappointment. Had I not been in the secret of the joint enterprise I suppose he would not have opened his mouth to me; but being so, the comedy was read to my Molly and me last Wednesday night, and our concern, for that it is not likely to be finished and represented, equalled the delight we had in hearing the piece: I cannot help thinking there is but one person in the world capable of playing Lord Ogleby, *et hinc illae Lachrymae!* but who can help it?

(The Private Correspondence of David Garrick with
the Most Celebrated Persons of his Time; . . . In
two volumes. London, 1831, vol. I, pp. 206-7)

The most interesting evidence both in regard to this quarrel and in regard to the authorship of ***The Clandestine Marriage*** is to be found in a letter written by Colman to Garrick, December 4, 1765. It corroborates in every detail the conclusions drawn from the play itself:

> Since my return from Bath I have been told, but I can hardly believe it, that, in speaking of **'The Clandestine Marriage,'** you have gone so far as to say, 'Colman lays a great stress on his having written this character on purpose for me, suppose it should come out that *I wrote it!*' That the truth should come out is my earnest desire; but I should be extremely sorry, for your sake, that it should come out by such a declaration from you. Of all men in the world, I believe I may venture to say that I should be one of the last to take any thing to myself of which I was not the author . . . but you know that it was not I, but yourself, who desired secrecy in relation to our partnership, and you may remember the reasons you gave for it. You know, too, that on the publication of the play the whole affair was to come out, and that both our names were to appear together on the title-page. . . . In your letter to Clutterbuck . . . you tell him, 'that you had formed a plan of a comedy called *The Sisters*; that if the piece did not succeed, you had promised to take your part, with the shame that might belong to it, to yourself.' I cannot quote the words of your letter, but I am sure I have not misrepresented the purport of it, though the whole is diametrically opposite to my notion of the state of the partnership subsisting between us. You have the plan of 'The Sisters' by you; read it, and see if there are in it any traces of the story of **'The Clandestine Marriage.'** You returned me the rough draught which I drew out of that story, and thinking it might be of use in conducting the plot I happened to preserve it: let them be compared, and see what is the resemblance between them. The first plate of Hogarth's 'Marriage à la Mode' was the ground I went upon: I had long wished to see those characters on the stage, and mentioned them as proper objects of comedy, before I had the pleasure of your acquaintance, in a letter written expressly in your defence against the attacks of your old arch enemy Shirley. . . . I understood it was to be a joint work, in the fullest sense of the word; and never imagined that either of us was to lay his finger on a particular scene, and cry, 'This is mine!' It is true, indeed, that by your suggestion, Hogarth's proud lord was converted into Lord Ogleby, and that, as the play now stands, the levee-scene, at the beginning of the second act, and the whole of the fifth act, are yours: but in the conduct as well

as dialogue of the fourth act, I think your favourite, Lord Ogleby, has some obligations to me.

(*The Private Correspondence of David Garrick,*
vol. I, pp. 209-210)

In Garrick's reply to this letter there is no attempt to deny Colman's assertions. Soon, however, the quarrel was over. On the one hand, the actor was able to prove to Colman's satisfaction that he had not intended to injure him; on the other hand, Colman was reconciled to the thought of having King take the part of Lord Ogleby. In less than three months after this letter was written, the play was on the stage.

From an examination of the preceding evidence certain facts are clear. In the first place, the story that Colman burned Garrick's manuscript is absurd. There is absolutely no indication of friction between the men before the play was finished. Had Colman been guilty of such an outrage there would undoubtedly have been some mention of it in their correspondence. In the next place, as has been suggested, the charge of plagiarism falls to the ground (1) because Garrick was not in London during the production of *False Concord* (2) because Colman's plans for the play were conceived before *False Concord* was produced, and (3) because contemporary writers were silent in regard to any hint of plagiarism.

In regard to the play itself it is evident that the draft which has been quoted and that mentioned in Colman's letter of December 4, 1765, are one and the same, and that the conception of **The Clandestine Marriage** as a whole must be credited to Colman. The characters, also, with the exception of the Swiss valet, Canton, and his comrade Brush, owe their individuality largely to him.

The evidence all points toward Garrick's authorship of Act V and the levee-scene in Act II. If he was the author of these portions of the play, it is probable that he was at least largely concerned in the other scenes where Ogleby and Canton appear. Their dialogue is so distinctive and so unvarying that it could not well have been written by two hands. Apparently Garrick had more share in writing Act IV than he had had in writing the preceding acts, but it is clear from the letter of December 4 and a comparison of the play with the draft, that Colman should be given credit for much of the ground-work. Because of its connection with Act V, we may assume that the scene in which Melvil rallies Lovewell for his nocturnal wanderings is due largely to Garrick.

Further than this we cannot go. It would not be safe to assume that every departure from Colman's early plan is traceable to the superior stagemanship of Garrick. Act V, it is true, is the best act in the play, but Garrick was always at his best in short flights. Unlike Colman, he had not written any long original plays: he delighted in sketches, in re-

workings, in short adaptations. Yet in spite of these facts, in those portions of the play where there has been a definite shifting of scenes for dramatic effect, it is probable that Garrick's brain, if not his pen, was the determining factor in the change.

George Winchester Stone, Jr. (essay date 1934)

SOURCE: Stone, George Winchester, Jr. "Garrick's Long Lost Alteration of *Hamlet*." *PMLA* 49.3 (1934): 890-921. Print.

[*In the following excerpt, Stone discusses Garrick's highly controversial and much-disparaged alterations to* Hamlet. *Contrary to previous accounts of the play's contemporary reception, Stone provides evidence that Garrick's* Hamlet *was in fact hugely successful for Drury Lane.*]

One incident in the life of David Garrick—Shakespeare's Priest—has subsequently evoked the harshest kind of criticism even from his professed admirers, namely, his alteration of *Hamlet*. James Boaden, who prefaced an edition of the actor's letters in 1831 with a biographical sketch, wrote:

> If there be any one act of his management which we should wish to blot out from these pages it is his *rash violation of the whole scheme of Shakespeare's Hamlet . . . All the contrivances* of Shakespeare by which he added absence from the scene to the melancholy irresolution of the character *were rendered abortive*. It became as much a monodrame as *Timon;* and the passive Hamlet was kept on the rack of perpetual exertion. *His very speeches were trimmed up with startling exclamations and furious resolves:* even Yoric himself was thrown out of the play to render the wit and pathos of Sterne inapplicable and unintelligible. *It was an actor's mutilation of all parts but his own.*

Davies, Garrick's first biographer, gave a general view of this changed version in his *Dramatic Miscellanies,*[1] and remarked the injudiciousness of cutting out the Gravediggers, Osric, and the fencing match, of leaving the audience in suspense with regard to the fate of Ophelia, and of adding a new ending. Of this ending Boaden wrote: "All is written in a mean and trashy commonplace manner, and, in a word sullied the page of Shakespeare and disgraced the taste and judgment of Mr. Garrick."[2]

Isaac Reed, in his continuation of Dr. Baker's *Biographia Dramatica,* considered the Alteration made in the true spirit of Bottom the Weaver who wished to play not only the part assigned to him, but all the rest in the piece: "Mr. Garrick in short has reduced the consequence of every character but that represented by himself."[3]

Jesse Foot in his *Life of Arthur Murphy* printed an unpublished manuscript entitled *Hamlet with Alterations,* a dramatic satire directed by Murphy against Garrick. The whole is a parody of *Hamlet,* Act I. Shakespeare's ghost visits Drury Lane Theater and chides Garrick in the following manner:

GHOST:

> ... my works have made your fortune,
> And *Hamlet* brought to you the mere reciter,
> The organ of another's sense, more money
> Than ere it did to me who wrought the tale.
> Yet on my scenes by ages sanctified,
> In evil hour thy restless spirit stole
> With juice of cursed nonsense in an inkhorn
> And o'er my fair applauded page did pour
> A manager's distillment, whose effect
> Holds such an enmity with wit of man
> That each interpolating word of thine
> Annihilates the sense ...
> Thus was I ev'n by thy unhallow'd hand
> Of both my gravediggers at once dispatch'd,
> Cut off in the luxurience of my wit,
> Unstudied, undigested, and bemawled:
> No critic ask'd—but brought upon the stage
> With all your imperfections on my head!
>
> ....
>
> Attempt no more, nor let your soul conceive
> Aught 'gainst my other plays: I leave thee now
> To the just vengeance critics will inflict ...
>
> ....

GARRICK:

> ... His plays are out of joint,—O cursed spite
> That ever I was born to set them right.[4]

The younger Boswell in the Prologomena to his edition of Malone's *Shakespeare* printed what he supposed to be the ending of Garrick's Alteration in order to show how prevalent and how damning was the influence of French dramatic criticism in the eighteenth century.[5] He used as his text a 1703 player's quarto altered in the hand of William Hopkins, Garrick's prompter, entitled *Hamlet as Altered by David Garrick, Esq. 1777.*[6]

Genest sums up the adverse critiques, and then quotes from a letter by Benjamin Victor, treasurer of Drury Lane, to Tate Wilkinson, who wished to have a copy of Garrick's *Hamlet* to play at the York Theater, in which Victor writes:[7]

> It is not in my power to send you the corrections lately made in *Hamlet.* No such favor can be granted to anyone. I presume the play will never be printed with alterations, as they are far from being universally liked; nay they are greatly disliked by the million, who love Shakespeare with all his glorious absurdities, and will not suffer a bold intruder to cut him up.[8]

In 1868 Percy Fitzgerald wrote: "There was one act of folly in his life to which Garrick might look back with compunction. That was his famous and Gothic mutilation of *Hamlet,* the outrageous hewing to pieces of the noble play, which

seems inconceivable in one who had such reverence."[9] Again in 1886, prompted by finding in a London bookstore the supposed original alteration which he thought was given to Kemble by Mrs. Garrick, he contributed an article to the *Theater* attacking the "mutilation."[10] But what Fitzgerald had was the prompter's copy already referred to by Boswell and Boaden.[11]

In 1890 Frank A. Marshall, in his edition of the *Henry Irving Shakespeare,* inserted the following note: "In an evil moment it occurred to Garrick to try to improve this matchless tragedy. Happily this version was so indifferently received that he never ventured to print it."[12]

At the turn of the century Professor Lounsbury gave a long account of the alteration, based on Davies, Boaden, and Reed. He admitted that he had never seen a copy of the play, yet elaborated Reed's point that Garrick cut the subordinate characters in order to emphasize the importance of the title rôle.[13]

In a very stimulating book, *Garrick and his French Friends,* Dr. F. A. Hedgcock continued this tradition of criticism, calling the "travesty of *Hamlet*" the most celebrated of all Garrick's nefarious attempts on Shakespeare's pieces, and substantiating his points by quotations from Davies, Fitzgerald, and from one of Garrick's own letters.[14]

The impression given by this accumulation of criticism is bitter and, I am persuaded, unjust to Garrick both as a dramatist and as an admirer of Shakespeare. The reason for so much misapprehension is that the Alteration was never printed, and had never been seen in its true form by any of the commentators.[15]

Garrick's alteration was made sometime before December 18, 1772, when it first appeared on the stage at Drury Lane. That at one time he intended to print it is evident from his letter to M. De La Place, March 7, 1773, in which he wrote:[16]

> I should be glad to know what pieces you have of mine that I might compleat them—I shall collect them together next winter in four vols and then you shall see the full measure of my iniquity! My alteration of *Hamlet* is not yet printed, when it is you shall have it directly with the rest, *en attendant* till the whole shall be publish'd together ...[17]

Garrick had been planning this alteration for a long time, and, moreover, had been encouraged in the attempt by Dr. Hoadly[18] and George Steevens.[19] He realized that it was a bold undertaking, and that it would evoke unfavorable criticism, yet he persisted and was proud, in a way, of the result. He wrote to Sir William Young: "It was the most imprudent thing I ever did in my life; but I had sworn I would not leave the stage till I had rescued that noble play from all the rubbish of the fifth act. ... The alteration was received with general approbation, beyond my most warm expectations."[20]

There can be little doubt that one motivating factor in this alteration was the significance Garrick attached to French criticism. He wrote four letters to French friends in which he tried to impress upon them the success of his effort. On December 3, 1773, he wrote again to La Place:

> I am still upon the stage and am so flattered by my country's partiality to me, that I have not yet been able to retire—just before Christmas I appeared in the character of the young Hamlet, [Garrick was then fifty-seven], and received more applause than when I acted it at five and twenty. . . . I must tell you that I have ventured to alter *Hamlet* and have greatly succeeded; I have destroyed the gravediggers (those favourites of the people) and almost all of the fifth act—it was a bold deed, but the event has answered my most sanguine expectations: if you correspond with any of the journalists this circumstance will be worth telling, as it is a great anecdote in our theatrical history.[21]

The next day while this train of thought was still in his mind he wrote to Morellet:[22]

> I have play'd the devil this winter, I have dar'd to alter *Hamlet,* I have thrown away the gravediggers, and all the fifth act, and notwithstanding the galleries were so fond of them, I have met with more applause than I did at five and twenty—this is a great revolution in our theatrical history, and for which 20 years ago instead of shouts of approbation, I should have had the benches thrown at my head.

Contrary to the statements of the critics and in accord with Garrick's observations the Alteration was well received. It held the stage for eight years and was played thirty-seven times. In the previous eight years Shakespeare's *Hamlet* had been played but twenty-six times. Garrick received during his four remaining years on the stage £3426.14.10 for this alteration alone. Scarcely any other play brought in more box receipts. An average full house brought the managers £160. Garrick's first three performances of this altered version brought £284.5.6, £272, and £264.13. respectively.[23] It would seem that it was hardly lack of interest or receipts that made him perform it no more that season. I append the statistics with regard to this alteration gathered from the Treasurer's Books of Drury Lane.[24] The fact that it was such a valuable piece for the Drury Lane company was doubtless the reason that Garrick refused to print it or give it to Tate Wilkinson, who so greatly desired to have it in his repertoire that he imitated Garrick and made a new ending of his own to the play.[25]

I am glad to announce that Garrick's alteration of *Hamlet,* with notes, cuts, and emendations in his own hand, has at last come to light in the Folger Shakespeare Library. Its history from the time of the actor's death in 1779 until the opening of the Folger Library in 1933 shows why none of the critics had been able to consult the original.

After Garrick's death his library came into the hands of his wife, where this volume remained for forty-three years until her death in 1822. Her will, proved October 30 of that year by her executors, the Reverend Thomas Rackett and George Frederick Beltz, provided for certain legacies and stated that the residuary estate was to be sold, and the income from the profits given to Elizabeth de Saar, Mrs. Garrick's niece, during her life and to any of her grandchildren living at her death. In accordance with this provision the greater part of Garrick's library was sold at auction by Saunders in 1823. But the volume with which we are concerned, together with a number of other Garrick relics, was overlooked or considered of insufficient value to be included. The executors sometime after this left a box of relics in the hands of the solicitors Coulthurst and Van Sommer, 13 New Inn, Strand, to be sold. There the box remained with the names of Rackett and Beltz upon it until the year 1900 when the office at New Inn was to be pulled down, and the firm had to move into new quarters. The present Mr. Van Sommer of the firm Van Sommer, Chillcott, and Kitcat, found the box, recognized its value, which had increased considerably during the last eighty years of the nineteenth century, turned it over to the auctioneers Puttick and Simpson, who sold its contents, and sent the profits to Elizabeth de Saar's three grandchildren living at the time. Lot number 136 of the sale, including the alteration of *Hamlet,* was bought by Pearson for Mr. Folger, and the volume then changed its quarters from 13 New Inn to Mr. Folger's Brooklyn storehouse, where it remained until its transference in 1932 to the Folger Shakespeare Library in Washington.[26]

Now that through the kindness of the authorities of the Folger Library it has been made available for study, it is time that Garrick's character be vindicated on the basis of the Alteration itself.

The *Hamlet* that Garrick used as a foundation for his alteration is a duodecimo,[27] one of the many reprintings of the text of "the accurate Mr. Hughs." The nature and the history of this text are important for an understanding of Garrick's version.

At the beginning of the eighteenth century Betterton was the only Hamlet the London audience wished to see, despite the fact that he was an old man. He acted an altered version of *Hamlet* prepared by Sir William D'Avenant in 1676 from a 1637 quarto.[28] The first eighteenth-century issue of Betterton's version is a quarto printed in 1703 for Richard Wellington, etc., with the stage cuts indicated by inverted quotation marks. Betterton died in 1710, having played Hamlet for the last time at the Haymarket on September 20, 1709, when he was well over seventy years of age. Robert Wilks succeeded to the title rôle, which he had begun as early as January 15, 1708, at Drury Lane. Until his death in 1732 he was the accepted Hamlet of the London stage, although Booth and Powell occasionally played the part. Each great Hamlet, wishing to be distinctive in the character, has tried to improve or to change the method of his predecessor sufficiently to make his an individualized performance. Wilks changed the Betterton performance by restoring two notable passages that the earlier player had cut from the stage presentation; namely, the whole of the "Angels and Ministers of Grace defend us" speech, and Hamlet's words to the Players, "Speak the speech I pray you." He also was interested in a version of the play which was closer to the Shakespeare text than the D'Avenant alteration.

> Accordingly he sought the help of his friend Mr. John Hughs, and the result was an edition of the play printed in 1718 which may be called the Hughs-Wilks' *Hamlet*. The presumption is that Wilks dictated the cuts and that Hughs restored the text, for although some blots remain, yet in very many cases Hughs with a copy of Rowe's edition before him restored the old readings where Betterton and D'Avenant had unnecessarily departed therefrom. From Rowe he inserted part of the folio text which did not occur in the quartos. It cannot claim to be a good text judged by present-day standards, but for 1718 compared with what was then available it was no doubt an excellent work. Hughs edited this again, and it was finally printed in 1723 after his death. It is to this latter edition that Theobald refers in his *Shakespeare Restored* when he mentions the text of "the accurate Mr. Hughs." It ran into nineteen editions before 1761, and the subsequent ones developed a mass of printer's errors.[29]

After Wilks' death there were a number of Hamlets at the different theaters; but neither Ryan at Covent Garden, nor Giffard at Goodman-Fields, nor Mills, and subsequently Milward at Drury Lane, equaled their predecessors in the rôle of the Danish Prince. Although many generalizations have been written about their performances there is no evidence that they played any other than the Hughs-Wilks text. The year 1741 found Denis Delane as a rising young star in *Hamlet* at Drury Lane; but his presentation was quickly eclipsed by that of David Garrick, who almost immediately after his first appearance in the part in Ireland, August 12, 1742, became the accepted Hamlet of the English theater.

Garrick received many letters from friends and anonymous correspondents advising him of possible improvements in his performance of the part. He began with the Hughs-Wilks text, its cuts and its stage directions, then gradually revised his presentation and created his own text. He seldom allowed his texts and revisions to be printed. The close of the season of 1763, however, found him in poor health, suffering from a temporary period of unpopularity, and severely attacked by Fitzpatrick. He sought escape and rest in a journey to France, and took with him the resolution of never appearing on the stage again unless a two years' absence should prove a remedy for his unpopularity.[30] The theater was left in charge of George Colman. Inasmuch as Garrick in all probability would not play again, Colman allowed Garrick's acting text of **Hamlet** to be printed. This edition, issued by Haws and Company in 1763, materially differs from the Hughs-Wilks text. The cuts, instead of being marked for excision, are omitted, thus making a very short play. Some lines cut by Wilks are restored, others retained by him are eliminated by Garrick.[31]

Garrick returned from France in 1765 in fine spirits, went back to the stage, and was eminently successful. In 1772 he gave the altered version of *Hamlet* we are now discussing; but instead of using as a foundation for this alteration a copy of his own 1763 edition he employed the 1747 edition of the Hughs-Wilks text. A glance at this text makes clear his reason: he was not interested in merely leaving out the Grave-Diggers and Osric, as the critics suppose; having cut the greater part of the fifth act he had to restore almost as much in the preceding part of the play, and in restoring some six hundred and twenty-nine lines he succeeded in giving the eighteenth-century audience a new interpretation of almost all the characters in the play.

His own statement in an unpublished letter to Madam Necker tells accurately and concisely the formal changes that he made:

> It has been resolv'd that I shall perform the character of Hamlet tomorrow—the copy of the play you have got from the bookseller will mislead you without some direction from me—the first act which is very long in the original is by me divided into two acts—the third act, as I act it, is the second in the original—the third in the original is the fourth in mine, and ends with the famous scene between Hamlet and his mother—and the fifth act in my alteration consists of the fourth and fifth of the original with some small alterations, and the omission of some scenes, particularly the Gravediggers.[32]

Cuts in altered plays are, perhaps, worth more study than critics have heretofore given them. Those who have blamed Garrick for his omissions have neglected to mention the fact that each eighteenth-century stage version of Shakespeare has omitted many lines and even scenes. Would it not be fair, before Garrick is condemned, to review the cuts made by other actors, and to study his in relation to them?

Betterton cut entirely the characters Voltimand and Cornelius; the King's address to the Court in the first act; the advice of Polonius to Laertes, and a large portion of Laertes' advice to Ophelia; most of the "Angels and Ministers of Grace" speech; eleven lines of the Ghost's speech; the entire scene between Polonius and Reynaldo; thirty-eight lines of the first conversation with the Players; Hamlet's advice to the Players; twenty-three lines of the Mouse Trap; forty-seven lines of the scene between Hamlet and his mother after the death of Polonius; and Fortinbras's army, Hamlet's converse with the Captain, and the soliloquy so important in the development of Hamlet's character, "How all occasions do inform against me." These are but the major cuts. Many of the King's lines, as well as those of Rosencrantz and Guildenstern, Marcellus, and Horatio were also omitted.

This made for a much more swiftly-moving play, and, in the words of Dr. Hazelton Spencer, substantiates "the historical critic's view of Hamlet as the beau ideal of active young manhood rather than a dreamsick weakling pining for the ministrations of Freud."[33]

Wilks restored the "Angels and Ministers of Grace" speech and Hamlet's advice to the Players; cut out the Dumb Show, the Fortinbras ending; and in other respects, except for small changes, followed the Betterton version. And so the acting text remained (with the exception of the minor changes noted in Garrick's 1763 edition) for fifty years.

The theater-goers who had been accustomed to this interpretation saw from the stage of Drury Lane on December 18, 1772, a radically different play.

Inasmuch as Garrick's first act ended when Horatio and Marcellus plan to meet on the parapet the following night, all the speeches cut in the Betterton version had to be restored to give substance to an otherwise short and thin act. The act thereby gained numerous descriptive passages, and some purple patches, notably Horatio's lines on Rome:

> A little ere the mightiest Julius fell
> The graves stood tenantless and the sheeted dead
> Did squeak and gibber in the Roman streets . . .

With this restoration the subordinate characters become something more than mere puppets to start the show going. Ninety-four lines were restored, including the scene in which Cornelius and Voltimand are sent as ambassadors to Norway. It was necessary to return those men to the play because Garrick wished later to restore the soliloquy, "How all occasions do inform against me," which refers to the Fortinbras episode, and to the very material about which these men give us knowledge.

In Garrick's second act Laertes is allowed to speak twenty-eight more lines of advice to Ophelia, and Polonius is allowed fifteen lines of admonishment to his son for the first time in the century. Garrick's brain furnished him with two more. The description of Danish drunkenness is cut as usual. The whole of the Ghost's speech is restored, and the exclamation, "O horrible, most horrible," is given to Hamlet in order to break the length of the speech.[34] The Ghost only once urges Horatio and Marcellus to swear as Hamlet presents the hilt of his sword. Seventeen lines are here cut from the Hughs-Wilks version.

Garrick was deeply interested in the character of Polonius. One of the things which indicates that the old courtier is a part of the rotten morass which forms the Danish court is his sending Reynaldo to spy upon Laertes. This scene is here for the first time restored to Act Three, as is also the material relating to the Fortinbras sub-plot. As usual there is much excision in the conversation between Hamlet, Rosencrantz, and Guildenstern. The description of the Players is cut considerably, that part being omitted which in Shakespeare's time referred to the boy actors ("an Aery of children, little Eyases"), and the sole reason for the players' travelling is the change for the worse in the administration of Denmark under Claudius. In the earlier version the Players' speech concerning Pyrrhus and Priam had been cut almost entirely. Garrick restored twenty lines in order to give some point to Polonius's "This is too long." The earlier actors, perhaps, had taken the hint literally and applied the shears with vigor. Garrick gave the soliloquy, "O what a rogue and peasant slave am I," as Betterton gave it, except that he supplied *Wretch* for *rogue,* as had Wilks.

Inasmuch as the conspiracy between the King and Laertes was to be cut, Garrick was careful to restore each aside and speech in which the King displayed his character and the workings of his conscience.[35]

Garrick omitted the Dumb Show, but for the first time included the whole of the Mouse Trap play. This, especially the restoring of lines to the Player Queen, gives point to the line, "The lady doth protest too much, methinks." The conversation between the King, Rosencrantz, and Guildenstern, when the plot is first made to send Hamlet to England, is restored. The king's whole prayer, and Hamlet's meditation are retained, though they had been cut from Garrick's 1763 text. An appreciable number of lines is restored to the scene between Hamlet and his mother, especially such lines as show the state of Hamlet's emotional conflict.

I give only a brief discussion of Garrick's fifth act inasmuch as I append the act to this article, now for the first time printed entire and annotated. It seems quite certain that this is the text that Garrick planned to print. And his work in restoring little words and phrases such as *Metals* for *metal, Seas* for *Sea, the Wind at help* for *the Wind sits fair; repast them with my blood* for *relieve them with my blood,* using for his sources the scholarly apparatus that had been built up by 1772, and Johnson's edition chiefly, indicates that he was something more than a mere Harlequin player, as Lamb so thoughtlessly called him. It indicates also that he was interested in presenting to his audiences a more correct text than had been customary. A man whose interest was only in playing need not have bothered himself with such minute details, for with the rapidity with which words cross the footlights the essential correctness of small phrases passes unnoticed.

Garrick changed the text to the original reading in twenty cases, altered it in eleven, restored one hundred and seventeen lines, including the scene in which Hamlet soliloquizes, "How all occasions do inform against me," and introduced thirty-five of his own for an ending. To the King's part he restored thirty-eight lines; and to the Queen, Ophelia, Laertes, and a Gentleman he gave from one to seven lines more than they had hitherto spoken in the century.

There is here no evidence of Bottom the Weaver—an actor mutilating all parts but his own. With the exception of Osric and the Grave-diggers, every character in the play is made richer by restorations.

What now of the character of Hamlet? There is ample testimony from contemporary writers of the powerful effect of Garrick's Hamlet upon his audience. Lichtenberg saw him play the Prince in 1775, and remarked on the power of the conception. Garrick's Hamlet was no "sick weakling pining for the ministrations of Freud," nor was he the "beautiful flower" about which Goethe speaks. He was vital, he was active; and the inner workings of his mind, and the conflicts that faced the thinker driven on by deep and active emotions were apparently presented in an unforgettable manner. Such psychological delineation was Garrick's stronghold. It was what made him stand head and shoulders above his contemporaries in the characters of Richard III and Macbeth. And all the passages which he restored to the Danish Prince were those which showed the conflicts within Hamlet's being.

I find no evidence that Hamlet's speeches were "trimmed up with startling exclamations and furious resolves," and that he was "kept on the rack of perpetual exertion," if by that the critic means physical exertion. The ending is swift but it is not "trashy and commonplace."

The omission of the Grave-diggers and of Osric calls for comment. Garrick by his own statement was here bowing to the force of French criticism; and the French were pleased. On November 21, 1774, Mrs. J. Henrietta Pye wrote to Garrick:

> I imagine Mr. Pye told you I had been to pay a visit to Voltaire, where I met with a most gracious reception. We talked of your alteration of *Hamlet*, which he very greatly approves, and exprest himself very highly in your praise.[36]

In his caustic letter to the French Academy, August 25, 1776, Voltaire quoted Marmontel on the subject:

> M. Marmontel dans un de ses ouvrages en a félicité la nation anglaise. "On abrège tous les jours Shakespeare," dit-il, "on le châtie; le célèbre Garrick vient tout nouvellement de retrancher sur son théâtre la scène des Fossoyeurs, et presque tout le cinquième acte. La pièce et l'auteur n'en ont été que applaudés."[37]

The word "rubbish" is a harsh term to apply to the Grave-diggers, unless perchance the parts were made crudely farcical, as Professor Adams suggests they were,[38] the first digger divesting himself of half-a-dozen waistcoats to the eternal delight of the groundlings. He quotes from a letter of a French visitor in England in 1811; but a letter from Tom King to Tate Wilkinson October 12, 1796, seems to prove that no such thing was done on the eighteenth-century stage, or at least not within the forty-eight years during which King was associated with it.[39] So the English admirers of Garrick must in this case accept the fact that for once French theory overcame his English allegiance.

Garrick's last performance of **Hamlet** was on May 30, 1776. In the Drury Lane Record Book there is the following note relative to it:

> Pit and boxes were put together, most of the tickets were sold for a guinea apiece, very few under half a guinea, and the whole quantity sold in about two hours.

Garrick's **Hamlet** closed in a blaze of glory.

In 1774 Gentleman Smith had come to Drury Lane and had played the Garrick alteration twice to much smaller audiences than did Garrick himself. But with Garrick's retirement in 1776 the part fell to Henderson, who came to Drury Lane the following year. He had played the Hughs-Wilks *Hamlet* with success at Bath, but as long as Garrick lived the Garrick version kept the stage at Drury Lane. The 1703 quarto with alterations in the hand of Hopkins, and entitled *Garrick's Alteration of Hamlet, 1777,* is doubtless the copy from which Henderson played, and shows evidence of his trying to maintain in general Garrick's scheme, but at the same time of attempting to make his own additions and subtractions.

Henderson went to Covent Garden in 1779, and the part fell to young Bannister, who on April 21, 1780, returned the Grave-diggers to the stage; he restored, that is, the Hughs-Wilks *Hamlet*.[40] After that, according to Genest and Adolphus, Garrick's alteration was never called for. Kemble took up the play, and after some experimenting, produced in 1796 a version which has held the stage until today.

While Garrick was playing **Hamlet** he would not suffer his alteration to be printed or to be used at other theaters for the obvious reason that in it he had a gold mine for Drury Lane. But why he did not print it, as he apparently planned, after his retirement is another question. I find nothing in his correspondence bearing on this. Yet in his letters there is plenty of wrath expressed against Voltaire's *Letter to the Academy,*[41] and against all Frenchmen who criticised and seemed to misunderstand Shakespeare, and there is as much praise of Mrs. Montagu and her *Essay on the Genius and Writings of Shakespeare.*[42] It may be conjectured that after Voltaire's attack the qualms of conscience that struck him when he first altered *Hamlet* returned, and rendered him unwilling to print what at that particular moment would seem to make him recreant to the English and Shakespearian cause, and align him with the French neo-classical theorists.

In any event since the copy has after these many years finally come to light it may not be improper to reprint the last act as an example of alteration which is seldom found among the tamperers with Shakespeare. It is worth study, for in it Garrick has made an effective play, has lost as few "drops of that immortal man" as was consistent with his scheme, has restored hundreds of lines to enrich every part, has with care adopted Shakespeare's text in many cases, and has added but thirty-seven lines of his own.

A Comparison of Cuts in Acting Copies of *Hamlet*

Major Cuts	1703 Betterton	1723 Wilks	1737 Milward Ryan Mills	1747 Wilks	1763 Garrick	1772 Garrick's Alteration	
							Act I[43]
Marcellus' Christmas speech ...	entire	entire	entire	entire	entire	restored	
King's address I, ii.	25 ll.	25 ll.	25 ll.	25 ll.	25 ll.	restored	
Voltimand Cornelius ...	entire	entire	entire	entire	entire	restored	
Solid Flesh ...	10 ll.	13 ll.	12 ll.	13 ll.	4 ll.	11 ll.	
							Act II
Laertes' advice	26 ll.	26 ll.	26 ll.	26 ll.	26 ll.	restored	
Polonius' to Laertes ...	entire	entire	entire	entire	entire	restored 15 ll.; cut 11; added 2.	
Danish Drunkenness	22 ll.	22 ll.	22 ll.	22 ll.	22 ll.	22 ll.	
"Angels and Ministers of ..."	12 ll.	restored	retained	retained	retained	retained	
Ghost's speech.	11 ll.	16 ll.	15 ll.	16 ll.	12 ll.	restored	
			Act II[43]				Act III
Polonius to Reynaldo ...	entire	entire	entire	entire	entire	restored	
First speech to Players ...	38 ll.	38 ll.	38 ll.	40 ll.	40 ll.	20 ll.	
"Rogue and peasant slave."	25 ll.	22 ll.	22 ll.	22 ll.	11 ll.	22 ll.	
			Act III				Act IV
"Speak the speech."	entire	restored	retained	retained	retained	retained	
Dumb show ...	present	entire	entire	entire	entire	entire	
Mouse trap ...	23 ll.	39 ll.	39 ll.	39 ll.	38 ll.	restored	
Ham. as K. prays.	present	present	present	present	entire	present	
Ham. and mother ...	47 ll.	50 ll.	50 ll.	54 ll.	80 ll.	36 ll.	
			Act IV				Act V
Fort. and Ham. sol.							
"How all occasions."	entire	entire	entire	entire	entire Act V	changed Almost entire	
Fort. ending	present	entire	entire	entire	entire	entire	

Record of Performances of Garrick's Alteration of *Hamlet* December 18, 1772-April 21, 1780
(Gathered from Record Books of Drury Lane Theatre, in Possession of the Folger Shakespeare Library)

1772-73
    December:
        No. 68. Fry.   18. *Hamlet* £ 284.5.6
           70. Mon. 21. *Hamlet* £ 272././
           72. Wed. 23. *Hamlet* £ 264.13./

    February:
        No. 109. Wed. 10. *Hamlet* £ 268.13.6

1773-74
    February:
        No. 113. Tues. 8. *Hamlet* £ 287.12./

    May:
        No. 170. Fry.   6. *Hamlet* £ 261.11.6

Feb. 17, and May 26, **King
Lear** brought £286. It was the only play whose single performances brought in more than *Hamlet.*

Xmas Tale, author's n. £298.

Jane Shore £267././

Ev'y Man in h.h. [*Every Man in His Humour*] £267././

May 13. **Zara.** bt. £304././

May 19. **Lear.** bt. £300././

1774-75
    October:
        No. 8. Tues.   4. *Hamlet*   *Wonder* £266.14.6
                      Mr. Smith £ 135.5./   *Maid of Oaks* £263.14.6
    December: **Macbeth** £281.9.6
        No. 57. Fry.   2. *Hamlet* £ 264.1.6
            65. Mon.   12. *Hamlet* £ 259.6./
1775-76
    October:
        No. 18. Mon.   23. *Hamlet*   *Much Ado* £280.1
                      Smith, as usual . . .
                           £ 183.3./
    November:
        No. 50. Wed.   29. *Hamlet* £ 286.14.6   *Meas. for Meas.* £288.5
    December:
        No. 58. Fry.   8. *Hamlet* £ 276./.6   *Discovery* £283.6.6
    April:
        No. 159. Sat.   27. *Hamlet* £ 297.6.6   **Provok'd Wife** £286.10
    May:
        No. 184. Thurs. 30. *Hamlet* £ 85.3.   *Lear* £305.13.6
          Garrick's receipts   £3426.14.10
1776-77
        No. 16. Wed. Oct.   3. *Hamlet* £ 243.13.6   **Tempest, Macbeth, Cymbeline,**
                                            Way of the World, School for
                                            Scandal (May 8, 17) at some
                                            performances brought more than **Hamlet.**
           48. Sat. Nov.   30. *Hamlet* £ 106.11./
           72. Wed. Jan.   1. *Hamlet* £ 172.12./
           99. Mon. Feb.   3. *Hamlet* £ 157.11.6
          104. Sat. Feb.   8. *Hamlet* £ 105.10.6
          159. Mon. May   5. *Hamlet* £ 59.12.6
1777-78
        No. 5. Tues. Sept.   30. *Hamlet* £ 228.4./   *School for Scandal* most popular
                                              single play. Shakespeare out-topped
                                            other dramatists.
           7. Sat. Oct.   4. *Hamlet* £ 234.18./
           17. Thur. Oct.   23. *Hamlet* £ 204.11./
           25. Mon. Nov.   3. *Hamlet* £ 173.5./
           54. Sat. Dec.   6. *Hamlet* £ 145.7./
           71. Mon. Dec.   29. *Hamlet* £ 174.18.
          132. Tues. Mar.   17. *Hamlet* £ 160.19./
1778-79
        No. 2. Sat. Sept.   19. *Hamlet* £ 157.17.6.   *School for Scandal* most popular
                                              single play. *Trip to Scarborough*
                                            ran high once. Sh. clear ahead.
           14. Fry. Oct.   16. *Hamlet* £ 224.6/
           65. Tues. Dec.   15. *Hamlet* £ 220.11./
           87. Tues. Jan.   12. *Hamlet* £ 220.11./
          107. Sat. Feb.   6. *Hamlet* £ 150.17./
1779-80
        No. 4. Sat. Sept.   18. *Hamlet* £ 173.18.6   *School for Scandal; Critic.*
          21. Sat. Oct.   30. *Hamlet* £ 243.1.6   Sh. clear ahead.
                    (First night of *Critic*)
          D. L. receipts.   £ 3498.14.6
        148. Fry. Apl. 21, 1780 *Hamlet* restored by Bannister
                         £105././

Notes

1. III, 86.

2. *Life of Kemble* (1825), I, 110-113.

3. (London, 1782), II, 144. Charles Dibdin repeated much of this condemnation in a paragraph of criticism in his *Complete History of the English Stage* (London, 1800), V, 240.

4. *Life of Arthur Murphy* (London, 1811), pp. 252-274.—It is worth noting that at the time Murphy wrote this he was suffering from a fit of spleen brought on by Garrick's refusal to produce his play *Alzuma*.

5. (London, 1821), II, 691-695.

6. It is this version, too, that Boaden prints from in his life of Kemble.

7. (London, 1830), V, 343-350.

8. The complete letter is in Wilkinson's *Memoirs,* IV, 360.

9. *Life of David Garrick,* II, 288.

10. New Series, ed. by Clement Scott (May, 1886), pp. 252 ff.

11. Note 6, above.

12. VIII, Introduction, 12-13.

13. *Shakespeare as a Dramatic Artist* (1901), pp. 161-173.

14. English translation (N.Y., 1912), pp. 77-78.

15. Professor G. C. D. Odell alone, in his *Shakespeare from Betterton to Irving,* I, 385-390, refrains from passing judgment on a text he has not seen.

16. Unpublished MS. is in Folger Library, Case II, folder 4, 880.

17. I. Reed, *Biographia Dramatica,* II, 144, gives a further note on Garrick's intention to publish the Alteration.

18. Boaden, *Private Correspondence of David Garrick,* I, 514, 573.

19. *Ibid.,* 451.

20. Boaden, *op. cit.,* II, 126.—The date is January 10, 1773.

21. The original is in the Folger Library, Case I, folder 5, 786.

22. December 4, 1773. Unpublished. Folger Case I, folder 2, 1132.

23. *King Lear* alone that entire year brought in more receipts than *Hamlet*. Twice its amounts came to £286. The Drury Lane Record Books furnish a mine of reference material of this sort.

24. Records of performances, dates, and box receipts. Folger Library.

25. Printed in *The Wandering Patentee* (London, 1795), I, 166-173.—A comparison of the two will show, as Professor Odell suggests, that to Wilkinson's bombast Garrick's ending is simplicity itself.

26. It is my privilege here to acknowledge the aid I received from M. Seymour de Ricci, Mr. W. Roberts, Mr. W. Geoffrey Horsman, of Puttick and Simpson, and Mr. Van Sommer in tracing the location of this volume during the last one hundred and fifty-four years.

27. Printed in 1747, of 96 pages, bound in boards along with a copy of Beaumont and Fletcher's *Humorous Lieutenant.*

28. Hazelton Spencer, *Shakespeare Improved* (Cambridge, 1927), p. 175 ff.

29. I wish to thank Mr. Henry N. Paul for the use of this quoted material. It is from his unpublished article on the Hughs' *Hamlet.*

30. Fitzgerald, *Life of Garrick,* II, 113.

31. This text was issued again by Haws and Company, n. d., and by T. Whitford, 1765 (wrongly dated 1755), by Woodfall in 1767 and 1768. Richardson is supposed to have reprinted it in 1768 and again in 1770.—I am indebted to Mr. Henry N. Paul for this information.

32. Folger Library, Case I, folder 10, 1009.—This letter is undated, but according to Hedgcock, *op. cit.,* p. 344: "Madam Necker was amongst those who came to London in 1776 to witness the actor's last public appearances." I take it that the letter was written at that time by way of explanation of one of his last performances of Hamlet.

33. *Op. cit.,* p. 9.

34. This suggestion is often credited to Mrs. Montagu and to Dr. Johnson. It was given to Garrick, however, by the Reverend Peter Whalley in a letter, February 20, 1748. (Boaden I, 23, wrongly dated 1744.)

35. An example in point is the dialogue between Polonius and Ophelia, to which the King is also a party:

POL.:

 . . . 'tis too much proved that with Devotion's visage and pious action, we do sugar o'er the Devil himself.

KING:

 O 'tis too true. How smart a lash that speech doth give my conscience . . .

This part, which immediately precedes the soliloquy "To be or not to be," had been cut since the time of Betterton.

36. Unpublished, Folger Library, Correspondence IV, 34.

37. *Œuvres Complètes,* XLIX, 316 (1785).

38. J. Q. Adams, *A Life of William Shakespeare* (New York, 1923), p. 13.

39. Quoted in an article by Dr. W. J. Lawrence, *The Stage* (June 5, 1924).—The original letter is in the Folger Library.

40. Adolphus, John, Esq., *Memoirs of John Bannister* (London, 1839), I, 55-59.

41. August 25, 1776.

42. *An Essay on the Genius and Writings of Shakespeare,* compared with the Greek and French dramatic poets, with some remarks on the misrepresentations of Voltaire, L., 1769.

43. In this table the first column of act numerals refers to the acts as divided in the versions preceding the Alteration; the second column to act divisions in the Alteration.

Elizabeth P. Stein (essay date 1938)

SOURCE: Stein, Elizabeth P. "Social Satires" and "Preludes, Interludes, and Burlesques." *David Garrick, Dramatist.* New York: MLA, 1938. 23-65; 157-93. Print.

[*In the following essays, Stein offers a survey of Garrick's dramatic works arranged by genre. The first essay is devoted to afterpieces; the second deals with interludes, burlesque rehearsal plays, and a musical prelude. Stein offers a reading of each piece that attends to topical context, source texts, plot, and character while demonstrating Garrick's antagonism toward the conventions of the sentimental comedy then in vogue.*]

LETHE

Garrick's first play, *Lethe,* a one-act "dramatic satire," as he described it, was presented at Drury Lane April 15, 1740.[1] In form it is like the French *pièce à tiroir,* a play that has no definite plot but consists merely of a series of episodes, or in this instance studies of a group of characters that the dramatist wishes to hold up to ridicule. *Lethe* is based on James Miller's (1706-1744) *An Hospital for Fools* (1739), the plot of which may be briefly outlined as follows:

Mercury, by Jupiter's command, proclaims to all mortals afflicted with any sort of folly to betake themselves to Æsculapius who will render them aid without compensation of any kind. Receiving no response, Mercury asks that mortals bring friends, relatives, or acquaintances who are "troubled with Folly of whatever kind, . . . and they shall be cur'd without Fee or Reward." Immediately fools of all descriptions come crowding in upon Mercury and Æsculapius. There are old fools and young fools, niggardly fools and extravagant ones, philosophical fools, poetical fools, prosaic fools, and a foolish songstress. When Mercury reverses the order and calls for all the wise men "to range themselves upon the Right-hand, and distinguish themselves from the rest," the entire mob with the exception of one, Wiseman, flocks to the right side. It is Wiseman who now proposes to Æsculapius a method by which to distinguish the wise man from the fool. "[Call] those Men Wise, who know themselves to be Fools; and those Men Fools, who think themselves to be Wise."[2] "A Grand Dance of Fools" follows, after which Mercury sends all home as wise as they came.

When this dramatic trifle was produced, it was hissed off the stage merely because Miller, who had offended the Town with his play *The Coffee House* (1737), was its author. *Lethe* shows some indebtedness also to Vanbrugh's *Æsop* (1697), in which the old Greek philosopher is called upon by a number of his neighbors to help each of them, through his sage counsel, to carry out some selfishly ambitious plan. Finding, however, that the advice Æsop offers is contrary to their expectations, they refuse to accept it.

The flexibility of the framework of *Lethe* permitted Garrick not only to drop various characters that did not conform to popular taste, but, in later revivals, to add characters. The most interesting of these proved to be Lord Chalkstone, for the interpretation of which Garrick was famous. Chalkstone was the miniature presentment of the later celebrated Lord Ogleby in Garrick's and Colman's *The Clandestine Marriage.* The plot of Garrick's *Lethe* proceeds thus:

To commemorate the anniversary of his abduction of Proserpine, Pluto has, at her request, granted to all mortals who wish to forget their cares permission to drink of the waters of Lethe. Mercury is to conduct them to the Styx; Charon is to ferry them over to Elysium; and Æsop is to distribute Lethe's water to all those whose complaints justify their partaking of it. Charon grumbles over the new task set him by Proserpine, declaring that the difference in weight between souls and bodies renders his work too difficult. He promises, however, to relieve many mortals of their cares even before they reach Lethe by leaving "Half of 'em in the Styx." Mercury announces the arrival of some mortals who clamor for Charon to ferry them across to Elysium. Charon goes off to do the bidding of these, and Æsop asks Mercury to usher in the mortals as they arrive in the kingdom of shadows.

A Poet enters and tells his tale of woe. He wrote a play and dedicated it to a young nobleman, but before he "could taste of his Bounty," the "Piece was unfortunately damn'd."[3] He confides to Æsop that the failure of his play was due to the mutilation of it before its presentation upon the stage.

ÆSOP:

How so, pray?

POET:

Why, Sir, some squeamish Friends of mine prun'd it of all the Bawdy and Immorality, the Actors did not speak a Line of Sense or Sentiment, and the Manager (who writes himself)[4] struck out all the Wit and Humour, in Order to lower my Performance to a Level with his own.[5]

The Poet wishes to drink of the waters of oblivion to forget his unfortunate play, the ghost of which haunts him constantly. Æsop, however, informs him that, in drinking to the forgetfulness of his own play, he might, unfortunately, forget the works of others so that his next piece would in all probability fare even worse than the first.

ÆSOP:

Suppose you could prevail upon the Audience to drink the Water; their forgetting your former Work, might be of no small Advantage to your future Productions.

POET:

Ah, Sir! if I could but do that—but I am afraid—*Lethe* will never go down with the Audience.

ÆSOP:

Well, since you are bent upon it, I shall indulge you . . .[6]

And with a promise to remember Æsop in the preface to his next play, the Poet takes his leave of the old philosopher.

"Enter an Old Man supported by a Servant." Although he is over ninety and "has buried his wife and forgotten her long ago," this gentleman wishes to forget that he is some day to die and leave his money behind. Æsop informs him that the water has no power over matters of the future but only of the past. The philosopher, however, suggests his drinking of Lethe's water to forget that he has any money at all. The old miser is horrified at this suggestion, but compromises with Æsop. He agrees to drink to forget how he acquired his money if only his servant, who now knows of his master's strong-box, will drink to forget that money. The old Greek consents to this plan and bids the miser walk into the grove to rest himself until the waters are distributed.

A Fine Gentleman comes to drink of the waters of Lethe to forget two of his qualities, namely, his modesty and his good-nature. He wishes to overcome his modesty so that he can fare better than heretofore in his various *amours,* and as for his good-nature, he possesses so much of this quality that, whenever he is affronted by a man, he runs away. Æsop advises him "to drink to the forgetfulness of everything he knows."

FINE GENT.:

The Devil you would; then I should have travell'd to a fine Purpose, truly; you don't imagine, perhaps, that I have been three Years abroad, and have made the Tour of Europe?

ÆSOP:

Yes, Sir, I guess'd you had travell'd by your Dress and Conversation: But, pray, (with Submission) what valuable Improvements have you made in these Travels?[7]

The fop now proceeds to describe all that he has acquired through his travels on the Continent and concludes thus:

In short, I have skim'd the Cream of every Nation, and have the Consolation to declare, I never was in any Country in my Life, but I had Taste enough thoroughly to despise my own.[8]

In this Garrick holds up to ridicule those Englishmen who Gallicized and Italianized themselves to the extent of forgetting their native land. The dialogue which follows contains Garrick's criticism of the behavior of the gallants at the theatre. This has already been referred to.[9] The Fine Gentleman, impatient at Æsop's delay, threatens to throw him into the river and help himself to the water if he does not bottle some of it off for him. Æsop answers that he has no great inclination to put the Fine Gentleman's valor to the test and asks him to walk into the grove to wait his turn.

Having sent his satellite, Mr. Bowman, beforehand to announce his visit, Lord Chalkstone, the most interesting and amusing of all the characters with which Garrick has peopled this playlet, enters with great *éclat.* He does not desire any water of forgetfulness. He comes merely for a conversation with Æsop and to see the Elysian Fields. In this Chalkstone episode Garrick points out several prevailing follies of the time. The practice of wagering is satirized in these words of Chalkstone's:

Wagers are now-a-days the only Proofs and Arguments that are made Use of by People of Fashion: All Disputes about Politics, Operas, Trade, Gaming, Horse-racing, or Religion, are determined now by *Six to Four,* and *Two to One*; and Persons of Quality are by this Method most agreeably releas'd from Hardship of Thinking or Reasoning upon any Subject.[10]

On the question of marriage, Chalkstone, like a true gentleman of quality, believes in marriage of convenience. In relating his matrimonial experiences, Chalkstone states:

I married for a Fortune; she for a Title. When we both had got what we wanted, the sooner we parted the better—We did so; and are now waiting for the happy Moment, that will give to one of us the Liberty of playing the same Farce over again.[11]

Landscape gardening carried to extremes, as was done by "Capability" Brown, is ridiculed in the following words of the old lord's:

I came merely for a little Conversation with you, and to see your *Elysian* Fields here—[*Looking about through his Glass*] which by the bye, Mr. Æsop, are laid out most detestably—No Taste, no Fancy in the whole World!—Your River there—what d'ye call—

ÆSOP:

Styx—

LORD CH.:

Ay, Styx—why 'tis as strait as Fleet-ditch.—You should have given it a Serpentine Sweep, and slope the Banks of it.—The Place, indeed, has very fine Capabilities; but you should clear the Wood to the Left, and clump the Trees upon the Right: In short the Whole wants Variety, Extent, Contrast, and Inequality—[11]

After this little tête-à-tête with Æsop, Lord Chalkstone, supported by his valet and by Bowman, prepares to go into the grove to meet his nephew, the Fine Gentleman, whom he has espied gallanting, as he wagers, with some of the "Beauties of Antiquity—Helen or Cleopatra." Joyfully anticipating a little coquetry with these beauties, he leaves for the grove, but his valet's stepping on his gouty toes spoils this pleasure for him.

A newly married pair arrive, Mr. and Mrs. Tatoo, who ask for some of Lethe's water "to forget one another and to be unmarried again." Æsop informs them that the water cannot effect a divorce. Mrs. Tatoo confides to the old Greek that several of her friends have advised her to procure a "separate Divorcement" if she expects to be a fine lady. Already acquainted with the character of the fine gentleman, Æsop asks for a definition of a fine lady, and in the following account, Garrick satirizes this type.

MRS. TAT.:

A fine Lady, before Marriage, lives with her Papa and Mamma, who breed her up till she learns to despise 'em and resolves to do Nothing they bid her; this makes her such a prodigious Favourite, that she wants for Nothing.

ÆSOP:

So, Lady.

MRS. TAT.:

When once she is her Mistress, then comes the pleasure!—

ÆSOP:

Pray let us hear . . .

MRS. TAT.:

She lies in Bed all Morning, rattles about all Day, and sits up all Night; she goes every where, and sees every Thing; knows every body, and loves no body; ridicules her Friends, coquets with her Lovers, sets 'em together by the Ears, tells Fibs, makes Mischief, buys China, cheats at Cards, keeps a Pug-dog, and hates the Parsons; she laughs much, talks loud, never blushes, says what she will, does what she will, goes where she will, marries whom she pleases, hates her Husband in a Month, breaks

his Heart in four, becomes a Widow, slips from her Gallants, and begins the World again.—There's a Life for you; what do you think of a fine Lady now?[12]

Æsop advises the young woman to drink a large quantity of Lethe to forget her acquaintances.

A Frenchman, who has come to England "pour polir la Nation," enters upon the scene and asks Æsop for some twenty or thirty "Douzains" of Lethe's water to distribute among his creditors to make them forget his debts. Unless he obtains that quantity of water, he will be obliged to leave England before he has married the fortune of a certain English lady, who in turn is in love with his "Qualité and Bagatelles." Æsop proposes that he "marry the Lady" as soon as possible, pay off his "Debts with Part of her Portion, drink the Water to forget his Extravagance, retire with her to his own Country, and be a better Oeconomist for the future."[13]

FRENCH.:

Go to my own Contré!—Je vous demande Pardon, I had much rather stay vere I am;—I cannot go dere, upon my Vard.—

ÆSOP:

Why not, my Friend!

FRENCH.:

Entre nous, I had much rather pass for one French Marquis in Inglande, keep bonne Compagnie, manger des Delicatesse, and do no ting at all; dan keep a Shop en Provence, couper and frisser les Cheveux, and live upon Soupe and Sallade de rest of my Life.—

ÆSOP:

I cannot blame you for your Choice; and if other People are so blind not to distinguish the Barber from the fine Gentleman, their Folly must be their Punishment—and you shall take the Benefit of the Water with them.[14]

This episode hints at the Mascarille-Magdelon plot of Molière's Les Précieuses ridicules. The fact, however, that Garrick's Frenchman is a barber masquerading as a nobleman who is paying court to a wealthy Englishwoman brings this episode nearer to the La Roche-Mrs. Fantast plot of Shadwell's Bury Fair than to the one in Molière.

Much to Æsop's discomfort, another fine lady, the vulgar tradesman's wife, Mrs. Riot, makes her appearance. The character of this personage, the commotion she stirs up upon her entrance, and the amusements the ladies of quality of Garrick's day enjoyed, are excellently set forth in the dialogue of this episode.

MRS. RIOT:

A Monster! a filthy Brute! Your Watermen are as unpolite upon the Styx as upon the Thames.—Stow a Lady of Fashion with Tradesmens Wives and Mechanics.—Ah!

123

what's this? *Serbeerus,* or *Plutus!* [*seeing* ÆSOP] am I to be frighted with all the Monsters of this *internal* World![15]

Of course, by "Serbeerus" Mrs. Riot means Cerberus, and she speaks of the "internal" instead of the infernal world. She calls Charon "Scarroon" and threatens to "die with temerity" if she sees any more ugly creatures in the nether regions. She considers herself "the very *Quincettence* and *Emptity* of a fine Lady" and informs Æsop that she has an "Anecdote" to counteract any of the poisons in his receipts for the vapours. In the mispronunciation of her words Mrs. Riot anticipates Mrs. Heidelberg in Garrick's and Colman's **The Clandestine Marriage,** and in her misuse of them she heralds the approach not only of Mrs. Heidelberg but also of the better known Mrs. Malaprop.

In the conversation between Mrs. Riot and Æsop Garrick touches upon a number of absurdities in the life of the people of fashion. The pleasures enjoyed by the *beau monde,* particularly by the fine lady, are here given in greater detail than in the Mrs. Tatoo episode. Garrick also takes occasion to thrust a passing hit at Italian opera. For instance, Mrs. Riot says to Æsop:

> Shew me to the glittering Balls, enchanting Masquerades, ravishing Operas, and all the polite Enjoyments of *Elysian.*

ÆSOP:

> This is a Language unknown to me, Lady.—No such fine Doings here, and very little good Company (as you call it) in *Elysium.*—

MRS. RIOT:

> What! no Operas! eh! no *Elysian* then! [*Sings fantastically in Italian.*] 'Sfortunato Monticelli! banished *Elysian,* as well as the *Hay-Market!* Your Taste here, I suppose, rises no higher than your *Shakespears* and your *Johnsons*; oh you *Goats* and *Vandils!* in the Name of Barbarity take 'em to yourselves, we are tir'd of 'em upon Earth.—[16]

Mrs. Riot laughs at Æsop's even supposing that she had any cares to forget, but upon second thought the lady decides that she has one great care that she wishes to drown in the waters of oblivion, and that is her husband.

ÆSOP:

> I thought, Madam, you had Nothing to complain of.—

MRS. RIOT:

> One's Husband, you know, is almost next to Nothing.[17]

Mrs. Riot then gives an account of her nightly revels and concludes her narration with a song, an invitation to the card table. Mrs. Riot was played by the inimitable Kitty Clive (1711-1785), one of the greatest comic geniuses of the English stage, an actress who excelled particularly in broad comedy parts.

A drunken man (Mrs. Riot's husband) and his tailor are the next solicitors for Lethe's water, but after a conversation with Mr. Riot, Æsop discovers that his fables were written to very little purpose. All mortals are finally summoned from the grove to appear before Æsop, who, in true eighteenth-century manner, preaches the moral of the play. He asks them "to drink to the Forgetfulness of Vice.—"

> 'Tis *Vice* alone disturbs the human Breast;
> Care dies with Guilt; be virtuous, and be blest.[18]

As in Miller's *An Hospital for Foods* so in Garrick's **Lethe,** there is scarcely any plot, but Garrick's is by far the brighter little piece. When compared with the dialogue of Garrick's play, Miller's seems dull. Garrick's is vivacious and fairly bubbling over with fun. His characterization shows him to have had a good knowledge of human nature. His satire is keen but not cutting. It is tempered with humor and kindliness. His aim is not to lash but to laugh out of fashion the foibles of society.

When **Lethe** was produced for the first time in 1740, the account of the life of the fine lady was given in a song, instead of in prose as in the later versions of this play. John Payne Collier (1789-1883), who had access to the Larpent Manuscripts (the MS. copies of the plays sent to the Lord Chamberlain from 1737 to 1824) and had seen, as he states, the 1740 manuscript of **Lethe,** introduced this song into his account of this play in *The New Monthly Magazine.*[19] This 1740 version, Collier informs us, included a character which the later versions (except the one produced in 1741) omitted, that of an attorney who wishes to forget his gratitude to a benefactor in distress. This episode is somewhat heavy and too decidedly didactic. It lacks the sprightliness and humor of the rest of the piece, and it is probably for this reason that Garrick abandoned it.

In 1741 a Frenchman and an Irishman were added to the list of *dramatis personæ,* but the Irishman was soon dropped and not included again in the play until 1772. In the 1749 version Garrick presented three additional characters—the Poet, the Old Man, and the Tailor. In 1756 Garrick introduced Lord Chalkstone, and on January 11, 1772, **Lethe** was revived with "two additional characters, viz., a *Fribble,* played by Mr. Dodd[20] and an *Irishman* by Mr. Moody," who performed all the Irish characters at Drury Lane. The Fine Gentleman was omitted in this performance, and "Mr. Tatoo was changed to a horsegrenadier."[21] **Lethe** was first published in 1749, although it had appeared surreptitiously in 1745, while Garrick was playing in Dublin. In the *dramatis personæ* of the 1749 edition of **Lethe,** we find that the characters of the Poet, the Frenchman, and the Drunken Man were taken by Garrick. Later he relinquished the playing of these parts for the rôle of Lord Chalkstone. In 1777, a year after his retirement from the stage, Garrick was invited to read his **Lethe** before the King and Queen. For this occasion, Collier tells us, Garrick added an entirely new character, a Jew, but his reading was so coldly received at court that he never again attempted to read before royalty.

Lethe was one of Garrick's most successful afterpieces. Apart from the fact that the characters here are excellently depicted and the situations in which they appear highly amusing, *Lethe* becomes important also for the fact that it provided characters and situations for later Garrick plays. Particularly is this true of Lord Chalkstone, who served as the model for his more famous kinsman, Lord Ogleby, in Garrick's and Colman's *The Clandestine Marriage.* The Chalkstone episode furnished a good part of the material for the Ogleby garden scene. Moreover, Bowman is the prototype for Ogleby's cajoling valet, Canton, and Mrs. Riot, as has already been pointed out, is the forerunner of Garrick's Mrs. Heidelberg and also of Sheridan's Mrs. Malaprop. Thus *Lethe* proved useful as well as popular.

LILLIPUT

Another satire, somewhat more serious in tone than *Lethe,* a seriousness that the dramatist caught from his source material is *Lilliput,* a one-act comedy of manners, founded on incidents in the fifth, sixth, and seventh chapters of the first part of Swift's *Gulliver's Travels.* Garrick entered particularly well into the mood that dominates the Lilliput portion of Swift's tale and carried it over successfully into his play. In details of background and in general tendencies he follows the original implicitly. Also the characters, in their journey from Swift's story into Garrick's play, do not undergo changes. They retain the traits, temperaments, and pettinesses that are theirs in the original story. The dramatist does, however, deviate in several respects from the narrative. Gulliver, for instance, both in the tale and in the play is the proud recipient of the title of nardac, but whereas in the original we are told that the honor is conferred upon the hero for his prevention of an invasion of the Blefuscudians into Lilliput, in the play the reason for the bestowing of the title is not mentioned. Garrick also omits the entire episode of the fire in the apartments of the Lilliputian empress, as he does, too, Swift's discussion of the laws and customs of her subjects as well as the recital of the manner in which they educate their children. Throughout the Gulliver episodes Garrick, because of his more limited scope, gives us in lesser detail than does Swift the hero's mode of living in the diminutive kingdom.

The most important change by Garrick occurs in his retelling of that part of the story which concerns Lady Flimnap. First of all, the high admiral Bolgolam, who in the original tale bears no kinship to Lady Flimnap, becomes in Garrick's play a brother of hers. The dramatist also provides her with another brother in the person of Fripperel, a fine gentleman, who has no counterpart in Swift's story. Lady Flimnap herself is converted into a fashionable lady of quality of Garrick's own day. In the original narrative Gulliver vindicates the reputation of this "excellent lady," of whom Lord Flimnap, the treasurer of Lilliput, "took a fancy to be jealous." Some malicious persons had informed the husband that, to quote Gulliver's words:

> her grace had taken a violent affection for my person; and the court scandal ran for some time, that she once came privately to my lodging. This I solemnly declare to be a most infamous falsehood, without any grounds, further than that her grace was pleased to treat me with all innocent marks of freedom and friendship. I own she came often to my house, but always publicly, nor ever without three more in the coach, who were usually her sister and young daughter, and some particular acquaintance: but this was common to many other ladies of the court.[22]

In the preface to his *Lilliput,* which Garrick introduced in the form of a letter to his publisher, Paul Vaillant, and which, in order to avoid detection and, hence, abuse from critics and fellow-playwrights, he signed fictitiously "W. C.," the dramatist discusses the change he made in the Lady Flimnap episode of the original story. "W. C.," the friend of a Mr. Jacob Wilkinson, "an old Gentleman" who was an "Intimate of Gulliver's," informs us that this Mr. Wilkinson frequently related to him "many Anecdotes of his Friend," and particularly late one summer's night Mr. Wilkinson narrated to a group of four fellow-members of the *Sunday* Evening Club, "W. C." among them, "the following curious Circumstance."

> My good Friend the Captain (said he, with some Emotion) protested to me, upon his Death-Bed, that tho' he was a great Traveller, and a Writer of Travels, he never published but one Falsehood, and that was about the Lady *Flimnap.* He acknowledged, that notwithstanding his Endeavours to justify her Innocence in his Book, she had really confessed a Passion for him, and had proposed to elope with him, and fly to *England*; and as he thought the Knowledge of this Fact, which lay heavy upon his Conscience, could not, after so long a Time, sully the Honour of the *Flimnap*-Family, he begg'd of me to publish it to the World—I have obey'd my Friend's Command in Part—I have told it in Conversation to a Multitude of People; but I think it also incumbent upon me to print it—Pray give me your Opinion, Gentlemen, in what Manner shall I usher it into the World?[23]

After the four had suggested their plans, "W. C.'s" proposal that the story of Gulliver's resisting Lady Flimnap's advances be cast into dramatic form was agreed upon as the best, and he was, moreover, urged by Mr. Wilkinson to undertake the writing of it.

Lady Flimnap's violent love for the English "man-mountain," Garrick's own version of the Gulliver-Lady Flimnap relationship, serves as the nucleus around which he builds his entire playlet. Besides, it is this enormous passion which the Lilliputian lady manifests for the foreign monster, and Lord Flimnap's subsequent demand that Gulliver satisfy his honor, that become in Garrick's play the cause for Gulliver's escape from Lilliput. As in Swift's story, the "man-mountain" in the play seeks refuge from the irate Lilliputians among the latter's enemy, the Blefuscudians.

In the Lady Flimnap episodes of his piece, Garrick protests against the utter disregard of the sanctity of the marriage vows and the laxity of morals in general prevalent among the members of the *beau monde*. Except for the character of Gulliver, which was played by Bransby, one of the members of Garrick's company, the piece was presented by a company of child players at Drury Lane on Friday, December 3, 1756.[24] The plot proceeds as follows:

Lord Flimnap, one of the most powerful noblemen in Lilliput, suspects his wife of carrying on an intrigue with the monster, Gulliver. To assist and advise him as to his future procedure with his wife and her lover, Lord Flimnap sends for her ladyship's brothers, Fripperel, a fine gentleman, who heartily approves of his sister's doings, and Bolgolam, lord high admiral of the Lilliputian navy and lover of honor and virtue. Fripperel chooses to have no hand in the counseling of his brother-in-law and leaves him with the admiral in order to attend the ceremonies in honor of Gulliver's attaining the title of nardac of the kingdom. The sound of the trumpets, which announce the mustering of the guards for the procession, breaks up the conversation between Flimnap and Bolgolam. Left alone, Flimnap indulges in a soliloquy. This one as well as the one with which Flimnap opens the play savor very strongly in tone and substance of the first soliloquy (I, i) of Sir John Brute (*The Provok'd Wife,* 1697), a character which was a great favorite with Garrick and one which he very frequently interpreted. Part of Flimnap's soliloquy runs to this effect:

> . . . why shou'd I disturb myself about my Lady's Conduct, when I have not the least Regard for my Lady herself?— However, by discovering her Indiscretions, I shall have an Excuse for mine; and People of Quality shou'd purchase their Ease at any Rate.

And true to the Restoration code of love and social behavior, which did not recognize or tolerate jealousy, this Lilliputian rake concludes:

> Let Jealousy torment the lower Life,
> Where the fond Husband loves the fonder Wife,
> Ladies and Lords should their Affections smother,
> Be always easy, and despise each other:
> With us no vulgar Passions should abide;
> For none become a Nobleman but—Pride.
>
> [*Exit.*][25]

Lady Flimnap now enters with Fripperel, who discloses to her the contents of a *billet-doux* sent to her husband by his mistress. They arrange to have Flimnap receive this letter when in their company, so that they can observe his behavior upon his perusal of it. Lady Flimnap then confides to her brother her love for Gulliver. Fripperel cannot understand her taste, but "so much the better; for I wou'd have a Woman of Quality always a little incomprehensible."[26] These two also leave to attend the ceremonies in honor of Gulliver.

The next important scene takes place in a room of Gulliver's house. Here Lady Flimnap comes to wish Gulliver joy of the honors which he has received. She declares her love for him, but when he slights her, plans to avenge herself on him. Flimnap, Bolgolam, and Fripperel enter at this moment. Lady Flimnap explains to her husband that it was curiosity that brought her to the monster's dwelling. She informs him also that Gulliver had evil designs upon her and even proposed taking her away with him to his own country. Flimnap thereupon demands reparation for his sullied honor. He draws his sword upon Gulliver, who, however, demands a public trial. Flimnap promises to summon him before the king and the peers to answer for the wrongs he had done him. As Gulliver's noble visitors are about to take leave of him, a letter is brought to Flimnap. The contents of this greatly disturb him. Lady Flimnap now discloses to her lord the fact that she knows of his intrigue with the lady of the letter; whereupon Flimnap confesses his guilt. During this altercation between husband and wife, Gulliver makes his escape, and when his flight is discovered, he is already far out at sea. Lord and Lady Flimnap agree to permit each other to follow personal inclinations as people of rank and fashion should do. Bolgolam is horrified at the conduct of his sister and her husband. Fripperel, the fine gentleman, however, has this to say of the entire matter:

> A queer Dog my Brother [Bolgolam] is, that's positive— But come—let me once again join your Hands upon this your second happier Union—
>
> Let Love be banish'd—We of Rank and Fashion, Should ne'er in Marriage mix one Grain of Passion.[27]

To which Lord Flimnap adds:

> Let low-bred Minds be curb'd by Laws and Rules,
> Our higher Spirit leaps the Bounds of Fools;
> No Law or Custom shall to us say nay;
> We scorn Restriction—*Vivè la Liberté.*[28]

Not only does Garrick voice here his objections to the frivolity, loose morals, and distorted views on marriage of the fashionable folk; but again, as in **Lethe,** he takes the opportunity to hold up to scorn the fine gentleman of the day. In the following dialogue between Flimnap and Bolgolam, who, as the commentator in the play, gives expression to Garrick's sentiments, the dramatist presents the eighteenth-century beau.

BOLGOLAM:

> *He* [FRIPPEREL] advise you! What can he advise you about! He was bred to nothing but to pick his Teeth, and dangle after a Court: So, unless you have a Coat to lace, a Feather to choose, or a Monkey to buy, *Fripperel* can't assist you.

FLIMNAP:

> But he is the Brother of my Wife, Admiral.

BOLGOLAM:

> So much the worse for her and you too, perhaps—If she has listened to him, I shan't be surprised that you have a

bad Time of it: Such Fellows as he, who call themselves fine Gentlemen, forsooth, corrupt the Morals of a whole Nation.[29]

Flimnap, who is himself a fine gentleman, cannot quite tolerate this criticism of the beaux. "Indeed, Admiral, you are too severe." To which Bolgolam retorts:

> Indeed, my Lord *Flimnap,* I speak the Truth—Time was when we had as little Vice here in *Lilliput* as any where; but since we imported Politeness and Fashions from *Blefuscu,* we have thought of nothing but being fine Gentlemen; and a fine Gentleman, in my Dictionary, stands for nothing but Impertinence and Affectation, without any one Virtue, Sincerity, or real Civility.

FLIMNAP:

> But, dear Brother, contain yourself.

BOLGOLAM:

> 'Zounds! I can't—we shall be undone by our Politeness— Those cursed *Blefuscudians* have been polishing us to destroy us—While we kept our own rough Manners, we were more than a Match for 'em; but since they have made us fine Gentlemen—we don't fight the better for't, I assure you.[30]

By Blefuscu Garrick, like Swift, of course, means France.

Garrick put his scene of action in Lilliput so that he could the better ridicule the follies and vices of London's ladies of quality. In his epistolary preface, he states in mirthful mockery:

> Many, you tell me, think the Performance too *satyrical* upon the Ladies—of *Lilliput,* I hope they mean—for I defy any of the Objectors to produce me a Woman of Fashion of their Acquaintance, who has any Follies in common with those in the following Piece; the Ingredients that compose the Ladies of the two Nations are as different ... as those which are to be found in the Powders of Dr. *James,* and those of the late Baron *Schwanberg.*[31]

In Lady Flimnap's conversation with Gulliver, the fashionable view on the rights and privileges of a woman of quality regarding her household duties is thus set forth:

LADY FLIMNAP:

> Bless me! how different People are in different Nations! I must confess to your Lordship, tho' I have some Children, I have not seen one of them these six Months; and tho' I am married to one of the greatest Men in the Kingdom, and, as they say, one of the handsomest, yet I don't imagine that I shall ever throw myself into a Fit of Sickness, by too severe an Attention to him or his Family.

GULLIVER:

> What a profligate Morsel of Nobility this is! [*Aside.*] I must own your Ladyship surprizes me greatly; for in *England* I have been so much used to see the Ladies employ'd in Matters of Affection and Oeconomy, that I cannot conceive, without these, how you can possibly pass your Time, or amuse yourself.

LADY FLIMNAP:

> What! are not tormenting one's Husband, and running him into Debt, tolerable Amusements!—It is below a Woman of Quality to have either Affection or Oeconomy; the first is vulgar, and the last is mechanic ...[32]

The mob scene, a Shakespearean device which Garrick, like the Elizabethan dramatist, employs to present the views of the ordinary man, shows the Lilliputians deploring the vast amount of food consumed by the giant. They fear that, unless Gulliver leaves the kingdom, his Gargantuan appetite will bring on famine. In the dialogue that follows is found Garrick's criticism of party quarrels and the pettiness of these. Moreover, the privileges that persons of quality either enjoyed, or took unto themselves in the belief that their rank carried those with it, are laughed at in bits of dialogue such as this:

LALCON:

> [*to* GULLIVER] It wou'd be Death to disturb you now—by our Laws no-body can make free with a Lord, but your Lordship may make free with any Body.[33]

Lalcon, the Chamberlain, announces to Gulliver that the tailors, who for six weeks had been working on the newly created nardac's ceremonial robes, have now brought their bills and hope for his lordship's "indulgence, for the sake of their Wives and Families."

GULLIVER:

> I am so much fatigu'd, that I must desire 'em to give me till Tomorrow, and assure them, that notwithstanding my Titles and Privileges, I shall give 'em very little Trouble.[34]

The playlet was well acted by the company of children, whom Garrick had instructed. Murphy, the biographer of Garrick, declares that "the parents of not less than a hundred were most liberally rewarded." With reference to this, the dramatist, at the close of his epistolary preface, explains that if the play was "the Means of helping so many poor Children (as you tell me are employ'd in the Piece) to some Mince-Pies this *Christmas,* tho' your printed Copies of it should be found at the Bottom of 'em, I shall not think that I have spent some leisure Hours unprofitably."[35]

Lilliput, with alterations by Garrick and a "burlesque pageant in the characters of cards, Gulliver appearing as the knave of Clubs,"[36] was produced on May 15, 1777.[37] On this occasion it served as the afterpiece to *The English Merchant,* the play with which George Colman, after securing the Haymarket Theatre from Samuel Foote, opened that playhouse under his own management.

THE MALE-COQUETTE

The two-fold purpose of this little comedy of manners, which was first called **The Modern Fine Gentleman,** but whose title, after the second performance, was changed to **The Male-Coquette,** is thus set forth in the introductory notice:

> The following Scenes were written with no other View than to serve Mr. *Woodward* last Year at his Benefit; and to expose a Set of People, (the *Daffodils*) whom the Author thinks more prejudicial to the Community, than the various Characters of *Bucks, Bloods* [rakish gallants], *Flashes* [blusterers], and *Fribbles* [effeminate gallants], which have by Turns infected the Town, and have been justly ridicul'd upon the Stage. He expects no Mercy from the Critics.[38]

This play, as Garrick continues to inform us, was planned, written, and acted in less than a month. It was produced at Drury Lane Thursday, March 24, 1757.[39] The following is the plot:

Sophia is beloved by Mr. Tukely, but she has set her heart upon Daffodil, the Male-Coquette. To find out whether this Daffodil is the wretch he is reported to be, Sophia assumes male attire, introduces herself to Daffodil as an Italian nobleman, "Il Marchese di Maccaroni," and is, moreover, successful in obtaining a second interview with him wherein she determines to probe his integrity to its fullest extent. So successful is Sophia's disguise that even Mr. Tukely fails to recognize her until she discovers herself as well as her plan regarding Daffodil to him. Here Garrick introduces a delightful bit of humor, and at the same time a hit at the affectations that young Englishmen acquired during their "grand tour." Sophia addresses herself to Tukely with all the familiarity and impertinence at the command of a fine gentleman. Tukely is amazed.

TUKELY:

> I don't understand this!

SOPHIA:

> I presume, Sir, you never was out of *England*—
> [*Picking her Teeth.*]

TUKELY:

> I presume, Sir, that you are mistaken—I never was so foolishly fond of my own Country, to think that nothing good was to be had out of it; nor so shamefully ungrateful to it, to prefer the Vices and Fopperies of every other Nation, to the peculiar Advantages of my own.[40]

Tukely informs Sophia that he has asked five ladies to meet him at Widow Dampley's. To each of these, as to Sophia, Daffodil has "presented his heart." Arabella, Sophia's cousin, believes Daffodil to be as faithful a lover as he is an accomplished gentleman, and she chuckles over the thought of how dumbfounded all of them will be when they discover that he has artfully pretended a regard for them to conceal his real love for her.

In the next scene we are ushered into Daffodil's apartment. We now learn of his long list of women admirers, all of whom he pretends to love. His greatest pleasure, in fact his

aim in life, is to be known as a man of many *affaires de cœur.* But Ruffle, his valet, does not understand this sort of pleasure.

RUFFLE:

> I don't understand it—What do you intend to do with 'em all? Ruin 'em?

DAFFODIL:

> Not I, faith.

RUFFLE:

> But you'll ruin their Reputations.

DAFFODIL:

> That's their Business—Not mine.

RUFFLE:

> Will you marry any one of 'em?

DAFFODIL:

> O, no; that wou'd be finishing the Game at once—If I preferr'd one, the Rest wou'd take it ill; so because I won't be particular, I give 'em all Hopes, without going a Step further.

RUFFLE:

> Widows can't live upon such slender Diet.

DAFFODIL:

> A true Sportsman has no Pleasure but in the Chace; the Game is always given to those who have less Taste, and better Stomachs.[41]

In Daffodil, therefore, we have the typical Restoration rake who is ever ready for the pursuit.

Apart from his various *amours,* the horse-races also play an important rôle in Daffodil's small life. Ruffle enters laden with cards and messages.

RUFFLE:

> There's the Morning's Cargo, Sir.
> [*Throws 'em down upon the Table.*]

DAFFODIL:

> Heigh Day! I can't read 'em in a Month; prithee, *Ruffle,* set down my Invitations from the Cards, according to their Date, and let me see 'em Tomorrow Morning—So much Reading wou'd distract me.

RUFFLE:

> And yet these are the only Books that Gentlemen read Now-a-Days.
> [*Aside.*][42]

Daffodil then orders that the "Marchese di Maccaroni" be admitted whenever he calls.

DAFFODIL:

> Where is my List of Women, *Ruffle,* and the Places of their
> Abode, that we may strike off some, and add the new
> Acquisitions?

RUFFLE:

> What, alter again! I wrote it out fair but this Morning—
> There are quicker Successions in your Honour's List, than
> the Court-Calendar.

DAFFODIL:

> Strike off Mrs. *Dotterel,* and the Widow *Damply.*[43]

And as Ruffle strikes these ladies off the list, Mrs. Dotterel
is announced. Daffodil asks Ruffle to admit her but orders
him also to admit anyone else who calls, regardless of Mrs.
Dotterel's presence. After an unsuccessful *tête-à-tête* with
Daffodil, Mrs. Dotterel denounces him as a deceiver. Hearing someone approach, Daffodil throws himself on his
knees before her and declares in most ardent terms his
love for her. In this attitude the "Marchese di Maccaroni"
finds them. Mrs. Dotterel leaves.

In the course of her conversation with Daffodil, Sophia
discovers his attitude toward women; to trifle and to
make love to them amuses him, particularly to her and to
her cousin. The Marchese asks for an introduction to some
of his lady-loves. At this moment a letter, which Sophia
has written to him as from the country, is brought to him.
Daffodil thereupon proposes to acquaint the Marchese
with two fine girls—

> Cousins, who live together; this is a Letter from one of
> 'em, *Sophia* is her Name—I have address'd 'em both, but
> as Matters become a little serious on their Side, I must
> raise a Jealousy between the Friends; discover to one the
> Treachery of the other; and so in the Bustle steal off as
> quietly as I can.[44]

But Daffodil is determined, before he brings this about, to
introduce the Marchese at the club where he will meet
more "men of figure and fashion." As Daffodil goes off
to dress for the club, he directs the Marchese into his study,
where, he informs him, he will find a "guitar and some
Venetian Ballads," or, if he prefers, some "Infidelity and
Bawdy Novels" with which to while his time away.

Tukely forms a plan to expose Daffodil's double-dealing to
a number of women, all of whom are victims of Daffodil's
duplicity. They meet at Widow Damply's house, whither
Sophia, having refused to accompany Daffodil to the club,
also comes. There she meets Tukely, whom she now consents to marry. She offers also to assist him in exposing
Daffodil and proposes that he introduce her to the ladies
with whom, she promises, she will cut as fine a figure as
ever Daffodil did. Arabella still clings to the belief that
Daffodil is strongly attached to her and "when Daffodil's
real Inclinations are known, how those poor Wretches will
be disappointed."

In the next scene Garrick gives a graphic picture of the
proceedings at a fashionable gentlemen's club. Here the
practice of wagering is vigorously attacked. To ridicule
this custom among the gentlemen of the *beau monde,*
Garrick introduces the following:

> Lord *Racket* has betted 70 Pounds to 50, with the Hon-
> ourable *George Daffodil*—that the Latter does not walk
> from *Buckingham-Gate,* to the *Bun-house,* at *Chelsea*—
> eat a Bun there, run back to the Turnpike, and from thence
> hop upon one Leg, with the other tied to the Cue of his
> Wig, to *Buckingham-Gate* again, in an Hour and Half.[45]

The gentlemen at the club are more than certain that Daffodil will lose the wager. "Consider your Women—you'll
never do it, *George,*"[46] Sir William cautions. So the wagering continues until the waiter enters and reports that Mr.
Dizzy, Daffodil's cousin, has fallen down the stairs, and
that the cook has carried him behind the bar. Mr. Dizzy's
legacy to Daffodil will bring him two thousand pounds a
year. The extreme callousness of the fashionable gentlemen is excellently exemplified in the episode which ensues.

DAFFODIL:

> Lay him upon a Bed, and he'll come to himself.
>   [*Exit* WAITER.]

LORD RACKET:

> I'll bet Fifty Pound, that he don't live till Morning.

SIR WILLIAM:

> I'll lay Six to Four, he don't live a Week.

DAFFODIL:

> I'll take your Fifty Pound.

SPINNER:

> I'll take your Lordship again.

LORD RACKET:

> Done, with you both.

SIR TAN-TIVY:

> I'll take it again.

LORD RACKET:

> Done, done, done;—but I bar all Assistance to him—Not
> a Physician, or Surgeon sent for—or I am off.

DAFFODIL:

> No, no; we are upon Honour—There shall be none, else it
> wou'd be a bubble Bet.—There shall be none.

SIR WILLIAM:

> If I were my Lord, now, the Physicians should attend
> him.[47]

At this moment Daffodil receives a letter from an "Incognita," requesting a *rendez-vous* with him. Daffodil agrees to meet her, provided his friends will surprise him with her. Sir William here, as in the instance with Dizzy, is opposed to all dishonorable dealing.

SIR WILLIAM:

> There's a Gallant for you!

DAFFODIL:

> Prithee, Sir *William,* be quiet—must a Man be in Love with every Woman that invites him!

SIR WILLIAM:

> No; but he should be honourable to 'em, *George*—and rather conceal a Woman's Weakness, than expose it—I hate this Work—so, I'll go to the Coffee-house.
>
> > [*Exit* SIR WILLIAM.]

LORD RACKET:

> Let him go—don't mind him, *George*; he's married, and past fifty—this will be a fine Frolic—Devilish high—[48]

The scene in the park is richly humorous. All of Daffodil's professed loves are gathered behind the bushes, while Tukely, disguised as the "Incognita" of the letter, forces from Daffodil his sentiments regarding his ladies. His comments on these are none too flattering. Among his various *amours* Sophia and Arabella also figure. Suddenly Sophia, wrapped in a large coat and slouched hat, comes upon this amorous pair and demands an explanation from Daffodil for decoying "his wife." Daffodil is all a-flutter with fear. When Sophia is about to draw upon Daffodil, his fashionable comrades appear and offer to throw Sophia into the pond. At this moment the disguised Tukely snatches the sword from Sophia's hand. The ladies now advance from behind the bushes and in their turn ridicule Daffodil. To his consternation and surprise, he learns that the fair lady with whom he had conversed is none other than Tukely, and that the lady's husband is Sophia herself. The fashionable gentlemen, among whom is also Dizzy, who survived despite the wager upon his life, demand an explanation of the entire matter.

TUKELY:

> The Mystery will clear in a Moment.

DAFFODIL:

> Don't give yourself any Trouble, Mr. *Tukely,* Things are pretty clear as they are—The Night's cool, and my Cousin *Dizzy,* here, is an Invalid—If you please, another Time, when there is less Company, [*Ladies laugh*]—The Ladies are pleas'd to be merry, and you are pleas'd to be a little angry; and so, for the Sake of Tranquility—I'll go to the Opera. [DAFF. *sneaking out by Degrees.*][49]

Wagering that Daffodil will never intrigue again, the fashionable gentlemen follow after him.

Tukely, in the closing lines of the play, points out the moral of it.

> As my Satisfaction is compleat, I have none to ask of Mr. *Daffodil.* I forgive his Behaviour to me, as it has hasten'd and confirm'd my Happiness here; [*to* SOPHIA.]—But as a Friend to you, Ladies, I shall insist upon his making you ample Satisfaction—However, this Benefit will arise, that you will hereafter equally detest and shun these Destroyers of your Reputation—
>
> In *You* Coquettry *is a* Loss of Fame;
> But *in Our* Sex, 'tis that detested Name,
> That marks the Want of Manhood, Virtue, Sense, and
> > Shame.[50]

The dialogue of this play is vivacious, and the action moves along briskly. The situations, a number of which follow situations in various Restoration comedies, are highly amusing, and the characters are exceedingly well drawn. Much of the success of this play upon the stage was due to the superb interpretation of the character of Daffodil by Henry Woodward (1714-1777), who was one of the excellent comedians of the Garrick era: an admirably fine Harlequin, an unsurpassed Mercutio, and a successful Captain Flash in Garrick's *Miss in Her Teens.*

Genest's statement that "the character of Daffodil is in a great degree stolen from that of Capt. Spark in the *Universal Gallant*"[51] (Fielding) is entirely unfounded. Spark is merely a conceited fool and fabricator of stories of conquests of which he boasts but which he never won. There is not a single instance in which Spark is presented as actually carrying on an *amour.* When, however, this coxcomb, through no efforts of his own, finally does succeed in securing a part in an assignation with an *inamorata,* supposedly Lady Raffler, the beloved one turns out to be the lady's husband disguised in woman's clothes. Daffodil, on the other hand, although he is a despicable wretch, is no fool. It is not folly that leads him to his undoing, but rather the fact that he has at last met a woman who, unlike all the others, refuses to accept him without testing the honesty of his intentions toward her. Not to the ridiculous Captain Spark does Daffodil bear any kinship, but rather to the heartless Dorimants, Horners, and Archers of Restoration comedy. Although he lacks the sparkle that we associate with Dorimant, the subtlety of Horner, and the dashing vivacity of Archer, still in his readiness for the chase, in his power to attract women to himself, and in his faithlessness to them, he is the typical Restoration rake. In his cruelty to women, that is, in his utter disregard for their feelings when they discover his perfidy, he is most like Dorimant. One has but to watch him in the *levée* scene as he coldly and calculatingly orders Ruffle to strike off Mrs. Dotterel and the Widow Damply from his list of conquests in order to add new acquisitions, to discover a miniature presentment of the Dorimant of the scene wherein he discusses his two cast mistresses and the qualifications and possibilities of his two new ones.[52] In so far as Daffodil's quarrel with Mrs. Dotterel is concerned, one can almost apply Dorimant's summation of his own code of love; namely, "next to coming to a good understanding with a new mistress, I love a quarrel with an old one."[53] In his soullessness, in his power to "assume Passions he never feels, and sport with the Sex's Frailties,"[54] Daffodil is related to Horner; and in his cowardice, he resembles Sir John Brute.

Although Daffodil is drawn in the tradition of the Restoration rake, Sophia is the typical daughter of the practical and moral eighteenth-century *bourgeoisie.* Her interest lies not in the pursuit but in contracting a happy and lasting marriage. With this end in view, she determines to convince herself of Daffodil's desirability of character, and to carry out her plan assumes male garb, a device that dates back to Elizabethan drama. Of all the disguised ladies in Elizabethan and Restoration plays, Sophia may best be compared to Sylvia, the heroine of Farquhar's *The Recruiting Officer.* Like Sylvia, she dons male attire to test the constancy of her lover; but whereas Sylvia, to win the love of Plume, presents herself as his rival in his intrigue with the country-girl Rose, Sophia, on discovering Daffodil's profligacy, casts him off and aids Tukely in exposing his contemptible philandering. We find, also, that the heroine of the eighteenth-century play is not so outspoken as her sister of a half century earlier. At any rate, Sophia was an excellent breeches part, the type made popular by the lovely Peg Woffington when she appeared in the rôle of Sir Harry Wildair in Farquhar's *The Constant Couple.* In the Widow Damply we have again the elderly coquette, the Lady Cockwood-Lady Wishfort type, enamored and in pursuit of the younger gallant. Mrs. Dotterel is a foolish and amorous young woman married to a jealous old man (the Pinchwife-Margery union). She has been carrying on an intrigue with Daffodil, and, discovering his treachery, decides to visit him at his lodgings. In her solicitude for her honor Mrs. Dotterel is not unlike Lady Cockwood or the ladies of Horner's coterie, but in her wounded pride and in her indignant rage at Daffodil's deception of her, she suggests Mrs. Loveit of the Dorimant-Loveit quarrel scene.[55] A humorous bit of dialogue that Garrick injected into this scene reveals excellently the folly of the deluded young woman on the one hand and Daffodil's evasiveness on the question of his love for her on the other. Mrs. Dotterel is attempting to discover whether Daffodil still loves her. He is elusive and decides suddenly to change the subject.

DAFFODIL:

As you say, Madam, Fire is a catching; 'tis dangerous to play with it; and as I am of the Tinder-Kind,—as one may say,—we had better,—as you say—Madam,—change the Subject—Pray did you ever hear of the Pug-dog that you advertis'd? It was a very pretty Creature—what was his Name, Madam?

MRS. DOTTEREL:

Daffodil, Sir!

[*Stifling her Passion.*]

DAFFODIL:

Madam!

MRS. DOTTEREL:

Could I love and esteem any Thing, and not call it *Daffodil?*—What a Wretch!

[*Aside.*]

DAFFODIL:

You do me Honour, Madam . . .[56]

This is a highly dramatic little scene.

Although the last scene of **The Male-Coquette** bears some likeness to the assignation scene between Captain Spark and the disguised Sir Simon Raffler of Fielding's *The Universal Gallant* (1735), it is more probable that Garrick, when writing this comedy, had in mind scenes of plays current in the repertory of his theatre rather than one that had been dropped after its third presentation more than twenty years before. The *rendez-vous* of "Incognita" and Daffodil resembles, therefore, the one that takes place between Lady Brute and Constant in Vanbrugh's *The Provok'd Wife,* a play that was a great favorite with Garrick, and one in which he played frequently. Like Vanbrugh's scene, this *rendez-vous* scene in **The Male-Coquette** has its setting out-of-doors, and like it, too, Garrick's has interested eavesdroppers. The *tête-à-tête* of the clandestine pair in both plays is interrupted by the arrival of a person in disguise: in the Restoration play it is the husband, Sir John Brute in woman's clothes; in Garrick's it is Tukely's *fiancée,* Sophia, dressed as a man. Like Constant, the lover of Lady Brute's assignation, Daffodil, is ready, when the drunken husband suddenly comes upon him, to surrender his *inamorata.* The fact that the lady in the case is the disguised Tukely and also the rival of Daffodil, brings this scene close also to the one in which Alderman Smuggler, disguised as Lady Lurewell's nurse, in order, as he supposes, to carry out his assignation with the lady more effectively, meets instead his nephew, Vizard, his rival in the love of Lurewell.[57] Moreover, when Garrick, in his *dénouement,* permits Daffodil's cast mistresses to taunt and jeer at him, we get a scene that is somewhat reminiscent of the one where Mistress Ford and Mistress Page make merry at the expense of the bewildered Falstaff. Then again, Daffodil's words as he runs sword in hand to meet his friends who were to have interrupted the *rendez-vous* between him and "Incognita"-Tukley, savor of the swaggering Falstaff, although it is the Falstaff of the earlier play (*1 Henry IV*).

O, my Friends, I have been wishing for you this half Hour. I have been set upon by a dozen Fellows—They have all made their Escape, but this—My Arm is quite dead—I have been at Cart and Tierce with 'em all, for near a Quarter of an Hour.[58]

Sophia's query, "in Buckram, my Lord," banishes all doubts as to Garrick's source for this particular moment in his play.

In the course of this same scene Daffodil, in his *tête-à-tête* with "Incognita"-Tukley, passes judgment upon his various mistresses. This is a typical Restoration inquest scene, such as is found in the Olivia-Novel-Lord Plausible scene of *The Plain Dealer,* and such as Sheridan was later to introduce so successfully into *The School for Scandal.* Contrary to the usual procedure in comedy of manners, Garrick permits Daffodil's relations with his various mistresses to be discovered. Moreover, although the dramatist allows these same mistresses to overhear Daffodil express in none too flattering terms his opinions of them, there does not result any reformation of character by eavesdropping, a trick so typical of sentimental comedy. Daffodil's revelation of his true feelings towards the women who thought themselves secure in his affection rouses rather their indignation. They realize the folly of their ways, but when we leave these five ladies, they do not hold out any promise of change. It is Tukely who, in concluding the play, informs us that these ladies will hereafter mend their ways. *The Male-Coquette* is significant, therefore, not only because it was one of the successful afterpieces of the time, but even more important than this, for its many backward links with the comedy of manners of the Restoration era.

BON TON; OR, HIGH LIFE ABOVE STAIRS

According to Garrick's introductory notice to **Bon Ton,** this two-act comedy of manners was written "many years" before its *première* on Saturday, March 18, 1775.[59] On this particular evening **Bon Ton** was presented, as Garrick continues to state in his prefatory remarks:

> with some alterations, for the benefit of Mr. King, as a token of regard for one, who, during a long engagement, was never known, unless confined by real illness, to disappoint the Public, or distress the Managers—The Author is sincerely apprehensive that the excellence of the performance upon the stage, will greatly lessen its credit with the readers in the closet.[60]

Prompter Hopkins' entry of this performance of **Bon Ton** in the *MS. Diaries of the Drury Lane Theatre* confirms three of Garrick's statements:[61] that the play had been written long before its first presentation; that it was given for King's benefit; and that it was excellently performed; but it includes also a comment on its reception at the hands of the audience, and the extremely interesting bit of information that Garrick had entrusted the staging of the piece to Thomas King (1730-1805), a player of outstanding ability. That Garrick should have done so is not at all surprising, for at this date—fifteen months prior to his retirement from the stage—his poor health forced him not only to appear less frequently on the stage, but also to relinquish all extra responsibilities connected with it. For King, the manager of Drury Lane had the highest regard both as a man and as an artist. It was to him that Garrick granted the privilege of creating the rôle of Lord Ogleby, a part that he had written for himself, in his own

and Colman's **The Clandestine Marriage** (1766). It was King, too, who was later to be the original Sir Peter Teazle in Sheridan's *The School for Scandal* (1777). In **Bon Ton** he played Sir John Trotley.

In this play of Garrick's Lord Minikin, one of the pillars of the state, a man of rank, wit, and fashion, possessing also the virtues befitting such a gentleman—a love for gaming, drinking, and *affaires de cœur*—is carrying on an *amour* with Miss Lucretia Tittup, his wife's cousin. On the other hand, Lady Minikin, like a true lady of quality, bears a consummate contempt for her husband. At the moment she is busily engaged in a love affair with Colonel Tivy, Miss Tittup's *fiancé.* This family, like all fashionable families, has been abroad. Of these travels Miss Tittup speaks thus:

> What a great revolution in this family, in the space of fifteen months! We went out of England a very awkward, regular, good English family! but half a year in France, and a winter passed in the warmer climate of Italy, have ripen'd our minds to every refinement of ease, dissipation, and pleasure.[62]

It is, therefore, these foolish French and Italian manners aped by the English fashionable set that Garrick attacks in this play.

To this ultra-fashionable household, Miss Tittup's uncle, Sir John Trotley, a staid and honest country-gentleman, comes on a visit. He is shocked at the change that has come over the family and finds that he cannot reconcile himself to the fashionable mode of living.

> My niece Lucretia is so be-fashioned and be-devil'd, that nothing I fear, can save her; however, to ease my conscience, I must try; but what can be expected from young women of these times, but sallow looks, wild schemes, saucy words, and loose morals!—they lie a-bed all day, sit up all night; if they are silent, they are gaming, and if they talk, 'tis either scandal or infidelity; and that they may look what they are, their heads are all feather, and round their necks are twisted, rattle-snake tippets—O Tempora, O Mores.[63]

At another time when his servant tells him that the London women look healthier and rosier than the country-girls, Sir John exclaims, "they are painted Jezabels."[64]

The *levée* scene which follows these remarks presents Lord Minikin at the *toilette*-table. His drinking and the loss of his money at the gaming-table the night before make him irritable beyond the patience of Mignon, his French *friseur.* Miss Tittup enters to tell him that Lady Minikin saw them together in a hackney-coach, but that her ladyship failed to recognize her. She also informs him that his wife hates him unalterably but that, at the same time, her pride is alarmed that he should prefer any woman to her. Tittup does not fear Lady Minikin's discovery of her little *amour* with her lord as much as she does Sir John's, for to incur his displeasure means disinheritance. Worst of all is the fact that there is no hope of his leaving his fortune behind him so soon, for the "Barbarian lives so regularly, and never makes use of a physician that he may live these twenty years."[65]

Sir John's knocking at the door interrupts the conversation between Minikin and Miss Tittup. His lordship hides Tittup behind a large chair and admits the uncle. Finding no one in the room with Minikin, Sir John asks him the reason for the loud talking which he had heard. Minikin answers that he was studying a speech and speaking it aloud for the sake of tone and action. "One must do it for the sake of the nation," says Minikin. His lordship's invitation to dinner is declined thus by Sir John:

> You must know, my Lord, that I love to know what I eat;— I hate to travel, where I don't know my way; and since you have brought in foreign fashions and figaries, every thing and every body are in masquerade; your men and manners too are as much fritter'd and fricasi'd, as your beef and mutton; I love a plain dish, my Lord.[66]

The conversation then turns upon Miss Tittup. Sir John objects to the immodesty of Tittup's dress and suggests a reform. "I wou'd have her begin with lengthening her petticoats, covering her shoulders, and wearing a cap upon her head."[67] Minikin, however, prefers Tittup just as she is. Sir John is beside himself with rage.

LORD MINIKIN:

> But why in a passion, Sir John?—
>   [MY LORD *nods and laughs at* MISS TITTUP, *who peeps from behind.*]
> Don't you think that my lady and I shall be able and willing to put her into the right road?

SIR JOHN:

> Zounds! my Lord, you are out of it yourself; this comes of your travelling; all the town knows how you and my lady live together . . .[68]

To Sir John's question as to the reason for his marrying Lady Minikin, the nobleman answers,

> Convenience! Marriage is not now-a-days, an affair of inclination, but convenience; and they who marry for love, and such old-fashion'd stuff, are to me as ridiculous as those who advertise for an agreeable companion in a post-chaise.[69]

Lady Minikin and Miss Tittup also speak of marriage in a somewhat similar way.

On discovering Minikin's views on marriage, Sir John decides that Miss Tittup shall either return with him to the country immediately or be disinherited. Tittup is frightened at this, but Minikin remains unconcerned. Sir John continues:

> Pray, my Lord, what husband is this you have got for her?

LORD MINIKIN:

> A friend of mine; a man of wit, and a fine gentleman.

SIR JOHN:

> May be so, and yet make a dam'd husband for all that. You'll excuse me!—What estate has he, pray?

LORD MINIKIN:

> He's a Colonel; his elder brother, Sir Tan Tivy, will certainly break his neck, and then my friend will be a happy man.

SIR JOHN:

> Here's morals!—a happy man when his brother has broke his neck!—a happy man—Mercy on me!

LORD MINIKIN:

> Why he'll have six thousand a year, Sir John—[70]

Sir John is now fully determined to leave them all and go back to his country estate. In great rage he leaves the room. But he returns immediately, only to find Lord Minikin on his knees before Miss Tittup. She explains that Minikin was persuading her to marry his friend and that, having at last wrung from her her consent, he fell upon his knees to wish her joy. But no explanation avails to appease Sir John's anger. Singing most gaily, Lord Minikin takes his leave to attend Lady Filligree's masquerade. Sir John resolves to inform Lady Minikin of the entire matter.

The scene now changes to Lady Minikin's apartments. Colonel Tivy, Miss Tittup's *fiancé,* is discovered exacting from Lady Minikin a promise that she will leave the masquerade with him earlier than the rest of the company. When she consents to this, he falls upon his knees and kisses her hand. In this attitude does Sir John find them when he enters to inform her of her husband's doings. All three are amazed. When Lady Minikin recovers her wits enough to tell him that his rudeness deserves death, Sir John retorts, "Death indeed! for I shall never recover myself again! All pigs of the same stye!"[71] Lady Minikin then explains that her promise to the Colonel to interfere no longer with his plans regarding Miss Tittup "threw him into such rapture" that he fell upon his knees. But Sir John turns a deaf ear to all these explanations. Lady Minikin leaves in a flood of tears, and Colonel Tivy, declaring that "the lady's tears must be dried and his honour satisfied," challenges Sir John to a duel. Sir John decides to take to his heels betimes.

Miss Tittup and Lord Minikin return home from the masquerade before Lady Minikin and Colonel Tivy. Their scene is broken in upon by a servant who announces Lady Minikin's arrival. Miss Tittup dares not go to her own room for fear of meeting with her ladyship. She, therefore, hides in a closet while Lord Minikin goes to his apartment. Lady Minikin, accompanied by Colonel Tivy, now enters. Their conversation is interrupted by Lord Minikin's approach. The Colonel hides behind the chimney board, and Lady Minikin is left to face her lord. After a brief and none too affectionate conversation, in which Lady Minikin chides her husband for his attentions at the masquerade to a lady in crimson, they bid each other good-night most ceremoniously and, taking the candles with them, leave the room in total darkness. This leave-taking scene is most delightful in its humor and satire. It is strongly reminiscent of the scene in Etherege's *She Wou'd if She Cou'd* (Act III), in which Sir Oliver Cockwood and his philandering wife, each out on a private little spree, meet face to face in the Bear Tavern.

Minikin, to rid himself of his wife in order to continue his love-making with Tittup, suggests to Lady Minikin that they "have a family *tête-à-tête*, by way of novelty." He orders a servant to remove the chimney-board behind which, unknown to him, Tivy is hidden.

LADY MINIKIN:

> What shall I do? [*Aside.*]—Here, Jessamy, there is no occasion—I am going to my own chamber, and my Lord won't stay here by himself.
>
> <div align="right">[<i>Exit</i> JESSAMY.]</div>

LORD MINIKIN:

> How cruel it is, Lady Minikin, to deprive me of the pleasure of a domestic duetto—a good escape, faith! [*Aside.*]

LADY MINIKIN:

> I have too much regard for Lord Minikin, to agree to any thing that would afford him so little pleasure—I shall retire to my own apartments.

LORD MINIKIN:

> Well, if your Ladyship will be cruel, I must still, like the miser, starve and sigh, tho' possessed of the greatest treasure—[*Bows.*] I wish your Ladyship a good night—
> <div align="right">[<i>He takes one candle, and</i> LADY MINIKIN <i>the other.</i>]</div>
> may I presume— [*Salutes her.*]

LADY MINIKIN:

> Your Lordship is too obliging—nasty man! [*Aside.*]

LORD MINIKIN:

> Disagreeable woman! [*Aside.*]
> [*They wipe their lips, and exeunt ceremoniously.*][72]

The scene that follows is excellent not only in its conception but in its humor and dramatic effectiveness. Miss Tittup and Colonel Tivy come forth from their hiding-places, and Lord and Lady Minikin return to seek out their individual loves. All four grope about in the dark until Lord Minikin enfolds his own lady in his arms and Colonel Tivy Miss Tittup. Thus Sir John finds them when, believing the house to be infested with robbers, he enters with candle and blunderbuss to ferret them out.

SIR JOHN:

> Well, but hark'ee my dear cousins, have you not got wrong partners?—here has been some mistake in the dark;—I am mighty glad that I have brought you a candle,

to set all to rights again—you'll excuse me, gentlemen and ladies![73]

On being informed that Miss Tittup is disinherited, Colonel Tivy renounces her and departs. Lady Minikin and Miss Tittup consent to accompany Sir John into the country, and Lord Minikin is left to face his lawyers and creditors and to learn that "dissipation of fortune and morals must be followed by years of parsimony and repentance." Turning to the audience, Sir John points the moral of the play:

> Thus then, with the wife of one under this arm, and the mistress of another, under this, I sally forth a Knight Errant, to rescue distress'd damsels from those monsters, foreign vices, and *Bon Ton,* as they call it; and trust that every English hand and heart here, will assist me in so desperate an undertaking—*You'll excuse me, Sirs!*[74]

Lady Minikin sees the folly of her ways and hints that a change in her mode of living is not impossible. She does not, however, specifically promise such a change.

LADY MINIKIN:

> However appearances have condemn'd me, give me leave to disavow the substance of those appearances: My mind has been tainted, but not profligate—your kindness and example may restore me to my former natural English constitution.[75]

Miss Tittup, too, realizes the impropriety of her conduct and confesses herself guilty—

> Of consenting to marry one, whom my heart could not approve, and coquetting with another which friendship, duty, honour, morals, and every thing, but fashion, ought to have forbidden.[76]

But Tittup does not even hold out, as Lady Minikin does, a possibility of reformation. And so these ladies of London's fashionable life accompany Sir John into the quiet of the country, where, he hopes, "a little country air might perhaps do well." Despite these hopes on Sir John's part, the play, in general, remains absolutely true to the mode of the comedy of manners.

Bon Ton is one of the most brilliant afterpieces in the English language. It is replete with sparkling conversation and witty repartee much in the manner of Congreve. The playlet proved a tremendous success upon the stage and continued to be played long after Garrick's death. The satire of the piece is keen. It exposes to contemptuous merriment the extravagant and ridiculous foreign fashions which the English had adopted. Like ***Lilliput, Bon Ton*** satirizes also fashionable marriages of convenience and the attitude of persons of quality on marriage in general.

The prologue, which conformably hits at the follies of the fashionable world, was written by George Colman and spoken by Thomas King, who thenceforth was obliged to repeat it occasionally to gratify the public demand for it. An almost tragic incident that occurred on the first presentation of **Bon Ton** in Dublin, which illustrates the very thing Garrick attacked in the piece—the absurdity of prevailing fashions—is thus described by the dramatist and actor John O'Keeffe (1747-1833):

> Brereton[77] spoke the prologue to it; and at the words "Bon Ton's the thing," the feathers of a lady's head-dress caught fire, from the chandelier hanging over the box; it was soon in a blaze, and her life hardly saved. At this time a lady in full dress could not go in a coach; a sedan-chair was her carriage, and this had a cupola. The seat was in grooves, to be raised or lowered according to the altitude of the head-dress.[78]

Another interesting description, and at the same time a criticism of a fashionably dressed lady, occurs in Garrick's **Harlequin's Invasion.** Dolly Snip, in anticipation of becoming a fine lady, plans her mode of dress:

> Then I'll carry my Head as high, and have as High a Head as the best of 'em, and it shall be all set out with Curls—It shall be too high to go in at any Door, without Stooping, and so broad that I must always go in Sideways; Then I shall Keep a Chair with a Cupola o'top to hold my Feather Head in, and I shall be carried in it by Day, and by Night, Dingle, Dangle, Bobbing and Nodding, all the way I go ... What a Life I shall lead, when I'm a fine Lady, I'll be as fine as any of 'em.[79]

That Garrick was determined to laugh the extravagant headdress of the ladies of the day out of fashion is evident also from the manner in which he dressed the part of Sir John Brute for a performance of **The Provok'd Wife** about a fortnight after the first presentation of **Bon Ton.** For that evening, October 31, 1775, Prompter Hopkins records this entry in the *MS. Diaries of the Drury Lane Theatre*:

> M[r] Gr. never play'd better, & when he was in the Woms Cloths [*sic*] he had a head drest with Feathers Fruit etc. as extravag[n] as possible to Burlesque the present Mode of dressing—it had a monstrous Effect.

It was such foolish fashions as these that Garrick satirized and attempted to reform, not through tears, however, unless through tears provoked by laughter.

The characters in **Bon Ton** are well delineated. Lord Minikin is the man of quality, of wit, of extravagance, of many *amours,*—in fact, the reckless, dissolute, although lovable rake in the typical Restoration mode, with all the fascinations and vices that go to make up that interesting creature. Lady Minikin is the lady of quality with her intrigues and her round of pleasures: "*Pantheons, Operas, Festinos, Coteries, Masquerades, and all the Devilades in this town.*" She affects a contempt for her husband merely because it is the fashionable thing to do, and is, nevertheless, not a little jealous when she discovers her husband in a "hackney-coach with a minx in a pink cardinal" or "in a *tête-à-tête* with a Lady in crimson" at Lady Filligree's masquerade.

A brilliant, witty, and altogether delightful creature is Miss Lucretia Tittup, a lady who comes to us from the circle of the Millamants and Harriets. A true heroine of the comedy of manners, she is ready for the chase just for the pleasure it will afford her. She does not permit her emotions to get the better of her; in fact, she is always complete mistress of herself. She is not deeply in love but merely coquets with her lovers:

> my Lord likes me, and I like my Lord; however, not so much as he imagines, or to play the fool so rashly as he may expect; she must be very silly indeed, who can't flutter about a flame, without burning her wings—[80]

She is jealous of her independence, is loath to surrender it, and, in a brilliant verbal fencing match with her *fiancé* Colonel Tivy, which suggests the proviso scene between Mirabell and Millamant, gives him to understand that she will permit no one to domineer over her either before or after her marriage: "Look'ee, Sir, I will command before marriage, and do what I please afterwards, or I have been well educated to very little purpose."[81] Like Harriet in Etherege's *The Man of Mode,* Tittup is packed off posthaste to the country by a virtue-loving relative, but unlike Harriet, she goes to her exile with no Dorimant to look forward to.

Sir John Trotley, the healthy, English, moral-preaching country knight, who cannot tolerate the follies and vices of the town, represents plain sound judgment. He acts here in the capacity of a commentator, a figure familiar in the comedies of Jonson and later also in those of his follower, Shadwell. It is the commentator, a character that appears in almost every play in which Garrick points out social follies, who serves as the spokesman for the dramatist's criticism. Such is the function of Sir John Trotley in **Bon Ton**; and such is also the service that Æsop renders in **Lethe,** Bolgolam in **Lilliput,** and Sir William in the club scenes, and Tukely at the conclusion of **The Male-Coquette.** Not only does the commentator point out the vices and extravagances of the age but also suggests the reform.

In Colonel Tivy we have the younger son of an aristocratic English family. He lives in constant hopes that the first-born will "break his neck" and make him a "happy man," for only then can the Colonel come into his brother's estate of six thousand pounds a year. But since his elder brother has no particular desire to leave this earth, Colonel Tivy does the next best thing, turns fortune-hunter and determines to secure Miss Tittup's "fine fortune." He, too, like Minikin, is the typical rake. He is engaged to the cousin (Tittup) of his friend, Lord Minikin, and, at the same time, also carries on an intrigue with the latter's wife. When he discovers that Sir John will disinherit Tittup, the Colonel bids farewell to the family and takes his leave.

Not only the characters of the drawing-room but also those of the servants-quarters are delineated with a deft hand. Particularly fine is the country bumpkin Davy, Sir John's servant, who, on his one holiday in London, adopts some of the fashionable absurdities of the town, and worst of all (that is, in so far as Sir John is concerned) acquires all the impertinence and the iniquities common to servants of London's *beau monde.* In this episode we find Garrick's hit at the servant class.

Bon Ton is one of the best miniature comedies in English dramatic literature. It is strictly in the tradition of the Restoration comedy of manners. It proved to be one of the most successful afterpieces on the English stage and was played well into the nineteenth century.

From our examination of these social satires, we discover that Garrick's attitude toward human frailties is not the sympathetic one of the fashionable sentimental vogue but rather the critical one of the comedy of manners. Although he laughs good-humoredly at prevailing follies, he attacks with all the seriousness he can command the social vices of the time. Himself an indefatigable worker and man of high moral principles, he refuses to tolerate the social parasite and idler as these are exemplified in the fine lady, the equally fine gentleman, the despicable philanderer, the Englishman who adopts the extravagant fashions of foreign countries, and the various other contemptible characters about town. These he holds up to scorn wherever the opportunity presents itself.

Not only Garrick's attitude, but his plots and characters, are strongly reminiscent of those of Restoration comedy. Moreover, from the Jonsonian comedy of humour he has borrowed the commentator, who, in his criticisms of the characters and of their doings and in his moral pronouncements, reflects the standards of the dramatist.

As for the plays themselves, they are excellent in their character delineations. The plots—except in ***Lethe,*** which is a series of satirical portraits presented in dialogue form—move briskly and are excellently constructed. The dialogue, too, is sprightly and rarely lags in interest. These plays of Garrick's serve, therefore, not only as attacks on the foibles and vices of contemporary society, but as excellent entertainment.

. . . . .

THE FARMER'S RETURN FROM LONDON

The Farmer's Return from London (1762) and ***Linco's Travels*** (1767) constitute Garrick's interludes, the form of entertainment which, as stated in Chapter I, was given between the principal play of the evening and the afterpiece. The first of these interludes was written, as the dramatist informs us in his introductory notice, "with a view of assisting Mrs. Pritchard at her benefit"; but this admirable actress, who was great not only in tragedy but also in high comedy, did not appear in it. Garrick played the Farmer. The piece, only ninety-four lines in length, was presented on the evening of March 20, 1762,[82] between Vanbrugh's *The Mistake* (1705), which served as the chief

attraction, and Murphy's *The Old Maid* (1761), the *petite-pièce.* Garrick's interlude is an account given by a farmer to his family of what he had seen in London on a visit there at the time that the city was celebrating the coronation of the new king and queen, George III and Queen Charlotte. This, naturally, afforded Garrick an excellent opportunity to satirize the prevailing follies of the day.

The scene is laid in a farmhouse kitchen. The Farmer has just returned home. His wife and children, after ministering to the needs of the travel-worn head of the house, gather about him wide-eyed and open-mouthed to listen to his report of the wonders he had seen in London during the coronation festivities. He describes first of all the vast multitudes of spectators that thronged the streets, windows, and housetops to see the king and queen pass. "'Twas thof all the World had been there with their Spouses."[83] Scaffolding with seats for spectators were built against the houses in those streets through which the procession was to pass on its way to Westminster Abbey. Places on these were purchased at most exorbitant prices and filled long before the dawn of the coronation day. There was tier upon tier of faces, and it is this spectacle to which the Farmer refers when he says:

> There was Street within Street, and Houses on Houses!
> I thought from above, (when the Folk fill'd the Pleaces)
> The Streets pav'd with Heads, and the walls made of
> Feaces![84]

His visit to the theatre is the next matter of interest. In the upper gallery "'twas like *Bedlam,* all roaring and rattling," and in the boxes "the fine Folk were all curts'ying and pratling."[85] As for the play itself:

> I saw a new Pleay too—they call'd it *The School*—
> I thought it pure Stuff—but I thought like a Fool—
> 'Twas *The School of*—pize on it!—my Mem'ry is
> naught—
> The Greaat ones disliked it—they heate to be taught:
> The Cratticks too grumbled—I'll tell you for whoy,
> They wanted to laugh—and were ready to croy.[86]

In this last line Garrick directs a sly hit at sentimental comedy, a *genre* to which he was never reconciled. *The School* that the Farmer mentions was William Whitehead's (1715-1785) sentimental comedy, *The School for Lovers,* which had had its first production at Garrick's theatre only a month before (February 10, 1762) the presentation of this interlude. In it Garrick played Sir John Dorilant, a "too delicately sensible" guardian in love with Caelia, his equally hypersensitive ward. The sentimentally romantic guardian was a character not new to Garrick, for he had portrayed just such a one in his own little comedy, ***The Guardian*** (1759), an adaptation of Fagan's *La Pupille.*[87] But whereas Fagan and Whitehead treat sentimentally the situation wherein the guardian and his young ward have too much delicacy to acknowledge their love for each other, Garrick, by exaggerating this very supersensitiveness in his two chief characters, turns away from the sentimental vogue toward the comic.

Having mentioned the "Cratticks," the Farmer's wife is anxious to know just what sort of creatures these are, and Garrick's views regarding the critics of his day follow.

> like Watchmen in Town,
> Lame, feeble, half-blind, yet they knock Poets down.
> Like old Justice *Wormwood,*—a Crattick's a Man,
> That can't sin himself,—and he heates those that can.[88]

The Farmer continues:

> I ne'er went to *Opras*!—I thought it too grand,
> For *poor* Folk to like what they don't understand.
> The top Joke of all, and what pleas'd me the moast,
> Some Wise ones and I sat up with a Ghoast.[89]

And thus the incident of the Cock Lane Ghost, which in 1762 stirred all London, also finds its way into the Farmer's narration.

The Cock Lane Ghost had its origin in the sudden death of a certain Miss Fanny, a young woman whose spirit, it was supposed, haunted the twelve-year-old daughter of a William Parsons, a clerk of St. Sepulchre. Miss Fanny, several months prior to her death, had ventured into London to take up lodgings with her widowed brother-in-law, a William Kent, erstwhile postmaster of a Norfolk town, with whom she had formed a *liaison.* It happened that Kent, during his residence at this house, was forced to have Parsons arrested for a debt of twenty pounds. Kent and Fanny presently moved to other lodgings in the same street, where, shortly after, she died of small-pox. Out of revenge for the insult that Kent had brought upon him, Parsons caused a report to be circulated about town that, through the medium of knockings and scratchings, the troubled spirit of Fanny manifested itself to his daughter, and, moreover, demanded that Kent be punished for administering poison to her during her illness. Fanny's scratchings were now heard over entire London. The town was all agog. To hear the ghost, for it was "not an *apparition* but an *audition,*"[90] became the reigning fashion.

> By Truth inspir'd, we numbers see
> Of each Profession and degree,
> Gentle and Simple, Lord and Cit,
> Wit without wealth, wealth without wit;
> When PUNCH and SHERIDAN have done,
> To Fanny's *Ghostly Lectures* run.[91]

To the *beau monde* it was of as much consequence to be seen at Fanny's as it was to attend the opera. And Fanny herself, "... great in Reputation grown, Keeps the best company in Town."[92]

A particularly interesting description of one of the then fashionable ghosting parties to the haunted house is given by Horace Walpole.

We set out from the Opera, changed our clothes at Northumberland House, the Duke of York, Lady Northumberland, Lady Mary Coke, Lord Hertford, and I, all in one hackney coach, and drove to the spot; it rained torrents; yet the lane was full of mob, and the house so full we could not get in—at last they discovered it was the Duke of York, and the company squeezed themselves into one another's pockets to make room for us. The house, which is borrowed, and to which the ghost has adjourned, is wretchedly small and miserable; when we opened the chamber, in which were fifty people, with no light but one tallow candle at the end, we tumbled over the bed of the child to whom the ghost comes, and whom they are murdering there by inches in such insufferable heat and stench. At the top of the room are ropes to dry clothes—I asked, if we were to have rope-dancing between the acts?—we had nothing; they told us, as they would at a puppet-show, that it would not come that night till seven in the morning—that is, when there are only prentices and old women. We stayed, however, till half an hour after one ... provisions are sent in like forage, and all the taverns and alehouses in the neighbourhood make fortunes. The most diverting part is to hear the people wondering *when it will be found out*—as if there was anything to find out—as if the actors would make their noises where they can be discovered.[93]

Fanny's popularity grew to such enormous proportions that Drury Lane and Covent Garden, too, took advantage of the ghostly fashion and revived Addison's *The Drummer; or, The Haunted House,* which they played to capacity audiences.

Parsons' daughter was examined and questioned by various persons of importance and authority both of the clergy and laity, but the girl clung tenaciously to her story and, moreover, proved it through exhibitions of Fanny's antics. But whether or not Fanny scratched, depended largely upon the importance of the visitors who "sat up" with her. She usually reserved her performances for the simple and the more credulous folk. One night, after much questioning, Fanny indicated through her knockings that, if Kent would venture into the burial vault under the church of St. John, Clerkenwell, she would by a knock upon her coffin give proof of her presence there. And so a party of prominent persons, among them the Reverend Stephen Aldrich, the rector of the church, descended into the vault. But Fanny was not true to her promise. Finally, after much experimenting with and close watching of the Parsons girl by a group of distinguished men, Samuel Johnson and the Reverend Mr. Aldrich among them, who were suspicious of the veracity of these ghostly visitations and, therefore, undertook to investigate the matter, the hoax was detected. In his account in the *Gentleman's Magazine* of the discovery of the imposture, Johnson reported that it was the "opinion of the whole assembly, that the child has some art of making or counterfeiting particular noise, and that there is no agency of any higher cause."[94] For his part in the hoax Parsons was set in the pillory, and after this punishment he and his accomplices were sent for terms of varying lengths to prison.

In the Garrick playlet the delusion of the Cock Lane Ghost is treated most ludicrously in the Farmer's recital of the London sights. When he tells of his having "sat up with a Ghoast," his wife and children exclaim:

A Ghoast! [*Starting*]

FARMER:

Yes, a Ghoast!

WIFE:

I shall swoond away, Love!

FARMER:

Odzooks!—thou'rt as bad as thy Betters above!
With her Nails, and her Knuckles, she answer'd so noice!
For *Yes* she knocked *Once,* and for *No* she knock'd
Twoice.
I ask'd her *one* Thing—

WIFE:

What Thing!

FARMER:

If yo', Dame, was true?

WIFE:

And the poor Soul knock'd *One.*

FARMER:

By the Zounds, it was *Two.*

WIFE:

I'll not be abus'd, *Jahn.* [*Cries.*]

FARMER:

Come, prithee no Croying,
The Ghoast, among Friends, was much giv'n to Loying.

WIFE:

I'll tear out her Eyes—

FARMER:

I thought, Dame, of matching
Your Neails [*sic*] against hers—for you're both good at
scratching.[95]

But the Farmer and his wife are soon reconciled.

In spite of Genest's assertion that **The Farmer's Return from London** is "not worth notice," it is a delightful little piece; full of good humor, excellent in its ridicule of the prevailing follies, and really fine in its presentation of realistically and sympathetically delineated characters in the humbler walks of life. Notwithstanding the favorable reception that was accorded the playlet, Garrick, as he sets forth in his introductory note, "would not have printed it, had not his Friend, Mr. *Hogarth,* flattered him most agreeably, by thinking *The Farmer and his Family* not unworthy

of a Sketch of his Pencil."[96] In reciprocation for the compliment Hogarth paid him, Garrick inscribed the playlet to him.

LINCO'S TRAVELS

To reward Thomas King for his excellent acting of the character of Linco in Garrick's play **Cymon,** the actor-manager presented his fellow-player for his benefit night with a dramatic trifle called **Linco's Travels** in which King again played Linco. So anxious was Garrick "for a full house at King's benefit" that in a letter sent on "Good Friday, 1767" (April 10),[97] from Bath, where he was taking the waters, he urged his brother, George, whom he had left in charge of affairs at Drury Lane, "to put a puff about **Linco's Travels** into the paper," and, moreover, in closing this letter, made the same plea that he did in the beginning, "Pray puff **Linco's Travels** for Tom."[98] But when Garrick asked for this "puff" for King, **Linco's Travels** had already been presented on the previous Monday. A possible explanation for this discrepancy is that King's benefit performance might have been pushed ahead of the date for which it had originally been scheduled before Garrick was apprised of the change. It might also be that Garrick, without his calendar of events before him on his spring holiday sojourn at Bath, confused the date of King's benefit performance with one of the numerous others that usually took place during the latter part of the theatrical season.

Whatever the explanation, the piece was presented April 6, 1767,[99] after the principal dramatic event of the evening, which, on this occasion, was Shakespeare's *Cymbeline* with King in the part of Cloten. **Linco's Travels** was probably given as an interlude[100] between Shakespeare's play and the concluding farce, for it is much too insignificant to have served as the afterpiece. What the *petite-pièce* was on this particular night, Genest does not state; nor can we glean this information from the *MS. Diaries of the Drury Lane Theatre* in the Folger Shakespeare Library, for these records are at this point incomplete.

As for the playlet itself, **Linco's Travels** has no plot. Garrick himself calls it a "hodge-podge." It tells merely of Linco's return to Arcadia after his travels abroad. He describes to his neighbors, who gather about him, the customs and peculiarities of the French, the Italians, the Germans, and, finally, and, in particular, of the English. This plan, like that of **The Farmer's Return from London,** gives Garrick free scope to ridicule, which he does in a most diverting manner. Here again, as in numerous other instances, he pokes fun at the Englishman who, during his travels abroad, learns to ape the manners and absurd fashions of his foreign neighbors and returns to his mother country a ridiculous creature of hybrid nature, which is neither foreign nor native. Michael Arne, who had done the music for **Cymon,** also composed for this playlet some music, which, we are told by O'Keeffe, one of the younger dramatists of the day, was "very beautiful."[101]

With the afterpiece, *A Peep Behind the Curtain* (1767), we come upon one of Garrick's contributions to the burlesque-rehearsal type of play. In it he gives us more than a peep not only behind but also before the curtain. In general, Garrick ridicules almost everything connected with the theatre; in particular, in the burletta of *Orpheus,* which is rehearsed in the second act of the play, he directs a thrust at the musical dramas, especially Italian opera then in vogue.

The play within a play as a medium for satire upon the reigning follies of the day had been long a favorite method with English dramatists. Peele, for instance, in *The Old Wives' Tale* uses this device to laugh at the extravagant absurdities of the then popular romances of folk-lore and of chivalry. This latter *genre* is parodied also in *The Knight of the Burning Pestle.*[102] But the satire here is more pointed than in Peele's play. Not only the heroical romances but also the dramas of *bourgeois* knight-errantry, as these are exemplified in Thomas Heywood's *Foure Prentises of London,* are held up to ridicule in *The Knight of the Burning Pestle.* But despite the fact that this play and Peele's *The Old Wives' Tale* present the performance of a burlesque play within another, and show us, moreover, the reactions to and the comments of the player-spectators on the performance, neither of these is an actual rehearsal play. For this sort of thing we must turn to Shakespeare's *A Midsummer Night's Dream* in which a group of "hempen homespuns" rehearse on the "green plot" near to where the dainty Titania lies asleep, the "most lamentable comedy, and most cruel death of Pyramus and Thisby." In the finished product which these mechanics enact before Theseus and his Amazon bride, we feel that Shakespeare is laughing good-humoredly at such performances as he, for instance, as a boy had perhaps seen presented by the guild players at Coventry or by the strolling actors that visited Stratford, performances whose crudity and attempts to depict concretely such details as should have been left to the imagination of the spectators made them notoriously ridiculous. In Bottom's speeches in the "tyrant's vein," Shakespeare pokes fun at the bombast of the tragedies in the Senecan style, and in Bottom himself, the perennial actor who, in his own opinion, is capable of doing not only his own part but also all the others in the play. The early Bottom episodes, therefore, contain the most important element of the rehearsal play, one which is not found in either *The Old Wives' Tale* or *The Knight of the Burning Pestle*—the rehearsal itself—during which Puck is auditor and actor, too.

The first outstanding example of the burlesque-rehearsal play as we come to know this form during the eighteenth century—that is, a drama wherein the rehearsal of a piece is presented before player-spectators who comment and pass judgment upon it as it unfolds itself before them—is *The Rehearsal* (1671) by George Villiers, second Duke of Buckingham, who, it is believed, had as his coadjutors in its composition, Martin Clifford, Thomas Sprat, and perhaps also Samuel Butler of Hudibrastic renown. *The Rehearsal,* in turn, became the famous ancestor to a long and distinguished line of satires by the hands of wits of such eminence as Fielding, Foote, Garrick, and, perhaps the most celebrated of them all, Sheridan. In *The Rehearsal* Buckingham, like his Elizabethan predecessor (or predecessors), lampoons the extravagance of the drama of his age. Whether the satire in *The Rehearsal* was originally leveled at Sir William Davenant, or at Dryden, or at the latter's brother-in-law, Sir Robert Howard, is not certain. Judging from the fact, however, that Bayes, the hero of the play, is obliged, after his accidental fall upon the stage, to wear a patch of wet paper on his broken nose, it seems possible that the dramatist is in this instance alluding to Davenant, who was afflicted with a deformity similar to Bayes's. *The Rehearsal* was long in preparation, and Davenant died before it was produced. With Davenant gone, it is possible that Buckingham now turned more directly to Sir Robert Howard and to Dryden himself as the objects for his shafts of raillery.

In the character of Bayes Buckingham painted a portrait in colors and perspective most startling and ridiculous, in which the Restoration audiences recognized perhaps their recently departed poet-laureate and also Dryden, then a dramatist of ever increasing popularity. To make his portrait of Dryden more complete and more recognizable, Buckingham personally instructed John Lacy (d. 1681), the actor who played Bayes, to mimic Dryden's abominably bad method of delivery and also his peculiarities of dress and manner. It was this by-play of Lacy's that initiated a vogue, carried on by later actors, particularly by Garrick, which made of the part of Bayes a vehicle for actors to introduce into it imitations of the idiosyncrasies of their fellow-players.

In the absurdly grandiloquent play of his dramatist-hero, Bayes, Buckingham satirizes the rhyming and bombastic heroic school of plays of which Davenant was the founder, and of which Dryden became the leading exponent. He parodies from Dryden's plays, particularly from *The Conquest of Granada* (1670/71), passage after passage of mouth-filling stuff. Nor does Buckingham forget to aim a thrust at Dryden's theories of play-writing as these are expounded in the latter's essay *Of Heroic Plays.* So that, although there are some seventeen plays ridiculed in this burlesque by Buckingham, and a number of these by dramatists other than Dryden, still the weight of the Duke's lampooning fell most heavily and most decidedly on Dryden. But the latter bided his time and retaliated in his *Absalom and Achitophel,* where, in a masterly fashion, he satirizes Buckingham in the character of Zimri.

Like the theatre of the preceding periods, that of the eighteenth century offered ample material for the satirist. Dramatic art was at a low ebb. In tragedy the pompously dull prevailed; in comedy, farce, intrigue, and the lachrymose held sway. The audiences preferred Harlequin to Shakespeare and demanded spectacle, Italian opera, and musical pieces in general. The skill of the stage-carpenter vied with that of the scene-painter, and the artistry of both of these often helped many a wretched play to financial success. Moreover, as the demand for spectacle increased, the importance of the property man grew to such tremendous proportions that he, together with his many mechanical contrivances for effecting the numerous stage displays, became one of the topics for burlesque. Sentimentalism, too, the opera, pantomime, the fashionable late-comers to the theatre, their inattentiveness to the proceedings on the stage, the noise in the upper gallery, the critics in the pit, the gallants on the stage (although these disappear from their stage-seats and, hence, from burlesques after 1762, the year in which Garrick enlarged the seating capacity of Drury Lane), green-room activities, rehearsals, quarrels between actors, managerial woes, among which were playwrights who refused to have their plays rejected and actors who demanded parts for which they were wholly unsuited, the thunder-trunk, the devices for making clouds and rain, the extravagances in the fashions of the day, and the grand tour—all these and many more came in for a goodly share of ridicule in the burlesques of the eighteenth century, particularly in the rehearsal plays of Fielding and Garrick and later in Sheridan's *The Critic*.

In Fielding's rehearsal plays the shafts of ridicule fly thick and fast, and although the extravagances of the theatre of the time come within the range of many of these, the greater number are directed with dexterous and unfailing aim at Sir Robert Walpole. But whether it is the drama or politics that Fielding is attacking, he is almost always dealing in personalities. It is the individual that he seeks out and ridicules rather than the thing.

In so far as Garrick is concerned, his satire is never personal. In every instance it is the thing rather than the individual that Garrick ridicules. Matters theatrical found their way into a considerable number of his plays, but in *A Peep Behind the Curtain* and in his two preludes, *The Meeting of the Company* (1774) and *The Theatrical Candidates* (1775), both of which we shall consider in this chapter, Garrick gives himself over almost entirely to a criticism of the extravagances prevalent in the theatre of his time. His two-act playlet, *A Peep Behind the Curtain; or, The New Rehearsal,* presented at Drury Lane on October 23, 1767,[103] served as the afterpiece to Lillo's *The London Merchant*. All but its first scene takes place on and about the stage of the Drury Lane Theatre.

The first scene deals with Wilson, a young man, who is in love with Miss Fanny Fuz, the daughter of Sir Toby and Lady Fuz, "ridiculous pretenders to taste and virtu." Failing as a poor relation to win the favor of Fanny's parents, Wilson now poses as a strolling player and as such gains ready admittance into their house. The lovers plan to elope

while Sir Toby and Lady Fuz are witnessing a rehearsal of a new burletta at the Drury Lane Theatre.

The next scene takes us to the playhouse where two women are discovered sweeping the stage. Despite their good wages, they air their complaints about their long hours of work and the "hurry and bustle from morning to night." Garrick now takes the opportunity to hit a thrust at his erstwhile friend and joint-author of *The Clandestine Marriage* (1766), George Colman, who, in the spring of 1767, had bought a share in Garrick's rival house, Covent Garden, and, at the time of the writing of *A Peep Behind the Curtain,* had already assumed his managerial duties.

2D WOMAN:

> . . . the folks say about us, that the other house will make them [the managers of Drury Lane] stir their stumps, and they'll make us stir ours: if they're in motion, we must not stand still, Mrs. Besom.

1ST WOMAN:

> Ay, ay, girl, they have met with their match, and we shall suffer for it—[104]

Johnston, the housekeeper, sends them off to sweep the other parts of the theatre. The prompter appears and inquires whether the beasts that are to be used in the burletta have been completed. Saunders, the carpenter, assures him that everything is ready but the dancing cows.

PROMPTER:

> Bless my heart, man, the Author depends most upon his Cows.

SAUNDERS:

> His Cows!—How came they to be his; they are *my* Cows—[105]

The rehearsal is consequently to take place without the dancing cows.

The prompter confides to the manager, who has just arrived, that the actors murmur greatly at being compelled to come to a full rehearsal of only one completed act. In the dialogue that follows Garrick criticizes the petty bickerings of the players.

PATENT:

> When do the performers not murmur, Mr. Hopkins?—Has any morning pass'd in your time without some grievance or another?

PROMPTER:

> I have half a dozen now in my pocket for you. [*Feeling in his pockets for papers.*]

PATENT:

> O pray let's have 'em, my old breakfast— [PROMPTER *gives 'em.*] And the old story—Actresses quarrelling about

parts; there's not one of 'em but thinks herself young enough for any part; and not a young one but thinks herself capable of any part—but their betters quarrel about what they are not fit for, So our Ladies have at least great precedents for their folly.

PROMPTER:

The young fellow from Edinburgh won't accept of the second Lord; he desires to have the first.

PATENT:

I don't doubt it—Well, well, if the Author can make him speak English, I have no objection.[106]

Glib, the author of the burletta, finally arrives. He informs Patent that he has invited some friends to witness the rehearsal. These are Sir Toby and Lady Fuz, Miss Fuz, and Sir Macaroni. The Fuz family, Glib assures the manager, will be at the theatre "in the drinking of a cup of tea," but as for Sir Macaroni, "he's too polite to be punctual." In this last remark Garrick holds to ridicule the lateness of the smart set in arriving at the theatre. The conversation here turns upon the play to be rehearsed, and the manager proceeds to discuss the plan of the second act. Glib impresses upon the manager the fact that part of his scheme is to bring Orpheus into hell, and since Orpheus in the infernal regions is to be represented as a man of fashion, the play thus tends to depict a sort of high life below stairs. The manager, however, fears for the effects of such a piece upon the patrons of the boxes.

AUTHOR:

Empty boxes!—I'll engage that my *Cerberus* alone shall fill the boxes for a month.[107]

Glib informs Patent that Cerberus is to be one of the characters in his play. "He shall be a comical dog too."

AUTHOR:

... I have thrown all my fancy and invention into his mouth, or rather mouths—there are three of 'em, you know.

PATENT:

Most certainly, if there are three heads.

AUTHOR:

Poh, that's nothing to what I have in petto for you—Observe me now—when Orpheus comes to the gates of hell—Cerberus stops him—but how, how—now for it—guess—

PATENT:

Upon my soul I can't guess.

AUTHOR:

I'll make his three heads sing a *trio*.

PATENT:

A *Trio*!

AUTHOR:

A trio! I knew I shou'd hit you—a trio, treble, tenor and bass—and what shall they sing? nothing in the world but, *Bow, wow, wow!*—Orpheus begins—

O bark not, Cerberus, nor grin—
A stranger sure to pass within,
Your goodness will allow?
Bow, wow, wow—

Treble, tenor, and bass—Then Orpheus shall tickle his lyre, and treble, tenor and bass, shall fall asleep by degrees, and one after another, fainter and fainter—*Bow, wow, wow*—fast—You understand me?

PATENT:

Very ingenious, and very new—I hope the critics will understand it.[108]

Garrick is here laughing at the duets, trios, quartets, and all other forms of ensemble singing that proved so popular in the Italian operas. In fact, this entire scene between Glib and Patent as well as the rehearsal itself, includes Garrick's satire upon the ridiculous and extravagant musical productions that the theatre-going populace of his day enjoyed and demanded. Incidentally, Garrick slyly aims a thrust at the critics, too.

The arrival of Glib's guests interrupts his conversation with the manager, who now goes off to prepare some tea and chocolate, while the guests are left to entertain themselves. Lady Fuz thereupon relates an incident that occurred at the theatre one evening. Sir Toby was the hero. Having fallen asleep against the box-door, he caused great merriment among the spectators in the pit and galleries as he lay there "his wig half off, his mouth wide open, and snoring like a Rhinoceros." Lady Fuz continues, "if the Box-keeper had not luckily open'd the door, and Sir Toby fell head-long into the passage, I should have died with shame."[109] This is another of Garrick's hits at the behavior of some of the fashionable gentlemen at the theatre. The lady proceeds to tell Sir Macaroni how she "adores Shakespeare," and how she worships him to the extent that Sir Toby and she often act some of his best tragedy scenes together. Sir Toby, his lady, and Sir Macaroni betake themselves to the green room to see the actors and actresses, and Miss Fuz is left alone on the stage. Wilson enters and attempts to persuade her to elope with him immediately, but Miss Fanny's courage begins to fail her. She promises, however, to steal away with him during the rehearsal, when her father will be fast asleep, and her mother will be deaf, dumb, and blind to everything but Mr. Glib's wit. For this promise Wilson thanks her on his knees, and thus Lady Fuz finds him when she returns from the green room where she and Sir Toby had been acting some scenes from *Romeo and Juliet*. Upon being assured that Wilson is the very same strolling player whose benefit they attended the summer before, and that he is merely teaching her how to speak some lines in

Romeo and Juliet, Lady Fuz is comforted and asks him for tickets for his next benefit.

Everything is now in readiness for the rehearsal, except that Sir Macaroni has left the house. Glib pretends indifference to his absence. Sir Toby promises to be "very critical," and Lady Fuz calls for a prologue, whereupon Glib informs her that the manager has one in preparation. Glib gives final instructions to the musicians; the overture is played; and the curtain rises. Orpheus is discovered asleep upon a couch. He is haunted constantly by his wife's spirit which implores him to deliver her from Pluto's realm. Conscience-stricken, Orpheus determines to venture into the lower world in quest of his wife. When, however, Rhodope, his mistress, endeavors to dissuade him from doing so, Orpheus resorts to his lyre, strikes a few notes, and Rhodope is soon sound asleep. Orpheus now makes his escape. On his way to Hades he passes through a mountainous country where the shepherds seem to be greatly annoyed by his music. When they threaten to beat him with their crooks, a tune from his lyre sets them and their beasts a-capering, and Orpheus leads them all out in a grand chorus of singing and dancing.

During this rehearsal Miss Fuz, while her father is asleep and her mother is admiring the genius of Mr. Glib, steals away with her lover. This her ladyship discovers after Orpheus has led the dancing shepherds and beasts off the stage. She is greatly wrought up over the whole affair. To avenge herself upon the manager because one of his players has run off with her daughter, Lady Fuz threatens to close the theatre. The manager goes to inquire into the matter, and Sir Toby and Lady Fuz leave the theatre to pursue their daughter. The manager re-enters, declaring that the young lady had indeed run away but with no one from his company. Glib is vexed over the fact that Miss Fuz should have chosen the morning of the rehearsal of his burletta for her pranks. He then reminds the manager that he depends upon him for a prologue and informs him of a kind of address to the town that he himself has prepared by way of an epilogue, but that it must be spoken by an actor who is "a little smart and degageè." The manager proposes King.

AUTHOR:

> Thank, thank you, dear Mr. Patent,—the very man—is he in the house! I wou'd read it to him.

PATENT:

> O no!—since the audience receiv'd him in Linco, he is practising musick, whenever he is not wanted here.

AUTHOR:

> I have heard as much; and that he continually sets his family's teeth on edge, with scraping upon the fiddle.— Conceit, conceit, Mr. Patent, is the ruin of 'em all.—I would wish, when he speaks this Address, that he wou'd be more easy in his carriage, and not have that damn'd jerk in his bow, that he generally treats us with.

PATENT:

> I'll hint as much to him.

AUTHOR:

> This is my conception of the matter;—Bow your body gently, turn your head semicircularly, on one side and the other; and smiling, thus agreeably begin;[110]

and Glib proceeds to speak the epilogue. The humor of this situation lay in the fact that Glib, who criticizes King for his fiddle-scraping, was played by King. Garrick achieved another such humorous effect when he made Lady Fuz, who was personated by Kitty Clive, express a wish "to see that woman off the stage."

The characters in this playlet are excellently well conceived. In Lady Fuz Garrick holds up to ridicule the romanticizing elderly lady. Since this particular one affects a taste for and a critical insight into matters theatrical, her romanticizing takes expression in a fondness for enacting love scenes from the various tragedies she has seen presented at the theatre. Those from *Romeo and Juliet* are her favorites. Of course, she prefers to do them with the handsome young player for whose benefit she purchased tickets, but, since her wish cannot be fulfilled, she must of necessity content herself to play these scenes with Sir Toby, her obese and elderly husband, at times the none too willing victim of her caprices. As a woman of supposedly good taste, she professes to "adore Shakespeare," but her limited power of discrimination bids her look with like veneration upon Glib's nonsensical burletta, the rehearsal of which the stupid dramatist has invited her to witness. To pass the time profitably while she is waiting for the players to begin the rehearsal, Lady Fuz asks that the manager entertain her and her party with the "thunder and lightning," and begs, moreover, to be permitted to see "his traps, his whims, and harlequin pantomimes." "And a shower of rain, or, an eclipse," are the items Sir Toby adds to his wife's order.

To the world at large Sir Toby poses as a patron and connoisseur of the arts and also as a critic of no mean ability, but in reality, he much prefers his food and sleep to a worship of the muses. When, however, he is called upon by his wife to play opposite her in the love scenes from the tragedies, he, of course, acquiesces and goes through them with much ardor. In fact, he makes of those characters he plays, "parts to tear a cat in." The theatre to him is a most convenient place in which to take the little nap that a late dinner prevents him from indulging in at home. That Sir Toby was in his day a "great libertine" is a fact to which Lady Fuz points with no little pride.

Fanny, their daughter, is a romantic but sensible young woman, who laughs at the affectations of her parents. She is more interested in gaining for herself the man she loves than in adopting the vagaries of Sir Toby and his lady. As for Wilson, the idol of Fanny's heart, he is not only a lover but also a man of a practical bent of mind. He finds that in winning Fanny, he will also regain the fortune of which Sir Toby's uncle, "A good lawyer," cheated his father. By carrying off, during the rehearsal of Glib's burletta, the apprehensive but none the less willing Fanny, Wilson wins both a wife and a fortune.

The situation in the Fuz family is not unlike the one in the *ménage* of the weak-willed Parisian, Chrysale, in Molière's *Les Femmes savantes.* With the exception of the level-headed Henriette, Chrysale's younger daughter, the character through which Molière ridicules the blue stockings in the play and, in a wider sense, the salons of the day, all the women here forsake their domestic duties to engage in the discussion of philosophy, poetry, and the like. In the sound-minded Fanny there is the suggestion of Henriette of the French play. Again, like Henriette's mother, Philaminte, and also like Mrs. Snip in **Harlequin's Invasion** and Mrs. Heidelberg in **The Clandestine Marriage,** Lady Fuz dictates the policies of her household, to which, like the husband in *Les Femmes savantes* and also like Snip and like Sterling, Mrs. Heidelberg's brother, Sir Toby bows submissively. In a manner which again recalls Philaminte and also Mrs. Heidelberg, Lady Fuz affects the attitude of the woman of good taste and fine literary discernment who aims to gather about her men of distinction, culture, and fashion. The results of her strivings in this direction are the stupid Glib, the dramatist of the burletta, *Orpheus,* and Sir Macaroni, a gentleman who adopts the attitude of fashionable *ennui* to everything about him. The vulgar, illiterate woman with aspirations after social greatness and with pretensions to good taste appears frequently in Garrick's plays. Mrs. Riot in **Lethe** is one, and, as already indicated, Mrs. Snip in **Harlequin's Invasion** and Mrs. Heidelberg in **The Clandestine Marriage** are others.

Sir Macaroni Virtu, as his name suggests, is the foppish *dilettante* who dabbles somewhat in musical composition. We discover that he is responsible for two of the songs in the burletta. In Glib's opinion Sir Macaroni is "perhaps the most accomplished connoisseur in these three kingdoms." He is the fashionable late-comer at the playhouse and everywhere else. He "generally sits up all night, and if he gets up before two o'clock he only walks in his sleep all the rest of the day . . . he is never properly awake 'till other people go to bed . . ."[111] He is the type that has no great opinion of anybody but himself. He abominates the playhouse for the reason that his "ingenious countrymen" have cultivated a taste for soft sentimental plays to the exclusion of the "high seasoned comedies," the *genre* for which he expresses a preference. Although Sir Macaroni's fashionable vices are in general laughed at by Garrick, still, in this particular instance, the fop seems to be permitted to voice the dramatist's own sentiments regarding the comedy of the day. Moreover, in the burletta to be rehearsed before Sir Toby Fuz and his lady, Garrick pokes hearty fun at sentimental comedy when he represents Orpheus, the hero, as a man of fashion who keeps a mistress and "upon a qualm of con-

science, quits his mistress and sets out for hell with a resolution to fetch his wife." To the manager's question, "Is that too like a man of fashion, Mr. Glib?" the author of the burletta replies, and here Garrick ridicules the eleventh-hour reformation of the rake in the sentimental comedies.

> No, that's the *moral* part of him—He's a mix'd character— but as he approaches and gets into the infernal regions, his principles melt away by degrees, as it were, by the heat of the climate—and finding that his wife, Eurydice, is kept by Pluto, he immediately makes up to Proserpine, and is kept by her, then they all four agree matters amicably—Change partners, as one may say, make a genteel partie quarrée, and finish the whole with a song and a chorus—and a stinger it is—The subject of the song is—the old proverb, *exchange is no robbery*—[112]

In so far as Glib, the author of the burletta, is concerned, he is the usual Bayes type of dramatist of the rehearsal play. Bumptious and all-knowing, he is unalterable in his opinions and most unwilling to take suggestions of any sort from those who from experience know better than he. Glib dictates unrestrainedly to all about him, even to the manager, and demands that his orders, whether sound or otherwise, be carried out. He is profuse in his complaints to the manager about players and conditions on the stage and exacts from him assurances that all transgressions will be punished and all oversights remedied. In Glib's play, *Orpheus,* the *raison d'être* of the rehearsal, Garrick takes the opportunity to point out what to him was a ridiculous extravagance prevalent in the drama of the time—the burletta which he holds up to laughter.

In so far as the burletta is concerned, the definition of this form varies. To the younger Colman in the nineteenth century, the burletta was a "drama in rhyme, and which is entirely musical; a short comic piece, consisting of recitative and singing, wholly accompanied, more or less, by the Orchestra."[113] In the middle of the eighteenth century up to the nineteenth, the burletta was looked upon as a kind of "poor Relation to an Opera,"[114] and, as Professor Nicoll points out, "if eighteenth century audiences defined it at all, they thought of it as connected with recitative and aria. If this recitative is in ridicule of the recitative of serious opera, the application of the test seems justified, but in practice no such method or rule seems to have been employed."[115] But it is decidedly in ridicule not only of the recitatives and arias but also, as has been pointed out, of the duets, trios, and all the other divisions of group singing in the Italian operas, that Garrick wrote his burletta of *Orpheus,* with its dancing cows (a hit at the popular demand for the stage-carpenter's tricks), which forms the rehearsal portion of his burlesque, **A Peep Behind the Curtain.** Garrick's burletta conforms in every respect to the type that Professor Nicoll describes when he says:

> Technically the term burletta ought to be confined to the burlesque comic operas, to those for example which deal in a ludicrous way with classic legend or history, etc.[116]

In the pointedness of its ridicule of the popular pattern of the *genre* itself, the burletta of *Orpheus* is delightful. In its extravagance and incongruity of characters and situations, and in its rollicking and spontaneous good fun, it is really excellent. The fact that Garrick gives to the elegant Eurydice of classical legend the scratching traits so characteristic of the heroine of the notorious Cock Lane Ghost affair adds to the absurdity of a plot already replete with ludicrous situations. Particularly admirable in the burletta of *Orpheus* are the lyrics. The autobiographical nature of some of Orpheus' songs; the narrative strain of some others which helps in the unfolding of the plot; the metrical dexterity of all of them; their sprightliness, singability, their extravagant and lively good humor, which, as in the situations themselves, depends upon incongruity; the good-natured and mirth-provoking satire which becomes a part of the very texture of them; all these characteristics give to the lyrics which Garrick injected into the burletta a ring that at times heralds the lyrics of a later master of satire, William Schwenck Gilbert.

A Peep Behind the Curtain enjoyed great popularity. The music for the burletta was written by the violinist François Hippolite Barthélemon (1741-1808), from whose fee for this work, Boaden informs us, Garrick "struck off ten guineas from the fifty which he had promised, saying, that '*the dancing cows* had cost him so much money he could not really afford to give the composer *more*.'"[117] The play is in the typical Garrick vein. It is vivacious in its dialogue, swiftly-moving in action, and good-humored in its satire. The situations are interesting and highly amusing, and the characterization well executed. The play was brilliantly acted, and, besides King in the character of Glib, the cast also included, as has been already indicated, the great Kitty Clive, who played Lady Fuz. It was she who also created the other parts of the coarse *bourgeois* wife with fine lady aspirations, Mrs. Riot, Mrs. Heidelberg, and probably (although the actress who interpreted this part is mentioned neither in Genest nor in the *MS. Diaries of the Drury Lane Theatre*) also, since it is a typical Kitty Clive part, Mrs. Snip.

The Meeting of the Company; or, Bayes's Art of Acting

The prelude, ***The Meeting of the Company; or, Bayes's Art of Acting,*** is the third of the long-lost Garrick plays that appeared in print for the first time in the volume ***Three Plays by David Garrick.*** The manuscript of this play, like that of ***The Jubilee,*** was in the Kemble-Devonshire Collection before it passed into the Henry E. Huntington Library and Art Gallery where it is now. The scheduled date of presentation of this one-act playlet, according to Garrick's petition[118] to the Lord Chamberlain in which he requests this official's consent to its production, was September 5, 1774; but it was given some two weeks later. On Saturday evening, September 17,[119] taking the place of the usual prologue, it introduced the 1774-1775 season into Garrick's theatre.

The play has scarcely any plot. It deals largely with a lesson given by another of the opinionated, coxcombical Bayes type of dramatist to the company of Drury Lane players on the art of acting both in tragedy and in comedy. Here, then, is another burlesque-rehearsal play. The stage-spectators are, however, missing in this piece, but actors here take the place of these and just as these spectators usually do, they, too, comment and pass judgment on whatever Bayes says or does; "it is full of fine Satyr & an Excellent Lesson to all performers,"[120] says Hopkins, the prompter of Drury Lane, of this play. It served as a vehicle for burlesquing the faults and idiosyncrasies of bad players and bad playwrights.

That Garrick wrote ***The Meeting of the Company*** with an eye upon the older piece, Buckingham's *The Rehearsal,* becomes evident from the fact that he borrowed for his hero the name of the protagonist of the Restoration play; in fact, the Bayes of the Garrick burlesque is a copy of the Bayes of *The Rehearsal,* drawn in miniature. Like the original, the eighteenth century Bayes is puffed up with his own greatness and importance. Instead of setting out, however, as does the Bayes of *The Rehearsal,* to construct plots and to turn verse into prose and prose into verse according to the methods expounded in his book, *Drama Commonplaces,* the Bayes of Garrick's play, with his book, Bayes's *Art of Acting* in his hand, undertakes an entirely different task, that of remoulding actors, "making the worst equal to the best," and turning tragedians into comedians and vice versa. In the projects of their stupidly conceived heroes, the dramatists of both the Restoration and eighteenth century burlesques find mediums for satirizing some of the prevailing follies of the theatres of their respective periods, particularly the ranting tragedies and the manner in which these were presented.

The stage on the rising of the curtain represents the one of the Drury Lane Theatre at the opening of a theatrical season. Painters, carpenters, and gilders are at work. The chief carpenter orders one of the stage-hands "to lower the Clouds" and to "bid Jack Trundle sweep out the Thunder Trunk," and adds, "we had very slovenly Storms last season."[121] Singers are singing, the ballet-master and his dancers are practicing their steps, and actors and actresses greet each other on meeting again after a summer spent in the various provincial theatres. Parsons, one of the outstanding character actors in Garrick's company, informs Miss Platt, another member but of minor importance, that the manager wishes her to be ready in a part by the next night; "'tis very short, & very easy to study."

Miss Platt:

I have been harrass'd all the Summer, & now I must sit up all Night, to Study this dab of a thing—Managers never consider the wear & tear of a Constitution. [*Exit peevish-ly.*][122]

This, incidentally, is all her part consists of.

The prompter clears the stage of all non-essentials preparatory to the rehearsal which Bayes is to conduct. In a conversation between Parsons and Weston, the admirable low comedian of the company, we find Garrick's criticism of such players in his *troupe* as Mrs. Abington (1737-1815), who took particular delight in vexing him by sending to Hopkins, oftentimes only one hour before curtain time, a note offering the usual excuse that some indisposition prevented her appearance at the theatre. On the back of one such Abington missive, Garrick wrote the comment, "that worst of bad women Mrs. Abington."

Patent, the manager, enters and greets the players cordially. Weston's boast that he can play tragedy as well as the best in the company, and a tragedy actor's retort to Weston's remark, give Garrick an opportunity to ridicule the methods employed by some of the tragedians of that period.

WESTON:

I can set my arms so, take two strides, roar as well as the best of you, & look like an owl.

TR. ACTR:

Is there nothing else requisite to form a Tragedian?
[*with contempt*]

WESTON:

O yes, the perriwig maker to make me a bush, a Taylor a hoop petticoat, a carpenter a Truncheon, a Shoemaker high heels, & Cork Soles—and as for Strange Faces, & Strange Noises, I can make them my Self.[123]

One has but to look at the portrait of James Quin (1693-1766) as Coriolanus to discover the accuracy of Garrick's description of the costume of the eighteenth-century actor of tragedy. As a result of Weston's discourse on the requisites of a tragedian, a quarrel ensues between one of these and the comedian Weston. To settle the difference between the contending pair, the manager assures both that Bayes will teach them "that there is nothing in Acting Tragedy or Comedy." But their differences are soon forgotten when they learn that Bayes, in a letter to the manager, has referred to the players as "Smoaky Chimnies." With a common cause to fight for, they now unite to "Smoak him" when he comes.

PATENT:

... Tom don't be too Riotous but listen to him & Learn.

WESTON:

Rather too old for that.[124]

With much bustle and ado, Bayes makes his appearance, greets the various players, congratulates some on the suc-

cess achieved by them in their performances in the provinces, and then proceeds to ridicule the judgment and tastes of the provincial audiences. Here Baddeley, another actor, enters, and Bayes extends to him his good wishes on the success of his new play. He asks Baddeley whether he has produced any ridiculous characters, and in the player's reply we find Garrick's criticism of the stupidly boastful writers of the Bayes type.

BADDELEY:

O yes, a conceited old Fool, whose Vanity makes him ridiculous, even to the Lamp Lighters of the Theatre.[125]

When, after some bandying of words, Baddeley refers to his own and Bayes's writing as "Scribbling," the strutting coxcomb takes offense and believes it is time to complain to Patent of the disrespect shown him by the players of whom he expects nothing but "Submission & Civility." Patent finds a reason soon enough for their rudeness, and here, in the words which Garrick puts into Patent's mouth, he pokes fun at the vaingloriousness of some of the members of his company.

PATENT:

The Matter is this Mr Bayes—being Just return'd from the Country, where they Play Kings & Heroes, & they can't be lower'd immediately—In a few days by good Discipline & waking them from their dreams of Royalty, they'll be very Civil again, & very good Subjects.

BAYES:

Poor Fellows—their weak heads are easily turn'd, but we'll fix 'em. Do you about your Business M^r. Patent, and I'll to mine—When I have giv'n 'em a Lecture or two, you shall hear them.

PATENT:

I will prepare Matters for opening the Season, & you for carrying it on Successfully. [*Exit.*]

BAYES:

Leave that to me;—if I don't chip your Blocks into some Shape, Say I am no workman. [*Pulls out his book.*][126]

Bayes now holds forth on his ideas on acting as these are set forth in his work, *Bayes's Art of Acting or The Worst equal to the Best*. His instructions to the actors, as he informs them, will be given in "very Musical Numbers" (*i.e.*, in verse). His plan is to "oppose Nature." Moreover, he proposes "to make the worst equal to the best, to turn tragedians into Comedians, and *vice versa*," and although Shakespeare, "A Silly Empty Creature," cautions the player "never o'erstep the Modesty of Nature," Bayes advises against this dictum, for "No Modesty will do upon the Stage." He expects to extend his scheme to poetry, painting, and music as well as to the drama,

and in a few years make Genius of as little Consequence in this Nation, as a fine Complexion, which you know

Ladies is to be bought of any French Milliner in the Bills of Mortality.[127]

The lesson begins. Bayes insists that whenever he "comes to some striking forcible lines," the actors, "by way of a Greek Chorus, repeat and act them." With this he enters upon his task of instructing them in the "Art of Acting Comedy & Tragedy." Here follows Garrick's burlesque on the methods employed by the tragedians of the Quin school, whose artificial style of elocution, Garrick with his natural manner of delivery revolutionized entirely. This scene is uproariously funny.

BAYES:

> [*Reads*] First Gentlemen, turn Nature out of door,
> Then Rant away, 'till you can rant no more,
> Walk, talk, & look, as none walk'd, talk'd, & look'd before.[128]

And after some interchange of opinion between players and playwright on these instructions, Bayes continues,

> Would you in Tragedy Extort applause,
> Distort *Yourselves,*—now Rage, now Start—now pause,
> Beat breast, roll Eyes, stretch Nose, up brows, down Jaws,
> Then strut, stride, stare, Goggle, bounce, & Bawl,
> And when you're out of breath—pant, drag, & drawl.[129]

Weston, however, is not very much impressed, but Bayes disregards the comedian and proceeds thus:

> Be in extremes in Buskin, or in Sock,
> In action Wild—in attitude a Block!
> From the Spectator's Eye, your faults to hide,
> Be either Whirlwind,—or be petrify'd.[130]

And having now warmed up to the occasion, Bayes rants on in much the same bombastic strain of Buckingham's Drawcansir.

> I thurst for Vengeance, bring me Fiends, a Cup,
> Large as my Soul, that I may drink it up.[131]

In Weston, the *habitué* of the London taverns, this "drink it up" part of Bayes' recitation strikes a responsive note, and he involuntarily "licks his lips."

BAYES:

> But you must not drink it up with Joy, M[r]. Weston.

WESTON:

> I can't help it—You must alter the figure.

BAYES:

> Not for all the Wine in the Kingdom . . .[132]

and Bayes continues:

> 'Tis only blood can quench me—thus I draw
> My droughty Dagger—& thus Slake it—ha!
>
> [*Starts into an Attitude.*][133]

And mimicking Bayes, the players, too, "start into an Attitude."

Bayes proceeds to instruct them in a new point. "To heighten Terror," he advises:

> Thus pull your hair to add to your distress,
> What your face cannot, let your Wig Express.[134]

Bayes sets about to demonstrate how to "tear a passion to tatters." He growls and draws out his "r's," assuring the players that he can, if he so pleases, "make a word of Two Syllables, two & Twenty." He does all but chew up the scenery. "I shall reach their hearts one way or another," he asserts defiantly.

With his lesson on the method of acting tragedy concluded, Bayes sets to work to chip Garrick's "Blocks into some Shape" in comedy also.

> Observe in Comedy to frisk about,
> Never stand still—Jerk, work—fly in—fly out,
> Your faults conceal in flutter, & in hurry;
> And with Snip, snap, the Poets [*sic*] meaning worry,
> Like Bullies hide your wants in bounce & Vapour,
> If Mem'ry fail—take Snuff, laugh, Curse, & Caper;
> Hey Jack! what!—damn it! ha! ha! Cloud, dull, sad,
> Cuss it! Hell Devil! Woman, Wine, drunk, Mad![135]

At this point Bayes orders the players to repeat some lines after him and, like Bayes in *The Rehearsal,* who "ends each act with a dance," he sets the company of Drury Lane actors a-capering. The plan is for them to "caper off" during the recital of the lines. When, however, Bayes commands that they "caper in again," they refuse to obey him. With his rehearsal thus abruptly terminated, the stupid Bayes, "addressing himself to the House," appeals to the audience to drive such "Blockheads" as Weston and his colleagues from the stage. Should they, however, be permitted to continue in their profession, Bayes promises that "not a single author of merit will be found to write for it." Weston, who "capered off" the stage with the other players, now returns to take issue with Bayes. He declares, and this seems to be Garrick's warning, that if such writers as Bayes are not driven from the theatre, not a single competent author will be found willing to engage in playwriting.

> If Nature is to be turn'd out of doors, there will be nothing
> but ranting & roaring in Tragedy & Capering, & face
> making in Comedy—the Stage will go to Ruin the Publick
> will go to Sleep, & I shall go to Jail—[136]

With Weston's departure, Bayes, like his prototype in the Restoration play, is left all alone in the supposedly empty theatre (rehearsal time), and like the other, he, too, proceeds to give vent to his feelings. He curses the theatre that retains such disrespectful and inefficient actors. In Bayes' invective Garrick takes the opportunity to satirize his audiences and to give a picture of conditions in the theatre in general.

may this House be always as Empty as it is now; or if it must fill, Let it be with fine Ladies to disturb the actors, fine Gentlemen to admire themselves, & fat Citizens to Snore in the Boxes;—may the Pit be fill'd with Nothing but Crabbed Critics, unemploy'd Actors, & Managers Orders—May places be kept in the Green Boxes without being paid for; & may the Galleries never bring good humour & horse laughs with them again.[137]

And with the words "Sic transit Gloria Mundi," Bayes leaves the theatre.

The Meeting of the Company is an interesting and briskly-moving little play. The dialogue is vivacious, the characterization good, and the humor excellent. The fact that the scene of action of this play is the stage of Garrick's own theatre; that the characters are members of his company, each of whom appears in his own name; and that Garrick permits these players to engage in a discussion on matters relative to acting and to the stage in general, recalls Molière's practice in *L'Impromptu de Versailles* (1663). The actors who took part in *The Meeting of the Company*—Thomas King, Tom Weston, and William Parsons—were the outstanding ones in the comic forces of the Drury Lane Theatre. That Weston did not play the part of Thomas King, as Knight in his account of Weston in the *Dictionary of National Biography* erroneously states,[138] but that he spoke for himself, has already been pointed out in the "Introduction" to the text of *The Meeting of the Company* in *Three Plays by David Garrick*.[139] Thomas King as himself does not make his appearance but is merely alluded to in the conversation between Patent, the manager, and Bayes. The fact that King did a particularly fine piece of work in his interpretation of Glib, the author of the burletta in *A Peep Behind the Curtain,* leads to the supposition that he also interpreted the stupidly opinionated Bayes in *The Meeting of the Company.* The play itself is an effective little piece. It was extremely well presented and deserved the popularity that it achieved. Both *The Meeting of the Company* and *A Peep Behind the Curtain* are worthy forerunners of the brilliant Sheridan rehearsal play, *The Critic* (1779).

THE THEATRICAL CANDIDATES

During the summer of 1775 Garrick's theatre underwent extensive alterations. From the *MS. Diaries of the Drury Lane Theatre,* we learn that the house was now "fitted up in the most Elegant manner Possible by the Adams's etc. and is the most compleat of any Theatre in Europe. Great Applause to the House before the Curtain."[140] The theatre opened its doors on September 23; and, instead of the customary prologue, the theatrical season of 1775-1776, Garrick's last one on the stage, was ushered in with his musical prelude, *The Theatrical Candidates.* The plot of it runs thus:

Mercury is sent to Drury Lane to see the "House's transformation" and to

Ask if the Critics give their approbation,
Or as in other cases—"Yawn at alteration."[141]

He informs the audience also that Tragedy and Comedy, having heard of the renovation of Drury Lane, have asked Jove to grant them leave to visit the theatre in order to canvass for the interest and votes of the audiences. Tragedy enters and claims the votes of the spectators which she asserts are hers by right, for she swelled the hearts of the old Britons with glory and stirred their nobler passions. Since she can still achieve this, her rival must resign in order that she, Tragedy, may fix her empire and throne in Drury Lane Theatre. She thereupon challenges all who dare contend with her. Comedy responds to Tragedy's call with a counter challenge.

Think you, your strutting, straddling, puffy pride,
Your rolling eyes, arms kimbo'd, tragic stride,
Can frighten me?—Britons, 'tis yours to chuse,
That murd'ring lady, or this laughing muse?
Now make your choice;—with smiles I'll strive to win ye:
If you chuse Her, she'll stick a dagger in ye![142]

Comedy then describes her qualifications which entitle her to solicit the votes of the Drury Lane audiences. She emphasizes the fact that it is she and not Melpomene who has won the hearts of the Britons. A quarrel arises between the two ladies.

TRAG.:

You can be wise too; nay a *thief* can be!
Wise with stale sentiments all stol'n from me:
Which long cast off, from my heroic verses,
Have stuff'd your motley, dull sententious farces:
The town grew sick!

COM.:

For all this mighty pother,
Have you not laugh'd with one eye, cry'd with t'other?

TRAG.:

In all the realms of nonsense, can there be,
A monster, like your comic-tragedy?

COM.:

O yes, my dear!—Your tragic-comedy.[143]

And here Garrick directs a shaft at sentimental comedy as well as at the injecting of comic elements into tragedy. The dispute between the two muses continues until Tragedy, exasperated, turns to the audience thus, "Which will you chuse?"

COM.:

Sour Her, or smiling Me?
There are but two of us.
    [*Enter* HARLEQUIN, *etc.*]

HAR.:

O yes, we're three!
Your votes and int'rest, pray, for me
[*to the pit*]

T<small>RAG</small>.:

What fall'n so low to cope with thee?

H<small>AR</small>.:

Ouy, Ouy!

C<small>OM</small>.:

Alas, poor We!

[*shrugs her shoulders and laughs*][144]

Harlequin in his turn claims the votes of the audience.

Each friend I have above, whose voice so loud is,
Will never give me up for two such dowdies;
She's grown so grave, and she so cross and bloody,
Without my help, your brains will all be muddy:
Deep thought, and politicks, so stir your gall,
When you come here, you should not think at all;
And I'm the best for that; be my protectors!
And let friend *Punch* here talk to the electors.[145]

Upon the conclusion of Harlequin's description of his virtues which give him the right to lay claim to the votes of the audience, Mercury arrives to announce Apollo's decision in the contention between Tragedy, Comedy, and Pantomime. Here Garrick sets forth his opinion on the matter of sentimental and tragi-comedy. Except when combined in the plays of Shakespeare, comedy and tragedy must keep to their own respective provinces. As for Harlequin, he is to be tolerated only when farce and musical entertainments will fail to please. But even then, Harlequin, mute or loquacious, is not to be the principal attraction, but is merely to serve as an attendant upon comedy and tragedy.

The *MS. Diaries of the Drury Lane Theatre* inform us that *The Theatrical Candidates,* which "is wrote by D. G. Esq., was receiv'd with great Applause."[146] Clever in itself, the piece, except for its sprightly dialogue, has no particular value dramatically. It is interesting and important in the fact that it gives Garrick's views as to the functions of the various forms of drama. This playlet was published in 1775 together with his one-act musical piece, *May-Day; or, The Little Gipsy.*

Except for some shafts of ridicule directed at the Cock Lane Ghost affair and at the ludicrous results that the grand tour effected in the ultra-fashionable young Englishman of the day, these plays represent largely Garrick's views on matters theatrical. Again he voices in them his antagonism toward sentimental comedy and satirizes the last minute reclamation of the rake. He makes merry over the musical extravaganzas of the period and over the popularity of the Italian opera with its elaborate musical forms. Except for the plays of Shakespeare, Garrick maintains the classical attitude with regard to the intermingling of comedy and tragedy. He stands for the purity of the *genre*. As for pantomime, despite popular acclaim, his wish was to relegate it to a position of minor importance in the repertory of his theatre. He deplores the fact that the stage-carpenter, the scene-painter, and the singing and dancing masters had gained for themselves so prominent a place in the theatre of his day. Of his actors he demands that they "hold the mirror up to nature"; of the critics he asks fair play. His exasperation over the ranting tragedies and over the persistence with which the dramatists of such plays forced them upon him knew no bounds. As for his attitude toward his audiences, these plays show him to have had no regard for the fashionable late-comer who visited the theatre merely to be seen. He has great admiration for those who frequented the playhouse because they enjoyed it. He scoffs at pretenders to good taste such as Lady Fuz; he respects such humble, honest, and simple folk as the Farmer and his family in *The Farmer's Return from London.* In all, these plays are replete with suggestions which convey vividly the conditions in and about the theatre of Garrick's day.

Notes

1. Genest, <small>III</small>, 609.

2. James Miller, *An Hospital for Fools* (1737), I, p. 26.

3. *Lethe* (1767), Act I, p. 8. The 1767 edition of *Lethe* is used in the discussion of the play.

4. A facetious little hit by Garrick at himself.

5. *Lethe,* Act I, p. 9.

6. *Ibid.,* p. 10.

7. *Ibid.,* p. 16.

8. *Ibid.,* pp. 16-17.

9. See Chapter I, note 14.

10. *Lethe,* Act I, p. 22.

11. *Ibid.,* pp. 23-24.

12. *Ibid.,* p. 30.

13. *Ibid.,* pp. 34-35.

14. *Ibid.,* p. 35.

15. *Ibid.,* pp. 35-36.

16. *Ibid.,* pp. 36-37. For the rest of Mrs. Riot's speech, see Chapter I, note 5. By "Johnsons" Mrs. Riot means, of course, Ben Jonson.

17. *Lethe,* Act I, p. 38.

18. *Ibid.,* p. 51.

19. *The New Monthly Magazine,* <small>XXXIV</small>, Part 1 (June, 1832), 568.

20. James William Dodd (1740-1796) was so particularly effective in his portrayal of fops that he was looked upon as a worthy successor to Colley Cibber. His interpretation of Sir Andrew Aguecheek some years later won the warm praise of Charles Lamb.

21. W. C. Oulton, *History of the Theatres of London* (1796), I, 4.

22. Swift, *Lilliput*, Chapter III.

23. *Lilliput* (1757), p. iv.

24. *MS. Diaries of the Drury Lane Theatre.*

25. *Lilliput,* I, i, p. 10.

26. *Ibid.,* p. 15.

27. *Ibid.,* I, iv, p. 39.

28. *Ibid.*

29. *Ibid.,* I, i, p. 3.

30. *Ibid.,* pp. 3-4.

31. *Ibid.,* p. iv.

32. *Ibid.,* I, iv, pp. 23-24.

33. *Ibid.,* p. 19.

34. *Ibid.,* p. 21.

35. *Ibid.,* p. vi.

36. Oulton, *History of the Theatres of London,* I, 61.

37. *Ibid.,* I, 59.

38. *The Male-Coquette* (1757), [Introduction].

39. *MS. Diaries of the Drury Lane Theatre.*

40. *The Male-Coquette,* I, i, p. 8.

41. *Ibid.,* I, ii, pp. 14-15.

42. *Ibid.,* p. 17.

43. *Ibid.,* p. 18.

44. *Ibid.,* pp. 25-26.

45. *Ibid.,* II, ii, p. 32.

46. *Ibid.*

47. *Ibid.,* pp. 37-38.

48. *Ibid.,* p. 39.

49. *Ibid.,* II, iii, p. 52.

50. *Ibid.*

51. Genest, IV, 482. Professor Nicoll, too, holds this opinion in his *Late Eighteenth Century Drama* (1927), p. 116.

52. Etherege, *The Man of Mode,* I, i.

53. *Ibid.*

54. *The Male-Coquette,* II, i, p. 28.

55. Etherege, *The Man of Mode,* II, ii.

56. *The Male-Coquette,* I, ii, p. 21.

57. Farquhar, *The Constant Couple,* IV, iii.

58. *The Male-Coquette,* II, iii, p. 50.

59. *MS. Diaries of the Drury Lane Theatre.*

60. *Bon Ton* (1775), Introduction.

61. Prompter Hopkins' entry reads: "Bon Ton is a Comedy in Two Acts written 15 or 16 years ago. M^r G out of Friendship for Mr King gave it him to get up for his Benefit—It was very well perform'd & receiv'd with highest Applause."

62. *Bon Ton,* I, i, p. 6.

63. *Ibid.,* p. 12.

64. *Ibid.,* p. 10.

65. *Ibid.,* I, ii, p. 15.

66. *Ibid.,* p. 17.

67. *Ibid.,* pp. 18-19.

68. *Ibid.,* p. 19.

69. *Ibid.,* pp. 20-21.

70. *Ibid.*

71. *Ibid.,* I, iii, p. 25.

72. *Ibid.,* II, ii, pp. 39-40.

73. *Ibid.,* p. 41.

74. *Ibid.,* p. 44.

75. *Ibid.,* p. 43.

76. *Ibid.,* p. 44.

77. William Brereton (1741-1787) played the part of Colonel Tivy in the presentation at Drury Lane.

78. John O'Keeffe, *Recollections* (1826), I, 162-163.

79. *Harlequin's Invasion,* II, ii *(Three Plays by David Garrick),* pp. 32-33.

80. *Bon Ton,* I, i, p. 6.

81. *Ibid.,* p. 8.

82. Genest, IV, 642. The entries in the *MS. Diaries of the Drury Lane Theatre* for the period between September, 1760, and September, 1762, are missing as are also those covering the period between September, 1764, and September, 1768. We have, therefore, no evidence from that source as to the date of the first performance of *The Farmer's Return from London.*

83. *The Farmer's Return from London* (1762), p. 11.

84. *Ibid.*

85. *Ibid.,* p. 12.

86. *Ibid.*

87. See Chapter III.

88. *The Farmer's Return from London,* pp. 12-13.

89. *Ibid.,* p. 13.

90. Walpole, *Letters* (to George Montague), V, 170, the letter of February 2, 1762.

91. Charles Churchill, *The Ghost,* in *Poems* (1764), I, 165.

92. *Ibid.,* 166.

93. Walpole, *Letters,* V, 170-171.

94. *Gentleman's Magazine* (February, 1762), XXXII, 81.

95. *The Farmer's Return from London,* pp. 13-14.

96. *Ibid.* [Introduction].

97. Garrick, *Correspondence,* I, 253.

98. *Ibid.,* 253-254.

99. Genest, V, 125. *Linco's Travels* is printed in Garrick's *Poetical Works,* II, 227-234.

100. For King's benefit night three years later (March 22, 1770), *Linco's Travels,* according to Genest (V, 269), did serve as the interlude of the evening's entertainment. It is interesting to note that the dramatic fare for that night was made up entirely of Garrick's works. The principal play was *The Clandestine Marriage,* which is predominantly Garrick's. Here King played Lord Ogleby. The interlude was Garrick's *Linco's Travels* with King as Linco; and the afterpiece proved to be the manager's dramatic burlesque *A Peep Behind the Curtain* in which King played the author, Glib. Prompter Hopkins' entry in the *MS. Diaries of the Drury Lane Theatre* for March 22, 1770 agrees with Genest as to the principal play and the afterpiece, but it makes no mention of a performance that evening of *Linco's Travels.* This does not necessarily mean that the playlet was not presented on that particular occasion. The general practice in the *MS. Diaries* was to record no other portions of the evening's program but the principal play and the afterpiece.

101. O'Keeffe, *Recollections of my Life,* I, 150.

102. Opinion is divided as to the respective shares of Beaumont and Fletcher in the authorship of this play.

103. Genest, V, 158. *The MS. Diaries of the Drury Lane Theatre* are incomplete here.

104. *A Peep Behind the Curtain,* I, ii, p. 6.

105. *Ibid.,* p. 9.

106. *Ibid.,* p. 11.

107. *Ibid.,* p. 15.

108. *Ibid.,* p. 16.

109. *Ibid.,* p. 20.

110. *Ibid.,* II, i, p. 45.

111. *Ibid.,* I, ii, p. 13.

112. *Ibid.,* p. 14.

113. Richard B. Peake, *Memoirs of the Colman Family* (1841), II, 398.

114. Catherine Clive, *The Rehearsal; or, Bayes in Petticoats* (1753), I, i, p. 14.

115. Allardyce Nicoll, *Late Eighteenth Century Drama* (1927), p. 195.

116. *Ibid.,* p. 194.

117. Garrick, *Correspondence,* I, 307 (note).

118. *The Meeting of the Company (Three Plays by David Garrick),* p. 123. Garrick's petition to the Lord Chamberlain reads:

   Sir.

   If the following little Piece call'd *The Meeting of the Company or Bayes's Art of Acting,* meets the Approbation of the Lord Chamberlain we shall have it perform'd at the Theatre Royal in Drury Lane 5 Sept[r] 1774.

   D. Garrick

   After his signature, Garrick added the note, "for M[r] Lacy & himself." This is Willoughby Lacy, who, upon the death of James Lacy, his father (January, 1774), stepped into the co-partnership with Garrick of the Drury Lane Theatre.

119. *MS. Diaries of the Drury Lane Theatre.*

120. *Ibid.,* Saturday, September 17, 1774.

121. *Three Plays by David Garrick,* p. 125.

122. *Ibid.*, p. 126.

123. *Ibid.*, p. 131.

124. *Ibid.*, p. 133.

125. *Ibid.*, p. 134.

126. *Ibid.*, p. 135.

127. *Ibid.*, p. 137.

128. *Ibid.*, p. 139.

129. *Ibid.*, pp. 139-140.

130. *Ibid.*, p. 140.

131. *Ibid.*

132. *Ibid.*

133. *Ibid.* "Attitude" was borrowed from pantomime terminology.

134. *Ibid.*, p. 141.

135. *Ibid.*, p. 142.

136. *Ibid.*, p. 144.

137. *Ibid.*, pp. 144-145.

138. *Dictionary of National Biography*, xx, 1287.

139. See page 117.

140. *MS. Diaries of the Drury Lane Theatre*, September 23, 1775.

141. *The Theatrical Candidates* (1775), I, i, p. 33.

142. *Ibid.*, p. 35.

143. *Ibid.*, p. 36.

144. *Ibid.*, p. 37.

145. *Ibid.*, pp. 37-38.

146. September 23, 1775.

Bibliography

VARIOUS EDITIONS OF GARRICK'S PLAYS

Bon Ton; or, High Life above Stairs. London: T. Becket, 1775. pp. viii + 44.

Farmer's Return from London, The. London: Printed by Dryden Leach for J. and R. Tonson, 1762. pp. 15.

────── *Three Plays by David Garrick,* ed. by Elizabeth P. Stein. New York: William Edwin Rudge, 1926. pp. 1-53.

Lethe. London: Paul Vaillant, 1767. pp. iv + 51.

Lilliput. London: Paul Vaillant, 1757. pp. viii + 39.

Linco's Travels. The Poetical Works of David Garrick. London: George Kearsley, 1785. 2. pp. 227-34.

Male-Coquette, The; or, Seventeen Hundred and Fifty-Seven. London: P. Vaillant, 1757. pp. viii + 52.

Meeting of the Company, The; or, Bayes's Art of Acting. Manuscript in the Henry E. Huntington Library and Art Gallery [1774]. pp. 31.

────── *Three Plays by David Garrick,* ed. by Elizabeth P. Stein. New York: William Edwin Rudge, 1926. pp. 113-51.

Peep Behind the Curtain, A; or, The New Rehearsal. London: T. Becket and P. A. De Hondt, 1767. pp. iv + 46.

Theatrical Candidates, The. With *May-Day; or, The Little Gipsy.* London: T. Becket, 1775. pp. 31-40.

Helmut E. Gerber (essay date 1957)

SOURCE: Gerber, Helmut E. "*The Clandestine Marriage* and Its Hogarthian Associations." *Modern Language Notes* 72.4 (1957): 267-71. Print.

[*In the following essay, Gerber addresses the issue of* The Clandestine Marriage's *debt to the painter William Hogarth. Gerber describes a set of indirect Hogarthian associations surrounding the genesis and development of the play, including Garrick and Colman the Elder's familiarity with two works of literature known to be modeled on Hogarth's art: John Shebbeare's novel* The Marriage Act *(1754) and James Townley's farce* False Concord *(1764).*]

Robert E. Moore, in his book on Hogarth, comments briefly on **The Clandestine Marriage** (1766) as a play that draws its idea from Hogarth's *Marriage à la Mode* (1745). Moore quotes from Garrick's prologue, "which announces the source of the play and pays tribute to the late Hogarth, one of his closest friends," and, he comments, "Hogarth's pictures do not really have very much to do with the action of the play except that the situation revolves around a marriage of convenience. ..."[1] Perhaps so, but the Colman-Garrick play owes a little to several sources which themselves owe much to Hogarth. In any event, Mr. Moore's perhaps too narrowly limited comments warrant expansion, for more evidence on the subject does exist.[2]

First, that Colman, like Garrick, was well-known to Hogarth and also had direct access to Hogarth's influence is plain.[3] Furthermore, Colman, unaided, produced a work which is specifically based on one of Hogarth's prints.[4] Austin Dobson lists this "musical entertainment" and, quoting from the stage directions, says that the ending of the piece comes "as near as possible to *Hogarth's* Print of

THE ENRAGED MUSICIAN [1741]."[5] More pertinently, the younger Colman prints the elder Colman's "Papers relative to a plan of Clandestine Marriage," which is addressed to Garrick.[6] Under the sub-heading "Loose Hints of Acts and Scenes," the author reveals that he had a specific type of scene from Hogarth's series in mind: "a short lawyer scene (*à la* Hogarth), with some family strokes on mortgages, settlements, etc. ..."[7] Such a scene does appear in *The Clandestine Marriage* (III, i). The younger Colman, without referring to this scene, then credits his father with "the outlines of the plan, and of the principal characters."[8]

Still another element also may have contributed to the genesis and development of *The Clandestine Marriage* in its Hogarthian connections. Rev. James Townley, "former Master of Merchant Taylor's School," writes the younger Colman, had written a farce called *False Concord* (acted 20 March 1764). The elder dramatist's son adds, quoting from *Biographia Dramatica*,[9] "that in this farce were three characters (Lord Lavender, Mr. Sudley, an enriched soap-boiler, and a pert valet,) which were afterwards transplanted, with the dialogue of some scenes, nearly *verbatim,* into the '**Clandestine Marriage,**' ... under the names of Lord Ogleby,[10] Mr. Sterling, and Brush." The same writer then adds that Townley's play "was only acted one night ... , and he did not print it." Townley's farce, at any rate, contained two of the chief characters (the old Lord and the old Cit) that are especially prominent in Hogarth's first plate. Although Garrick is usually credited with developing the Ogleby part, Colman also knew Garrick's friend Townley.[11]

As much to the purpose as both Colman's and Garrick's friendship with Townley and Hogarth is Townley's own close relationship with Hogarth. Austin Dobson writes that Hogarth knew "the Rev. Mr. Townley of 'High Life Below Stairs'"[12] and that the latter wrote a complimentary poem to Hogarth. Two lines of this poem, I find, are echoed in Garrick's prologue (lines 21-22). Townley and James Ralph, Dobson says, "are reported to have been among the number of the artist's volunteer assistants. ..."[13] While we cannot say with certainty how much *False Concord* owed to Hogarth, we do know that the farce contained at least two of the major characters shared by Hogarth's prints and the Colman-Garrick play.

Still another indirect Hogarthian connection with *The Clandestine Marriage* is Dr. Shebbeare's novel, *The Marriage Act* (1754), which, Moore says, "found inspiration in *Marriage à la Mode*."[14] Although Moore notes the very close parallel between the novel and Hogarth's first plate,[15] neither Moore nor Dobson connects the novel with *The Clandestine Marriage*. Boaden, however, prints two letters from Shebbeare to Garrick, one of which (November 10, 1766) has particular bearing on the play. Shebbeare gratefully reminds Garrick that "in the advertisement prefixed to your comedy of '**The Clandestine Marriage,**' you have acknowledged some little obligation to one of my novels. ..."[16] However small Garrick's obligation, it is nevertheless a fact that the play and the novel include the same central situation and a number of the chief characters of Hogarth's prints.

Hogarth's prints, then, stimulated a number of authors to write plays and novels containing at least the core of Hogarth's idea and many of his vividly delineated characters. Colman and Garrick, mainly relying on the first plate of Hogarth's series, retain the gouty, dissipated, and financially embarrassed nobleman (Ogleby), his younger kinsman (Sir John Melvil), the wealthy, avaricious citizen (Sterling),[17] and the latter's daughter (Miss Sterling). Colman and Garrick surely retain the essential characterization of these persons as they are depicted in the artist's first plate. Hogarth, of course, develops the characters much further, particularly in showing the almost complete dissipation of the young nobleman. Hogarth's young wife, in the later plates, is perhaps also more sympathetically portrayed than Colman and Garrick's jealous and vain Miss Sterling. Of Hogarth's supernumeraries one finds only somewhat slight reflections in the play. In Hogarth's pictures there is no one quite like Brush, the pert valet, unless he is faintly seen in the yawning footman (Plate II), and Canton, Lord Ogleby's Swiss yes-man, is perhaps slightly evident in the Swiss valet who curls the young countess' hair (Plate IV).

Of Hogarth's story, there is little more in the play than the marriage contract scene, with the attendant lawyers (Plate I). What is not in Hogarth's pictures and what is significantly introduced into the play is at least partly responsible for the difference in tone of the two works. Colman and Garrick add the sentimental story of Fanny and Lovewell. It would perhaps strain the comparison to suggest the possible reflection of the victimized young girl (Plate III) in Fanny, who is legitimately pregnant and not otherwise ill. One might also find some general similarity between Hogarth's discovery scene (Plate V) and the revelations that occur in the play (V, ii).

As far as the setting is concerned, Colman and Garrick have shifted the scene from the nobleman's estate, where Hogarth's action (Plate I) takes place, to the citizen's home. So, also, Colman and Garrick have shifted most of the bad taste from the nobleman to the citizen. As Hogarth satirizes the fashionable taste in art by means of the pictures on the wall (Plate I), so Colman and Garrick make fun of the prevailing taste in architecture (II, ii). Closely related to this is the dialogue on the "most excellent serpentine" in landscaping (II, ii), which is apparently a humorous reflection on Hogarth's line of beauty.

These, then, make up the mélange of "clandestine" Hogarthian associations that at least stimulated Colman and Garrick to write a comedy which, however much it departs from the Hogarthian tree, is certainly an organically connected branch.

Notes

1. R. E. Moore, *Hogarth's Literary Relationships* (Minneapolis, 1948), pp. 57-58. H. B. Wheatley, *Hogarth's London* (London, 1909), p. 107, dismisses the connection between the play and the pictures much more easily.

2. Many of the essentials are given in *Memoirs of the Colman Family,* ed. R. B. Peake (London, 1841, 2 vols.). Although much of Peake's material is drawn from *Posthumous Letters . . . to Francis Colman, and George Colman, the Elder,* ed. George Colman, the younger (London, 1820), the *Memoirs* are more useful because wider in scope.

3. *Memoirs,* I, 71, 74, 103 (Townley, of whom more later, is also mentioned), and 124.

4. Peake, in a note, identifies this as "*Ut Pictura Poesis*; or, the Enraged Musician." According to A. Dobson, *William Hogarth* (N.Y., London, 1907), p. 167, the pantomime was printed in 1789. Also see *Memoirs,* II, 202.

5. Dobson, *op. cit.,* 168; also see pp. 64-65, 245.

6. Reproduced in *Memoirs,* I, 162-68, from *Posthumous Letters,* pp. 333-47.

7. *Memoirs,* I, 165.

8. *Ibid.,* 169.

9. Only in *Posthumous Letters,* p. 346, is it clear that the younger Colman is quoting. In *Memoirs,* I, 172, the passage is given as though it were young Colman's.

10. Other writers suggest that Ogleby is developed from Garrick's own Chalkstone in *Lethe* (1740), who in turn was founded on Foppington in Colley Cibber's *Careless Husband* (1704) (See F. A. Hedgcock, *David Garrick and His French Friends,* N.Y., n. d., p. 89). This does not exclude Garrick's awareness of the traditional character as portrayed by Hogarth. Curiously, in April, 1733, Colley Cibber's play was produced together with Theophilus Cibber's "Grotesque Pantomime" *The Harlot's Progress, or, The Ridotto Al'Fresco,* the latter being dedicated to Hogarth. See the summary and discussion of this piece in Moore, *op. cit.,* pp. 36-40.

11. *Posthumous Letters,* p. 264.

12. Dobson, *op. cit.,* p. 89. Arthur Murphy, *The Life of David Garrick* (London, 1801, 2 vols.), I, 343, says Garrick was responsible for this piece and that he allowed Townley's name to be whispered in connection with it. Townley, in his poem, wrote, "Our sons, in time to come, shall strive / Where the chief honour they shall give, / Or to your pencil, or your pen. . . ."

13. *Ibid.,* p. 112. That Townley assisted Hogarth in preparing the *Analysis* is reported in *William Hogarth,* ed. A. P. Oppé (N.Y., 1948), Cat. 108.

14. Moore, *op. cit.,* pp. 56-57. Shebbeare appears in the third *Election* print (1755). Garrick bought the *Four Pictures of an Election* (see Dobson, *op. cit.,* p. 204).

15. Moore, *op. cit.,* pp. 56-57. In connection with the reference to "the fellow holding the mortgage," the reader may recall my earlier citation of Colman's remark about introducing "a short lawyer scene (*à la* Hogarth), with some family strokes on Mortgages," into *The Clandestine Marriage* (see *Memoirs,* I, 65). Dobson, *op. cit.,* pp. 7, 119, also comments on Shebbeare's connections with Hogarth.

16. *The Private Correspondence of David Garrick,* ed. J. Boaden (London, 1831-32, 2 vols.), I, 246. For Garrick's advertisement see *The Dramatic Works of George Colman* (London, 1777, 4 vols.), I, 152.

17. Note that in Hogarth's sixth plate this person prudently removes a ring from his dying daughter's finger before *rigor mortis* can prevent this economy. Mr. Sterling is no less prudent.

Fred L. Bergmann (essay date 1959)

SOURCE: Bergmann, Fred L. "Garrick's *Zara.*" *PMLA* 74.3 (1959): 225-32. Print.

[*In the following essay, Bergmann attributes the longevity of the Drury Lane revival of* Zara *(1766) to Garrick's alterations to Aaron Hill's text, itself an adaptation of a play by Voltaire. Noting that Garrick played the role of Lusignan for several of* Zara's *twenty-three seasons at Drury Lane, Bergmann provides a careful study of his acting, describing the changes as a conscious attempt to restore the Voltaire reading.*]

In recent works on eighteenth-century drama and theatrical practices, Aaron Hill's *Zara* has received passing attention because of its notable longevity.[1] The play did make theatrical history of a sort in that it was one of only three which were presented for more than twenty consecutive years during David Garrick's tenure at Drury Lane as manager (1747-76). *Zara,* with its twenty-three consecutive seasons, was surpassed only by *Hamlet* and Benjamin Hoadly's *Suspicious Husband* in unbroken performance, both of the latter having achieved twenty-nine consecutive seasons.[2] But mere longevity and consecutiveness of performance cannot force the play upon the attention of today's students of the history of the drama. What perhaps can, however, is the hitherto unrecorded fact that for a considerable portion of its history in Garrick's theater and for years afterward it was not Hill's play but Garrick's own adaptation that was popular. Furthermore, it is an adaptation which sheds interesting light on Garrick's dramatic methods and increases his stature as a careful reviser of older plays.

Exactly when Garrick made his alterations to Hill's play is not easily determined. And the fact that there has been no indication of the alteration in the products of dramatic research—it is not included in the collections of Garrick's works, nor is it listed as his by Thomas Davies,[3] the *CBEL,* Allardyce Nicoll, or today's writers on the Garrick period[4]—does not simplify the problem. Yet alter it he did, as evidenced by a prompt copy in Garrick's hand which is preserved in the Folger Shakespeare Library. The prompt is made from Hill's printed edition of 1763. Garrick never published the play as he emended it, but the acting version in the 1776 Bell's *British Theatre* is clearly based on the alterations in his copy, although the alterer is not named.[5]

The fact that the play, after Garrick's alterations, continued to be popular during the remainder of his career as an actor and for a considerable time afterward and that it drew lucrative houses suggests that some attention be given to it as a theatrical phenomenon of the period. But because the play has long since passed into oblivion, it will be well to review briefly its stage history before discussing the nature of Garrick's alterations.

I. STAGE HISTORY

The English *Zara* is an adaptation of Voltaire's *Zaïre,* which was first presented in Paris on 13 August 1732, and soon thereafter was brought to the English stage. A translation by a Mr. Johnson was advertised, as printed for J. Stone, in May 1735, and is duly noted in the play lists.[6] Aaron Hill's "elegant liberal Translation"[7] appeared in 1736. There has been some confusion among the earlier writers on the period as to the first presentation of the English version. Davies says that Hill translated the play "to relieve the distress" of the actor William Bond, "then aged and infirm," and relates that Bond, who played Lusignan, "expired almost upon the stage, and at the very time when the people were applauding him for his natural exhibition of an aged and dying monarch."[8] The *Biographia Dramatica* (III, 430), apparently basing its account on one in *L'Observateur François à Londres,* a Paris periodical, calls Bond a gentleman who, "collecting a party of his friends, got up the play of *Zara* (which a friend had translated for him) . . ." and maintains that the actor actually died on the stage, a circumstance which is supported by Dr. Doran.[9] Joseph Reed, in the preface to *Madrigal and Turlletta,* relates the claim of one Thomas Hudson to the effect that Hill stole the translation from him after it had been sent to London for criticism. Hudson, an usher in a Durham grammar school, supposedly was told that his tragedy was unfit for presentation, but the pilfered play appeared on the stage the next season as by Hill.[10] Hill himself, in his preface to the printed text (1736), does not mention the early production with Bond, but in No. 60 of his *Prompter* (1735) he had told the story of Bond's death during its first run.

The newspaper bills help to clarify the matter. An item in the *Daily Journal* for 6 May 1735 indicates that a translation of *Zaïre* was to be acted "by Subscription, for the Benefit of a Gentleman" who would play Lusignan, and continues, "all the Parts in the Play are to be perform'd by Gentlemen and Ladies of Taste, and Capacity that way, without Mixture of any Persons who make Acting their Profession." The papers announced the first performance on 29 May "At the Great Room in Villars-Street, York-Buildings" as a benefit for Bond, "the Proprietor, who brings it on at a great Expence (tho' all who act in it are so good to appear Gratis for him) He having lain deplorably ill of the Gout, and Rheumatism, upwards of four Years."[11] Bond played Lusignan, but no mention was made of the translator, who may very well have been the Johnson of the May 1735 edition. The play was repeated the next night, was canceled on Saturday because of the opera at the King's Theatre,[12] and then returned for four more nights,[13] the "Gentleman who plays Osman" taking over the role of the ill-fated Bond beginning with the fourth night. For a final performance that season the play moved to the New Haymarket on 9 July with the same Lusignan.[14]

Hill, in his preface to the 1736 edition, says that his play was first presented by Fleetwood at Drury Lane to test Hill's thesis that true tragedy could be revived by "Young Actors, and Actresses, beginning, unseduc'd by Affected Examples," who were "not disabled, by Custom, and obstinate Prejudice, from pursuing the Plain Track, of Nature." It was performed with notable success in January 1736. Colley Cibber's prologue charges that Voltaire borrowed from *Othello* and tells us that "Zara's Success his utmost Hopes outflew, / And a twice twentieth Weeping-Audience drew." *Zara* was notable, too, as the play which first introduced Mrs. Cibber as a dramatic actress. It had a continuous run of fourteen nights, beginning 12 January, with Mrs. Cibber in the title role, Hill's nephew playing Osman in the initial presentation, and Milward the role Garrick was later to make memorable—Lusignan. Supporting them were Mrs. Pritchard as Selima, Cibber as Nerestan, Berry as Chatillon, Turbutt as Orasmin, and Cross as Melidor.[15] An advance notice in the *Daily Advertiser* for 7 January said that Osman would be played "by a Gentleman, during the first Run only, he not designing to continue on the Stage," which fact was repeated in the bill for the first night on 12 January. Davies tells us that the nephew had "a certain stiffness in action, and too laboured and emphatical an emphasis in speaking" which "disgusted the critics, who too severely corrected the young performer, whom, on the first night of his acting, they cruelly exploded."[16] Thus the second night's notice in the *Daily Post and General Advertiser* informed the public that the gentleman had declined to continue in the part and that it would be "read till one of the Players could be studied in it." On the seventh night (19 January) it was announced in the same paper that William Mills would play the part of Osman.

During the run of fourteen nights (12-27 January) Mrs. Cibber received great acclaim and established herself firmly as a tragic actress, having been coached in her role, according to Davies (I, 137), by Hill himself, who "interlined her part with a kind of commentary upon it; he marked every accent and emphasis; every look, action, and deportment proper to that character, in all its different situations, he critically pointed out." Such was her success that Rich at Covent Garden was forced to run *Zara* concurrently at his house, with old Mrs. Porter in the title role. So firmly was Mrs. Cibber's reputation established in this and succeeding roles that her enforced, though temporary, departure from the stage soon afterward did no permanent injury to her career as an actress.

After its initial success *Zara* experienced a decline. Two editions of the play had been printed in 1736 and one was published in Dublin the following year; thereafter it was not reprinted until 1752, during a revival at Covent Garden. Later, at Drury Lane on 25 March 1754, as a benefit for Mossop, Garrick played Lusignan for the first time, Mrs. Cibber again taking the title role. It had not been acted at that theater for seventeen years[17] but had very likely been chosen for the benefit because of interest in the play created by its Covent Garden run that season and for the two preceding. *Zara* had been performed at the latter house on 16 March 1751 for Mrs. Cibber's benefit. She was supported in the title role by Sparks as Lusignan and Barry as Osman. Covent Garden repeated the play twice that spring (19 March and 3 May), ran it three times the following season, and again twice during that of 1752-53 before Drury Lane, noting its popularity and now having Mrs. Cibber in its company, revived it.

Thereafter *Zara* received a permanent place in Garrick's repertoire. Although there were no long runs in any one season—the longest was five performances in both the 1756-57 and the 1758-59 seasons—it was repeated steadily on an average of almost three times a year for the next twenty-two seasons. Even when Garrick was absent on the Continent (1763-65) the play was performed, Powell taking the role which Garrick had made a permanent fixture of his theater. And as its revival in 1754 had been for a successful benefit (in his *Diary* Richard Cross, the prompter, estimated the house at £225),[18] *Zara* continued to be chosen through the years for benefit nights, not only for the actors and the authors of the accompanying farces, but also for the General Lying-In Hospital (20 December 1758)[19] and the Marine Society (5 December 1759). In fact, nineteen of its sixty-four performances during the twenty-three years of presentation under Garrick were benefits.

Except for the two seasons when Garrick was on the Continent and two performances following his return, during which time Powell continued the part, the actor-manager

played the role of Lusignan throughout the period here being considered—fifty-six times in a total of sixty-four presentations. Mrs. Cibber was almost as hardy: of the thirteen seasons of acting between her resumption of the role at Drury Lane in 1754 and her death in January 1766, she missed only two seasons of playing in *Zara*—that of 1763-64 and two seasons later, when she was fatally ill. Altogether she played her part twenty-nine times at Drury Lane during the Garrick period, being spelled in the role by Mrs. Yates ten times and by Mrs. Palmer once.

After Garrick's alteration, the play continued to draw lucrative houses at Drury Lane. Receipts were consistently high throughout the twenty-three seasons. During its first season (two performances) the average gross was slightly more than £208, according to Cross's figures; and in its last season (four performances) the average, according to the figures in the Treasurer's Account Books, was something above £225.[20] These receipts speak well for Garrick's production of *Zara,* which, when the actor last played Lusignan on 7 March 1776, had been holding the interest of the playgoers for forty-one years. After Garrick's day it continued to be played, carrying over into the drama of the nineteenth century and being frequently reprinted.

II. GARRICK'S ALTERATION

Exactly when Garrick made his alteration cannot be established with certainty. The prompt copy in the Folger Shakespeare Library is a 1763 edition of Hill's play, altered in ink in Garrick's hand. In addition to the omissions and changes in text to be detailed below, the prompt gives the stage setting for each act (the palace, the garden, the palace gates), directs the entrances and exits for each character (prompt side, opposite prompt), calls for music at appropriate times, names some props and gives stage directions (three letters, the "Redarm'd Chair," two carpets; "Sink Lamps," "Rattle Chains"), and notes when each character should be readied for his entrance and when each new scene must be in readiness. Sometimes Garrick's revisions and additions are interlinear or added to the bottom of a page, and in some instances new lines have been carefully written out and pasted over Hill's printed text. The care with which the prompt copy was prepared suggests that it was a final version for a performance of the play.

It is highly unlikely that Garrick altered the play for the 1763-64 or following season, when he was abroad and Powell was taking his role. By way of conjecture, however, there are two possible performances which were of sufficient importance to occasion the alteration, for on these nights Garrick would have wanted to put his best foot forward. The first is the performance of 23 January 1766, when *Zara* was commanded by Their Majesties. This was shortly after Garrick resumed acting upon his return from the Continent; it was, moreover, a period when Garrick was especially desirous of making a strong impression, of giving the best performances of which Drury Lane was capable. The presence of Rousseau in Garrick's box[21] would have been another incentive for the most careful kind of presentation of Voltaire's play.

The other possibility for the date of alteration is the performance of 11 October 1768, when **Zara** was again presented "by particular desire," this time of the King of Denmark. So important was the occasion of the royal presence that the play, as a result of the king's late arrival, was held up until 7:35 P.M. at the express desire of the audience (MacMillan, p. 135).

Of the two possibilities the most likely date of alteration centers on the performance of 23 January 1766, for at that time Garrick had not only the presence of Rousseau but also the importance of his comeback to suggest the revision of the old play. Furthermore, Susannah Cibber, the original Zara, lay dying; she had played the part for the last time on 6 February 1765, and was not to play it again before her death on 30 January the next year. It is unlikely that while she acted Garrick would have made extensive alterations in a role she had played since she had changed from singer to dramatic actress in 1736. But now Zara was Mrs. Yates's role, and after her it was to be Mrs. Dancer's and Miss Younge's. The time was propitious for whatever alterations Garrick felt it desirable to make.

Still another clue to the date of alteration is to be found in a textual change which Garrick made in the play. For some reason he felt it necessary to drop Nerestan's bitter line, "Paris, the Refuge, still, of ruin'd Kings!" (II, 208).[22] The statement itself would not necessarily be offensive to the reigning monarch, but it would perhaps be displeasing to die-hard Jacobites, especially when one remembers that James Edward, the Old Pretender, who had made an unsuccessful attempt to return to the throne in 1715 and who was involved in the uprising of 1745, did not die until 1766, and that his son, Charles Edward, lived until 1788. The reference might have proved embarrassing at the performance of 23 January 1766, for this was the first after the death of the Old Pretender, who had died on 1 January. It is reasonable to suppose that Garrick would not have wanted to call attention to a spot on the British conscience by using Nerestan's line, however apt an epitaph it would have been for James.

Turning now to the alteration itself, it may be said that Garrick, in preparing stylized tragedies for his stage, was well aware of the fact that there was a saturation point for declamation and high-flown rhetoric. He knew also that his audience admired plays in the French classical vein and that Voltaire's had been hardy on English soil. For despite the outbursts of patriotic ire which led Englishmen to express contempt for "that insolent *French* Panegyrist"[23] who had dared to attack Shakespeare, Voltaire's plays found their way to the English stage throughout the Garrick period, some of them meeting with exceptional suc-

cess. Although by no means all of these English renderings and adaptations achieved the acclaim of **Zara,** *The Orphan of China, Alzira,* and *The English Merchant,* none can be called an out-and-out failure, even though their creator was a "carping superficial Critic" and "low paltry Thief."[24] Garrick's task was therefore to trim a line here, cut a speech there, eliminate some ranting at another spot in order to preserve the genre yet not assault the ears of the playgoers.[25] To preserve this delicate balance his method was in the majority of instances to eliminate a line or two at a time. Altogether he reduced the bulk of *Zara* by 305 3/5 lines, not a great number, indeed, but impressive enough when one notes the skill with which he extracted them. Garrick also knew his cast intimately; some of the speeches were very likely shortened when their forcible expression *in toto* would have unduly strained an actor's histrionic ability.

Study of Garrick's alteration makes evident the fact that the adapter kept his eye on Voltaire's text as he prepared his acting version, frequently eliminating lines of the Hill translation which go beyond the spirit or intent of the original. This attempt to make the play more nearly Voltaire's—an attempt which gives some point to the conjecture that the alteration was made for the performance which Rousseau attended—is yet more striking in Garrick's emendations and additions, which, although slight in bulk, are interesting in the frequency with which they recapture the intention of the original author. In the five acts of the play emendations occur in only twenty-two lines and total but 15 4/5 verse lines and five single words. Garrick added only seven new lines to the play and made brief additions to two other lines. Yet in fourteen instances these emendations and additions either restore or approximate much more closely the original reading of Voltaire. Of the lines omitted, 18 2/5 have no basis in Voltaire's text and many others contain material only partially in the original *Zaïre.*

The deletion of 226 of the lines omitted by Garrick serves to shorten and speed up the play. Some of the omitted passages are clearly unnecessary to the action, as for example the introduction of Osman in the first act:

SELIMA:

> Hark! the wish'd Music sounds!—'Tis he—he comes—
> [*Exit* SELIMA.]

ZARA:

> My Heart prevented him, and found him near: Absent, two whole long Days, the slow-pac'd Hour At last, is come—and gives him, to my Wishes!

> (139-142)

Here Garrick merely substitutes a flourish off stage and permits Osman to enter without the help of the women. Other speeches he trims, sometimes drastically, as in a soliloquy of Osman in Act IV, where only five lines of a twenty-seven-line speech are retained. This passage will illustrate Garrick's method of tightening the play, the lines retained being italicized:

OSMAN:

> [*Alone*] It shou'd be, yet, methinks, too soon to fly me!
> Too soon, as yet, to wring my easy Faith;
> *The more I think, the less I can conceive,*
> *What hidden Cause shou'd raise such strange Despair!*
> Now, when her Hopes have Wings, and ev'ry Wish
> Is courted to be lively!—When I love,
> And Joy, and Empire, press her to their Bosom;
> When, not alone belov'd, but, ev'n, a Lover;
> Professing, and accepting; bless'd, and blessing;
> To see her Eyes, thro' Tears, shine mystick Love!
> 'Tis Madness! and I were unworthy Power,
> To suffer, longer, the capricious Insult!
> *Yet, was I blameless?—No—I was too rash;*
> *I have felt Jealousy, and spoke it, to her;*
> *I have distrusted her——and, still, she loves:*
> Gen'rous a tonement, that! and 'tis my Duty
> To expiate, by a Length of soft Indulgence,
> The Transports of a Rage, which, still, was Love.
> Henceforth, I, never, will suspect her false;
> Nature's plain Power of Charming dwells about her,
> And Innocence gives Force to ev'ry Word;
> I owe full Confidence to All, she looks,
> For, in her Eye, shines Truth, and ev'ry Beam
> Shoots Confirmation round her:—I remark'd,
> Ev'n, while she wept, her Soul, a thousand times,
> Sprung to her Lips, and Long'd to leap to mine,
> With honest, ardent, Utt'rance of her Love.——
> Who can possess a Heart, so low, so base,
> To look such Tenderness, and, yet, have none?

(183-211)

Later in the same act Garrick retains only seven lines of a thirty-line exchange between Osman and Orasmin, omitting a great deal of repetitious ranting by the sultan over Zara's apparent defection (245-274). Garrick seems to be especially wary of the ranting. In one instance in Act v he eliminates eleven lines which put the *Spanish Tragedy* to shame:

> *Orasmin!* Prophet! Reason! Truth! and Love!
> After such Length of Benefits to wrong me!
> How have I over-rated, how mistaken,
> The Merit of her Beauty!—Did I not
> Forget I was a Monarch? Did I remember,
> That *Zara* was a Slave?—I gave up all;
> Gave up Tranquility, Distinction, Pride,
> And fell, the shameful Victim of my Love!

ORASMIN:

> Sir! Sovereign! Sultan! my Imperial Master!
> Reflect on your own Greatness, and disdain
> The distant Provocation.—

(109-119)[26]

In other instances in which Osman out-Herods Herod, Garrick likewise tempers the passages by omission.

Some of Garrick's omissions reveal his interest in proper development of character. For example, he eliminates a passage at the beginning of the play in which Zara refers to Nerestan with unnecessary disparagement and thereby loses something of the nobility of her character (37-39), and later in the first act he cuts down on she-tragedy sentimentality with another omission (161-167). Of Osman's character he is even more careful, for it had been Voltaire's, and thus Hill's, tendency to bring out the essential goodness of the Sultan of Jerusalem. Garrick, keeping the types more distinct, prefers that Osman remain simply a heathen villain. He therefore eliminates such passages as the following, designed to stress Osman's tragic grandeur: "I think, with Horror, on these dreadful Maxims, / Which harden Kings, insensibly, to Tyrants" (I, 217-218); or this one, in which Osman reveals his greatness of soul in mourning the fate which has made Lusignan, last of the Christian kings of Jerusalem, his captive:

> Such is the Law of States, had I been vanquish'd,
> Thus had *He* said of *Me*:——I mourn his Lot,
> Who must, in Fetters, lost to Day-light, pine,
> And sigh away old Age, in Grief, and Pain.

(I, 247-250)

Nor is Osman allowed to say that he loves Lusignan "for his virtue and his blood" (III, 19). In fact, Garrick cuts out the moralizing element which Voltaire, and Hill to an even greater degree, had scattered through Osman's speeches. He no longer may say that "Friends should *part, kind,* who are to meet no more" (III, 42), nor, after he has ranted at Nerestan's presumption in pressing a second interview with Zara, to reflect, "I feel, that I descend, below my self" (III, 318). Other moralizing passages not necessarily reflecting on Osman's character are likewise omitted, as in Act I, where Garrick omits lines not in Voltaire's play which Hill had added to dress up his own version: Osman's parenthetical ". . . Monarchs, like the Sun, / Shine but in vain, unwarming, if unseen" (212-213) and the couplets closing Hill's first act:

> Monarchs, by Forms of pompous Misery, press'd
> In proud, unsocial Solitude, unbless'd
> Wou'd, but for Love's soft Influence, curse their Throne,
> And, among crowded Millions, live, *alone.*

Likewise interesting is the care Garrick exercises in handling lines of a religious nature, a tendency seen throughout the plays he altered for the theater. Here one finds such omissions as Osman's calling upon Heaven "to blast that unbelieving Race," the Christians (I, 168); Chatillon's reference to Nerestan as a "Christian Saviour! by a Saviour sent" (II, 3); Zara's swearing by "the dread Presence" of Heaven's "living Author" (III, 94);[27] and Nerestan's line condemning Zara for quitting her God (III, 141). There are other omissions of a similar nature, which need not be cited here. One more deletion of a different nature is worth stating: the description which Chatillon, the French officer, gives of Lusignan near the beginning of Act II, shortly before the old Christian makes his first appearance. Garrick omits the passage, probably in order that the impact of Lusignan's entrance will not be diminished by Chatillon's word picture:

> Yet, Great, amidst his Miseries, he look'd,
> As if he could not feel his Fate, himself,
> But, as it reach'd his Follower:—And shall we,
> For whom our gen'rous Leader suffr'd This,
> Be, vilely, safe? and dare be bless'd, without him?

(78-82)

After all, Garrick was protecting his own role!

Garrick's few additions to the Hill text, except for a slight one in Act IV and another in the last act, are to be found in Act II. To Lusignan's account of how he lost his wife and children Garrick adds four lines, two of them from Voltaire, to improve the effect of the narration. Hill's version is as follows:

> And, there, beheld'st my Wife, and Two dear Sons
> Perish, in Flames—They did not *need* the Grave,
> Their Foes wou'd have deny'd 'em! I beheld it;
> *Husband!* and *Father!* helpless, I beheld it!
> Deny'd the mournful Privilege, to die!

(II, 233-237)

Voltaire's passage has some slight differences:

LUSIGNAN:

> ... Tes yeux virent périr mes deux fils & ma femme.

CHATILLON:

> Mon bras chargé de fers ne les put secourir.

LUSIGNAN:

> Hélas! & j'étais pére, & je ne pus mourir!
> Veilliz du haut des Cieux, chers enfans que j'implore
> Sur mes autres enfans, s'ils sont vivans encore.

Now Garrick, using only a part of the Hill version, restores something of Voltaire's intent in his addition:

And, there, beheld'st my Wife, and Two dear Sons Perish in flames.

CHAT.:

> A captive & in fetters I could not help 'em.

LUSIG.:

> I know thou could'st not,—
> O 'twas a dreadful Scene! these Eyes beheld it
> Husband & Father! helpless I beheld it!
> Deny'd the mournful priviledge to die.
> O my dear Children! whom I now deplore.

Later in the same act Garrick again adds to and emends Hill's text. When Lusignan is about to discover that Nerestan is his long-lost son he cries, in Hill's version,

> O, thou! who, thus, canst bless my life's last sand!
> Strengthen my heart, too feeble for this joy.
> Madam! Nerestan!——Help me, Chatillon! [*Rising*]
> Nerestan! if thou ought'st to own that name,
> Shines there, upon thy noble breast, a noble scar

(281-285)

and so on. Garrick rewrites to improve the effect of Lusignan's prayer and to tone down the accent on nobility:

> O God! who see'st my Tears, & knows my thought
> Do not forsake me at this dawn of hope—
> Strengthen my heart too feeble for this Joy!
> Madam! Nerestan—help me Chatillion [sic]!—
> Nerestan, hast thou on thy breast a Scar.[28]

Following closely upon this speech Garrick adds another line, again taking it directly from Voltaire: Lusignan's "I cannot tear you from my Arms my Children"[29] is Voltaire's "De vos bras, mes enfans, je ne puis m'arracher," which Hill had ignored.

As for the other additions, a very slight one in Act IV again shows us that Garrick worked closely with Voltaire's text. To Hill's line for Osman, "It is too true, my *Fame* requires it" (117), Garrick adds "of me" as substantiated by Voltaire's "l'honneur me l'ordonne." A final one in Act V, the addition of the single word *hark!* (108), takes care of an omission of eleven lines and makes a neat suture with Osman's following query, "Heard'st thou nothing?" (120).

Most of Garrick's emendations are likewise to be found in Act II, and again the chief reason for emending is to restore Voltaire's reading. Nine lines of the act contain such changes. Upon Lusignan's first entrance the nearly blind old man cries out, in Hill's version, "Where am I! What forgiven Angel's Voice / Has call'd me, to revisit long-lost Day?" (168-169). Voltaire's line had been, "Du séjour du trépas quelle voix me rapelle?" Whereupon Garrick emends Hill to restore the original reading, substituting "from the dungeon's depths what Voice" for Hill's phrase about the forgiven angel. Some lines later, in another speech of Lusignan, Garrick again corrects Hill's translation, restoring *Coucy* (Voltaire's *Couci*) for Hill's erroneous *Courcy* in the old king's list of French warriors (212) and supplying "ask the recompence / For" in place of Hill's "move Remembrance, there, / Of" (217-218) as translation of Voltaire's "Je vais au Roi des Rois demander aujourdhui / Le prix de tous les maux que j'ai soufferts pour lui." The alterer also takes exception to Hill's translation of Lusignan's agonized lines when he learns that his new-found daughter, Zara, is not a Christian. Voltaire had written, "Que la foudre en eclats ne tombe que sur moi! / Ah, mon fils! A ces mots j'eusse expire sans toi." These lines, powerful in their simplicity, Hill had embellished thus.

> Oh! my misguided child!—at that sad word,
> The little life, yet mine, has left me, quite,
> But that my death might fix thee, lost for ever.

(303-305)

Garrick's version restores the simplicity of the original: "Her words are Thunder bursting on my head. / Wer't not for thee, my son, I now should die." Near the end of the same speech Garrick, again careful of minute details, restores Voltaire's reading once more by substituting *renounce* for *betray* in Hill's line, "Shame not thy Mother—nor betray thy God" (329), as called for by Voltaire's *renier.*

Of the few remaining emendations, an interesting one is Garrick's revision of Hill's ending for the fourth act. Hill's closing lines are lame:

> I feel, I must confess, a kind of shame,
> And blush, at my own tenderness;—but, faith,
> Howe'er it seems deceiv'd, were weak, as I am,
> Cou'd it admit distrust, to blot its face,
> And give appearance way, till proof takes place.

Garrick knew, as an actor would, that the final words of Act IV should be more compelling; the closing speech of the penultimate act is invaluable in summing up the suspense which is to be resolved in the final act. And so Garrick strengthens the play at this point:

> On this last Tryal all my hopes depend,
> Prophet for once thy kind Assistance lend,
> Dispell the doubts, that rank my Anxious breast
> If Zara's Innocent, thy Osmans blest.

The alterations summarized above reveal Garrick's care in preparing plays for his stage. Judging from the evidence of his own prompt book, it may be said that in altering *Zara* he wanted to reduce as much as possible the unnaturalness of neoclassical tragedy by cutting down on long speeches and dramatic narration and by breaking up lengthy, yet necessary, speeches with lines for other players; he wanted to clarify obscure lines, maintain suspense, and restore the intent of the original author whenever he felt that the English translator had strayed too far from the text. The result is a play which, although somewhat shorter than Hill's, differs outwardly but little from it; but when it does differ it backs up the changes with either the authority of the original playwright or that of the experienced actor-producer.

Thomas Davies, in his *Memoirs of the Life of David Garrick,* comments on Hill's French adaptations without, however, making reference to Garrick's alteration of *Zara.* Yet his account has direct application to the play here being considered in that he makes a distinction between French and English tragedy and in so doing points up one of the basic changes which Garrick made in Hill's text. Says Davies (I, 142-143):

> Mr. Hill, in adapting French plays to the English stage, forgot the distinguishing character of the two nations. The Frenchman, when he goes to a play, seems to make his entertainment a matter of importance. The long speeches in the plays of Corneille, Racine, Crebillon, and Voltaire, which would disgust an English ear, are extremely pleasing to our light neighbours: they sit in silence, and enjoy the beauty of sentiment, and energy of language; and are taught habitually to cry at scenes of distress. The Englishman looks upon the theatre as a place of amusement; he does not expect to be alarmed with terror, or wrought up by scenes of commiseration; but he is surprised into the feeling of these passions, and sheds tears because he cannot avoid it. The theatre, to most Englishmen, becomes a place of instruction by chance, not by choice.
>
> Hill, in translating Zara and Alzira, forgot the genius of the two nations; he should have interrupted, by an easy interposition, those long speeches which are equally tiresome to the speaker and the hearer.

That Garrick understood the "genius" of his nation is borne out by his alteration. Hill had made a French play for the English stage; Garrick made it, insofar as he was able within the framework of the original, an English tragedy.

After Garrick had prepared his alteration of *Zara* in the prompt copy the text continued to be changed as the years passed. But it may be noted that the changes are, on the whole, based on Garrick's alteration. Some of Hill's lines were restored, and new excisions were made—the standard fate of the alterations performed in that day. A hint as to what could happen to a play is indicated in a letter of George Steevens to Garrick on 2 January 1775. "I think you never played Lusignan so happily as on Saturday night; at least you never affected me in it so much before," he wrote. But he complained of the others in the cast: "Are there words to be found that can convey any adequate idea of their incomparable badness? Had I been a cannibal, I think I could scarce have ventured to sup upon them, so surely should I have been sick with gorging such cat's meat and dog's meat." He also complained of severe pruning: "The play was so cut, at that, though we stayed it out, we were here at supper by half an hour after nine. Every line not absolutely necessary to the action seemed to be omitted."[30]

The version published in Bell's *British Theatre,* 1776 ("Regulated from the prompt-books" of Drury Lane and Covent Garden), serves as an example of later versions of the play. Although it reduces the number of lines omitted from the 305 3/5 in Garrick's prompt to 216, of which 42 2/5 are new omissions, it retains all of Garrick's additions and revisions except for five single words. Two changes which Garrick had originally made in the prompt copy but which he had decided not to keep (marked "stet" in the margin) are observed in the Bell version.[31] These may have been deleted at any time after Garrick made his prompt copy. All these later deletions are the usual ones made during the long run of an already altered play; yet some importance must be attached to the fact that, in retaining Garrick's revised and added lines, the later versions are based on the actor-manager's alteration rather than on Hill's original translation. The 1791 Bell edition, for example, remains basically Garrick's, as does Mrs. Inchbald's reprint of the play in her *British Theatre* of 1808.

For years after Garrick's retirement from the stage **Zara** remained standard theatrical fare, and the public saw the great actors and actresses of the moment try their skill in the roles of Lusignan and Zara. Isaac Reed, the inveterate play-goer, thought well enough of the she-tragedy to see it five times between 1766 and 1784.[32] And although minor changes in the acting version were made during the course of time, Garrick's alteration had made an indelible imprint on the text during the remainder of *Zara*'s theatrical history.

Notes

1. Harry W. Pedicord (*The Theatrical Public in the Time of Garrick,* New York, 1954), for example, notes its 64 performances in 23 seasons.

2. Several other plays were performed without a break during their runs under Garrick's supervision, but for much shorter periods. *The Clandestine Marriage,* acted for 10 consecutive seasons, and *A Peep Behind the Curtain,* acted for 8, were the closest competitors of the hardy three. Among other long-run plays at Drury Lane during Garrick's managership, 10 were presented annually except for a single year's break in continuity. These include *Macbeth* and *Much Ado About Nothing,* Rowe's *Tamerlane, The Beggar's Opera, The Conscious Lovers,* Coffey's *The Devil to Pay,* Murphy's *The Way to Keep Him,* Colman's *The Jealous Wife,* Vanbrugh's *The Provok'd Wife,* and Farquhar's *The Beaux' Stratagem.* See Dougald MacMillan, *Drury Lane Calendar, 1746-1776* (Oxford, 1938).

3. In the appendix to his *Memoirs of the Life of David Garrick,* 3rd ed. (London, 1781), II, 414-419.

4. E.g., Pedicord's excellent book (n. 1, above) and James J. Lynch's *Box, Pit, and Gallery* (Berkeley, 1953).

5. All of Garrick's revisions of lines and additions are included but for 5 single words, even though not all of his omissions are followed. See below, p. 232.

6. *Gentleman's Mag.,* V (May 1735), 279; *Biographia Dramatica* (London, 1812), III, 429; *Barker's Complete List of Plays* (London, 1803), p. 336; John Egerton's *Theatrical Remembrancer* (London, 1788), p. 171.

7. Preface to *Zara* in Bell's 1791 *British Theatre,* XIII, xi.

8. *Memoirs of the Life of David Garrick,* 1st ed. (London, 1780), I, 136.

9. *Annals of the English Stage from Thomas Betterton to Edmund Kean* (London, 1864), I, 323-324.

10. *Biographia Dramatica,* III, 430-431.

11. *Daily Journal, Daily Post and General Advertiser, Daily Advertiser.*

12. *Daily Post and General Advertiser,* 2 June 1735.

13. Allardyce Nicoll lists only 5 performances for this group between 29 May and 18 June (*History of Early Eighteenth-Century Drama, 1700-1750,* Cambridge, 1925, p. 336).

14. *Daily Post and General Advertiser,* 9 July 1735.

15. Although the first edition of *Zara* (1736) lists Este as Orasmin, each of the 14 bills in *Daily Post and General Advertiser* lists Turbutt for that part.

16. *Life of Garrick,* I, 137.

17. "Drury Lane Chronicle During Garrick's Management, 1747-1776," in Percy Fitzgerald's *Life of David Garrick* (London, 1868), II, 475.

18. MS *Diary* in the Folger Shakespeare Library.

19. Cross estimated a house of £320 for this benefit, one of the highest recorded for the period.

20. How well *Zara* fared under Garrick's management may be seen by comparing its average annual receipts with representative average annual receipts at Drury Lane. The selected monthly receipts given by Pedicord (*Theatrical Public,* Appendix B, p. 185) include 4 seasons which are useful for comparison. Pedicord's figures (all in round numbers) for 1758-59 average just over £157, whereas *Zara* that season (Treasurer's Account Books) averaged more than £202. For 1763-64 the year's average (round numbers) is £164 as compared with *Zara*'s £236; for 1772-73 the average is £183 to *Zara*'s £202; for 1774-75 the house average is £194 to *Zara*'s £219.

21. William Hopkins' *Diary* No. 12, reprinted by MacMillan, *Drury Lane Calendar,* p. 117 (n. 2, above). James Cradock tells an anecdote of the performance which Rousseau witnessed. After Garrick had played both Lusignan in *Zara* and Lord Chalkstone in his own *Lethe* as the afterpiece, Rousseau complimented the actor by saying, "I have cried all through your Tragedy, and laughed through all your Comedy, without being at all able to understand the language" (*Literary and Miscellaneous Memoirs,* London, 1826-28, I, 206).

22. Voltaire's line is, "Et la Cour de Louis est l'azyle des Rois."

23. Samuel Foote, *The Roman and English Comedy Consider'd and Compar'd* (London, 1747), p. 21.

24. Ibid., p. 22. George H. Nettleton, in the bibliography appended to Ch. iv, Vol. X, of the *CHEL* lists 13 separate Voltaire adaptations between 1734 and 1776, most of which thrived (pp. 493-494).

25. I have used as basic texts Garrick's prompt copy, Hill's edition of 1763, the Bell edition of 1776, and *Zaïre,* in the *Collection complète des œuvres de M. de Voltaire,* 1st ed. ([Geneva], 1756), Vol. VIII. I have also examined the texts of 1736, 1752, 1759, 1760 (in Hill's 2-vol. *Dramatic Works,* Vol. II), 1762 (Dublin), 1769, 1775, the Bell edition of 1791, and Mrs. Inchbald's *British Theatre* version of 1808. In my text Roman numerals indicate acts, Arabic numerals, lines.

26. Voltaire's passage is as follows:

> Zayre! … l'infidelle … après tant de bienfaits!
> J'aurais d'un oeil serein, d'un front inaltérable,
> Contemplé de mon rang la chûte épouvantable:
> J'aurais su, dans l'horreur de la captivité,
> Conserver mon courage & ma tranquilité;
> Mais me voir à ce point trompé par ce que j'aime! …

CORASMIN:

> Eh! que prétendez-vous dans cette horreur extrême?
> Quel est votre dessein?

27. The line is not in Voltaire.

28. Voltaire's text is as follows:

> Oui, grand Dieu, tu le veux, tu permets que je voye;
> Dieu, ranime mes sens trop faibles pour ma joye.
> Madame … Nerestan … Soutien-moi, Chatillon …
> Nerestan, si je dois nommer encor ce nom,
> Avez-vous dans le sein la cicatrice heureuse
> Du fer dont à mes yeux une main furieuse. …

29. Following Hill's l. 293.

30. *The Private Correspondence of David Garrick,* ed. James Boaden (London, 1831-32), II, 35.

31. The Bell text uses Garrick's emendation, "My Miseries have worn me, more than Age," for Hill's "Yet, *Misery* has worn me, more than Age" (II, 172) and Garrick's "O my Misguided daughter" for Hill's "Oh my misguided child!" (II, 303). In the prompt version Garrick had in both instances decided to retain Hill's reading.

32. *Isaac Reed Diaries,* 1762-1804, ed. Claude E. Jones (Berkeley, 1946), p. 44 and passim.

Lillian Gottesman (essay date 1967)

SOURCE: Gottesman, Lillian. "Garrick's *Institution of the Garter.*" *Restoration and 18th Century Theatre Research* 6.2 (1967): 37-43. Print.

[*In the following essay, Gottesman focuses on Garrick's* Institution of the Garter *(1771), a production dramatizing the 1348 festival hosted by King Edward III to receive candidates into England's highest order of chivalry. Gottesman compares the play with Garrick's source text, Gilbert West's dialog poem "The Institution of the Order of the Garter," to highlight Garrick's skill at staging extravagant spectacles.*]

David Garrick's *Institution of the Garter, or Arthur's Round Table Restored* was performed at Drury Lane. It is listed in the *Winston MS.* as a "New Masque" in the entry for Monday, October 28, 1771, and Dibdin is named as the composer of the music. This entertainment had at least twenty-six performances,[1] a good run for its day.

That this piece was fairly successful is not surprising. As a dramatist and theatre manager, Garrick was cognizant of his audience's love of pageantry and its increasing interest in history. We should perhaps note briefly that the latter half of the eighteenth century witnessed a revived interest in England's past and a patriotic concern for England's heritage. This was the time of Burke, Rousseau, and Godwin. These were the years immediately preceding the American and French Revolutions, and the theatre public must have done some political thinking. Then, too, authors such as Percy, Chatterton, and Macpherson paved the way for a medieval revival in literature. Little wonder that Garrick combined politics, history, and medieval tradition in one stage masque.

We have available two texts of the *Institution of the Garter.* One is an unpublished, hand-written, complete manuscript.[2] The other is an abridged printed edition entitled *The Songs, Choruses, and Serious Dialogue of the Masque Called The Institution of the Garter, or, Arthur's Round Table Restored.*[3] From a study of the two manuscripts, from comments made by Garrick, and from contemporary criticism, we may conclude that the stage version was the complete text or something very close to it. The abridged printed text is of value to us primarily because of its preface written by Garrick, which the unpublished text does not contain.

In this preface or "Advertisement" Garrick discloses his purpose and sources. He tells us that a recent installation of the Knights of the Order excited a curiosity in the public.[4] That installation was, therefore, a fruitful and justifiable opportunity for a stage pageant on a subject of immediate interest. It was difficult, says Garrick, to bring to the people an adequate representation of this solemn installation, procession, and feast. Whenever possible, Garrick sought to facilitate his work by adapting and altering rather than creating. He found a plot in a poem called "The Institution of the Order of the Garter," which had been published almost thirty years earlier, in 1742, by Gilbert West. Garrick regarded this poem as rich in machinery, but only a poem, in dialogue, without action, and so not stage material. It was apparent to our dramatist that some sections, with the necessary alterations and the addition of comic scenes, would make a proper vehicle for stage presentation. Garrick adapted parts, altered, and added comic scenes. The comic scenes, however, were omitted from the printed text. Garrick intended them as a preparation for the principal scenes, and they would lose much of their effect, he felt, if they were separated from the action of the performers. Some liberties were necessary, Garrick explains, in order to render the piece more theatrical, and he trusts that the public will overlook these liberties if the entertainment is otherwise acceptable. Garrick introduces the procession, a pageant of knights crossing the stage; this scene is not in West's poem at all. He takes poetic license with the chronology and portrays the Black Prince as nine years younger than he actually was when knighted; West, on the other hand, postpones the installation nine years in order to allow for the presence of King John of France. Both authors celebrate the 1348 festival given by Edward III. The time of the action is during the reign of Edward, "who was the Founder of the Order, after having restored that of the *Knights of the Round Table,* which we have supposed with Writers, to be continued at the Institution of the Garter."[5]

All this information is supplied in the preface. From the masque proper,[6] we gather that Edward III is holding a solemn session at Windsor to receive candidates who seek the glory of the Garter. The king is to choose the worthiest and organize a princely brotherhood dedicated to honor, virtue, and truth. He will be its chief, and Saint George its patron. The Genius of England calls upon the spirits, bards, and druids to clear the air of evil sprites and to guide Edward's choices, for posterity will evaluate his judgment by them. We see only the Prince of Wales knighted, but the procedure is the same for all accepted candidates. We see also the procession of knights to Saint George's Hall, where the knights enjoy a feast. Edward is summoned by Genius and is shown the influence his Order will have upon the future. The play closes with a chorus of bards, druids, and spirits hailing Britain's great king.

The masque is divided into three parts. The first presents the setting of mood through the medium of song. Preceding the first part is a comic opening scene in which Needle the tailor, his wife, and Dingle the court fool drown their differences in drink. This scene is followed by an overture.

When the curtain rises after the overture, the setting discloses Windsor Park with a view of the castle in the distance. The stage direction indicates elaborate workmanship and props. The Genius of England is in a "Machine" which descends slowly in response to the songs of two Spirits. In his right hand the Genius holds the Wand of Enfranchisement and in his left, a parchment bearing the words Magna Charta. One spirit summons all immortal spirits to guard Britannia's Genius. Another Spirit calls to the Bards to attend and "sooth the toiling hero's pains." The Genius, in turn, summons the Druids from their "sequester'd vallies, pensive groves, and dark recesses" and explains that "a great event" demands their presence in this "grosser atmosphere." They must protect Edward and his noble train on this solemn day. With the work so assigned, the enchanting scene closes.

Part Two opens in the Chapel of Saint George, where the knights are seated in stalls. Edward steps forward to dub the Prince of Wales. His speech to the Prince (II.i) is the first serious dialogue in the play and is suggestive of the installation procedure:

> Thus I admit three, Edward Prince of Wales,
> First Founder of the order of *St. George* ...
> United to maintain the Cause of truth
> And Justice only. ...[7]

The Prince accepts the honor and hopes to be guided rightly so as never to soil the luster of the Order.

Prior to the procession of the knights to Saint George's Hall, which closes Part Two, there is a lengthy comic scene among low characters who have come to see the "Extallation" and are unable to enter the castle gates. Roger, one of these characters, will not give up in the attempt to see the king and, if necessary, will speak treason in order to be brought before the king. Sir Dingle approaches, and all crowd around him in the hope that he will help them in. He is much too busy, however, to bother with inferior people or to remember his promise or to return a courtesy. His job is to "talk much, say little, do nothing, & be paid for it ... the very quintessence of a Court Life." The function of these commoners is to provide not only comedy, but also commentary. The element of satire is present. As in the *Jubilee,* for instance, a play which celebrates the Shakespeare festival at Stratford, Garrick satirizes the attitude of the commoners towards the formal ceremony.

Part Three is devoted to the feast and to a prophecy of England's future. The knights are seated at the Round Table, and Sir Dingle enters and implores King Edward to admit the "mighty Power the Mob *without*" so that they may partake of the food. Edward consents. In the last scene, the Genius of England unfolds the future and shows Edward a vision of the precious fruit his tree shall bear. The bards, druids, and spirits join in a chorus to hail Britannia's matchless king, and the play closes as it opened—in song of praise.

We are aware that this entertainment must have been an extravagant production with little to its credit as a literary accomplishment. Many of the scenes are languid, and the poetry is bad. The common folk in the comic scenes are portrayed with artistic accuracy, but this is to be expected since Garrick excelled as a creator of comedy. The dialogue and songs of the commoners provide a contrast with those of the dignified cast. The characters are types; there is no individual delineation. We no longer have the musical score, but if we turn to contemporary criticism, we find that both script and score were poorly reviewed.

One eighteenth-century critic thought that the public had enough of *The Jubilee* to want anything more like it and called Garrick's statement that the *Institution of the Garter* was inspired by public curiosity a "jesuitical insinuation" which is "as contemptible as it is false."[8] Mr. Potter considered the first comic scene "tolerable, but owes much of its success to the eminent Abilities of Messrs. *King, Weston,* and *Parsons.*" The second comic scene he thought "intolerable," and the spectacle scenes "showy." He thought the vehicles of ascending and descending coarse and producing odd effects. Of the music, only the overture was worth notice. The poor review of the music was substantiated by at least one other commentator, who called the music poor, flat, and lacking in enthusiasm.[9]

The only commendation which we can allow the piece is its excellent staging and stage directions. The changes of scene must have been accomplished through the use of shutters and transparencies. The place of action moves back and forth from the main platform to the back of the stage.[10] An outer curtain, we are told, rises after the overture, and the spirits are discovered. There is rare mention of an outer curtain in English drama at this time. The only machinery employed is the device used in the ascending and descending of the spirits; this was suggested in West's poem and is retained in the masque by Garrick.[11]

A comparison between Garrick's masque and his source poem reveals just what Garrick thought essential to rendering theatrical a poem which was not fit for the stage. Though Garrick retains the situation, most of the characters, and many speeches, he simplifies by omitting and condensing. Garrick omits Philippa, Edward's queen, and King John, monarch of France. In West's poem, Philippa performs no function other than that of guest at the installation and is dispensable; so is John. Garrick omits the shape-shifting quality of the druids who, in West, appear in borrowed shapes at Windsor Castle and present themselves as candidates for knighthood. Garrick omits the long succession of rejected candidates and presents only the last one to receive the honor. Garrick simplifies staging by cutting down on the descriptions and costuming. There is no indication in the masque of what was worn, but West specifies luxurious costumes. John Potter noticed that if the dresses of the spirits had been a little longer they would have been "more consistent with decency." Garrick shortens speeches, particularly Genius' explanatory ones.

On the subject of speeches, there is one which we should not overlook. That is the speech (I.ii) made by Genius to Druid explaining why Edward's choices must be guided. It is a warning against the granting titles and honor to the undeserving; to do so would bring shame to the throne and to the Order and would invite false glitter to adorn the Court. The speech is significant because it is an amplification rather than a condensation. It is more significant for its very presence because it is political in tone and Garrick seldom is. Garrick was particularly careful to steer clear of politics after the affair with Junius,[12] but this masque preceded the Junius episode by less than one month.

A student once misquoted amusingly that "digression is the better part of valor." At the risk of slight digression, some comment on the medieval tradition here utilized is in order. My reference is, of course, to King Arthur and to the legends surrounding him and his knights of the Round Table.

The Arthurian romance has not produced a single great play.[13] It may be stated further that first-rate dramatists were not usually attracted to this cycle of stories and when a major figure such as Garrick adapted the subject for stage use, he dis so for a timely political purpose. Even then, his Arthurian play did not equal his other plays in quality. Perhaps there is an explanation for this scarcity of Arthurian plays. Romance literature is mythological; its incidents are extravagant; its heroes are superhuman; it creates a tapestry effect which the stage cannot fully capture. Dryden chose the medium of opera for his *King Arthur; or, the British Worthy* (1691), setting precedent for the eighteenth century to follow. He undoubtedly felt that the romance was not suited to another kind of drama, for in his preface to *Albion and Albanius,* he wrote:

> An opera is a poetical tale, or fiction, represented by vocal and instrumental music, adorned with scenes, machines, and dancing. The supposed persons of this musical drama are generally supernatural, as gods, and goddesses, and heroes, which at least are descended from them, and are in due time to be adopted into their number. The subject, therefore, being extended beyond the limits of human nature, admits of that sort of marvellous and surprising conduct, which is rejected in other plays.[14]

The eighteenth century was ripe for a play such as Dryden's dramatic opera. Opera was popular throughout the century, and English productions had to rival the phenomenal success of Italian imports. Garrick adapted Dryden's work in his own *King Arthur: or, The British Worthy* (1770)[15] and a year later produced the **Institution of the Garter.** We may conclude that the dramatic value of this latter piece lies in its skilfully staged pageantry. Its historical value lies in that it is the only obtainable dramatic work on the subject of this supposed Arthurian society, that it is a patriotic interpretation and glorification of a theme associated with Arthurian tradition, and that it embodies the Elizabethan concept of the divine guidance of monarchs. We find the patriotism, the echoes of man's rights to liberty, and the statement of government's responsibility timely and typical of late eighteenth-century drama.

Notes

1. David Erskine Baker, Biographia Dramatica; or, a Companion to the Playhouse (London, 1812), II, 327. Dougald MacMillan, Drury Lane Calendar, 1747-1776 (Oxford, 1938), lists 34 performances.

2. Larpent 327, Huntington Library.

3. London, 1771. Available at the Folger Shakespeare Library, Washington, D.C.

4. Ceremonies of the Order were held on July 25, 1771, in honor of the installation of the Prince of Wales.

5. See "The History and Antiquities of Windsor Castle . . . with the Institution, Laws and Ceremonies of the Most Noble Order of the Garter," *Monthly Review,* I (August 1749), 251-270. The opinion voiced by Garrick that the Order of the Garter grew out of Round Table festivals is expressed also in Ashmole's *The Institution, Laws, and Ceremonies of the Most Noble Order of the Garter,* p. 182, and in Selden's *Titles of Honor,* p. 658. Both Elias Ashmole and John Selden accept Froissart's statement that Edward III was the founder of the Order of the Garter. Both references were known to Garrick; so he tells us in his preface to the masque. The real meaning of the word "garter" is uncertain. Selden quotes the story about the garter lost by Lady Joan, which was found and worn by Edward, who replied either to his jealous queen or to observant lords: "Honi foit noto "soit" qui mal y pense." Ashmole denies this story entirely. It has been suggested that the garter was Edward's symbol in successful battle. Cf. "Sir Gawain and the Green Knight."

6. Discussion is based on the unabridged Larpent manuscript.

7. The opening lines of Edward's speech are in substance from Ashmole's *The Institution . . . of the Order of the Garter,* p. 357. Additional lines are quoted directly from West's poem.

8. John Potter, *The Theatrical Review; or New Companion to the Play-House* (London, 1772), I, 121-141.

9. *"The Songs, Choruses, and serious Dialogue of the Masque called The Institution of the Garter, or Arthur's Round Table restored"* (anon. rev.), *Critical Review,* XXXII (October 1771), 310.

10. See Allardyce Nicoll, *The English Theater: A Short History* (New York, 1936), p. 127. Garrick's reorganization in stage illumination, which placed the candles behind the side wings instead of over the apron, contributed to the gradual fading of the apron stage and improved illumination of the portion of the stage behind the proscenium arch. This change contributed also to the popularity of pageant and spectacle because these were better seen and heard by the audience.

11. West's poem indicates such elaborate machinery that the use of it in staging would be impractical. Note, for example, how much more complex than Garrick's the following description is:

> *Chorus of Bards descends, drest in long flowing Sky-colour'd Robes spangled with Stars, with Garlands of oaken Boughs upon their Heads, and golden Harps in their Hands, made like the* Welsh *or old* British *Harp. Before they appear, they sing the Chorus, and afterwards, as they descend, the following Songs; at the last Stanza of which, the Chariot of* Genius *appears, and*

> *descends gradually all the while that and the grand Chorus is singing.*

12. Junius, an unknown author who wrote under a pen name in order to remain unknown, stood politically in opposition to Edmund Burke. Garrick attempted to determine Junius' identity. The following note was sent on November 10, 1771, by Junius to H. S. Woodfall for transmission to Garrick:

> I am very exactly informed of your impertinent inquiries. . . . Now mark me, vagabond.—Keep to your pantomimes, or be assured you shall hear of it. Meddle no more, thou busy informer!—It is my power to make you curse the hour in which you dared to interfere with.

> JUNIUS *Monthly Review,* LXXI
> (August 1813), 370

13. Prior to 1500 no play utilizing the Arthurian romance was produced. Only one such play of the Tudor period is extant—Thomas Hughes' *Misfortunes of Arthur* (1587), a tragedy. Dating to the first half of the seventeenth century are Thomas Middleton's *Mayor of Queenborough,* a comedy, and *The Birth of Merlin,* a tragi-comedy by Rowley and possibly Middleton. In 1691 Dryden produced his *King Arthur,* an opera for which Purcell wrote the music. The eighteenth century, in addition to a couple of adaptations of Dryden's opera, produced Lewis Theobald's *The Vocal Parts of an Entertainment, Call'd Merlin* (1734), a musical interlude of a pantomime; Aaron Hill's *Merlin in Love* (1759), a pantomime opera; Abraham Portal's *Vortimer,* a tragedy printed in 1796; William Ireland's *Vortigern* (1796), a history play and forgery; and William Hilton's *Arthur* (1759), a tragedy.

14. *The Works of John Dryden,* ed. Scott (London, 1808), VII, 216.

15. The *Winston MS.* gives the exact date of the play's first performance as Thursday, December 13, 1770, and supplies the initials D. G. Genst (V, 295) gives the same date and names Garrick as the author, as does the *Biographia Dramatica* (II, 39). *The British Museum Catalogue of Printed Books* lists the play as a Garrick alteration.

Lillian Gottesman (essay date 1972)

SOURCE: Gottesman, Lillian. "Garrick's *Lilliput.*" *Restoration and 18th Century Theatre Research* 11.2 (1972): 34-7. Print.

[*In the following essay, Gottesman discusses* Lilliput's *reworking of the portion of Jonathan Swift's* Gulliver's Travels *(1726) dealing with Lady Flimnap's passionate attraction to Gulliver. Gottesman illustrates that Garrick adapted Swift's account to suggest the mutual marital indiscretions of Lady Flimnap and her husband, a modification that allowed Garrick to better satirize the upper-class marriage of convenience and exploit its theatrical possibilities.*]

David Garrick, the talented actor whom Pope considered outstanding, was, in addition to actor and theater manager, a playwright of distinction. For the subject matter of his plays, he often looked to literary or dramatic works which he could adapt or utilize. The source of *Lilliput* is clear not only from the title and names of characters and places, but also from a prefatory letter addressed to Mr. Vaillant, dated December 8, 1756, and signed W. C.[1]

In this letter W. C. replies to adverse criticism of the play. One such criticism was that Fripperel speaks of *"firing a broadside;* when it may be seen in *Gulliver's Travels,* that the people of *Lilliput* had not the use of gun-pouder." To answer this charge, W. C. quotes from a "Lilliputian manuscript": *"Udel mis Aleph penden tapadel quif menef duren."* He hopes he has satisfied his critic. But the strongest objection was to the alteration in the character of Lady Flimnap, whom Swift's Gulliver described as "innocent." However, says W. C., an old man and friend of the late Gulliver, a Mr. Jacob Wilkinson, told him and others present at an evening meeting that Gulliver on his death-bed disclosed the following: Gulliver

> never published but one falsehood, and that was about the lady Flimnap. He acknowledged, that notwithstanding his endeavours to justify her innocence in this book, she had really confessed a passion for him, and had proposed to elope with him, and fly to England.

W. C. suggested "throwing the story into a little *Drama.*"

The "little drama," a comedy of manners and satire on the "loose morals of the age," appeared anonymously and was performed at Drury Lane. It ran for fifteen performances, the first on December 3, 1756.[2] After its initial publication by Vaillant (1757), it was printed in the *Dramatic Works of David Garrick* in 1768, 1774, and 1798. It was included, also, in *A Collection of the Most Esteemed Farces,* 1786 and 1792. Except for Gulliver, who was played by Bransby, the performers were children.[3] It was, therefore, possible to create the illusion of one giant surrounded by tiny people, even if the exact mathematical proportions set by Swift could not be accomplished.

After the Prologue with "magic ring" and "taper wand" transports spectators to the pygmy commonwealth, the action focuses on one episode—Lady Flimnap's conduct. As the play opens in Lord Flimnap's apartment, he complains about the misery of having a wife. He has sent for his wife's brothers Bolgolam and Fripperel.[4] Bolgolam does not believe that Fripperel can offer useful advice, for "such fellows as he, who call themselves fine gentlemen, forsooth, corrupt the morals of a whole nation."[5] Furthermore, Bolgolam adds: "Time was when we had as little vice here in Lilliput as any where; but since we imported politeness and fashions from Blefuscu, we have thought of nothing but

being fine gentlemen."[6] Finally, Flimnap discloses his problem: "Your sister has dishonour'd me." She has fallen in love with the man-mountain Gulliver, whom she visits and "takes great familiarities."[7] Bolgolam is ready to "cut her to pieces," but Fripperel considers these things "trifles."

The discussion is cut short because Gulliver is about to enter the metropolis to be made a Nardac. Bolgolam and Flimnap vow to get him out of the country; Flimnap, because of jealousy; Bolgolam, because he does not trust him.[8] Persons in the mob gathered to witness the ceremony discuss Gulliver. One person says that he is to be made a Nardac because of his service, but what kind of service is not indicated. Another fears that he consumes too much food and will create a shortage. They refer to Gulliver's country where people are "brave and free" and they "quarrel." Don't they have laws? "Laws, ay, laws enough; but they never mind laws, if they are brave and free."[9]

Following the procession, the scene shifts to Gulliver's room, where Gulliver, in a soliloquy, wishes himself in his own country: "Every thing is in miniature here but vice, and that is so disproportioned, that I'll match our little rakes at Lilliput, with any of our finest gentlemen in England."[10] Lady Flimnap interrupts, ostensibly to congratulate Gulliver. She admits that she has not seen her children for six months and that she amuses herself by "tormenting" her husband and "running him in debt." Gulliver replies that he cannot offer his "services" because he has a family: "I, madam, not having the good fortune to be born and bred in high life, am a slave to vulgar passions ... I really love my wife and children."[11]

In the confrontation which follows of Lord and Lady Flimnap, Fripperel, Bolgolam, and Gulliver, the lady accuses Gulliver of indecency, Flimnap receives a letter from his mistress, and Gulliver escapes to Blefuscu. The lord and lady resolve their difficulties. He gives her complete freedom "to follow your inclinations," and she will not interfere in his affairs. Bolgolam is alarmed at these "politenesses," but Fripperel is pleased.

The portrayal of Lady Flimnap is a major difference between Swift's *Lilliput* and Garrick's. There are other differences. Garrick was not interested in political or religious issues. He was not interested in following his literary predecessors in voyage literature. He felt no need to explain how Gulliver arrived in Lilliput or to discuss the problems of the court or of education. He did not describe the fire at the palace or the extinguishing of it. He did not argue the advantages of breaking the egg at one end or the other. He was not anxious about war with Blefuscu although he was critical of the "imported politeness and fashions from Blefuscu." His characters did not symbolize particular political persons. He added Fripperel to the cast of major characters and also Moretta, or, at least, a letter from Moretta, to underscore his satire in that Flimnap's conduct hardly enabled him to be critical of his wife. As a result of these differences, Garrick's satire is limited and it seems to be more good-natured and less biting than Swift's.

Like Swift, Garrick was critical of the socially elite. Like Swift, he censured their follies and hypocrisy and exposed them in order to achieve reform.[12] Like Swift, he allowed Gulliver to escape to Blefuscu (France), thus indicating that one acquires "politenesses" in addition to those he already has. As we would expect of Garrick, he made skillful use of theatrical devices, e.g., prologue, epilogue, procession, pageantry, soliloquies, confrontation, character foils, mob opinion, scenery, and costumes. If Swift turned his microscope[13] on the state and on the pettiness of man's existence, Garrick focused his on the one foible in which he recognized theatrical possibility—[14] the upper-class marriage of convenience—and he set this comic and yet serious and relevant subject on stage. He magnified and altered the Lady Flimnap-Gulliver relationship and juxtaposed Fripperel and Bolgolam, whom he made brothers of the lady, as voices of differing points of view. Bolgolam, a mouthpiece for reason and for Garrick, speaks for the sanctity of marriage. The words of caution spoken in the Prologue to the audience are sustained:

> Beware you lay not to the conjurer's charge,
> That those in miniature, are you in large.

Notes

1. Printed as a preface to the play.

2. Dougald MacMillan, *Drury Lane Calendar, 1747-1776* (Oxford, 1938), p. 272.

3. See W. C.'s letter. MacMillan, p. 272, lists names of performers.

4. Fripperel is a Garrick addition to the story, probably to serve as a counterpart to Bolgolam, who, in Swift's work, is the Admiral. In Garrick's play, he is Lady Flimnap's brother and is married to Flimnap's sister.

5. David Garrick, "Lilliput," *The Dramatic Works,* 2 vols. (London, 1774), I, 187. All references are to this text.

6. P. 187.

7. P. 188.

8. In Swift's work, Bolgolam is jealous of Gulliver's success in defeating the fleet of Blefuscu, a service for which Gulliver was made a Nardac.

9. Garrick, p. 193.

10. P. 194.

11. P. 197.

12. Garrick wrote other social comedies: *Lethe* (1740), *Male-Coquette* (1757), *Bon Ton* (1775). See Elizabeth P. Stein, *David Garrick, Dramatist* (New York, 1938).

13. Marjorie Nicolson, "The Microscope and English Imagination," *Smith College Studies in Modern Languages,* XVI (July 1935), 1-92.

14. Garrick is not the only dramatist to have used a portion of *Gulliver's Travels.* Some other plays are: Harry Paulton's *Grand Christmas Pantomime Entitled Gulliver's Travels,* 1885; Mary Barnard Horne's *Gulliver and the Lilliputians up to Date,* 1903; Antonio Paso's *Los viajes de Gulliver,* 1911.

Ralph G. Allen (essay date 1974)

SOURCE: Allen, Ralph G. "*A Christmas Tale,* or, Harlequin Scene Painter." *Tennessee Studies in Literature* 19 (1974): 149-61. Print.

[*In the following essay, Allen focuses on the sets created by P. J. de Loutherbourg for Garrick's five-act story of love and magic,* A Christmas Tale *(1773). Allen observes that de Loutherbourg imposed his own personal and fantastic vision onto Garrick's play through the use of unusual paintings and bizarre lighting effects.*]

As I write, it is nearing the two-hundredth anniversary of P. J. De Loutherbourg's first important production for Drury Lane, Garrick's five-act romance **A Christmas Tale.** The occasion should not pass unnoticed if only because recent commentaries on the career of this enigmatic artist have both overemphasized his technical achievements and undervalued the content of his special vision of the world.[1] Let others praise De Loutherbourg the proto-realist, the facile creator of new stage spaces, the forerunner of Charles Kean and Clarkson Stanfield. I celebrate, instead, De Loutherbourg, the fantastic, the Harlequin seer whose private fancies transformed a public art.

Not that technique is unimportant. Indeed in one sense De Loutherbourg's skill was often its own subject, requiring only the slightest of literary supports. **A Christmas Tale** is a case in point. The play almost certainly was based on [some] designs created by De Loutherbourg almost a year before Garrick prepared a script to display them.

In this connection two letters which De Loutherbourg wrote to Garrick and Lacy at the beginning of the artist's association with Drury Lane deserve at least passing attention here. Both, though undated, clearly refer to the terms of his employment during the 1772-1773 season.[2]

In the first, De Loutherbourg proposes that he devote three months to preparing some models and "little paintings" as a "project" for the theatre, in return for which he asks a salary of £300. The project, we learn, will contain "seven scenes … paint[ed] in miniature." In the second letter, having apparently completed his initial task to the manager's satisfaction, the painter submits a more ambitious series of proposals. In return for an annual salary of £600 ("what was formerly given at the opera to Servandoni"), he agrees to undertake the following obligation:

1. I will take care of all which concerns the decorations and the machines dependent upon them, the way of lighting them and their manipulation.

2. to devise them [the scenes] and to prepare them for execution by your painters, and in this to treat your interests as my own, if you decide to charge me with the task.

3. to give you every winter a beautiful play with grandiose new effects, concerning which we will agree between ourselves upon the outline, or if you prefer, something smaller that will be your choice.

4. to give you when it is necessary—ideas and designs of costumes for both the dance as well as for the actors.

5. to devote the whole year to matters concerning all these courses, by preparing during the summer for the winter season so you will not be a moment behind at the opening.[3]

The first of these propositions is perhaps the most interesting of all. In the eighteenth century as many as five or six scene painters were frequently employed independently on the same play or pantomime. Seldom, if ever, was there any attempt to give a unity of tone or style to a performance. Consequently it must have seemed very radical indeed to suggest that all the visual elements in a production should be brought under the direction of one man.[4]

Scholars have searched in vain for any mention of De Loutherbourg's name in connection with one of the new pieces of the 1772-1773 season. The account books record that he was paid the £300 for the seven miniature scenes which he mentions in his first letter.[5] But no one can give with any authority the name of the entertainment for which the scenes were intended.

The most likely possibility, however, is *A Christmas Tale,* first presented on December 27, 1773, midway through the following season. A note in Hopkins' *Diary* confirms our suspicion that Garrick's text postdated the designs. "This piece, was written by Mr. G. which he wrote in a hurry and on purpose to Shew Some fine Scenes which were design'd by Mons DeLoutherberg particularly a Burning Palace &c. which was extreamly fine indeed."[6] Shortly after the decorations appeared, De Loutherbourg's name became a decided commercial asset to the theatre, worth every bit of the £500 which he annually charged for his services. Indeed the scenery for *A Christmas Tale* made such a strong impression on its first audience that for many years it remained closely identified with the artist's name. Angelo and Dibdin, for example, mistakenly assume that De Loutherbourg made his London debut with this production.[7]

But if De Loutherbourg's success in *A Christmas Tale* was complete, Garrick's certainly was not. The scheme for the entertainment was suggested by Favart's comedy *La Fée urgèle.* Garrick borrowed from his French source not only the pervading tone of his work, but also the central situation in the last act—the miraculous transformation of an apparently old and ugly woman into a lovely young girl, as a result of the reluctant and disinterested love of a handsome young knight.[8] Garrick's version, however, lacks the wit of the original, and Horace Walpole's reaction sums up the opinion of most serious critics. The play, he observes, is a "dire mixture of opera, tragedy, comedy and pantomime." De Loutherbourg's designs are "the most beautiful scenes next to those in the opera at Paradise," but "they have much to do to save the piece from being thrown to the devil."[9]

The author of the *Biographia Dramatica* agrees with Walpole. *A Christmas Tale,* he notes, is a "performance yet more contemptible in its composition than *Cymon,* which led the way to this childish and insipid species of entertainment. The success ... though moderate, was chiefly owing to the assistance of Lutherburgh."[10]

That "moderate" success amounted to seventeen performances in the first season, a run which, although hardly a failure, was unquestionably disappointing to Garrick.[11] The play was a substitute for the annual holiday spectacle, and the manager had invested no little money in its preparation. According to Genest, Garrick's crucial mistake was in conceiving of his romance as a full-length play: "[A]s an afterpiece and a spectacle it might have passed without censure, but such things when produced as first pieces must excite the indignation of all but barren spectators."[12]

The reviewer for the *London Magazine* (December 1773) agrees with Genest. He condemns the piece as a "representation of what never did and indubitably never will happen." He speaks contemptuously of scenes that must "frequently break into pieces ... [so that] a grand spectacle ... [may] immediately present itself." He compares the story to "Jack the Giant-Killer" and derides Garrick's plot in which a virtuous young man must show his valor, honor, and constancy to win a fair lady by conquering a wicked and powerful magician. He calls the comic incidents in the subplot "sacrifices to the galleries," but is forced to admit that the "machinery is admirable, the scenery almost entirely new and for the most part very beautiful." He particularly admires some of De Loutherbourg's lighting effects, as well as a "palace which tumbles into ruin," a grand garden scene, "and the sea prospect which bounds it." The scenery, he concludes, "is a sort rarely seen in this country, and reflects infinite credit on the artists." Henry Angelo, writing some years later, puts the matter even more strongly. De Loutherbourg, he tells us, "astonished the audience by the beautiful coloring and designs, far superior to what they had been accustomed to."[13]

What were the innovations which so excited the audience of *A Christmas Tale*? Why did the designs seem more impressive than anything previously exhibited? Part of the answer lies in De Loutherbourg's ability to provide an increased illusion of depth through the employment of set pieces and ground rows irregularly spaced on the stage. The design for Part IV, scene iii, of the play is the earliest surviving *pictorial* evidence of his use of the "broken" scene (more correctly called a set scene), the invention of which is attributed to De Loutherbourg by O'Keeffe.[14] The reviews of *A Christmas Tale* clearly indicate that Malton's famous condemnation of English designers (for their "inability to proportion one part to another on detached scenes") was not meant to include the new painter at Drury Lane.

Moreover, *A Christmas Tale* contained some unusual lighting effects. Instead of settling for the neutral illumination of scenes that audiences had come to expect, De Loutherbourg spread his light unevenly. He also made spectacular use of colored light not only to reflect nature in pictures of moonlight and sunrise, but also to contradict nature in fantastic and allegorical scenes.

The subject matter of De Loutherbourg's designs was innovative as well. His exotic style gave a sense of strangeness to the paintings, particularly in the two Eastern scenes which appear in the last part of the play. These scenes foreshadow a major element in the artist's later work, an element which was to be prominent in such important productions as *Sethona* (1774), *The Sultan* (1775), *Selima and Azor* (1776), *Semiramis* (1777), *Zoraida* (1779), and *The Fair Circassian* (1781).

A Christmas Tale might be described as a speaking pantomime, that is, a serious play which employs all the devices and illogicalities of the traditional harlequinade. Its influence on the dramatic repertory of the nineteenth century (especially in the works of Planché) can hardly be overestimated. And most of the influence derives from the contributions of De Loutherbourg rather than from those of the musician or scenarist.

A description of the settings for *A Christmas Tale* must depend primarily on the text of that production, published by T. Becket shortly after the first performance.[15] As might be expected in a play especially designed to exhibit scenery, the stage directions are unusually detailed. By supplementing these with excerpts from the newspapers, one can obtain a fairly accurate impression of the designs which so astonished the Drury Lane audience. For the first part of the play only, our reconstruction receives some additional help in the form of a surviving prompt-copy with some corrections in Garrick's own handwriting.[16]

The play is divided into five parts. Altogether, ten separate designs were employed. Three of these were part of complicated transformation effects.

Before the curtain rose, the actor Palmer came on the stage to deliver the prologue. He was dressed, according to the stage directions, "in the character of Christmas." The text of the prologue concerns itself with a description and explanation of his costume, which consisted of a long robe with holly and ivy twined around it. The robe, padded to show that he was "not ill-fed," was divided with "mince pies by way of belt." At his side was a carving knife in place of a sword. There is no indication that De Loutherbourg designed this costume, but in later years, he did create many of a similarly fantastical nature. Palmer's address concludes by instructing the audience to be "merry and not wise," an excellent suggestion considering the intellectual level of the entertainment.

Part I contains two scenes. The first of these is described in the stage directions simply as a "beautiful landskip." From that description it would appear that a shallow scene of some kind was employed, especially since the scene following is an elaborate, full-stage garden. Our conjecture is confirmed by an entry in the prompt-copy, which reads:

Scene #1   a   [New[17]]   Short Landscape   #1 gr.[18]

The first groove (#1 gr.) was, of course, not more than a few feet behind the downstage curtain line. Two characters appear in the scene, and the action is simple and straightforward. Only one minor piece of business required special attention from the designer. Tycho, the comic servant of the hero, is spying on his inamorata, Robinette. At one point, he appears "peeping out of a tree," an action which suggests a fairly sturdy, practicable set piece, or at least a profiled downstage wing.

Clearly, however, most of the scene was painted on a pair of flats. The mood is comic and pastoral, and the "landskip" must have exhibited a gentle, restful picture. The reviewer for the *London Chronicle* of December 25-28, 1773, describes it as "a river with a castle at a distance."

Scene i concludes with a comic song called "The Freaks of Woman Kind," after which the flats part to reveal "Camilla's beautiful garden" (I, ii). The depth of this setting is indicated by an entry in the prompt-copy (Part I, scene ii) which describes it as a "long garden" and adds "5 Entrance." There are two garden scenes in the play. The first one, "Camilla's Garden" (described by the *London Chronicle* as "a gentleman's seat, seen through an avenue arched with trees"[19]), was used again for Part III, scene i.

Camilla, the heroine of the play, is the orphaned daughter of a benign magician, from whom she has inherited some footling supernatural powers. During Part I, scene ii (Prompt-copy), her lover, Floridor, whose father is also a magician, begs her to marry him. She points, by way of reply, to an enchanted laurel and tells Floridor that she has promised her father she will not marry unless the suitor can "give proofs of what this inchanted laurel will unfold," whereupon, according to the stage direction, the laurel does unfold to discover *"the words* valor, constancy, and Honour, in letters of Gold." This effect must have been more spectacular than the text indicates, for both the *Whitehall Evening Post* (December 28-30) and the *London Packet* (December 27-29) mention it prominently in their descriptions of the production.

At the conclusion of this first part, the following note appears in the prompt script:

> drop Green Curtain
> Cor cur.[20]

In *Alfred,* De Loutherbourg had used a painted drop scene to mask the stage during the act intermissions. In *A Christmas Tale,* however, he apparently reverted to the older and more customary practice of lowering a neutral curtain to signal the end of each act of his entertainment.

In Part II one scene appears; it is described in the text as "Bonoro's Cell with Prisons around it," and in the *London Chronicle* as "a cave with separate dungeons enclosed with grates" (December 25-28). The *Whitehall Evening Post* for December 28-30 adds that the dungeons have "talismans upon the doors."

Bonoro, as his name suggests, deals in white magic, and his cells contain a chorus of evil spirits, who are the servants of the wicked sorcerer, Nigromant. Tycho, the comic servant, is given Bonoro's wand and told to watch the imprisoned spirits. The female spirits sing a song and charm him to sleep, whereupon he drops the wand. At this point, according to the stage directions: *"it thunders, the dens burst open, and various evil spirits of both sexes enter promiscuously, and riotously express their joy."*

The etching which De Loutherbourg contributed to the printed edition of the play shows Tycho, as played by Weston, immediately after he has fallen asleep.[21] To his left is a cell containing the spirits, who are shown in the act of escaping from their confinement. The etching, needless to say, gives very little information about the scenery. However, it does clearly show a wing downstage left, cut out to represent some kind of tall rock, and from behind the wing, the prison grate (presumably a set piece) extending obliquely upstage.

Most of the reviewers mention this moment in the play as particularly spectacular, and the *London Packet* is impressed with the fact that "the stage is darkened suddenly" (December 27-29). Unfortunately, the terror created by the darkness was considerably dissipated on the opening night of the production. One reviewer complains that "the spirits . . . are supposed to rend the air with yells and howls enveloped with fire; but the intent of this scene is destroyed by the inaction and silence of most of the performers."[22]

In Part III, two scenes are needed, both of them repeated from the beginning of the play. Scene i is a second view of Camilla's garden, and scene ii shows the outside of Bonoro's cell, its cages now empty of their tenants.

The text of III, i, clearly shows the singleness of purpose with which Garrick arranged the action of his entertainment to display the talents of his new designer. The logic is perhaps a trifle strained. Camilla and Floridor are alone in the garden; suddenly Camilla says:

> My fancy teems with a thousand apprehensions, all my senses are in disorder. I heard or thought I heard strange noises in the air; even now my eyes are deceiv'd, or this garden, the trees, the flowers, the heav'ns change their colours to my sight, and seem to say something mysterious which is not in my heart to expound.

The stage direction immediately following this speech confirms Camilla's apprehension, for indeed "The objects in the garden vary their colours." This is the effect which made such an impression on the reviewer for the *London Magazine.* Equally impressed is the critic of the *London Chronicle* who reports with something approaching wonder that the "trees change colour alternating from green to Red, resembling fire" (December 25-28).

The importance of this scene is much greater than would first appear. The English audience was not accustomed to the spectacular possibilities of unevenly spread colored light, and the device created by De Loutherbourg had a sensational and startling effect. The novelty of the scene was remembered long after its inventor had retired from the stage. Indeed Angelo, writing in 1830, describes it in some detail:

> It was a sudden transition in a forest scene, where the foliage varies from green to blood colour. This contrivance was entirely new; and the effect was produced by placing different coloured silks in the flies, or side scenes, which turned on a pivot, and, with lights behind, which so illumined the stage, as to give the effect of enchantment. This idea probably was taken from the magical delusions as represented in the story and print of the enchanted forest where Rinaldo meets with his frightful adventures.
>
> (Vol. II, 326-27)

While the trees are changing color, Camilla appropriately sings a song about mutability.

Part IV contains four scenes. The first setting is described in the text as "a dark Wood." A certain difficulty presents itself here: the same scene is mentioned in the *London Chronicle* as "a piece of ruins with a sarcophagus" (December 25-28). Possibly, the reviewer listed the scene out of the proper order and was actually referring to a design (the burned palace) which was used later in the action. Or perhaps, and this seems more likely, De Loutherbourg's picture of the wood actually contained some suggestion of a stone ruin.

Floridor, having lost his sword and shield, is wandering in a forest. Camilla, disguised as an old woman, enters and promises to recover his weapons if he will consider himself bound to her in the future. Floridor reluctantly promises, whereupon, "*She waves her wand, the wood opens and discovers his sword and shield hung upon the stem of a tree.*" The account of this effect in the *London Packet* tells us that "the trees on each side *withdraw.*"[23] Without question, a pair of back-flats were used, but whether these flats formed a continuous prospect or were cut in profile it is impossible to say. De Loutherbourg frequently used profiled flats in later productions.

Scene ii of Part IV is Bonoro's cell again; Bonoro is dispatching a troop of spirits to help his son. Scene iii exhibits what the stage direction calls "*a prospect of Rocks*" in the domain of Nigromant. Floridor approaches these rocks and calls on Tycho to sound his horn, "the horn of defiance." As soon as Tycho obeys, a remarkable transformation appears: "*The rocks split and discover the castle of Nigromant and the Fiery Lake.*"

A curious confusion seems to have troubled the critic of the *London Chronicle* at this point. His version of the scene differs considerably from the one noted in the stage direction above. Instead of reporting that the fiery lake appeared after the rocks had split, the *Chronicle* reviewer describes the scene as composed of "distant rocks, with a river of (very unnatural) fire, which at the blowing of Tycho's horn, *disappears* and discovers a beautiful bay."

There is no indication in the text that Tycho blew his horn twice; therefore we must conclude that the reviewer for the *Chronicle* is mistaken. His description is also at odds with the stage direction which follows shortly after the blowing of the horn: "*The magician appears in a fiery lake into which Floridor jumps, and fights and sinks with him*" (Part IV, scene iii).

It is impossible to say with any certainty how this effect was managed. Perhaps some sort of glowing transparency was employed, in conjunction with a trap in the floor of the stage. After Nigromant and Floridor sink into the lake, Tycho is left alone; he is joined shortly by a chorus of demons, and a comic dance ensues. The stage direction indicates no scene change at this point, but certainly the shallow flats of "distant Rocks" must have closed again in front of the lake and palace. Room was needed to set up triumphal arches for the procession of victory in the fourth scene, a procession which undoubtedly required the entire depth of the stage.

Our suspicion concerning the reappearance of the "distant Rocks" is confirmed by a drawing of this scene which was apparently executed by De Loutherbourg himself.[24] In the design the actor Weston, as Tycho, is seen preparing for his comic battle with the demons. In the background, on the stage-left side of the sketch, a huge rock rises out of sight. The design is a perfect example of "sublime" painting. The landscape is rugged and wild, and its execution is reminiscent of that of Salvatore Rosa.

The drawing of the rock is, of course, an idealized picture of the stage setting, and therefore of very limited value to the theatre historian. Nevertheless there seems to be an unmistakable indication of ramps and ground rows in the design. The scene is clearly "broken" in the manner described by O'Keeffe. On one of the ramps downstage left, Tycho is standing, sword in hand. Masking the ramp is a raking piece painted to resemble rocks. Literally a new dimension had been added to the stage, or so it must have seemed to an audience accustomed to the monotonous settings of the eighteenth century.

At the beginning of Part IV, scene iv, the text reads:

> (*The Castle Gates*
> *The triumphal entry of* FLORIDOR
>   *to martial musick*
> *With* NIGROMANT *and* EVIL SPIRITS
>   *in chains*
> *Then enter* TYCHO *attended with the female*
>   *evil spirits.*)

The *London Chronicle* describes this scene as "the front of a castle with a triumphal entry of spirits in chains followed by Tycho riding on a rhinoscerous" (December 25-28). The *Morning Chronicle* also mentions this beast and adds that the procession contained "every addition likely to be an allurement to the numerous idolators of stage pageantry" (December 28).

The most spectacular effects of the play, however, were reserved for the final act. Part V, scene i, is "*A grand apartment in the Seraglio,*" containing a "triumphal Turkish throne."[25] Up until this point in the action, there has been no suggestion of Eastern scenery, either in the stage directions or in the newspaper accounts of the production. The only faint foreshadowing of the seraglio was the rhinoceros in Part IV and the costume of Tycho, which in the print appears to be vaguely Oriental.

The first scenes in the play—the castles, the gentleman's seat, the garden—were almost certainly European. We are forced to conclude that any attempt at architectural unity was abandoned in this production in favor of an eclecticism which permitted the designer to display his versatility.

During the scene in the seraglio, Floridor receives a letter from Camilla's alter ego, the old woman who had befriended him in the dark wood. He tears the letter, whereupon a violent storm occurs:

> It thunders and the stage is darkened at which all the women attendants and Camilla shriek and run off. Tycho enters in horror; says that the palace is in flames which are seen through the windows of the seraglio. Tycho runs off; Floridor braves it; the flames come on; the seraglio is on fire and falls down. Daemons enter and run away with different things in flames. The scene changes to a moonlight prospect with the moon rising.

> (*London Packet,* December 27-29)

This startling transformation was undoubtedly aided greatly by the colored light which De Loutherbourg was able to throw on his setting. Thus in the *London Chronicle* the destruction of the palace is described as "a horrid scene of fire with the ebullition of blood and the stage darkened," while the prospect which follows is "a blue scene . . . [with] the rising of the moon."

The old woman now appears, and Floridor reluctantly agrees to marry her. At this moment, *"The stage grows light, and Camilla quitting at once the form of the old woman, assumes her real character and dress"* (v, i). No sooner has Floridor recognized his mistress than (according to the *London Chronicle*) *"a cloud descends, and opening discovers the Hermit within them."* The Hermit is, of course, Bonoro, who immediately gives his blessing to the lovers.

The cloud was obviously large enough to conceal a change of scenery behind it, for when it ascends, it *"Discovers a fine distant prospect of the sea and a castle at a distance with the sun rising"* (v, i).

With this final transformation *A Christmas Tale* comes to its predictably happy conclusion. As a playwright Garrick is always predictable, and here his white magicians practice a very pallid sorcery indeed. There was nothing pallid, however, about the sorcery of Garrick's new designer, who clearly had a Harlequin gift for making tame fancies seem unpredictable and strange. De Loutherbourg's "brick-dust foregrounds, red fields, brass trees, and . . . copper horizon[s],"[26] which Williams so much despised, were in fact the touchstones of his genius. For De Loutherbourg was no simple realist. His vision of the world was fantastic, special, not bound to an "association of palpable objects."[27] We can see in these early designs the same restless imagination which, in a less controlled form, prompted De Loutherbourg's later search for occult secrets and magical cures. In an age that still professed to admire reason, he created irrational entertainments, and in so doing, gave form to the buried life of an entire generation. Not since Inigo Jones had any designer so successfully imposed a personal vision upon a collective art.

Notes

1. Among the many recent accounts of De Loutherbourg's career, mention should be made of Lillian Elvira Preston's "Phillipe Jacques de Loutherbourg, Eighteenth Century Romantic Artist and Scene Designer," Diss. Univ. of Florida 1957. Russell Thomas' "Contemporary Taste in the Stage Decorations of London Theatres, 1770-1800," *MP* 42 (Nov. 1944), 65-78, is also valuable, as are the following articles by the present writer: "The Eidophusikon," *Theatre Design & Technology,* No. 7 (Dec. 1966), 12-16; "De Loutherbourg and Captain Cook," *Theatre Research* 4 (1962), 195-211; and "Topical Scenes for Pantomime," *Educational Theatre Journal* 17 (1965), 289-300.

2. The first letter is preserved at the Harvard Library; the second is at the Victoria and Albert. A photostatic copy of the French text of both letters is available in the Yale-Rockefeller Theatrical Prints Collection.

3. Second MS. Letter to Garrick and Lacy. All these propositions proved acceptable to Garrick and Lacy except the one concerning salary. Angelo, for example, indicates in *Reminiscences* (London: H. Colburn, 1828), II, 15 g, that De Loutherbourg was paid £500 annually for his services, rather than the £600 which he had requested.

4. In his earlier letter De Loutherbourg's suggestions had been even more startling. In order to achieve "a new sensation," the artist proposed changing not only the method of lighting the theatre but also "the method of withdrawing the scenes" (First MS. Letter to Garrick). However, Charles Dibdin tells us that Garrick's penury prevented De Loutherbourg from effecting this last reform. *A Complete History of the Stage* (London: Charles Dibdin, 1799?), v, 243.

5. George Winchester Stone, Jr., *The London Stage, 1747-1776* (Carbondale: Southern Illinois Univ. Press, 1962), IV, 1731.

6. Entry for Dec. 27, 1773. The manuscript is at the Folger Library.

7. Angelo, II, 326. The first scene specifically attributed to De Loutherbourg in the playbills was not *A Christmas Tale* but instead a topical design of a recent naval review at Spithead, inserted somewhat illogically into a revival of *The Masque of Alfred* (Oct. 9, 1773). For a detailed account of this production, see my article, "Topical Scenes for Pantomime" (note 1).

8. Albert Iacuzzi, *The European Vogue of Favart* (New York: Publications of the Institute of French Studies, 1932), gives an excellent account of *La Fée urgèle.*

9. *The Letters of Horace Walpole,* ed. Mrs. Paget Toynbee (Oxford: Clarendon Press, 1903-1905), VIII, 398.

10. David Erskine Baker and others (London: Longman, Hurst, Rees, Orme and Brown, 1812), II, 101.

11. *The London Stage,* pp. 1773-1827.

12. John Genest, *Some Account of the English Stage from the Restoration in 1660 to 1830* (Bath: H. E. Carrington, 1832), v, 401. *A Christmas Tale* was later successfully converted into an afterpiece by Sheridan. The first performance of the play in its abridged form took place on Oct. 11, 1776.

13. II, 326-27.

14. *Recollections of the Life of John O'Keeffe* (London: H. Colburn, 1826), II, 114.

15. *A New Dramatic Entertainment Called A Christmas Tale, In Five Parts, Embellished with an Etching by*

De Loutherbourg (London: T. Becket, 1774). Hereafter, this edition will be referred to as *A Christmas Tale.* It is interesting to note that De Loutherbourg's name appears on the title page of this edition, despite the fact that the author receives no credit. This clearly shows, I think, how closely the reputation of the designer was linked to the production.

16. *A Christmas Tale,* 1st part, MS. in an unknown hand with corrections in Garrick's autograph, Folger Library, MS. D.a. 69. This copy will hereafter be referred to as Prompt-copy, Part I.

17. In the original copy, "New" was crossed out.

18. Part I, scene i. In the original copy, "New" was crossed out. The fact that the word "new" is crossed out in the Prompt-copy raises some interesting questions. Although the newspaper accounts imply that all the scenery for *A Christmas Tale* was designed especially for the occasion, it is possible that at the last moment a refurbished stock scene was substituted for a new design in the opening scene of the play.

19. Dec. 25-28, 1773.

20. I, ii. The Prompt-copy ends with the conclusion of Part I.

21. This etching appears in the Yale-Rockefeller Theatrical Prints Collection (BH2800).

22. *London Chronicle,* Dec. 25-28, 1773.

23. Dec. 27-29; italics mine.

24. A photograph of this drawing appears in the Yale-Rockefeller Theatrical Prints Collection (BH 3500).

25. *London Chronicle,* Dec. 25-28, 1773.

26. John Williams (Anthony Pasquin, pseud.), *An Authentic History of the Professors of Painting, Sculpture, & Architecture, Who Have Practiced in Ireland ... To Which Are Added, Memoirs of the Royal Academicians, Being an Attempt to Improve the Taste of the Realm* (London: H. D. Symonds, 1796), II, 78-80.

27. Ibid.

M. A. Goldsmith and J. D. Hainsworth (essay date 1978)

SOURCE: Goldsmith, M. A., and J. D. Hainsworth. "James Townley and *The Clandestine Marriage.*" *Review of English Studies* ns 29.114 (1978): 169-77. Print.

[In the following essay, Goldsmith and Hainsworth review the charge that The Clandestine Marriage *is a plagiarism of Townley's farce* False Concord. *They find no evidence to support the claim that* False Concord *is the source for several of the characters in Garrick's play, but they highlight the personal and professional friendship of Garrick and Townley to account for the surface similarities between the two works.]*

Discussion of ***The Clandestine Marriage*** has largely been concerned with the question of which parts of the play are to be attributed to each of its co-authors, George Colman and David Garrick.[1] The question of the play's relationship to the Reverend James Townley's farce, *False Concord,* first raised by J. P. Roberdeau, Townley's son-in-law, has never been adequately considered.

Roberdeau's comments on *False Concord,* made in the course of an account of James Townley, appeared first in his *Fugitive Verse and Prose* (Chichester, 1803), and were given wider currency when reprinted in the *Gentleman's Magazine* of February 1805:

> It is to be remarked, that False Concord contains three characters of Lord Lavender, Mr. Suds, an enriched soap-boiler, and a pert valet, who are not only the exact Lord Ogelby [*sic*], Mr. Sterling, and Brush, of the **Clandestine Marriage,** brought out in 1767 by Garrick and Colman conjointly; but that part of the dialogue is nearly *verbatim.*[2]

For a number of years, no one was in a position either to confirm or to deny Roberdeau's assertions, since *False Concord,* which had been performed only once, at Covent Garden on 20 March 1764, had never been published and there was no manuscript copy accessible. About 1832,[3] however, John Payne Collier and Thomas Amyot purchased from the widow and executors of John Larpent, late Examiner of Plays, the manuscripts of plays submitted for censorship between 1737 and January 1824, which included a manuscript of *False Concord.* In an article, 'New Facts regarding Garrick and his Writings,'[4] based on an examination of manuscripts in this collection, Collier briefly discusses the relationship between ***The Clandestine Marriage*** and *False Concord.* His conclusion is that, although Roberdeau's charge regarding the transplantation of characters and plagiarism of dialogue, 'is by no means borne out by the fact,' nevertheless, there is 'sufficient resemblance, both in the characters, plot, and execution of the two pieces, to make it clear that Garrick, when he wrote his portion of ***The Clandestine Marriage,*** had *False Concord* in his eye, if not actually in his hand.'[5]

Collier is, so far, the only writer on the relationship between the two plays actually to have seen a copy of *False Concord,* but, unfortunately, the discussion by which he supports his conclusions is too cursory to carry conviction. The fact that subsequent writers on ***The Clandestine Marriage*** have not had Collier's advantage has not deterred some of them from a more unqualified rejection of Roberdeau's charge. Beatty rejects it on three grounds: because Garrick was not in London during the production of *False Concord*; because Colman's plans for the play[6] were conceived before *False Concord* was produced; and because contemporary writers were silent in regard to any hint of plagiarism.[7] Page rejects it on the grounds that the characters of ***The Clandestine Marriage*** 'were so representative of their day that it would be easy to assign assumed sources without proving any plagiarism.'[8] Stein reaffirms Beatty's arguments and points to evidence that the first three acts of **The Clandestine Marriage,** and not just a general plan of it, were written by the time Garrick left London on his European tour, six months before the performance of *False Concord.* The manuscript of *False Concord* once owned by Collier and Amyot has, in fact, been in the possession of the Huntington Library, with the other Larpent manuscripts, since 1917.[9] It is possible, therefore, to check Collier's assertions and to enlarge upon his cursory comparison of the two plays.

A comparison of the plays confirms Collier's assertion that there is no substance in Roberdeau's charge that some of the dialogue in **The Clandestine Marriage** is taken 'nearly *verbatim*' from the earlier play. There are, however, similarities of a more general nature. Both the five-act comedy and Townley's two-act farce start from a situation in which the daughter of a wealthy city merchant is to be married to an aristocrat who is short of money. In each case, the projected marriage has the character of a business transaction: social status is being offered in exchange for money. Such a situation is, of course, to be found elsewhere in the art, literature, and drama of the period and can hardly be cited as proof of plagiarism. The particular source to which the 'Advertisement' to the first edition of the play, Garrick in his prologue to the play, and Colman in a letter to Garrick of 4 December 1765, acknowledge indebtedness is, in fact, Hogarth's series of paintings, 'Marriage à la Mode' (1745). Colman specifies the first plate in the engravings made from the paintings:

> The first plate of Hogarth's 'Marriage à la Mode' was the ground I went upon: I had long wished to see those characters on the stage. ...[10]

This plate shows a gouty old lord drawing attention to his pedigree and ignoring the unpaid mortgages being shown him by an anxious clerk, a younger aristocrat admiring himself in the glass while his bride-to-be engages in intimate conversation with a young lawyer, and a wealthy merchant examining closely the details of the marriage contract. The painting could also have been in Townley's mind when he wrote *False Concord,* although the younger aristocrat is absent from his play, where it is the old lord who is to marry the merchant's daughter. Like Colman and Garrick, Townley was a friend of Hogarth's.[11]

As far as individual characters in the two plays are concerned, the first of the comparisons suggested by Roberdeau is the most interesting. Although it is far from the truth to say, as he does, that Townley's Lord Lavender is 'the exact Lord Ogleby,' there are resemblances between these two elderly and decrepit fops. Lavender's name suggests his fondness for perfume. His room smells so strongly of it that Sudley feels an urgent need to smoke tobacco when he and his wife are invited there to drink chocolate. Ogleby's chocolate is itself 'charmingly perfum'd'—or so Sterling's Chambermaid finds it (II. i; p. 19).[12] Sterling himself reacts less favourably to the perfumed letter he

receives from Ogleby (I. ii; p. 9). In each play there is a memorable scene between the lord and his valet in which the lord is made ready for the activities of the day.[13] Lord Ogleby does not have recourse to artificial hips, calves, teeth and eyebrows, as Lord Lavender does, but, in the words of his valet: 'he must have a great deal of brushing, oyling, screwing, and winding up to set him a going for the day' (II. i; p. 18). Both lords employ rouge. The superiority of **The Clandestine Marriage** in comic inventiveness is seen in the use made of this detail. In *False Concord,* Jasper, Lavender's valet, assembles the rouge and all the other items necessary for his master's toilet. Lord Ogleby, however, imagines that he can conceal the use of rouge even from his servants. Dismissing them on the pretext that he is about to read a pamphlet, he unlocks the drawer in which the rouge is hidden and applies it in secret. More important, however, than any similarity of detail between the two scenes involving the lord and his valet is the similarity in their position and function in their respective plays. They are the means by which the noble lord enters the play; and they establish the comic tone appropriate to his character—in *False Concord,* one of acid satire, in **The Clandestine Marriage,** one in which the satire is mild and humour predominates.

In his *Dramatic Censor* of 1770, Francis Gentleman notes that Lord Ogleby has been 'pronounced a very near relation to Lord Chalkstone.'[14] Chalkstone is an elderly and decrepit lord whom Garrick introduced into his farce **Lethe** on its revival in 1756. He has come to visit the underworld, taking advantage of an invitation that has been issued to mortals to enable them to drink of the waters of Lethe and so forget their troubles. Certainly Ogleby resembles Chalkstone more than he does Lavender. As with Chalkstone, the spirit with which he transcends his physical infirmities arouses admiration as well as laughter in the audience, whereas Lavender's attempts to conceal his physical defects seem merely grotesque and foolish. Ogleby resembles Chalkstone, too, in his susceptibility to female charm. At the end of his scene in **Lethe,** Chalkstone, although requiring physical support from his servant Bowman, sets out to 'coquet a little' with some of the beautiful women of antiquity. Ogleby believes that, despite his advanced age, all women find him irresistibly attractive. Lavender, on the other hand, shows no sign of any feeling for the opposite sex.

Both the Sudley and Sterling families are abused for their bad taste and ignorance. For Lord Lavender, the Sudleys are 'Goths,' 'Cannibals,' 'Barbarians,' 'Hottentots,' and Mr. Sudley is 'a downright Negro.'[15] Lord Ogleby's abuse of the Sterlings excludes only Fanny, apart from whom they are 'Goths and Vandals' (IV. ii; p. 58). For their bad taste in respect of their gardens both Sudley and Sterling are satirized. They are satirized, however, for quite opposite reasons. Sudley has no notion of contemporary fashions in gardening and disapproves of his lawn because it is too bare and of his canal because it has no practical function.

He plans to fell some 'Venerable Oaks' because they encourage rooks, whose cawing he dislikes, and to sell the timber for shipbuilding. Sterling, on the other hand, is satirized because he has uncritically embraced popular notions of landscape gardening and has spent £150 on putting his ruins in repair (II. ii; p. 30). Stein sees this aspect of Sterling as deriving from Lord Chalkstone in *Lethe,* who, similarly obsessed with contemporary notions of gardening, holds forth on the unrealized '*capabilities*' of the *Elysian Fields*.[16]

Apart from their bad taste in gardening, Sudley and Sterling differ sharply. Thus, Sudley would be perfectly happy for his daughter to marry Raymond, with whom she is in love, if his wife were not so determined that she should marry Lord Lavender. Sterling, on the other hand, although he likes Lovewell, is opposed to his daughter's marrying him, his attitude being entirely determined by financial considerations. Sudley, too, has an idiosyncracy for which there is no counterpart in Sterling—he is fond of showing off his Latin. Trimmer, Lavender's lawyer, calls him 'a Barbaric Murderer of the Latin tongue,' and, connecting him with Mrs. Slipslop in Fielding's novel *Joseph Andrews* (1742), 'a Slip Slop in Latin.' It is because of his fondness for Latin that Sudley describes 'Unequal Wedlock' by the grammatical term 'False Concord,' thus giving Townley's play its title.

It is surprising that Roberdeau has not suggested Mrs. Sudley in *False Concord* as a source for Mrs. Heidelberg, the sister of Mr. Sterling in *The Clandestine Marriage,* for Mrs. Sudley dominates her husband just as effectively as Mrs. Heidelberg does her brother, and both ladies are ruthless in their determination that the marriage which has been planned shall actually take place. Both regard themselves, too, quite erroneously, as well equipped to take their places in high society. 'Nobody knows the *qualaty* better than I do,' asserts Mrs. Heidelberg (I. ii; p. 15), but cannot even pronounce the word 'quality' correctly. Mrs. Sudley has grotesque notions of the behaviour appropriate to the social position to which she aspires:

> Oh! I shall take a prodigious deal of Pains to be Easy—Then I will be near sighted and Rude, and know Nobody. Then I'll be gracefull and smile;—Then I'll have a Violent Head Ach, and take out my Smelling Bottle;—then I'll talk very loud, and say something exceeding Smart, and go off in an Horse laugh. Ha, ha, ha!

It is also possible, however, that, for the character of Mrs. Heidelberg, *The Clandestine Marriage* may again be indebted to Garrick's *Lethe.* Stein[17] has suggested a connection with Mrs. Riot in that play. Mrs. Riot is equally forceful, regards herself as a fine lady, enjoys the pursuits of fashionable society, and deplores her husband's unwillingness to 'leave off his nasty merchandizing.'[18] Like Mrs. Heidelberg, too, she mispronounces words.

Roberdeau suggests that Brush in *The Clandestine Marriage* derives from the 'pert valet' in *False Concord,* whose name is given as Jasper in the Larpent manuscript. Jasper, however, except for his assistance in the daily resuscitation of his lord, has no significant similarities to Brush. A more likely source for Brush are the servants, especially the Duke's Servant, in *High Life Below Stairs,* first acted at Drury Lane in 1759. The servants in this farce pride themselves on following their own inclinations, rather than their employers' commands. They usurp the titles and adopt the airs of their masters and mistresses. They also appropriate to their own use their employers' supplies of food. Brush behaves in just this way. 'The moment my Lord wakes,' he tells the Sterlings' Chambermaid, whom he has invited to partake of Lord Ogleby's chocolate, 'he rings his bell, which I answer sooner or later, as it suits my convenience' (II. i; p. 18). Of the projected marriage of Miss Sterling into the aristocracy, he remarks loftily: 'we don't consider tempers—we want money, Mrs. Nancy—give us enough of that, we'll abate you a great deal in other particulars—ha, ha, ha' (II. i; p. 19). Later on, when news circulates that Sir John Melvil now wants to marry Fanny, instead of her elder sister, Brush initiates a celebration for the servants at which Sterling's butler dispenses his master's port. The similarity between Brush and the Duke's Servant must have been evident to the first audiences of *The Clandestine Marriage,* for Brush was played by Robert Palmer, who had made the Duke's Servant in *High Life Below Stairs* one of his most popular roles; and *High Life Below Stairs,* with Palmer as the Duke's Servant, was in the repertoire at Drury Lane during the season in which *The Clandestine Marriage* was first performed.

The apparent indebtedness of *The Clandestine Marriage* to *High Life Below Stairs* is of especial interest, for the authorship of *High Life Below Stairs* has been ascribed both to David Garrick and to James Townley. Arthur Murphy's account of its authorship in his *Life of David Garrick* (1801) is as follows:

> Early in October [1759], Garrick brought forward that excellent farce, called *High Life Below Stairs.* For some private reasons he wished to lie concealed, and, with that design, prevailed on his friend, Mr. Townly [*sic*], master of Merchant Taylor's [*sic*] school, to suffer his name to be circulated in whispers. The truth, however, was not long suppressed.

> (i. 343)

Such behaviour on Garrick's part would not be unusual. Indeed, prior to his quarrel with Colman he had intended that his participation in the writing of *The Clandestine Marriage* should be kept secret until the play was printed. Garrick explains why he thought such secrecy necessary in a letter to the Earl of Bute of 11 February 1759, which relates to his farce *The Guardian*:

> Prince Edward ask'd me last Night, who was the Author of yᵉ Farce; I was in great Confusion at yᵉ Question, because I happen'd to be the Guilty person Myself, But I have so many Enemies among the Writers on Account of my refusing so many of their Performances Every Year, that I

am oblig'd to conceal Myself in order to avoid the Torrent of abuse that their Malice would pour upon Me—I thought it proper (and I hope Your Lordship will Excuse Me) to discover this; lest his Royal Highness should be angry at my not answering his Question directly, as I ought to have done . . .[19]

Murphy's account of the authorship of *High Life Below Stairs* is, however, contradicted in a letter from Thomas Clare in the *Gentleman's Magazine* of May 1801 (p. 389). Clare claims that Townley really was the author of the play. He gives as the source of his information his friend the Rev. Samuel Bishop, who, he says, 'had obtained his knowledge of it from the repeated communications of Mr. Townley himself.' Bishop was an under-master at Merchant Taylors' School at a time when Townley was high master, and, according to Clare, 'they mutually submitted their several literary productions to each other's judgement.' Clare asserts also that Townley's surviving sons 'know and have satisfactory proof that their father was really the author of the little dramatic piece in question.' In a postscript to his letter, he says that one of these sons has now convinced Arthur Murphy that he was in error in ascribing *High Life Below Stairs* to Garrick. This statement of Clare's cannot be considered conclusive, however. His assertion that Arthur Murphy changed his mind cannot be verified elsewhere and his sources of information are people who might be prejudiced in Townley's favour. A difficulty in accepting Townley's authorship is the vast superiority of this farce to either of his two later and undisputed plays, *False Concord* and *The Tutor*.[20] The *Biographia Dramatica*,[21] which accepts Clare's account, gets round the difficulty by suggesting that Dr. Benjamin Hoadly, author of the highly successful comedy *The Suspicious Husband* (1747), had a hand in the farce, citing as its authority Charles Dibdin, 'who professes some particular knowledge as to this subject.' There is, however, no confirmation elsewhere of this assertation. It may well be that the question of the authorship of *High Life Below Stairs* will never be resolved with certainty.

The most significant resemblances between *The Clandestine Marriage* and *False Concord* would seem to be in the scenes involving master and valet; in the position and function which these have in their respective plays; in the similar manner in which the two noble lords abuse the merchant and his family; in the satire, in both plays, of the merchant's taste in landscape gardening; and in the similarities in character and behaviour of Mrs. Heidelberg and Mrs. Sudley. These resemblances by no means afford conclusive proof of *The Clandestine Marriage*'s indebtedness to *False Concord* but they make it seem likely that at least one of the co-authors of *The Clandestine Marriage* had *False Concord* 'in his eye,' as J. P. Collier expresses it. It would seem that he had other plays 'in his eye' as well, however, such as *Lethe* and *High Life Below Stairs*.

While there have been differences of opinion amongst scholars as to the contributions to *The Clandestine Mar-*

riage of its two co-authors, there is general agreement that Garrick was responsible for the opening scene of Act II, involving Lord Ogleby and his valet. Indeed, this is a scene of which Colman himself admitted Garrick's authorship in the quarrel they had about the play two-and-a-half months before it opened.[22] This is one of the scenes in which *The Clandestine Marriage* comes closest to *False Concord*. There remains, therefore, the difficulty raised by Beatty that Garrick was out of the country on the one night on which *False Concord* was performed. What has been overlooked here is the friendship between Garrick and Townley which was clearly already well established as early as July 1757, when Garrick recommended Townley for the living of Clavering, a parish in Essex.[23] Several of Garrick's letters to Colman[24] during his absence abroad (1763-65) ask that affectionate greetings be passed on to Townley, who appears to have been an associate of Colman's as well. Thomas Clare, who wrote the letter to the *Gentleman's Magazine* asserting Townley's authorship of *High Life Below Stairs,* claims, in his memoirs of the Reverend Samuel Bishop, that 'Mr. Garrick had so high an opinion of Mr. Townley's judgment, that he submitted all his own works to his correction.'[25] On his side, Garrick took an interest in Townley's writings. This is shown by his enquiries about Townley's farce *The Tutor* in letters written from Paris to Colman and James Love.[26] Garrick often gave practical help to other playwrights. Richard Cumberland, for instance, tells how he sought out Garrick's assistance when he was writing *The West Indian*:

> I resorted to him again and again with the manuscript of my comedy; I availed myself of his advice, of his remarks . . .[27]

The *Biographia Dramatica* goes so far as to say that

> among the several dramatic pieces which made their first appearance on the theatre in Drury Lane, there are very few whose authors have not acknowledged themselves greatly indebted to this gentleman [Garrick] for useful hints or advantageous alterations, to which their success has in great measure been owing.'

> (i. 266)

If *High Life Below Stairs* is by Townley, then its striking superiority to his other two plays, which were performed when Garrick was overseas, may well be due in part to the extent of the advice and assistance which Garrick was able to give him.

There is evidence, then, that Garrick and Townley were accustomed to consult each other about their writings. It seems clear that, by the time Garrick left London for the Continent on 17 September 1763, the first three acts of *The Clandestine Marriage* had been completed.[28] It is not known how far the writing of *False Concord*, which was to be performed six months later, was advanced by this time. It is quite possible, however, that Garrick was able to exert some influence on Townley's conception of his play. It is also possible that talks with Townley may have influenced Garrick's contributions to **The Clandestine Marriage.** The fact that Garrick and Townley are known to have discussed their writings with each other and that both plays are likely to have been in preparation at the same time provides a satisfactory explanation of the similarities between them.

Notes

1. See Joseph M. Beatty, Jr., 'Garrick, Colman, and *The Clandestine Marriage*,' *M.L.N.,* xxxvi (1921), 129-141; Eugene R. Page, *George Colman the Elder* (New York, 1935), pp. 118-28; Elizabeth P. Stein, *David Garrick, Dramatist* (New York, 1938), pp. 203-47; Frederick L. Bergmann, 'David Garrick and *The Clandestine Marriage*,' *P.M.L.A.,* lxvii (1952), pp. 148-62; Ann T. Straulman, 'George Colman and David Garrick, *The Clandestine Marriage*: A critical edition' (unpublished Ph.D. thesis, University of Wisconsin, 1968), pp. iv-lxxx.

2. *Gentleman's Magazine* (February 1805), p. 110. Roberdeau's 'Mr. Suds' is actually called 'Mr. Sudley' in *False Concord,* and 1766, not 1767, was the year in which *The Clandestine Marriage* was first performed.

3. On the date of this transaction, see Dougald MacMillan, *Catalogue of the Larpent Plays in the Huntington Library* (San Marino, 1939), p. v.

4. *New Monthly Magazine,* xxxiv (1832), 568-75.

5. *New Monthly Magazine,* xxxiv (1832), 572. In his reference to Garrick's portion of the play Collier is assuming that 'Garrick was the author of the part of Lord Ogleby, and of what relates to him.'

6. A suggested outline for the play sent by Colman to Garrick and published by his son, George Colman, Jr., in his *Posthumous Letters, from Various Celebrated Men; addressed to Francis Colman, and George Colman, the Elder* (London, 1820), pp. 333-42.

7. Op. cit., p. 140.

8. Op. cit., pp. 127-8.

9. See Dougald MacMillan, op. cit., p. vi. Although MacMillan's *Catalogue* was not published until 1939, Allardyce Nicoll mentions the presence of the Larpent Collection in the Huntington Library and makes specific reference to the manuscript of *False Concord* in his *History of Late Eighteenth Century Drama* (Cambridge, 1927). He indicates that he has not himself seen the copy of *False Concord.* Strangely, he nevertheless remarks of Roberdeau's charge: 'The accusation has justice, but there can be no comparison between Townley's farcical characters and Colman's finished portraits' (p. 169). Even more strangely, he also notes that *False Con-*

cord is 'Based on G. Colman, *The Clandestine Marriage*' (p. 312).

10. *The Private Correspondence of David Garrick* [ed. James Boaden] (London, 1831-2), i. 210.

11. See Ronald Paulson, *Hogarth, His Life, Art, and Times* (New Haven and London, 1971), ii. 84, 157, 158, 365, etc.

12. Page references are to the 1st edition of the play (London, 1766).

13. Cf. Collier, op. cit., p. 573: 'Of the various scenes in "False Concord," the only one at all resembling any part of "The Clandestine Marriage," is that in which Lord Lavender converses with Jasper his valet.' He quotes part of the scene from *False Concord* to demonstrate the inferiority of its dialogue.

14. i. 250.

15. Quotations from the manuscript of *False Concord* are included with the permission of The Huntington Library, San Marino, California.

16. *The Dramatic Works of David Garrick* (London, 1798), i. 16.

17. Op. cit., pp. 219-20. Stein also sees a connection between Mrs. Heidelberg and Mrs. Snip in Garrick's *Harlequin's Invasion* (1759).

18. *Dramatic Works of David Garrick,* i. 24.

19. *The Letters of David Garrick,* ed. D. M. Little and G. M. Kahrl (Cambridge, Mass., 1963, No. 224.

20. First performed Drury Lane, 4 February 1765.

21. By David Erskine Baker, Isaac Reed and Stephen Jones (London, 1812), ii. 302-3.

22. '. . . as the play now stands, the levee-scene, at the beginning of the second act, and the whole of the fifth act, are yours . . .' (*Private Correspondence of David Garrick,* i. 210).

23. See *Letters of David Garrick,* ed. cit., No. 188.

24. Ibid., Nos. 323, 329, 336, 341.

25. Cited by H. B. Wilson, *The History of Merchant-Taylor's School* (London, 1814), p. 506. Clare's memoirs are prefixed to *The Poetical Works of the Rev. Samuel Bishop* (London, 1796). There is an intriguing letter (*Letters of David Garrick,* No. 387) which Garrick wrote to Colman shortly after he had returned to London from the Continent. In it he mentions a 'Farce' which Townley has read but will not comment on until he sees Garrick. The context suggests that the 'Farce' in question is *The Clandestine Marriage.*

26. *Letters of David Garrick,* Nos. 341, 348.

27. *Memoirs of Richard Cumberland, written by himself* (London, 1806), p. 216.

28. Amongst the evidence on which this statement is based is Garrick's remark to Colman in a letter from Naples of 24 December 1763: 'I have not yet wrote a word of ye 4th or 5th of the Clandestine Marriage ...' (*Letters of David Garrick*, No. 321).

Dane Farnsworth Smith and M. L. Lawhon (essay date 1979)

SOURCE: Smith, Dane Farnsworth, and M. L. Lawhon. "David Garrick." *Plays about the Theatre in England, 1737-1800; or, The Self-Conscious Stage from Foote to Sheridan.* Lewisburg: Bucknell UP, 1979. 38-63. Print.

[*In the following essay, Smith and Lawhon survey a cluster of satires that document the back-and-forth feuding among Garrick and his peers on such subjects as managing, casting, acting, and audience participation. They focus on three of Garrick's own satires and describe the controversy surrounding the Shakespeare Jubilee of 1769, which also provoked several topical dramas.*]

THE LONDON THEATRE

As the greatest actor of his time, David Garrick lent his name to an age that was characterized in English theatrical history by conservatism regarding production of new comedies or tragedies,[1] matched with perfervid interest in innovative acting styles, production methods, and theatrical gossip. Although the practitioners of sentimental comedy had some success with their productions, the creative energies of many of the period's writers seem to have been devoted to the composition of shorter forms, such as the farce or the dramatic prelude, interlude, or afterpiece; or "semi-literary" forms such as pantomime, ballad opera, and entertainment.[2] The age also had an obvious taste for the topical and satiric, and this taste, coupled with intense interest in the theatre and the prevalence of shorter, less traditional dramatic forms, accounts largely for the number of pieces written then about the theatre. Prevented by the Licensing Act from addressing political issues, a satirist could always revert to theatrical ones and be assured of an interested audience. Likewise, managers could "puff" their own productions and burlesque their rivals on the stage in preludes or pantomimes, knowing that their allusions would be understood and appreciated.

Garrick himself wrote seven dramatic pieces in which he employed the theatre as primary subject matter and presented his own concerns: a new naturalistic style of acting instead of the traditional artificial and oratorical mode; needed reforms in taste and audience behavior; and, of course, Shakespeare. Even before his official debut as Richard III in 1741, the young Garrick had demonstrated his preoccupation with players and the stage by writing a short "dramatic satire" bearing on matters theatrical, which proved to be his first success as a playwright.[3] Entitled

Lethe; or, Esop in the Shades, the piece was performed first as an afterpiece for Henry Giffard's benefit at Drury Lane, April 15, 1740, and a second time a year later in Giffard's theatre in Goodman's Fields. Finally revised and enlarged, and with the subtitle of *A Dramatic Satire, Lethe* was again produced under Garrick's own management at Drury Lane, January 2, 1749,[4] and continued at the theatre, ranking sixth in the repertoire in total number of performances for the period 1747-76.[5] In his earlier version of *Lethe,* Garrick had composed a loose dramatic sketch in which a number of "fashionable mortals" about to pass over the River Styx encounter the philosopher Aesop,[6] who, out of the generosity of Pluto, distributes "the waters of Lethe as a sovereign remedy" for the complaints of mankind. The revised 1749 version was, according to its title page, "strengthened ... with several additional characters," among them, "a Poet and a Fine Gentleman,"[7] both of whose activities involve the theatre.

Garrick's method in the farce is a simple one; each character presents himself to Aesop, who questions him about his past life and troubles. The poet arrives first, complaining of a "Whistling" in his head that has troubled him ever since his play was "damn'd" by an audience that included his patron, who "Played the best Cat-call the first Night, and was the merriest Person in the whole Audience."[8] Garrick's mention here of the catcall, an instrument popularly used by mid-eighteenth-century playgoers to indicate their disapproval, is particularly interesting, since he would later direct to the "town," but never publish, a treatise "designed as preparatory to the use of the Cat-call."[9] The Poet then explains further that the failure of his play resulted from its being "terribly handled, before it appear'd in publick." His friends removed all its "Bawdy and Immorality"; the players spoke not a "line of Sense or Sentiment"; and, worst of all, "the Manager (who writes himself) struck out all the Wit and Humour, in Order to lower my Performance to a level with his own."[10] Although similar complaints against managers are frequently met in the plays of the period, the poet's criticism here is comically involved because the author of the play in which he appears—and, therefore, his creator—is also a manager who was often accused of "over-altering" other dramatists' works.[11] Such allusive connections tend, however, not to destroy dramatic illusion in *Lethe,* or in the typical play about the theatre, but, rather, to develop a particular, self-conscious tone in the characters regarding that illusion. Here, the poet as character is aware of being both on the banks of the Styx and on the stage of Drury Lane, a situation that, instead of diminishing Garrick's dramatic illusion, seems somehow to double it. When Aesop, for example, suggests that the Poet persuade his audience to drink some of Lethe's water and thus forget his first play, the Poet, referring both to his fictional circumstances and to the literal fact that he is a character in a play entitled *Lethe,* replies: "If I could but do that—but I am afraid— *Lethe* will never go down with the Audience."

Later in the farce, Garrick shifts his satire directly to a certain species of playgoer in his characterization of the "Fine Gentleman," who, among his many self-professed talents, is a "Critick at the Theatres ... The Delight of the Ingenious, the Terror of Poets, the Scourge of Players, and the Aversion of the Vulgar."[12] As a satiric portrait, the Fine Gentleman functions on Garrick's stage as a kind of mirror to at least part of the audience whom he addresses, for he describes himself as going to the playhouse not for the play, but "to intrigue, and shew myself." He stands "upon the Stage, talk[s] loud, and stare[s]-about—which confounds the Actors, and disturbs the Audience." The resentment occasioned by such behavior is underscored by his explanation that his exaggerated scorn of hissing and shouts of "off!" from the galleries "exasperates the Savages" and leads to "Vollies of suck'd Oranges, and half-eaten pippins."[13] Garrick's problems with the presence of the *beau monde* upon the stage and the ultimate solution of such problems are well known and well documented,[14] but his reference here is particularly interesting in the satiric relationship it establishes between a dramatic character and the real audience, some of whom may have been seated on the stage as the lines were delivered.

Given Garrick's importance and the prevalence of plays about the theatre at the time, it is hardly surprising to discover that he was himself the subject of various dramatic pieces. *Lethe,* for instance, occasioned two such topical reactions: *Lethe Rehears'd,* a dramatic dialogue published in 1749, and *The Anniversary, Being a Sequel to Lethe,* a farce performed at Covent Garden, March 29, 1758.[15] Despite its title, the latter work does not actually discuss Garrick's play, but does indicate the fairly rigid customs of social distinctions observed in the seating of the eighteenth-century audience[16] when it compares the socially stratified theatre to a masquerade where "there is no pit nor galleries, no hisses nor cat-calls; ... no distinction of persons." *Lethe Rehears'd,* on the other hand, praises Garrick's acting abilities, notes his services to the town, and concentrates on the educational value of his dramatic satires.[17] During a conversation among certain followers of the theatre in London, praise of Drury Lane's actor-manager is motivated by the criticisms of Mr. Snip-Snap, a gentleman who later admits that his adverse remarks have only been a trick to force his companions to express themselves feelingly about Garrick, whom he admires also. Basically, *Lethe Rehears'd* deals less with purely theatrical questions than with fairly conventional literary ones, for it favorably presents Garrick as a satirist bent on improving through his plays the taste and mores of his audience, who, according to Dr. Heartfree, "are sure to leave the *House* with something *worth remembering.*"[18]

Not all topical theatrical references to Garrick, however, were as complimentary as *Lethe Rehears'd.* In 1751 an anonymously printed "Dramatic Satire" written by Thomas Lowndes accused the actor-manager of personal arrogance, plagiarism, contempt for his own actors, and, especially, ill-will toward other playwrights.[19] In *The Theatrical Manager,* Garrick is satirized in the character of Vaticide (killer of prophets), an actor turned manager who resents a summons to rehearse *Richard III* from his co-manager, Lacy, and refuses to hire his old actor friends.[20] Worst of all, he revels in egotistically motivated bad taste and boasts that he can make *Miss in Her Teens* and *The Lying Valet* (two of Garrick's more successful farces) "succeed as well under my Directions, as the Works of immortal Shakespear."[21] Garrick himself had taken comic note of frequent complaints that he was unfair in his rejection of contemporary plays in *Lethe,*[22] a criticism that is repeated here quite vituperatively, since it insults Garrick's known veneration of Shakespeare. As Vaticide, he is made to vindicate his rejection of his contemporaries' plays by cynically explaining: "I have ... saved many a poor Bard from sharing the destructive Fate of their worthless Predecessor."[23]

In its *ad hominem* satire and slanderous tone, *The Theatrical Manager* anticipates by five years Arthur Murphy's *The Spouter; or, The Triple Revenge,*[24] a play so vulgar that it was never acted, was denied by Murphy himself,[25] and excluded from his collected works. Published in 1756, this piece borrowed its title and its negligible framing-plot about the conflicts between a young would-be actor and his father from Henry Dell's *The Spouter; or, The Double Revenge* (1756), but here similarities cease. Murphy's primary concern is not genial satire of "spouters" but the presentation of somewhat malicious portraits of leading theatrical figures of the day and the avenging of personal and professional injuries committed by Foote and Theophilus Cibber. Murphy's *Spouter* claims even more interest upon recognition of the part that Garrick, for whom Murphy was then acting and writing, played in its composition.[26] Only recently, in November 1755, Garrick had suffered humiliation in the Noverre riots at Drury Lane and was naturally eager to end any adverse influence that threatened his success. In 1756 the chief menace would have been Theophilus Cibber, who, because the patent houses opposed his founding a new theatrical company in competition with them, was attacking Garrick both personally and artistically.[27] That Murphy's play represents an attempt on Garrick's behalf to curtail Cibber's increasing influence was recognized even in its own time, for the *Critical Review,* in March 1756, charged *The Spouter's* author with writing and publishing "this motley performance"[28] for just that purpose.

Apart from his desire to aid his employer against young Cibber, Murphy wanted to redress an injury that he thought he had received from Samuel Foote, his former mentor and personal friend. Because Foote had used the basic idea of Murphy's *Englishman from Paris* in a slightly earlier work of his own, Murphy's piece, written for his benefit night at Drury Lane, survived only one night and was never published.[29] Murphy, of course, blamed Foote for the failure, and, perhaps to conceal these motives and Garrick's intensely personal one in *The Spouter,* he includes satirical references to himself and to the actor-manager. The machinery of anonymity begins in the preface, which casts doubt on the judgment and integrity of Garrick and attacks the author of *The Apprentice* (Murphy himself), calling him a "*Smatterer in Letters*" and a plagiarist of Dell's *Spouter.* Much later in the play he has Squint-Eyed Pistol (T. Cibber) say that "*M—phy*" is "the damn'dest Actor, and damn'dest Author. . . . I wonder he'd think of Writing—such damn'd Stuff as that *Apprentice* is . . . *M—phy's an Idiot.*"[30] Of course, these comments, coming from the mouth of such a fool as Murphy makes of Pistol, really only prove the speaker's lack of acumen and suggest his jealousy of a better playwright. In contrast to his treatment of himself in *The Spouter,* Murphy attempts to set his readers off Garrick's track by presenting him as Patent, a manager delighted by his full houses because of his self-confessed "Love of Money" and "Love of Fame." Candidly admitting that "I'm no Actor at all, only they [the audiences] have not Sense enough to find it out," Patent nevertheless shows little sympathy for the plight of real actors.[31] How much of a hand Garrick had in this depiction of himself is uncertain, but one of his nineteenth-century biographers perhaps committed an unconscious irony when he remarked that in *The Spouter* "Garrick . . . in his customary fashion, aimed some harmless ridicule at himself."[32] Harmless it is, and, compared to the treatment given John Hill, Cibber, and Foote in the following scenes, Garrick's "portrait" seems quite benign.

Structurally, *The Spouter* consists of a series of visits to various managers and writers by a young "Spouter" or would-be actor named Slender, a representation of Dr. John Hill, with whom Murphy had exchanged attacks in the periodical and pamphlet warfare of the time. An enemy also of Garrick, "Sir John," as he called himself, had used his influence to have Rich at Covent Garden "set actors to mimick Garrick."[33] He was passionately interested in acting, as evidenced by his authorship of a treatise on the subject drawn in part from Rémond de Sainte-Albine's *Le Comédien* (Paris 1747), but had failed twice as an actor at Covent Garden and at the Little Theatre in the Haymarket, a fact Murphy no doubt had in mind when he cast him as an out-of-work amateur in *The Spouter.* Hill's friend, John Rich, with whom he later quarreled, appears briefly in Murphy's play under his familiar stage name, "Lun," and surrounded by his legendary casts. Seemingly anxious to proceed to his real satiric targets, Murphy contents himself in his presentation of Lun-Rich with the usual satiric thrusts aimed at the manager: his penurious production habits, his ignorance in pronouncing words, and his somewhat misplaced pride in his ability to "larn" young amateurs to act.[34] Lun does, however, introduce a running sight gag[35] into the play when he describes Pistol as "sans *Nose,* sans *Teeth,* sans *Taste,* sans *ev'ry Thing,*"[36] for the very next scene introduces Pistol in his quarters, "*his Nose and a Set of Teeth lying on the Table.*"

In his interview with Slender, Pistol calls Garrick (Patent) "a vile Tragedian—Horrid Little Fellow"[37] and goes on to say that the Drury Lane manager once broke the heart of "a good-natur'd actor," thereby causing his death through the abusiveness of his imitations. Here Murphy no doubt refers to Garrick's alteration in the acting tradition of Buckingham's *Rehearsal,* the young innovator's greatest comic triumph during his first season at Goodman's Fields.[38] In this production, according to Murphy's biography of Garrick, the actor "seized the opportunity to make *The Rehearsal* a keen and powerful criticism on the absurd stile of acting that prevailed on the stage."[39] Such burlesque could hardly have suited Cibber, a detractor of Garrick's "new" naturalistic style. Cibber's father, Colley, was famous for his "intoning" manner of delivery, while Theophilus's own predilections for the old method are evinced by frequent stage directions for Pistol that indicate that he "tremulates his voice."[40]

Next in Murphy's series of unflattering portraits comes Foote, who, as Dapperwit, is first seen contemplating plagiarism. The allusion here to the affair of Murphy's *Englishman from Paris* again seems obvious, for Dapperwit muses over a new farce and confesses: "It's true, a Gentleman told me of the Subject first; and, in Confidence too! by way of Consulting my Judgment. . . . To consult me!— A Blockhead!—He might know me better."[41] His subsequent conversation with Slender, though it promises to be courteous, is foreshortened by Dapperwit's decision to give some unintelligible imitations, the last of which—that of a dog—delights him so much that he totally confuses his visitor with his endless barking. Murphy returns to this depiction of Foote-Dapperwit as a foolish and pointless mimic in *The Spouter*'s penultimate scene. In a coffeehouse Squint-Eyed Pistol and Dapperwit come together to repeat their follies of earlier scenes and to demonstrate even more of them. "Tremulating his voice," Pistol repeats for the company an attack on Garrick he had made the night before in his playhouse. He is interrupted by hissing but goes on unperturbed[42] to praise his own father's failures:

> Such was the Hiss that spoke the great Applause
> Our mighty Father met with, when he brought
> His Riddle on the Stage: such was the Hiss
> Welcom'd his Caesar to the Egyptian Shore:
> Such was the Hiss, in which King John should have expired[43]
> Such were the Hisses, which from Age to Age
> Our Family has born triumphant on the Stage.[44]

Still barking, laughing, and now mimicking "Mia Spiletta,"[45] Dapperwit joins Pistol and tells him that Murphy's *Apprentice* is "All Trash," and that Murphy himself "is the most ridiculous Son of a _____." He goes on to mention having given Murphy a temporary home and having instructed him in acting in the summer of 1754[46] and then offers to read his own new farce to the patrons of the coffeehouse. Meeting with no enthusiasm, Dapperwit defends his own histrionic ability, a defense that Murphy adroitly turns into a kind of compliment to his own work:

> It [*The Apprentice*] will never be acted. . . . If I could do all the Parts, it would be fine. The actors can't do it—I wonder at their Impudence to pretend to Act at all—Not one of 'em can read—by G-d—*Garrick,* he can't. . . .[47]

Murphy's last hit at Foote is a personal and telling one, for he has Dapperwit, who acts the best of friends to Pistol's face, turn on him when he departs and mimic him unmercifully, an unpleasant habit of Foote's even toward old friends. Yet Murphy evidently dissipated some of his personal anger at Foote in *The Spouter,* because he soon became reconciled with his former mentor and remained friends with him until Foote's death in 1777.[48]

Garrick's troubles with Theophilus Cibber were soon resolved also, but in a less felicitous way than were Murphy's with Foote, for the younger Cibber perished in a storm while traveling to Ireland in 1758. Not all of Garrick's theatrical problems ended so definitively. Audiences were still rowdy, and public taste often drove the manager into competing for spectators with Covent Garden's John Rich on his own level. Rich's success with pantomime, for instance, had led Garrick in 1750 to introduce it at his own theatre, using Woodward as Harlequin, and in 1759 Garrick wrote a pantomime himself. Borrowing his general theme from an earlier piece in which he had played Harlequin,[49] he introduced speech into his work and produced **Harlequin's Invasion** (Drury Lane, December 31, 1759) from written dialogue instead of from the usual scenario.[50] A great success at the time and in later revivals, **Harlequin's Invasion** displays the conjunction of allegorical "plot" and harlequinade common to pantomimes of the time, but also reveals Garrick's interests in its allegorical treatment of the threat posed to the production of Shakespeare by the popularity of pantomime.

In Garrick's piece, as in his source, Harlequin invades the dramatic realm, and Comedy and Tragedy, the defenders of the legitimate stage, are urged to rally against him. Their mobilization is superfluous, however, since the "*Powers of Pantomime*" are easily wafted away with a wave of Mercury's Caduceus and the verse

> Now let immortal Shakespear rise
> Ye Sons of Taste Adore him
> As from the Sun each Vapour flies
> Let Folly sink before him.[51]

Mercury's directions take effect immediately as "*Shakespear Rises: Harlequin Sinks,*"[52] and the pantomime ends with a song that adjures the audience to remain faithful to Reason and Shakespeare:

> Ye Britons may Fancy ne'er lead you astray
> Nor e'er through your Senses your Reason betray
> By your Love to the Bard may your wisdom be known
> Nor injure his Fame to the loss of your own.[53]

Although Garrick seems to have intended some identification of the defeat of Harlequin with that of the French, who were at the time losing the war with England,[54] he capitalizes on these topical allusions by associating the implied patriotism of "Ye Britons" not only with reason but also with Shakespeare, and anticipates his apotheosis of Shakespeare at the Stratford Festival ten years later.

Garrick returns to the defense of Shakespeare against pantomime, spectacle, and foreign imports like opera in his Epilogue to Colman the Elder's **Clandestine Marriage,**[55] a most successful play of which Garrick is now considered the principal author.[56] In the Epilogue several persons of quality discuss the theatre as they play cards. Their attitude toward legitimate drama is derogatory, and, except for Sir Patrick Mahoney, they agree with Colonel Trill's declaration that "nasty plays are [only] fit for Goths and Vandals." To Sir Patrick's exclamation that "Shakespeare was no fool!" the Colonel replies with a song:

> I hate all their nonsense,
> Their Shakespeares and Jonsons
> Their plays, and their playhouses and bards;
> 'Tis singing not saying;
> A fig for all playing
> But playing, as we do, at cards![57]

The colonel makes an exception of theatrical spectacle because he loves "their tricks and their cheating!" Sir Patrick continues to defend Shakespeare and finally moves his opponents to laughter with a topical allusion to recent alterations in the very theatre in which he is now appearing when he says: "I love the play-house now—so light and gay, / With all those candles, they have ta'en away!"[58]

This widening of the illusionary boundaries of the Epilogue to include its literal as well as dramatic setting continues with the entrance of Miss Crotchet, who has just returned from Drury Lane, where she and a party of fashionable friends have been unsuccessful in their attempt to damn **The Clandestine Marriage,** the play that her own audience has just seen. Like the Fine Gentleman of **Lethe,** she complains about the rudeness of the "city folks," who "fell a swearing" whenever her party hissed.[59] Miss Crotchet then gives a deprecating account of the performance, and she and her friends, the several detractors of the playhouse, cry out each in turn: "Damn it!" "Damn it!" "Damn it!"

Garrick, annoyed from the first, as evidenced in **Lethe,** by the fashionable set, whose superior attitudes in public places often degenerated into rudeness and crude behavior, has here tried to forestall their possible criticism of **The Clandestine Marriage** by presenting characters whose adverse opinions are obviously ludicrous and inconsistent with their supposed social and intellectual superiority. By showing them themselves in the persons of Miss Crotchet and party, he not only performs the generalized mirroring of society common to satirists but also intensifies his satire through the extension of dramatic illusion to include the actual theatre and present time as well as fictional setting and stage time. His audience may damn *The Clandestine Marriage,* but in so doing, they join the party of Miss Crochet.

In the nine years following the Epilogue to the *Clandestine Marriage,* Garrick produced two longer pieces that deal in even more detail with the theatre and the problems facing a manager. The first of these, *A Peep behind the Curtain; or, The New Rehearsal,* was acted at Drury Lane on October 23, 1767,[60] and represented a combination on Garrick's part of his usual satire of the fashionable world, a playhouse-wedding plot, and a rehearsal in the manner of Buckingham. Rather than simply have characters make topical references to theatrical affairs, as in his earlier pieces, Garrick, perhaps influenced by Foote's *Occasional Prelude,* which appeared in May of the same year, now sets his farce[61] on the stage at Drury Lane and peoples it with members of his own staff. Comedian Thomas King and Kitty Clive, popular favorites who took the leading parts of Glib and Lady Fuz, are mentioned by name; Hopkins, the Prompter, and Saunders, the Carpenter, appear, played by Bannister and Moody. After a scene introducing the characters of the playhouse-wedding plot—Sir Toby Fuz, Lady Fuz, Miss Fanny Fuz, and Wilson—Garrick moves his audience directly to the stage of Drury Lane, where two cleaning women complain about the incessant "hurry and bustle" that has plagued the company ever since the "house open'd."[62] In keeping with this strenuous activity, Mr. Hopkins, the Prompter, hurries in to speed completion of the scenery for the first act of the burletta of Orpheus by Glib, Garrick's counterpart of Bayes. Saunders, the Carpenter, assures him that, having sat up all night, his men "have now finish'd every thing but the Dancing Cows" and complains against technical knowledge of authors who ask for "a flying Devil, or a dancing Bear."[63] The Prompter commiserates with Saunders and then tells him that the managers wish to fire a drunken scene-man who, in discharging the stage lightning, has, according to the Carpenter, "burnt a hole in the new cascade, and set fire to the shower of rain."[64]

Garrick next introduces the company's manager under the name of "Patent," the same title used for Garrick in Murphy's *Spouter.* Like Garrick himself, he is bedeviled with the idiosyncracies and ambitions of his actors. The actresses quarrel about their roles, with the oldest thinking "herself young enough for any part"; one "young fellow" won't accept the part assigned him; and Mr. Rantley, obviously a tragedian, has sent word that he is too ill to play.[65] Patent's list of daily woes is cut short by the arrival of author Glib, who, because his burletta is to be rehearsed, has also invited Sir Macaroni Virtu, a fashionable "critic," and the members of the Fuz family. Before they arrive, however, Glib confides to Patent that his greatest stroke of genius, one that alone "shall fill the boxes for a month," is his conception of Cerberus as a canine monster whose three heads will "sing a trio, treble, tenor and bass." Garrick here continues his satire on theatrical extravagance, begun with the "Dancing Cows," and extends it to the types of ensemble singing found in the Italian opera.[66] But his favorite satiric targets—the Londoners of fashion—are about to appear.

When Glib's visitors arrive, Garrick is on familiar ground, for in Sir Macaroni Virtu one encounters again the fashionable pretender-critic from whom the name of Shakespeare evokes but a yawn[67] and who eventually leaves, wishing the theatre and all its people "at the bottom of the Thames." Sir Toby Fuz can only laugh, request that the manager entertain them with his stage machinery, and—that being impracticable—finally fall asleep. Lady Fuz, on the other hand, is so entranced with the "wit" of Mr. Glib and the aura of the theatre that she fails even to notice when her daughter elopes with young Wilson. At last the remaining guests settle down, and Glib begins the rehearsal of his fantastic burletta, coaching the musicians instrument by instrument, note by note, just as Bayes had stressed the accent on words in Buckingham's *Rehearsal.* The *Rehearsal* tradition, however, does not necessarily explain Glib's tutoring or his constant interruptions of the performers, for some authors—Macklin, T. Sheridan, and Foote, for example—occasionally did direct their own plays at Drury Lane.[68] Here Garrick most likely intends no satire of those authors who were actors as well, but rather, aims his comedy at intrusive writers who had no knowledge of theatrical production. For Garrick's satire, unlike that of his predecessors, is general, not personal, amusing, not vitriolic. Glib's burletta itself is the usual rhymed nonsense and ends with Orpheus leading out a grand chorus of singing and dancing shepherds followed by a procession of beasts, each of whom is "upon his hind legs."[69] After some flurry as the Fuzes depart to find their runaway daughter, Glib recites the epilogue, and one learns that Patent will continue the rehearsal just as soon as the author completes the burletta. Exaggerated as it may seem, such piecemeal delivery of plays was not unheard of at Drury Lane, as Garrick's experience with the scene-by-scene delivery of Jephson's *Braganza* in 1775 amply illustrates.[70]

Besides the insight it gives into the workings of a theatre and into David Garrick's opinions of the *beau monde* and popular taste, *A Peep behind the Curtain* also provides an example of his compositional method in his plays about the theatre. Just as he had based *Harlequin's Invasion* on an older pantomime, *Harlequin Student,* Garrick here draws his ideas from two earlier sources with which he had had some theatrical experience: Kitty Clive's *Rehearsal; or, Bays in Petticoats* and Buckingham's *Rehearsal.* He would again rely heavily upon Buckingham—and Foote as well—in his next play about the theatre, *The Meeting of the Company; or, Bayes's Art of Acting,* a prelude hastily written for the opening of the Drury Lane season on September 17, 1774. For this piece Garrick borrowed from Buckingham the name, figure, and stage business of Bayes, but modified the character so that the prelude focuses almost entirely on casting and acting. From Foote he borrowed the prelude form itself and its use of the theatre's stage-as-stage for its setting.

The Meeting of the Company opens, in a manner similar to the previous ***Peep behind the Curtain,*** with Mr. William Hopkins, Drury Lane's prompter, attempting to clear the stage so that the carpenters can ready the settings. Through Phill, the carpenter, Garrick admits his own compliance with the popular taste for spectacle, for this stage is no temple of Shakespeare. "Coronations—Installations, Portsmouth Reviews, Masquerades, Jubilees—Fete Champetres & the Devil," Phill complains, "we have no rest at all— Master's head is always at work."[71] Almost immediately, Parsons, played by Parsons,[72] enters, soon to be followed by Weston and Patent, again the manager, who decries the vicissitudes of the newspapers, which, he says, "kill'd me one day & reviv'd me the next."[73] Weston,[74] playing himself, then provokes a controversy with a tragic actor by declaring that he can "play Tragedy" as well as the best of them. When asked if nothing but wild gesticulation and roaring is requisite to the making of a tragedian, Weston satirizes extravagant acting styles by contemptuously answering:

> O yes; the perriwig maker to make me a bush, a Taylor a hoop petticoat, a carpenter a Truncheon, a Shoe-maker high heels, & Cork Soles—and as for Strange Faces, & Strange Noises, I can make them my Self.[75]

The patentee begs the two not to begin the season with a quarrel, and the discussion naturally fades at the arrival of Bayes, the playwright.

Bayes has decided, despite his conviction that manager and players have treated him badly, to perfect their acting by instructing them in "a method to make the worst Actors equal to the best" in return for their promise to perform his piece.[76] His plans, in which talent, ability, and experience are to play no part, he explains to the company by using Garrick's satiric criticism of unnatural and formulaic acting:

> First Gentlemen, turn Nature out of door,
> Then Rant away, 'till you can rant no more,
> Walk, talk, & look, as none have walk'd.
>   talk'd, & look'd before.
>
> . . . .
>
> Would you in Tragedy Extort applause,
> Distort *Yourselves,*—now Rage, now Start, now pause,
> Beat breast, roll Eyes, stretch Nose, up brows, down Jaws,
> Then strut, stride, stare, Goggle, bounce, & Bawl,
> And when you're out of breath—pant, drag & drawl.
>
> . . . .
>
> Be in extremes in Buskin, or in Sock,
> In action Wild—in attitude a Block!
> From the Spectator's Eye, your faults to hide,
> Be either Whirlwind, or be petrify'd.
>
> . . . .
>
> To heighten Terror—be it wrong or right,
> Be black your Coat, your handkerchief be white,

> Thus pull your hair to add to your distress,
> What your face cannot, let your Wig Express.[77]

Weston and Parsons comment all the while, striking attitudes and comically "obeying" Bayes's commands until, ordered to "Curse & Caper," they run offstage and refuse to tolerate any further nonsense. Weston returns to exchange insults with Bayes and to appeal to the audience for support, but Bayes, like Buckingham's author, is finally left alone to curse Drury Lane with malicious wishes that represent a compendium of the worst of any manager's nightmares:

> May this House be always as Empty as it is now; or if it must fill, Let it be with fine Ladies to disturb the actors, fine Gentlemen to admire themselves, & fat Citizens to Snore in the Boxes;—may the Pit be fill'd with Nothing but Crabbed Criticks, unemploy'd Actors, & Managers Orders—May places be kept in the Green Boxes without being paid for; & may the Galleries never bring good humours & horse laughs with them again.[78]

Bayes's curses, standing as they do at the end of ***The Meeting of the Company,*** serve as a kind of summary of many annoyances with patrons that Garrick had expressed in previous pieces about the theatre. Similarly, the foolish author's unconsciously satiric instructions on acting bring together and emphasize Garrick's earlier satiric hits at the "old style." In short, the prelude can be seen almost as an abstract of Garrick's dramatic writings about the theatre except that one major interest of Garrick's is missing— Shakespeare. And it is to Shakespeare that he will turn in his musical prelude, ***The Theatrical Candidates,*** for a resolution of the strife between the two allegorical figures of Tragedy and Comedy. Written for the seasonal opening of the Drury Lane Theatre, September 23, 1775,[79] this occasional libretto extols the thorough refurbishing and remodeling of the house by presenting Drury Lane's opening as an event that has attracted even the gods' attention. Mercury, for instance, has been dispatched by Apollo "to see this House's transformation" and to "ask if the Critics give their approbation."[80] Comedy and Tragedy, too, have been sent by Jove to dwell in the house, but they fall into contention for the approval of the audience. Through these exchanges, Garrick, who was no lover of sentimental drama despite his production of it, elucidates his attitude toward the genre:

COMEDY:

> Have you not laugh'd with one eye, cry'd with t'other?

TRAGEDY:

> In all the realms of nonsense can there be,
> A Monster, like your comic-tragedy?

COMEDY:

> O Yes, my dear!—your tragic-comedy![81]

In the midst of their argument, Harlequin suddenly appears and claims the audience's votes, for he has, he maintains, supported the two candidates, especially since Comedy has "grown so grave" and Tragedy is "so cross and bloody." Without his aid, the only "consequence" would be "empty houses." The issue is settled abruptly by Mercury, who arrives with the message that each Muse must keep her proper place; comedy must not turn "prude," and tragedy must not "engross" the stage. Each is forbidden to "encroach" upon the other's right "unless that Shakespear bring you both together." Finally, even Harlequin is allowed a place in Drury Lane, but his office is only to carry the "train" of muses.[82] Here, as in *Harlequin's Invasion*, Garrick has used mythological allegory, frequently associated with pantomime, to put pantomime gently in its place. Whatever the content of its speeches regarding the primacy of tragedy and comedy may reveal about Garrick's tastes, *The Theatrical Candidates* nevertheless does not state any conclusion. The decrees of Apollo are declared "vain" until "confirmed" by the audience, and even here Garrick admits, as in his earlier plays about the theatre, the necessity of playing to the public taste. Shakespeare may have been the personal "God of his idolatry," but in his seven pieces about his profession, Garrick contends what any successful theatre manager of the century would know—namely, that the audience's favor pays the bills.

THE STRATFORD JUBILEE

Of all the events in eighteenth-century theatrical history, perhaps only the initial run of *The Beggar's Opera* produced more reaction than Garrick's Shakespeare Jubilee of 1769. Though some of the festivities planned for this three-day celebration in honor of Shakespeare did not even take place because of inclement weather, the Jubilee and its possible significance almost immediately became subjects of controversy among Garrick's contemporaries. The festival proved an excellent touchstone for topical drama; one could gather together highly diverse characters, comment upon Shakespeare, criticize Garrick, or discuss the theatre in general—all through reference to a single event. Even if the attractions of topicality soon disappeared, the Great Shakespeare Jubilee—or "Garrick's Folly," depending on one's viewpoint—continued to attract attention, but from scholars of theatre history, not playwights, so that documentation of its origins and events is now vast and thorough.[83] The influence exerted by the Jubilee on the actual theatrical works in its own time, however, can be assessed only by examining those works themselves.

Four pieces based directly upon the Shakespeare festival appeared in 1769; and of these, the one most involved in the issues surrounding the event is an anonymous pamphlet in play form entitled *Garrick's Vagary; or, England Run Mad.*[84] Published on September 18, 1769,[85] the pamphlet, despite the tone of its title, represents an attempt to treat fairly both sides of the controversy that arose over the Shakespeare celebration. The varied reactions provoked

by the Jubilee are presented here through a series of dialogues, with little attempt made to establish any continuity, except perhaps a vague geographical progression from London to Stratford and back again to London.

In the opening scene at the Bedford Coffee-House in London, "*three critical Play-house Frequenters,*" all of whom bear the tag names of regular drama, discuss the coming event at Stratford and indulge at length in "a little etymologizing" of the word *Jubilee*. The religious associations of the term lead to comparisons between Garrick and the Pope in which Garrick's supposed egotism and extravagance are unfavorably viewed.[86] Adverse criticism is somewhat neutralized, however, since the most vehement of Garrick's detractors is Nettle, a stock type of the disgruntled author motivated more by lack of success than by critical acumen. His insistence that the term *Jubilee* is being "perverted, to notify [announce] and misdecorate a new Species of Bacchanalian Revelling at Stratford upon Avon"[87] is answered judiciously by Lurcher, who indicates the possibilities for stage reform offered by the celebration. "Mr. Garrick, and his Brother Managers" would be justified in using the term, he contends, if their return to Shakespeare would procure "the Stage's *Deliverance* from the many undramatic Beasts of Lumber under which it now groans." Such a return could also bring a "*Remission*" of all that "critically candid Resentment" that arises when managers prefer the work of the carpenter and designer to that of the playwright and poet.[88]

An inn on the road to Stratford provides the setting for the next scene, where one encounters an entirely new pair of characters: Hemlock, the failed writer of tragedies, and Crotchet, an equally unsuccessful comic author. Piqued at Garrick's rejection of their work, the two plot to interrupt the Jubilee but differ on the question of method. Hemlock, falling back on the legal prejudices that had frustrated actors since Elizabethan times, plans to evoke an old edict against actors that states:

> Every Person who shall ... perform, or cause ... to be represented ... any Entertainment of the Stage ... in Case such a Person shall not have any legal Settlement in the Town ... without Authority ... or without Licence ... shall be deemed ... a Rogue and Vagabond ... and Shall be liable ... to all ... Punishments ... as are inflicted on ... Rogues and Vagabonds ... wandering, begging, and misordering themselves. ...[89]

Crotchet's scheme, on the other hand, is more "modern" in the eighteenth-century sense, for, rather than resorting to law, he plans to attack the "Pride of the Performers" and "raise a spirit of Mutiny and Revolt amongst them" by hinting that their processions in the streets of Stratford have reduced "them too nearly on a Level with the formerly despised Paraders before the Booths of Bartholomew Fair."[90] Both plans, however farcically presented, reflect two major problems that had plagued the theatre in its past, and Crotchet's reference to an actor's mutiny perhaps is intended to evoke memories of Garrick's part in a similar "revolt" at Drury Lane in 1743.

Crotchet, the less extreme of the two plotters, finally reneges on the planned interruption after Hemlock delivers a rather traditional denunciation of actors. To answer the charge that the players are authors' "Parrots . . . as Ignorant as Dirt, yet vain as Peacocks,"[91] Crotchet, supporting the general bipartisan spirit of the play, gives an opposing, as well as approbatory, viewpoint. "What . . . of the Words and Writings of Authors," he asks, "if there were not such Parrots . . . to give Utterance and Energy to their Meaning? . . . Several among them . . . I esteem as Valuable Members in private Life, and admire their Talents in a public Capacity."[92]

Having touched upon issues such as the reputation of the acting profession and the possible value of the Jubilee to the theatre, the author of *Garrick's Vagary* turns, in the remaining scenes, to exposition of conflicting opinions of Garrick himself. A third group of characters is introduced in order to describe the Jubilee, and in the course of their discussion, which is set now at Stratford, a laudatory defense of both Garrick and his project is offered by two critics less prejudiced than Crotchet and Hemlock:

Sɪʀ Bᴇɴᴊᴀᴍɪɴ:

> . . . No other Individual could have been the principal Agent here, with so much Propriety. This Project too may be considered . . . as the discharging a Debt of Gratitude . . . to the immortal Bard's Writings. The Admirable Performer at his first launching on the Stage, in the Characters of Richard, Lear, & tc. owed [to Shakespeare] the establishment of that Fame, which has since procured to him an ample Fortune; a Part whereof cannot, surely, be better employed than on an Occasion like this.

Lᴏʀᴅ Cʜᴀʀʟᴇs:

> . . . For my Part, I am not only pleased with, but obliged to Mr. Garrick, for his having been chiefly instrumental in so commendable, nay so patriotic an Institution.[93]

This tribute sets the tone for the remainder of the pamphlet, and, except for some incidental criticism of the Jubilee's use of fireworks as inappropriate to honor a man of Shakespeare's genius, the dominant attitude is one of commendation of Garrick.

Plays merely capitalizing upon the topicality of the Shakespeare festival, however, were far more common in 1769 than works that attempted, as did *Garrick's Vagary,* to discuss the theatrical issues it raised. One such opportunistic piece was Francis Gentleman's *Stratford Jubilee,* a rather typical comedy of amorous intrigue set in Stratford during the festival.[94] For the most part, Gentleman's references to contemporary theatrical matters are incidental to his plot, although he does at one point comment upon the general public's lack of dramatic taste and literary sophistication. In an exchange with Longcork, a fairly knowledgeable waiter, neither Scrapeall, a middle-class London businessman, nor Sir John Hearty, a city gentleman, emerges as a very creditable critic of Shakespeare:

Sᴄʀᴀᴘᴇᴀʟʟ:

> Shakespeare! what was he? the first woolcomber!

Lᴏɴɢᴄᴏʀᴋ:

> Woolcomber! what do not you know Shakespeare, Sir?

Sɪʀ Jᴏʜɴ:

> No! how the devil should we—he never lived in our neighborhood.

Lᴏɴɢᴄᴏʀᴋ:

> Nor the sign of him in Covent-Garden, where I have the honor to reside? . . . This Shakespeare was a writer of plays.

Sᴄʀᴀᴘᴇᴀʟʟ:

> I hate plays.

Sɪʀ Jᴏʜɴ:

> Now I like them! . . . Whittington and his cat . . . Punch in the suds, and two or three more make me laugh by the hour; . . .[95]

Later in the play, the popular taste for opera and his lavish entertainment is mildly satirized through the character of Lady Spangle, a fashionable gentlewoman whose interest in horse racing so outweighs her appreciation of drama that she thinks that a jubilee would better befit her favorite jockey than "the old musty scribbler Shakespeare."[96] Her husband, equally fashionable and just as obtuse, agrees completely:

Lᴏʀᴅ Sᴘᴀɴɢʟᴇ:

> . . . No critic of any delicacy can bear the fellow's hum drum pieces now.

Lᴀᴅʏ Sᴘᴀɴɢʟᴇ:

> Quite intolerable.—Though if some of them were turned into singing affairs they might be endured well enough, the opera of Hamlet; the opera of Othello; the opera of Richard; in short, the opera of every thing, to banish that antiquated barbarous word Tragedy.[97]

However exaggerated Lady Spangle's preferences may seem, the reality of a popular demand for extravagant theatrical spectacle in this period can hardly be denied; another of the 1769 festival plays, George Colman the Elder's *Man and Wife; or, The Shakespeare Jubilee,* illustrates this fad quite literally.[98] Like Gentleman's *Stratford Jubilee,* Colman's piece is primarily a romantic comedy set at Stratford during the celebration; its plot is a frame or perhaps an excuse for the presentation of a lavish stage version of the procession and pageant originally planned for the festival itself. With its first production on October 7,

1769, Colman and the management of Covent Garden successfully anticipated the Drury Lane opening of *The Jubilee,* a similar spectacle planned by Garrick. *Man and Wife* was acted twelve times[99] and thereafter, with Colman's prelude and the festival pageant removed, was played as a farce or afterpiece.

The prelude, or induction, is of particular importance to a discussion of plays about the theatre because it provides an early example of the dialogue-form prelude later to become characteristic of Colman,[100] and represents a conversation set on the stage of the theatre itself. In this short dialogue, Dapperwit, a manager and author identified as Colman,[101] discusses the Jubilee with two gentlemen of London and manages, at the same time, both to wittily defend Garrick's Festival *Ode* and to "advertise" the pageant that will be presented in the play to follow:

TOWNLY:

Ay Sir; but an ode without poetry—

DAPPERWIT:

... It had one capital fault, I must confess. ... Why ... I understood every word of it.—Now, an ode ... to be very good, should be wholly unintelligible.

. . . .

JENKINS:

Well—but you intend to give it us here, I suppose?

DAPPERWIT:

No—the ode can no where be heard to so much advantage as from the mouth of the author—and indeed it was so happily calculated for the time and place, for which it was originally intended, and the speaker so truly felt a noble enthusiasm on the occasion, that you have lost a very exquisite pleasure ... by not hearing it at Stratford Upon-Avon.

TOWNLY:

... But the pageant and the masquerade—

DAPPERWIT:

Those you shall see ... and perhaps they may appear to more advantage ... at the Theatres Royal, than they could have been at Stratford itself.[102]

Throughout the comic plot that frames the Jubilee procession, Colman discusses the contemporary theatre, and especially Shakespeare's place in it, as a means of differentiating the characters of Kitchen and Marcourt, the two young suitors for the hand of Charlotte, the romantic heroine. Asked if he prefers the "puns and quibbles" of Shakespeare to the "wit and humour" of Molière, Kitchen, torn, like many an eighteenth-century critic, between admiration of Shakespeare and respect for neoclassical critical strictures, defends the playwright by ascribing such "faults" to the "vicious taste of the times."[103] His rival, Marcourt, untroubled by any lingering fondness for the Bard, evokes the

judgment of "foreigners," none of whom "can endure him." They understand Shakespeare well enough, he explains,

to be shocked at his absurdities. A baby in the first act become a grown person in the last—plays made out of halfpenny ballads—ghosts and grave-diggers, witches and hobgoblins! ... Hamlet killing a rat—and Othello raving about an old pocket-hankerchief.—There's your Shakespeare for you![104]

Marcourt hardly need assign the discovery of these supposed absurdities to foreign critics, for one can find English objections to them appearing in works as early as Ben Jonson, from whose prologue to *Every Man in His Humour* Marcourt's specific reference here to a first-act baby "become a grown person in the last" may well be borrowed.[105] Whatever Colman's literary sources are, his characterization of Marcourt provides a clearly drawn satiric portrait of the literary Francophile whose regard for the rules of neoclassical decorum leads him to dismiss even the greatest dramas of his native tradition as "barbarous farces."[106]

A few years before the development of the rivalry between theatres that grew up in London as an aftermath of the Stratford celebration, Covent Garden had, in utilizing the pomp and circumstance of the Coronation for a spectacle in September 1761, scored a decisive victory over Drury Lane.[107] David Garrick, looking back on his comparative failure at that time, was therefore determined to make his new London Shakespearean pageant, which would follow the Stratford Jubilee, a lavish entertainment. He succeeded, for the afterpiece became "one of the most magnificent Spectacles ever exhibited on the stage,"[108] running to more than ninety performances and bringing in a rich harvest of admissions.[109]

Long in preparation, Garrick's *Jubilee* opened at Drury Lane on October 14, 1769, only a week after Colman's *Man and Wife* at Covent Garden.[110] For a week the rival company at Covent Garden had been giving its account of the affair, and the public was at the moment eager for the slightest additional detail. Garrick, reflecting upon the whole experience with amused acceptance of his dampened celebration, catered to the curiosity of the public and gave the town what its appetite at the time would relish most. Instead of taking his stay in Stratford seriously, he treated the whole Jubilee with the utmost hilarity compatible with his real purpose of honoring Shakespeare.[111] The result was that though his version surpassed all other dramatic reproductions of the festival,[112] his manner and tone varied little from the comic felicities achieved by George Colman in the Jubilee scene of *Man and Wife.*

Unlike Colman, however, Garrick did not frame his pageant with a separate, unified comic plot, but, rather, augmented it with a series of disconnected scenes of local color and musical entertainment. The discomforts experienced by visitors to Stratford, the befuddlement of unenlightened rustics, even the extravagant claims of souvenir peddlers are all depicted in these random scenes in the same good-humored manner. The scenes are entertaining, surely, but incidental, for their whole *raison d'être* is the pageant or spectacle itself. Originally planned as the high point of the Stratford celebration and canceled there because of the weather, this pageant consists primarily of an elaborately costumed parade of characters from twenty of Shakespeare's plays led by Garrick as Benedick and Miss Jane Pope as Beatrice.[113] The three Graces also participate as an escort for "Apollo with his Lyre," and the procession reaches its climax with the appearance of the "Statue of Shakespear supported by ye Passions and Surrounded by the seven Muses with their Trophies." As the parade ends, "the Bells ring 'em off & the Scene changes to a street in Stratford."[114]

Despite direct competition from Covent Garden's rival pageant, Garrick's *Jubilee* proved successful beyond all expectation, scoring the longest theatrical run of the century.[115] The universal popularity of theatrical spectacles in the age accounts perhaps for a great deal of the work's success; but Garrick too deserves much credit, for his characteristic lightness of touch and gentle humor make *The Jubilee* by far the best play to come down to us from the ample dramatic reaction to the festival.

In an age when relatively minor theatrical events could be the basis for a play about the theatre, it is hardly surprising that an occurrence of the magnitude of the Stratford Jubilee would elicit a number of plays and entertainments like those of Garrick and Colman, which would capitalize on the topical interest of the celebration. What is unusual, however, is that a play about the Jubilee was to bring forth another dramatic piece about itself. Later in the 1769-70 season, Henry Woodward, undoubtedly inspired by the phenomenal success of Garrick's *Jubilee,* produced a satire of it entitled *Harlequin's Jubilee* at Covent Garden on January 27, 1770.[116]

Although only Woodward's songs are extant, they and contemporary accounts of the performance are sufficient to indicate that Woodward produced in *Harlequin's Jubilee* another of those most curious eighteenth-century plays about the theatre—a pantomime whose function was to criticize pantomime. The afterpiece opens with "a ballad of magpies"[117] representing the London theatrical managers as having appropriated the materials of the Shakespeare Jubilee to keep their houses going. In an apparent reference to the contradiction inherent in Garrick's earlier "borrowing" of the pantomime form from John Rich and his present complaints against managers and writers who were in turn using "his" Jubilee as subject matter, Woodward says of these theatrical magpies:

> Like wits of the stage they will crib for relief,
> And he that cribs most is the first that cries Thief. ...
> (The mag of all mags is the Jubilee mag.)

Through the use of mythological and allegorical characters typical of the "serious" portion of pantomimes, Woodward

presents "Pantomime" as enslaved and wrongly forced to participate in the Stratford celebration. Juno dispatches Iris, identified here as the goddess of pageantry and show, to rescue Pantomime from Stratford and to ruin the planned pageant by thunderstorms. With this whimsical explanation of the rain that had spoiled Garrick's actual pageant in the previous September, Woodward moves *Harlequin's Jubilee* back to Covent Garden, the house built by "Lun" (John Rich) and, consequently, the proper setting for spectacle, and ends his pantomime with a parody of the current Jubilee pageant at Drury Lane. In obvious ridicule of Garrick's apotheosizing of Shakespeare—the crowning of his statue by Tragedy and Comedy[118]—in the final act of his *Jubilee,* Woodward's pantomime concludes with the "descent of the statue of the late Mr. Rich under the name of Lun" to which "the Harlequins all pay ... honour."[119]

Interest in the Jubilee and in the spectacle it generated on the London stage was strong enough in the 1769-70 season to allow Woodward's pantomime a successful run of thirty performances, while Garrick's *Jubilee* was continuing its own run, undiminished in popularity.[120] The topic of the Jubilee waned, necessarily, but its creator, David Garrick, remained controversial. Even in death he was not safe from critics, for shortly after his demise in 1779 an anonymous dialogue appeared in which his ghost figures as the central character. This piece, *Garrick in the Shades; or, A Peep into Elysium,* describes itself as "A Farce: Never Offered to the Managers of the Theatres-Royal,"[121] and its subject matter, though hardly farcical, more than adequately explains why it was "never offered," or considered, for public performance. Set in Elysium, the dialogue concerns the arraignment of the newly arrived Garrick by the "Judges of the Infernal Regions" as well as the shades of well-known actors, such as James Quin and Samuel Foote.

Garrick first faces a charge of vanity and love of money, which he answers with the damning excuse that he had been "ambitious of being received well amongst the great" and that to succeed there he had had to be both "a good actor" and "a rich one."[122] Far more disturbing to Garrick, however, than this accusation is the revelation that his beloved Shakespeare is convinced that, in organizing the Stratford Jubilee:

> Thou madest his name a stalking horse to wealth
> And freely borrow'd'st from his lib'ral store.
> . . . .
> That, thy fam'd Jubilee, was a mean device
> To gull the people—And to cram thy well-fill'd purse.[123]

Accused of venality by Quin, denounced for greed by Shakespeare, and informed by Ben Jonson that he should not presume to consider himself a writer, Garrick is finally judged and handed over to his rivals, Quin and Foote, to be purged of vanity and avarice. He is allowed some commendation, however, for Rhadamanthus, his judge, praises his art and honesty. None, Rhadamanthus explains, will dispute his claim to "histrionic fame," and Garrick, at last given his due, is told to

> Take thy seat of actors first:
> For such thy art, thou seem'dst as thou wert born
> For the stage only—yet thy manners such,
> Thy probity so great, thou seem'dst unfit
> To have been there—[124]

Quite apart from the criticism expressed in this piece, presumably from a disappointed author, and the questionable taste in allowing it to appear in print the very year of Garrick's death, this playlet holds some interest for its final admission in his own time of Garrick's character[125] and genius,[126] and for its closing appraisal which approximates the estimate prevailing in literary circles today. Furthermore, from scholarly research of the present day Garrick emerges also as an able playwright and as a sensitive and careful manager, as well as unquestionably the greatest English actor of his century and "undisput'd Monarch of the English Stage."[127]

Notes

1. Cecil Price, in noting that "the same comedies and tragedies went on appearing year by year," views the works of Hoadly, Colman, Goldsmith, and Sheridan as "the only ones that came to terms with the age and showed it itself from a particular angle." *Theatre in the Age of Garrick* (Totowa, N.J.: Rowman and Littlefield, 1973), pp. 196-97.

2. See Elizabeth Stein, *David Garrick: Dramatist* (New York: Modern Language Association: 1938), pp. 15-21; Stone, ed., *The London Stage,* pt. 4, l:cxlv-clii; Price, *Age of Garrick,* pp. 170-73.

3. Scouten, ed., *The London Stage,* pt. 3, 2.831. See n. 5.

4. Stone, ed., *The London Stage,* pt. 4, 1:86.

5. Harry William Pedicord, *The Theatrical Public in the Time of Garrick* (New York: King's Crown Press, 1954; reprinted., Carbondale, Ill.: Arcturus Books, 1966), pp. 198-99. Pedicord classifies *Lethe* as a farce, as does Price, *Age of Garrick,* p. 1. This farce "attracted the company's finest comedians including Garrick himself." Iain Mackintosh and Geoffrey Ashton, *The Georgian Playhouse: Actors, Artists, Audiences and Architecture,* Catalogue of Exhibition at Hayward Gallery, London, 1975 (London: Arts Council of Great Britain, 1975), II, no. 29.

6. In the spelling of *Aesop,* there is a variation between title and text.

7. David Garrick, *Lethe: A Dramatic Satire* (London: P. Vaillant, 1749). Garrick took the part of the Poet; Woodward, of the Fine Gentleman. Stone, ed., *The London Stage,* pt. 4, 1:86.

8. Garrick, *Lethe,* p. 8.

9. For a detailed discussion of eighteenth-century references to the catcall, see Leo Hughes, *The Drama's Patrons* (Austin: University of Texas Press, 1971), pp. 35-42.

10. Garrick, *Lethe,* p. 9.

11. Kalman A. Burnim, *David Garrick: Director* (Pittsburgh, Pa.: University of Pittsburgh Press, 1961), pp. 17-19.

12. Garrick, *Lethe,* p. 17.

13. Ibid., p. 18; for documentation of actual incidents of "pelting" in the theatre, see Hughes, *The Drama's Patrons,* pp. 45-52.

14. Pedicord, *Theatrical Public,* pp. 59-60; Hughes, *The Drama's Patrons,* pp. 23-26; p. 25 n.

15. Larpent MS no. 144, MacMillan, *Catalogue of Larpent Plays,* p. 25. For the authorship by two Friends of Lacy Ryan, see Stone, ed., *The London Stage,* pt. 4, 2:656-57.

16. See Price, *Age of Garrick,* pp. 86-96.

17. *Lethe Rehears'd: A Critical Discussion* (London: Roberts, 1749).

18. Ibid., p. 35.

19. *The Theatrical Manager* (London: Printed for Thomas Lowndes, 1751). Harvard College Library gives Lowndes as the author.

20. Actually, Garrick and Lacy's management of Drury Lane (1747-74) was "distinguished by its remarkable harmony in artistic endeavors." Burnim, *David Garrick: Director,* p. 5.

21. Lowndes, *The Theatrical Manager,* p. 44.

22. See text above.

23. Lowndes, *The Theatrical Manager,* p. 44.

24. [Arthur Murphy], *The Spouter; or, The Triple Revenge* (London: Reeve, 1756); Nicoll *Late Eighteenth Century Drama,* p. 289; Stone, ed., *The London Stage,* pt. 4, 2:540.

25. "The play has been attributed to Mr. Murphy." Stone, ed., *The London Stage,* pt. 4, 2:540. Nicoll enters it under Murphy. *Late Eighteenth Century Drama,* p. 289.

26. "It seems mainly to have been written with the aid of Garrick to satirize Cibber . . . who was trying to break a monopolistic hold on the London stage by . . . Covent Garden and Drury Lane." Trefman, "Arthur Murphy's Long Lost Englishman from Paris," p. 139. See

also Genest, *English Stage,* 4:461; Dunbar, *Dramatic Career of Murphy,* pp. 26-30.

27. Cibber sharply criticized Garrick's "new style" of acting in *Two Dissertations on the Theatres* (1756). Price, *Age of Garrick,* pp. 15, 19, 23.

28. Quoted by Trefman, "Arthur Murphy's Long Lost Englishman from Paris," p. 140.

29. Nicoll, *Late Eighteenth Century Drama,* p. 289; Stone, ed., *The London Stage,* pt. 4, 1:536. See chap. 1, n. 48.

30. [Murphy], *The Spouter,* pp. 37-38.

31. Ibid., pp. 16-17.

32. Joseph Knight, *David Garrick* (London: Kegan Paul, 1894), pp. 157-8.

33. Ibid., p. 147.

34. [Murphy], *The Spouter,* pp. 21-22.

35. Pistol's artificial nose and teeth are the subjects of comic action in at least four instances: Ibid., pp. 23, 24-25, 39, 41.

36. Ibid., p. 23. An obvious echoing of Jaques's speech on the seven ages of man in *As You Like It* (2.7.166).

37. Ibid., p. 24.

38. February 3, 1742. Scouten, ed., *The London Stage,* pt. 3, 2:965.

39. Arthur Murphy, *Life of David Garrick,* 2 vols. (London: Wright, 1801), 1:51-52.

40. [Murphy], *The Spouter,* pp. 23, 33. For the "old style" of "quavering" tragic speech, see Price, *Age of Garrick,* pp. 14-15, 15 n.

41. [Murphy], *The Spouter,* p. 26.

42. The Cibbers were well known for their equanimity onstage in the face of audience disapproval. See Hughes, *The Drama's Patrons,* p. 8 n.

43. Three of Colley Cibber's unsuccessful plays were *Love in a Riddle* (1729), *Caesar in Ægypt* (1724), and *Papal Tyranny in the Reign of King John* (1745).

44. [Murphy], *The Spouter,* p. 36. Pistol's speech on hissing is lifted from Fielding's *Historical Register for the Year 1736* (2.1).

45. Ibid., p. 39. Spiletta, the stage name of Nicolina Giordani, was a popular burletta singer.

46. Ibid., p. 40. See Trefman, *Sam. Foote, Comedian,* p. 67.

47. [Murphy], *The Spouter,* p. 40.

48. Trefman, *Sam. Foote, Comedian,* pp. 79-80.

49. This was a performance of *Harlequin Student; or, The Fall of Pantomime,* at Goodman's Fields on March 3, 1741. Scouten, ed., *The London Stage,* pt. 3, 2:894.

50. Stone, ed., *The London Stage,* pt. 4, 2:765; MacMillan, *Catalogue of Larpent Plays,* p. 29.

51. David Garrick, *Harlequin's Invasion,* in *Three Plays by David Garrick,* ed. Elizabeth Stein (New York: W. E. Rudge, 1926), p. 46.

52. Ibid.

53. Ibid., p. 47.

54. See Stein, ed., *Three Plays by Garrick,* p. 51.

55. David Garrick, Epilogue to *The Clandestine Marriage,* by George Colman the Elder and David Garrick. Drury Lane, February 20, 1766. Stone, ed., *The London Stage,* pt. 4, 2:1153. See George Colman the Elder, *The Dramatic Works of George Colman,* 4 vols. (London: T. Becket, 1777), vol. 4.

56. Garrick agreed to write both prologue and epilogue. Eugene R. Page, *George Colman the Elder* (New York: Columbia University Press, 1935), p. 124. All of act 5 is by Garrick. Stein (*David Garrick: Dramatist,* pp. 208-35, 246) concludes that Garrick did practically the whole play. Frederick L. Bergman supports her views in showing that Garrick wrote the Ogleby scenes and in finding also that a large proportion of the play is by Garrick. See Bergman, "David Garrick and *The Clandestine Marriage,*" *PMLA* 67 (1952): 148 ff.

57. Epilogue to *Clandestine Marriage,* In *The Poetical Works of David Garrick,* 2 vols. (London: Kearsley, 1785; reprinted New York: Benjamin Blom, 1968, 1:206-7.

58. Ibid., p. 208. Note in the text: "The chandeliers which used to hang from the ceiling were this Season taken away." Lights elsewhere improved the general visibility.

59. Ibid., pp. 209-11. Here Garrick has continued his satire of the manners of the fashionable set as expressed earlier in his *Harlequin's Invasion,* where he has the socially ambitious Dolly remark:

> I won't be stuff'd up . . . at Holiday Time at the Top of the Playhouse among Folks that laugh and cry, just as they feel. . . . Then I shall sit in the side Boxes, among my equals, Laugh, talk loud—mind nothing—Stare at the low People in the Galleries.
>
> (p. 32)

60. Stone, ed., *The London Stage,* pt. 4, 3:1285. The play was based on Mrs. Kitty Clive's *Rehearsal; or, Bays in Petticoats.* See Chap. 7.

61. An afterpiece, *A Peep behind the Curtain* is variously labeled. Its contemporaries called it "a farce." *Theatrical Monitors,* quoted by Stone, ed., *The London Stage,* pt. 4, 3:1285; Stein identifies it as a "burlesque-rehearsal type of play," *David Garrick: Dramatist,* pp. 166-67; Pedicord, "Burlesque," *Theatrical Public,* pp. 200-1; and Price settles for "short comedy," *Age of Garrick,* p. 145.

62. David Garrick, *A Peep behind the Curtain; or, The New Rehearsal* (London: Becket, 1767), p. 6.

63. Ibid., p. 9.

64. Ibid., p. 10.

65. On the problems of actors and actresses failing to appear for scheduled performances at Drury Lane, see Burnim, *David Garrick: Director,* pp. 25-27.

66. Stein, *David Garrick: Dramatist,* p. 174.

67. Garrick, *Peep behind the Curtain,* p. 21.

68. Burnim, *David Garrick: Director,* p. 40.

69. A humorous stage direction for an exit that may have suggested Puff's "exeunt praying" in Sheridan's *Critic* (2.2).

70. For a full account, see Burnim, *David Garrick: Director,* pp. 48-49.

71. David Garrick, *The Meeting of the Company; or, Bayes's Art of Acting,* in *Three Plays by Garrick,* ed. Stein, p. 125.

72. A member of the Drury Lane company who specialized in old men.

73. Garrick, *Meeting of the Company,* p. 130.

74. Thomas Weston, a comic actor famous for his unchangeable expression and slow, flat speech. Price, *Age of Garrick,* pp. 35-36.

75. Garrick, *Meeting of the Company,* p. 131.

76. Ibid., p. 132.

77. Ibid., pp. 139-41.

78. Ibid., pp. 144-45.

79. Stone, ed., *The London Stage,* pt. 4, 3:1912-13.

80. David Garrick, *The Theatrical Candidates: A Musical Prelude,* in *The Dramatic Works of David Garrick,* 3 vols. (London: Millar, 1798), 3:246.

81. Ibid., p. 248.

82. Ibid., p. 250.

83. Christian Deelman, *The Great Shakespeare Jubilee* (New York: Viking Press, 1964); Martha W. England, *Garrick's Jubilee* (Columbus: Ohio State University Press, 1964); Johanne M. Stochholm, *Garrick's Folly:*

The Shakespeare Jubilee of 1769 (London: Methuen; New York: Barnes & Noble, 1964).

84. Stochholm, *Garrick's Folly,* pp. 135 ff.

85. Its appearance was announced by the *London Chronicle.* Ibid., p. 135.

86. *Garrick's Vagary; or, England Run Mad, with Particulars of the Stratford Jubilee* (London: Bladon, 1769), pp. 1-21.

87. Ibid., pp. 1-7.

88. Ibid., p. 10.

89. Ibid., pp. 27-28.

90. Ibid., pp. 30-31.

91. Ibid., p. 32.

92. Ibid., pp. 32-33.

93. Ibid., pp. 37-38.

94. Francis Gentleman, *The Stratford Jubilee. To Which Is Prefixed Scrub's Trip to the Jubilee* (London: Lowndes, 1769). No author was given originally. Manager Samuel Foote, to whom it was dedicated, would not consider this anonymous comedy. Stochholm, *Garrick's Folly,* p. 140. It received journalistic notice on Sept. 19. Ibid., p. 139.

95. Gentleman, *Stratford Jubilee,* p. 3.

96. Ibid., pp. 10-11; during the planning period for the Jubilee, it was rumored that Garrick had selected a date coinciding with the annual Stratford Race Meeting in order to attract the "local nobility and gentry." Deelman, *Great Shakespeare Jubilee,* p. 106.

97. Gentleman, *Stratford Jubilee,* p. 12.

98. George Colman the Elder, *Man and Wife; or, The Shakespeare Jubilee,* in *The Dramatic Works of George Colman,* 4 vols. (London: T. Becket, 177, vol. 2; Nicoll, *Late Eighteenth Century Drama,* p. 246; Page, *George Colman the Elder,* pp. 175-76.

99. Stone, ed., *The London Stage,* pt. 4, 3:1419, 1427.

100. For Colman's development of the occasional prelude, see chap. 3.

101. England, *Garrick's Jubilee,* p. 87.

102. Colman, *Man and Wife,* prelude.

103. Colman, *Man and wife,* 2: 248-51.

104. Ibid.

105. "To make a child now swaddled, to proceed / Man, and then shoot up, in one beard and weed, / Past threescore years; or, with three rusty swords, / And help of some few foot and half-foot words, / Fight over York and Lancaster's long jars" (11. 7-11).

106. For Colman's characteristic tendency to "blame" foreign affectation for the decline of English taste, see chap. 3.

107. Thomas Davies, contemporary historian, had nothing but praise for Mr. Rich, whose Coronation "fully satisfied their (the public's) warmest imagination" (*Memoirs of the Life of David Garrick,* 2 vols. [London: Davies, 1780], 1:328-30), but he called Garrick's Coronation "the meanest, and most unworthy of a theatre I ever saw" (ibid., p. 329).

108. Genest, *English Stage,* 5:257.

109. Stein, ed., *Three Plays by Garrick,* p. 64; Stein, *David Garrick: Dramatist,* p. 132; England, *Garrick's Jubilee,* p. 114.

110. Stone, ed. *The London Stage,* pt. 4, 3:1419, 1427, 1429-39.

111. England observes: "The Jubilee was a private joke made public, a closed inner circle open to all. All were really and truly idolators." *Garrick's Jubilee,* p. 103. Stein comments: "Garrick could now sit back and laugh heartily at the whole Jubilee venture and at himself!" *David Garrick: Dramatist,* p. 132.

112. While Colman paraded representative characters from Shakespeare's plays, "Garrick presented each play as a dramatic unit" and "gave brief mime performances of the major scenes" of about nineteen plays. Deelman, *Great Shakespeare Jubilee,* pp. 283-84.

113. Stein, *Three Plays by Garrick,* p. 64.

114. Ibid., pp. 89-92. The whole idea of the Jubilee was first precipitated by the Stratford Council, which requested from Garrick a contribution of some ornament for the new Town Hall. Garrick gave two portraits—of himself and of Shakespeare—and a bust of Shakespeare. See Deelman, *Great Shakespeare Jubilee,* chap. 3.

115. England, *Garrick's Jubilee,* p. 114; Stochholm, *Garrick's Folly,* p. 165.

116. See MacMillan, *Catalogue of Larpent Plays,* p. 52; Stone, ed., *The London Stage,* pt. 4, 3:1451. The text is from the printed version of the songs in *Harlequin's Jubilee* (London, 1770).

117. In the prologue to Garrick's *Jubilee,* Drury Lane and Covent Garden described as two rival taverns named the Old Magpye and the New Magpye. Deelman, *Great Shakespeare Jubilee,* p. 280.

118. Stone, ed., *The London Stage,* pt. 4, 3:1430.

119. *Town and Country Magazine,* quoted in ibid., p. 1451.

120. Ibid., p. 1419.

121. *Garrick in the Shades; or, A Peep into Elysium* (London: J. Southern, 1779), title page. Nicoll, *Late Eighteenth Century Drama,* p. 329.

122. *Garrick in the Shades,* p. 15. The charges are not altogether unfounded. Deelman describes Garrick as a "born snob" who "loved fame," was susceptible to flattery, valued the company of famous men, and "moved in circles far removed from those of other actors." *Great Shakespeare Jubilee,* pp. 85-86.

123. *Garrick in the Shades,* p. 25. Yet his correspondence amply verifies that he was "one of the most generous and open-handed men of his day" but "did not make his charity public." The rumor that he was a miser was started by Macklin and furthered by Foote. Deelman, *Great Shakespeare Jubilee,* p. 85.

124. *Garrick in the Shades,* p. 43.

125. Deelman states that there was no hint of scandal ever attached to Garrick's reputation. *Great Shakespeare Jubilee,* pp. 84-85.

126. For tributes from contemporaries such as Alexander Pope, Edmund Burke, James Boswell, and Dr. Johnson, who called him a "master both in tragedy and comedy" but "liked him best in comedy," see Mackintosh and Ashton, *Georgian Playhouse,* II, III.

127. Ibid., II.

Bibliography

PLAYS ABOUT THE THEATRE

The Anniversary, Being a Sequel to Lethe. Larpent MS no. 144, 1758.

Clive, Mrs. Kitty. *The Rehearsal; or, Bays in Petticoats.* London: Dodsley, 1753.

Colman, George the Elder. *Man and Wife; or, The Shakspeare Jubilee.* In *The Dramatic Works of George Colman.* 4 vols. London: T. Becket, 1777.

Dell, Henry. *The Spouter; or, The Double Revenge.* London. S. Crowder, 1756.

Foote, Samuel. *An Occasional Prelude.* In *Memoirs of Samuel Foote.* Edited by William Cooke. 3 vols. London: Phillips, 1805.

Garrick, David. Epilogue to *The Clandestine Marriage.* In *The Dramatic Works of George Colman.* 4 vols. London: T. Becket, 1777.

————. *Harlequin's Invasion.* In *Three Plays by David Garrick.* Edited by Elizabeth Stein. New York: W. E. Rudge, 1926. Reprint. New York: Benjamin Blom, 1967.

————. *The Jubilee.* In *Three Plays by David Garrick.* Edited by Elizabeth Stein. New York: W. E. Rudge, 1926. Reprint. New York: Benjamin Blom, 1967.

———. *Lethe; A Dramatic Satire.* First Authorized Edition. London: For Paul Vaillant, 1749.

———. *The Meeting of the Company; or, Bayes's Art of Acting.* In *Three Plays by David Garrick.* Edited by Elizabeth Stein. New York: W. E. Rudge, 1926. Reprint. New York: Benjamin Blom, 1967.

———. *A Peep behind the Curtain; or, The New Rehearsal.* London: T. Becket, 1767.

———. *The Theatrical Candidates: A Musical Prelude.* In *The Dramatic Works of David Garrick.* 3 vols. London: Millar, 1798.

Garrick in the Shades; or, A Peep into Elysium. London: J. Southern, 1779.

Garrick's Vagary; or, England Run Mad, with Particulars of the Stratford Jubilee. London: Bladon, 1769.

Gentleman, Francis. *The Stratford Jubilee. To Which Is Prefixed Scrub's Trip to the Jubilee.* London: Lowndes, 1769.

Introductory Scene of *The Beggar's Opera* [*The Lady's Opera*]. Larpent MS no. 572, 1781.

Lethe Rehears'd: A Critical Discussion. London: J. Roberts, 1749.

Lowndes, Thomas. *The Theatrical Manager.* London: Printed for the Author, 1751.

The Managers: A Comedy. London: Nokes, 1768.

Murphy, Arthur. *The Apprentice.* London: P. Vaillant, 1756.

[Murphy, Arthur.] *The Spouter; or, The Triple Revenge.* London: W. Reeve, 1756.

[Wilson, Richard?] *A Peep into Elysium; or, Foote, Shuter, and Weston in the Shades.* Larpent MS no. 667, 1784.

Woodward, Henry. *Harlequin's Jubilee.* London: For W. Griffin, 1770.

Works Consulted

Bergman, Frederick L. "David Garrick and *The Clandestine Marriage.*" *PMLA* 67 (1952).

Burnim, Kalman A. *David Garrick: Director.* Pittsburgh, Pa.: University of Pittsburgh Press, 1961.

Davies, Thomas. *Memoirs of the Life of David Garrick.* 2 vols. London: Davies, 1780.

Deelman, Christian. *The Great Shakespeare Jubilee.* New York: Viking Press, 1964.

Dunbar, Howard Hunter. *The Dramatic Career of Arthur Murphy.* New York: Modern Language Association, 1946.

England, Martha W. *Garrick's Jubilee.* Columbus: Ohio State University Press, 1964.

Genest, John. *Some Account of the English Stage, from the Restoration in 1660 to 1830.* 10 vols. Bath: H. E. Carrington, 1832.

Hughes, Leo. *The Drama's Patrons.* Austin: University of Texas Press, 1971.

Knight, Joseph. *David Garrick.* London: Kegan Paul, 1894.

The London Stage. Edited by William Van Lennep, Emmett L. Avery, Arthur H. Scouten, George Winchester Stone, Jr., and Charles Beecher Hogan. 5 pts. (1660-1800). Carbondale: Southern Illinois University Press, 1960-68.

Mackintosh, Iain, and Ashton, Geoffrey. *The Georgian Playhouse: Actors, Artists, Audiences and Architecture, 1730-1830.* Catalogue of Exhibition at Hayward Gallery, London, 1975. London: Arts Council of Great Britain, 1975.

MacMillan, Dougald. *Catalogue of the Larpent Plays in the Huntington Library.* San Marino, Calif., 1939.

Murphy, Arthur. *Life of David Garrick.* 2 vols. London: Wright, 1801.

Nicoll, Allardyce. *A History of Early Eighteenth Century Drama, 1700-1750.* 2d ed. London: Cambridge University Press, 1929.

———. *A History of Late Eighteenth Century Drama, 1750-1800.* 2d ed. London: Cambridge University Press, 1927.

———. *The World of Harlequin.* New York: Cambridge University Press, 1963.

Page, Eugene R. *George Colman the Elder.* New York: Columbia University Press, 1935.

Pedicord, Henry William. *The Theatrical Public in the Time of Garrick.* New York: King's Crown Press, 1954. Reprint. Carbondale, Ill.: Arcturus Books, 1966.

Price, Cecil. *Theatre in the Age of Garrick.* Totowa, N.J.: Rowman and Littlefield, 1973.

Stein, Elizabeth, *David Garrick: Dramatist.* New York: Modern Language Association, 1938.

———, ed. *Three Plays by David Garrick.* New York: W. E. Rudge, 1926. Reprint. New York: Benjamin Blom, 1967.

Stochholm, Johanne M. *Garrick's Folly: The Shakespeare Jubilee of 1769.* London: Methuen; New York: Barnes & Noble, 1964.

Trefman, Simon. "Arthur Murphy's Long Lost *Englishman from Paris*: A Manuscript Discovered." *Theatre Notebook* 20, no. 4 (Summer 1966): 137-41.

———. *Sam. Foote, Comedian, 1720-1777.* New York: New York University Press, 1971.

Charles Conaway (essay date 2004)

SOURCE: Conaway, Charles. "'Thou'rt the Man': David Garrick, William Shakespeare, and the Masculinization of the Eighteenth-Century Stage." *Restoration and 18th Century Theatre Research* 19.1 (2004): 22-42. Print.

[*In the following essay, Conaway discusses Garrick's* Catharine and Petruchio *(1754), an adaptation of Shakespeare's* The Taming of the Shrew *(1590-91). Noting that Petruchio revises his original promise of a marriage of mutual love and regard, ultimately demanding that Catharine consent to his domination, Conaway contends that Garrick similarly asserted male hegemony in the English theater, thereby freeing himself and the stage from the charge of homoeroticism.*]

I

By the middle of the eighteenth century, David Garrick was recognized as an expert interpreter of Shakespeare's plays. This expertise, as Michael Dobson has noted, authorized Garrick's efforts "to replace the adapted texts of his plays still in the repertory with their originals" (167). Shakespeare's originals, however, were perceived to be in need of some occasional polishing, and so Garrick's expertise also gave him the authority, paradoxically, to alter Shakespeare's plays when supposedly restoring the originals to the stage. Such alterations, as Dobson writes, attempted to "promot[e] decency and inspir[e] virtue" (177) in an effort to promote English nationalism.

I will argue that Garrick's 1754 adaptation of *The Taming of the Shrew,* titled **Catharine and Petruchio,** attempts to promote certain "virtues" because it is concerned, not primarily with English nationalism, but with gender relations. Specifically, I will show how Garrick's farce follows the lead of Sir Richard Steele's report of an undoubtedly fictitious shrew-taming incident recorded in a 1710 edition of the *Tatler.* Both of these eighteenth-century texts, I contend, seem to offer egalitarian gender relations in marriage but effectively reinscribe male dominion over spouses. Steele and Garrick seize the discourse of what Lawrence Stone has since termed the "companionate marriage" in order to reassert male hegemony, and Garrick's effort, when set alongside his other work, can be seen as part of a larger mid-eighteenth-century effort to legitimize the stage by showing that it is a locus of masculine virtue. Following the work of Lawrence Senelick and Kristina Straub, I will demonstrate that Garrick participated in an attempt to masculinize, professionalize, and legitimize the stage by trying to reign in audience suspicions about the sexualities of actors and actresses. Garrick's adaptation of *Shrew,* I will argue, aims not only to promote male supremacy in marriage, but also, as Straub might say, to domesticate the sexuality of its lead actress, and other works in Garrick's canon, along with his reaction to being implicated in a same-sex affair, demonstrate his efforts to free himself and the stage from the taint associated with homoeroticism. Thus, Garrick's **Catharine and Petruchio** can

be said to construct Shakespeare's emerging cultural authority, first and foremost, in accord with dominant misogynist and homophobic agendas.

II. "... TAKING A WOMAN DOWN IN HER WEDDING SHOES": GENDER HIERARCHIES AND POLITE SOCIETY

In the Saturday, September 30, 1710 edition of the *Tatler,* Steele's Isaac Bickerstaff reports on a series of events related to the "Proverbial Expression of *taking a Woman down in her Wedding Shoes,* if you would bring her to Reason" (3.196).[1] The article owes more to the oral tradition of shrew-taming narratives than it does to Shakespeare's play. Jan Harold Brunvand demonstrates that Folk Tale Type 901 indicates that "the secret of the successful taming is the husband's trick of administering excessively severe punishment to an animal in order to frighten his bad wife" (1966, 347), and such is the case in Steele's essay.[2] The daughter of a gentleman in Lincolnshire, Bickerstaff reports, had "so imperious a Temper ... that it continually made great Uneasiness in the Family, became her known Character in the Neighbourhood, and deterred all her Lovers from declaring themselves" (3.196). Eventually, however, she is approached by "a Gentleman of plentiful Fortune and long Acquaintance" who manages to obtain "her Consent in due Form" (3.196). Lawyers draw up the marriage contract—"in which, by the Way, there was no Pin-Money," Bickerstaff interjects—and the couple is wed without ado (3.196). After a "decent Time" spent at the house of the bride's father, the groom departs, and returns, not so much in Petruchio-like madcap attire, but "without a Servant, mounted on the Skeleton of a Horse which his Huntsman had the Day before brought in to feast his Dogs on the Arrival of their new Mistress, with a Pillion fixed behind, and a Case of Pistols before him, attended only by a Favourite Hound" (3.197). As the couple rides home, they find their way barred by a gate. The bridegroom commands the dog to open the gate, and when it doesn't, he shoots it dead. Soon after that, the horse stumbles, rights itself after being threatened by the groom, but stumbles again. The groom therefore runs the animal through with his sword: "Then says to his Wife, Child, prithee take up the Saddle; which she readily did, and tugged it Home, where they found all Things in the greatest Order, suitable to their Fortune and the present Occasion" (3.197-98). Not long thereafter, the bride and groom return to her father's house where, after the women retire to another room, a wager is made to see who was "the most Master at Home" (3.198). The bride and groom win the wager, after which the husband takes his wife in his arms and confesses that he had only temporarily taken on the illusory appearance of a man with an "Impatien[t] ... Temper," and he "assures her, That since she could now command her Temper, he would no longer disguise his own" (3.197, 198).

The proverbial expression of "*taking a Woman down in her Wedding Shoes*" suggests that the *Tatler*'s readers should prevent ill-habits at the moment when those habits first appear: a wife's behavior should be addressed at the very beginning of a marriage if her supposed ill-habits are to be corrected. But it also suggests that by taking a woman down in her wedding shoes, a husband can bring his wife to "Reason." Bickerstaff's bride, it seems—whose "High Spirit" makes "great Uneasiness in the Family" and deters "all her Lovers from declaring themselves" to her—is not a reasonable person (3.196). Conversely, his shrew-taming husband is clearly marked as a "Man of the most equal Temper" and a "careful Husband" (3.197). Although he ruthlessly shoots his favorite dog, slays his horse, and practices psychological violence upon his wife, he is explicitly depicted as a person who puts on a "disguise" that he wears over his own good nature and that he vows to put off after his wife learns to "command her Temper"—that is, after she is brought to "Reason."

One of the implicit and often explicit aims of the *Tatler* and *Spectator* essays of Joseph Addison and Richard Steele was to fashion a polite society, and the very ground on which they based the notion of that polite society was "Reason." They argued that polite, eighteenth-century English culture was primarily constituted in, by, and through, relations based on the kind of rational arguments that were associated with the notion of "Universal Reason." According to Jürgen Habermas this polite and reasonable discourse proceeded through a theatre or an arena he labels the "public sphere"—an institution through which the eighteenth-century bourgeoisie attempted to exercise its power and hold the government accountable to its citizens. Access to this discursive arena no longer depended, according to Addison and Steele, on social standing or political affiliation, but instead relied on the ability to argue reasonably. The public sphere was thus, supposedly, an egalitarian sphere, and the process of bringing a woman to reason, then, coming as it does in the pages of Steele's *Tatler*, appears analogously to argue that the process of taming a shrew, or taking a woman down in her wedding shoes, will lead to egalitarian relations between a husband and wife. That is, just as reason renders social and political differences insignificant in the public sphere, it might also erase gender hierarchies in the domestic sphere.

However, as Nancy Fraser argues, "the full utopian potential ... of the public sphere was never realized in practice" (113), and as Joan Landes claims in her analysis of the public sphere in the age of the French Revolution that utopian potential was not achieved in France because the public sphere there was constructed in opposition to women who had been politically influential in salon culture. The English public sphere in the eighteenth century, despite its egalitarian pretensions, likewise excluded women from access to power. In Steele's essay, for example, Bickerstaff's bride is denied pin-money—a kind of "independent fixed income," according to Lawrence Stone, "at [the bride's] exclusive disposal" (221). In the *Tatler* and *Spectator* es-

says, as Erin Mackie notes, Addison and Steele argue that woman of polite society should *not* indulge in the kind of fashionable items that were often purchased by women with their pin-money. She claims that Addison and Steele often demonize fashion in their essays: "fashion becomes an object for the containment and rationalization of bad, often "feminine" forces present both in the marketplace and on the domestic scene" (1997, 27). For Addison and Steele, then, pin-money serves in part as the grounds through which femininity can be marked as unreasonable, justifying any effort to exclude women from the public sphere.

In such a light, however, the fact that Bickerstaff's bride is denied pin-money would seem to indicate that, provided she can be brought to reason, she might be able to enter polite society. But as Timothy Breen argues, "the consumer market may have been a source of female empowerment. ... The acquisition of goods by women in this economy was an assertive act, a declaration [or, at least, an appropriation] of agency" (cited in Mackie, 1997, 23). In light of Breen's argument, then, Bickerstaff's bride is denied the opportunity to negotiate or transact business on her own behalf. The denial of pin-money in that sense constitutes a denial to participate in the market economy of the public sphere.

The inclusion or exclusion of pin-money also had an impact on gender relations in the domestic sphere. Stone defines the "companionate marriage" as one that "equalize[es] relationships between husband and wife" (217). He explicitly sets companionate marriage against the idea of marrying for income or status, claiming that spouses "began to put the prospects of emotional satisfaction before the ambition for increased income or status" (217). Stone argues that men and women who began to choose their own marriage partners selected spouses for the kind of companionship they might offer rather than for the economic or social capital they might bring to an alliance. Men who sought companionate spouses presumably were not interested in treating their wives as pieces of property that were subject to their authority, and one of the most salient pieces of evidence indicating that the husband's seemingly absolute authority over the wife was in a state of decline during the eighteenth century, according to Stone, could be found in the fact that, in "the propertied classes ... an admittedly limited series of changes in the power of the former to control the latter's estate and income" was underway (221). That is, the clauses that were occasionally inserted into marriage contracts guaranteeing pin-money for the wife are regarded by Stone as evidence of the fact that hierarchical relations in marriage were in a state of decline.

However, Susan Staves cautions us against reading the emergence of pin-money clauses in marriage contracts as evidence of any kind of sweeping changes in marital gender hierarchies. Regarding clauses that secured pin money as a kind of separate maintenance agreement, Staves argues that they were not a cause for any kind of feminist celebration because they were private contracts and not necessarily endorsed by society—as, for example, they were certainly not endorsed by Addison and Steele—or enforced to the letter by the courts:

> Marriage itself, though often called a contract, and in some ways treated as contractual, has not been contractual in the sense that the two parties could negotiate whatever provisions were dictated by their individual wills. ... Wives' access to pin-money and other forms of married women's separate property within on-going marriage were repeatedly said to be bad for them, bad for marriage, and disruptive of society.

(168)

For Staves, then, the *inclusion* of pin-money in the marriage contract does not necessarily prove a lessening of male dominion in marriage. But the explicit *exclusion* of pin-money, as is found in the parenthetical aside in Steele's shrew-taming narrative, can surely be read as an effort to deny the wife the means by which male dominance *might* be lessened. Bickerstaff's bride remains dependant on her husband's income.

Even if a husband attempts to bring a wife to reason, then—or to put it more generously, perhaps—even if a husband marries for intellectual and/or emotional companionship, egalitarian gender relations do not necessarily follow, and Steele's narrative conforms to this seeming paradox of a marriage that is companionate yet hierarchical. In addition to denying the bride the material means—the pin-money—by which she might be able to lessen her husband's dominion over her, and despite the fact that, unlike Shakespeare's *The Taming of the Shrew,* it does not include a submission speech arguing that women should be submissive to their husbands, the *Tatler* essay aims to prop up male dominion in marriage. The purpose of the taming process, for example, is to render the wife "meek and humble" like an obedient "Child," rather than an equal marriage partner who is capable of rational argument.[3] What is worse, perhaps, Bickerstaff's bride is reduced to a beast of burden. After the groom slays his own horse, he politely asks (but more or less compels) his bride to take up his saddle and tug it home, treating her as though she was, as Shakespeare's Petruchio says, his goods, his chattels, his house, his household stuff, his field, his barn, his horse, his ox, his ass, his anything.[4] Whereas Shakespeare's Katherina spiritedly argues that "Asses are made to bear, and so" is Petruchio (2.1.199), Steele bestializes and infantilizes his bride, turning *her* into an ass that is made to bear. Finally, the purpose of the bridegroom's "Tryal" is not only to demonstrate that the "World [was] mistaken as to the Temper of his Lady" but also to prove which of the men was "most Master at Home" (3.198). The cruelty of Bickerstaff's bridegroom, then, may be part of a disguise that he agrees no longer to employ once his wife

comes to Reason, but it is also put to the service of securing his mastery over his wife. Despite the fact that Steele's narrative implies that a wife may be brought to reason and companionship in marriage, then, it also quite clearly indicates that male dominion in both the domestic and public sphere will be a part of that marriage.

III. "THOU'RT THE MAN, THE MAN OF CATH'RINE, AND HER FATHER TOO": MALE DOMINION IN MARRIAGE

The ideological work of Garrick's **Catharine and Petruchio** follows closely that of Steele's narrative. Garrick eliminated Shakespeare's Induction and the Bianca-and-her-suitors subplot in order to write a three-act farcical afterpiece that showcases Shakespeare's wooing scene (Act One), the wedding day—including both Petruchio's madcap return to Padua and his outrageous behavior on his arrival with Catharine at his country house (Act Two)—and a sequence of scenes, all of which take place at Petruchio's home, including the tailor's visit, the Sun/Moon dialogue, and a visit from Baptista, Hortensio and his wife, Bianca, wherein Catharine utters an abbreviated and interrupted submission speech (Act Three). Like Steele's essay, Garrick's farce appears to call for an egalitarian-like companionate marriage but ultimately serves only to secure male dominion.

Garrick's Petruchio is a gentleman—that is, he is depicted as a gentle man, a member of polite society. He demonstrates no predisposition to violence: there is no scene, for example, in which Petruchio knocks Grumio soundly when they first come to Padua. In fact, it is Garrick's Grumio who makes the argument that his master is really a gentleman who puts on a disguise in order to tame Catharine, telling Curtis, on his return to Petruchio's country house, that "we must look for another-guise master than we have had" (2.110-11). Not only is Petruchio's expected ill-temperedness "another guise," according to Grumio, it is also only temporary: Petruchio will appear to be "more shrew than she," but only "for the nonce—" (2.283-84). Presumably, then, the *undisguised* Petruchio is so even-tempered that no sort of coil would erupt between himself and his bride, an idea that is further emphasized when, after Petruchio razes the dinner table, the servant Peter apologizes for his master's actions, saying that "He kills her in her own humor. I did not think so good and kind a master could have put on so resolute a bearing" (2.371-72). The notion that Petruchio disguises his constitution in order to tame Catharine is finally confirmed by Petruchio himself, who confesses, after Catharine's submission, that the role of "the lordly husband ... [is] An honest mask" that he will no longer wear (3.269-70).

Such a seemingly gentle groom appears to put his disguise to the service of securing a marriage of mutual companionship. After doffing his mask, for example, Petruchio announces:

Far hence all rudeness, wilfulness, and noise,
And be our future lives one gentle stream
Of mutual love, compliance, and regard.

(3.271-73)

Brian Morris argues that this promise of mutual love, compliance, and regard "marks a distinct shift of Shakespeare's emphasis, towards a conventional, genial eighteenth-century comedy resolution of the problems of marriage" (95). Elizabeth Schafer agrees, arguing that the eighteenth-century notion of "sentiment ... reigns as Petruchio says he will 'doff' the 'mask' he has assumed of "lordly husband" (3.269-70), [and] promises Catharine" a marriage based on mutual love and respect (11).

But the play does not *end* on Petruchio's promise. Instead, it continues with Petruchio's claim that wives are bound to obey their husbands:

PETRUCHIO:

> Good Kate, no more. This is beyond my hopes.
> (*Goes forward with* CATHARINE *in his hand.*)
> Such duty as the subject owes the prince,
> Even such a woman oweth to her husband.
> And when she's froward, peevish, sullen, sour,
> And not obedient to his honest will;
> What is she but a foul contending rebel
> And graceless traitor to her loving lord?
> How shameful 'tis when women are so simple
> To offer war where they should kneel for peace;
> Or seek for rule, supremacy, and sway,
> Where bound to love, to honor and obey.
> (*Finis*)

(3.276-86)

Tori Haring-Smith notes that, when Garrick parcels out to Petruchio these lines from Katherina's submission speech, Catharine "loses the spotlight in the last scene" (16), and Catharine's loss is Petruchio's gain. The final word belongs to him, and Catharine functions here merely to demonstrate her consent. She is deprived of the opportunity to speak—either with or without an ironic tone—and is instead led forth and presented, as Dobson argues, "as an exhibit" (197). It is possible, of course, that, in performance, the actress who portrays Catharine might go forward reluctantly with Petruchio—or even not at all—in order to register disapproval of his words: the actress who plays Catharine is not necessarily silenced simply because Garrick's text does not give Catharine any words to speak. But Garrick's text, in and of itself, directs Petruchio to go forward with Catharine. It places her figuratively in the very palm of her husband's hand as he elaborates on his notion of mutual love, compliance, and regard—a notion which insists, despite its seeming egalitarianism, that a woman should not "seek for rule, supremacy, and sway" in relation to her husband (3.285). Such efforts mark her as rebellious, peevish, sullen, sour, graceless, shameful, and traitorous. As Dobson notes, then, "the companionate mar-

riage *Catharine and Petruchio* celebrates, proves, despite Garrick's cosmetic alteration, to be based as squarely as ever on the husband's absolute dominion over the wife" (197), and as Jean Marsden writes, Garrick "expose[s] the hierarchical foundation on which such an ideal of egalitarian marriage is built" (82). According to Garrick's farce, marital relations are mutual and reciprocal relations, but they are not egalitarian.

Not only is Petruchio's call for companionate marriage thus *revised,* but it had already been *conditioned* on Catharine's obedience. It is only after Catharine has demonstrated, or at least performed, compliance with the idea of male sovereignty that Petruchio's chimerical promise of mutual love, compliance and regard is offered. Catharine scolds Bianca, for example, and tells her that her husband is her lord, her king, and her governor (3.239) *before* Petruchio promises such a seemingly congenial notion of marital relations. It is possible, though perhaps unlikely, that the actress who played Catharine spoke ironically here suggesting that she did not necessarily mean what she said to Bianca, but again Garrick's play text in and of itself not only suggests that Catharine's compliant behavior bodes "peace ... and love, and quiet life / And awful rule and right supremacy" (3.212-13), it also argues that peace and love and quiet life *depend* upon lawful rule and right supremacy. As Marsden writes, Petruchio "'doffs' the mask of brutish masculinity only after Catharine has proclaimed that a husband is a wife's rightful 'keeper,' 'head,' and 'sovereign' (*CP* [*Catharine and Petruchio*], 3.1.250-51)" (82).[5]

This assertion of male dominion over women is perhaps more clearly demonstrated in the marriage negotiations that take place between Petruchio and Baptista. Unlike Bickerstaff's bridegroom, Garrick's Petruchio is portrayed as a mercenary who has "thrust [himself] into the world, / Haply to wive and thrive as best [he] may" (1.11-12). There is no wager scene in Garrick's adaptation, but Petruchio's fortune-hunting status is nonetheless reinforced when Grumio tells Baptista that Petruchio will have no problem winning Catharine's consent to be married: "Though she had as many diseases as two and fifty horses, why nothing comes amiss, so money comes withal" (1.29-31). In Shakespeare's play, Grumio utters these lines to Hortensio,[6] but in Garrick's farce, he says them directly to the bride's father, thus telling Baptista outright that nothing matters to Petruchio but the money that comes with Catharine. In fact, Petruchio himself has already told Baptista the same thing: in Shakespeare's play, Petruchio tells Hortensio that he has come "to wive and thrive as best I may" (1.2.56), that he has "come to wive it wealthily in Padua; / If wealthily, then happily in Padua" (1.2.75-76). In Garrick's farce, however, these lines are delivered by Petruchio to Baptista (1.12 and 1.73-74), and he tells his future father-in-law that his "business," as he refers to his efforts to marry, "asketh haste" (1.13). For Garrick's Petruchio, then, marriage is a transaction and a bride is a commodity to be exchanged and possessed.[7] Petruchio does not search for a companion to marry. He seeks a dowry, and his attitudes about the role and nature of women in the marriage transaction are in line with ideologies that are traditionally used to help justify male dominion in marriage.

Garrick's Baptista seems to share those sentiments. Like Shakespeare's father of the bride, Garrick's Baptista tells Petruchio that he must win "My daughter's love, for that is all in all" (1.18), but his concern for Catharine's consent is quickly exposed as pretence and dropped as a condition for marriage in the negotiations with Petruchio:

BAPTISTA:

> As I have showed you, Sir, the coarser side,
> Now let me tell you she is young and beauteous,
> Brought up as best becomes a gentlewoman.
> Her only fault (and that is fault enough)
> Is that she is intolerably forward.
> If that you can away with, she is yours.

> (1.32-37)

Garrick borrows the first five lines from Shakespeare's play. But there, they are uttered by Hortensio to Petruchio. Garrick gives them to Catharine's father and adds the last line, thus changing Baptista's line of argument: instead of claiming that Catharine's consent needs to be won, he now tries to win *Petruchio*'s consent to marry his daughter by more or less selling Catharine's assets of youth and beauty. Still, Baptista cannot forget his daughter's supposed forwardness and thus tells Petruchio that if he can "away with" that, if he can tolerate Catharine's forwardness, then he can marry her.[8] Petruchio claims that despite these supposed faults he will woo her—after all, he has "heard lions roar" (1.49) and is thus not afraid of Catharine. At this point, the bargain is sealed:

BAPTISTA:

> Then thou'rt the man,
> The man of Cath'rine, and her father too.
> That shall she know, and know my mind at once.
> I'll portion her above her gentler sister,
> New-married to Hortensio.
> And if with scurril taunt and squeamish pride
> She make a mouth and will not taste her fortune,
> I'll turn her forth to seek it in the world;
> Nor henceforth shall she know her father's doors.

> (1.59-67)

Convinced that Petruchio is not afraid to woo and wed his daughter, Baptista determines that the marriage will proceed: by claiming that Petruchio is "the man of Cath'rine, and her father too," Baptista indicates that, as far as he is concerned, Petruchio has won Catharine's consent because he has won her father's consent, and if Catharine refuses to obey her father, Baptista will put her out of doors. Just as Petruchio's call for companionate marriage seems to indi-

cate this his notion of marital relations are not hierarchical when in fact they are, Baptista's claim that Catharine's love must be won seems to indicate that his notion of his relationship with his daughter is not hierarchical, when in fact it is—her will, in the matter of her own marriage, matters not.

If the men in the play assume that Catharine's will is negligible, however, Catharine herself does not. She responds to her father's ultimatum, for example, by claiming that she will turn it to her advantage:

> How! Turned adrift nor know my father's house?
> Reduced to this, or none, the maid's last prayer,
> Sent to be wooed like the bear unto the stake?
> Trim wooing like to be! And he be the bear,
> For I shall bait him—

> (1.135-39)

Rejecting the possibility of a celibate life, Catharine sets her sights for the man her father insists she must marry, and she vows, in the process, *not* to be reduced to Petruchio's prey. Realizing that her father's wishes seem to render her something like a baited bear, Catharine claims that she will instead make Petruchio such a bear at whom she will figuratively snap and into whom she will tear—which she does, following the example of Shakespeare's Katherina in the wooing scene. And when Baptista tells her that it will be better to be married to "this jack [ie—Petruchio] than starve, and that's your portion" (1.227), Catharine comments in an aside, "I'm vexed; / I'll marry my revenge, but I will tame him" (1.244-45). Again, Catharine notes her vexed position—she acknowledges that her duty must follow her father's command (1.273), but she declares her own motivation to marry, vowing that she will take revenge on her father's disregard for her will by taming her husband.

In marrying Petruchio, Catharine also aims to settle a score with her sister, Bianca:

CATHARINE:

> Why, yes: sister Bianca now shall see
> The poor abandoned Cath'rine, as she calls me,
> Can hold her head as high, and be as proud,
> And make her husband stoop unto her lure,
> As she, or e'er a wife in Padua.
> As double as my portion be my scorn;
> Look to your seat, Petruchio, or I throw you.
> Cath'rine shall tame this haggard; or, if she fails,
> Shall tie her tongue up and pare down her nails.

> (1.278-86)

Here, Garrick develops the idea expressed in Shakespeare's play that Katherina may never find a husband, that she may be destined to "lead apes in hell" (2.1.34). It is unclear, in Shakespeare's play, whether Katherina genuinely fears spinsterhood or whether she simply uses that idea as leverage in an argument with her sister and her father, but Garrick suggests that such fears have been a genuine concern for his Catharine. He situates her fear or shame of spinsterhood in a rivalry with Bianca, in which Catharine seems historically to have been on the losing end: she seems to have been taunted for being "the poor abandoned Cath'rine." But Catharine also hopes to gain the upper hand in that rivalry as a result of her marriage to Petruchio. She borrows, from Petruchio's soliloquy in Shakespeare's play, the claim that she will tame a hunting bird, that she will make Petruchio "stoop unto her lure," that she will occupy the dominant position in her marriage, and thus avenge not only her father's disregard for her will, but her sister's apparent mockery of her. Though suggesting, then, that the wills of fathers and husbands are absolute in relation to daughters and wives, Garrick's farce also demonstrates that Catharine can negotiate within the limits of such male-imposed restrictions in order to gain an advantage for herself.

Apart from her spirited arguments in the wooing scene and these vows she makes to herself, however, Garrick's Catharine never follows through on her pledge to tame her husband. In fact, her claim that if she does not tame her husband, she will "tie her tongue up and pare down her nails" (1.286) seems to be all too sadly prophetic. In the comedy's third act, for example, Baptista, Hortensio, and Bianca arrive at the home of Catharine and Petruchio just after the Sun/Moon dialogue. Upon witnessing his daughter's performance of obedience—demonstrated when she addresses him, at Petruchio's direction, as a "Young budding virgin" (3.190) and then as her "reverend father" (3.202)—Baptista adds, "Ar't not altered, Kate?" (3.206). Catharine confesses that she has been "transformed to stone" so that her "master cannot choose but mend" her (3.207-09). Bianca then urges Catharine to "Hold up thy head, / Nor lose our sex's best prerogative, / To wish and have our will" (3.216-18), praying, "Lord, never let me have a cause to sigh, / 'Till I be brought to such a silly pass" (3.222-23), and swearing that Petruchio's "eyes and ears had felt these fingers e'er / He should have moped me so" (3.227-28). Catharine, Bianca seems to feel, has been robbed of her womanly spirit, her willfulness, her desire to rule her husband. And when Catharine begins her submission speech, Bianca pleads with her to "be quiet" (3.248), but Catharine, at Petruchio's bidding, continues. Her husband appears to have mended her so that she is now a mouthpiece for female submission.

Whereas Bianca once provided motivation for Catharine to marry Petruchio and take revenge by making her husband "stoop unto her lure" (1.281), she now serves as a foil to a Catharine who is transformed. Bianca remains willful—insofar as the text is concerned, inappropriately so—whereas Catharine seems to have learned that her desire to gain the upper hand over her husband was misplaced. She now "look[s] with blushes on [her] former self" (3.275). She has, in fact, "tie[d] her tongue up and pare

[d] down her nails" (1.286). Garrick's farce, then, circulates the possibility of Catharine's resistance in order to dramatize her reformation and make the point that lawful rule and right supremacy leads to a happy marriage.

Finally, it might be argued that Catharine does not follow through on her motivation to take revenge in her marriage, because she has genuinely fallen in love with Petruchio. Garrick's farce certainly suggests such a possibility when it implies that Catharine is physically attracted to her husband. Upon first eyeing him, for example, immediately after stating that she shall make him the baited bear, she exclaims, "yet the man's a man" (1.139). This attraction for Petruchio helps to make a supposedly genial, romantic-comedy-like ending to the action more plausible. It helps to suggest that Catharine has loved Petruchio from the first moment she met him—that she and, perhaps, Petruchio engage in a battle of wits until they finally realize their love for each other. Such a reading suggests that Catharine and Petruchio can be seen as a Beatrice and Benedick-like couple—lovers who, whether they realize it or not, participate in a "merry war" wherein they profess to hate each other but are actually, as is obvious to everyone else in the play and in the audience, very much attracted to each other. Beatrice and Benedick were very popular among eighteenth-century audiences, and Shakespeare's *Much Ado About Nothing* was one of Garrick's favorite plays. He began acting the part of Benedick in 1748, six years prior to penning **Catharine and Petruchio,** and appeared in the role until very late in his career—as late as 1776. It is thus quite possible that Garrick altered Shakespeare's shrew and shrew-tamer to fit the mold of one of his own most popular and successful productions.

But if such is the case, it is odd that Garrick did not exploit the success of his own performances as Benedick by casting himself in the role of Petruchio. That role went instead to Henry Woodward. Thus Garrick did not use his own fame in order to suggest that his Petruchio should be read as a Benedick-like character. In fact, the production's casting ultimately suggested that Catharine and Petruchio were far less genial than Beatrice and Benedick. A well-known and very strained relationship existed between the two stars of Garrick's farce—Catharine Clive, who replaced Hannah Pritchard in 1756, and Henry Woodward. According to Elizabeth Schafer, "Clive and Woodward were known to dislike each other and stories circulated suggesting that they used onstage fights to settle offstage scores" (9). There was, as James J. Lynch writes, a "known antipathy that existed between the two chief actors" of Garrick's farce (105), and audiences apparently flocked to see it represented onstage. Thomas Davies writes:

> Mrs. Clive, though a perfect mistress of Catherine's humour, seemed to be overborne by the extravagant and triumphant grotesque of Woodward; she appeared to be overawed as much by his manner of acting, as Catherine is represented to be in the fable. In one of his mad fits, when

he and his bride are at supper, Woodward stuck a fork, it is said, in Mrs. Clive's finger; and in pushing her off the stage he was so much in earnest that he threw her down: as it is well known that they did not greatly respect one another, it was believed that something more than chance contributed to these excesses.

(1.312)

The fork-stabbing incident in Davies's report is supported only by hearsay, but it nevertheless suggests that Clive and Woodward were regarded as being genuinely hostile to each other. Furthermore, Davies suggests that their relationship, wherein Clive was "overawed" by Woodward's acting, is similar to the relationship between Catharine and Petruchio, wherein Catharine—according to Davies's interpretation—is overawed by Petruchio. In such a light, a Beatrice-and-Benedick-like reading of Garrick's Catharine and Petruchio seems inappropriate. Perhaps Catharine is attracted to her husband, and perhaps Petruchio, beneath his "guise," loves his young and beautiful wife, but there is more here than just a merry war: Garrick's play is not simply concerned with the fact that Catharine and Petruchio fail to realize that they love each other—though that can be part of the production's appeal, provided that actors other than Clive and Woodward portray Catharine and Petruchio. Garrick's play is ultimately concerned with the fact that what is "sweet and happy" in a marriage depends on female submission (3.214).

Finally, as Kristina Straub notes, popular actresses in the eighteenth century, including Clive, were often "claimed, in popular representations, as the social or sexual pets of the aristocracy" (92). Such representations troubled efforts to secure dominant notions of femininity and female sexuality in the eighteenth century. In response to the troubling nature of such depictions, Straub argues, and as part of an effort to secure the legitimacy of the theatre as a cultural institution, writers attempted to recuperate the sexuality of actresses by trying "to fit their subjects' sexual lives into domestic roles" (93). The effort to domesticate the sexuality of actresses proceeded through reports in theatrical memoirs and histories as well as the associations that were made between actresses and their stage personas—star images that were based on the characters that the actresses played. Surely, Catharine Clive's turn as the ultimately submissive Catharine in Garrick's play can be seen as part of the eighteenth-century theatre's effort to reign in popular misconceptions about the supposedly wanton nature of the sexuality of actresses, and, although as Straub rightly contends such efforts to domesticate the actresses' sexualities were never able to achieve coherence and closure, Garrick's farce is nevertheless committed to the attempt to do so. It aims to secure male dominion in the home and resituate Clive/Catharine in the domestic sphere, not just for the sake of gender relations in marriage, but ultimately in order to demonstrate that the theatre is a locus of masculine virtue and female submissiveness.

IV. "IF YOU KNEW HOW LITTLE I CARE FOR THE WHOLE SEX ...": GARRICK'S SUPPRESSION OF SAME-SEX DESIRE FROM THE EIGHTEENTH-CENTURY STAGE

It was not only the sexuality of actresses that was of concern in the effort to legitimize and professionalize the eighteenth-century stage. Straub writes that, as a result of "long-implicit associations of actors with [what we now call] homosexuality" (48), actors in the middle of the eighteenth century "were increasingly vulnerable to the charge of sodomy" (47). As a result, she continues, "professionals of the theater were more and more likely to distance themselves from a suspect male effeminacy" (47). This spread of homophobia led, as Straub notes, to "a discursive impetus to 'masculinize' the theater, to expel the ambiguities that were increasingly subject to disconcertingly unambiguous labels" (48). Lawrence Senelick traces the history of this gradual effort to masculinize the theatre, noting that the theatrical representation of sodomites changed during the Restoration and eighteenth century from the Restoration rake who explicitly entertained desires for men, boys, and women, to fops, who signified same-sex desire only through an exaggerated, comical, and stereotyped effeminacy, until, by the end of the eighteenth century, they were by and large de-sexualized as they "dwindled into a mere-clothes horse" (67).

Garrick's participation in the reformation of the theatre is not limited to his revision of *Shrew*. In his 1757 farce, *The Male-Coquette; or, Seventeen Hundred Fifty-Seven,* for example, Garrick presents in the character of Daffodil exactly the kind of fop whose effeminacy signifies the kind of same-sex desire that is demonized and held out for ridicule by the theatre.[9] Daffodil is clearly attractive to members of the opposite sex, and he enjoys the reputation that accrues to him as a result of his numerous "affairs," but he is nevertheless depicted as a rather effeminate man who is more devoted to Italian opera and fashion than he is to the women whom he pursues. As the Prologue to *The Male-Coquette* indicates, it is "Ye slaves to fashion, dupes of chance, / Whom fortune leads her fickle dance" (18-19) to whom the play is addressed, and these slaves to fashion and dupes of chance are not women, but men such as Daffodil who clearly prefers to spend his time at his men's club among his circle of male friends, making absurd wagers such as whether or not he can "walk from Buckingham-Gate to the Bun-House at Chelsea, eat a bun there, run back to the turnpike, and from thence hop upon one leg, with the other tied to the cue of his wig, to Buckingham-Gate again, in an hour and half" (2.2.17-21).

In fact, Daffodil prefers the pleasure of male company because he finds women sexually repugnant, claiming, for example, that "To ruin women would be troublesome; to trifle and make love to 'em amuses one. I use my women as daintily as my tokay. I merely sip of both, but more than half a glass palls me" (1.2.256-59). Daffodil "makes love" to or flirts with women, but the idea of consummating a physical relationship with them would be troubling and appalling to him. One potential female lover reviles him as a "wretch who can assume passions he never feels and sport with our sex's frailties" (2.1.8-10), and after the insincerity of his attentions are discovered in the farce's denouement, he states that "if you knew how little I care for the whole sex, you would not be so furious with an innocent man" (2.3.162-64). As Robert Fahrner notes, echoing Senelick's claim that the fop's effeminacy signifies same-sex desire, Daffodil is clearly depicted as a man who "publicly expressed interest in women to hide [his] real inclinations" (9).[10]

For Garrick, illicit sexualities were fodder for obvious jokes, and he repeatedly exploited the contentious debates related to the politics of sex, gender, and desire, as Katherine S. Green notes, as part of his "customary attempts at self promotion" (21). But in what was perhaps the most notorious incident involving Garrick and illicit sexualities, he fought almost tooth and nail to dissociate himself from sexual scandal. In 1772, William Kenrick published *Love in the Suds,* a pamphlet that implicated Garrick in a same-sex love affair with Isaac Bickerstaff. Unlike the fictional Isaac Bickerstaff of Jonathan Swift and Sir Richard Steele, Isaac John Bickerstaff wrote numerous comic operas for the mid-eighteenth-century stage. He was prolific, successful, and well-acquainted with Garrick, having produced work for his theatre. While there is no evidence to suggest that Garrick and Bickerstaff were intimately acquainted in a same-sex relationship, however, Kenrick's eclogue portrayed them as lovers.

Bickerstaff's troubles began in late April, 1772. On April 30 and May 1 of that year, *The Daily Advertiser* ran the following ad:

> *Whereas* on Tuesday Night last [April 28], between the hours of Eight and Ten, A Gentleman left with a Centinel belonging to Whitehall Guard, a Guinea and a half, and a Metal Watch with two Seals, the one a Cypher, the other a Coat of Arms, a Locket, and a Pistol Hook. The Owner may have it again by applying to the Adjutant of the first Battalion of the first Regiment of Foot-Guards at the Savoy Barracks, and paying for this Advertisement.
>
> (quoted in Tasch, 222)

Apparently, Bickerstaff became enamored of a soldier who wanted nothing to do with him. After being threatened with immediate arrest, Bickerstaff attempted to buy off the soldier by giving him his watch and most, if not all, other valuables he had in his possession. The soldier was more or less happy with the deal, but ran the ad, presumably, to run Bickerstaff out of town and thus prevent any future entanglements or liabilities. Bickerstaff, apparently aware that the soldier and his officers had discovered his identity, fled the country for France.

Shortly thereafter, presumably bearing a long-term grudge against Garrick, William Kenrick published *Love in the Suds,* an eclogue casting the actor as Bickerstaff's heartbroken lover, who laments for his lost Nyky—a common diminutive for Isaac—and defends same-sex desire, asking, for example, "Of manly love ah! why are men asham'd?" (6). Thomas J. Campbell writes:

> By most accounts a thorough-going scoundrel, William Kenrick was very likely the most notorious literary libeler of his age. ... He seemed to fancy himself more a playwright than a mere miscellaneous reviewer, though he never achieved even a moderate success. And for this he blamed Garrick.

(iii)

Garrick produced two of Kenrick's comedies, *Falstaff's Wedding* (1766) and *The Widow's Wife* (1767), but this does not seem to have had any beneficent impact on, what is by all accounts, Kenrick's professional jealousy.

More important for this argument than Kenrick's motivation for writing *Love in the Suds* is Garrick's response to it. When Kenrick in 1765 attacked Samuel Johnson's edition of Shakespeare, Johnson refused to respond in public and later prevented Boswell from attempting to defend him. But Johnson's refusal to stir even more controversy was a lesson lost on Garrick. Instead of letting the matter die quietly, Garrick sued Kenrick for libel and later refused to drop the suit or settle out of court, even when it seemed unlikely that he might win. And it was only in November 1772, after Kenrick's public apology to Garrick, that the matter was finally settled. For Garrick, being associated with supposedly deviant or illicit sexualities such as same-sex desire seems to have been so distasteful that it was worth his time and effort to respond to Kenrick's eclogue. Garrick was adamant in his efforts to clear himself from the taint associated with same-sex desire, and his **Catharine and Petruchio** can be seen as being motivated by related reformist concerns. When Garrick's adaptation of Shakespeare's *Shrew* rewrites the eighteenth-century notion of companionate marriage as male dominion in marriage, then, it constructs Shakespeare's cultural authority in line with the misogynistic and homophobic efforts to domesticate the sexuality of actresses and suppress same-sex desire from the stage.

Notes

1. Steele's fictional Isaac Bickerstaff is appropriated from Jonathan Swift who employed him as a writer of pamphlets, including the satiric tract entitled *Predictions for the Year 1708* wherein he predicts, among other things, the death of an actual quack astrologer and prognosticator, John Partridge. When Partridge, having survived beyond the supposed appointed hour of his death, called attention to this fact in an effort to discredit Swift's Bickerstaff, Steele's Bickerstaff, in *The Tatler* number one, contradicts

Partridge's rebuttal, assuring the quack that, whether he realizes it or not, he is, in fact, dead. In borrowing Swift's fictional narrator/pamphleteer, Steele gains, as Bickerstaff writes in *The Tatler*'s Dedication to Arthur Maynwaring, "an Audience of all who had any Taste of Wit" (Reprinted in Mackie, 1998, 47). A non-fictional Isaac John Bickerstaff was born, presumably in Dublin, on September 26, 1733. He wrote comic operas for the English stage during the middle of the eighteenth century and was acquainted with Boswell, Samuel Johnson, and David Garrick. In the 1770s, he fled England after being accused of homosexuality, a "crime" in which, as discussed below, Garrick was implicated.

2. In its most reduced form, the 901 subtype appears as a joke, titled "That's Once," which Brunvand records as follows:

> A newly married couple were leaving the church they were married in, in a horse-drawn carriage. The horse stumbled on a rock. "That's one," said the groom. Later on the horse stumbled again. "That's two," he said. A short while later the horse tripped on a rock, "That's three," the man said as he pulled out a gun and shot the horse. His wife said he was too cruel. "That's one," said the man, and they lived happily ever after.

(1991, 217-18)

3. In *The Taming of a Shrew* (1594), Kate invokes divine order in her submission speech. And in *The Taming of the Shrew* (1623) Katherina's submission speech argues that a wife owes to her husband a duty similar to that which a subject owes to his sovereign. Whether or not *A Shrew* or *The Shrew* (or even the submission speeches themselves) ultimately argue that a wife ought to submit herself to her husband's rule is an issue that continues to be debated by critics. I believe that there is ample evidence to throw into question an argument for female submission. In any event, my point in mentioning the submission speech here is that even though Steele's narrative does *not* include a speech that might argue that women should submit themselves to their husband's rule, his essay still promotes such a point of view.

4. Cf Petruchio's comments about Katherina in Shakespeare's *Shrew*: "She is my goods, my chattels, she is my house, / My household stuff, my field, my barn, / My horse, my ox, my ass, my any thing" (3.2.230-32).

5. In contrast, Haring-Smith argues that Garrick's Petruchio "rules his household, but he is no longer a tyrant: Catharine is tamed, but she is not humiliated" (17). I would add that if Petruchio is no longer a tyrant it is only because Catharine is tamed. If she were to reject her submissive status, her husband

would no doubt be resolved to put on another guise and oppressively and violently bring her to a submissive status once again. As Haring-Smith also notes, the prompt book for J. P. Kemble's 1786 revival of Garrick's adaptation provides "the earliest evidence we have of Petruchio carrying the now traditional whip" (24), a prop that profoundly indicates how readily his shrew-taming guise might be taken off, or put back on again.

6. See Shakespeare's *Shrew* 1.2.77-82.

7. Such a notion is ambiguously represented in Petruchio's response to Baptista's offer of a second dowry:

BAPTISTA:

> Then, my now gentle Cath'rine,
> Go home with me along, and I will add
> Another dowry to another daughter.
> For thou art changed as thou hadst never been.

PETRUCHIO:

> My fortune is sufficient, Her's my wealth.

(3.262-66)

Whereas Shakespeare's Petruchio accepts Baptista's offer of a second dowry by claiming "I will win my wager better yet" (5.2.116), Garrick's equally-mercenary bridegroom refuses Baptista's offer, but insists that his wife is his wealth. Insofar as Garrick's Petruchio is concerned, then, Catharine remains his property. She is a commodity before and after marriage.

8. Baptista's line might also mean that if Petruchio can do away with or tame Catharine's forwardness, he can marry her. But subsequent comments indicate that no such prerequisite is placed on the marriage.

9. The full title of Garrick's farce suggests that it addresses issues pertaining to more than just Daffodil, the male-coquette, and Robert Fahrner argues that the farce is in dialogue with the Reverend John Brown's *An Estimate of the Manners and Principles of the Times* (1757). Garrick knew Brown professionally, having previously produced two of his plays, and seems to have exploited not only the popularity of Brown's treatise—the *Estimate* reached a seventh printing as early as one year later in 1758—but its ideologies as well. Brown argues that mid-eighteenth-century England's most pressing problem was "*vain, luxurious,* and *selfish* EFFEMINACY" (cited in Fahrner, 2). Like Addison and Steele, he is concerned with the manners and mores of English society, but he repeatedly places the blame for the nation's problems on male effeminacy. My discussion of Garrick's *Male-Coquette* is very much indebted to Fahrner's essay.

10. Fahrner relies on Randolph Trumbach's essay which refers to the *Love-Letters between a Certain Late Nobleman and the Famous Mr. Wilson* (1723) and argues that "sodomites chased women only to protect themselves from infamy" (1990, 121).

Works Cited

Anonymous. *A Pleasant Conceited Historie, Called the Taming of A Shrew.* Eds. Graham Holderness and Bryan Loughrey. Lanham, Maryland: Barnes & Noble Books, 1992.

Brunvand, Jan Harold. *The Taming of the Shrew: A Comparative Study of Oral and Literary Versions.* New York: Garland Publishing, 1991.

———. "The Folktale Origin of *The Taming of the Shrew.*" *Shakespeare Quarterly* 17 (1966): 345-59.

Campbell, Thomas J. "Introduction." *Love in the Suds: A Town Eclogue. Being the Lamentation of Roscius for the Loss of his Nyky.* (1772) Los Angeles: University of California, Los Angeles, 1987. iii-xi.

Davies, Thomas. *Memoirs of the Life of David Garrick.* 2 Vols. (1808) New York: Benjamin Blom, Inc., 1969.

Dobson, Michael. *The Making of the National Poet: Shakespeare, Adaptation, and Authorship, 1660-1769.* Oxford: Clarendon Press, 1992.

Fahrner, Robert. "A Reassessment of Garrick's *The Male-Coquette; or, Seventeen-Hundred-Fifty-Seven* as Veiled Discourse." *Eighteenth-Century Life* 17 (1993): 1-13.

Fraser, Nancy. "Rethinking the Public Sphere: A Contribution to the Critique of Actually Existing Democracy." *Habermas and the Public Sphere.* Ed. Craig Calhoun. Cambridge MA: The MIT Press, 1992. 109-42.

Garrick, David. *Catharine and Petruchio: A Comedy.* (1756) *The Plays of David Garrick.* Volume 3: Garrick's Adaptations of Shakespeare, 1744-1756. Eds. Harry William Pedicord and Fredrick Louis Bergmann. Carbondale: Southern Illinois UP, 1981. 187-220.

———. *The Male-Coquette; or, Seventeen Hundred Fifty-Seven.* (1757) *The Plays of David Garrick.* Volume 1: Garrick's Own Plays, 1740-1766. Eds. Harry William Pedicord and Fredrick Louis Bergmann. Carbondale: Southern Illinois UP, 1980. 133-67.

Green, Katherine S. "David Garrick and the Marriage Habitus: The Clandestine Marriage Revisited." *Restoration and Eighteenth Century Theatre Research* 13:2 (1998): 17-34.

Habermas, Jürgen. *The Structural Transformation of the Public Sphere: An Inquiry into a Category of Bourgeois Society.* Trans. By Thomas Burger with Frederick Lawrence. Cambridge MA: The MIT Press, 1991.

Haring-Smith, Tori. *From Farce to Metadrama: A Stage History of The Taming of the Shrew, 1594-1983.* Westport CT: Greenwood, 1985.

Holderness, Graham, and Bryan Loughrey. Eds. "Introduction." *A Pleasant Conceited Historie, Called The Taming of A Shrew.* Lanham, Maryland: Barnes & Noble Books, 1992. 13-36.

Kenrick, William. *Love in the Suds: A Town Eclogue, Being the Lamentation of Roscius for the Loss of his Nyky.* 3rd Edition. (1772) Ed. Thomas J. Campbell. Los Angeles: University of California, Los Angeles, 1987.

Landes, Joan. *Women and the Public Sphere in the Age of the French Revolution.* Ithaca: Cornell UP, 1988.

Lynch, James J. *Box, Pit, and Gallery: Stage and Society in Johnson's London.* Berkeley: U of California P, 1953.

Mackie, Erin. Ed. *The Commerce of Everyday Life: Selections from* The Tatler *and* The Spectator. Boston: Bedford/St. Martin's, 1998.

Mackie, Erin. *Market à la Mode: Fashion, Commodity, and Gender in* The Tatler *and* The Spectator. Baltimore: The Johns Hopkins Press, 1997.

Marsden, Jean I. *The Re-Imagined Text: Shakespeare, Adaptation, and Eighteenth-Century Literary Theory.* University of Kentucky Press, 1995.

Morris, Brian. "Notes." *The Taming of the Shrew.* By William Shakespeare. Methuen & Co., 1981.

Schafer, Elizabeth. Ed. "Introduction" and "Notes." *The Taming of the Shrew.* By William Shakespeare. Cambridge UP, 2002.

Senelick, Laurence. "Mollies or Men of Mode?: Sodomy and the Eighteenth-Century London Stage." *Journal of the History of Sexuality* 1 (1990): 33-67.

Shakespeare, William. *Much Ado About Nothing. The Riverside Shakespeare.* Ed. G. Blakemore Evans. Boston: Houghton Mifflin Company, 1974. 327-64.

———. *The Taming of the Shrew. The Riverside Shakespeare.* Ed. G. Blakemore Evans. Boston: Houghton Mifflin Company, 1974. 106-42.

Staves, Susan. *Married Women's Separate Property in England, 1660-1833.* Cambridge MA: Harvard UP, 1990.

Stone, Lawrence. *The Family, Sex, and Marriage in England 1500-1800.* Abridged Edition. New York: Harper Torchbooks, 1979.

Straub, Kristina. *Sexual Suspects: Eighteenth-Century Players and Sexual Ideology.* Princeton: Princeton UP, 1992.

Tasch, Peter A. *The Dramatic Cobbler: The Life and Works of Isaac Bickerstaff.* Lewisburg: Bucknell UP, 1971.

The Tatler. Ed. Donald F. Bond. 3 vols. Oxford: Clarendon Press, 1987.

Trumbach, Randolph. "Sodomy Transformed: Aristocratic Libertinage, Public Reputation and the Gender Revolution of the 18th Century." *Journal of Homosexuality* 19:2 (1990): 105-24.

Raphael Shargel (essay date 2004)

SOURCE: Shargel, Raphael. "The Devolution of *The Alchemist*: Garrick, Gentleman, and 'Genteel Comedy.'" *Restoration and 18th Century Theatre Research* 19.2 (2004): 1-21. Print.

[*In the following essay, Shargel provides examples from the texts of the Garrick and Francis Gentleman versions of Jonson's* The Alchemist *to prove that these adaptations are travesties of the original. Shargel complains that both authors diluted language, simplified character, and sterilized nuance in order to make Jonson's play conform to the tastes of eighteenth-century audiences. Shargel considers Garrick's cutthroat strategy symptomatic of Jonson's waning reputation.*]

Although eighteenth-century dramatists routinely altered the texts of earlier works when reviving them for the stage, it is nevertheless ironic that the plays of Ben Jonson were transformed into entertainments that but shallowly reflected the originals. In his own age, Jonson professed himself the reformer and corrector of the English theater; after his death in 1637, his "sons" and admirers continued to articulate this sentiment. But by the middle of the eighteenth century, Shakespeare was solidly established as the national poet amid increasingly hostile rumors regarding his rivalry with Jonson.[1] As a result, Jonson's popularity suffered in print and his success on the boards from the 1740s onward was due almost entirely to David Garrick, who popularly adapted two of his comedies. Garrick's scripts and the contemporary accounts of their performances prove them to be fascinating travesties. Substituting many of Jonson's most impressive linguistic passages with comic "mugging," stage "business," and theatrical spectacle, they provide evidence of intense changes in stagecraft over a 150 year period. Just as significantly, they register a contempt for the dramatic integrity of Jonsonian drama that is lacking in Garrick's adaptations of Shakespeare.

Yet surprisingly, these playtexts, and particularly that of *The Alchemist,* have been regarded by modern critics as generally faithful to their source, judiciously streamlining lengthy works by eliminating obscurities and obscenities that would have bewildered and offended Garrick's audiences.[2] Garrick's adaptation of *The Alchemist* is indeed shorter and more brisk than Jonson's, but its vast cuts

and strategic additions alter the source in ways that go far beyond the period's formal demands for polite dialogue. Indeed, Garrick preserves some of Jonson's crassest language and innuendo even as he flattens the Jonsonian panorama, polarizing complex ambiguities and sexual politics that, unlike those in the era's most popular Shakespearean texts, refuse to incorporate the centrality of character and plot that the age found appealing. A later crib of *The Alchemist* by Francis Gentleman entitled *The Tobacconist* has long been scorned as a trivialization of Jonson's original. Yet it merely follows the path that Garrick paved to a logical and mediocre end.

The radicalism of Garrick's transformation can perhaps best be understood by comparing his approach to *The Alchemist* with his treatments of Shakespeare. Although Garrick modified Shakespeare's texts intensively, his efforts were seen as a part of the century's grand project of rescuing Shakespeare from the hands of earlier corrupters, both in the page and on the stage. Despite the extensive changes he rung upon *A Midsummer Night's Dream* and *Cymbeline* on the one hand and the fact that, on the other hand, *Much Ado About Nothing* and *The Tempest* (in its second incarnation under Garrick's revisionist pen) were performed with relatively minimal alterations,[3] Garrick generally sought to translate Shakespeare's dramas into a form that preserved as much of his language as possible. His contemporaries saw him as the "restorer of Shakespeare."[4]

To win this title, he adopted a number of imaginative approaches. Garrick's **Hamlet**[5] and **King Lear** imported many of the plot alterations of earlier versions. With the latter, he followed the lead of Nahum Tate's 1681 adaptation: the fool is eliminated, Edgar and Cordelia are lovers, and the play ends happily. But inside Tate's overall structure, he repaired much, putting back many passages that had been cut.[6] Recasting *The Winter's Tale,* whose generation-crossing narrative was considered too lugubrious for contemporary audiences, Garrick focused on the second generation of Acts IV and V, crystallizing the play into a dramatic pastoral that showcased the sheep-shearing scene and the resurrection of Hermione. And while his **Romeo and Juliet** is severely altered and his **Catharine and Petruchio** a much-trimmed version of *The Taming of the Shrew,* both are still more faithful to the originals than the versions that had appeared since the Restoration.

Even as he took his liberties, Garrick proved deeply invested in preserving the depth of Shakespeare's characters, particularly the ones he deemed central. Reshaping *Antony and Cleopatra,* Shakespeare's second longest play, he dropped and consolidated minor figures and folded short scenes together, but retained a great deal of the dialogue spoken by the title couple, showcasing as much of their linguistic and personal complexity as possible. His addition of a death speech for Macbeth perhaps erroneously fleshes out and ennobles the protagonist, but permits him to mourn the errors of his ways before he dies in the tradition of tragic heroes that stretches from Sophocles to Marlowe's Faustus.[7]

To create a performable text of the admittedly lengthy *Alchemist,* abbreviation was unavoidable, but it is possible to imagine a shortened revision that, in line with Garrick's stance toward much of Shakespeare as well as other authors he adapted, simplifies plot and even eliminates some characters in order to give free and faithful reign to memorable scenes, speeches, and persons.[8] Yet with Jonson, Garrick tread on less sacred ground. He thus had the liberty to approach him with the cutthroat strategy of the Restoration adapters from whose hands he claimed to be rescuing Shakespeare. Like Tate picking over each speech in *Lear,* Garrick doctored *The Alchemist* at every point, sterilizing its nuances. His extensive omissions trivialize all but one of Jonson's characters, turning them into the "flat" figures which some contemporary and many later critics read into his texts, even when unadulterated. His aversion to the vividness of Jonson's language, even when it is not obscure or obscene, converts one of the most complex of Renaissance plays into a light piece.

Perhaps the most remarkable aspect of Garrick's revision is that he manages to alter the play's meaning almost entirely by cutting. Examples of Garrick's textual ruthlessness can be seen in the metamorphosis of Sir Epicure Mammon into a relatively ordinary voluptuary, of Face into a less perceptive con-artist who becomes the most sympathetic of the play's cozening triumvirate, and of Dol Common from an independent and canny whore into an object for her male partners to manipulate.

Garrick—and later, Gentleman—thus participated in the critical turn against Jonson which rejected his unique representation of plot and character, sociology and politics. In doing so, both adapters followed the model of what Henry Fielding, just as Garrick was first preparing his *Alchemist,* denigrated as the modern vogue of "genteel" comedy, which he defined as a diversion that touches but obliquely upon serious issues while avoiding the hard, direct expression uncompromising satirists believe to be at the root of the genre.

A brief summary of Jonson's eighteenth-century reception will help put Garrick's and Gentleman's versions in their context. The number of theatrically viable works in the Jonson canon decreased as the century wore on. Robert Gale Noyes notes that from the Restoration, only six Jonson dramas continued to be performed regularly. Of these, *Catiline* fell from the boards before the beginning of the eighteenth century. Productions of *Bartholomew Fair* in anything resembling its original state ceased after 1731, and it was not professionally revived until 1921. *Epicoene* fared poorly after 1752, having two brief revivals in 1776 and 1784, and was not seen again until an 1895 adaptation. *Volpone,* arguably the most accessible of Jonson's major plays, held the stage infrequently after the middle of the eighteenth century and was never acted in the next.[9]

The state of Jonson's texts also stagnated. The one new complete edition of his works that appeared in the 1700s was edited by Peter Whalley and published in 1756.[10] And Whalley could not make the same excuses for his author's flaws as his Shakespearean peers. Unlike Shakespeare, Jonson prepared most of his own texts for publication. No one could argue that later hands had corrupted them before they saw print. Any "errors" in taste or judgment were directly attributable to the author and Whalley, at best a dispassionate editor, took pains to do just that.[11]

By contrast, adapters and editors of Shakespeare (with Garrick, as I have noted, chief among them) often claimed to be rescuing him from corruption. Because editions of Shakespeare's works were available in many versions in every year of the century and because theatrical adaptations were produced throughout the era, Shakespeare's texts, both in print and on the boards, remained fluid. Readers as well as audiences, comparing the different versions they read and saw, participated in a debate about works that were continually recreated and redefined.

But if Garrick, in adapting Jonson, succeeded in making Jonson serve his talents and the needs of his theater, he risked little by cutting much. Garrick acted in his versions of *The Alchemist,* first performed in 1743, and *Every Man in His Humor,* first performed in 1751, throughout his subsequent career at Drury Lane.

In his dilution of *Every Man Out of His Humor,* where he took the role of Kitely, Garrick may be forgiven for wishing to shorten a long comedy. He removed many of its local references, place-names, and forgotten histories that would be meaningless to his audience. He also softened Jonson's coarseness, pruning the roles of low characters like Cob, Tib, Matthew, Bobadill, and even Justice Clement.[12] His additions, particularly in Act IV, highlighted the importance of Kitely to such a degree that many who witnessed the production believed him to be the central figure.[13] He thus retooled the Jonsonian panorama as a personal showcase.

His revision of *The Alchemist* is even more lopsided. While this play has no central figure, a performer shining in one of its more prominent roles might appear to be the protagonist. But rather than assume the part of Subtle or Face—who, with Dol Common, comprise the comedy's brilliant triad of con artists—or make the idiosyncratic but interesting choice of Mammon, Ananias, or Tribulation Wholesome, its most quixotic gulls, he conceded to developing theatrical tradition and took on the character of the dimwitted tobacconist Abel Drugger, a relatively minor figure whose role he expanded considerably.

Drugger's comic potential had already been exploited in the strolling "drolls" of the Interregnum[14] and continued, in Garrick's time, with the popular mugging of Theophilus Cibber, who preceded Garrick in the role and to whom his Drugger was sometimes compared.[15] Rather than "restore" the original balance to the play or attempt to dignify it—as he had **Macbeth** as well as **Every Man in His Humor**—by curtailing lowly figures and focusing on the follies of the higher classes, he instead capitalized upon one of **The Alchemist**'s most vulgar roles. Indeed, over the decades, as the play became a staple of Garrick's theater, Drugger's dialogue and stage "business" expanded. In all, he gave Drugger 28 additional speeches, many of them lines so insubstantial and exclamatory—"Oh, fie for shame, Captain" (I.392), "Yes, very strange" (I.427) "Will ye?" (I.471), "I don't understand it ... And so it is ... Captain Face, Captain Face, your worship" (II.617-35), "Is he? ... Has he? ... Will he?" (II.685-92) "Yes, what is it? ... Ay; what is it?" (III.232-40)—that they provide little more than wind for the performer's histrionics. At least one contemporary spectator found no line more memorable in Garrick's production than Drugger's exclamation, "My name!" an insertion of Garrick's (II.625), made just after Subtle advises him to construct a sign outside his shop whose pictorial symbols will spell out the words "Abel Drugger." The spectator reports that Garrick spoke his line while "hugging his delight to himself for a few moments, so that he actually gets those red rings round his eyes which often accompany great joy."[16]

To give time and space for those red rings to emerge, Garrick cut the play by about a third, omitting almost 1000 lines and eliminating character speeches at their most revealing and expository.[17] He removed anything that might steal Drugger's fire. He struck scores of Subtle's lines, virtuoso displays of alchemical expertise. He pared down Dapper in Acts I and V, Mammon in Acts II and IV, Tribulation and Ananias in Act III, sequences which expose the humors of these characters most powerfully.

And to great success. "The history of **The Alchemist**," writes Noyes, "was virtually the history of the rôle of Abel Drugger, about whom, I believe, more was written up to Garrick's death than about any other comic character except Falstaff" (103). With Drugger, and Garrick, at the center of the play, Jonson's comedy became a vehicle for a player rather than for a company, and by extension, a society.

And the metamorphosis of **The Alchemist** continued. Toward the end of Garrick's career, Drugger became such a popular figure that in the early 1770s, characters called Drugger began to appear in original playlets. These appearances were due in great part to the popularity of the actor Thomas Weston, who began to impersonate Drugger alternately with Garrick when the impresario reached his later years. Francis Gentleman's *The Pantheonites* (1773), which concerns the foolish fantasy life of an eighteenth-century descendant of Drugger's, and Weston's declamatory speech, *Abel Drugger's Return from the Fête Champêtre*

at Marybone Gardens (1774)[18] were liberated entirely from the plot of **The Alchemist.** But the most telling of such trifles was Gentleman's *The Tobacconist*. This two act afterpiece premiered in 1770 and held the stage long after performances of **The Alchemist** in any other form had ceased, which they did shortly after Garrick's retirement in 1776. In the Romantic period, the only version of *The Alchemist* an audience could have seen on the professional stage was this one, and when Edmund Kean played Drugger in 1815, he read Gentleman's lines, not Jonson's.

To compare these several versions of *The Alchemist* is to study an aesthetic that is being drained of its variety and vastness. Garrick and Gentleman wring the enormity of the Jonsonian humor from his characters' diction, tying a rein around the turbulent structure of his drama.

Parallel examples from the texts of each version will demonstrate the extent to which the play's language was watered down. In Act II of Jonson's *Alchemist,* Mammon anticipates the day when the schemers' science will at last produce the stone that will enable him to work magical transformations and turn base metal into gold. Consumed by the desire to dominate all others, the knight fantasizes elaborately about drowning himself in narcissistic luxury. This magnificent passage is worth quoting in full, so that we can see in detail what Garrick and Gentleman do to it:

> I will have all my beds blown up, not stuffed:
> Down is too hard. And then mine oval room
> Filled with such pictures as Tiberius took
> From Elephantis, and dull Aretine
> But coldly imitated. Then, my glasses
> Cut in more subtle angles, to disperse
> And multiply the figures as I walk
> Naked between my succubae. My mists
> I'll have of perfume, vapoured 'bout the room,
> To loose our selves in; and my baths like pits
> To fall into; from whence we will come forth
> And roll us dry in gossamer and roses.—
> Is it arrived at ruby?—Where I spy
> A wealthy citizen, or rich lawyer,
> Have a sublimed pure wife, unto that fellow
> I'll send a thousand pound to be my cuckold.

FACE:

> And I shall carry it?

MAMMON:

> No. I'll ha' no bawds
> But fathers and mothers. They will do it best.
> Best of all others. And my flatterers
> Shall be the pure and gravest of divines,
> That I can get for money. My mere fools,
> Eloquent burgesses; and then my poets
> The same that writ so subtly of the fart,
> Whom I will entertain, still, for that subject.
> The few that would give out themselves to be
> Court and town-stallions, and each where belie
> Ladies who are known most innocent, for them,
> These will I beg to make me eunuchs of,

And they shall fan me with ten ostrich tails
Apiece, made in a plume to gather wind.
We will be brave, Puff, now we ha' the med'cine.
My meat shall all come in in Indian shells,
Dishes of agate, set in gold, and studded,
With emeralds, sapphires, hyacinths, and rubies.
The tongues of carps, dormice, and camels' heels,
Boiled i' the spirit of Sol, and dissolved pearl
(Apicius's diet, against the epilepsy)
And I will eat these broths with spoons of amber,
Headed with diamond and carbuncle.
My footboy shall eat pheasants, calvered salmons,
Knots, godwits, lampreys. I myself will have
The beards of barbels, served instead of salads;
Oiled mushrooms; and the swelling unctous paps
Of a fat pregnant sow, newly cut off,
Dressed with an exquisite and poignant sauce;
For which, I'll say unto my cook, "There's gold,
Go forth, and be a knight."

(II.ii. 41-87)[19]

Many of Jonson's characters talk hyperbolically, but this speech holds a special place in his *oeuvre* and indeed in English theatrical history. Even William Hazlitt, who read Jonson with notorious distaste, declared that these lines are "the finest example I know of dramatic sophistry."[20] In them, the play uncovers the luxuriance of Mammon's imagination and satirizes its mad impossibility, the corruption of an outrageously greedy mind. After hearing this diatribe, audience members will be hard pressed to forget those broken mirrors Mammon means to set up so that he can multiply the image of himself walking among his lovers. Equally memorable are the obscene poets he will command to entertain and possibly pimp for him and the dishes he intends to have prepared from unconventional parts of uncommon animals. Mammon will lift his attendants into higher classes and pay the parents of his young lovers such inordinate sums to bed their daughters that they'll be happy to pander them. No one else in the play could, or does, speak like this. With these words, Mammon not only distinguishes his greed from that of the play's other figures, but also adds to *The Alchemist*'s magnificently multifaceted catalogue of bloated imaginations.

In his version, Garrick preserves the greedy parents, the elevated servants, some of the dishes, and a few pieces of fancy cutlery, but leaves out the highlights. He mows Mammon down at his most hilarious, extracting the exacting sensuality that might overshadow Drugger's less articulate gestures and grimaces. Here is what the speech becomes:

I will have all my beds blown up, not stuffed;
Down is too hard.
(Is it arrived at ruby?)—Where I spy
A wealthy citizen or a rich lawyer
Have a sublimed pure wife, unto that fellow
I'll send a thousand pounds to be my cuckold.

FACE:

And shall I carry it?

MAMMON:

No, I'll have no bawds,
But fathers and mothers. They will do it best,
Best of all others. And my flatterers
Shall be the pure, and gravest of divines
That I can get for money, my meet fools
Eloquent burgesses.
We will be brave, Puffe, now we have the med'cine.
My meat shall all come in in Indian shells,
Dishes of agate set in gold and studded
With emeralds, saphirs, hyacinths, and rubies.
My foot-boy shall eat pheasants, calvered salmons,
Knots, goldwits, lampreys. I myself will have
The beards of barbels served instead of salads;
Oiled mushrooms
Dressed with an exquisite and poignant sauce,
For which, I'll say unto my cook, "There's gold;
Go forth and be a knight."

(II. 114-37)

Turning 46 lines into 23 (and some of these but half lines), Garrick manages to retain the gist of Mammon's dreams: he will be pampered; he will have a harem; he will dole out rewards to those who serve him. But though the words that remain were all written by Jonson, their effect is softer, less manic than the original. Importantly, Garrick's cuts are not all for the sake of his audience's allegedly refined sensibilities. He does strike distasteful words like "paps" and "fart," but retains the speech's most potentially shocking ideas: Garrick's Mammon still pays parents to pimp their daughters; landowners and clergymen, equally enthralled by the showers of gold he rains upon them, fall adoringly at his feet.

Still, Mammon's lasciviousness, the pleasure he takes in coddling himself, the egotism which wishes to blot out any other authority, is seriously diminished. The fantastic heights of fancy which distinguish his greedy egotism from that of the Puritans, Kastril, Subtle, Face, and the others, which make him unique as well as unforgettable, have been removed. So have the grandest opportunities the actor playing Mammon might have to hug himself with the joys of his fantasies, as we know Garrick's Drugger did. When Mammon, toward the end of this play, utters his succinct lament—"O, my voluptuous mind!"[21]—his words have far less resonance than they do in Jonson.[22] With the play's humors reduced in order to highlight a single character's idiosyncrasies, it is not surprising that the very audiences who were losing interest in Jonson's lengthy and highly referential playtexts were amused by this production.

The Tobacconist's version of this speech deviates from Jonson's text entirely, crushing it into bare summary:

Well, after this day, all that art can frame, or luxury can desire, is mine; I'll have a seraglio, to put the grand seignior's out of countenance; for where's that beauty can withstand a knight of gold?—my very slaves shall live on such viands as monarchs now call rarities.

(23-24)

Gentleman's adaptation pales before the least accurate memorial reconstruction of any Renaissance "bad" quarto—and Gentleman could have held Jonson's text before him as he wrote! In the adaptations, Mammon is a saner, more tolerable, and less disturbing creature than he is in Jonson. Following the lead of Garrick's changes, Gentleman's version forbids him and his audience from reveling in the blind hunger of his humor, from indulging an omnivorous fantasy in intense tactile detail.

Garrick was of course writing for a stage over which he had more technical control than Jonson. He would have been able to direct the performance of the actor playing Mammon as Jonson never could. In Garrick, the unveiling of a character's persona relies, as the expansion of Drugger's role suggests, more on the performer than on dialogue. The adaptation thus marks a colossal shift in theatrical convention from Jonson's time to Garrick's, the de-emphasis of language in favor of stagecraft. It comes as no surprise that in Garrick's best known discussion of the challenges of acting Drugger, he does not discuss the delivery of dialogue but the dropping of a urinal, a piece of stage business he inherited from Theophilus Cibber.[23]

By the same token, Garrick seemed determined to rely on his technicians, rather than Jonson's diction, to create a sensational effect.[24] For example, in Act IV, after Mammon fails to seduce Dol Common, a great crack is heard, signifying that the alchemical efforts on his behalf have gone up in flames. Garrick has Face say,

> Oh, Sir, we are defeated; all the works
> Are flown *in fumo*:
> Retorts, receivers, pellicanes, bolt-heads
> All struck in shivers.

> (IV.ii.68-71)

In Jonson, the lines read,

> O sir, we are defeated! All the works
> Are flown *in fumo,* every glass is burst.
> Furnace and all rent down, as if a bolt
> Of thunder had been driven through the house.
> Retorts, receivers, pelicans, bolt-heads,
> All struck in shivers!

> (IV.v.64-69)

Garrick may have felt no need for Jonson's bursting glass, rent furnaces, and bolt of thunder, but the absent lines do more than merely offer a verbal substitute for a great sound. They also demonstrate how well Face understands his patsy. It is likely that Face tailored his apocalyptic description both to persuade and to humiliate a figure who carries a heroic sense of his own worth and imagines himself as a kind of demented epic hero. Just as Garrick deboned Mammon, he also incinerated this additional dimension of Face's character.

Garrick's and Gentleman's changes further simplify Jonson's characters by eliminating passages that might complicate audience sympathies. Perhaps because it is Face who will oust his partners in the end, Garrick chose to elevate him over them, making him more sympathetic and therefore more worthy of his concluding triumph. In the comedy's first scene, Face and Subtle quarrel, each insisting that he has done the other a service by bringing him into a con-game that made him rich. Garrick retains almost all of Face's harangue, where he recalls discovering Subtle starving in the street, his alchemical quackery earning nothing until he entered Lovewit's house (Jonson I.i.24-49; Garrick I.33-58). Yet he preserves only three of Subtle's 38 line riposte regarding Face's corresponding wretchedness before the two teamed up (Jonson I.i.49-87; Garrick I.61-63). Bleeding Subtle (who loses more lines than any other character in the play) of his equal standing in the quarrel, Garrick makes Face's conclusive cozening of his partners more morally defensible, more poetically just, than it is in Jonson.[25]

While he retains Dol's mention of the "venter tripartite" (Jonson I.i.135; Garrick I.103), the term loses much of its meaning in the adaptation. Dol's interventions in this scene are also snipped; her telling and politically pointed line about avoiding "civil war" (I.i.82) has been removed. Gentleman summarizes a bit of Subtle's self-defense, but the opening spat lasts only a few speeches and "Doll Tricksey" is not even present for most of it. Garrick cuts Dol's warning that she will abandon the quarrelers if they don't make up and Gentleman has her cry that she will turn them in to the authorities if they don't "live peaceably" and "cheat industriously."[26] This threat sounds absurd; if she ratted on her comrades, she would almost certainly be jailed as well, rather than rewarded, as she predicts. Gentleman's nonsensical addition does little more than invoke the power of outside political forces that Jonson's text makes less central and foreboding,[27] further limiting the scope of the con artists' power and ambition.

The "tripartite" relationship is not the only one that becomes polarized in the adaptations. Surly, the "gamester" who accompanies Mammon into Lovewit's house, has a personality that suits his name, but Garrick eradicates many of his rancorous tendencies. In Jonson and Garrick, it is good of Surly to refuse to debauch Dame Pliant after the sharpers shut them in together, but Garrick removes his unkind admonition: "Y'are a handsome woman; would you were wise too!" (IV.vi.7). In the same scene, he lifts most of Surly's vicious invective against Face. The result is an elevation of Pliant's deliverer into a more gallant figure than he is in Jonson. Gentleman removes the characters of Surly and Pliant entirely, along with any hint of rescue and romance that might add generic confusion to his rigidly straightforward farce.

Garrick's paring of Dapper's part is one of his most pardonable decisions; if the play must be cut, this least interesting of the gulls is probably the most expendable. But by extracting so much, particularly in Act V, Garrick removes an element of Jonsonian plot construction crucial to his work: the development and resolution of intrigue even during the denouement. The commencement of a new trial in *Volpone,* the masquerade of Otter and Cutbeard in *Epicoene,* the puppet show in *Bartholomew Fair* are all executed in the fifth act, defying more modern conventions of rising action, climax, and conclusion. In Jonson's *Alchemist,* it is astonishing that, even as Lovewit and the play's victims are knocking at the door, Subtle and Dol, dressed as the Queen of Fairy, continue to toy with Dapper, and just for the fun of it. They have already taken his money. In Garrick, the two hustle him out of the house quickly, thus allowing the action to cruise more gently to a stop. Gentleman, again following the potential Garrick's changes created, loses interest in Subtle and Doll toward the end of the play, allowing Drugger to enlarge business Garrick added to his role in Act IV and physically assault the quarrelsome Kastril and other figures in the house. In the end, Gentleman concentrates almost exclusively on the pact between Face and "Knowlife" (Gentleman's Lovewit, who enters just minutes before the end of the play) and a concluding speech and rhymed ditty of Drugger's, where he condemns alchemy and marriage and then begs for the audience's applause.

Garrick's and Gentleman's devotion to a neater, less dynamic play includes the transformation of Dol Common from the autonomous and powerful figure she is in Jonson into a lowbrow and servile tool of the males. As we have already seen with reference to Mammon and despite his critical reputation, Garrick does not always remove sexually explicit dialogue. In fact, he retains many Jonsonian vulgarities. For example, he holds on to the nudity and buttocks jokes in Face's opening tirade (Jonson I.i.33 37; Garrick I.42-46) as well as Subtle's teasing remarks to Dame Pliant to the effect that she is melancholy because suffering post-coital depression after bedding Surly (Jonson IV.vi.20-24; Garrick IV.iii.19-23). And while Garrick plucks out Face's assertion that Dol has the power to "milk" Mammon's "epididymis" (III.iii.22), he lets stand the bawdy innuendo that suggests her sexual malleability at the hands of the pimps who control her. According to Face, Dol is "*our* castle, *our* cinque port, / *Our* Dover pier, *our* what thou wilt" (Jonson III.iii.18-19; Garrick III.109-10; italics mine). When Face sets her upon Mammon, Garrick has no problem retaining his pander-like goading: "To him, Dol, suckle him" (Jonson IV.i.32; Garrick IV.i.27). Garrick is happy to preserve the men's confidence that if they cannot make gold, they can at least coin Dol's attractions into a fortune for themselves.

But he silences them and Dol whenever anyone mentions *her* ability to master others by manipulating them with her body and mind. Gone is the passage where Subtle claims Dol will dominate Mammon, having her way with him as

he is thrown helplessly before her on a huge down bed (III.iii.41-49). Absent too is Face's faith in her sensual versatility when it relies on her own will. He claims, in Jonson, that she can, with regards to Mammon, "firk like a flounder; kiss like a scallop, close; / And tickle him with thy mother-tongue" (III.iii.69-70). Garrick eliminates Face's notation of Dol's great strength: when he prepares Mammon to meet her, he warns him that if she should go into her fit, "six men will not hold her down" (IV.i.11). Also lopped are references to Dol's intellect, her ability to discourse on "physic, or mathematics, / Poetry, state, or bawdry" (IV.i.15-16). Predictably, Garrick does not permit Mammon to go into a rapturous outburst inspired by her beauty, which climaxes with his greedily lustful desire that together they will "*concumbre* gold" (IV.i.30). Also removed is Face's very funny line about how seeing Dol as a great lady is a kind of "modern happiness" (IV.i.23), a joke that pays tribute to the brilliance with which she appeals to and deceives her customers.

This suggestive bawdry is not as sexually explicit as the dialogue Garrick retains. But in cutting it, Garrick does further his project of diminishing the equality of the triumvirate and of domesticating female autonomy. In Gentleman's even more chaste version, Doll Tricksey finds her admirers irritating. Unlike her earlier incarnation, she fears that Headlong (Gentleman's Kastril) may beat her when they meet. At one point, she admits that she is mentally inferior to Mammon: "Sir Epicure . . . batters my ears with such pomposity of phrase, that I should always have a dictionary at hand to understand him" (16). This speech turns Jonson directly on his head, for in the original it is Dol who, in her mock insanity, speaks with such high allusiveness that Mammon cannot follow her.

As Dol's intellectual capacities dwindle from adaptation to adaptation, her prudishness increases. Jonson's Mammon puts Dol Common into her fit because he "talked / Of a fifth monarchy I would erect / With the philosopher's stone, by chance, and she / Falls on the other four straight" (IV.v.33-36). Garrick removes this passage, which attests to her learning, and cuts most of her ravings. In Gentleman, Doll's paroxysm takes the form of a chastisement that makes her sound like a third rate imitation of the mad Ophelia—and just because poor Mammon offered to kiss her![28] Gentleman's Doll is a dull coward, a pedestrian witness whose principal occupation, like most of the play's other characters, is to give the actor playing Drugger a breather.

On the whole, the adaptive energies of Gentleman and Garrick import convention into an unconventional play. They insist that Jonsonian tensions, merrymaking, and extravagance must be toned down or eliminated in order to please eighteenth-century tastes. Garrick and Gentleman may have believed that to make an old comedy newly popular with audiences, they must satisfy the refined appetites of their contemporaries. But we ought to note that Garrick began acting **The Alchemist** six years after the passage of the Licensing Act of 1737, which restricted London dramas almost entirely to two theaters, subjected it to government censure, and effectively barred playwrights like Henry Fielding from presenting more of their experimental, politically savage, and often popular works on the stage.

Fielding expressed open disappointment with the tame fare that was applauded in the theater. He articulated his frustration in the preface to a translation of Aristophanes's *Plutus,* which he and William Young adapted in 1742. It was one of his very last works to take dramatic form, though it was written for the closet rather than the stage.

Introducing the play, Fielding invited his audience to think in the neoclassical terms that he associated not only with Aristophanes but also with Jonson. He shaped his critique of contemporary theater as an assault against Colley Cibber, who preceded Garrick as one of the managers of Drury Lane and took the role of Subtle in the early decades of the century. Cibber, who also adapted earlier dramas, falls under Fielding's lash because he favors "pretty, dapper, brisk, smart, pert Dialogue" rather than the simple style of earlier writers. In his critique, Fielding recommends Jonson as an antidote for the mild repartee to which dramatic audiences have become accustomed:

> This sort of stuff, which is, I think, called genteel comedy, in which our laureate succeeded so excellently well as both author and actor, had some years ago taken almost sole possession of our stage, and banished Shakespeare, Fletcher, Jonson, &c. from it; the last of whom, of all our English poets, seems chiefly to have studied and imitated Aristophanes ... To such therefore of our readers, whose palates are vitiated with the theatrical diet I have above-mentioned, I would recommend a play or two of Jonson's, to be taken as a kind of preparative before they enter on this play; for otherwise the simplicity of style, for want of being sweetened with modern quaintness, may, like old wine after sugar-plumbs, appear insipid, and without any flavor. But our readers of a purer taste and sounder judgment, will be able, we apprehend, to digest good sense, manly wit, just satire, and true humor, without those garnishments which we could with infinitely greater ease have supplied (as others have done) in the room of our author's meaning, than have preferred it in his own plain simplicity of style.[29]

Fielding asserts that contemporary audiences have developed such an appetite for sweets that they no longer savor them as something that enhances a repast, but rather crave them as a main course. He contrasts the "simple" style, which he associates with Aristophanes, Jonson, and himself, to "genteel comedy," which he claims has dulled the dramatic tastebuds of contemporary audiences.[30] The sweet tooth of theatergoers sinks into "garnishments," distracting elaborations that Fielding asserts are a hallmark of lesser writers. By asserting the triumvirate of Renaissance playwrights, whom John Dryden had earlier associated

with "the giant race, before the flood,"[31] over Cibber's brand of comedy, Fielding claims to prefer punchingly direct, open satire to the niceties of expression and empty wit he associates with the eighteenth-century's diluted inheritance of Restoration comedy.[32]

In his preface, Fielding admits that while he had to take some liberties in translating Aristophanes, an adapter must avoid allowing his language to become corrupted by the mild rambling that passes for modern cleverness. What he says about translation may also apply to Garrick's theories of adaptation, at least with reference to Jonson. While Fielding and Garrick "enjoyed each other's company and admired each other's talents,"[33] Fielding was far more impressed with Garrick the actor than he was with the adapter.[34] Under Fielding's definition, Garrick's additions and omissions rob the text of the open, forceful satire that he, delightfully, associates with simplicity. For Fielding, Jonson's simplicity lies not in his brevity but in his directness, the specifics of language and character that Garrick took pains to mute.

In their place, we have "garnishments" in the form of windy additions and stage business: Drugger huffing Garrick's vacuous lines; Drugger hugging himself with delight; Drugger dropping the urinal; Drugger beating Kastril. Such "business," when it overshadows the stagecraft in the text, serves the same distracting purpose Fielding found in Cibber's innuendo: it celebrates crowd-pleasing antics over the "sense, wit, satire, and humor" enjoyed by audiences "of a purer taste and sounder judgment." Much had changed between the ages of Jonson and Fielding, but, for better or worse, each claimed a willingness to be martyred in the battle between playwrights who make noble use of edgy satire and audiences more eager to be tickled than scourged.[35]

It is significant that the only passages of Jonson's Drugger that Garrick cut are those in the last act of the play, where his ignominious entrance and exit must have felt like anticlimax after the bellows Garrick applied to the role. For scholars who read *The Alchemist* as social satire as well as those who see the play in grand metaphorical terms—as a revisionist morality play, a disquisition upon plague years, a treatise on early modern conceptions of republic and monarchy, a discourse upon wisdom and science, a self-conscious diatribe on the tenuousness and risk of theatrical productions[36]—Garrick's and Gentleman's drive to rid the play of ambiguity and danger grinds such notions to powder, preserving Jonsonian drama in their century only because they dilute the potent aspects of his work for which he wished to be remembered and for which he is still studied today.

Notes

1. Discussions of how Jonson's fall corresponded to Shakespeare's rise are numerous. See, for example,

Barish, 1-13; Craig, "Introduction," 9-37; Donaldson, 162-97.

2. "The chief problems encountered by Garrick in altering *The Alchemist* to suit the eighteenth-century stage were the necessity of cutting down the playing time of this enormous comedy, of eliminating Jonson's references to contemporary persons and events long since forgotten, of omitting technical details of alchemy which would no longer be interesting to the audience, and of scrubbing up the Jacobean diction no longer considered fit for the nice ears of Garrick's public—and all this without spoiling the superb unity and coherence of the plot ... Garrick's achievement is that he was able to reduce the length of the play by more than one-third, and to do this by trimming, not butchering" (Pedicord and Bergmann, vol. 5, 320). (Hereafter, this edition will be cited as P&B.)

In his introduction to the Revels edition of *The Alchemist,* F. H. Mares says Garrick's adaptation "is in the main a careful abridgement. No characters are lost, and the intrigue is preserved clear in all its complexities" (lxviii). Garrick biographer Ian MacIntyre is equally forgiving, noting that in contending with *The Alchemist* Garrick had to simplify "the complications of the plot" and delete "some of Jonson's more sexual and scatological passages" (69). Of the critics who have discussed Garrick's *Alchemist* over the last century, Robert Gayle Noyes is the most severe, observing rightly that the adapter destroyed "much of the literary greatness of the satire and ruined the greatest character, Sir Epicure Mammon." But even he asserts that "the alteration was ... on the whole, dramatically more compact and more modern" (146).

Alvin Kernan offers some insight into the gentle assessment of these scholars when he notes that *The Alchemist* "is still played rather infrequently for despite its obvious greatness it is a most difficult play to perform on the modern stage, and actors and directors are always forced to make some adjustment in the play's language and to its obscure allusions if its vitality and ultimate power are to be successfully conveyed" (244).

As I will argue, Garrick sacrifices the play's vitality and its power in his skeletal adaptation.

3. Garrick collapsed the plots of *Cymbeline*'s first three acts and rewrote the fourth and fifth. In 1756, he adapted *The Tempest* into an opera, as he had *A Midsummer Night's Dream* the year before. The texts were drastically cut and many songs added. When the operatic version of *The Tempest* failed, he quickly moved to put a more faithful version on the stage, to much greater success (P&B III, 444).

4. For the information here and in the two surrounding paragraphs, I am indebted to the excellent and informative texts and notes of Pedicord and Bergmann, particularly *Lear* (III, 306-90; 443-52), *Antony and Cleopatra* (IV, 7-92; 395-401), *Florizel and Perdita* (III, 227-66; 431-35), *Catharine and Petruchio* (193-220; 427-30), *Romeo and Juliet* (III, 82-149, 406-13; see also Copeland, *passim*) and *Macbeth* (III, 5-74; 398-402).

5. Garrick's *Hamlet* (which Pedicord and Bergmann cover in IV, 245-323; 431-37), is a special and complex case. For much of his career, Garrick relied heavily on earlier revisions, as his 1751 and 1763 playtexts attest. The truncation of the play he published in 1773 restores hundreds of lines in the first three acts but severely condenses the fourth and fifth. It was quite controversial. See Burnim, 153-65 and Jeffrey Lawson Laurence Johnson, *passim.*

6. Garrick's *Lear* grew from Tate's. When he took on the role in 1742 (at the age of 24), he performed Tate's text, gradually adding more Shakespearean lines over time. By 1756, he advertised that he would act a version he had "restored." Garrick's rendition, which he probably continued to "restore" after 1756, was published in 1773. For a brief history and summary of the analysis done on Garrick's *Lear,* see Freeman, 11.

> 'Tis done! the scene of my life will quickly close.
> Ambition's vain, delusive dreams are fled,
> And now I wake to darkness, guilt, and horror;
> I cannot bear it! let me shake it off—
> 'Tw'o not be; my soul is clogg'd with blood—
> I cannot rise! I dare not ask for mercy—
> It is too late, hell drags me down; I sink,
> I sink—Oh!—my soul is lost for ever!
> Oh!
>
> [*Dies*]

7. (This citation is from Vickers, 34.)

8. In the strolling drolls of the Interregnum, which featured probably the first truncations of *The Alchemist,* an adapter did just that, turning scenes with Drugger and Ananias into a short playlet called "The Imperick" (see Elson, 229-36).

9. See Noyes, particularly his chronology of Jonson's plays in performance, pp. 319-33.

10. It would not be superseded until William Gifford's edition of 1816.

11. See, particularly, Whalley's half-hearted defense of the Jonsonian humor, which he applies not to all humankind but only to the low classes, for whom he registers contempt. See also his admission that much of Jonson's satire is outdated, modern civilization having grown beyond the primitive appetites of the figures he lampoons (pp. xix and xvi).

12. For commentaries on Garrick's revision, see Noyes, 258-65; P&B VI, 364-73. Interestingly, when Charles Dickens acted in *Every Man in His Humor* a century later, he played Bobadill (John Forster acted Kitely), shifting the emphasis of the text toward the low comedy that Garrick showcased in *The Alchemist*. See Edgar Johnson, 301-02.

13. Thomas Wilkes, a friend of Garrick's, observed that the "main design" of *Every Man in His Humor* "is to cure a wrong-headed husband of a ridiculous, ill-grounded jealousy; we never lose sight of the husband and wife through the whole Play, until we find them made friends, and the husband cured of his folly in the catastrophe" (Craig 483). In fact, there are plenty of scenes in Garrick's adaptation that do not concern Kitely or his plot, but the strength of Garrick's performance seems to have emphasized Kitely's concerns over all others.

14. See P&B V, 318. *The Imperick* does not pretend to adapt the whole of *The Alchemist* and takes fewer liberties with Jonson's text than Garrick.

15. See Noyes, 121-22 and 132-33; Craig, 483-84.

16. See Georg Christoph Lichtenberg's review in Craig, 533.

17. See P&B V, 320-321. For further commentary on the revision of *The Alchemist,* see 318-26 and Noyes, 143-53.

18. See Craig, 27 and Noyes, 153-61. Gentleman made something of a career in mutilating Jonson. He adapted *Sejanus* in 1752 and *Epicoene,* as *The Coxcombs,* in 1771.

19. Citations from *The Alchemist* are from Kernan's edition.

20. Hazlitt VI, 45.

21. Jonson, IV.v.82; Garrick, IV.ii.87.

22. In Gentleman, Mammon promises personal reform that is foreign to both Jonson and Garrick: "Ooons, if this be the case, I'll never trust the stars again, and every man that speaks a hard word, in my mind shall be a cheat" (Gentleman 42).

23. The passage, from Garrick's *Essay on Acting,* is cited in Craig, 406 and McIntyre, 70.

24. Anne Barton declares that "*The Alchemist* is the funniest play Jonson ever wrote" in part because it "stands out from the rest of his work for the number of bizarre and hilarious stage situations it invents" (142). Garrick, mistrusting the comic potential of these very situations, emphasizes spectacle at the expense of the play's other qualities.

25. The error of giving Face moral prominence over Subtle has alas become something of a theatrical tradition, as recent accounts continue to attest. See, for example, Peter Happé's review of a 1996 production of the play (182-84).

26. Here, in full, is the cap to Dol's speech which Garrick removes:

> 'Sdeath, you perpetual curs,
> Fall to your couples again, and cozen kindly,
> And heartily, and lovingly, as you should,
> And lose not the beginning of a term,
> Or, by this hand, I shall grow factious too,
> And take my part and quit you.

(I.i.136-41)

Gentleman substitutes the dialogue of the scene with the following:

> You sputter at one another, and yet have as little courage as honesty; I know your high words and big looks; you spend your lungs to bawl, and strain your limbs to stride, without any meaning ... Ads my life, shake hands, live peaceably, and cheat industriously, or tremble at my vengeance; I'll expose ye—get a genteel reward for apprehending such notorious rogues.

(14)

27. Ian Donaldson, commenting upon the closed space of the play's action, notes that the sharpers constantly remind one another to speak softly, lest they be overheard. "A single cry might suffice to destroy the conspiracy." But while the visitors to the house fear and call upon officers of the law, the cozening triad seem more concerned with their potentially meddling neighbors and the gulls waiting in other rooms who, overhearing, might learn they are being tricked (75). See also Barton, 142-43. In Jonson, when Dol warns her companions that she may leave them, she cries, "I'll not be made a prey unto the marshal" (I.i.120). But her wariness of political authority is a very small piece of the original author's cosmos. Gentleman enlarges it.

David Bevington remarks that in this play's world, "the satirist reigns supreme, unchallenged by any authority figures of law and order" (85).

28. "Thy cousins, Etna and Vesuvius, vomit not combustibles more destructive than are winged on thy infectious breath—come, if thou hast courage, I'll lead the way from off the sky-crowned rock, and headlong plunge into yon roaring deep—thou tremblest—guilt makes a coward of thee, and thou must remain a prey to self-consuming flames; while white-winged doves wait to bear me to the fields of bliss, where such as thou can never, never come" (28).

29. Fielding and Young, *xii.* The passage is also cited in Craig, 400.

30. Fielding cites Cibber and Vanbrugh's *The Provoked Husband* as an example of how theatrical dialogue has "denigrated into ... pleasantry" (*xi*). Yet it is Richard Steele who claimed, in *The Spectator* no. 65, that with *The Conscious Lovers* he had arrived at the "Pattern of Gentile Comedy" (see Kenny, 24 and 22-37 *passim*).

31. See his dedicatory poem to Congreve's *The Double-Dealer*, l. 5 (in Dryden, 455).

32. Fielding's phrase "genteel comedy" should be distinguished from "sentimental comedy," the more common generic designation applied to the work of Cibber and his successors. The latter term would not come into full vogue until after Goldsmith published his "Essay on the Theater" in 1772 where the author in fact praised "the laughing, and even low comedy, which seems to have been last exhibited by Vanbrugh and Cibber." In the preface to *Plutus*, Fielding shows small interest in denouncing what Goldsmith calls "weeping sentimental comedy ... in which the virtues of private life are exhibited, rather than the vices exposed." The gentility he attacks is a gentility of language. See Hynes for an interesting overview of the critical controversies that surround the genre.

33. Battestin, 363.

34. This point is driven home in the famous interchanges between Garrick and Fielding during Garrick's rehearsals and production of Fielding's *The Wedding-Day*, the only one of his works that premiered in his lifetime after the Licensing Act of 1737. For this 1743 production, Arthur Murphy, in his *Life of David Garrick*, reports that Fielding would not bow to Garrick's keener sense of what audiences were willing to tolerate and allow select lines to be cut. For discussions of Murphy's anecdote and this failed production's impact on both figures' careers, see Battestin, 361-63 and McIntyre, 66.

35. Harry Levin concludes that Jonson, enlarging upon Cicero's reputed definition of comedy as the imitation of life, the mirror of custom, and the image of truth, added "the metaphor of a scourge" in his early comedies (129). While Levin claims that Jonson was later in his career "more successful when he gave up his didactic asperity for good-natured realism" (130), the sharp satire that remained in Jonson's mature work must have appealed to Fielding, who, fitting himself within the camp and tradition of both Aristophanes and Jonson, eagerly directed his own comic spirit to lean, as occasion demanded, toward geniality or savagery.

36. For examples of such analyses, see, respectively, Riggs, 172 ("In its broad outline, *The Alchemist* resembles an old fashioned morality play"); Ross, *passim*; Sanders, 68-88; Barton, 136-53; Donaldson, 82 ("The theater in the "Blackfriars . . . [and] Lovewit's house . . . are in fact the same house, and the charlatans who arouse and exploit the fantasies of their victims are [when all is said and done] members of the company of the King's Men, who use similar arts to somewhat similar ends").

Works Cited

Barish, Jonas. "Introduction." *Ben Jonson: A Collection of Critical Essays.* Ed. Barish. Englewood Cliffs, New Jersey: Prentice Hall, 1963. 1-13.

Barton, Anne. *Ben Jonson: Dramatis.* Cambridge: Cambridge UP, 1984.

Battestin, Martin C. with Ruthe R. Battestin. *Henry Fielding: A Life.* London: Routledge, 1989.

Bevington, David. "The Major Comedies." *The Cambridge Companion to Ben Jonson,* Eds. Richard Harp and Stanley Stewart. Cambridge: Cambridge UP, 2000.

Burnim, Kalman A. *David Garrick: Director.* Pittsburgh: U of Pittsburgh P, 1961.

Copeland, Nancy. "The Sentimentality of Garrick's *Romeo and Juliet*." *Restoration and Eighteenth-Century Theatre Research,* 2d ser, IV, no. 2 (Fall/Winter, 1989), 1-13.

Craig, D. H., ed. *Ben Jonson: The Critical Heritage.* London: Routledge, 1990.

Donaldson, Ian. *Jonson's Magic Houses.* Oxford: Clarendon, 1997.

Dryden, John. *The Major Works.* Ed. Keith Walker. Oxford: Oxford UP, 2003.

Elson, John James, ed. *The Wits: Or, Sport Upon Sport.* Ithaca: Cornell UP, 1932.

Fielding, Henry and William Young. *Plutus: The God of Riches.* London: T. Waller, 1742.

Freeman, John. "Beyond Bombast: David Garrick's Performances of Benedick and King Lear." *Restoration and Eighteenth-Century Theatre Research,* 2d ser., XIV, no. 2 (Winter, 1999), 1-21.

Gentleman, Francis. *The Tobacconist; A Farce.* Boston: Wells and Lilly, 1823.

Happè, Peter. "*The Alchemist* and *Le Bourgeois Gentilhomme*: Folly and Theatrical Illusion." *The Ben Jonson Journal* 4 (1997), 181-86.

Hazlitt, William. *The Complete Works of William Hazlitt.* Ed. P. P. Howe. 20 vol. London: J. W. Dent and Sons, Ltd., 1920.

Hynes, Peter. "Richard Steele and the Genealogy of Sentimental Drama." *Papers on Language and Literature,* 40, no. 2 (Spring 2004), 142-65.

Johnson, Edgar. *Charles Dickens: His Tragedy and Triumph.* Harmondsworth: Penguin, 1977.

Johnson, Jeffrey Lawson Laurence. "Sweeping up Shakespeare's 'Rubbish': Garrick's Condensation of Acts IV and V of *Hamlet.*" *Eighteenth Century Life* VIII, n.s., no. 3, (May 1983), 14-25.

Kenny, Shirley Straum. "Richard Steele and the 'Pattern of Genteel Comedy.'" *Modern Philology* 70, no. 1 (August 1972), 22-37.

Kernan, Alvin B. "Introduction." In Ben Jonson. *The Alchemist.* New Haven. Yale UP, 1974. Citations from the text of *The Alchemist* are from this edition.

Harry Levin. "Notes toward a Definition of City Comedy." *Renaissance Genres.* Ed. Barbara Kiefer Lewalski. Cambridge, MA: Harvard UP, 1986. 126-46.

Mares, F. H. "Introduction." In Ben Jonson, *The Alchemist.* Cambridge, MA: Harvard UP, 1967.

MacIntyre, Ian. *Garrick.* Harmondsworth: Penguin, 1999.

Noyes, Robert Gayle. *Ben Jonson on the English Stage.* Cambridge, MA: Harvard UP, 1935.

Pedicord, Henry William and Frederick Louis Bergmann, eds. *The Plays of David Garrick.* 7 vols. Carbondale: Southern Illinois UP, 1982 (cited in this article as P&B). Citations from Garrick's adaptation of *The Alchemist* are from volume V of this edition.

Riggs, David. *Ben Jonson: A Life.* Cambridge, MA: Harvard UP, 1989.

Ross, Cheryl Lynn. "The Plague of *The Alchemist.*" *Renaissance Quarterly* 41 (1988), 439-58.

Sanders, Julie. *Ben Jonson's Theatrical Republics.* New York: St. Martin's, 1998.

Vickers, Brian, ed. *Shakespeare: The Critical Heritage, Volume 3: 1733-1752.* London and Boston: Routledge and Kegan Paul, 1975.

Whalley, Peter. *The Dramatic Works of Ben Jonson.* London: John Stockdale, 1811.

Judith Milhous and Robert D. Hume (essay date 2007)

SOURCE: Milhous, Judith, and Robert D. Hume. "*A Bundle of Prologues* (1777): The Unpublished Text of Garrick's Last Rehearsal Play." *Review of English Studies* ns 58.236 (2007): 482-99. Print.

[*In the following essay, Milhous and Hume describe the circumstances surrounding the production of* A Bundle of Prologues *(1777), a brief entertainment written for the annual benefit in support of aged and infirm actors and Garrick's last dramatic composition for Drury Lane. Never before published and performed only once, the work survives in manuscript and is reprinted in full with explanatory notes by Milhous and Hume.*]

On Monday 28 April 1777, David Garrick's last dramatic composition for Drury Lane received its only performance. The occasion was the company's annual benefit for the 'theatrical fund, for the support of such performers as should be obliged, through age, infirmity, or accident, to retire from the stage.'[1] Garrick had retired from acting and management the previous June, but he remained deeply committed to the fund, to which he left a substantial bequest when he died in 1779. The entertainment was advertised in the newspaper bills for the day as *A Bundle of Prologues,* without attribution or performers' names.[2] The text was not published. There is no Larpent manuscript, so either no copy was submitted to the censor or it was lost. The work is never mentioned in the modern edition of Garrick's dramatic writing or in the standard modern biography.[3] Modern scholarly attention to this *pièce d'occasion* has been virtually nil—which seems odd, given that Henry Folger bought a manuscript copy at a Sotheby sale (18-21 June 1928, lot 340).[4] The manuscript now reposes in the Folger Shakespeare Library, shelfmark W.b. 461. It was accurately entered in Mary E. Knapp's *A Checklist of Verse by David Garrick,*[5] with the explanation 'Folger, transcript.' Knapp's revised edition of 1974 emends this to 'transcript with autograph lines.' Two generations of scholars have made use of the Folger's extensive Garrick holdings, but so far as we can determine no one has ever bothered to investigate this manuscript—which is the stranger since it is a fine example of the 'peep behind the curtain' rehearsal playlets of which Garrick had made something of a speciality.[6] We present here a complete transcription (with explanatory notes) and some discussion of attribution issues, the manuscript itself, and the circumstances of production.

What has been known of *A Bundle of Prologues* comes entirely from the playbill and a bit of notice in the newspapers of the day. It was given as a curtain-raiser, with *Twelfth Night* as the mainpiece and Garrick's *The Jubilee* (1769) as the after-piece. The advertisement states that 'The Words of the Songs will be given at the Theatre,' though apparently no copy has survived. The little prelude was described in some detail in the *Public Advertiser* of 30 April.

SOME ACCOUNT OF THE **BUNDLE OF PROLOGUES,**
PERFORMED ON MONDAY FOR THE THEATRICAL FUND

When the curtain drew up Mr Bannister was discovered seated as President of a Club of supposed Pensioners upon the Theatrical Fund; around the table sat Mr and Mrs Davies, Mr Moody, Mr Parsons, Mrs Bradshaw, and several other performers, habited as veterans and joining Mr Tragedy Truncheon (the President) in a glass of gratitude to their benefactors the public, for furnishing them with the means of thus comfortably enjoying themselves, when old age and infirmities had rendered them incapable of retaining their station in the theatre, and discharging the duties of their profession. As soon as the toast had gone round, the president called in some musical assistants, and was joined by two of his brethren in a three part song.

This over, the president called on the several members of the club to rehearse what they intended to say to the publick on the night of their annual benefit. Mr Quaver, Mrs Ranter, Mrs Stately, Mr Smirk, and Patrick Boosely, followed the President's order, each delivering something humourous and pertinent to the occasion. As soon as they had ended their several prolocutory addresses, the President left his chair, and, coming forward began the following Vaudeville, the rest of the performers bearing a bob by way of chorus [followed by some 50 lines of the words of the concluding song].

The 'Vaudeville' was printed in the May 1777 issue of the *Sentimental Magazine,* and the benefit was similarly noticed in the *London Chronicle* (29 April to 1 May), the *Whitehall Evening-Post* (29 April to 1 May), with excerpts in the *London Magazine* (Dublin) for June 1777. The text of the 'Vaudeville' was included in *The Poetical Works of David Garrick, Esq.*[7] The identity of the composer is not known and the music is lost. From published sources not much can be guessed about *A Bundle of Prologues,* but the neglected manuscript gives us a vivid picture of the occasion.

Two obvious questions arise at this point. Exactly what is W.b. 461, and is it what it purports to be? The Sotheby's catalogue reproduces the title page description ('An Entertainment of Dialogue & Singing . . .') plus its statement of date, venue, and attribution to 'D.G.,' and adds '16 pp. 4to. With 10 alternative readings in Garrick's hand.' The Folger catalogue entry is substantively identical, though it says merely 'Some additions in Garrick's hand.' The manuscript comprises 16 folios of fair copy, originally occupying rectos only, but with interpolations written on three of the versos, each with a point of insertion marked on the facing recto. Corrections and additions have been written throughout the text. We agree with the Sotheby cataloguer that several of them appear to be in David Garrick's late-life hand, ranging from the alteration of a couple of words to a four-line insertion. Others are written in pencil in a crude hand that we are unable to identify. Four stages of composition and revision are evident. (1) The original contriver of the text (presumptively Garrick himself) produced a rough draft, now lost. (2) The draft was fair-copied in what we take to be the hand of the prompter William Hopkins, yielding the uncorrected state of W.b. 461. (3) Garrick then made a variety of improvements, large and

small, in his own hand.[8] (4) Further changes were written in by two people. The pencil-annotator made a series of insertions and substituted Smirkin for Mildby at line 19. One additional speech (lines 148-9) was added in a fourth hand not present elsewhere in the manuscript, which resembles Hopkins's backhand.[9] Many of the corrections are probably just the copyist catching his own errors (e.g. altering 'brisky' to 'brisk' at line 106).

When the copyist began work on this manuscript, he picked up a sheet of unwatermarked paper, folded it in half, and numbered the upper right corner. He transcribed only onto the recto of each folio, without numbering the second one. He did the same thing six more times. Hence, only every other recto is numbered, and no verso is. After he had finished the text, he added the title on an unnumbered half sheet and wrote the incomplete cast on the verso. Then he sewed the sheets together between two rough paper covers. Few texts prepared by eighteenth-century prompters have survived intact, since collectors usually had them rebound. Because this one was boxed rather than rebound, it is a good exemplar of how texts were prepared circa 1777. However, it also raises questions: why did a manuscript apparently found among Garrick's papers show interim, but not final, corrections in so many hands? And does Garrick's hand among the correctors imply that he supervised rehearsal of the piece? We can only speculate as to answers. Corrections in multiple hands suggest to us that the prompter recorded all agreed changes in his copy and that complete manuscripts were collected and updated periodically after rehearsals. Actors were probably responsible for updating their own sides, unless extensive additions were proposed. We doubt that Garrick rehearsed the prelude (he was not on comfortable terms with the new management of Drury Lane), but he may have attended a first reading, and at some point he made numerous changes in his own hand. We hypothesise that the prompter sent him this semi-final copy, either for last minute adjustments or for his files. The Folger manuscript represents a penultimate phase of revision, to judge from discrepancies with newspaper reports of the performance. We should emphasise that it represents several layers of textual revision but was not marked up to serve as a 'prompt' copy.

Before presenting the text, we need to address the issue of attribution. What grounds have we for believing that Garrick wrote the piece, and if he did so, why was it not loudly advertised as his work? The case for Garrick's authorship rests essentially on the 'by D.G.' on 2r; on the extensive addenda and corrigenda in his handwriting; on his passionate devotion to the Theatrical Fund and its benefits (about which more later); and on the publication of the 'Vaudeville' in his posthumous *Poetical Works* (1785). Failure to use his name in the playbill is in no way surprising: Garrick customarily did *not* permit use of his name on playbills advertising his plays, adaptations, afterpieces, or preludes. Given the slight and occasional nature of the piece, we may presume that he was willing to help out by concocting the little entertainment, but not to violate his usual policy of insisting on anonymity. We accept the attribution, with the caveat that the piece as performed underwent further adjustments not recorded in this manuscript, as for example the further transformation of Mildby into Quaver.

In the transcription of Folger MS W.b. 461 below we have followed copy exactly, with a few exceptions. We have reformatted to put speech tags at the beginnings of lines (rather than centred on their own lines), italicised them, and followed them with a period. Stage directions have been put in *italic,* and italic has been substituted for underlining throughout. We have lowered superscript letters and expanded abbreviations involving them (e.g. 'y^r' becomes 'your' at line 26). Where the principal scribe formed lower case and capital letters identically for nouns, adjectives, and verbs, we have silently capitalised the first word of a sentence and internal nouns only. Where he is inconsistent, we have silently interpolated periods after Mr and Mrs. This text presents what we judge to have been the cumulative intention of Garrick and at least two subsequent revisers; changes, cancellations, and earlier versions of lines have been presented in the textual notes rather than in a diplomatic text. Cancelled text cannot always be deciphered with complete confidence. We have underlined the additions and emendations that we believe are in Garrick's own hand. Some of the alterations do not offer sufficient evidence to make a good judgement, and we have refrained from claiming that they are Garrick's, though they may be his. Textual notes are collected together in note 10; the presence of a textual note in a line is indicated with an asterisk (*).[10]

A
Bundle of Prologues
1777
An
Entertainment
of Dialogue & Singing
Among the Old & Infirm
Actors & Actresses
Who may be suppos'd to be
Pensioners upon the Charity
This is design'd to be perform'd at

THE FUND BENEFIT THE 28TH[11] OF
APRIL 1777 BY D.G.

Persons
Men[12]

Crotchet	Mr. Vernon
Truncheon	Mr. Bannister
Smirkin	Mr. Parsons
Patrick Boozely	Mr. Moody
Mildby	[blank]

Women

Mrs. Stately	Mrs. Bradshaw
Mrs. Rantum	Mrs. Davies

Players Singers &c

(The Scene represents a Room where the suppos'd Pensioners of The Theatrical Fund are sitting with a Table & Bowl before them.)

TRUNCHEON:

First Gentlemen & Ladies fill your Glasses, and let us prove our Gratitude before we proceed to Business— come Ladies dont mince the matter—We have done with our Profession &* are old enough to have worn out our Hypocrisy and therefore let us take our Liquor freely, & with it remember our kind Benefactors *(they drink)* now what have you to say Mr. Mildby—*   5

MILDBY*:

I think it right* Brother Truncheon—

TRUNCHEON:

Hold Mr. Mildby,* as we are met here, and are to take our places according to our Rank in our Profession—less Freedom would become us—you are not upon the Tragedy List[13]—when we have done our Business, & precedency & Degree are lost in the Familiarity & Merriment of the Table, you may Brother me as much as you please— 'till then I beg that you will address me in the Chair with the Appellation of Mr. Truncheon or Mr. President   10

MILDBY*:

Mr. President Truncheon the Tragedian you are right &* shall be obey'd—

PATRICK BOOZELY:

O fye for Shame! What the Devil are you Brothering & Bothering about—are we not all Singers & Dancers, & Comic, & Tragic and therefore all Brothers alike, as we are not* a kin—Let honest Patrick Boozely beseech you, that we may be all harmony and concord, and not have the least discord among us, 'till we come to the Music.   15

SMIRKIN*:

Well said Brother Boozely—No Offence I hope to call *him* Brother—& therefore to tune our minds to peace & happiness, & prepare them for the Business of this meeting—Let us not forget our Annual Song, which will give us, and the Ladies Spirits for the work in hand—there are* some Musical Friends[14] without* to assist us—shall we call them in Mr. President the Tragedian Truncheon*   20

TRUNCHEON:

By all Means—who is there desire ye Gentlemen to walk in & set chairs for ye Gentlemen—   25

SMIRKIN:

Gentlemen Tune several [?]* now clear up* your pipes* my Boys—hem!—& away with it.

TRUNCHEON:

Not a note yet Gentlemen—Before you proceed to Singing, & more drinking (for I very well know the Consequences) it will be proper to remind you of the Subject & Cause of our meeting.—   30

BOOZELY:

(*fuddled*) Right Mr. Truncheon—Business should be done before we get any Vapours into our pates—for my part, I am never affected with Liquor—I only speak as a prudent Caution for those Gentlemen that have weak heads—proceed Mr. Truncheon—nobody speaks better.—

TRUNCHEON:

In a few days our Benefit Play for the continuing these Comforts unto us, will be Exhibited—It is therefore thought proper that at that time we should shew both our Wit & Gratitude to our noble & generous Benefactors then assembled—   35

BOOZELY:

Brava!—I will shew 'em both never fear Boy

TRUNCHEON:

You, my Brothers & Sisters therefore, who are prepar'd with a Grateful Address, must now Rehearse your parts—We will suppose this great Room the Playhouse—I wish it was better furnish'd that the Similitude might be more Compleat—   40

SMIRKIN:

Well said Master Truncheon!—tho you *are* a Tragedian, you are no Fool, I'll say that for you—

BOOZELY:

Can't you take a Sample by me Mister Smirkin and not say one word to Bother the Gentleman—   45

TRUNCHEON:

This Room is the Playhouse—the fine China in those Glass Cases, shall represent the Ladies—those Roman figures in the Tapistry shall stand for the Gentlemen in the Pit & Boxes & Hogarth's Prints of the good & bad Prentice we will suppose the upper Gallery[15]—& now Mr Mildby you had the smallest Salary & must march first—I shall bring up the rear—[16]   50

MILDBY*:

I beg your pardon Mr. Truncheon*—we must first strike up with a little Musical Gratitude

SMIRKIN:

To be [sure?]—what's a Man without Gratitude—he had better be without his head—Gratitude first & then* to Prologues Epilogues & Speeches, or whatever you please to call them.   55

TRUNCHEON:

With all my heart—away with it.
(*Song in three parts*)[17]
    When, old boys, we are Young,

    We are Vigorous, & Strong;
The Sight of sweet Beauty alarms us,
      But now that we're Old,   60
      And our hearts growing Cold
There's nought but good Liquor that warms us.

2

    Here is Joy to each heart,
    That will Rapture impart,
And Joy to our hearts who will give Boys;   65
    Tho' pulses slowly move,
    And we cannot live to Love,
Still, still we Love to Laugh, & Live Boys.

BOOZELY:

Bravissimo—ye Sweet Singers—

TRUNCHEON:

Now begin Mr Mildby—and make your Reverence & speak as well, as if you had the first audience, in the World before you.   70
(MILDBY *goes forward*.)[18]
      I was a Play'r of small Renown,*
      Not much applauded by the Town,
      I got but little by the Week,
      And therefore little had to Speak;   75

      No help I needed from Apollo,
      To speak such Sentences as follow—
"Master Manly my Lord desires to know
*"If you're at home";**[19] this said then off I go—.
In Richard thus—*"Moreton my Lord is fled"***[20]   80
Then in Macbeth—*"The Queen my Lord is dead"***[21]
But what did most my Pow'rs awaken—
*"My Liege the Duke of Buckingham is taken"***[22]
      A Line & half was oft my due,
      They seldom trusted me with two;   85
      I could not for a* Hero pass
      For want of Lungs & want of Brass.
      I could not dare—a Sheepish Creature
      Oerstep the Modesty of Nature—
      Tho' I could then no pow'rs reveal—   90
      Warm'd by your Bounty now I feel—

TRUNCHEON:

Mrs. Stately—Madam—be pleas'd to step forward.
(MRS. STATELY *goes forward*)[23]
      Behold in me, tho Old, I hope not homely,
      What once the Critics said was fair & Comely;
      You, and your Sires good Sirs—I've kindly
      serv'd;   95
      Nor from my Occupation ever swerv'd;
      Here all my Charms most* Gratefully I lavish'd
      Was for your pleasure poysond, stabb'd &
      Ravish'd;—
      Nor yet past Service—tho' perhaps my Prime,
      You shall command me still at any time:
(*She turns off*)   100

TRUNCHEON:

Are you ready Mr. Smirkin?—

SMIRKIN:

Always ready to follow the Ladies Sir—and to obey your
Commands—hem!—

TRUNCHEON:

Pass on then—and Address the Audience—

SMIRKIN:

I'll be at the Tapistry in a Moment[24]   105
(SMIRKIN *comes forward*)
  Tho' Old, I'm brisk* as any Bee,
  No Mortal has more Mirth & Glee—
  With Mirth, Life's always on the Wing,
  The Wise may pout—to Laughs the thing
  Shew me a Lass with Shape & Chest,   110
  And my heart dances in my breast,—
  If she but ogle—my Eye Twinkles
  My Love & Spirit have no Wrinkles
  Sound Wind, & Limb no rusty hinges
 (*Turns round quick*)
  No pains—a few Rheumatic twinges;—   115
  Sweet Youth to Age will give a Spring,
  Say what we will—Beauty's the thing—*
  When I was young, I found Grimace
  Much better pleas'd, than Nature's face;
  Thus merrily dispos'd* within,   120
  To gain Applause I thought no Sin,
  So Grinn'd & Laugh'd, to make you* laugh & Grin.
  Getting a habit of this trick
  I soon made real Judges sick
  For habits bad are like Dram-drinking,   125
  You must go on, or heart is sinking;
  Without Grimace I could not please,
  You kept me up, with Drams like these—
   (*Clapping his hands to the Upper Gallery*)
  But now to all a grateful Debtor,
  You keep me up with something better
 (*points to the Bowl*)   130
  To have the Audience in a String
  I know the plan—Nature's the thing—
  No grinning, noddling, wriggling, Jercking—
  So thinks, yours ever, Sammy Smirkin   (*turns off*)

TRUNCHEON:

Take the Field Mrs. Rantum   135
(MRS. RANTUM—*comes forward*)[25]
  Tho' by your Bounty, I can never starve,
  Yet sure tho' Nervous, not too Old to serve;
  With red & white, & dark'ning what is grey,
  And with some Cork supplying Time's decay,
  My head work'd up with Cushion, paste, &
  Curls,   140
  Still I could frisk the Ladies, & Young Girls*
  But Managers such fools are—chuse the Young,
  And think at sixty five—we stay too long—
  Tho my Eyes fail me, & I've lost some Teeth;
  And to be sure this Astma stops my
  breath,   145
  Yet let me say, humbly to you appealing,
  My Judgments riper—& I still have *feeling*.
  And why not act—you see in me no Ruin,

  My Spirit's good, & still I would be doing.*
  For spite of Cough, the loss of teeth, &
  blindness   150
  None can more warmly* feel a loving kindness

TRUNCHEON:

If you can speak Mr Boozely now is your time—
(BOOZELY *comes forward*)
  Yes, yes, I can speak,[26] & I hope to some
  purpose—
  Ladies & Gentlemen—both low, & high,—
  A faithful steady Servant, here am I!   155
  In Five & twenty years, be this my Glory,
  I never toxicated came before you.
  But led a Decent, & a sober Life;
  Would I could say as much for my sweet Wife;
  She's gone,[27] thank Heav'n—I'd follow the
  poor dear,   160
  But that you've made my Life so happy here.
  For which I hope to thank you many a year;
  I for your sport play'd Teague in many a play,
  And Blunder'd on from Youth, 'till I grew grey;*
  Now that they say my Life is in declension,   165
  Tis best not play—that's work—but have a
  pension*
  Who long have Blunder'd, are at last discarded,
  Then have a pension, & am well rewarded
  Whether I ate or no—I'd make no rout—
  But that I cannot fait,[28] well live without;   170
  Sweet Ladies if you Smile, then I am blest,
  O you've a littler Friend here in this breast;*
  Poor Play'rs will bless your hearts—how well
  you trate[29] 'Em
  Good things you give 'Em—but no Teeth to Ate
  'Em.
  Faith I'm content—Patrick will ne'er say nay,   175
  Whether I'm paid to play, or not to play,—
  For that's the Question—If this Corporation
  Will not afford me proper Consolation;
  But starve Your Servant—then will I be here
  Or if I die—why then I can't appear   180
  So thank you for it now, lest I can't come*
  next year
(TRUNCHEON *comes forward*)[30]
Stand by!
  I trod this Stage—tho' now my fire is cool'd,
  When David call'd the Little—Liv'd & Rul'd;[31]
  I fought abreast with him, & mighty Barry,[32]   185
  In Bloody Field of Richard and Fifth Harry;[33]
  I fought, and three times breath'd on Severn's
  brink,[34]
  And glad I was three times to stop & drink;
  No year roll'd by, but I was deep in Treason,
  I fiffty times was murder'd in one Season;[35]   190
  To Kill, or to be kill'd with Joy I flew,
  For Ev'ry drop of Blood was Spilt for *you*

BOOZELY:

O well said i'faith Mr. Truncheon upon my Soul but when
you come to deliver it with your Grace and figure before an Audience, but you'll make their blood run cold
in the hottest Month of the year and now Gentlemen &
Ladies, as we have spoken together singly for our own 195
Emoluments and seperate Consideration, so now for the

good of the Community, we will all Join, not only Every one for himself, but all together each individually for the good of the Community, and to shew our benevolence to our most grateful Benefactors;* so strike up my Old Boys, & Girls, for the honour of Musick, ourselves, & our Noble Patrons the Public   200

Vaudeville[36]

1

My Brothers & Sisters of Buskin & Sock,
We now are not Actors to feign & to mock,
    We give you no* passions
    No Humours* & Fashions,
Save only our own Native Stock,   205
For the Bounty with which you o'erflow
Makes the sweet plant of Gratitude grow

CHORUS: In our Bosoms our merry hearts leap,
    We now are no Play'rs
    But send up our Pray'rs   210
That the Blessings you sow, you may reap;

2

My Sisters & Brothers who oft trod the Stage,
Who now are declining with Sickness & Age,
    You now see before ye,
    The Charms that restore ye   215
Whose Bounty your Griefs will asswage,
    Tender Beautie* is fairest to view
As a Rose is when sprinkled with dew

CHORUS: In our Bosoms &c

3D

The King & the Cobler by turns was my Lot,   220
I mended old Soals, & wore Crowns on this Spot;
    What ever my Station
    Or high Occupation
My Duty I never forgot
    When a Tyrant with Death in my Stride   225
    My Dependance on you was my pride

CHORUS: In our Bosoms &c

4

PATRICK: I beg your Old Servant may throw in his mite,
Who loves, and, would serve you by day & by night,
    For you my dear Craters,[37]   230
    And you with sweet Fateres*
I'm ready to Sing or to fight,
    As by you all distress I defy,*
    So for you while I live, will I* die—

CHORUS: In our Bosoms &c   235

5

In the Change of each Year, as this day will come round
Our Duty we'll pay, as in Duty we're bound.
    Our old hearts with pleasure
    Their thanks without measure

From Earth to the Sky will resound   240
    In our Faces your Bounty is seen
    Smiles of Age speak the Comfort within

CHORUS: In our Bosoms &c

Lightweight as this *pièce d'occasion* unquestionably is, we judge that it should have proved effective in the theatre. Garrick always had a flair for simulating rehearsals and back-stage conditions. By placing the table upstage, Garrick arranged for the actors to rehearse adopting their on-stage personae as they moved downstage, and he provided hints as to how they might vary. Mildby/Quaver has to be directed to bow to the audience, whereas Truncheon begins with a cue to the supernumeraries to rise and follow him (*ll.* 70 and 182 above). Garrick of course knew the performers he wrote for, and on some of them he turned his considerable powers of satiric mimicry.[38]

The actors were veteran second-rank members of the company, not even close to retirement. The men had all served on the committee to incorporate the Theatrical Fund. Charles Bannister (Truncheon) played character parts in comedy, such as Major Sturgeon in *The Mayor of Garratt* (a role created by Foote), and Tugg in *The Waterman.* He sang as Tugg, as Caliban in **The Tempest,** and as Hecate in **Macbeth** (a part new for him in November).[39] Because of his tall, imposing figure, he gradually acquired a few minor tragic roles, but mimicry and singing were always his strengths. Over the course of 32 seasons beginning in 1762, William Parsons (Smirkin) performed more than 200 small roles at Drury Lane.[40] Obadiah in Sir Robert Howard's *The Committee* and Waitwell in William Congreve's *The Way of the World* were typical. He was very thin and asthmatic, so he offered a visual contrast to Bannister's height and Moody's bulk. John Moody (Boozely) had come to Drury Lane in 1759 and was a favourite with Garrick as well as with the public. Teague in *The Committee* was one of his enduringly popular characters, and Garrick wrote Sir Patrick O'Neale in **The Irish Widow** for him. Moody played five other Irish roles this season, as well as Adam in *As You Like It,* the Tartuffe character in *The Hypocrite,* and Sir Tunbelly Clumsey in Sheridan's adaptation called *A Trip to Scarborough,* from Vanbrugh's *The Relapse.* A big, sloppy man, Moody was a good, if untrained, singer whose vocal abilities were often employed in characters written for him.[41] William Davies (Mildby/Quaver) had the hardest job in this piece, since he stepped into a role written for someone else and not, in this manuscript at any rate, adjusted to him. The audience had seen him in such supporting parts as Sebastian in *Twelfth Night,* 'Rosencrans' in **Hamlet,** and doubling Mercury and the Old Woman in **Harlequin's Invasion.** However, he could not sing, so he would have needed to find his own ways to make amusing a role written for Vernon, a singer. Although we can only speculate about Vernon's withdrawal, he may have begged off because, once plays were chosen for the evening, he found he was to play the

Clown in *Twelfth Night* and sing the *Epilogue Song.* The decision not to use him might also have been made by management, since variety was a key feature of benefits.

Garrick devoted little effort to characterising the women in this piece. Mary Bradshaw (Mrs Stately) had been performing secondary roles in London since 1743, among them one he wrote for her in *The Farmer's Return from London* (1762). She played half a dozen nurse-housekeepers this season, but also the flirtatious Jiltup, who is married to Commodore Flip in the course of *The Fair Quaker of Deal,* and Mrs Over-done in *Measure for Measure.* Garrick looked out for her personally and gave her money from time to time.[42] Elizabeth Davies (Mrs Rantum), William's wife, first performed in London in 1770. Probably under 30 at the time of this benefit, she was advertised for only eight roles this season, including Sukey Chitterlin in *Harlequin's Invasion* and Phoebe in *As You Like It.* On the latter performance the prompter Hopkins commented, 'La! La!,' meaning that he was not impressed, but she was pretty and 'spirited,' so she offered a contrast to the much older Mrs Bradshaw.[43]

On the rare occasions when Garrick's dramatic compositions receive critical scrutiny, it is generally devoted to *The Clandestine Marriage* (1766, with Colman), to the popular afterpiece farces (*Lethe, Miss in Her Teens*), or to his numerous adaptations of seventeenth-century dramas. Garrick was, however, an extremely skilled and prolific contriver of small, lightweight entertainments, often of an occasional sort. He was a famous prologue writer and speaker with a genius for catchy, witty, couplet teasing. From time to time, he employed this talent in petite pieces designed simply as extras in a night's entertainment. Some were intended only as benefit one-offs for favoured actors; others were clearly written in the hope that they would attract the fancy of the audience—and a few of them got revived now and again. Some were vehicles for Garrick himself (*The Farmer's Return* [*The Farmer's Return from London*] is a notable example), though in most of them he acted no part. If they were published, they appeared without attribution, though his authorship must have been an open secret around the theatre and is generally recorded in the prompter's records—as for example with *The Theatrical Candidates* in 1775.[44]

Garrick had no set pattern for constructing his preludes, interludes, and additional entertainments, but in practical ways *A Bundle of Prologues* reflects his habits in this sort of piece. Its length, flip couplets, small cast, and essentially static structure are all very much the norm. Garrick occasionally composed in prose (*The Meeting of the Company,* 1774, is an instance), but as a rule he seems to have relished virtuoso exposition in couplets—dazzlingly exhibited in *The Enchanter* (1760), *The Farmer's Return, Linco's Travels* (1767), and *The Theatrical Candidates.* Some of the pieces are essentially just assemblages of cheerful bits of satire—on naïve reactions to Londoners and their entertainments in *The Farmer's Return,* on national foibles in *Linco's Travels.* Others serve principally as vehicles for small bouquets of songs (*The Enchanter, The Theatrical Candidates,* and, of course, *A Bundle of Prologues*). Garrick seems to have made a clear distinction between comic afterpieces and these prelude/interlude sorts of entertainments. Compare, for example, *A Peep Behind the Curtain* (1767) with *The Meeting of the Company*: both are satiric pictures of the theatre behind the scenes, but the two are entirely different in structure and substance. In the context of his other petite pieces, *A Bundle of Prologues* can be seen as a final exemplar of Garrick's talent for witty verse turned to the service of a *pièce d'occasion.*

His willingness to write this little piece for the Theatrical Fund benefit of 1777 should be recognised as a continuation of a serious commitment on his part.[45] Early in his managerial career Garrick had firmly resisted pleas from the Drury Lane actors for the establishment of a fund for assisting elderly actors in distress.[46] Exactly what changed his mind and when we will probably never know. Davies says that such a fund was set up at Covent Garden while Garrick was on the Continent in 1765, and that he was embarrassed and annoyed at not having been consulted. Close study of the chronology, however, suggests that Davies was twisting the story to make Garrick look as good as possible. Davies goes on to date the first meeting of contributors to the rival theatre's charity as 22 December 1765, not anticipating that scholars would find out that Garrick had in fact returned to London late in the previous April.[47] As the leading actor and co-manager of Drury Lane, Garrick must have learned what was afoot at the other theatre before the general public did, and at some point he evidently persuaded his partner Lacy that public relations and company morale compelled them to institute a similar scheme. Garrick then set up a trust fund, established a supervisory committee, and instituted a heavily subsidised annual benefit in support of the charity. The first Covent Garden benefit was given on 13 May 1766; Drury Lane followed suit on 22 May with Garrick playing Kitely in *Every Man in His Humour* and speaking a special 'Occasional Prologue' of his own composition.[48] This plea for support he repeated annually (sometimes as prologue, sometimes as epilogue), with topical variants introduced as appropriate.[49]

Garrick also contributed his labours in a principal role at the Fund benefit every year from 1766 to his retirement 10 years later. In his final season, he not only played Hamlet on 30 May 1776 but donated the proceeds of his last public performance, in which he played Don Felix in *The Wonder, or A Woman Keeps a Secret* on 10 June. Gross receipts are known for 6 of the 12 benefit performances, and they average close to £300. The theatre deducted only incidental nightly charges (which ran from £16 to £36), while management covered the 'constant charge' (which at this period was normally calculated at £73 per night). Davies reports that Garrick 'gave to the proprietors of the fund a house situate in Drury Lane, for the conveniency of assembling to transact business: this house, some time before his death, the committee sold to him for a sum of £370. By his will, he bequeathed the same back again to the fund.'[50] Garrick's support of the fund can only be called extraordinary. Davies continues, 'It is computed, that, by the product of his labours in acting annually capital parts, and by donations of one kind or another, he gained for this beneficial institution a capital of near £4,500.' Dizzying as this total seems, it is plausible. Twelve benefits at upwards of £300 each would amount to about £3500, which plus the houses and some other gifts would bring the total to what Davies reports. The present-day value of £4500 cannot be computed with any precision, but depending on the multiplier one uses, a total somewhere between £900,000 and £1,350,000 might be estimated.[51]

Garrick had become a rich man (he sold his share in Drury Lane to the Sheridan consortium for £35,000 in 1776),[52] and he had always been a tough and hard-headed businessman. His post-1765 commitment to the welfare of elderly and distressed actors cannot be questioned, and it gained him a lot of good will.[53] He had donated his valuable services, administrative assistance, and quite a lot of money. In the spring of 1776 he encouraged the directors to solicit Parliament for a special act incorporating the Theatrical Fund and paid the costs of the bill out of his own pocket.[54] His leaving *A Bundle of Prologues* anonymous we attribute to his customary insistence on anonymity for his dramatic writing, but one might wonder why he did not offer to speak the special Address. Any answer must be speculative, but we would point to the prompter's diary entry for Garrick's last performance on 10 June 1776. Hopkins wrote that Garrick 'went forward and address'd the Audience in so pathetic a Manner as drew Tears from the Audience & himself & took his leave of them forever.'[55] We deduce that Garrick meant to make a clean break and stuck to his resolve. To judge from a tart letter he wrote to Sheridan on 29 October 1778, he was treated as 'an interloper' when he attended a rehearsal to which he had received a 'very particular' invitation.[56] Even just a year after he retired, he may already have felt unwelcome at Drury Lane. He remained willing, however, to concoct a Prelude for the 1777 benefit—and he put together his usual slickly constructed, highly performable vehicle for the occasion.

Notes

1. As described by Thomas Davies in *Memoirs of the Life of David Garrick, Esq.*, rev. ed., 2 vols (London, 1808), vol. II, 331.

2. See *The London Stage, 1660-1800*, Part 5: 1776-1800, ed. Charles Beecher Hogan, 3 vols (Carbondale, 1968), vol. I, 76.

3. *The Plays of David Garrick,* ed. Harry William Pedicord and Fredrick Louis Bergmann, 7 vols (Carbondale, 1980-82); George Winchester Stone, Jr. and George M. Kahrl, *David Garrick: A Critical Biography* (Carbondale, 1979).

4. Formerly 'the Property of Mrs M. A. Carew, Combe Hill, Lustleigh, Devon.' The price was £16. A large collection of Garrick-related material was dispersed at this auction, parts of it bought by Henry Folger and the Yale University Library. On some of the material that went to Yale, see Louis L. Martz and Edwine M. Martz, 'Notes on Some Manuscripts Relating to David Garrick,' *RES*, 19 (1943), 186-200. The Martzes point out that Mary Carew's first husband was Charles Carrington Hensley, whose mother was Catharine Payne Garrick, daughter of Christopher Philip Garrick, who was the son of Carrington Garrick (Vicar of Hendon), who was the son of David Garrick's brother George. The early provenance of the manuscript is entirely uncertain. We note that David Garrick predeceased George by only 2 weeks.

5. (Charlottesville, 1955), item 435.

6. Heather Wolfe, Curator of Manuscripts at the Folger, has kindly informed us that the Folger has no record in its files of anyone having ever worked on this manuscript.

7. 2 vols (London, 1785), vol. II, 336-37.

8. Garrick had apparently conceived Crotchet and Mildby as separate characters, since at line 49 Truncheon refers to Mildby. However, at some point after this manuscript had been copied out, Crotchet was combined with Mildby, changing a number of speech tags.

9. See for example Folger W.a. 104 (13), the final volume of Hopkins's Diary, where he has written 'Command' in backhand beside the 18 October 1775 performance entry, to make it stand out from the rest of the text.

10. Lines 2-3 Have done with our Profession &] <Careted insertion in Garrick's hand> 4-5 (they drink) ... Mildby] <Added in Garrick's hand, replacing 'fill your Glass' after 'Benefactors'; 'your Glass' cancelled; 'fill' evidently meant to be cancelled> 6 Mildby] Crotchet 6 I think it right] Right <Replacement in Garrick's hand> 7 Mildby] Crotchet 13 Mildby] Crotchet 13 are right &] <Pencil interpolation in unidentified hand> 16 as we are not] <Replacement of 'without being' in Garrick's hand> 19 Smirkin] <In pencil, replacing 'Mildby,' which had replaced 'Crotchet'> 22-6 there are ... Truncheon] <'There are' in Garrick's hand replaces 'we have got'; 'without' in Garrick's hand replaces 'here.' On

the preceding verso is interpolated in Garrick's hand 'shall we call them in Mr. President'; the unknown writer in pencil adds 'the Tragedian Truncheon.' Garrick's addition continues with '*Truncheon*. By all means … Gentlemen.' The speech he assigns to Mildby is changed to 'Smirkin' in pencil. Garrick's addition finishes with 'Gentlemen … your pipes.' Reading of 'Tune several' very doubtful; 'old' dropped out of overlapping phrase 'your old pipes' in the interpolation.> 51 Mildby] Crotchet 51 Truncheon] Crotchet <Copyist caught his own error> 53-4 *Smirkin* … Then] <Added in smudged pencil on preceding verso; reading of 'sure' doubtful; 'your' dropped out of overlapping phrase 'your Prologues and Epilogues'> 72 Renown] Degree 79"] *eds.* 81"] *eds.* 83"] *eds.* 86a] the 97 most] mostle 106 brisk] brisky 116-17 Sweet … thing—] <Couplet bracketed in left margin, possibly to indicate omission> 120 dispos'd] <Written after 'deposit'> 122 you] Fools 138-41 With … Girls] <Passage added by Garrick on preceding verso> 148-9 And … doing.] <Couplet added on preceding verso in a hand unlike any other in the MS, though it may be William Hopkins's backhand> 151 warmly] wantonly [?] 163-4 I … grey;] <These two lines are bracketed in the left margin, but the bracket is cancelled> 165-6 Now … pension] <Couplet bracketed in left margin> 171-2 Sweet … breast;] <Couplet bracketed in left margin> 181 come] <Word obscured by an ink blot> 195-9 and now … Benefactors;] <Lines boxed in MS with a single diagonal stroke through the passage, which probably indicates omission.> 199 grateful] <Does not make sense; could be a copyist's mistake or an authorial slip for a word like 'generous'> 203 We give you no] No humours & 204 Humours] manners 217 Beautie] Beauties 231 Fateres] Features <emended to indicate Irish accent and rhyme with 'Craters' (= Creatures)> 233 all distress I defy] I have lived & felt[?] Joy 234 will I] I will.

11. As of 24 March 1777, the projected date for this benefit was 21 April: see *The Letters of David Garrick,* ed. David M. Little and George M. Kahrl, 3 vols (Cambridge, MA, 1963), vol. III, no. 1085. Nothing indicates why the date was changed. This letter and no. 1094 document Garrick's ticket-selling activities on behalf of the Fund among his wealthy contacts.

12. We print this list as it appears in the manuscript, but this was not the cast reported in the *Public Advertiser* of 30 April 1777. In the event, Joseph Vernon (*c.* 1731?-1782), the company's principal singer, did not participate. The name of his character was changed from Crotchet to Mildby in the script, and changed again to Quaver by the time the prelude was staged. That role was played by William Davies (1751-1809). Information about performers not other-

wise credited is from Philip H. Highfill, Jr., Kalman A. Burnim, and Edward A. Langhans, *A Biographical Dictionary of Actors, Actresses, Musicians, Dancers, Managers and Other Stage Personnel in London, 1660-1800,* 16 vols (Carbondale, 1973-93).

13. Management often kept reference lists of major plays in each genre that the current company was prepared to do with minimal notice, annotated with the names of key actors. Davies had in fact appeared in many more tragedies than Charles Bannister (1741-1804) this season. We see here the first of many joking reversals and inversions in this prelude.

14. The 'Musical Friends' are members of the orchestra brought on stage to play for the trio.

15. From the initial stage direction, we deduce that the 'table and bowl,' possibly with several straight chairs, were to be placed upstage of the theatre's curtain line, so that participants would make their way down and onto the forestage to recite. We suggest that this description is meant to represent allegorically the three physical and social levels of the theatre: the 'glass cases' standing for the on-stage and side boxes, the 'tapestry' indicating the pit and back boxes, and the Hogarth prints suggesting the galleries. The enumerated elements of décor may or may not have graced rehearsal rooms in the theatre, about which we know little except that they existed. On the 1778 site plan for Drury Lane, see the parcels marked 'U,' 'Old Green room and New Green room Building,' in the discussion of Robert Adam's 1775 reconstruction of the theatre in *Survey of London,* vol. 35, ed. F. H. W. Sheppard (London, 1970), 34 and 47-48.

16. The pretense is that the hierarchy of the company was being maintained among the retired actors. Since Davies—who had replaced Vernon as Mildby—had the smallest salary of the four men, £3 a week, this direction was factual, not funny, as it might have been when said to Vernon, who made £8 a week. The line still foretells the shape of the piece: each will recite, beginning with Mildby and ending with Truncheon.

17. This song was evidently designed for Vernon, Bannister, and John Moody (1727-1812). Who replaced Vernon in this song when he left the cast is not clear; Davies was not a good singer.

18. Originally, the joke was that Vernon would pretend to be a minor actor of limited vocal power who could hope only to deliver messages and was unable to end a longer speech. In fact, much of what Davies did was deliver messages, but the roles cited are not his. For example, in Colley Cibber's *Tragical History of King Richard III* (1699; pub. 1700), he played

Tressel, who delivers to Henry VI the news that Gloster has murdered his son. He had performed the role this season on 12 October and 6 December.

19. This is a slightly mangled version of a speech by an unnamed servant to Mr Manly in Act IV of the Cibber-Vanbrugh *Provok'd Husband*: 'Sir, my Lord desires to speak with you.' *The Provok'd Husband* (London, 1728), 79. The play remained a staple in the Drury Lane repertory. It had been performed on 20 March and 5 April this spring, and was to be performed again on 8 and 28 May. The part was too minor to be credited to a performer in the playbills.

20. 'Bad News, my Lord, *Morton* is fled to *Richmond*': Catesby in Act IV of Cibber's *Richard III,* 40. The title role had been one of Garrick's ten most-performed parts. Catesby was being played by John Packer at this time.

21. *Macbeth,* line 1997, in William Shakespeare, *The Complete Works, Original Spelling Edition,* ed. Stanley Wells and Gary Taylor (Oxford, 1986). Seyton to Macbeth in Act V, Scene v.

22. Spoken by Catesby later in Act IV of Cibber's *Richard III,* p. 45. This report provokes from Richard the most famous of Cibber's additions to Shakespeare: 'Off with his head. So much for Buckingham.'

23. Mary Bradshaw (*d.* 1780) was definitely cast against type here: she was a minor actress who appeared in neutral or comic roles, not tragic ones, so this was a chance for her to burlesque tragedy queens. She often played older women, nurses and companions, and she was close to or over 50 herself, though she was still playing Audrey in *As You Like It.*

24. William Parsons (1736-1795) was only 41, but his forte had long been old men. As Smirkin, he evidently took some time to move forward to speak. He was later criticised for the faults Smirkin admits to: grimacing, face-making, and playing to the upper gallery. Garrick appears to be sketching a theory of comic acting here.

25. Only a death date is known for Elizabeth Davies (*d.* 1782), but in view of her husband's age, she must have been less than half the 65 her character claims. She played minor soubrette roles, so Mrs Rantum is a great departure from type for her.

26. There is not a word, even in some distinctly hostile late notices, about Moody himself being drunk at the theatre. The role shows off the mood swings of his drunken Irishman speciality.

27. Mrs Moody did not actually die until 1805.

28. Spelling indicates an Irish pronunciation of 'faith.'

29. Spelling indicates an Irish pronunciation of 'treat.'

30. Bannister, who had a bass voice but also a good falsetto, was only 36 in 1777, and most of his roles at this time were comic, so his Tragedy Truncheon is very much against type. The audience was of course in on the joke, and he no doubt made a flourish as he strode downstage to begin his speech.

31. Garrick's small stature was a sore point with him, and had been a problem for him as an actor. This acerbic touch at his own expense is a nice in-joke.

32. Spranger Barry (1717?-1777), one of the principal tragedians of the third quarter of the 18th century. He had worked extensively with and for Garrick at Drury Lane, though they had a difficult relationship. He died on 10 January 1777, about 3 months before Garrick composed this piece.

33. That is, *Henry V* at Covent Garden against *Richard III* at Drury Lane, between 1769-70 and 1772-73. The contest is exaggerated, however. Covent Garden also performed *Richard III,* but Barry was not in either production, and Garrick had largely given up Richard before he retired.

34. This is a mangled reference to a speech by Hotspur to the King in *1 Henry IV,* Act I, Scene iii about Mortimer's fighting Glendower: 'on the gentle Seuerns siedgie banke ... Three times they breathd, & three times did they drinke' (*Complete Works,* lines 414-8). Bannister had played the title role, not Hotspur (for example, on 23 October 1769).

35. Another comic exaggeration: comedies were performed much more often than tragedies—and in 1777, the closest Bannister got to tragedy was to play Hecate in *Macbeth.* Truncheon would obviously go on spouting, if Boozely did not cut him off.

36. Garrick is using the word in the first (older) sense given in the *OED*: 'A light popular song, commonly of a satirical or topical nature; *spec.* a song of this nature sung on the stage.' The *OED* quotes a 1739 letter by Horace Walpole: 'I will send you one of the vaudevilles or ballads which they sing at the comedy after their *petites pièces*.' The term usually implies a different singer for each verse, which was presumably the intention in this instance, though the description in the *Public Advertiser* seems to imply that Bannister had to take the first verse in addition to the third. Internal references suggest that Mrs Davies, the prettiest woman onstage and the only young one, sang verse 2 as herself, and 'The King and the Cobler' in verse 3 attaches that one to Bannister, who had played the title role in Charles Dibdin's *The Cobler* (9 December 1774). Verse 4 is explicitly assigned to 'Patrick' (Moody). Because the late addition to the cast, Davies, was a poor singer, we doubt

37. As at lines 170 and 173 we have here stage-Oirish orthography and pronunciation. 'Craters' = creatures; 'Fateres' = features.

38. For discussion of Garrick's mimicry of other actors in *The Rehearsal,* see *Plays, Poems, and Miscellaneous Writing associated with George Villiers, Second Duke of Buckingham,* 2 vols, ed. Robert D. Hume and Harold Love (Oxford, 2007), vol. I, 373-76.

39. *Biographical Dictionary,* vol. I, 259-65.

40. *Biographical Dictionary,* vol. XI, 218-27.

41. *Biographical Dictionary,* vol. X, 288-96.

42. 'Mrs Bradshaw wrote to Garrick on 11 October 1778 about her financial distress. . . . She thanked Garrick for £50 he had sent her, but she had to repay Hull £20 which he had loaned her while she was on a sick bed, and the rest had gone to release her 'goods' which she had pawned. . . . She asked Garrick for another £50' (*Biographical Dictionary,* vol. II, 288). Bradshaw's letter is not in *The Private Correspondence of David Garrick,* 2 vols [ed. James Boaden] (London, 1831-32), and we do not know the whereabouts of the manuscript. To judge from an undated note from Garrick to Mrs Bradshaw (*Private Correspondence,* vol. II, 361) she was a personal favourite and family friend, lowly though her status remained. Her weekly salary never exceeded £2.

43. *Biographical Dictionary,* vol. IV, 214. When John Philip Kemble excerpted Hopkins's comments onto his playbill for *Rule a Wife* for 11 October 1775, he converted 'la-la' to 'so-so' (see *The London Stage* entry under date).

44. See *The London Stage,* Part 4: 1747-1776, ed. George Winchester Stone, Jr., 3 vols (Carbondale, 1962), vol. III, under 23 September 1775, citing Folger MS W.a. 104.

45. The source of much of what we know about the history of what Garrick calls in his will 'the fund for decayed Actors of the Theatre' is Davies, *Memoirs of the Life of David Garrick,* vol. II, 331-42.

46. In the 1780 edition of the *Memoirs,* Davies (II, 305) implies that 'talk of establishing a theatrical fund' started about 1750. In the 1784 edition he alters his phrasing to 'more than thirty years since.'

47. Davies, vol. II, 335. For Garrick's return, see the *Biographical Dictionary,* vol. VI, 42. The first public notice of the Covent Garden fund in *The London Stage* alerts the audience that Richard Cumberland had promised the fund the profits of his benefit for *The Summer's Tale* on 29 January 1766.

48. For the prologues given on each occasion, see Pierre Danchin, *The Prologues and Epilogues of the Eighteenth Century,* Part IV, 1761-1776 (Paris, 2001), vol. VII, 279-81.

49. On Garrick's involvement in the charity and the textual variants of the personal appeal in five extant manuscripts, see J. D. Hainsworth, 'David Garrick's Address to the Audience on Behalf of the Drury Lane Theatrical Fund,' *RES,* n.s. 26 (1975), 50-55. The partial manuscript at Yale was published by the Martzes ('Notes on Some Manuscripts,' 192-93). On the multiple printed texts and variants, see Danchin, vol. VIII, 866-7.

50. Davies, vol. II, 340-41. The passage in his will actually specifies more than one house. See *Letters of David Garrick,* vol. III, 1365.

51. On the calculation issues involved, see Robert D. Hume, 'The Economics of Culture in London, 1660-1740,' *Huntington Library Quarterly,* 69 (2006), 487-533.

52. *Letters of David Garrick,* vol. III, no. 978.

53. On 25 March 1777, a 'Testimony of Duty and Affection' to him was dictated by the Fund committee (*Letters,* vol. III, no. 1094, n. 3), and benevolence was one attribute of the gentleman he aspired to be.

54. Davies, vol. II, p. 340.

55. Hopkins's Diary, printed in *The London Stage,* Part 4, vol. III, under 10 June 1776. The farewell address is printed by Danchin, vol. VII, 867.

56. *Letters,* vol. III, no. 1204.

Peter Holland (essay date 2007)

SOURCE: Holland, Peter. "Hearing the Dead: The Sound of David Garrick." *Players, Playwrights, Playhouses: Investigating Performance, 1660-1800.* Ed. Michael Cordner and Holland. Houndmills: Palgrave Macmillan, 2007. 248-70. Print.

[*In the following essay, Holland observes that theater history is preoccupied with the visual rather than the aural. He seeks to redress this imbalance with respect to Garrick's career by retrieving evidence attesting to how the actor sounded on the stage. Holland presents a wealth of contemporary testimony describing Garrick's choices of pronunciation, inflection, timbre, tempo, and accent.*]

Could *how* Betterton spoke be as easily known as *what* he spoke; then might you see the Muse of *Shakespear* in her Triumph, with all her Beauties in their best Array, rising into real Life, and charming her Beholders. But alas! since all this is so far out of the reach of Description, how shall I shew you *Betterton*?[1]

I began with a desire not to speak with the dead in Stephen Greenblatt's fashion but simply to listen to them, to hear the voices of eighteenth-century actors. It is not a new wish. In 1775 Joshua Steele wrote with the same regretful awareness that I have been feeling throughout this project, about the sound of these voices which cannot be heard:

> We have heard of Betterton, Booth, and Wilks, and some of us have seen Quin; the portraits of their person are probably preserved, but no models of their elocution remain; ... Had some of the celebrated speeches from Shakespeare been noted and accented as they spoke them, we should now be able to judge, whether the oratory of our stage is improved or debased.[2]

Steele's wish to hear—or at least to have a visual notation for what the audiences of the past heard—was a desire to value, a Whiggish search for proof of progress or decline. My aim is to see what can be recovered, through Steele's own method and the contexts provided by many others' writings, of what David Garrick sounded like. There is no wish here to value, simply to attempt to reconstruct a way of hearing.

This article is, of course, doomed to failure. I shall assemble some fragments, make some claims, chart some details. I shall, of necessity, find myself arguing over tiny matters, for, as Richard Warner suggested, in publishing as a letter to Garrick his proposal for a Shakespeare glossary, Garrick was the deserved recipient, given '[t]he intimate acquaintance you have had with his writings, the very *minutiæ* of which you have made your study.'[3] But it is also a necessity as I resist the bland generalizations that usually characterize such analysis, the clichés that then and now too often pass for accounts of voices. To be told the following is not really to be told very much of use:

> Mr. Garrick's voice was clear, impressive, and affecting; agreeable, though not harmonious; sharp, though not dissonant; strong, tho' not extensive. In declamation uncommonly forcible, in narrative unaffectedly simple.[4]

I shall at the end explore the conflicting accounts of exactly what Garrick sounded like when as Lear he cursed Goneril. I shall, perhaps with worthwhile results, try to foreground some undervalued parts of the Garrick literature, that vast mass of pamphlets that his career generated (not least ones written by himself against himself), drawing attention to items in the Garrick bibliography that have been surprisingly ignored. But it is still going to be hopeless.

Why even try? In part, this is a conventional academic gesture of asking us to look at some materials we have not noted as strongly or as often as the article-writer believes we should have done. My delight in my discoveries of what came out of Garrick's mouth (Look on him, look,

his lips) generates the 'look there, look there' gesture of the scholar. I was surprised how rarely the standard modern studies of Garrick have anything much to say about the sound of Garrick, even though his contemporaries said a good deal.[5] I shall also, inevitably, be suggesting further directions for future research for others with more finely-honed skills, particularly in historical phonology and in the history of elocution, as ways that would enhance the image I will be sketching.

But I want, too, to point to a fundamental flaw in theatre history's concerns, one that it shares with much that recounts or accounts for performance, for our discipline is apparently, at times I have come to fear irretrievably, tied to the visual rather than the aural. Visual evidence tends to survive and our exploration of the physical shape of theatres, the evidence that can be retrieved from paintings of actors or handbooks of gesture, from the accounts for costumes and sets, have become the basis for our work. A longer account of this problem would need to investigate the nature of acoustic memory, why it should be that, say, theatre reviewers always tell us what a production looks like but rarely what it sounded like, why I should find, as I leave the theatre, that I can minutely describe set, costumes, movement and gesture but cannot recall much of how an actor sounded at a particular point, how s/he inflected a line, even when I have been intrigued by the inflection at its moment. Our recall of music is strong and our recall of the speaking voice is weak. In addition, even where we do recall, we cannot describe. We have strikingly failed to develop a vocabulary to record in prose (unlike recording on audio cassette) precisely what an actor has sounded like. We can describe pauses but not tonality, volume but not inflection, other than by using complex devices of linguistic analysis beyond all except experts.

But something has changed between Garrick and now in that regard. That there was minute dissection of Garrick's way of speaking particular lines is in itself remarkable, a sign of a theatre history, specifically a history of audience response as listening, marked now by discontinuity. As early in his acting career as 16 December 1741, Garrick received a letter from one of his greatest fans, the Rev. Thomas Newton, like Garrick Lichfield-born and an heir to an alcohol merchant. Newton, while concerned for Garrick's health ('I hope in the mean time you will spare yourself as much as you can, till you are recovered from your cold, and your voice may appear in perfection'), is also unable, as Boaden puts it, to allow a 'trivial error to sully long the general merit of his performance' as Richard III:

> In the last scene between Richard and Lady Ann, there is one thing that I think you did not speak quite properly, though I am somewhat doubtful. She says
>
> What have I done? What horrid crime committed?
>
> RICH. To me the worst of crimes—outliv'd my liking.

In the latter part, *outliv'd my liking,* you spoke with the same voice, only exalting it; whereas I imagine it should have been with an alteration of voice, more peevishly and angrily.[6]

Did Antony Sher receive similar letters when he played Richard III? Or was Toby Stephens as Hamlet told in the summer of 2004, by an anonymous correspondent,

> something that seems to me wrong about the pronunciation of a single word ... It is tropically. That o, I imagine, should be pronounced short, as we pronounce the o in logical; and both for the same reason, because the vowel in the original words, from whence they are derived, is in both an o, not an ω—a short o, not a long one. I believe you will find custom to be on this side of the question ...[7]

Or was Simon Russell Beale, when he was playing Macbeth, informed, as Garrick was in January 1744, that 'I see no reason for pronouncing the speech that begins with "Blood hath been shed ere now," aside'?[8] Even more striking is the fact that Garrick seems to have kept the letters, for, while most of the correspondence Boaden included in his 1831 edition of Garrick's correspondence, still the major printed source for letters *to* Garrick, is from the 1770s, the early letters that survive in his collection are, apart from the ones to and from Garrick's family, predominantly the ones of complaint about such matters of delivery. Rather than throwing them in the bin, Garrick seems to have cared enough to answer them, when not anonymous, and keep them. His answers were often detailed and strikingly apologetic in tone. In other words, Garrick engaged with this kind of detailed analysis of delivery, more evidence of his concern with 'the very *minutiæ* of which you have made your study' when it comes to the sound (here rhythm, syntax, pronunciation and stage-focus) of Shakespeare.

There is an implicit parallel to the investigation into the sound of long-dead actors in the acoustic history of music, for the recreation of the sound of earlier performances, once only of early music, now of Berlioz, Wagner and even Elgar, has been one of the most marked meetings between historical research and performance in recent years. Bach not performed on reproductions of early instruments is beginning to sound odd. The technologies of performance, the scale of surviving evidence, and the interest of performers have made such work desirable. But the recreation of an earlier human spoken voice has been relatively unexplored. There have been attempts across the late twentieth-century to perform Shakespeare in early modern pronunciation, most recently and elaborately in the performances at Shakespeare's Globe in London in June 2004 of *Romeo and Juliet* and in the summer of 2005 of *Troilus and Cressida,* spoken in a style coached by David Crystal.[9] Reflecting on that experiment, Crystal wonders:

> Why stop with Early Modern English? ... What about Restoration dramatists? ... It has always struck me as

curious that a play from the eighteenth or nineteenth centuries is faithfully presented using its dialect grammar and vocabulary, because this is reflected in the text, but its associated pronunciation is not, because it is hidden by the standard English spelling. Why not Sheridan in OP?[10]

But, even if I found the recreations of early modern pronunciation more convincing than is the case, I do not believe it to be significantly effective or desirable to perform in the vocal style of Garrick, though performances in the gestural style might well be revealing and though modern actors certainly have much to learn from the evidence for eighteenth-century actors' ability to work in a more rhetorically aware and metrically sophisticated tradition. Reconstruction of performance is a quite different aim from reconstruction for performance and the old complaint about lacking eighteenth-century eyes and ears is far more potently relevant here than for 'authentic' music performances. I do not want to hear someone pretending to be Garrick; I want to hear Garrick.

What I am centrally concerned with is our refusal or at least reluctance to be historians of sound, even in the aftermath of Bruce Smith's ground-breaking study of early modern soundscapes.[11] We have, for instance, nothing about the sound of eighteenth-century performance to set beside Dene Barnett's study of gesture.[12] Robert Hume's mapping account of our territory in this volume speaks of the state of our research in the physical conditions of costume and scenery and movement but, apart from theatre music, not of sound. The complex sensescape of theatre, the interaction of vision and hearing, has been only half explored. This chapter merely asks, by using Garrick as the inevitable example, that we might start to look at the other half more closely. I begin the enquiry at the level of the phoneme, move through speed, silence and syntax to end with a single example of interpretation and the performance of character, Lear's curse.

* * *

When Garrick was in Dublin in August 1742, he received yet another anonymous letter of complaint, this time over 'your false pronunciation of several words':

> The words that I chiefly remember are these:—*matron, Israel, villain, appal, Horatio, wind*; which you pronounced, *metron, Iserel, villin, appeal, Horetio*; and the word *wind* you pronounced short. I cannot imagine what your objection can be to the letter *a*, that you should change it into an *e*, both in the English language and the Latin ...[13]

Since the correspondent suggests that *matron* is made 'Greek,' Garrick may have made the *e* long in Greek style (equivalent to a Greek eta) or the writer may have made the *a* of *matron* short as in *mat*—anonymous letter-writers are not always clear. Though the correspondent was writing in Dublin it does not follow that his accent is Irish. Here, as elsewhere, the material is rebarbative and needs further analysis.

The attack on Garrick's orthoepy, his choice of pronunciation, reappeared again in 1759 when John Hill, author of *The Actor* (1750 and 1755), published *To David Garrick, Esq; The Petition of I. In behalf of herself and her Sisters.* Boaden comments that '[t]hey who have critically examined the English vowels, are not to be told that the letter *i* is sometimes allowably an usurper upon the letter *u.* Dr. Hill, however, maintained otherwise.'[14] For Hill, 'the indelicate and indeterminate sound *u*' had 'taken the place of most of the vowels and dipthongs' (9). If the choices were simply, say, 'ungrateful' over 'ingrateful,' it might not be so intriguing, but Hill's complaint was over words like *virtue, Hercules, earth* and *heard,* in each of which, he complained, Garrick sounded the first vowel as a *u* (7, 15) and:

> Your Petitioner does, and must conceive, the original and natural Pronunciation of the good word Firm, to be at least as elegant, and expressive of the Sense, as the coarse boggy Furm, which you have introduced into its place, and which your many Excellencies, fixing the Stamp of Judgment upon Folly, have forced into the Throats of others.
>
> (6)

My difficulty, of course, is that I cannot pronounce the words any other way. Modern RP will not allow me to distinguish *firm* and *furm* at all; Michael Cordner could distinguish them if he switched from RP to his native Northern Irish. It is easy to hear what Hill was on about when he complains that Garrick's 'Delicacy, disgusted at the broad Roman Accent' pronounced the vowel *a* 'as others speak *ey* in *they,* a soft and civil Diphthong' so that Cleopatra became Cleopeytra (11). But the rest of the complaining is a mark of a historical distance and a strikingly different soundworld. Garrick responded to the petition with an epigram:

> If 'tis true, as you say, that I've injured a letter,
> I'll change my note soon, and I hope for the better:
> May the just right of letters, as well as of men,
> Hereafter be fix'd by the tongue and the pen;
> Most devoutly I wish that they both have their due,
> And that *I* may be never mistaken for yo*U*.[15]

A link between the two men was also voiced by Garrick as Roscius in Samuel Pratt's pamphlet on his retirement: 'Not Sir John Hill, so much has wrote, / As I have spoken through my throat.'[16]

None of these complaints about Garrick's speech specifically identify his accent as regional, though there are signs that he may have had some Lichfield tinges to particular words. Thomas Sheridan made some of the some points as Hill, in his elementary guide to teaching reading and pronunciation, *Elements of English,* in 1786, pointing out, as he defined the correct pronunciation of *ir* forms, that Garrick pronounced words like *gird, birth,* and *firm* with a *u* vowel plus /r/ sound where Sheridan demanded a short *e*

plus /r/ sound.[17] Sheridan called this 'a very improper pronunciation' which 'has of late gained ground, owing to a provincial dialect with which Mr. Garrick's speech was infected' (note here the conceptualization of a sanitized orthodoxy that leads Sheridan to dub this an infection). Garrick made these errors 'according to Staffordshire custom': 'Nay he did the same where the vowel *e* preceded the *r*' and Sheridan gives as examples *heard, earth* and *interr'd.* But, while Garrick might be forgiven for failing to eradicate the pernicious traces of his provincial roots, Sheridan adds that 'His example was followed by many of his imitators on the stage, who would do well to correct this impropriety, as it is now easily in their power.'[18]

Though Sheridan's description definitely places the effect as a regional burr, Michael MacMahon suggests, in his outstanding account of English phonology from the late eighteenth-century to the present, 'Whether this reflected an aspect of phonological reality—not just in Staffordshire but also in London—rather than some socially induced pretence is impossible to judge.'[19] MacMahon's 'phonological reality' effectively divides the stage voice from the social voice. None of the accounts of Garrick's particularities of pronunciation have anything to do with his off-stage speaking, only the voice of the performer, and we accept that stage voices are and were necessarily distinct from others, not least through the need to project and fill the increasingly substantial acoustic volumes of theatre spaces, producing vowels often rounder and fuller than those in use off-stage.

The phonology of London English in Garrick's time was not hugely different from that of the present. Insofar as it is possible to reconstruct that sound (and MacMahon is my professional guide here), there are distinctions that would be striking. The initial letter of *humble* or *hospital* was silent, as in the current US pronunciation of *herb.* The second vowel of *oblige* was a long *e, obleege. China* was nearer to *chaynee.* And there are other examples. It is less the search for distinctions—as if we would hear Garrick's speech as belonging to another country—than the period's search for an orthodoxy that is striking. What, in turn, is most significant about the move towards the orthoepical doctrine and prescription that marks lexicography after Dr Johnson is the intimate connection between that movement and the theatre.

There are three crucial figures in the late-eighteenth century publication of books on elocution and pronunciation (dictionaries, guides, manuals, rhetorics and courses of lectures). All three were closely connected with Garrick's Drury Lane. The most combative was William Kenrick (1729/30-79), author of *Falstaff's Wedding* (1766) and *The Widowed Wife* (1767), would-be editor of Shakespeare and the man who, angry about the distribution of the profits, accused Garrick of a homosexual relationship with Bickerstaff in the poem *Love in the Suds* (1772). Kenrick had attacked Johnson's dictionary too and published in

1773 *A New Dictionary of the English Language,* prefaced by a substantial *Rhetorical Grammar,* later published separately in 1784.

Like the others Kenrick was concerned with defining rules for pronunciation but he was far less influential than John Walker (1732-1807) who joined the Drury Lane company in 1757, rising to the rank of second-level roles in tragedy before leaving the stage in 1768 to start a school and begin the series of publications on pronunciation that defined the 'mechanical school' of elocution; rule-bound, fiercely constricting and placing all its emphasis on analysis over feeling.[20] Walker dedicated his *Dictionary of the English Language* to Garrick in 1775, announcing that if either of his works (the *Dictionary* or his proposal for it)

> have a sufficient degree of merit to recommend them to the attention of the public, it is in a great measure owing to the early opportunities I have had of observing your pronunciation on the stage . . .

> (sig. π2r-v)

This was a reverse dictionary, alphabetized by the final letters and including a long index of rhymes, defined as 'perfect and allowable,' so that it is 'allowable' imperfectly to rhyme *cab* with *babe, made* with *dead, safe* with *deaf* or *laugh* (402f). Its quotation sources are not drama but the corpus of poetry. In his *Critical Pronouncing Dictionary and Expositor of the English Language* of 1791, a work reprinted over a hundred times by 1904, Walker set out not only meanings and sounds but, as the title-page put it, 'where Words are subject to different Pronunciations, the Reasons for each are at large displayed, and the preferable Pronunciation is pointed out.'

In his *Elements of Elocution* (1781), Walker regrets that he has to rely on his own experience 'to convey such turns and inflexions of voice as accompanied the pauses and emphasis of a good speaker; and this, had that great actor and excellent citizen Mr. Garrick lived, I should have exemplified in some of his favourite speeches' (1:xii). Garrick, then, functions for Walker as a model for elocution both as outstanding thespian but also because his social status and civic pride make him a social hero. He must, then, implicitly lie somewhere behind Walker's *The Melody of Speaking Delineated* of 1787 which sets out to teach elocution 'like music' (title-page) and which prints a number of Shakespeare speeches on facing pages with the clean text confronted by one divided into feet with light, heavy and equal stresses marked and with the mood and tone defined. I do not mean that Garrick's voice is what Walker is here recording but rather that the modelling is theatrical before it is socially elocutionary. The effect is a careful encoding of the vocal effects of various stratified forms of speech (high, middle, low; plaintive, didactic, grand, and so on). John of Gaunt's set-piece speech in *Richard II,* for instance, opens on a 'High plaintive tone of voice,' moving to a 'Lower tone, simple and didactic' at 'His rash fierce

blaze of riot,' on to a 'Low, solemn monotone' for 'This royal throne of kings,' 'Rapture; higher plaintive tone' at 'This blessed plot,' 'Grand description; lower and more solemn tone' at 'Renowned for their deeds,' 'Lower and more familiar tone' at 'Is now leased out,' and various other increasingly rapid switches, four in the last six lines alone, ending on 'Lower and reproaching tone' (50-4).

I emphasize that I am not suggesting that Walker's prescription here is a description of Garrick, not least because the whole rise of elocution at the end of the century is bound up with educational practice in schools and universities, not with stage performance. Yet elocution is profoundly performative and the pervasive presence of Shakespeare and other dramatists within these systems warrants attention.

If Walker was a minor actor, the same cannot be said for Thomas Sheridan (1719?-1788), actor and manager in Dublin and London.[21] Sheridan's lectures on elocution were given at both Oxford and Cambridge, earning him honorary MAs from both universities in 1758 and 1759. In 1762 he published his *Course of Lectures on Elocution,* following it with, among other works, a two-volume *Lectures on the Art of Reading,* one on prose and one on verse, in 1775, directed primarily at the clergy and at schoolteachers, and in 1780 his *General Dictionary of the English Language,* a work which paved the way for Walker's dictionary later. Sheridan's dictionary was, according to Robin Alston, 'the first attempt to provide for the whole vocabulary an accurate indication of the way words should be pronounced.'[22] Sheridan, incidentally, like Garrick's Dublin correspondent, opts for a long *i* in *wind,* a word he sees as in dispute, 'upon this principle, that there is no monosyllable in the English language terminating in *ind* in which the vowel *i* is not pronounced long' (58). Sheridan, as a Dubliner, was particularly concerned to help 'the Natives of Ireland' to 'attain a just Pronunciation of English' (59) and, in so doing, highlights some intriguing forms for London English with *cheerful* and *fearful* sounded as *cherful* and *ferful,* while *beard* is *berd* (60). Sheridan, like many a pioneer, was criticized by those who followed for errors in his choices, for, as Walker gleefully complained, he sounds the *t* of *creature, nature, tune and tumult* as *tsh* or *tch.*[23]

The work of these three has been extensively investigated by historical phonologists but not by theatre historians and the pickings would be rich. It would be possible to go through a speech and check each word against Sheridan's and Walker's prescriptions for pronunciation—and, indeed, against other accounts of mid- to late-eighteenth century forms and against the identifiable features of Garrick's diction in order to reconstruct both Garrick's and a possibly more normative form of such speech. But research in the materials on late eighteenth-century theories of elocution could go far beyond such phonological concerns. Sheridan, in particular, minutely explicates the meaning of a number of Shakespeare passages in his *Course of Lectures on Elocution* as part of his concern about where emphasis should be placed, a dissection of disagreements over rhythm and punctuation at the level of sound in intimate interconnection with the semantics of dramatic meaning. He is sure that phrasing Macbeth's line 'Making the green one, red' is 'flat nonsense,' urging 'Making the green—one red':

> Here is a most sublime idea conveyed, ... Nor, if we consider the disturbed state of his imagination at that time, will this thought, hyperbolical as it may seem at first view, appear at all unnatural. For it is highly probable that his fancy at that instant presented all objects about him as of that sanguine hue; nay converted the very atmosphere that surrounded him, into a sea of blood.
>
> (65)[24]

If Sheridan's recommendation to Othello to say 'Put out the light, and then put out *the* light' or 'Perdition catch my soul but I dò love thee'—'the emphasis ... marks the vehemence of his affection much better than any emphasis on the verb love could' (65-6)—sound distinctly odd, they are thoughtfully argued and come from someone with a profound experience of eighteenth-century theatre. They also bring an awareness of character and imagination to bear on processes of rhythm and emphasis. While these texts in elocution are not designed for the stage, they are nonetheless at a performative intersection between theatre and education, as in, for instance, *The Sentimental Spouter or Young Actor's Companion* (1774) with its 'Treatise on Oratory' or the precise evidence of the modes of speaking Thomas Sheridan and another actor and elocutionist John Henderson (1747-1785) demonstrated in a pamphlet *Sheridan's and Henderson's Practical Method of Reading and Reciting English Poetry ... and the manner pointed out in which they were read or recited by the above Gentlemen* (1796), with numerous examples from Shakespeare. We can, for instance, carefully compare Lichtenberg's and others' accounts of Garrick's Hamlet meeting the Ghost and the speech 'As repeated by the late Mr. Sheridan' who began it 'With a *low, solemn, awful* voice, as if repeating a short prayer' for 'Angels and ministers of grace, defend us': 'Then pausing ere you proceed, you raise your voice a little, not forgetting the greatest solemnity of *tone* and *manner*' and so on and on, requiring many pages for the one speech, a bulk of evidence that is well worth considering.[25] It is striking that in 1753 Sheridan, then still an actor, was praised—at least I think it is praise—for being 'very judicious in his Delivery ... Perhaps a truer Orator never trod the Stage.'[26] In terms of the long shadow this casts, it is worth remembering that Sheridan was the preferred private coach for Sarah Siddons.

Sheridan's preference for a natural delivery and a feeling style aligned him closely with the 'School of Garrick' against the mechanized rule-bound prescriptive elocutionary practice of Walker. Apart from the words I have explored above, Garrick seems also to have chosen '*sism*' as the pronunciation for *schism* and '"burial" the *u* long, instead of the way often made use of, as if it were spelt "*berrial.*"'[27] These last two examples come from an extraordinary pamphlet called *The Manner Pointed out in which the Common Prayer was Read in Private by the Late Mr Garrick* published by J. W. Anderson in 1797 and, as far as I can see, completely ignored by Garrick scholars. Anderson describes Garrick's gesture, movement, rhythms and voice, line by line through the service, from 'Dearly beloved brethren' onwards:

> Mr. Garrick recommended a look, expressive of the utmost *suitable gravity*, to be cast slowly around the congregation, the voice rather *low,* and denoting, together with the whole manner, that *solemn* and *reverential respect* which is due to the place of public worship ... Here make a pause much longer than the comma, or, indeed, than the time which is thought to be necessary after a semicolon.
>
> (9)

As a detailed study of Garrick's performance of a part it is unequalled, even by, say, Lichtenberg's familiar accounts of Garrick as Hamlet.[28] The only comparable text until we reach recordings would be James Hackett's detailing of Kean's performance as Richard III.[29] It appears that Garrick instructed a young clergyman in the right way of speaking divine service and Anderson compiled his pamphlet from manuscript notes. There is no reason to suspect the report as fake, even if its status as evidence needs careful evaluation. Intriguingly, it provides a precise intersection between Garrick's mode of elocution and that advocated by Thomas Sheridan who in his *Lectures on the Art of Reading* (1775) had set out his mode of speaking the service. Anderson contrasts the two methods:

> In the one [i.e. Garrick's], a *suitable fervour* of *exterior devotion* on the part of the Clergyman, as well as on that of the people, appears to be the chief thing endeavoured to be inculcated; in the other, the grand objects seem to be those of finding out the word upon which the emphasis should be placed ... while the *pious energy* and *spiritual animation* ... are left almost entirely unrecommended. The one speaks more to the *heart,* the other to the *understanding* ...
>
> (7-8)

Speaking to the heart is, of course, that emphasis on the natural and the affective which has always been defined as Garrick's most characteristic mode of speaking. At the same time, Garrick was praised—and occasionally blamed—for the speed and energy of his delivery. As early as his first triumphant performances of *Richard III,* there was a speed that startled the audience who were used to the measured pace of Quin. Among the many passages in the performance that might have surprised the audience in the 1740s I would not have suspected these lines to figure: 'The North!—what do they in the North, / When they should serve their Sovereign in the West.'[30] But

Arthur Murphy, in his 1801 biography, reported that 'The rage and rapidity, with which he spoke [the lines] made a most astonishing impression on the audience.'[31] Murphy, praising Garrick waking up from the ghosts, the next passage he describes, emphasizes the realism, 'Every thing he described was almost reality,' but also the variety:

> He was a spectacle of horror: He called out in a manly tone,
>> Give me another horse;
> He paused, and, with a countenance of dismay, advanced, crying out in a tone of distress,
>> Bind up my wounds;
> and then, falling on his knees, said in the most piteous accent,
>> Have mercy Heaven;
> In all this, the audience saw an exact imitation of nature . . .[32]

Macklin was less inclined to admire this:

> Garrick huddled all passions into strut and quickness—bustle was his favourite. In the performance of a Lord Townly he was all bustle. In Archer, Ranger, Don John, Hamlet, Macbeth, Brute—all bustle! bustle! bustle! The whole art of acting, according to the modern practice, is compriz'd in—bustle! 'Give me a Horse!'—'Bind up my Wounds!'—'Have mercy Jesu!'—all bustle!—everything is turned into bustle![33]

Something of the bustling speed is apparent in the exact representation of Garrick's voice that was included in Joshua Steele's analysis of 'To be or not to be,' his one attempt to recover from the past 'some of the celebrated speeches from Shakespeare . . . noted and accented as [actors] spoke them.' Steele, in his attempt to define the 'melody and measure of speech,' set out rhythm, metre and inflection for the speech 'as I pronounced it' but then, '[s]ince writing the foregoing treatise, I have heard Mr. Garrick in the character of Hamlet' and he marks the differences 'that I can remember' between Garrick and himself.[34] It is the most extraordinary document to have survived to demonstrate the sound of an eighteenth-century actor, even though we have no means of knowing how accurate Steele is.[35] Where Steele spoke it 'in the stile of a ranting actor, swelled with *forte* and softened with *piano,* he [Garrick] delivered with little or no distinction of piano and forte, but nearly uniform; something below the ordinary force, or, as a musician would say, *sotto voce,* or *sempre poco piano.*' But comparing Steele's version of the first line with Garrick's it is clear too that Garrick's is about speed. In every case where the quantity of the syllable is different, Garrick is shorter: 'or' is a crotchet length (US quarter-note) where Steele has a dotted minim (half-note) and Steele gives it a whole foot where Garrick gives it a light stress after the pause; 'that is' is dotted crotchet and quaver (eighth-note) where Steele has a dotted minim and minim, lightening the stress on 'is' considerably from Steele's ponderous mode.[36] At the very end of the speech, Steele notes that Garrick pronounced the last word, 'orisons,' with a short *i,* where Steele himself had made it

'long and heavy, by supposing the word to have been originally Norman French, *oraison.*'[37] But Garrick did without the pause after 'Nymph,' just as his pauses after 'To die' and 'to sleep' were markedly shorter than Steele's. This is not just bustle but a search for the through-line of the speech, its architecture as important as its momentary effect. Steele, incidentally, particularly praises Garrick for the clarity of his diction: he and Mrs Cibber 'are distinctly heard even in the softest sounds of their voices; when others are scarcely intelligible, though offensively loud.'[38]

Steele consulted with Garrick about his complex system of notation and Garrick wondered '[s]upposing a speech was noted, according to these rules, in the manner he spoke it, whether any other person, by the help of these notes, could pronounce his words in the same tone and manner exactly as he did' (54). Steele attempted to reassure him but letters Steele received after publication and which he answered in the second edition of his work, *Prosodia Rationalis* (1779), kept returning to the point. At the core of the disagreement was the crucial difference between the notation of music and Steele's notation of speech, the former lacking the precision of gracing, inflection and stresses that Steele included.[39] Difficult and abstruse though Steele's system may be, it is the most complex and considered notation of a moment of theatre speech available and Garrick's lightness and speed are conspicuously apparent.

Aaron Hill, whose writings defined an approach to performance in the 1730s, the years just before the Garrick sonic revolution, warned against speed and encouraged the careful use of pauses. In a letter he recommends,

> The actor, who pauses judiciously, will be sure to appear in earnest, like the conceiver of what he utters; whereas, without pausing, the words, arising too fast for the thought, demonstrate him but a repeater of what he should seem to invent, before he expresses it.[40]

For Hill, language takes time to be understood:

> For, without those restings, our understanding, wanting time to receive impressions from the ear, retains, but defectively, the image of the meaning, being continually hurried forward, to a *new* idea, while the *old* is unformed and imperfect.[41]

How long is a pause? For Hill, in a wonderful phrase that any actor would relish, 'the measure of time, in a pause, should vary according to the sense. But it will, in general, be enough to rest, as long as might suffice, to pronounce such a word as *power.*'[42]

Roger Pickering put the motto 'tacere qui nescit, nescit loqui' ('whoever doesn't know how to be silent, doesn't know how to speak') on the title-page of his pamphlet *Reflections upon Theatrical Expression in Tragedy* (1755), commenting that 'the best Construction of the motto . . . is Mr. Garrick's Pause' after the first line of

Richard III's speech after waking, the same passage that Murphy considered, though Murphy does not mention a decisive pause: 'A Man, awaken'd in Surprize, requires *Time* to recover himself for coherent Speech.'[43] But, more often than Pickering's praise, Garrick's pauses attracted regular criticism. The bustle was, it seems, carefully, even obsessively and certainly idiosyncratically offset and balanced by the frequent pauses in his delivery.

But it was less the frequency than the length and placing that drew sharp responses throughout Garrick's career. Even the most fervent fans were dubious about his tendency to pause too long or in the wrong place. Writing to Reverend Peter Whalley in 1748, the year Whalley published his study *On the Learning of Shakespeare,* Garrick worried whether Whalley

> have mistook me in the Prologue to Henry the 5th—surely the little Pause was made at *Fire!* And I connected the subsequent Relative, Verb, and Accusative Case (*that would ascend the brightest Heav'n,* &c.) in one Breath? I know in the general I speak it so, but may have fail'd the Night you heard me.[44]

Garrick here defends himself on syntactic grounds, the analysis of sentence structure defining the moment to pause. Whalley's criticism suggests that Garrick's pause was metrical, a pause at the line-ending. Fundamental to speaking Shakespearean verse is the tension between syntax and metrics, between the demands of the sentence and the rhythm of the verse-line. It is a contradictory pull, requiring the drawing out of an acutely discriminatory sense of the balance between the two. But the reason to pause may also be a different kind of artistic sensibility, as Garrick points out to another correspondent in 1767:

> In the speaking of Soliloquys, the great art is to give variety, & which only can be obtain'd by a strict regard to y[e] pauses—the running the different parts of a Monologue togeather, will necessarily give a Monotony & take away y[e] Spirit, & Sense of y[e] Author.[45]

John Hill, in a passage in *The Actor* in 1750, offered a further explanation for the intrusive pause:

> we observ'd in Mr. *Garrick,* a fault from his very first appearance on the stage, which is grown up with him, and now much worse than at first; it is a way of resting in the middle of a line where the sense is continued; such a pause is unnatural and hateful. We can easily see that the reason of this is, that this actor has an ambition to give a peculiar emphasis to every word of a sentence where he would be particularly great in his part; the force of voice which he uses on this occasion requires so much breath to every syllable, that he cannot pronounce more than half a line together. We first observ'd this in him in King *Richard*; where, in the heat of his fury, he calls out to the archers,
>
> Draw, archers, draw, your arrows to the head.
>
> It is easy to see that a line like this ought to be spoken with rapidity, and the whole force of the voice reserv'd for the last word; instead of this, Mr. *Garrick* bestows so much

breath on the three first, that he is forc'd to pause to get in more to speak the rest with, and accordingly he always pronounces the line with an unnatural gap in the middle,

> Draw, archers, draw—your arrows to the head.[46]

Garrick was defended in 1753 by the author of *The Present State of the Stage*:

> In this Place 'tis proper to obviate an Objection made against him by some superficial Critics, of stopping falsly; which from the most minute Observation I find to be groundless: 'Tis true, that sometimes he pauses in Places, where, critically speaking, there is no Pause, in order to collect his Breath, to give additional Force to what ensues; but his Tone of Voice shews plainly the Connection uninterrupted.[47]

In *The Theatrical Review* (1763), the problem is again defined as a consequence of a more general vocal limitation:

> Wanting power at the top, it sometimes sinks where the passions meet with any violent agitation. Mr. Garrick has so peculiar a method of adapting it, that we scarcely perceive it is unhappily limited; and we are almost induced to believe, that it ought to rise no farther . . . than the particular key to which he has the power of extending it.
>
> (76)

Garrick is indicted for using 'a sort of hesitating stammering, when there is no natural obstacle to occasion it, merely to strike a seeming shew of something out of nothing' (79)—this is presumably the kind of thing Foote attacked in mocking Garrick's performance of Lothario's death speech in Rowe's *The Fair Penitent*: 'Adorns my fall / And chea-chea-chea-chea-chea-chears / My heart in dy-dy-dying.'[48] Here too the pauses are seen as caused 'by the too great length of a period, where he would have rendered himself absolutely inarticulate' if he had not paused. But Garrick is also indicted for using pauses 'as a trap for applause where he could reasonably expect none.'[49]

Laurence Sterne mocked the objections to the Garrickian pause in *Tristram Shandy*:

> And how did *Garrick* speak the soliloquy last night?—Oh, against all rule, my Lord,—most ungrammatically! betwixt the substantive and the adjective, which should agree together in *number, case* and *gender,* he made a breach thus,—stopping, as if the point wanted settling;—and betwixt the nominative case, which your lordship knows should govern the verb, he suspended his voice in the epilogue a dozen times, three seconds and three fifths by a stop-watch, my Lord, each time.—Admirable grammarian!—But in suspending his voice—was the sense suspended likewise? Did no expression of attitude or countenance fill up the chasm?—Was the eye silent? Did you narrowly look?—I look'd only at the stop-watch, my Lord.—Excellent observer![50]

Sterne may be referring to a specific moment for Garrick had had to explain at length in a letter why there appeared one night to be a false division between the substantive 'single' and the adjective 'state' in Macbeth's line 'My thought, whose murder yet is but fantastical / Shakes so my single state of man' (1.3.139-40):

> *Shakes so my single*—If I stop at yᵉ last word, it is a glaring fault, for the Sense is imperfect—but my Idea of that passage is this—Macbeth is absorb'd in thought, & struck with yᵉ horror of yᵉ Murder, tho but in Idea (*fantastical*) and it naturally gives him a slow—tremulous—under tone of voice, & tho it might appear that I stop'd at Every word in yᵉ Line, more than Usual, yet my intention, was far from dividing the Substantive from its adjective, but to paint yᵉ horror of Macbeth's Mind, & keep yᵉ voice suspended a little—wch it will naturally be in such a Situation.[51]

Garrick goes on at length to explain what he means by 'suspending the voice … Which in many cases I reckon a Beauty in the Speaker, when a Stop would be a great fault,' using as an example a pause after 'see' in Hamlet's line 'I think it was to see my mother's wedding,' 'for Hamlet's Grief causes yᵉ break & with a Sigh, he finishes yᵉ Sentence … I really could not from my feelings act it otherwise.'[52] The appeal to emotion ('my' here used intriguingly as a shorthand for 'Hamlet's,' a complex marker of the sympathetic identification between the actor's emotional state and the role) is crucial here, with feeling dominating over syntax or metrical, rhythmic structures.

It was not only onstage that Garrick could misaccent. Dr Johnson accused Garrick, Giffard, manager of Goodman's Fields, and other actors of having 'a kind of rant, which they run on, without regard either to accent or emphasis.' Garrick and Giffard protested and Johnson asked them to repeat the ninth commandment, 'Thou shalt not bear false witness against thy neighbour':

> Both tried it … and both mistook the emphasis, which should be upon *not* and *false witness.* Johnson put them right, and enjoyed his victory with great glee.[53]

The most sustained analysis of Garrick's pauses and his tendency to misaccent a line was in a series of letters to journals by Thaddaeus Fitzpatrick (possibly with others), gathered together as *An Enquiry into the Real Merit of a Certain Popular Performer* (1760), an attack to which Garrick replied in his satire *The Fribbleriad* (1761) but whose detailed charges he completely ignored.[54] Fitzpatrick's main targets included Garrick as Pierre in *Venice Preserved,* a role he had not played for six years. It was not, then, exactly news. Of course it is an exaggeration, though some of its examples had been or would be mentioned elsewhere (e.g. 'I think it was to see—my mother's wedding') and hence may well have been valid. But its lists and dissections are an extraordinary satiric demonstration of Garrick's vocal mannerisms, whether accurate or not. Here are some of the twenty examples from **Hamlet,** recorded, Fitzpatrick claimed, during a performance, for 'as our memories did not serve us to clear up the point, it was agreed that we should go to the tragedy of Hamlet this

evening, each man, furnished with a printed play and a pencil, mark such improprieties, in respect of speaking, as Mr. G——might possibly fall into':

> Oh that this too too solid—flesh would melt.
> He would drown—the stage with tears.
> I'll have these players
> Play something like—the murther of my father.
> Lay not that flattering—unction to your soul.[55]

Garrick is here shown separating adjective from substantive, and another group shows a tendency to emphasize the last word in a line with a pause before the next, in a fashion of which Sir Peter Hall might now approve but which Fitzpatrick opposed:

> Or that the everlasting had not *fixt*—
> His canon 'gainst self-slaughter.
> Whether it is nobler in the mind, to *suffer*—
> The stings [*sic*] and arrows.[56]

Another twenty examples from *Richard III* distinguish between 'the words printed in Italics, [which] are those he thought fit to lay emphasis on; … such as are in Small Capitals, I apprehend he ought to have spoken emphatically' (27), for example:

> Now *are* our brows bound with VICTORIOUS wreaths,
> Our STERN alarms are *changed* to MERRY meetings;
> Our DREADFUL *marches* to DELIGHTFUL measures …
> I, that *am* CURTAIL'D of man's FAIR proportion,
> Deform'd unfinish'd, *sent* BEFORE my time—
> Into this breathing world, *scarce* HALF made up …

> (28)

One need not of course think that Fitzpatrick is necessarily right in his suggestions to recognize that Garrick may have been wrong in his. Michael Cordner rightly suggests to me that one might want to point up 'proportion' rather than 'fair.' But, if Fitzpatrick's report is accurate, Garrick's emphasis of 'am' in the line is distinctly odd.

For many of his examples, there are detailed explanations of why Garrick's choice was mistaken, for example, for Richard's line to Lady Anne 'Then bid me *kill* MYSELF, and I will do it':

> By his former conduct, and confession, it appears, that he was sufficiently ready to kill, and therefore the verb might have escaped the emphasis; but as he seemed willing to change the object, if she ordered him, he should have marked *himself.*

> (32)

It is a fair note to an actor and I for one often make similar mental notes when listening to actors at the RSC and elsewhere. The intelligence of Fitzpatrick's analysis of such cases as well as its compatibility with the substance of numerous letters to and by Garrick enhances the probability that, as an account of Garrick's errors, it is not far off the mark. Garrick's silence in reply, keeping his attack to a mockery of Fitzpatrick's camp style, may also be a kind of admission of fault.

The Fitzpatrick pamphlet can in some respects be seen as part of the pamphlet culture wars that surrounded Garrick's management, a sign of the cultural investment—and the profit for publishers—in such wars of words focused on the institution of the theatre. Yet its detail also suggests a quite different concern, with the drama as an act of semantic communication, for, while the complaint is about emphases and caesuras, it is not an argument about the speaking of verse and the problems of metrics. Instead it is firmly concentrated on the meaning of the lines and Garrick's apparent failure to allow the movement of thought to emerge from an accurate delivery of the syntactic forms of the language. It is not a matter of tone, of character, of interpretation, for the concerns are far more fundamentally semantic than that. It is a matter of a straightforward—or at least comparatively simple—argument about how the phrase fits the action of the play, its argument through dialogue. The investment in meaning is primary and Garrick's perceived failure is a failure not only of style but also of intelligence, a failure to understand the meaning of the lines he speaks.

Yet Garrick's performances also demonstrated a sustained critical intelligence, a concern to read a role and find a way through it. I want to pursue a single passage in this respect, the curse on Goneril in ***King Lear***, the speech that in Tate's version as adapted by Garrick ended Act 1 without the brief exchange between Goneril and Albany that Tate had included:

> Hear, Nature! hear, dear goddess, hear a father!
> If thou didst intend to make this creature fruitful,
> Suspend thy purpose.
> Into her womb convey sterility!
> Dry up in her the organs of encrease,
> That from her derogate body never spring
> A babe to honour her! If she must teem,
> Create her child of spleen, that it may live,
> And be a thwart, disnatur'd torment to her!
> Let it stamp wrinkles in her brow of youth;
> With candent tears fret channels in her cheeks;
> Turn all her mother's pains and benefits,
> To laughter and contempt;
> That she may curse her crime, too late; and feel,
> How sharper than a serpent's tooth it is,
> To have a thankless child!—Away, away.[57]

After Garrick's initial lack of success as Lear, he was coached by Macklin who praised a later performance: 'the curse he particularly admired; he said it exceeded all his imagination; and had such an effect, that it seemed to electrify the audience with horror.'[58] It continued to do so for nearly thirty years. Over and over again, people commented on the effectiveness of this moment but there were also complaints. Samuel Foote argued in 1747 that the curse

should be utter'd with a Rage almost equal to Phrenzy, quick and rapid as a Whirlwind, no Mark of Malice, no Premeditation, no Solemnity; the Provocation, the Persons against whom the Curse is denounced, *Lear's* Character, all conspire to render such a Behaviour absurd: nor can I easily pardon the Tears shed at the Conclusion ... that strange Mixture of Anger and Grief is to me highly unnatural; this unmanly Sniveling lowers the Consequence of *Lear*; this Practice may, with Propriety, be introduced in the Imitation of a vex'd Girl, who cries because she can't (in the vulgar Tongue) gain her Ends.[59]

Foote implicitly seems to have preferred Barton Booth's performance years earlier, for Thomas Davies reports that

Booth was more rapid than Garrick, his fire was ardent and his feelings were remarkably energetic, but they were not attended with those strugglings of parental affection, and those powerful emotions of conflicting passions, so visible in every look, action, and attitude of our great Roscius.[60]

The same assumption of the dominating emotion of energetic passion underpins Charles Gildon's recommendation in 1710, couched in the voice of Betterton, that the curse 'must be spoke with an elevated Tone and enraged Voice, and the Accents of a Man all on Fire, and in a Fury next to Madness.'[61] Davies goes on at length about this sense of conflict in Garrick's performance here:

I have heard certain critics complain, that, in pronouncing this denunciation, Garrick was too deliberate, and not so quick in the emission of his words as he ought to have been, that he did not yield to the impetuosity which his particular situation required. But we should reflect that Lear is not agitated by one passion only, that he is not moved by rage, by grief, and indignation, singly, but by a tumultuous combination of them all together, where all claim to be heard at once, and where one naturally interrupts the progress of the other ... Shakspeare [*sic*] ... wrote them for the mouth of one who was to assume the action of an old man of fourscore, for a father as well as a monarch, in whom the most bitter execrations are accompanied with extreme anguish, with deep sighs, and involuntary tears.[62]

Davies was a fan writing with a long experience of the performance. But Garrick's approach was immediately defended against Foote by an anonymous pamphleteer:

you begin

Hear Nature, Dear Goddess!—

with a *broken, inward, eager* utterance; from thence rising every Line in Loudness and Rapidity of Voice, 'till you come to [the serpent's tooth]. Then you are struck at once with your Daughter's Ingratitude; and bursting into Tears, with an almost sorrowful Heart-breaking Tone of Voice, you say

—*go, go, my People.*[63]

If the report is accurate, Garrick moved the final line from earlier in the scene in order to provide a totally different kind of exit, less abrupt, perhaps, than Shakespeare's and Tate's 'Away, away.' This increase in speed and volume was, for Francis Gentleman, writing notes to the published edition of Garrick's text, one of the two ways of playing the speech:

> This execration is conceived and expressed in such a nervous climax of resentment, that it requires great abilities to give it due force. There are two justifiable modes of delivering it: one is, beginning low, as if speech was for a moment benummed; and rising to the conclusion; the other is, commencing with a burst of passion, and repressing a swell of grief, till the two last lines; then melting into a modulated shiver of utterance, watered with tears. We prefer the latter.[64]

Theophilus Cibber agreed. In 1756 he analysed the passage and Garrick's performance at length, preferring Barry for his majesty and grace:

> Can the Actor be too rapid in the Delivery?—Do not long Pauses damp the Fire of it, like cold Water dropp'd thereon? ... too long a Preparation for it, seems not consistent with *Lear*'s Character: 'Tis here unnatural. Such long Pauses give him Time to reflect, which the hasty *Lear* is not apt to do 'till 'tis too late.—This philosophic Manner would become a Man, who took Time to recollect;—which if Lear did, would not the good King, the o'er-kind Father, change this dire Curse into a fervent Prayer, for his Child's Repentance and Amendment? ... so dire is the Curse, Nature can scarce endure it, unless delivered in the rapid Manner, the wild Transport of the choleric King, with sudden and unchecked Passion, would surely give it:— when it appears premeditated,—it speaks Rancour, Spleen, and Malice; a cool Revenge; not a Burst of Passion, from an o'er-charged Heart.[65]

I am deliberately ignoring here the long descriptions of Garrick's preparation for the speech, the kneeling, the clenching of the teeth and all the other physical, non-vocal devices which Garrick used. By 1755 John Shebbeare could praise Garrick at this moment above all for that dignity Cibber felt Barry had over Garrick:

> This all other Actors speak with that kind of Rage, with which a drunken shoemaker curses his daughter that has secretly taken his Money from him, and prevented his going to the ale-house; it is indeed a sheer scolding. In Mr. Garrick it is a prince in anger.[66]

The effect must have been immensely powerful and Edward Taylor in 1774 used the moment as the means of resisting Johnson's assumption that all spectators are always in their right mind:

> Whoever at such a critical moment can turn aside to view any other object, or not forget his own situation, and be wholly wrapt up in that of the inimitable performer, is to be pitied, not envied, for his composure and sang froid.[67]

With more space, it would be possible to analyse these conflicting accounts but, to a very large extent, the conflict is neither surprising nor troubling. The understanding of meaning in vocal inflection is necessarily imprecise. One

thing is clear, however: Garrick's form of speaking allowed for multiple and complex emotions both to succeed each other rapidly and to co-exist within a single moment. His aim was to represent that density of emotional state that most fully accorded with the differing social, familial, political, rational and cultural dynamics of the character across the play and at the precise moment.[68] If this has the kind of complexity that, say, Strindberg famously argued for in the preface to *Miss Julie*, it is a sign of the multiplicity which Garrick saw as a consequence of that 'natural' style which he and Macklin created. John Shebbeare commented, in a standard phrase of praise, '[i]t is not possible to decide which is superior in the knowledge of nature, the poet who wrote, or the player who animates these passages.'[69] Hence Garrick's recommendation to the actors in the character of Bayes in his short play **The Meeting of the Company**:

> First, gentlemen, turn nature out of door,
> Then rant away 'till you can rant no more.
> Walk, talk and look as none walked, talked and looked before.[70]

I have ended in a familiar place, with a sense of Garrick as a natural actor, as a stylized representation of a complex cultural formation of assumptions about behaviour, affective emotion and the mind. But I start to hear him better, not yet clearly but no longer quite so inaudible.

Notes

1. Colley Cibber, *An Apology for the Life of Mr. Colley Cibber, Comedian* (London, 1740), 60.

2. Joshua Steele, *An Essay Towards Establishing the Melody and Measure of Speech* (London, 1775), 14.

3. Richard Warner, *A Letter to David Garrick, Esq., concerning a Glossary to the Plays of Shakespeare* (London, 1768), 92.

4. *The Theatrical Review, or Annals of the Drama* (1763), p. 76, reprinted in *The Life and Death of David Garrick, Esq.,* Anon. (2nd edn., 1779), 11.

5. There is oddly little in the two excellent standard biographies, George Winchester Stone, Jr., and George M. Kahrl, *David Garrick: A Critical Biography* (Carbondale, Ill.: Southern Illinois University Press, 1979) and Ian McIntyre, *Garrick* (London: Allen Lane, 1999); a little more in Jean Benedetti, *David Garrick and the Birth of Modern Theatre* (London: Methuen, 2000). The best account is still probably the chapter in Bertram Joseph, *The Tragic Actor* (London: Routledge and Kegan Paul, 1959).

6. James Boaden, ed., *The Private Correspondence of David Garrick*, 2 vols (London, 1831-2), 1:3-4.

7. Boaden, *Private Correspondence,* 1:11.

8. Boaden, *Private Correspondence,* 1:20.

9. See David Crystal, *Pronouncing Shakespeare* (Cambridge: Cambridge University Press, 2005). See, or rather hear, also the material on Crystal's website, www.shakespeareswords.com.

10. Crystal, *Pronouncing Shakespeare,* 171.

11. Bruce R. Smith, *The Acoustic World of Early Modern England* (Chicago: Chicago University Press, 1999).

12. Dene Barnett, *The Art Of Gesture: The Practices and Principles of 18th Century Acting* (Heidelberg: Carl Winter, 1987).

13. Boaden, *Private Correspondence,* 1:12.

14. Boaden, *Private Correspondence,* 1:xxxv.

15. Boaden, *Private Correspondence,* 1:xxxv.

16. S. J. Pratt, *Garrick's Looking-Glass* (Dublin, 1776), 4.

17. See also Francis Gentleman's complaint: 'we have often regretted an adulteration of language, by changing the *e* and *i* into *u*; this gentleman, and several after him, have pronounced *stern, sturn, mirth, murth, birth, burth,* which is really rendering our language, already sufficiently dissonant, still more so' (Francis Gentleman, *The Dramatic Censor,* 2 vols (1770), 2:483).

18. Thomas Sheridan, *Elements of English* (1786), 28-9.

19. Michael K. C. MacMahon, 'Phonology,' in Suzanne Romaine, ed., *The Cambridge History of the English Language. Vol. 4 1776-1997* (Cambridge: Cambridge University Press, 1998), 373-535 (417).

20. On Walker, in addition to the fine entry by Joan C. Beal in the *Oxford Dictionary of National Biography,* see also Bryan K. Brown, 'John Walker (1732-1807)' in Michael G. Moran, ed., *Eighteenth Century British and American Rhetorics and Rhetoricians* (Westport, Conn.: Greenwood Press, 1994), 230-4. See also Joseph R. Roach, *The Player's Passion* (Newark: University of Delaware Press, 1985), 76-87, for his thoughtful work on emotion in eighteenth-century acting and the work of John Walker (especially *Elements of Elocution* (1787)), James Burgh (in *The Art of Speaking* (1761)); and Aaron Hill, *The Works,* 4 vols (London, 1753), 1:140; and on Burgh, Donald E. Hargis, 'James Burgh and *The Art of Speaking,*' *Speech Monographs,* 24 (1957): 275-84.

21. Peter Thomson's *ODNB* entry has virtually nothing to say about Sheridan the orthoepist and Esther K. Sheldon's impressive biography of his theatrical career has little more (*Thomas Sheridan of Smock-Alley* (Princeton, NJ: Princeton University Press, 1967). But see Wallace A. Bacon, 'The Elocutionary Career

of Thomas Sheridan (1719-88),' *Speech Monographs,* 31 (1964), 1-53; W. Benzie, *The Dublin Orator* (Menston: University of Leeds School of English, 1972); and Wilbur Samuel Howell, *Eighteenth-Century British Logic and Rhetoric* (Princeton: Princeton University Press, 1971), 214-43 as attempts to rectify the balance.

22. Robin C. Alston, prefatory note to facsimile reprint (Menston: Scolar Press, 1967), vol. 1.

23. Benzie, *The Dublin Orator,* 103.

24. The same passage, always a bone of contention in eighteenth-century Shakespeare editing, is discussed in the context of Garrick's pronunciation, in Arthur Murphy's article in *The Gray's Inn Journal* for 27 January 1752 (see *The Gray's Inn Journal,* 2 vols (1756), 1:100-1).

25. Thomas Sheridan and John Henderson, *Sheridan's and Henderson's Practical Method,* (1796), 14-15.

26. *The Present State of the Stage in Great-Britain and Ireland* (1753), 51.

27. J. W. Anderson, *The Manner Pointed out in which the Common Prayer was Read in Private by the Late Mr Garrick* (London, 1797), 43-4. A more elaborate edition with further notes was published in 1840 as *Garrick's mode of reading the liturgy of the Church of England* (London, 1840).

28. See G. C. Lichtenberg, *Lichtenberg's Visits to England,* ed. Margaret L. Mare and W. H. Quarrell (Oxford: Clarendon Press, 1938), 1-30.

29. See Alan S. Downer, ed., *Oxberry's 1822 edition of King Richard III: With descriptive notes recording Edmund Kean's performance made by James Hackett* (London: Society for Theatre Research, 1959).

30. The first line in Cibber's adaptation reads 'The North! Why, what do they in the North' (*The Tragical History of King Richard III* (1700), 44) but Murphy may be misquoting.

31. Arthur Murphy, *The Life of David Garrick, Esq.* (Dublin, 1801), 16.

32. Murphy, *Life of David Garrick,* 16-17.

33. Quoted McIntyre, *Garrick,* 2.

34. Steele, *An Essay,* 39 and 47.

35. David Thomas's comment that it is 'impossible to interpret meaningfully' is unduly cautious. See David Thomas and Arnold Hare, eds, *Restoration and Georgian England, 1660-1788* (Theatre in Europe: A Documentary History, Cambridge: Cambridge University Press, 1989), 353.

36. Steele, *An Essay,* 40 and 47.

37. Ibid., 48.

38. Ibid.

39. Joshua Steele, *Prosodia Rationalis* (1779), 203-6.

40. Aaron Hill, *The Works,* 4 vols (London, 1753), 1:140.

41. Hill, *Works,* 1:139.

42. Hill, *Works,* 1:140.

43. Roger Pickering, *Reflections upon Theatrical Expression in Tragedy* (London, 1755), 51.

44. David M. Little and George M. Kahrl, eds, *The Letters of David Garrick,* 3 vols (London: Oxford University Press, 1963), 1:93.

45. Ibid., 2:559-60.

46. John Hill, *The Actor* (1750), 309. The passage is repeated, unacknowledged, as one of the few criticisms of Garrick allowed into the first biography, *The Life and Death of David Garrick, Esq.,* 16.

47. *The Present State of the Stage,* 20.

48. Quoted by Alan S. Downer, 'Nature to Advantage Dressed: Eighteenth-Century Acting,' *PMLA,* 58 (1943): 1002-37 (1017).

49. *The Theatrical Review,* 79.

50. Quoted in Ronald Hafter's excellent article, 'Garrick and *Tristram Shandy,*' SEL, 7 (1967): 475-89 (484-5).

51. Letter to Hall Harston, *The Letters of David Garrick,* 1:350.

52. *Letters,* 1:350-1.

53. James Boswell, *The Life of Samuel Johnson,* ed. George Birkbeck Hill, revised L. F. Powell, 6 vols, (Oxford: Clarendon Press, 1934-50), 1.168-9. Michael Cordner suggests to me that Johnson is not necessarily persuasive here and that a reader might not wish to emphasize 'not' every time.

54. See Stone and Kahrl, *David Garrick,* 149-50.

55. Thaddeus Fitzpatrick, *An Enquiry into the Real Merit of a Certain Popular Performer* (1760), 21.

56. Ibid. See also Boswell's account of Colonel Pennington's complaint of Garrick's failure of emphasis in *Hamlet*: 'I will speak *daggers* to her; but use *none,*' instead of 'I will *speak* daggers to her; but *use* none' (Boswell, *Life of Samuel Johnson,* 5:127).

57. The principal printed text of Garrick's version of *King Lear* is the one in Bell's Shakespeare, 'as performed at the Theatre-Royal, Drury-Lane. Regulated from the prompt-book, with permission of the managers,

by Mr. Hopkins, Prompter.' The speech is in *Bell's Edition of Shakespeare's Plays,* 9 vols (London, 1774), 2:20. The standard account of Garrick's production is still George Winchester Stone, Jr., 'Garrick's Production of *King Lear*: A Study in the Temper of the Eighteenth-Century Mind,' *SP,* 45 (1948): 89-103. See also the edition of Garrick's adaptation in Harry W. Pedicord and Frederick L. Bergmann, eds, *The Plays of David Garrick,* 7 vols (Carbondale: Southern Illinois University Press, 1980-2), vol. 3.

58. William Cooke, *Memoirs of Charles Macklin, Comedian* (1804), 107. See also John Hill's praise: 'It is impossible to say whether Mr. Garrick expresses in this passage more fire or more feeling. Each is carried to the height, and they cast a new lustre upon one another' (*The Actor* (London, 1755), 129-30).

59. Samuel Foote, *A Treatise on the Passions* (London, 1747), p. 17; see also J. T., *A Letter of Compliment to the Ingenious Author of a Treatise on the Passions* (London, 1747), 18-21 for an elaborate description of Lear's feelings and emotional state.

60. Thomas Davies, *Dramatic Miscellanies,* 3 vols (London, 1784), 2:279.

61. Charles Gildon, *The Life of Mr. Thomas Betterton* (London, 1710), 115-16.

62. Davies, *Dramatic Miscellanies,* 2:279-80.

63. *An Examen of the New Comedy, Call'd The Suspicious Husband* (London, 1747), 31-2.

64. *Bell's Edition,* 2:20.

65. Theophilus Cibber, *Cibber's Two Dissertations of the Theatres* (London, 1756), Second Dissertation, 31.

66. John Shebbeare, *Letter to the English Nation,* 2 vols (London, 1755), 2:286-7. Joseph Pittard steals the passage in his *Observations on Mr. Garrick's Acting* (London, 1758), 10.

67. Edward Taylor, *Cursory Remarks on Tragedy* (London, 1774), 16, quoted Stone, 'Garrick's Production of *King Lear,*' 102.

68. See, for his overall view of King Lear, his letter of 1770, *The Letters of David Garrick,* 2:682-3.

69. Shebbeare, *Letter to the English Nation,* 2:288.

70. Pedicord and Bergmann, *The Plays of David Garrick,* 2:247.

John Pruitt (essay date 2008)

SOURCE: Pruitt, John. "David Garrick's Invisible Nemeses." *Restoration and 18th Century Theatre Research* 23.1 (2008): 2-18. Print.

[*In the following essay, Pruitt examines the profusion of dramatic satires of Garrick by his peers, some of them written by unemployed actors and playwrights whose work he had rejected. As Pruitt notes, Garrick's critics frequently charged him with sacrificing his artistic integrity to business management, refusing new plays and inscribing gentility onto established ones in his pursuit of wealth and the accolades of polite society.*]

In an interesting look at biographies of David Garrick, Cheryl Wanko poses an intriguing question. On discovering that Garrick had inspired more than five hundred critical commentaries during his lifetime, she asks, "[W]hy was Garrick important enough to provoke this swarming press?" (188).[1] As early as 1748, only one year into Garrick's management of Drury Lane, one commentator observed that "The Press swarms with Pamphlets address'd to you; and, how the Authors or Printers can find it worth their while to publish 'em, is a Matter of Some Wonder."[2] Wanko's question and the commentator's observation entice us to delve into this abundance of primary sources in order to uncover popular opinions about the man who transformed the eighteenth-century theater. Scholars and biographers, including Ian McIntyre and his collaborating forebears George Winchester Stone, Jr., and George M. Kahrl, have spent an impressive amount of energy singing his praises and analyzing the histrionic and dramaturgical contributions of this immortalized and energetic thespian, theater manager, philanthropist, and playwright; subject of numerous paintings; disciple of Shakespeare. When mourning Garrick's retirement, Hannah More even composed an *Ode to Dragon, Mr. Garrick's House-Dog, at Hampton*, begging the animal to "change with me thy fate, / To me give up they place and state, / And I will give thee mine" (7). Indeed, Garrick is certainly entitled to such accolades, but I find an investigation into the obvious though obscured equally important: Garrick's peers, especially those in the theater, also publicly (although more often than not anonymously) loathed and denounced him. As Garrick's contemporary John Hall-Stevenson made apparent, many of his "envious crew [...] / felt a satire in his merit" (12).

During his management of Drury Lane from 1747 to 1776, unrestrained contentions arose between Garrick, theater enthusiasts, and the population of unemployed performers he rejected for roles on the stage. In fact, in an impressively large number of letters, his critics alleged "what ten thousand people beside wish you should hear, (whether it be right or wrong)," that he ultimately rejected the spirit of the theater and petitions for novel productions because he had surrendered the better part of himself, that is, the sensibility vital for acting, in favor of management.[3] In the context of these tensions and among the five hundred critical commentaries, the occasional anonymous dramatic satire emerged berating him for lacking the emulative sensibility an actor should possess and for adopting commercial standards in its place.

In his defense, despite public entreaties for novelty in the stifling climate of the Stage Licensing Act of 1737 and afterwards, experimenting with new plays required available funds, risk, and time, and theater managers often panicked about the Lord Chamberlain abruptly banning performances and about rejection by an audience on opening night. This predicament forced the managers to work from a steady body of drama—often re-adaptations of established plays—muting overt censure against the government and to select appropriate entertainments to attract and captivate audiences. The town unfortunately reminded Garrick that it staunchly dismissed this business practice. Even more than thirty years following the passing of the Licensing Act, critics continued to reprimand him for refusing to stage new productions. Ideally, one author argues, "What I would earnestly recommend to you is, to represent as many new plays as possible, and let them stand or fall by their own merit." In fact, the same author argues, the theater manager, as "an inferior member of the republic of letters," regrettably "is possessed of a right of regulating the public diversions according to his will and pleasure, and of deciding the fate of the most important branch of literature."[4] In the spirit of such splenetic eruptions, Garrick served as an emblem of the unethical entrepreneur, shifting from object on stage to subject of topical satires blatantly epitomizing and embodying gross economic inequality and social jealousies dissociated from bourgeois merit, diligence, and industry. In Garrick's first year as manager, the author of *A Letter to Mr. Garrick, on His Having Purchased a Patent for Drury-Lane Play-House* pilloried Garrick as a plutocrat or parvenu whose veins and arteries circulate cash and whose very life depends on commerce:

> It is said of you, that as few Men at your Years ever attained to so much Perfection in the Capacity of an Actor, so scarce ever any Man at your Years, was so well acquainted with the Value of Money.—That every Addition to the Sum [of] your Abilities, and the almost unexampled Favour of the Town, has filled your Coffers with, gives you Extasies inexpressible; and on the least Diminution, tho' for the necessary Expences of Life, you feel Agonies like those of parting with your Vital Blood.

(7-8)

Throughout his tenure as a businessman, Garrick became such a target of abuse as a means of illustrating, preserving, and extending specific moral ideals and class values. According to Jürgen Habermas, such polite and reasonable discourse circulated through the eighteenth-century public sphere, where the bourgeoisie eagerly sought to exercise its power. Although the idea of the public sphere idealized an egalitarian utopia, in practice it failed because it excluded many professionals, such as actors, from access to power despite income and connections. The energy that Garrick spent to secure his reputation, while a tribute to his vivacity and fortitude, portended the difficulty of becoming an acclaimed actor and manager, especially among polite circles who marginalized performers.[5]

NEGOTIATING SENSIBILITY AND COMMERCIAL ENDEAVORS

The satires on Garrick's abuse of his management suggest the conflicts that beset the degradation of the theater as an institution and exemplify the anxieties about movement through social channels. As Jacob Viner argues in an early essay on eighteenth-century satirical approaches to economic disparity, although the English continually attempted to label and classify relative merit based on social standing, they recognized the impossibility of organizing and fixing the class hierarchies thought necessary for maintaining political order and authority. Despite the futility of stabilizing these structures in the existing market economy, critics and satirists did argue that Garrick, a former wine merchant affected and advantaged by a commercial economy, exploited his talent for acting with sensibility in order to persuade polite society, which sentenced the majority of actors to survive on the cusp of gentility, to attend the theater and therefore line his own pockets.

Such a compromise between commerce and sensibility calls into question contemporary assertions about the compatibility of the two. Although many of Garrick's critics and their forebears found commerce and sensibility mutually exclusive,[6] it actually is possible to situate this convergence of mutually determining spheres within the paradigm of contemporary social and political theory identified by J. G. A. Pocock. Pocock argues that commerce engaged in important dialogues with concepts of virtue, manners, politeness, and sensibility: "The social psychology of the age declared that encounters with things and persons evoked passions and refined them into manners; [and] it was pre-eminently the function of commerce to refine the passions and polish the manners" (49).[7] Despite this reality, the eighteenth-century propertied members of society, compulsively purchasing the status of lady and gentleman in London's growing culture of conspicuous consumption, stridently dismissed the unpropertied classes as irritably and pompously seeking to emulate the mannerly conduct necessary to business, credit, and gentility. In practice, though, politeness equated not only with "an orgy of spending" (McKendrick 9) and the accumulation of material acquisitions. Politeness also aligned with urbane manners and social connections offered by London's public spaces such as coffee houses, parks and gardens, and shops and markets where the masses practiced cultivating proper etiquette. Indeed, in London's expanding economy and upwardly mobile society, anyone with disposable income could participate in the fashionable display of the urban elites; once combined, rituals of social engagement including "[c]ivilized conduct, taste, aesthetics, and deportment conveyed affluence" (Berg 205).[8]

As merchant-turned-entrepreneur rehearsing and performing gentility on all stages, Garrick had become one of them.[9]

Through this line of thinking, Garrick's fluid social status actually evolved from his ability to perform with sensibility, which provided his talent for beguiling his fans and infuriating his critics. In his own criticism, Garrick deemed sensibility to be paramount to the acting and spectating experiences. In a 3 January 1769 letter to Helfric Peter Sturz on the performance of Mme Clairon, Garrick wrote about her remarkably natural style but abysmal dearth of sensibility, which alienated her audience: "She has every thing that Art and a good understanding, with great Natural Spirit can give her—But then I fear [...] the Heart has none of those instantaneous feelings, that Life blood, that keen Sensibility, that bursts at once from Genius, and like Electrical fire shoots thro' the Veins, Morrow, Bones and all, of every Spectator" (qtd. in Stone and Kahrl 45).[10] To Garrick, sensibility is a discrete facet of performance that the actor must integrate to become a commodity worthy of public consumption, that is, as a means of emblematizing and reflecting the habits of the polite members of his audience. By the mid-eighteenth century, many writers had undermined the myth that those not born of the nobility might still achieve gentility through social performance, that "a range of middling sorts in London assumed modes of politeness within their reach" (Klein 374).[11] Still, because of his proletariat background and position as common (yet venerated) actor, his magnetism among the upper ranks spawned a great deal of anxiety among the socially aspiring classes who considered themselves to be members of a polite theater audience. In 1742, Horace Walpole, later Lord Orford, voiced this perspective by effusing that "all the run is now after Garrick, a wine-merchant, who is turn'd player at Goodman's Fields" (qtd. in Woods 19). Although Walpole later fraternized with Garrick the theater manager, it appears that the basis for his initial criticism stemmed from the degeneration of tastes—signs of civility and socialized desire—among a larger playgoing public who permitted a wine merchant to explode suddenly into their graces. Such remarks haunted Garrick nearly until the end of his career, when critics attacked not only him but also "those *fools of quality* ... led by fashion to pay an implicit belief to whatever comes from the *dear mouth of the wonderful Garrick*."[12] It appears that his talent for acting attracted the upper classes both to his performances on stage and to his capacity to create and maintain relations and exchanges with those whose patronage he sought. The upper ranks generally permitted arbitration of public taste to Garrick because, as a compulsive performer on all stages, he displayed the refined attributes of a gentleman, which defined his mastery of the dynamics of theatrical production and reception and his recognition of both the power and the vulnerabilities of the institution that would legitimate him as an actor and manager. Indeed, although Garrick's censurers found his behavior inexcusable, Jean

Benedetti suggests that the manager actually fitted perfectly into this culture requiring men to control their emotions while catering to the needs and feelings of others, for polite society demanded nothing less (28-29). While voices as prominent as those of Samuel Johnson fumed over the actor's ability to assume the identity of "an easy, fine-bred gentleman" (qtd. in Woods 21) both on and off stage, by this means Garrick retained a form of patronage necessary for the endurance of Drury Lane and his livelihood in a highly competitive market.

GARRICK CHARACTERIZED

In the context of Garrick's fawning admirers and critics alike treating the stage as a space for inscribing politeness and the theater as a legitimate, civilized diversion and refuge from the depredations of the masses, satirists began to evaluate Garrick by both social criteria and business endeavors: they investigated and questioned his identity as a virtuous gentleman and his business ethics as a perversion of true commerce. Such lies the purpose behind *The Theatrical Manager* (1751), the first dramatic satire lodged directly against Garrick, made apparent in the author's dedication "To all the Aspiring Genius' and pretended Commentators," explaining that "I have only *privately* attempted to reform the Manners of him, who *publicly* dared to reclaim the Customs of the World" (vi, original emphasis). As Charles Knight suggests, satirists generally "attack for a commanding reason which they openly articulate or cunningly apply" (13). Here, by portraying the debilitating consequences of emulation and consumption through excessive desire to raise one's social status, the satire illustrates how the actor-manager surrenders his integrity through performance outside the theater and explains the means by which he culturally and ideologically partakes in the discourse of politeness.

The Theatrical Manager centers around Vaticide, the ruthless, tightfisted, and hypocritical caricature of Garrick, currently an actor aspiring to become theater manager, who receives a note requesting his presence at a rehearsal of *Richard III* (incidentally the play that made Garrick famous). The decision to comply seems difficult for the player seeking social elevation, for "what Torture do I labour under, to be forced to act thus against my Inclinations—but my Hopes are now within my Reach, and let any one find me the Man that would not betray his Conscience for such a glorious Prospect" (2). En route to the theater, Vaticide encounters the indigent and starving Buck, ruthlessly pursued by creditors; Buck's equally suffering and emaciated Welsh servant Ap Meagre; and Buck's acquaintance Dangle, financially spent from indulging his beloved (prostitute) Lucinda. On Vaticide's quick departure from Buck's complaints and paranoid surveillance of the vicinity, Buck attempts to persuade Dangle to recognize his poor decision to waste money on contemptible women and encourages him to mimic Vaticide, to "pretend to like every Body, and never suffer yourself to

be ensnared by any one, and live in Contempt of all lawful Conjunctions, where your Interest is not directly concerned" (12).

In order to amend their financial situations, Buck requests from Vaticide a loan of one hundred pounds, which the newly appointed manager declines with advice simply to "make the best of a bad Market" (28); on this rejection, they decide to pursue acting careers. Finally gaining access to Vaticide's rooms in order to audition, Buck and Dangle plead their case to seek employment by arguing that "tho' we have lost our Fortunes, we would not willingly throw away our Reputations" (59). The statement obviously confounds Vaticide, who wonders "what the Plague is Reputation worth without a Fortune?" (59) and, after dismissing the men, vows to "guard against falling into the same Absurdity for the future, for I'll only make a Friend of those that have Wealth to continue so" (62). Satiated himself by an early career of destitution and servility, Vaticide surrenders gentlemanly charity, humility, and benevolence as leading qualities of the eighteenth-century man of commerce.

The Theatrical Manager chiefly contrasts Vaticide with Buck, who lost his fortune and honor through emulating the upper ranks and failed to meet his debts. Rather than balancing his accounts to establish his credit publicly, Buck professes that he surrendered his virtue by relying on the performance of gentility to gain a favorable public reputation: "wanting Virtue to enjoy what I possessed, I was deluded by outward Appearances, and fell a Prey to those gaudy Villains who infest public Places to catch the Unwary, and live in all the Splendour and Gaiety of Men of Fortune, without any visible Means of supporting it" (28). The author's endorsement of maintaining one's credit through financial meticulousness exposes the complexity of the relationship between credit and consumption. The offense of emulating the upper ranks for preferment discloses an alternative identity for Buck and Vaticide as it does for Garrick: whereas Buck ultimately becomes a model of social and ethical virtues, Vaticide intensifies the tensions between the defense of the gentleman and the condemnation of the new man of commerce. Although Vaticide appears to embrace Buck's advice to Dangle by performing with politeness to one's creditors and customers, contemporary commercial culture has actually razed systems of integrity and sensibility, for, as Vaticide admits, "if you trust to Honour and Honesty now-a-days, let me tell you, you build your Dependence upon a rotten Foundation, for that has been a Maxim long since exploded" (15).

Accordingly, the sensibility vital for acting with gentility among one's peers in *The Theatrical Manager* conflicts with the sensibility for performing on stage. As Buck contends, "That sprightly turn is owing to the Multitude of People [Vaticide] converses with, that he borrows from all sorts a Rhapsody of uncommon Expressions, and pours them out as incoherently as a Parrot; which false Wit, by many People is mistaken for Sense, but in Fact he is nothing more than an Eccho of the Public" (36). The public sphere as a site where the commercial classes uphold their reputations through performance of civility signifies not only the importance of credit and profit. It also suggests that the capacity to act with sensibility is detrimental to the middle classes who frantically struggle to rise in social status but neglect to monitor personal spending and consumption. Buck admits that his decline from gentleman to highwayman "agrees not with my Constitution; for being outlawed from all Society must essentially destroy our Reputation.—And what must I do?—The Credit by which I so long maintained my Character is entirely blasted" (23). He has therefore lost his honor, for he is unable to pay his debts to uphold his credit. However, countering Vaticide's philosophy to refrain from assisting his friends, Buck delivers thanks and financial compensation to Ap Meagre and to Dangle's Irish servant, O Bragg, thus illustrating the proper ends for teaching moral lessons about charity and economy: "I am not like many People, condemn you, because I cannot serve you, but will assist you as far as I am able; here take all we have, and divide between you, and let me advise you, return to your Countries, settle in some Employment, and live honest" (34-35).

Vaticide, himself opposed to contributing charitably, to his own dismay remains trapped in his role as manager, unprepared for the vigilance required to manage a theater and for the anxieties of pending financial ruin: "what an unthinking Wretch was I, to let Fancy, that active Daemon to an ambitious Mind, so infatuate my Understanding, as to lead me blindfold into the misty Road of Preferment, without consulting my Abilities" (57-58). Vaticide's concern for his talents echoes a caustic warning that Garrick received on purchasing the patent to Drury Lane in 1747, a warning of the perils of theater management and the inanity of relinquishing his own celebrated art of acting to pursue a capitalist venture. "Permit me to ask you, in the Name of Common Sense, what possibly could induce you to such an Undertaking?" the anonymous author asks, insisting that Garrick's impressive salary will never compensate for the impending emotional anguish of coordinating successful performances and directing scoundrel actors who manipulate managers in order to procure public notoriety and profit.[13] In light of such a harbinger of impending misery, Vaticide realizes that self-interest has "become the Standard of Politeness" (62) and acknowledges that he irrecoverably abrogated his acting sensibility to reach a higher social status. Buck, on the other hand, seeks to become an actor in Vaticide's company to regain his reputation, which will reinforce his lower social status but allow him to recover his credit by earning wages: "as you know my Abilities from our former Intimacy, [I] would gladly embrace the Opportunity of serving under you in the Capacity of an Actor, and endeavour to acquire by Merit what I am denied by Fortune" (61). Vaticide,

however, to uphold his own credit, declines Buck's request because he suspects that only famous actors, which he himself has become, will attract the upper classes to the theater.

Consequently, in a final apostrophe to the country, Buck identifies England as a macrocosmic theater where fortune and credit negate virtue: "O *England! England!* how art thou degenerated! from a Theatre of Virtue and Benevolence, to a Receptacle of Pride and Luxury" (62-63, original emphasis). Buck's contention echoes that of Garrick's critics who vocally recognize the new theater's national disruption, that Garrick had transformed the stage from a pedagogical tool only to "misapply the Power that is plac'd in you, for your Countrymens Service" by "Plot[ting] upon the Understandings of the younger Part of the Nation, in order to make the future Age all *Lunaticks.*"[14] With the identification of economic self-interest rather than merit and morality as the driving force of Garrick's activity, both of the author of *The Theatrical Manager* and Garrick's patriotic critic determine that the theater thrives on the regulation of money and manners.

With explicit footnotes so as not to confound the reader (by unambiguously labeling the satire's target as "G—k"), the author continues in the epilogue the imagery of a nation in peril by identifying a new world order under a capitalist monarch who has commodified acting and dramaturgy: "King David," an object of vilification, has captured the theater by "Diffusing Fear thro' all the captive Band, / And breath'd Destruction o'er the Mimic Land" and now "Spurns at the Precepts that his Friends advise, / And vainly thinks his Merit will suffice" (64). Thus Garrick has built his new empire in Drury Lane through financial accumulation and development under the aegis of meeting his debts and living up to his credit. The epilogue also justifies the author's use of satire to respond publicly to Garrick's abhorrent action of surrendering his acting sensibility to pursue commercial endeavors: "When Kings (dramatic) prove such dastard Rogues, / And quit the Sword to fight with Epilogues, / What must we Subjects do?—Not cringe and bow; / But zealous in our Cause, give Blow for Blow" (64). Through these means the satirist, asking Garrick to embrace the community of performers that spawned such a successful entrepreneur, makes his or her presence felt within the parameters of social; political, and economic power but not necessarily with malicious intent:

> If you our noble Spirits will defend,
> And crown our Labour with triumphant End,
> We'll boast no Titles, free from Pride's Disease,
> With the Reflection, we will rest at Ease?
> —He merits most, who studies most to please.

(64)

This strategy of emphatically centering the text's argument on the theater community's attitude toward the manager's (lack of) merit when hiring actors and poets suggests that all relationships, personal qualities, values, and entire persons are assigned monetary worth in a market-oriented society, and that all employments are reducible to one's self interests and pursuit of wealth. According to the satirist, to become prosperous and therefore reach a safe haven in which moral uprightness is merely possible, one may have to turn to dishonorable means.

Following the publication of *The Theatrical Manager,* presses erupted forth with a number of dramatic satires against Garrick, creating an arsenal of paper bullets aimed directly at the manager's inability to satisfy the nation, maintain a playhouse, and uphold his role as both actor and manager.[15] Although these assaults provide only an indirect criticism of the separation between Garrick's management style and artistic sensibilities, a brief account of their contributions to the undermining of his career provides a compelling narrative on perceptions of his self-promotion and image construction. The anonymous *A Dialogue in the Green-Room upon a Disturbance in the Pit* (1763), for example, suggests that the fractious public, rather than the theater's timorous manager, actually controls the playhouse. The dialogue imagines a conversation between Drury Lane's manager, his cashier, and his entourage as the audience prepares to riot if the manager refuses to lower ticket prices for revived plays. As a critique concerned centrally with the subject's connection to property, the imaginary *Dialogue* evaluates the social mechanisms that account for riots spawned by the public's perception of its rights to dictate and administer theater policy and repertoire. According to the satirist, as the furniture in the auditorium flies, we discover that Fitzgig, the leader of this affair, has resorted to violence because his notices against rising ticket prices have remained unaddressed. In fact, the riot leaves Sir Charles Easy to ask the manager rhetorically, "Who cou'd have thought such an insignificant paper as this cou'd have had so great an effect, when so much has been written against you without having the least operation[?]" (23). The following night, when the manager finally meets the demands of the audience—"In my fright, to be sure, I did say *Yes,* and agreed to what they proposed" (31, original emphasis)—it leaves us to wonder if Garrick ever controlled what he was doing in a realm where he was distinguished by his capacity for mastering, rather than abandoning himself to, the passions.

Francis Gentleman's anonymously published *The Stratford Jubilee* (1769) also questions Garrick's ability to control performance venues, here by satirizing the effects of the Shakespearean revelry on the public. Rather than commemorating the Bard's contribution to the English theater, the Jubilee congregates the aristocracy, ignorant of Shakespeare's existence, seeking casual sexual encounters by displaying both their bodies and wealth:

> To the market, old dowagers also repair
> With borrowed complexions, teeth, eye-brows, and hair;

> Each wooes with her purse,
> For better or worse,
> The female that's wealthy must surely be fair.
> . . . .
> Smart beaux, whom stern cynics call rational apes,
> Haste hither to shew their fine cloaths and fine shapes,
> They know *Shakespeare*'s name,
> And have heard of his fame,
> Though his merit their shallow conception escapes.

(5, original emphasis)

Under the pseudonym Nicholas Nipclose, Gentleman followed this satire with *The Theatres. A Poetical Dissection* (1772), to chastise Garrick as "the polluted source of all Theatrical dullness and deficiency" (vii). On the title page we find Matthew Darley's caricature of Garrick's showmanship, a parody of Joshua Reynolds' painting *Garrick between Tragedy and Comedy* (1760-61) carrying the poetic caption "Behold the Muses Roscius sue in Vain, / Taylors & Carpenters usurp their Reign." A seemingly complaisant Garrick, straddled between the muses Thalia and Melpomene battling with Drury Lane's scene-makers for his undivided attention while the works of Shakespeare, Jonson, and Rowe lie trampled underfoot, appears to express a predilection for pleasing both audiences and the theater's stakeholders.

The tranquility Garrick sought in his own playhouse also could not be sustained in the fallen world of the afterlife, for the satires continued even after his death. Of course, when Garrick died, the press erected forth numerous elegies praising his resurrection of Shakespeare. The author of *An Elegy on the Death of David Garrick* (1779) observes that "With Shakespeare's Fire his Breast was fraught, / 'Twas he embodied Shakespeare's Thought" (8); the author of "To the Memory of David Garrick, Who Died in the Year 1779, at the Age of 63" remarked that "To paint fair nature, by divine command, / Her magic pencil in his glowing hand, / A Shakespeare rose: Then to expand his fame, / Wide o'er this breathing world, a Garrick came" ("Garrick's Monument" 375); and the lugubrious author of the untitled dedication to Garrick in *The Literary Fly* (30 Jan. 1779) tearfully asks the reader to "picture to himself, the subject will require all his colours, what kind of meeting it was, if spirits indeed know each other in their world, between Garrick and Shakespeare" (13). The author of the satire appropriately titled *Garrick in the Shades; or, A Peep into Elysium* (1779) took this final request literally. Published the same year as Garrick's death, the satire concludes the assaults on the manager's career by arraigning him in the underworld before the testimony delivered by an assembly of actors and authors he rejected. Framing the satire as a trial, the author intimates that there is something inherently criminal in Garrick's business strategy. Although Garrick steered clear of legal trouble, it appears that the author registers a general hostility to Garrick's aristocratic pretensions to taste and contests his authority to ascribe value to dramaturgical talents. As "King David" on earth, Garrick must submit to classical, mythical authorities for a critique of his moral degeneracy.

Elysium, a theater itself, is managed by Rhadamanthus, one of the ancient Greek judges of the dead who presides over the court and, unlike Garrick, objectively determines the fates of the actors who appear before him: "These realms of govern'd by a manager, / Severe, and scrutinizing, Rhadamanthus call'd; / Who with a balance nice, weighs each offence, / And deals out punishment proportionate" (35). Elysium subverts the Drury Lane monarchy and the theatrical social order and becomes a site of legal regulation under the unbiased management of Rhadamanthus where actors from Antiquity and modernity interact, partake in the distractions they were accused of while living (such as Thomas Weston, who drank himself into debtor's prison, now in Elysium drinking with one of the Furies), and become Garrick's tormentors.

On their long-awaited confrontation with the "little King of Drury" (15), former rivals and acquaintances, particularly the giddy Samuel Foote and James Quin,[16] notice when they welcome him into his new kingdom, "thou paragon of actors! thou that wast the living comment on thy beloved Shakespeare" (13-14), that he maintains his poise despite the tension, that "With what composure of muscle he hears all this flattery" (14). However, the accusations run quickly, for Quin promises Garrick that Rhadamanthus will scour him in Phlegethon, a river of fire surrounding Hades, "to cleanse thee from thy vanity, and love of money" (15). Garrick justifies his motives for getting a fortune by equating his merit with his affluence, a confessional act suturing gaps in Garrick's persona as both artist and capitalist: "If I coveted riches, it was, because I perceived they removed every obstacle in the path that led to honours.—I was, besides, ambitious of being well received amongst the great, and I well knew, that being a good actor was no title to their acquaintance, unless I was a rich one" (15). Garrick's motives here echo those of Vaticide, motives that critics viewed as consistent throughout his career, and his composure during the attacks on his character evinces his security as an esteemed actor in the perspective of his patrons. But Garrick is no longer protected by the company of his aristocratic coterie, and his sensibility for acting, he discovers, fails to save him from his vituperative detractors.

Garrick's associations within this theater of dead actors and poets confirm his final demise, for the introductions of those who welcome versus those who denounce him reveal this dynamic as the mode of operation in the satire. The flustered shades of Charles Holland, Henry Mossop, and Spranger Barry welcome Garrick as a god whose realms he "Controul'd, with staff of pow'r manageric" (17). Although Garrick revels in the flattery, Foote explains to Quin that these performers actually managed less than admirable careers. Mossop, although a fine actor, transferred to man-

agement in Dublin but ended his life in debtors prison; Barry acted alongside Garrick but ruined his career by playing Macheath in *The Beggar's Opera* without the ability to sing; and Holland became Garrick's protégé. Before Garrick left England to travel through France from 1763 to 1765, he trained Holland to play his chief roles, and audiences gathered at Drury Lane to see him perform. In return, Garrick hosted Holland's benefits by staging Otway's *Venice Preserv'd* in 1760 and Joseph Reed's tragedy *Dido* in 1767, and most interestingly allowed him to play Richard III, the role that launched Garrick's acting career, to the audience's elation in 1776. Foote, however, defines Holland as "a fellow of no feeling, that being just able to read, and having a tolerable stage-figure, strutted, stared, and started, just as he had received from his master, and learnt by rote" (*Shades* 18), implying that Garrick denied Holland agency to interpret each character and desired the audiences to see an icon of himself on stage by projecting his image even *in absentia*.

I devote significant space to Holland because he serves as messenger between Garrick and his forebears. In return for his favoritism, Garrick expects his student to play the compassionate sycophant: "But tell me, my Holland!—inform me, my favourite pupil—whom I instructed in emphasis, tone, and pause—to whom I imparted my own stare—my own stamp—my own fall—in short, whom I taught to read—tell me, hast thou no comfort for thy friend, and master—" (*Shades* 27). But, as the sympathetic Holland claims, only his lack of education prompts him to admire his trainer: "All simple as I am, with letters unimbu'd, / I thought thee greatest, at one time, of bards, / As thou of actors surely art the first— / But that's nor here, nor there" (28). Like Garrick's patrons, even Holland reveals that Garrick's career is now insignificant and his behavior unredeemable.

The final blow to Garrick's ego manifests itself between scenes, for we discover that the shades of his idols and theatrical ancestors scoff at and dismiss him:

FOOTE:

> Did you observe, my soul of sarcasm, how cooly Shakespeare received him?—Johnson [sic] surveyed him from head to foot—then turning from him, Ben stalked surlily away.——

QUIN:

> I did observe all this, my worthy publisher of private scandal;—and moreover, that Beaumont, Fletcher, Massinger, Southern, Otway, Lee, Dryden, Rowe, all behaved with great indifference.

(23-24)

Shakespeare, it seems, deft himself at exposing the corruption inherent to human nature through his own villains such as Iago, Claudius, Macbeth, and Goneril and Regan, insightfully uncovers through Holland his knowledge that

Garrick exploited his reputation and chastises Garrick for his insolence:

> hence he knows,
> Thou madest his name a stalking horse to wealth,
> And freely borrow'd'st from his lib'ral store,
> . . . That, thy fam'd Jubilee, was a mean device
> To gull the people—and to cram thy well-fill'd purse."

(Shades 25)

The reprimand suggests not only Shakespeare's disgust with Garrick's intentions, but also the space of dramatic talent between them. At the same time, although Shakespeare's name survives because of the statues Garrick erected and portraits he sat for, Garrick's audiences have already forgotten his performances. In a message that the elusive Ben Jonson relays through Holland, Garrick learns that an actor's reputation never flourishes, for the memory of a performance collapses immediately afterward:

> Frail and imperfect is the actor's fame—
> He lives but to the age, that sees him act.
> The well-tim'd pause—the thrilling tone
> That harrows up the soul—the emphasis
> That rightly plac'd, conveys a meaning,
> Strong, full, and clear, beyond a comment's reach—
> The expressive look, that draws the sympathetic tear—
> —These excellencies all are lost—
> Buried within the grave that shrouds his corse;
> Or if they live—
> Live only in the faint memorials of the times[.]

(Shades 30)

In Elysium, Garrick's wealth, credit, and sensibility for acting become insignificant, but he strives to prolong his fame in the underworld by applying to perform as Abel Drugger (one of his most celebrated roles) for Jonson, who shows appreciation for the revival of *The Alchemist,* thus securing only the persistence of Jonson's own fame as a poet.

The satirist's picture of Garrick's demise into ridicule highlights the superficiality on which his career was supposedly founded, particularly when previous authors attack the dignity of his dramatic works, which Jonson describes as:

> Without intrigues, scenes jumbled and confus'd
> And characters which nature never own'd;
> Which, like a bantling drop'd at rich men's doors,
> Compassion foster'd, until bolder grown,
> The spurious offspring claim'd as lawful right,
> That patronage by charity bestow'd.

(Shades 32)

Whereas Jonson suggests that Garrick received patronage through pity, Garrick's contemporaries and members of his social circle—Lord George Lyttleton and Lord Philip Stanhope Chesterfield—admit that they attended plays at Drury Lane because, they regret, it was fashionable:

> We, whilst on earth, did sacrifice to fashion;
> Fashion, the deity of fools ever worship;
> To honour whom they give up ease and health,
> And blindly think and act as she dictates;
> By fashion led, we then frequented him,
> As others did; and here such vanities,
> With greivous pains have expiated.

(Shades 34)

The "fashionable" aristocratic culture that supplied Garrick with his livelihood and credit in the public sphere divests Garrick of his honor, for his career has been commissioned by the congregation of "the deity of fools." By casting himself into public circulation to augment his fame, Garrick has ironically entered into a debased circulation. Fashionable culture, denounced by its own disciples, supplies the cache of artifice that supported Garrick's transgression of the class structure and imitation of those of higher rank.

The distressed and nameless actors and poets who testify against Garrick complain that they are the best judges of their sensibility in acting and of their talent for writing. In their own search for fame, they denounce Garrick for denying them further opportunity to pursue their artistic endeavors and to solicit laudable reputations with the audiences they admit abominated their plays and performances. The "Second Player, whom nobody now remembers," was deprived of a major role "because he had tried me in two parts, and the town did not just then happen to approve of me" (*Shades* 39). Moreover, another player complains that he "made me [the Fourth Player] appear in trifling characters, which I was not approved in by the town, notwithstanding I was always firmly of opinion, that if I had acted capital parts I should have been well received" (40). Garrick snubbed the authors for similar reasons: the "Third Poet, whom nobody ever heard of," "for no earthly reason, but because I failed in two or three I had written before—and they chanced to be damned" (39-40). But the Fifth Poet gives Garrick an ounce of credit, for "I submitted my piece to his correction; to which I intirely [sic] attribute its miscarriage on the stage, though, to be sure, the parts best received were what he had altered" (41). Here, Garrick is attacked for being a slave to public opinion and for being a critic himself because he determined the careers of those who professed to best understand the terms of their own authorship. Their testimony suggests that Garrick's progress as theater manager actually debased his character and finally his body and spirit, the first expired, the second sentenced to eternal ablution of sycophancy and cupidity by means of "a hearty scouring in Phlegethon" (*Shades* 15). Finally, the actor's texts and body are set outside his control. Whereas Garrick exploited both his sensibility and body in order to operate within the polite modes of social discourse, the backstage of the post-mortem theater world disfigures the tools that made him a star and trivializes the theme of acting sensibility with a ludic consistency and cruelty.

In the words of Martin Price, "The satirist is always demonstrating a failure" (16). For Garrick's satirists who charge the manager with inauthenticity of all sorts, the failure resides in his social and economic fluidity. Indeed, Garrick's opponents are no more insightful about the "realities" of their (and his) situation than is Garrick himself; they don't chronicle the degradation of the theater, but assert that position to justify their own opposition to Garrick and what he supposedly represents. Although Garrick tried to raise the social standing of actors by setting himself up as a model of polite affability and modern refinement while striving to maintain profits and thus keep himself and his current actors employed, his thespian opponents saw his need for commercial success and favorable reputation as cutting away from the novel perception of theater as embodying sensibility: Garrick, they argued, commercialized his craft and thus degraded the actors.

These openly belligerent satires purportedly expose Garrick's inability to retain the kind of sensibility integral to the acting profession, which set him at odds with what made him the great actor he supposedly was. Whereas Melinda Rabb suggests that satire contributes to unearthing what many wish to conceal, the satirist "a purveyor of confounding hidden truths, a restless malcontent who rakes the filth from dark corners," Garrick's anonymous satirists open the secret world of the theater to audiences seeking to confirm what they already apparently believe truthful (326). They argue that Garrick, motivated by his recent potential for social mobility and profit, abandoned his artistic license to solicit a reputation as a highly regarded public figure among the upper ranks, a status that many actors wished to achieve themselves. In a way, they seem to be holding out against the possibilities that a burgeoning economy in leisure offers, and see actors as a repository for values that may be ignored or even destroyed as the theater grows more "politely" commercial. However, it is actually Garrick's acting sensibility that enabled him to become a respected associate of the gentility and a successful manager.

Notes

1. Wanko cites her source as Stone's "David Garrick and the Eighteenth-Century Stage," 9.

2. *D[rur]y-L[a]ne P[la]yh[ou]se Broke Open. In a Letter to Mr. G[arrick]*, 1-2.

3. *A Letter to Mr. Garrick on the Opening of the Theatre, with Observations on the Conduct of Managers to Actors, Authors, and Audiences: And Particularly to New-Performers* (London, 1758) 5.

4. H. W., *A Letter to David Garrick, Esq; on Opening the Theatre. In Which, with Great Freedom, He Is Told How He Ought to Behave* (London, 1769) 11, 5.

5. For an extensive investigation into the conflation of acting and social class, see Straub, 151-73.

6. In the early 1700s, for example, Bernard Mandeville and Anthony Ashley Cooper, Third Earl of Shaftesbury, dialogued about the implications of the arts among contemporary debates about culture, ethics, and socioeconomic power. While Shaftesbury observed a virtuous polity, Mandeville directed his contemporaries to recognize that neither culture nor society shaped morality. The sooner they grasped the reality of this separation, the quicker England could realize its potential as a great commercial nation. See Solkin, 1-26.

7. Also see Langford, who contends that "The alliance of money and gentility was calculated to maintain the morale and sense of superiority of propertied people" (60) and discovers evidence of the collusion of politeness and consumption in the expansion of the book trade, in the rise of tourism to spa towns and resorts, and in the management of servants. Barker-Benfield expands Langford's evidence to include a fascination with self-fashioning through sermons, books of courtly behavior, and apparition narratives (77-98).

8. Berg's section on "A Nation of Shoppers" (195-325) is one of many valuable resources on the social and economic construction of the middle-class consumer. See Klein, "Politeness for Plebes," Berry 199-242, James 129-228, and Finn 25-63.

9. For a recent delineation of the evolution of politeness and sensibility both on and off of the eighteenth-century stage, see Goring, 114-41. In his chapter on conflicting acting styles, Goring reviews criticism from Jeremy Collier's *A Short View of the Immorality of the Profaneness of the English Stage* (1698) to Aaron Hill's *The Art of Acting* (1746) in order to trace the gradual civilizing of the theater through the impression of morality on the minds of the audience via the stage presence of actors.

10. For detailed discussions about eighteenth-century theories of acting, see Roach and Freeman.

11. Both Klein and Raven (83-111) provide copious reviews of sixteenth- and seventeenth-century conduct literature and its impact on eighteenth-century trade and on the moral imperatives for the entrepreneur.

12. *A Letter to David Garrick, Esq. on His Conduct as Principal Manager and Actor at Drury-Lane* 12, original emphasis.

13. *A Letter to Mr. Garrick, on His Having Purchased a Patent for Drury-Lane Play-House*, 5.

14. *A Letter to Mr. G[arric]k, Relative to His Treble Capacity of Manager, Actor, and Author* (London, 1749) 6-7, original emphasis.

15. See Fisher, who details a number of satires such as *The Theatrical Manager, A Dialogue in the Green Room,* and Arthur Murphy's *Life of Hamlet, with Alterations,* in order to illustrate the tension between Garrick's multiple roles both on and off stage.

16. According to biographers, Foote reveled in undermining Garrick's authority. For example, he inserted satirical allusions to Garrick's *Jubilee* into his own performance of *The Devil upon Two Sticks,* playing at the Haymarket the summer of 1769, and wrote the following paragraph for a provincial newspaper: "It is said our English Aristophanes has declared his Intention of going to Stratford, at the Time of the Jubilee, in order to collect Incidents for a humorous Piece, which he will lay before the Public, for their Amusement next Winter, under a very odd Title." In order to prevent Foote from publicizing additional false rumors, Garrick confirmed comfortable lodgings for Foote in Stratford during the event. Quin, a famously cantankerous actor well before Garrick took to the stage, resented Garrick's novel acting style and perceived the performer as a threat. See McIntyre 62-64, 417.

Works Cited

Barker-Benfield, G. J. *The Culture of Sensibility: Sex and Society in Eighteenth-Century Britain.* Chicago: U of Chicago P, 1992.

Benedetti, Jean. *David Garrick and the Birth of Modern Theatre.* London: Methuen, 2001.

Berg, Maxine. *Luxury and Pleasure in Eighteenth-Century Britain.* Oxford: Oxford UP, 2005.

Berry, Christopher J. *The Idea of Luxury: A Conceptual and Historical Investigation.* Cambridge: Cambridge UP, 1994.

A Dialogue in the Green-Room upon a Disturbance in the Pit. London, 1763.

D[rur]y-L[a]ne P[la]yh[ou]se Broke Open. In a Letter to Mr. G[arrick]. London, 1748.

An Elegy on the Death of David Garrick, Esq. 2nd ed. London, 1779.

Finn, Margot C. *The Character of Credit: Personal Debt in English Culture, 1740-1914.* Cambridge: Cambridge UP, 2003.

Fisher, Judith W. "Actor and/or Manager? David Garrick Off Stage." *Restoration and Eighteenth-Century Theatre Research* 21.1 (2006): 2-17.

Freeman, Lisa A. *Character's Theater: Genre and Identity on the Eighteenth-Century English Stage.* Philadelphia: U of Pennsylvania P, 2002.

Garrick in the Shades; or, A Peep into Elysium. London, 1779.

"Garrick's Monument, in Westminster-Abbey." *European Magazine* June 1797: 375.

[Gentleman, Francis]. *The Stratford Jubilee. A New Comedy of Two Acts.* London, 1769.

Goring, Paul. *The Rhetoric of Sensibility in Eighteenth-Century Culture.* Cambridge: Cambridge UP, 2005.

H. W. *A Letter to David Garrick, Esq; On Opening the Theatre. In Which, with Great Freedom, He Is Told How He Ought to Behave.* London, 1769.

Habermas, Jürgen. *The Structural Transformation of the Public Sphere: An Inquiry into a Category of Bourgeois Society.* Trans. Thomas Burger with Frederick Lawrence. Cambridge: MIT Press, 1991.

Hall-Stevenson, John. *The Sick Monkey, a Fable.* London, 1765.

Hunt, Margaret R. *The Middling Sort: Commerce, Gender, and the Family in England, 1680-1780.* Berkeley: U of California P, 1996.

James, Lawrence. *The Middle Class: A History.* London: Little, 2006.

Klein, Lawrence E. "Politeness for Plebes: Consumption and Social Identity in Early Eighteenth-Century England." *The Consumption of Culture, 1600-1800: Image, Object, Text.* Ed. Ann Bermingham and John Brewer. London: Routledge, 1995. 362-82.

Knight, Charles A. *The Literature of Satire.* Cambridge: Cambridge UP, 2004.

Langford, Paul. *A Polite and Commercial People: England, 1727-1783.* Oxford: Clarendon, 1989.

A Letter to David Garrick, Esq. on His Conduct as Principal Manager and Actor at Drury-Lane. London, 1772.

A Letter to Mr. Garrick, on His Having Purchased a Patent for Drury-Lane Play-House. London, 1747.

A Letter to Mr. Garrick on the Opening of the Theatre, with Observations on the Conduct of Managers to Actors, Authors, and Audiences: And Particularly to New-Performers. London, 1758.

A Letter to Mr. G[arric]k, Relative to His Treble Capacity of Manager, Actor, and Author. London, 1749.

McIntyre, Ian. *Garrick.* London: Allen Lane, 1999.

McKendrick, Neil. "The Consumer Revolution of Eighteenth-Century England." *The Birth of a Consumer Society: The Commercialization of Eighteenth-Century England.* By McKendrick, John Brewer, and J. H. Plumb. Bloomington: Indiana UP, 1985. 9-33.

More, Hannah. *Ode to Dragon, Mr. Garrick's House-Dog, at Hampton.* London, 1777.

Nipclose, Nicholas [Francis Gentleman]. *The Theatres. A Poetical Dissection.* London, 1772.

Pocock, J. G. A. *Virtue, Commerce, and History: Essays on Political Thought and History, Chiefly in the Eighteenth Century.* Cambridge: Cambridge UP, 1985.

Price, Martin. *To the Palace of Wisdom: Studies in Order and Energy from Dryden to Blake.* New York: Doubleday, 1964.

Rabb, Melinda. "The Secret Memoirs of Lemuel Gulliver: Satire, Secrecy, and Swift." *ELH* 73 (2006): 325-54.

Raven, James. *Judging New Wealth: Popular Publishing and Responses to Commerce in England, 1750-1800.* Oxford: Clarendon, 1992.

Reynolds, Joshua. *Garrick between Tragedy and Comedy.* British Museum, London.

Roach, Joseph. *The Player's Passion: Studies in the Science of Acting.* Newark: U of Delaware P, 1985.

Solkin, David H. *Painting for Money: The Visual Arts and the Public Sphere in Eighteenth-Century England.* New Haven: Yale UP, 1993.

Stone, Jr., George Winchester. "David Garrick and the Eighteenth-Century Stage: Notes toward a New Biography." *In Search of Restoration and Eighteenth-Century Theatrical Biography.* Ed. Stone and Philip H. Highfill, Jr. Los Angeles: U of California P, 1976. 1-31.

Stone, Jr., George Winchester, and George M. Kahrl. *David Garrick: A Critical Biography.* Carbondale: Southern Illinois UP, 1979.

Straub, Kristina. *Sexual Suspects: Eighteenth-Century Players and Sexual Ideology.* Princeton: Princeton UP, 1992.

The Theatrical Manager: A Dramatic Satire. London, 1751.

Viner, Jacob. "Satire and Economics in the Augustan Age of Satire." *The Augustan Milieu: Essays Presented to Louis A. Landa.* Ed. Henry Knight Miller, Eric Rothstein, and G. S. Rousseau. Oxford: Clarendon, 1970. 77-101.

Wanko, Cheryl. *Roles of Authority: Thespian Biography and Celebrity in Eighteenth-Century Britain.* Lubbock: Texas Tech UP, 2003.

Woods, Leigh. *Garrick Claims the Stage: Acting as Social Emblem in Eighteenth-Century England.* Westport, CT: Greenwood, 1984.

Jenny Davidson (essay date 2008)

SOURCE: Davidson, Jenny. "Why Girls Look like Their Mothers: David Garrick Rewrites *The Winter's Tale.*" *Shakespeare and the Eighteenth Century.* Ed. Peter Sabor and Paul Yachnin. Aldershot: Ashgate, 2008. 165-80. Print.

[*In the following essay, Davidson examines* Florizel and Perdita *(1756), Garrick's version of Shakespeare's* The Winter's Tale *(1609-10), within the context of the science of human reproduction. Davidson points to eighteenth-century developments in theories concerning inheritance, breeding, and identity to explain why Garrick modified Shakespeare's focus on the paternal lineage of both male and female children to emphasize the daughter's descent from the mother.*]

Summing up the results of a major recent conference on heredity, two historians of science concluded that "no general concept of heredity was underlying the discourse on life (including medicine, anthropology and the moral sciences) in the eighteenth century and that such a concept was only slowly emerging in the first half of the nineteenth century" (Rheinberger and Müller-Wille 3). Environmental accounts of people, plants, and animals dominated eighteenth-century writing, with some scientific authorities arguing that culture could change one species of grain into another and accounting for the resemblance between a child and its father by invoking a maternal imagination so powerful (according to the 1684 sex-advice manual *Aristoteles Master-Piece*) "that though a Woman be in unlawful Copulation, yet if fear or any thing else causes her to fix her mind upon her husband, the Child will resemble him, tho' he never got it" (25). Meanwhile, theorists of education from Locke to Rousseau emphasized the power of education to transform the self, and most writers concluded that external influences (described in a constellation of terms that include habit, custom, and climate) rather than any nature inherent to the individual had the most profound effects in determining that person's character.

Despite the lack of a persuasive scientific account of how parents pass on traits to their children, however, the hereditary entered into eighteenth-century European literature and culture in all kinds of ways, and this essay represents a small piece of the complex picture of how people thought and wrote about breeding—an umbrella term that can refer to nature or nurture, generation, pregnancy, hereditary resemblance, manners, moral character, social identity, or all of the above—in the several hundred years that preceded the coinage of the modern nouns *biology* (c. 1802), *heredity* (c. 1830), and *genetics* (c. 1906), telling a little-known story that offers a new perspective on the language with which we now explore and explain the fundamentals of human nature. One way of thinking about the topic of breeding is to say that the word itself (often used by eighteenth-century British writers as a synonym for "manners," "education," or "upbringing") sets a place for nature at culture's table.

The genre of romance often features a young person whose mysteriously good breeding belies a lowly upbringing, and the working-out of the plot in such cases reveals breeding to be the result of blood rather than education: part of the job of romance is to argue that education doesn't much matter, except insofar as a rustic upbringing may save a young prince or princess from corruption by courtly manners.[1] Even among romances, with their structural interest in reuniting families and their celebration of values associated with the natural and the hereditary, *The Winter's Tale* (first performed in 1611 and published in the 1623 Folio) is striking for its obsessiveness about inheritance and generation. This late play of Shakespeare's explores the transmission of properties from parent to offspring, observing and interpreting the resemblances by which familial relationships are discerned and patterns of inheritance regulated. (The play investigates inheritance in gardens as well as palaces, with King Polixenes famously defending the art that lets one "marry / A gentler scion to the wildest stock, / And make conceive a bark of baser kind / By bud of nobler race": a charged topic, given that the projected marriage between prince and shepherdess—closely analogous to the grafting he endorses in the garden—seems to threaten a social order Polixenes believes to be natural and wants to protect [4.4.92-95]. If the gardener's art allows for the propagation of new fruits and flowers of mixed lineage, problems may surface for the stability of inheritance in Sicilia and Bohemia, and possibly in seventeenth-century England as well.)

The Winter's Tale essentially dropped out of the theatrical repertory following Shakespeare's death, and for the first half of the eighteenth century, the play held relatively little appeal for theatrical companies and audiences.[2] The first eighteenth-century revivals of the play were staged at Goodman's Fields in the 1740-1741 season and at Covent Garden in 1741-1742, and it is likely that the playtext of both productions adhered fairly closely to what was printed in the First Folio of 1623 (Pedicord and Bergmann 435). But *The Winter's Tale* underwent a striking surge in popularity at mid-century, and was acted about a hundred times in several different adaptations between 1750 and 1800.[3] Both the choice of plays to adapt and stage and the nature of those adaptations offer significant indicators of cultural changes since Shakespeare's day, and the evidence suggests that *The Winter's Tale* offered mid-eighteenth-century adapters a uniquely valuable opportunity to revise older ideas about breeding, birth, and upbringing.

The Winter's Tale was seen most frequently in the second half of the eighteenth century in one of three versions: Macnamara Morgan's *The Sheep-Shearing: Or, Florizel and Perdita,* first staged in 1754 and published in 1762; David Garrick's ***Florizel and Perdita,*** first staged in 1756 and published in 1758; and George Colman's *The Sheep-Shearing,* published in 1777. One theater historian has described Morgan's as the main version, Garrick's as the main competitor (Bartholomeusz 31), and this essay will concentrate on Garrick's version as well as on the intervening developments in the science of human reproduction that facilitated Garrick's transformation of Shakespeare's account of aristocratic inheritance under threat into an endorsement of a new model of English breeding, one that emphasized middle-class manners and values and insisted that daughters inherit more from their mothers than their fathers. Where lineage in Shakespeare's time was frequently understood as transmitting likeness regardless of the sex of the offspring, in other words, the model adopted by Garrick suggests that sex largely trumps descent from the father as characters discover their true identities.

Especially interesting is Shakespeare's treatment of the physiology of resemblance in people and plants, for *The Winter's Tale* contains a rich set of observations and speculations about the bodily mechanisms that support, complement, or sometimes run counter to the operations of social and political inheritance. Garrick makes a small but significant pair of changes to Shakespeare's account of familial resemblance, and the puzzle at the center of this essay concerns the motivation behind those changes and what they reveal about mid-eighteenth-century understandings of identity and inheritance. In Shakespeare's play, both male and female children are described in terms of their resemblance to the father: Shakespeare's Perdita may also resemble Hermione (see for instance 5.1.225-27 and 5.2.30-39), but nobody comments as directly on her resemblance to her mother as on how much she looks like her father. Paulina notes the baby Perdita's resemblance to Leontes when she asks the court to behold in Perdita, "Although the print be little, the whole matter / And copy of the father" (2.3.99-100), and for Shakespeare, it is fathers, not mothers, whose form stamps their offspring, as when Leontes later compliments the grown-up Florizel by telling him that his mother must have been true to her husband, "For she did print your royal father off / Conceiving you" (5.1.124-25).

Garrick makes an extraordinary revision to Shakespeare's language, one that would seem inexplicable without knowledge of the investigations into generation conducted during the intervening years but that has broader social and cultural implications as well. Shakespeare's focus on the child's resemblance to the male rather than the female parent makes sense within the conceptual framework of early seventeenth-century theories of generation: not, of course, that observers from Aristotle onwards had not *noticed* the puzzle that a child may look like any one of his or her forebears, male or female, but the dominant theories of generation did not offer a satisfactory account of that fact. In sharp contrast, Garrick's Leontes observes of Perdita that "whilst I gaze upon / This pretty abstract of *Hermione,* / So truly printed off, I can't forget / My blemishes in them" (57). This sentence could scarcely have been written in Shakespeare's time: in the preferred theories of generation, the daughter could not have been printed off the mother, for the father provided the form for both sons and daughters. In other words, Garrick's phrasing echoes Shakespeare's, but he departs radically from the tradition of Aristotelian thought on generation, in which there is no real mechanism for the daughter to be printed off the mother, except insofar as the power of the mother's imagination (jokingly referred to in *The Winter's Tale* when Autolycus invokes the ballad of the usurer's wife who gave birth to moneybags) acts as a wild card, introducing unexpected physical traits in the offspring.

Garrick's transformation of the image cannot be careless or accidental, moreover, for he does it *again*: at the unveiling of Hermione's "statue," Garrick's Perdita comments that twenty years would not be too long a time to stand and admire it, and Florizel adds, "So long cou'd I / Admire her royal image stampt on thee, / Heiress of all her qualities" (62). Here, Garrick adopts the more conventional word "stampt," as opposed to Shakespeare's very distinctive conflation of physical reproduction with the terminology of the new technology of print, but the revision of Shakespeare's trope is unmistakable.[4] Why does Garrick change the image in this way, and what does the alteration tell us about the ways that he and his contemporaries had come to interpret resemblance, identity, and inheritance?

All human societies must have rules for regulating the passage of property and power from one generation to the next, and anthropologists take kinship structures and patterns of inheritance to be two of the most significant and interesting features of the societies they study. These can be expressed in a wide range of different forms, from customs, legal instruments, and prescriptions for how to choose a new ruler, to scientific theories about natural relationships, and myths, legends, and religious beliefs about blood and its properties. The kingdom of Sicilia in *The Winter's Tale* is no exception to this generalization, but one of the most striking facts about kinship and inheritance is the extent to which Sicilia's king himself understands them to have been disrupted: most immediately by the threat of female infidelity, more generally by the frightening, even monstrous aspects of reproduction.

Leontes's greatest anxieties surround the question of whether the children of his marriage to Hermione are really his own. "Art thou my boy?" he asks Mamillius, in a painful scene of obsessive questioning (1.2.119-35). Commenting of the boy's "smutch'd" nose that "[t]hey say it is a copy out of mine," Leontes harps on the likeness at disturbing length, showing that likeness is not in itself enough to assure him of his wife's fidelity. "How now, you wanton calf," Leontes continues, "Art thou my calf?"

MAMILLIUS:

> Yes, if you will, my lord.

LEONTES:

> Thou want'st a rough pash and the shoots that I have,
> To be full like me; yet they say we are
> Almost as like as eggs; women say so—
> That will say any thing. But were they false
> As o'er-dy'd blacks, as wind, as waters, false
> As dice are to be wish'd by one that fixes
> No bourn 'twixt his and mine, yet were it true
> To say this boy were like me.

Perplexed by how to interpret this likeness in a world of falsehood, Leontes reverses the order of resemblance, emphasizing the father's likeness to his son rather than the son's to his father:

> Looking on the lines
> Of my boy's face, methoughts I did recoil
> Twenty-three years, and saw myself unbreech'd
> In my green velvet coat, my dagger muzzled,
> Lest it should bite its master, and so prove
> (As [ornament] oft does) too dangerous.
> How like (methought) I then was to this kernel,
> This squash, this gentleman.

> (1.2.153-60)

According to the second edition of the *Oxford English Dictionary* (1989), the kernel is the pip or seed of a fruit, the squash the unripe pod of the pea. Looking at Mamillius, Leontes sees only himself, and the "recoil" to the days of his youth stimulates something like the rewinding of a time-lapse film in which buds blossom into leaves and flowers, the grown man in this case folding himself back up into potential rather than actual being. The king's choice of words makes it hard to imagine that this kernel will undergo the processes of development that lead to maturity: the image of the dagger "muzzled, / Lest it should bite its master" implies some failure of the phallus, and the death of Mamillius in Act Three thus only makes real a failure of succession that is already implicit in the distortions of generation and growth expressed by these analogies.

While Leontes's uncertainty about the parentage of his son is equivocal, he is quite sure that Perdita cannot be his child, and he renounces any claim to the baby after Hermione gives birth:

> This brat is none of mine,
> It is the issue of Polixenes.
> Hence with it, and together with the dam
> Commit them to the fire!

> (2.3.93-96)

His language is profoundly depersonalizing (Perdita is a "brat," "issue" of Polixenes, and Hermione only "the dam," like a brood-mare), and the outraged waiting-woman Paulina counters it by pointing out the resemblance between the baby and its father. She offers a metaphor of "printing off" a child (the same image Leontes himself will use to Florizel in Act Five) that is studded with print's technical vocabulary:

It is yours:
And might we lay th' old proverb to your charge,
So like you, 'tis the worse. Behold, my lords,
Although the print be little, the whole matter
And copy of the father—eye, nose, lip,
The trick of's frown, his forehead, nay, the valley,
The pretty dimples of his chin and cheek, his smiles,
The very mould and frame of hand, nail, finger.

(2.3.96-103)

Though the image of the mold or stamp is a common one for writers on reproduction, Shakespeare seems to have been the first to come up with this particular twist on the idea of the copy, his imaginative updating of the Aristotelian conceit embedding generation in seventeenth-century print culture.

What does it mean to say in early seventeenth-century England that a child resembles his or her father? Despite some interesting conceptual discussions of generation in medieval writing, historians of European medicine (Cole, Needham) generally agree that there were no major developments in embryology between the body of Greek writing that includes the Hippocratics, Aristotle, and Galen (roughly from the fifth century BCE to the second century CE) and the late sixteenth century, when Fabricius and others used dissection and experimentation to expand the boundaries of knowledge about the development of the fetus. The terms of debate in the early modern period continued to rely heavily on elements (some of them incompatible) drawn from Galen's model of conception as well as from Aristotle's; Galen argued that both male and female semen contributed to form the body of the child, while Aristotle emphasized the dominance of the father. Aristotle argues in the *Generation of Animals* that the mother contributes only the material out of which the child is formed, while the father determines the shape or form it will take: "The male provides the 'form' and the 'principle of the movement,' the female provides the body, in other words, the material" (1.20 [109]); and see also Laqueur). The analogy he offers is that the male semen acts in the female body as fig-juice or rennet works to set milk into cheese, and he suggests later that the child is formed from the male and female "only in the sense in which a bedstead is formed from the carpenter and the wood, or a ball from the wax and the form" (1.21 [113]). The male makes his contribution to generation from outside the female body, and the child develops within the mother's body simply because that's where the material is: "nothing passes from the carpenter into the pieces of timber, which are *his* material, and there is no part of the art of carpentry present in the object which is being fashioned: it is the shape and the form which pass from the carpenter, and they come into being by means of the movement in the material" (1.22 [121]).[5]

This does not mean that children always and only resemble their fathers: Aristotle comments more than once on the fact that a child may resemble the father, the mother, or a more remote ancestor.[6] He also remains agnostic on the question of whether acquired traits can be passed on to children, a question crucial to determining whether the semen is drawn from the whole body—in which case traits *would* be passed on—or just from a part of it—meaning that the seed would not be affected by modifications to or mutilations of other parts of the body. But the paramount importance of the father's contribution is clear, and despite being challenged by Galen's theory of the two semens (which emphasized the mother's contribution of form as well as matter to the embryo), Aristotle's discussion of generation continued to set the terms of European investigations into generation well into the seventeenth century. Increasingly, though, investigators turned to a new mechanism for explaining the unpredictable patterns of resemblance between children and their forebears, a theory of resemblance premised on the assumption that the mother's imagination somehow transmitted to the fetus whatever sights or thoughts struck her most forcefully: a desire for strawberries might produce a strawberry birthmark, the sight of a mutilated beggar a child with missing limbs.[7]

It is not only by means of her imagination that the mother was supposed to affect the child. The breastfeeding mother or nurse "was believed to transmit to the child, along with her ideas, beliefs, intelligence, intellect, diet, and speech, all her other physical and emotional qualities" (Fildes, *Breasts, Bottles and Babies* 189), and Leontes invokes this belief when he says to Hermione, "Give me the boy. I am glad you did not nurse him. / Though he does bear some signs of me, yet you / Have too much blood in him" (2.1.56-58). Mamillius was not breastfed by Hermione but by a wet-nurse, in other words (though attacks on wet-nursing began in England during the Reformation, it would not become fashionable for upper-class women to breastfeed their own children until the eighteenth century); the "blood" Hermione contributed to Mamillius (perhaps an allusion to Galen's argument that the mother's menstrual blood tipped the balance of likeness away from the father) cannot efface the "signs" of the father (Fildes, *Wet Nursing* 68, 88; and see also Prytula 15-17; Trumbach 197-208; and Myers 56). The prenatal influence of the imagination on the body and mind of the child, however, was believed to be even more powerful than the effects of breastfeeding, and popular fascination with the potentially monstrous effects of the maternal imagination is explicitly invoked later on in Shakespeare's play, when Autolycus hawks his wares to the naïve Mopsa, who says earnestly, "I love a ballet in print, a-life, for then we are sure they are true" (4.4.260-61). Autolycus's pitch is typical of contemporary broadsheet and ballad accounts of monstrous births: "Here's one to a very doleful tune, how a usurer's wife was brought to bed of twenty money-bags at a burthen, and how she long'd to eat adders' heads, and toads carbonado'd," he says (4.4.262-65; and see Kitch).

In his treatise on monsters (first published in 1573), the French surgeon Ambroise Paré attributes monstrous births to many different causes, but mainly to the power of the imagination: it should not surprise us that a pregnant woman with a craving for cherries might give birth to a child with a birthmark in the shape of a cherry, he says, "given the force of the imagination being joined with the conformational power, the softness of the embryo, ready like soft wax to receive any form" (38, 54).[8] The story in the Book of Genesis of Jacob and Laban's sheep, cited by Paré and given here in the King James translation, provided key evidence in support of the hypothesis of the maternal imagination: in response to Laban's reluctant donation to his son-in-law of all the spotted or parti-colored sheep in his herd:

> Jacob took him rods of greene poplar, and of the hasel and chesnut tree, and pilled white strakes in them, and made the white appeare which was in the rods. And he set the rods which he had pilled, before the flockes in the gutters in the watering troughes when the flocks came to drinke, that they should conceive when they came to drinke. And the flockes conceived before the rods, and brought forth cattell ringstraked, speckled and spotted."
>
> (Genesis 30: 37-39)[9]

"And if Brutes are stigmatized or mark'd by the Force of Imagination," writes one eighteenth-century authority on midwifery, "What then must be the Effects of it in *rational Beings,* whose Memories are more lasting?" (Bracken 40). The mother's imagination thus has the potential to counter or even undermine the physical mechanism by which a father transmits properties to his children, leaching the value from resemblance as a test for paternal kinship and constantly threatening to disrupt the patrilineal forms of inheritance on which many societies depend.

Because theatrical adapters are charged with tailoring older texts to contemporary tastes, eighteenth-century adaptations are often very revealing about widely held assumptions and attitudes. Morgan's and Garrick's versions of *The Winter's Tale* are no exception. Morgan's *Sheep-Shearing* rather cleverly confines the action of the play to the fourth act, eliminating the characters of Leontes and Hermione; there are accordingly no scenes of jealousy and no statue to be resurrected. While Garrick's adaptation retains more of the original play than Morgan's, including Leontes's jealous tirades (the part was one of Garrick's showcase roles) and the statue scene at the end, it is in many ways a less intelligent version of *The Winter's Tale* than Morgan's; Michael Dobson has called it "a priggish, corrective revision of Macnamara Morgan's bawdier adaptation" and deplores its "full-scale celebration of the sanctified nuclear family" (190, 192; and see also Pedicord and Bergmann 431-35).

While Garrick substitutes for Morgan's sexually explicit language a rather coy innuendo, he shares Morgan's vision of love in a cottage. Under his father's threat to disinherit him, Florizel promises Perdita that they will fly together to a place "[w]here no base views our purer minds shall move; / And all our wealth be innocence and love" (41). When all is happily resolved, he asks Perdita to "[b]e still my queen of *May,* my shepherdess, / Rule in my heart; my wishes be thy subjects, / And harmless as thy sheep" (66). Quite literally, then, he subjects his own desires to his wife's governance, rendering them harmless as her flock of sheep; Perdita's authority within the house and the marriage must compensate her for the loss of the power to rule in her own right which accompanies her marriage to Florizel.

What are the broad implications of these changes in family, breeding, inheritance? And how might Garrick's choice to emphasize the daughter's descent from her mother let us mark those changes and understand their significance? The century and a half between Shakespeare's time and Garrick's saw many major discoveries in the physiology of reproduction in both plant and animal worlds. Even the most imaginative and inspired scientists of the day, however, were unable to come up with an account of the mechanics of reproduction that would make sense in modern scientific terms. Generation was thus a topic both of central, indeed obsessive, interest and of telling misprision.

One of the major intellectual controversies of eighteenth-century Europe concerned the question of whether reproduction took place by epigenesis (the fresh development of the embryo) or preformation (the unfolding of preexistent structures). Preformation (also known as "evolution" before Darwin and others claimed the word for a very different purpose) was also sometimes called *emboîtement* or encasement, and is summed up well in the Dutch investigator Jan Swammerdam's statement that "[i]n nature, there is no generation but only propagation, the growth of parts. Thus original sin is explained, for all men were contained in the organs of Adam and Eve. When their stock of eggs is finished, the human race will cease to be" (qtd. in Needham 170). This is the ovist version of preformation, in which the germs that contain all future descendants reside in the egg or ovum: there is also an animalculist version, following Leeuwenhoek's microscopic observation of the sperm (which he terms "animalcules," worms, or eels) in the 1670s.

The prestige and popularity of preformation underwent rapid changes, decade by decade, at times the cutting edge of science, at times the much-mocked and unwanted legacy of prior investigators. One setback for preformation in the early eighteenth century was that the animalculist version implied immense wastefulness on God's part, given how many germs perished with each emission of semen; also, in the words of one early nineteenth-century translator of Lucretius, acceptance of animalculism meant that "[e]very anatomist, and indeed every man who pretended to the smallest portion of medical science, was convinced that his children were no more related, in point of actual generation, to his own wife, than they were to his neighbours" (Good 2: 197). Ovists had to reckon with the problem that vexed all preformationists: how to explain the resemblance of children to both parents rather than simply to the mother (Roger, *Life Sciences* 308-12). Yet preformation regained legitimacy in the 1760s on the basis of some important new experimental work and dominated accounts of reproduction through the end of the eighteenth century (Gasking 107). Each theory of generation is also associated with a range of political and cultural positions. In her idiosyncratic but fascinating book on preformation, for instance, Clara Pinto-Correia argues that by imagining tiny preformed descendants all encased within the ovary of a progenitor, preformation tended to justify the status quo: "By putting lineages inside each other, preformation could function as a 'politically correct' antidemocratic doctrine, implicitly legitimating the dynastic system" (4; and see also Keller). Another way of thinking about it is to say that by reconceiving daughters' relationships to their fathers, scientific investigators contributed to an increasing tendency in Britain to disinherit daughters at the expense of sons, a disenfranchisement that ironically heightened the culture's investment in stories about fathers and daughters (Perry 40-41).

The theory of the maternal imagination, a useful complement to preformationist theories of reproduction dogged by the problem of how to explain a child's relationship to both parents, directly displaced the father from the task of printing off his children. While literary critics have recently been especially fascinated with the theory as it pertains to monstrous births, it was also very often invoked to explain ordinary resemblances between a child and its parents and/or more distant forebears. The maternal imagination comes, for the theory's most passionate advocates, to provide the best explanation not just for the child's resemblance to a particular parent but even for species' remaining consistent from one generation to the next. Nicolas Malebranche, the late seventeenth-century French scientist whose name is strongly associated with both preformation and the theory of the maternal imagination, asserted that without the communication between the brains of mother and child, "women and animals could not easily bring forth young of the same species" (117; II.i.7). (A wonderful late seventeenth-century translation of Malebranche makes the thought even more vivid: we need the maternal imagination, suggests the translator, in order to "explain why a Mare does not produce a Calf, and a Hen an Egg which contains a little Partridge, or some other Bird of a new *Species*" [Taylor 59].) Indeed, as suggested in the opening paragraph of this essay, for some seventeenth- and eighteenth-century theorists of generation, a child comes to resemble his or her father primarily because the mother is thinking about the father at the moment of conception, and the significance of resemblance as a proof of legitimacy is thereby eroded: resemblance might perfectly well come about because the mother, lying in her lover's arms, feared discovery by her real husband (*Aristoteles Master-Piece* 25; Venette 525; Maubray 64-65).

Advocates of preformation adopted tactics that may seem undignified to modern readers: Leeuwenhoek assured the editors of *Philosophical Transactions of the Royal Society* (about to publish the letter he had written describing the appearance of animalcules in the male semen) that the human semen he examined "was not obtained by any sinful contrivance on my part, but the observations were made upon the excess with which Nature provided me in my conjugal relations" (the translation can be found in Cole 9-12). But the evident appeal for forward-looking eighteenth-century investigators of the idea that all of the essential parts of the fetus are already present in the egg is particularly clear when we consider that even the brilliant experimentalist Lorenzo Spallanzani—who pioneered techniques of artificial insemination and dressed male frogs in tiny taffeta breeches to demonstrate that while they continued to have sex with the females, none of the eggs could be fertilized—understood his own experiments, though they seem to modern audiences to provide incontrovertible evidence for the major role played by the sperm in reproduction, to offer undeniable proof of the ovist version of preformation (Gasking 136; Pinto-Correia 183-210; Spallanzani 43).

Garrick's revision of Shakespeare can be seen in this sense to generate a kind of "soft" ovism.[10] His imagination—powerful but also highly conventional—seems not to encompass the idea that his pastoral princess looks more like her father than her mother, if only because the shared fact of femaleness trumps other relations of resemblance. Indeed, if we turn outwards and look at some other popular fictions of later eighteenth-century Britain, we see a new preoccupation (amounting almost to an obsession) with the idea that daughters must look like their mothers (Greenfield 51-56; Perry 77-78; Campbell 654-56). Frances Burney's first novel *Evelina,* published in 1778, tells the history of a young lady's entrance into the world, including her attempt to claim her identity as the legitimate daughter of Sir John Belmont, who has never acknowledged her. It emerges that Evelina has been displaced by an imposter: a wet-nurse substituted her own child for the baby Evelina, a child subsequently raised privately by Sir John as his own daughter. Yet Sir John's conviction that Evelina herself must be the imposter is exploded when they meet face to face and he sees her resemblance to her dead mother: "My God! does Caroline Evelyn still live! ... lift up thy head, thou image of my long-lost Caroline!" he tells Evelina in their third-volume reunion (372-74). Here Burney patterns her novel on *The Winter's Tale,* with the economical reformulation that the reconciliation of the father with the daughter he cast off is united with the coming-to-life of the dead mother in the person of the daughter. Now that the truth has emerged, the reader learns that Sir John Belmont "had *always* observed that his daughter bore no resemblance of either of her parents, but, as he had never doubted the veracity of the nurse, this circumstance did not give birth to any suspicion." The novel solves the problem of having two pretenders to the same role by having "both the real and the fictitious daughter married without delay" (377).

Elizabeth Inchbald's *A Simple Story* (1791) is even more clearly indebted than Burney's novel to *The Winter's Tale*, as its title suggests. A story of separation and reconciliation over two generations, the novel is split into two halves, the first following the misfortunes of the mother, the second those of the daughter. The Catholic priest Dorriforth, appointed guardian of the charming but wayward Miss Milner, inherits the title of Lord Elmwood and is then released from his vows for the sake of the greater good of the Catholic Church in England. The ex-priest's marriage to his ward Miss Milner is doomed from the start. The second part begins with the revelation that after giving birth to their child, Lady Elmwood committed adultery and was cast out, along with their legitimate daughter Matilda, by Lord Elmwood, who swore to banish Matilda forever from his sight. A deathbed request from her mother to her father finds Matilda living under her father's roof but only on the condition that she literally stay out of his sight. Deprived of any contact in person, Matilda feels an extraordinary affinity for her father's painted portrait:

> In the features of her father she was proud to discern the exact moulds in which her own appeared to have been modelled; yet Matilda's person, shape, and complexion were so extremely like what her mother's once were, that at the first glance she appeared to have a still greater resemblance to her, than of her father—but her mind and manners were all Lord Elmwood's; softened by the delicacy of her sex, the extreme tenderness of her heart, and the melancholy of her situation.

(207)[11]

Inchbald seems to be torn here between the general propriety of a daughter resembling her mother more than her father (the Georgian middle-class consensus, underwritten by contemporary theories of generation and by the socio-economic transformations that nudged Britain away from blood kinship towards a conjugal model in which a woman's identity was defined more clearly by her husband than her father) and the need to insist that Matilda looks like her father in order to ensure that Miss Milner's adultery casts no retroactive shadows on Matilda's legitimacy. This leads to some awkward contortions. In an accidental encounter some chapters later, Matilda faints into her father's arms. He catches her and tries to rouse her: "Her name did not however come to his recollection—nor any name but this—'Miss Milner—Dear Miss Milner'" (255). Yet Inchbald also writes that Matilda's features have "the most striking resemblance" to her father's (294). In reality, of course, a child can bear a striking resemblance to both parents, but we expect novels to streamline such facts, to simplify and make sense of them for us. In the end, Inchbald uses the mother-daughter pair to perform a kind of experiment in the interplay of nature and nurture: the adultery and inevitable unhappy death of Miss Milner demonstrate "the pernicious effects of an improper education," in

contrast to the happier product of "that school of prudence—though of adversity—in which Matilda was bred" (318).

For writers of the 1790s, the novel becomes the genre most suited to working out systematic arguments about the effects of education on innate character: indeed, it is hardly an exaggeration to identify novels like *A Simple Story* as one point of origin of the now familiar opposition between nature and nurture that would be articulated and consolidated by Francis Galton and others later in the nineteenth century. Charles Darwin's list of his own reading in 1840 included not just *A Simple Story* but *Mansfield Park* (1814) and *Sense and Sensibility* (1811), the two novels of Jane Austen's that most obviously play with the interactions of nature and nurture.[12] One historian of theories of generation observes that "while modern genetics is, logically, the successful heir to the seventeenth and eighteenth century investigations into generation, there is not much historical connection between the two enquiries. The gap during the early nineteenth century was too great" (Gasking 164-65). When the old problems concerning the science of inheritance resurface late in the nineteenth century, most scientists are ignorant of the earlier theories: Thomas Huxley is an exception, as are a few others, but Darwin knew little or nothing of the seventeenth-and eighteenth-century controversies alluded to here. Literary texts, though, retained a palimpsest of these arguments, a means by which Darwin and others gained access to the knowledge of earlier generations.

Notes

1. The term "romance" is not Shakespeare's, but was applied to several of his late plays by subsequent editors. Parker offers a particularly thoughtful account of romance and its vagaries.

2. Between 1700 and 1750, it was staged only a few more times than such perennially unpopular plays as *Coriolanus, The Comedy of Errors, Troilus and Cressida,* and *Pericles* (Hogan 1: 457-58). In terms of stage performance, Shakespeare's popularity remained roughly the same in the second half of the eighteenth century as it had been in the first: approximately one-sixth of all documented plays performed in London were by Shakespeare (Hogan 2: 715).

3. It was roughly comparable in popularity to *Twelfth Night* or *Henry V* (Hogan 2: 716-19). The number refers to total performances, not separate productions; for purposes of comparison, during the same period, *Romeo and Juliet* was acted 399 times, *Hamlet* 343, and *Antony and Cleopatra* only six.

4. In an invaluable treatment of the stamp metaphor in "theories of both knowledge and generation," de Grazia points to the pervasiveness of the trope of the child as imprint of the father and the ways it was affected

by the introduction of printing (72, 75). Thanks to David Kastan for this reference.

5. On the idea (shared by the Egyptians and the Greeks) that the father is the sole parent of the child, see Needham 43-46. The best-known exposition of this idea can be found in the *Oresteia,* where Orestes is absolved of the blood guilt for killing his mother on the grounds (in Apollo's words) that "[t]he mother is no parent of that which is called / her child, but only nurse of the new-planted seed / that grows. The parent is he who mounts" (Aeschylus lines 658-60).

6. See Aristotle 4.3 (401-03). In conjunction with an argument that "anyone who does not take after his parents is really in a way a monstrosity," he notoriously goes on to identify "[t]he first beginning of this deviation [as] when a female is formed instead of a male"; and see also the assertion that "we should look upon the female state as being as it were a deformity, though one which occurs in the ordinary course of nature" (4.6 [461]).

7. Ballantyne remains an excellent survey of primary sources on maternal impression (esp. 24-46 and the bibliography given at 47-62); more recent discussions of maternal impression and its effects on children, mostly concentrating on the special case of the monstrous birth, include Rousseau; Park and Daston; Boucé; Stafford 313; Huet; Porter and Hall 48; Todd 45-48 and 282-83; Finucci; Wilson; Adams 186-89; and Crawford.

8. The treatise was first published in 1573; this translation follows the text given in the posthumous 1598 edition of Paré's *Oeuvres complètes,* but also refers to the 1585 edition (see Pallister's note on the text at xxvii). For another roughly contemporary discussion of the power of the imagination, see Montaigne 1: 100.

9. Shylock invokes the story of Jacob and Laban's sheep as a metaphor for his own generation of money in *The Merchant of Venice,* 1.3.77-90, first performed c. 1598 and published in quarto in 1600.

10. It is very likely that Garrick knew the rough outlines of Buffon's celebrated theories, whether or not he had himself read the *Natural History.* Prints from Buffon's *Natural History* were catalogued in Garrick's collections, and he had a taste for natural history (Stone and Kahrl 456).

11. It is possible that the word "moulds" invokes Buffon's controversial but influential suggestion that reproduction worked by a mechanism of *moules intérieures* or interior molds; on this theory of Buffon's, see Roger, *Buffon* 129-31, 133-34.

12. Darwin's reading list for 1840 is quoted in Beer, *Darwin's Plots* 27; and see also the discussion of Darwin's reading of Montaigne and Shakespeare in Beer, "Darwin's Reading" 551-52, 587.

Works Cited

Adams, Rachel. *Sideshow U.S.A.: Freaks and the American Cultural Imagination.* Chicago: University of Chicago Press, 2001.

Aeschylus. *Eumenides. Oresteia.* Trans. Richmond Lattimore. Chicago: University of Chicago Press, 1953.

Aristotle's Master-Piece, or the Secrets of Generation Displayed in All the Parts Thereof. London, 1684.

Aristotle. *Generation of Animals.* Trans. A. L. Peck. 1942. Cambridge: Harvard University Press, 1990.

Ballantyne, J. W. *Teratogenesis: An Inquiry into the Causes of Monstrosities.* Edinburgh, 1897.

Bartholomeusz, Dennis. The Winter's Tale *in Performance in England and America, 1611-1976.* Cambridge: Cambridge University Press, 1982.

Beer, Gillian. *Darwin's Plots: Evolutionary Narrative in Darwin, George Eliot and Nineteenth-Century Fiction.* 2nd ed. Cambridge: Cambridge University Press, 2000.

———. "Darwin's Reading and the Fictions of Development." *The Darwinian Heritage.* Ed. David Kohn. Princeton: Princeton University Press, 1985. 543-88.

Boucé, Paul-Gabriel. "Imagination, pregnant women, and monsters in eighteenth-century England and France." *Sexual Underworlds of the Enlightenment.* Ed. G. S. Rousseau and Roy Porter. Chapel Hill: University of North Carolina Press, 1988. 86-100.

Bracken, Henry. *The Midwife's Companion; or, A Treatise of Midwifery.* London, 1737.

Burney, Fanny [Frances]. *Evelina: Or the History of a Young Lady's Entrance Into the World.* 1778. Ed. Edward A. Bloom and Lillian D. Bloom. New York: Oxford University Press, 1984.

Campbell, Jill. " 'The Exact Picture of His Mother': Recognizing Joseph Andrews." *ELH* 55 (1988): 643-64.

Cole, F. J. *Early Theories of Sexual Generation.* Oxford: Clarendon Press, 1930.

[Colman, George]. *The Sheep-Shearing: A Dramatic Pastoral in Three Acts. Taken from Shakespeare. As it is performed at the Theatre Royal in the Haymarket.* London, 1777.

Crawford, Julie. *Marvelous Protestantism: Monstrous Births in Post-Reformation England.* Baltimore: Johns Hopkins University Press, 2005.

Daston, Lorraine J., and Katharine Park. "Unnatural Conceptions: The Study of Monsters in Sixteenth- and Seventeenth-

Century France and England." *Past and Present* 92 (1981): 20-54.

———. *Wonders and the Order of Nature, 1150-1750.* New York: Zone Books; Cambridge,: MIT Press, 1998.

de Grazia, Margreta. "Imprints: Shakespeare, Gutenberg, and Descartes." *Alternative Shakespeares.* Ed. Terrence Hawkes. Vol 2. London: Routledge, 1996. 63-94.

Dobson, Michael. *The Making of the National Poet: Shakespeare, Adaptation and Authorship, 1660-1769.* Oxford: Clarendon Press, 1992.

Fildes, Valerie A. *Breasts, Bottles and Babies: A History of Infant Feeding.* Edinburgh: Edinburgh University Press, 1986.

———. *Wet Nursing: A History from Antiquity to the Present.* Oxford: Basil Blackwell, 1988.

Finucci, Valeria. "Maternal Imagination and Monstrous Birth: Tasso's *Gerusalemme liberata.*" *Generation and Degeneration: Tropes of Reproduction in Literature and History from Antiquity through Early Modern Europe.* Ed. Finucci and Kevin Brownlee. Durham and London: Duke University Press, 2001. 41-77.

Garrick, David. *Florizel and Perdita: A Dramatic Pastoral in Three Acts. Alter'd from* The Winter's Tale *of Shakespear.* London, 1758. London: Cornmarket, 1969.

Gasking, Elizabeth B. *Investigations into Generation, 1651-1828.* Baltimore: Johns Hopkins University Press, 1967.

Good, John Mason. *The Nature of Things: A Didactic Poem.* 2 vols. London, 1805.

Greenfield, Susan C. *Mothering Daughters: Novels and the Politics of Family Romance, Frances Burney to Jane Austen.* Detroit: Wayne State University Press, 2002.

Hogan, Charles Beecher. *Shakespeâre in the Theatre, 1701-1800.* 2 vols. Oxford: Clarendon Press, 1952-1957.

Huet, Marie-Hélène. *Monstrous Imagination.* Cambridge and London: Harvard University Press, 1993.

Inchbald, Elizabeth. *A Simple Story.* 1791. Ed. Pamela Clemit. London: Penguin, 1996.

Keller, Eve. "Embryonic Individuals: The Rhetoric of Seventeenth-Century Embryology and the Construction of Early-Modern Identity." *Eighteenth-Century Studies* 33:3 (2000): 321-48.

Kitch, Aaron. "Bastards and Broadsides in *The Winter's Tale.*" *Renaissance Drama* 30 (2001): 43-71.

Laqueur, Thomas. *Making Sex: Body and Gender from the Greeks to Freud.* Cambridge: Harvard University Press, 1990.

[Leeuwenhoek, Antoni van]. "Observationes D. Anthonii Lewenhoeck, De Natis E Semine Genitali Animalculis." *Philosophical Transactions of the Royal Society* 12 (1679): 1040-1046.

Malebranche, Nicolas. *The Search after Truth.* Trans. and ed. Thomas M. Lennon and Paul J. Olscamp. Cambridge: Cambridge University Press, 1997.

Maubray, John. *The Female Physician, Containing All the Diseases Incident to that Sex, in Virgins, Wives, and Widows.* London, 1724.

Montaigne, Michel de. "Of the Force of Imagination." *The essays of Montaigne done into English by John Florio anno 1603.* Ed. George Saintsbury. 3 vols. London, 1892. New York: AMS, 1967.

[Morgan, Macnamara]. *The Sheep-Shearing: Or, Florizel and Perdita. A Pastoral Comedy Taken from Shakespear.* London, 1762. London: Cornmarket, 1969.

Myers, Mitzi. "'Servants as They are now Educated': Women Writers and Georgian Pedagogy." *Essays in Literature* 16 (1989): 51-69.

Needham, Joseph. *A History of Embryology.* 1934. 2nd ed. Rev. with Arthur Hughes. Cambridge: Cambridge University Press, 1959.

Paré, Ambroise. *On Monsters and Marvels.* 1573. Trans. Janis L. Pallister. Chicago and London: University of Chicago Press, 1982.

Parker, Patricia A. *Inescapable Romance: Studies in the Poetics of a Mode.* Princeton: Princeton University Press, 1979.

Pedicord, Harry William, and Fredrick Louis Bergmann, eds. *Garrick's Adaptations of Shakespeare, 1744-1756.* Carbondale and Edwardsville: Southern Illinois University Press, 1981.

Perry, Ruth. *Novel Relations: The Transformation of Kinship in English Literature and Culture, 1748-1818.* Cambridge: Cambridge University Press, 2004.

Pinto-Correia, Clara. *The Ovary of Eve: Egg and Sperm and Preformation.* Chicago: University of Chicago Press, 1997.

Porter, Roy, and Lesley Hall. "Medical Folklore in High and Low Culture: *Aristotle's Masterpiece.*" *The Facts of Life: The Creation of Sexual Knowledge in Britain, 1650-1950.* Ed. Porter and Hall. New Haven: Yale University Press, 1995. 33-53.

Prytula, Nina Adriane. "'The soul stark naked': The Female Breast and the Anatomy of Character in the Eighteenth-Century Novel." PhD disseraration, Yale University, 2001.

Rheinberger, Hans-Jörg, and Staffan Müller-Wille. Introduction. *A Cultural History of Heredity II: 18th and 19th*

Centuries, Preprint 247. Berlin: Max Planck Institute for the History of Science, 2003. 3-6.

Roger, Jacques. *Buffon: A Life in Natural History.* Trans. Sarah Lucille Bonnefoi. Ed. L. Pearce Williams. Ithaca: Cornell University Press, 1997.

————. *The Life Sciences in Eighteenth-Century French Thought.* Ed. Keith R. Benson. Trans. Robert Ellrich. 1963. Rev. ed. Stanford: Stanford University Press, 1997.

Rousseau, G. S. "Pineapples, Pregnancy, Pica, and *Peregrine Pickle.*" *Tobias Smollett: Bicentennial Essays Presented to Lewis M. Knapp.* Ed. Rousseau and Paul-Gabriel Boucé. New York: Oxford University Press, 1971. 79-109.

Shakespeare, William. *The Winter's Tale. The Riverside Shakespeare.* 2nd ed. Ed. G. Blakemore Evans. Boston: Houghton Mifflin, 1997. 1617-1655.

Spallanzani, Abbé. *An Essay on Animal Reproductions.* [Trans. M. Maty.] London, 1766.

Stafford, Barbara Maria. *Body Criticism: Imaging the Unseen in Enlightenment Art and Medicine.* Cambridge: MIT Press, 1991.

Stone, George Winchester, Jr., and George M. Kahrl. *David Garrick: A Critical Biography.* Carbondale and Edwardsville: Southern Illinois University Press; London: Fetter and Simons, 1979.

Taylor, T., trans. *Father Malebranche's Treatise concerning The Search after Truth.* Oxford, 1694.

The Bible in English (990-1970). *Literature Online.* 15 Dec. 2003 <http://collections.chadwyck.com/bie>.

Todd, Dennis. *Imagining Monsters: Miscreations of the Self in Eighteenth-Century England.* Chicago: University of Chicago Press, 1995.

Trumbach, Randolph. *The Rise of the Egalitarian Family: Aristocratic Kinship and Domestic Relations in Eighteenth-Century England.* New York: Academic Press, 1978.

Venette, Nicolas. "Si les enfans sont bâtards ou legitimes quand ils ressemblent à leur pere ou à leur mere." *De la generation de l'homme, ou tableau de l'amour conjugal.* 1686. 7th ed. Cologne, 1696.

Wilson, Philip K. "Eighteenth-Century Monsters and Nineteenth-Century 'Freaks': Reading the Maternally Marked Child." *Literature and Medicine* 21.1 (2002): 1-25.

FURTHER READING

Bibliography

Berkowitz, Gerald M. *David Garrick: A Reference Guide.* Boston: Hall, 1980. Print.
> A thorough and well-organized work covering all but the least substantial writings about Garrick from 1741 to 1979. Berkowitz's annotations are brief and helpful.

Biographies

Davies, Thomas. *Memoirs of the Life of David Garrick.* 2 vols. 1780. New York: Blom, 1969. Print.
> The first of many biographies of Garrick, written by a supportive actor and originally published in 1780. Focused more on defending Garrick's career than documenting his personal life, Davies's account is nonetheless thorough and interesting.

Stone, George Winchester, Jr., and George M. Kahrl. *David Garrick: A Critical Biography.* Carbondale: Southern Illinois UP, 1979. Print.
> The authoritative modern biography of Garrick. Stone and Kahrl's richly detailed book is essential reading for anyone interested in Garrick's life and works.

Criticism

Bergmann, Fredrick L. "David Garrick and *The Clandestine Marriage.*" *PMLA* 67.2 (1952): 148-62. Print.
> Uses *The Clandestine Marriage* to illustrate that Garrick's conception of dramatic comedy was deeply influenced by his natural method of acting. Bergmann contends that Garrick's contributions to *The Clandestine Marriage* and his selection and adaptation of plays for Drury Lane represent "a modification both of the sentimental comedy then reigning on the stage and of the older comedy of manners."

Burnim, Kalman A. *David Garrick: Director.* Pittsburgh: U of Pittsburgh P, 1961. Print.
> Provides an account of Garrick's directorial techniques that emphasizes theatricality by highlighting Garrick's staging methods and development of actors. Using various contemporary documents, Burnim reconstructs several of Garrick's productions.

Copeland, Nancy. "The Sentimentality of Garrick's *Romeo and Juliet.*" *Restoration and 18th Century Theatre Research* 2nd ser. 4.2 (1989): 1-13. Print.
> Details Garrick's various changes to the plot, language, and characterization of *Romeo and Juliet.* Copeland asserts that all of Garrick's alterations are designed to enhance the pathos of the lovers' crisis and result in a "radical sentimentality" that successfully catered to contemporary expectations of affective tragedy.

Cunningham, Vanessa. *Shakespeare and Garrick*. Cambridge: Cambridge UP, 2008. Print.

> Provides a thorough examination of Garrick's Shakespearean adaptations, arranged chronologically. Cunningham also discusses the relationship between text and performance in the eighteenth century and evaluates Garrick's influence on Shakespeare's legacy.

Dircks, Phyllis T. "Garrick's Fail-Safe Musical Venture, *A Peep behind the Curtain,* an English Burletta." *The Stage and the Page: London's "Whole Show" in the Eighteenth-Century Theatre.* Ed. Geo. Winchester Stone, Jr. Berkeley: U of California P, 1981. 136-47. Print.

> Evaluates Garrick's contributions to the burletta (comic opera) form. Identifying *A Peep behind the Curtain* as Garrick's first use of music as a substantive rather than decorative element, Dircks observes that Garrick's clever insertion of a burletta fragment into the second act of the play makes the burletta both the agent and the object of the satire.

———. "David Garrick, George III, and the Politics of Revision." *Philological Quarterly* 76.3 (1997): 289-312. Print.

> Analyzes the satiric intentions of Garrick's interlude *The Farmer's Return from London* (1762) and concludes that Garrick censored his own play to prevent offense. Dircks includes the full text of Garrick's manuscript.

England, Martha Winburn. *Garrick's Jubilee*. Columbus: Ohio State UP, 1964. Print.

> Provides an account that comprehensively reconstructs the Shakespeare Jubilee of 1769, which was organized by Garrick. England maintains that the jubilee was a major force in the elevation of Shakespeare's reputation.

Gentleman, Francis. "*The Clandestine Marriage.* A Comedy. By Mess. Garrick and Colman." *Dramatic Censor; or, Critical Companion.* Vol. 1. London: Bell and Etherington, 1770. 239-55. Print.

> Provides a scene-by-scene account of the plot intricacies of Garrick's collaboration with Colman the Elder, followed by an assessment of the actors' performances. Gentleman concludes that *The Clandestine Marriage* fares better on the stage than on the page.

Green, Katherine S. "David Garrick and the Marriage *Habitus*: *The Clandestine Marriage* Revisited." *Restoration and 18th Century Theatre Research* 2nd ser. 13.2 (1998): 17-34. Print.

> Maintains that the production and staging of *The Clandestine Marriage* carefully exploited the contemporary debate concerning underage and secret marriages, specifically as codified by the Hardwicke Marriage Act of 1753. Arguing that the act valued money and property over romantic love, Green interprets the sexual politics of the play in terms of class-inflected interests and prevailing notions of cultural and symbolic capital.

Hainsworth, John. "David Garrick, Poet of the Theatre: A Critical Survey." *Studies in the Eighteenth Century II: Papers Presented at the Second David Nichol Smith Memorial Seminar, Canberra 1970.* Ed. R. F. Brissenden. Toronto: U of Toronto P, 1973. 359-76. Print.

> Argues that Garrick's achievement as a poet rests on his prologues and epilogues. Citing various examples, Hainsworth demonstrates that Garrick transcended the hackneyed devices of these forms through wit, imagery, and his own acting talents.

Knapp, J. Merrill. "English Theatrical Music in Garrick's Time: *The Enchanter* (1760) and *May Day* (1775)." *The Stage and the Page: London's "Whole Show" in the Eighteenth-Century Theatre.* Ed. Geo. Winchester Stone, Jr. Berkeley: U of California P, 1981. 123-35. Print.

> Provides a detailed analysis of the pieces Garrick wrote for the purpose of introducing fresh singing talent to the stage. Knapp analyzes the afterpieces from two works: The first is the two-act opera *The Enchanter* (1760), scored by John Christopher Smith, who was a pupil of George Frideric Handel; the second is the one-act playlet *May Day* (1775), with songs by Thomas Arne.

Levenson, Jill L. "Early Revivals: David Garrick versus Charlotte Cushman." *Romeo and Juliet.* Manchester: Manchester UP, 1987. 17-45. Print.

> Contends that Garrick altered *Romeo and Juliet* to make it conform to eighteenth-century tastes in tragedy, which frowned upon excesses of lyricism and rhymed verse, vulgar language and punning, and any plot complexities that might detract from the idealization of the victimized protagonists. Levenson also describes how stage, scene, costume, and acting conventions had changed since Elizabethan times.

Ribes, Purificación. "Country Wives and Country Girls in Eighteenth-Century England: A History of Theatrical Rewriting." *Sederi* 16 (2006): 91-108. Print.

> Considers the rewritings of William Wycherley's *The Country Wife* (1675), a play that was judged too sexually explicit to be performed and only survived into the eighteenth century through adaptation. Ribes focuses on two of these adaptations: John Lee's version, originally performed in 1765, and Garrick's version, first brought to the stage in 1766 as *The Country Girl.*

Roach, Joseph R., Jr. "Garrick, the Ghost and the Machine." *Theatre Journal* 34.4 (1982): 431-40. Print.

> Focuses on the remarkable fright wig Garrick used in his performance of *Hamlet.* Roach discusses Garrick's approach to his craft and its consequences for the understanding of eighteenth-century theatrical practice.

Scouten, A. H., ed. *The London Stage, 1660-1800: A Calendar of Plays, Entertainments and Afterpieces. Part 3, 1729-1747.* 2 vols. Carbondale: Southern Illinois UP, 1961. Print.

Provides an invaluable account of all aspects of eighteenth-century theatrical practice during the early years of Garrick's career. The volumes are part of one of the most important reference works on Restoration theater.

Sherman, Stuart. "Garrick among Media: The '*Now* Performer' Navigates the News." *PMLA* 126.4 (2011): 966-82. Print.
Traces the vexed and complex relationship between Garrick and the print culture of his day to suggest a rethinking of the traditional separation of the evanescence of stage performance from the permanence of press coverage. Sherman posits a reciprocal relationship between live theater and its documentation, "where diurnality and immortality converge," using as his example the publicity surrounding two famous episodes from Garrick's career.

Stone, George Winchester, Jr. "Shakespeare's *Tempest* at Drury Lane during Garrick's Management." *Shakespeare Quarterly* 7.1 (1956): 1-7. Print.
Suggests that Garrick's version of *The Tempest* was one of the best eighteenth-century adaptations of Shakespeare.

———. "A Century of *Cymbeline*; or Garrick's Magic Touch." *Philological Quarterly* 54.1 (1975): 310-22. Print.
Documents the stage history of Garrick's version of *Cymbeline* (1761) and details the specifics of his alterations to the original. Stone attributes the play's longevity to "David Garrick, for [his] acting text, inspired acting, and direction which showed the possibilities of the play and of the parts not only to a succession of actors, actresses and managers but also to scene painters, and costumers."

———, ed. *The London Stage, 1660-1800: A Calendar of Plays, Entertainments and Afterpieces. Part 4, 1747-1776.* 3 vols. Carbondale: Southern Illinois UP, 1962. Print.
Covers Garrick's years at Drury Lane. Stone's lengthy introduction, like that of Scouten (see above), offers a wealth of information regarding all aspects of London theatrical practice throughout Garrick's career.

Additional information on Garrick's life and works is contained in the following sources published by Gale: *Dictionary of Literary Biography,* Vols. 84, 213; *DISCovering Authors Modules: Dramatists*; *Literature Criticism from 1400 to 1800,* Vols. 15, 156; *Literature Resource Center*; and *Reference Guide to English Literature,* Ed. 2.

Angels in America
Tony Kushner

(Full name Anthony Robert Kushner) American playwright.

The following entry provides criticism of Kushner's two-part play *Angels in America: A Gay Fantasia on National Themes* (1991). For additional information about Kushner's complete dramatic career, see *DC*, Volume 10.

INTRODUCTION

Angels in America is a Pulitzer Prize-winning two-part play sequence by Tony Kushner (1956-) that explores issues of gay identity and their intersection with other national themes. The narrative focuses on the lives of a cast of interconnected characters in mid-1980s New York City, each of whom is affected, directly or indirectly, by the AIDS crisis. In addition to the struggle for gay equality, the play addresses a wide range of contemporary topics, including the rise of Reagan-era conservative politics, environmental catastrophes, and racial and religious bigotry. Kushner employs experimental techniques rooted in the political theater of Bertolt Brecht, specifically his *Verfremdungseffekt,* or estrangement effect, by which the familiar is made to seem strange in order to provoke critical reflection. Critics have praised the ambition, complexity, and breadth of Kushner's play, and they continue to examine how it interlaces various philosophical, theological, and moral visions of the world.

Angels in America, which takes seven hours to perform, is divided into two parts, *Millennium Approaches* and *Perestroika,* each of which can be staged separately as a complete play. According to Kushner's directions, most of the actors who assume major roles also play other minor characters. As indicated in the work's subtitle, *A Gay Fantasia on National Themes,* it also shifts between realistic action and dreamlike sequences, with some scenes involving disjointed action being performed on opposite ends of the stage. *Millennium Approaches* was commissioned in 1990 as a workshop, premiered in May 1991 in San Francisco, and opened on Broadway two years later. *Perestroika,* under development when *Millennium Approaches* was first performed, received its world premiere in November 1991 and opened on Broadway in November 1993. Both plays received numerous Tony Awards, four in 1993 for *Millennium Approaches* and three in 1994 for *Perestroika,* including best play both years, and *Millennium Approaches* received the Pulitzer Prize in 1993. In 2003, HBO presented an adaptation of the works as a television miniseries, which was directed by Mike Nichols and received multiple honors, including eleven Emmys and five Golden Globe awards.

PLOT AND MAJOR CHARACTERS

Millennium Approaches shifts between the stories of Louis Ironson, whose lover, Prior Walter, is dying of AIDS, and Mormon lawyer Joe Pitt, a closeted homosexual who is married to Harper, a troubled woman addicted to Valium. The play begins with the funeral of Louis's grandmother, a Jewish woman who had escaped the Holocaust and is described by Kushner as a representative of Old World values. After the funeral, Prior confesses to Louis that he has AIDS. Deeply distressed by the news that his lover is dying and terrified by the threat to his own health, Louis tries, at first, to care for Prior, but is eventually overcome by depressive dread. After Louis leaves Prior, the drag-queen nurse Belize becomes Prior's main caregiver. Prior, meanwhile, has a series of spectral visions, including two ghosts, called Prior I and II, who had died in earlier plagues in the thirteenth and seventeenth centuries. They inform Prior that he is being prepared for important work.

Joe and Harper are at odds over a job offer Joe has received from his bigoted mentor, Roy Cohn, to be Cohn's aide at the Justice Department. Harper does not want to move to Washington. As he is considering his options, Joe meets Louis at the courthouse where they both work, and they strike up a friendship based on an unspoken sexual attraction. In a subsequent dream sequence, Harper imagines that she and Prior meet, and Prior tells her that her "husband's a homo." In real life, she confronts Joe, and he admits that he is conflicted. Meanwhile Cohn, in his doctor's office, is told he has AIDS, a disease, according to Cohn, of "homosexuals and drug addicts." He insists that he isn't a homosexual—gay men have "no clout," he says—and claims that he has liver cancer. In a later scene at a bar, Joe tells Cohn about Harper's reluctance to move to Washington. Cohn presses him to come without her, promising to be like a father to him, and confides that he is dying. When Joe rejects his job offer, Cohn calls him a "sissy" and brags about being responsible for the execution of Ethel Rosenberg, convicted of conspiracy to commit espionage three decades earlier. In another dream sequence that occurs after Joe leaves, Rosenberg's ghost appears to witness Cohn's last days.

Tensions increase between the two couples, Joe and Harper and Louis and Prior, and both relationships deteriorate. In a late-night phone call Joe admits his homosexuality to his mother, Hannah, who makes plans to come to New York from Utah to help with his situation. Before she arrives, Harper kicks Joe out of their house. Soon afterward, Joe and Louis meet in Central Park and consummate their relationship, as Prior has a terrifying yet strangely exciting vision of an Angel who announces, "The Great Work begins."

Perestroika continues the story. Harper, after having gone missing for a few days wandering around Central Park in her nightgown, is picked up at the police station by Hannah, who takes her to the Mormon Visitor Center. In a dream there, Harper imagines that the dummies of a diorama portraying the great crossing of the desert come to life, and the mother of the group gives a critical speech about the harsh reality of female sacrifice in the name of the millennial faith. Harper's hallucination amounts to a critique of the Mormon worldview and, more specifically, women's roles in it.

Cohn's physical health deteriorates, and he checks into a hospital, where Belize is his nurse and suffers his homophobic hostility. When political pressures mount for Cohn's disbarment on charges of malfeasance, he turns to Joe as a confidante, but when he learns that Joe has been living with Louis, he once again explodes with anger. After his disbarment and death, Belize, in an afterlife scene, asks Louis, a Jew, to recite the Kaddish, the Jewish prayer for the dead, and the scene ends with Rosenberg leading him in the prayer.

Prior is visited by and wrestles with the Angel in his hospital room. On a second visitation, he goes with the Angel up to heaven, which is like San Francisco after the 1906 earthquake. There he meets the other Angels, all named after continents, and the Angel America explains their predicament. With the creation of man, God created time and history itself, which shook up heaven and eventually lured God away to attend to progress on earth. Abandoned, the Angels have turned to Prior, who himself is suffering the consequences of "progress," to make mankind "STOP MOVING!" Eventually, towards the end of the play, Prior rejects this mission, claiming that he wants "more life." He advises the Angels to stop waiting for God and to "sue Him" if he ever returns. Prior says he feels abandoned by God. When he returns to consciousness, he has accepted his fate and says a final goodbye to a repentant Louis. In a similarly emancipatory move, Harper then leaves for San Francisco and a new phase of her life.

The play ends with an epilogue taking place four years after the main action of the play, in which Louis, Prior, Belize, and Hannah meet at the Bethesda fountain in Central Park and plead for a continuation of the Great Work.

MAJOR THEMES

Prior, at one point in the play, proclaims, "This disease will be the end of many of us, but not nearly all. And the dead will be commemorated, and we'll struggle on with the living, and we are not going away. We won't die secret deaths anymore. The world only spins forward. We will be citizens. The time has come." This moment encapsulates important themes of the play: dealing with AIDS, which the work often connects to earlier plagues and environmental disasters, and the gay community's struggle for acceptance, which also reflects the prejudice and discrimination experienced by the Jews, Mormons, and African Americans in the work. The tension between the individualism and the isolation that discrimination encourages and the community and solidarity that it inhibits is at the heart of the play.

Prior's insistence that "the world only spins forward" indicates another central thematic focus of the play: history. As Michelle Elkin-Squitieri (1998) pointed out, the Angel attempts to transcend history by picturing its end, which is countered by a focus on the "immediate historical moment," as demonstrated in Prior's rejection of the Angel's emphasis on stasis. Critics, including James Corby (2010), have suggested that the Angel is an allusion to Marxist philosopher Walter Benjamin's description of the "angel of history" in his *Über den Begriff der Geschichte* (1942).

As Corby observed, for Benjamin, "one only actively moves forward by looking ... in a backwards glance that freezes time ... just long enough to view the past" and judge it. In *Angels in America,* Corby noted, Kushner advances "the idea that, in that moment of flux, society can be reconfigured to allow it to move forward on a more equitable basis, better prepared to face the as-yet unknown challenges that lie ahead." The play is thus, as many scholars have pointed out, thematically committed to the ideas of hope, progress, and revolution in the face of catastrophe and struggle.

Critics have argued that central scenes of the play, such as when Louis and Rosenberg recite the Kaddish for Cohn or when Prior wrestles the Angel, not only insist on history moving forward, but do so in a way that emphasizes very diverse people working together as a community. The presence of various minority communities—homosexuals, Jews, and Mormons—in Kushner's play thus highlights the conflict between restrictive traditions and the pressing need for greater inclusiveness. In *Angels in America,* group alignments ultimately cross the boundaries of gender, sex, religion, politics, and race.

CRITICAL RECEPTION

Initial reaction to the play was overwhelmingly positive, as attested by its many awards. Much of the praise focused on the experimental techniques and encompassing scope of the play. Boris Vejdovsky (2011) reported that theater critics declared it "the authoritative achievement of a radical dramatic artist" and "the broadest, deepest, most searching American play of our time."

One of the main strands of critical response has traced the development in the play of what Jennifer Glaser (2009; see Further Reading) called a "queer consciousness." Glaser argued that Kushner presented the gay perspective as one that stands at a critical distance from mainstream American society. Daniel Kiefer (1994) found that the play ends with "smooth good wishes" rather than the acerbic camp humor that dominates the rest of the text, and he considered this shift an artistic flaw.

Though critics have generally agreed that the play encourages community, forgiveness, and forward movement, some have argued that it does not necessarily resolve the tension between community and individualism. Joshua Takano Chambers-Letson (2012) contended that the play fails to adequately address issues of class and race. He claimed that the work disregards "the subordination of the working classes" and features only one black character, Belize, who resembles the "archetype of the mammy." Alex J. Tuss (1996), on the other hand, argued that the play shows a spiritual transformation from a "gospel of clout" preached by Cohn to a personal revival that suggests a rejuvenation of society.

Critics continue to untangle Kushner's many religious references in the play, particularly to Judaism and Mormonism. Critics such as Ranen Omer-Sherman (2007) have argued that "the ethical imperative of community" in Judaism makes it an ideal fit for the ethical stance of the play, although Joshua Pederson (2009) remarked that Kushner chose fairly archaic forms of Jewish mysticism, which, in his view, reflects the playwright's own troubled relationship with the religion. Elkin-Squitieri suggested that there are two competing apocalyptic visions in the play, one represented by the Angel, who attempts to transcend history, and the other by Prior, who focuses on the "immediate historical moment."

In *Angels in America* Kushner often refers to intellectual and philosophical figures, including Benjamin, Georg Wilhelm Friedrich Hegel, Ernst Bloch, Raymond Williams, and various Enlightenment philosophers. In his overview of these influences, Corby suggested that Kushner used these sources to help him grasp the importance of community and to forge a radical adherence to hope. In his 2006 study (see Further Reading) of the neo-Hegelian elements of the play, David Krasner agreed that the play focuses on the need to move past abstract individualism, adding that this movement requires "understanding of the body, flesh, and the responsibility freedom entails."

Abigail Mann

PRINCIPAL WORKS

Plays

The Age of Assassins. Newfoundland Theatre, New York. 1982.

La fin de la Baleine: An Opera for the Apocalypse. Ohio Theatre, New York. 1983.

Last Gasp at the Cataract. The Yard, Inc., Martha's Vineyard. 1984.

The Umbrella Oracle. The Yard, Inc., Martha's Vineyard. 1984.

A Bright Room Called Day. Theatre 22, New York. 22 Apr. 1985. New York: Theatre Communications Group, 1994.

The Heavenly Theatre. Tisch School of the Arts, New York. 1986.

In Great Eliza's Golden Time. Repertory Theatre of St. Louis, St. Louis. 1986.

*Yes, Yes, No, No: The Solace-of-Solstice, Apogee/Perigee, Bestial/Celestial Holiday Show. Repertory Theatre of St. Louis, St. Louis. 1986.

Hydriotaphia; or, The Death of Dr. Browne. Home for Contemporary Theatre and Art, New York. 1987.

Stella. Adapt. from *Stella,* by Johann Wolfgang von Goethe. New York Theatre Workshop, New York. 1987.

The Illusion. Adapt. from *L'illusion comique,* by Pierre Corneille. New York Theatre Workshop, New York. 19 Oct. 1988. New York: Theatre Communications Group, 1994.

In That Day (Lives of the Prophets). Tisch School of the Arts, New York. 1989.

Angels in America: A Gay Fantasia on National Themes. Part One: Millennium Approaches. Eureka Theatre, San Francisco. May 1991.

Angels in America: A Gay Fantasia on National Themes. Part Two: Perestroika. Eureka Theatre, San Francisco. May 1991. London: National Theatre/Hern, 1994.

Widows. With Ariel Dorfman. Adapt. from *Viudas,* by Dorfman. Mark Taper Forum, Los Angeles. 24 July 1991. London: Hern, 1997.

Slavs! Thinking about the Longstanding Problems of Virtue and Happiness. Actors Theatre of Louisville, Louisville. 8 Mar. 1994. New York: Broadway Play, 1999.

The Good Person of Szechuan. Adapt. from *Der gute Mensch von Sezuan,* by Bertolt Brecht. La Jolla Playhouse, La Jolla. July 1994.

A Dybbuk; or, Between Two Worlds. Adapt. from *Tsvishn tsvey veltn—der dibek,* by Solomon Ansky. Hartford Stage Company, New Haven. Feb. 1995. New York: Theatre Communications Group, 1998.

†*Angels in America: A Gay Fantasia on National Themes.* New York: Theatre Communications Group, 1995.

Notes on Akiba. Jewish Museum of New York, New York. 1995.

Thinking about the Longstanding Problems of Virtue and Happiness: Essays, a Play, Two Poems, and a Prayer. New York: Theatre Communications Group, 1995. (Essays, play, and poems)

Reverse Transcription: Six Playwrights Bury a Seventh. A Ten-Minute Play That's Nearly Twenty Minutes Long. Actors Theatre of Louisville, Louisville. Mar. 1996.

Terminating; or, Sonnet LXXV; or, "Lass meine Schmerzen nicht verloren sein"; or, Ambivalence. Guthrie Theater Lab, Minneapolis. 7 Jan. 1998.

Henry Box Brown; or, The Mirror of Slavery. Royal National Theatre, London. 1998.

Homebody/Kabul: A Monologue for Kika Markham. Chelsea Theatre Centre, London. July 1999. New York: Theatre Communications Group, 2002.

‡*Death and Taxes: Hydriotaphia and Other Plays.* New York: Theatre Communications Group, 2000.

Angels in America. HBO. 2003. (Teleplay)

Brundibar. Adapt. from *Brundibár,* by Hans Krása and Adolf Hoffmeister. Chicago Opera Theatre, Chicago. 2003. (Libretto)

Caroline; or, Change. Public Theater, New York. 2003. New York: Theatre Communications Group, 2004. (Libretto)

The Comedy on the Bridge. Adapt. from *Veselohra na mostě,* by Bohuslav Martinů and Václav Kliment Klicpera. Berkeley Repertory Theatre, Berkeley. 2005. (Libretto)

Munich: The Screenplay. With Eric Roth. North Hollywood: Script Fly, 2005. (Screenplay)

The Intelligent Homosexual's Guide to Capitalism and Socialism with a Key to the Scriptures. Guthrie Theater, Minneapolis. 2009. Theatre Communications Group, 2012.

Lincoln. Dream Works, 2012. (Screenplay)

Mother Courage and Her Children: A Chronicle of the Thirty Years' War. By Brecht. Trans. Tony Kushner. London: Methuen Drama, 2009.

Tiny Kushner: Five One-Act Plays. Guthrie Theater, Minneapolis, 2009. New York: Theatre Communications Group, 2011.

Lincoln: The Screenplay. New York: Theatre Communications Group, 2013. (Screenplay)

Other Major Works

Tony Kushner in Conversation. Ed. Robert Vorlicky. Ann Arbor: U of Michigan P, 1998. (Interviews)

The Art of Maurice Sendak: 1980 to the Present. New York: Abrams, 2003. (Nonfiction)

Brundibar. Adapt. from *Brundibár,* by Krása and Hoffmeister. New York: Michael di Capua, 2003. (Children's fiction)

Save Your Democratic Citizen Soul!: Rants, Screeds, and Other Public Utterances for Midnight in the Republic. New York: New, 2003. (Speeches)

Wrestling with Zion: Progressive Jewish-American Responses to the Israeli-Palestinian Conflict. Ed. Kushner and Alisa Solomon. New York: Grove, 2003. (Essays)

*This play was first published in *Three Plays for Young Audiences.* New York: Theatre Communications Group, 1987.

†This is the first combined edition of the play.

‡Includes published versions of the plays *Hydriotaphia; or, The Death of Dr. Browne*; *Notes on Akiba*; *Reverse Transcription: Six Playwrights Bury a Seventh. A Ten-Minute Play That's Nearly Twenty Minutes Long*; and *Terminating; or, Sonnet LXXV; or, "Lass meine Schmerzen nicht verloren sein"; or, Ambivalence.*

ANGELS IN AMERICA (1991)

AUTHOR COMMENTARY

Tony Kushner and Craig Lucas (interview date 1993)

SOURCE: Kushner, Tony. "Tony Kushner." Interview by Craig Lucas. *BOMB* 43 (1993): 30-5. Print.

[*In the following interview with playwright Craig Lucas, conducted as auditions were being held for the Broadway premiere of* Millennium Approaches, *Kushner talks about the process of writing the play and his intentions regarding the portrayal of Roy Cohn as a redeemed villain. He also discusses contemporary political and social issues that are relevant to the work.*]

[*Craig Lucas*]: *It must all be overwhelming.*

[Tony Kushner]: Yeah, it is. It's been a very, very strange time. I feel very lost and confused and sort of unclear about what I should be doing with the play, where I should be going with it and where I should be going after the play is done, and it's not going to be done for quite a while because we're not even going to open *Perestroika* until October of next year, and then it'll be opening in London at the same time.

Will you get a chance to work on a production of **Perestroika** *before it comes to New York?*

I'm going to workshop it with some NYU graduate students. And I think that's probably all I'll do with it. I'm beginning to run out of steam, because I've been working on the play pretty much since 1988; I wrote one play in the middle of working on *Angels* [*Angels in America*], but that was an adaptation [Corneille's *The Illusion*]. So I feel like it's time to move on. I don't want this to be the only thing that I ever write. And I have a lot of plays that I've backlogged in the meanwhile, so I wanted a director that I could just give the play to for New York and not really have to sit and watch very closely. I hope that I am banned from rehearsals. It's like being in therapy with somebody for a long time. I've done as much work with these people as I can possibly do. It's time to go and find another gig.

It can turn into a cottage industry, and you don't want to be that mother hen following it around.

And the question of whether you want to make it into a film, or whether writing a screenplay is a good idea. You can spend years and years and years, and it's probably a terrible mistake. One thing the play's taught me is that I can let it go.

What you have in your favor is the force of your clarity, a lucidity. So much modern art is about ambiguity and what one is going to read into it. You've created a moral universe which allows audiences to watch your characters run 180 degrees in the wrong *direction. It's enjoyable to watch Roy Cohn, and at the same time even the most right wing fundamentalist homophobe would not suspect that you were endorsing this man's values.*

Yeah, I hope not. I mean, I still feel—especially in *Perestroika*—there were people in the audience in LA who cried when Roy Cohn died. And the audience was kind of shifting in their seats and thinking, "Well, *should* we be crying?" Which is, I guess, the point. I mean, I'd like to explore being ambiguous a little bit more in the future. I feel sometimes that that's kind of a flaw in the work.

It's not that there are no contradictions. I simply mean there's this sense of mastery. For a seven-hour play, it's very economical. There's not a lot of fat.

Yeah. *Millennium* [*Millennium Approaches*] was about 40 pages longer in its first draft and *Perestroika* was literally twice the length, so they've both been boiled down. I don't think that there is actually a great deal of fat. I've listened to *Millennium* now for a long time, and I'm a very fat writer in several senses of the word. (*laughter*) I've been working with a lot of very good editors and directors, and because we knew that the ultimate thing was going to be as prodigiously long as it is, we couldn't really afford to be sentimental about anything, everything that could possibly go would go. One of the things that worries me about the play is that everybody in it, except for Roy, is sort of a decent person trying their best. And that's part of the appeal of the play, but it's the part of me that I worry about being excessively liberal, that I genuinely believe people are primarily motivated by the good. And I wonder if that makes everything a little bit vanilla. There's a certain kind of writing that starts with a more cynical set of assumptions about people, that produces a harsher picture of reality. And the world is a harsh place, so I'm trying to figure out what it is in myself that resists seeing the world that way. Excessive optimism or sentimentality or something ... I don't know.

Well, I'm here to dissuade you from this delusion. I think you picture a complex universe.

I'm not sure that I'm explaining myself correctly. You want to believe that people are usually behaving according to standards that they've set for themselves that are assigned qualifications like good and bad. And the thing that works about Roy is that I proceeded from the assumption that his world made sense to him and that he wasn't operating with conscious knowledge of being a bad man. And I think that people do proceed, for the most part, from that assumption. But—

Hitler.

Hitler. Well, yeah, but then there, *exactly.* Where does evil come from? Is Bush really proceeding from just a very bad ideological system that he's being true to, that he's consequently doing very bad things because of his fidelity to that? Or is there something else at work? Because when you look at somebody like Bush, you see a monstrously cynical man, or one reading of Bush might be that. He'd be an interesting character for a play because the question is whether or not people that do really terrible things are always self justifying in the way that I have Roy self justify, or whether or not there's more clarity about the malevolence that they're creating.

Like Richard the Third.

Yeah. Which is a very daring ... or Iago ... There are characters in Shakespeare which at some point say to the audience: "There is no human justification for what I am, and I represent a kind of evil that's more radical and more profound than human evil." That's the question that Hannah Arendt asks or gets asked when she puts forth the notion of the banality of evil in *Eichman in Jerusalem.* For somebody like Eichman, for a petty demon, that seems a sufficient explanation, but for somebody that really does immense historical damage, not a Roy Cohn, but an Adolf Hitler, how do you describe that evil, what do you call it, and how do you account for it in a system that doesn't have a very clear spiritual dimension? If there isn't a devil, then what is that evil? I mean, I feel that maybe the plays are a little too forgiving. But I don't know.

Do you think there is a devil?

I just had a big argument with a friend of mine who was telling me (she's a very political radical feminist, Kimberly Flynn who **Perestroika** is dedicated to, and very smart) that she fears the devil and believes in the existence of the Satanic. And I guess I don't. But then maybe I just don't want to believe it. That's what I mean by saying that I worry about being too liberal. I mean, so much of what we've lived through in the last 12 years has shown us that these people really are murderers. I mean, they're very, very, very evil people.

Yes, I agree. But you know you can be a murderous villain simply by virtue of leading an unexamined life.

Yeah . . . you can be that. But do you want to say then that all evil is to be ascribed to ignorance and a lack of examination and a lack of analysis? There's something very comforting about believing that, because it suggests a continuity between yourself, the people that you know and love and have conversations with and reason with, and those people who are doing this terrible thing. It suggests that Bush or Reagan or a Hitler or the neo-Nazi skinheads who are now beating up disabled people in Germany, that these people are really just part of the human community, and that there's some way . . . if their *system* is bad, as long as they're basically faithful adherents to a system in the way that you are faithful to a moral vision that you have, then you should be able to convince them of the inappropriateness of their system and reason them out of their evil behavior. But that may in fact be wrong. There may be something at work, and I don't know what that something is, but there may be a kind of active malevolence that's beyond . . . that has to be resisted, I *think,* finally with force. So you have writers like Larry Kramer, for instance, whose anger clearly goes in the direction—I don't know whether Larry has actually ever advocated violence or not (but I guess he sort of has) but certainly people who have no real problem saying, "These people are our enemies, and there is no community between us." I think that may be the difference between being a radical and being a liberal. You're not sentimental about letting go of that continuum.

I think that abuse, whether it comes in the form of poverty or ignorance or sexual molestation, can actually twist a mind and a psyche to such a degree that you have Jeffrey Dahmers on a mass scale.

Yeah.

Witness the fascists in Germany. Those are, I believe, sociologically induced psychoses.

Yeah.

They're not going to be changed in individuals who are over a certain age.

Right.

But perhaps the way the next generation is raised can be changed. By force, I agree. It's a curious contradiction, though. In your play, **A Bright Room Called Day,** *you call the Gulf War a misadventure, or your character Zillah does, and she states that the U.S. is trying to start World War III. But then another character, Paz, is held up to criticism for* not *shooting Hitler when he has the opportunity. I sometimes drop my liberalism when I think about Hussein or Milosovec who through the force of their will and hatred would certainly annihilate you and me. How far are they from Hitler? I'm not sure that* I'm *so far from Mr. Bush, though he may have had different goals in mind, surely he did, when he used force against a murderous dictator. What are your feelings about Serbia and Bosnia? Do we have any responsibility there?*

I think that those situations are terribly difficult. It's very hard for me to ever say that I think unilateral military action on the part of the United States can be a great thing at this point. The idea of the United States armed forces going in and suppressing and controlling a population of any sort is so fraught with history. And I don't trust our government, I don't trust our motives, so I don't think that I would ever really be . . . I mean, it's like in Somalia. It's hard to believe that the United States ever would act out of—or that any government really ever acts out of altruism. One would really like to see somebody go in and just kick the shit out of the Serbs in Bosnia; the situation is horrible, and it's terrible to watch a Holocaust unfolding, and to feel that we're sitting around and doing nothing, but it's also hard to feel that once you let that thing out . . . I mean, you're a fool to think that you're going to be able to control it. Congress doesn't control it. We don't know what we've been using; in Iraq they were using what I consider nuclear weapons—bullets covered with radioactive waste. There's those Tomahawk missiles which don't work and which basically are happier hitting things in cities than flying off into the ether. I think we've completely lost the possibility of limited warfare.

By the same token, if there had been a way for us to militarily intervene in Germany in 1933, we might have prevented . . .

Right, and there would have been a catastrophe if Roosevelt had not been President and we had not broken out of isolationism and stood up against Hitler. And so I'm not a pacifist in any way, I just think that in terms of this particular situation it's very complicated. And I think that ethnic cleansing and the progressive Balkanization of that entire part of the world has to stop somehow. I think Saddam is a danger, but I don't believe economic sanctions were given a chance. I think that what the *real* New World Order . . . One thing that the Cold War seems to have eliminated is an ideological wall that prevented a certain kind of discussion. There's the possibility now of the countries of the world acting in concert to manipulate trouble spots out of military conflict. And I think that could have worked in Iraq. And of course that's also very problematic, because you wind up with kids not getting medicine and people dying of starvation in countries that are sanctioned, but the end of the Cold War doesn't mean the end of American Imperialism. And what one doesn't want to see is a failure to compete economically transformed into our becoming a bully with our weapons.

This is the whistle Noam Chomsky keeps blowing. The more our economy fails to produce anything anybody needs or can afford, the more we put all of our eggs in the military basket and become this international arsenal, selling weapons to Iran and Iraq so that neither side can win, and all we see are dollar signs, and nobody's even looking past next month.

Dollar signs and this national sense of failed virility, so that the minute we start dropping bombs on anybody, everybody feels very good for five minutes. And there is a fantasy sense that we're still the number one country on earth because we can go in there and kick this person, and we forget we're talking about this completely decimated country that was annihilated two years ago and has never rebuilt and has no military machine at this point, and what we're doing is going in and ineptly trying to bomb a couple of—I mean, they announce that we've gone in and it was very quick and here are a couple of videotapes, and then the next day it turns out they didn't hit any of their targets and they dropped bombs on hotels and on private buildings and orphanages, and everybody's shuffling and saying, "Well, we're *trying* to hit our targets." I mean, in addition to the fact that we're not much of an economic superpower, in point of fact, although we have the ability to destroy millions of lives, the army doesn't seem to be very good any more. It seems to be run by people who don't know how to run the technology that we've created. We spent so much money building machines, and none of these people really know how to work them. Which is one of the reasons that Desert Storm evaporated as an exploitable issue within

days after the first shot was fired; it became clear that we were killing our own people, that we were doing things no civilized nation would ever want to admit to doing, like burying people alive in trenches. And, in addition to being an unsuccessful war, because we didn't really get rid of Saddam, it was an ineptly handled one against a vastly inferior enemy.

While you were in auditions today we swore in a new President.

Yeah, did you watch him? I heard the speech was like hot air.

Maya Angelou was so moving. . . . How do you feel about Clinton?

I don't know, I mean, I'm really thrilled that he won, and I'm really thrilled that those bastards are out and I'm really thrilled at the way in which it's becoming a simple fact now that the whole twelve years of Reaganism was a horrendous mistake; it says a great deal about the American people, and about the way that this weird amalgam of different populations and this very troubled history, still produces a country that's committed to participatory democracy of some sort. And to *not* finding easy, ugly solutions . . . Because the British couldn't get rid of Thatcher, they still have Major around. I thought the Republican National Convention was a watershed event. They saw that Reaganomics was failing, and they pulled out their witchiest stuff, and you could just feel it not working. Feel people sort of curdling.

In **A Bright Room Called Day,** *Zillah says of our much-touted 'great communicator,' "what Reagan communicated was that you can be even more divorced from History and Reality and Language than he was from Jane Wyman and STILL BE THE MOST POWERFUL MAN ON EARTH!" So many of my friends and I are critical of the status quo, and yet there isn't an explicit or articulated vision of how things . . .*

How to improve it.

I often wish that there was a party I could belong to. Or a school. And I'm embarrassed and afraid sometimes to say that I am attracted to Marx, that I think there is something wrong with the division of wealth in our society, and I feel very vulnerable when I say this. I fear I may lose the ability to make a living as a writer and be vilified as a socialist—which certainly happened to many writers during McCarthy. Do you worry about these things?

Oh yeah. I know exactly what you mean when you said you wished there was a party to belong to. The idea of socialism is still completely valid, and the collapse of the Soviet system doesn't in any way mean that capitalism has succeeded. Capitalism is always going to be successful economically in the sense that about 10% of the population will have a lot of money and 1% will have immense amounts of money and everybody else will live lives that are either full of fear or full of poverty, and there'll be huge numbers of people out of work. Socialism is simply the idea that people are better off if we work collectively and that the economic system we live in is made by people and therefore can be controlled intelligently rather than let loose. There's no way that can't be true. As long as there are decent people in the world, there's going to be a demand for socialism. I mean, the demand for health care right now, which is a demand that 80% of the people in this country share, is a demand for a certain kind of socialism. People wanted to get rid of Bush because they wanted the restitution of the social net that FDR put into place. We don't want to live in an outlaw, in a bandit country anymore.

At the same time they want to see the end of welfare.

Yeah, well, welfare is the demon and people don't even think about what it means. What it is basically is the fear and terror of being poor. Fear of the notion of being dependent in a country where dependency is a shameful thing. Everyone recognizes their potential for being homeless, for being on welfare, so we hate people that are because they frighten us. David Duke made great political hay out of welfare expenditures in Louisiana which, when it was examined, amounted to 5% of the state budget. So it's a complete, idiotic fantasy. What really makes you nuts is that people want health care and they don't want to pay taxes. But then again they don't get anything for their taxes. In Europe you pay a huge amount, but you actually get services that you would want. Here all you get are Tomahawk missiles. Here all you're doing is bailing out savings and loan associations. You don't get anything back. So you need to hold onto your money, because you're not going to get anything from the government. It's very embarrassing and difficult to say that you're a socialist at this point in history, but lots of people, I think, really still are.

Another thing in your work that makes me feel less alone in the world is that it doesn't share the kneejerk, dismissive attitude towards Freud. Have you been analyzed?

Oh, yes, endlessly ... I sound like Woody Allen, I really have been analyzed virtually all of my adult life. ... And I've just gone back in. And I absolutely believe that the people of the Frankfurt school were on the right track in trying to come up with some political theory that incorporated Freud and Marx, because it seems to me that there's much consonance between the two world views. There's a direction you can take Freud in that's anti-collective, just as there's a direction you can take Marx in that's anti-psychoanalytic, but neither of them need to be seen that way. And the deepest Freudians, including Freud himself, have acknowledged the existence of the collective, and have not seen people as being hermetically sealed entities, just as

the best Marxists were very sophisticated and believed in psychoanalysis; Trotsky sent his own daughter into psychoanalysis. One has to acknowledge the profoundly antisocial dimension in people and recognize that it isn't truer—you don't want to privilege it above the social dimension, but recognize that these two things are thesis and anti-thesis, that they're in constant struggle with one another, and that a real collective doesn't annihilate the idea of people being differentiated from one another and having specific detail. The thing that I find so moving about Brecht's plays, especially some of his early plays before he went into exile, is that it was obvious to him because of the discourse in which his work was situated in Germany where psychoanalysis was seen as being incredibly bourgeois, and being a Communist at that point and not being a Leninist and not really spending too much time worrying about the internal, but Brecht was very, *very* clear and was struggling with the question of how the individual is transmuted into the socialist subject. Because here's this guy who's clearly a genius and who knows himself to be one of the greatest writers of the century, believing also very deeply in the need to be part of a mass, of a group. And I think obviously in great pain and agony, trying to figure out how to kill off this glorious ego or to make this glorious ego function in the services of a collective will without losing what makes it glorious. And you can sort of rewrite the whole arc of his career thinking of the characters in his plays as all struggling with that. It's the great failure, again, of socialism: they crushed those people, but they didn't make them better. There's this great thing from Bulgakov in like 1920: "People keep talking about the new Muscovites after the revolution; they seem to me much like the old Muscovites except the housing shortage has made them sour."

Your plays are filled with visions and angels, devils and revelations. Do you hold a belief system about God?

I'm an honest to god agnostic. I think that agnosticism really is a tough position and it isn't a shoulder shrug, you know, "I don't know and I don't care." If you don't care, you're really an atheist, you just don't want to call yourself that because you don't want people to think you're Madeline Murray O'Hare or something (who I think is one of the great, *fabulous* Americans). I'm in a position of constant confusion about it. I don't understand how to incorporate the existence of evil into any theological system, I just don't. I don't feel comfortable saying that evil is a part of life, because I don't know how you then become anything other than complacent in the face of it, and justice is something that I do believe in. Louis says in **Angels** that justice is God. That's the one thing that I feel, you know, that when justice wins, when you're reading history, that's what feels the best to you. Or to me anyway. But I also really can't say that I am sure that there isn't a God, and there are many smart people like Martin Luther King who believed in God. And I have a sense that the material world is not all that there is. When one loses people that one loves, one's inability to accept that life ends with the material body ... sort of punches holes in the walls of one's resistance to the notion of something beyond.

The magician at the end of **The Illusion** *suggests something which Christian theologists have been trying to articulate for 2000 years, that time and the physical universe are illusions which are created in the separation, and our belief in this world is the dream.*

Yeah.

And he says it very beautifully in terms of love being perhaps the only reality.

I also believe that it has a lot to do with being in theater ... the whole thing of the real and the unreal, the uncertainty about which is which. I decided I really wanted to be a playwright and be in theater when my Shakespeare professor at Columbia read for us the Theseus/Hyppolita debate at the top of Act Five of *Midnight*. This sounds incredibly corny, but it's true ... it's the closest thing that I've ever come to magic. And also to a sense of collectivity and a sense of energy that's not bound by physical bodies. Because sex, of course, requires a certain degree of ... I mean, it's *better* when there's contact ... but in the way that an audience and actors create something, and they really do create something. It isn't just an old theater cliché, the event that takes place on any given night is something that a bunch of people who are not speaking to one another and don't know each other make almost before the first line gets spoken ... there's a kind of thing that will happen. And some of it you can tease out and say: "Well, this person coughed on that line and so he didn't get his laugh and so the whole play fell apart," but it's never reducible to that. There's something in the air ... I feel in a certain sense that the theater is the closest that I come to a religion.

The afternoon that my lover and I saw **Millennium Approaches** *at the National, we were so invigorated. As you know he has AIDS, and I worried that the play was going to send him into a tailspin. We were so elated, and so sorry when it was over, we were on such a theater high, we went and saw* Heartbreak House *that night. Which was how I came to be reminded that your subtitle,* A Gay Fantasia on National Themes, *comes from Shaw—something which nobody seems to have noted. How do you feel about Shaw?*

Oh, I love Shaw. Yeah, you're the first person. John Bellucci, the actor who played Roy Cohn in San Francisco ... And *I* didn't know what it had come from ... kept saying, "Something else is called that." It strikes terror in your veins because you're going to find out that someone else ...

Oscar Hammerstein.

Or somebody your own age. And then he said it was *Heartbreak House.* I wanted a title that had a musical sound to it. Every playwright probably wants their plays to have a kind of musical structure, its themes and interweaving.

Did you work from an outline? The design is so ingenious.

I started to, but it just fell apart completely, and I had never really been successful at doing an outline. Because I really didn't know what I wanted it to say; I had no idea what the second part was supposed to be about. When I first started writing it, it didn't have a second part; it was three acts, they each had like 56 scenes in them, and I could tell that I was heading into trouble, but by the time I got past the end of the second act, and there were things that happened in the second act that I hadn't planned for ...

Such as?

Well, Joe's mother coming out at the end of the act and selling her house in Salt Lake. And I didn't know why she was selling her house or what she was doing. ...

I love that the first part ends, she arrived in New York, it's a promise and it's completely unanswered and unaddressed. To me ... obviously it throws you into the second play, but it also has the feeling of life lived. Change. And so much of the play is about change and how painful it is (I love what Harper says in **Perestroika** *about God slitting you open with his thumb and pulling all your guts out and rearranging them and stuffing them back in, and that's how change happens) ... It must have cost you an enormous amount of pain to shape these plays.*

Well, yeah. *Millennium* has been shaped a good deal, but the first draft of it and this draft are within shooting distance of one another. *Perestroika* has just changed and changed and changed and changed, and it's still changing, and that's appropriate, because that's what the play's about. It's a little miracle of compression at this point. *Millennium* introduces eight major characters, only five of which are dealt with substantively, and nothing happens in *Millennium.* And in *Perestroika* everything happens. Probably there could have been a third play. It was originally five acts long and a 293 page manuscript that I've had to just crush down. It's a little uncomfortable that it's happened in such a public way, because now the critics in San Francisco who saw the really long version wrote that I had ruined it, that I'd cut too much out, and I think that when people who saw it in LA—it's going to lose some more before it gets to New York—will say, "But what about that?" And everybody will say how their favorite things were lost. And that's been hard, but it's nothing compared to the thrill of getting it done. I can't think of any other play where there were two parts, and the first half went out and did its thing, and then the second part has to sort of live up ... it's a really weird situation.

Are you at all struck by the irony of those who saw nothing in **A Bright Room Called Day** *now jumping up and down and screaming about* **Angels***? I mean, the same person wrote these two plays.*

I know that while **Bright Room** would never be a big success, if you took Zillah out of it, and just did the German scenes, people would say, "Well, it's a nice play." Or they'd say it's not a good play, but it would be this tepid little non-event. But having this character get up and say Ronald Reagan and Adolf Hitler are virtually the same thing, and that fascism starts at home and whatever it is that Zillah's saying, just made people ballistic. Even though Zillah comprises about six pages out of a 130 page manuscript ... I didn't read any of the reviews in New York, because when it got trashed in London I stopped reading reviews forever.

You don't read them now.

No. I can't. I was reading Michael Billington's review in the *Guardian* of **Bright Room** in London, and it was so angry and he was so incredibly contemptuous of everything in the play, that I felt like if I read this all the way through and read any more of these, I'll never write again. And this isn't fair because I just started, and I don't think that these people are getting what's good about the play. It's sort of amazing to me that, from what I've understood of the critical response to **Bright Room,** virtually no separation was made between me and Zillah, and no one noticed that she is in fact a character, she *speaks to people,* and that she's full of contradictions and that she herself says to the audience that this is deliberately overstated, you need to overstate. Not five months later after everybody got hysterical, John Frohnmayer was standing in front of the National Press Club saying, "What's happening at the NEA will lead to fascism in America." By the time the Republican National Convention was getting reviewed and the farther reaches of Iran Contra, you had Murray Kempton and all the poobahs of the press saying this is fascism. All of a sudden it became sayable.

Not to Al D'Amato.

Well, he doesn't know how to pronounce the word. Dale Collins did this great column where she went to all the Senate Candidates in the fall and asked them to name the two books that they had read in the last year and liked the best and she cornered D'Amato without any of his aides around and he came up with one that clearly didn't exist, and then he said, "Oh yes, another book, *The Rise and Fall of the Second Reich.*" Collins said, "Well, what's a Reich or two between friends." (*laughter*)

... To get back to change, I was thinking how it was within the last ten years that John Simon felt free to call a play "faggot nonsense" in New York Magazine. *Things can seem to go along one way for so long and then be trans-*

formed ... I don't think AIDS is the only force that has shoved homophobia and homosexuality out into the open, but it is nonetheless dazzling to me that now I can pick up the paper and read articles about gay people whereas ten years, fifteen years ago I could not. I'm frightened for what's going to come because I feel we're a very visible target now—

Yeah.

We're not so very different from European Jewry in the '30s. We're accepted in certain sophisticated urban quarters, in our ghettos, and nice people don't openly say mean things about us, but lots of people would like to see us dead. Do you have thoughts about why homophobia holds on and what is under the surface now and ...

What one must understand is that when one examines any great social phobia, one will be examining really the heart of the society that hates. Sexual politics is the eye of the storm, and racism is the eye of the storm even though blacks are 11% of the population. That the oppressed minorities in this country's history, or anywhere in the world, are the thing by which the majority defines itself, and that it has no identity except as not being the thing that it's despising. The Catholic Church is an enormously complicated institution; it represents one of the biggest stumbling blocks that the progress of gay rights faces. Because how do you get around fundamentalism, how do you get around doctrine?

With a certain amount of learning. John Boswell writes that early Christians honored gay marriage and that the earliest existing Christian marriage ceremony is between people of the same sex.

Right.

The Vatican may wish to tear the page out of the books.

Well, they do destroy stuff, but they don't really need to. They're not like the Mormons who actually do have to put things in their secret vaults. The fact of the matter is that the Holy Texts of Christianity contain passages that clearly anathematize homosexuality as a practice. And if you believe in a fundamental reading of those texts or if you believe that the Vatican, that the Cardinals and Pope interpret doctrine, which they do, which is part of the doctrine of Catholicism, then you can't do anything about it. You either have to go for a reformation which is, I think, coming in this country, or you just sign on for the whole nine yards. I mean, Boswell's great, but a lot of what he's talking about is Christianity as it was practiced before Paul, before the gospels were really codified, and yes, there was a tremendous—Elaine Pagel's book also shows there was a tremendously weird bunch of religions going around back then that were all sort of vaguely Christian or Jewish or something.

But so many Catholics are willing to put aside notions on contraception. They're just not willing to put other—

I think that women are going to be the great beach heads for the church, because I don't think that women are really interested in back-room abortion anymore, or in having 50 babies in a row. They're really tired of watching successions of uninspired male priests tell them what the church is about. They clearly are the life force of the church. Just like the third world, there's going to be people of color in the church (who are far and away the most populous element) who are going to get tired of an endless succession of Europeans. And the first time there's a Latin American pope or an African pope, we can hope for certain kinds of incursions into church reactionary thinking that we're not seeing. I do feel, like you, things are changing remarkably. I mean, the plays you've written, *Angels,* there's a space for us now, and a way that straight critics and straight audiences can listen, that just didn't exist ten years ago. And it is going to make life better and also more difficult because there are going to be backlashes like what's happened in Colorado, all over the place.

Well, I feel very strongly that you have opened that space out. Thank you.

PRODUCTION REVIEW

Joshua Takano Chambers-Letson
(review date 2012)

SOURCE: Chambers-Letson, Joshua Takano. "The Principle of Hope: Reflections on a Revival of *Angels in America.*" Rev. of *Angels in America,* by Tony Kushner. *Drama Review* 56.1 (2012): 143-49. Print.

[*In the following review of the 2010 production of* Angels in America *by the Signature Theater Company in New York City, Chambers-Letson reflects on the ways in which the "performative force" of the play focuses the audience's attention on the work's message of hope, particularly as that force contrasts with the portrayal of the Angel, who is locked in time and unable to create.*]

> I'm scared. And also full of, I don't know, Joy or something.
>
> Hope.

Prior Walter, *Angels in America*
(Kushner 1995:154)

When Signature Theatre Company announced that its 2010/2011 season would include a Michael Greif-helmed pro-

duction of Tony Kushner's *Angels in America: A Gay Fantasia on National Themes,* it was much remarked that this would be the first major professional production of *Angels* in New York City since it first debuted. *Angels in America* is one of the most produced contemporary plays and is also the source of a compendium of critical attention.[1] It has been heralded and critiqued as a lyrical meditation on the question of America; a heartbreaking interrogation of personal and political loss; and a sometimes-cloying documentation of a specific vision of urban, middle-class, white, queer intellectual liberalism at the end of the millennium. Signature's return to *Angels* 20 years after the play's debut is more than just all of the above: it manifests the performative force of *Angels,* drawing attention less to what *Angels* means and more to what it does.

Beyond all else, Signature's *Angels does* the labor of hope. As philosopher Ernst Bloch spent a lifetime arguing, hope is the powerful and inexhaustible fuel of human progress (Bloch 1988, 1996a, 1996b, 1996c, 2000). As such, hope's labor is to insist that the present is not enough and that the future can and must be better. In dark times such as these, characterized by a range of hope's disappointments—from war without end to the economic and political failures of the Obama presidency—it seems ever more critical that we investigate and affirm the political potentiality of hope. As *Angels* stages and *does* the labor of hope, Signature's production provides an opportunity to consider the political potentiality of hope alongside the critical questions raised by Bloch and by hope's disappointment.

Hope's labor has often been overlooked in critical assessments of *Angels in America.* Many critics have noted that Kushner's Angel bears a resemblance to the Angel of History described by Walter Benjamin in the "Theses on the Philosophy of History" (1988).[2] Few, if any, have noted another of Kushner's sources, Ernst Bloch's three-volume encyclopedia of hope's role in human progress, *The Principle of Hope* (1996a, 1996b, 1996c).[3] This is a surprising oversight given that Bloch is literally cited by the playwright, who titles the third act of *Millennium Approaches* "Not-Yet-Conscious, Forward Dawning" (Kushner 1995:91).[4] This phrase is lifted from Bloch's contention that humanity is gifted with "a Not-Yet-Conscious, one that has never been conscious and has never existed in the past, therefore itself a forward dawning, into the New. It is the dawning that can surround even the simplest daydreams; from there it extends into further areas of negated deprivation, and hence of hope" (1996a:77). This hope is not the empty promise articulated by national politicians, nor is it the escapist fantasy sold for consumption in the romantic comedies and melodramas of the culture industries. Rather, it is a hope critically rooted in the knowledge that the world in which we live is insufficient and that something better must and can be attained.

Two scenes from Signature's production exemplify the dialectical structure of deprivation and dawning that characterizes hope's labor: the Angel's arrival (in which the Angel delivers to the AIDS-stricken prophet Prior Walter an epistle commanding the end of human progress), and Prior's ascent to Heaven (in which he refuses the command). In May of 1991, an Angel burst through the ceiling of Prior's apartment in the Eureka Theatre Company's San Francisco production, descending from above attached to theatrical rigging; in April of 1993 she delivered her epistle to the chosen prophet on the stage of Broadway's Walter Kerr Theatre; and in the Winter of 1995, as a 15-year-old, I watched her descend from the rafters during a performance by the national touring company (directed by Michael Mayer) in Denver, Colorado. Now, on 9 October 2010, in a small theatre on 42nd Street, I sit next to a beloved friend. She is gripping my hand and Prior Walter (Christian Borle) is once again manifest before our eyes, alone in bed, abandoned by his lover Louis, and terrified of facing this future alone.

The back of the stage rips apart, a caesura that cuts across history as a blinding white light pours out across the stage from behind the shadow of this Angel, resurrected by Robin Weigert and suspended on visible wires, to deliver the Word. A slight jerk as the mechanics whir into motion and she moves forward, toward us, her left arm extended to her side, the right crooked above her, palm exposed and fingers extended, lifting upwards in heavenly gesture. It occurs to me in this instant that most previous productions got it wrong: their Angels descended from above, from the heavens, from the uppermost regions of the stage. But Benjamin told us that the Angel of History does not come down from above; instead it is facing forward, wings blasted open by the violence of history, a storm that "irresistibly propels him into the future to which his back is turned" (1988:258). As the Angel is coming toward us, then, we in the audience are facing the future. But what kind of future can we hope to have in times such as these?

This 2010 Angel is not Ellen McLaughlin's divine 1993 New York incarnation, dressed in regal gowns and replicating the stony faced dignity of the Bethesda Fountain in Central Park; this Angel is not Carolyn Swift's metallic and neurotic celestial being who spoke to me across Wagner's mystic gulf in Denver in 1995; this Angel is not the elegantly confused cinematic impression of Emma Thompson in the 2003 television adaptation; Weigert's 2010 Angel is different from those who have come before her. Although she is a messenger from the Heavens, Weigert's Angel, before all else—and like the most human amongst us—suffers from a broken heart. And instead of descending from above, she comes forward in supplicant gesture, and it is we, in the audience, who look toward the horizon of the future.

The wires relax and her body lowers, the heavy apparatus of the wings pulled by gravity to the ground as Weigert balances herself in an act of physical endurance. (Indeed,

throughout the run the actress suffered bruises and strained muscles as a result of the wing's harness.) Her foot hits the earth and she tells her prophet a story: In God's infinite order of creation, he produced humans, and from humans came progress, and progress shook the heavens. Enamored of his creation and bored of Angels, who neither create nor progress, "He left."

PRIOR:

Abandoned.

ANGEL:

And did not return.
We do not know where HE has gone. He may *never* . . .

(Kushner 1995:177)

She has brought herself to her prophet's level. Sitting on the edge of his bed with tears streaming down her face she reaches out a hand to him as if, perhaps, he might comfort her. He can't. Because, paralyzed, he hears in her words the echo of the loss of his lover Louis. She could not speak it, her abandonment unutterable, so she cuts short the admission with an ellipsis: "He may *never* . . ." Words falter. I'll write it here: He will *never* return.

Abandoned, the present tears at us and still the future rests in our hands. Is it at last the hour to abandon hope and cease the work of progress? In a later sequence, the Angel returns and Prior wrestles her to the ground to demand her blessing. The actress looks exhausted by the apparatus that clings to her back; so too is the character who, drained by the emotional demands of her defeat, relents and grants Prior entrance to Heaven. An industrial ladder slides onstage and projections of flames take residence on the steps, transforming it into the divine vision of Jacob's ladder for Prior's ascent.

The Angels wanted him to deliver the epistle and the epistle demands that humans stop progressing, stop moving, and stop hoping for more. When he arrives in Heaven, every actor (save Prior) is transformed into a different Angel, huddling together on the left side of the stage to hear his response, delivered from stage right. The Angels don ridiculous-looking judicial robes and crouch in preposterous positions likely meant to look ethereal and otherworldly. But the stunning exchange between Borle's Prior and the host of Angels compensates for Greif's unfortunate stage picture. Stephen Spinella's 1993 Prior was tall, commanding, elegant, and superhuman in his delicate but admirable humanity. Borle is less regal, slight and vulnerable, someone you might otherwise overlook in a crowded room. This is precisely what makes his defiance of the Angels crack with a resounding force. From a body marked by a physical fragility, Prior speaks a truth that Heaven's minions cannot themselves articulate:

We can't just stop. We're not rocks—progress, migration, motion is . . . modernity. It's *animate,* it's what living things do. We desire. Even if all we desire is stillness, it's still desire *for*. Even if we go faster than we should. We can't *wait*. And wait for what? God . . . He isn't coming back.

(Kushner 1995:263-64)

The Angel argues with him. She tells him the end is near, "It is Not-to-Be Time." "Still," he says, "Still. Bless me anyway. I want more life. I can't help myself. I do" (266).

To the Angels, the end is nigh; the Angel of America muses, "Oh, who asks of the Order's Blessing / With apocalypse Descending?" (266). The Angel's nihilism stages the difference between Angels and prophets. As Prior describes the Angels, "they're basically incredibly powerful bureaucrats, they have no imagination, they can *do* anything but they can't invent, create, they're sort of fabulous and dull all at once" (175). This is the reason that the Angels require a prophet. In the words of Giorgio Agamben,

> There are two kinds of work or praxis in God: the work of redemption and that of creation. To the former corresponds the prophets, who serve as mediators in order to affirm the work of salvation; to the latter correspond the angels, who mediate the work of creation. The work of salvation precedes in rank that of creation, hence the superiority of the prophets over angels.

(2009:107)

Angels can only execute God's design; they are incapable of creating the New. Without God's creative force, Angels can only see cessation, as they are unable to imagine or create its alternative. But humans have the capacity to be agents of change, to hope for, imagine, and enact other possibilities.

In this scene, Bloch's resilient politics of hope surges forth; hope is revealed as a trait that is unique to humanity and that makes the construction of an alternative future possible, even in a world without a God. "We live past hope," Prior says, "It's so much not enough, so inadequate but . . . Bless me anyway. I want more life" (Kushner 1995:267). Here, then, in Prior's refusal we see the Principle of Hope as that which refuses negation and demands movement towards something better and Not-Yet-Here. As he utters this refusal, "Bless me anyway. I want more life," my companion grips my hand harder. In this grasp she and I become part of a larger We—the members of the audience (including Kushner, who is seated directly behind us) watching this moment together, a fabulous collectivity in an otherwise alienating age of anomie. And in this moment We are reminded that even in times such as these, We desire to live *together*. We progress *together*. We hope for more *together*. As Bloch wrote in 1918: "I am. We are. That is enough. Now we have to begin" (2000:1).

Where do We begin? Already we have seen how hope constitutes itself against its negation. Prior, abandoned and dying, says, "still." "Still" is an exceptional word. It asks for a pause, for a caesura, for a break, and a moment in which we suspend ourselves and acknowledge that life's imperfections, as they are, are rife with potential. The hope that appears onstage before me is not a foolish hope that distracts from the suffering of the Now; rather, it is a hope that guides me towards something better. A German-Jewish, Marxist philosopher in the mid-20th century, Bloch knew something of hope's failure. So after decades of hope's negation, in 1961 Bloch posed a necessary question: "Can Hope be disappointed?"

Hope, he said, "can and will be disappointed" (1998:340). Transformation and change are born directly out of the dialectical battle between hope and its disappointment:

> Above all, hope knows—by its own definitions, so to speak—not only that danger implies salvation, but that wherever salvation exists, danger increases. Hope knows, too, that defeat pervades the world as a function of nothingness; and that futility is latent in objective-real possibility, which carries both redemption and perdition, unreconciled, within itself.

(345)

It is not simply that hope draws us into the horizon of possibility, but that the disappointments of the present spur us toward this horizon at breakneck speed. In Heaven, we find this aphorism affirmed when Prior encounters another heartbroken figure, Harper, a Mormon housewife who has been abandoned by her husband Joe. (Indeed, Joe has left her for Louis, the man that left Prior.) Harper, played by Zoe Kazan, is young, not much older than 23 or 24. Mousey, long, thin, blonde hair, a slightly red nose as if she's been out in the cold. Her voice shakes as she nervously confirms the catalytically charged relationships between destruction, disappointment, hope, and progress: "I've finally found the secret of all that Mormon energy. Devastation. That's what makes people migrate, build things. Heartbroken people do it, people who have lost love" (Kushner 1995:253).

How do we reconcile the heartbreak of our present disappointment with Prior's insistence on hope and More Life? Mounted on the 20th anniversary of the play's debut, Signature's production can't escape the quality of being a retrospective, allowing us to place the progress of the past 20 years on trial. Directly engaged with the politics of the late 1980s and early '90s, the play is a document of political failure and disappointment, reminding us with all the more ferocity of the need to "migrate, build things." Hollywood actor Zachary Quinto plays Louis, reinventing the self-absorbed character with a surprisingly effective, hipsterlike, confident masculinity. In a passionate fight with Joe (Bill Heck), Louis decries Joe's role in crafting judicial decisions that legitimized the expulsion of gay and lesbian soldiers from the army. When *Angels* debuted, the legal regulation of queer sexuality was the law of the land, supported by the Supreme Court's infamous *Bowers v. Hardwick* ruling (*Bowers v. Hardwick* 1986). By 2010, sodomy laws had been stricken from the books in a stunning 2003 reversal, delivered the same year that Kushner's marriage to his husband was the first gay nuptial announced in the *New York Times* (*Lawrence v. Texas* 2003; Brady 2003). During the years in which the play takes place, the president was Ronald Reagan—that shining symbol of reactionary and devastatingly dangerous, backward-looking nostalgia—who could speak of homosexuals only as "still outside the law" (Reagan 2003:796). At the time of Signature's revival the nation is guided by the first black president, Barack Obama, who signed the repeal of "Don't Ask, Don't Tell" into law on 22 December 2010. But is this progress? Is this real change, or simply a reorganization of America to include *some* formerly excluded subjects as we mobilize against new enemies? With gays and lesbians serving openly in the military, their services can now be utilized in one of three (illegal) wars that rage with no end in sight.[5]

Angels contains, within its own structures of representation, documents of the disappointments of liberalism's promise. Though inspired by Marxist theorists of progress and change, class difference is barely acknowledged and the subordination of the working masses is all but invisible in *Angels in America.* Women are represented as wives and mothers, neurotics and caretakers. And as I watch the performance, I am painfully aware of the whiteness of the actors onstage and the audience around me as I feel my own racial difference from them. Indeed, race is a radically interiorized exterior in a play about the US in which the only character of color has the name of a foreign country: Belize. And this character is a black nurse who spends most of the play caring for white people in a fashion not unlike the archetype of the mammy.

Billy Porter breathes defiant and willful life into Belize, however, as in a scene with Louis where Porter's Belize surges up against the forces that would reduce him to an idealized racial foil. Critiquing Louis's idealization of America, he stands up from the café table around which they argue and sharply reminds his interlocutor (and the audience) that the failings of our ideals have material consequences on those who *live* with the results: "I *live* in America, Louis," he spits with a cool rage, "that's hard enough, I don't have to love it" (Kushner 1995:228). America may be a lofty idea and an ideal, but its weight is felt on the ground level for those who have to live under the burden of its failures.

Isn't it precisely the sting of disappointment that makes us dream of a better world? Does this wall of whiteness onstage stop me from wanting a world of difference and complexity, or does it challenge me to construct one that would liberate us from the class, gender, and race limitations contained within and reproduced by the play? For all the beauty contained in *Angels,* might we not learn even more from its failings? I see in *Angels'* shortcomings and omissions the powerfully inspiring fact that, as Bloch once said in conversation with Adorno, quoting Brecht, "Something's missing." This realization inspires me to ask and answer, as Bloch did before me, "What is this 'something?'" (Bloch and Adorno 1988:15). That question is the beginning of change, messy and imperfect, but no less necessary.

In the final scene, set in 1990, Prior and his friends gather at the Bethesda Fountain to debate the politics of the moment: AIDS, the potential for peace in occupied Palestine, the collapse of the Cold War. A projection of the fountain shimmers behind the actors and Prior stands at the front of the stage directly addressing us, reminding us again that we are facing the future: the Angel, now frozen statuary, once more looking towards us, wings blasted open by history rushing at her. Louis enthusiastically remarks on the hopeful signs of progress, "Look! Perestroika! The Thaw! ... The whole world is changing!" (Kushner 1995:277). Another character responds, "I wonder what'll happen now in places like Yugoslavia." We, in Signature's audience, don't need to wonder: we know. Hope, once more, has been disappointed, beat back by Bosnia and Srebrenica; Perestroika in Russia displaced by the reformation of authoritarian oligarchy under Putin; progress in the Middle East collapsed into the Second Intifada; Palestinian suffering exacerbated by the Israeli blockade; the peace of the Cold War overshadowed by the explosion of the War on Terror; the seemingly permanent invocation of the state of exception; and AIDS ... In 1990, AIDS was an epidemic disproportionately affecting queers. Today it is a pandemic with devastating effects on the global South.

Watching *Angels* at the end of the first decade of the new millennium reminds us that the many disappointments that we have seen, that we will continue to see, are not hope's end, but the future's beginning. A friend complained that this final scene of *Angels* is its most unsatisfying. Midway through the performance she attended the lights failed and the actors were interrupted, forced to restart the scene a few moments later. Strangely, she remarked, it was the glitch that made her long for more—she wanted to see what would happen and how the rupture could be overcome. So performance, like hope, is also predicated on its failure. It is imperfect, inadequate—but necessary. This is, in fact, the point. The play, like the march of history, must leave us unsatisfied and longing for more; it must remind us of the work that remains to be done. Standing at the front of the stage in a winter coat, surveying the audience and making eye contact with many of us, Prior commissions us to do just this: "Bye now. You are fabulous creatures, each and every one. And I bless you: *More Life.* The Great Work Begins" (280). The future is in *our* collective hands (as Prior says goodbye, my companion is still holding mine) and its content is not yet determined. The failed hope of the past two decades—indeed, of the past 50 millennia—must not be met with resignation, but instead with hopeful defiance. As Bloch maintained in his 1961 address:

The world-process has not yet achieved victory anywhere; but it just as surely has not yet been defeated anywhere. And humans on earth can alter course toward a destination that has not yet been decided—toward redemption or perdition. The world remains, in its entirety, very much a working laboratory *possibilis salutis.*

(1998:345)

Notes

1. *Angels,* a play in which New York is as much a character as any of Kushner's flesh-and-blood figures, first belonged to other places. Commissioned by Eureka Theatre Company, its first half (*Millennium Approaches*) debuted in San Francisco in 1991. The complete *Angels* (including its second half, *Perestroika*) was first produced in Los Angeles at the Mark Taper Forum in 1992, before it emigrated later that year to London's Royal National Theatre. *Angels* only manifested on the New York stage in 1993 under the direction George C. Wolfe, releasing the play into endless migration across the globe's dramatic landscape. For critical responses, see, for example, Geis and Kruger (1997).

2. Benjamin's Angel is, of course, drawn from the philosopher's description of Paul Klee's painting *Angelus Novus.*

3. Benjamin receives 40 references in Geis and Kruger's anthology on the play; Bloch isn't mentioned once.

4. Bloch has generally received less attention than his contemporaries and friends, including Benjamin and Theodor Adorno. Bloch was introduced to American Marxist literary theory primarily in the work of Fredric Jameson and has recently been engaged by queer theorist José Esteban Muñoz (see Jameson 1972; Muñoz 2009).

5. As Jasbir Puar has argued, the folding of queers into the national body politic has been concurrent with a surge in nationalism in order to enact and sustain states of exception at use in the global War on Terror (see Puar 2007).

References

Agamben, Giorgio. 2009. *The Signature of All Things: On Method.* Trans. Luca D'Isanto with Kevin Attell. New York: Zone Books.

Benjamin, Walter. [1968] 1988. "Theses on the Philosophy of History." In *Illuminations: Essays and Reflections,* ed. Hannah Arendt, trans. Harry Zohn, 253-65. New York: Harcourt.

Bloch, Ernst. 1988. *The Utopian Function of Art and Literature: Selected Essays.* Trans. J. Zipes and F. Mecklenburg. Cambridge, MA: MIT Press.

———. [1986] 1996a. *The Principle of Hope.* Trans. N. Plaice, S. Plaice, and P. Knight. 3 vols. Vol. 1. Cambridge, MA: MIT Press.

———. [1986] 1996b. *The Principle of Hope.* Trans. N. Plaice, S. Plaice, and P. Knight. 3 vols. Vol. 2. Cambridge, MA: MIT Press.

———. [1986] 1996c. *The Principle of Hope.* Trans. N. Plaice, S. Plaice, and P. Knight. 3 vols. Vol. 3. Cambridge, MA: MIT Press.

———. 1998. "Can Hope Be Disappointed?" In *Literary Essays,* trans. Andrew Joran et al., 339-45. Stanford, CA: Stanford University Press.

———. 2000. *The Spirit of Utopia.* Trans. Anthony Nassar. Stanford, CA: Stanford University Press.

Bloch, Ernst, and Theodor W. Adorno. 1988. "Something's Missing: A Discussion between Ernst Bloch and Theodor Adorno on the Contradictions of Utopian Longing." In *The Utopian Function of Art and Literature: Selected Essays,* trans. Zack Zipes and Frank Mecklenburg, 1-18. Cambridge, MA: MIT Press.

Bowers v. Hardwick. 478 US 186 (1986).

Brady, Lois Smith. 2003. "Weddings/Celebrations: Vows; Mark Harris and Tony Kushner." *New York Times,* 4 May.

Geis, Deborah R., and Steven F. Kruger, eds. 1997. *Approaching the Millennium: Essays on Angels in America.* Ann Arbor: University of Michigan Press.

Jameson, Fredric. 1972. *Marxism and Form: Twentieth-Century Dialectical Theories of Literature.* Princeton, NJ: Princeton University Press.

Kushner, Tony. 1995. *Angels in America: A Gay Fantasia on National Themes.* New York: Theatre Communications Group.

Lawrence v. Texas. 539 US 558 (2003).

Muñoz, José Esteban. 2009. *Cruising Utopia: The Then and There of Queer Futurity.* New York: New York University Press.

Puar, Jasbir K. 2007. *Terrorist Assemblages: Homonationalism in Queer Times.* Durham: Duke University Press.

Reagan, Ronald. 2003. *Reagan: A Life in Letters.* Eds. Kiron K. Skinner, Annelise Graebner Anderson, and Martin Anderson. New York: Free Press.

CRITICAL COMMENTARY

Daniel Kiefer (essay date 1994)

SOURCE: Kiefer, Daniel. "*Angels in America* and the Failure of Revelation." *American Drama* 4.1 (1994): 21-38. Print.

[*In the following essay, Kiefer provides an overview of the plot, characters, themes, and allusions in* Angels in America. *He also examines aspects of performance and drama in the play, particularly in its repeated references to camp and drag. The play falters, Kiefer argues, because it takes itself too seriously at the end rather than continuing as camp.*]

Last year's most celebrated play (actually two plays) is Tony Kushner's seven-hour extravaganza, *Angels in America: A Gay Fantasia on National Themes.* With high-spirited theatricality and real compassion for human suffering, the plays represent the complicated interactions of religion, sexuality, and politics in America. "The magic of the theatre or something" (*Perestroika* 69) is certainly on display here: dream visions come true, drug fantasies approach "the very threshold of revelation," and concurrent scenes are superimposed on each other. There are insistent ghosts, ancestors returning from the dead, and one spectacular angel. A stunning mixture of theatrical tonalities, the work intercuts bombast with camp, deceit with sudden honesty, sitcom skits with allegory, realism with magic—all in strange combinations. The mixture anticipates an ending where the tragic, the comic, and the bitterly ironic would converge. Instead, the resolution smooths away the antagonisms of these conflicting styles to present a unified optimism.

Part One, *Millennium Approaches,* brings an angel down from heaven, while **Part Two,** *Perestroika,* repudiates her message. When the great promise offered by the angel's descent cannot be realized, because her message turns out to be deathly, the work pleads for more life. Instead of mustering the courage to go down with its own dark forces, like traditional tragedy, *Angels* [*Angels in America*] lets our pity and fear dissipate under the sun of cheerful determination. It refuses to see the longing for stillness represented by the angel's command as the desire for annihilation, and therefore it substitutes the death of Roy Cohn, the demi-devil, for the inevitable ruin of the AIDS sufferer who receives the angel's message.

Kushner's writing is very funny and vividly satirical, zinging out epigrams and one-liners. The humor is both Jewish and gay, pursuing two strains of American humor that emerge from the experience of oppression and even self-oppression. The Jewish strain is rueful and self-lacerating. When Louis wants to unburden himself of the crimes he may commit, the rabbi says, "You want to confess, better you should find a priest." Louis says, "But I'm not a Cath-olic, I'm a Jew," and the rabbi retorts, "Worse luck for you, bubbulah. Catholics believe in forgiveness. Jews believe in Guilt" (*Millennium* [*Millennium Approaches*] 25). The gay strain of humor can be sardonic and bitter, scornful of any kind of pretense, and very dark, as when the AIDS sufferer looks at his Kaposi's Sarcoma lesions and says, "I'm a lesionnaire. The Foreign Lesion. The American Lesion. Lesionnaire's disease" (*Millennium* 21). But it is usually joyful and outrageous in its mockery—that is to say, campy. The whole audience is invited into the irony that gay men feel when we look at how we really are. The figures on stage stand for the audience because each one is, as the rabbi says at the start, "not a person but a whole kind of person" (*Millennium* 10). But each one is also highly individual, with details of speech and action so highly inflected as to make the allegorical representation very powerful.

The task of *Angels in America* may be, as Louis proclaims in **Part II,** "Exploration. Across an unmapped terrain. The body of the homosexual human male" (72). The plays see the homosexual body, in all its forms, as the body politic of America, ruined not by AIDS but by the collective repression of homosexuality. There is plenty of queer talk in the scripts, and one sodomitical act performed on stage, but the only completely unclothed body we see is the infected body of the AIDS sufferer, the body most difficult to behold and most resistant to platitudes.

The chief characters in the plays are gay men, and a list of them in order of appearance also happens to show an advancing order of self-acceptance. The range represents men from the most "closeted," macho, and politically powerful (at the top of the social heap) to the most despised, effeminate, and fully "out" (at the bottom); from the omnipotent Roy Cohn to the hired nurse Belize:

Roy Cohn—political wheeler-dealer, famous anti-Communist, Jewish

Joe Pitt—married, Republican, Mormon

Louis Ironson—the central character, intellectual, Jewish

Prior Walter—Louis' boyfriend, AIDS patient, visited by the angel

Belize—nurse, former drag-queen, African-American

In marking out this range, the plays make an incisive political analysis of the sexual resentment lodged in the heart of power-politics. A character's acceptance of queer sexual pleasure is inversely proportional to his love of the America that Ronald Reagan commands. Or rather, patriotism is constructed out of the denial of queerness.

Roy Cohn epitomizes such denial, and the Roy Cohn we see here is the real one made theatrical. He was a prosecutor in the 1951 case that sent Julius and Ethel Rosenberg to the electric chair for treason. His friendship with the judge in that trial secured the death sentence for Ethel and was the highest demonstration of his illicit influence. He was chief committee counsel for Senator Joseph McCarthy's anti-Communist hearings in the 1950s. Those hearings made McCarthy and Cohn invincible, until they ran into the lawyer defending the Army, Joe Welch. (As the name for both Roy Cohn's father-protector and his nemesis, "Joe" is the perfect name for his protege in these plays, although there is a recognition of Mormon founder Joseph Smith, as well.) It was Joe Welch who uttered the famous entreaty: "Senator, may we not drop this? ... You have done enough. Have you no sense of decency, sir, at long last? Have you no sense of decency?" (Hoffman 236). Kushner's use of this line is quite stunning. Shouted into Joe's face by Louis it becomes, in effect, an outcry against the attack on queers by the all-powerful triumvirate who would not admit their queerness: J. Edgar Hoover, Joseph McCarthy, and Roy Cohn. Here is Kushner's most trenchant criticism of American culture. In the character of Roy Cohn he brings to life the great American traitor in matters sexual, racial, and political. The Roy Cohn of history was the perfect example of the closeted homosexual who reviles homosexuals, the Jew who hates Jews, and the patriot who scorns the law of the land. He became a prominent figure in New York in the 1960s, and throughout his notorious public career he was a crony of people like Ronald and Nancy Reagan, Francis Cardinal Spellman, Donald Trump, and Barbara Walters. He died of AIDS in 1986, refusing to admit publicly that it was in fact AIDS, and his lies still fester in our political body.

There are actually three intertwined stories in *Angels in America,* each worth a long play in itself. One story is Roy Cohn's decline into illness and AIDS dementia, and his obdurate defiance of heaven and hell. Another story follows Joe Pitt, who tries to accept Roy's commission to infiltrate the U.S. Department of Justice, and who struggles to leave his wife and come out as gay. In this story we see the constraints of religious repression most clearly, and witness the suffering that a gay man causes his wife and his mother in the fight against his own desires.

It is very astute of Kushner to depict the Mormon religion as *the* American religion. As the Church of Latter-day Saints, it represents the spiritual lateness of America's civilization. In making their Great Migrations westward, the Mormons trace the expansion of the nation in pursuing its manifest destiny all the way to the Pacific shore. Their ceaseless evangelism marks a restlessness in their faith. Their eschatological beliefs make them eager for positions of secular power, for they need to be in place when the millennium comes. And in its denial of pleasure and its horror of homosexuality the church seeks to crush gays and lesbians.

The central story involves Prior Walter, the faithlessness of his lover, Louis, and the comradeship of his friend Belize. It is Prior to whom the angel comes, because he suffers most unjustly and because his wonderful sense of humor expresses deep longings for happiness. But it is Belize who has the greatest moral authority in the plays, because he is black, and because he has guided so many patients to their final rest. He speaks a more humane truth than anyone else on stage. Hegel understood that the slave knows the master far better than the master can know the slave, and in the theater masters come to hear what slaves have no other way of expressing. We attend to what Belize says about America, for he combines theory and practice with his snappy drag-queen delivery.

Louis stands for the playwright, in part, because he is Jewish, articulate, and deeply interested in how America works. He has a brash intelligence, and he says whatever comes to mind. As Joe says to him, "Whatever you feel like saying or doing, you don't care, you just ... do it" (*Millennium* 71, ellipsis Kushner's). Louis stands in the middle of the five main figures, connecting the closeted Joe to the openly gay Prior, and yet he cannot see as far as Belize can from the bottom of the heap. The women on this stage stand primarily in relation to the men—as wife married to a homosexual, as nurse, as heroic figure in history, as angel, as mother. But there are indications of their own inner life, full of pathos. Joe's wife. Harper, spins Valium-induced fantasies so necessary to her sanity that they come to life. She sees herself clearly, and she sees the ruin of the natural world and the ruin of her own marriage as one. Joe's mother, Hannah comes as a ministering angel to assist Prior, and she is wonderfully drawn—savvy, loving, and fearless.

But it is Roy Cohn who is truly reckless. He revels in the gore of political battle: "This is gastric juices churning, this is enzymes and acids, this is intestinal is what this is, bowel movement and blood-red meat—this stinks, this is *politics,* Joe, the game of being alive" (*Millennium* 68). As bloody as his talk is, it is luscious too, and we are compelled against our will to admire his love of the game. He is heroically ruthless, aspiring to the amoral ecstatic realm beyond the divine or the demonic. Roy speaks the truth most brutally, in vulgar and extravagant words. He believes what he says in **Part II,** that "lawyers are ... the High Priests of America. We alone know the words that made America. Out of thin air. We alone know how to use The Words" (89; ellipsis Kushner's). His misanthropy displays a foul mouth, hurling angry curses with a fury that comes of self-scorn, and it is marvelous to hear. Louis says, "He's like the polestar of human evil" (*Perestroika* 95). This villain, this fallen angel, this Iago, is one superb character.

At one point Cohn launches into a tirade of contempt for queers—really a tirade of self-loathing—as he describes the difference between himself and the homosexual. He is taunting his doctor into applying to him the labels "homosexual" or "gay," words which the straight characters in these plays cannot bring themselves to utter. And then he says:

> Like all labels they tell you one thing and one thing only: where does an individual so identified fit in the food chain, in the pecking order? Not ideology, or sexual taste, but something much simpler: clout. Not who I fuck or who fucks me, but who will pick up the phone when I call, who owes me favors. This is what a label refers to. Now to someone who does not understand this, homosexual is what I am because I have sex with men. But really this is wrong. Homosexuals are not men who sleep with other men. Homosexuals are men who in fifteen years of trying cannot get a pissant anti-discrimination bill through City Council. Homosexuals are men who know nobody and who nobody knows. Who have zero clout. Does this sound like me, Henry?
>
> (*Millennium* 45)

The doctor must reply, "No," and Roy is exultant: "No. I have clout." The exuberance of his language in boasting of his power is itself a theatrical triumph. He exults in the ruthless potency of his speech. By refusing the term "homosexual" he lays claim to the phallus, that token of sexual and political power wielded by straight men; and his decline represents the decline of American phallic tyranny.

The Angel, the Continental Principality of America, comes as a messenger from heaven, a kind of fierce Archangel Gabriel announcing the dreadful news to the Virgin Mary, namely Prior. This Angel tells a more poignant version of the Fall of the Angels and the Fall of Adam and Eve. She breaks with Genesis and Milton's *Paradise Lost* when she describes God the Father as a *deus absconditus,* who has abandoned both heaven and earth, both angels and human beings, and cannot be found. The Angel comes to enlist Prior in the search for the Master and commands him to sit quietly, without seeking to fathom the world. She wants us human beings to stop our roving and sit still: "*YOU HAVE DRIVEN HIM AWAY! YOU MUST STOP MOVING!*" (*Perestroika* 52). It is an old religious practice that she urges on us, as old as eremitic contemplation. In Isaiah 30:15 the prophetic message is similar: "In returning and rest shall ye be saved; in quietness and in confidence shall be your strength: and ye would not"; but the scriptural message depends on divine involvement in human affairs and human sin. She comes in such dramatic glory that we expect a real revelation, but Prior resists it from the start, making campy jokes about the special effects she has at her command: "*Very* Steven Spielberg" (*Millennium* 118). Her message, "On you in you in your blood we write have written: STASIS!" (*Perestroika* 54), is later repudiated by Prior: "I want more life. I can't help myself. I do" (*Perestroika* 135). The repudiation makes human sense, for we follow with great sympathy the yearnings of Prior, and Harper too, for some kind of happiness. Their unhappiness impels their restlessness. The repudiation makes dramatic and moral sense, too, if divine providence has really abandoned us.

As the playwright has pointed out, the Angel bears some resemblance to the Angel of History described by Walter Benjamin in a passage on history as a catastrophe beyond our human imagining:

> A Klee painting named "Angelus Novus" shows an angel looking as though he is about to move away from something he is fixedly contemplating. His eyes are staring, his mouth is open, his wings are spread. This is how one pictures the angel of history. His face is turned toward the past. Where we perceive a chain of events, he sees one single catastrophe which keeps piling wreckage upon wreckage and hurls it in front of his feet. The angel would like to stay, awaken the dead, and make whole what has been smashed. But a storm is blowing from Paradise; it has got caught in his wings with such violence that the angel can no longer close them. This storm irresistibly propels him into the future to which his back is turned, while the pile of debris before him grows skyward. This storm is what we call progress.
>
> (Benjamin 257-58)

Benjamin's angel, or his version of Klee's angel, has no chance of resisting the forces of change and divine chaos. He would like to bring comfort, but he cannot; he is fixed, although he stands amid constant fluctuation. This figure stands for the inevitability of suffering that the plays confront. Kushner has said that *Perestroika* is the mountain of detritus piling up at the angel's feet in Benjamin's image, the collapse of the expectation of divine intervention (Letter 2). Act 5 and the Epilogue of *Perestroika* deny this vision of wreckage in order to find a happy ending, and the result is a diminishment of dramatic force.

Angels in America wants to relieve the overwhelming sorrow that gay men have endured from watching our lovers and friends die, while powerful closeted homosexuals have repudiated us and glorified our enemies. The first play longs for divine intervention, and yet the second one understands that no such intervention is possible. As Louis tells Belize: "There are no gods here, no ghosts and spirits in America, there are no angels in America, no spiritual past, no racial past, there's only the political" (*Millennium* 92). The absence of angels is more than our inability to see the angelic beings like Prior who walk among us; it is a fact which the plays confront.

To perceive the transcendent in the material is not enough of a lesson to learn, for the plays bring a tremendous angel down to earth with a fervor that is more than theatrical. Like the moment in Act 5 of Shakespeare's *The Winter's Tale* when Hermione's statue comes to life, the moment of the angel's descent at the end of *Millennium Approaches* affects us beyond the trickery of staging. It would continue to astonish us, had Kushner let it. In preparing the final script of *Perestroika* he has moved the angel's revelation from Act 1 to Act 2 and made the re-enactment, in Prior's narrative, a past event. The angel's status has been made suspect, more recollected than experienced, more hallucinated than real. She is more like the ghost Horatio describes than the one Hamlet addresses. Already the angel has begun to falter; and in purely theatrical terms, once the angel's message is refuted we need some dramatic recompense for that failed revelation.

With plentiful allusion to the Hebrew scriptures, turned ironically, so that the human ridicules the divine, *Angels* nevertheless misses its chances to stage a fragmented, postmodern kind of prophecy. Jacob wrestling with the angel is Joe's picture for his own wrestling with homosexual desire, and for good reason, since the Genesis passage is full of erotic possibilities:

> And Jacob was left alone; and there wrestled a man with him until the breaking of the day. And when he saw that he prevailed not against him, he touched the hollow of his thigh; and the hollow of Jacob's thigh was out of joint, as he wrestled with him. And he said, Let me go, for the day breaketh. And he said, I will not let thee go, except thou bless me.
>
> (Genesis 32:24-26, AV)

In that damaging touch to the hollow of the thigh, the interior of the phallus, as it were, the scene feels erotic in its violence. Prior's wrestling with the actual angel refers directly to this passage as well, with effective jokes about the angel's vulnerability. While the Genesis passage is mysterious and compelling, *Angels* disperses the solemnity and displaces the eroticism between men, as the female angel turns her kisses upon Hannah instead.

Another version of the Genesis story occurs when Louis accuses Joe of political betrayal and Joe beats him up. It's "like a sex scene in an Ayn Rand novel," as Louis says (*Perestroika* 112). The violence of queer love, in disrupting what is expected, is here represented as introjected violence, like the ongoing fights between Joe and Harper, Louis and Prior, Roy and Joe, Louis and Belize, and even Hannah and Harper. Joe plunges into the violence that Roy has been urging on him: "Transgress a little, Joseph. There are so many laws; find one you can break" (*Millennium* 110). But now *Perestroika* repudiates him, as if his violence were the end rather than the start of his humanity. Although he has overcome his tempting angel by bloodying his lover, he is denied the playwright's blessing, and his story gives way to Roy's.

The blessing that Jacob exacts of the angel hearkens back to the blessing he wins from his father by subterfuge: "And Jacob went near unto Isaac his father; and he felt him, and said, The voice is Jacob's voice, but the hands are the hands of Esau" (Genesis 27:22). Roy Cohn speaks of Jacob with topmost admiration. "A ruthless motherfucker," he calls him, "some bald runt, but he laid hold of his birthright with his claws and his teeth" (*Perestroika* 83). Roy acts out the sentimental scene of getting Joe as Jacob to ask for his fatherly blessing. Sentimentality is at the heart of Roy's violence, and he is overjoyed to make heartfelt speeches

about his own filial devotion to Joe McCarthy and the necessity that Joe Pitt pledge himself to a surrogate father. Whether in tenderness or spite, Roy's performance always views itself as performance, and we cannot resist that theatrical self-awareness.

When Roy in his madness sings "The Battle Hymn of the Republic" while sitting in his hospital bed, we pity him against our will. When Belize compels Louis to recite Kaddish over Roy's body, with the vengeful ghost of Ethel Rosenberg prompting every line, we wonder if the playwright hasn't gone too far. Why must Roy Cohn be forgiven? Why is the villain of the piece mourned so extravagantly? The reason Belize gives is dramatic but not satisfactory:

> He was a terrible person. He died a hard death. So maybe. ... A queen can forgive her vanquished foe. It isn't easy, it doesn't count if it's easy, it's the hardest thing. Forgiveness. Which is maybe where love and justice finally meet. Peace, at least. Isn't that what the Kaddish asks for?
>
> (*Perestroika* 124, ellipsis Kushner's)

But Roy is not vanquished, merely dead, and his spirit lives on in the virulent hatred of a Pat Buchanan. Jewish custom would expect Kaddish to be recited over his body, as the decent thing to do for anyone who has died, even someone as despicable as Cohn. But it skews the moral structure of the plays to have so much grief poured out upon his passing. Roy Cohn is no human being but a demon, a satanic force. He represents the tyranny of the American state in its sexual hypocrisy, especially its repression of homosexuality. Even the brutal eloquence of his speech makes him supernaturally evil. Kushner maintains that the real issue of *Perestroika* is personal and political forgiveness, that Roy as PWA is the hard thing about the play, not the clever demon of *Millennium,* but the very sick man with an evil past (Letter 1). *Perestroika* goes too far in its tenderness for Roy's illness and death, making him a representative of all those who have died of AIDS. It wants above all to grieve for him, as if our humanity depended on our mourning for the most vicious, hateful, reactionary American ever to deny his queerness.

And yet, Scene 3 of Act 5 deserves to be the arrival point of both plays because it marks Louis's induction into human sympathy. Love and justice cannot meet in Roy Cohn, but they can start to mix better in Louis. More than any physical injury he has endured, by doing what Belize wants Louis follows Belize into human kindness: "Expiation for your sins" (*Perestroika* 124). Louis's consciousness of his own transformation is not shown, but the mere performance of grief softens his heart.

The plays emphasize the power of various kinds of performance. We see many different self-conscious actors do their bit for an admiring, reluctant, bewildered, or heckling audience on stage. It is a brilliant turn to have Roy in his illness fall into the capable hands of Belize. We get to see two master performers, two fierce queens, at work with each other. There is also a great scene in the Diorama Room of the Mormon Visitors' Center, with the diorama enacting the Great Migrations and Harper singing out from the audience. She derides the Mormon faith in divine providence: "They drag you on your knees through hell and when you get there the water of course is undrinkable. Salt. It's a Promised Land, but what a disappointing promise" (***Perestroika*** 66). She expresses the truth of her own bitterness by assailing the lies she sees on that stage, and she speaks for us in our disappointment with the angel's revelation.

Throughout the plays we see ourselves as audience members witnessing the performance of political, historical, or sexual roles. Beyond the mocking references to the magic of the theater we hear lines mimicking the great movie divas beloved by gay men, and we watch all too many renditions of scenes from *The Wizard of Oz*. We are given to believe that the energy of queer life in America, if it can rescue America from heartlessness, will do so by demonstrating that all action, even moral action, is performed by actors, who must never take themselves too seriously. Of course, we know that all the world's a stage. Nor is it much revelation to discover that Prior can write his own part as prophet. These plays do not know where to find full revelation, and their belief in human forgiveness is not sufficient recompense.

Once the drama of supernatural descent has been rejected, we need another kind of drama, perhaps the Brechtian drama of alienation and accusation, demanding that the audience take up the role of divine messenger, now in materialist terms. Bertolt Brecht in *The Good Woman of Setzuan* makes the gods laughable from the start. In the end, the woman they have blessed with money (of all things!) and ordered to be good, tells them that their injunction was a thunderbolt, tearing her in two. The mockery directed at the angel in Kushner's second play is almost as trenchant as Brecht's irony, proceeding as it does from the madness that pain produces. In Harper's valium dreams and Prior's AIDS-dementia visions we see a kind of human revelation. The two characters literally cross over into each other's madness and become allies. The theatrical brilliance of this intersection cannot reach full spiritual enlightenment because it is an intersection of lunacies. As Harper says to Prior in the Diorama scene: "Crazy time. The barn door's open now, and all the cows have fled" (***Perestroika*** 71). They reach what they call the "threshold of revelation" and cannot step over.

The montage effect when scenes intercut each other, echoing and re-echoing each other visually, is another possible replacement for the drama of divine revelation. This technique superimposes one character or pair of characters upon another, doubling or squaring the emotional impact of uncoupling and recoupling, loss and ministration. It enhances the energy of one scene with the charge of another, as electromagnetic coils raise the voltage of electricity. The best example is the scene in Act 2 of ***Millennium*** where Louis is leaving Prior and Harper is sending Joe away without her. Here the permutations of betrayal and abandonment are worked to show Louis and Joe as united in their violation of those who love them. In ***Perestroika*** Harper's delirious invasion of the sex-scenes between Joe and Louis becomes meta-theatrical. She is like an ineffectual ghost flying in from some higher realm, or a director trying to rework the staging. She warns her husband: "You can't save him. You never saved anyone. . . . You're turning into me" (***Perestroika*** 40, ellipsis mine), indicating how the characters in ***Angels*** become versions of each other and warning us against trying to alter their fates, for she cannot hold him back.

But the greatest possibility for a new dramatic substitute for divine revelation is camp. Camp mocks the phallus, even the phallic priority of the divine. Prior's mockery of the angel's descent becomes a mockery of his own assumption into the phallic power that the angel offers him. When he gets an erection as the angel approaches, he even makes fun of that. Moe Meyer has described "camp" as embracing the strategies and tactics of queer parody. He says that "Camp appears, on the one hand, to offer a transgressive vehicle yet, on the other, simultaneously invokes the specter of dominant ideology within its practice, appearing, in many instances to actually reinforce the dominant order" (Meyer 11).

The phallus is another name for that specter of dominant ideology, and Prior's camping certainly invokes the specter without reinforcing it. In Act 2 of ***Millennium*** Belize visits the sick Prior and brings rollicking possibilities as these two sisters camp it up together. Belize administers what he calls magic goop:

PRIOR:

    (*Opening a bottle, sniffing*): Pooh! What kinda crap is that?

BELIZE:

    Beats me. Let's rub it on your poor blistered body and see what it does.

PRIOR:

    This is not Western medicine. These bottles . . .

BELIZE:

    Voodoo cream. From the botanica 'round the block.

PRIOR:

    And you a registered nurse.

                        (59, ellipsis Kushner's)

Here death is the phallic power that is effectively mocked. The friendship between Belize and Prior has a light-hearted intimacy that holds stronger than any supernatural intervention. When *Perestroika* transfers Belize from Prior's bedside to Roy Cohn's instead, it opens up the darker possibilities of camp. The battle royal joined in earnest by Belize and Roy sets queer parody against closeted power, with death still the target. If Roy is tough, declaiming, "Pain's ... nothing, pain's life," Belize is funnier: "Sing it, baby" (*Perestroika* 27, ellipsis Kushner's).

What is forgotten in Prior's scene in heaven is just this kind of campy ridicule. He cannot see that he is delivering a Broadway set-piece that youngsters will memorize for auditions:

> I don't know if it's not braver to die. But I recognize the habit. The addiction to being alive. We live past hope. If I can find hope anywhere, that's it, that's the best I can do. It's so much not enough, so inadequate but. ... Bless me anyway. I want more life.

> (*Perestroika* 136, ellipsis Kushner's)

The language is as thin as the sentiment is thick. And the epilogue preserves the same tone of solemn yearning:

> This disease will be the end of many of us, but not nearly all, and the dead will be commemorated and will struggle on with the living, and we are not going away. We won't die secret deaths anymore. The world only spins forward. We will be citizens. The time has come.

> (148)

The risk of speaking now without irony is that all the hilarious mockery echoing through the plays will undermine the speaker without his knowledge. No sentimental plea for more life, no proclamation of emancipation can have the theatrical force of the ridiculous. Even the drama of alienation and accusation that Prior represents has been all camped up. The play cannot pull itself up into pathos now, when what it needs is even more sardonic tragedy and mock-tragedy. As Harold Beaver says about camp, "But at its best, the laugh is on homosexuals themselves. For the real trick is not merely to don a mask; it is to mask the masquerade." He quotes Christopher Isherwood from *The World in the Evening*: "You can't camp about something you don't take seriously. ... You're expressing what's basically serious to you in terms of fun and artifice and elegance" (106). The mock-serious reaches deeper into the destitution of AIDS suffering than the real, because it speaks to a queer audience immersed in camp.

Angels in America should conclude with its irreverent mixture of violence, delirium, and queer mockery. Instead, we get a fade-out ending, neither comic nor tragic, as rough irony is planed down into smooth good wishes. The question of how we might receive divine help has been presented theatrically, and we deserve a theatrical answer, not a declamatory one. It is not enough to decry the super-

natural power represented before our eyes. The great works of Euripides, Shakespeare, Brecht, and Beckett do more than that. They provide understanding—in dramatic action—of how human beings recover from the loss of divine guidance, or how they do not.

Works Cited

Beaver, Harold. "Homosexual Signs (In Memory of Roland Barthes)." *Critical Inquiry* 8 (1981): 99-119.

Benjamin, Walter. "Theses on the Philosophy of History." *Illuminations.* Ed. and intro. Hannah Arendt. Trans. Harry Zohn. New York: Schocken, 1969. 253-64.

Hoffman, Nicholas von. *Citizen Cohn: The Life and Times of Roy Cohn.* New York: Bantam, 1988.

Kushner, Tony. *Angels in America: A Gay Fantasia on National Themes. Part One: Millennium Approaches.* New York: Theatre Communications Group, 1993.

———. *Angels in America: A Gay Fantasia on National Themes. Part Two: Perestroika.* New York: Theatre Communications Group, 1994.

———. Letter to the author. 1 July 1993.

Meyer, Moe. "Reclaiming the Discourse of Camp." Introduction. *The Politics and Poetics of Camp.* Ed. Moe Meyer. London: Routledge, 1994. 1-22.

Alex J. Tuss (essay date 1996)

SOURCE: Tuss, Alex J. "Resurrecting Masculine Spirituality in Tony Kushner's *Angels in America*." *Journal of Men's Studies* 5.1 (1996): 49-63. Print.

[*In the following essay, Tuss traces spiritual transformation in* Angels in America *from a "gospel of clout," where dominant masculine achievement is the most prized commodity, to a gay valorization of interpersonal bonds. "In contrast to the spiritual sterility of Cohn's gospel of clout,"* Tuss writes, "Angels in America *offers an alternative that involves both personal revival and a societal reinvigoration.*"]

The American credo of rugged individualism and the self-made man combines significant elements of American culture. Icons from the American West, Wyatt Earp and Wild Bill Cody among them, and political icons such as Theodore Roosevelt and Ronald Reagan have all drawn on these facets of America's cultural history. They embody a masculine image that continues to exercise great influence on American males. That influence persists, at least in part, because these elements of American culture surface throughout society, including religious faith and practice. Even given Robert Alter's (1992) sense that "a great deal has changed in this country since that distant era when the Pilgrim founders habitually thought of America as the

New Israel" (p. 191), Norman Vincent Peale's power of positive thinking and Robert Schuller's telegenic testament on the individual bear witness to the impact of such notions on American religious and civic sensibilities.

Indeed, American culture has often relied on a public religious faith that externalizes the New Israel in terms of icons, with the proliferation of televangelists being merely the latest incarnation of the phenomenon. At the same time, however, as William G. McLoughlin (1978) rightly contends, American culture also contains a history of "great awakenings" and religious revivalism that "have been the shaping power of American culture from its inception" (p. 1). These awakenings, "periods of cultural revitalization" marked by "a general crisis of beliefs and values," produce "a profound reorientation" of America's cultural values (McLoughlin, 1978, p. xiii).

Cultural rebirth and personal resurrection in that culture constitute the cornerstones of Tony Kushner's (1993, 1994) drama *Angels in America.* Set in the middle of the Ronald Reagan presidency, the play appropriates these concepts in a manner that parallels McLoughlin's argument that "revivals alter the lives of individuals; awakenings alter the world view of a whole people or culture" (p. xiii). Kushner portrays the crisis of beliefs and values in the America of the 1980s through the lives of Roy Cohn, the personification of the iconic power system the play criticizes as a spiritual wasteland, and those of a number of gay men whose personal revivals intertwine with the larger awakening that the drama builds toward. Kushner constructs what the play's subtitle calls "a gay fantasia on national themes" so as to contrast the arid gospel of clout personified by the solitary figure of Roy Cohn with the community of characters, primarily gay men, who represent for Kushner the sort of awakening McLouglin sees as revitalizing, therapeutic, and cathartic (p. 2).

In doing so, Kushner reflects a pluralistic religious faith that arises in America from what Alter identifies as "the persisting cultural presence of the Bible" (p. 191). That pluralism draws on the evident diversity of American culture and the variety of people in American society who make significant contributions to it. *Angels in America,* with its mixture of Judaism and Mormonism, focuses on the contributions of its gay male characters to a spiritual regeneration that drives the "great awakening" in the play. What proves intriguing is the manner in which Kushner transcends the socially corrosive attitudes of Roy Cohn through the revivals that occur in the hearts of seemingly marginal and politically ineffectual homosexual men. It is these men who reshape the perceived notions of masculine spirituality and serve as the forerunners of the play's "great awakening."

THE TRADITIONAL MALE SPIRIT

When Kushner's acerbic Roy Cohn wishes "I was an octopus, a fucking octopus. Eight loving arms and all those

suckers. Know what I mean?" (*Millenium* [*Millennium Approaches*], p. 11), he aspires to a level of individual power and accomplishment that personifies the Reagan era's equivalent of the American Robber Barons of the Gilded Age. And when Cohn describes for Joe Pitt, his earnest acolyte, a vision of the universe as "a kind of sandstorm in outer space with winds of mega-hurricane velocity, but instead of grains of sand it's shards and splinters of glass" (*Millenium,* p. 13), he delineates the landscape of the rugged individual, the arena of Charles E. Rosenberg's (1980) Masculine Achiever (p. 230). It is this arena that Cohn seeks to dominate, although doubly excluded from it by virtue of being Jewish and a closeted homosexual. "Only in America" (*Millenium,* p. 14), Cohn declares, echoing the bromide that underscores the American spirit of Cohn's Horatio Alger story.

But Cohn also realizes that the "genteel gentleman Brahmin lawyers" see him as "some sort of filthy little Jewish troll" (*Millenium,* p. 67). Given such opposition, Cohn understands that success in the arena of the Masculine Achiever may also depend upon the emergence of what Rosenberg identifies as "aggressive masculinity" (p. 23). Cohn espouses such an approach when he advises Joe Pitt to "learn at least this: What you are capable of. Let nothing stand in your way" (*Millenium,* p. 58). The brutal aspect of such Social Darwinism does not escape Cohn. As he observes to his doctor after being diagnosed with AIDS, "labels" such as homosexual "tell you one thing and one thing only: where does an individual so identified fit in the food chain, in the pecking order? Not ideology, or sexual taste, but something much simpler: clout" (*Millenium,* p. 45). The spirituality of clout, the capacity to command, and the triumph of the individual will—these are the chief tenets of the American Gospel according to Cohn, tenets that underscore the crisis of belief and values in America that Kushner seeks to highlight.

THE POWER OF THE ALMIGHTY

And what of the role of God in such a gospel? Cohn makes clear his attitude in response to Joe Pitt's earnest request that he not take the Lord's name in vain: "No, principles count, I respect principles, I'm not religious but I like God and God likes me" (*Millenium,* p. 15). What Cohn particularly likes about God is the exercise of power, a divine attribute Jack Miles (1995) perceives in God's somewhat multifaceted, ever-changing persona. In Genesis, Miles sees God as a "masterful, inscrutable being" who manifests both a "radically unpredictable creator and destroyer" aspect and that of the human family's "loyal advocate" (p. 66). Cohn's explosive dialogue demonstrates both aspects of the God of Genesis. He angrily dismisses Harry, an underling, by phone, telling him, "You hold. I pay you to hold fuck you Harry you jerk. (*Button*) Half-wit dick-brain" (*Millenium,* p. 13). Later, intent on enlisting Joe Pitt in the effort to save his career as a lawyer, Cohn enthuses about his closeness to Pitt: "I want to be family. Familia, as my Italian friends call it. La Familia. A lovely word. It's important for me to help you, like I was helped" (***Millenium,*** p. 58).

Further paralleling the God of Genesis, Cohn describes himself and all lawyers as "the High Priests of America. We alone know the words that made America. Out of thin air. We alone know how to use the Words" (***Perestroika,*** p. 89). This secular priesthood of the Law, this gospel of power and privilege, resides in the men with clout, those public ministers in the Temple of the State, the courthouse. They alone possess the power of the words that galvanize the great judicial institution. They alone can pass on that power, in a manner Cohn compares to the father-son relationship. "I've had many fathers," Cohn observes. "I owe my life to them, powerful, powerful men" such as Walter Winchell, J. Edgar Hoover, and Joe McCarthy, fathers who push their sons "farther than they otherwise would go" (***Millenium,*** p. 56).

FATHERS AND SONS

Such fathers carry out what John W. Miller (1989) identifies from the talmudic tractate Kiddishun as the essential role of the father "as teacher of Torah and a trade," matters "essential to the son's future well-being" (p. 89). Cohn instructs Pitt in just such matters so that he understands that "the most precious asset in life ... is the ability to be a good son" (***Millenium,*** p. 56). Such a son, Cohn insists, "offers the father his life as a vessel for carrying forth his father's dream" (***Millenium,*** p. 56), and when Pitt remarks that "I had a hard time with my father," Cohn concedes that "sometimes that's the way. Then you have to find other fathers, substitutes" (***Millenium,*** p. 56). For in finding and in imitating such men, Pitt will be educated as Cohn was.

This education in the power and priesthood of The Law patterns itself on what Miller detects as the educational mode of fathers and sons in the Hebrew culture of the Bible (p. 82). The father inculcates in the son a full appreciation for the deeds and the power of God so that the son might "in turn pass this knowledge on to the next generation (hence also education, pedagogy)" (p. 83). Cohn offers that same education in power to Pitt if he agrees, as a good son ought, to aid Cohn's fight to avert being disbarred. "Without the light of the [legal] sun, Joe," Cohn purrs, "these cases ... will wither and die. A well-placed friend ... can turn off the sun. Cast a deep shadow on my behalf. Make them shiver in the cold. If they overstep. They would fear that" (***Millenium,*** p. 67).

Even in death and after being disbarred, Cohn strives to remain among the priests of The Law, offering to represent God in a potential lawsuit stemming from God's abandonment of the world in ***Perestroika,*** the second part of the play. "Yes I will represent you, King of the Universe," Cohn tells God. "I will bully and seduce, I will win for you and make the plaintiffs, those traitors, wish they had never heard the name of ... (*Huge thunderclap*)" (***Pere-***

stroika, p. 139). But Cohn also envisions the continued exercise of his power in the afterlife from an unchanged and cynical point of view:

> Is it a done deal, are we on? Good, then I gotta start by telling you you ain't got a case here, you're guilty as hell, no question, you have nothing to plead but not to worry, darling, I will make something up.

(***Perestroika,*** p. 139)

THE PRODIGAL SON

Joe Pitt, the closeted and repressed Mormon that Cohn wishes to promote as his spiritual son and protector from the disbarment proceedings, shares Cohn's faith in the power of The Law. Pitt tells his wife Harper that Cohn's offer of a job in the Justice Department in Washington will enable him to be a part of a change in the world. He too invokes the solemn, hieratic position of a lawyer. The lawyer-priest can be an agent of "change for the good. America has rediscovered itself. Its sacred position among the nations. And people aren't ashamed of that like they used to be. The truth restored. Law restored" (***Millenium,*** p. 26). But like his patron and father-figure Cohn, who steals money from a client, Pitt equivocates on his oath as an attorney, just as he does with his wife and his Mormon faith when he wanders the Ramble in Central Park, seeking homosexual sex. Pitt secretly writes and then signs the opinions of a judge that Cohn aptly terms "a good man. Not the brightest man on earth, but he has manners. And a nice head of silver hair" (***Millenium,*** p. 13). Pitt writes decisions that condemn him as well as those the decisions unfairly punish. Such legal bashing goes undetected until Louis Ironson confronts Pitt and is literally bashed by him. In the Gospel according to Cohn, a gospel that ultimately undoes Joe Pitt, the only sin is being caught, being exposed, and so being banished from the Temple of the Law, a further indication of the "crisis of legitimacy" (McLoughlin, 1978, p. 179) that precedes a revitalization of American culture.

THE PERIL OF EXPOSURE

Exposure and its attendant embarrassment before the other High Priests constitute the gravest consequences for both Cohn and his gullible protégé. When Cohn insists to Pitt that "I'm gonna be a goddamn motherfucking legally licensed member of the bar lawyer ... until the day I die" (***Millenium,*** p. 69), he expresses a ferocious resolve to avert the public humiliation that David Leverenz (1989) believes "lies in a man's fear that other men will see him as weak and therefore vulnerable to attack" (p. 73). For both Cohn and Pitt, exposure as homosexuals as well as apostates of The Law, poses an equally threatening possibility. Such a possibility requires every effort to maintain secrecy, to remain closeted, a situation Eve Kosofsky Sedgwick (1990) sees as consistent with a "whole cluster of the most crucial sites for the contestation of meaning in the twentieth-century Western culture" (p. 72). Secrecy/disclosure and private/public emerge as two of Sedgwick's "epistemologically charged pairings" (p. 72).

Kushner's play dramatizes this point in Pitt's strenuous but finally futile effort to suppress his homosexuality, in the tense banter about anyone saying the word "homosexual," and most pointedly in Cohn's exchange with his doctor about publicly disclosing the fact the Cohn is a homosexual with AIDS:

HENRY:

This is absurd.

ROY:

Say it.

HENRY:

Say what?

ROY:

Say, "Roy Cohn, you are a . . ."

HENRY:

Roy.

ROY:

"You are a . . ." Go on. Not "Roy Cohn you are a drug fiend." "Roy Marcus Cohn, you are a . . ." Go on, Henry, it starts with an "H."

HENRY:

Oh I'm not going to . . .

ROY:

With an "H," Henry and it isn't Hemophiliac." Come on . . .

HENRY:

What are you doing Roy?

ROY:

No say it. I mean it. Say: Roy Cohn, you are a homosexual. (*Pause*)
And I will proceed, systematically, to destroy your reputation and your practice and your career in New York State, Henry. Which you know I can do.

(*Millenium,* p. 44)

Cohn's unflinching willingness to ruin his doctor in order to preserve his clout manifests the sort of "autonomy and aggression" Anthony Rotundo (1987) depicts as essential in the "intense competition for success in the marketplace" (p. 37). Cohn's command of The Law as a weapon exemplifies the corporate ethos of a man whose spiritual development has been channeled towards a career that submerges all human feeling in the effort to carve out a position in the "hierarchies of competition" (Pleck & Pleck, 1980, p. 39). Since disclosure of his homosexuality imperils that posi-

tion, Cohn stands prepared to do all he can to prevent it. His cold-blooded threat underscores Cohn's loathing of homosexuals as "men who know nobody and who nobody knows. Who have zero clout" (*Millenium,* p. 45). As an imitator of the mysterious and inscrutable God that Miles sees as capable of both creation and utter annihilation (p. 46), Cohn, faithful to the spirituality of clout, admits no one who wavers, as Pitt does, in the exercise of power. The Temple in which Cohn serves as High Priest does not include such potential defectives.

A SPIRITUAL DILEMMA

Joe Pitt realizes this requirement for initiation. He mistakenly perceives priesthood in The Law as something he needs, as "something big to lift me up" (*Millenium,* p. 26). Pitt applies all the energy he possesses to insure that "my behavior is what I know it has to be. Decent. Correct. That alone in the eyes of God" (*Millenium,* p. 40). And so Joe Pitt writes opinions antithetical to his orientation because he believes that he will thus be correct and decent in the eyes of God, fit for service in the secular Temple. Pitt's dilemma echoes Sedgwick's reflection on conversations she held after the Supreme Court ruled in Bowers v. Hardwick that homosexual activity conducted in private was not protected under the law. Sedgwick speculates about "what it could have felt like to be a closeted gay court assistant, or clerk, or justice" who played some part in the framing of the decision (p. 75).

Kushner's drama parallels Sedgwick's scenario, even mirroring her analysis of Racine's play *Esther,* in which Esther saves the Jews by revealing her Jewish descent to her husband Assuerus, just as Pitt reveals himself to Cohn in hopes of being saved as Esther was. But as Sedgwick notes, Assuerus (Cohn) may also be in disguise, and so Pitt discovers "that a homophobic figure in power has, if anything, a disproportionate likelihood of being gay and closeted" (p. 81). Consequently, Cohn rejects the label "homosexual," reviling such men as powerless. And when Pitt, needing Cohn's blessing, reveals his affair with a man, he receives instead Cohn's brusque command: "I want you home. With your wife. Whatever else you got going, cut it dead" (*Perestroika,* p. 87).

Pitt seeks Cohn's compassion for his situation. Instead, he experiences Cohn's wrath over the fact that Pitt, or anyone else, does not totally submit to Cohn's all-consuming desire to maintain power and position in the world. Even at the moment of death, Cohn displays his rapacious tendencies, his utter fidelity to the gospel of clout. Informed by the ghost of Ethel Rosenberg that he has been disbarred, Cohn dies gasping, "Next time around: I don't want to be a man. I want to be an octopus. Remember that, OK? A fucking . . . (*Punching an imaginary button with his finger*) Hold. (*He dies*)" (*Perestroika,* p. 115).

Consistent with his belief, Cohn dies grasping for the control he perpetually sought to exercise in an effort to embody his gospel of clout, resisting to the very end any attempt to label him as a pariah, an outcast from the temple of The Law. Kushner writes Cohn's death in terms that emphasize the moral bankruptcy of his life, the failure of his lifelong quest to remain atop the pecking order of the powerful. Cohn's unceasing bargaining with God in the hereafter further underscores this failure. While the play musters a grudging admiration for Cohn's relentless drive for dominance in his hope that "they have something for me to do in the Great Hereafter, I get bored easy" (*Perestroika,* p. 127), his horrifying and solitary death agony counters any admiration with the sense of the barren legacy Cohn leaves behind.

UNLIKELY ALTERNATIVES

In contrast to the spiritual sterility of Cohn's gospel of clout, *Angels in America* offers an alternative that involves both personal revival and a societal reinvigoration. But the play does so through the most unlikely of agents: the one-time lovers and drag queens Prior Walter and Norman Arriaga, also known as Belize, and Louis Ironson, who deserts Prior due to his illness. Prior and Belize's transvestism, Louis's cowardice in the face of AIDS, and the publicly proclaimed homosexuality of all three men make them the incarnation of the homosexuals that Cohn sneers at, the fullest expression of the powerless population at the bottom of the food chain in Cohn's gospel of clout. They represent a line of literary characters who trace their origins to Jim Willard, whose coming out as a gay man in Gore Vidal's (1948) *The City and the Pillar* first provided "an unsensationalized portrait of the flourishing gay subcultures" (Summers, 1990, p. 113).

Like Jim Willard, Prior Walter, Belize, and Louis are part of a subculture that Kushner will not moralize about or hold up "as the villain of the piece" (Summers, 1990, p. 113). As Claude Summers notes about Vidal's novel, Prior, Belize, and Louis may exhibit the neurosis that accompanies "being gay in an unaccepting society," but they also demonstrate that "the expression of being gay" can result in "healthy introspection and valuable social criticism" (p. 115), both factors in the personal revival and social revitalization in the play. The introspection leading to a "great awakening" sharpens after Prior realizes that he has AIDS, a fact that causes Louis, his lover, to desert him because "he isn't so good with death" (*Millenium,* p. 25). At the same time, Belize, a registered nurse, assumes the caregiver's role for Prior. Belize dispenses medication and a social commentary that both nurtures Prior and provides the means for Louis's spiritual renewal. In combination with Prior's prophetic vision, Belize's caregiving forms the basis of the transformation of masculine spirituality in *Angels in America.* That new-found spirituality culminates in the gathering of a nascent community at Bethesda fountain at the play's conclusion, the characters all awaiting, along with the authence, the healing angel's touch.

Before that dramatic conclusion, however, Prior, Belize, and even Louis must develop as individuals and as self-made men who personify Kushner's transformed and transforming spirituality. Initially, Prior and Belize appear to be the quintessential objects of Cohn's contempt. Prior searches for his lost cat, doing "my best Shirley Booth . . . 'Come back, Litüe Sheba, come back'" (*Millenium,* p. 21), and then later, in drag, impersonates Gloria Swanson in Sunset Boulevard, lamenting that "you know you've hit rockbottom when even drag is a drag" (*Millenium,* p. 31). Belize, arriving to visit Prior in the hospital, launches into high camp in French, quotes from *Streetcar Named Desire,* and engages Prior in politically incorrect "girl-talk shit" (*Millenium,* p. 61). Politically incorrect though it may be, the talk, and the characters' comfort with such talk, emphasized Kushner's intent, like Gore Vidal's in his Afterword (1965) to the revised *The City and the Pillar,* "to take risks, . . . and in the process show the 'naturalness' of homosexual relations" (p. 245). The very naturalness of Prior and Belize demonstrates the ways in which they have already cultivated a life in defiance of Cohn's gospel of clout.

Kushner undertakes an even greater risk in depicting the "naturalness" of homosexuals in the ambivalence of Louis Ironson, someone Cohn would also despise for his lack of worldly achievements. Though openly gay, Louis cannot summon the fidelity necessary to remain with Prior. Early in the play, tormented by fears of what may lie ahead, he asks Prior, "What if I walked out on this? Would you hate me forever?" (*Millenium,* p. 40). Then, when Prior suffers a seizure, Louis cries out, "Oh God help me I can't I can't I can't" (*Millenium,* p. 48). Louis's fear of AIDS places his character in a middle role in the drama, someone who can embrace his relationship with Prior but only if it entails no ultimate commitment. Louis senses this shortcoming when he compares himself to Queen Mathilde, the wife of William the Conqueror, in whose army Prior's ancestor served. Mathilde awaited William's return, Louis speculates, without ever praying, as he does, that Prior the "if he can't return to me whole and healthy and able to live a normal life. . . . If he had died, she would have buried her heart with him. So what the fuck is the matter with me?" (*Millenium,* p. 52).

Prior perceptively sums up what is wrong when he observes, "Apartment too small for three? Louis and Prior comfy but not Louis and Prior and Prior's disease?" (*Millenium,* p. 78), and Louis, still struggling internally, continues to focus on himself: "I have to find some way to save myself" (*Millenium,* p. 79). Louis ultimately discovers a way to remove "the Mark of Cain" (*Millenium,* p. 99), his sense of having betrayed what is truest in himself when he betrays Prior and deserts him. But before he can remove the telltale stain, Louis must acknowledge Prior's prophetic pronouncement to Louis "that you endanger nothing in yourself. It's like that idea of crying when you do it. Or the idea of love" (*Perestroika,* p. 85). Equally crucial is Prior's insistence that Louis manifest the internal bruises he carries as a result of his failure. "Come back to me when they're visible," Prior commands Louis. "I want to see black and blue, Louis, I want to see blood" (*Perestroika,* p. 89). The enlightened Prior confronts a horrified Louis with the disturbing truth of Louis's dis-ease even as Prior and Belize seek to contend with the actual disease that also marks Prior and those who associate with him as untouchables in the world of Roy Cohn.

THE PROPHET'S ROLE

Paradoxically, it is by means of the disease that Prior and Belize then reclaim the spiritual desert Cohn depicts. The disease that takes Cohn's life irrevocably transfigures Prior, Belize, and Louis. The AIDS virus leads Prior to develop as the reluctant prophet, not unlike Isaiah and Jeremiah, both of whom actively resist the role. Just as Isaiah resists proclaiming God's word, crying out that he is a wretch with unclean lips (Isaiah 6:5) and Jeremiah hopes to escape God's call because of his inability to speak (Jeremiah 1:6), Prior responds to the call of the messenger angel, "What the fuck ...? (He holds himself) Poor me. Poor me. Why me?" (*Millenium,* p. 35). When the angel actually approaches, Prior beseeches "Oh don't come in here don't come in. ... I'm talking nonsense, I ... No more mad scene, hush, hush. ..." (*Millenium,* p. 115).

But like his Hebrew counterparts, Prior gains privileged spiritual insight, the "threshold of revelation" (*Millenium,* p. 33). Similar to Isaiah, whose lips are cleansed by an angel bearing a burning coal (6:6-7), and Jeremiah, who is assured that he will be given the words to speak (1:9), Prior experiences spiritual renewal through his affliction with AIDS, enabling him to prophesy. Harper Pitt, Joe's Valium-addicted wife and another of the play's afflicted prophets, sees this truth when she tells Prior "there's a part of you, the most inner part, entirely free of disease" (*Millenium,* p. 35). The angel of annunciation also tells Prior he will not die, for "a marvelous work and a wonder we undertake, an edifice awry we sink plumb and straighten, a great Lie we abolish, ... with the rule, sword, and broom of Truth!" (*Millenium,* p. 62).

Belize, ostracized both as an African-American and a gay man, shares with Prior this capacity for insight. Though Belize never calls it revelation, he senses the shift from the "ruination" of autumn to the white blanket of life-giving snow (*Millenium,* p. 100). Coming as it does after a particularly acrimonious and humorous exchange with Louis about race and oppression, Belize's smelling the approach of "softness, compliance, forgiveness, grace" (*Millenium,* p. 100) foreshadows the biblical reversal that occurs in *Angels in America.*

And Louis, after learning of Joe Pitt's "legal fag-bashing" in authoring Judge Wilson's decision against a homosexual serviceman, saves himself at the price of being battered by Joe (*Perestroika,* p. 110). Louis echoes Joseph Welch's encounter with Senator Joseph McCarthy, asking Joe and, in effect, himself, "Have you no decency at long last sir, have you no decency at all?" (*Perestroika,* p. 110). Bloodied, Louis has finally endangered himself for someone, has committed himself for the sake of the gay man discriminated against by Joe's decision, thereby placing himself among those who can participate in the reversal Belize senses.

Quite literally, as in the gospel of Luke, "some are last [Prior, Belize, and Louis] who will be first, and some are first [Cohn and Pitt] who will be last" (13:30). The gospels also provide a reason for the reversal in *Angels in America.* As Jesus teaches in Matthew, "where your treasure is, there your heart will be also" (6:21). Prior, Belize, and Louis's hearts transform them due to their ability to sustain or rediscover affective relationships, something Michael Pollak (1985) identifies as crucial in the homosexual milieu (p. 43). Outlawed as unacceptable, homosexuality becomes separated from the affective aspects of relationship, becomes a clandestine activity "that minimizes risks and optimizes effectiveness" (p. 43). Such "isolation of the homosexual act in time and space" (p. 43) constitutes the very essence of Roy Cohn and Joe Pitt's secret world, divorced from "the constraints imposed by stable and lasting relationships" (p. 43), but also devoid of any human comfort. Instead, their hearts are corroded by the gospel of clout, rendering them indeed last in the regenerated spirituality of *Angels in America.*

MORE LIFE

Nowhere is this regeneration more evident than in Prior's visit to heaven in *Perestroika.* In this tumbled-down, post 1906 San Francisco earthquake paradise, Prior realizes that "I have to choose. I can return to the world. If I want to" (*Perestroika,* p. 121). To return to the world, to immerse himself in affective relationships, becomes the essence of Prior's truest revelation, a revelation that directly opposes the express desire of the celestial host that Prior stop trying to progress. For human progress, the angels say, will lead to a "last dreadful daybreak" when "a tidal wave of Protean fire" will bare the Earth clean as a bone in the cosmic firestorm that Cohn envisioned at the play's opening (*Perestroika,* p. 135). Because God has abandoned the universe and cannot be found, the angels hope that the cessation of human activity may result in God's return.

But Prior cannot accept such homeostasis. He insists that, should God return to view "all the terrible days of this terrible century," the angels "should sue the bastard. That's my only contribution to all this Theology" (*Perestroika,* p. 133). Prior's defiance reflects Miles's interpretation of the complicated relationship between God and human beings. Miles argues that God is often "surprised" by the effects of his actions "and inclined to repudiate them" (p. 88). In many cases, Miles continues, "God relies on man even for the working out of his own intentions, and is, to this extent, almost parasitic on human desire. If man wanted nothing, it is difficult to imagine how God would discover what God wanted" (p. 89).

And, despite his obstreperous challenge to God, Prior seems to grasp this fact, seizing on it as the centerpiece of his reinvigorated spirit. "Bless me anyway," he tells the angels; "I want more life. I can't help myself. I do" (***Perestroika,*** p. 135). Prior wants to return to life, to return to work out the intentions of a God so confused by what he has wrought that he has left it altogether. For, even if his return to Earth is no more than an "addiction to being alive," Prior also realizes that humans can live "past hope." "If I can find hope anywhere, that's it, that's the best I can do. It's so much not enough, so inadequate but ... Bless me anyway. I want more life" (***Perestroika,*** p. 136).

LOVE AND JUSTICE

At the same time that Prior chooses more life, Belize makes another significant contribution to the resurrection of the spirit. Roy Cohn, dying of AIDS, becomes Belize's patient, a situation Cohn wants changed: "I want a white nurse. My constitutional right" (***Perestroika,*** p. 26). To which Belize responds, "You're in a hospital. You don't have any constitutional rights" (***Perestroika,*** p. 26). The irascible Cohn and the unflappable Belize achieve a moment of honesty when Belize concedes that Cohn is dying. Building on that initial contact, Belize goes on to warn Cohn against treatment that may kill him, prompting Cohn to retort, "You're just a fucking nurse. Why should I listen to you over my ... very expensive WASP doctor?" (***Perestroika,*** p. 29). Belize's answer that "he's not queer. I am. (*He winks at Roy*)" (***Perestroika,*** p. 29) tentatively establishes a connection between Belize and the man he first describes to Prior as "The Killer Queen Herself. New York's number-one closeted queer" (***Perestroika,*** p. 26). Although Belize readily admits to Cohn that he hates him, Belize does not adhere to Cohn's gospel of clout and its hierarchical human food chain.

The ultimate proof of Belize's fidelity to an alternative spirituality comes once Cohn has died. Intent on removing the cache of AZT Cohn has locked at the foot of his bed, Belize summons Louis Ironson to be his "packmule," telling him that the deed constitutes "expiation for your sins" (***Perestroika,*** pp. 123-124). Belize and Louis join together to endanger themselves for others, to risk themselves for human beings with whom they share relationship. Louis's personal revival becomes a part of the great awakening symbolized in Belize's humane efforts. Belize also acknowledges the human being who has just died, insisting that Louis recite Kaddish, the Jewish prayer for the dead, for Roy Cohn. When Louis balks at the notion, Belize persists:

> He was a terrible person. He died a hard death. So maybe ... A queen can forgive her vanquished foe. It

isn't easy, it doesn't count if it's easy, it's the hardest thing. Forgiveness. Which is maybe where love and justice finally meet. Peace, at least.

(***Perestroika,*** p. 124)

Belize enacts the foremost principle in affective relationships, the capacity to forgive. In doing so, he carries out the teaching of Jesus that his disciples should forgive, not seven times, a perfect number, but seventy times seven (Matthew 18:22). In the same way, Louis's recitation of Kaddish, guided by the ghost of Ethel Rosenberg, effects a double act of forgiveness, incarnating the forgiveness that lies at the heart of the resurrected spirituality in the play. Louis receives that forgiveness even as he prays for Roy Cohn, his fallen foe.

Like Prior, who seeks more life despite the horrible suffering that may lie ahead, Belize and Louis do not shirk from "the hardest thing," merging love and justice in the desire for peace. Though scorned by the High Priests who preach the gospel of clout as merely an insignificant African-American gay man and an ethnic Jew of no real substance, Belize and Louis refuse to accept "the limitations of those categories that naturalize the power to name our [homosexual] experience as 'unnatural'" (Cohen, 1989, p. 199). Because the characters refuse limitations and prejudicial categories, they too partake in Prior's spirituality, eschewing clout and simply asking for more life. And since their rejection of the gospel of clout takes the form of a prayer for a "vanquished foe," Belize and Louis can join Prior and the other survivors at Bethesda fountain in what the Rabbi Isidor Chemelwitz, one of the play's wisdom-figures, indicates as the best method for working out the intentions of God: "You should struggle with the Almighty!" (***Perestroika,*** p. 138).

That Joe Pitt, alone among the play's characters, has no opportunity to make that struggle poses a problem in the conclusion. Apparently, forgiveness is the hardest thing since the play does not admit of that possibility in Pitt's case. The guilt-ridden neophyte of the Temple of the Law receives only this advice from his wife, Harper: "Get lost, Joe. Go exploring" (***Perestroika,*** p. 143). She hands him two Valium and then leaves him in order to catch a flight to San Francisco to search out the unspeakably beautiful.

FAITH'S ASSURANCE

Yet the play does not end there. Prior, Belize, Louis, and Hannah Pitt, Joe's mother and another caregiver for Prior—all of them people who recognize the power of affective relationships—gather on a cold January day at the Central Park fountain to await its flowing. And when the original Bethesda fountain flows again, they will all bathe in it and be made clean. Certain of new life even in the midst of winter and courageous even in the face of the devastation of AIDS, Prior, Belize, and Louis reflect William James's (1916) assertion that the converted manifest "the joyous conviction itself, the assurance that all is well" (p. 247). Prior, the prophet of more life, embodies James's convert, who displays "the peace, the harmony, the willingness to be, even though the outer conditions should remain the same" (p. 248). Prior describes the fountain in summer as "a sight to see. I want to be around to see it. I plan to be. I hope to be" (*Perestroika,* p. 148).

Serene in himself, Prior closes the play by encouraging the audience to "organize the secular world in the direction of the holy" (Frymer-Kensky, 1992, p. 116). His parting words reiterate the new spiritual imperative to struggle on together because "the world only spins forward. We will be citizens. The time has come" (*Perestroika,* p. 148). The individual revivals of the characters merge in the great awakening that ends the play. As Prior Walter gently instructs and challenges the audience, "The Great Work Begins" (*Perestroika,* p. 148), when men in America can depart from the gospel of clout and espouse a pattern of affective relationships that will renew their lives.

References

Alter, J. (1992). *The world of biblical literature.* New York: Basic Books.

Cohen, E. (1989). *Legislating the norm: From sodomy to gross indecency.* In R. R. Butters, J. M. Clum, & M. Moon (Eds.), *Displacing homophobia: Gay male perspectives in literature and culture* (pp. 169-205). Durham, NC: Duke University Press.

Frymer-Kensky, T. (1992). *In the wake of the goddesses: Women, culture, and the biblical transformation of pagan myth.* New York: The Free Press.

Holy Bible. *The New Revised Standard Version.* (1989). Nashville: Thomas Nelson Publishers.

James, W. (1916). *The varieties of religious experience: A study in human nature.* New York: Longman, Green, and Co.

Kushner, T. (1993). *Angels in America. Part one: Millenium approaches.* New York: Theatre Communications Group.

———. (1994). *Angels in America. Part two: Perestroika.* New York: Theatre Communications Group.

Leverenz, D. (1989). *Manhood and the American renaissance.* Ithaca, NY: Cornell University Press.

McLoughlin, W. G. (1978). *Revivals, awakenings, and reform: An essay on religion and social change in America, 1607-1977.* Chicago: The University of Chicago Press.

Miles, J. (1995). *God: A biography.* New York: Knopf.

Miller, J. W. (1989). *Biblical faith and fathering: Why we call God "Father."* New York: Paulist Press.

Pleck, E. H., & Pleck, J. H. (1980). Introduction. In E. H. Pleck & J. H. Pleck (Eds.), *The American man* (pp. 1-49). Englewood Cliffs, NJ: Prentice-Hall.

Pollak, M. (1985). *Male homosexuality.* In P. Aries & A. Béjin (Eds.), *Western sexuality: Practice and precept in past and present times* (A. Forster, Trans.; pp. 40-61). Oxford: Basil Blackwell.

Rosenberg, C. E. (1980). *Sexuality, class and role in 19th century America. In E. H. Pleck & J. H. Pleck (Eds.), The American man* (pp. 219-54). Englewood Cliffs, NJ: Prentice-Hall.

Rotundo, E. A. (1987). *Learning about manhood: Gender ideals and the middle-class family in nineteenth century America.* In J. A. Mangan & J. Walvin (Eds.), *Manliness and morality: Middle-class masculinity in Britain and America, 1800-1940* (pp. 35-51). New York: St. Martin's Press.

Sedgwick, E. K. (1990). *Epistemology of the closet.* Berkeley: University of California Press.

Summers, E. K. (1990). *Gay fictions: Wilde to Stonewall.* New York: The Continuum Publishing Company.

Vidal, G. (1965). *The city and the pillar revised.* New York: E. P. Dutton.

Michelle Elkin-Squitieri (essay date 1998)

SOURCE: Elkin-Squitieri, Michelle. "'The Great Work Begins': Apocalyptic and Millenarian Vision in *Angels in America.*" *Anglophonia* 3 (1998): 203-12. Print.

[*In the following essay, Elkin-Squitieri focuses on two competing apocalyptic visions in* Angels in America: *that of the "literary genre," which attempts to transcend history by picturing its end (as represented by the Angel), and an "oral" or "ephemeral" vision focused on the "immediate historical moment" (mirrored in Prior's eventual rejection of the Angel's prophecy).*]

Angels in America is Tony Kushner's extraordinarily successful pair of plays about the lives of five homosexual men in New York City during the mid-1980s.[1] Or rather, it is a single, seven-hour long play in two parts, the first half titled *Millenium Approaches,* the second, *Perestroika.* It was commissioned by the Eureka Theatre Company with the help of the National Endowment for the Arts, and it was just the sort of project that motivated the recent Republican attack on the N.E.A. in the U.S. Congress: it portrays gay men sympathetically, though not uncritically, and with considerable psychological sophistication; sexual acts between men are not only referred to but represented on stage; there is a good deal of religious parody which playfully, but also very seriously insists on the erotic dimension of religious experience, the unity of flesh and spirit; and included among the characters are two self-hating, closet homosexuals who are also flag-waving, conservative Republican lawyers. Because of the N.E.A. funding for an ambitious work by an openly gay playwright dealing explicitly with gay themes, the play received a lot of publicity even before the first part was finished. As a major work of American theater written by, for and about the gay community, *Angels in America,* it was hoped, would finally bring that community out of the cultural closet. The remarkable thing is that Kushner seems to have pulled it off. The play largely fulfilled expectations, even surpassed them, if you can judge from the success of the productions in Los Angeles, London, New York and San Francisco—and the numerous awards it received, including the Pulitzer Prize for Drama for *Millenium Approaches* in 1993.

It is a wonderful play, very funny and very moving. Its context, of course, is the AIDS epidemic, and its pathos and its humor respond to that collective suffering. My husband first read it while working as a teaching assistant with Professor Bill Nestrick at U.C. Berkeley. Bill was a very distinguished gay professor in the English and Film Departments at Berkeley. He died last year of a heart attack at the age of 50, and at the memorial service, people talked about his learning, his eclecticism, his love of movies and food, his sardonic humor and his emotional reserve—he was not given to public displays of feeling. But Victor recalled that in the middle of a class on *Angels in America,* Bill broke down and cried right in front of his students because the play so powerfully reminded him of friends who had died from AIDS.

That response was not unusual, probably in part because the play portrays the physiological and emotional effects of AIDS in such painful, graphic details, symptoms with which audiences in San Francisco, Los Angeles and New York would have been only too familiar. It also evokes other disturbing recollections of Reagan's second term: the late twentieth-century disintegration of families and communities, the apparent triumph of the far right-wing's politics of ruthless self-interest, the growing population of homeless people on the streets, the diminishing quantity of ozone in the outer atmosphere, Chernobyl. But the harsh realism of the play is balanced by a certain playful, spiritual dimension: it is packed full of ghostly apparitions, angelic visitations, supernatural insights, telepathic communions and prophetic visions, both apocalyptic and millenarian.

Those visions are the subject of this article, which will focus on the most theatrically dramatic and thematically central example of this recurrent motif, the scene in which an Angel crashes through the protagonist's bedroom ceiling with great pomp and circumstance to appoint him Prophet for the latter days and bestow on him, or rather, instill *in* him, a huge prophetic Book with an apocalyptic

message. (The capitalized nouns are a stylistic feature of the play which contribute to an effect of portentousness that is always playful, never solemn, yet somehow very serious.) I want to try to explain the function of this scene, its relevance to the characters' stories and to the larger historical processes which Kushner sees as inseparable from those individual experiences. As we shall see, Kushner distinguishes between two kinds of prophecy. There is the Apocalyptic prophecy of the Book, literally imposed from above by an angelic politburo horrified by the volatility and destructiveness of human affairs. This is an attempt to stop history which Kushner's protagonist ultimately rejects. And there is the Millenial prophecy on which the play concludes: this is a promise of healing and renewal, explicitly drawn from an historical tradition and orally transmitted by the characters within and between the shifting and attenuating parameters of their communities. This distinction suggests to me that Kushner is very much in touch with what Steven Goldsmith has identified in *Unbuilding Jerusalem*[2] as an historical tension dating back to the prophetic texts of the New and Old Testaments: between the highly literary genre of apocalypse, which attempts to transcend history by representing the end of history, and the (more or less) oral, or perhaps more accurately, ephemeral tradition of millenial prophecy which speaks directly to the immediate historical moment.

It would be difficult to imagine a more unlikely prophet than the play's protagonist, Prior Walter. A gay man and sometime transvestite living in New York City, Prior is the scion of an Anglo-American family that dates back to the Mayflower and beyond; in fact, one of his thirty ancestors by the same name is said to be represented in the Bayeux Tapestry. His lover is Louis Ironson, a Jewish son of "New Deal Pinko Parents in Schenectady," who works as a word processor for the Brooklyn Federal Court of Appeals. When we first meet Prior and Louis, they have just attended the funeral of Louis's Eastern European immigrant grandmother whom he guiltily admits he never visited. Prior takes this occasion to tell Louis that he has recently been diagnosed with AIDS and shows him his first Kaposi's sarcoma lesion. Knowing that Louis has a phobic terror of disease and death, Prior admits that he postponed giving Louis the painful news because he feared Louis might abandon him. That fear will turn out to be well-founded. Not long after, while Prior is in the hospital with his first medical crisis, Louis disappears, then returns briefly in an explosive scene to tell Prior that he has moved out. Soon, Louis is involved in an affair with a young, married Mormon lawyer who is a clerk for an appeals court judge. Throughout the play, Louis is tormented by anxiety and guilt, even as he holds forth on the nature of Democracy in America, the Palestinian Question, the Race Question, etc. His foil is Prior's closest friend Belize, a black transvestite nurse whose loyalty to Prior, down-to-earth wit and daily familiarity with disease and death are the antithesis of Louis' bad faith and wordy evasions.

This, the story of Prior, Louis and Belize, is the main plot of the play and the context of the visitations by Prior's Angel. It is interwoven with two other stories: the disintegration of the marriage of Joe and Harper Pitt, and the diagnosis, disease and death of another AIDS victim, Roy Cohn. Joe Pitt is the conservative young Mormon law clerk from Utah who, after trying unsuccessfully for years to suppress his homosexuality, finally falls in love with Louis. His wife, Harper, suffers from agoraphobia, a "mild valium addiction," and hallucinations, or visions (depending on your point of view). Attorney Roy Cohn is one of two historically based characters in the play. The real Roy Cohn was an assistant to Joe McCarthy in the fifties and a power broker for conservative politicians in subsequent decades until he was finally disbarred, shortly before his death in 1986. Until the end, he maintained the fiction that the disease that killed him was liver cancer. In Kushner's play this corrupt attorney, self-hating Jew, closet homosexual, and behind-the-scenes Washington wheeler dealer has an irrepressible frenetic energy. He plays the telephone like a set of drums in a heavy metal band, carrying on four or five conversations at once punctuated by savage jabs at the hold button. He is haunted by the ghost of Ethel Rosenberg, the other historical character in the play, whose execution for treason he engineered by illegal contacts with the judge while serving as Assistant U.S. Attorney in her trial.

Kushner often makes use of split scenes to emphasize thematic relations between the interwoven plots. For example, Louis tells Prior he has moved out in a scene that intersperses their dialogue with a similar conversation on the other side of the stage between Joe and Harper. Not only do the private domestic spaces and traumas of these characters overlap, so do their imaginative spaces. Prior and Harper meet in a dream before they ever meet in person (and argue about whose dream or hallucination they are in). Later, they share a vision of their respective former partners at the diorama of the Mormon Visitors Center in Brooklyn, and they meet again one last time in Heaven.

Prior has intimations of the Angel's approach throughout part one, but she does not actually arrive until the final lines of the last scene of *Millenium Approaches.* Her arrival is reenacted in Act 1, Scene 1 of *Perestroika,* but we don't actually learn what happens after her arrival until Act 2, when Prior tells Belize about the visitation while simultaneously reenacting it with the Angel onstage. Although this scene alludes to the story of another angel who bestowed another book on Joseph Smith, prophet and founder of the Mormon Church 170 years ago, Kushner's Angel is very unlike Smith's angel or any other angel in the literature of angels. She is powerful but clumsy, wreaking havoc in Prior's bedroom when she crashes through the ceiling. She is bald like the American bald eagle, she is nonetheless beautiful, in a sort of postmodernist way, with an extraordinarily resonant, bell-like voice and "magnificent steel-gray wings." She seems to be less in control of the situation than we might expect of an angel; she is annoyed and

embarrassed when Prior does not respond according to script and she is forced to improvise. Above all, she is a very material, fleshly, sexual creature: her contacts with Prior are always signaled by his erection, and in this scene, their communion culminates in a mutual orgasm. When Prior complains that his creation makes it hard to concentrate on the Book she has commanded him to read, she replies,

> READ!
> You are Mere Flesh. I I I I am Utter Flesh,
> Density of Desire, the Gravity of Skin [. . .].[3]

The expererience of reading the Book is identified with that of hearing the Angel's words and boths are inseparable from what is subsequently described as a sexual union:

BELIZE:

> Whoa whoa whoa wait a minute excuse me please. You fucked this angel?

PRIOR:

> She fucked me. She has [. . .] well, she has eight vaginas.

Angels, we learn, are actually hermaphrodites, equipped with eight full sets of male and female sexual organs. The cosmic order, as the Angel describes it, is no less a union of flesh and spirit, its motor driven by the orgasmic energy of continual angelic copulation:

> What makes the Engine of Creation Run?
> Not Physics but Ecstatics Makes The Engine Run.[4]

God is a "male Hebrew letter"; "Heaven is a City much like San Francisco"; and "The Body is the Garden of the Soul."[5] The wit of such aphoristic pronouncements has a great deal to do with the context in which they are delivered. As the Angel's description of a universe sustained by angelic sex becomes more erotic and ecstatic, Prior, in Kushner's stage directions, "*starts to hump the book,*" and the orgasmic culmination of her speech is immediately followed by a moment of post-coital stillness:

> (*Pause. If they had cigarettes they'd smoke them now.*)

PRIOR:

> Oh. Oh God.

ANGEL:

> The Body is Garden of the Soul.

PRIOR:

> What *was* that?

ANGEL:

> Plasma Orgasmata.

PRIOR:

> Yeah well no doubt.

For all their power and passion, angels do have certain important limitations. Prior explains to Belize that

Each angel is an infinite aggregate myriad entity, they're basically incredibly powerful bureaucrats, they can do anything but they can't invent, create, they're sort of fabulous and dull all at once.

God became bored with his Angels' limitations ("Made for His Pleasure, We can only ADORE") and so he "split the World in two" to invent "Human beings, Uni-Genitaled: Female, Male." From an Angel's point of view, there is something fatally unbalanced about a creature with only one set of genitals, and the result was catastrophic: "In creating You, Our Father-Lover unleashed / Sleeping Creation's Potential for Change. / In YOU the Virus of TIME began!"

She explains that constant human explorations, migrations and inventions caused disturbances in the universe so terrible that the shocks were felt in Heaven, which resembles San Francisco not only in its topography but in being subject to earthquakes "or rather, heaven-quakes." Worse, God became so fascinated by his human creatures that he began to imitate them by wandering to unknown destinations. On April 18, 1906, the day of the great San Francisco earthquake, he left and hasn't been heard from since.

Not exactly Joseph Smith. All this is very playful, very delightful, but what the Angel has to say next is deadly serious. Since God disappeared and left humans to their own devices, the cosmos has been coming apart at the seams.

ANGEL:

> Surely you see towards what We are Progressing:
> The fabric of the sky unravels:
> Angels hover, anxious fingers worry
> The tattered edge.
> Before the boiling of blood and the searing of skin
> Comes the Secret Catastrophe:
> Before Life on Earth becomes finally merely impossible,
> It will for a long time before have become completely
> unbearable.
> (*Coughs*)
> YOU HAVE DRIVEN HIM AWAY! YOU MUST STOP MOVING!

PRIOR:

> (*Quiet, terrified*): Stop moving.

ANGEL:

> (*Softly*) Forsake the Open Road:
> Neither Mix Nor Intermarry: Let Deep Roots Grow:
> If you do not MINGLE you will Cease to Progress:
> Seek Not to Fathom the World and its Delicate Particle
> Logic:
> You cannot Understand, You can only Destroy.
> You do not Advance, You only Trample.
> Poor blind Children, abandoned on the Earth,
> Groping, terrified, misguided, over
> Fields of Slaughter, over bodies of the Slain:
> HOBBLE YOURSELVES!
> There is No Zion Save Where You Are!
> If you Cannot find your Heart's desire [. . .].

PRIOR:

> In your own backyard [. . .].

ANGEL, PRIOR AND BELIZE:

> You never lost it to begin with.
> (*The* ANGEL *coughs.*)

ANGEL:

> Turn back. Undo.
> Till HE returns again.[6]

Prior, initially puzzled and frightened, then angry, challenges her: "Stop Moving. That's what you want. Answer me! You want me dead." The Angel's reply is confused: "YES. NO. NO. / (*Coughs*) / YES. / This is not in the Text. We deviate [. . .]."

In an early, and generally appreciative review of ***Perestroika***,[7] *New Yorker* reviewer John Lahr complained that Kushner's "verbose Angel [. . .] takes up a lot of time broadcasting a deadly simple, reactionary message of cosmic collapse."[8] He saw the Angel's prophecies in this speech as a distraction from what he views as the real center of interest in the play, the human characters. "But, once the characters get back on the narrative track of the plot," he remarked, "***Perestroika*** finds its feet and its wisdom." I will argue that Lahr missed the point here: in my view Kushner's Angel and her message are absolutely central, not tangential, to the "narrative track of the plot," that is, to the emotional lives of the characters.

It is certainly true that this Angel, indeed all the angels in the play, are reactionaries; the question is how Kushner wishes us to understand that characterization. It is Belize who, upon hearing this story, uses that term to describe the Angel, and it is Belize who points out the relevance of her message to Prior's personal life, the "motif" of abandonment, "the man who got away." When Prior insists that either he has seen a real angel or he is suffering from AIDS-related dementia, Belize angrily replies that this vision is neither dementia or reality: "This is just you, Prior, afraid of the future, afraid of time. Longing to go backwards so bad you made this angel up, a cosmic reactionary." It is the Angel, not Belize, who has the last word in this scene, and she seems a lot more materially real than Belize wants to admit (although repeated allusions to *The Wizard of Oz* keep this ambiguity unresolved). Still, Belize's assessment is consistent with the Angel's own parting words to Prior just before she transforms him, with a kind of sacramental embrace, into a "Vessel of the BOOK" with the word "STASIS" written "On you in you in your blood" and reascends through the ravaged ceiling:

ANGEL:

> You can't Outrun your Occupation, Jonah.
> Hiding from Me one place you will find me in another.
> I I I I stop down the road, waiting for you.
> (*She touches him, tenderly, and turns him, cradling him
> with one arm.*)

You Know Me Prophet: Your battered heart,
Bleeding Life in the Universe of Wounds.[9]

These lines emphasize the Angel's connection with the essentially fleshly conservatism of human desire, the almost childlike way in which the self, the bodily, passionate self, simply refuses to accept loss and pain, no matter how clearly the mind sees the inevitability of that loss. In another variation on this theme, Harper, still overcome with grief over her discovery of Joe's homosexuality and his subsequent abandonment of her, fully aware that he is incapable of loving her, reflects on the infantile absurdity of her continuing obsession with him:

HARPER:

I don't understand why I'm not dead. When your heart breaks, you should die.
But there's still the rest of you. There's your breasts, and your genitals, and they're amazingly stupid, like babies or faithful dogs, they don't get it, they just want him. Want him.[10]

From the beginning, all the main characters, with the exception of Belize, have something in common: they are driven by fear and rage, and consequently they are stuck, unable to accept change and loss, unable to grow.[11] Prior is both terrified and enraged at his disease and at Louis's abandonment of him; Louis is overwhelmed by the same feelings compounded by self-hatred and guilt. Joe is horrified by his own homosexual desires and enraged by the mutual dependency of a marriage which has not enabled him to banish those desires but only intensified his frustration. Like Louis, Joe uses the language of politics, first to suppress and disguise his self-disgust, and later to rationalize his abandonment of his wife and his new dependency on Louis. Louis's left-wing, utopian fantasies of social progress are shown to have something in common with Joe's right-wing rhetoric of capitalist self-interest: both function to deny the painful chasm between desire and reality, between idealized self-images and actual behavior. Harper is furious at Joe for his inability to love and reassure her, yet terrified of finding herself alone in the world. Roy Cohn's compulsive need to wield power is manifestly a defense against a profound self-hatred, evident in his need to annihilate Ethel Rosenberg, who "reminded us of all our little Jewish mamas,"[12] and his insistence that his identity is defined by his power, not his sexual behavior. He demands that his doctor maintain the charade that the disease which is killing him is not AIDS but liver cancer. Finally, Joe's mother, who will later sell her home in Salt Lake City and come to New York looking for her son and daughter-in-law, initially responds with fear and denial to his troubled phone call in the early hours of the morning to tell her about his homosexuality: "You really ought to go home now to your wife. I need to go to bed. This phone call [...] We will just forget this phone call."[13]

Kushner links these personal dilemmas to larger historical dilemmas. Both plays begin with an apparently tangential nostalgic tribute to an heroic past. In *Millenium Approaches,* the first scene portrays the funeral of Sarah Ironson, Louis's grandmother, in late October. Rabbi Isidor Chemelwitz of the Bronx Home for Aged Hebrews commemorates not so much the individual woman whom he never spoke with, but the generation of immigrants she represents:

She was [...]

(*He touches the coffin*)

[...] not a person but a whole kind of person, the ones who crossed the ocean, who brought with us to America the villages of Russia and Lithuania—and how we struggled, and how we fought, for the family, for the Jewish home, so that you would not grow up *here,* in this strange place, in the melting pot where nothing melted. Descendants of this immigrant woman, you do not grow up in America, you and your children and their children with the goyische names. No such place exists. Your clay is the clay of some Litzvak shtetl, your air the air of the steppes—because she carried the old world on her back across the ocean, in a boat, and she put it down on Grand Concourse Avenue, or in Flatbush, and she worked that earth into your bones, and you pass it on to your children, this ancient, ancient culture and home.

You can never make that crossing that she made, for such Great Voyages in this world do not any more exist. But every day of your lives the miles that voyage between that place and this one you cross. Every day. You understand me? In you that journey is.

So [...] She was the last of the Mohicans, this one was. Pretty soon [...] all the old will be dead.[14]

Although the speech commemorates and honors a journey, it also mourns the inevitable consequences of that journey: the loss of the old world; the scattering of communities and families; the alienation from children and grandchildren with goyische names as those children are increasingly assimilated into the larger American culture and detached from the Jewish families that those immigrants worked so hard to preserve. For all their courage and hardships, in some sense those immigrants never really left the old world and never fully arrived in the new. The promise of this promised land was broken, and they too were trapped, incapable of transcending that loss.

There is a speech at the beginning of *Perestroika* which parallels the rabbi's elegy for the dying immigrant generation in *Millenium Approaches.* Aleksii Antedilluvianovich Prelapsarianov, the World's Oldest Living Bolshevik, described as "unimaginably old and totally blind," addresses the younger generations of Russian Soviet functionaries in the Kremlin in 1986. With a nostalgia oddly reminiscent of the rabbi's, Prelapsarianov celebrates an heroic past, castigates the diminished present and repudiates attempts to move into an unknown future without the reassurance of a powerful and coherent ideology:

ALEKSII ANTEDILLUVIANOVICH PRELAPSARIANOV:

[…] How are we to proceed without *Theory*? What System of Thought have these Reformers to present to this mad swirling planetary disorganization, to the Inevident Welter of fact, event, phenomenon, calamity? Do they have, as we did, a beautiful Theory, as bold, as Grand, as comprehensive a construct […]? You can't imagine, when we first read the Classic Texts, when in the dark vexed night of our ignorance and terror the seed-words sprouted and shoved incomprehension aside, when the incredible bloody vegetable struggle up and through into Red Blooming gave us Praxis, True Praxis, True Theory married to Actual Life […] You who live in this Sour Little Age cannot imagine the grandeur of the prospect we gazed upon: like standing atop the highest peak in the mighty Caucasus, and viewing in one all-knowing glance the mountainous, granite order of creation […]. And what have you to offer now, children of this Theory? […] Market Incentives? American Cheeseburgers? Watered-down Bukharinite stopgap makeshift Capitalism? NEPmen! Pygmy children of a gigantic race! […] Show me the words that will reorder the world, or else keep silent.[15]

Although this scene is utterly tangential as far as the plot is concerned (it is a vestige of what was formerly another subplot in the play), it recaps the themes of loss, disillusionment and broken promises from the first play and suggests a similarity between the political convulsions going on in Eastern Europe in the late eighties and the emotional convulsions which will lead to a different kind of Perestroika, or restructuring, in the characters' lives.

The Angel's command to Prior and to the human race, "STOP MOVING!," recapitulates the nostalgia of the Rabbi's funeral sermon and the old Bolshevik's speech; both characters would like nothing more than for history to stop and go *backwards,* and the same is true for most or all of the main characters in the play. But of course, these two speeches also suggest the impossibility of such a return to the past; immigrant Jews and Russian revolutionaries themselves did not necessarily embrace their futures without ambivalence; they too were driven by powerful historical exigencies to leave or destroy an old world and find or create a new one. As Belize says to Prior, "Some of us didn't exactly choose to migrate, know what I'm saying." Later in *Perestroika,* Kushner makes the same point about the Mormon migration when the manikin of the Mormon mother in the diorama at the Mormon Visitor Center magically comes to life and takes Harper out in the middle of the night to the Brooklyn Heights Promenade:

HARPER:

In your experience of the world. How do people change?

MORMON MOTHER:

Well it has something to do with God so it's not very nice. God splits the skin with a jagged thumbnail from throat to belly and then plunges a huge filthy hand in, he grabs hold of your bloody tubes and they slip to evade his grasp but he squeezes hard, he insists, he pulls and pulls till all your innards are yanked out and the pain! We can't even talk about that. And then he stuffs them back, dirty, tangled and torn. It's up to you to do the stitching.[16]

The play suggests that change and growth in human life are not, for the most part, chosen; rather they are the result of loss and grief and pain. That pain is unavoidable and yet we all try to avoid it, and it was no less a fact of life for those apparently imperturbable Mormon pioneers than it is for their descendants, Harper and Joe.

This is why Prior ultimately rejects the Book and the prophecy he has been given. On the advice of Hannah, who took him to the hospital after he collapsed at the Mormon Visitor Center, he confronts and wrestles with the Angel and wins the right to return the Book to Heaven, There, he tells the Angelic Politburo that their demand is impossible to fulfill, and he asks for their blessing, a demand for "more life" in the most literal sense of the word.[17] Why would you want to continue to live? they ask. Horrible suffering is the only thing you and the rest of the human race have to look forward to. The Apocalypse is descending. But Prior insists that he wants to go on living, even with his illness and the suffering it entails, as long as possible. He has finally arrived at an acceptance of his disease, although his anger is not gone. If God should return, he advises them, "take Him to court. He walked out on us. He ought to pay."

The angels' grim forecast is frightening, but the play offers an alternative point of view. Walking down the streets of Heaven, trying to find his way home, Prior runs into Sarah Ironson playing cards with the rabbi. He asks them why people play cards in Heaven, and the rabbi, formerly a spokesman for pessimism and nostalgia, replies:

Because mister, with the Angels, those makhers, may their names be always worshipped and adored, it's all gloom and doom and give up already. But still is there Accident, in this pack of playing cards, still is there the Unknown, the Future. You understand me? It ain't all so much mechanical as they think.[18]

Prior returns home with a message of hope from the rabbi and a message of forgiveness to Louis from his grandmother. On his way, he sees Roy Cohn engaged in a professional consultation with God; the angels have apparently taken Prior's advice, and God now finds himself in need of a lawyer.

In the Epilogue, Prior and his friends address the audience directly with one final prophecy. Although Prior has rejected the Angel's Book, he has learned about the promised Millenium from Hannah. It was she who told him to reject the vision, never imagining that she would find herself in orgasmic communion with an all-too-real angel, and it is she who has explained to Prior the story of Joseph Smith's angelic vision on which Kushner's playful variation was based. In the Epilogue, this middle-aged Mormon woman from Utah who, during the intervening years has been transformed into a rather sophisticated, urban-looking New Yorker, is a spokesperson for restructuring, and for a new version of the Mormon Millenial promise that includes Prior, and by implication, all gay men and women.

Kushner's parody of Mormon beliefs may seem harsh at moments but it is also compassionate. He seems to see the rigidities of Mormon traditions and values, like those of Judaism, Marxism and the ideologies of American left-wing progressivism and right-wing capitalist self-interest, as understandable, if not always effective or humane, defenses against tragedy and suffering. The contrast between apocalyptic and millenarian prophecy in this play is analogous to the contrast between the relatively static conventions of modern theater and Kushner's dynamic use of split scenes and shared surrealistic vision to reveal the shared sufferings that underlie the apparently irreconcilable differences between cultures, races and individuals, and to suggest a fusion of political, social, psychological and spiritual significance. Just as Prior rejects the Angel's impossible demand that human beings stop the historical clock and substitutes for that deathly message a millenarian promise of spiritual healing and political renewal, so Kushner rejects the cult of the autonomous, ahistorical artwork and substitutes a theater that is engaged—politically and spiritually—in the historical moment.

Notes

1. All citations will refer to the following editions. *Part One: Millenium Approaches* (New York: Theatre Communications Group, Inc., 1992, 1993). *Part Two: Perestroika* (New York: Theatre Communications Group, Inc., 1992, 1994).

2. Steven Goldsmith, *Unbuilding Jerusalem* (Ithaca, New York: Cornell UP, 1993) 27-84.

3. Kushner, *Perestroika* 47.

4. Kushner, *Perestroika* 47.

5. Kushner, *Perestroika* 48-50.

6. Kushner, *Perestroika* 52-53.

7. John Lahr, "Beyond Nelly." *New Yorker* 68 (November 23, 1992): 126-130.

8. Lahr, "Beyond Nelly" 129.

9. Kushner, *Perestroika* 54.

10. Kushner, *Perestroika* 20.

11. Belize expresses a good deal of racial and personal anger, and some fear for Prior's sanity, but does not seem driven by anxiety in the same way as the other characters.

12. Kushner, *Millenium approaches* 108.

13. Kushner, *Millenium approaches* 76.

14. Kushner, *Millenium approaches* 10-11.

15. Kushner, *Perestroika* 13-14.

16. Kushner, *Perestroika* 79.

17. In the Afterword to *Perestroika* (157), Kushner says he owes this idea to Harold Bloom who, in an introduction to Olivier Revault d'Allones' *Musical Variations on Jewish Thought*, suggested "more life" as a literal translation of the Hebrew word for blessing.

18. Kushner, *Perestroika* 137.

Allen J. Frantzen (essay date 1998)

SOURCE: Frantzen, Allen J. "Alla, Angli, and *Angels in America.*" *Before the Closet: Same-Sex Love from* Beowulf *to* Angels in America. Chicago: U of Chicago P, 1998. 264-92. Print.

[*In the following essay, Frantzen argues that Kushner rewrites an important dynamic in medieval texts by which angels are associated with Anglo-Saxons as a means of claiming racial purity and superiority. Frantzen contends that by pitting Prior, the most prominent WASP in the play, against the angels, Kushner denies "the power of race to unify a people."*]

Rome, not Northumbria, is the center of *The Man of Law's Tale,* and celibacy, not marital bliss, is the Man of Law's preferred mode for Christ's holy ministers. Chaucer's text looks neither to the vernacular tradition of married clergy that the Wycliffites sought nor to the celibate clerical world demanded by Roman canon law and espoused earlier by the Anglo-Saxon church of Ælfric and by Norman reformers. Instead, the Man of Law's heroine is a product of Chaucerian compromise. She practices what might be thought of as serial chastity. Custance marries Alla, but after she becomes pregnant she lives without his company for all but the last year of his life. Clerical ideals dominate *The Man of Law's Tale,* much of its domestic sentiment notoriously devalued not only by the narrator's self-dramatizing interruptions but by Chaucer's debt to the work of a great reforming cleric, Pope Innocent III, whose "De miseriis humane conditionis" (On the misery of the human condition) is quoted in the prologue to the tale and elsewhere in the text.[1]

Chaucer makes much of the dependence of the English church on Rome. His reform-minded contemporaries, the Lollards, regarded Rome as a dangerous influence; in the Reformation the city became a symbol used to attack Catholicism. But for the Anglo-Saxons and for orthodox Christians of Chaucer's time, Rome was the center of the Church on earth. Correspondence with the pope and travel to and from Rome were means by which the church of the frontier established its authenticity. In this chapter I examine one small part of this traffic, an episode from Bede's *Ecclesiastical History of the English People,* which describes the sale of angelic English boys in Rome, a story subsequently retold by Wace, Laȝamon, and others, including John Bale, a Reformation historian. I compare the juxtaposition of angels and Angli, meaning "English," in these texts to angelic powers in Tony Kushner's *Angels in America,* a play in which the Anglo-Saxons, embodied in the stereotype of the WASP, play a small but significant role. For a moment, however, I return to Chaucer's Alla and a scene in which he too meets a boy in Rome.

ALLA AND ÆLLE

Alla registers a dim presence in *The Man of Law's Tale.* He is heard about after Custance converts Hermengyld and her husband but otherwise, except for letters to his mother, not heard from until a young boy (who proves to be his son) is set before him at a feast. This act is part of Custance's plan. She too has arrived in Rome but has refused to identify herself to the senator who rescued her from the ship on which she was set adrift from Northumbria. Now, in her husband's presence, she speaks through her son. "[A]t his moodres heeste / Biforn Alla, durynge the metes space, / The child stood, lookynge in the kynges face" (1013-15).[2] The child does not look like him, however, but "as lyk unto Custance / As possible is a creature to be" (1030-31). Because Alla has kept the faith (he is on a pilgrimage of repentance for killing his wicked mother), he realizes that Christ might have sent Custance to Rome just as he sent her to Northumbria. Shortly thereafter Alla and Custance are reconciled. Only then does she reveal herself to her father, the emperor, explaining for the first time who she is (1105-13).

The story of Custance reminds many readers of a saint's life and recalls some of the dynamics of stories about cross-dressed women saints recounted in chapter 2.[3] Like Euphrosyne, Custance is betrothed, in Custance's case to a sultan who becomes a Christian in order to marry her. His mother, outraged, kills him and sends Custance out to sea, a scenario repeated when Custance is expelled from Northumbria. Unlike Euphrosyne, Custance marries and has a child. But in many ways her life as a missionary is similar to the lives of the evangelizing saints commemorated in Anglo-Saxon texts. The moment at which Custance reveals herself to her father recalls the revelation made by both Euphrosyne and Eugenia to theirs. And, like Eugenia, Custance preaches the word of God from within a same-sex community. It is, of course, a tiny one, just Custance and Hermengyld, but their same-sex love, symbolized by the bed they share, is genuine and more warmly demonstrated than such love is in the Anglo-Saxon texts.

Having been reunited in Rome, Custance and Alla return to Northumbria for a year of wedded bliss. After Alla's death, Custance goes back to Rome and takes up a life of virtue

and good works, never again parting from her father (1156-57). Chaucer rejoined his roving heroine to patriarchal structures identical to those governing the lives of Eugenia and Euphrosyne. The difference is that Chaucer's holy woman is not just a daughter but also a wife and mother—a married evangelist. To a surprising degree *The Man of Law's Tale* conforms to what might have been a Lollard vision of evangelism in the true church. Custance's language, for example, recognized as "a maner Latyn corrupt" in Northumbria, is what the Lollards thought Italians spoke—that is, a vernacular, albeit not English. The tale discreetly hints of controversies building in the Church in Chaucer's time by effecting a radical redescription of the origins of the Church in the Anglo-Saxon period. According to the Man of Law, Northumbria was converted by a woman who arrives from Rome by way of Syria, directed only by God's will and the winds. But as Bede's *Ecclesiastical History* makes clear, the territory was converted by Irish missionaries and by holy men who came at the pope's behest from Rome—Augustine sent by Gregory the Great in 596, Theodore and Hadrian sent by Pope Vitalian over half a century later. Equally bold is the Man of Law's revised account of Alla, Chaucer's version of the Northumbrian king Ælle, the only English character in the text who is known to have been a historical person. Chaucer's Alla is converted to Christianity by Custance and with her has a son, Maurice, who was crowned emperor by the pope (1122). Bede's Ælle was not Christian but rather served as a symbol of pagan kingship awaiting redemption. Ælle's son, Edwin, converted to Christianity because he wished to marry Æthelburh, the daughter of the Christian king Æthelberht.[4] Thereafter Edwin "held under his sway the whole realm of Britain, not only English kingdoms but those ruled over by the Britons as well."[5]

Ælle's role in Bede is much smaller on the historical level but much greater on the symbolic level. He appears in Bede's text but once, in a description of some boys who, like Maurice, ended up in Rome through circumstances not of their own choosing. They too looked into the face of an important man, Pope Gregory. Or I should say, rather, that he looked into their faces, and what he saw there, depending on whose account we accept, was either the image of a chosen people waiting to be converted (the preferred explanation)—or love.[6]

> It is said that one day, soon after some merchants had arrived in Rome, a quantity of merchandise was exposed for sale in the market place. Crowds came to buy and Gregory too amongst them. As well as other merchandise he saw some boys put up for sale, with fair complexions, handsome faces, and lovely hair. On seeing them he asked, so it is said, from what region or land they had been brought. He was told that they came from the island of Britain, whose inhabitants were like that in appearance. He asked again whether those islanders were Christians or still entangled in the errors of heathenism. He was told that they were heathen. Then with a deep-drawn sigh he said, "Alas that the author of darkness should have men so bright of face in his grip, and that minds devoid of inward

grace should bear so graceful an outward form." Again he asked for the name of the race. He was told that they were called *Angli.* "Good," he said, "they have the face of angels, and such men should be fellow-heirs of the angels in heaven." "What is the name," he asked, "of the kingdom from which they have been brought?" He was told that the men of the kingdom were called *Deiri.* "*Deiri*," he replied, "*De ira!* good! snatched from the wrath of Christ and called to his mercy. And what is the name of the king of the land?" He was told that it was Ælle; and playing on the name, he said, "Alleluia! the praise of God the Creator must be sung in those parts."[7]

The story of the Anglian boys in Rome is found at the start of book 2 of the *Ecclesiastical History,* where Bede encloses a summary of Gregory's life within a larger narrative of the origins of the English nation. Like Gildas, Bede portrayed the early British as a Chosen People who violated their covenant with God and were destroyed as a result.[8] Bede effected a complete break between the histories of the lapsed early Christian communities of the British—the community that Custance encounters when she lands in Northumbria and reads a "Britoun book"—and the heathen tribes, the Anglo-Saxons, whom Gregory's missionaries would convert. Bede located his own origins in the Anglo-Saxons, the new rather than the old chosen people.

The boys whom Gregory saw in the marketplace were descendants of Anglo-Saxons who, 150 years after coming to Britain, were still pagan. Gregory and Bede call the boys "Angli," a term that generally means "English."[9] But Bede had a more particular understanding of the term, as his description of the settlements of Germanic tribes makes clear. Bede located the Jutes where the people of Kent live, and the Saxons where the West, East, and South Saxons live. He continued: "Besides this, from the country of the Angles, that is, the land between the kingdoms of the Jutes and the Saxons, which is called *Angulus,* came the East Angles, the Middle Angles, the Mercians, and all the Northumbrian race (that is those people who dwell north of the river Humber) as well as the other Anglian tribes. *Angulus* is said to have remained deserted from that day to this."[10] Bede seems to have meant "Anglian" in the more specific sense of "Northumbrian." He himself was born in the territory of Monkwearmouth-Jarrow, in Northumbria, and so was "Angli" in three senses—Northumbrian, Anglian, and English.[11] "Angli" also means "angels," of course, but Bede carefully understates this meaning, which in the anecdote is better left to Gregory. That the boys' beauty should make Gregory think of angels is significant, for it suggests a purely symbolic meaning for "angli" otherwise rare in Bede's *Ecclesiastical History.*

Bede affirms a natural affinity between Gregory and the Anglo-Saxons. It might seem curious that Gregory should find the boys attractive, since his admiration suggests that he prefers their unfamiliar appearance (light-complected and light-haired) to that of his own people. The discrepancy strongly suggests that the anecdote originates with an English author whose views Gregory is made to express. The episode is a pretext for witty verbal play that valorizes the boys' race, their nation, and their king. Young, innocent, and beautiful, the boys themselves represent a benign and neglected heathendom. When Gregory recognizes all the signs of a chosen people awaiting God's blessing, Bede is permitted to foresee the new Christian age of the English people that arrived in England with Gregory's missionaries.

For all its piety, the encounter between Gregory and the boys reflects earthly and political concerns. Bede shows us Gregory's interest in establishing the Church in England and in complementing the churches that Rome had already fostered so successfully elsewhere in western Europe. Bede's chief aim was to bolster the success of that Church especially in the land of his birth; he dedicated the work to the Northumbrian king Ceolwulf.[12] The reference to angels promotes this aim, symbolically affiliating the Anglo-Saxon church with Rome. When Gregory announced that the people of Anglia, represented by angelic youth, were ready to be changed into "fellow-heirs of the angels in heaven," a new age—the history of Bede's own beginnings—came into being. But these unhappy boys were not its heralds, any more than they were angels. Other messengers—missionaries brought to England by Augustine at Gregory's command, long after the boys had been forgotten—were charged with bringing the faith to the Anglo-Saxons. That the boys could be compared to angels was not testimony to their proximity to the divine, a role Bede reserved for real angels, but to the angel-like state of their descendants, who would be newly baptized, newly converted, and newly saved.

The boys, Bede notes, were "put up for sale." Gregory saw them amid stacks of other merchandise. What were they doing there? Peter Hunter Blair warned that readers should not "jump to the romantic conclusion that the boys whose purchase was envisaged by Gregory were English slaves on sale in a market-place." The boys might also have been held in service, he suggested, as four English boys were held in the service of Jews at Narbonne, or prisoners of war, mercenaries, or "merely young men in some way bound to the soil on Merovingian estates."[13] A letter survives from Gregory to the priest Candidus (written in September 595), asking him to buy "English boys who are seventeen or eighteen years old, that they may be given to God and educated in the monasteries" ("pueros Anglos qui sunt ab annis decem et septem vel decem et octo, ut in Monasteriis dati Deo proficiant comparet").[14] The boys Gregory sees in the marketplace are not destined for education and clerical status, however. Those who have looked closely at the episode, including Bertram Colgrave, R. A. B. Mynors, and David Pelteret, identify the boys as slaves—although Bede does not—and relate the episode to the well-documented practice of slavery by the Anglo-Saxons.[15] "The custom of buying or ransoming slaves to turn them into missionaries was known," according to Colgrave, and both Aidan and Willibrord observed it.[16]

In the later Anglo-Saxon period opposition to slavery seemed to intensify. In 1014 Wulfstan denounced those who sold their children into foreign servitude.[17] But foreign trade in slaves persisted until the Norman Conquest, after which opposition to slavery continued. The Council of London of 1102 criticized the custom, even as servile tenure was becoming a more prevalent form of bondage.[18] In almost all cases in Anglo-Saxon sources the slaves in question are penal slaves forced into slavery because they could not pay debts or because they were being punished for some offense. The boys' status depended on their age; if they were seventeen or eighteen, they could have been sold as slave labor. But it is also possible that the boys Gregory saw in Rome were captives who were too young to be penal slaves and who merely represented a benign and neglected heathendom. Bede's narrative exalted their innocence, youth, and beauty, even though its real subject was their race, their nation, and Ælle, their king. What was their value in the market place? Ruth Mazo Karras points out that sexual exploitation was among the many unfortunate facts of life for women slaves. It is possible that boys were also sexually exploited and that their commercial value was directly related to their beauty and fairness, underscored by Gregory's focus on their faces (they are "bright of face," they have "the face of angels").[19] The boys would have been exploited by men, obviously, a kind of same-sex sex that, as we saw in chapter 4, was of particular concern to the Anglo-Saxons.

Any sexual resonance in the anecdote is, of course, suppressed by Bede and, in turn, by all those who retold the episode after him. In the version found in Laȝamon's *Brut*, the "angli" are men, not boys, whose response anticipates Gregory's discovery and spoils the drama of his curiosity and his good heart. "We are heathen men," they say, "and have been brought here, and we were sold in England, and we seek baptism from you if you would only free us" ("We beoð heðene men and hider beoð iladde, / and we weoren ut isalde of Anglene lond; / and fulluht we to þe ȝeorneð ȝef þe us wult ifreoiȝen," 14707-9). Gregory's reply is obliging. "[O]f all the peoples who live on earth, you English are assuredly most like angels; of all men alive your race is the fairest" ("Iwis ȝe beoð Ænglisce englen ilicchest / of alle þan folke þa wunieð uppen uolde; / eouwer cun is feȝerest of alle quike monnen," 14713-15).[20] Neither Laȝamon's nor other versions subsequent to Bede's include all of the episode's verbal play. Instead these versions overtly state points implied in Bede's account, showing, first, that the Angli desired baptism and requested it of Gregory, and, second, that they were captives who yearned to be free. But an ironic reading is also possible. Laȝamon's version, which makes nothing of Gregory's insight, might suggest that the Anglo-Saxons use the pope to effect a cynical exchange of baptism for freedom; conversion is their idea, not his.

The first modern reader to comment on the sexual subtext of Bede's story was John Boswell, who documented the Church's concern that abandoned children would be sold into slavery and used for sexual purposes. Some writers protested this practice, but not for the reasons we might expect. Their concern was that fathers who abandoned their children might later accidentally buy them as slaves and commit incest by having intercourse with them. Boswell noted that the public sale of slaves continued in Rome long after the empire was Christianized and illustrated the practice with the episode as Bede recounted it.[21] In the 1540s, some seven hundred years after Bede's death, Boswell's point was vividly anticipated by a remarkable figure named John Bale, the first reader to see a same-sex shadow in the story that has charmed so many.

BEDE AND BALE

Bale (1495-1563) was a Carmelite priest who left the Church of Rome in the 1530s. The author of several large-scale surveys of English authors and the first biographer of Chaucer, Bale was also a collector of early manuscripts, including those in Anglo-Saxon.[22] According to John N. King, Bale was "the most influential English Protestant author of his time."[23] He was also a prodigious instrument in the propaganda efforts of Thomas Cromwell.[24] Bale recounted the episode of Gregory and the slave boys in a revisionist narrative of English ecclesiastical history called *The Actes of Englysh Votaryes*.

> And as thys Gregorye behelde them fayre skynned and bewtyfullye faced, with heare upon their heades most comelye, anon he axed, of what regyon they were. And answere was made hym, that they were of an yle called Englande. Wele maye they be called *Angli* (sayth he) for they have verye Angelych vysages. Se how curyose these fathers were, in the wele eyenge of their wares. Here was no cyrcumstaunce unloked to, perteynynge to the sale. Yet have [has] thys Byshopp bene of all writers reckened the best sens hys tyme.[25]

Bale mockingly urged his readers to "[m]arke thys ghostlyc mysterye, for the prelates had than no wyves." He plainly implied that Gregory had sexual designs on the boys. "[T]hese fathers" were "curyose" in the "wele eyenge" of the boys as "wares," he wrote, using an expression with strong sexual overtones. In sixteenth-century English, "ware" could mean "piece of goods" (an expression "jocularly applied to women," according to the *OED*) and "the privy parts of either sex."[26] Because priests were unmarried, Bale observes, with much sarcasm, "other spirytuall remedyes were sought out for them by their good prouvders and proctours, we maye (yf we wyll) call them apple squyres." "Apple-squires," according to the *OED*, means "pimp" or "panderer," thus further underscoring Bale's sexual innuendo. Stressing that this sale was not unique, Bale produces another witness, Machutus, who saw a similar event in Rome in AD 500 and bought the boys to protect them (23a). We are meant to conclude that Gregory, deprived of a wife by the Church's demand for clerical celibacy, sought out "other spirytuall remedyes" by purchasing boys for sex.

Bale's rewriting of the story of Gregory and the Anglian boys takes place in the context of an elaborate revision of England's Anglo-Saxon Christian history proposed in *The Actes of Englysh Votaryes* and *The Image of Bothe Churches*. In *The Actes of Englysh Votaryes* Bale boldly revised English history in order to describe the nation's struggles against the corrupt influences of the Church of Rome. The chief instrument of Roman domination, Bale argued, was clerical celibacy, which permitted the clergy to degrade marriage and advocate virginity, all the while using its own religious houses for immoral purposes. Bale vigorously defended the right of the clergy to wed and believed that the Roman clergy who claimed to be celibate had in fact indulged in every form of sexual corruption. In *The Image of Bothe Churches,* Bale set forth a thesis about the Church in England that, as it was later developed by his better-known contemporary, John Foxe, became a foundational strategy for Reformation anti-Roman polemic.[27] Bale argued that the Church had been divided during the reign of Constantine and that the See of Saint Peter stemmed from the corrupt division, while an isolated community of the faithful, who retained belief in the true Church, reestablished the true Church in England. Bale argued that the false Church of Rome had taken on the image of the true Church of antiquity and that from the time of St. Augustine's mission to the English (597) to the rejection of papal authority by Henry VIII (1533) the Church in England had been corrupt. Bale was among the historians who looked back to the Anglo-Saxon period, skipping over an internal period in which they perceived England as dominated by the Church of Rome to a point that they erroneously saw as a free, "native," English church unencumbered by Roman influence. This was an exercise in self-justification. Having recently thrown off Roman rule itself, the new "English" or "Anglican" church was searching for its origins in the Anglo-Saxon period, which was perceived as another time when England's Christians governed themselves justly and righteously.

For Bede, the mission of Augustine marked the permanent conversion of Britain. Bale reversed the significance of this event. He claimed that the English church had survived pure and uncorrupted until the coming of Roman missionaries. With them they brought pernicious doctrines such as clerical celibacy, and as a result they transformed the once-pure land and its church into a new Sodom. Seeking to open his readers' eyes to the false miracles used by "obstynate hypocrytes" still living under the pope's rules, Bale wrote *The Actes of Englysh Votaryes* in order to accuse Catholics of portraying "whoremongers, bawdes, brybers, idolaters, hypocrytes, traytors, and most fylthye Gomorreanes as Godlye men and women" (2a). His diatribes are laced with references to Sodom and Gomorrah. Although his definitions of the sins of these unholy places remain vague, they encompass theological error as well as sexual excess, including, at certain points, male homosexual intercourse.

Marriage, Bale wrote in *The Actes,* was the "first order of religion," created in order to protect against "beastlye abusyons of the fleshe that shuld after happen" if men and women disobeyed God's command to increase and multiply (7b). The Church sought to dissuade holy men and women from marriage, broke up existing marriages, venerated only unmarried saints, and demonized women as "spretes" ("sprites," 3a); these were the acts of "the Sodomytycall swarme or brode of Antichrist" (4a). According to Bale's extraordinary revision of the history of Anglo-Saxon holy men and women, clergymen fornicated with cloistered nuns and produced a race of bastards who were then venerated as saints, Cuthbert, Dunstan, Oswald, Anselm, and Becket among them (2b). Some did worse, since they refrained from women but "spared not to worke execrable fylthyness among themselves, and one to pollute the other," an obvious reference to male homosexual acts (12b). Devout in his praise of Mary, Bale was eager to insist that she was not abused by the clergy and that she was not a professed nun, "as the dottynge papystes have dreamed, to couer their sodometrye with a most precyouse coloure, but an honest mannys wyfe" (13a). Bale attacked "spirituall Sodomytes and knaves" who wrote the lives of these sinful saints (18a): "Come out of Sodome ye whoremongers and hypocrytes, popysh byshoppes and prestes" (18b). Bale used "sodometrie"—an obsolete word for sodomy, first used in 1530, according to the *OED*—to attack clergy who took the required vows of celibacy but who were unable to remain celibate: either men who had sex with each other because they could not have sex with women, or men who did have sex with cloistered nuns who were virtually the male clergy's sexual slaves. Shortly before he recounts the story about Gregory, Bale tells of a large group of women who joined a pilgrimage only to find that they had been taken from England to be forced to prostitute themselves to the clergy on the Continent (21a).

In leading up to his account of the boys, Bale followed Geoffrey of Monmouth, who embroidered Gildas's account into a claim that sodomy was pervasive among the early Britons, practiced by two of their kings (Malgo and Mempricius) and the cause of their overthrow by the Saxons. Gildas's version contains no hint of sexual slander, as we saw in chapter 5. Bale wrote that Malgo, who was possibly fashioned on William Rufus, was "the most comelye persone of all hys regyon," someone to whom God had given great victories against the "Saxons, Normeies, and Danes." But he was a sodomite. He imitated the ways of his predecessor Mempricius, who was "geuen to most abhomynable sodometrye, which he had lerned in hys youthe of the consecrate chastyte of the holie clergye" (21b-22a).[28] Thus the British were weak and were easily conquered by the Saxons. Bale believed that Roman Christianity entered England with the Saxons, who renamed the land England. "Then came therein a newe fashyoned christyanyte yet ones agayne from Rome with many more heythnysh yokes than afore." Bale then immediately introduced

Gregory and told the story about the boys (22a-b, a section entitled "The Saxons entre with newe Christyanyte").

Elsewhere Bale underscored the charges of sodomy among Catholic clergy made in *The Image of Both Churches*. In his *Apology against a Rank Papist* (1550), Bale asked, "Whan the kynges grace of England by the autorite of Gods wurd, discharged the monkish sectes of his realme, from their vowed obedience to the byshop of Rome, did he not also discharge them in conscience of the vowe of Sodometry, whyche altogether made them Antichristes creatures?"[29] Catholic clergy had set marriage and virginity "at variance" and replaced them with "two unhappy gestes, called whoredom and buggery."[29] In *The Pageant of Popes*, published in 1574 (after Bale's death), Bale recounted visitations to monasteries ordered by Henry VIII, which found "such swarmes of whoremongers, ruffians, filthie parsouns, giltye of sinne against nature, Ganimedes, and yet votaries and unmaryed all, so that thou wouldest thincke that there were a newer Gomorrah amonge them." At Battle Abbey, according to Bale, there were nearly twenty "gilty of sinne against nature" (their crimes included bigamy and adultery); at Canterbury there were eleven.[30] *The Pageant of Popes* shows that Bale saw another side to Gregory, casting him as the creator of a policy opposing clerical celibacy (no one could ever accuse Bale of consistency). Gregory was informed that priests "accompanied not only with virgins and wyves, but also even with their owne kindred, with mankind, yea and that whiche is horrible to be sayde, with brute beastes." ("Accompanied" is an obsolete euphemism for "cohabit with," according to the *OED*. Note that Bale regards bestiality as worse than same-sex acts.) Appalled at this conduct, Gregory revoked the canon requiring that priests not marry.[31] Gregory was given credit for being "the best man of all these Romaine Patriarkes, for learning and good life," and Bale praised his humility and his learning.[32]

Like many polemicists, Bale was an idealist. His attack on the Roman clergy can be explained by his high regard for marriage and his ardent defense of women's position. When he was a Carmelite priest, in the 1520s, Bale carried out extensive research into Carmelite archives and took special interest in the Church's view of women, in part at least because of his interest in Mary, the patron of the Carmelite order.[33] His recruitment to the Church of England came in the 1530s, when he lived in London and could see the drastic impact of Henry's marriage and decrees on all monastic orders, including his own. It was also at this time—in 1536—that Bale married, and undoubtedly this change in his life fueled his polemics about the Roman Church's demand for clerical celibacy.[34] Bale identified the ideal of marriage for the clergy as an Anglo-Saxon custom that had been brought to an end with the Norman Conquest. "I omit to declare for lengthe of the matter," he wrote in *Apology against a Rank Papist* (xiii), "what mischefe and confusion, vowes [vows] brought to this realme by the Danes and Normannes, whan the lyves of the vowers in

their monasteries were more beastlye than eyther amonge paganes or Turkes." Bale, who was unaware that the Danes were not Christian, believed that the monks and clergymen, once forced to give up wives, turned to "bestlye" lives worse than those lived by pagans or Turks. In other words, he thought they had become sodomites.

Sodomy also figured in Bale's plays, his best known works. In *A Comedy concernynge Thre Lawes, of Nature, Moses, & Christ, Corrupted by the Sodomytes, Pharysees, and Papystes* (1538), written before the historical studies just sampled, Bale created a character named Sodomismus, an allegorical figure unique in sixteenth-century English drama.[35] Sodomismus is one of six vice characters in the play. Attired "lyke a monke of all sectes," according to Bale,[36] Sodomismus repeatedly associates himself with both monks and the pope.

> I dwelt amonge the Sodomytes,
> The Benjamytes and Madyantes
> And now the popish hypocrytes
>   Embrace me every where.
> I am now become all spyrytuall [i.e., taken over by spiritual leaders],[37]
> For the clergye at Rome and over all
> For want of wyves, to me doth fall,
>   To God they have no feare.
>
>   (2:571-78)

Pederastic unions are listed among the forms of sodomy he promotes.

> In Rome to me they fall,
> Both byshopp and cardynall,
> Monke, fryre, prest and all,
>   More ranke they are than antes.
> Example in Pope Julye,
> Whych sought to have in hys furye
> Two laddes, and to use them beastlye,
>   From the Cardinall of Nantes.
>
>   (2:643-50)

Had he known about Gregory's letter to Candidus, Bale would have had an even more pertinent example of how a Roman pope allegedly abused innocent boys.

In *King Johan*, which casts the king as an opponent of clerical corruption, the king speaks for Bale's position. Johan (King John) regrets that the clergy

> Shuld thus bynd yowre selfe to the grett captyvyte
> Of blody Babulon the grownd and mother of whordom—
> The Romych Churche I meane, more vyle than ever was Sodom.[38]

For Bale, "sodomites" were not only the unjust and impious but also those who turned from the lawful union of marriage and had illicit intercourse either with the opposite sex or with their own. In *A Comedy concernynge Thre Lawes*, Sodomismus claims to have inspired all manner of sexual sinners, ranging from the fallen angels who fornicated with the daughters of men (Genesis 6:1-4) to Onan (Genesis 38:9; see *A Comedy*, 580-610). The offense that seems most closely connected to sodomy in Bale's mind is idolatry, represented in the play as Idolatria, an old woman. Idolatria is the companion of Sodomismus, who speaks to her in terms of endearment, calling her "myne owne swetehart of golde" (481). Sodomismus is sexually profligate, not exclusively or even primarily interested in same-sex intercourse. His accusations against monks and popes, however, conform precisely to those Bale himself made in his nondramatic works.

The inference that Bale had accused Gregory of sodomy was drawn by Bale's Catholic opponent, who recognized the unacknowledged source of Bale's story in Bede's *Ecclesiastical History*. In 1565, in the first translation of Bede's *Ecclesiastical History* in modern English, Thomas Stapleton listed "a number of diuersities between the pretended religion of Protestants, and the primitive faith of the english Church" (he counted forty-five points of difference in all). Stapleton contrasted the authority of Bede, who wrote without prejudice, with that of Bale, Foxe, and other "pretended refourmers." Stapleton discussed the episode involving Gregory and the Anglian boys in his preface. Bede, who was close to this event, had told a story contrasting outer beauty with inner lack of belief. Bale had deliberately misread the event in order to charge Gregory "with a most outrageous vice and not to be named." Stapleton obviously understood Bale to have accused Gregory of sodomy. Bede was a bee who made honey (beautiful meaning) out of this episode, said Stapleton, but Bale was a "venimous spider being filthy and uncleane himself," an "olde ribauld," and "another Nero" who found "poisonned sence and meaning" therein.[39]

To be fair, Bale's interpretation, admittedly harsh, is somewhat better than Stapleton allowed. Bale forces us to reconsider Bede's treatment of the anecdote and calls our attention to its dark side, its shadow. The episode about Gregory and the boys is animated by the contrast between light and dark, outside and inside. Gregory calls Satan "the author of darkness" who holds "men so bright of face in his grip." He finds the Anglians "devoid of inward grace" while admiring their "graceful . . . outward form[s]." Gregory's language clearly recognizes that physical and moral beauty exist in close proximity to the evil and the ugly. Bede did not look beyond Gregory's words for these malignant forces. Instead he saw the brightness of the episode, which marked the "Angli" as a people elevated by their likeness, at least in Gregory's mind, to angels. Bale saw around Gregory's words and, like Gregory himself, recognized how near evil was to the good. But Bale reversed the field of Gregory's vision, casting Gregory into the darkness where Gregory himself saw Satan. What lived in that darkness was same-sex desire, the unholy appetite of Gregory and other reluctant celibates for the sexual favors of young Englishmen. Such shadows, dark places of evil and corruption, are not the only kind of shadows

where same-sex relations can be seen. They are not the kinds of shadows I think of when I think of the presence of same-sex love in a heterosexual world. All the same, Bale's vision of the shadow, however distasteful it might seem, is, in context, accurate. The sexual abuse of young boys was a danger to which life in the monastery exposed them, as the penitentials show. Slavery was another danger, not unrelated, that lurked in the episode Bede describes. It is difficult to deny that the shadows seen by Bale are places where "the author of darkness," as Gregory called him, held sway.

Bale's recasting of Anglo-Saxon history had a prominent sexual aspect, if not a primary sexual character. He saw the Anglo-Saxons as a people who naturally observed God's lawful commandment to be fruitful and multiply. Their Roman oppressors, on the other hand, were those who denied clergy the right to marry and, as a result, spread sexual corruption wherever they were to be found. Gregory's "wele eyenge" of the slave boys' "wares" vividly emblematizes this exploitation and situates it in the heart of Rome. For Bale, Anglo-Saxon identity was continuous with British identity that predated the arrival of the Anglo-Saxons. English identity emerged out of this combined British-Anglo-Saxon identity in a struggle against the enslaving bonds of Roman and then Norman domination. Racial differences are but vaguely registered by Bale, and his chronology, not unexpectedly, is confused. Malgo won victories over "Saxons, Normeies, and Danes," for example, even though it was the Saxons who subverted the realm (22a). Bale's historical discourse, punctuated with numerous references to Sodom and allegations of homosexual acts among the clergy, is entirely free of allegory (his plays, obviously, are not). Bale did not need a figurative discourse about angels or origins to celebrate what was, for him, the distinguishing feature of his sources. His sense of who was Saxon, Norman, or Dane was imprecise, but Bale unquestionably understood that Gildas, Bede, Geoffrey of Monmouth, Chaucer, and others, were not mythical figures but were instead his predecessors, righteous as he was himself.[40] He was sure that the history he chronicled was as English as he was. His association of corrupt sexual practices with foreign powers—Roman and Catholic especially—is therefore easily explained, however disagreeable we find it. His polemical use of sodomy strongly resembles that of the Anglo-Norman historians and chroniclers on whose work he drew. But whereas they directed their diatribes against their own princes and rulers, Bale directed his at the princes of the Catholic Church. Among their agents he numbered the Norman conquerors of England, the despoilers of the True Church of the British.

ANGELS AND ANGLI

Another polemicist and dramatist with a vague sense of the Anglo-Saxon past and strong views on its significance is Tony Kushner. His celebrated two-part drama, *Angels in*

America: A Gay Fantasia on National Themes, approaches the Anglo-Saxons through the stereotype of the WASP. Kushner correlates same-sex relations with racial stereotypes and national heritage and makes revealing use of Anglo-Saxon culture that is seldom noticed by the play's admirers. Kushner's AIDS-infected hero is the play's only WASP, the thirty-second Prior Walter in a line traced to the Norman Conquest so that it can represent the Anglo-Saxon hegemony of the West. But *Angels* reverses a dynamic that operates in all the other texts I have examined throughout this study. Anglo-Saxon penitentials, histories, poems, and commentaries ultimately side with the angels. And so, for that matter, do Chaucer and Bale, Custance being Chaucer's angel, the English boys being Bede's and Bale's. Angels are pure, either above sex or, if involved with sexual relations, chastely married; they are on the side of order. Sodomites, however they have been defined, are not. They and same-sex relations are stigmatized and repressed because they subvert order, lack shame, and threaten to lead others into sin.

In order to express Kushner's millennial vision, *Angels in America* rewrites the social history of England (and America) in order to enable a new era in which same-sex relations thrive while heterosexual relations wither. Kushner does not take the side of the angels but rather represents them as weak, lost, and prejudiced. Amid their confusion, paradoxically, their saving grace is that they retain their sexual prowess. The Angel of America, as she will be known, enters the play as a messenger to a white, Anglo-Saxon, Protestant but exits taking advice because the WASP is also a PWA, a "person with AIDS," prophet of a new homosocial order and herald of a revolution so sweeping that it offers redemption even for angels.

Rich in references to migratory voyages and the Chosen People, *Angels in America* advances a broad argument about history and progress. The play is a multicultural juxtaposition of WASP, Jewish, black, and Mormon traditions, among others. David Savran has argued that the "spiritual geography" of Mormonism is central to the play's "conceptualization of America as the site of a blessed past and a millennial future." Savran demonstrates that Mormonism was among the evangelical, communitarian sects formed in reaction to the individualism fostered by Jacksonian democracy and the ideology of Manifest Destiny.[41] A key element in the racial basis of Manifest Destiny, which claimed for the chosen people "a preeminent social worth, a distinctively lofty mission, and consequently unique rights in the application of moral principles,"[42] is Anglo-Saxonism. The premise of Anglo-Saxonism (familiar in earlier forms in the works of Gildas, Bede, Chaucer, and Bale, as we have seen, and many others, of course) is that the English are a Chosen People and a superior race.[43] Numerous nineteenth-century accounts used the racial purity of the Anglo-Saxons to justify westward expansion and empire building. Anglo-Saxon culture was thought to have been inherently democratic and the Anglo-Saxons

egalitarian, self-governing, and free. The descendants of a people who so perfectly embodied the principles of American democracy had, it appeared, natural rights over lesser peoples and their lands. Anglo-Saxonism enters *Angels in America* through the lineage of Prior Walter. He is a token of the WASP culture—the only white Anglo-Saxon Protestant in the play, according to Kushner[44]—against which the oppressed peoples of the play, Jews and blacks in particular, strive.

The Anglo-Saxon subtext of *Angels* emerges in both parts of the drama, *Millennium Approaches* and *Perestroika,* through the association of Prior Walter with the angel. Kushner locates Prior's origins in the mid-eleventh century, but the Anglo-Saxon characteristics that Prior represents are prior to the Normans, whose conquest of England constitutes a particularly troubled originary moment for the chief Anglo-Saxon of the play. An early scene in each of the three acts of *Millennium Approaches* reveals something about Prior's Anglo-Saxon identity (act 1, scene 4; act 2, scene 3; and act 3, scene 1). In the first of the scenes about his lineage, Prior jokes with Louis, his Jewish lover, after a funeral service for Louis's grandmother. Prior comments on the difficulties that their relatives present for gay men: "Bloodlines," he says. "Jewish curses are the worst. I personally would dissolve if anyone ever looked me in the eye and said 'Feh.' Fortunately WASPs don't say 'Feh'" (**1** [*Millennium Approaches*]:20).[45] A few moments later he reveals his first AIDS lesions to Louis, who is horrified both by the lesions and by Prior's mordant jocularity about them. This scene establishes Prior's AIDS status and his WASP identity and introduces the largest of the cultural themes of *Angels in America*: the resistance that biological descent and inherited tradition, embodied here in the body of the WASP, pose to political change. Bloodlines are curses because they carry the past into the present, creating resistance to the possibilities of change that the present raises. WASP blood resists change because WASPs, as they are presented in this play, exist in a culture of stasis, while other races and creeds, denied that stability and permanence and driven by persecution and need from place to place, have developed migratory and transitional cultures open to, and indeed dependent on, change.

Having inherited a distinguished past, Prior faces an uncharacteristically grim future (for a WASP) because he carries a fatal new element in his bloodline, AIDS. The virus paradoxically reverses the deadening flow of WASP tradition and prepares for a new social order whose values the WASP himself will eventually espouse. The virus he bears is both literal (HIV) and figurative; it is eventually identified as "the virus of time," the "disease" of change and progress. The angel who appears to Prior at the end of *Millennium Approaches,* and who punctuates the play with intimations of her arrival, claims to herald a new age. When Prior receives his first intimation of the angelic, a feather drops into his room and an angelic voice ("an incredibly beautiful voice," the text specifies) commands,

"Look up! ... Prepare the way!" (**1**:34-35). But the side of the angels is not what we expect it to be. The angel is not pointing to a new age but instead calling for a return to a previous one. The tradition and stasis that constitute Prior's Anglo-Saxon heritage draw her. She believes that Prior will be a worthy prophet precisely because he is a worthy WASP.

Kushner happened on Prior's name when looking "for one of those WASP names that nobody gets called any more." Discussing Walter Benjamin with a friend so interested in the philosopher that she sometimes "thought she was Walter Benjamin reincarnated," Kushner referred to the real Benjamin as the "prior" Walter.[46] The significance of Prior's name unfolds in a subsequent dialogue between Louis and Emily, a nurse, after Prior has been hospitalized. "Weird name. Prior Walter," says Emily. "Like, 'The Walter before this one.'" Louis replies: "Lots of Walters before this one. Prior is an old old family name in an old old family. The Walters go back to the Mayflower and beyond. Back to the Norman Conquest. He says there's a Prior Walter stitched into the Bayeux tapestry" (**1**:51). The oldest medieval record mentioned in *Angels in America,* the tapestry would seem designed to surround Prior's origins with an aura of great antiquity.

The appearance of Prior Walter's name on the tapestry validates Louis's claim that the Walter name is indeed an "old old" one. But the Bayeux tapestry is a record of the political and military events surrounding the Norman Conquest of Anglo-Saxon England in 1066. The tapestry testifies to the subjugation of the Anglo-Saxons and marks the point at which the government and official vernacular language of England were no longer English. Generations of Anglo-Saxonizing historians and writers regarded the arrival of the Normans as the pollution of the pure stock of the race.[47] Thus Kushner's announced aim of portraying Walter as a WASP is more than a little complicated by this decision to trace Walter's ancestry to a tapestry long accepted as a lucid statement of Norman claims to the English throne.[48] Notoriously ironic throughout *Angels in America,* Kushner might have chosen the tapestry to register precisely this compromised aspect of Prior's lineage.[49] But one's view of that lineage would seem to depend on the uses to which it is put in *Angels in America,* where it seems intended to represent the Anglo-Saxons as a monolithic, triumphant culture that has reached a symbolic end point in Prior's blood.

Emily (played by the actress who plays the angel) is somewhat baffled by Louis's high regard for Prior's ancient name and for the tapestry itself. Louis believes that the queen, "La Reine Mathilde," embroidered the tapestry while William was away fighting the English. In the long tradition of French historians and politicians who used the tapestry to arouse public sentiment to support nationalistic causes, including the Napoleonic wars against the English,[50] Louis pictures Mathilda waiting at home, "stitch[ing] for years,"

waiting for William to return. "And if he had returned mutilated, ugly, full of infection and horror, she would still have loved him," Louis says (**1**:52). He is thinking penitently of Prior, who is also "full of infection and horror," whom Louis will soon abandon for Joe, the married Mormon lawyer with whom Louis has an affair. Louis's view of when and where the tapestry was made is popular, but wrong. The tapestry was made in England, under the patronage of William's half-brother Odo, bishop of Bayeux and vice-regent of England, within a generation of 1066, not during the Conquest itself, and then taken to the Bayeux Cathedral.[51]

Kushner's mistaken ideas of when, where, and by whom the Bayeux tapestry was made have significant implications for his definition of "WASP." Kushner invokes the Conquest as if its chief force were to certify the antiquity and authenticity of Prior's Anglo-Saxon credentials and heritage, a point of origin for *English* identity, although, as I have shown, it traditionally represented the very betrayal of the racial purity that "Anglo-Saxon" came to represent. Louis's assertion that the name of a "Prior Walter" is stitched into the tapestry is also without foundation. Only four minor characters are named in the tapestry, none of them Anglo-Saxons ("Turold," "Ælfgyva," "Wadard," and "Vital"). The rest are important figures (Harold, William, and others), most of them Norman and well-known from contemporary sources.[52] If Prior Walter were an Anglo-Saxon, it is highly unlikely that he would be commemorated in the tapestry, although it is possible he could have been an English retainer of Harold (who was defeated by William).

But "Prior Walter" is a singularly inappropriate name for an Anglo-Saxon. It strongly suggests an ecclesiastical, monastic context, as if "Prior Walter" were "Walter, prior of" some abbey, instead of the secular and heroic ethos usually called to mind by "Anglo-Saxon." Apart from the tapestry, there is no evidence either for or against an argument about Prior's origins. Although it is possible that his ancestors were Anglo-Saxon, it is more likely that they were Normans who, after the Conquest, settled in England and established the line from which the Walters descended. Few Anglo-Saxons would expect to find their ancestors mentioned in the tapestry, while Normans would want to boast of this testimony to a family's distinguished history. The original Prior Walter might have been a Norman who took part in the conquest of the English. His family would have been prosperous. As we saw in the last chapter, the Anglo-Saxons were less well-to-do than their conquerors and resented the superiority of French into the fourteenth century. If so, as the last in a line of thirty-one men of the same name (or, by an alternative count, if bastard sons are included, thirty-three [**1**:86]), Prior Walter claims Norman rather than Anglo-Saxon ancestry, or, more likely, a heritage in which Norman and Anglo-Saxon blood is mixed—in other words, Anglo-Norman. His long genealogy, to which Louis proudly points, is hybrid at its origins. Kushner's stereotype of the WASP is itself a further hybrid, obviously, since it is a post-Reformation construct in which P ("Protestant") is a new element. WASP, we can see, is not only a recent vehicle for the representation of "Anglo-Saxon" culture, but an exceedingly shallow one.[53]

We learn more about Prior's ancestry at the start of the third act, when two prior Priors appear to him in a dream (**1**:85-89). The first to appear, the "fifth of the name," is the thirteenth-century squire who is known as "Prior 1." He tells of the plague that wiped out whole villages, the "spotty monster" that killed him (**1**:86). (This is another sign of Kushner's shaky historical sense; the first outbreak of the Black Death in England was a century later, in 1348.)[54] They are joined by "Prior 2," described as "an elegant 17th-century Londoner" (**1**:86), who preceded the current Prior by some seventeen others and also died of the plague, "Black Jack." Priors 1 and 2 are not merely ancient ancestors, however. They are also the forerunners of the angel whose arrival spectacularly concludes the play. To "distant, glorious music," they recite the language later used by the angel; her messengers, they are "sent to declare her fabulous incipience." "They [the angels] chose us," Prior 2 declares, "because of the mortal affinities. In a family as long-descended as the Walters there are bound to be a few carried off by plague" (**1**:87). Neither Prior 1 nor Prior 2 understands why Prior is unmarried and has no wife, although the second Prior understands that the plague infecting Prior is "the lamentable consequence of venery" (**1**:87). Only later, when they see him dancing with Louis, does Prior 1 understand: "Hah. Now I see why he's got no children. He's a sodomite" (**1**:114). Prior Walter is, therefore, the end of his line. After him the WASP hegemony of the Walters, apparently unbroken from the mid-eleventh century to the present, will cease to exist.

The vague and portentous sense of these genealogical relations is clarified in the next scene (**1**:89-96), in which Louis engages in a long, confused, and painfully naïve monologue about race and identity politics in America, much to the disgust of his friend Belize, a black nurse and ex-drag queen.[55] Louis describes a difference between American and European peoples that encapsulates the tension between Anglo-Saxons and other races. "Ultimately what defines us [in America] isn't race, but politics," he says. "Not like any European country where there's an insurmountable fact of a kind of racial, or ethnic, monopoly, or monolith, like all Dutchmen, I mean Dutch people, are, well, Dutch, and the Jews of Europe were never Europeans, just a small problem" (**1**:90). Significantly, Kushner chooses England as site for a scene in which, according to Louis, the "racial destiny," not the "political destiny," matters (**1**:91). A Jew in a gay bar in London, Louis found himself looked down upon by a Jamaican man who still spoke with a "lilt," even though his family had been in England for more than a century. At first this man, who complained that he was still treated as an outsider, struck Louis as a fellow traveler: "I said yeah, me too, these people

are anti-Semites." But then the man criticized British Jews for keeping blacks out of the clothing business, and Louis realized how pervasive racial stereotypes could be (**1**:91). In America, Louis believes, there is no racial monopoly; in America the "monolith is missing," so "reaching out for a spiritual past in a country where no indigenous spirits exist" is futile (**1**:92). The native peoples have been killed off: "there are no angels in America, no spiritual past, no racial past, there's only the political and the decoys and the ploys to maneuver around the inescapable battle of politics, the shifting downwards and outwards of political power to the people" (**1**:92). Wiped clean of its indigenous spirits, the nation as Louis sees it would seem to be a blank slate not unlike England before the Anglo-Saxons, ready for migratory peoples (including Jews and Mormons) who bring their past with them as they seek to build a new future. Belize holds Louis's liberal interpretation of American government and culture in utter contempt. Kushner ensures that the naiveté of the Jew's liberalism will be exposed and contained by Belize's furious reply that in America race is more important than anything else.

Louis's speech reveals the meaning of Anglo-Saxon that is encapsulated in Prior's WASP identity. Even though Prior's mixed Norman and Anglo-Saxon genealogy contradicts Louis's point about the monolith of racial purity that the WASP supposedly represents, Prior is singled out as the recipient of the angel's visit because he is made to represent the cultural monolith of WASP America, fixed and unchanging, embodying what Louis calls "an insurmountable fact of a kind of racial, or ethnic, monopoly, or monolith" (**1**:90). WASP heritage stands conveniently juxtaposed both to Louis's vision and to Louis's own heritage of many small groups, "so many small problems" (**1**:90). Although Kushner might have wished to represent the Anglo-Saxons only as a hybrid people, and hence introduced evidence that points to the eleventh-century intermingling of Norman blood, it seems evident to me that the racial dynamics of the play require that the Anglo-Saxons represent the "monolith" about which Louis speaks. Only then can other races and groups be set up in opposition to them.

Indeed, even in motion, the Anglo-Saxons of *Angels in America* are oppressors. One of the most harrowing moments in *Millennium Approaches* is Prior's account of his ancestor, a ship's captain, who sent whale oil to Europe and brought back immigrants, "Irish mostly, packed in tight, so many dollars per head." The last ship he captained sank off Nova Scotia in a storm; the crew loaded seventy women and children onto an open boat but found that it was overcrowded and began throwing passengers overboard: "They walked up and down the longboat, eyes to the waterline, and when the boat rode low in the water they'd grab the nearest passenger and throw them into the sea" (**1**:41). The boat arrived in Halifax carrying nine people. Crewmen are the captain's agents; the captain is at the bottom of the sea, but his "implacable, unsmiling men, irresistibly strong, seize . . . maybe the person next to you, maybe you"

(**1**:41-42). The agents of the Anglo-Saxons arbitrarily decide the fates of the Irish in their care. The episode is a stark political allegory, a nationally rendered reminder of the rights of one group to survive at the expense of another, a deft miniature that reveals the power of the conquerors over the conquered, the interrelation of commerce and the immigration patterns of impoverished nations, and, most of all, "unique rights in the application of moral principles," a signature belief of Manifest Destiny.[56]

The point of the association of stasis with Anglo-Saxon heritage—the grand design of *Angels in America*—emerges fully in *Perestroika,* when the Angel of America articulates her ambitions for the WASP and discloses the assumed affiliations between the Anglo-Saxons and the angels. The angel attempts to persuade Prior to take up her prophecy. "I I I I / Am the Bird of America," she proclaims, saying that she has come to expose the fallacy of change and progress (**2** [*Perestroika*]:44), "the Virus of TIME" that God released in man (**2**:49), enabling humans to explore and migrate. Angels do not migrate; instead, they stand firm (**2**:49). God himself found time irresistible and began to prefer human time to life in heaven. The angel says:

> Paradise itself Shivers and Splits
> Each day when You awake, as though WE are only the
>   Dream of YOU.
> PROGRESS! MOVEMENT!
> Shaking *HIM.*
>
> (**2**:50)

A few moments later she shouts, "*YOU HAVE DRIVEN HIM AWAY! YOU MUST STOP MOVING!*" (**2**:52). God became so bored with the angels that he abandoned them on the day of the 1906 San Francisco earthquake. And who could blame him? In the one scene that Kushner gives performers the permission to cut, if only in part (act 5, scene 5; see **2**:9), the angels are shown sitting around heaven listening to a malfunctioning 1940s radio over which they hear the broadcast of the meltdown of the Chernobyl reactor. Their real concern, however, is the radio's malfunctioning vacuum tube (**2**:130). They are a picture of feckless paralysis, obviously unable to respond to the changes forced on them by human or heavenly time. "More nightmare than utopia, marooned in history," Savran writes, "Heaven commemorates disaster, despair, and stasis."[57] The purpose of the angel's visitation is to recruit Prior as the angels' prophet on earth. Angels, we see, are not messengers from the divine or heralds of change, although that is how we conventionally think of them, and how Kushner and the play's publicity represent them. Angels are instead associated with stasis and with the power of ancient spirits to resist change. Opposed to the flow of power "downward and outward," as Louis puts it, of "power to the people," the angels want God to return to his place so that they can return to theirs.

The angel's visit is not intended to save Prior from his disease but to use his disease against him, to try to persuade this "long descended" man (like the angel in this) to stop the phenomenon of human progress, to get him to turn back the clock. The angel says to him that she has written "The End" in his blood. This could mean that the AIDS virus is supposed to ensure his desire to stop time—stop the progress of the disease—and prompt him to proclaim her message (**2**:53), although what is written in his blood could also be his homosexuality, which writes "The End" in a different sense, since it means that he is the last of his line. Later in the scene in which the angel commands Prior to stand still, symbolically appealing to his Anglo-Saxon love of stability and tradition, Belize dismisses the vision as Prior recounts it: "This is just you, Prior, afraid of the future, afraid of time. Longing to go backwards so bad you made this angel up, a cosmic reactionary" (**2**:55). Prior and Belize were once lovers; Belize knows him well. Like Prior, three other figures—the angel, Sister Ella Chapter (a friend of Joe's mother in Salt Lake City), and the nurse (all played by the actress who plays the angel)—are fearful of movement. Emily does not want Louis to leave the hospital room (**1**:52). Before Joe's mother moves to New York to help Joe cope with his schizophrenic wife, Harper, Ella reminds her that Salt Lake City is "the home of the saints" and "the godliest place on earth," and then cautions, "Every step a Believer takes away from here is a step fraught with peril" (**1**:83). But Ella's is not a view that the play endorses. Joe's mother leaves anyway. All the chosen people do.

Like her, Prior rejects the advice to stay put. He ignores the angel's command precisely because "The End" is written in his blood. He interprets these words as the angel's wish that he die: "You want me dead" (**2**:53). No longer the Prior who joked fatalistically about his lesions outside the funeral home in act 1 of *Millennium Approaches,* he refuses to die. Because he has contracted "the virus of time," the WASP, who has the most to lose, turns from the past to the future. All the "good" characters in the play are already on the move, already evolving, even Joe's drug-maddened wife, just as all the valorized nations and races in the play have migrated. The prominence of migration and the movement away from racial purity are basic elements of Kushner's thesis about change, which is based on an idea of the Anglo-Saxons, the WASPS, as static, permanent, and fixed. Politics change racial makeup and break down pure races and their racism. Kushner explains:

> Prior is the only character in the play with a Yankee WASP background; he can trace his lineage back for centuries, something most Americans can't reliably do. African-American family trees have to start after ancestors were brought over as slaves. Jews emigrated from a world nearly completely destroyed by European genocide. And most immigrant populations have been from poor and oppressed communities among which accurate genealogy was a luxury or an impossibility. ... a certain sense of rootlessness is part of the American character.[58]

Anglo-Saxon history prior to the Normans shows that "a certain sense of rootlessness" is also part of the Anglo-

Saxon character. American rootlessness was inherited from the nation's Anglo-Saxon founders; the Anglo-Saxons in America were hardly a people who wanted to stay put. It is because of their restlessness and their desire to move westward that Louis, as Kushner's surrogate, can assert that there are no angels in America.[59]

Kushner's association of WASPs with stasis is his most interesting—but least accurate—reinterpretation of the historical record. Kushner seems to think that Anglo-Saxons—WASPs at least—are not a migratory people. At this point his play helps us see a truth in Bede's *Ecclesiastical History* that Bede himself did not acknowledge. Bede reported that after the migration of the Angles to Britain, the land of "Angulus" remained empty "from that day to this." Are there no angels in America? There are no angels in Angulus, either, because the entire population moved to Britain. Thus the Angles took *their* ancient spirits with them, just as did blacks, Jews, and other migrant peoples. Already in the eighth century the immigrants to Britain were known as Anglo-Saxons.[60]

Louis's tendentious view of history is easily discredited, and not only by Belize. The intermarrying of Anglo-Saxon and Norman families ended the pure monolith of "the English" that Prior Walter supposedly represents. What is true of Prior Walter and all WASPS was true for people in England even before the Conquest. "Apartheid is hard enough to maintain," Susan Reynolds writes, "even when physical differences are obvious, political control is firm, and records of births, deaths, and marriages are kept. After a generation or two of post-Roman Britain not everyone, perhaps comparatively few people, can have been of pure native or invading descent. Who can have known who was descended from whom?" Reynolds draws the inescapable conclusion that "those whom we call Anglo-Saxons were not consistently distinguishable from everyone else."[61] After the Conquest, of course, the Anglo-Saxons became less "Anglo-Saxon" than they had been earlier, but at no time were bloodlines in Anglo-Saxon England pure; like most bloodlines, they were even then more the consequence of politics than they were of race.

This severing of biological descent and culture is a denial of the power of race to unify a people. That is the good news of *Angels in America* for homosexuals, the new Chosen People of this epic (what epic does not have one?). Like Mormons, Jews, and other racial groups, gay people too are oppressed, without a homeland, and on the move. But unlike those groups, gays are, first of all, a *political* people, not bound by nation or race. They have no common descent; there is no link between their sexual identity, which the play sees as their central affiliation, and either their biological or their cultural ancestry. So seen, gays serve as a perfect prophetic vehicle for Kushner's newly multicultural America. Prior succeeds in subverting the angels' design and persuading them to become his messenger; he has refused to become theirs. Their message is that the

clock should be turned back to old values and stasis, staying put. His message is that change is good. Won over to humanity's view of time and place, the angels sue God, resorting to time-bound human processes (litigation) to redress grievances. The joke apparently is that the angels' heavenly wishes are inferior to the desires of humanity. The new angels of America know better than the Angel of America because Prior, their WASP spokesman, resoundingly refutes the angel's call for stasis. God, however, will probably win; his lawyer is Roy Cohn, the demon in *Angels.* Discredited at this point, God is a disloyal lover who has abandoned his angels for (the men of?) San Francisco. The angels, in turn, are also discredited, for they have accepted Prior's suggestion that those who abandon their lovers should not be forgiven, just as Prior will not forgive or take back Louis (**2**:133, 136).

So Prior moves ahead, not in spite of AIDS but rather *because* of AIDS. The "virus of time" has jolted him out of torpor and self-pity and eventually transforms him into the play's strongest character, a position from which he waves an affectionate goodbye to the audience. This is an AIDS play with a difference—with a happy ending.[62] Because he is a WASP the angel singled him out, but because he is a PWA he rejects her. In *Angels in America,* AIDS retains its deadly force (Cohn and others die of it) without killing the play's central character. Obviously weakened, but strong nonetheless, Prior survives. Having been visited by an angel, Prior all but becomes one. "You are fabulous creatures, each and every one," he says to the audience. "And I bless you: *More Life.* The Great Work begins" (**2**:148). He recapitulates the last lines of *Millennium Approaches,* in which the Angel declares, "Greetings, Prophet. The Great Work begins. The Messenger has arrived" (**1**:119). Another messenger has arrived at the end of *Perestroika,* and his name is Prior Walter. Prior's farewell to the audience, however moving, is a remarkable banality to which I will return.

Savran argues that the play, like *The Book of Mormon,* "demonstrates that there are angels in America, that America is in essence a utopian and theological construction, a nation with a divine mission."[63] It is possible to suggest that Bede and Kushner share a political purpose, which is to create the idea of a unified people. Bede does this with the term—the concept—"Angli," which comes to mean "the English," a people elevated by their likeness to angels. Like Chaucer and Bale, Kushner is also out to unify a people, but more ambitiously and inclusively, and not a people to be compared to angels, but a people to replace them. The threat that unifies the English in Bede's work is the heathen past. The same might be said for Chaucer's ancient British Christians, at least as the Man of Law imagines them. Bale too imagined the British as overwhelmed by Roman Catholicism as brought by the Anglo-Saxons; he saw the British of his own time triumphing over the same evil force. The threat that unifies Kushner's new angels is not AIDS, which only menaces a small percentage of them, but the old regimes of race that divide and weaken people and prevent change, the very forces of conservative national and religious identity that Bede, Chaucer, and Bale advocated so powerfully. Those forces are routed at the end of *Angels in America,* and the boards are clear for a new age. The promised land of *Angels in America* is a multicultural, tolerant world in which biological descent counts for little (there are no successful marriages in the play) and cultural inheritance imparts defining characteristics to people without imposing barriers among them.

Millennium Approaches

I began thinking about this study in 1993, when I saw *Angels in America* for the first time. I was troubled by the conflation of Anglo-Saxon and Norman identities and unclear about how Kushner meant to align his vaguely sketched history of Prior's family with the play's sexual politics. It seemed obvious that he had merely used the WASP as a rhetorical trope and that he had not thought about the Anglo-Saxonism contained in that acronym or how Anglo-Saxonism might be related to his historical thesis about Mormons or, for that matter, angels in America. Kushner ignored the hybrid nature of WASP identity. Likewise, he missed the prominence of same-sex friendships in the nineteenth-century Mormon tradition. D. Michael Quinn has noted that Mormons, although sometimes seen as clannish and isolated, participated fully in what Quinn describes as the "extensive homocultural orientation among Americans generally" a century ago.[64] Same-sex relations, sexual and otherwise, figure prominently in the history of early Mormon leaders, male and female alike. Kushner's representation of the Mormons would lead one to believe otherwise, however, since his Mormons seem hardly aware that homosexuality exists.

In not knowing much about the Anglo-Saxons, Kushner shares a great deal with the authors I have examined in part 3 of this book. The Anglo-Norman chroniclers knew next to nothing about the Anglo-Saxons that they did not get from Bede's *Ecclesiastical History.* A few later writers, including thirteenth-century scholars, struggled to recover the Anglo-Saxons' language, but their efforts mostly reveal how quickly knowledge of the Anglo-Saxons' culture, even their ecclesiastical culture, had faded. Chaucer and his contemporaries knew even less, relying again on French chronicles to conjure images of the Anglo-Saxon past. For all his testy and repetitive declarations, Bale was closer than any of his predecessors to real knowledge of the Anglo-Saxons. Despite his errors and confusion, his knowledge of a continuous historical tradition and its sources shames both earlier and especially later efforts. The "scholarly recovery" of Anglo-Saxon language and texts advanced rapidly after Bale's time but did not, for many years, produce a representation of Anglo-Saxon culture any more accurate than his.

Kushner, unfortunately, did no better than the other authors I have named. I take *Angels in America* as a

reasonable, if regrettable, reflection on popular understanding of Anglo-Saxon culture. Kushner seems to be more respectful of Mormon traditions than of Anglo-Saxon traditions. The play contains a diorama portraying the Mormons' westward journey but nothing about the migration of the Anglo-Saxons (2:62-72). Mormon culture seems alien to him and hence multiculturally significant; its history needs to be recaptured and represented. WASP culture, evidently, is familiar and does not need to be elaborated. But at least in the extended historical sense that Kushner evokes through his use of the Bayeux tapestry, WASP culture too is alien to him. Its multicultural significance is ignored, homogenized into stereotypical patterns and ideas. Absent the oversimplified WASP, would *Angels in America* have had a culture to demonize and denounce?

Angels in America is unique among the works I have discussed in not taking the side of the angels. More important, it is also unique in its perspective on same-sex love. As I showed in part 1, it is possible to glimpse satisfying moments of same-sex love—if not same-sex sex—in opera and dance, and even in a few Anglo-Saxon narrative texts. Gays and lesbians hoping to find representations of love as they know it can find it in these works, sometimes at a small cost (i.e., closing our eyes at the opera), often at no cost. But when we go to *Angels in America,* we have no need to deprive our senses in any way. This is a work that, like many others, not only aims to show gays and lesbians what the author assumes we want to see but even blesses its audience for showing up. There are many differences between the power of such a work and that of *Dido and Aeneas,* as danced by Mark Morris, and the power of *Der Rosenkavalier,* with its use of the convention of the trouser role. The central difference, it seems to me, conforms to the difference between liberation and legitimation as approaches to gay and lesbian rights. Kushner and Morris liberate a same-sex perspective; they emphasize the sexual—the homosexual—in a transgressive manner. That is one way to see homosexual sensibility in the modern world, demanding its due. But finding same-sex love in works that are not about homosexual desire—for example, in operas using trouser roles—also legitimates same-sex love by pointing out that it can exist, plainly if unobtrusively, as the shadow of heteronormative desire.

The second time I saw *Angels in America* was New Year's Eve, 1995. My partner and I had bought tickets at a premium because the theater advertized a "party" to follow the performance, which concluded shortly before midnight. The "party" turned out to be glasses of cheap fizzy wine hurriedly passed out by staff members eager to clear the house. The cast reappeared to mock the management's fleecing of the audience and to lead us in "Auld Lang Syne," gracefully lifting the occasion above the circumstances provided for it. Shortly before midnight, in a light snowfall, we walked down a street filled with people who were rushing into bars and restaurants. It was a relief to board the train. The cars were also full—some couples, some groups, some singles, some straight, some gay—but oddly quiet, a capsule of greater Chicago heading to parties or to bed. Between one stop and another the new year arrived. The car's little communities acknowledged the moment without ceremony. Gay, straight, alone, together, we rode happily along. For me the calm—the indifference—made a welcome change from the excitement and intensity of the play and the hustle of the street. No angels crashed through the roof, no heterosexuals were chastised, no homosexuals turned into saints (or demons), no call to a great work of liberation sounded. This is all right, I thought to myself. This is how the millennium, Kushner's and any other, will come, and go.

That is also how I think same-sex love goes along in the world, how it works best for some of us at least—love that belongs in the picture, always there, an ever-present shadow. Political and social work will always be needed to win equal treatment for gays, lesbians, bisexuals, and others who make up sexual minority groups. But there are many ways in which that work can be undertaken. I know that many activists cannot see themselves resting until the difference between heterosexual and homosexual is obliterated and such institutions as marriage and the family are transformed and open partnerships and public sex become the new norms. These people see no reason why the institutions of heterosexual desire should be their institutions. Neither do I. Nor do I see why the institutions of homosexual desire should be mandated for all. My vision of same-sex love might seem tepid and diffuse, devoid of passion and revolutionary fervor, not queer enough. Perhaps it is. But I strongly believe that same-sex love cannot be reduced to genital sex, and I will always believe that life is more interesting, pleasurable, and meaningful if its erotic potential can be realized across a spectrum that includes but is not restricted to the sexual. A world that slowly gets used to that idea would seem a better home to me than any queer planet I have yet to see described.

Notes

1. See Robert P. Miller, ed., *Chaucer: Sources and Backgrounds* (New York: Oxford University Press, 1977), 484. On the narrator's many apostrophes, see the explanatory notes by Patricia J. Eberle in Geoffrey Chaucer, *The Riverside Chaucer,* ed. Larry D. Benson, 3d ed. (Boston: Houghton Mifflin, 1987), 856-58. Innocent's treatise was addressed to a deposed cardinal; Chaucer reported that he had translated this work himself. See the G Prologue to the *Legend of Good Women,* lines 414-15, in Benson, *Riverside Chaucer,* 600.

2. References to *The Man of Law's Tale* are given by line number from *Riverside Chaucer,* 89-103.

3. For an analysis of hagiographical tropes in *The Man of Law's Tale,* see Melissa M. Furrow, "The Man of Law's St. Custance: Sex and the Saeculum," *Chaucer Review* 24 (1990): 223-35.

4. Æthelburh was allowed to marry Edwin because he promised to allow her to worship as she wished and agreed to consider accepting her faith as his own. Eventually he did so, but only after letters to him and his wife from Pope Boniface and persuasions of other forms, including victory over his assailants, a vision, and the sage counsel of his wise men. See Bertram Colgrave and R. A. B. Mynors, eds. and trans., *Bede's Ecclesiastical History of the English People* (Oxford: Oxford University Press, 1969), book 2, where the saga of Edwin's conversion occupies chaps. 9-14, pp. 162-89.

5. Colgrave and Mynors, *Bede's Ecclesiastical History,* book 2, chap. 9, pp. 162-63.

6. Some of the Anglo-Saxon evidence discussed in this chapter appears in my essay "Bede and Bawdy Bale: Gregory the Great, Angels, and the 'Angli,'" in *Anglo-Saxonism and the Construction of Social Identity,* ed. Allen J. Frantzen and John D. Niles (Gainesville: University of Florida Press, 1997), 17-39.

7. Colgrave and Mynors, *Bede's Ecclesiastical History,* book 2, chap. 1, pp. 132-35. Gregory's puns were not original with Bede; a version of the story is found the anonymous Whitby *Life of St. Gregory,* probably written between 704 and 714 but unknown to Bede when he finished the *Ecclesiastical History* in 731. See Bertram Colgrave, ed. and trans., *The Earliest Life of Gregory the Great* (Cambridge: Cambridge University Press, 1985), 49, 144-45.

8. Gildas, *The Ruin of Britain and Other Documents,* ed. and trans. Michael Winterbottom (London: Phillimore, 1978). See Nicholas Howe, *Migration and Myth-Making in Anglo-Saxon England* (New Haven: Yale University Press, 1989), 33-49, for a discussion of Gildas and the pattern of prophetic history.

9. Colgrave, *Earliest Life,* 144-45 note 42. See "Angles" and variants in the index to Colgrave and Mynors, *Bede's Ecclesiastical History,* 596. Recent studies on the meaning of "angli" in Bede's *Ecclesiastical History* do not discuss Gregory's role in choosing the name, presumably because it is seen as merely symbolic. See D. P. Kirby, *The Earliest English Kings* (London: Unwin Hyman, 1991), 13-15; and H. E. J. Cowdrey, "Bede and the 'English People,'" *Journal of Religious History* 11 (1981): 501-23. See also Patrick Wormald, "Bede, the *Bretwaldas,* and the Origins of the *Gens Anglorum,*" in *Ideal and Reality in Frankish and Anglo-Saxon Society,* ed. Patrick Wormald with Donald Bullough and Roger Collins (Oxford: Basil Blackwell, 1983), 121-24.

10. Colgrave and Mynors, *Bede's Ecclesiastical History,* book 1, chap. 15, p. 51. For an analysis of the ethnography operating in Bede's analysis, see John Hines, "The Becoming of the English: Identity, Material Culture, and Language in Early Anglo-Saxon England," *Anglo-Saxon Studies in Archaeology and History* 7 (1994): 49-59.

11. Colgrave and Mynors, *Bede's Ecclesiastical History,* book 5, chap. 24, pp. 566-67. Although Bede clearly wished to present the Angles (the angels) as the primary group in the migration, there was never a consensus about which group, the Angles or the Saxons, was primary, or even about where in England they settled. D. P. Kirby notes that Gregory believed that the Saxons settled in the north and the Angles in the south, reversing the usual assumptions about the pattern of distribution and pointing to its arbitrary nature. The *Life* of Wilfrid, who came from York, describes him as a Saxon bishop. See Kirby, *Earliest English Kings,* 12-13.

12. Colgrave and Mynors, *Bede's Ecclesiastical History,* preface, 2-3.

13. Peter Hunter Blair, *The World of Bede* (Cambridge: Cambridge University Press, 1970), 45. See also Hunter Blair, *An Introduction to Anglo-Saxon England* (Cambridge: Cambridge University Press, 1956), 116-17.

14. Colgrave and Mynors, *Bede's Ecclesiastical History,* 72 note 1; the letter is found in Arthur West Haddan and William Stubbs, eds., *Councils and Ecclesiastical Documents Relating to Great Britain and Ireland,* 3 vols. (Oxford: Clarendon, 1871), 3:5 (quoted here), and is translated in Dorothy Whitelock, ed., *English Historical Documents, c. 500-1042* (London: Eyre Methuen, 1979), no. 161, p. 790.

15. David Pelteret, "Slave Raiding and Slave Trading in Early England," *Anglo-Saxon England* 9 (1981): 104. See also Pelteret, *Slavery in Early Mediaeval England: From the Reign of Alfred until the Twelfth Century* (Woodbridge, Suffolk: Boydell Press, 1995).

16. Colgrave, *Earliest Life,* 145 note 43.

17. Dorothy Whitelock, *The Beginnings of English Society* (Harmondsworth, Middlesex: Penguin, 1952), 111. The church allowed penitents to free or manumit slaves as a form of penance or as an act of mercy.

18. On the Council of London of 1102, dominated by Anselm, see the discussion in chapter 6. On the question of selling women who were wives of the clergy into slavery, see A. L. Poole, *From Domesday Book to Magna Carta, 1087-1216,* 2d ed. (Oxford: Oxford University Press, 1955), 40. The Normans' decrees did not affect the status of those who were already

slaves, and it continued to be possible for individuals to volutarily surrender their freedom when compelled by necessity to do so; see Marjorie Chibnall, *Anglo-Norman England, 1066-1166* (Oxford: Basil Blackwell, 1986), 188.

19. Ruth Mazo Karras comments on prostitution and female slaves in "Desire, Descendants, and Dominance: Slavery, the Exchange of Women, and Masculine Power," in *The Work of Work: Servitude, Slavery, and Labor in Medieval England,* ed. Allen J. Frantzen and Douglas Moffat (Glasgow: Cruithne, 1994), 16-29. See also Elizabeth Stevens Girsch, "Metaphorical Usage, Sexual Exploitation, and Divergence in the Old English Terminology for Male and Female Slaves," in *Work of Work,* 30-54. I raise the possibility that the Anglian boys were intended for sexual purposes in *Desire for Origins: New Language, Old English, and Teaching the Tradition* (New Brunswick: Rutgers University Press, 1990), 47.

20. G. L. Brook and R. F. Leslie, eds., *Laȝamon: "Brut,"* 2 vols., EETS, OS, 250, 277 (London: Oxford University Press, 1963, 1978), 2:770. For commentary on versions of the anecdote by Wace and Geoffrey of Monmouth, see Lawman, *Brut,* trans. Rosamond Allen (London: Dent, 1992), 463, notes to lines 14695-923.

21. John Boswell, *Christianity, Social Tolerance, and Homosexuality: Gay People in Western Europe from the Beginning of the Christian Era to the Fourteenth Century* (Chicago: University of Chicago Press, 1980), 144.

22. For an informative survey of Bale's achievement, see Leslie P. Fairfield, *John Bale: Mythmaker for the English Reformation* (West Lafayette, Ind.: Purdue University Press, 1976). See also Hugh A. MacDougall, *Racial Myth in English History: Trojans, Teutons, and Anglo-Saxon* (Hanover, N.H.: University Press of New England, 1982), 33-37. On Bale's Anglo-Saxon manuscripts, see David Dumville, "John Bale, Owner of St. Dunstan's Benedictional," *Notes and Queries* 41 (1994): 291-95.

23. John N. King, *English Reformation Literature: The Tudor Origins of the Protestant Tradition* (Princeton: Princeton University Press, 1982), 56. For recent commentary on Bale in the context of Renaissance humanism, see Alan Stewart, *Close Readers: Humanism and Sodomy in Early Modern England* (Princeton: Princeton University Press, 1997), 38-83.

24. See Fairfield, *John Bale,* 55-56, 121.

25. John Bale, *The Actes of Englysh Votaryes* (London, 1548), 22a-22b. Stewart comments briefly on this episode, *Close Readers,* 42.

26. Contemporary sources invite wordplay on "Angles" and "Ingles." In the sixteenth century "Ingles" meant both "English" and "a boy-favourite (in bad sense): a catamite" (*OED*), and was used to pun both on "angle" and on "angel." "Ingle" was also a term of abuse for boys who played women on the stage. See Patricia Parker, *Shakespeare from the Margins: Language, Culture, Context* (Chicago: University of Chicago Press, 1996), 143-46.

27. John Bale, *The Image of Bothe Churches* (Antwerp, 1545 or 1546). For Foxe's views, see William Haller, *The Elect Nation: The Meaning and Relevance of Foxe's "Book of Martyrs"* (New York: Harper and Row, 1963).

28. Ultimately these stories derive from Geoffrey of Monmouth, *History of the Kings of Britain,* trans. Sebastian Evans, revised by Charles W. Dunn (New York: Dutton, 1958), book 11, chap. 7, p. 238, for Malgo. Bale indicates a variety of sources, ranging from Gildas to Geoffrey of Monmouth, "Florence" (John) of Worcester, and others, including William Tyndale (22a). Bale's immediate source is probably the *Nova legenda Angliae* of John Capgrave, whose narratives of saints' lives he grossly distorted. See Fairfield, *John Bale,* 114, 121-22.

29. John Bale, *Apology against a Rank Papist* (London, 1550), xxvii, xii (v).

30. John Bale, *The Pageant of Popes* (London, 1574), 36.

31. Bale cites Gregory's "Epistle to Nicolas" (*Pageant of Popes,* 34v-35r).

32. Bale, *Pageant of Popes,* 32.

33. Fairfield, *John Bale,* 17-18, 42-43.

34. This summary is based on Fairfield's analysis, *John Bale,* 31-49.

35. Donald N. Mager, "John Bale and Early Tudor Sodomy Discourse," in *Queering the Renaissance,* ed. Jonathan Goldberg (Durham: Duke University Press, 1994), 141-61. See also Stewart, *Close Readers,* 52-62.

36. John Bale, *A Comedy concernynge Thre Lawes, of Nature, Moses, & Christ, Corrupted by the Sodomytes, Pharysees, and Papystes,* ed. Peter Happé, in *The Complete Plays of John Bale,* 2 vols. (Cambridge: D. S. Brewer, 1986), 2:65-121. References to act and line number are for quotations from this text. On the attire for Sodomismus, see 121.

37. See Happé, *Complete Plays of John Bale,* 165, note to line 575.

38. Bale, *King Johan,* lines 368-70, in Happé, *Complete Plays of John Bale,* 1:39.

39. Thomas Stapleton, *The History of the Church of England Compiled by Venerable Bede, Englishman* (1565; reprint, Menston, England: Scolar, 1973), 3b. Stapleton's translation is used in the Loeb Classical Library, *Baedae opera historica,* ed. J. E. King (New York: Putnam, 1930).

40. John Bale, *Scriptorum illustrium Maioris Brytanniae* ("Ipswich," but really Wesel, 1548). For a list of Bede's works, including an English translation of the Gospel of John ("in patriam transtulit linguam"), see 50v-52r; for Chaucer's, see 198, unhelpfully alphabetized under *G* for "Galfridus Chaucer").

41. David Savran, "Ambivalence, Utopia, and a Queer Sort of Materialism: How *Angels in America* Reconstructs the Nation," *Theatre Journal* 47 (1995): 218. Some of the following material appears in my essay "Prior to the Normans: The Anglo-Saxons in *Angels in America,*" in *Approaching the Millennium: Essays on Tony Kushner's Angels in America,* ed. Deborah A. Geis and Steven F. Kruger (Ann Arbor: University of Michigan Press, 1997), 134-50.

42. Manifest Destiny had its roots in a theory of natural rights for a particular race that translates into nationalism and then imperialism. See Albert K. Weinberg, *Manifest Destiny* (1935; reprint, Chicago: Quadrangle, 1963), 8 (for the quote), 41.

43. Reginald Horsman, *Race and Manifest Destiny: The Origins of American Racial Anglo-Saxonism* (Cambridge: Harvard University Press, 1981); the phrase "Manifest Destiny" was not coined until 1845; see 219. On Anglo-Saxonism, see Frantzen, *Desire for Origins,* 15-18, and 27-61, where I comment on the phenomenon as a force in Anglo-Saxon studies from the Renaissance to the present.

44. Tony Kushner, "The Secrets of 'Angels,'" *New York Times,* 27 March 1994, H5.

45. Tony Kushner, *Angels in America: A Gay Fantasia on National Themes,* part 1, *Millennium Approaches* (New York: Theatre Communications Group, 1993); part 2, *Perestroika* (New York: Theatre Communications Group, 1994). References to volume and page number are given in the text (vol. 1 for *Millennium Approaches* and vol. 2 for *Perestroika*).

46. Savran, "Ambivalence," 212 note 14.

47. For an excellent summary of this issue, see Clare A. Simmons, *Reversing the Conquest: History and Myth in Nineteenth-Century British Literature* (New Brunswick: Rutgers University Press, 1990), 13-41.

48. The earl Harold was elected king of England at the death of Edward the Confessor in 1066; he was said to have given an oath of allegiance to William, duke

of Normandy, and betrayed that oath when he claimed the throne of England. Harold was defeated at the Battle of Hastings by William the Conqueror. See Frank Stenton, *Anglo-Saxon England,* 3d ed. (Oxford: Oxford University Press, 1971), 576-80.

49. According to Savran, "The opposite of nearly everything you say about *Angels in America* will also hold true" ("Ambivalence," 208; see also 222).

50. David J. Bernstein, *The Mystery of the Bayeux Tapestry* (Chicago: University of Chicago Press, 1986), reports that Hitler, like Napoleon, studied the tapestry when he contemplated an invasion of England, 28-30.

51. Bernstein, *Mystery of the Bayeux Tapestry,* 8, 14.

52. Bernstein, *Mystery of the Bayeux Tapestry,* 30.

53. The term was originally used to describe American Protestantism. See E. Digby Baltzell, *The Protestant Establishment: Aristocracy and Caste in America* (New Haven: Yale University Press, 1964). Kushner's elaborate genealogy for Prior Walter attaches a far more ambitious historical and international sense to the term.

54. May McKisack, *The Fourteenth Century, 1307-1399* (Oxford: Oxford University Press, 1959), 219.

55. See Savran, "Ambivalence," 223-24, for an analysis of Kushner's treatment of identity politics and race in this scene.

56. Weinberg, *Manifest Destiny,* 8.

57. Savran, "Ambivalence," 213.

58. Kushner, "Secrets of 'Angels,'" H5.

59. Several reviewers have commented on the identification of Louis with Kushner's own views. See, for example, John Simon, "Angelic Geometry," *New York,* 6 December 1993, 130. Savran says that Louis is "constructed as the most empathetic character in the play" ("Ambivalence," 223).

60. Susan Reynolds, "What Do We Mean by 'Anglo-Saxon' and 'Anglo-Saxons'?" *Journal of British Studies* 24 (1985): 397-98.

61. Reynolds, "What Do We Mean by 'Anglo-Saxon'?" 402-3.

62. On the need for narratives that reverse the usual trajectory of the experience of AIDS, see Steven F. Kruger, *AIDS Narratives: Gender and Sexuality, Fiction and Science* (New York: Garland, 1996), 73-81.

63. Savran, "Ambivalence," 222-23.

64. D. Michael Quinn, *Same-Sex Dynamics among Nineteenth-Century Americans: A Mormon Example* (Urbana: University of Illinois Press, 1996), 2.

Ranen Omer-Sherman (essay date 2007)

SOURCE: Omer-Sherman, Ranen. "Jewish/Queer: Thresholds of Vulnerable Identities in Tony Kushner's *Angels in America.*" *Shofar* 25.4 (2007): 78-98. Print.

[*In the following essay, Omer-Sherman examines the ways in which Jewish traditions inform the ethics of* Angels in America. *Omer-Sherman characterizes the play as a reaction to the failure of a community response to AIDS and to the larger problem of rampant American individualism. Omer-Sherman suggests that in its examination of vulnerable identities, however, the play ultimately opens the door to ideas of restoration and reconciliation.*]

> The model I used in the process of coming out was everything I knew about the Jewish experience in the twentieth century.
>
> Tony Kushner[1]

For many, it has long seemed apparent that in his two-part "gay fantasia," *Angels in America,*[2] Kushner aspired to forge some vital but unspoken alliance between Judaism and gay struggle. For many, this remains one of the play's most interesting and yet not altogether coherent arguments. Yet when one considers the myriad of ways that Judaism always presumes a community of believers and more importantly, ethical adherents bound to one another and God by covenant, the politics of *Angels* cannot be isolated from its relation to Judaism's understanding of the sacred status of the stranger. By considering Judaism's intrinsic relation to "prophecy" as a rigorous mission of social progress, the coherence of Kushner's vision of men and angels emerges with greater clarity. In recasting the biblical outsider as AIDS victim, Kushner sought to reconfigure the encoded tribalism of liberation, to ensure that the prophetic message of the sacred texts was restated in the most inclusive terms possible.

By the time HBO aired Mike Nichols' two-part television adaptation of Tony Kushner's *Angels in America* (*Millennium Approaches* and *Perestroika*) as a star-studded spectacle in December 2003, it seemed manifestly apparent that the work had not lost its reputation as one of the most provocative dramatic statements of the late 20th century. An ambitious (some have said unwieldy) work, almost unprecedented in scale, *Angels in America* encompasses narrative complexities, including a richly multicultural spectrum of ethnic identities and religions that have sometimes obscured its profoundly Jewish sensibility. In fact, few critics have been attentive to *Angels*' striking indebtedness to post-as-similationist skepticism in the canon of Jewish-American literature, an affinity that this essay addresses. While *Angels* is rightly appreciated, or criticized, for its unabashed liberal paean to multicultural tolerance and understanding, a closer examination of the text reveals a surprisingly conservative approach to the moral gains and losses incurred by Jews in their American success story.

While in some ways *Angels* can be viewed as an appreciation of the successful acculturation and intermingling of America's disparate groups, early in the work it is strikingly evident that Kushner's epic can most productively be understood as bearing a distinct relation to portrayals of the dangers of thoughtless assimilation in much earlier literary works such as Anzia Yezierska's moral fables of tenement life in the nineteen-twenties, Budd Schulberg's *What Makes Sammy Run?* (1941), and most recently Philip Roth's *American Pastoral* (1997). First however, a brief introduction to its characters and prominent themes seems in order.

For those unfamiliar with the drama, *Angels in America*'s two parts reveal the intersecting lives of a cluster of individuals living in New York City whose destinies are profoundly shaped by the nineteen-eighties' AIDS epidemic. There is Prior Walter, whose body already exhibits the ravages of his disease. His lover, Louis Ironson, cannot bear to witness Prior's bodily humiliations or, for that matter, the fact of mortality and vulnerability in *any* human being, a failure that I will return to because it forms the drama's critical moral focus. Louis works as a clerk in a courthouse where he discovers the welcome distraction of wholesome Joe, a resolute lawyer of conservative politics who serves as chief clerk to a presiding judge. A once steadfast Mormon, Joe finds himself struggling in his marriage to Harper as long-suppressed homosexual desires begin to overcome his will. For her part, Harper struggles with her addiction to Valium, bouts with anxiety, and increasingly surreal hallucinations. Her husband Joe's mentor, Roy Cohn, whose blustering character is etched close to the historical figure, is an infamous red-baiter and corrupt lawyer now struggling to suppress the manifest calamity of his AIDS even as he distances himself from other homosexuals. Through Cohn's obdurate refusal to identify with other victims, the drama makes some of its most compelling statements about image vs. reality, power, and the egalitarian institution of death. A character named Belize serves as a gay mediator for Prior and Louis during their separation, as well as the hospital nurse for Cohn, and is one of the most humane voices of the drama.

Though *Angels* has a staggering range that encompasses weighty and imaginative treatment of such disparate matters as the historical migration of the Mormons, the McCarthy hearings, historical figures such as Roy Cohn and Ethel Rosenberg, the politics of the Reagan era, the supernatural presence of ghosts and angels, and even the nature of Heaven, its pivotal character is Louis. Kushner himself asserts that "Louis carries the biggest burden of the play."[3] We first encounter this young, disaffected Jew at his grandmother's funeral, where he confesses to his gentile boyfriend Prior, recently diagnosed with Kaposi's sarcoma, that he has had no contact with his grandmother over the past decade. This guilty admission of the abnegation of responsibility provides a critical ethical context for a subsequent betrayal when he chooses to flee Prior at the latter's most acute moment of need. While capable of delivering sweeping judgments about the historical culpability of nations and groups, he is a moral failure in his own relations with others. In fact, Louis resembles nothing so much as the rebellious protagonists of Philip Roth's novels, for whom the sovereign authority is the Self, an ascendancy that marks a departure from what was once an inescapable framework of identity—familial, communal, traditional, even the Jewish neighborhood—inherited at birth. Ultimately, Louis's responses to those around him are an essential conduit for the drama's spiritual approach to redemption, which presumes that the fate of the nation and even the cosmos depends on the individual's assumption of responsibility.

In *Angels* Kushner forges a vital (but often ignored) alliance between Judaism and gay struggle. The drama's constant allusions to an underlying affiliation between gays and Jews may strike some as merely irreverent whimsy, but it seems to owe more to Kushner's sincere outrage toward the bigotry of his co-religionists: "I'm very critical of Jews because I am one and . . . Jewish homophobia makes me angrier than Goyische homophobia . . . good God, after what we've gone through for the last six hundred years and before . . . surely suffering should teach you compassion."[4] Elsewhere in a dialogue with another prominent American dramatist, Craig Lucas, Kushner endorsed his colleague's view that: "We're not so very different from European Jewry in the '30s. We're accepted in certain sophisticated urban quarters, in our ghettos, and nice people don't openly say mean things about us, but lots of people would like to see us dead."[5] Nevertheless, the profound ways that gay and Jewish identities inflect one another remains one of the play's most interesting and yet not altogether coherent features (perhaps because Kushner himself claims to have been taken by surprise when he discovered the degree to which the work is permeated by Judaism).[6] In a special service held on Yom Hashoah at the Hebrew Union College in New York, he elaborated on the intertwined strands of Judaism and homosexuality in the nascent stages of his out-of-the-closet identity:

> The model I used in the process of coming out was everything I knew about the Jewish experience in the twentieth century. What I mean is, and I think this has been true of most gay Jewish men, that in being Jewish one is born into a history of oppression and persecution, and a history that offered, at various points, a sort of false possibility of a kind of assimilation that demanded as one of its prerequisites that you abandon your identity as a Jew. The possibility of passing which is not, let's say, available to people whose oppression stems from racial difference or gender difference. For me, as I think is true for most Jewish homosexuals, the business of claiming an identity, the business of coming out of the closet, the business of learning one of the central lessons of the Holocaust . . . is that, as Hannah Arendt says, it's better to be a pariah than a parvenu. If you're hated by a social order, don't try and make friends with it. Identify yourself as other, and identify your determining characteristics as those characteristics which make you other and unliked and despised.[7]

While for some this linkage between European genocidal history and America's homophobia may seem nevertheless incongruous, those who accept liberal denominations of Judaism's understanding of "prophecy" as a demonstrably *inclusive* mission of social progress will fully appreciate the coherence of Kushner's vision of an enlarged sense of human community in the face of bureaucratic angels and an altogether absent deity. To grasp this essence, it is critical to consider the figure of the "prophet" Prior, whose drug-induced hallucinations bring visions of apocalypse to the stage and screen, including images of burning books, an angel crashing through a ceiling, and eventually Heaven itself, which seems to function as a Kafkaesque bureaucracy. Prior himself is modeled after the ancient Hebraic prophet as not so much a "seer" (understood as one who merely predicts the future) but a marginal outsider who has the capacity to level a severe critique at society, and to warn against dire consequences if that polity does not correct its path. Recasting the biblical outsider as AIDS victim, Kushner radically translates the notion of salvation to the inclusive terms that American society requires in its indifferent response to the plight of the Other.

In addressing the question of *Angels'* current relevance it is important to note that, while the AIDS crisis is by no means over (its once-alarming expansion in North America has shifted to inflict a greater catastrophe in Africa and perhaps Asia), its victims are no longer treated with indifference in the United States. Perhaps for that reason other dimensions of *Angels'* moral universe are now more apparent. It is easier to grasp that Kushner's visionary achievement is greatly indebted to Kushner's liberal Jewish renderings of exile, *mentshlichkeit, tikkun olam,* and *t'shuva,* or as Sarah Ironson proclaims in the streets of Heaven, "*Azoi toot a Yid*" (it's the Jewish way) (*Perestroika,* 135).[8] *Angels* unsparingly exhibits the failure of abstract ideology, so that Louis's failure of responsibility is as heinous as Roy Cohn's betrayal of Ethel Rosenberg (Cohn regards her execution in the electric chair as his loftiest legal achievement in spite of the manifest illegality of his actions in the proceedings). Kushner wants us to recognize in both betrayals disturbing symptoms of the larger culture's inauthentic response to suffering, calling on us to replace indifference with the traditional principle of compassion. Neither liberalism nor conservatism (both ideologies are eloquently voiced throughout the drama) proves redemptive when conduct and conscience fail. Kushner seems to want the audience to recognize Louis and Roy as moral *doppelgangers,* for "Louis lives outside Jewish communal life, whereas Roy is completely acommunal."[9] In Prior's stern censure of Louis, he declares: "There are thousands of gay men in New York City with AIDS and nearly every one of them is being taken care of by . . . a friend or by . . . a lover who has stuck by them. . . . Everyone got that, except me. I got you" (*Perestroika,* 87). What the hauntingly *insistent* name "Prior" has always conveyed is a shared sensibility with that of the late French Jewish intellectual and Talmudist

Emmanuel Levinas (1906-1995). In the latter's severe formulation of obligation, "ethical anteriority of responsibility" or demand of being-for-the-other must always exceed the mutuality of Buber's ethical parameters established in his famous formulation of the I—Thou relation, because responsibility has no limits: "I am thrown back toward what has never been my fault or deed."[10] This is a condition that always predates the individual's own subjectivity and well-being: an instant burden beyond reciprocity, and *prior* to ethics. Judaism's intrinsic relation to exile establishes the archetypal grounds for this orientation to the Other's acute vulnerability. Abraham's desert wanderings have important implications for prophetic Judaism's emphasis on the human Other as well:

> Above all Abraham is the one who knows how to receive and feed men, the one whose tent was open to the four winds. Through all these openings he watched out for passersby he could welcome. The meal offered by Abraham? We know of one above all: the meal he had offered to the three angels. Without being aware that they were angels. . . . Abraham must have taken the three passers-by for three Bedouins, three nomads from the Negev desert—three Arabs indeed! He runs to meet them and calls them "My Lords." Abraham's descendents are men to whom their ancestor bequeathed a difficult tradition of duties toward the other, which we have never finished fulfilling, an order from which we are never released, but where duty takes on above all the form of obligation toward the body, the duty to feed and shelter. . . . Abraham's descendents are men of all nations: every man who is truly a man is probably a descendant of Abraham.[11]

What concerns Levinas here is what he views as the western world's relentless repugnance toward the Other ("an insurmountable allergy" he calls it) archetypally manifested in the story of Ulysses. In his analysis of Greek and Hebraic attitudes toward wandering, Levinas argues that whereas Ulysses returns home to himself, a one-way movement embodying the West's perpetual self-sufficiency and self-satisfaction, the Abraham of Genesis leaves his homeland forever for the unknown, thus embodying a movement without return.[12] I dwell on this point because, far more than any other discursive paradigm of responsibility (spiritual or legal), the overarching vision of Kushner's *Angels* most closely resembles Levinas's emphasis that the exilic world needs a radical conception of absolute responsibility for the Other. His archetype of responsiveness derives from the apparent etymological relation of the word "responsibility" in Hebrew, *achraiyut,* to the root *acher,* "other," someone who is not me. There is a gravity in our relation to the alterity of the stranger, and it is this enormity which Levinas calls responsibility or obligation, a reality in which we are always already obligated to the Other, *prior* to any action (or failure of action) we might perform.[13] In Kushner's universe of an absconded God and careless angels, there is a strikingly similar urgency in human agency. The notion of unending struggle has long been a consistent feature of Kushner's vision, and in a work whose range is so encompassing this theme of radical human responsibility and action-for-the-other is the feature that most underlies the moral trajectory of *Angels*.[14] With this paradigm in mind, it seems clear that Kushner wants his audience to understand that precisely when Louis fails in his personal responsibilities as a gay man or a lover, he ultimately fails in his identity as a Jew as well.

For Kushner, it seems clear that the Jew's role as morally and spiritually sensitive outsider and victim has largely been supplanted by other vulnerable identities, but that centuries of oppression place a special sense of obligation on Jews in this regard. In terms reminiscent of his earlier response to Harold Bloom, he continues to insist on a view of Judaism as largely a "political tradition": "I'm an inheritor of at least a 2,500-year-tradition of oppression and murder and holocaust, and so I know, like all Jews know in a bone-deep way, what political mischief, bigotry, and xenophobia lead to. The only thing that we can actively do to speak to the Holocaust now is to make sure no other holocaust happens, and if we do make sure that no holocaust happens—of course they're happening all the time—but if we struggle against that, every time we're successful, in some way I believe the dead are comforted."[15] Interestingly, even Kushner's memories of his antagonistic relationship with his father (over his early intimations of a nonconforming sexual identity) reveal a precocious awareness of the strategic solidarity that can be forged under the shadow of this terrible vulnerability: "My father and I had a very complicated, difficult relationship for most of my childhood. His sense of my sexual difference, my preferential difference, was all channeled into a lot of political hostility. So we screamed and fought about everything. But one thing that we both agreed [on] was that Jews do badly when they try to pretend to not be Jews. And so it was a way of making inroads into something that was emotionally very, very difficult for him."[16] In this crucial sense, Kushner's post-Holocaust consciousness encompasses the prophetic relationship between Judaism and social change as well as the violent consequences that always follow when the dominant culture fails in its empathy with the Other within.

The title of the first part of his drama, *Millennium Approaches*, strongly suggests that, at the beginning of the 1990s, the dramatist was anxious about both the apocalyptic traditions and anxieties that would be unpredictably expressed across a broad spectrum of global and American culture as the year 2000-2001 approached. Perhaps the theme of "Judgment Day" (which since antiquity encodes both anxiety and hope) was a perfect motif for the inclusive framework that Kushner's social vision required.[17] It is not difficult to glean the way Kushner's postmodern drama about afflicted individuals represents a similar conversion from pessimism in the present into a more redemptive narrative of history. That *Angels* has at its heart a very serious commitment to life, as violent process and painful but necessary transformation, is evident in a bittersweet speech that relates the apocalyptic necessity, and pain, of transformation:

God splits the skin with a jagged thumbnail from throat to belly and then plunges a huge filthy hand in, he grabs hold of your bloody tubes and they slip to evade his grasp but he squeezes hard, he *insists*, he pulls and pulls till all your innards are yanked out and the pain! We can't even talk about that. And then he stuffs them back, dirty, tangled and torn. It's up to you to do the stitching.

HARPER:

And then get up. And walk around.

MORMON MOTHER:

Just mangled guts pretending.

HARPER:

That's how people change.

(*Perestroika*, 77-78)

Just as traditional apocalyptic narratives seek to unify the course of history to create meaning, it might be said that *Angels* presses toward its own agenda, in the form of a renewed unification of present-day humanity united by a common plight with the angels, dwelling in a cosmos that God has abandoned. In a revealing speech, Prior's words wryly combine Borscht Belt shtick with the Hebraic tradition of arguing with God that can be traced back to Abraham's pleas for compassion: "If he ever did come back, if he ever *dared* to show His face . . . if after all this destruction, if after all the terrible days of this terrible century He returned to see . . . how much suffering His abandonment had created, if all He has to offer is death, you should *sue* the bastard. . . . Sue the bastard for walking out. How dare He" (*Perestroika*, 130). But no character has more painful awareness than Prior that amidst the AIDS crisis, God is not the only one who abandons those in need.

Inevitably, in a work of such complexity, *Angels* can seem conflicted in certain moments. While unwavering in its attention to the ethical blemishes of its nomadic urban characters, *Angels* also manages to affirm the imaginative triumphs of exile and the tenacity of the exiled. Aside from his eloquent gestures to the historical displacements of Jews and Mormons, Kushner's troubled souls include a woman who sojourns in Antarctica (or at least a hallucinatory version), two wayward lovers, a Mormon mother who pursues her drifting son, and an AIDS victim who travels to Heaven and returns with a revised sense of human destiny. Perhaps the motif most visible throughout the drama is that of transformation, a state which seems to enable greater sensitivity to the neediness of others. In describing the unified condition of the Mormons, Blacks, and Jews of the play (aside from Cohn), Allen Frantzen observes that they are "denied . . . stability and permanence and driven by persecution and need from place to place"; these "migratory and transitional cultures" are "open to, and indeed dependent on, change."[18] Interestingly, when asked about *Angels*' unusual emphasis on Mormon identity, Kushner remarks that Mormonism is the quintessential American religion ("a theology that I think could only really have come from America") but it seems characteristic of Kushner's restless search for common ground that he makes this striking observation of Mormonism: "it reminds me of Judaism in that they have an interesting ambivalence toward sensuality and the flesh."[19]

In this vital sense, each of Kushner's memorable characters will experience change, but more importantly, they also come to embrace dramatic transformations in their identities and values. Even the structure of *Angels* is organized around the theme of a universe and a human society receptive to the change that brings about redemption; nearly all the desperate flights from responsibility in *Millennium Approaches* are resolved in the various reconcilations in *Perestroika.* Only Cohn seems to remain utterly unredeemable. Cocooned in selfishness and bigotry, he dies a lonely and miserable death.[20] Unlike virtually every other character who in one form or another embraces some confidence in historical and individual progress, Cohn's fatal indifference to all but his own jungle struggle is signaled by a devastatingly morbid Social Darwinism that infects his vision of eternity: "I see the universe, Joe, as a kind of sandstorm in outer space with winds of mega-hurricane velocity, but instead of grains of sand it's shards and splinters of glass" (*Millennium,* 13). He advises his apprentice to learn to "live in the raw wind, naked, alone" (*Millennium,* 58). In submitting to this nightmare of the cosmos and indifferent human society, entrenched in his contempt for progress and redemptive social struggle, Cohn, forgiven by Belize and the ghost of Ethel Rosenberg, remains obdurately indifferent to the fate of others, is set apart, the drama's sole Cain. Disbarred just before his death, he remains unrepentant in his isolation. In contrast, Joe, who initially thinks he will go to hell for succumbing to homoerotic leanings and thinks he must kill off that buried identity, learns to live with the messiness of his once-opposed Republican and homosexual selves. In *Angels,* radically disavowing either Self or Other wreaks terrible violence on the individual and society.

In fact, this crucial theme is strategically established early in the first scene of *Millennium Approaches,* where the ancient East European immigrant Rabbi Isidor Chemelwitz presides at a funeral (in the HBO production this resonant figure is played by Meryl Streep in yet another milestone of her astonishingly versatile career). This first speech of the play reveals Sarah Ironson, grandmother of Louis, as the embodiment of a dormant world of Jewish values, a communal consciousness repressed by the comfortable arrogance of her grandchild's generation, and yet merely quiescent, not erased. She

> was ... not a person but a whole kind of person, the ones who crossed the ocean, who brought with us to America the villages of Russia and Lithuania—and how we struggled, and how we fought, for the family, for the Jewish home, so that you would not grow up *here,* in this strange place, in the melting pot where nothing melted. Descendants of this

> immigrant woman, you do not grow up in America, you and your children and their children with the goyische names. You do not live in America. No such place exists. Your clay is the clay of some Litvak Shtetl, your air the air of the steppes—because she carried the old world on her back across the ocean, in a boat, and she put it down on Grand Concourse Avenue, or in Flatbush, and she worked that earth into your bones, and you pass it to your children, this ancient, ancient culture and home.

> (*Millennium,* 10)

Here Kushner seems to be thinking about the immigrant generations that arrived until the mid-century. In this almost-liturgical speech (it is, after all, a eulogy) *Angels* reaches out to implicate the audience: How do you understand yourself? How is the journey of your ancestors valorized in your actions? With this in mind it is worth noting that during an interview given not long after *Angels'* first production he confesses that "[i]t's a very distressing thing to me that American Jews have lost contact with the traditions of socialism and humanism ... there are important progressive and radical European traditions that arrived with Jews in the U.S. from Germany to Russia that really informed American Jewish consciousness all the way up to the 1950s," but it seems particularly telling when the dramatist emphasizes that it was "Roy [Cohn]'s generation ... that succeeded in beginning the severance of that."[21] Moreover, the placement of the rabbi's eulogy seems to lay the foundation for the audience's experience for all the painful transformations that are to follow. In the multicultural, urban world that is *Angels'* milieu, Chemelwitz's stirring elegy resonates anachronistically with the imperative continuum of Judaism's diasporic origins and exilic identity as its foundational movement in God's command to Abraham recalls: "Get thee out of thy country, and from thy kindred, and from thy father's house, unto a land that I will show thee" (Genesis 12:1). Speaking directly to the drifting young generation "with the goyische names," the aged rabbi sternly reminds them that "[y]ou can never make that crossing that she made, for such Great Voyages in this world do not any more exist. But every day of your lives the miles that voyage between that place and this one you cross. Every day. You understand me? In you that journey is" (*Millennium,* 10-11). But obviously, Kushner's drama does not exclusively address the Jews in its theater audience itself. Instead, it creates a space in which Diaspora serves to unify the human condition as a whole. In part this is achieved through the device of the second-person "you," the rabbi implicates the alienated Diaspora Jew as well as all others in the audience who might be estranged from the world of values represented by their origins, ethnic or otherwise. Kushner's entire epic affirms this imperative to remember and to honor the "journey," for the drama's Jewish and non-Jewish characters alike.

In prophetic fashion, the rabbi indicates that the genuine home of humanity is always in an exiled space, at once a realm of continuity and a corridor for future displacements.

After all, it is ultimately the play's gay characters who carry forward the rabbi's term—the charged dialectical crisis of Jewish modernity, its incessant debates over power vs. powerlessness, memory vs. forgetting—into a universal future. For example, whereas many intellectuals have celebrated the Jewish Diaspora for its tenacity and resilient adaptability under oppression, it is Prior who utters these lines: "I can handle pressure, I am a gay man and I am used to pressure, to trouble, I am tough and strong" (*Perestroika,* 117). On the other hand, in the stark moral logic of *Angels,* the very existence of a virulent figure such as Roy Cohn, the drama's Cain-like figure, seems to confirm the danger of forgetfulness, when Jews are all too much "at home." Signaling his lack of self-knowledge and sense of origins ("the clay of some Litvak shtetl" [*Millennium,* 10]), Cohn strangely later echoes Chemelwitz's prophetic utterance: "The immutable heart of what we are that bleeds through whatever we might become" (*Perestroika,* 80), but without achieving true self-knowledge. As such utterances suggest, *Angels* represents Kushner's alliance, not only with a multicultural and liberal ethos but with a well-established tradition of Jewish-American writers whose antagonistic works offer profound, sometimes disturbing iterations of the imperative to overcome the erasure of memory and the Jewish individual's submission to the values, or indifference, of the state.

The character whose betrayal most resembles Cohn's odious actions against the Rosenbergs and others is the likeable Louis, but unlike Cohn, who has fossilized into a calculating monster beyond redemption long before the action unfolds, *Angels* examines Louis as a sort of Everyman whose moral journey toward repentance is essential to Kushner's examination of responsibility. Approaching the rabbi immediately after his grandmother's funeral, Louis sets forth the self-serving rationale for his irresponsibility:

LOUIS:

> Rabbi, what does the Holy Writ say about someone who abandons someone he loves at a time of great need?

RABBI ISIDOR CHEMELWITZ:

> Why would a person do such a thing?

LOUIS:

> Because he has to.
> Maybe because this person's sense of the world, that it will change for the better with struggle, maybe a person who has this neo-Hegelian positivist sense of constant historical progress towards happiness or perfection or something, who feels very powerful because he feels connected to these forces, moving uphill all the time … maybe that person can't, um, incorporate sickness into his sense of how things are supposed to go. Maybe vomit … and sores and disease … really frighten him, maybe … he isn't so good with death.

> (*Millennium,* 25)

Kushner astutely contrasts Louis's faith in Hegel's myth of progress with the naked fact of his abandonment of a loved one in a terrible time of need. This will prove to be the crux, the moral center of *Angels* as a whole. In the face of Louis's faltering solipsistic and intellectual rationalizations, the rabbi responds with stark sadness: "The Holy Scriptures have nothing to say about such a person" (p. 25). Interestingly, both the rabbi's speech and Louis' subsequent moral vacillations seem strongly inflected by Kushner's awareness of Walter Benjamin's evocative sense of memory as a redemptive storehouse for future action and responsibility: "There is a secret agreement between past generations and the present one. Our coming was expected on earth. Like every generation that preceded us, we have been endowed with a *weak* Messianic power, a power to which the past has claim."[22]

If, as I have argued, Kushner's emphasis on the trials faced by gay characters never diminishes the play's provocative focus on the diminished spirit of Jewish conscience and identity, it should also be noted there are times when even the Mormon characters seem to channel a Jewish sensibility, perhaps because, as Steven Kruger notes, "both religions' … originary movement is a conversional one that involves a movement of dis- and relocation."[23] That underlying consciousness emerges in unexpected moments. For instance, it rings false that Hannah Pitt, the mother of Joe, who has left Utah to come to New York to settle the chaos in her son's life, says that "angels are beliefs with wings," for this belies the literal core of the Mormon faith even while it affirms progressive Judaism's more relaxed relationship with metaphor. Even the identity of the angel that visits Prior and would proclaim him as a biblical prophet owes to the Jewish tradition. When she visits Prior she admonishes that she has come to liberate the universe from "the virus of TIME" that God released in humanity (2:42) which enabled humans to transcend their fixed position in the natural order. The angel complains that God himself began to find time seductive and preferred human life to the stasis of heaven; all of which is consistent with midrashic traditions.[24] As Daniel Mendelsohn observes, "the drama takes the side of churning, complex, ultimately redemptive forces of 'life'—suffering, change, emotional evolution, even politics (as distinguished from stultifying ideology)."[25]

For Kushner, writing in a time that many perceived as a failure of the collective American will in response to its victims of AIDS, the "absolute triumph of Reaganite ideology" required substituting "the social human, the communal human, with this little sealed monad of an ego fragment that has no connection, or is at least not willing to admit to any connection, to any other living being."[26] That is why *Angels* draws on the mystical rabbinical imagination, which posited that angels were nostalgic, conservative beings who felt threatened by the introduction of humanity, but the play ultimately applies that to human society's resistance to new paradigms of community. Ultimately, the ethical imperative of community that Kushner expresses in the "Afterword" to *Perestroika* also derives from Jewish tradition. For how are we to understand this sentiment if not as a midrashic reworking of the law requiring ten men as the minimum required for a *minyan*?[27] On the other hand, Kushner's sense of the role of Jewishness in America is much more aligned to a system of values and a shared sense of destiny than to a tribal sense of community, as his utter disavowal of identity politics in this declaration eloquently underscores:

> I have a kind of dangerously romantic reading of American history. I do think there is an advantage to not being burdened by history the way Europe is. This country has been, in a way, an improvisation of hastily assembled groups that certainly have never been together before and certainly have a lot of trouble being together, but who recognize that our destiny is not going to be a racial destiny. Anyone who thinks that completely self-interested politics is going to get you anywhere in America is making a terrible mistake. Which is why I object to Louis Farrakhan. Which is why I object to gays and lesbians ... who say "I hate straights." Or to Jews who think that the only thing that matters is Israel and defense against anti-Semitism. People who don't recognize common cause are going to fail politically in this country. Movements that capture the imagination of people are movements that deny racism and exclusion.[28]

In a similar spirit, *Angels* expresses the dramatist's condemnation of the terrible price paid by Americans "for maintaining the Myth of the Individual." As Kushner declares in his Afterword, "the smallest indivisible human unit is two people, not one; one is a fiction. From such nets of souls societies, the social world, human life springs" (*Perestroika,* 155). Though resisting an exclusively ethnocentric triumphalism, seeking out "community" in the widest possible sense, the life-affirming spirit of the minyan seems to inflect Kushner's heartfelt coda to the written text. As Alisa Solomon points out, Kushner's intentions for *Angels* are greatly illuminated by the Talmudic imperative: "When a man appears before the Throne of Judgment, the first question he will be asked is not 'Have you believed in God?' or 'Have you prayed and observed the ritual?'— but 'Have you dealt honorably with your fellow man?'[29] Kushner construes Louis as a modern Jewish Everyman, at least insofar as that identity encompasses the limits of the self-serving Jewish American liberal conscience.

In the drama's tense opposition between diasporic and Zionist identities, it is clear that Kushner privileges the expansive, open-ended identity of wandering over the narrowly proscribed politics and monolithic identity that accompanies territorialism. Indeed, to understand the primacy the Jewish dramatist places on paradigm shifts and expanded human consciousness (the true gifts born of movement), the Jewish tradition's rich and creatively productive relation to exile bears mentioning. One need only return to the Book of Genesis, beginning with the pervasive sense of *felix culpa* that accompanies the exile from the Garden, the command given to Abraham, *Lech Lacha* ("Get you gone from your country and from your birthplace and from your father's

house"), the expulsion of Ishmael into the desert, the narrative of Ruth the Moabite, all of which offer a richly circuitous terrain, repetitions of wandering that haunt the certainties of the present. Indeed, it is this primordial, sadly neglected essence of Hebrew monotheism (often vilified as the source of global violence), that offers the richest counter-traditions to rebuke those who would root themselves in blood-drenched soil. The radical monotheism that engendered Jewish writers as disparate as Yehudah Halevi, Franz Kafka, and Tony Kushner, after all, evolved as a cultural strategy for being-at-home wherever one was— learning the discipline demanded of moving fluidly between disparate worlds.

Kushner's affinity for progressive Judaism's commitment to *tikkun* (global healing) is explicitly stated in his introduction to the printed text of *Perestroika.* Aside from refusing the temptation of a maudlin closure to the traumas of the first part ("It shouldn't be easy"), the language nonetheless affirms the merit of struggle against daunting odds:

> *Perestroika* is essentially a comedy, in that issues are resolved, mostly peaceably, growth takes place and loss is, to a certain degree, countenanced. But it's not a farce; all this happens only through a terrific amount of struggle, and the stakes are high. ... There is also a danger in easy sentiment. Eschew sentiment! Particularly in the final act— metaphorical though it may at times be (or maybe not), the problems the characters face are finally among the hardest problems—how to let go of the past, how to change and lose with grace, how to keep going in the face of overwhelming suffering.
>
> (*Perestroika,* 8)

The second part of *Angels* features memorable acts of reconciliation that underscore the overarching theme of overcoming the barriers of faith, culture, identity, and ideology to integrate America's disparate communities into a compassionate society. For instance, Belize, the gay, black nurse on the AIDS ward, despises Roy Cohn but gives him crucial advice about how to make the best of his deteriorating condition; Hannah Pitt, who in the first part is repulsed when her son Joe reveals he is gay, tenderly cares for Prior when he is at his lowest ebb; and most spectacularly of all, the ghost of Ethel Rosenberg appears to say Kaddish for Cohn, the metaphoric son who abandoned her just as he betrays his gay brethren "by always fucking in a locked closet."[30] Most important, Louis and Prior are reconciled after Louis shows genuine remorse. Of Louis's moral journey, Rabbi Norman J. Cohen observes that Kushner's flawed character embodies not only "the impulse to walk away" but by the end of Perestroika, "the ability slowly and with great difficulty of coming back. ... That ultimately it's through our relation with other people and in community that we come to some higher sense of existence ... that sense of something divine in other people that can make you even more whole."[31] It is precisely due to this affirmation of an enlarged community that (in spite of Kushner's disavowal of sentiment), the final scene of *Perestroika,* set in Central Park with the Bethesda Fountain in the background, gravitates toward a utopian closure wherein its outcast blacks, Jews, Mormons, and gays learn to reconcile the messy reality of human existence. The Mormon mother Hannah intends to celebrate the *new* millennium Prior in the waters that sprang up in Jerusalem when the angel Bethesda appeared amidst Romans and Jews in the previous one, a distant age of strife and upheaval mirroring the present one. Suddenly, Louis interrupts to interject "Not literally in Jerusalem, I mean we don't want this to have sort of Zionist implications—" to which Belize rejoins:

BELIZE:

Right on.

LOUIS:

But on the other hand we *do* recognize the right of the state of Israel to exist.

BELIZE:

But the West Bank should be a homeland for the Palestinians, and the Golan Heights should . . .

LOUIS:

Well not both the West Bank and the Golan Heights, I mean no one supports Palestinian rights more than I do but . . .

BELIZE:

(*Overlapping*) Oh yeah right, Louis, like not even the Palestinians are more devoted than . . .

                (*Perestroika,* 145-146)

Belize's gentle but uncompromising demonstration of the limits of Louis's liberalism (and by extension that of the audience!) serves as a necessary respite from the wounding encounters with suffering that dominate the drama. But at the same time, the satire offers a barbed rejection of exclusively tribal narratives of truth and the violent logic of territorial destiny encoded in sacred texts. In this sense, Belize's compassionate but critical perspective strengthens the midrashic way the play both feeds off of, and fends off, the Jewish apocalyptic tradition of recovery and sovereignty. After the grave seriousness of betrayal, madness, and disease that hitherto dominate the text, the barbed and catty exchange that ensues between these adversaries, whether on stage or film, is experienced as a tender respite of comic relief—an acknowledgement of the sheer unresolved messiness of the world that will always defy messianic resolution. Here is where Kushner struggles to reconcile his manifestly Jewish identity with his refusal to spare any tribe from assuming its full responsibility for the disastrous state of the world. For Jewish American readers, this barbed exchange, though revealing that the parties that have wounded one another have moved on, places ironic emphasis on what Kushner perceives as the

limits of Jewish American liberal pieties in the face of the Israel and Palestine conflict. For the record he has stated plainly his distaste for uncritical Jewish American support for Israel—"I really believe that the Israel lobby has pulled American Jews into bed with some really awful people"— while insisting that he is "incapable of . . . rejecting a Jewish yearning for a homeland."[32]

"In you that journey is." Returning to Prior, shouldering his ethical burden, Louis at last realizes the rabbi's admonition to *remember* by acting compassionately. But though Louis is the character that most resembles the identity and politics of Kushner, we have seen that the dramatist remains ruthless in exposing the shallow hypocrisy of the Jewish liberal zeitgeist. If one considers the trajectory from Rabbi Isidor Chemelwitz's opening, elegiac speech to the liberal bickering that culminates in *Perestroika*'s happy conclusion, one gleans the significance of the provocative bookend device that Kushner offers the Jews in his audience. For *Angels* begins and ends with the recitation of the Kaddish, Judaism's ostensible prayer of mourning that is really a reaffirmation of the living's proper orientation to the world. If the first is an aging rabbi's elegiac farewell to a vanished world, the final (recited by a confused and forgetful Louis prompted by Ethel's ghost) is a cautionary nod to the lost values of Jews of the post-assimilation era.[33]

The heart of the matter, for Jews and Gentiles, constituents of the Right and Left, is how a democratic society treats its outsiders—as well as how its individuals contribute to shaping that process. As Steven Kruger puts it, *Angels* conscientiously presents identity "as social and relational: one is not oneself in isolation but only in contrast to, in solidarity and negotiation with a variety of other selves . . . even a character's fantasies and imaginations are conceived of as not solely his or hers. These gather their full meaning only in relation to, even interpenetration with, one another—just as, in Kushner's stagecraft, the 'split scenes' suggest that discrete actions must, if we are to understand them fully, be read together."[34] As one character comes to understand, "Freedom is where we bleed into one another. . . . Freedom is the far horizon where lines converge" (*Perestroika,* 73). For it is clear that the self-hatred of both Jews and homosexuals produces some of *Angels*' most powerful examinations of moral failure. Though Felman's reading of the fallen secular world of self-loathing revealed by the first play also seems apt—"*Angels* is about Jewish male self-loathing in the twentieth century held tightly within the ever expanding embrace of Miss Liberty's very tired, porous hands"[35]—it seems clear that something restorative *has* transpired. Indeed above all else, *Angels* posits an imaginatively porous America of open-mindedness and open-endedness, gracefully allowing the audience to exit through a door of hope. Loneliness, betrayal, and banishment are supplanted by increasing prospects for cultural and individual stamina, reconciliation, and reconstruction of America's lost promise.

Like other self-consciously Jewish writers, Kushner is never free "intertextually"—he can never invent a new prophetic language out of nothing. Instead, he toils, patching together fragments of the Bible's contradictory and multiple strands to respond to the urgent needs of the present. Kushner has long been convinced of theater's political potential, once remarking to an interviewer that his early exposure to Brecht persuaded him that "really good theater had the potential for radical intervention."[36] Hence, in Prior's return from Heaven to the mundane world of earthly politics, there is an implicit burden laid by Prior on the audience/reader, requiring that when s/he emerges blinking into the sunlight, s/he accept the arduous ethical journey, with all its lurching and messy uncertainties, toward *Tikkun*: "The world only spins forward. We will be citizens. The time has come. Bye now. You are fabulous creatures, each and every one. And I bless you: *More Life*. The Great Work Begins" (*Perestroika,* 146).[37] In Kushner's rendering of Jewish identity, survival at any price is simply not a part of the Jewish bargain. His *Angels* is informed by Deuteronomy's vision of "Justice, justice shalt thou pursue, that thou mayest live" (16:20), which may depend on the notion that it is a moral imperative not to be too much at home in one's home, that a people's humanity and moral energy is best marshaled in the face of uncertainty rather than belonging and satiation. In this vital sense, ***Angels in America*** delivers Judaism's prophetic message about the plight of the stranger, his/her vulnerability in the face of the state's destructive indifference.

Notes

1. Quoted in Norman J. Cohen, "Wrestling With Angels" (Interview with Tony Kushner), in Robert Vorlicky, ed., *Tony Kushner in Conversation* (Ann Arbor: University of Michigan Press, 1998), p. 217.

2. Tony Kushner, *Angels in America: A Gay Fantasia on National Themes. Part One: Millennium Approaches* (New York: Theatre Communications Group, 1993); Kushner, *Angels in America, A Gay Fantasia on National Themes. Part Two: Perestroika* (Revised Version) (New York: Theatre Communications Group, 1996).

3. Adam Mars Jones, "Tony Kushner at the Royal National Theatre of Great Britain," in Vorlicky, ed., *Tony Kushner in Conversation,* p. 26.

4. Jones, "Tony Kushner at the Royal National Theatre," p. 27.

5. Craig Lucas, "The Eye of the Storm," *Bomb,* No. 43 (Spring 1993): 34.

6. Jones, "Tony Kushner at the Royal National Theatre," p. 26. It seems of some significance that Kushner insists on embracing both identities, that to him these seem interrelated and intrinsic to his role as a political artist: "It's great to be part of a community. I

want to be thought of as a Jewish writer. I want to be thought of as a gay writer—mostly as a gay writer, because I experience in my life a lot more homophobia than I do anti-Semitism. There may come a time when I feel that it's more important to be thought of as a Jew than as a gay person" (Michael Cunningham, "Thinking About Fabulousness," in Vorlicky, ed., *Tony Kushner in Conversation,* p. 69).

7. Cohen, "Wrestling with Angels," p. 218.

8. "Mentshlichkeit" derives from the German *mensch* and the Yiddish *mentsh,* both denoting a human being or person. However in Yiddish, there is no greater compliment than to say that someone behaves as a *mentsh,* demonstrating personal integrity and moral uprightness. Hence, *mentshlichkeit* is the quality of being a *mentsh.* "Tikkun Olam" is ethical action oriented toward the repair or restoration of the world. "T'shuva," denotes "turning" in Hebrew and is essential to the Jewish reverence for human life; the notion of turning to God, or to the right ethical path, derives from the Jewish conception of human redemption and underlies both the intrinsic hopefulness about humankind, and the ceaseless yearning for messianic salvation.

9. Jyl Lynn Felman, "Lost Jewish (Male) Souls: A Midrash on *Angels in America*," *Tikkun,* Vol. 10, No. 3 (1995): 29.

10. Emmanuel Levinas, *Otherwise than Being or Beyond Essence,* trans. Alphonso Lingis (Pittsburgh: Duquesne University Press, 1999), p. 157.

11. Emmanuel Levinas, *Du sacré au saint. Cinq nouvelles lectures talmudiques* (Paris: Minuit, 1977), p. 19.

12. For an overview of Levinas's engagement with the rabbinic tradition, see *Difficult Freedom: Essays on Judaism,* trans. Seán Hand (Baltimore: The Johns Hopkins University Press, 1990) and *Nine Talmudic Readings,* trans. Annette Aronowicz (Bloomington: Indiana University Press, 1994).

13. For my perspective on the usefulness of Levinas for addressing the Jewish narrative imagination, see Ranen Omer-Sherman, *Israel in Exile: Jewish Writing and the Desert* (Champaign: University of Illinois Press, 2006).

14. Kushner's evocative remarks to the opening night cast at the Mark Taper Forum in May of 1992 (the first American production of *Millennium*) underscore this disavowal of divine comfort and insistence on a fully-awakened sense of human obligation: "If we are to be visited by angels we will have to call them down with sweat and strain, we will have to drag them out of the skies" (John Lahr, "After Angels," *The New Yorker* [January 3, 2005]: 49).

15. Sara Marcus, "Staging Change: The Revolutionary Rigor of Tony Kushner" (Interview), *Heeb,* Vol. 4 (Fall 2003): 60.

16. Cohen, "Wrestling with Angels," p. 218.

17. Jewish, Christian, and even Muslim strains of apocalyptic traditions have wielded a considerable influence on the aesthetics of Western culture, engendering not only the startling visions of works such as the Book of Daniel and the Dead Sea Scrolls but also the literary and visual art of masterpieces such as Dante's *Divine Comedy,* Michelangelo's fresco of *The Last Judgment,* and William Blake's *America: A Prophecy.* It seems that whenever a society is preoccupied by the trauma of change, apocalyptic narratives, not unlike conspiracy theories, offer a structure of history and a sense of purpose behind bewildering events.

18. Allen J. Frantzen, *Before the Closet: Same-Sex Love from* Beowulf *to* Angels in America (Chicago: University of Chicago Press, 1998), p. 280.

19. Jones, "Tony Kushner at the Royal National Theatre," p. 25.

20. Ironically, Kushner seems to associate Cohn's lack of *Yiddishkayt,* or human ethics, with the fate of his "Jewish nose" in early infancy: "See this scar on my nose?" asks Roy. "When I was three months old, there was a bony spur, she made them operate, shave it off. They said I was too young for the surgery, I'd outgrow it but she insisted. I figure she wanted to toughen me up. And it worked" (*Perestroika,* 81).

21. Bruce McLeod, "The Oddest Phenomena in Modern History" (Interview with Tony Kushner), *Iowa Journal of Cultural Studies,* Vol. 14, No. 1 (Spring 1995): 152.

22. Walter Benjamin, "Theses on the Philosophy of History," in Walter Benjamin, *Illuminations,* trans. and ed. Harry Zohn (New York: Schocken, 1973), p. 254. For a remarkably insightful discussion of Kushner's indebtedness to Benjamin's theory of history, see David Savran's "Ambivalence, Utopia, and a Queer Sort of Materialism: How *Angels in America* Reconstructs the Nation," in Deborah R. Geis and Steven F. Kruger, eds., *Approaching the Millennium: Essays on* Angels in America (Ann Arbor: University of Michigan Press, 1997), pp. 13-39.

23. Steven F. Kruger, "Identity and Conversion in *Angels in America,*" in Geis and Kruger, eds., *Approaching the Millennium,* p. 156.

24. Though it is Hannah who wisely explains that mortals must transcend the danger of angelic entrapment if it means succumbing to life-smothering dogma: "An angel is just a belief, with wings and arms that can carry you. It's naught to be afraid of. If it lets you down, reject it. Seek for something new" (*Perestroika,* 103).

25. Daniel Mendelssohn, "Winged Messages," *The New York Review of Books* (February 2, 2004): 44.

26. Marcus, "Staging Change," p. 59.

27. *Minyan* (from a Hebrew root meaning to count or to number) translates as prayer quorum. In Judaism, prayer is largely conceived as a group activity rather than an individual activity. Certain prayers and religious activities cannot be performed without a minyan. This need for a minyan has often helped to keep the Jewish community together in isolated areas. Although it is generally permissible to pray alone, the individual Jew must always make every effort to pray with a group.

28. Tom Szentgyorgyi, "Look Back—and Forward—in Anger" (Profile of Tony Kushner), *Theater Week,* Vol. 6, No. 1 (January 14-21, 1991): 19.

29. Alisa Solomon, "Wrestling with *Angels*: A Jewish Fantasia," in Geis and Kruger, eds., *Approaching the Millennium,* p. 124). The Talmudic precept is quoted in *Leo Rosten's Treasury of Jewish Quotations* (New York: McGraw Hill, 1972), p. 279.

30. Felman, "Lost Jewish (Male) Souls," p. 29.

31. Cohen, "Wrestling with Angels," p. 229.

32. McLeod, "The Oddest Phenomena," pp. 152-53. Together with theater critic Alisa Solomon, Kushner later went on to co-edit a collection of essays and creative works, titled *Wrestling With Zion: Progressive Jewish American Responses to the Israeli-Palestinian Conflict* (New York: Grove Press, 2003), a project that began with a letter of invitation sent out to roughly sixty Jewish writers which reads in part: "A widespread but relatively recent conflation of Judaism and Jewish identity with Israel and Israeli nationalist identity has done a grave disservice to the heterogeneity of Jewish thought, to the centuries-old Jewish traditions of lively dispute and rigorous, unapologetic skeptical inquiry. As a consequence of this artificial flattening and deadening of discourse, enforced by rage and even violence, the vital connection between Jewish culture and the struggle for social and economic justice is coming apart. . . . [B]ecause American foreign policy has a tidal effect on the politics of the region, the Jewish-American community can play a pivotal role in the pursuit of a just and lasting peace. We hope this book will help liberate American voices of negotiation for the end of the occupation, for justice for the Palestinians, for peace and security for both nations" (*Wrestling with Zion,* p. 8).

33. For Kushner himself "the most moving scene in both parts [of *Angels*] is where Ethel Rosenberg says the Kaddish for Roy Cohn. ... And I do believe—I wouldn't be in theater if I didn't believe this—that certain forms of ritual practice can transform one's consciousness through gestures and through design and through ritual" (Cohen, "Wrestling with Angels," p. 228).

34. Kruger, "Identity and Conversion," p. 154.

35. Felman, "Lost Jewish (Male) Souls," p. 27.

36. Carl Weber, "I Always Go Back to Brecht" (Interview with Tony Kushner), *Brecht Yearbook/Das Brecht-Jahrbuch,* Vol. 25 (Madison: The International Brecht Society, 1995), p. 68.

37. In declaring that gays "will be citizens," Prior effectively intensifies *Angels'* layered approach to Jewish and queer struggles, by evoking the Enlightenment dream of civic belonging that the Jews of 18th-century France pursued.

Joshua Pederson (essay date 2009)

SOURCE: Pederson, Joshua. "'More Life' and More: Harold Bloom, the J Writer, and the Archaic Judaism of Tony Kushner's *Angels in America.*" *Contemporary Literature* 50.3 (2009): 576-98. Print.

[*In the following essay, Pederson argues that "much of the play's religious mythology and, by extension, its portrayal of Judaism" relies upon Bloom's explication of a strand of "archaic Jewish myth" that is one of the sources of the Torah. According to Pederson, Kushner's reliance on Bloom results in his celebration of a religious ethos that is anthropomorphic and dynamic, ultimately enhancing the play's humanism.*]

> Even sick. I want to be alive. ...
>
> I want more life. I can't help myself. I do.
>
> I've lived through such terrible times, and there are people who live through much much worse, but. ... You see them living anyway. When they're more spirit than body, more sores than skin, when they're burned and in agony, when flies lay eggs in the corners of the eyes of their children, they live.
>
> Tony Kushner, *Perestroika*
> (second ellipsis in original)

In Genesis 32, Jacob—son of Isaac, grandson of Abraham, and third patriarch—sets out with his wives, his children, and his entourage to meet his estranged brother Esau. On the eve of that reunion, by the shores of the river Jabbok, Jacob grapples with an angel—or more specifically, a mysterious man. Though they wrestle until near dawn, neither bests his opponent. As the sun is about to rise, the angel demands that Jacob release him. Jacob agrees, on one

condition: "I will not let you go, unless you bless me" (32:26). The angel assents, and Jacob receives both his blessing and a new name, Israel.

Prior Walter, the AIDS-stricken hero of Tony Kushner's *Angels in America,* whom the author explicitly and implicitly likens to Jacob, also wrestles with an angel. And upon being admitted into the angelic council in one of the last scenes of *Perestroika,* the play's second part, he demands his own blessing: "more life." "More life"—as Kushner acknowledges in his notes to *Perestroika* (10, 154-55)—is a translation of the Hebrew word for "blessing" taken from Harold Bloom and expanded upon in *The Book of J,* Bloom's attempt (with translator David Rosenberg) to tease out and interpret one of the multiple voices that contemporary scholarship suggests constitute the Torah narrative. Though courteous, this nod toward Bloom is enigmatic in its solitude, for it is the only one that the playwright makes, even though the imaginative fabric of *Angels* features the ideas of many great thinkers, including Walter Benjamin, Bertolt Brecht, and Ernst Bloch, to name a few. It is, therefore, downright peculiar that Kushner would mention just the seemingly minor influence of Bloom.[1] But a closer look at the text itself proves Bloom's presence to be more significant than the gift of a two-word phrase. It seems that Kushner is indebted to Bloom not only for two crucial words—"more life"—but also for much of the play's religious mythology and, by extension, its portrayal of Judaism.

According to Bloom, *The Book of J* provides readers with glimpses of what he calls an "archaic Judaism" (*Book* 14), a freer, more dynamic cultic practice unconstrained by the rite and ritual of the temple-centered Judaism of Solomon, during whose reign the J text was putatively written. In what follows, I will argue that Kushner injects *Angels* with significant doses of J's (or Bloom's) archaic Jewish myth. Indeed, I will suggest that Bloom's J gives Kushner much of the religiosity of his play. But why Bloom? And why, especially for the self-professed agnostic Kushner, the archaic Judaism of J? The answer has something to do with Kushner's own conflicted relationship with his Jewish heritage. A close reading of the speech that opens the play—Rabbi Isidor Chemelwitz's eulogy for Sarah Ironson, the grandmother of Prior's boyfriend Louis—yields some insight:

> She was ... (*He touches the coffin*) not a person but a whole kind of person, the ones who crossed the ocean, who brought with us to America the villages of Russia and Lithuania—and how we struggled, and how we fought, for the family, for the Jewish home, so that you would not grow up *here,* in this strange place, in the melting pot where nothing melted. Descendants of this immigrant woman, you do not grow up in America, you and your children and their children with the goyische names. You do not live in America. No such place exists. Your clay is the clay of some Litvak shtetl, your air the air of the steppes—because she carried the old world on her back across the ocean, in a boat, and she put it down on Grand

Concourse Avenue, or in Flatbush, and she worked that
earth into your bones, and you pass it to your children, this
ancient, ancient culture and home.

(*Little pause*)

You can never make that crossing that she made, for such
Great Voyages in this world do not any more exist. But
every day of your lives the miles that voyage between that
place and this one you cross. Every day. You understand
me? In you that journey is. . . .

She was the last of the Mohicans, this one was. Pretty
soon . . . all the old will be dead.

> (***Millennium*** 10-11; first and
> third ellipses in original)

It is apparent that Chemelwitz's is an atavistic brand of
Judaism, a European diasporan Judaism, a religious sensibility that holds on to the ideals of an intrinsically exilic
faith when the establishment of the state of Israel and assimilation of Jews into American culture render such sentiments retrograde. God molds Chemelwitz's Jews from "the
clay of some Litvak shtetl," from the soil of an eternally
foreign country. Always strangers in strange lands, Jews
are Jews because they make journeys to struggle in homes
that are not their own, so many journeys, in fact, that journey itself—and not destination—becomes constitutive of
the Jewish soul; "In you that journey is," he intones. His is a
Judaism of eternal movement, of movement enshrined in a
forever dynamic Jewish identity. Motion, not situatedness,
is key—homelessness, not home.

Such a figuration of Judaism lines up almost perfectly with
Kushner's own understanding of what is—or was—best
about the Jewish faith. As he said in a 1995 interview, "I
think the Diasporan Jewish culture has a magnificent history of progressive involvement with the cultures that Jews
have found themselves in and interacting with." Such involvement, according to Kushner, put Judaism in touch
with "traditions of socialism and humanism" (*Tony Kushner* 82). For Kushner, much of Judaism's diasporan progressivism has been lost since the establishment of the state
of Israel: "[T]here was this tremendous support for Israel
and that's been part of this calamity—it's driven international Jewish culture from its progressive basis . . .
[because] there are important progressive and radical
European traditions that arrived with Jews in the U.S. . . .
that really informed American Jewish consciousness all the
way up to the 1950s." It is as if, for Kushner, as for his
character Chemelwitz, the placelessness of diasporan Judaism kept it in contact with progressive, tolerant social
trends, while the establishment of stable Jewish homelands
in Israel and the United States led to the slow attrition of
such positive cultural forces. More simply, Judaism is at its
best when it is in constant motion, when it is without the
ultimately stultifying safeties of temple, state, or homeland.
It is for this reason, I suggest, that Kushner takes up
Bloom's J narrative of the development of an archaic Jewish faith, for J's tales provide him with an even purer my-

thology of Jewish dynamism. Chemelwitz's age—indeed,
he is so near death that we see him later in heaven—seems
to suggest that diasporan Judaism, despite all its positive
qualities, is condemned to the dustbin of history for Kushner. In attempting to restore to Judaism its spirit of progressivism, Kushner reaches further back into Jewish history
for an even more dynamic portrait of the ancient religious
faith: J's archaic Judaism, as interpreted by Harold Bloom.
In what follows, I hope to uncover the elements of this
archaic Judaism as they appear in ***Angels in America***.
Kushner's appropriation of the imaginative world of J—
as interpreted by the ubiquitous Bloom—is neither whole-
sale nor without its ironies. Indeed, the playwright puts his
own stamp on the religious imagery that Bloom has—not
always unproblematically—teased from the Torah;[2] Kushner occasionally slants or even inverts elements of the J
text. But the influence of Bloom's reading of J is undeniable, and generative of a more complete understanding of
the unique religiosity of ***Angels***.

BLOOM'S J: THE CREATION OF AN AUTHOR

The majority of modern biblical scholarship supports what
has come to be known as the "documentary hypothesis,"
initially proposed by Julius Wellhausen in nineteenth-
century Germany. This theory suggests that the Torah or
Pentateuch—the first five books of the Bible—is the collective composition of no fewer than five writers living at
various times in the first millennium before the common
era. Scholars have settled on a shorthand for identifying
these five writers, referring to them by the letters J, D, P, E,
and R. According to the theory, J, D, P, and E are several
producers of text; R—or the redactor—is the editor who
gathered, molded, and arranged the work of the four other
writers to produce a composite text very similar to today's
Torah. In *The Book of J*, Harold Bloom attempts to cull
from the composite work of the Torah the writing of one
particular author—J, or the Yahwist.[3] Bloom works in tan-
dem with David Rosenberg, whose new translation of the
putative writing of J Bloom reads and interprets.

It's worth emphasizing the eccentricity of Bloom's method.
Bloom is a very readerly critic, and his interpretation of the
J text is typical of his brand of "strong misreading." "Since
we cannot know the circumstances under which the work
was composed, or for what purposes," he observes, "ultimately we must rely upon our experience as readers to
justify our surmises as to what it is that we are reading"
(*Book* 9). Strong misreading assumes that texts possess
only illusory being, and the strong misreader strives not
to arrive at a text's truth or essence but instead to "usurp"
meaning, to forcefully take hold of a text and use it to
establish a position in a lineage of readers and poets.[4] Unable to arrive at the "truth" of a text, one instead tries to
"make something happen" with it. That which Bloom tries
to "make happen" with the text of the J writer is—in essence—the production of an author:

For reasons that I will expound, I am assuming that J lived at or nearby the court of Solomon's son and successor, King Rehoboam of Judah, under whom his father's kingdom fell apart soon after the death of Solomon in 922 B.C.E. My further assumption is that J was not a professional scribe but rather an immensely sophisticated, highly placed member of the Solomonic elite, enlightened and ironic. But my primary surmise is that J was a woman, and that she wrote for her contemporaries as a woman, in friendly competition with her only strong rival among those contemporaries, the male author of the court history narrative in 2 Samuel.

(*Book* 9)

The figure of J that Bloom teases out of *The Book of J*—who remains an imagined authorial construct—serves to guide us back into the text, fueling further readings and (mis)interpretations.[5]

Bloom believes that J's is both the most powerful Hebrew text and the earliest. Thus he asserts that J gives us a glimpse of the religious ethos that preceded the Judaism of Solomonic Israel: "What J portrays, with loving irony, is an archaic Judaism now largely lost to us, though to call it a Judaism at all is bound to be an error" (*Book* 14). For Bloom, the portrait J provides of this religion remains so vibrant that it forms the imaginative foundation for a variety of scriptures: "J mixes everything available to her and produces a work so comprehensive and so universal that the entire Hebrew Bible, Greek New Testament, and Arabic Koran could be founded upon it" (18). In brief, her version of religion provides the seed material for all the main Western traditions. This archaic Judaism—strongly misread by Bloom—also shapes the religious message of Kushner's play. Broadly speaking, five aspects of J's Judaism appear in Kushner's text, though not without some irony: J's vision of Yahweh, intensely dynamic and strikingly anthropomorphic; her portrait of Jacob, equally dynamic and somewhat theomorphic; her concept of the blessing "more life"; her glorification of sex and sexuality; and her thoroughly unlegalistic attitudes toward divine law. It is important to note, for reasons explored below, that these five elements never resolve into a theological system; the dynamic Yahweh who sneaks into and out of Kushner's play will not consent to his own assimilation into such a confining matrix. They do, however, come together in privileging anthropology (as opposed to theology), and the religion that the playwright borrows from Bloom and J only strengthens his own vibrant humanism.

In taking on the documentary hypothesis, Bloom wades into muddy waters. Without engaging modern biblical criticism too technically, one may nonetheless note that the theory has changed significantly since Wellhausen first articulated it well over a century ago. Today, many would make no distinction between the J and E sources, opting instead to distinguish between only a priestly (P) author and a nonpriestly author.[6] Thus some would argue that Bloom's narrative features only half a voice. Further, schol-

arly consensus is moving toward the position that these multiple authors were not indeed authors at all, but schools of authors—that the Torah is not the product of four or five writers, but of perhaps hundreds spaced over centuries.[7] So others may contend that Bloom is dealing not with a voice but with a chorus. Finally, Robert Alter points out that while it is helpful to assert the multiple authorship of the Torah, it is impossible—and perhaps harmful—to pull apart those authors' respective contributions:

> But even if we assume that we know confidently in all significant instances what is J, E, and P [and we frequently do not], there remains the intractable problem of what Sir Edmund Leach has called "unscrambling the omelette." Perhaps there once was a splendid J narrative from Adam to Moses, but all that is left of it is what R decided to splice with E and P. The J texts that have come down to us . . . are an intermittent, inadequate story, a poor thing compared to the wonderful orchestration that R has made of all his sources.

(162-63)

Hence it is very likely that we—and more importantly, Bloom—have only part of J and can never remake her whole. Bloom's J is therefore an almost imaginary text, as much the creation of the critic as of an ancient author.

In the following analysis, I do not presume that Kushner is privy to such intricate scholarly debates. The playwright is intellectually curious, and his work confirms that he is intimately familiar with Bloom's J. I do not wish to argue that Kushner is similarly familiar with the contemporary landscape of biblical scholarship or the lively debates that have sprung up around Bloom's work. Many of the historical discoveries mentioned above came to light only after the publication of *Angels* in 1993 and 1994, and while two intervening decades have allowed us ample time to fully interrogate Bloom's theses, the layman Kushner, exploring them in the first several months after the 1990 publication of *The Book of J,* had no such luxury.[8]

REVELING IN ANTHROPOMORPHISM: J'S YAHWEH, KUSHNER'S GOD

Bloom hopes, in extracting J's narrative from the composite work of the Torah, to remove her writing from a normative interpretive tradition that stifles the dynamism of her text. Bloom scorns the rest of the contributors to the Pentateuch, assuming that they soften or even bastardize the genius of J. Nowhere is this more obvious than in the complex figure of Yahweh. Bloom believes that traditional biblical writing—beginning with the E, D, and P authors—has obscured the contours of J's Yahweh, rendering him amorphous. The divergence between this figure and the God of the rest of the Torah begins with a debate over Yahweh's anthropomorphism—the extent to which he resembles his human creations. Not without some petulance, Bloom contends that while later, more traditional writers try to obscure Yahweh's human elements, J revels in his dynamic similarity to his greatest creation, humankind. Bloom delights in the apparent anthropomorphism of J's Yahweh, noticing how J brings the deity and his creatures into close, intimate association. Indeed, J's account of the creation of man blurs the distinction between creator and creature, god and man, eternal and carnal. It is this blurring that renders Yahweh such a compelling figure. J's Yahweh alters and even transcends the terms of the anthropomorphism debate: "[H]er Yahweh is both more and less than anthropomorphic: he is wild and free, an almost unconditioned impulse. There is a glint in J's eye whenever we receive a portrait of Yahweh, for his restless dynamism will not consent to be confined" (*Book* 291). Dynamism is Yahweh's hallmark. He is irascible, impish, changeable, intimate, dirty. He has hands and a mouth and grime under his fingernails. In his relations with humankind, he is capable of moments of touching intimacy and fits of childish wrath. His physical and emotional distance from his human creation varies wildly. A lip's breadth away from humanity in the book's first verses, Yahweh suffers a seeming crisis of confidence as the writing continues, pulling away to mountaintops and distant heavens: "Yahweh is presence, is the will to change, is origination and originality. His leading quality is not holiness, or justice, or love, or righteousness, but the sheer energy and force of becoming, of breaking into fresh being" (294).

Maybe not so coincidentally, for Bloom this "sheer energy" describes not only the Yahweh of J's text but the god of Joseph Smith's brand of Mormonism. Though in the following I will treat only Bloom's influence on the Jewish—or "archaic" Jewish—content of Kushner's play, I would be remiss if I did not acknowledge the critic's likely influence on the play's characterization of Mormonism, another of the important religious influences in *Angels*. (Three main characters—Hannah, Joe, and Harper—are all Mormons and originally from Utah.) In *The American Religion,* Bloom identifies Mormonism as one of the three major strands of an authentically American national religion. Further, he considers Smith, its founder, to be one of this country's very few religious geniuses: "He was an authentic religious genius, and surpassed all Americans, before or since, in the possession and expression of what could be called the religion-making imagination" (*American Religion* 96-97). For Bloom, there are striking similarities that connect Smith's deity to J's Yahweh:

> I think transumptively of the Prophet Joseph's God when I read the text of the Yahwist, or J Writer, author of the earliest tales of the Pentateuch. The Yahweh who closes Noah's ark with his own hands, descends to make on-the-ground inspections of Babel and Sodom, and who picnics with two angels under Abram's terebinth trees at Mamre is very close, in personality and dynamic passion, to the God of Joseph Smith, far closer than to the Platonic-Aristotelian divinity of Saint Augustine and Moses Maimonides.

> (101)

Perhaps Bloom's understanding of the dynamism of Smith's God partially accounts for the principal role that Mormonism plays in Kushner's religious vision in *Angels,*

and for the strong bond that quickly develops between Hannah and Prior, the standard-bearer for J's archaic Judaism.

This remarkable dynamism—the eternal changeability of J's deity, be he Mormon, archaic Jewish, or otherwise—fuels the creation of Kushner's cosmology in *Angels in America.* The epigraph with which Kushner opens the second half of the play—Ralph Waldo Emerson (in "On Art") on the nature of the soul—could as well apply to J's Yahweh and Kushner's God: "Because the soul is progressive, it never quite repeats itself, but in every act attempts the production of a new and fairer whole" (*Perestroika* 11). This quotation gestures toward the continual breaking into newness that characterizes J's Yahweh. Kushner's play explores the dialectical relationship that exists between dynamism—so effectively embodied by J's Yahweh—and its polar opposite, stasis. The first conversation between Prior and the Angel—who breaks through the ceiling of Prior's bedroom to enlist him as a new prophet for stasis—helps to flesh out this relationship. Prior, who is recounting his revelation to his ex-lover Belize, provides his own version of the Angel's tale: "In making people God apparently set in motion a potential in the design for change, for random event, for movement forward" (*Perestroika* 42). God, bored or uninterested with his first, angelic creation—"they're basically incredibly powerful bureaucrats" (41), mutters Prior—creates humanity in order to introduce an aleatory spark into what must have become a staid, if fabulous, universe.

At least before the play's cosmic present, Kushner's God—though possessing enough of a sense of change and randomness to instill it within humans—remains a stable heavenly presence. Nonetheless, God's creation of a changeable humanity paves the way not only for "Sleeping Creation's Potential for Change" (*Perestroika* 42) but also for his own revitalization. After the creation of humanity, Kushner's God begins to develop. The Angel continues:

> He began to leave Us!
> Bored with His Angels,
> Bewitched by Humanity,
> In Mortifying imitation of You, his least creation,
> He would sail off on Voyages, no knowing where.

> (*Perestroika* 43)

Belize, savvy interpreter that he is, "smell[s] a motif" (44), likening God to all the play's departing lovers and positing a time before the creation of humanity, before God's relationship with his angelic harem, when the Divine reveled in his own dynamic, cosmic bachelorhood. The deity's midnight wanderings—and ultimate departure—signify the changeability innate in his being. His flight mimics that of J's Yahweh, who is quite intimate with Adam and his nameless wife but eventually moves away, becoming for Moses a distant voice, an occasional presence given to flights of violence.

For Bloom there is something innately contradictory about J's efforts to represent Yahweh, for to do so "is to compromise his relentless dynamism. For J's Yahweh, . . . as for J, everything that matters most is perpetually new" (*Book* 311). The textual representation of Yahweh partially reifies him and perhaps pins him down in the midst of—and almost in spite of—his changes. Hence it is not unimportant that Kushner's God is gone. Unwilling to have his dynamism compromised by artistic depiction, Kushner's God leaves the stage before the play begins, rendering the situation of the angels who hope for his return downright Beckettian.[9] Of course, to say that God is absent from the play is not entirely true. He appears once—a pulsing, red aleph—in a nonspeaking role, addressed by the deceased Roy Cohn, who offers to represent him in some sort of cosmic court. (Cohn, Kushner's fictionalized version of the crooked McCarthy-era prosecutor and Reagan-era power broker, has recently died of AIDS.) But what may be more important about this scene than its presence in the play is Kushner's insistence in the notes that it be optional.[10] Though the scene may provide posthumous redemption for Cohn, it also compromises the dynamism of an otherwise unrepresented God. Another optional scene— act 5, scene 6—also weakens the play's dynamism. In it, Prior and the now-deceased Rabbi Chemelwitz have a chat in heaven. The rabbi is playing cards with Louis's grandmother and explains to Prior how card-playing brings joy to the afterlife: "Cards is strategy but mostly a game of chance. In Heaven, everything is known. To the Great Questions are lying about here like yesterday's newspaper all the answers. So from what comes the pleasures of Paradise? *Indeterminacy!*" (*Perestroika* 134). Like Kushner's representation of God in conversation with Cohn, the rabbi's speech compromises the dynamism of humanity. Dead, it appears as if humanity becomes subject to the same stasis that the angels represent, stealing from them their defining characteristic along with their life.

AN IRONIC JACOB: THE UNTHEOMORPHIC LAST WALTER AND A DUBIOUS BLESSING

In the "playwright's notes" to **Perestroika** (7), Kushner confirms his "indebtedness to Harold Bloom's reading of the Jacob story" (10). In contrast to his appropriation of J's Yahweh, however, Kushner's use of her Jacob is playful, even ironic. If, for J, Yahweh lowers himself and comes to resemble his creation, Jacob is the patriarch who most boldly lifts himself up to meet God halfway; put differently, Yahweh's anthropomorphism is dialectically matched with Jacob's theomorphism. Bloom explains, "Indeed, [Jacob] is theomorphic precisely because J's Yahweh is so outrageous; Jacob is as cunning as Yahweh, and like Yahweh possesses in abundance . . . subtle, naked consciousness" (*Book* 209).[11] Jacob proves his theomorphic cunning in his pursuit of the blessing. But J's blessing is different from that of the other Torah authors. First, J's blessing deals not only with the imperative or privilege of fruitfulness and multiplication ("Be fruitful and multi-

ply") but also with the proliferation of one's *name,* which it "preserves and extends" (*Book* 210). But on a more comprehensive level, the blessing has something to do with life itself, and more of it. In this respect, the blessing is less a guarantee than a burning spur that drives its possessors to a relentless pursuit of vitality and change.

Though Kushner may well be indebted to Bloom for the latter's reading of Jacob, his indebtedness is subtle and complex. Kushner's play acts as a prism that separates the aspects of J's Jacob, distilling them in different amounts in different characters. I want to suggest that Prior—the character whom critics have most frequently likened to Jacob—is at best an ironic patriarch, an unwilling participant in the divine plan. (I maintain that the play's true Jacob is Roy Cohn, who is every bit as dynamic, irascible, and cunning as J's Jacob or, for that matter, J's God.) However, Prior and Roy aside, it is Joe Pitt—the Mormon appellate-court clerk who is also Roy's protégé—who introduces Jacob into the play's narrative by comparing himself to Jacob in the patriarch's struggle with the angel:

> It's me. In that struggle. Fierce, and unfair. The angel is
> not human, and it holds nothing back, so how could any-
> one human win, what kind of a fight is that? It's not just.
> Losing means your soul thrown down in the dust, your
> heart torn out from God's. But you can't not lose.

> (*Millennium* 49)

A far cry from J's Jacob, who is persistent and hungry for the blessing the angel will yield, Joe wrestles only to avoid the pain of loss. (For Joe, Jacob's bout with the angel serves as a metaphor for his own struggle with homosexual urges he can no longer ignore; Joe eventually leaves his wife Harper and takes up with Louis.) If J defines the struggle between Jacob and the angel in terms of possibility and blessing, Joe defines it in terms of disparity and injustice.

Prior, who before ascending to heaven in the play's last act actually wrestles angels (and who, unlike Joe, begs for a blessing), also differs from J's Jacob.[12] Though sometimes wily and dynamic, Prior (unlike J's Jacob) is not theomorphic; he neither resembles nor wishes to resemble God. For Kushner's vision of the divine is just another version of Belize's unreliable male. Joe abandons Harper; Louis abandons Prior; God abandons his angels and his creation. But Prior does no such thing. Prior is mature, steadfast, and emotionally stable. He rails against changeable lovers who slip out the back door when the going gets rough. Furthermore, the blessing sought by the angel-wrestling Prior has nothing to do with either genetic transmission or generational continuity. Barring adoption or in vitro fertilization (an option that, although mentioned, remains unlikely given Prior's AIDS-tainted blood), Prior will be the last of the Walters, Kushner puns. Prior's plea for more life at play's end is ironic at the expense of J's Jacob. More life for Prior means more susceptibility to contagion, more disease, more pain. When Prior pleads with the angels—"I still want. . . . My blessing. Even sick. I want to be alive" (*Perestroika* 131)—he does so in spite of the pain implicit in the additional life he will ultimately receive. Prior's vitriol in addressing the angels proves just how un-theomorphic he is, just how fervently he wishes to embrace humanity's plight:

> We can't just stop. We're not rocks—progress, migration, motion is … modernity. It's *animate,* it's what living things do. We desire. Even if all we desire is stillness, it's still desire *for.* Even if we go faster than we should. We can't *wait.* And wait for what? God …

> (*Perestroika* 130; ellipses in original)

He ends his most impassioned speech with this cynical evocation of the departed Divine, and the pause that surely sits between "what?" and "God" shows just how grounded Prior is in the mortal lot, in pain, in a desire to distance himself from an absentee creator who leaves when things get tough. Indeed, Prior's appropriation of J's blessing—"more life"—is a barb fired at heaven and a plea that Prior be allowed to stick around even when God will not.

THE FLAMING ALEPH: SEX AND MONISM IN *ANGELS*

The view of sex that Kushner provides in *Angels* also betrays the influence of Bloom and J. Kushner's play is filled with sex; whether it be gay sex, straight sex, married sex, or unfaithful sex, Kushner injects heaven and earth with a dynamic libidinal energy. However, it is the eroticization of God and his heavenly court that is most likely to rile the conservative reader of *Angels,* for indeed they have sex too. As Prior explains it, sex is constitutive of God's relationship with the angels. The orgasmic energy—or, more bluntly, the "Spooj"—that their coupling produces powers the creation and maintenance of the cosmos. Moreover, the erotic plays an important role in divine-human relations. Joe's vision of Jacob and the wrestling angel is undeniably erotic (and specifically homoerotic): "Jacob is young and very strong. The angel is … a beautiful man, with golden hair and wings, of course. I still dream about it" (*Millennium* 49; ellipsis in original). Prior's first encounter with the Angel involves him humping the book of the angelic prophecy while the Angel climaxes. (In director Mike Nichols's film version of the play, Prior and the Angel actually copulate.) It seems as if, at least in Prior's case, sex serves as a necessary stage in a mystical quest. Further, before returning to heaven near the end of *Perestroika,* the Angel gives Joe's mother Hannah what one can only assume is her first orgasm in many years. For Kushner, sex and the flesh—human, angelic, or even godly—are undoubtedly divine.

All of this erotic theological play is a very far cry from the Pauline dualistic mode that raises up the spirit only at the expense of the flesh (or, for that matter, the degradation of sex and sexuality in Augustine). Only the spirit is holy; the flesh—which becomes synecdoche for body and sexual activity—is an obstacle, a temptation whose allures must be overcome if salvation is to be attained. As Paul writes, "Live by the Spirit, I say, and do not gratify the desires of the flesh. For what the flesh desires is opposed to the Spirit, and what the Spirit desires is opposed to the flesh; for these are opposed to each other, to prevent you from doing what you want" (Gal. 5:16-17). In *Angels,* such a negative valuation of the body is absent, and the distinction between flesh and spirit is immaterial. The Angel's description of herself takes up Paul's language—referring to the body as "flesh"—and confirms Kushner's glorification of the carnal and the corporeal:

> You are Mere Flesh. IIII am Utter Flesh,
> Density of Desire, the Gravity of Skin:
> What makes the Engine of Creation Run?
> Not Physics But Ecstatics Makes the Engine Run.

> (*Perestroika* 39)

The Angel is humanity's own bodily nature rendered ultimate. Hence, contra Paul, Kushner seems to suggest that individual "spiritual" progress requires not the destruction of the flesh but its fulfillment. It is almost as if what is required of us is not that we abstain from sex but perfect it, learn to do it correctly. Kushner's depiction of God also serves as a tacit critique of Pauline dualism. Kushner describes God as "a flaming Hebrew letter, but a male flaming Hebrew letter" (*Perestroika* 49).[13] Paul as frequently distinguishes between the spirit and the flesh as he does between the spirit and "the letter," and famously suggests in 2 Corinthians that "the letter kills, but the Spirit gives life" (3:6). In his vision of God, Kushner elevates—nay, deifies—both the letter and the flesh, making his version of God a fiery *aleph* fully capable of satisfying the sexual needs of a countless host of hermaphroditic (and, candidly speaking, randy) angels. Thus does God destroy the imaginary distinctions that exist among flesh, letter, and spirit.[14]

Such distinctions are similarly lost on J. In fact, Bloom attributes to the J writer the seminal development of monism, the theological opposite of Paul's dualism: "A monistic vitalism that refuses to distinguish between flesh and spirit is at the center of J's vision, which is thus at the opposite extreme from either the Gnostic or the Pauline Christian dualism" (*J* 277). Bloom goes so far as to suggest that J *invents* monism—a theological and anthropological system based not on distinctions and binaries but on unity and wholeness. For Bloom, only the priestly writer (P, in the shorthand of Biblical scholarship) and later redactors are interested in degrading the flesh; J accepts it and glories in it, acknowledging the integral role the body plays in human progress. Indeed, if Saint Augustine suggests that sex is the sin that led to Adam's (and Eve's) Fall, for J, *there is no fall,* because "for J there is nothing fallen about nature, earthly or human" (Bloom, *Book* 176). The same can be said of Kushner's *Angels,* in which sex is not that which drives us from God, but instead that which makes us more like him.

MAKING LAW IN A LAWLESS LAND: ROY COHN AS JACOB

Modern Judaism is most simply identified as the religion of the Law. When the Jewish temple in Jerusalem—the physical and spiritual center of Judaism—was destroyed by the Romans in 70 CE (never to be rebuilt), Judaism lost its core and largely transformed itself from a religion of ritual sacrifice to a religion of the Book. For Jews ever since, the Book is the Torah, and the Torah is the Law.

In the absence of the Temple, Rabbinic Jews rebuilt their religion from text, and from a textual reverence of the Jewish Law as found in the Torah. However, the archaic Judaism of pre-Davidic Israel was not a legalistic religion; in fact, rigid adherence to Law is anathema to J's Yahweh and his children. In J's narrative, though there is mention of the production of the Commandments at Sinai, it is greatly truncated. In fact, J's recitation of the commandments—and for her, there are fewer than ten—is delightfully beside the point; it pales in comparison to the drama of the the theophany that precedes it. Additionally, within the commandments themselves, Bloom suggests that "J's emphasis is much more pragmatic than ethical" (*Book* 260). Therefore, the notion of sin—at least insofar as one might define it as transgression of the Law—is irrelevant to J's religious universe. Indeed, those who "sin" in J merely fail to attain the same kind of vital dynamism that Yahweh embodies. And if there is no sin in J, then there is also no judgment—evaluation before the strictures of the Law (though there certainly is punishment). Yahweh and his fortunate sons (and daughters) all interact on the same level, and neither he nor his offspring may serve as fit judge for the other.

Kushner's, too, is just such an amoral (though not necessarily immoral) fictional realm. And his "Law"—or lack thereof—also shows the influence of J. Though Louis and Joe, both employees of the local district court, occasionally pontificate on the nature of the Law, it is Roy Cohn who best expatiates upon its Bloomian aspects in *Angels.* For Roy, one does not follow the law or prostrate oneself before it. One uses it, subverts it, transcends it, and remakes it in one's own image. As Roy puts it: "You want to be Nice, or you want to be Effective? Make the law, or subject to it" (*Millennium* 108). (Roy overreaches in "making" the law; shortly before his death, he is disbarred for ethical breaches.) Law, sin, and judgment are, for Roy and J, paper tigers. There is no Law; there is only God, that breathlessly dynamic, ever-changing imp-of-a-deity. Compare, for instance, such a description of God with Roy's understanding of the Law: "I don't see the Law as a dead and arbitrary collection of antiquated dictums, thou shall, thou shalt not, because, because I know the Law's a pliable, breathing, sweating ... *organ*" (*Millennium* 66; ellipsis in original).

All this is not to suggest that for Roy and J there is no standard for correct behavior. A man is successful (and J

and Roy both measure strength in terms of success, not morality) insofar as he is a good son—insofar as he receives, or occasionally steals, a blessing from his father. In a scene markedly similar to Isaac's blessing of Jacob in Genesis 27, Roy blesses Joe shortly before his death. Earlier in the play, Roy lists the many fathers from whom he wrested his own blessing:

> The most precious asset in life, I think, is the ability to be a good son. You have that, Joe. Somebody who can be a good son to a father who pushes them farther than they would otherwise go. I've had many fathers, I owe my life to them, powerful, powerful men. Walter Winchell, Edgar Hoover. Joe McCarthy most of all. He valued me because I am a good lawyer, but he loved me because I was and am a good son.

> (*Millennium* 56)

For J as for Roy, the blessing is a generational gift passed on, if not by blood, at least by a metaphorical lineage. Shortly before blessing Joe, Roy makes explicit reference to Jacob, that "heel-grabber" who, more than any of J's other characters, validates relentless and occasionally unscrupulous pursuit of the blessing. As Roy describes him, Jacob is "[a] ruthless motherfucker, some bald runt, but he laid hold of his birthright with his claws and his teeth" (*Perestroika* 81). From this description, it is clear that Roy shares Bloom's unorthodox understanding of Jacob. As Bloom and others point out, J's Jacob does not succeed because he follows a law; instead, he thrives because of his single-minded, grasping pursuit of his goals and, often, by the subversion of widely accepted customs and traditions. Such a description also applies to Roy. In fact, even more than the always sympathetic Prior or the weak, indecisive Joe, Roy stands in as Kushner's resident Jacob, indefatigable and sometimes despicable in the pursuit of blessing. In the Bloomian zone of Kushner's play, heroes may distinguish themselves by passionate action, by dynamic transformation that heeds no legalistic requirements. Roy, though sometimes repulsive, remains an unrelenting anti-hero, a protagonist who is seldom nice but frequently effective.[15] Perhaps it is this relentlessness, this dynamic drive, that draws Belize—serving as Roy's nurse—to this "ruthless motherfucker" that he should detest. How else can one explain why Belize urges Roy to use his connections to acquire a stash of a new anti-AIDS drug (AZT, still in experimental trials), or why he demands that a Kaddish be spoken over the man's corpse?

In *Millennium Approaches,* Joe apprehensively dreams about the abolition of the Law:

> Maybe the court won't convene. Ever again. Maybe we are free. To do whatever. Children of the new morning, criminal minds. Selfish and greedy and loveless and blind. Reagan's children. You're scared. So am I. Everybody is in the land of the free. God help us all.

> (*Millennium* 74)

However, evidence suggests that in Kushner, the Law has already been abolished, and that only the weak still cling to antiquated notions of it. If, as in J, the Law is irrelevant in *Angels in America,* then all the play's residents live in a state of vertiginous freedom. And perhaps the only character who is bold enough—or brutal enough—to act on that freedom is Roy, Kushner's own despicable heel-grabber.[16] Of course, freedom from the Law is not the only type of freedom, and there are those who may compellingly argue that in Kushner's "Gay Fantasia," the closeted Roy is anything but "free." Jonathan Freedman, for one, calls the historical Cohn "spectacularly self-denying" (93). But at least according to Roy's own understanding of sexual identity, sexual distinctions disintegrate under the solvent force of individual power, or "clout." As Roy explains to his doctor, Henry:

> [Y]ou are hung up on words, on labels. ... AIDS. Homosexual. Gay. Lesbian. You think these are names that tell you who someone sleeps with, but they don't. ... [T]hey tell you one thing and one thing only: where does an individual so identified fit in the food chain, in the pecking order? Not ideology, or sexual taste, but something much simpler: clout.

> (*Millennium* 45)

Though the real Roy Cohn may have suffered for his sexual self-denial, Kushner's Roy never does. Further, even AIDS cannot fully eradicate the stubborn Roy. Cohn survives Kushner's multiple efforts to kill him off; Freedman counts four death scenes for Roy and cites Kushner's "profound fascination with this character" as one of the reasons for his persistence (96). After these assassination attempts, a hell-bound Roy is still practicing his profession, gearing up for a legal defense of God. Just as J's Yahweh blesses Jacob, so does Kushner reward Roy's dogged obstinance, granting him a fiery immortality despite his many crimes.

From Theology to Anthropology

Likely by design, these five pieces borrowed from Bloom—Yahweh, Jacob, the blessing, sex, the Law—never coalesce into a discernible theology. That is to say, they remain an array of discrete effects that enliven Kushner's text without imposing a new religious order upon it. However, that they do so remains a direct effect of Bloom's influence. For as the critic repeatedly argues, J "is an author who tells stories, and not a theologian" (*Book* 301). Her Yahweh possesses a "restless dynamism [that] will not consent to be confined" (291), and she defines him in terms of the incommensurate and the inassimilable. Hence to make of Yahweh a field of study—to identify his theology—is impossible; it is to systematize and institutionalize him out of existence. Moreover, it is unlikely that Kushner would have allowed a theologized, theologizing vision into his most significant play. In a 2005 *New Yorker* feature, John Lahr recounts an episode during which, "in a debate sponsored by the Classic Stage Company, one of Kushner's great champions, the critic Harold Bloom, spent the better part of two hours trying in vain to get Kushner to admit that he was a theo-

logical writer" (42). Had Bloom remembered his own work in the *Book of J,* perhaps he would have given up this vain effort. For Kushner—like Bloom—is not a theological writer at all, at least insofar as theologizing tends to involve imposing regulations upon the vital dynamism of the divine.[17] Kushner's God—as with J's and Bloom's—will not be confined; in fact, he will walk off the stage and never return if he sees fit.

But ultimately, for Kushner, God is not the point. In all of his sundry borrowings from J's religious vision, Kushner never lets his gaze stray too far from his very earthly characters. His musings on the nature of a vital, incommensurate divine (and the mythological ramifications of these musings) do not obscure Kushner's basic humanism. Thus Kushner leaves his reader at the end of *Perestroika* not with some Dantean revelation of his idiosyncratic God but with a utopic vision of human community. Indeed, Kushner's channeling of J only *enhances* his humanism. After all, if Bloom calls J's "exaltation of men and women" unique in the ancient world (*Book* 275), in *Angels,* Kushner revels in this exaltation. Both J and Kushner lift humanity up while at the same time endowing it with an attractive power that pulls God and his heavens down (recall God's "Mortifying imitation" of humanity in *Perestroika*). From J, Kushner learns that God looks (and wants to look) like humans; he learns that earthly life, and more of it, is a divine blessing; he learns that the flesh is sacred; and he learns that one is free to explore the earth unrestrained by divine Law. In sum, he learns that to be human is to be holy, and very nearly divine. For as Bloom reminds us, "Man" is one of the "ancient rabbinical names for God" (*Book* 292).

Notes

1. Or perhaps this brief reference is just a symptom of Bloom's "anxiety of influence"—an instance of what Bloom calls *apophrades,* or "the return of the dead": "The strong dead return, in poems as in our lives, and they do not come back without darkening the living" (*Anxiety* 139). James Miller, however, comments on Kushner's surprising freedom from such anxiety: "When I saw Part I on Broadway in 1993, ... I recall feeling oddly anxious that Kushner was evincing no anxiety of influence—as if he had a moral obligation to acknowledge somewhere in his work the profound political impact of that other gay Jewish Reagan-hating playwright from New York [Larry Kramer] on all serious AIDS drama produced in the second decade of the epidemic" (62).

2. Early reviews of Bloom's volume both praise its ingenuity and identify significant shortcomings. Jack Miles suggests that Bloom's method is, at times, "brilliantly brought off" but that some of his theses are not new (640). Walter Brueggemann calls his commentary "rich and suggestive" but "undisciplined and quixotic" (236). Yehoshua Gitay believes

that the J text is "brightly illuminated" (413) by Bloom's reading but also condemns that reading as "fragmentary" (411). It is not my intent in this essay to defend Bloom's scholarship but only to show its influence on the development of Kushner's play.

3. She is called J—not Y, after Yahweh—because the first scholars who distinguished the J author from other authors were German, who transliterated the divine name "Jahweh."

4. The culmination of Bloom's thoughts concerning "strong misreading" appears in *Agon.*

5. Bloom's method finds a precedent in Sigmund Freud's *Moses and Monotheism,* in which Freud strongly misreads Exodus in suggesting that the biblical figure of Moses is an amalgamation of historical figures, the most important of which is an Egyptian disciple of the first monotheist, the pharaoh Akhenaton.

6. Most prominent among these commentators is Richard Elliott Friedman, who points out the stylistic similarities between J and E in *Who Wrote the Bible?*

7. Michael D. Coogan's introduction to the Pentateuch in *The New Oxford Annotated Bible* outlines this position (6).

8. Additionally, one should not take Kushner's indirect engagement with the documentary hypothesis as a significant challenge to biblical authority. Even given its contemporary fluidity, the theory has been an accepted part of biblical scholarship for decades in both religious and secular, conservative and liberal circles. Only a small minority of traditional hermeneutists still contend that the Torah was written by Moses alone.

9. David Savran numbers the Beckettian hints in Kushner's play among many nods to figures from the "long history of Western dramatic literature" (15).

10. Ironically, this optional scene allows readers of the play to read Kushner's God as an actual character in *Angels in America.* Though some may choose to treat God's departure in the play's prehistory as purely symbolic—as Kushner's indication that *Angels* is set in a post-theistic or post-religious world—his fleeting appearance onstage allows us to follow Bloom in treating this enigmatic God as a literary figure deserving of characterological analysis.

11. On a related note, Bloom credits Joseph Smith with restoring the "Bible's sense of the theomorphic" in nineteenth- and twentieth-century religious practice (*American Religion* 99).

12. James Miller and Alisa Solomon both recognize Prior's likeness to Jacob. As Solomon puts it, "Like Jacob, Prior wrestles with the Angel and seeks the blessing of more life. And, like Jacob, the struggle leaves him limping. . . . Most importantly, Prior takes on a new, collective identity by holding out against the Angel" (131). Miller figures him as a sort of gay revolutionary patriarch: "Prior is the Jacob who must wrestle with . . . the Angel herself. Fortunately, his physical frailty is offset by a spiritual toughness reminiscent of the fighting spirit of the drag queens who kicked off the Stonewall Riots in 1969" (61-62).

13. David Savran wittily notes the (homo)sexual figuration of Kushner's God: "After his visitation by the Angel, Prior explains that 'God . . . is a man. Well, not a man, he's a flaming Hebrew letter, but a male flaming Hebrew letter.' In comparison with this masculinized, Old Testament-style, 'flaming' (!) patriarch, the Angels are decidedly hermaphroditic" (22-23).

14. Kushner's language—and more specifically, the status of the word itself in *Angels in America*—may reflect Bloom's influence. In *The Book of J,* Bloom cites Ephraim Urbach's understanding of J's "words": "When Urbach explains that the word for 'word' stands also for 'substance' or 'thing,' we are very much in J's sense of the truth, for 'the Hebrew tongue' here actually means J" (*Book* 276). Bloom seems to join Urbach in placing J in a moment before the development of a semiotic distinction between symbol and referent—Derrida's *différance.* For J, at least in Bloom's conception, the fact that "word" and "thing" are one and the same points to a primal identity of symbol and referent. Such is certainly the case with Kushner's God, the flaming *aleph* who is both letter (word) and thing, signifier and referent.

15. It should be understood that, in likening Roy to Jacob, I do not wish to suggest that Roy is somehow redeemed. The Torah narrative, taken as a whole, smoothes over some of Jacob's rough edges; in J's tale, by contrast, Jacob is relentless, immoral, brutal, and frankly unlikable—he is the most unexpected of Yahweh's chosen. Therefore, Kushner can see Jacob in Roy without depicting the latter as anything other than morally reprehensible. It should be noted that the characters most closely associated with the Law and legal institutions—Roy, Joe, and Louis—are ethically dubious characters.

16. This understanding of Roy may at least partially counteract Jonathan Freedman's description of him as a nexus of negative Jewish (and queer) stereotypes. To characterize Roy in terms of an (unironic) reflection of one of the Jewish patriarchs is to suggest a more positive connection with Jewish tradition, if an "archaic" one.

17. If critics agree with Kushner's assertion that he is not a theological writer—and many do—they nonetheless ought not take his words as tacit permission to ignore or reduce the *religious* elements of his plays, and of *Angels* in particular. A more recent strain in Kushner criticism—whose ranks include Anthony Lioi, Amy Schindler, and Matthew Wilson Smith—distinguishes itself by engaging his religious content on its own terms.

Works Cited

Alter, Robert. *The World of Biblical Literature.* New York: Basic, 1992.

Bloom, Harold. *Agon: Towards a Theory of Revisionism.* Oxford: Oxford UP, 1982.

———. *The American Religion: The Emergence of the Post-Christian Nation.* New York: Simon, 1992.

———. *The Anxiety of Influence: A Theory of Poetry.* New York: Oxford UP, 1973.

———. *The Book of J.* Trans. David Rosenberg. New York: Grove, 1990.

Brueggemann, Walter. Rev. of *The Book of J,* by Harold Bloom. *Theology Today* 48.2 (1991): 234-40.

Coogan, Michael D. Introduction. *New Oxford Annotated Bible* 3-7.

Freedman, Jonathan. "Angels, Monsters, and Jews: Intersections of Queer and Jewish Identity in Kushner's *Angels in America.*" *PMLA* 113.1 (1998): 90-102.

Freud, Sigmund. *Moses and Monotheism.* Trans. Katherine Jones. New York: Vintage, 1955.

Friedman, Richard Elliott. *Who Wrote the Bible?* Englewood Cliffs, NJ: Prentice-Hall, 1987.

Geis, Deborah R., and Steven F. Kruger, eds. *Approaching the Millennium: Essays on Angels in America.* Ann Arbor: U of Michigan P, 1997.

Gitay, Yehoshua. "J in Bloom." Rev. of *The Book of J,* by Harold Bloom. *Cross Currents* 41.3 (1991): 410-13.

Kushner, Tony. *Angels in America: Millennium Approaches.* New York: Theater Communications, 1993.

———. *Angels in America: Perestroika.* 1994. Rev. ed. New York: Theater Communications, 1996.

———. *Tony Kushner in Conversation.* Ed. Robert Vorlicky. Ann Arbor: U of Michigan P, 1998.

Lahr, John. "After Angels: Tony Kushner's Promethean Itch." *New Yorker* 3 Jan. 2005: 42-52.

Lioi, Anthony. "The Great Work Begins: Theater as Theurgy in *Angels in America.*" *Cross Currents* 54.3 (2004): 96-117.

Miles, Jack. "The Book of B: Bloom, Bathsheba, and the Book." Rev. of *The Book of J,* by Harold Bloom. *Commonweal* 117.9 (1990): 639-42.

Miller, James. "Heavenquake: Queer Anagogies in Kushner's America." Geis and Kruger 56-77.

The New Oxford Annotated Bible: New Revised Standard Version with the Apocrypha. Ed. Michael D. Coogan. Oxford: Oxford UP, 2001.

Nichols, Mike, dir. *Angels in America.* 2003. DVD. HBO Home Video, 2004.

Savran, David. "Ambivalence, Utopia, and a Queer Sort of Materialism: How *Angels in America* Reconstructs the Nation." Geis and Kruger 13-39.

Schindler, Amy. "Angels and the AIDS Epidemic: The Resurgent Popularity of Angel Imagery in the United States of America." *Journal of American Culture* 22.3 (1999): 49-61.

Smith, Matthew Wilson. "*Angels in America*: A Progressive Apocalypse." *Theater* 29.3 (1999): 153-65.

Solomon, Alisa. "Wrestling with *Angels*: A Jewish Fantasia." Geis and Kruger 118-33.

Wellhausen, Julius. *Prolegomena zur Geschichte Israels.* 2nd ed. Berlin: G. Reimer, 1883.

James Corby (essay date 2010)

SOURCE: Corby, James. "The Audacity of Hope: Locating Kushner's Political Vision in *Angels in America.*" *Forum for Modern Language Studies* 47.1 (2010): 16-35. Print.

[*In the following essay, Corby examines* Angels in America *within several contexts, including Enlightenment philosophy, Raymond Williams's socialist vision of progress, and Benjamin's materialist conception of history. Corby claims that Kushner's "radical" brand of hope is "detached from utopian notions of perfectibility," depending on "praxis" and "how society collectively reconfigures itself."*]

Tony Kushner's ***Angels in America*** is a deeply political play that dramatizes various forms of political philosophy, rehearsing recognizable political positions as well as exploring less familiar, more radical political ideas in a context that is as distinctly and unapologetically American as it is apocalyptically millennial. Kushner himself makes no secret of the fact that he is, as a writer, politically engaged, announcing in the Afterword to ***Angels in America*** that he continues to believe in 'the effectiveness of activism.'[1] It is entirely reasonable, then, that critics should seek to identify the political and philosophical position that, ultimately, is being advocated in the play.[2] On the evidence of the already sizeable amount of criticism to which ***Angels in America*** has given rise, this has proved to be no straightforward task. Among the largely very positive reviews of early productions, *Variety* critic Greg Evans, in November 1992, judged the play to be 'weighed down by a lack of focus'[3] and, writing in the *New York Times* of 10 November 1992, Frank Rich called the 'dense imagery and baroque spiritual, political and historical metaphor' 'mind-exploding.'[4] In a subsequent article dated 24 November 1993, Rich remarked on Kushner's 'refusal to adhere to any theatrical or political theory.'[5] Less forgivingly, Leo Bersani, writing in 1996, called the play a 'muddled and pretentious play.'[6]

Subsequent criticism has on the whole been more considered, often going to great lengths to try to do justice to the political import of the play; and yet, more often than not, critics remain content simply to accommodate, excuse or make concessions towards the play's tangled, multi-faceted politics rather than attempting to resolve them. Thus, in 2002, James Fisher comments on Kushner's 'Shavian affection for political digression,' and notes the 'unabashedly sprawling' play's 'enormous thematic challenges' and how it 'crosses over into controversial terrain on several fronts.'[7] James Berger, in 1999, asserts that '[t]he play's politics [...] are confusing.'[8] Christopher Bigsby, also writing in 1999, concludes, not entirely incorrectly, that *Angels in America* is 'a serious play which begs the audience not to take it too seriously since its very confusions, its disorientations, its sometimes camp ostentation, are a part of the antidote it offers to the sombre regularity of those who prefer order to vitality.'[9] David Savran, writing two years earlier, is one of the few critics to attempt to clarify the play's political complexities. However, in so doing, he swings to the opposite extreme, and dispels them. Like the majority of critics, he acknowledges *Angels in America*'s 'ambivalence,' judges it to be 'a promiscuously complicated play,' and notes that it is 'filled with political disputation.'[10] But he then goes on to argue that, really, in terms of its political allegiance, 'the play is not ambivalent at all.'[11] Despite all of the gestures to a more radical politics, *Angels in America* is at root, Savran concludes, a paean to a kind of 'liberal humanism' that is 'fundamentally conservative.'[12] Again, this is not entirely incorrect, but it makes the mistake of conflating the political position of Louis, one of the key characters, with that of the play as a whole, thus neglecting the play's affinity with a more messianic, speculative politics.

Certainly, one of the difficulties confronting any attempt to locate and explain the view of politics that the play might be said to endorse is the sheer wealth of diverse political references contained in the play. *Angels in America* is thoroughly immersed in political discourse of various tones and registers and this can make it difficult to distinguish the political stance that Kushner is promoting. But this need not mean that one cannot produce an ordered account of how these different discourses interact with each other. In what follows, I want to locate the main political currents in the play in a way that is not reductive. Whilst I make no attempt to take account of the play's entire political genealogy, I will examine Kushner's presentation of the politics of Reagan-era America, attempt to unpick some of the

debts that this presentation owes to the Enlightenment philosophies out of which, ideologically, the United States of America developed, and then, finally, identify and explore Kushner's radical political vision of America's future, arguing that *Angels in America,* more than simply being steeped in political philosophy, warrants consideration as politically interventionist.

RIGHT IS WRONG; LEFT IS RIGHT?

The most obvious way of categorizing the political positions articulated in the play is in terms of Left and Right. Kushner's broad portrayal of right-wing Republican characters such as Joe and Roy and the whole pointed evocation of Reagan-era capitalism on the one hand, and the comparatively disfranchised left-wing characters such as Louis, Prior and Belize on the other, invite just such an approach. What is perhaps significant about Kushner's treatment of this familiar political terrain is his ability to show, by means of allusive echoes, the extent to which both Left and Right ideologies are strongly rooted in various aspects of Enlightenment thought. Through exploring the inadequacies of both ends of the classical American political spectrum as represented by various characters in the play, Kushner connects the political with the personal and opens an ethically motivated space for his own radical position.[13]

Joe—lawyer, Mormon, closeted homosexual and husband to Harper—is presented as a naïve and idealistic ideologue of the Right. Although his idealism is tempered by a belief in the 'world's unperfectibility' (*AA* [*Angels in America*], p. 204) capable of excusing the iniquitous status quo, he believes he perceives '[c]hange for the good' (*AA,* p. 32) being brought about by the Republican administration. He preaches this message to Harper:

> America has rediscovered itself. Its sacred position among nations. And people aren't ashamed of that like they used to be. This is a great thing. The truth restored. Law restored. That's what President Reagan's done, Harper. He says 'Truth exists and can be spoken proudly.' And the country responds to him. We become better. More good.

> (*AA,* p. 32)

When sitting on Jones Beach with Louis, Joe exclaims: 'The whole country was like this once. A paradise' (*AA,* p. 203). It seems unlikely that this echoing of Locke's claim, '[I]n the beginning all the World was *America*,' is inadvertant.[14] Locke's account in *Two Treatises of Government* of how personal rights and individual ownership of property develop out of what he takes to be the state of nature—a state of freedom and equality, according to him—is, and always has been, an all-pervasive influence on American political culture. Even the most famous line of the Declaration of Independence, the one about life, liberty and the pursuit of happiness, is taken from Locke, albeit with one important alteration. Locke speaks of 'Life, Health, Liberty [and] Possessions,'[15] but in composing the Declaration, Thomas Jefferson and the other Founding Fathers—

perhaps struck by the dissonance of claiming that all men are created equal and are free to pursue, among other things, property, when at the time the most important form of property was enslaved man—substitute 'property' with the anodyne word 'happiness.'[16] Joe too, at least at the outset of the play, seems to be confusing the ideology of capitalism, the pursuit of private wealth, with happiness. It gradually becomes apparent, however, that his desire to 'become better' and '[m]ore good' (*AA*, p. 32) masks the true motivation of his adherence to Republicanism, which has little to do with the pursuit of happiness and a lot to do with his reluctance to confront his homosexuality. He confesses to Louis:

> I just wondered what a thing it would be ... if overnight everything you owe anything to, justice, or love, had really gone away. Free.
>
> It would be ... heartless terror. Yes. Terrible, and ...
>
> Very great. To shed your skin, every old skin, one by one and then walk away, unencumbered, into the morning.

(*AA*, pp. 78-79)

The Republican emphasis on rights-based individualism offers Joe the framework within which to effect at least a degree of the detachment from other people and from society that he secretly fantasises about. In the words of another character in the play, to be a child of the Reagan era is to have 'No connections. No responsibilities' (*AA*, p. 77). It seems reasonable to assume that Joe is so desirous of the safety of distance from other people because the closer his relations with society the more compelled he feels either to act out a role and conform, or to confront the person he really is. He feels comfortable with neither option.

Roy Cohn, whom Kushner bases on the real-life Roy Cohn, is a closeted homosexual of the Right too, but his adherence to right-wing ideology springs from a different source entirely, namely his belief that society is malevolent and that the only thing worth attaining (that is, the only thing of any value) is power. It is entirely plausible to understand this view of the world as originating in the deep self-loathing that develops from his confused sexual identity (he is not a homosexual, he says, he is 'a heterosexual man [...] who fucks around with guys' [*AA*, p. 52]), but there can be little doubt that Kushner roots Roy's worldview in Hobbesian political philosophy, contrasting him with the Lockean Joe. Unlike Locke's state of nature, the primal state Hobbes envisages is not one of peace but one of war in which the life of man is, famously, 'solitary, poor, nasty, brutish, and short.'[17] As far as Roy is concerned, any accurate and unflinching account of human nature cannot but come to this conclusion. Boastingly, he says to Joe:

> My generation, we had *clarity*. Unafraid to look deep into the miasma at the heart of the world, what a pit, what a nightmare is there—*I* have looked, I have searched all my life for absolute bottom, and I found it, *believe* me: *Stygian*. How tragic, how brutal and short life is. How sinful people are.

(*AA*, pp. 213-14)

Roy, whom Louis calls 'the polestar of human evil' (*AA*, p. 217), is for the left-wing characters in the play (and, we can safely assume, for Kushner himself) the essential distillation of everything wrong with Republican America in the mid-1980s. Indeed, Roy himself says: 'if you want to look at the heart of modern conservatism, you look at me' (*AA*, p. 213). It is unsurprising, then, that Belize, in rejecting Louis's professed love for the *idea* of America, provides a further echo of Hobbes when he says: 'You come with me to room 1013 over at the hospital, I'll show you America. Terminal, crazy and mean' (*AA*, p. 228). The message is clear: America, in veering towards the Right, allowing individual participation in an unregulated free-market economy to shape society, has descended into something approximating the warlike conditions of the Hobbesian state of nature. Hobbes tells us that in such a state, 'every man is enemy to every man' and so 'men live without other security, than what their own strength, and their own invention shall furnish them withal.'[18] In the Reagan era, Roy calls this sort of strength 'clout.' 'Invention' becomes an ability to bend, break and, most importantly, make the rules ('Make the law, or subject to it,' he tells Joe [*AA*, p. 114]). Roy chastises his physician Henry for his literal-mindedness, the antithesis of inventiveness: 'Your problem, Henry, is that you are hung up on words, on labels, that you believe they mean what they seem to mean' (*AA*, p. 51). He boasts that he does not abide by rules because he knows that the law is 'a pliable, breathing, sweating ... *organ*' and that 'Lawyers are ... the High Priests of America' (*AA*, p. 72): 'We alone,' says Roy, 'know the words that made America. Out of thin air. We alone know how to use The Words' (*AA*, p. 221). As one might expect, then, in a society seemingly bereft of other forms of security, clout, guile and influence have become all-important. Self-interest gives rise to a stark individualism that prompts Roy to advise Joe in a father-to-son-style talk: 'Whatever pulls on you, whatever needs from you, threatens you [...], don't be afraid to live in the raw wind, naked, alone' (*AA*, p. 64).

But Hobbesian man, hell-bent on self-preservation, has limited dramatic value. Kushner brings depth and perhaps a glimpse of pathos to Roy's character by tying him, by means of a form of vanity, to the very thing he disdains—society. His great badge of distinction is that he has clout. But this differs from Hobbesian strength inasmuch as an attachment to clout, unlike simple strength, implies an investment in how others see you. By way of proving his clout, Roy tells Henry: 'I can pick up this phone, punch fifteen numbers, and you know who will be on the other end in under five minutes, Henry?' (*AA*, p. 51). For Roy, clout amounts to having the President or, 'even better,' the President's wife regard you as important enough to accept a telephone call from you. It is this desire for recognition from others that prevents him from ever being able to accept the term 'homosexual': in his view homosexuals do not have (that is, are not regarded as having) clout. In presenting this misanthropic figure who, quite pathetically, places so much importance on how he appears to others, Kushner might be said to be adding to Hobbesian man aspects of Rousseauian political thought. For Rousseau, writing explicitly in opposition to Hobbes, life in the state of nature was solitary but idyllic. Our savage ancestors living in such a state felt only *amour de soi-même* (an impulse to preserve one's life) and *pitié* (compassion when confronted by the suffering of others). However, once in society man is susceptible to *amour propre,* vanity, which Rousseau describes as 'a sentiment that prompts each individual to set greater store by himself than by anyone else [and this] triggers all the evil they do to themselves and to others.'[19] So, whereas from a Hobbesian perspective Roy's vanity would have to be explained as growing out of his bleak, hopeless, view of mankind—with Roy's ability to thrive in such an environment being an achievement of which he is proud to the extent of craving its acknowledgement by others—from a perhaps more plausible Rousseauian perspective this bleak, agonistic view of the world does not so much lead to vanity as arise out of it.

Rousseau was committed to the idea of *perfectibility,* a term he introduced into the discourse of philosophy. It is this capacity to change which, when misapplied, can lead to the degradation of human nature—from *amour de soi-même* to *amour propre,* for instance. When applied correctly, however, this principle of change can lead to the improvement and, in theory, the perfection of mankind. Louis, Prior's and then Joe's boyfriend, believes passionately in this Rousseauian idea of perfectibility. One of the most stridently political characters in the play, forever spouting what other characters consider overly intellectualized political theory, Louis is as far Left as Roy is Right. Joe, seeing that Louis's belief in perfectibility is the source of his sense of disappointment with society, counsels him to think otherwise:

> You believe the world is perfectible and so you find it always unsatisfying. [...] You have to reconcile yourself to the world's unperfectibility [...]. The rhythm of history is conservative.
>
> *(AA,* p. 204)

Louis himself readily admits to 'a neo-Hegelian positivist sense of constant historical progress towards happiness or perfection or something' *(AA,* p. 31). But it becomes clear that he is not able to live up to his own radical political beliefs. Indeed, the key to understanding the character of Louis is to understand him as a liberal in radical clothing, torn between the progressive politics to which he aspires and the liberalism he professes to despise but that he, in spite of himself, in fact affirms. In the American context, liberalism and radicalism are not always easily distinguishable because America came into being by means of a *revolutionary* event that proclaimed an allegiance to a *liberal* ideology of equality and freedom. Gordon Wood persuasively argues that although this is not the sort of thing we tend to think of when we hear the word radical,

'it was as radical and social as any revolution in history.'[20] However, the radicalism that Louis affirms—characterized by his vision of 'radical democracy spreading outward and growing up'—is very different from the rather sober, pre-Marxian radicalism of the Founding Fathers.[21] Nevertheless, his connection with the liberalism that has long defined the mainstream political culture in America can clearly be seen in his belief in the *idea* of America, even when he feels revulsion at the contemporary state of America. Belief in America as an idea or an ideology has been identified by Gunnar Myrdal, Louis Hartz, Seymour M. Lipset, Anatol Lieven and others as the characteristic that distinguishes American nationalism from other, older (particularly European) models of nationalism which traditionally were more rooted in ethnicity.[22] American national identity, it is argued, in contrast to these older forms of nationalism, is held together not by ethnicity but by a general allegiance to a set of beliefs. Influenced by G. K. Chesterton's observation that 'America is the only nation in the world that is founded on a creed,'[23] but drawing also on an understanding of America that stretches all the way back to Toqueville's *Democracy in America* (which, according to Belize, Louis is struggling to get through),[24] this form of American civic nationalism is frequently referred to as 'creedal' nationalism. Myrdal asserts that the 'American Creed is a humanistic liberalism developing out of the epoch of the Enlightenment.'[25] It is, he suggests, 'the cement in the structure of this great and disparate nation.'[26] Hartz speaks of 'the national acceptance of the Lockean creed [...] enshrined in the constitution,'[27] and, more recently, Lieven has reaffirmed this idea:

> The essential elements of the American Creed and American civic nationalism are faith in liberty, constitutionalism, the law, democracy, individualism and cultural and political egalitarianism. They have remained in essence the same through most of American history. They are chiefly rooted in the Enlightenment and are also derived from English traditions: the liberal philosophy of John Locke as well as much older beliefs in the law and in the 'rights of freeborn Englishmen.'[28]

Although Louis would certainly never admit to sharing the particular rights-based, Locke-inspired creed of liberal America (indeed, he makes reference to Thomas Paine's most famous work of political philosophy, pouring scorn on what he calls 'these bourgeois property-based Rights-of-Man-type rights' [*AA,* p. 96]), he does clearly subscribe to the notion that America's identity is creedal. He infuriates Belize, the black, gay, former drag queen who now works as a nurse, precisely by suggesting that in America '[i]t's not really about race' *(AA,* p. 98). Indeed, for Louis, this is what gives America radical potential and why he continues to believe in America: without a 'monolith' *(AA,* p. 96) such as race to overcome, America exists as a mutable idea of democracy. At present this democracy might be far from satisfactorily realized, but the point is that the creed of America can be changed and refined by popular political participation in a way that would be impossible in other countries. Unlike old Europe, in other words, America is perfectible. Understandably, Belize has nothing but contempt for Louis's thoughts. Far from being radical, this idea that America is essentially different from other countries because of the way it came into existence actually serves further to align Louis with mainstream liberalism in so far as the idea of American exceptionalism has long been held dear by the liberal hegemony.[29]

Even though Louis's belief that American nationalism is civic rather than ethnic and that America is in this regard exceptional shows him to be closer to the liberal tradition than he realizes, it does not bring us to the heart of Louis's self-contradiction. Louis reserves some of his most vituperative disgust for 'bourgeois tolerance,' which he calls 'the worst kind of liberalism' (*AA,* p. 96). Revealingly, he suggests that AIDS acts as a limit case which reveals how narrow such tolerance actually is: '[W]hat I think is that what AIDS shows us is the limits of tolerance, that it's not enough to be tolerated, because when the shit hits the fan you find out how much tolerance is worth. Nothing' (*AA,* p. 96). The accusation is that liberal tolerance is merely a self-serving mask disguising what is really little more than self-interested individualism and power. Louis's great internal contradiction and the source of his bountiful sense of guilt is the fact that he too, *in extremis,* resorts to just such a position of self-interest, readily adopting the discourse of liberal humanism to serve his own ends. So, for instance, when, in **Perestroika,** he attempts to make up with Prior, he appeals to him saying: 'There are limits. Boundaries. And you have to be reasonable' (*AA,* p. 216). Similarly, when Belize reveals to him that he went with Prior to the courthouse to see Joe, Louis snaps at him: '*You had no right to do that.*' To which Belize mockingly responds: 'Oh did we violate your *rights*?' (*AA,* p. 226).

It might be said that Louis is a person for whom, in John Ashbery's words, 'tomorrow is easy, but today is uncharted.'[30] He has grand visions of what radical democracy will one day achieve, yet cannot bring himself to confront contemporary obstacles such as the problem of racism in American society. Belize accuses him of being 'Up in the air, just like that angel, too far off the earth to pick out the details. Louis and his Big Ideas' (*AA,* p. 228). That which does not fit into Louis's grand scheme is ignored. However, when confronted by an aspect of social reality that can neither be accommodated by his idea of how the world ought to be, nor be simply ignored, Louis resorts to the language of liberalism. So he neutralizes the problem of race by turning to traditional notions of consensus-based creedal nationalism, for instance. This contradiction is most sharply drawn in his response to Prior's illness. Unlike Joe, who admits that what attracts him to Harper is her faults ('the part of her that's farthest from the light' [*AA,* p. 59]), Louis simply cannot deal, intellectually or emotionally, with human frailty. Prior sees this and confronts him, saying: 'Apartment too small for three? Louis and Prior comfy but not Louis and Prior and Prior's disease?' (*AA,* p. 84). Louis, too, is very

aware of his failing, confessing it early on in the play to Rabbi Isidor Chemelwitz, presenting the difficulty as an impersonal hypothesis:

> Maybe because this person's sense of the world, that it will change for the better with struggle, maybe a person who has this neo-Hegelian positivist sense of constant historical progress towards happiness or perfection or something, who feels very powerful because he feels connected to these forces, moving uphill all the time ... maybe that person can't, um, incorporate sickness into his sense of how things are supposed to go. Maybe vomit ... and sores and disease ... really frighten him, maybe ... he isn't so good with death.

> (*AA,* p. 31)

Clearly, then, AIDS is a limit case not only for 'bourgeois tolerance' but for Louis's radical politics as well. It marks the point at which the world-view he professes breaks down and he retreats full of self-disgust to the safety of mainstream liberal ideology. Although this contradiction in Louis's behaviour is evident and clearly amounts to a failing of Prior, his more general echoing of the liberal tradition might be accounted for as a reflection of Kushner's own sympathy towards a liberal tradition that all too often stands at odds with his own radical politics. Interviewed, Kushner has said:

> The strain in the American character that I feel the most affection for and that I feel has the most potential for growth is American liberalism, which is incredibly short of what it needs to be and incredibly limited and exclusionary and predicated on all sorts of racist, homophobic and classist prerogatives.[31]

HOPE FROM ITS OWN WRECK: THE MESSAGE OF THE APOCALYPSE

In **Angels in America,** of course, Kushner does more than simply rehearse the well-worn and perhaps rather predictable ideological contradictions and peculiarities of the American Left and Right. **Angels in America** invites the audience to reconsider this relatively familiar political landscape in a new, all-transfiguring, apocalyptic and messianic light. Society, the environment, man himself, teeter on the edge of catastrophe.[32] Harper, who has something of the idiot savant about her (recall her insights from the 'threshold of revelation' [*AA,* p. 39]), paints a picture straight out of Yeats's 'Second Coming.' Where Yeats speaks of the 'widening gyre,' Harper describes the 'old fixed orders spiralling apart'; matching Yeats's centre that 'will not hold,' Harper has a feeling 'that something's going to give'; echoing Yeats's 'Things fall apart,' she says at one point, 'something just ... fell apart'; and where Yeats, in horror, says 'Surely some revelation is at hand, / Surely the second coming is at hand,' Harper, more bluntly, says: 'The end of the world is at hand.' In a bold extension of Hobbes's body-politic metaphor, Kushner seems to be presenting AIDS as symptomatic of this more general collapse—the failure of Prior's immune system being somehow commensurate with what Harper, troubled by news of the hole in the ozone layer, describes as 'everywhere [. . .] systems of defense giving way' (*AA,* p. 23).

The symbol or, rather, the messenger of this impending disaster is the Angel, who comes with tales of abandonment by God and urging stasis as the only possible recourse in the face of what will otherwise befall mankind:

> YOU MUST STOP MOVING! [. . .]
> Forsake the Open Road:
> Neither Mix Nor Intermarry: Let Deep Roots Grow:
> If you do not MINGLE you will Cease to Progress:
> Seek Not to Fathom the World and its Delicate Particle
>   Logic:
> You cannot Understand, You can only Destroy,
> You do not Advance, You only Trample.
> Poor blind Children, abandoned on the Earth,
> Groping blind Children, abandoned on the Earth,
> Groping terrified, misguided [. . .]
> Turn Back. Undo.

(*AA,* pp. 178-79)

In spite of how theatrically bold such announcements appear in performance, there is at least one sense, discernable here, in which the Angel is merely the manifestation of a temptation that Prior himself has already considered. Early on in the play he says to Louis: 'While time is running out I find myself drawn to anything that's suspended, that lacks an ending' (*AA,* p. 48). But he realizes that this is something to which he cannot, in good conscience, allow himself to give in. The catch, he suggests, is 'it seems to me that it lets you off scot-free' (*AA,* p. 48). Here, then, long before the Angel has made an appearance, Prior seems to reject stasis as a form of escape. Once he encounters the Angel, this feeling is only reinforced: 'ever since She arrived, ever since, I have been consumed by this ice-cold, razor-blade terror that just shouts and shouts "keep moving! Run!"' (*AA,* p. 235). But if accepting stasis does indeed, at least on some level, equate with 'being let off scot-free,' then conversely the implication is that in rejecting it and embracing change and forward movement there is a price to pay and it is our responsibility to pay it. In this dawning realization Prior is possessed by fear, but also by something which he cannot as easily identify: 'I'm scared. And also full of, I don't know, Joy or something. Hope' (*AA,* p. 154). It is tempting—indeed one is almost invited—to try to discern here in the lure of stasis, its rejection and the subsequent affirmation of hope, something that might qualify as the play's political or perhaps philosophical message. But how should it be interpreted and how does it modify the Leftist political stance presented by Louis? The Angel is of course a complex figure who performs a number of different functions in the play and who evokes intertextual resonances with other literary angels. But perhaps the most important precursor angel for any attempt to understand ***Angels in America*** as a form of political intervention is the angel in Walter Benjamin's 1940 essay 'On the Concept of History.' Benjamin writes:

> There is a picture by Klee called *Angelus Novus.* It shows an angel who seems about to move away from something he stares at. His eyes are wide, his mouth is open, his wings are spread. This is how the angel of history must look. His face is turned toward the past. Where a chain of events appears before *us, he* sees one single catastrophe, which keeps piling wreckage upon wreckage and hurls it at his feet. The angel would like to stay, awaken the dead, and make whole what has been smashed. But a storm is blowing from Paradise and has got caught in his wings; it is so strong that the angel can no longer close them. This storm drives him irresistibly into the future, to which his back is turned, while the pile of debris before him grows toward the sky. What we call progress is *this* storm.[33]

In this elliptical passage, Benjamin presents in kernel form his particular conception of historical materialism. In opposition to the historicist or historiographic perspective that views history as one long transitionary chain that exists in what Benjamin calls 'homogeneous, empty time,'[34] he imagines the historical materialist as having to freeze a moment in history from which position the past can be appropriated and, in that revolutionary moment, judged.[35] The latter position, represented by the Angel in Benjamin's piece, takes hold of the past and frames it, but 'only as an image that flashes up at the moment of its recognisability' as it is swept along into the future.[36] The crucial point seems to be that in occupying this position, even though time cannot be permanently halted, the '*Jetztzeit*' (now-time) of the momentary arrest allows one to orient or reorient oneself so that, instead of simply being passively carried along by the dominant ideology's version of progress, one takes hold of one's fate and moves forward with purpose.[37] In other words, one only actively moves forward by looking backwards—not, of course, in nostalgia and not in fear of the future, but in a backwards glance that freezes time in a 'tremendous abbreviation' just long enough to view the past as a monad which can be judged in a manner that releases from it that which historiography suppresses. Benjamin interprets this moment as 'a messianic arrest of happening, or (to put it differently) a revolutionary chance in the fight for the oppressed past'; but how does one 'blast open the continuum of history' in this way?[38] How does one accede to such a messianic perspective? At one point Benjamin suggests that 'it is our task to bring about a real state of emergency,'[39] the idea being that it would provide the right conditions in which to, as it were, momentarily step outside history or, as Benjamin puts it, 'to blast a specific era out of the homogeneous course of history.'[40]

Benjamin's Angel is not, of course, Kushner's Angel, but the latter also heralds the rupture of history. As the Ethel Rosenberg character says: 'History is about to crack wide open. Millennium approaches' (*AA,* p. 118). Furthermore, it seems clear that Prior is positioned as a historical materialist who in the messianic zero-hour gains a deeper understanding of humankind and is, with that knowledge, able to face the future by rejecting stasis. The disturbing implication of this interpretation is that Kushner, rather audaciously, seems to be presenting catastrophe—environmental meltdown and the AIDS epidemic, in this case—as an *opportunity*. Furthermore, it seems Kusher is suggesting that there is an ethical obligation to seize this 'emergency' as an opportunity, since not to do so would be an abnegation of responsibility amounting to 'getting off scot-free.' An opportunity for what, though? Following Benjamin, one would have to interpret it as an opportunity to open up what has been suppressed by American historiography, with the idea that, in that moment of flux, society can be reconfigured to allow it to move forward on a more equitable basis, better prepared to face the as-yet unknown challenges that lie ahead.

An important influence on Kushner in this regard, besides Benjamin, is Raymond Williams. Kushner has on numerous occasions spoken of the importance of Williams' short essay from 1985, 'Walking Backwards into the Future,'[41] and has even used a line from it as the title of one of his books, *Thinking About the Longstanding Problems of Virtue and Happiness.*[42] Williams begins the essay by asking: how exactly are we to face the future?[43] Traditionally, he suggests, socialism drew confidence in the future from two main sources: firstly, from 'older ideas of a millennium: a moment in history when the world would be changed'; and secondly, from a notion of progress rooted in a belief in the dialectical movement of history.[44] Williams points out that in 1985 such ideas, far from inspiring confidence in the future, produce 'the exact opposite, despair and pessimism; the millennium as apocalypse; the final crisis as nuclear holocaust.'[45] Despite this, Williams still finds reasons to be heartened:

> What is most surprising about contemporary socialism, haunted as it is by these dark ideas, is the resilience, the energy and in surprising ways the confidence of those most committed to it. The reasons for this are important. The central reason is that however much we may have been affected by these other ideas—of the coming millennium or of a historically inevitable socialism—we have always drawn our real strength from very different sources: from our actual relationships and class experiences in our own lives.[46]

In the moment of threatened catastrophe, then, when systems of defence seem least able to cope, there remains a resilience that develops out of our relationships with others: a resilience rooted not in theory, but in praxis. Thus presented, the real threat to such resilience is the individualism of capitalism with which historiography is complicit. In order to move forwards into the future without succumbing to false ideas of progress, one must 'face the difficulties' of the present 'but only as a challenge.'[47] In so doing we discover 'a more general resilience, learned more from ourselves under pressure than simply from ideas'; and 'In this sense,' Williams continues, 'we can face the future as we really get to know ourselves in the present: a confidence in ourselves that is always our leading resource.'[48]

It seems not at all improbable that Kushner is recommending just such a course of action. The change and forward

movement that Prior endorses are certainly presented as something quite distinct from the models of progress represented by Louis and Aleksii Antedilluvianovich Prelapsarianov (described as 'the world's oldest Bolshevik' [*AA,* p. 138]). As we have seen, the only way Louis can face the future is precisely by refusing to 'face the difficulties' of the present, preferring instead to focus on a utopian notion of perfectibility. Aleksii represents a different, more traditional aspect of socialism, but one which is no better equipped to deal with the challenge of how one faces the future whilst dealing with the present. Failing to see the full value of praxis, Aleksii is paralysed by his dogmatic attachment to theory:

> The Great Question before us is: Are we doomed? The Great Question before us is: Will the Past release us? The Great Question before us is: Can we Change? In Time? And we all desire that Change will come.
>
> And *Theory*? How are we to proceed without *Theory*?
>
> [...]
>
> Change? Yes, we must change, only show me the Theory, and I will be at the barricades, show me the book of the next Beautiful Theory, and I promise you these blind eyes will see again, just to read it [...].
>
> If the snake sheds his skin before a new skin is ready, naked he will be in the world, prey to the forces of chaos. Without his skin he will be dismantled, lose coherence and die.
>
> (*AA,* pp. 147-48)

As one might expect, then, the conviction that Prior develops towards the end of the play, after he has brought under control his fear of the unknown future, and after he has decided to reject stasis, believing, with Belize, that the world 'only spins forward' (*AA,* p. 178), is that one has no choice but to move forward into the future and that, crucially, one does so without the assurances of a belief in perfectibility or a theory of material change. The only way to move forward affirmatively, he seems to believe, is by drawing strength from relationships with other people and from an understanding of society as it is in the present moment. This rootedness in the everyday allows one to dare to hope, even when hope seems hopelessly misplaced. In this sense, Kushner, along with Benjamin and Williams, seems to be suggesting that in moments of extreme crisis there is the possibility, determined by the manner in which one responds when challenged, of a type of progress—a progress wholly detached from utopian notions of perfectibility and dogmatic historical materialism; a form of progress contingent on praxis, on how society collectively configures itself. It is in this sense that Kushner seems to urge us to view catastrophe as an opportunity, as a revolutionary chance.[49]

This reading of *Angels in America* as promoting a radical message of hope in circumstances that, it would seem, could barely be more hopeless is lent support by evidence in the play suggesting Voltaire as an influence. Earthquakes feature significantly in the play. The Angel believes that mankind's constant movement has led God to abandon his creation. The moment of this abandonment was marked by the San Francisco earthquake of 18 April 1906, a sign of everything coming 'unglued.' It was in response to the even more devastating Lisbon earthquake of 1755 that Voltaire, in 1759, wrote *Candide,* his famous critique of Leibnizian theocracy—the idea that belief in God is enough to assure us that all is for the best in the best of all possible worlds. The position that Voltaire seems to validate in *Candide* is one that rejects grand but ultimately ineffective philosophizing in favour of a more modest, praxis-based approach to life ('let us dig in our garden' is the oft-repeated refrain[50]). Furthermore, it is suggested that because our knowledge of the world is always limited and finite, we have no option but to embrace social and religious tolerance simply on the grounds that we can never know enough to be assured that we are justified in persecuting those with whom we disagree on such matters. Related to this is the fact that although Voltaire roundly criticizes the idea that everything in the world is for the best, thus acknowledging the presence of evil in the world, he holds out the possibility that one might continue to hope for a better future. When Candide says 'Pangloss was in the right—everything is for the best,' the sceptical Martin says, 'I hope it may be.'[51] This endorsement of hope against hope can be seen even more clearly in Voltaire's 'Poem on the Lisbon Disaster,' written immediately after the earthquake: 'All will be well one day—so runs our hope. / All *now* is well, is but an idle dream.'[52] Unmitigating, unappeasing acknowledgement of disaster or the threat of catastrophe, aligned with an indeterminate hope in the future and a belief in the possibility of progress, is something that clearly informs Kushner's intellectual vision, too. Indeed, Kushner has asserted that '[i]t is an ethical obligation to look for hope; it is an ethical obligation not to despair,'[53] but, as he says elsewhere, 'it has to be hope that has been filtered through the most lamentable conditions of real existence.'[54] In this light Prior seems, in spirit at least, a rather Beckettian figure: he must go on, he can't go on, he'll go on.[55] He affirms what Harper at the end of the play calls 'painful progress' (*AA,* p. 275). Like Jacob, Prior wrestles with the angel for a blessing, or 'more life,' but he does so knowing that more life will mean more pain, more suffering and no prospect of redemption.[56] But clinging to life is what humans do. Prior tries to convince the Angels:

> We can't stop. We're not rocks—progress, migration, motion is … modernity. It's *animate,* it's what living things do. We desire. Even if all we desire is stillness, it's still desire *for.*

> (*AA,* pp. 263-64)

Not to request more life, then, would be almost *inhuman.* He goes on:

> I still want … My blessing. Even sick. I want to be alive.
> […]

I want more life. I can't help myself. I do.

> I've lived through such terrible times, and there are people who live through much worse, but … You see them living anyway. When they're more spirit than body, more sores than skin, when they're burned and in agony, when flies lay eggs in the corners of the eyes of their children, they live. Death usually has to *take* life if it's not braver to die. But I recognise the habit. The addiction to being alive. We live past hope. If I can find hope anywhere, that's it, that's the best I can do. It's so much not enough, so inadequate but … Bless me anyway. I want more life.

> (*AA,* pp. 265-67)

Williams' essay 'Walking Backwards into the Future' was published in the 1989 collection *Resources of Hope.* Clearly, for Kushner, the resources of hope available as America approached the millennium were not in themselves sufficient, and it was no longer possible to base hope on an unthinking confidence in the future or in progress. We live on, he seems to suggest, in the hope of some as-yet unspecified, unforeseeable event that would redeem the pain and suffering currently endured in the world. As Cassirer, writing on Voltaire, says:

> It is foolish self-deception to close our eyes to the evils which everywhere confront us; all we can do is turn our eyes to the future hoping it will bring the solution of the riddle which is now insoluble.[57]

To accept what Kushner seems to be advocating in *Angels in America* would be to wait, in hope, for such an event; always in the knowledge, however, that it might never happen. Such hope would have to enlist what Benjamin calls our '*weak* messianic power' which would allow us to remain open towards the future in expectation of an unspecified moment that would suspend the flow of history in a way that would retrospectively redeem our hope.[58]

So have we located and, at least to some degree, explained what might be considered the political 'stance' promoted by *Angels in America*? Can we conclude that Kushner's message is one of messianic hope, rooted in aspects of Enlightenment thought but strengthened and radicalized by the resilience of present-day socialist experience? I think we perhaps can, but only with the proviso that there is precious little about this conclusion that is conclusive. At the heart of Kushner's vision is a rejection of political theory and a concomitant avowal of hope predicated upon an indeterminate future event that is hardly likely, let alone certain. Louis, in the final scene of *Perestroika,* contradicting both his earlier position and that of Alekseii, says: 'You can't wait around for a theory [...]. It's all too much to be encompassed by a single theory now' (*AA,* p. 278). Instead he speaks admiringly of politicians who are capable of 'making a leap into the unknown.' He even makes the uncharacteristic and rather messianic suggestion that 'only in politics does the miraculous occur.' But this cannot be concluded so quickly, either. Belize responds, objecting: 'But that's a theory' (*AA,* p. 278). Hannah, in turn, suggests that in a sense you still need a theory of some sort: 'You can't live in the world without an idea of the world, but it's living that makes the ideas' (*AA,* p. 278). They are unable to reach a final agreement, but their discussion remains amicable, tolerant and open. As such, the final scene performs and preserves the open-endedness that seems to be at the heart of Kushner's political vision. This, of course, is why *Angels in America* cannot simply be reduced to a political message, and yet it is also why it should be understood as politically interventionist. Political philosophy can make such arguments for pluralism and urge resistance to easy resolution, but these arguments risk being undermined by the univocal and conclusive manner of their presentation. The distinct advantage of drama for Kushner is that it is able to perform the ultimate lack of resolution so central to the political heart of the play. The Angel, then, as the symbol of rupture, signifies not only that which holds open history or ideology, but also that which holds open the text, guarding the indeterminacy out of which hope is able to emerge, resisting the temptation to ossify into an ideological position or utopian belief. As such, *Angels in America* might be considered activist drama of the most thoroughgoing kind.

AFTERWORD: LOOKING BACK ON AMERICA'S POLITICAL FUTURE

Knowing, as we do now with what one might call twenty-twenty 9/11 hindsight, what was just around the corner for New York, Kushner's millenarianism is prescient and troubling in a way that he surely never intended and that forces a reconsideration of his political philosophy. Lines such as 'I feel like something terrifying is on its way [...] like a missile from outer space, and it's plummeting down towards the earth, and I'm ground zero' (*AA,* p. 104), spoken by Prior, carry a shudder-inducing resonance that they simply lacked prior to the Al-Qaeda attacks on New York. 9/11, as these events have come to be known, can be described as an unforeseeable event that momentarily ruptured the flow of American historiography and forced a reconfiguration of society. Not a million miles, then, from the sort of catastrophe of which Kushner seems to be urging his audience to be ready to take revolutionary advantage. It is an intriguing question whether considerations such as these have inclined Kushner to temper the radical political view he sets forth in *Angels in America.* No such chastening is evident in the exuberant and highly successful 2003 HBO mini-series adaptation, but then that had been in preparation long before the 2001 attacks and so was hardly the most likely vehicle for a *volte face.*[59] However, the Afterword to *Homebody/ Kabul* suggests that 9/11 did have a profound effect on Kushner's politics. Writing just months after 9/11, he says: 'What time in human history is comparable to this? It's nearly impossible to locate plausible occasions for hope.'[60] Nearly impossible, but still it remains imperative that one finds hope somewhere. Without it life becomes unbearable: 'Hope dies, the imagination withers and with it the human heart.'[61] What changes in Kushner's post-9/11 articulation of his political philosophy is the source from which hope springs. Articulating the belief that seems to motivate *Angels in America,* Kushner writes: 'Tragedy is the annihilation from whence new life springs, the Nothing out of which Something is born. Devastation can be a necessary prelude to a new kind of beauty.'[62] But he is now more hesitant, more questioning: 'Are cataclysm and catastrophe the birth spasms of the future, is the mass grave some sort of cradle, does the future always arrive borne on a torrent of blood?'[63] Evidently unable to answer in the affirmative, Kushner now locates hope in a different source that would seem to mark both a departure from his radical pre-millennial stance and a chastening of the audacity of hope. At the close of the Afterword, he writes:

> I read the following sentence, which suggests another kind of prologue to creation, perhaps offers hope for some prelude other than destruction, some other way for the future to commence; from the Talmud:
>
> Repentance preceded the world.[64]

Notes

1. T. Kushner, *Angels in America* (London, 2007), p. 286. (Subsequent references to *AA* appear parenthetically.) Kushner's political commitment is further demonstrated by his declaration that 'all theatre is political. I cannot be a playwright without having some temptation to let audiences know what I think when I read the newspaper in the morning.' J. Fisher, *The Theater of Tony Kushner: Living Past Hope* (New York and London, 2002), p. 60.

2. By 'political and philosophical position,' I wish to indicate broadly an ideological stance affiliated with particular established political discourses which carries an implied commitment to an ethical vision of how things ought to be. When discussing the political implications of Kushner's play, the terms 'position,' 'stance' and 'vision' will be used synonymously to evoke this idea.

3. Fisher, *The Theater of Tony Kushner,* p. 87.

4. F. Rich, 'Marching Out of the Closet, Into History,' *New York Times,* 10 November 1992, available online at <http://www.nytimes.com/1992/11/10/theater/review-theater-marching-out-of-the-closet-into-history.html> [last accessed 22 April 2010].

5. F. Rich, 'Following an Angel for a Healing Vision of Heaven on Earth,' *New York Times,* 24 November 1993, available online at <http://www.nytimes.com/1993/11/24/arts/review-theater-perestroika-following-angel-for-healing-vision-heaven-earth.html> [last accessed 22 April 2010].

6. L. Bersani, *Homos* (Harvard, 1996), p. 69.

7. Fisher, *The Theater of Tony Kushner,* pp. 58, 92 and 59.

8. J. Berger, *After the End: Representations of Post-Apocalypse* (Minneapolis and London, 1999), p. 224, n. 11.

9. C. Bigsby, *Contemporary American Playwrights* (Cambridge, UK, 1999), p. 113.

10. D. Savran, 'Ambivalence, Utopia, and a Queer Sort of Materialism: How *Angels in America* Reconstructs the Nation,' in *Approaching the Millennium: Essays on 'Angels in America,'* ed. by D. R. Geis and S. F. Kruger (Ann Arbor, 1997), pp. 13-39 (pp. 14, 15 and 29).

11. Ibid., p. 36.

12. Ibid., pp. 31 and 32.

13. It might be said, rather broadly, that the inadequacies of Left and Right have, for Kushner, a common root in individualism. This might be taken to suggest a move towards a communitarian politics. Whilst such an expectation would not be entirely disappointed, it does not take into account the influence of secular Judaism that draws Kushner towards Walter Benjamin's writings on history.

14. J. Locke, *Two Treatises of Government,* ed. by P. Laslett (Cambridge, UK, 2004), p. 301.

15. Ibid., p. 271.

16. For close textual analysis of the Declaration and its indebtedness to antecedent texts, see P. Maier, *American Scripture: How America Declared its Independence from Britain* (London, 1999), pp. 104-36, and G. Wills, *Inventing America: Jefferson's Declaration of Independence* (New York, 2002), especially pp. 229-55. A particularly important precedent with regard to the inclusion of the word 'happiness' was set by George Mason's choice of wording in the Virginia Declaration of Rights, drafted in 1776, which refers to 'the enjoyment of life and liberty, with the means of acquiring and possessing property, and pursuing and obtaining happiness and safety,' repr. in *Roots of the Republic: American Founding Documents Interpreted,* ed. by S. L. Schechter (Oxford, 1990), pp. 150-65 (p. 154). This can be contrasted with similar documents such as the Declaration and Resolves of the First Continental Congress of 1774, which uses the more familiar Lockean phrase 'life, liberty and property,' repr. in *Documentary Source Book of American History: 1606-1898,* ed. by W. MacDonald (New York, 1908), pp. 162-66 (p. 164). The apparently aberrant departure from Lockean ideology in the use in the Declaration of Independence of the word 'happiness' instead of 'property' has puzzled many people. Howard Mumford Jones writes: 'As for the unalienable right to pursue happiness, no one, so far as I know, has ever understood why Jefferson substituted the phrase for John Locke's comprehensible trilogy

[sic], life, liberty, and property, except that Jefferson may have had in the back of his mind an imperfect recollection of a passage which George Mason wrote into the Virginia Declaration of Rights of June 1776' (quoted by Wills in *Inventing America,* p. 230). Indeed, the phrasing of the Declaration of Independence is so close to Mason's text that it has occasionally been judged to 'detract from his achievement' (Maier, *American Scripture,* p. 104). Gilberd Chinard, for instance, in *Thomas Jefferson: The Apostle of Americanism,* comments: 'The only fault that could be found is that he did not more clearly acknowledge his indebtedness to George Mason' (quoted by Wills in *Inventing America,* p. 240). Although most commentators identify the Declaration of Independence as a thoroughly Lockean text in which the word 'happiness' appears misplaced, Wills mounts a spirited defence of the intellectual integrity of the text, distancing it from Locke's influence. Gunnar Myrdal suggests that '[w]hen Jefferson changed "property" to "pursuit of happiness," he followed the more inclusive French idealism, and stuck a radical tone'; see G. Myrdal, *An American Dilemma: The Negro Problem and Modern Democracy* (New York, 1944), p. 1182, n. 12. It is interesting that the substitution of 'happiness' for 'property' seems to have had the support of Benjamin Franklin. In *The Compleated Autobiography,* Mark Skousen writes: 'From several sources, it appears that Franklin was in league with Jefferson in emphasising the defence of "life, liberty, and the pursuit of happiness" as the goal of government, and downplaying the right to "property."' B. Franklin, *The Compleated Autobiography,* ed. by M. Skousen (Washington D.C., 2006), p. 413.

17. T. Hobbes, *Leviathan,* ed. by J. C. A. Gaskin (Oxford, 1998), p. 84.

18. Ibid., p. 84.

19. J. J. Rousseau, *Discourse on Inequality,* trans. by Franklin Philip (Oxford, 1999), p. 115.

20. G. S. Wood, *The Radicals of the American Revolution* (New York, 1993), p. 5.

21. Throughout this article, it is the more recognisably post-Marxian understanding of 'radical' that I intend to signify by the term. Attempting to answer the question 'what *is* radical politics today?,' Zygmunt Bauman provides what might serve as a useful working definition of radicalism: 'Acts, undertakings, means and measures may be called "radical" when they reach down to the *roots*: of a problem, a challenge, a task. Note, however, that the Latin noun "radix," to which the metaphorical uses of "radical" trace their pedigree, refers not only to *roots,* but also to *foundations* and to *origins.*' Bauman observes that implicit

in this definition is the recognition that violence may be necessary to destroy the 'outgrowth' in order to reach the roots. Z. Bauman, 'Getting to the Roots of Radical Politics Today' in *What is Radical Politics Today?*, ed. by Jonathan Pugh (Basingstoke, 1999), p. 25, n. 1.

22. Lipset, for instance, comments: 'Born out of revolution, the United States is a country organised around an ideology which includes a set of dogmas about the nature of a good society. [. . .] In Europe, nationality is related to community, and thus one cannot become un-English or un-Swedish. Being an American, however, is an ideological commitment. It is not a matter of birth. Those who reject American values are un-American'; S. E. Lipset, *American Nationalism: A Double-Edged Sword* (New York, 1997), p. 31. As the historian Richard Hofstadter famously remarked: 'It has been our fate as a nation not to have ideologies, but to be one' (quoted by Lipset in *American Nationalism*, p. 18). See also G. Myrdal, *An American Dilemma*, pp. 3-9; L. Hartz, *The Liberal Tradition in America* (New York, 1955), pp. 3-14, and A. Lieven, *America Right or Wrong: An Anatomy of American Nationalism* (London, 2005), pp. 4-5, 48-52.

23. Chesterton adds: 'That creed is set forth with dogmatic and even theological lucidity in the Declaration of Independence.' G. K. Chesterton, *What I Saw in America* (New York, 1922), p. 7.

24. A. de Tocqueville, *Democracy in America*, trans. by G. E. Bevan (London, 2003). For Belize's criticism of Louis's reading habits, see *AA*, p. 102.

25. Myrdal, *An American Dilemma*, p. 8.

26. Ibid., p. 3.

27. Hartz, *The Liberal Tradition in America*, p. 9.

28. Lieven, *America Right or Wrong*, p. 49.

29. The notion that America is qualitatively different from other nations because of its ideological origins can be traced back to Tocqueville, who referred to the American position as 'entirely exceptional' (*Democracy in America*, p. 519). In light of Louis's comments on race and his unwitting proximity to liberalism, it is worth noting that the influential interpretation of American identity as unique in so far as it is constituted, first and foremost, by a general adherence to a liberal creed, has also come under fire for neglecting the question of race. Alan Wolfe, for instance, points out that criticisms aimed at Hartz for his 'insufficient treatment of race, have stuck'; A. Wolfe, *The Future of Liberalism* (New York, 2009), p. 4.

30. J. Ashberry, 'Self-Portrait in a Convex Mirror,' in *Selected Poems* (Manchester, 2002), p. 192.

31. Savran, 'Ambivalence, Utopia, and a Queer Sort of Materialism,' p. 39, n. 47.

32. Although this may in fact have been the case, there seems anyway to have been an ideological connection between Reaganism and apocalypse. See Berger's chapter, '"Achieved Utopias": The Reaganist Post-Apocalypse,' in *After the End*, pp. 133-68.

33. W. Benjamin, 'On the Concept of History,' in *Walter Benjamin: Selected Writings*, Vol. 4: *1938-1940*, trans. by Edmund Jephcott and others (Cambridge, MA, and London, 2006), pp. 389-400 (p. 392).

34. Ibid., p. 395.

35. This is in stark contrast with Louis, who does not like judgement (see *AA*, p. 44-45). He likes ongoing transitional history without the sacrifice of the catastrophe.

36. Benjamin, 'On the Concept of History,' p. 390.

37. Ibid., p. 395.

38. Ibid., p. 396 (both quotations).

39. Ibid., p. 392.

40. Ibid., p. 396.

41. R. Williams, 'Walking Backwards Into the Future,' in *Resources of Hope: Culture, Democracy, Socialism* (London and New York, 1989).

42. T. Kushner, *Thinking About the Longstanding Problems of Virtue and Happiness: Essays, A Play, Two Poems, and a Prayer* (London, 1995).

43. Williams, 'Walking Backwards Into the Future,' p. 281.

44. Ibid., p. 281.

45. Ibid., p. 282.

46. Ibid., pp. 282-83.

47. Ibid., p. 286.

48. Ibid., p. 287.

49. Of course, in doing so, Kushner is, on one level, simply adapting an established template of radical thought. Bauman writes: 'Taking a "radical" stance signals an intention to *destroy*—or, at any rate, the readiness to *take the risk* of destruction; more often than not, a radical stance aims at a "*creative* destruction"—destruction in the sense of "site-clearing," or

turning over and loosening the soil, in order to prepare for another round of sowing or planting and make the ground ready to accommodate another type of root.' Bauman, 'Getting to the Roots of Radical Politics Today,' p. 25, n. 1.

50. Voltaire, *Candide,* trans. by N. Cameron (London, 2001), p. 104.

51. Ibid., p. 91.

52. Voltaire, 'Poem on the Lisbon Disaster,' in *Selected Works of Voltaire,* ed. by Joseph McCabe (London, 1911), pp. 1-7 (p. 7).

53. <http://www.wrestlingwithangelsthemovie.com/content/view/32/36/> [last accessed 22 April 2010].

54. Bigsby, *Contemporary American Playwrights,* p. 121.

55. See S. Beckett, *The Unnameable* (New York, 1970), p. 179. Intriguing comparisons may be made with Shelley's affirmation of hope as expressed in the final lines of 'Prometheus Unbound': 'to hope till Hope creates/From its own wreck the thing it contemplates.' P. B. Shelley, *The Major Works,* ed. by M. O'Neill (Oxford, 2003), p. 313.

56. Kushner writes: 'I want to acknowledge my indebtedness to Harold Bloom's reading of the Jacob story, which I first encountered in his introduction to Olivier Revault D'Allonnes's *Musical Variations on Jewish Thought,* in which Bloom translates the Hebrew word for "blessing" as "more life." Bloom expands on his interpretation in *The Book of J' (AA,* p. 144).

57. E. Cassirer, *The Philosophy of the Enlightenment,* trans. by F. C. A. Koelln and J. P. Pettegrove (Princeton, 1951), p. 147.

58. Benjamin, 'On the Concept of History,' p. 390.

59. K. Nielsen, *Tony Kushner's 'Angels in America'* (London, 2008), p. 88.

60. T. Kushner, *Homebody/Kabul* (London, 2002), p. 148.

61. Ibid., p. 148.

62. Ibid., p. 150.

63. Ibid., p. 150.

64. Ibid., p. 151.

Boris Vejdovsky (essay date 2011)

SOURCE: Vejdovsky, Boris. "Hidden Truths and Open Lies: The Performance of U.S. History and Mythography in Tony Kushner's *Angels in America* and Its Film Adaptation." *American Secrets: The Politics and Poetics of Secrecy in the Literature and Culture of the United States.* Ed. Eduardo Barros-Grela and José Liste-Noya. Madison: Fairleigh Dickinson UP, 2011. 73-84. Print.

[*In the following essay, Vejdovsky connects the act of coming out with the play's emphasis on history to argue that* "Angels in America *becomes the performance in which America declares publicly its true nature, confesses some of its crimes, and reveals some of its dark secrets." However, according to Vejdovsky, the play also emphasizes the more difficult task of preventing revealed knowledge to degenerate into "open lies."*]

Millennium Approaches, the first part of Tony Kushner's ***Angels in America: A Gay Fantasia on National Themes,*** premiered in 1991 at the Eureka Theater in San Francisco. Part Two, ***Perestroika,*** opened the following year, at the Mark Taper Forum in Los Angeles. San Francisco has been, at least since Robert Duncan's 1944 controversial article "The Homosexual in Society," a pivotal locus for U.S. gay cultural expression, while Los Angeles, the "city of angels," evokes the themes of the play and suggests that what happens in the play and what happens around the play mix the audiences' experience of historical and political reality with such stuff as dreams are made of.

Kushner's play hinges upon unveiling, but also preserving, the secrecy of American history and mythography. It presents thereby, as this essay proposes to show, a paradoxical reversal of truth and lies, which operates in the play as a reversal of the visible and the invisible. The play reverses the Platonic assumption that secrets and truth need to be unveiled or revealed. It may be that one of the functions of art, of political drama certainly, is to reveal secrets and the truth, and this seems to be confirmed by Kushner, who has stated that he saw his play as "a complicated relationship . . . between politics and aesthetics" (Bernstein). Kushner's "gay fantasia" proposes to open some U.S. closets and perform America's cultural coming out. Such a "coming out" is predicated on the metaphor of someone's declaring their hitherto hidden sexual orientation. America's coming out is epitomized by Joe's confession of his homosexuality to his mother (***Millennium*** [***Millennium Approaches***] I, 8). ***Angels in America*** becomes the performance in which America declares publicly its true nature, confesses some of its crimes, and reveals some of its dark secrets.

Thus, U.S. indifference to gay men dying of AIDS in the 1980s and 1990s and the hidden agendas of that indifference are revealed. Simon Watney reminds us how "In 1986 a small group of gay men who called themselves the SILENCE = DEATH Project designed and began to fly-post a poster that appeared all over downtown New York" (94). Kushner's play dramatizes the feeling of the time that "a catastrophe was taking place" and "that nothing was being said in public, and not enough was being done" (Watney, 94). The play, not unlike the Project referred to by Watney, "declares that silence about the oppression of gay people . . . must be broken as a matter of [their] survival" (94). It is undoubtedly this form of historical revelation that has secured the success of the play, as it is one of the functions of theater to present a mirror, or a sounding chamber, to its audience and allow it to see that which would otherwise remain hidden, or to hear that which would otherwise be silenced.

But Kushner's *Angels in America* also suggests that revealing these American secrets is not enough to make them harmless. When they are revealed, hidden truths can turn into open lies: they no longer lurk in the dark, but stare the audience in the eyes, so much so that they become invisible. Thus, Kushner's play can be read as reversing the usual pattern of hiding and revelation, and as showing that disclosing America's historical secrets and debunking its myths is not as hard as keeping them from becoming open and therefore invisible and even more dangerous lies.

* * *

Theater critics have called the play "the authoritative achievement of a radical dramatic artist with a clear voice," and it has been welcomed as the "the broadest, deepest, most searching American play of our time" (quoted by Savran, 207). John Clum, the author of the influential *Acting Gay*, has declared that the play "marks a turning point in the history of gay drama, the history of American drama, and of American literary history" (quoted by Savran, 208). This phenomenal critical appraisal was confirmed by a Pulitzer Prize for drama that Kushner received for *Millennium.* The play also won two Tony Awards when it was staged in the United States, while its film adaptation by HBO as a miniseries earned it five Golden Globes, and eleven Emmy Awards. Another form of lionization came from one of America's most influential literary critics, Harold Bloom, who included *Angels* [*Angels in America*] in his 1995 *Western Canon* (567), alongside Milton, Shakespeare, and the Bible. It is impossible to supplement or detract from the hyperbolic chanting of praise that has accompanied the play for almost twenty years. It is crucial, on the other hand, to interrogate the way history and myths are represented and aestheticized in the play and in its cinematographic adaptation to examine what forms of revelation and concealment it offers. It is essential, in other words, to see whether the revelation of America's historical and mythographical secrets may not lead to a new form of blindness, and to ask the question with Savran: "Why is [*Angels in America*] both popular and 'radical'?" (208). It may be that something there is in American culture that is always prompt to assimilate radical narrative strategies to

include them into mainstream culture, this turning revelation into the reiteration of consent and possibly lie.

Angels in America is a "promiscuously complicated play" (Savran, 209) that has become popular partly because of its complexity. The play has an impressive array of more than thirty characters played by only eight actors. As the characters are male and female, gay and straight and bisexual, Jewish and Mormon and WASP, angelic and human, historical and fictional, this complicates the identity of each character, disputes the validity of binary oppositions, and explicitly places the play in the current American conflict over identity politics. The multiplication of characters and the combination of fictional characters with historical ones turns *Angels in America* into a revisiting of American history, with emphasis on McCarthyism, immigration, Western expansion, and the myth of the melting pot. The play calls into question this central trope, one of the most significant "national themes" of the American democratic ethos. The play opens with Rabbi Chemelwitz speaking of America as "the melting pot where nothing melted" (*Millennium* I, 1) and invoking and rejecting the St. John de Crèvecoeur assertion that America is the place where "individuals of all nations are melted into a new race of men" (70). This first apparent ironic debunking of a national fantasy is an important clue for the reading of the play, as it suggests that this debunking is going to be insufficient.

Early on, Kushner reveals his obsession with history and suggests that *Angels in America* is "not just about AIDS as a major medical crisis, but somehow incorporate[s] into [its] debate the whole state of America" (Watney, 184). Thus, the play is really about the confusion of the world and its hermeneutical reading. As Patrick Brantlinger has it, "The play brilliantly expresses the mood of the contemporary United States and perhaps other Western societies . . . that no longer believe in their manifest destinies" (77-78). Complexity and confusion are important aspects of Kushner's aesthetics and maybe even its necessary condition, and he does not perceive this as detrimental to the sense of community that he seeks to foster.

The sense of confusion of the world is represented in the play by millennial thought and eschatology that appear as "a long heritage stretching back through Christian Apocalypticism and Jewish Messianism" (Gardner, 174). Stanton Gardner points out that "after World War II, a darker vision of America's millenarian role has prevailed," forming "the apocalyptic rhetoric . . . that characterized the Cold War" (174). While *Millennium Approaches* debunks America's mythopoeic sense of history, *Perestroika* anchors it in the political history of the turn of the twentieth century and projects it into the future.

The action of the play is projected against a backdrop of anxious expectation of either catastrophe or regeneration. *Angels in America* consciously and conspicuously plays with the apocalyptic historical sense that developed in the

1990s and that George W. Bush, Sr. famously sought to capture in an address to Congress in March 1990: "Now, we can see a new world coming into view. A world in which there is the very real prospect of a new world order."[1] President Bush's speech resonated with buzzwords of U.S. mythical history. The "new world order" chanted by the president was also a sort of "fantasy on national themes," though there was nothing gay—in any sense of that word—about it. When the play was first staged, the Berlin Wall had been down for two years, and the dichotomous world of the Cold War was indeed about to change. *Angels in America* thematizes the major crises that came to darken the lyrical prospects evoked by President Bush, and as a "sweeping indictment of the Reagan era" (Greenman), the play denounces and exposes the hidden agendas and lies of the hegemonic neoconservative Reaganite right.

To the threats on the climate, on the military poise between the East and the West, and on the economy, was added the explosion of the epidemic of AIDS. The disease had been identified in the previous decade, and not unlike the means of global communication—in particular the Internet—that sprawled over the whole world, the HIV virus infected people globally, irrespective of national borders, cultural identities, sexual orientation, or racial definition. The play refers to the disease as a defining element of the historical situation of the United States at the turn of the millennium, and relates it to the plague, or Black Death, and to the way the latter had determined European history. This also places the gay community at the center of the play and proposes thereby a displacement of the perception of history. By placing gay men at the center of his reconstruction of the American democratic ethos, Kushner makes of a social group that has been discriminated against the depository of a special kind of knowledge and potential for regeneration. The play thus points to the secret or hidden construction of history and to the changes that happen in that construction when history is no longer told from the point of view of the hegemonic group in a culture. Kushner exposes, in particular, the process by which the "political, which ostensibly drives history ... intersects with the personal and sexual, which ostensibly are no more than footnotes to history" (Savran, 227).

Just after the funeral of Sarah Ironson that opens the play, Prior shows Louis the first lesions caused by AIDS and tells him that he has received the kiss of "the angel of death" (*Millennium* I, 4). Thus, the first part of *Angels in America* begins with an annunciation, but this is no "Good News," as in the Bible where these words promise redemption. On the contrary, the first act, set in "Fall 1985," is titled "Bad News," and the funeral sets the plays under the aegis of death and the *Göttersdämerung* of a culture and a new American Fall.

Characteristically, the opening scene bridges past and present when the rabbi pays respect to Louis's grandmother and says:

In her was—not a person but a whole kind of person, the ones who crossed the ocean, who brought with us to America the villages of Russia and Lithuania—and who struggled, and how we fought, for the family, for the Jewish home, so that you would not grow up *here,* in this strange place, in the melting pot where nothing ever melted. Descendents of this immigrant woman, you do not grow up in America, you and your children with goyische names. You do not live in America. No such place exists.

[...]

She was the last of the Mohicans, this one was. Pretty soon ... all the old will be dead.

(*Millennium* I, 1)

Having him call Prior's grandmother "the last of the Mohicans" is facetious, but his joke also "resonates with America's past, a complex past that Kushner grapples with throughout *Angels in America* and that melds both the myth and reality of American notions of racism and xenophobia" (Minton). The rabbi tells the assembled mourners that Sarah Ironson "fought for the Jewish home," and he goes on to explain the reasons for that fight: "so that you would not grow up here, in this strange place, in the melting pot where nothing ever melted" (*Millennium* I, 1). "This brilliant ironic inversion of the American credo of integration and American race" (Minton) debunks the myth of the American melting pot, and it is the first statement of the central theme of the play, "namely that the myth and the reality of democratic America are two different, and often contradictory, entities" (Minton). It is the divorce between myth and reality that the play seeks to overcome by displacing the perception of history—that is, by queering history and making the United States come out of its closet. It does so by challenging the tenets of Ronald Reagan's all-American neoconservative ideology, and by subverting the conventions of American realistic theater.

To achieve this, Kushner's "gesture of defiance" is to "anoint Prior, a gay man suffering from AIDS, as the prophet who will ostensibly lead America into the new millennium" (Minton). Prior does not only represent the future of the nation; he is also the descendant of a family of immigrants, and his, too, is the story of a haunted American past:

PRIOR: One of my ancestors was a ship captain who made money by bringing whale oil back to Europe and returning with immigrants—mostly Irish ... , so many dollars per head. The last ship he captained foundered off the coast of Nova Scotia ... and went to the bottom. ... [H]is crew took seventy women and children into the ship's only longboat, ... and when the weather got too rough, and when they thought the boat was overcrowded, the crew started ... hurling people into the sea. ... The boat was leaky, see; seventy people; they arrived in Halifax with nine people on board.

[...]

PRIOR: I think of that story a lot now. People in a boat, waiting, terrified, while implacable, unsmiling men, irresistibly strong, seize . . . maybe the person next to you, maybe you, and with no warning at all, with time only for a quick intake of air you are pitched into freezing, turbulent water and salt and darkness to drown.

(***Millennium*** I, 8)

This episode is the first of Prior's reflections on his situation and his family's past, and his story becomes a metaphor for the unpredictability of AIDS. Prior's narrative also establishes a link to the rabbi's story of immigration; America is a precarious boat on the ocean. In Prior's story, the boat is full—*das Schiff ist voll,* as others have said under not so different circumstances.[2] In Kushner's allegory, America is a boat on a stormy sea; anybody can be hurled into the ocean at any time, and nobody will help. This is the way Prior feels in an America that rejects homosexuals and presents the disease as a scourge inflicted by God.

Kushner "cannily depicts Prior as a figure that simultaneously epitomizes the stereotypical gay male and confounds essential characteristics of that very stereotype" (Minton). Kushner thus challenges the stereotypes of heterosexual masculinity, and at the end of the play Prior is a paradoxically strong man despite his illness, and he is determined to pursue "more life" (***Perestroika,*** Epilogue). He proposes a new masculine model for the new millennium, a model that denounces the ostensible models of heterosexual masculinity represented by Joe, Roy Cohn, or even Henry, Joe's doctor. To the false strength or the "clout" they pretend to have, he opposes a different form of resilience: "I am a gay man and I am used to pressure, to trouble, I am tough and strong" (***Millennium*** 3, 8), he poignantly declares.

The clearest emblem of Kushner's queering of politics and aesthetics is, however, the angel who comes to visit Prior in a mock evocation of the annunciation to Mary, or of Jacob wrestling with the angel. The angel's blundering arrival definitively destroys the realistic setup of the play, even as Kushner's hermaphroditic angel (equipped with eight vaginas and a bouquet of phalli) subverts gender and sexual definitions. The angel is both (super)human and angelic, male and female, gay and straight, maternal and paternal, protective and threatening, oracular and blundering. Prior's struggle with the angel takes the form of graphic sexual intercourse and there is nothing immaculate about the conception of that scene.

At the end of ***Millennium,*** when the angel arrives, Prior, who is lying in his sickbed, is awestruck, and before the angel that comes crashing through the ceiling of his kitchen, he mutters: "God almighty! . . . *Very* Steven Spielberg!" (III, 8). Prior's quip suggests that Kushner is aware that his subversive gesture consisting in using and abusing the figure of the angel is always already culturally and historically determined, and that it is in danger of being accommodated by mainstream culture, of which Spielberg was the epitome in the 1980s. The implicit reference to movies with stunning special effects, such as *E.T.* or *Close Encounters of the Third Kind,* projects us into an era of technological progress, consumerism, and neo-liberalism typical of the time where the play is set.

In his "Note About the Staging," Kushner specifies that "The moments of magic . . . are to be fully realized as bits of *theatrical* illusion which means that it's OK if the wires show, and maybe it's good that they do, but the magic should at the same time be thoroughly amazing" (***Millennium*** xi). Kushner's note takes us in the direction of meta-theatricality and fosters in the audience a reflection on the relationship between art and reality, history and aesthetics, and on the capacity of drama to reveal the truth or simply to mimic such a revelation.

However, Kushner's note also presents the theater as the locus of historical possibility and suggests that by taking distance from historical reality—by showing its "wires"—we may be able to affect that reality. In the utopia of the theater, we become better readers of the world, and we can hope for change. Kushner's play purports to show the "wires" of the story it tells and thereby the "wires" of history to disclose its secrets. Techniques such as parallel montage, or characters that enter a scene where they normally do not belong, reinforce the spectators' awareness that this is all *playing* with history.

However, this utopian and subversive vision of the theater also always already makes of the play a commodity for mainstream culture. Savran cunningly writes that "not *despite but because of these endeavors,* [has] the play been accommodated with stunning ease to the hegemonic ideology not just of the theater-going public, but of the democratic majority—an ideology that has become the *new* American religion: liberal pluralism" (219). Kushner's theater where the "wires" of history and politics are revealed is thus commensurate with the ideology of liberal pluralism, which has become, in turn, the new American utopia.

In Kushner's utopian world, ostensibly opposed views on America are confronted. Thus, Joe, the closeted gay Mormon Republican, tells his wife Harper:

JOE:

I think things are starting to change in the world.

HARPER:

But I don't want . . .

JOE:

Wait. For the good. America has rediscovered itself. Its sacred position among nations. . . . The truth restored. The law restored. This is what President Reagan's done,

HARPER:

He says "Truth exists and can be spoken proudly." And the country responds to him. We become better. More

good. ... I mean six years ago the world seemed in decline, horrible, hopeless, full of unsolvable problems and
crime and confusion and hunger and ...

HARPER:

But it still seems that way. More now than before. They
say the ozone layer is ...

JOE:

Harper ...

HARPER:

And today out of the window on Atlantic Avenue there
was a schizophrenic traffic cop who was making these

[...]

JOE:

Stop it! I'm trying to make a point.

HARPER:

So am I.

JOE:

You aren't even making sense, you ...

HARPER:

My point is the world seems just as ...

JOE:

It only seems that way because you never go out in the
world, Harper, and you have emotional problems.

(*Millennium* I, 5)

The play is full of political disputation—all of it between
men, since women are excluded from the public sphere, or
silenced like Harper in the passage above. Actual dissent is
banned from this male utopian world. Harper notes this
when she visits the Mormon Visitors' Center; in words
that resound in the play with bitter irony, she comments
on the female characters on display: "They don't have any
lines, the sister and the mother. And only their faces move.
That's not really fair" (*Perestroika* III, 2). The "truth" according to Joe has been revealed, and can be spoken in the
apocalyptic rhetoric of Bush's "new world order," or Reagan's "evil empire" rhetoric. But this simplification of the
world, this ending of "unsolvable problems" or "confusion," is a male fantasy out of which Harper and the
other women of the play are excluded by a rhetoric that
claims to reveal the truth and put an end to confusion.

One of the play's pivotal scenes from this point of view is
Louis's enunciation of his political views, which seem radically opposed to those of Joe. This takes place in a conversation with Belize, whom Louis offends by telling him

that there is "no race problem in America." Louis's diatribe
begins with a rhetorical question: "Why has democracy
succeeded in America?" His wishy-washy noncommittal
declaration climaxes when he ejaculates:

[T]his reaching out for a spiritual past in a country where
no indigenous spirits exist—only the Indians, I mean Native American spirits and we killed them off so now, there
are no gods here, no ghosts and spirits in America, there
are no angels in America, no spiritual past, no racial past,
there's only the political ...

(*Millennium* III, 2)

Through the character that probably resembles him most,
Kushner exposes the central idea of his play, but ironically,
in the negative. Indeed, if there is one thing that comes out
of the play, it is that there *are* angels in America; America
is haunted by ghosts; America *is* tragically inhabited by its
racial, sexual, and religious past. Louis speaks about politics all the time to forget or repress that he too is haunted by
guilt about forsaking Prior. Belize responds to Louis's
torrent of words by telling him that "instead of spending
the rest of [his] life trying to get through *Democracy in
America*" (*Millennium* III, 3), he should try to understand
what loving someone really means. Louis, Roy Cohn, and
Joe have in common that the "truth" they speak is dominated by some superior ideal that makes them unable to
relate to people around them, and so ultimately, the truth
they reveal is really a political open lie.

Although the political visions of America of Prior, Joe,
Louis, and even Roy Cohn, the arch-villain, seem antithetical and irreconcilable, they are all actually united by a
utopian vision of "America." This vision of "America"
is essentially a theological construction subordinated to
utopian fantasies that Sacvan Bercovitch calls "harmony-
in-diversity and diversity-in-harmony" ("Problem," 649,
quoted in Savran 220). All these utopian visions are dominated by patriarchy where surrogate fathers replace biological fathers, patriarchy that remains remarkably efficient
when it comes to excluding dissent from its utopian visions.
In this respect, Gardner is right to say that "For Roy Cohn
the Republican tradition is patriarchal at heart, and it per-
petuates itself through the relationship of fathers and sons."
Patriarchal authority "resonates deep [or *haunts*] the American historical imagination" and "it is central to the masculinist tradition of American drama against which Kushner
writes" (Gardner, 181). In the end, "***Angels in America*** sets
forth a liberal pluralist vision of America in which all, not
in spite but because of their diversity, will be welcomed in
the New Jerusalem" (Savran, 221). This is where the hidden truths of patriarchy and masculinity become open lies,
and where rhetoric and aesthetics make patriarchal consensus and hegemony *masquerade* as dissent.

The pretense of showing the wires of the hidden machina-
tion of the rhetoric of patriarchy is further reinforced when

the play is transposed to another medium, and for the audience of cable television, which represents the actual American melting pot, or rather, the American "smorgasbord" (Savran, 220). Indeed, the interplay between revelation and secrets is particularly striking in Mike Nichols adaptation of the play for television.[3] The movie was almost unanimously well received, and Saul Austerlitz credits "Nichols for . . . not interfering with what was already perfect about *Angels in America*: the beauty of its language." Austerlitz rightly points to the linguistic and poetic qualities of the play and its rendition in the movie, but it is interesting to contrast what the words unveil with what the camera openly conceals.

This contrast between the wires of rhetoric and the wires of the theater—which Kushner insists on showing—and their smooth rendition in the movie appears most interestingly in the credits. The credits are an extra-diegetic element of the movie, an element that seems to belong to its "facts," rather than to the fiction it tells; however, they too constitute a reading of the play. As the film consists of two parts, the credits are shown twice, and Thomas Newman's obsessive musical theme further enhances their impact. The credits roll over heavenly music and display a bird's-eye view, or maybe angelic view, of America. The camera pans the nation from West to East catching on the way sights of U.S. symbolic and historical landmarks from the Golden Gate Bridge in San Francisco, to the Mormon Temple in Salt Lake City, the Gateway Arch in Saint Louis, Missouri, and the Sears Tower in Chicago. Finally, the camera swoops over the Manhattan skyline, soars into Central Park, and is arrested mid-air in front of an angel's statue that stands on the top of the Bethesda Fountain in Central Park. As the camera fixedly stares at the angel's bronze face, the latter comes alive, lifts her chin and gazes heavenward. Austerlitz rightly points out that, "This sequence establishes two of the film's major tropes, extended, played with and stretched like taffy over the course of its six hours: forward motion, and the relationship of humanity with the spiritual world." Nichols' film presents an angelic vision of America, a vision that is contested but also elicited by the play.

Sacvan Bercovitch identifies how Puritan America "has provided . . . the United States with a useful, flexible, durable and compelling fantasy of American identity" (*Rites*, 7). He also insists that "America is a controlling metaphor, a synonym for human possibility" (quoted in Savran, 26). Nichols' adaptation of *Angels in America* shows how Kushner's subversive strategies are effectively disarmed by what Bercovitch calls a "controlling metaphor" and how Kushner's revealing of truth becomes an open lie.

The "controlling metaphor" gives birth in Nichols' movie to a spiritual geography in which America is both point of origin and the locus of the meaning of history. The opening of the film is a reaffirmation of the nation's motto—*e*

pluribus unum—even as it unconsciously evokes the lyrics of *America the Beautiful,* sometimes called the second national anthem:

> America! America!
> God shed his grace on thee
> And crown thy good with brotherhood
> From sea to shining sea!

Nichols' camera takes us indeed from sea to shining sea, and the God-like perspective on the nation directly evokes the address to the nation recited by many schoolchildren: "I pledge allegiance to the flag of the United States of America, and to the Republic for which it stands, *one Nation under God, Indivisible,* with Liberty and Justice for all" (emphasis added). These words, which the play shows to be a series of open lies, resonate as truth in Nichols' credits. Indeed, the counter-chronological and regressive movement of the camera takes us from West to East that brings the spectators to a theological point of origin. But the magisterial gaze of the camera also becomes a latter-day expression of America's belief in its manifest destiny, which was, "to overspread the American continent." The aesthetics of the camera presents as truth the open lie of the melting pot that the play rejected. Now, "the place where nothing ever melted" becomes on the contrary one seamless fabric of unconscious and oblivious national community and identity. The celestial voyage becomes a Hollywood Boulevard of sorts and the sky is strewn with the names of the (movie) stars who act in the movie. These stars are the heroes of modern America even more than the characters they interpret; they are the figures around which the populace rallies and unites.

The one flight over the nation and the compression of time, which makes it possible to cover the distance coast to coast in just a few seconds, the angelic digitalized clouds, the animation of the statue, and the stunningly sharp pictures and saturated colors all proclaim the technological mastery over time and space, a mastery that Nichols' camera (which substitutes for the spectator's eye) embodies and endows America with. The credits end with the fountain of Bethesda, named after the biblical fountain of health in the Gospel of John (5:1). Not unlike Christ who travels back to Jerusalem, Nichols' camera travels back in time and space to the miraculous fountain of health and to the four figures around the fountain's base that symbolize Temperance, Purity, Health, and Peace. These are now the figures that are to reunite the nation. The play sought to disclose many a hidden truth about the ideological and historical construction of the United States, but in the movie the American continent becomes again the embodiment of the melting pot.

When called upon, the angel responds with a conniving wink of the eye, and directs its gaze toward heaven, thus establishing the privileged link between the nation and God. The only sign that this may all be fake, that this may be indeed an open lie, is the music that goes eerily off tune as the camera zooms in on the angel's face—but that is the only false note, one that many may choose to over-hear.

Nichols' flight over the nation is reminiscent of that desire for flying that Sigmund Freud interprets in "Leonardo da Vinci and a Memory of his Childhood" as the desire for sexual potency. Thus the debunking of patriarchal myths and the revelation of their secrets in *Angels in America* eventually leads to their reaffirmation in Nichols' adaptation of the play. Harold Bloom suggests that for Freud "flight is the metaphor for repression, for unconscious yet purposeful forgetting." And, he adds, "The purpose is clear enough . . . : to assuage displaced guilt. Forgetting, in an aesthetic context, is ruinous, for cognition . . . always relies on memory" (*Canon,* 17-18). Such is also the performance of Kushner's play: it awakens the guilt and the repressed of the nation by revealing its secrets, but at the same time it awakens the anxiety to control that guilt by turning them into open lies in which the nation can believe.

Notes

1. President Bush famously continued his speech by appealing to a sense of historical justice and equity, and by quoting Winston Churchill, who had advocated a "'world order' in which the principles of justice and fair play . . . protect the weak against the strong." "A world," President Bush concluded, "where the United Nations, freed from cold war stalemate, is poised to fulfill the historic vision of its founders. A world in which freedom and respect for human rights find a home among all nations." Don Oberdorfer, in the *Washington Post,* notes that "[Bush] actually had spoken of a 'new world order' at least once before, in a February 1990 political speech hailing the crumbling of the Iron Curtain the year before. By August 30, the phrase became a central feature of Bush's public oratory, including an address to the U.N. General Assembly and three speeches to joint sessions of Congress. According to a search of presidential documents published by the White House, Bush referred publicly to a 'new world order' at least 42 times from last summer [1990] to the end of March [1991]" (May 26, 1991).

2. Literally, "The boat is full." The phrase was used in several countries, particularly in Switzerland, to justify their refusal to harbor Jewish refugees fleeing from Nazi repression and the death camps.

3. The play was to have been adapted to the silver screen by Robert Altman. Finally, as Kushner commented, "Studio executives had concerns—about the material, about the budget, about the length—and it fell apart" (Greenman). Interestingly, Kushner remarks.

"There's something about TV that's much more like theater." . . . It's primarily a dialectical medium, alternating between two cameras. It's limited—but in an interesting way" (Greenman).

Bibliography

Austerlitz, Saul. "We Have Heard on High: Mike Nichols's *Angels in America*." Reverse Shot online. http://reverseshot.com/janfeb04/angels.html.

Bercovitch, Sacvan. *The Rites of Assent: Transformations in the Symbolic Construction of America.* New York and London: Routledge, 1993.

Bernstein, Andrea. Interview with Tony Kushner, July/August 1995. *Mother Jones: Smart, Fearless Journalism.* http://www.motherjones.com/arts/qa/1995/07/bernstein.html.

Bloom, Harold. *The Western Canon: The Books and the Schools of the Ages.* New York: Harcourt & Brace, 1994.

Brantlinger, Patrick. "Apocalypse 2001; Or, What Happens After Posthistory?" *Cultural Critique* 39 (spring 1998): 59-83.

Bush, George H. W. Address Before a Joint Session of the Congress on the Cessation of the Persian War. March 6, 1991. *Washington Post,* March 7, 1991.

Clum, John. *Acting Gay: Male Homosexuality in Modern Drama.* New York: Columbia University Press, 1994.

Crèvecoeur, J. Hector St. John de. *Letters from an American Farmer* and *Sketches of Eighteenth-Century America.* Edited by Albert E. Stone. New York: Penguin Books, 1981.

Gardner, Stanton B., Jr. "*Angels in America*: The Millennium and Postmodern Memory." In *Approaching the Millenium: Essays on Angels in America,* edited by Deborah R. Geis and Steven F. Kruger, 173-84. Ann Arbor: University of Michigan Press, 1997.

Greenman, Ben. Interview with Tony Kushner, November/December 2003. *Mother Jones: Smart, Fearless Journalism.* http://www.motherjones.com/arts/qa/2003/11/ma_586_01.html.

Kushner, Tony. *Angels in America: A Gay Fantasia on National Themes. Part One: Millennium Approaches.* London: Nick Hern Books, 1992.

———. *Angels in America: A Gay Fantasia on National Themes. Part Two: Perestroika.* London: Nick Hern Books, 1994.

Minton, Gretchen E. "*Angels in America*: Adapting to a New Medium in a New Millenium." http://findarticles.com/p/articles/mi_qa4129/is_200601/ai_n15971929.

Savran, David. "Ambivalence, Utopia, and a Queer Sort of Materialism: How *Angels in America* Reconstructs the Nation." *Theatre Journal* 47, no. 2, Gay and Lesbian Queeries (May 1995): 207-27.

Watney, Simon. *Imagine Hope: AIDS and Gay Identity.* London and New York: Routledge, 2000.

FURTHER READING

Bibliographies

Fisher, James. "Select Bibliography." *The Theatre of Tony Kushner: Living Past Hope.* New York: Routledge, 2001. 233-65. Print.

> A detailed bibliography of criticism about Kushner's life and works.

———. "Bibliography." *Understanding Tony Kushner.* Columbia: U of South Carolina P, 2008. 173-87. Print.

> Provides an updated bibliography of works by and about Kushner.

Criticism

Barnett, Claudia. "AIDS = Purgatory: Prior Walter's Prophecy and *Angels in America*." *Modern Drama* 53.4 (2010): 471-94. Print.

> Maintains that the many religious parallels in *Angels in America* allow Kushner to explore the idea of purgatory as marked by possibility rather than finality. The play, Barnett suggests, sets up binaries such as life and death, and heaven and hell, not simply to suggest opposite choices but, rather, to suggest that the nature of those choices should be examined carefully.

Benjamin, Walter. "On the Concept of History." *Walter Benjamin: Selected Writings.* Trans. Edmund Jephcott et al. Ed. Howard Eiland and Michael W. Jennings. Vol. 4. Cambridge: Harvard UP, 2003. Print.

> Includes Benjamin's often-quoted description of the "angel of history." Critics have frequently interpreted the character of the Angel in *Angels in America* to be an allusion to the backward-looking angel that appears in Benjamin's critique of the idea of historical progress. This essay was originally published in German in 1942.

Byttebier, Stephanie. " 'It Doesn't Count If It's Easy': Facing Pain, Mediating Identity in Tony Kushner's *Angels in America*." *Modern Drama* 54.3 (2011): 287-309. Print.

> Discusses *Angels in America* within a larger argument about whether suffering elicits sympathy or detachment. Kushner's play, Byttebier claims, exposes the different ideologies of suffering, and ultimately asks the audience to reevaluate theatrical and political practices of identification.

Ceballos Muñoz, Alfonso. "Tony Kushner's *Angels in America* or How American History Spins Forward." *BELLS: Barcelona English Language and Literature Studies* 15 (2006): 1-14. Print.

> Argues that *Perestroika* offers two competing visions of history: the Angel's belief in history as stasis, and Prior's prophetic belief in the individual mission of history. According to Ceballos Muñoz, the play presents an optimistic vision that depends on communities of diverse individuals: although all of the male characters are gay, they differ in race, religion, and ethnic background.

Fujita, Atsushi. "Queer Politics to Fabulous Politics in *Angels in America*: Pinklisting and Forgiving Roy Cohn." *Tony Kushner: New Essays on the Art and Politics of the Plays.* Ed. James Fisher. Jefferson: McFarland, 2006. 112-26. Print.

> Argues that Kushner created a "fabulous politics," which seeks to avoid excluding any minority. Fujita suggests that Kushner depicts the historical character of Cohn as evil in order to expose and subvert the frequent homophobic "pinklisting" of gay identity, ultimately criticizing "what Cohn did and not what he was."

Geis, Deborah R. "Not '*Very* Steven Spielberg'?: *Angels in America* on Film." *Interrogating America through Theatre and Performance.* Ed. William W. Demastes and Iris Smith Fischer. New York: Palgrave Macmillan, 2007. 243-55. Print.

> Addresses differences in dialog and production style between the 2003 HBO version of *Angels in America* and Kushner's script. Geis suggests that several factors, including audience expectations of "the possibility of the supernatural," viewers' different historical knowledge and context, and particularly the aftereffects of 11 September 2001, led to subtle differences in staging key moments.

Geis, Deborah R., and Steven F. Kruger, eds. *Approaching the Millennium: Essays on Tony Kushner's* Angels in America. Ann Arbor: U of Michigan P, 1997. Print.

> Collects an authoritative and ambitious group of essays on *Angels in America*. The volume contains the work of leading theater scholars on the play's treatment of politics, philosophy, religion, sexuality, race, gender, and disability. It also offers various considerations of the play's performance contexts.

Glaser, Jennifer. "Queer Politics and the Politics of the Queer in Kushner's *Angels in America.*" *Human Sexuality.* Ed. Harold Bloom and Blake Hobby. New York: Infobase, 2009. 1-8. Print.

Contends that "Kushner's characters are able to 'queer' America, gaining an outsider's awareness that allows them to look at the nation from an appropriate critical distance." This distance, Glaser suggests, applies not just to gender and sexuality but also to race and religion. She ultimately argues that *Angels in America* offers an optimistic vision of an "increasingly inclusive" nation.

Hogan, Katie. "Green *Angels in America*: Aesthetics of Equity." *Journal of American Culture* 35.1 (2012): 4-14. Print.

Takes notice of an important yet often overlooked aspect of Kushner's aesthetic: its sympathy for the environmental justice movement. Hogan offers an analysis of Kushner's treatment of AIDS, racism, queer citizenship, and environmental destruction as coextensive social and national injustices.

Jones, Anderson. "'Angels' Deserves Its Hyperbole." Rev. of *Angels in America,* by Tony Kushner. *Philadelphia Inquirer* 14 Nov. 1995: 31. Print.

Declares *Angels in America* "the most important play of this modern age" and still "relevant." Jones praises the production, which included both *Millennium Approaches* and *Perestroika,* as "magnificently staged."

King, Emily. "The Overlooked Jewish Identity of Roy Cohn in Kushner's *Angels in America*: American Schmucko." *Studies in American Jewish Literature* 27 (2008): 87-100. Print.

Examines Kushner's treatment of the paradox that Cohn's power and influence pose in the context of rampant anti-Semitism in America in the 1950s. King argues that *Angels in America* suggests that instead of choosing among the identities available to him, those of "the pariah or the parvenu," Cohn "occupies and exploits to his benefit the liminal space of the trickster, and as such, he achieves voice, visibility, and power."

Krasner, David. "Stonewall, 'Constant Historical Progress,' and *Angels in America*: The Neo-Hegelian Positivist Sense." *Tony Kushner: New Essays on the Art and Politics of the Plays.* Ed. James Fisher. Jefferson: McFarland, 2006. 98-111. Print.

Suggests that Louis's explanation that he cannot handle Prior's illness because of his "neo-Hegelian positivist sense of constant historical progress" is central to understanding *Angels in America*'s treatment of post-Stonewallian freedom. According to Krasner, Kushner's plays show that in order to meaningfully progress and participate in an AIDS-ravaged world, Louis needs to move from an abstract, Hegelian rationalism to an idea of struggle reconciling "the flesh and the ideal."

Kushner, Tony. "Thinking about Fabulousness." Interview by Michael Cunningham. *Tony Kushner in Conversation.* Ed. Robert Vorlicky. Ann Arbor: U of Michigan P, 1998. 62-76. Print.

Discusses his influences, his major themes, and the current state of theatrical production. On a more personal level, Kushner talks about growing up gay, wanting to have children of his own, fame, his identification with characters in his play, and what is called "gay sensibility."

Minton, Gretchen E., and Ray Schultz. "*Angels in America*: Adapting to a New Medium in a New Millennium." *American Drama* 15.1 (2006): 17-42. Print.

Argues that HBO's adaptation of *Angels in America,* although well received, compromised the "epic scope and queer sensibility" of the play. Minton and Schultz focus on the reduction of Louis's role, the muting of Prior's "flamboyance," and the reduced meta-theatricality of the production. These cuts, Minton and Schultz argue, flatten Kushner's vision of history in a way that is antithetical to the play's message.

Montgomery, Benilde. "*Angels in America* as Medieval Mystery." *Modern Drama* 41.4 (1998): 596-606. Print.

Discusses *Angels in America*'s similarity in structure, roles, and thematic interest in redemptive history to medieval mystery plays. Montgomery argues that such a comparison offers an intellectual context other than the Enlightenment, of which Kushner has sometimes been called, by some of his more critical commentators, "the unwitting heir."

Neumann, Claus-Peter. "Theo/teleological Narrative and the Narratee's Rebellion in Tony Kushner's *Angels in America.*" *Codifying the National Self: Spectators, Actors and the American Dramatic Text.* Ed. Barbara Ozieblo and María Dolores Narborna-Carrión. Brussels: Lang, 2006. 153-67. Print.

Argues that *Angels in America,* contrary to what most critics have argued, exposes how both theological and teleological visions of history preserve an "inequitable status quo." Kushner accomplished this, Neumann claims, through the use of multiple narrators and "rebelling narratees," for example, Harper, who refuses to let Joe tell her that he is gay.

Nielsen, Ken. *Modern Theatre Guides: Tony Kushner's Angels in America.* London: Continuum Intl., 2008. Print.

Contextualizes Kushner and *Angels in America,* offers a plot summary and analysis of characters and key scenes, and discusses the play's production history. Nielsen also provides exercises for workshops and includes a brief list of suggested articles for further reading.

Pearl, Monica B. "Epic AIDS: *Angels in America* from Stage to Screen." *Textual Practice* 21.4 (2007): 761-79. Print.

> Assesses the role of the film adaptation of Kushner's play in the normalization of the story of AIDS in twenty-first-century America. Pearl discusses the contextual shift that has given new meaning to the story of *Angels in America,* but she also lists the similarities between the play and the film.

Posnock, Ross. "Roy Cohn in America." *Raritan* 13.3 (1994): 64-77. Print.

> Focuses on the "problematic" centrality of Cohn in *Millennium Approaches.* Posnock's study is helpful for those seeking more information about the real-life Cohn and about the discrepancy between Kushner's stated intentions for this character in the play and the achieved effect. [Reprinted in *DC,* Vol. 10.]

Quinn, John R. "*Corpus Juris Tertium*: Redemptive Jurisprudence in *Angels in America.*" *Theatre Journal* 48.1 (1996): 79-90. Print.

> Analyzes Kushner's fascination with law in *Angels in America.* With recourse to American legal history, Quinn explains the law's thematic status in the play as a secular religion.

Rogoff, Gordon. "*Angels in America,* Devils in the Wings." *Theater* 24.2 (1993): 21-9. Print.

> Reviews *Angels in America*'s journey to Broadway, and its effect on the play's form as well as its subversiveness and resonance. [Reprinted in *DC,* Vol. 10.]

Savran, David. "Ambivalence, Utopia, and a Queer Sort of Materialism: How *Angels in America* Reconstructs the Nation." *Theatre Journal* 47.2 (1995): 207-27. Print.

> Covers a wide range of topics, from Kushner's interest in Benjamin's philosophy of history to the play's engagement with ideas of the Enlightenment, Progressivism, and Expansionism, and Kushner's use of the religious symbolism of the Jewish and Mormon faiths. Savran provides a useful guide to the playwright's complex vision of America. [Reprinted in *DC,* Vol. 10.]

Smith, Matthew Wilson. "*Angels in America*: A Progressive Apocalypse." *Theater* 29.3 (1999): 153-65. Print.

> Examines the play's deep philosophical engagement with two radically different visions of history, identified as the apocalyptic and the progressive worldviews.

Additional information on Kushner's life and works is contained in the following sources published by Gale: *American Writers Supplement,* **Vol. 9;** *Authors and Artists for Young Adults,* **Vol. 61;** *Concise Major 21st-Century Writers; Contemporary American Dramatists; Contemporary Authors,* **Vol. 144;** *Contemporary Authors New Revision Series,* **Vols. 74, 130;** *Contemporary Dramatists,* **Eds. 5, 6;** *Contemporary Literary Criticism,* **Vols. 81, 203, 297;** *Dictionary of Literary Biography,* **Vol. 228;** *DISCovering Authors Modules: Dramatists; DISCovering Authors 3.0; Drama Criticism,* **Vol. 10;** *Drama for Students,* **Vol. 5;** *Encyclopedia of World Literature in the 20th Century,* **Ed. 3;** *Gale Contextual Encyclopedia of American Literature; Gay and Lesbian Literature,* **Ed. 1;** *Literature and Its Times,* **Vol. 5;** *Literature Resource Center; Major 20th-Century Writers,* **Ed. 2;** *Major 21st-Century Writers; Modern American Literature,* **Ed. 5;** *Reference Guide to American Literature,* **Ed. 4;** *Reference Guide to Holocaust Literature;* **and** *Something about the Author,* **Vol. 160.**

How to Use This Index

The main references

> **Calvino, Italo**
>   1923-1985 .... CLC 5, 8, 11, 22, 33, 39,
>   73; SSC 3, 48

list all author entries in the following Gale Literary Criticism series:

AAL = *Asian American Literature*
BG = *The Beat Generation: A Gale Critical Companion*
BLC = *Black Literature Criticism*
BLCS = *Black Literature Criticism Supplement*
CLC = *Contemporary Literary Criticism*
CLR = *Children's Literature Review*
CMLC = *Classical and Medieval Literature Criticism*
DC = *Drama Criticism*
FL = *Feminism in Literature: A Gale Critical Companion*
GL = *Gothic Literature: A Gale Critical Companion*
HLC = *Hispanic Literature Criticism*
HLCS = *Hispanic Literature Criticism Supplement*
HR = *Harlem Renaissance: A Gale Critical Companion*
LC = *Literature Criticism from 1400 to 1800*
NCLC = *Nineteenth-Century Literature Criticism*
NNAL = *Native North American Literature*
PC = *Poetry Criticism*
SSC = *Short Story Criticism*
TCLC = *Twentieth-Century Literary Criticism*
WLC = *World Literature Criticism, 1500 to the Present*
WLCS = *World Literature Criticism Supplement*

The cross-references

> See also CA 85-88, 116; CANR 23, 61;
> DAM NOV; DLB 196; EW 13; MTCW 1, 2;
> RGSF 2; RGWL 2; SFW 4; SSFS 12

list all author entries in the following Gale biographical and literary sources:

AAYA = *Authors & Artists for Young Adults*
AFAW = *African American Writers*
AFW = *African Writers*
AITN = *Authors in the News*
AMW = *American Writers*
AMWR = *American Writers Retrospective Supplement*
AMWS = *American Writers Supplement*
ANW = *American Nature Writers*
AW = *Ancient Writers*
BEST = *Bestsellers*
BPFB = *Beacham's Encyclopedia of Popular Fiction: Biography and Resources*
BRW = *British Writers*
BRWS = *British Writers Supplement*
BW = *Black Writers*
BYA = *Beacham's Guide to Literature for Young Adults*
CA = *Contemporary Authors*
CAAS = *Contemporary Authors Autobiography Series*
CABS = *Contemporary Authors Bibliographical Series*
CAD = *Contemporary American Dramatists*
CANR = *Contemporary Authors New Revision Series*
CAP = *Contemporary Authors Permanent Series*
CBD = *Contemporary British Dramatists*
CCA = *Contemporary Canadian Authors*

CD = Contemporary Dramatists
CDALB = Concise Dictionary of American Literary Biography
CDALBS = Concise Dictionary of American Literary Biography Supplement
CDBLB = Concise Dictionary of British Literary Biography
CMW = St. James Guide to Crime & Mystery Writers
CN = Contemporary Novelists
CP = Contemporary Poets
CPW = Contemporary Popular Writers
CSW = Contemporary Southern Writers
CWD = Contemporary Women Dramatists
CWP = Contemporary Women Poets
CWRI = St. James Guide to Children's Writers
CWW = Contemporary World Writers
DA = DISCovering Authors
DA3 = DISCovering Authors 3.0
DAB = DISCovering Authors: British Edition
DAC = DISCovering Authors: Canadian Edition
DAM = DISCovering Authors: Modules
    DRAM: Dramatists Module; **MST:** Most-studied Authors Module;
    MULT: Multicultural Authors Module; **NOV:** Novelists Module;
    POET: Poets Module; **POP:** Popular Fiction and Genre Authors Module
DFS = Drama for Students
DLB = Dictionary of Literary Biography
DLBD = Dictionary of Literary Biography Documentary Series
DLBY = Dictionary of Literary Biography Yearbook
DNFS = Literature of Developing Nations for Students
EFS = Epics for Students
EW = European Writers
EWL = Encyclopedia of World Literature in the 20th Century
EXPN = Exploring Novels
EXPP = Exploring Poetry
EXPS = Exploring Short Stories
FANT = St. James Guide to Fantasy Writers
FW = Feminist Writers
GFL = Guide to French Literature, Beginnings to 1789; 1789 to the Present
GLL = Gay and Lesbian Literature
HGG = St. James Guide to Horror, Ghost & Gothic Writers
HW = Hispanic Writers
IDFW = International Dictionary of Films and Filmmakers: Writers and Production Artists
IDTP = International Dictionary of Theatre: Playwrights
LAIT = Literature and Its Times
LAW = Latin American Writers
JRDA = Junior DISCovering Authors
MAICYA = Major Authors and Illustrators for Children and Young Adults
MAICYAS = Major Authors and Illustrators for Children and Young Adults Supplement
MAWW = Modern American Women Writers
MJW = Modern Japanese Writers
MTCW = Major 20th-Century Writers
NCFS = Nonfiction Classics for Students
NFS = Novels for Students
PAB = Poets: American and British
PFS = Poetry for Students
RGAL = Reference Guide to American Literature
RGEL = Reference Guide to English Literature
RGSF = Reference Guide to Short Fiction
RGWL = Reference Guide to World Literature
RHW = Twentieth-Century Romance and Historical Writers
SAAS = Something about the Author Autobiography Series
SATA = Something about the Author
SFW = St. James Guide to Science Fiction Writers
SSFS = Short Stories for Students
TCWW = Twentieth-Century Western Writers
WLIT = World Literature and Its Times
WP = World Poets
YABC = Yesterday's Authors of Books for Children
YAW = St. James Guide to Young Adult Writers

Literary Criticism Series
Cumulative Author Index

See also CA 85-88; CANR 45; DLB 20, 36, 100, 149; LMFS 2; RGEL 2

Aldiss, Brian W. 1925- .... **CLC 5, 14, 40, 290; SSC 36**
See also AAYA 42; BRWS 19; CA 5-8R, 190; CAAE 190; CAAS 2; CANR 5, 28, 64, 121, 168; CN 1, 2, 3, 4, 5, 6, 7; DAM NOV; DLB 14, 261, 271; MTCW 1, 2; MTFW 2005; SATA 34; SCFW 1, 2; SFW 4

Aldiss, Brian Wilson
See Aldiss, Brian W.

Aldrich, Ann
See Meaker, Marijane

Aldrich, Bess Streeter
1881-1954 .... **TCLC 125**
See also CLR 70; TCWW 2

Alegria, Claribel 1924- .... **CLC 75; HLCS 1; PC 26, 150**
See also CA 131; CAAS 15; CANR 66, 94, 134; CWW 2; DAM MULT; DLB 145, 283; EWL 3; HW 1; MTCW 2; MTFW 2005; PFS 21

Alegria, Claribel Joy
See Alegria, Claribel

Alegria, Fernando 1918-2005 .... **CLC 57**
See also CA 9-12R; CANR 5, 32, 72; EWL 3; HW 1, 2

Aleichem, Sholom 1859-1916 .. **SSC 33, 125; TCLC 1, 35**
See also CA 104; DLB 333; TWA

Aleixandre, Vicente 1898-1984 ...... **HLCS 1; TCLC 113**
See also CANR 81; DLB 108, 329; EWL 3; HW 2; MTCW 1, 2; RGWL 2, 3

Alekseev, Konstantin Sergeivich
See Stanislavsky, Constantin

Alekseyev, Konstantin Sergeyevich
See Stanislavsky, Constantin

Aleman, Mateo 1547-1615(?) .... **LC 81**

Alencar, Jose de
1829-1877 .... **NCLC 157**
See also DLB 307; LAW; WLIT 1

Alencon, Marguerite d'
See de Navarre, Marguerite

Alepoudelis, Odysseus
See Elytis, Odysseus

Aleshkovsky, Joseph
See Aleshkovsky, Yuz

Aleshkovsky, Yuz 1929- .... **CLC 44**
See also CA 121; 128; DLB 317

Alexander, Barbara
See Ehrenreich, Barbara

Alexander, Lloyd 1924-2007 .... **CLC 35**
See also AAYA 1, 27; BPFB 1; BYA 5, 6, 7, 9, 10, 11; CA 1-4R; 260; CANR 1, 24, 38, 55, 113; CLR 1, 5, 48; CWRI 5; DLB 52; FANT; JRDA; MAICYA 1, 2; MAICYAS 1; MTCW 1; SAAS 19; SATA 3, 49, 81, 129, 135; SATA-Obit 182; SUFW; TUS; WYA; YAW

Alexander, Lloyd Chudley
See Alexander, Lloyd

Alexander, Meena 1951- .... **CLC 121, 335**
See also CA 115; CANR 38, 70, 146; CP 5, 6, 7; CWP; DLB 323; FW

Alexander, Rae Pace
See Alexander, Raymond Pace

Alexander, Raymond Pace
1898-1974 .... **SSC 62**
See also CA 97-100; SATA 22; SSFS 4

Alexander, Samuel 1859-1938 .... **TCLC 77**

Alexander of Hales
c. 1185-1245 .... **CMLC 128**

Alexeiev, Konstantin
See Stanislavsky, Constantin

Alexeyev, Constantin Sergeivich
See Stanislavsky, Constantin

Alexeyev, Konstantin Sergeyevich
See Stanislavsky, Constantin

Alexie, Sherman 1966- ... **CLC 96, 154, 312; NNAL; PC 53; SSC 107, 189**
See also AAYA 28, 85; BYA 15; CA 138; CANR 65, 95, 133, 174; CLR 179; CN 7; DA3; DAM MULT; DLB 175, 206, 278; LATS 1:2; MTCW 2; MTFW 2005; NFS 17, 31, 38; PFS 39; SSFS 18, 36

Alexie, Sherman Joseph, Jr.
See Alexie, Sherman

al-Farabi 870(?)-950 .... **CMLC 58**
See also DLB 115

Alfau, Felipe 1902-1999 .... **CLC 66**
See also CA 137

Alfieri, Vittorio 1749-1803 .... **NCLC 101**
See also EW 4; RGWL 2, 3; WLIT 7

Alfonso X 1221-1284 .... **CMLC 78**

Alfred, Jean Gaston
See Ponge, Francis

Alger, Horatio, Jr.
1832-1899 .... **NCLC 8, 83, 260**
See also CLR 87, 170; DLB 42; LAIT 2; RGAL 4; SATA 16; TUS

Al-Ghazali, Muhammad ibn Muhammad
1058-1111 .... **CMLC 50, 149**
See also DLB 115

Algren, Nelson 1909-1981 .... **CLC 4, 10, 33; SSC 33**
See also AMWS 9; BPFB 1; CA 13-16R; 103; CANR 20, 61; CDALB 1941-1968; CN 1, 2; DLB 9; DLBY 1981, 1982, 2000; EWL 3; MAL 5; MTCW 1, 2; MTFW 2005; RGAL 4; RGSF 2

al-Hamadhani 967-1007 .... **CMLC 93**
See also WLIT 6

al-Hariri, al-Qasim ibn 'Ali Abu Muhammad al-Basri 1054-1122 .... **CMLC 63**
See also RGWL 3

Ali, Ahmed 1908-1998 .... **CLC 69**
See also CA 25-28R; CANR 15, 34; CN 1, 2, 3, 4, 5; DLB 323; EWL 3

Ali, Monica 1967- .... **CLC 304**
See also AAYA 67; BRWS 13; CA 219; CANR 158, 205, 240; DLB 323

Ali, Tariq 1943- .... **CLC 173, 323**
See also CA 25-28R; CANR 10, 99, 161, 196

Alighieri, Dante
See Dante

al-Kindi, Abu Yusuf Ya'qub ibn Ishaq
c. 801-c. 873 .... **CMLC 80**

Allan, John B.
See Westlake, Donald E.

Allan, Sidney
See Hartmann, Sadakichi

Allan, Sydney
See Hartmann, Sadakichi

Allard, Janet .... **CLC 59**

Allen, Betsy
See Harrison, Elizabeth (Allen) Cavanna

Allen, Edward 1948- .... **CLC 59**

Allen, Fred 1894-1956 .... **TCLC 87**

Allen, Paula Gunn 1939-2008 .... **CLC 84, 202, 280; NNAL**
See also AMWS 4; CA 112; 143; 272; CANR 63, 130; CWP; DA3; DAM MULT; DLB 175; FW; MTCW 2; MTFW 2005; RGAL 4; TCWW 2

Allen, Roland
See Ayckbourn, Alan

Allen, Sarah A.
See Hopkins, Pauline Elizabeth

Allen, Sidney H.
See Hartmann, Sadakichi

Allen, Woody 1935- .... **CLC 16, 52, 195, 288**
See also AAYA 10, 51; AMWS 15; CA 33-36R; CANR 27, 38, 63, 128, 172; DAM POP; DLB 44; MTCW 1; SSFS 21

Allende, Isabel 1942- .... **CLC 39, 57, 97, 170, 264, 350; HLC 1; SSC 65; WLCS**
See also AAYA 18, 70; CA 125; 130; CANR 51, 74, 129, 165, 208; CDWLB 3; CLR 99, 171; CWW 2; DA3; DAM MULT, NOV; DLB 145; DNFS 1; EWL 3; FL 1:5; FW; HW 1, 2; INT CA-130; LAIT 5; LAWS 1; LMFS 2; MTCW 1, 2; MTFW 2005; NCFS 1; NFS 6, 18, 29; RGSF 2; RGWL 3; SATA 163; SSFS 11, 16; WLIT 1

Alleyn, Ellen
See Rossetti, Christina

Alleyne, Carla D. .... **CLC 65**

Allingham, Margery (Louise)
1904-1966 .... **CLC 19**
See also CA 5-8R; 25-28R; CANR 4, 58; CMW 4; DLB 77; MSW; MTCW 1, 2

Allingham, William 1824-1889 ..... **NCLC 25**
See also DLB 35; RGEL 2

Allison, Dorothy E. 1949- .... **CLC 78, 153, 290**
See also AAYA 53; CA 140; CANR 66, 107; CN 7; CSW; DA3; DLB 350; FW; MTCW 2; MTFW 2005; NFS 11; RGAL 4

Alloula, Malek .... **CLC 65**

Allston, Washington 1779-1843 ...... **NCLC 2**
See also DLB 1, 235

Almedingen, E. M. 1898-1971 .... **CLC 12**
See also CA 1-4R; CANR 1; SATA 3

Almedingen, Martha Edith von
See Almedingen, E. M.

Almodovar, Pedro 1949(?)- ... **CLC 114, 229; HLCS 1**
See also CA 133; CANR 72, 151; HW 2

Almqvist, Carl Jonas Love
1793-1866 .... **NCLC 42**

al-Mutanabbi, Ahmad ibn al-Husayn Abu al-Tayyib al-Jufi al-Kindi
915-965 .... **CMLC 66**
See also RGWL 3; WLIT 6

Alonso, Damaso
1898-1990 .... **CLC 14; TCLC 245**
See also CA 110; 131; 130; CANR 72; DLB 108; EWL 3; HW 1, 2

Alov
See Gogol, Nikolai

al'Sadaawi, Nawal
See El Saadawi, Nawal

al-Shaykh, Hanan
See Shaykh, Hanan al-

Al Siddik
See Rolfe, Frederick (William Serafino Austin Lewis Mary)

Alta 1942- .... **CLC 19**
See also CA 57-60

Alter, Robert B. 1935- .... **CLC 34**
See also CA 49-52; CANR 1, 47, 100, 160, 201

Alter, Robert Bernard
See Alter, Robert B.

Alther, Lisa 1944- .... **CLC 7, 41**
See also BPFB 1; CA 65-68; CAAS 30; CANR 12, 30, 51, 180; CN 4, 5, 6, 7; CSW; GLL 2; MTCW 1

Althusser, L.
See Althusser, Louis

Althusser, Louis 1918-1990 .... **CLC 106**
See also CA 131; 132; CANR 102; DLB 242

Altman, Robert
1925-2006 .... **CLC 16, 116, 242**
See also CA 73-76; 254; CANR 43

Alurista 1947- .... **HLCS 1; PC 34**
See also CA 45-48R; CANR 2, 32; DLB 82; HW 1; LLW

Alvarez, A. 1929- .... **CLC 5, 13**
See also CA 1-4R; CANR 3, 33, 63, 101, 134; CN 3, 4, 5, 6; CP 1, 2, 3, 4, 5, 6, 7; DLB 14, 40; MTFW 2005

Auster, Paul 1947- ... **CLC 47, 131, 227, 339**
See also AMWS 12; CA 69-72; CANR 23, 52, 75, 129, 165; CMW 4; CN 5, 6, 7; DA3; DLB 227; MAL 5; MTCW 2; MTFW 2005; SUFW 2; TCLE 1:1

Austin, Frank
See Faust, Frederick

Austin, Mary Hunter 1868-1934 ... **SSC 104; TCLC 25, 249**
See also ANW; CA 109; 178; DLB 9, 78, 206, 221, 275; FW; TCWW 1, 2

Avellaneda, Gertrudis Gomez de
See Gomez de Avellaneda, Gertrudis

Averroes 1126-1198 .... **CMLC 7, 104**
See also DLB 115

Avicenna 980-1037 .... **CMLC 16, 110**
See also DLB 115

Avison, Margaret 1918-2007 .... **CLC 2, 4, 97; PC 148**
See also CA 17-20R; CANR 134; CP 1, 2, 3, 4, 5, 6, 7; DAC; DAM POET; DLB 53; MTCW 1

Avison, Margaret Kirkland
See Avison, Margaret

Axton, David
See Koontz, Dean

Ayala, Francisco 1906-2009 .... **SSC 119**
See also CA 208; CWW 2; DLB 322; EWL 3; RGSF 2

Ayala, Francisco de Paula y Garcia Duarte
See Ayala, Francisco

Ayckbourn, Alan 1939- .... **CLC 5, 8, 18, 33, 74; DC 13**
See also BRWS 5; CA 21-24R; CANR 31, 59, 118; CBD; CD 5, 6; DAB; DAM DRAM; DFS 7; DLB 13, 245; EWL 3; MTCW 1, 2; MTFW 2005

Aydy, Catherine
See Tennant, Emma

Ayme, Marcel (Andre)
1902-1967 .... **CLC 11; SSC 41**
See also CA 89-92; CANR 67, 137; CLR 25; DLB 72; EW 12; EWL 3; GFL 1789 to the Present; RGSF 2; RGWL 2, 3; SATA 91

Ayrton, Michael 1921-1975 .... **CLC 7**
See also CA 5-8R; 61-64; CANR 9, 21

Aytmatov, Chingiz
See Aitmatov, Chingiz

Azorín
See Martinez Ruiz, Jose

Azuela, Mariano 1873-1952 .... **HLC 1; TCLC 3, 145, 217**
See also CA 104; 131; CANR 81; DAM MULT; EWL 3; HW 1, 2; LAW; MTCW 1, 2; MTFW 2005

Ba, Mariama 1929-1981 .... **BLC 2:1; BLCS**
See also AFW; BW 2; CA 141; CANR 87; DLB 360; DNFS 2; WLIT 2

Baastad, Babbis Friis
See Friis-Baastad, Babbis Ellinor

Bab
See Gilbert, W(illiam) S(chwenck)

Babbis, Eleanor
See Friis-Baastad, Babbis Ellinor

Babel, Isaac
See Babel, Isaak (Emmanuilovich)

Babel, Isaak (Emmanuilovich)
1894-1941(?) .... **SSC 16, 78, 161; TCLC 2, 13, 171**
See also CA 104; 155; CANR 113; DLB 272; EW 11; EWL 3; MTCW 2; MTFW 2005; RGSF 2; RGWL 2, 3; SSFS 10; TWA

Babits, Mihaly 1883-1941 .... **TCLC 14**
See also CA 114; CDWLB 4; DLB 215; EWL 3

Babur 1483-1530 .... **LC 18**

Babylas
See Ghelderode, Michel de

Baca, Jimmy Santiago
1952- .... **HLC 1; PC 41**
See also CA 131; CANR 81, 90, 146, 220; CP 6, 7; DAM MULT; DLB 122; HW 1, 2; LLW; MAL 5; PFS 40

Baca, Jose Santiago
See Baca, Jimmy Santiago

Bacchelli, Riccardo 1891-1985 .... **CLC 19**
See also CA 29-32R; 117; DLB 264; EWL 3

Bacchylides
c. 520B.C.-c. 452B.C. .... **CMLC 119**

Bach, Richard 1936- .... **CLC 14**
See also AITN 1; BEST 89:2; BPFB 1; BYA 5; CA 9-12R; CANR 18, 93, 151; CPW; DAM NOV, POP; FANT; MTCW 1; SATA 13

Bach, Richard David
See Bach, Richard

Bache, Benjamin Franklin
1769-1798 .... **LC 74**
See also DLB 43

Bachelard, Gaston 1884-1962 ..... **TCLC 128**
See also CA 97-100; 89-92; DLB 296; GFL 1789 to the Present

Bachman, Richard
See King, Stephen

Bachmann, Ingeborg 1926-1973 ... **CLC 69; PC 151; TCLC 192**
See also CA 93-96; 45-48; CANR 69; DLB 85; EWL 3; RGHL; RGWL 2, 3

Bacigalupi, Paolo 1973- .... **CLC 309**
See also AAYA 86; CA 317; SATA 230

Bacon, Francis 1561-1626 ... **LC 18, 32, 131**
See also BRW 1; CDBLB Before 1660; DLB 151, 236, 252; RGEL 2; TEA

Bacon, Roger
1214(?)-1294 .... **CMLC 14, 108, 155**
See also DLB 115

Bacovia, G.
See Bacovia, George

Bacovia, George 1881-1957 .... **TCLC 24**
See Bacovia, George
See also CA 123; 189; CDWLB 4; DLB 220; EWL 3

Badanes, Jerome 1937-1995 .... **CLC 59**
See also CA 234

Badiou, Alain 1937- .... **CLC 326**
See also CA 261

Bage, Robert 1728-1801 .... **NCLC 182**
See also DLB 39; RGEL 2

Bagehot, Walter 1826-1877 .... **NCLC 10**
See also DLB 55

Bagnold, Enid 1889-1981 .... **CLC 25**
See also AAYA 75; BYA 2; CA 5-8R; 103; CANR 5, 40; CBD; CN 2; CWD; CWRI 5; DAM DRAM; DLB 13, 160, 191, 245; FW; MAICYA 1, 2; RGEL 2; SATA 1, 25

Bagritsky, Eduard
See Dzyubin, Eduard Georgievich

Bagritsky, Edvard
See Dzyubin, Eduard Georgievich

Bagrjana, Elisaveta
See Belcheva, Elisaveta Lyubomirova

Bagryana, Elisaveta
See Belcheva, Elisaveta Lyubomirova

Bail, Murray 1941- .... **CLC 353**
See also CA 127; CANR 62; CN 4, 5, 6, 7; DLB 325

Bailey, Paul 1937- .... **CLC 45**
See also CA 21-24R; CANR 16, 62, 124; CN 1, 2, 3, 4, 5, 6, 7; DLB 14, 271; GLL 2

Baillie, Joanna 1762-1851 **NCLC 71, 151; PC 151**
See also DLB 93, 344; GL 2; RGEL 2

Bainbridge, Beryl 1934-2010 .... **CLC 4, 5, 8, 10, 14, 18, 22, 62, 130, 292**
See also BRWS 6; CA 21-24R; CANR 24, 55, 75, 88, 128; CN 2, 3, 4, 5, 6, 7; DAM NOV; DLB 14, 231; EWL 3; MTCW 1, 2; MTFW 2005

Baker, Carlos (Heard)
1909-1987 .... **TCLC 119**
See also CA 5-8R; 122; CANR 3, 63; DLB 103

Baker, Elliott 1922-2007 .... **CLC 8**
See also CA 45-48; 257; CANR 2, 63; CN 1, 2, 3, 4, 5, 6, 7

Baker, Elliott Joseph
See Baker, Elliott

Baker, Nicholson 1957- .... **CLC 61, 165**
See also AMWS 13; CA 135; CANR 63, 120, 138, 190, 237; CN 6; CPW; DA3; DAM POP; DLB 227; MTFW 2005

Baker, Ray Stannard
1870-1946 .... **TCLC 47**
See also CA 118; DLB 345

Baker, Russell 1925- .... **CLC 31**
See also BEST 89:4; CA 57-60; CANR 11, 41, 59, 137; MTCW 1, 2; MTFW 2005

Baker, Russell Wayne
See Baker, Russell

Bakhtin, M.
See Bakhtin, Mikhail Mikhailovich

Bakhtin, M. M.
See Bakhtin, Mikhail Mikhailovich

Bakhtin, Mikhail
See Bakhtin, Mikhail Mikhailovich

Bakhtin, Mikhail Mikhailovich
1895-1975 .... **CLC 83; TCLC 160**
See Bakhtin, Mikhail Mikhailovich
See also CA 128; 113; DLB 242; EWL 3

Bakshi, Ralph 1938(?)- .... **CLC 26**
See also CA 112; 138; IDFW 3

Bakunin, Mikhail (Alexandrovich)
1814-1876 .... **NCLC 25, 58**
See also DLB 277

Bal, Mieke 1946- .... **CLC 252**
See also CA 156; CANR 99

Bal, Mieke Maria Gertrudis
See Bal, Mieke

Baldwin, James 1924-1987 .... **BLC 1:1, 2:1; CLC 1, 2, 3, 4, 5, 8, 13, 15, 17, 42, 50, 67, 90, 127; DC 1; SSC 10, 33, 98, 134; TCLC 229; WLC 1**
See also AAYA 4, 34; AFAW 1, 2; AMWR 2; AMWS 1; BPFB 1; BW 1; CA 1-4R; 124; CABS 1; CAD; CANR 3, 24; CDALB 1941-1968; CN 1, 2, 3, 4; CPW; DA; DA3; DAB; DAC; DAM MST, MULT, NOV, POP; DFS 11, 15; DLB 2, 7, 33, 249, 278; DLBY 1987; EWL 3; EXPS; LAIT 5; MAL 5; MTCW 1, 2; MTFW 2005; NCFS 4; NFS 4; RGAL 4; RGSF 2; SATA 9; SATA-Obit 54; SSFS 2, 18; TUS

Baldwin, William c. 1515-1563 ... **LC 113, 209**
See also DLB 132

Bale, John 1495-1563 .... **LC 62, 228**
See also DLB 132; RGEL 2; TEA

Ball, Hugo 1886-1927 .... **TCLC 104**

Ballard, James G.
See Ballard, J.G.

Ballard, James Graham
See Ballard, J.G.

Ballard, J.G. 1930-2009 .... **CLC 3, 6, 14, 36, 137, 299; SSC 1, 53, 146**
See also AAYA 3, 52; BRWS 5; CA 5-8R; 285; CANR 15, 39, 65, 107, 133, 198; CN 1, 2, 3, 4, 5, 6, 7; DA3; DAM NOV, POP; DLB 14, 207, 261, 319; EWL 3; HGG; MTCW 1, 2; MTFW 2005; NFS 8; RGEL 2; RGSF 2; SATA 93; SATA-Obit 203; SCFW 1, 2; SFW 4

Ballard, Jim G.
See Ballard, J.G.

Balmont, Konstantin (Dmitriyevich)
1867-1943 .... **PC 149; TCLC 11**
See also CA 109; 155; DLB 295; EWL 3

Barres, (Auguste-)Maurice
1862-1923 .... **TCLC 47**
See also CA 164; DLB 123; GFL 1789 to the
Present
Barry, Mike
See Malzberg, Barry N(athaniel)
Barry, Philip 1896-1949 .... **TCLC 11**
See also CA 109; 199; DFS 9; DLB 7, 228;
MAL 5; RGAL 4
Barry, Sebastian 1955- .... **CLC 282**
See also CA 117; CANR 122, 193, 243;
CD 5, 6; DLB 245
Bart, Andre Schwarz
See Schwarz-Bart, Andre
Barth, John 1930- ...... **CLC 1, 2, 3, 5, 7, 9,**
10, 14, 27, 51, 89, 214; SSC 10, 89
See also AITN 1, 2; AMW; BPFB 1; CA 1-
4R; CABS 1; CANR 5, 23, 49, 64, 113,
204; CN 1, 2, 3, 4, 5, 6, 7; DAM NOV;
DLB 2, 227; EWL 3; FANT; MAL 5;
MTCW 1; RGAL 4; RGSF 2; RHW; SSFS
6; TUS
Barth, John Simmons
See Barth, John
Barthelme, Donald 1931-1989 .... **CLC 1,**
2, 3, 5, 6, 8, 13, 23, 46, 59, 115; SSC 2,
55, 142
See also AMWS 4; BPFB 1; CA 21-24R;
129; CANR 20, 58, 188; CN 1, 2, 3, 4;
DA3; DAM NOV; DLB 2, 234; DLBY
1980, 1989; EWL 3; FANT; LMFS 2;
MAL 5; MTCW 1, 2; MTFW 2005; RGAL
4; RGSF 2; SATA 7; SATA-Obit 62;
SSFS 17
Barthelme, Frederick 1943- .... **CLC 36, 117**
See also AMWS 11; CA 114; 122; CANR
77, 209; CN 4, 5, 6, 7; CSW; DLB 244;
DLBY 1985; EWL 3; INT CA-122
Barthes, Roland 1915-1980 ...... **CLC 24, 83;**
TCLC 135
See also CA 130; 97-100; CANR 66, 237;
DLB 296; EW 13; EWL 3; GFL 1789 to
the Present; MTCW 1, 2; TWA
Barthes, Roland Gerard
See Barthes, Roland
Bartram, William 1739-1823 ...... **NCLC 145**
See also ANW; DLB 37
Barzun, Jacques 1907- .... **CLC 51, 145**
See also CA 61-64; CANR 22, 95
Barzun, Jacques Martin
See Barzun, Jacques
Bashevis, Isaac
See Singer, Isaac Bashevis
Bashevis, Yitskhok
See Singer, Isaac Bashevis
Bashkirtseff, Marie 1859-1884 ...... **NCLC 27**
Basho, Matsuo
See Matsuo Basho
Basil of Caesaria c. 330-379 .... **CMLC 35**
Basket, Raney
See Edgerton, Clyde
Bass, Kingsley B., Jr.
See Bullins, Ed
Bass, Rick
1958- .... **CLC 79, 143, 286; SSC 60**
See also AMWS 16; ANW; CA 126; CANR
53, 93, 145, 183; CSW; DLB 212, 275
Bassani, Giorgio 1916-2000 .... **CLC 9**
See also CA 65-68; 190; CANR 33; CWW
2; DLB 128, 177, 299; EWL 3; MTCW 1;
RGHL; RGWL 2, 3
Bassine, Helen
See Yglesias, Helen
Bastian, Ann .... **CLC 70**
Bastos, Augusto Roa
See Roa Bastos, Augusto
Bataille, Georges
1897-1962 .... **CLC 29; TCLC 155**

See also CA 101; 89-92; EWL 3
Bates, H(erbert) E(rnest)
1905-1974 .... **CLC 46; SSC 10**
See also CA 93-96; 45-48; CANR 34; CN 1;
DA3; DAB; DAM POP; DLB 162, 191;
EWL 3; EXPS; MTCW 1, 2; RGSF 2;
SSFS 7
Batiushkov, Konstantin Nikolaevich
1787-1855 .... **NCLC 254**
See also DLB 205
Bauchart
See Camus, Albert
Baudelaire, Charles 1821-1867 .... **NCLC**
6, 29, 55, 155; PC 1, 106, 150; SSC 18;
WLC 1
See also DA; DA3; DAB; DAC; DAM MST,
POET; DLB 217; EW 7; GFL 1789 to the
Present; LMFS 2; PFS 21, 38; RGWL 2, 3;
TWA
Baudouin, Marcel
See Peguy, Charles (Pierre)
Baudouin, Pierre
See Peguy, Charles (Pierre)
Baudrillard, Jean 1929-2007 .... **CLC 60**
See also CA 252; 258; DLB 296
Baum, L. Frank 1856-1919 .... **TCLC 7, 132**
See also AAYA 46; BYA 16; CA 108; 133;
CLR 15, 107, 175; CWRI 5; DLB 22;
FANT; JRDA; MAICYA 1, 2; MTCW 1,
2; NFS 13; RGAL 4; SATA 18, 100; WCH
Baum, Louis F.
See Baum, L. Frank
Baum, Lyman Frank
See Baum, L. Frank
Bauman, Zygmunt 1925- .... **CLC 314**
See also CA 127; CANR 205
Baumbach, Jonathan 1933- .... **CLC 6, 23**
See also CA 13-16R, 284; CAAE 284; CAAS
5; CANR 12, 66, 140; CN 3, 4, 5, 6, 7;
DLBY 1980; INT CANR-12; MTCW 1
Baumgarten, Alexander Gottlieb
1714-1762 .... **LC 199**
Bausch, Richard 1945- .... **CLC 51**
See also AMWS 7; CA 101; CAAS 14;
CANR 43, 61, 87, 164, 200; CN 7; CSW;
DLB 130; MAL 5
Bausch, Richard Carl
See Bausch, Richard
Baxter, Charles 1947- .... **CLC 45, 78**
See also AMWS 17; CA 57-60; CANR 40, 64,
104, 133, 188, 238; CPW; DAM POP; DLB
130; MAL 5; MTCW 2; MTFW 2005;
TCLE 1:1
Baxter, Charles Morley
See Baxter, Charles
Baxter, George Owen
See Faust, Frederick
Baxter, James K(eir) 1926-1972 .... **CLC 14;**
TCLC 249
See also CA 77-80; CP 1; EWL 3
Baxter, John
See Hunt, E. Howard
Bayer, Sylvia
See Glassco, John
Bayle, Pierre 1647-1706 .... **LC 126**
See also DLB 268, 313; GFL Beginnings
to 1789
Baynton, Barbara
1857-1929 .... **TCLC 57, 211**
See also DLB 230; RGSF 2
Buchner, (Karl) Georg 1813-1837 .... **DC 35;**
NCLC 26, 146; SSC 131
See also CDWLB 2; DLB 133; EW 6; RGSF
2; RGWL 2, 3; TWA
Becquer, Gustavo Adolfo 1836-1870 .. **HLCS**
1; NCLC 106, 285; PC 113
See also DAM MULT

Bodker, Cecil 1927- .... **CLC 21**
See also CA 73-76; CANR 13, 44, 111; CLR
23; MAICYA 1, 2; SATA 14, 133
Beagle, Peter S. 1939- .... **CLC 7, 104**
See also AAYA 47; BPFB 1; BYA 9, 10, 16;
CA 9-12R; CANR 4, 51, 73, 110, 213;
DA3; DLBY 1980; FANT; INT CANR-4;
MTCW 2; MTFW 2005; SATA 60, 130;
SUFW 1, 2; YAW
Beagle, Peter Soyer
See Beagle, Peter S.
Bean, Normal
See Burroughs, Edgar Rice
Beard, Charles A(ustin)
1874-1948 .... **TCLC 15**
See also CA 115; 189; DLB 17; SATA 18
Beardsley, Aubrey 1872-1898 .... **NCLC 6**
Beatrice of Nazareth
1200-1268 .... **CMLC 124**
Beattie, Ann 1947- .... **CLC 8, 13, 18,**
40, 63, 146, 293; SSC 11, 130
See also AMWS 5; BEST 90:2; BPFB 1; CA
81-84; CANR 53, 73, 128, 225; CN 4, 5, 6,
7; CPW; DA3; DAM NOV, POP; DLB
218, 278; DLBY 1982; EWL 3; MAL 5;
MTCW 1, 2; MTFW 2005; RGAL 4;
RGSF 2; SSFS 9; TUS
Beattie, James 1735-1803 .... **NCLC 25**
See also DLB 109
Beauchamp, Katherine Mansfield
See Mansfield, Katherine
Beaumarchais, Pierre-Augustin Caron de
1732-1799 .... **DC 4; LC 61, 192**
See also DAM DRAM; DFS 14, 16; DLB
313; EW 4; GFL Beginnings to 1789;
RGWL 2, 3
Beaumont, Francis 1584(?)-1616 .... **DC 6;**
LC 33, 222
See also BRW 2; CDBLB Before 1660; DLB
58; TEA
Beauvoir, Simone de 1908-1986 ...... **CLC 1,**
2, 4, 8, 14, 31, 44, 50, 71, 124; SSC 35;
TCLC 221; WLC 1
See also BPFB 1; CA 9-12R; 118; CANR
28, 61; DA; DA3; DAB; DAC; DAM MST,
NOV; DLB 72; DLBY 1986; EW 12; EWL
3; FL 1:5; FW; GFL 1789 to the Present;
LMFS 2; MTCW 1, 2; MTFW 2005;
RGSF 2; RGWL 2, 3; TWA
Beauvoir, Simone Lucie Ernestine Marie
Bertrand de
See Beauvoir, Simone de
Becker, Carl (Lotus) 1873-1945 .... **TCLC 63**
See also CA 157; DLB 17
Becker, Jurek 1937-1997 .... **CLC 7, 19;**
TCLC 287
See also CA 85-88; 157; CANR 60, 117;
CWW 2; DLB 75, 299; EWL 3; RGHL
Becker, Walter 1950- .... **CLC 26**
Becket, Thomas a 1118(?)-1170 ... **CMLC 83**
Beckett, Samuel 1906-1989 ..... **CLC 1, 2, 3,**
4, 6, 9, 10, 11, 14, 18, 29, 57, 59, 83; DC
22; SSC 16, 74, 161; TCLC 145; WLC 1
See also BRWC 2; BRWR 1; BRWS 1; CA
5-8R; 130; CANR 33, 61; CBD; CDBLB
1945-1960; CN 1, 2, 3, 4; CP 1, 2, 3, 4;
DA; DA3; DAB; DAC; DAM DRAM,
MST, NOV; DFS 2, 7, 18; DLB 13, 15,
233, 319, 321, 329; DLBY 1990; EWL 3;
GFL 1789 to the Present; LATS 1:2; LMFS
2; MTCW 1, 2; MTFW 2005; RGSF 2;
RGWL 2, 3; SSFS 15; TEA; WLIT 4
Beckett, Samuel Barclay
See Beckett, Samuel
Beckford, William
1760-1844 .... **NCLC 16, 214**
See also BRW 3; DLB 39, 213; GL 2; HGG;
LMFS 1; SUFW

Benn, Gottfried
1886-1956 .... **PC 35; TCLC 3, 256**
See also CA 106; 153; DLB 56; EWL 3;
RGWL 2, 3

Bennett, Alan 1934- .... **CLC 45, 77, 292**
See also BRWS 8; CA 103; CANR 35, 55,
106, 157, 197, 227; CBD; CD 5, 6; DAB;
DAM MST; DLB 310; MTCW 1, 2;
MTFW 2005

Bennett, (Enoch) Arnold
1867-1931 .... **TCLC 5, 20, 197**
See also BRW 6; CA 106; 155; CDBLB
1890-1914; DLB 10, 34, 98, 135; EWL 3;
MTCW 2

Bennett, Elizabeth
See Mitchell, Margaret

Bennett, George Harold 1930- .... **CLC 5**
See also BW 1; CA 97-100; CAAS 13;
CANR 87; DLB 33

Bennett, Gwendolyn B. 1902-1981 ... **HR 1:2**
See also BW 1; CA 125; DLB 51; WP

Bennett, Hal
See Bennett, George Harold

Bennett, Jay 1912- .... **CLC 35**
See also AAYA 10, 73; CA 69-72; CANR
11, 42, 79; JRDA; SAAS 4; SATA 41, 87;
SATA-Brief 27; WYA; YAW

Bennett, Louise 1919-2006 .... **BLC 1:1;
CLC 28**
See also BW 2, 3; CA 151; 252; CDWLB 3;
CP 1, 2, 3, 4, 5, 6, 7; DAM MULT; DLB
117; EWL 3

Bennett, Louise Simone
See Bennett, Louise

Bennett-Coverley, Louise
See Bennett, Louise

Benoit de Sainte-Maure
fl. 12th cent. .... **CMLC 90**

Benson, A. C. 1862-1925 .... **TCLC 123**
See also DLB 98

Benson, E(dward) F(rederic)
1867-1940 .... **TCLC 27**
See also CA 114; 157; DLB 135, 153; HGG;
SUFW 1

Benson, Jackson J. 1930- .... **CLC 34**
See also CA 25-28R; CANR 214; DLB 111

Benson, Sally 1900-1972 .... **CLC 17**
See also CA 19-20; 37-40R; CAP 1; SATA
1, 35; SATA-Obit 27

Benson, Stella 1892-1933 .... **TCLC 17**
See also CA 117; 154, 155; DLB 36, 162;
FANT; TEA

Benet, Stephen Vincent 1898-1943 ... **PC 64;
SSC 10, 86; TCLC 7**
See also AMWS 11; CA 104; 152; DA3;
DAM POET; DLB 4, 48, 102, 249, 284;
DLBY 1997; EWL 3; HGG; MAL 5;
MTCW 2; MTFW 2005; RGAL 4; RGSF
2; SSFS 22, 31; SUFW; WP; YABC 1

Benet, William Rose 1886-1950 .... **TCLC 28**
See also CA 118; 152; DAM POET; DLB
45; RGAL 4

Bentham, Jeremy
1748-1832 .... **NCLC 38, 237**
See also DLB 107, 158, 252

Bentley, E(dmund) C(lerihew)
1875-1956 .... **TCLC 12**
See also CA 108; 232; DLB 70; MSW

Bentley, Eric 1916- .... **CLC 24**
See also CA 5-8R; CAD; CANR 6, 67;
CBD; CD 5, 6; INT CANR-6

Bentley, Eric Russell
See Bentley, Eric

ben Uzair, Salem
See Horne, Richard Henry Hengist

Beolco, Angelo 1496-1542 .... **LC 139**

Beranger, Pierre Jean de
1780-1857 .... **NCLC 34; PC 112**

Berceo, Gonzalo de
c. 1190-c. 1260 .... **CMLC 151**
See also DLB 337

Berdyaev, Nicolas
See Berdyaev, Nikolai (Aleksandrovich)

Berdyaev, Nikolai (Aleksandrovich)
1874-1948 .... **TCLC 67**
See also CA 120; 157

Berdyayev, Nikolai (Aleksandrovich)
See Berdyaev, Nikolai (Aleksandrovich)

Berendt, John 1939- .... **CLC 86**
See also CA 146; CANR 75, 83, 151

Berendt, John Lawrence
See Berendt, John

Berengar of Tours
c. 1000-1088 .... **CMLC 124**

Beresford, J(ohn) D(avys)
1873-1947 .... **TCLC 81**
See also CA 112; 155; DLB 162, 178, 197;
SFW 4; SUFW 1

Bergelson, David (Rafailovich)
1884-1952 .... **TCLC 81**
See also CA 220; DLB 333; EWL 3

Bergelson, Dovid
See Bergelson, David (Rafailovich)

Berger, Colonel
See Malraux, Andre

Berger, John 1926- .... **CLC 2, 19**
See also BRWS 4; CA 81-84; CANR 51, 78,
117, 163, 200; CN 1, 2, 3, 4, 5, 6, 7; DLB
14, 207, 319, 326

Berger, John Peter
See Berger, John

Berger, Melvin H. 1927- .... **CLC 12**
See also CA 5-8R; CANR 4, 142; CLR 32;
SAAS 2; SATA 5, 88, 158; SATA-Essay 124

Berger, Thomas 1924- .... **CLC 3, 5, 8, 11,
18, 38, 259**
See also BPFB 1; CA 1-4R; CANR 5, 28,
51, 128; CN 1, 2, 3, 4, 5, 6, 7; DAM NOV;
DLB 2; DLBY 1980; EWL 3; FANT; INT
CANR-28; MAL 5; MTCW 1, 2; MTFW
2005; RHW; TCLE 1:1; TCWW 1, 2

Bergman, Ernst Ingmar
See Bergman, Ingmar

Bergman, Ingmar
1918-2007 .... **CLC 16, 72, 210**
See also AAYA 61; CA 81-84; 262; CANR
33, 70; CWW 2; DLB 257; MTCW 2;
MTFW 2005

Bergson, Henri(-Louis)
1859-1941 .... **TCLC 32**
See also CA 164; DLB 329; EW 8; EWL 3;
GFL 1789 to the Present

Bergstein, Eleanor 1938- .... **CLC 4**
See also CA 53-56; CANR 5

Berkeley, George 1685-1753 .... **LC 65**
See also DLB 31, 101, 252

Berkoff, Steven 1937- .... **CLC 56**
See also CA 104; CANR 72; CBD; CD 5, 6

Berlin, Isaiah 1909-1997 .... **TCLC 105**
See also CA 85-88; 162

Bermant, Chaim (Icyk)
1929-1998 .... **CLC 40**
See also CA 57-60; CANR 6, 31, 57, 105;
CN 2, 3, 4, 5, 6

Bern, Victoria
See Fisher, M. F. K.

Bernanos, (Paul Louis) Georges
1888-1948 .... **TCLC 3, 267**
See also CA 104; 130; CANR 94; DLB 72;
EWL 3; GFL 1789 to the Present; RGWL
2, 3

Bernard, April 1956- .... **CLC 59**
See also CA 131; CANR 144, 230

Bernard, Mary Ann
See Soderbergh, Steven

Bernard of Clairvaux 1090-1153 ... **CMLC 71**
See also DLB 208

Bernard Silvestris
fl. c. 1130-fl. c. 1160 .... **CMLC 87**
See also DLB 208

Bernart de Ventadorn
c. 1130-c. 1190 .... **CMLC 98**

Berne, Victoria
See Fisher, M. F. K.

Bernhard, Thomas 1931-1989 .... **CLC 3,
32, 61; DC 14; TCLC 165**
See also CA 85-88; 127; CANR 32, 57;
CDWLB 2; DLB 85, 124; EWL 3; MTCW
1; RGHL; RGWL 2, 3

Bernhardt, Sarah (Henriette Rosine)
1844-1923 .... **TCLC 75**
See also CA 157

Berni, Francesco c. 1497-1536 .... **LC 210**

Bernstein, Charles 1950- .. **CLC 142; PC 152**
See also CA 129; CAAS 24; CANR 90; CP
4, 5, 6, 7; DLB 169

Bernstein, Ingrid
See Kirsch, Sarah

Béroul fl. c. 12th cent. .... **CMLC 75, 148;
PC 151**

Berriault, Gina 1926-1999 ...... **CLC 54, 109;
SSC 30**
See also CA 116; 129; 185; CANR 66; DLB
130; SSFS 7,11

Berrigan, Daniel 1921- .... **CLC 4**
See also CA 33-36R; 187; CAAE 187;
CAAS 1; CANR 11, 43, 78, 219; CP 1,
2, 3, 4, 5, 6, 7; DLB 5

Berrigan, Edmund Joseph Michael, Jr.
1934-1983 .... **CLC 37; PC 103**
See also CA 61-64; 110; CANR 14, 102; CP
1, 2, 3; DLB 5, 169; WP

Berrigan, Ted
See Berrigan, Edmund Joseph Michael, Jr.

Berry, Charles Edward Anderson
See Berry, Chuck

Berry, Chuck 1931- .... **CLC 17**
See also CA 115

Berry, Jonas
See Ashbery, John

Berry, Wendell 1934- .... **CLC 4, 6, 8, 27,
46, 279; PC 28**
See also AITN 1; AMWS 10; ANW; CA 73-
76; CANR 50, 73, 101, 132, 174, 228; CP
1, 2, 3, 4, 5, 6, 7; CSW; DAM POET; DLB
5, 6, 234, 275, 342; MTCW 2; MTFW
2005; PFS 30; TCLE 1:1

Berry, Wendell Erdman
See Berry, Wendell

Berryman, John 1914-1972 ..... **CLC 1, 2, 3,
4, 6, 8, 10, 13, 25, 62; PC 64**
See also AMW; CA 13-16; 33-36R; CABS
2; CANR 35; CAP 1; CDALB 1941-1968;
CP 1; DAM POET; DLB 48; EWL 3;
MAL 5; MTCW 1, 2; MTFW 2005; PAB;
PFS 27; RGAL 4; WP

Berssenbrugge, Mei-mei 1947- .... **PC 115**
See also CA 104; DLB 312

Bertolucci, Bernardo 1940- ..... **CLC 16, 157**
See also CA 106; CANR 125

Berton, Pierre (Francis de Marigny)
1920-2004 .... **CLC 104**
See also CA 1-4R; 233; CANR 2, 56, 144;
CPW; DLB 68; SATA 99; SATA-Obit 158

Bertrand, Aloysius 1807-1841 .... **NCLC 31**
See also DLB 217

Bertrand, Louis oAloysiusc
See Bertrand, Aloysius

Bertran de Born c. 1140-1215 .... **CMLC 5**

Besant, Annie (Wood) 1847-1933 ... **TCLC 9**
See also CA 105; 185

Bessie, Alvah 1904-1985 .... **CLC 23**
See also CA 5-8R; 116; CANR 2, 80; DLB 26

Bestuzhev, Aleksandr Aleksandrovich
1797-1837 .... NCLC 131
See also DLB 198

Bethlen, T.D.
See Silverberg, Robert

Beti, Mongo 1932-2001 ... BLC 1:1; CLC 27
See also AFW; BW 1, 3; CA 114; 124;
CANR 81; DA3; DAM MULT; DLB
360; EWL 3; MTCW 1, 2

Betjeman, John 1906-1984 .... CLC 2, 6,
10, 34, 43; PC 75
See also BRW 7; CA 9-12R; 112; CANR 33,
56; CDBLB 1945-1960; CP 1, 2, 3; DA3;
DAB; DAM MST, POET; DLB 20; DLBY
1984; EWL 3; MTCW 1, 2

Bettelheim, Bruno 1903-1990 .... CLC 79;
TCLC 143
See also CA 81-84; 131; CANR 23, 61;
DA3; MTCW 1, 2; RGHL

Betti, Ugo 1892-1953 .... TCLC 5
See also CA 104; 155; EWL 3; RGWL 2, 3

Betts, Doris 1932-2012 .. CLC 3, 6, 28, 275;
SSC 45
See also CA 13-16R; CANR 9, 66, 77; CN
6, 7; CSW; DLB 218; DLBY 1982; INT
CANR-9; RGAL 4

Betts, Doris Waugh
See Betts, Doris

Bevan, Alistair
See Roberts, Keith (John Kingston)

Bey, Pilaff
See Douglas, (George) Norman

Beyala, Calixthe 1961- ... BLC 2:1; CLC 329
See also EWL 3

Beynon, John
See Harris, John (Wyndham Parkes Lucas)
Beynon

Bhabha, Homi K. 1949- .... CLC 285

Bohme, Jakob 1575-1624 .... LC 178
See also DLB 164

Bialik, Chaim Nachman 1873-1934 ... TCLC
25, 201
See also CA 170; EWL 3; WLIT 6

Bialik, Hayyim Nahman
See Bialik, Chaim Nachman

Bickerstaff, Isaac
See Swift, Jonathan

Bidart, Frank 1939- .... CLC 33
See also AMWS 15; CA 140; CANR 106,
215; CP 5, 6, 7; PFS 26

Bienek, Horst 1930- .... CLC 7, 11
See also CA 73-76; DLB 75

Bierce, Ambrose 1842-1914(?) .... SSC 9, 72,
124, 169; TCLC 1, 7, 44; WLC 1
See also AAYA 55; AMW; BYA 11; CA
104; 139; CANR 78; CDALB 1865-1917;
DA; DA3; DAC; DAM MST; DLB 11, 12,
23, 71, 74, 186; EWL 3; EXPS; HGG;
LAIT 2; MAL 5; RGAL 4; RGSF 2; SSFS
9, 27; SUFW 1

Bierce, Ambrose Gwinett
See Bierce, Ambrose

Biggers, Earl Derr 1884-1933 .... TCLC 65
See also CA 108; 153; DLB 306

Bilek, Anton F. 1919-
See Rankin, Ian
See also CA 304

Billiken, Bud
See Motley, Willard (Francis)

Billings, Josh
See Shaw, Henry Wheeler

Billington, Lady Rachel Mary
See Billington, Rachel

Billington, Rachel 1942- .... CLC 43
See also AITN 2; CA 33-36R; CANR 44,
196, 242; CN 4, 5, 6, 7

Binchy, Maeve 1940- .... CLC 153
See also BEST 90:1; BPFB 1; CA 127; 134;
CANR 50, 96, 134, 208; CN 5, 6, 7; CPW;
DA3; DAM POP; DLB 319; INT CA-134;
MTCW 2; MTFW 2005; RHW

Binyon, T(imothy) J(ohn)
1936-2004 .... CLC 34
See also CA 111; 232; CANR 28, 140

Bion 335B.C.-245B.C. .... CMLC 39

Bioy Casares, Adolfo 1914-1999 ..... CLC 4,
8, 13, 88; HLC 1; SSC 17, 102
See also CA 29-32R; 177; CANR 19, 43, 66;
CWW 2; DAM MULT; DLB 113; EWL 3;
HW 1, 2; LAW; MTCW 1, 2; MTFW
2005; RGSF 2

Birch, Allison .... CLC 65

Bird, Cordwainer
See Ellison, Harlan

Bird, Robert Montgomery
1806-1854 .... NCLC 1, 197
See also DLB 202; RGAL 4

Birdwell, Cleo
See DeLillo, Don

Birkerts, Sven 1951- .... CLC 116
See also CA 128; 133, 176; CAAE 176;
CAAS 29; CANR 151, 243; INT CA-133

Birney, (Alfred) Earle
1904-1995 .... CLC 1, 4, 6, 11; PC 52
See also CA 1-4R; CANR 5, 20; CN 1, 2, 3,
4; CP 1, 2, 3, 4, 5, 6; DAC; DAM MST,
POET; DLB 88; MTCW 1; PFS 8; RGEL 2

Biruni, al 973-1048(?) .... CMLC 28

Bishop, Elizabeth 1911-1979 .... CLC 1,
4, 9, 13, 15, 32; PC 3, 34, 150; SSC 151;
TCLC 121
See also AMWR 2; AMWS 1; CA 5-8R; 89-
92; CABS 2; CANR 26, 61, 108; CDALB
1968-1988; CP 1, 2, 3; DA; DA3; DAC;
DAM MST, POET; DLB 5, 169; EWL 3;
GLL 2; MAL 5; MBL; MTCW 1, 2; PAB;
PFS 6, 12, 27, 31, 44; RGAL 4; SATA-
Obit 24; TUS; WP

Bishop, George Archibald
See Crowley, Edward Alexander

Bishop, John 1935- .... CLC 10
See also CA 105

Bishop, John Peale
1892-1944 .... TCLC 103
See also CA 107; 155; DLB 4, 9, 45; MAL
5; RGAL 4

Bissett, Bill 1939- .... CLC 18; PC 14
See also CA 69-72; CAAS 19; CANR 15;
CCA 1; CP 1, 2, 3, 4, 5, 6, 7; DLB 53;
MTCW 1

Bissoondath, Neil 1955- .... CLC 120, 285
See also CA 136; CANR 123, 165; CN 6, 7;
DAC

Bissoondath, Neil Devindra
See Bissoondath, Neil

Bitov, Andrei (Georgievich) 1937- .... CLC 57
See also CA 142; DLB 302

Biyidi, Alexandre
See Beti, Mongo

Bjarme, Brynjolf
See Ibsen, Henrik

Bjoernson, Bjoernstjerne (Martinius)
1832-1910 .... TCLC 7, 37
See also CA 104

Black, Benjamin
See Banville, John

Black, Robert
See Holdstock, Robert

Blackburn, Paul 1926-1971 .... CLC 9, 43
See also BG 1:2; CA 81-84; 33-36R; CANR
34; CP 1; DLB 16; DLBY 1981

Black Elk 1863-1950 .... NNAL; TCLC 33
See also CA 144; DAM MULT; MTCW 2;
MTFW 2005; WP

Black Hawk 1767-1838 .... NNAL

Black Hobart
See Sanders, Ed

Blacklin, Malcolm
See Chambers, Aidan

Blackmore, R(ichard) D(oddridge)
1825-1900 .... TCLC 27
See also CA 120; DLB 18; RGEL 2

Blackmur, R(ichard) P(almer)
1904-1965 .... CLC 2, 24
See also AMWS 2; CA 11-12; 25-28R;
CANR 71; CAP 1; DLB 63; EWL 3;
MAL 5

Black Tarantula
See Acker, Kathy

Blackwood, Algernon
1869-1951 .... SSC 107; TCLC 5
See also AAYA 78; CA 105; 150; CANR
169; DLB 153, 156, 178; HGG; SUFW 1

Blackwood, Algernon Henry
See Blackwood, Algernon

Blackwood, Caroline (Maureen)
1931-1996 .... CLC 6, 9, 100
See also BRWS 9; CA 85-88; 151; CANR
32, 61, 65; CN 3, 4, 5, 6; DLB 14, 207;
HGG; MTCW 1

Blade, Alexander
See Hamilton, Edmond; Silverberg, Robert

Blaga, Lucian 1895-1961 .... CLC 75
See also CA 157; DLB 220; EWL 3

Blair, Eric
See Orwell, George

Blair, Eric Arthur
See Orwell, George

Blair, Hugh 1718-1800 .... NCLC 75
See also DLB 356

Blais, Marie-Claire 1939- .... CLC 2, 4, 6,
13, 22
See also CA 21-24R; CAAS 4; CANR 38,
75, 93; CWW 2; DAC; DAM MST; DLB
53; EWL 3; FW; MTCW 1, 2; MTFW
2005; TWA

Blaise, Clark 1940- .... CLC 29, 261
See also AITN 2; CA 53-56; 231; CAAE
231; CAAS 3; CANR 5, 66, 106; CN 4, 5,
6, 7; DLB 53; RGSF 2

Blake, Fairley
See De Voto, Bernard (Augustine)

Blake, Nicholas
See Day Lewis, C.

Blake, Sterling
See Benford, Gregory

Blake, William 1757-1827 .... NCLC 13,
37, 57, 127, 173, 190, 201; PC 12, 63;
WLC 1
See also AAYA 47; BRW 3; BRWR 1;
CDBLB 1789-1832; CLR 52; DA; DA3;
DAB; DAC; DAM MST, POET; DLB 93,
154, 163; EXPP; LATS 1:1; LMFS 1;
MAICYA 1, 2; PAB; PFS 2, 12, 24, 34,
40; SATA 30; TEA; WCH; WLIT 3; WP

Blanchot, Maurice 1907-2003 .... CLC 135
See also CA 117; 144; 213; CANR 138;
DLB 72, 296; EWL 3

Blasco Ibanez, Vicente
1867-1928 .... TCLC 12
See also BPFB 1; CA 110; 131; CANR 81;
DA3; DAM NOV; DLB 322; EW 8; EWL
3; HW 1, 2; MTCW 1

Blatty, William Peter 1928- .... CLC 2
See also CA 5-8R; CANR 9, 124, 226; DAM
POP; HGG

Bleeck, Oliver
See Thomas, Ross (Elmore)

Bleecker, Ann Eliza 1752-1783 .... LC 161
See also DLB 200

Blessing, Lee 1949- .... CLC 54
See also CA 236; CAD; CD 5, 6; DFS 23, 26

Blessing, Lee Knowlton
See Blessing, Lee
Blight, Rose
See Greer, Germaine
Blind, Mathilde 1841-1896 .... **NCLC 202**
See also DLB 199
Blish, James 1921-1975 .... **CLC 14**
See also BPFB 1; CA 1-4R; 57-60; CANR 3;
CN 2; DLB 8; MTCW 1; SATA 66; SCFW
1, 2; SFW 4
Blish, James Benjamin
See Blish, James
Bliss, Frederick
See Card, Orson Scott
Bliss, Gillian
See Paton Walsh, Jill
Bliss, Reginald
See Wells, H. G.
Blixen, Karen 1885-1962 .... **CLC 10, 29,**
95; SSC 7, 75, 191; TCLC 255
See also CA 25-28; CANR 22, 50; CAP 2;
DA3; DLB 214; EW 10; EWL 3; EXPS;
FW; GL 2; HGG; LAIT 3; LMFS 1;
MTCW 1; NCFS 2; NFS 9; RGSF 2;
RGWL 2, 3; SATA 44; SSFS 3, 6, 13;
WLIT 2
Blixen, Karen Christentze Dinesen
See Blixen, Karen
Boll, Heinrich
See Boell, Heinrich
Bloch, Robert (Albert)
1917-1994 .... **CLC 33**
See also AAYA 29; CA 5-8R, 179; 146;
CAAE 179; CAAS 20; CANR 5, 78; DA3;
DLB 44; HGG; INT CANR-5; MTCW 2;
SATA 12; SATA-Obit 82; SFW 4; SUFW
1, 2
Blok, Alexander (Alexandrovich)
1880-1921 .... **PC 21; TCLC 5**
See also CA 104; 183; DLB 295; EW 9;
EWL 3; LMFS 2; RGWL 2, 3
Blom, Jan
See Breytenbach, Breyten
Bloom, Harold 1930- .... **CLC 24, 103, 221**
See also CA 13-16R; CANR 39, 75, 92, 133,
181, 238; DLB 67; EWL 3; MTCW 2;
MTFW 2005; RGAL 4
Bloomfield, Aurelius
See Bourne, Randolph S(illiman)
Bloomfield, Robert 1766-1823 .... **NCLC 145**
See also DLB 93
Blount, Roy, Jr. 1941- .... **CLC 38**
See also CA 53-56; CANR 10, 28, 61, 125,
176; CSW; INT CANR-28; MTCW 1, 2;
MTFW 2005
Blount, Roy Alton
See Blount, Roy, Jr.
Blowsnake, Sam 1875-(?) .... **NNAL**
Bloy, Leon 1846-1917 .... **TCLC 22**
See also CA 121; 183; DLB 123; GFL 1789
to the Present
Blue Cloud, Peter (Aroniawenrate)
1933- .... **NNAL**
See also CA 117; CANR 40; DAM MULT;
DLB 342
Bluggage, Oranthy
See Alcott, Louisa May
Blume, Judy 1938- .... **CLC 12, 30, 325**
See also AAYA 3, 26; BYA 1, 8, 12; CA 29-
32R; CANR 13, 37, 66, 124, 186; CLR 2,
15, 69, 176; CPW; DA3; DAM NOV, POP;
DLB 52; JRDA; MAICYA 1, 2; MAI-
CYAS 1; MTCW 1, 2; MTFW 2005; NFS
24; SATA 2, 31, 79, 142, 195; WYA; YAW
Blume, Judy Sussman
See Blume, Judy
Blunden, Edmund (Charles)
1896-1974 .... **CLC 2, 56; PC 66**

See also BRW 6; BRWS 11; CA 17-18; 45-
48; CANR 54; CAP 2; CP 1, 2; DLB 20,
100, 155; MTCW 1; PAB
Bly, Robert 1926- .... **CLC 1, 2, 5, 10,**
15, 38, 128, 325; PC 39
See also AMWS 4; CA 5-8R; CANR 41, 73,
125, 235; CP 1, 2, 3, 4, 5, 6, 7; DA3; DAM
POET; DLB 5, 342; EWL 3; MAL 5;
MTCW 1, 2; MTFW 2005; PFS 6, 17;
RGAL 4
Bly, Robert Elwood
See Bly, Robert
Boas, Franz 1858-1942 .... **TCLC 56**
See also CA 115; 181
Bobette
See Simenon, Georges
Boccaccio, Giovanni 1313-1375 ... **CMLC 13,**
57, 140; SSC 10, 87, 167
See also EW 2; RGSF 2; RGWL 2, 3; SSFS
28; TWA; WLIT 7
Bochco, Steven 1943- .... **CLC 35**
See also AAYA 11, 71; CA 124; 138
Bock, Charles 1970- .... **CLC 299**
See also CA 274
Bode, Sigmund
See O'Doherty, Brian
Bodel, Jean 1167(?)-1210 .... **CMLC 28**
Bodenheim, Maxwell 1892-1954 ... **TCLC 44**
See also CA 110; 187; DLB 9, 45; MAL 5;
RGAL 4
Bodenheimer, Maxwell
See Bodenheim, Maxwell
Bodker, Cecil
See Bodker, Cecil
Boell, Heinrich 1917-1985 .... **CLC 2, 3, 6,**
9, 11, 15, 27, 32, 72; SSC 23; TCLC 185;
WLC 1
See also BPFB 1; CA 21-24R; 116; CANR
24; CDWLB 2; DA; DA3; DAB; DAC;
DAM MST, NOV; DLB 69, 329; DLBY
1985; EW 13; EWL 3; MTCW 1, 2;
MTFW 2005; RGHL; RGSF 2; RGWL
2, 3; SSFS 20; TWA
Boell, Heinrich Theodor
See Boell, Heinrich
Boerne, Alfred
See Doeblin, Alfred
Boethius c 480-c. 524 .... **CMLC 15, 136**
See also DLB 115; RGWL 2, 3, WLIT 8
Boff, Leonardo (Genezio Darci)
1938- .... **CLC 70; HLC 1**
See also CA 150; DAM MULT; HW 2
Bogan, Louise 1897-1970 .... **CLC 4, 39,**
46, 93; PC 12
See also AMWS 3; CA 73-76; 25-28R;
CANR 33, 82; CP 1; DAM POET; DLB
45, 169; EWL 3; MAL 5; MBL; MTCW 1,
2; PFS 21, 39; RGAL 4
Bogarde, Dirk 1921-1999 .... **CLC 14**
See also CA 77-80; 179; DLB 14
Bogat, Shatan
See Kacew, Romain
Bogomolny, Robert L. 1938- .... **SSC 41;**
TCLC 11
See also CA 121, 164; DLB 182; EWL 3;
MJW; RGSF 2; RGWL 2, 3; TWA
Bogomolny, Robert Lee
See Bogomolny, Robert L.
Bogosian, Eric 1953- .... **CLC 45, 141**
See also CA 138; CAD; CANR 102, 148,
217; CD 5, 6; DLB 341
Bograd, Larry 1953- .... **CLC 35**
See also CA 93-96; CANR 57; SAAS 21;
SATA 33, 89; WYA
Boiardo, Matteo Maria
1441-1494 .... **LC 6, 168**
Boileau-Despreaux, Nicolas
1636-1711 .... **LC 3, 164**

See also DLB 268; EW 3; GFL Beginnings
to 1789; RGWL 2, 3
Boissard, Maurice
See Leautaud, Paul
Bojer, Johan 1872-1959 .... **TCLC 64**
See also CA 189; EWL 3
Bok, Edward W(illiam)
1863-1930 .... **TCLC 101**
See also CA 217; DLB 91; DLBD 16
Boker, George Henry 1823-1890 ... **NCLC 125**
See also RGAL 4
Boland, Eavan 1944- .... **CLC 40, 67, 113;**
PC 58
See also BRWS 5; CA 143, 207; CAAE 207;
CANR 61, 180; CP 1, 6, 7; CWP; DAM
POET; DLB 40; FW; MTCW 2; MTFW
2005; PFS 12, 22, 31, 39
Boland, Eavan Aisling
See Boland, Eavan
Bolano, Roberto 1953-2003 .... **CLC 294**
See also CA 229; CANR 175
Bolingbroke, Viscount
See St. John, Henry
Bolt, Lee
See Faust, Frederick
Bolt, Robert (Oxton) 1924-1995 .... **CLC 14;**
TCLC 175
See also CA 17-20R; 147; CANR 35, 67;
CBD; DAM DRAM; DFS 2; DLB 13, 233;
EWL 3; LAIT 1; MTCW 1
Bolivar, Simon 1783-1830 .... **NCLC 266**
Bombal, Maria Luisa
1910-1980 .... **HLCS 1; SSC 37**
See also CA 127; CANR 72; EWL 3; HW 1;
LAW; RGSF 2; SSFS 36
Bombet, Louis-Alexandre-Cesar
See Stendhal
Bomkauf
See Kaufman, Bob (Garnell)
Bonaventura .... **NCLC 35, 252**
See also DLB 90
Bonaventure 1217(?)-1274 .... **CMLC 79**
See also DLB 115; LMFS 1
Bond, Edward
1934- .... **CLC 4, 6, 13, 23; DC 45**
See also AAYA 50; BRWS 1; CA 25-28R;
CANR 38, 67, 106; CBD; CD 5, 6; DAM
DRAM; DFS 3, 8; DLB 13, 310; EWL 3;
MTCW 1
Bonham, Frank 1914-1989 .... **CLC 12**
See also AAYA 1, 70; BYA 1, 3; CA 9-12R;
CANR 4, 36; JRDA; MAICYA 1, 2; SAAS
3; SATA 1, 49; SATA-Obit 62; TCWW 1,
2; YAW
Bonnefoy, Yves
1923- .... **CLC 9, 15, 58; PC 58**
See also CA 85-88; CANR 33, 75, 97, 136;
CWW 2; DAM MST, POET; DLB 258;
EWL 3; GFL 1789 to the Present; MTCW
1, 2; MTFW 2005
Bonner, Marita
See Occomy, Marita (Odette) Bonner
Bonnin, Gertrude 1876-1938 .... **NNAL**
See also CA 150; DAM MULT; DLB 175
Bontemps, Arna 1902-1973 .... **BLC 1:1;**
CLC 1, 18; HR 1:2; TCLC 292
See also BW 1; CA 1-4R; 41-44R; CANR 4,
35; CLR 6; CP 1; CWRI 5; DA3; DAM
MULT, NOV, POET; DLB 48, 51; JRDA;
MAICYA 1, 2; MAL 5; MTCW 1, 2; PFS
32; SATA 2, 44; SATA-Obit 24; WCH; WP
Bontemps, Arnaud Wendell
See Bontemps, Arna
Boot, William
See Stoppard, Tom
Booth, Irwin
See Hoch, Edward D.

Camden, William 1551-1623 .... **LC 77**
See also DLB 172
Cameron, Carey 1952- .... **CLC 59**
See also CA 135
Cameron, Peter 1959- .... **CLC 44**
See also AMWS 12; CA 125; CANR 50,
117, 188, 239; DLB 234; GLL 2
Camoes, Luis de 1524(?)-1580 .... **HLCS 1;**
LC 62, 191; PC 31
See also DLB 287; EW 2; RGWL 2, 3
Camoens, Luis Vaz de 1524(?)-1580
See Camoes, Luis de
Camp, Madeleine L'Engle
See L'Engle, Madeleine
Campana, Dino 1885-1932 .... **TCLC 20**
See also CA 117; 246; DLB 114; EWL 3
Campanella, Tommaso 1568-1639 ..... **LC 32**
See also RGWL 2, 3
Campbell, Bebe Moore
1950-2006 .... **BLC 2:1; CLC 246**
See also AAYA 26; BW 2, 3; CA 139; 254;
CANR 81, 134; DLB 227; MTCW 2;
MTFW 2005
Campbell, John Ramsey
See Campbell, Ramsey
Campbell, John W.
1910-1971 .... **CLC 32**
See also CA 21-22; 29-32R; CANR 34; CAP
2; DLB 8; MTCW 1; SCFW 1, 2; SFW 4
Campbell, John Wood, Jr.
See Campbell, John W.
Campbell, Joseph
1904-1987 .... **CLC 69; TCLC 140**
See also AAYA 3, 66; BEST 89:2; CA 1-4R;
124; CANR 3, 28, 61, 107; DA3; MTCW 1, 2
Campbell, Maria 1940- ...... **CLC 85; NNAL**
See also CA 102; CANR 54; CCA 1; DAC
Campbell, Ramsey 1946- ... **CLC 42; SSC 19**
See also AAYA 51; CA 57-60, 228; CAAE
228; CANR 7, 102, 171; DLB 261; HGG;
INT CANR-7; SUFW 1, 2
Campbell, (Ignatius) Roy (Dunnachie)
1901-1957 .... **TCLC 5**
See also AFW; CA 104; 155; DLB 20, 225;
EWL 3; MTCW 2; RGEL 2
Campbell, Thomas 1777-1844 ...... **NCLC 19**
See also DLB 93, 144; RGEL 2
Campbell, Wilfred
See Campbell, William
Campbell, William 1858(?)-1918 .... **TCLC 9**
See also CA 106; DLB 92
Campbell, William Edward March
See March, William
Campion, Jane 1954- .... **CLC 95, 229**
See also AAYA 33; CA 138; CANR 87
Campion, Thomas 1567-1620 .... **LC 78, 221;**
PC 87
See also BRWS 16; CDBLB Before 1660;
DAM POET; DLB 58, 172; RGEL 2
Camus, Albert 1913-1960 .... **CLC 1, 2, 4, 9,**
11, 14, 32, 63, 69, 124; DC 2; SSC 9, 76,
129, 146; WLC 1
See also AAYA 36; AFW; BPFB 1; CA 89-92;
CANR 131; DA; DA3; DAB; DAC; DAM
DRAM, MST, NOV; DLB 72, 321, 329; EW
13; EWL 3; EXPN; EXPS; GFL 1789 to the
Present; LATS 1:2; LMFS 2; MTCW 1, 2;
MTFW 2005; NFS 6, 16; RGHL; RGSF 2;
RGWL 2, 3; SSFS 4; TWA
Canby, Vincent 1924-2000 .... **CLC 13**
See also CA 81-84; 191
Cancale
See Desnos, Robert
Canetti, Elias 1905-1994 ...... **CLC 3, 14, 25,**
75, 86; TCLC 157
See also CA 21-24R; 146; CANR 23, 61, 79;
CDWLB 2; CWW 2; DA3; DLB 85, 124,
329; EW 12; EWL 3; MTCW 1, 2; MTFW
2005; RGWL 2, 3; TWA

Canfield, Dorothea F.
See Fisher, Dorothy (Frances) Canfield
Canfield, Dorothea Frances
See Fisher, Dorothy (Frances) Canfield
Canfield, Dorothy
See Fisher, Dorothy (Frances) Canfield
Canin, Ethan 1960- .... **CLC 55; SSC 70**
See also CA 131; 135; CANR 193; DLB
335, 350; MAL 5
Cankar, Ivan 1876-1918 .... **TCLC 105**
See also CDWLB 4; DLB 147; EWL 3
Cannon, Curt
See Hunter, Evan
Cao, Lan 1961- .... **CLC 109**
See also CA 165
Cape, Judith
See Page, P.K.
Capella, Martianus
fl. 4th cent. .... **CMLC 84**
Capote, Truman 1924-1984 ..... **CLC 1, 3, 8,**
13, 19, 34, 38, 58; SSC 2, 47, 93; TCLC
164; WLC 1
See also AAYA 61; AMWS 3; BPFB 1; CA
5-8R; 113; CANR 18, 62, 201; CDALB
1941-1968; CN 1, 2, 3; CPW; DA; DA3;
DAB; DAC; DAM MST, NOV, POP; DLB
2, 185, 227; DLBY 1980, 1984; EWL 3;
EXPS; GLL 1; LAIT 3; MAL 5; MTCW 1,
2; MTFW 2005; NCFS 2; RGAL 4; RGSF
2; SATA 91; SSFS 2; TUS
Capra, Frank 1897-1991 .... **CLC 16**
See also AAYA 52; CA 61-64; 135
Caputo, Philip 1941- .... **CLC 32**
See also AAYA 60; CA 73-76; CANR 40,
135; YAW
Caragiale, Ion Luca
1852-1912 .... **TCLC 76**
See also CA 157
Card, Orson Scott
1951- .... **CLC 44, 47, 50, 279**
See also AAYA 11, 42; BPFB 1; BYA 5, 8;
CA 102; CANR 27, 47, 73, 102, 106, 133,
184; CLR 116; CPW; DA3; DAM POP;
FANT; INT CANR-27; MTCW 1, 2;
MTFW 2005; NFS 5; SATA 83, 127,
241; SCFW 2; SFW 4; SUFW 2; YAW
Cardenal, Ernesto 1925- .... **CLC 31, 161;**
HLC 1; PC 22
See also CA 49-52; CANR 2, 32, 66, 138,
217; CWW 2; DAM MULT, POET; DLB
290; EWL 3; HW 1, 2; LAWS 1; MTCW
1, 2; MTFW 2005; RGWL 2, 3
Cardinal, Marie 1929-2001 .... **CLC 189**
See also CA 177; CWW 2; DLB 83; FW
Cardozo, Benjamin N(athan)
1870-1938 .... **TCLC 65**
See also CA 117; 164
Carducci, Giosue (Alessandro Giuseppe)
1835-1907 .... **PC 46; TCLC 32**
See also CA 163; DLB 329; EW 7; RGWL
2, 3
Carew, Thomas 1595(?)-1640 ... **LC 13, 159;**
PC 29
See also BRW 2; DLB 126; PAB; RGEL 2
Carey, Ernestine Gilbreth
1908-2006 .... **CLC 17**
See also CA 5-8R; 254; CANR 71; SATA 2;
SATA-Obit 177
Carey, Peter 1943- .... **CLC 40, 55, 96,**
183, 294; SSC 133
See also BRWS 12; CA 123; 127; CANR 53,
76, 117, 157, 185, 213; CN 4, 5, 6, 7; DLB
289, 326; EWL 3; INT CA-127; LNFS 1;
MTCW 1, 2; MTFW 2005; RGSF 2;
SATA 94
Carey, Peter Philip
See Carey, Peter
Carleton, William 1794-1869 ... **NCLC 3, 199**
See also DLB 159; RGEL 2; RGSF 2

Carlisle, Henry 1926-2011 .... **CLC 33**
See also CA 13-16R; CANR 15, 85
Carlisle, Henry Coffin
See Carlisle, Henry
Carlsen, Chris
See Holdstock, Robert
Carlson, Ron 1947- .... **CLC 54**
See also CA 105, 189; CAAE 189; CANR
27, 155, 197; DLB 244
Carlson, Ronald F.
See Carlson, Ron
Carlyle, Jane Welsh
1801-1866 .... **NCLC 181**
See also DLB 55
Carlyle, Thomas
1795-1881 .... **NCLC 22, 70, 248**
See also BRW 4; CDBLB 1789-1832; DA;
DAB; DAC; DAM MST; DLB 55, 144,
254, 338, 366; RGEL 2; TEA
Carman, (William) Bliss
1861-1929 .... **PC 34; TCLC 7**
See also CA 104; 152; DAC; DLB 92;
RGEL 2
Carnegie, Dale 1888-1955 .... **TCLC 53**
See also CA 218
Caro Mallén de Soto, Ana
c. 1590-c. 1650 .... **LC 175**
Carossa, Hans 1878-1956 .... **TCLC 48**
See also CA 170; DLB 66; EWL 3
Carpenter, Don(ald Richard)
1931-1995 .... **CLC 41**
See also CA 45-48; 149; CANR 1, 71
Carpenter, Edward 1844-1929 ...... **TCLC 88**
See also BRWS 13; CA 163; GLL 1
Carpenter, John 1948- .... **CLC 161**
See also AAYA 2, 73; CA 134; SATA 58
Carpenter, John Howard
See Carpenter, John
Carpenter, Johnny
See Carpenter, John
Carpentier, Alejo 1904-1980 ...... **CLC 8, 11,**
38, 110; HLC 1; SSC 35; TCLC 201
See also CA 65-68; 97-100; CANR 11, 70;
CDWLB 3; DAM MULT; DLB 113; EWL
3; HW 1, 2; LAW; LMFS 2; RGSF 2;
RGWL 2, 3; WLIT 1
Carpentier y Valmont, Alejo
See Carpentier, Alejo
Carr, Caleb 1955- .... **CLC 86**
See also CA 147; CANR 73, 134; DA3;
DLB 350
Carr, Emily 1871-1945 .... **TCLC 32, 260**
See also CA 159; DLB 68; FW; GLL 2
Carr, H. D.
See Crowley, Edward Alexander
Carr, John Dickson 1906-1977 .... **CLC 3**
See also CA 49-52; 69-72; CANR 3, 33, 60;
CMW 4; DLB 306; MSW; MTCW 1, 2
Carr, Philippa
See Hibbert, Eleanor Alice Burford
Carr, Virginia Spencer 1929-2012 ... **CLC 34**
See also CA 61-64; CANR 175; DLB 111
Carrier, Roch 1937- .... **CLC 13, 78**
See also CA 130; CANR 61, 152; CCA 1;
DAC; DAM MST; DLB 53; SATA 105, 166
Carroll, James Dennis
See Carroll, Jim
Carroll, James P. 1943(?)- .... **CLC 38**
See also CA 81-84; CANR 73, 139, 209;
MTCW 2; MTFW 2005
Carroll, Jim 1949-2009 .... **CLC 35, 143**
See also AAYA 17; CA 45-48; 290; CANR
42, 115, 233; NCFS 5
Carroll, Lewis 1832-1898 .... **NCLC 2, 53,**
139, 258; PC 18, 74; WLC 1
See also AAYA 39; BRW 5; BYA 5, 13;
CDBLB 1832-1890; CLR 18, 108; DA;
DA3; DAB; DAC; DAM MST, NOV, POET;

Cayrol, Jean 1911-2005 .... **CLC 11**
See also CA 89-92; 236; DLB 83; EWL 3

Cela, Camilo Jose
See Cela, Camilo Jose

Cela, Camilo Jose 1916-2002 ..... **CLC 4, 13, 59, 122; HLC 1; SSC 71**
See also BEST 90:2; CA 21-24R; 206; CAAS 10; CANR 21, 32, 76, 139; CWW 2; DAM MULT; DLB 322; DLBY 1989; EW 13; EWL 3; HW 1; MTCW 1, 2; MTFW 2005; RGSF 2; RGWL 2, 3

Celan, Paul 1920-1970 .... **CLC 10, 19, 53, 82; PC 10**
See also CA 85-88; CANR 33, 61; CDWLB 2; DLB 69; EWL 3; MTCW 1; PFS 21; RGHL; RGWL 2, 3

Cela y Trulock, Camilo Jose
See Cela, Camilo Jose

Cellini, Benvenuto 1500-1571 .... **LC 7**
See also WLIT 7

Cendrars, Blaise
See Sauser-Hall, Frederic

Centlivre, Susanna 1669(?)-1723 ...... **DC 25; LC 65, 221**
See also DLB 84; RGEL 2

Cernuda, Luis 1902-1963 .. **CLC 54; PC 62; TCLC 286**
See also CA 131; 89-92; DAM POET; DLB 134; EWL 3; GLL 1; HW 1; RGWL 2, 3

Cernuda y Bidon, Luis
See Cernuda, Luis

Cervantes, Lorna Dee 1954- .... **HLCS 1; PC 35**
See also CA 131; CANR 80; CP 7; CWP; DLB 82; EXPP; HW 1; LLW; PFS 30

Cervantes, Miguel de 1547-1616 ...... **HLCS; LC 6, 23, 93; SSC 12, 108; WLC 1**
See also AAYA 56; BYA 1, 14; DA; DAB; DAC; DAM MST, NOV; EW 2; LAIT 1; LATS 1:1; LMFS 1; NFS 8; RGSF 2; RGWL 2, 3; TWA

Cervantes Saavedra, Miguel de
See Cervantes, Miguel de

Cesaire, Aime
See Cesaire, Aime

Cesaire, Aime Fernand
See Cesaire, Aime

Chaadaev, Petr Iakovlevich 1794-1856 .... **NCLC 197**
See also DLB 198

Chabon, Michael 1963- .... **CLC 55, 149, 265; SSC 59**
See also AAYA 45; AMWS 11; CA 139; CANR 57, 96, 127, 138, 196; DLB 278; MAL 5; MTFW 2005; NFS 25; SATA 145; SSFS 36

Chabrol, Claude 1930-2010 .... **CLC 16**
See also CA 110

Chairil Anwar
See Anwar, Chairil

Challans, Mary
See Renault, Mary

Challis, George
See Faust, Frederick

Chambers, Aidan 1934- .... **CLC 35**
See also AAYA 27, 86; CA 25-28R; CANR 12, 31, 58, 116; CLR 151; JRDA; MAICYA 1, 2; SAAS 12; SATA 1, 69, 108, 171; WYA; YAW

Chambers, James .... **CLC 21**
See also CA 124; 199

Chambers, Jessie
See Lawrence, D. H.

Chambers, Maria Cristina
See Mena, Maria Cristina

Chambers, Robert W(illiam) 1865-1933 .... **SSC 92; TCLC 41**
See also CA 165; DLB 202; HGG; SATA 107; SUFW 1

Chambers, (David) Whittaker 1901-1961 .... **TCLC 129**
See also CA 89-92; DLB 303

Chamisso, Adelbert von 1781-1838 .... **NCLC 82; SSC 140**
See also DLB 90; RGWL 2, 3; SUFW 1

Chamoiseau, Patrick 1953- ... **CLC 268, 276**
See also CA 162; CANR 88; EWL 3; RGWL 3

Chance, James T.
See Carpenter, John

Chance, John T.
See Carpenter, John

Chand, Munshi Prem
See Srivastava, Dhanpat Rai

Chand, Prem
See Srivastava, Dhanpat Rai

Chandler, Raymond 1888-1959 ...... **SSC 23; TCLC 1, 7, 179**
See also AAYA 25; AMWC 2; AMWS 4; BPFB 1; CA 104; 129; CANR 60, 107; CDALB 1929-1941; CMW 4; DA3; DLB 226, 253; DLBD 6; EWL 3; MAL 5; MSW; MTCW 1, 2; MTFW 2005; NFS 17; RGAL 4; TUS

Chandler, Raymond Thornton
See Chandler, Raymond

Chandra, Vikram 1961- .... **CLC 302**
See also CA 149; CANR 97, 214; SSFS 16

Chang, Diana 1934-2009 .... **AAL**
See also CA 228; CWP; DLB 312; EXPP; PFS 37

Chang, Eileen 1920-1995 ...... **AAL; SSC 28, 169; TCLC 184**
See also CA 166; CANR 168; CWW 2; DLB 328; EWL 3; RGSF 2

Chang, Jung 1952- .... **CLC 71**
See also CA 142

Chang Ai-Ling
See Chang, Eileen

Channing, William Ellery 1780-1842 .... **NCLC 17**
See also DLB 1, 59, 235; RGAL 4

Chao, Patricia 1955- .... **CLC 119**
See also CA 163; CANR 155

Chaplin, Charles Spencer 1889-1977 .... **CLC 16**
See also AAYA 61; CA 81-84; 73-76; DLB 44

Chaplin, Charlie
See Chaplin, Charles Spencer

Chapman, George 1559(?)-1634 .... **DC 19; LC 22, 116; PC 96**
See also BRW 1; DAM DRAM; DLB 62, 121; LMFS 1; RGEL 2

Chapman, Graham 1941-1989 .... **CLC 21**
See also AAYA 7; CA 116; 129; CANR 35, 95

Chapman, John Jay 1862-1933 .... **TCLC 7**
See also AMWS 14; CA 104; 191

Chapman, Lee
See Bradley, Marion Zimmer

Chapman, Maile .... **CLC 318**

Chapman, Walker
See Silverberg, Robert

Chappell, Fred 1936- .... **CLC 40, 78, 162, 293; PC 105**
See also CA 5-8R, 198; CAAE 198; CAAS 4; CANR 8, 33, 67, 110, 215; CN 6; CP 6, 7; CSW; DLB 6, 105; HGG

Chappell, Fred Davis
See Chappell, Fred

Char, Rene 1907-1988 ... **CLC 9, 11, 14, 55; PC 56**
See also CA 13-16R; 124; CANR 32; DAM POET; DLB 258; EWL 3; GFL 1789 to the Present; MTCW 1, 2; RGWL 2, 3

Char, Rene-Emile
See Char, Rene

Charby, Jay
See Ellison, Harlan

Chardin, Pierre Teilhard de
See Teilhard de Chardin, (Marie Joseph) Pierre

Chariton fl. 1st cent. (?) .... **CMLC 49**

Charlemagne 742-814 .... **CMLC 37**

Charles I 1600-1649 .... **LC 13, 194**

Charriere, Isabelle de 1740-1805 .... **NCLC 66**
See also DLB 313

Charron, Pierre 1541-1603 .... **LC 174**
See also GFL Beginnings to 1789

Chartier, Alain c. 1392-1430 .... **LC 94**
See also DLB 208

Chartier, Emile-Auguste
See Alain

Charyn, Jerome 1937- .... **CLC 5, 8, 18**
See also CA 5-8R; CAAS 1; CANR 7, 61, 101, 158, 199; CMW 4; CN 1, 2, 3, 4, 5, 6, 7; DLBY 1983; MTCW 1

Chase, Adam
See Marlowe, Stephen

Chase, Mary (Coyle) 1907-1981 .... **DC 1**
See also CA 77-80; 105; CAD; CWD; DFS 11; DLB 228; SATA 17; SATA-Obit 29

Chase, Mary Ellen 1887-1973 .... **CLC 2; TCLC 124**
See also CA 13-16; 41-44R; CAP 1; SATA 10

Chase, Nicholas
See Hyde, Anthony

Chase-Riboud, Barbara (Dewayne Tosi) 1939- .... **BLC 2:1**
See also BW 2; CA 113; CANR 76; DAM MULT; DLB 33; MTCW 2

Chateaubriand, Francois Rene de 1768-1848 .... **NCLC 3, 134**
See also DLB 119, 366; EW 5; GFL 1789 to the Present; RGWL 2, 3; TWA

Chatterje, Saratchandra -(?)
See Chatterji, Sarat Chandra

Chatterji, Bankim Chandra 1838-1894 .... **NCLC 19**

Chatterji, Sarat Chandra 1876-1936 .... **TCLC 13**
See also CA 109; 186; EWL 3

Chatterton, Thomas 1752-1770 ... **LC 3, 54; PC 104**
See also DAM POET; DLB 109; RGEL 2

Chatwin, Bruce 1940-1989 .... **CLC 28, 57, 59**
See also AAYA 4; BEST 90:1; BRWS 4; CA 85-88; 127; CANR 228; CPW; DAM POP; DLB 194, 204; EWL 3; MTFW 2005

Chatwin, Charles Bruce
See Chatwin, Bruce

Chaucer, Daniel
See Ford, Ford Madox

Chaucer, Geoffrey 1340(?)-1400 .... **LC 17, 56, 173, 210, 213; PC 19, 58; WLCS**
See also BRW 1; BRWC 2; CDBLB Before 1660; DA; DA3; DAB; DAC; DAM MST, POET; DLB 146; LAIT 1; PAB; PFS 14; RGEL 2; TEA; WLIT 3; WP

Chaudhuri, Nirad C(handra) 1897-1999 .... **TCLC 224**
See also CA 128; 183; DLB 323

Chaviaras, Strates 1935- .... **CLC 33**
See also CA 105

Chayefsky, Paddy 1923-1981 .... **CLC 23**
See also CA 9-12R; 104; CAD; CANR 18; DAM DRAM; DFS 26; DLB 23; DLBY 7, 44; RGAL 4

Chayefsky, Sidney
See Chayefsky, Paddy

Chedid, Andree 1920-2011 .... **CLC 47**
See also CA 145; CANR 95; EWL 3

Circus, Anthony
See Hoch, Edward D.

Cisneros, Sandra 1954- .... **CLC 69, 118, 193, 305, 352; HLC 1; PC 52; SSC 32, 72, 143, 187**
See also AAYA 9, 53; AMWS 7; CA 131; CANR 64, 118; CLR 123; CN 7; CWP; DA3; DAM MULT; DLB 122, 152; EWL 3; EXPN; FL 1:5; FW; HW 1, 2; LAIT 5; LATS 1:2; LLW; MAICYA 2; MAL 5; MTCW 2; MTFW 2005; NFS 2; PFS 19; RGAL 4; RGSF 2; SSFS 3, 13, 27, 32; WLIT 1; YAW

Cixous, Helene 1937- .... **CLC 92, 253**
See also CA 126; CANR 55, 123; CWW 2; DLB 83, 242; EWL 3; FL 1:5; FW; GLL 2; MTCW 1, 2; MTFW 2005; TWA

Clair, Rene
See Chomette, Rene Lucien

Clampitt, Amy 1920-1994 ... **CLC 32; PC 19**
See also AMWS 9; CA 110; 146; CANR 29, 79; CP 4, 5; DLB 105; MAL 5; PFS 27, 39

Clancy, Thomas L., Jr.
See Clancy, Tom

Clancy, Tom 1947- .... **CLC 45, 112**
See also AAYA 9, 51; BEST 89:1, 90:1; BPFB 1; BYA 10, 11; CA 125; 131; CANR 62, 105, 132; CMW 4; CPW; DA3; DAM NOV, POP; DLB 227; INT CA-131; MTCW 1, 2; MTFW 2005

Clare, John 1793-1864 .... **NCLC 9, 86, 259; PC 23**
See also BRWS 11; DAB; DAM POET; DLB 55, 96; RGEL 2

Clare of Assisi 1194-1253 .... **CMLC 149**
Clarin
See Alas (y Urena), Leopoldo (Enrique Garcia)

Clark, Al C.
See Goines, Donald

Clark, Brian (Robert)
See Clark, (Robert) Brian

Clark, (Robert) Brian 1932- .... **CLC 29**
See also CA 41-44R; CANR 67; CBD; CD 5, 6

Clark, Curt
See Westlake, Donald E.

Clark, Eleanor 1913-1996 .... **CLC 5, 19**
See also CA 9-12R; 151; CANR 41; CN 1, 2, 3, 4, 5, 6; DLB 6

Clark, J. P.
See Clark-Bekederemo, J. P.

Clark, John Pepper
See Clark-Bekederemo, J. P.

Clark, Kenneth (Mackenzie)
1903-1983 .... **TCLC 147**
See also CA 93-96; 109; CANR 36; MTCW 1, 2; MTFW 2005

Clark, M. R.
See Clark, Mavis Thorpe

Clark, Mavis Thorpe 1909-1999 .... **CLC 12**
See also CA 57-60; CANR 8, 37, 107; CLR 30; CWRI 5; MAICYA 1, 2; SAAS 5; SATA 8, 74

Clark, Walter Van Tilburg
1909-1971 .... **CLC 28**
See also CA 9-12R; 33-36R; CANR 63, 113; CN 1; DLB 9, 206; LAIT 2; NFS 40; RGAL 4; SATA 8; TCWW 1, 2

Clark-Bekederemo, J. P. 1935- ..... **BLC 1:1; CLC 38; DC 5**
See also CA 79; AFW; BW 1; CA 65-68; CANR 16, 72; CD 5, 6; CDWLB 3; CP 1, 2, 3, 4, 5, 6, 7; DAM DRAM, MULT; DFS 13; DLB 117; EWL 3; MTCW 2; MTFW 2005; RGEL 2

Clark-Bekederemo, John Pepper
See Clark-Bekederemo, J. P.

Clark Bekederemo, Johnson Pepper
See Clark-Bekederemo, J. P.

Clarke, Arthur
See Clarke, Arthur C.

Clarke, Arthur C. 1917-2008 ...... **CLC 1, 4, 13, 18, 35, 136; SSC 3**
See also AAYA 4, 33; BPFB 1; BYA 13; CA 1-4R; 270; CANR 2, 28, 55, 74, 130, 196; CLR 119; CN 1, 2, 3, 4, 5, 6, 7; CPW; DA3; DAM POP; DLB 261; JRDA; LAIT 5; MAICYA 1, 2; MTCW 1, 2; MTFW 2005; SATA 13, 70, 115; SATA-Obit 191; SCFW 1, 2; SFW 4; SSFS 4, 18, 29, 36; TCLE 1:1; YAW

Clarke, Arthur Charles
See Clarke, Arthur C.

Clarke, Austin 1896-1974 .... **CLC 6, 9; PC 112**
See also BRWS 15; CA 29-32; 49-52; CAP 2; CP 1, 2; DAM POET; DLB 10, 20; EWL 3; RGEL 2

Clarke, Austin 1934- .... **BLC 1:1; CLC 8, 53; SSC 45, 116**
See also BW 1; CA 25-28R; CAAS 16; CANR 14, 32, 68, 140, 220; CN 1, 2, 3, 4, 5, 6, 7; DAC; DAM MULT; DLB 53, 125; DNFS 2; MTCW 2; MTFW 2005; RGSF 2

Clarke, Gillian 1937- .... **CLC 61**
See also CA 106; CP 3, 4, 5, 6, 7; CWP; DLB 40

Clarke, Marcus (Andrew Hislop)
1846-1881 .... **NCLC 19, 258; SSC 94**
See also DLB 230; RGEL 2; RGSF 2

Clarke, Shirley 1925-1997 .... **CLC 16**
See also CA 189

Clash, The
See Headon, (Nicky) Topper; Jones, Mick; Simonon, Paul; Strummer, Joe

Claudel, Paul (Louis Charles Marie)
1868-1955 .... **TCLC 2, 10, 268**
See also CA 104; 165; DLB 192, 258, 321; EW 8; EWL 3; GFL 1789 to the Present; RGWL 2, 3; TWA

Claudian 370(?)-404(?) .... **CMLC 46**
See also RGWL 2, 3

Claudius, Matthias 1740-1815 ...... **NCLC 75**
See also DLB 97

Clavell, James 1925-1994 ..... **CLC 6, 25, 87**
See also BPFB 1; CA 25 28R; 146; CANR 26, 48; CN 5; CPW; DA3; DAM NOV, POP; MTCW 1, 2; MTFW 2005; NFS 10; RHW

Clayman, Gregory .... **CLC 65**

Cleage, Pearl 1948- .... **DC 32**
See also BW 2; CA 41-44R; CANR 27, 148, 177, 226; DFS 14, 16; DLB 228; NFS 17

Cleage, Pearl Michelle
See Cleage, Pearl

Cleaver, (Leroy) Eldridge 1935-1998 ... **BLC 1:1; CLC 30, 119**
See also BW 1, 3; CA 21-24R; 167; CANR 16, 75; DA3; DAM MULT; MTCW 2; YAW

Cleese, John (Marwood) 1939- .... **CLC 21**
See also CA 112; 116; CANR 35; MTCW 1

Cleishbotham, Jebediah
See Scott, Sir Walter

Cleland, John 1710-1789 .... **LC 2, 48**
See also DLB 39; RGEL 2

Clemens, Samuel
See Twain, Mark

Clemens, Samuel Langhorne
See Twain, Mark

Clement of Alexandria
150(?)-215(?) .... **CMLC 41**

Cleophil
See Congreve, William

Clerihew, E.
See Bentley, E(dmund) C(lerihew)

Clerk, N. W.
See Lewis, C. S.

Cleveland, John 1613-1658 .... **LC 106**
See also DLB 126; RGEL 2

Cliff, Jimmy
See Chambers, James

Cliff, Michelle 1946- .... **BLCS; CLC 120**
See also BW 2; CA 116; CANR 39, 72; CDWLB 3; DLB 157; FW; GLL 2

Clifford, Lady Anne 1590-1676 .... **LC 76**
See also DLB 151

Clifton, Lucille 1936-2010 ..... **BLC 1:1, 2:1; CLC 19, 66, 162, 283; PC 17, 148**
See also AFAW 2; BW 2, 3; CA 49-52; CANR 2, 24, 42, 76, 97, 138; CLR 5; CP 2, 3, 4, 5, 6, 7; CSW; CWP; CWRI 5; DA3; DAM MULT, POET; DLB 5, 41; EXPP; MAICYA 1, 2; MTCW 1, 2; MTFW 2005; PFS 1, 14, 29, 41; SATA 20, 69, 128; SSFS 34; WP

Clifton, Thelma Lucille
See Clifton, Lucille

Celine, Louis-Ferdinand
1894-1961 .... **CLC 1, 3, 4, 7, 47, 124**
See also CA 85-88; CANR 28; DLB 72; EW 11; EWL 3; GFL 1789 to the Present; MTCW 1; RGWL 2, 3

Clinton, Dirk
See Silverberg, Robert

Clough, Arthur Hugh
1819-1861 .... **NCLC 27, 163; PC 103**
See also BRW 5; DLB 32; RGEL 2

Clutha, Janet
See Frame, Janet

Clutha, Janet Paterson Frame
See Frame, Janet

Clyne, Terence
See Blatty, William Peter

Cobalt, Martin
See Mayne, William

Cobb, Irvin S(hrewsbury)
1876-1944 .... **TCLC 77**
See also CA 175; DLB 11, 25, 86

Cobbett, William 1763-1835 .. **NCLC 49, 288**
See also DLB 43, 107, 158; RGEL 2

Coben, Harlan 1962- .... **CLC 269**
See also AAYA 83; CA 164; CANR 162, 199, 234

Coburn, D(onald) L(ee) 1938- .... **CLC 10**
See also CA 89-92; DFS 23

Cockburn, Catharine Trotter
See Trotter, Catharine

Cocteau, Jean 1889-1963 .... **CLC 1, 8, 15, 16, 43; DC 17; TCLC 119; WLC 2**
See also AAYA 74; CA 25-28; CANR 40; CAP 2; DA; DA3; DAB; DAC; DAM DRAM, MST, NOV; DFS 24; DLB 65, 258, 321; EW 10; EWL 3; GFL 1789 to the Present; MTCW 1, 2; RGWL 2, 3; TWA

Cocteau, Jean Maurice Eugene Clement
See Cocteau, Jean

Codrescu, Andrei 1946- .... **CLC 46, 121**
See also CA 33-36R; CAAS 19; CANR 13, 34, 53, 76, 125, 223; CN 7; DA3; DAM POET; MAL 5; MTCW 2; MTFW 2005

Coe, Max
See Bourne, Randolph S(illiman)

Coe, Tucker
See Westlake, Donald E.

Coelho, Paulo 1947- .... **CLC 258**
See also CA 152; CANR 80, 93, 155, 194; NFS 29

Coen, Ethan 1957- .... **CLC 108, 267**
See also AAYA 54; CA 126; CANR 85

Coen, Joel 1954- .... **CLC 108, 267**
See also AAYA 54; CA 126; CANR 119

Coetzee, J. M. 1940- .... **CLC 23, 33, 66, 117, 161, 162, 305**

LATS 1:1; LMFS 1; MTCW 1, 2; MTFW
2005; NFS 2, 16; RGEL 2; RGSF 2; SATA
27; SSFS 1, 12, 31; TEA; WLIT 4

Conrad, Robert Arnold
See Hart, Moss

Conroy, Donald Patrick
See Conroy, Pat

Conroy, Pat 1945- .... **CLC 30, 74**
See also AAYA 8, 52; AITN 1; BPFB 1;
CA 85-88; CANR 24, 53, 129, 233; CN 7;
CPW; CSW; DA3; DAM NOV, POP;
DLB 6; LAIT 5; MAL 5; MTCW 1, 2;
MTFW 2005

Constant (de Rebecque), (Henri) Benjamin
1767-1830 .... **NCLC 6, 182**
See also DLB 119; EW 4; GFL 1789 to the
Present

Conway, Jill K. 1934- .... **CLC 152**
See also CA 130; CANR 94

Conway, Jill Ker
See Conway, Jill K.

Conybeare, Charles Augustus
See Eliot, T. S.

Cook, Michael 1933-1994 .... **CLC 58**
See also CA 93-96; CANR 68; DLB 53

Cook, Robin 1940- .... **CLC 14**
See also AAYA 32; BEST 90:2; BPFB 1;
CA 108; 111; CANR 41, 90, 109, 181, 219;
CPW; DA3; DAM POP; HGG; INT CA-111

Cook, Roy
See Silverberg, Robert

Cooke, Elizabeth 1948- .... **CLC 55**
See also CA 129

Cooke, John Esten 1830-1886 .... **NCLC 5**
See also DLB 3, 248; RGAL 4

Cooke, John Estes
See Baum, L. Frank

Cooke, M. E.
See Creasey, John

Cooke, Margaret
See Creasey, John

Cooke, Rose Terry 1827-1892 ... **NCLC 110;
SSC 149**
See also DLB 12, 74

Cook-Lynn, Elizabeth 1930- **CLC 93; NNAL**
See also CA 133; DAM MULT; DLB 175

Cooney, Ray .... **CLC 62**
See also CBD

Cooper, Anthony Ashley 1671-1713 **LC 107**
See also DLB 101, 336

Cooper, Dennis 1953- .... **CLC 203**
See also CA 133; CANR 72, 86, 204; GLL 1;
HGG

Cooper, Douglas 1960- .... **CLC 86**

Cooper, Henry St. John
See Creasey, John

Cooper, J. California (?)- .... **CLC 56**
See also AAYA 12; BW 1; CA 125; CANR
55, 207; CLR 188; DAM MULT; DLB 212

Cooper, James Fenimore
1789-1851 ... **NCLC 1, 27, 54, 203, 279**
See also AAYA 22; AMW; BPFB 1; CDALB
1640-1865; CLR 105; DA3; DLB 3, 183,
250, 254; LAIT 1; NFS 25; RGAL 4;
SATA 19; TUS; WCH

Cooper, Joan California
See Cooper, J. California

Cooper, Susan Fenimore
1813-1894 .... **NCLC 129**
See also ANW; DLB 239, 254

Coover, Robert 1932- .... **CLC 3, 7, 15, 32,
46, 87, 161, 306; SSC 15, 101**
See also AMWS 5; BPFB 1; CA 45-48;
CANR 3, 37, 58, 115, 228; CN 1, 2, 3,
4, 5, 6, 7; DAM NOV; DLB 2, 227; DLBY
1981; EWL 3; MAL 5; MTCW 1, 2;
MTFW 2005; RGAL 4; RGSF 2

Copeland, Stewart 1952- .... **CLC 26**
See also CA 305

Copeland, Stewart Armstrong
See Copeland, Stewart

Copernicus, Nicolaus 1473-1543 .... **LC 45**

Coppard, A(lfred) E(dgar)
1878-1957 .... **SSC 21; TCLC 5**
See also BRWS 8; CA 114; 167; DLB 162;
EWL 3; HGG; RGEL 2; RGSF 2; SUFW
1; YABC 1

Coppee, Francois 1842-1908 .... **TCLC 25**
See also CA 170; DLB 217

Coppola, Francis Ford 1939- ... **CLC 16, 126**
See also AAYA 39; CA 77-80; CANR 40,
78; DLB 44

Copway, George 1818-1869 .... **NNAL**
See also DAM MULT; DLB 175, 183

Corbiere, Tristan 1845-1875 .... **NCLC 43**
See also DLB 217; GFL 1789 to the Present

Corcoran, Barbara (Asenath)
1911-2003 .... **CLC 17**
See also AAYA 14; CA 21-24R, 191; CAAE
191; CAAS 2; CANR 11, 28, 48; CLR 50;
DLB 52; JRDA; MAICYA 2; MAICYAS
1; RHW; SAAS 20; SATA 3, 77; SATA-
Essay 125

Cordelier, Maurice
See Giraudoux, Jean

Cordier, Gilbert
See Rohmer, Eric

Corelli, Marie
See Mackay, Mary

Corinna c. 225B.C.-c. 305B.C. ..... **CMLC 72**

Corman, Cid 1924-2004 .... **CLC 9**
See also CA 85-88; 225; CAAS 2; CANR
44; CP 1, 2, 3, 4, 5, 6, 7; DAM POET;
DLB 5, 193

Corman, Sidney
See Corman, Cid

Cormier, Robert 1925-2000 .... **CLC 12, 30**
See also AAYA 3, 19; BYA 1, 2, 6, 8, 9; CA 1-
4R; CANR 5, 23, 76, 93; CDALB 1968-
1988; CLR 12, 55, 167; DA; DAB; DAC;
DAM MST, NOV; DLB 52; EXPN; INT
CANR-23; JRDA; LAIT 5; MAICYA 1, 2;
MTCW 1, 2; MTFW 2005; NFS 2, 18; SATA
10, 45, 83; SATA-Obit 122; WYA; YAW

Cormier, Robert Edmund
See Cormier, Robert

Corn, Alfred (DeWitt III) 1943- .... **CLC 33**
See also CA 179; CAAE 179; CAAS 25;
CANR 44; CP 3, 4, 5, 6, 7; CSW; DLB
120, 282; DLBY 1980

Corneille, Pierre 1606-1684 .... **DC 21;
LC 28, 135, 212, 217**
See also DAB; DAM MST; DFS 21; DLB
268; EW 3; GFL Beginnings to 1789;
RGWL 2, 3; TWA

Cornwell, David
See le Carre, John

Cornwell, David John Moore
See le Carre, John

Cornwell, Patricia 1956- .... **CLC 155**
See also AAYA 16, 56; BPFB 1; CA 134;
CANR 53, 131, 195; CMW 4; CPW; CSW;
DAM POP; DLB 306; MSW; MTCW 2;
MTFW 2005

Cornwell, Patricia Daniels
See Cornwell, Patricia

Cornwell, Smith
See Smith, David (Jeddie)

Corso, Gregory 1930-2001 .... **CLC 1, 11;
PC 33, 108**
See also AMWS 12; BG 1:2; CA 5-8R; 193;
CANR 41, 76, 132; CP 1, 2, 3, 4, 5, 6, 7;
DA3; DLB 5, 16, 237; LMFS 2; MAL 5;
MTCW 1, 2; MTFW 2005; WP

Cortes, Hernan 1485-1547 .... **LC 31, 213**

Cortez, Jayne 1936- .... **BLC 2:1**
See also BW 2, 3; CA 73-76; CANR 13, 31,
68, 126; CWP; DLB 41; EWL 3

Cortazar, Julio 1914-1984 .... **CLC 2, 3, 5,
10, 13, 15, 33, 34, 92; HLC 1; SSC 7, 76,
156; TCLC 252**
See also AAYA 85; BPFB 1; CA 21-24R;
CANR 12, 32, 81; CDWLB 3; DA3; DAM
MULT, NOV, DLB 113; EWL 3; EXPS;
HW 1, 2; LAW; MTCW 1, 2; MTFW
2005; RGSF 2; RGWL 2, 3; SSFS 3,
20, 28, 31, 34; TWA; WLIT 1

Corvinus, Jakob
See Raabe, Wilhelm (Karl)

Corwin, Cecil
See Kornbluth, C(yril) M.

Coryate, Thomas 1577(?)-1617 .... **LC 218**
See also DLB 151, 172

Cosic, Dobrica 1921- .... **CLC 14**
See also CA 122; 138; CDWLB 4; CWW 2;
DLB 181; EWL 3

Costain, Thomas B(ertram)
1885-1965 .... **CLC 30**
See also BYA 3; CA 5-8R; 25-28R; DLB 9;
RHW

Costantini, Humberto
1924(?)-1987 .... **CLC 49**
See also CA 131; 122; EWL 3; HW 1

Costello, Elvis 1954(?)- .... **CLC 21**
See also CA 204

Costenoble, Philostene
See Ghelderode, Michel de

Cotes, Cecil V.
See Duncan, Sara Jeannette

Cotter, Joseph Seamon Sr.
1861-1949 .... **BLC 1:1; TCLC 28**
See also BW 1; CA 124; DAM MULT;
DLB 50

Cotton, John 1584-1652 .... **LC 176**
See also DLB 24; TUS

Couch, Arthur Thomas Quiller
See Quiller-Couch, Sir Arthur (Thomas)

Coulton, James
See Hansen, Joseph

Couperus, Louis (Marie Anne)
1863-1923 .... **TCLC 15**
See also CA 115; EWL 3; RGWL 2, 3

Coupland, Douglas 1961- .... **CLC 85, 133**
See also AAYA 34; CA 142; CANR 57, 90,
130, 172, 213; CCA 1; CN 7; CPW; DAC;
DAM POP; DLB 334

Coupland, Douglas Campbell
See Coupland, Douglas

Court, Wesli
See Turco, Lewis

Courtenay, Bryce 1933- .... **CLC 59**
See also CA 138; CPW; NFS 32

Courtney, Robert
See Ellison, Harlan

Cousteau, Jacques 1910-1997 .... **CLC 30**
See also CA 65-68; 159; CANR 15, 67, 201;
MTCW 1; SATA 38, 98

Cousteau, Jacques-Yves
See Cousteau, Jacques

Coventry, Francis 1725-1754 .... **LC 46**
See also DLB 39

Coverdale, Miles c. 1487-1569 .... **LC 77**
See also DLB 167

Cowan, Peter (Walkinshaw)
1914-2002 .... **SSC 28**
See also CA 21-24R; CANR 9, 25, 50, 83;
CN 1, 2, 3, 4, 5, 6, 7; DLB 260; RGSF 2

Coward, Noel 1899-1973 .... **CLC 1, 9, 29,
51; DC 45**
See also AITN 1; BRWS 2; CA 17-18; 41-
44R; CANR 35, 132, 190; CAP 2; CBD;
CDBLB 1914-1945; DA3; DAM DRAM;

DFS 3, 6; DLB 10, 245; EWL 3; IDFW 3,
4; MTCW 1, 2; MTFW 2005; RGEL 2;
TEA

Coward, Noel Peirce
See Coward, Noel

Cowley, Abraham 1618-1667 .... **LC 43;
PC 90**
See also BRW 2; DLB 131, 151; PAB;
RGEL 2

Cowley, Malcolm 1898-1989 .... **CLC 39**
See also AMWS 2; CA 5-8R; 128; CANR 3,
55; CP 1, 2, 3, 4; DLB 4, 48; DLBY 1981,
1989; EWL 3; MAL 5; MTCW 1, 2;
MTFW 2005

Cowper, William 1731-1800 .... **NCLC 8, 94;
PC 40**
See also BRW 3; BRWR 3; DA3; DAM
POET; DLB 104, 109; RGEL 2

Cox, William Trevor
See Trevor, William

Coyle, William
See Keneally, Thomas

Coyne, P. J.
See Masters, Hilary

Cozzens, James Gould
1903-1978 .... **CLC 1, 4, 11, 92**
See also AMW; BPFB 1; CA 9-12R; 81-84;
CANR 19; CDALB 1941-1968; CN 1, 2;
DLB 9, 294; DLBD 2; DLBY 1984, 1997;
EWL 3; MAL 5; MTCW 1, 2; MTFW
2005; RGAL 4

Crabbe, George 1754-1832 .... **NCLC 26,
121; PC 97**
See also BRW 3; DLB 93; RGEL 2

Crace, Jim 1946- .... **CLC 157; SSC 61**
See also BRWS 14; CA 128; 135; CANR 55,
70, 123, 180; CN 5, 6, 7; DLB 231; INT
CA-135

Craddock, Charles Egbert
See Murfree, Mary Noailles

Craig, A. A.
See Anderson, Poul

Craik, Mrs.
See Craik, Dinah Maria (Mulock)

Craik, Dinah Maria (Mulock)
1826-1887 .... **NCLC 38; 286**
See also DLB 35, 163; MAICYA 1, 2;
RGEL 2; SATA 34

Cram, Ralph Adams 1863-1942 ... **TCLC 45**
See also CA 160

Cranch, Christopher Pearse
1813-1892 .... **NCLC 115**
See also DLB 1, 42, 243

Crane, Harold Hart
See Crane, Hart

Crane, Hart 1899-1932 .... **PC 3, 99;
TCLC 2, 5, 80; WLC 2**
See also AAYA 81; AMW; AMWR 2; CA
104; 127; CDALB 1917-1929; DA; DA3;
DAB; DAC; DAM MST, POET; DLB 4,
48; EWL 3; MAL 5; MTCW 1, 2; MTFW
2005; RGAL 4; TUS

Crane, R(onald) S(almon)
1886-1967 .... **CLC 27**
See also CA 85-88; DLB 63

Crane, Stephen 1871-1900 ... **PC 80; SSC 7,
56, 70, 129, 194; TCLC 11, 17, 32, 216;
WLC 2**
See also AAYA 21; AMW; AMWC 1; BPFB
1; BYA 3; CA 109; 140; CANR 84;
CDALB 1865-1917; CLR 132; DA; DA3;
DAB; DAC; DAM MST, NOV, POET;
DLB 12, 54, 78, 357; EXPN; EXPS; LAIT
2; LMFS 2; MAL 5; NFS 4, 20; PFS 9;
RGAL 4; RGSF 2; SSFS 4, 28, 34; TUS;
WYA; YABC 2

Crane, Stephen Townley
See Crane, Stephen

Cranmer, Thomas 1489-1556 .... **LC 95**
See also DLB 132, 213

Cranshaw, Stanley
See Fisher, Dorothy (Frances) Canfield

Crase, Douglas 1944- .... **CLC 58**
See also CA 106; CANR 204

Crashaw, Richard 1612(?)-1649 .... **LC 24,
200; PC 84**
See also BRW 2; DLB 126; PAB; RGEL 2

Cratinus c. 519B.C.-c. 422B.C. .... **CMLC 54**
See also LMFS 1

Craven, Margaret 1901-1980 .... **CLC 17**
See also BYA 2; CA 103; CCA 1; DAC;
LAIT 5

Crawford, F(rancis) Marion
1854-1909 .... **TCLC 10**
See also CA 107; 168; DLB 71; HGG;
RGAL 4; SUFW 1

Crawford, Isabella Valancy
1850-1887 .... **NCLC 12, 127**
See also DLB 92; RGEL 2

Crayon, Geoffrey
See Irving, Washington

Crebillon, Claude Prosper Jolyot de (fils)
1707-1777 .... **LC 1, 28**
See also DLB 313; GFL Beginnings to 1789

Creasey, John 1908-1973 .... **CLC 11**
See also CA 5-8R; 41-44R; CANR 8, 59;
CMW 4; DLB 77; MTCW 1

Credo
See Creasey, John

Credo, Alvaro J. de
See Prado (Calvo), Pedro

Creeley, Robert 1926-2005 ...... **CLC 1, 2, 4,
8, 11, 15, 36, 78, 266; PC 73**
See also AMWS 4; CA 1-4R; 237; CAAS
10; CANR 23, 43, 89, 137; CP 1, 2, 3, 4, 5,
6, 7; DA3; DAM POET; DLB 5, 16, 169;
DLBD 17; EWL 3; MAL 5; MTCW 1, 2;
MTFW 2005; PFS 21; RGAL 4; WP

Creeley, Robert White
See Creeley, Robert

Crenne, Helisenne de
1510-1560 .... **LC 113**
See also DLB 327

Crevel, Rene 1900-1935 .... **TCLC 112**
See also GLL 2

Crews, Harry
1935-2012 .... **CLC 6, 23, 49, 277**
See also AITN 1; AMWS 11; BPFB 1; CA
25-28R; CANR 20, 57; CN 3, 4, 5, 6, 7;
CSW; DA3; DLB 6, 143, 185; MTCW 1,
2; MTFW 2005; RGAL 4

Crichton, John Michael
See Crichton, Michael

Crichton, Michael 1942-2008 .... **CLC 2, 6,
54, 90, 242**
See also AAYA 10, 49; AITN 2; BPFB 1;
CA 25-28R; 279; CANR 13, 40, 54, 76,
127, 179; CMW 4; CN 2, 3, 6, 7; CPW;
DA3; DAM NOV, POP; DLB 292; DLBY
1981; INT CANR-13; JRDA; LNFS 1;
MTCW 1, 2; MTFW 2005; NFS 34; SATA
9, 88; SATA-Obit 199; SFW 4; YAW

Crispin, Edmund
See Montgomery, Bruce

Cristina of Sweden 1626-1689 .... **LC 124**

Cristofer, Michael 1945(?)- .... **CLC 28**
See also CA 110; 152; CAD; CANR 150;
CD 5, 6; DAM DRAM; DFS 15; DLB 7

Cristofer, Michael Ivan
See Cristofer, Michael

Criton
See Alain

Croce, Benedetto 1866-1952 .... **TCLC 37**
See also CA 120; 155; EW 8; EWL 3;
WLIT 7

Crockett, David
See Crockett, Davy

Crockett, Davy 1786-1836 .... **NCLC 8**
See also DLB 3, 11, 183, 248

Crofts, Freeman Wills 1879-1957 **TCLC 55**
See also CA 115; 195; CMW 4; DLB 77;
MSW

Croker, John Wilson 1780-1857 ... **NCLC 10**
See also DLB 110

Crommelynck, Fernand
1885-1970 .... **CLC 75**
See also CA 189; 89-92; EWL 3

Cromwell, Oliver 1599-1658 .... **LC 43**

Cronenberg, David 1943- .... **CLC 143**
See also CA 138; CCA 1

Cronin, A(rchibald) J(oseph)
1896-1981 .... **CLC 32**
See also BPFB 1; CA 1-4R; 102; CANR 5;
CN 2; DLB 191; SATA 47; SATA-Obit 25

Cross, Amanda
See Heilbrun, Carolyn G.

Crothers, Rachel 1878-1958 .... **TCLC 19**
See also CA 113; 194; CAD; CWD; DLB 7,
266; RGAL 4

Croves, Hal
See Traven, B.

Crow Dog, Mary (?)- .... **CLC 93; NNAL**
See also CA 154

Crowfield, Christopher
See Stowe, Harriet Beecher

Crowley, Aleister
See Crowley, Edward Alexander

Crowley, Edward Alexander
1875-1947 .... **TCLC 7**
See also CA 104; GLL 1; HGG

Crowley, John 1942- .... **CLC 57**
See also AAYA 57; BPFB 1; CA 61-64;
CANR 43, 98, 138, 177; DLBY 1982;
FANT; MTFW 2005; SATA 65, 140; SFW
4; SUFW 2

Crowne, John 1641-1712 .... **LC 104**
See also DLB 80; RGEL 2

Crud
See Crumb, R.

Crumarums
See Crumb, R.

Crumb, R. 1943- .... **CLC 17**
See also CA 106; CANR 107, 150, 218

Crumb, Robert
See Crumb, R.

Crumbum
See Crumb, R.

Crumski
See Crumb, R.

Crum the Bum
See Crumb, R.

Crunk
See Crumb, R.

Crustt
See Crumb, R.

Crutchfield, Les
See Trumbo, Dalton

Cruz, Victor Hernandez 1949- .... **HLC 1;
PC 37**
See also BW 2; CA 65-68; 271; CAAE 271;
CAAS 17; CANR 14, 32, 74, 132; CP 1, 2,
3, 4, 5, 6, 7; DAM MULT, POET; DLB 41;
DNFS 1; EXPP; HW 1, 2; LLW; MTCW
2; MTFW 2005; PFS 16; WP

Crevecoeur, J. Hector St. John de
1735-1813 .... **NCLC 105**
See also AMWS 1; ANW; DLB 37

Crevecoeur, Michel Guillaume Jean de
See Crevecoeur, J. Hector St. John de

Cryer, Gretchen (Kiger) 1935- .... **CLC 21**
See also CA 114; 123

Cesaire, Aime 1913-2008 .... **BLC 1:1;
CLC 19, 32, 112, 280; DC 22; PC 25**

See also BW 2, 3; CA 65-68; 271; CANR 24, 43, 81; CWW 2; DA3; DAM MULT, POET; DLB 321; EWL 3; GFL 1789 to the Present; MTCW 1, 2; MTFW 2005; WP

Cesaire, Aime Fernand
See Cesaire, Aime

Csath, Geza
See Brenner, Jozef

Cudlip, David R(ockwell) 1933- ..... **CLC 34**
See also CA 177

Cuervo, Talia
See Vega, Ana Lydia

Cullen, Countee 1903-1946 ... **BLC 1:1; HR 1:2; PC 20; TCLC 4, 37, 220; WLCS**
See also AAYA 78; AFAW 2; AMWS 4; BW 1; CA 108; 124; CDALB 1917-1929; DA; DA3; DAC; DAM MST, MULT, POET; DLB 4, 48, 51; EWL 3; EXPP; LMFS 2; MAL 5; MTCW 1, 2; MTFW 2005; PFS 3, 42; RGAL 4; SATA 18; WP

Culleton, Beatrice 1949- .... **NNAL**
See also CA 120; CANR 83; DAC

Culver, Timothy J.
See Westlake, Donald E.

Cum, R.
See Crumb, R.

Cumberland, Richard 1732-1811 .... **NCLC 167**
See also DLB 89; RGEL 2

Cummings, Bruce F. 1889-1919 ... **TCLC 24**
See also CA 123

Cummings, Bruce Frederick
See Cummings, Bruce F.

Cummings, E. E. 1894-1962 ... **CLC 1, 3, 8, 12, 15, 68; PC 5; TCLC 137; WLC 2**
See also AAYA 41; AMW; CA 73-76; CANR 31; CDALB 1929-1941; DA; DA3; DAB; DAC; DAM MST, POET; DLB 4, 48; EWL 3; EXPP; MAL 5; MTCW 1, 2; MTFW 2005; PAB; PFS 1, 3, 12, 13, 19, 30, 34, 40; RGAL 4; TUS; WP

Cummings, Edward Estlin
See Cummings, E. E.

Cummins, Maria Susanna 1827-1866 .... **NCLC 139**
See also DLB 42; YABC 1

Cunha, Euclides (Rodrigues Pimenta) da 1866-1909 .... **TCLC 24**
See also CA 123; 219; DLB 307; LAW; WLIT 1

Cunningham, E. V.
See Fast, Howard

Cunningham, J. Morgan
See Westlake, Donald E.

Cunningham, J(ames) V(incent) 1911-1985 .... **CLC 3, 31; PC 92**
See also CA 1-4R; 115; CANR 1, 72; CP 1, 2, 3, 4; DLB 5

Cunningham, Julia (Woolfolk) 1916- .... **CLC 12**
See also CA 9-12R; CANR 4, 19, 36; CWRI 5; JRDA; MAICYA 1, 2; SAAS 2; SATA 1, 26, 132

Cunningham, Michael 1952- ... **CLC 34, 243**
See also AMWS 15; CA 136; CANR 96, 160, 227; CN 7; DLB 292; GLL 2; MTFW 2005; NFS 23

Cunninghame Graham, R. B.
See Cunninghame Graham, Robert Bontine

Cunninghame Graham, Robert Bontine 1852-1936 .... **TCLC 19**
See also CA 119; 184; DLB 98, 135, 174; RGEL 2; RGSF 2

Cunninghame Graham, Robert Gallnigad Bontine
See Cunninghame Graham, Robert Bontine

Curnow, (Thomas) Allen (Monro) 1911-2001 .... **PC 48**
See also CA 69-72; 202; CANR 48, 99; CP 1, 2, 3, 4, 5, 6, 7; EWL 3; RGEL 2

Currie, Ellen 19(?)- .... **CLC 44**

Curtin, Philip
See Lowndes, Marie Adelaide (Belloc)

Curtin, Phillip
See Lowndes, Marie Adelaide (Belloc)

Curtis, Price
See Ellison, Harlan

Cusanus, Nicolaus 1401-1464
See Nicholas of Cusa

Cutrate, Joe
See Spiegelman, Art

Cynewulf fl. 9th cent. .... **CMLC 23, 117**
See also DLB 146; RGEL 2

Cyprian, St. c. 200-258 .... **CMLC 127**

Cyrano de Bergerac, Savinien de 1619-1655 .... **LC 65**
See also DLB 268; GFL Beginnings to 1789; RGWL 2, 3

Cyril of Alexandria c. 375-c. 430 ... **CMLC 59**

Czaczkes, Shmuel Yosef Halevi
See Agnon, S. Y.

Dabrowska, Maria (Szumska) 1889-1965 .... **CLC 15**
See also CA 106; CDWLB 4; DLB 215; EWL 3

Dabydeen, David 1955- .... **CLC 34, 351**
See also BW 1; CA 125; CANR 56, 92; CN 6, 7; CP 5, 6, 7; DLB 347

Dacey, Philip 1939- .... **CLC 51**
See also CA 37-40R, 231; CAAE 231; CAAS 17; CANR 14, 32, 64; CP 4, 5, 6, 7; DLB 105

Dacre, Charlotte c. 1772-1825(?) .... **NCLC 151**

Dafydd ap Gwilym c. 1320-c. 1380 ... **PC 56**

Dagerman, Stig (Halvard) 1923-1954 .... **TCLC 17**
See also CA 117; 155; DLB 259; EWL 3

D'Aguiar, Fred 1960- ... **BLC 2:1; CLC 145**
See also CA 148; CANR 83, 101; CN 7; CP 5, 6, 7; DLB 157; EWL 3

Dahl, Roald 1916-1990 ... **CLC 1, 6, 18, 79; TCLC 173**
See also AAYA 15; BPFB 1; BRWS 4; BYA 5; CA 1-4R; 133; CANR 6, 32, 37, 62; CLR 1, 7, 41, 111; CN 1, 2, 3, 4; CPW; DA3; DAB; DAC; DAM MST, NOV, POP; DLB 139, 255; HGG; JRDA; MAICYA 1, 2; MTCW 1, 2; MTFW 2005; RGSF 2; SATA 1, 26, 73; SATA-Obit 65; SSFS 4, 30; TEA; YAW

Dahlberg, Edward 1900-1977 ...... **CLC 1, 7, 14; TCLC 208**
See also CA 9-12R; 69-72; CANR 31, 62; CN 1, 2; DLB 48; MAL 5; MTCW 1; RGAL 4

Dahlie, Michael 1970(?)- .... **CLC 299**
See also CA 283

Daitch, Susan 1954- .... **CLC 103**
See also CA 161

Dale, Colin
See Lawrence, T. E.

Dale, George E.
See Asimov, Isaac

d'Alembert, Jean Le Rond 1717-1783 .... **LC 126**

Dalton, Roque 1935-1975(?) .... **HLCS 1; PC 36**
See also CA 176; DLB 283; HW 2

Daly, Elizabeth 1878-1967 .... **CLC 52**
See also CA 23-24; 25-28R; CANR 60; CAP 2; CMW 4

Daly, Mary 1928-2010 .... **CLC 173**
See also CA 25-28R; CANR 30, 62, 166; FW; GLL 1; MTCW 1

Daly, Maureen 1921-2006 .... **CLC 17**
See also AAYA 5, 58; BYA 6; CA 253; CANR 37, 83, 108; CLR 96; JRDA; MAI-

CYA 1, 2; SAAS 1; SATA 2, 129; SATA-Obit 176; WYA; YAW

Damas, Leon-Gontran 1912-1978 .... **CLC 84; TCLC 204**
See also BW 1; CA 125; 73-76; EWL 3

Damocles
See Benedetti, Mario

Dana, Richard Henry Sr. 1787-1879 .... **NCLC 53**

Dangarembga, Tsitsi 1959- .... **BLC 2:1**
See also BW 3; CA 163; DLB 360; NFS 28; WLIT 2

Daniel, Samuel 1562(?)-1619 ...... **LC 24, 171**
See also DLB 62; RGEL 2

Daniels, Brett
See Adler, Renata

Dannay, Frederic 1905-1982 .... **CLC 3, 11**
See also BPFB 3; CA 1-4R; 107; CANR 1, 39; CMW 4; DAM POP; DLB 137; MSW; MTCW 1; RGAL 4

D'Annunzio, Gabriele 1863-1938 .... **TCLC 6, 40, 215**
See also CA 104; 155; EW 8; EWL 3; RGWL 2, 3; TWA; WLIT 7

Danois, N. le
See Gourmont, Remy(-Marie-Charles) de

Dante 1265-1321 .... **CMLC 3, 18, 39, 70, 142; PC 21, 108; WLCS**
See also DA; DA3; DAB; DAC; DAM MST, POET; EFS 1:1, 2:1; EW 1; LAIT 1; RGWL 2, 3; TWA; WLIT 7; WP

d'Antibes, Germain
See Simenon, Georges

Danticat, Edwidge 1969- .... **BLC 2:1; CLC 94, 139, 228; SSC 100**
See also AAYA 29, 85; CA 152, 192; CAAE 192; CANR 73, 129, 179; CN 7; DLB 350; DNFS 1; EXPS; LATS 1:2; LNFS 3; MTCW 2; MTFW 2005; NFS 28, 37; SSFS 1, 25, 37; YAW

Danvers, Dennis 1947- .... **CLC 70**

Danziger, Paula 1944-2004 .... **CLC 21**
See also AAYA 4, 36; BYA 6, 7, 14; CA 112; 115; 229; CANR 37, 132; CLR 20; JRDA; MAICYA 1, 2; MTFW 2005; SATA 36, 63, 102, 149; SATA-Brief 30; SATA-Obit 155; WYA; YAW

Dao, Bei
See Bei Dao

Da Ponte, Lorenzo 1749-1838 .... **NCLC 50**

d'Aragona, Tullia 1510(?)-1556 .... **LC 121**

Darko, Amma 1956- .... **BLC 2:1; CLC 341**

Darley, George 1795-1846 .. **NCLC 2; PC 125**
See also DLB 96; RGEL 2

Dario, Ruben 1867-1916 ..... **HLC 1; PC 15; TCLC 4, 265**
See also CA 131; CANR 81; DAM MULT; DLB 290; EWL 3; HW 1, 2; LAW; MTCW 1, 2; MTFW 2005; RGWL 2, 3

Darrow, Clarence (Seward) 1857-1938 .... **TCLC 81**
See also CA 164; DLB 303

Darwin, Charles 1809-1882 .... **NCLC 57**
See also BRWS 7; DLB 57, 166; LATS 1:1; RGEL 2; TEA; WLIT 4

Darwin, Erasmus 1731-1802 .... **NCLC 106**
See also BRWS 16; DLB 93; RGEL 2

Darwish, Mahmoud 1941-2008 .... **PC 86**
See also CA 164; CANR 133; CWW 2; EWL 3; MTCW 2; MTFW 2005

Darwish, Mahmud -2008
See Darwish, Mahmoud

Daryush, Elizabeth 1887-1977 .... **CLC 6, 19**
See also CA 49-52; CANR 3, 81; DLB 20

Das, Kamala 1934-2009 .... **CLC 191; PC 43**
See also CA 101; 287; CANR 27, 59; CP 1, 2, 3, 4, 5, 6, 7; CWP; DLB 323; FW

2; MSW; MTCW 1, 2; MTFW 2005; NFS 28; RGEL 2; RGSF 2; RHW; SATA 24; SCFW 1, 2; SFW 4; SSFS 2; TEA; WCH; WLIT 4; WYA; YAW

Doyle, Conan
See Doyle, Sir Arthur Conan

Doyle, John
See Graves, Robert

Doyle, Roddy 1958- .... **CLC 81, 178**
See also AAYA 14; BRWS 5; CA 143; CANR 73, 128, 168, 200, 235; CN 6, 7; DA3; DLB 194, 326; MTCW 2; MTFW 2005

Doyle, Sir A. Conan
See Doyle, Sir Arthur Conan

Dr. A
See Asimov, Isaac; Silverstein, Alvin; Silverstein, Virginia B.

Drabble, Margaret 1939- ..... **CLC 2, 3, 5, 8, 10, 22, 53, 129**
See also BRWS 4; CA 13-16R; CANR 18, 35, 63, 112, 131, 174, 218; CDBLB 1960 to Present; CN 1, 2, 3, 4, 5, 6, 7; CPW; DA3; DAB; DAC; DAM MST, NOV, POP; DLB 14, 155, 231; EWL 3; FW; MTCW 1, 2; MTFW 2005; RGEL 2; SATA 48; TEA

Drakulic, Slavenka 1949- .... **CLC 173**
See also CA 144; CANR 92, 198, 229; DLB 353

Drakulic, Slavenka
See Drakulic, Slavenka

Drakulic-Ilic, Slavenka
See Drakulic, Slavenka

Drakulic-Ilic, Slavenka
See Drakulic, Slavenka

Drapier, M. B.
See Swift, Jonathan

Drayham, James
See Mencken, H. L.

Drayton, Michael 1563-1631 ...... **LC 8, 161; PC 98**
See also DAM POET; DLB 121; RGEL 2

Dreadstone, Carl
See Campbell, Ramsey

Dreiser, Theodore 1871-1945 .... **SSC 30, 114; TCLC 10, 18, 35, 83, 277; WLC 2**
See also AMW; AMWC 2; AMWR 2; BYA 15, 16; CA 106; 132; CDALB 1865-1917; DA; DA3; DAC; DAM MST, NOV; DLB 9, 12, 102, 137, 361, 368; DLBD 1; EWL 3; LAIT 2; LMFS 2; MAL 5; MTCW 1, 2; MTFW 2005; NFS 8, 17; RGAL 4; TUS

Dreiser, Theodore Herman Albert
See Dreiser, Theodore

Drexler, Rosalyn 1926- .... **CLC 2, 6**
See also CA 81-84; CAD; CANR 68, 124; CD 5, 6; CWD; MAL 5

Dreyer, Carl Theodor 1889-1968 ... **CLC 16**
See also CA 116

Drieu la Rochelle, Pierre 1893-1945 .... **TCLC 21**
See also CA 117; 250; DLB 72; EWL 3; GFL 1789 to the Present

Drieu la Rochelle, Pierre-Eugene 1893-1945
See Drieu la Rochelle, Pierre

Drinkwater, John 1882-1937 .... **TCLC 57**
See also CA 109; 149; DLB 10, 19, 149; RGEL 2

Drop Shot
See Cable, George Washington

Droste-Hulshoff, Annette Freiin von 1797-1848 .... **NCLC 3, 133, 273**
See also CDWLB 2; DLB 133; RGSF 2; RGWL 2, 3

Durrenmatt, Friedrich 1921-1990 ... **CLC 1, 4, 8, 11, 15, 43, 102**
See also CA 17-20R; CANR 33; CDWLB 2; CMW 4; DAM DRAM; DLB 69, 124; EW

13; EWL 3; MTCW 1, 2; RGHL; RGWL 2, 3

Drummond, Walter
See Silverberg, Robert

Drummond, William Henry 1854-1907 .... **TCLC 25**
See also CA 160; DLB 92

Drummond de Andrade, Carlos 1902-1987 .... **CLC 18; TCLC 139**
See also CA 132; 123; DLB 307; EWL 3; LAW; RGWL 2, 3

Drummond of Hawthornden, William 1585-1649 .... **LC 83**
See also DLB 121, 213; RGEL 2

Drury, Allen (Stuart) 1918-1998 .... **CLC 37**
See also CA 57-60; 170; CANR 18, 52; CN 1, 2, 3, 4, 5, 6; INT CANR-18

Druse, Eleanor
See King, Stephen

Dryden, John 1631-1700 ... **DC 3; LC 3, 21, 115, 188; PC 25; WLC 2**
See also BRW 2; BRWR 3; CDBLB 1660-1789; DA; DAB; DAC; DAM DRAM, MST, POET; DLB 80, 101, 131; EXPP; IDTP; LMFS 1; RGEL 2; TEA; WLIT 3

du Aime, Albert
See Wharton, William

du Aime, Albert William
See Wharton, William

Du Bellay, Joachim 1524-1560 .... **LC 92; PC 144**
See also DLB 327; GFL Beginnings to 1789; RGWL 2, 3

Duberman, Martin 1930- .... **CLC 8**
See also CA 1-4R; CAD; CANR 2, 63, 137, 174, 233; CD 5, 6

Dubie, Norman (Evans) 1945- .... **CLC 36**
See also CA 69-72; CANR 12, 115; CP 3, 4, 5, 6, 7; DLB 120; PFS 12

Du Bois, W. E. B. 1868-1963 .... **BLC 1:1; CLC 1, 2, 13, 64, 96; HR 1:2; TCLC 169; WLC 2**
See also AAYA 40; AFAW 1, 2; AMWC 1; AMWS 2; BW 1, 3; CA 85-88; CANR 34, 82, 132; CDALB 1865-1917; DA; DA3; DAC; DAM MST, MULT, NOV; DLB 47, 50, 91, 246, 284; EWL 3; EXPP; LAIT 2; LMFS 2; MAL 5; MTCW 1, 2; MTFW 2005; NCFS 1; PFS 13; RGAL 4; SATA 42

Du Bois, William Edward Burghardt
See Du Bois, W. E. B.

Dubos, Jean-Baptiste 1670-1742 ...... **LC 197**

Dubus, Andre 1936-1999 .... **CLC 13, 36, 97; SSC 15, 118**
See also AMWS 7; CA 21-24R; 177; CANR 17; CN 5, 6; CSW; DLB 130; INT CANR-17; RGAL 4; SSFS 10, 36; TCLE 1:1

Duca Minimo
See D'Annunzio, Gabriele

Ducharme, Rejean 1941- .... **CLC 74**
See also CA 165; DLB 60

du Chatelet, Emilie 1706-1749 .... **LC 96**
See also DLB 313

Duchen, Claire .... **CLC 65**

Duck, Stephen 1705(?)-1756 .... **PC 89**
See also DLB 95; RGEL 2

Duclos, Charles Pinot- 1704-1772 .... **LC 1**
See also GFL Beginnings to 1789

Ducornet, Erica 1943- .... **CLC 232**
See also CA 37-40R; CANR 14, 34, 54, 82, 236; SATA 7

Ducornet, Rikki
See Ducornet, Erica

Dudek, Louis 1918-2001 .... **CLC 11, 19**
See also CA 45-48; 215; CAAS 14; CANR 1; CP 1, 2, 3, 4, 5, 6, 7; DLB 88

Duerrematt, Friedrich
See Durrenmatt, Friedrich

Duff Gordon, Lucie 1821-1869 ... **NCLC 262**
See also DLB 166

Duffy, Bruce 1951- .... **CLC 50**
See also CA 172; CANR 238

Duffy, Carol Ann 1955- .... **CLC 337**
See also CA 119; CANR 70, 120, 203; CP 5, 6, 7; CWP; PFS 25; SATA 95, 165

Duffy, Maureen 1933- .... **CLC 37**
See also CA 25-28R; CANR 33, 68; CBD; CN 1, 2, 3, 4, 5, 6, 7; CP 5, 6, 7; CWD; CWP; DFS 15; DLB 14, 310; FW; MTCW 1

Duffy, Maureen Patricia
See Duffy, Maureen

Du Fu
See Tu Fu

Dugan, Alan 1923-2003 .... **CLC 2, 6**
See also CA 81-84; 220; CANR 119; CP 1, 2, 3, 4, 5, 6, 7; DLB 5; MAL 5; PFS 10

du Gard, Roger Martin
See Martin du Gard, Roger

du Guillet, Pernette 1520(?)-1545 .... **LC 190**
See also DLB 327

Duhamel, Georges 1884-1966 .... **CLC 8**
See also CA 81-84; 25-28R; CANR 35; DLB 65; EWL 3; GFL 1789 to the Present; MTCW 1

du Hault, Jean
See Grindel, Eugene

Dujardin, Edouard (Emile Louis) 1861-1949 .... **TCLC 13**
See also CA 109; DLB 123

Duke, Raoul
See Thompson, Hunter S.

Dulles, John Foster 1888-1959 ..... **TCLC 72**
See also CA 115; 149

Dumas, Alexandre (père) 1802-1870 .... **NCLC 11, 71, 271; WLC 2**
See also AAYA 22; BYA 3; CLR 134; DA; DA3; DAB; DAC; DAM MST, NOV; DLB 119, 192; EW 6; GFL 1789 to the Present; LAIT 1, 2; NFS 14, 19, 41; RGWL 2, 3; SATA 18; TWA; WCH

Dumas, Alexandre (fils) 1824-1895 .... **DC 1; NCLC 9**
See also DLB 192; GFL 1789 to the Present; RGWL 2, 3

Dumas, Claudine
See Malzberg, Barry N(athaniel)

Dumas, Henry L. 1934-1968 .... **BLC 2:1; CLC 6, 62; SSC 107**
See also BW 1; CA 85-88; DLB 41; RGAL 4

du Maurier, Daphne 1907-1989 .... **CLC 6, 11, 59; SSC 18, 129; TCLC 209**
See also AAYA 37; BPFB 1; BRWS 3; CA 5-8R; 128; CANR 6, 55; CMW 4; CN 1, 2, 3, 4; CPW; DA3; DAB; DAC; DAM MST, POP; DLB 191; GL 2; HGG; LAIT 3; MSW; MTCW 1, 2; NFS 12; RGEL 2; RGSF 2; RHW; SATA 27; SATA-Obit 60; SSFS 14, 16; TEA

Du Maurier, George 1834-1896 .... **NCLC 86**
See also DLB 153, 178; RGEL 2

Dunbar, Alice
See Nelson, Alice Ruth Moore Dunbar

Dunbar, Alice Moore
See Nelson, Alice Ruth Moore Dunbar

Dunbar, Paul Laurence 1872-1906 ...... **BLC 1:1; PC 5; SSC 8; TCLC 2, 12; WLC 2**
See also AAYA 75; AFAW 1, 2; AMWS 2; BW 1, 3; CA 104; 124; CANR 79; CDALB 1865-1917; DA; DA3; DAC; DAM MST, MULT, POET; DLB 50, 54, 78; EXPP; MAL 5; PFS 33, 40; RGAL 4; SATA 34

Dunbar, William 1460(?)-1520(?) .... **LC 20; PC 67**
See also BRWS 8; DLB 132, 146; RGEL 2

Dunbar-Nelson, Alice
    See Nelson, Alice Ruth Moore Dunbar
Dunbar-Nelson, Alice Moore
    See Nelson, Alice Ruth Moore Dunbar
Duncan, Dora Angela
    See Duncan, Isadora
Duncan, Isadora 1877(?)-1927 ...... **TCLC 68**
    See also CA 118; 149
Duncan, Lois 1934- .... **CLC 26**
    See also AAYA 4, 34; BYA 6, 8; CA 1-4R;
    CANR 2, 23, 36, 111; CLR 29, 129; JRDA;
    MAICYA 1, 2; MAICYAS 1; MTFW 2005;
    SAAS 2; SATA 1, 36, 75, 133, 141, 219;
    SATA-Essay 141; WYA; YAW
Duncan, Robert 1919-1988 .... **CLC 1, 2,
    4, 7, 15, 41, 55; PC 2, 75**
    See also BG 1:2; CA 9-12R; 124; CANR 28,
    62; CP 1, 2, 3, 4; DAM POET; DLB 5, 16,
    193; EWL 3; MAL 5; MTCW 1, 2; MTFW
    2005; PFS 13; RGAL 4; WP
Duncan, Sara Jeannette 1861-1922 .. **TCLC 60**
    See also CA 157; DLB 92
Dunlap, William 1766-1839 .... **NCLC 2, 244**
    See also DLB 30, 37, 59; RGAL 4
Dunn, Douglas (Eaglesham) 1942- .. **CLC 6, 40**
    See also BRWS 10; CA 45-48; CANR 2, 33,
    126; CP 1, 2, 3, 4, 5, 6, 7; DLB 40; MTCW 1
Dunn, Katherine 1945- .... **CLC 71**
    See also CA 33-36R; CANR 72; HGG;
    MTCW 2; MTFW 2005
Dunn, Stephen 1939- .... **CLC 36, 206**
    See also AMWS 11; CA 33-36R; CANR 12, 48,
    53, 105; CP 3, 4, 5, 6, 7; DLB 105, 238; PFS
    21
Dunn, Stephen Elliott
    See Dunn, Stephen
Dunne, Finley Peter 1867-1936 .... **TCLC 28**
    See also CA 108; 178; DLB 11, 23; RGAL 4
Dunne, John Gregory 1932-2003 ... **CLC 28**
    See also CA 25-28R; 222; CANR 14, 50;
    CN 5, 6, 7; DLBY 1980
Dunne, Mary Chavelita
    See Egerton, George
Duns Scotus, John
    See Scotus, John Duns
Dunton, John 1659-1733 .... **LC 219**
    See also DLB 170
Duong, Thu Huong 1947- .... **CLC 273**
    See also CA 152; CANR 106, 166; DLB
    348; NFS 23
Duong Thu Huong
    See Duong, Thu Huong
du Perry, Jean
    See Simenon, Georges
Durang, Christopher 1949- .... **CLC 27, 38**
    See also CA 105; CAD; CANR 50, 76, 130;
    CD 5, 6; MTCW 2; MTFW 2005
Durang, Christopher Ferdinand
    See Durang, Christopher
Duras, Claire de 1777-1832 .... **NCLC 154**
Duras, Marguerite 1914-1996 ...... **CLC 3, 6,
    11, 20, 34, 40, 68, 100; SSC 40**
    See also BPFB 1; CA 25-28R; 151; CANR
    50; CWW 2; DFS 21; DLB 83, 321; EWL
    3; FL 1:5; GFL 1789 to the Present; IDFW
    4; MTCW 1, 2; RGWL 2, 3; TWA
Durban, (Rosa) Pam 1947- .... **CLC 39**
    See also CA 123; CANR 98; CSW
Durcan, Paul 1944- .... **CLC 43, 70**
    See also CA 134; CANR 123; CP 1, 5, 6, 7;
    DAM POET; EWL 3
d'Urfe, Honore
    See Urfe, Honore d'
Durfey, Thomas 1653-1723 .... **LC 94**
    See also DLB 80; RGEL 2
Durkheim, Emile 1858-1917 .... **TCLC 55**
    See also CA 249

Durrell, Lawrence 1912-1990 .... **CLC 1, 4,
    6, 8, 13, 27, 41; PC 142**
    See also BPFB 1; BRWR 3; BRWS 1; CA 9-
    12R; 132; CANR 40, 77; CDBLB 1945-
    1960; CN 1, 2, 3, 4; CP 1, 2, 3, 4, 5; DAM
    NOV; DLB 15, 27, 204; DLBY 1990; EWL
    3; MTCW 1, 2; RGEL 2; SFW 4; TEA
Durrell, Lawrence George
    See Durrell, Lawrence
Durrenmatt, Friedrich
    See Durrenmatt, Friedrich
Dutt, Michael Madhusudan
    1824-1873 .... **NCLC 118**
Dutt, Toru 1856-1877 .... **NCLC 29**
    See also DLB 240
Dwight, Timothy 1752-1817 ... **NCLC 13, 245**
    See also DLB 37; RGAL 4
Dworkin, Andrea 1946-2005 ... **CLC 43, 123**
    See also CA 77-80; 238; CAAS 21; CANR
    16, 39, 76, 96; FL 1:5; FW; GLL 1; INT
    CANR-16; MTCW 1, 2; MTFW 2005
Dwyer, Deanna
    See Koontz, Dean
Dwyer, K.R.
    See Koontz, Dean
Dybek, Stuart 1942- .... **CLC 114; SSC 55**
    See also AMWS 23; CA 97-100; CANR 39;
    DLB 130; SSFS 23
Dye, Richard
    See De Voto, Bernard (Augustine)
Dyer, Geoff 1958- .... **CLC 149**
    See also CA 125; CANR 88, 209, 242
Dyer, George 1755-1841 .... **NCLC 129**
    See also DLB 93
Dylan, Bob 1941- .... **CLC 3, 4, 6, 12,
    77, 308; PC 37**
    See also AMWS 18; CA 41-44R; CANR
    108; CP 1, 2, 3, 4, 5, 6, 7; DLB 16
Dyson, John 1943- .... **CLC 70**
    See also CA 144
Dzyubin, Eduard Georgievich
    1895-1934 .... **TCLC 60**
    See also CA 170; DLB 359; EWL 3
E. V. L.
    See Lucas, E(dward) V(errall)
Eagleton, Terence
    See Eagleton, Terry
Eagleton, Terence Francis
    See Eagleton, Terry
Eagleton, Terry 1943- .... **CLC 63, 132**
    See also CA 57-60; CANR 7, 23, 68, 115,
    198, 243; DLB 242; LMFS 2; MTCW 1, 2;
    MTFW 2005
Earl of Orrey
    See Boyle, Roger
Early, Jack
    See Scoppettone, Sandra
Early, Tom
    See Kelton, Elmer
East, Michael
    See West, Morris L(anglo)
Eastaway, Edward
    See Thomas, (Philip) Edward
Eastlake, William (Derry) 1917-1997 ... **CLC 8**
    See also CA 5-8R; 158; CAAS 1; CANR 5,
    63; CN 1, 2, 3, 4, 5, 6; DLB 6, 206; INT
    CANR-5; MAL 5; TCWW 1, 2
Eastland, Sam
    See Watkins, Paul
Eastman, Charles A(lexander)
    1858-1939 .... **NNAL; TCLC 55**
    See also CA 179; CANR 91; DAM MULT;
    DLB 175; YABC 1
Eaton, Edith Maude
    1865-1914 ... **AAL; SSC 157; TCLC 232**
    See also CA 154; DLB 221, 312; FW
Eaton, (Lillie) Winnifred 1875-1954 .... **AAL**
    See also CA 217; DLB 221, 312; RGAL 4

Eberhart, Richard 1904-2005 .... **CLC 3, 11,
    19, 56; PC 76**
    See also AMW; CA 1-4R; 240; CANR 2,
    125; CDALB 1941-1968; CP 1, 2, 3, 4, 5,
    6, 7; DAM POET; DLB 48; MAL 5;
    MTCW 1; RGAL 4
Eberhart, Richard Ghormley
    See Eberhart, Richard
Eberstadt, Fernanda 1960- .... **CLC 39**
    See also CA 136; CANR 69, 128
Ebner, Margaret c. 1291-1351 ..... **CMLC 98**
Echegaray (y Eizaguirre), Jose (Maria Waldo)
    1832-1916 .... **HLCS 1; TCLC 4**
    See also CA 104; CANR 32; DLB 329;
    EWL 3; HW 1; MTCW 1
Echeverria, (Jose) Esteban (Antonino)
    1805-1851 .... **NCLC 18**
    See also LAW
Echo
    See Proust, Marcel
Eckert, Allan W. 1931- .... **CLC 17**
    See also AAYA 18; BYA 2; CA 13-16R;
    CANR 14, 45; INT CANR-14; MAICYA
    2; MAICYAS 1; SAAS 21; SATA 29, 91;
    SATA-Brief 27
Eckhart, Meister
    1260(?)-1327(?) .... **CMLC 9, 80, 131**
    See also DLB 115; LMFS 1
Eckmar, F. R.
    See de Hartog, Jan
Eco, Umberto 1932- ... **CLC 28, 60, 142, 248**
    See also BEST 90:1; BPFB 1; CA 77-80;
    CANR 12, 33, 55, 110, 131, 195, 234;
    CPW; CWW 2; DA3; DAM NOV, POP;
    DLB 196, 242; EWL 3; MSW; MTCW 1, 2;
    MTFW 2005; NFS 22; RGWL 3; WLIT 7
Eddison, E(ric) R(ucker)
    1882-1945 .... **TCLC 15**
    See also CA 109; 156; DLB 255; FANT;
    SFW 4; SUFW 1
Eddy, Mary (Ann Morse) Baker
    1821-1910 .... **TCLC 71**
    See also CA 113; 174
Edel, (Joseph) Leon 1907-1997 .. **CLC 29, 34**
    See also CA 1-4R; 161; CANR 1, 22, 112;
    DLB 103; INT CANR-22
Eden, Emily 1797-1869 .... **NCLC 10**
Edgar, David 1948- .... **CLC 42; DC 44**
    See also CA 57-60; CANR 12, 61, 112;
    CBD; CD 5, 6; DAM DRAM; DFS 15;
    DLB 13, 233; MTCW 1
Edgerton, Clyde 1944- .... **CLC 39**
    See also AAYA 17; CA 118; 134; CANR 64,
    125, 195, 238; CN 7; CSW; DLB 278; INT
    CA-134; TCLE 1:1; YAW
Edgerton, Clyde Carlyle
    See Edgerton, Clyde
Edgeworth, Maria 1768-1849 .... **NCLC 1,
    51, 158, 279; SSC 86**
    See also BRWS 3; CLR 153; DLB 116, 159,
    163; FL 1:3; FW; RGEL 2; SATA 21;
    TEA; WLIT 3
Edmonds, Paul
    See Kuttner, Henry
Edmonds, Walter D(umaux)
    1903-1998 .... **CLC 35**
    See also BYA 2; CA 5-8R; CANR 2; CWRI
    5; DLB 9; LAIT 1; MAICYA 1, 2; MAL 5;
    RHW; SAAS 4; SATA 1, 27; SATA-Obit 99
Edmondson, Wallace
    See Ellison, Harlan
Edson, Margaret 1961- .... **CLC 199; DC 24**
    See also AMWS 18; CA 190; DFS 13; DLB
    266
Edson, Russell 1935- .... **CLC 13**
    See also CA 33-36R; CANR 115; CP 2, 3, 4,
    5, 6, 7; DLB 244; WP
Edwards, Bronwen Elizabeth
    See Rose, Wendy

Forrest, Leon (Richard)
1937-1997 .... **BLCS; CLC 4**
See also AFAW 2; BW 2; CA 89-92; 162;
CAAS 7; CANR 25, 52, 87; CN 4, 5, 6;
DLB 33

Forster, E. M. 1879-1970 .... **CLC 1, 2, 3,
4, 9, 10, 13, 15, 22, 45, 77; SSC 27, 96;
TCLC 125, 264; WLC 2**
See also AAYA 2, 37; BRW 6; BRWR 2; BYA
12; CA 13-14; 25-28R; CANR 45; CAP 1;
CDBLB 1914-1945; DA; DA3; DAB; DAC;
DAM MST, NOV; DLB 34, 98, 162, 178,
195; DLBD 10; EWL 3; EXPN; LAIT 3;
LMFS 1; MTCW 1, 2; MTFW 2005; NCFS
1; NFS 3, 10, 11; RGEL 2; RGSF 2; SATA
57; SUFW 1; TEA; WLIT 4

Forster, Edward Morgan
See Forster, E. M.

Forster, John 1812-1876 .... **NCLC 11**
See also DLB 144, 184

Forster, Margaret 1938- .... **CLC 149**
See also CA 133; CANR 62, 115, 175; CN
4, 5, 6, 7; DLB 155, 271

Forsyth, Frederick 1938- .... **CLC 2, 5, 36**
See also BEST 89:4; CA 85-88; CANR 38,
62, 115, 137, 183, 242; CMW 4; CN 3, 4,
5, 6, 7; CPW; DAM NOV, POP; DLB 87;
MTCW 1, 2; MTFW 2005

Fort, Paul
See Stockton, Francis Richard

Forten, Charlotte
See Grimke, Charlotte L. Forten

Forten, Charlotte L. 1837-1914
See Grimke, Charlotte L. Forten

Fortinbras
See Grieg, (Johan) Nordahl (Brun)

Foscolo, Ugo 1778-1827 ... **NCLC 8, 97, 274**
See also EW 5; WLIT 7

Fosse, Bob 1927-1987 .... **CLC 20**
See also AAYA 82; CA 110; 123

Fosse, Robert L.
See Fosse, Bob

Foster, Hannah Webster
1758-1840 .... **NCLC 99, 252**
See also DLB 37, 200; RGAL 4

Foster, Stephen Collins 1826-1864 .. **NCLC 26**
See also RGAL 4

Foucault, Michel
1926-1984 .... **CLC 31, 34, 69**
See also CA 105; 113; CANR 34; DLB 242;
EW 13; EWL 3; GFL 1789 to the Present;
GLL 1; LMFS 2; MTCW 1, 2; TWA

Fountain, Ben 1958- .... **CLC 354**
See also CA 254; CANR 254

Fouque, Friedrich (Heinrich Karl) de la Motte
1777-1843 .... **NCLC 2**
See also DLB 90; RGWL 2, 3; SUFW 1

Fourier, Charles 1772-1837 .... **NCLC 51**

Fournier, Henri-Alban
See Alain-Fournier

Fournier, Pierre 1916-1997 .... **CLC 11**
See also CA 89-92; CANR 16, 40; EWL 3;
RGHL

Fowles, John 1926-2005 .... **CLC 1, 2, 3, 4,
6, 9, 10, 15, 33, 87, 287; SSC 33, 128**
See also BPFB 1; BRWS 1; CA 5-8R; 245;
CANR 25, 71, 103; CDBLB 1960 to Present; CN 1, 2, 3, 4, 5, 6, 7; DA3; DAB;
DAC; DAM MST; DLB 14, 139, 207;
EWL 3; HGG; MTCW 1, 2; MTFW
2005; NFS 21; RGEL 2; RHW; SATA
22; SATA-Obit 171; TEA; WLIT 4

Fowles, John Robert
See Fowles, John

Fox, Norma Diane
See Mazer, Norma Fox

Fox, Paula 1923- .... **CLC 2, 8, 121**
See also AAYA 3, 37; BYA 3, 8; CA 73-76;
CANR 20, 36, 62, 105, 200, 237; CLR 1,
44, 96; DLB 52; JRDA; MAICYA 1, 2;
MTCW 1; NFS 12; SATA 17, 60, 120,
167; WYA; YAW

Fox, William Price, Jr.
See Fox, William Price

Fox, William Price 1926- .... **CLC 22**
See also CA 17-20R; CAAS 19; CANR 11,
142, 189; CSW; DLB 2; DLBY 1981

Foxe, John 1517(?)-1587 .... **LC 14, 166**
See also DLB 132

Frame, Janet 1924-2004 .... **CLC 2, 3, 6, 22,
66, 96, 237; SSC 29, 127**
See also CA 1-4R; 224; CANR 2, 36, 76,
135, 216; CN 1, 2, 3, 4, 5, 6, 7; CP 2, 3, 4;
CWP; EWL 3; MTCW 1,2; RGEL 2;
RGSF 2; SATA 119; TWA

Frame, Janet Paterson
See Frame, Janet

France, Anatole 1844-1924 .... **TCLC 9**
See also CA 106; 127; DA3; DAM NOV;
DLB 123, 330; EWL 3; GFL 1789 to the
Present; MTCW 1, 2; RGWL 2, 3; SUFW
1; TWA

Francis, Claude .... **CLC 50**
See also CA 192

Francis, Dick
1920-2010 .... **CLC 2, 22, 42, 102**
See also AAYA 5, 21; BEST 89:3; BPFB 1;
CA 5-8R; CANR 9, 42, 68, 100, 141, 179;
CDBLB 1960 to Present; CMW 4; CN 2,
3, 4, 5, 6; DA3; DAM POP; DLB 87;
INT CANR-9; MSW; MTCW 1, 2;
MTFW 2005

Francis, Paula Marie
See Allen, Paula Gunn

Francis, Richard Stanley
See Francis, Dick

Francis, Robert (Churchill)
1901-1987 .... **CLC 15; PC 34**
See also AMWS 9; CA 1-4R; 123; CANR 1;
CP 1, 2, 3, 4; EXPP; PFS 12; TCLE 1:1

Francis, Lord Jeffrey
See Jeffrey, Francis

Franco, Veronica 1546-1591 .... **LC 171**
See also WLIT 7

Frank, Anne 1929-1945 .... **TCLC 17;
WLC 2**
See also AAYA 12; BYA 1; CA 113; 133;
CANR 68; CLR 101; DA; DA3; DAB;
DAC; DAM MST; LAIT 4; MAICYA 2;
MAICYAS 1; MTCW 1, 2; MTFW 2005;
NCFS 2; RGHL; SATA 87; SATA-Brief
42; WYA; YAW

Frank, Annelies Marie
See Frank, Anne

Frank, Bruno 1887-1945 .... **TCLC 81**
See also CA 189; DLB 118; EWL 3

Frank, Elizabeth 1945- .... **CLC 39**
See also CA 121; 126; CANR 78, 150; INT
CA-126

Frankl, Viktor E(mil) 1905-1997 .... **CLC 93**
See also CA 65-68; 161; RGHL

Franklin, Benjamin
See Hasek, Jaroslav

Franklin, Benjamin 1706-1790 .... **LC 25,
134; WLCS**
See also AMW; CDALB 1640-1865; DA;
DA3; DAB; DAC; DAM MST; DLB 24,
43, 73, 183; LAIT 1; RGAL 4; TUS

Franklin, Madeleine
See L'Engle, Madeleine

Franklin, Madeleine L'Engle
See L'Engle, Madeleine

Franklin, Madeleine L'Engle Camp
See L'Engle, Madeleine

Franklin, (Stella Maria Sarah) Miles (Lampe)
1879-1954 .... **TCLC 7**
See also CA 104; 164; DLB 230; FW;
MTCW 2; RGEL 2; TWA

Franzen, Jonathan 1959- .... **CLC 202, 309**
See also AAYA 65; AMWS 20; CA 129;
CANR 105, 166, 219; NFS 40;

Fraser, Antonia 1932- .... **CLC 32, 107**
See also AAYA 57; CA 85-88; CANR 44,
65, 119, 164, 225; CMW; DLB 276;
MTCW 1, 2; MTFW 2005; SATA-Brief 32

Fraser, George MacDonald
1925-2008 .... **CLC 7**
See also AAYA 48; CA 45-48; 180; 268;
CAAE 180; CANR 2, 48, 74, 192; DLB
352; MTCW 2; RHW

Fraser, Sylvia 1935- .... **CLC 64**
See also CA 45-48; CANR 1, 16, 60; CCA 1

Frater Perdurabo
See Crowley, Edward Alexander

Frayn, Michael 1933- .... **CLC 3, 7, 31,
47, 176, 315; DC 27**
See also AAYA 69; BRWC 2; BRWS 7; CA
5-8R; CANR 30, 69, 114, 133, 166, 229;
CBD; CD 5, 6; CN 1, 2, 3, 4, 5, 6, 7; DAM
DRAM, NOV; DFS 22, 28; DLB 13, 14,
194, 245; FANT; MTCW 1, 2; MTFW
2005; SFW 4

Fraze, Candida 1945- .... **CLC 50**
See also CA 126

Fraze, Candida Merrill
See Fraze, Candida

Frazer, Andrew
See Marlowe, Stephen

Frazer, J(ames) G(eorge)
1854-1941 .... **TCLC 32**
See also BRWS 3; CA 118; NCFS 5

Frazer, Robert Caine
See Creasey, John

Frazer, Sir James George
See Frazer, J(ames) G(eorge)

Frazier, Charles 1950- .... **CLC 109, 224**
See also AAYA 34; CA 161; CANR 126, 170,
235; CSW; DLB 292; MTFW 2005; NFS 25

Frazier, Charles R.
See Frazier, Charles

Frazier, Charles Robinson
See Frazier, Charles

Frazier, Ian 1951- .... **CLC 46**
See also CA 130; CANR 54, 93, 193, 227

Frederic, Harold
1856-1898 .... **NCLC 10, 175**
See also AMW; DLB 12, 23; DLBD 13;
MAL 5; NFS 22; RGAL 4

Frederick, John
See Faust, Frederick

Frederick the Great 1712-1786 .... **LC 14**

Fredro, Aleksander 1793-1876 .... **NCLC 8**

Freeling, Nicolas 1927-2003 .... **CLC 38**
See also CA 49-52; 218; CAAS 12; CANR
1, 17, 50, 84; CMW 4; CN 1, 2, 3, 4, 5, 6;
DLB 87

Freeman, Douglas Southall
1886-1953 .... **TCLC 11**
See also CA 109; 195; DLB 17; DLBD 17

Freeman, Judith 1946- .... **CLC 55**
See also CA 148; CANR 120, 179; DLB 256

Freeman, Mary E(leanor) Wilkins
1852-1930 ..... **SSC 1, 47, 113; TCLC 9**
See also CA 106; 177; DLB 12, 78, 221;
EXPS; FW; HGG; MBL; RGAL 4; RGSF
2; SSFS 4, 8, 26; SUFW 1; TUS

Freeman, R(ichard) Austin
1862-1943 .... **TCLC 21**
See also CA 113; CANR 84; CMW 4;
DLB 70

French, Albert 1943- .... **CLC 86**
See also BW 3; CA 167

French, Antonia
See Kureishi, Hanif

French, Marilyn 1929-2009 ...... **CLC 10, 18,
60, 177**

See also BPFB 1; CA 69-72; 286; CANR 3,
31, 134, 163, 220; CN 5, 6, 7; CPW; DAM
DRAM, NOV, POP; FL 1:5; FW; INT
CANR-31; MTCW 1, 2; MTFW 2005

French, Paul
See Asimov, Isaac

Freneau, Philip Morin
1752-1832 .... **NCLC 1, 111, 253**
See also AMWS 2; DLB 37, 43; RGAL 4

Freud, Sigmund 1856-1939 .... **TCLC 52**
See also CA 115; 133; CANR 69; DLB 296;
EW 8; EWL 3; LATS 1:1; MTCW 1, 2;
MTFW 2005; NCFS 3; TWA

Freytag, Gustav 1816-1895 .... **NCLC 109**
See also DLB 129

Friedan, Betty 1921-2006 .... **CLC 74**
See also CA 65-68; 248; CANR 18, 45, 74;
DLB 246; FW; MTCW 1, 2; MTFW 2005;
NCFS 5

Friedan, Betty Naomi
See Friedan, Betty

Friedlander, Saul
See Friedlander, Saul

Friedlander, Saul 1932- .... **CLC 90**
See also CA 117; 130; CANR 72, 214;
RGHL

Friedman, Bernard Harper
See Friedman, B.H.

Friedman, B.H. 1926-2011 .... **CLC 7**
See also CA 1-4R; CANR 3, 48

Friedman, Bruce Jay 1930- ... **CLC 3, 5, 56**
See also CA 9-12R; CAD; CANR 25, 52, 101,
212; CD 5, 6; CN 1, 2, 3, 4, 5, 6, 7; DLB 2,
28, 244; INT CANR-25; MAL 5; SSFS 18

Friel, Brian 1929- .... **CLC 5, 42, 59, 115,**
253; DC 8, 49; SSC 76
See also BRWS 5; CA 21-24R; CANR 33,
69, 131; CBD; CD 5, 6; DFS 11; DLB 13,
319; EWL 3; MTCW 1; RGEL 2; TEA

Friis-Baastad, Babbis Ellinor
1921-1970 .... **CLC 12**
See also CA 17-20R; 134; SATA 7

Frisch, Max 1911-1991 .... **CLC 3, 9, 14, 18,**
32, 44; TCLC 121
See also CA 85-88; 134; CANR 32, 74;
CDWLB 2; DAM DRAM, NOV; DFS
25; DLB 69, 124; EW 13; EWL 3; MTCW
1, 2; MTFW 2005; RGHL; RGWL 2, 3

Froehlich, Peter
See Gay, Peter

Fromentin, Eugene (Samuel Auguste)
1820-1876 .... **NCLC 10, 125**
See also DLB 123, 366; GFL 1789 to the
Present

Frost, Frederick
See Faust, Frederick

Frost, Robert 1874-1963 ...... **CLC 1, 3, 4, 9,**
10, 13, 15, 26, 34, 44; PC 1, 39, 71;
TCLC 236; WLC 2
See also AAYA 21; AMW; AMWR 1; CA
89-92; CANR 33; CDALB 1917-1929;
CLR 67; DA; DA3; DAB; DAC; DAM
MST, POET; DLB 54, 284, 342; DLBD
7; EWL 3; EXPP; MAL 5; MTCW 1, 2;
MTFW 2005; PAB; PFS 1, 2, 3, 4, 5, 6, 7,
10, 13, 32, 35, 41; RGAL 4; SATA 14;
TUS; WP; WYA

Frost, Robert Lee
See Frost, Robert

Froude, James Anthony
1818-1894 .... **NCLC 43**
See also DLB 18, 57, 144

Froy, Herald
See Waterhouse, Keith

Fry, Christopher 1907-2005 .... **CLC 2, 10,**
14; DC 36
See also BRWS 3; CA 17-20R; 240; CAAS
23; CANR 9, 30, 74, 132; CBD; CD 5, 6;
CP 1, 2, 3, 4, 5, 6, 7; DAM DRAM; DLB

13; EWL 3; MTCW 1, 2; MTFW 2005;
RGEL 2; SATA 66; TEA

Frye, (Herman) Northrop
1912-1991 ...... **CLC 24, 70; TCLC 165**
See also CA 5-8R; 133; CANR 8, 37; DLB
67, 68, 246; EWL 3; MTCW 1, 2; MTFW
2005; RGAL 4; TWA

Fuchs, Daniel 1909-1993 .... **CLC 8, 22**
See also CA 81-84; 142; CAAS 5; CANR
40; CN 1, 2, 3, 4, 5; DLB 9, 26, 28; DLBY
1993; MAL 5

Fuchs, Daniel 1934- .... **CLC 34**
See also CA 37-40R; CANR 14, 48

Fuentes, Carlos 1928- ...... **CLC 3, 8, 10, 13,**
22, 41, 60, 113, 288, 354; HLC 1; SSC
24, 125; WLC 2
See also AAYA 4, 45; AITN 2; BPFB 1; CA
69-72; CANR 10, 32, 68, 104, 138, 197;
CDWLB 3; CWW 2; DA; DA3; DAB;
DAC; DAM MST, MULT, NOV; DLB
113; DNFS 2; EWL 3; HW 1, 2; LAIT
3; LATS 1:2; LAW; LAWS 1; LMFS 2;
MTCW 1, 2; MTFW 2005; NFS 8; RGSF
2; RGWL 2, 3; TWA; WLIT 1

Fuentes, Gregorio Lopez y
See Lopez y Fuentes, Gregorio

Fuentes Macias, Carlos Manuel
See Fuentes, Carlos

Fuertes, Gloria
1918-1998 .... **PC 27; TCLC 271**
See also CA 178, 180; DLB 108; HW 2;
SATA 115

Fugard, Athol 1932- .... **CLC 5, 9, 14,**
25, 40, 80, 211; DC 3
See also AAYA 17; AFW; BRWS 15; CA
85-88; CANR 32, 54, 118; CD 5, 6; DAM
DRAM; DFS 3, 6, 10, 24; DLB 225;
DNFS 1, 2; EWL 3; LATS 1:2; MTCW
1; MTFW 2005; RGEL 2; WLIT 2

Fugard, Harold Athol
See Fugard, Athol

Fugard, Sheila 1932- .... **CLC 48**
See also CA 125

Fuguet, Alberto 1964- .... **CLC 308**
See also CA 170; CANR 144

Fujiwara no Teika 1162-1241 ...... **CMLC 73**
See also DLB 203

Fukuyama, Francis 1952- ...... **CLC 131, 320**
See also CA 140; CANR 72, 125, 170, 233

Fuller, Charles (H.), (Jr.) 1939- .... **BLC 1:2;**
CLC 25; DC 1
See also BW 2; CA 108; 112; CAD; CANR
87; CD 5, 6; DAM DRAM, MULT; DFS 8;
DLB 38, 266; EWL 3; INT CA-112; MAL
5; MTCW 1

Fuller, Henry Blake 1857-1929 ... **TCLC 103**
See also CA 108; 177; DLB 12; RGAL 4

Fuller, John (Leopold) 1937- .... **CLC 62**
See also CA 21-24R; CANR 9, 44; CP 1, 2,
3, 4, 5, 6, 7; DLB 40

Fuller, Margaret
1810-1850 .... **NCLC 5, 50, 211**
See also AMWS 2; CDALB 1640-1865;
DLB 1, 59, 73, 183, 223, 239; FW; LMFS
1; SATA 25

Fuller, Roy (Broadbent)
1912-1991 .... **CLC 4, 28**
See also BRWS 7; CA 5-8R; 135; CAAS 10;
CANR 53, 83; CN 1, 2, 3, 4, 5; CP 1, 2, 3,
4, 5; CWRI 5; DLB 15, 20; EWL 3; RGEL
2; SATA 87

Fuller, Sarah Margaret
See Fuller, Margaret

Fuller, Thomas 1608-1661 .... **LC 111**
See also DLB 151

Fulton, Alice 1952- .... **CLC 52**
See also CA 116; CANR 57, 88, 200; CP 5,
6, 7; CWP; DLB 193; PFS 25

Fundi
See Baraka, Amiri

Furey, Michael
See Ward, Arthur Henry Sarsfield

Furphy, Joseph 1843-1912 .... **TCLC 25**
See also CA 163; DLB 230; EWL 3; RGEL 2

Furst, Alan 1941- .... **CLC 255**
See also CA 69-72; CANR 12, 34, 59, 102,
159, 193; DLB 350; DLBY 01

Fuson, Robert H(enderson) 1927- ... **CLC 70**
See also CA 89-92; CANR 103

Fussell, Paul 1924- .... **CLC 74**
See also BEST 90:1; CA 17-20R; CANR 8,
21, 35, 69, 135; INT CANR-21; MTCW 1,
2; MTFW 2005

Futabatei, Shimei 1864-1909 .... **TCLC 44**
See also CA 162; DLB 180; EWL 3; MJW

Futabatei Shimei
See Futabatei, Shimei

Futrelle, Jacques 1875-1912 .... **TCLC 19**
See also CA 113; 155; CMW 4

GAB
See Russell, George William

Gaberman, Judie Angell
See Angell, Judie

Gaboriau, Emile 1835-1873 .... **NCLC 14**
See also CMW 4; MSW

Gadda, Carlo Emilio 1893-1973 .... **CLC 11;**
TCLC 144
See also CA 89-92; DLB 177; EWL 3;
WLIT 7

Gaddis, William 1922-1998 ..... **CLC 1, 3, 6,**
8, 10, 19, 43, 86
See also AMWS 4; BPFB 1; CA 17-20R;
172; CANR 21, 48, 148; CN 1, 2, 3, 4, 5,
6; DLB 2, 278; EWL 3; MAL 5; MTCW 1,
2; MTFW 2005; RGAL 4

Gage, Walter
See Inge, William (Motter)

Gaiman, Neil 1960- .... **CLC 319**
See also AAYA 19, 42, 82; CA 133; CANR
81, 129, 188; CLR 109, 177; DLB 261;
HGG; MTFW 2005; SATA 85, 146, 197,
228; SFW 4; SUFW 2

Gaiman, Neil Richard
See Gaiman, Neil

Gaines, Ernest J. 1933- .... **BLC 1:2;**
CLC 3, 11, 18, 86, 181, 300; SSC 68, 137
See also AAYA 18; AFAW 1, 2; AITN 1;
BPFB 2; BW 2, 3; BYA 6; CA 9-12R;
CANR 6, 24, 42, 75, 126; CDALB 1968-
1988; CLR 62; CN 1, 2, 3, 4, 5, 6, 7; CSW;
DA3; DAM MULT; DLB 2, 33, 152;
DLBY 1980; EWL 3; EXPN; LAIT 5;
LATS 1:2; MAL 5; MTCW 1, 2; MTFW
2005; NFS 5, 7, 16; RGAL 4; RGSF 2;
RHW; SATA 86; SSFS 5; YAW

Gaines, Ernest James
See Gaines, Ernest J.

Gaitskill, Mary 1954- .... **CLC 69, 300**
See also CA 128; CANR 61, 152, 208; DLB
244; TCLE 1:1

Gaitskill, Mary Lawrence
See Gaitskill, Mary

Gaius Suetonius Tranquillus
See Suetonius

Galdos, Benito Perez
See Perez Galdos, Benito

Gale, Zona 1874-1938 ...... **DC 30; SSC 159;**
TCLC 7
See also CA 105; 153; CANR 84; DAM
DRAM; DFS 17; DLB 9, 78, 228; RGAL 4

Galeano, Eduardo 1940- .... **CLC 72;**
HLCS 1
See also CA 29-32R; CANR 13, 32, 100,
163, 211; HW 1

Galeano, Eduardo Hughes
See Galeano, Eduardo

Galiano, Juan Valera y Alcala
   See Valera y Alcala-Galiano, Juan
Galilei, Galileo 1564-1642 .... **LC 45, 188**
Gallagher, Tess 1943- ..... **CLC 18, 63; PC 9**
   See also CA 106; CP 3, 4, 5, 6, 7; CWP;
   DAM POET; DLB 120, 212, 244; PFS 16
Gallant, Mavis 1922- .... **CLC 7, 18, 38,
   172, 288; SSC 5, 78**
   See also CA 69-72; CANR 29, 69, 117;
   CCA 1; CN 1, 2, 3, 4, 5, 6, 7; DAC; DAM
   MST; DLB 53; EWL 3; MTCW 1, 2;
   MTFW 2005; RGEL 2; RGSF 2
Gallant, Roy A(rthur) 1924- .... **CLC 17**
   See also CA 5-8R; CANR 4, 29, 54, 117;
   CLR 30; MAICYA 1, 2; SATA 4, 68, 110
Gallico, Paul 1897-1976 .... **CLC 2**
   See also AITN 1; CA 5-8R; 69-72; CANR
   23; CN 1, 2; DLB 9, 171; FANT; MAICYA
   1, 2; SATA 13
Gallico, Paul William
   See Gallico, Paul
Gallo, Max Louis 1932- .... **CLC 95**
   See also CA 85-88
Gallois, Lucien
   See Desnos, Robert
Gallup, Ralph
   See Whitemore, Hugh (John)
Galsworthy, John 1867-1933 .... **SSC 22;
   TCLC 1, 45; WLC 2**
   See also BRW 6; CA 104; 141; CANR 75;
   CDBLB 1890-1914; DA; DA3; DAB;
   DAC; DAM DRAM, MST, NOV; DLB
   10, 34, 98, 162, 330; DLBD 16; EWL
   3; MTCW 2; RGEL 2; SSFS 3; TEA
Galt, John 1779-1839 .... **NCLC 1, 110**
   See also DLB 99, 116, 159; RGEL 2; RGSF 2
Galvin, James 1951- .... **CLC 38**
   See also CA 108; CANR 26
Gamboa, Federico 1864-1939 .... **TCLC 36**
   See also CA 167; HW 2; LAW
Gandhi, M. K.
   See Gandhi, Mohandas Karamchand
Gandhi, Mahatma
   See Gandhi, Mohandas Karamchand
Gandhi, Mohandas Karamchand
   1869-1948 .... **TCLC 59**
   See also CA 121; 132; DA3; DAM MULT;
   DLB 323; MTCW 1, 2
Gann, Ernest Kellogg
   1910-1991 .... **CLC 23**
   See also AITN 1; BPFB 2; CA 1-4R; 136;
   CANR 1, 83; RHW
Gao Xingjian
   See Xingjian, Gao
Garber, Eric
   See Holleran, Andrew
Garber, Esther
   See Lee, Tanith
Garcia Lorca, Federico 1898-1936 ..... **DC 2;
   HLC 2; PC 3, 130; TCLC 1, 7, 49, 181,
   197; WLC 2**
   See also AAYA 46; CA 104; 131; CANR 81;
   DA; DA3; DAB; DAC; DAM DRAM,
   MST, MULT, POET; DLB 108;
   EW 11; EWL 3; HW 1, 2; LATS 1:2;
   MTCW 1, 2; MTFW 2005; PFS 20, 31,
   38; RGWL 2, 3; TWA; WP
Garcia Marquez, Gabriel 1928- ...... **CLC 2,
   3, 8, 10, 15, 27, 47, 55, 68, 170, 254; HLC
   1; SSC 8, 83, 162; WLC 3**
   See also AAYA 3, 33; BEST 89:1, 90:4;
   BPFB 2; BYA 12, 16; CA 33-36R; CANR
   10, 28, 50, 75, 82, 128, 204; CDWLB 3;
   CPW; CWW 2; DA; DA3; DAB; DAC;
   DAM MST, MULT, NOV, POP; DLB 113,
   330; DNFS 1, 2; EWL 3; EXPN; EXPS;
   HW 1, 2; LAIT 2; LATS 1:2; LAW; LAWS
   1; LMFS 2; MTCW 1, 2; MTFW 2005;

NCFS 3; NFS 1, 5, 10; RGSF 2; RGWL 2,
3; SSFS 1, 6, 16, 21, 37; TWA; WLIT 1
Garcia Marquez, Gabriel Jose
   See Garcia Marquez, Gabriel
Garcia, Cristina 1958- .... **CLC 76**
   See also AMWS 11; CA 141; CANR 73,
   130, 172, 243; CN 7; DLB 292; DNFS 1;
   EWL 3; HW 2; LLW; MTFW 2005; NFS
   38; SATA 208
Garcilaso de la Vega, El Inca
   1539-1616 .... **HLCS 1; LC 127**
   See also DLB 318; LAW
Gard, Janice
   See Latham, Jean Lee
Gard, Roger Martin du
   See Martin du Gard, Roger
Gardam, Jane 1928- .... **CLC 43**
   See also CA 49-52; CANR 2, 18, 33, 54,
   106, 167, 206; CLR 12; DLB 14, 161, 231;
   MAICYA 1, 2; MTCW 1; SAAS 9; SATA
   39, 76, 130; SATA-Brief 28; YAW
Gardam, Jane Mary
   See Gardam, Jane
Gardens, S. S.
   See Snodgrass, W. D.
Gardner, Herb(ert George)
   1934-2003 .... **CLC 44**
   See also CA 149; 220; CAD; CANR 119;
   CD 5, 6; DFS 18, 20
Gardner, John, Jr. 1933-1982 ...... **CLC 2, 3,
   5, 7, 8, 10, 18, 28, 34; SSC 7; TCLC 195**
   See also AAYA 45; AITN 1; AMWS 6;
   BPFB 2; CA 65-68; 107; CANR 33, 73;
   CDALBS; CN 2, 3; CPW; DA3; DAM
   NOV, POP; DLB 2; DLBY 1982; EWL
   3; FANT; LATS 1:2; MAL 5; MTCW 1, 2;
   MTFW 2005; NFS 3; RGAL 4; RGSF 2;
   SATA 40; SATA-Obit 31; SSFS 8
Gardner, John 1926-2007 .... **CLC 30**
   See also CA 103; 263; CANR 15, 69, 127,
   183; CMW 4; CPW; DAM POP; MTCW 1
Gardner, John Champlin, Jr.
   See Gardner, John, Jr.
Gardner, John Edmund
   See Gardner, John
Gardner, Miriam
   See Bradley, Marion Zimmer
Gardner, Noel
   See Kuttner, Henry
Gardons, S.S.
   See Snodgrass, W. D.
Garfield, Leon 1921-1996 .... **CLC 12**
   See also AAYA 8, 69; BYA 1, 3; CA 17-
   20R; 152; CANR 38, 41, 78; CLR 21, 166;
   DLB 161; JRDA; MAICYA 1, 2; MAI-
   CYAS 1; SATA 1, 32, 76; SATA-Obit 90;
   TEA; WYA; YAW
Garland, (Hannibal) Hamlin
   1860-1940 ... **SSC 18, 117; TCLC 3, 256**
   See also CA 104; DLB 12, 71, 78, 186;
   MAL 5; RGAL 4; RGSF 2; TCWW 1, 2
Garneau, (Hector de) Saint-Denys
   1912-1943 .... **TCLC 13**
   See also CA 111; DLB 88
Garner, Alan 1934- .... **CLC 17**
   See also AAYA 18; BYA 3, 5; CA 73-76,
   178; CAAE 178; CANR 15, 64, 134; CLR
   20, 130; CPW; DAB; DAM POP; DLB
   161, 261; FANT; MAICYA 1, 2; MTCW 1,
   2; MTFW 2005; SATA 18, 69; SATA-
   Essay 108; SUFW 1, 2; YAW
Garner, Helen 1942- .... **SSC 135**
   See also CA 124; 127; CANR 71, 206; CN
   4, 5, 6, 7; DLB 325; GLL 2; RGSF 2
Garner, Hugh 1913-1979 .... **CLC 13**
   See also CA 69-72; CANR 31; CCA 1; CN
   1, 2; DLB 68

Garnett, David 1892-1981 .... **CLC 3**
   See also CA 5-8R; 103; CANR 17, 79; CN
   1, 2; DLB 34; FANT; MTCW 2; RGEL 2;
   SFW 4; SUFW 1
Garnier, Robert c. 1545-1590 .... **LC 119**
   See also DLB 327; GFL Beginnings to 1789
Garrett, George 1929-2008 .... **CLC 3, 11,
   51; SSC 30**
   See also AMWS 7; BPFB 2; CA 1-4R, 202;
   272; CAAE 202; CAAS 5; CANR 1, 42,
   67, 109, 199; CN 1, 2, 3, 4, 5, 6, 7; CP 1,
   2, 3, 4, 5, 6, 7; CSW; DLB 2, 5, 130, 152;
   DLBY 1983
Garrett, George P.
   See Garrett, George
Garrett, George Palmer
   See Garrett, George
Garrett, George Palmer, Jr.
   See Garrett, George
Garrick, David 1717-1779 .... **DC 50;
   LC 15, 156**
   See also DAM DRAM; DLB 84, 213; RGEL 2
Garrigue, Jean 1914-1972 .... **CLC 2, 8**
   See also CA 5-8R; 37-40R; CANR 20; CP 1;
   MAL 5
Garrison, Frederick
   See Sinclair, Upton
Garrison, William Lloyd
   1805-1879 .... **NCLC 149**
   See also CDALB 1640-1865; DLB 1, 43, 235
Garro, Elena 1920(?)-1998 .... **HLCS 1;
   TCLC 153**
   See also CA 131; 169; CWW 2; DLB 145;
   EWL 3; HW 1; LAWS 1; WLIT 1
Garshin, Vsevolod Mikhailovich
   1855-1888 .... **NCLC 257**
   See also DLB 277
Garth, Will
   See Hamilton, Edmond; Kuttner, Henry
Garvey, Marcus (Moziah, Jr.)
   1887-1940 .... **BLC 1:2; HR 1:2;
   TCLC 41**
   See also BW 1; CA 120; 124; CANR 79;
   DAM MULT; DLB 345
Gary, Romain
   See Kacew, Romain
Gascar, Pierre
   See Fournier, Pierre
Gascoigne, George 1539-1577 .... **LC 108**
   See also DLB 136; RGEL 2
Gascoyne, David (Emery)
   1916-2001 .... **CLC 45**
   See also CA 65-68; 200; CANR 10, 28, 54; CP
   1, 2, 3, 4, 5, 6, 7; DLB 20; MTCW 1; RGEL 2
Gaskell, Elizabeth 1810-1865 ...... **NCLC 5,
   70, 97, 137, 214, 264; SSC 25, 97**
   See also AAYA 80; BRW 5; BRWR 3;
   CDBLB 1832-1890; DAB; DAM MST;
   DLB 21, 144, 159; RGEL 2; RGSF 2; TEA
Gass, William H. 1924- ..... **CLC 1, 2, 8, 11,
   15, 39, 132; SSC 12**
   See also AMWS 6; CA 17-20R; CANR 30,
   71, 100; CN 1, 2, 3, 4, 5, 6, 7; DLB 2, 227;
   EWL 3; MAL 5; MTCW 1, 2; MTFW
   2005; RGAL 4
Gassendi, Pierre 1592-1655 .... **LC 54**
   See also GFL Beginnings to 1789
Gasset, Jose Ortega y
   See Ortega y Gasset, Jose
Gates, Henry Louis, Jr.
   1950- .... **BLCS; CLC 65**
   See also AMWS 20; BW 2, 3; CA 109;
   CANR 25, 53, 75, 125, 203; CSW; DA3;
   DAM MULT; DLB 67; EWL 3; MAL 5;
   MTCW 2; MTFW 2005; RGAL 4
Gatos, Stephanie
   See Katz, Steve
Gautier, Theophile 1811-1872 .... **NCLC 1,
   59, 243, 267; PC 18; SSC 20**

Gilman, Charlotte Perkins
1860-1935 .. **SSC 13, 62, 182; TCLC 9, 37, 117, 201**
See also AAYA 75; AMWS 11; BYA 11; CA 106; 150; DLB 221; EXPS; FL 1:5; FW; HGG; LAIT 2; MBL; MTCW 2; MTFW 2005; NFS 36; RGAL 4; RGSF 2; SFW 4; SSFS 1, 18

Gilmore, Mary (Jean Cameron)
1865-1962 .... **PC 87**
See also CA 114; DLB 260; RGEL 2; SATA 49

Gilmour, David 1946- .... **CLC 35**

Gilpin, William 1724-1804 .... **NCLC 30**

Gilray, J. D.
See Mencken, H. L.

Gilroy, Frank D(aniel) 1925- .... **CLC 2**
See also CA 81-84; CAD; CANR 32, 64, 86; CD 5, 6; DFS 17; DLB 7

Gilstrap, John 1957(?)- .... **CLC 99**
See also AAYA 67; CA 160; CANR 101, 229

Ginsberg, Allen 1926-1997 ...... **CLC 1, 2, 3, 4, 6, 13, 36, 69, 109; PC 4, 47; TCLC 120; WLC 3**
See also AAYA 33; AITN 1; AMWC 1; AMWS 2; BG 1:2; CA 1-4R; 157; CANR 2, 41, 63, 95; CDALB 1941-1968; CP 1, 2, 3, 4, 5, 6; DA; DA3; DAB; DAC; DAM MST, POET; DLB 5, 16, 169, 237; EWL 3; GLL 1; LMFS 2; MAL 5; MTCW 1, 2; MTFW 2005; PAB; PFS 29; RGAL 4; TUS; WP

Ginzburg, Eugenia
See Ginzburg, Evgeniia

Ginzburg, Evgeniia 1904-1977 .... **CLC 59**
See also DLB 302

Ginzburg, Natalia 1916-1991 .... **CLC 5, 11, 54, 70; SSC 65; TCLC 156**
See also CA 85-88; 135; CANR 33; DFS 14; DLB 177; EW 13; EWL 3; MTCW 1, 2; MTFW 2005; RGHL; RGWL 2, 3

Gioia, (Michael) Dana 1950- .... **CLC 251**
See also AMWS 15; CA 130; CANR 70, 88; CP 6, 7; DLB 120, 282; PFS 24

Giono, Jean 1895-1970 .... **CLC 4, 11; TCLC 124**
See also CA 45-48; 29-32R; CANR 2, 35; DLB 72, 321; EWL 3; GFL 1789 to the Present; MTCW 1; RGWL 2, 3

Giovanni, Nikki 1943- ..... **BLC 1:2; CLC 2, 4, 19, 64, 117; PC 19; WLCS**
See also AAYA 22, 85; AITN 1; BW 2, 3; CA 29-32R; CAAS 6; CANR 18, 41, 60, 91, 130, 175; CDALBS; CLR 6, 73; CP 2, 3, 4, 5, 6, 7; CSW; CWP; CWRI 5; DA; DA3; DAB; DAC; DAM MST, MULT, POET; DLB 5, 41; EWL 3; EXPP; INT CANR-18; MAICYA 1, 2; MAL 5; MTCW 1, 2; MTFW 2005; PFS 17, 28, 35, 42; RGAL 4; SATA 24, 107, 208; TUS; YAW

Giovanni, Yolanda Cornelia
See Giovanni, Nikki

Giovanni, Yolande Cornelia
See Giovanni, Nikki

Giovanni, Yolande Cornelia, Jr.
See Giovanni, Nikki

Giovene, Andrea 1904-1998 .... **CLC 7**
See also CA 85-88

Gippius, Zinaida 1869-1945 ... **TCLC 9, 273**
See also CA 106; 212; DLB 295; EWL 3

Gippius, Zinaida Nikolaevna
See Gippius, Zinaida

Guiraldes, Ricardo (Guillermo)
1886-1927 .... **TCLC 39**
See also CA 131; EWL 3; HW 1; LAW; MTCW 1

Giraldi, Giovanni Battista
1504-1573 .... **LC 220**

Giraldi, William .... **CLC 334**
See also CA 329

Giraudoux, Jean 1882-1944 .... **DC 36; TCLC 2, 7**
See also CA 104; 196; DAM DRAM; DFS 28; DLB 65, 321; EW 9; EWL 3; GFL 1789 to the Present; RGWL 2, 3; TWA

Giraudoux, Jean-Hippolyte
See Giraudoux, Jean

Gironella, Jose Maria (Pous)
1917-2003 .... **CLC 11**
See also CA 101; 212; EWL 3; RGWL 2, 3

Gissing, George (Robert) 1857-1903 ..... **SSC 37, 113; TCLC 3, 24, 47**
See also BRW 5; CA 105; 167; DLB 18, 135, 184; RGEL 2; TEA

Gitlin, Todd 1943- .... **CLC 201**
See also CA 29-32R; CANR 25, 50, 88, 179, 227

Giurlani, Aldo
See Palazzeschi, Aldo

Gladkov, Fedor Vasil'evich
See Gladkov, Fyodor (Vasilyevich)

Gladkov, Fyodor (Vasilyevich)
1883-1958 .... **TCLC 27**
See also CA 170; DLB 272; EWL 3

Gladstone, William Ewart
1809-1898 .... **NCLC 213**
See also DLB 57, 184

Glancy, Diane 1941- .... **CLC 210; NNAL**
See also CA 136, 225; CAAE 225; CAAS 24; CANR 87, 162, 217; DLB 175

Glanville, Brian (Lester) 1931- .... **CLC 6**
See also CA 5-8R; CAAS 9; CANR 3, 70; CN 1, 2, 3, 4, 5, 6, 7; DLB 15, 139; SATA 42

Glasgow, Ellen 1873-1945 .... **SSC 34, 130; TCLC 2, 7, 239**
See also AMW; CA 104; 164; DLB 9, 12; MAL 5; MBL; MTCW 2; MTFW 2005; RGAL 4; RHW; SSFS 9; TUS

Glasgow, Ellen Anderson Gholson
See Glasgow, Ellen

Glaspell, Susan 1882(?)-1948 .... **DC 10; SSC 41, 132; TCLC 55, 175**
See also AMWS 3; CA 110; 154; DFS 8, 18, 24; DLB 7, 9, 78, 228; MBL; RGAL 4; SSFS 3; TCWW 2; TUS; YABC 2

Glassco, John 1909-1981 .... **CLC 9**
See also CA 13-16R; 102; CANR 15; CN 1, 2; CP 1, 2, 3; DLB 68

Glasscock, Amnesia
See Steinbeck, John

Glasser, Ronald J. 1940(?)- .... **CLC 37**
See also CA 209; CANR 240

Glassman, Joyce
See Johnson, Joyce

Gluck, Louise 1943- .... **CLC 7, 22, 44, 81, 160, 280; PC 16**
See also AMWS 5; CA 33-36R; CANR 40, 69, 108, 133, 182; CP 1, 2, 3, 4, 5, 6, 7; CWP; DA3; DAM POET; DLB 5; MAL 5; MTCW 2; MTFW 2005; PFS 5, 15; RGAL 4; TCLE 1:1

Gluck, Louise Elisabeth
See Gluck, Louise

Gleick, James 1954- .... **CLC 147**
See also CA 131; 137; CANR 97, 236; INT CA-137

Gleick, James W.
See Gleick, James

Glendinning, Victoria 1937- .... **CLC 50**
See also CA 120; 127; CANR 59, 89, 166; DLB 155

Glissant, Edouard 1928-2011 ... **CLC 10, 68, 337**
See also CA 153; CANR 111; CWW 2; DAM MULT; EWL 3; RGWL 3

Glissant, Edouard Mathieu
See Glissant, Edouard

Gloag, Julian 1930- .... **CLC 40**
See also AITN 1; CA 65-68; CANR 10, 70; CN 1, 2, 3, 4, 5, 6

Glowacki, Aleksander
See Prus, Boleslaw

Glyn, Elinor 1864-1943 .... **TCLC 72**
See also DLB 153; RHW

Gomez de Avellaneda, Gertrudis
1814-1873 .... **NCLC 111, 264**
See also LAW

Gongora (y Argote), Luis de
1561-1627 .... **LC 72**
See also RGWL 2, 3

Gunter, Erich
See Eich, Gunter

Gobineau, Joseph-Arthur
1816-1882 .... **NCLC 17, 259**
See also DLB 123; GFL 1789 to the Present

Godard, Jean-Luc 1930- .... **CLC 20**
See also CA 93-96

Godden, (Margaret) Rumer
1907-1998 .... **CLC 53**
See also AAYA 6; BPFB 2; BYA 2, 5; CA 5-8R; 172; CANR 4, 27, 36, 55, 80; CLR 20; CN 1, 2, 3, 4, 5, 6; CWRI 5; DLB 161; MAICYA 1, 2; RHW; SAAS 12; SATA 3, 36; SATA-Obit 109; TEA

Godoy Alcayaga, Lucila
See Mistral, Gabriela

Godwin, Gail 1937- .... **CLC 5, 8, 22, 31, 69, 125, 331**
See also BPFB 2; CA 29-32R; CANR 15, 43, 69, 132, 218; CN 3, 4, 5, 6, 7; CPW; CSW; DA3; DAM POP; DLB 6, 234, 350; INT CANR-15; MAL 5; MTCW 1, 2; MTFW 2005

Godwin, Gail Kathleen
See Godwin, Gail

Godwin, William 1756-1836 .. **NCLC 14, 130, 287**
See also BRWS 15; CDBLB 1789-1832; CMW 4; DLB 39, 104, 142, 158, 163, 262, 336; GL 2; HGG; RGEL 2

Goebbels, Josef
See Goebbels, (Paul) Joseph

Goebbels, (Paul) Joseph
1897-1945 .... **TCLC 68**
See also CA 115; 148

Goebbels, Joseph Paul
See Goebbels, (Paul) Joseph

Goethe, Johann Wolfgang von
1749-1832 ..... **DC 20; NCLC 4, 22, 34, 90, 154, 247, 266, 270, 284, 287; PC 5, 147; SSC 38, 141; WLC 3**
See also CDWLB 2; DA; DA3; DAB; DAC; DAM DRAM, MST, POET; DLB 94; EW 5; GL 2; LATS 1; LMFS 1:1; RGWL 2, 3; TWA

Gogarty, Oliver St. John
1878-1957 .... **PC 121; TCLC 15**
See also CA 109; 150; DLB 15, 19; RGEL 2

Gogol, Nikolai 1809-1852 .. **DC 1; NCLC 5, 15, 31, 162, 281; SSC 4, 29, 52, 145; WLC 3**
See also DA; DAB; DAC; DAM DRAM, MST; DFS 12; DLB 198; EW 6; EXPS; RGSF 2; RGWL 2, 3; SSFS 7, 32; TWA

Gogol, Nikolai Vasilyevich
See Gogol, Nikolai

Goines, Donald 1937(?)-1974 .... **BLC 1:2; CLC 80**
See also AITN 1; BW 1, 3; CA 124; 114; CANR 82; CMW 4; DA3; DAM MULT, POP; DLB 33

Gold, Herbert 1924- .... **CLC 4, 7, 14, 42, 152**
See also CA 9-12R; CANR 17, 45, 125, 194; CN 1, 2, 3, 4, 5, 6, 7; DLB 2; DLBY 1981; MAL 5

Grade, Khayim
See Grade, Chaim
Graduate of Oxford, A
See Ruskin, John
Grafton, Garth
See Duncan, Sara Jeannette
Grafton, Sue 1940- .... **CLC 163, 299**
See also AAYA 11, 49; BEST 90:3; CA 108; CANR 31, 55, 111, 134, 195; CMW 4; CPW; CSW; DA3; DAM POP; DLB 226; FW; MSW; MTFW 2005
Graham, John
See Phillips, David Graham
Graham, Jorie 1950- **CLC 48, 118, 352; PC 59**
See also AAYA 67; CA 111; CANR 63, 118, 205; CP 4, 5, 6, 7; CWP; DLB 120; EWL 3; MTFW 2005; PFS 10, 17; TCLE 1:1
Graham, R. B. Cunninghame
See Cunninghame Graham, Robert Bontine
Graham, Robert
See Haldeman, Joe
Graham, Robert Bontine Cunninghame
See Cunninghame Graham, Robert Bontine
Graham, Tom
See Lewis, Sinclair
Graham, W(illiam) S(ydney)
1918-1986 .... **CLC 29; PC 127**
See also BRWS 7; CA 73-76; 118; CP 1, 2, 3, 4; DLB 20; RGEL 2
Graham, Winston (Mawdsley)
1910-2003 .... **CLC 23**
See also CA 49-52; 218; CANR 2, 22, 45, 66; CMW 4; CN 1, 2, 3, 4, 5, 6, 7; DLB 77; RHW
Grahame, Kenneth
1859-1932 .... **TCLC 64, 136**
See also BYA 5; CA 108; 136; CANR 80; CLR 5, 135; CWRI 5; DA3; DAB; DLB 34, 141, 178; FANT; MAICYA 1, 2; MTCW 2; NFS 20; RGEL 2; SATA 100; TEA; WCH; YABC 1
Granger, Darius John
See Marlowe, Stephen
Granin, Daniil 1918- .... **CLC 59**
See also DLB 302
Granovsky, Timofei Nikolaevich
1813-1855 .... **NCLC 75**
See also DLB 198
Grant, Skeeter
See Spiegelman, Art
Granville-Barker, Harley
1877-1946 .... **TCLC 2**
See also CA 104; 204; DAM DRAM; DLB 10; RGEL 2
Granzotto, Gianni
See Granzotto, Giovanni Battista
Granzotto, Giovanni Battista
1914-1985 .... **CLC 70**
See also CA 166
Grasemann, Ruth Barbara
See Rendell, Ruth
Grass, Gunter 1927- ..... **CLC 1, 2, 4, 6, 11, 15, 22, 32, 49, 88, 207; WLC 3**
See also BPFB 2; CA 13-16R; CANR 20, 75, 93, 133, 174, 229; CDWLB 2; CWW 2; DA; DA3; DAB; DAC; DAM MST, NOV; DLB 330; EW 13; EWL 3; MTCW 1, 2; MTFW 2005; RGHL; RGWL 2, 3; TWA
Grass, Gunter Wilhelm
See Grass, Gunter
Grass, Guenter
See Grass, Gunter
Gratton, Thomas
See Hulme, T(homas) E(rnest)
Grau, Shirley Ann 1929- ..... **CLC 4, 9, 146; SSC 15**
See also CA 89-92; CANR 22, 69; CN 1, 2, 3, 4, 5, 6, 7; CSW; DLB 2, 218; INT CA-89-92; CANR-22; MTCW 1

Gravel, Fern
See Hall, James Norman
Graver, Elizabeth 1964- .... **CLC 70**
See also CA 135; CANR 71, 129
Graves, Richard Perceval
1895-1985 .... **CLC 44**
See also CA 65-68; CANR 9, 26, 51
Graves, Robert 1895-1985 .... **CLC 1, 2, 6, 11, 39, 44, 45; PC 6**
See also BPFB 2; BRW 7; BYA 4; CA 5-8R; 117; CANR 5, 36; CDBLB 1914-1945; CN 1, 2, 3; CP 1, 2, 3, 4; DA3; DAB; DAC; DAM MST, POET; DLB 20, 100, 191; DLBD 18; DLBY 1985; EWL 3; LATS 1:1; MTCW 1, 2; MTFW 2005; NCFS 2; NFS 21; RGEL 2; RHW; SATA 45; TEA
Graves, Robert von Ranke
See Graves, Robert
Graves, Valerie
See Bradley, Marion Zimmer
Gray, Alasdair 1934- .... **CLC 41, 275**
See also BRWS 9; CA 126; CANR 47, 69, 106, 140; CN 4, 5, 6, 7; DLB 194, 261, 319; HGG; INT CA-126; MTCW 1, 2; MTFW 2005; RGSF 2; SUFW 2
Gray, Amlin 1946- .... **CLC 29**
See also CA 138
Gray, Francine du Plessix
1930- .... **CLC 22, 153**
See also BEST 90:3; CA 61-64; CAAS 2; CANR 11, 33, 75, 81, 197; DAM NOV; INT CANR-11; MTCW 1, 2; MTFW 2005
Gray, John (Henry) 1866-1934 ..... **TCLC 19**
See also CA 119; 162; RGEL 2
Gray, John Lee
See Jakes, John
Gray, Simon 1936-2008 .... **CLC 9, 14, 36**
See also AITN 1; CA 21-24R; 275; CAAS 3; CANR 32, 69, 208; CBD; CD 5, 6; CN 1, 2, 3; DLB 13; EWL 3; MTCW 1; RGEL 2
Gray, Simon James Holliday
See Gray, Simon
Gray, Spalding 1941-2004 ...... **CLC 49, 112; DC 7**
See also AAYA 62; CA 128; 225; CAD; CANR 74, 138; CD 5, 6; CPW; DAM POP; MTCW 2; MTFW 2005
Gray, Thomas 1716-1771 ..... **LC 4, 40, 178; PC 2, 80; WLC 3**
See also BRW 3; CDBLB 1660-1789; DA; DA3; DAB; DAC; DAM MST; DLB 109; EXPP; PAB; PFS 9; RGEL 2; TEA; WP
Grayson, David
See Baker, Ray Stannard
Grayson, Richard (A.) 1951- .... **CLC 38**
See also CA 85-88; 210; CAAE 210; CANR 14, 31, 57; DLB 234
Greeley, Andrew M. 1928- .... **CLC 28**
See also BPFB 2; CA 5-8R; CAAS 7; CANR 7, 43, 69, 104, 136, 184; CMW 4; CPW; DA3; DAM POP; MTCW 1, 2; MTFW 2005
Green, Anna Katharine
1846-1935 .... **TCLC 63**
See also CA 112; 159; CMW 4; DLB 202, 221; MSW
Green, Brian
See Card, Orson Scott
Green, Hannah
See Greenberg, Joanne (Goldenberg)
Green, Hannah 1927(?)-1996 .... **CLC 3**
See also CA 73-76; CANR 59, 93; NFS 10
Green, Henry
See Yorke, Henry Vincent
Green, Julian
See Green, Julien

Green, Julien 1900-1998 .... **CLC 3, 11, 77**
See also CA 21-24R; 169; CANR 33, 87; CWW 2; DLB 4, 72; EWL 3; GFL 1789 to the Present; MTCW 2; MTFW 2005
Green, Julien Hartridge
See Green, Julien
Green, Paul (Eliot) 1894-1981 .... **CLC 25; DC 37**
See also AITN 1; CA 5-8R; 103; CAD; CANR 3; DAM DRAM; DLB 7, 9, 249; DLBY 1981; MAL 5; RGAL 4
Greenaway, Peter 1942- .... **CLC 159**
See also CA 127
Greenberg, Ivan 1908-1973 .... **CLC 24**
See also CA 85-88; DLB 137; MAL 5
Greenberg, Joanne (Goldenberg)
1932- .... **CLC 7, 30**
See also AAYA 12, 67; CA 5-8R; CANR 14, 32, 69; CN 6, 7; DLB 335; NFS 23; SATA 25; YAW
Greenberg, Richard 1959(?)- .... **CLC 57**
See also CA 138; CAD; CD 5, 6; DFS 24
Greenblatt, Stephen J. 1943- .. **CLC 70, 334**
See also CA 49-52; CANR 115; LNFS 1
Greenblatt, Stephen Jay
See Greenblatt, Stephen J.
Greene, Bette 1934- .... **CLC 30**
See also AAYA 7, 69; BYA 3; CA 53-56; CANR 4, 146; CLR 2, 140; CWRI 5; JRDA; LAIT 4; MAICYA 1, 2; NFS 10; SAAS 16; SATA 8, 102, 161; WYA; YAW
Greene, Gael .... **CLC 8**
See also CA 13-16R; CANR 10, 166
Greene, Graham 1904-1991 .... **CLC 1, 3, 6, 9, 14, 18, 27, 37, 70, 72, 125; DC 41; SSC 29, 121; WLC 3**
See also AAYA 61; AITN 2; BPFB 2; BRWR 2; BRWS 1; BYA 3; CA 13-16R; 133; CANR 35, 61, 131; CBD; CDBLB 1945-1960; CMW 4; CN 1, 2, 3, 4; DA; DA3; DAB; DAC; DAM MST, NOV; DLB 13, 15, 77, 100, 162, 201, 204; DLBY 1991; EWL 3; MSW; MTCW 1, 2; MTFW 2005; NFS 16, 31, 36; RGEL 2; SATA 20; SSFS 14, 35; TEA; WLIT 4
Greene, Graham Henry
See Greene, Graham
Greene, Robert 1558-1592 .... **LC 41, 185**
See also BRWS 8; DLB 62, 167; IDTP; RGEL 2; TEA
Greer, Germaine 1939- .... **CLC 131**
See also AITN 1; CA 81-84; CANR 33, 70, 115, 133, 190; FW; MTCW 1, 2; MTFW 2005
Greer, Richard
See Silverberg, Robert
Gregor, Arthur 1923- .... **CLC 9**
See also CA 25-28R; CAAS 10; CANR 11; CP 1, 2, 3, 4, 5, 6, 7; SATA 36
Gregor, Lee
See Pohl, Frederik
Gregory, Lady Isabella Augusta (Persse)
1852-1932 .... **TCLC 1, 176**
See also BRW 6; CA 104; 184; DLB 10; IDTP; RGEL 2
Gregory, J. Dennis
See Williams, John A(lfred)
Gregory of Nazianzus, St.
329-389 .... **CMLC 82**
Gregory of Nyssa c. 335-c. 394 ... **CMLC 126**
Gregory of Rimini 1300(?)-1358 **CMLC 109**
See also DLB 115
Gregory of Tours 538?-594 .... **CMLC 158**
Gregory the Great c. 540-604 ... **CMLC 124**
Grekova, I.
See Ventsel, Elena Sergeevna
Grekova, Irina
See Ventsel, Elena Sergeevna

Grendon, Stephen
See Derleth, August (William)

Grenville, Kate 1950- .... **CLC 61**
See also CA 118; CANR 53, 93, 156, 220;
CN 7; DLB 325

Grenville, Pelham
See Wodehouse, P. G.

Greve, Felix Paul (Berthold Friedrich) 1879-
1948 .... **TCLC 4, 248**
See also CA 104; 141, 175; CANR 79;
DAC; DAM MST; DLB 92; RGEL 2;
TCWW 1, 2

Greville, Fulke 1554-1628 .... **LC 79**
See also BRWS 11; DLB 62, 172; RGEL 2

Grey, Lady Jane 1537-1554 .... **LC 93**
See also DLB 132

Grey, Zane 1872-1939 .... **TCLC 6**
See also BPFB 2; CA 104; 132; CANR 210;
DA3; DAM POP; DLB 9, 212; MTCW 1,
2; MTFW 2005; RGAL 4; TCWW 1, 2;
TUS

Griboedov, Aleksandr Sergeevich
1795(?)-1829 .... **NCLC 129**
See also DLB 205; RGWL 2, 3

Grieg, (Johan) Nordahl (Brun)
1902-1943 .... **TCLC 10**
See also CA 107; 189; EWL 3

Grieve, C. M. 1892-1978 .... **CLC 2, 4,**
11, 19, 63; PC 9, 122
See also BRWS 12; CA 5-8R; 85-88; CANR
33, 107; CDBLB 1945-1960; CP 1, 2;
DAM POET; DLB 20; EWL 3; MTCW
1; RGEL 2

Grieve, Christopher Murray
See Grieve, C. M.

Griffin, Gerald 1803-1840 .... **NCLC 7**
See also DLB 159; RGEL 2

Griffin, John Howard 1920-1980 ... **CLC 68**
See also AITN 1; CA 1-4R; 101; CANR 2

Griffin, Peter 1942- .... **CLC 39**
See also CA 136

Griffith, David Lewelyn Wark
See Griffith, D.W.

Griffith, D.W. 1875(?)-1948 .... **TCLC 68**
See also AAYA 78; CA 119; 150; CANR 80

Griffith, Lawrence
See Griffith, D.W.

Griffiths, Trevor 1935- .... **CLC 13, 52**
See also CA 97-100; CANR 45; CBD; CD 5,
6; DLB 13, 245

Griggs, Sutton (Elbert)
1872-1930 .... **TCLC 77**
See also CA 123; 186; DLB 50

Grigson, Geoffrey (Edward Harvey)
1905-1985 .... **CLC 7, 39**
See also CA 25-28R; 118; CANR 20, 33; CP
1, 2, 3, 4; DLB 27; MTCW 1, 2

Grile, Dod
See Bierce, Ambrose

Grillparzer, Franz 1791-1872 .... **DC 14;**
NCLC 1, 102, 245; SSC 37
See also CDWLB 2; DLB 133; EW 5;
RGWL 2, 3; TWA

Grimble, Reverend Charles James
See Eliot, T. S.

Grimke, Angelina Emily Weld
See Grimke, Angelina Weld

Grimke, Angelina Weld
1880-1958 .... **DC 38; HR 1:2**
See also BW 1; CA 124; DAM POET; DLB
50, 54; FW

Grimke, Charlotte L. Forten
1837(?)-1914 .... **BLC 1:2; TCLC 16**
See also BW 1; CA 117; 124; DAM MULT,
POET; DLB 50, 239

Grimke, Charlotte Lottie Forten
See Grimke, Charlotte L. Forten

Grimm, Jacob Ludwig Karl
1785-1863 .. **NCLC 3, 77, 288; SSC 36,**
88, 179
See also CLR 112; DLB 90; MAICYA 1, 2;
RGSF 2; RGWL 2, 3; SATA 22; WCH

Grimm, Wilhelm Karl
1786-1859 .. **NCLC 3, 77, 288; SSC 36,**
88, 179
See also CDWLB 2; CLR 112; DLB 90;
MAICYA 1, 2; RGSF 2; RGWL 2, 3;
SATA 22; WCH

Grimm and Grimm
See Grimm, Jacob Ludwig Karl; Grimm,
Wilhelm Karl

Grimm Brothers
See Grimm, Jacob Ludwig Karl; Grimm,
Wilhelm Karl

Grimmelshausen, Hans Jakob Christoffel von
See Grimmelshausen, Johann Jakob Christoffel von

Grimmelshausen, Johann Jakob Christoffel
von 1621-1676 .... **LC 6, 209**
See also CDWLB 2; DLB 168; RGWL 2, 3

Grindel, Eugene 1895-1952 .... **PC 38;**
TCLC 7, 41
See also CA 104; 193; EWL 3; GFL 1789 to
the Present; LMFS 2; RGWL 2, 3

Grisham, John 1955- .... **CLC 84, 273**
See also AAYA 14, 47; BPFB 2; CA 138;
CANR 47, 69, 114, 133; CMW 4; CN 6, 7;
CPW; CSW; DA3; DAM POP; LNFS 1;
MSW; MTCW 2; MTFW 2005

Grosseteste, Robert
1175(?)-1253 .... **CMLC 62**
See also DLB 115

Grossman, David 1954- .... **CLC 67, 231**
See also CA 138; CANR 114, 175; CWW 2;
DLB 299; EWL 3; RGHL; WLIT 6

Grossman, Vasilii Semenovich
See Grossman, Vasily

Grotius, Hugo 1583-1645 .... **LC 203**

Grossman, Vasily 1905-1964 .... **CLC 41**
See also CA 124; 130; DLB 272; MTCW 1;
RGHL

Grossman, Vasily Semenovich
See Grossman, Vasily

Grove, Frederick Philip
See Greve, Felix Paul (Berthold Friedrich)

Grubb
See Crumb, R.

Grumbach, Doris 1918- ...... **CLC 13, 22, 64**
See also CA 5-8R; CAAS 2; CANR 9, 42,
70, 127; CN 6, 7; INT CANR-9; MTCW 2;
MTFW 2005

Grundtvig, Nikolai Frederik Severin
1783-1872 .... **NCLC 1, 158**
See also DLB 300

Grunge
See Crumb, R.

Grunwald, Lisa 1959- .... **CLC 44**
See also CA 120; CANR 148

Gryphius, Andreas 1616-1664 ... **LC 89, 223**
See also CDWLB 2; DLB 164; RGWL 2, 3

Guare, John 1938- .... **CLC 8, 14, 29, 67;**
DC 20
See also CA 73-76; CAD; CANR 21, 69,
118; CD 5, 6; DAM DRAM; DFS 8, 13;
DLB 7, 249; EWL 3; MAL 5; MTCW 1, 2;
RGAL 4

Guarini, Battista 1538-1612 ... **DC 48; LC 102**
See also DLB 339

Gubar, Susan 1944- .... **CLC 145**
See also CA 108; CANR 45, 70, 139, 179;
FW; MTCW 1; RGAL 4

Gubar, Susan David
See Gubar, Susan

Gudjonsson, Halldor Kiljan
1902-1998 .... **CLC 25**

See also CA 103; 164; CWW 2; DLB 293,
331; EW 12; EWL 3; RGWL 2, 3

Guedes, Vincente
See Pessoa, Fernando

Guenter, Erich
See Eich, Gunter

Guest, Barbara 1920-2006 .... **CLC 34;**
PC 55
See also BG 1:2; CA 25-28R; 248; CANR
11, 44, 84; CP 1, 2, 3, 4, 5, 6, 7; CWP;
DLB 5, 193

Guest, Edgar A(lbert)
1881-1959 .... **TCLC 95**
See also CA 112; 168

Guest, Judith 1936- .... **CLC 8, 30**
See also AAYA 7, 66; CA 77-80; CANR 15,
75, 138; DA3; DAM NOV, POP; EXPN;
INT CANR-15; LAIT 5; MTCW 1, 2;
MTFW 2005; NFS 1, 33

Guest, Judith Ann
See Guest, Judith

Guevara, Che 1928-1967 .. **CLC 87; HLC 1**
See also CA 127; 111; CANR 56; DAM
MULT; HW 1

Guevara (Serna), Ernesto
See Guevara, Che

Guicciardini, Francesco 1483-1540 ... **LC 49**

Guido delle Colonne
c. 1215-c. 1290 .... **CMLC 90**

Guild, Nicholas M. 1944- .... **CLC 33**
See also CA 93-96

Guillemin, Jacques
See Sartre, Jean-Paul

Guillen y Alvarez, Jorge
See Guillen, Jorge

Guillevic, (Eugene) 1907-1997 .... **CLC 33**
See also CA 93-96; CWW 2

Guillen, Jorge 1893-1984 .... **CLC 11;**
HLCS 1; PC 35; TCLC 233
See also CA 89-92; 112; DAM MULT,
POET; DLB 108; EWL 3; HW 1; RGWL
2, 3

Guillen, Nicolas 1902-1989 .... **BLC 1:2;**
CLC 48, 79; HLC 1; PC 23
See also BW 2; CA 116; 125; 129; CANR
84; DAM MST, MULT, POET; DLB 283;
EWL 3; HW 1; LAW; RGWL 2, 3; WP

Guillen, Nicolas Cristobal
See Guillen, Nicolas

Guillois
See Desnos, Robert

Guillois, Valentin
See Desnos, Robert

Guimaraes Rosa, Joao
1908-1967 .... **CLC 23; HLCS 1**
See also CA 175; 89-92; DLB 113, 307;
EWL 3; LAW; RGSF 2; RGWL 2, 3;
WLIT 1

Guiney, Louise Imogen
1861-1920 .... **TCLC 41**
See also CA 160; DLB 54; RGAL 4

Guinizelli, Guido c. 1230-1276 .... **CMLC 49**
See also WLIT 7

Guinizzelli, Guido
See Guinizelli, Guido

Guma, Alex La
See La Guma, Alex

Gumilev, Nikolai (Stepanovich)
1886-1921 .... **TCLC 60**
See also CA 165; DLB 295; EWL 3

Gumilyov, Nikolay Stepanovich
See Gumilev, Nikolai (Stepanovich)

Gump, P.Q.
See Card, Orson Scott

Gunesekera, Romesh 1954- ..... **CLC 91, 336**
See also BRWS 10; CA 159; CANR 140,
172; CN 6, 7; DLB 267, 323

See also DLB 37

Hamilton, Clive
See Lewis, C. S.

Hamilton, Edmond 1904-1977 .... **CLC 1**
See also CA 1-4R; CANR 3, 84; DLB 8;
SATA 118; SFW 4

Hamilton, Elizabeth 1758-1816 ... **NCLC 153**
See also DLB 116, 158

Hamilton, Eugene (Jacob) Lee
See Lee-Hamilton, Eugene (Jacob)

Hamilton, Franklin
See Silverberg, Robert

Hamilton, Gail
See Corcoran, Barbara (Asenath)

Hamilton, (Robert) Ian
1938-2001 .... **CLC 191**
See also CA 106; 203; CANR 41, 67; CP 1,
2, 3, 4, 5, 6, 7; DLB 40, 155

Hamilton, Jane 1957- .... **CLC 179**
See also CA 147; CANR 85, 128, 214; CN
7; DLB 350; MTFW 2005

Hamilton, Mollie
See Kaye, M.M.

Hamilton, Patrick 1904-1962 .... **CLC 51**
See also BRWS 16; CA 176; 113; DLB
10, 191

Hamilton, Virginia 1936-2002 .... **CLC 26**
See also AAYA 2, 21; BW 2, 3; BYA 1, 2, 8;
CA 25-28R; 206; CANR 20, 37, 73, 126;
CLR 1, 11, 40, 127; DAM MULT; DLB
33, 52; DLBY 2001; INT CANR-20;
JRDA; LAIT 5; MAICYA 1, 2; MAICYAS
1; MTCW 1, 2; MTFW 2005; SATA 4, 56,
79, 123; SATA-Obit 132; WYA; YAW

Hamilton, Virginia Esther
See Hamilton, Virginia

Hammett, Dashiell 1894-1961 ...... **CLC 3, 5,
10, 19, 47; SSC 17; TCLC 187**
See also AAYA 59; AITN 1; AMWS 4;
BPFB 2; CA 81-84; CANR 42; CDALB
1929-1941; CMW 4; DA3; DLB 226, 280;
DLBD 6; DLBY 1996; EWL 3; LAIT 3;
MAL 5; MSW; MTCW 1, 2; MTFW 2005;
NFS 21; RGAL 4; RGSF 2; TUS

Hammett, Samuel Dashiell
See Hammett, Dashiell

Hammon, Jupiter
1720(?)-1800(?) .... **BLC 1:2;
NCLC 5; PC 16**
See also DAM MULT, POET; DLB 31, 50

Hammond, Keith
See Kuttner, Henry

Hamner, Earl (Henry), Jr. 1923- ..... **CLC 12**
See also AITN 2; CA 73-76; DLB 6

Hampton, Christopher 1946- .... **CLC 4**
See also CA 25-28R; CD 5, 6; DLB 13; MTCW 1

Hampton, Christopher James
See Hampton, Christopher

Hamsun, Knut
See Pedersen, Knut

Hamsund, Knut Pedersen
See Pedersen, Knut

Handke, Peter 1942- .... **CLC 5, 8, 10, 15,
38, 134; DC 17**
See also CA 77-80; CANR 33, 75, 104, 133,
180, 236; CWW 2; DAM DRAM, NOV;
DLB 85, 124; EWL 3; MTCW 1, 2;
MTFW 2005; TWA

Handler, Chelsea 1975(?)- .... **CLC 269**
See also CA 243; CANR 230

Handy, W(illiam) C(hristopher)
1873-1958 .... **TCLC 97**
See also BW 3; CA 121; 167

Haneke, Michael 1942- .... **CLC 283**

Hanif, Mohammed 1965- .... **CLC 299**
See also CA 283

Hanley, James 1901-1985 .... **CLC 3, 5, 8, 13**
See also BRWS 19; CA 73-76; 117; CANR
36; CBD; CN 1, 2, 3; DLB 191; EWL 3;
MTCW 1; RGEL 2

Hannah, Barry 1942-2010 .... **CLC 23, 38,
90, 270, 318; SSC 94**
See also BPFB 2; CA 108; 110; CANR 43,
68, 113, 236; CN 4, 5, 6, 7; CSW; DLB 6,
234; INT CA-110; MTCW 1; RGSF 2

Hannon, Ezra
See Hunter, Evan

Hanrahan, Barbara 1939-1991 ... **TCLC 219**
See also CA 121; 127; CN 4, 5; DLB 289

Hansberry, Lorraine 1930-1965 ... **BLC 1:2,
2:2; CLC 17, 62; DC 2; TCLC 192**
See also AAYA 25; AFAW 1, 2; AMWS 4;
BW 1, 3; CA 109; 25-28R; CABS 3; CAD;
CANR 58; CDALB 1941-1968; CWD;
DA; DA3; DAB; DAC; DAM DRAM,
MST, MULT; DFS 2, 29; DLB 7, 38; EWL
3; FL 1:6; FW; LAIT 4; MAL 5; MTCW 1,
2; MTFW 2005; RGAL 4; TUS

Hansberry, Lorraine Vivian
See Hansberry, Lorraine

Hansen, Joseph 1923-2004 .... **CLC 38**
See also BPFB 2; CA 29-32R; 233; CAAS
17; CANR 16, 44, 66, 125; CMW 4; DLB
226; GLL 1; INT CANR-16

Hansen, Karen V. 1955- .... **CLC 65**
See also CA 149; CANR 102

Hansen, Martin A(lfred)
1909-1955 .... **TCLC 32**
See also CA 167; DLB 214; EWL 3

Hanson, Kenneth O. 1922- .... **CLC 13**
See also CA 53-56; CANR 7; CP 1, 2, 3, 4, 5

Hanson, Kenneth Ostlin
See Hanson, Kenneth O.

Han Yu 768-824 .... **CMLC 122**

Harbach, Chad .... **CLC 334**
See also CA 327

Hardwick, Elizabeth 1916-2007 ...... **CLC 13**
See also AMWS 3; CA 5-8R; 267; CANR 3,
32, 70, 100, 139; CN 4, 5, 6; CSW; DA3;
DAM NOV; DLB 6; MBL; MTCW 1, 2;
MTFW 2005; TCLE 1:1

Hardwick, Elizabeth Bruce
See Hardwick, Elizabeth

Hardy, Thomas 1840-1928 .... **PC 8, 92;
SSC 2, 60, 113; TCLC 4, 10, 18, 32, 48,
53, 72, 143, 153, 229, 284; WLC 3**
See also AAYA 69; BRW 6; BRWC 1, 2;
BRWR 1; CA 104; 123; CDBLB 1890-
1914; DA; DA3; DAB; DAC; DAM MST,
NOV, POET; DLB 18, 19, 135, 284; EWL
3; EXPN; EXPP; LAIT 2; MTCW 1, 2;
MTFW 2005; NFS 3, 11, 15, 19, 30; PFS 3,
4, 18, 42; RGEL 2; RGSF 2; TEA; WLIT 4

Hare, David 1947- .... **CLC 29, 58, 136;
DC 26**
See also BRWS 4; CA 97-100; CANR 39,
91; CBD; CD 5, 6; DFS 4, 7, 16; DLB 13,
310; MTCW 1; TEA

Harewood, John
See Van Druten, John (William)

Harford, Henry
See Hudson, W(illiam) H(enry)

Hargrave, Leonie
See Disch, Thomas M.

**Hariri, Al- al-Qasim ibn 'Ali Abu
Muhammad al-Basri**
See al-Hariri, al-Qasim ibn 'Ali Abu
Muhammad al-Basri

Harjo, Joy 1951- ... **CLC 83; NNAL; PC 27**
See also AMWS 12; CA 114; CANR 35, 67,
91, 129; CP 6, 7; CWP; DAM MULT;
DLB 120, 175, 342; EWL 3; MTCW 2;
MTFW 2005; PFS 15, 32, 44; RGAL 4

Harlan, Louis R. 1922-2010 .... **CLC 34**
See also CA 21-24R; CANR 25, 55, 80

Harlan, Louis Rudolph
See Harlan, Louis R.

Harlan, Louis Rudolph
See Harlan, Louis R.

Harling, Robert 1951(?)- .... **CLC 53**
See also CA 147

Harmon, William (Ruth) 1938- ...... **CLC 38**
See also CA 33-36R; CANR 14, 32, 35;
SATA 65

Harper, Edith Alice Mary
See Wickham, Anna

Harper, F. E. W.
See Harper, Frances Ellen Watkins

Harper, Frances E. W.
See Harper, Frances Ellen Watkins

Harper, Frances E. Watkins
See Harper, Frances Ellen Watkins

Harper, Frances Ellen
See Harper, Frances Ellen Watkins

Harper, Frances Ellen Watkins
1825-1911 .... **BLC 1:2; PC 21;
TCLC 14, 217**
See also AFAW 1, 2; BW 1, 3; CA 111; 125;
CANR 79; DAM MULT, POET; DLB 50,
221; MBL; PFS 44; RGAL 4

Harper, Michael S. 1938- .... **BLC 2:2;
CLC 7, 22; PC 130**
See also AFAW 2; BW 1; CA 33-36R; 224;
CAAE 224; CANR 24, 108, 212; CP 2, 3,
4, 5, 6, 7; DLB 41; RGAL 4; TCLE 1:1

Harper, Michael Steven
See Harper, Michael S.

Harper, Mrs. F. E. W.
See Harper, Frances Ellen Watkins

Harpur, Charles 1813-1868 .... **NCLC 114**
See also DLB 230; RGEL 2

Harris, Christie
See Harris, Christie (Lucy) Irwin

Harris, Christie (Lucy) Irwin
1907-2002 .... **CLC 12**
See also CA 5-8R; CANR 6, 83; CLR 47;
DLB 88; JRDA; MAICYA 1, 2; SAAS 10;
SATA 6, 74; SATA-Essay 116

Harris, E. Lynn 1955-2009 .... **CLC 299**
See also CA 164; 288; CANR 111, 163, 206;
MTFW 2005

Harris, Everett Lynn
See Harris, E. Lynn

Harris, Everette Lynn
See Harris, E. Lynn

Harris, Frank 1856-1931 .... **TCLC 24**
See also CA 109; 150; CANR 80; DLB 156,
197; RGEL 2

Harris, George Washington
1814-1869 .... **NCLC 23, 165**
See also DLB 3, 11, 248; RGAL 4

Harris, Joel Chandler 1848-1908 .... **SSC 19,
103; TCLC 2**
See also CA 104; 137; CANR 80; CLR 49,
128; DLB 11, 23, 42, 78, 91; LAIT 2;
MAICYA 1, 2; RGSF 2; SATA 100; WCH;
YABC 1

**Harris, John (Wyndham Parkes Lucas)
Beynon** 1903-1969 .... **CLC 19**
See also BRWS 13; CA 102; 89-92; CANR 84;
DLB 255; SATA 118; SCFW 1, 2; SFW 4

Harris, MacDonald
See Heiney, Donald (William)

Harris, Mark 1922-2007 .... **CLC 19**
See also CA 5-8R; 260; CAAS 3; CANR 2,
55, 83; CN 1, 2, 3, 4, 5, 6, 7; DLB 2;
DLBY 1980

Harris, Norman .... **CLC 65**

Harris, (Theodore) Wilson 1921- ... **BLC 2:2;
CLC 25, 159, 297**
See also BRWS 5; BW 2, 3; CA 65-68;
CAAS 16; CANR 11, 27, 69, 114; CDWLB

3; CN 1, 2, 3, 4, 5, 6, 7; CP 1, 2, 3, 4, 5, 6, 7; DLB 117; EWL 3; MTCW 1; RGEL 2

Harrison, Barbara Grizzuti
1934-2002 .... **CLC 144**
See also CA 77-80; 205; CANR 15, 48; INT CANR-15

Harrison, Elizabeth (Allen) Cavanna
1909-2001 .... **CLC 12**
See also CA 9-12R; 200; CANR 6, 27, 85, 104, 121; JRDA; MAICYA 1; SAAS 4; SATA 1, 30; YAW

Harrison, Harry 1925- .... **CLC 42**
See also CA 1-4R; CANR 5, 21, 84, 225; DLB 8; SATA 4; SCFW 2; SFW 4

Harrison, Harry Max
See Harrison, Harry

Harrison, James
See Harrison, Jim

Harrison, James Thomas
See Harrison, Jim

Harrison, Jim 1937- .... **CLC 6, 14, 33, 66, 143, 348; SSC 19**
See also AMWS 8; CA 13-16R; CANR 8, 51, 79, 142, 198, 229; CN 5, 6; CP 1, 2, 3, 4, 5, 6; DLBY 1982; INT CANR-8; RGAL 4; TCWW 2; TUS

Harrison, Kathryn 1961- .... **CLC 70, 151**
See also CA 144; CANR 68, 122, 194

Harrison, Tony 1937- .... **CLC 43, 129**
See also BRWS 5; CA 65-68; CANR 44, 98; CBD; CD 5, 6; CP 2, 3, 4, 5, 6, 7; DLB 40, 245; MTCW 1; RGEL 2

Harriss, Will(ard Irvin) 1922- .... **CLC 34**
See also CA 111

Hart, Ellis
See Ellison, Harlan

Hart, Josephine 1942-2011 .... **CLC 70**
See also CA 138; CANR 70, 149, 220; CPW; DAM POP

Hart, Moss 1904-1961 .... **CLC 66**
See also CA 109; 89-92; CANR 84; DAM DRAM; DFS 1; DLB 7, 266; RGAL 4

Harte, Bret 1836(?)-1902 .... **SSC 8, 59; TCLC 1, 25; WLC 3**
See also AMWS 2; CA 104; 140; CANR 80; CDALB 1865-1917; DA; DA3; DAC; DAM MST; DLB 12, 64, 74, 79, 186; EXPS; LAIT 2; RGAL 4; RGSF 2; SATA 26; SSFS 3; TUS

Harte, Francis Brett
See Harte, Bret

Hartley, L(eslie) P(oles)
1895-1972 .... **CLC 2, 22; SSC 125**
See also BRWS 7; CA 45-48; 37-40R; CANR 33; CN 1; DLB 15, 139; EWL 3; HGG; MTCW 1, 2; MTFW 2005; RGEL 2; RGSF 2; SUFW 1

Hartman, Geoffrey H.
1929- .... **CLC 27**
See also CA 117; 125; CANR 79, 214; DLB 67

Hartmann, Sadakichi 1869-1944 ... **TCLC 73**
See also CA 157; DLB 54

Hartmann von Aue
c. 1170-c. 1210 .... **CMLC 15, 131**
See also CDWLB 2; DLB 138; RGWL 2, 3

Hartog, Jan de
See de Hartog, Jan

Haruf, Kent 1943- .... **CLC 34**
See also AAYA 44; CA 149; CANR 91, 131

Harvey, Caroline
See Trollope, Joanna

Harvey, Gabriel 1550(?)-1631 .... **LC 88**
See also DLB 167, 213, 281

Harvey, Jack
See Rankin, Ian

Harwood, Ronald 1934- .... **CLC 32**
See also CA 1-4R; CANR 4, 55, 150; CBD; CD 5, 6; DAM DRAM, MST; DLB 13

Hasegawa Tatsunosuke
See Futabatei, Shimei

Haslett, Adam 1970- .... **CLC 334**
See also CA 216; SSFS 24

Hass, Robert
1941- .... **CLC 18, 39, 99, 287; PC 16**
See also AMWS 6; CA 111; CANR 30, 50, 71, 187; CP 3, 4, 5, 6, 7; DLB 105, 206; EWL 3; MAL 5; MTFW 2005; PFS 37; RGAL 4; SATA 94; TCLE 1:1

Hassler, Jon 1933-2008 .... **CLC 263**
See also CA 73-76; 270; CANR 21, 80, 161; CN 6, 7; INT CANR-21; SATA 19; SATA-Obit 191

Hassler, Jon Francis
See Hassler, Jon

Hastings, Hudson
See Kuttner, Henry

Hastings, Selina 1945- .... **CLC 44**
See also CA 257; CANR 225

Hastings, Selina Shirley
See Hastings, Selina

Hastings, Lady Selina Shirley
See Hastings, Selina

Hastings, Victor
See Disch, Thomas M.

Hathorne, John 1641-1717 .... **LC 38**

Hatteras, Amelia
See Mencken, H. L.

Hatteras, Owen
See Mencken, H. L.; Nathan, George Jean

Hauff, Wilhelm 1802-1827 .... **NCLC 185**
See also CLR 155; DLB 90; SUFW 1

Hauptmann, Gerhart 1862-1946 ...... **DC 34; SSC 37; TCLC 4**
See also CA 104; 153; CDWLB 2; DAM DRAM; DLB 66, 118, 330; EW 8; EWL 3; RGSF 2; RGWL 2, 3; TWA

Hauptmann, Gerhart Johann Robert
See Hauptmann, Gerhart

Havel, Vaclav 1936-2011 .... **CLC 25, 58, 65, 123, 314; DC 6**
See also CA 104; CANR 36, 63, 124, 175; CDWLB 4; CWW 2; DA3; DAM DRAM; DFS 10; DLB 232; EWL 3; LMFS 2; MTCW 1, 2; MTFW 2005; RGWL 3

Haviaras, Stratis
See Chaviaras, Strates

Hawes, Stephen 1475(?)-1529(?) .... **LC 17**
See also DLB 132; RGEL 2

Hawk, Alex
See Kelton, Elmer

Hawkes, John 1925-1998 ..... **CLC 1, 2, 3, 4, 7, 9, 14, 15, 27, 49**
See also BPFB 2; CA 1-4R; 167; CANR 2, 47, 64; CN 1, 2, 3, 4, 5, 6; DLB 2, 7, 227; DLBY 1980, 1998; EWL 3; MAL 5; MTCW 1, 2; MTFW 2005; RGAL 4

Hawking, S. W.
See Hawking, Stephen W.

Hawking, Stephen W. 1942- ... **CLC 63, 105**
See also AAYA 13; BEST 89:1; CA 126; 129; CANR 48, 115; CPW; DA3; MTCW 2; MTFW 2005

Hawking, Stephen William
See Hawking, Stephen W.

Hawkins, Anthony Hope
See Hope, Anthony

Hawthorne, Julian 1846-1934 .... **TCLC 25**
See also CA 165; HGG

Hawthorne, Nathaniel 1804-1864 .... **NCLC 2, 10, 17, 23, 39, 79, 95, 158, 171, 191, 226; SSC 3, 29, 39, 89, 130, 166, 176, 185, 190, 195; WLC 3**
See also AAYA 18; AMW; AMWC 1; AMWR 1; BPFB 2; BYA 3; CDALB 1640-1865; CLR 103, 163; DA; DA3; DAB; DAC; DAM MST, NOV; DLB 1,

74, 183, 223, 269; EXPN; EXPS; GL 2; HGG; LAIT 1; NFS 1, 20; RGAL 4; RGSF 2; SSFS 1, 7, 11, 15, 30, 35; SUFW 1; TUS; WCH; YABC 2

Hawthorne, Sophia Peabody
1809-1871 .... **NCLC 150**
See also DLB 183, 239

Haxton, Josephine Ayres 1921-
See Douglas, Ellen

Hayaseca y Eizaguirre, Jorge
See Echegaray (y Eizaguirre), Jose (Maria Waldo)

Hayashi, Fumiko 1904-1951 .... **TCLC 27**
See also CA 161; DLB 180; EWL 3

Hayashi Fumiko
See Hayashi, Fumiko

Haycraft, Anna 1932-2005 .... **CLC 40**
See also CA 122; 237; CANR 90, 141; CN 4, 5, 6; DLB 194; MTCW 2; MTFW 2005

Haycraft, Anna Margaret
See Haycraft, Anna

Hayden, Robert
See Hayden, Robert Earl

Hayden, Robert E.
See Hayden, Robert Earl

Hayden, Robert Earl 1913-1980 ... **BLC 1:2; CLC 5, 9, 14, 37; PC 6, 123**
See also AFAW 1, 2; AMWS 2; BW 1, 3; CA 69-72; 97-100; CABS 2; CANR 24, 75, 82; CDALB 1941-1968; CP 1, 2, 3; DA; DAC; DAM MST, POET; DLB 5, 76; EWL 3; EXPP; MAL 5; MTCW 1, 2; PFS 1, 31; RGAL 4; SATA 19; SATA-Obit 26; WP

Haydon, Benjamin Robert
1786-1846 .... **NCLC 146**
See also DLB 110

Hayek, F(riedrich) A(ugust von)
1899-1992 .... **TCLC 109**
See also CA 93-96; 137; CANR 20; MTCW 1, 2

Hayford, J(oseph) E(phraim) Casely
See Casely-Hayford, J(oseph) E(phraim)

Hayley, William 1745-1820 .... **NCLC 286**
See also DLB 142

Hayman, Ronald 1932- .... **CLC 44**
See also CA 25-28R; CANR 18, 50, 88; CD 5, 6; DLB 155

Hayne, Paul Hamilton 1830-1886 .. **NCLC 94**
See also DLB 3, 64, 79, 248; RGAL 4

Haynes, Todd 1961- .... **CLC 313**
See also CA 220

Hays, Mary 1760-1843 .... **NCLC 114**
See also DLB 142, 158; RGEL 2

Haywood, Eliza (Fowler)
1693(?)-1756 .... **LC 1, 44, 177**
See also BRWS 12; DLB 39; RGEL 2

Hazlitt, William 1778-1830 ..... **NCLC 29, 82**
See also BRW 4; DLB 110, 158; RGEL 2; TEA

Hazzard, Shirley 1931- ... **CLC 18, 218, 325**
See also BRWS 19; CA 9-12R; CANR 4, 70, 127, 212; CN 1, 2, 3, 4, 5, 6, 7; DLB 289; DLBY 1982; MTCW 1

Hebert, Anne 1916-2000 ...... **CLC 4, 13, 29, 246; PC 126**
See also CA 85-88; 187; CANR 69, 126; CCA 1; CWP; CWW 2; DA3; DAC; DAM MST, POET; DLB 68; EWL 3; GFL 1789 to the Present; MTCW 1, 2; MTFW 2005; PFS 20

Head, Bessie 1937-1986 .... **BLC 1:2, 2:2; CLC 25, 67; SSC 52**
See also AFW; BW 2, 3; CA 29-32R; 119; CANR 25, 82; CDWLB 3; CN 1, 2, 3, 4; DA3; DAM MULT; DLB 117, 225; EWL 3; EXPS; FL 1:6; FW; MTCW 1, 2; MTFW 2005; NFS 31; RGSF 2; SSFS 5, 13, 30, 33; WLIT 2; WWE 1

Headley, Elizabeth
See Harrison, Elizabeth (Allen) Cavanna

Headon, (Nicky) Topper 1956(?)- ... **CLC 30**

Heaney, Seamus 1939- ... **CLC 5, 7, 14, 25, 37, 74, 91, 171, 225, 309; PC 18, 100; WLCS**
See also AAYA 61; BRWR 1; BRWS 2; CA 85-88; CANR 25, 48, 75, 91, 128, 184, 241; CDBLB 1960 to Present; CP 1, 2, 3, 4, 5, 6, 7; DA3; DAB; DAM POET; DLB 40, 330; DLBY 1995; EWL 3; EXPP; MTCW 1, 2; MTFW 2005; PAB; PFS 2, 5, 8, 17, 30, 41; RGEL 2; TEA; WLIT 4

Heaney, Seamus Justin
See Heaney, Seamus

Hearn, Lafcadio
1850-1904 .... **SSC 158; TCLC 9, 263**
See also AAYA 79; CA 105; 166; DLB 12, 78, 189; HGG; MAL 5; RGAL 4

Hearn, Patricio Lafcadio Tessima Carlos
See Hearn, Lafcadio

Hearne, Samuel 1745-1792 .... **LC 95**
See also DLB 99

Hearne, Vicki 1946-2001 .... **CLC 56**
See also CA 139; 201

Hearon, Shelby 1931- .... **CLC 63**
See also AITN 2; AMWS 8; CA 25-28R; CAAS 11; CANR 18, 48, 103, 146; CSW

Heat-Moon, William Least 1939- ... **CLC 29**
See also AAYA 9, 66; ANW; CA 115; 119; CANR 47, 89, 206; CPW; INT CA-119

Hebbel, Friedrich 1813-1863 .... **DC 21; NCLC 43, 287**
See also CDWLB 2; DAM DRAM; DLB 129; EW 6; RGWL 2, 3

Hebreo, Leon c. 1460-1520 .... **LC 193**
See also DLB 318

Hecht, Anthony (Evan)
1923-2004 .... **CLC 8, 13, 19; PC 70**
See also AMWS 10; CA 9-12R; 232; CANR 6, 108; CP 1, 2, 3, 4, 5, 6, 7; DAM POET; DLB 5, 169; EWL 3; PFS 6; WP

Hecht, Ben 1894-1964 ...... **CLC 8; TCLC 101**
See also CA 85-88; DFS 9; DLB 7, 9, 25, 26, 28, 86; FANT; IDFW 3, 4; RGAL 4

Hedayat, Sadeq 1903-1951 .... **SSC 131; TCLC 21**
See also CA 120; EWL 3; RGSF 2

Hoeg, Peter 1957- .... **CLC 95, 156**
See also CA 151; CANR 75, 202; CMW 4; DA3; DLB 214; EWL 3; MTCW 2; MTFW 2005; NFS 17; RGWL 3; SSFS 18

Hegel, Georg Wilhelm Friedrich
1770-1831 .... **NCLC 46, 151**
See also DLB 90, 366; TWA

Heidegger, Martin 1889-1976 .... **CLC 24**
See also CA 81-84; 65-68; CANR 34; DLB 296; MTCW 1, 2; MTFW 2005

Heidenstam, (Carl Gustaf) Verner von
1859-1940 .... **TCLC 5**
See also CA 104; DLB 330

Heidi Louise
See Erdrich, Louise

Heifner, Jack 1946- .... **CLC 11**
See also CA 105; CANR 47

Heijermans, Herman 1864-1924 ... **TCLC 24**
See also CA 123; EWL 3

Heilbrun, Carolyn G. 1926-2003 ... **CLC 25, 173, 303**
See also BPFB 1; CA 45-48; 220; CANR 1, 28, 58, 94; CMW; CPW; DLB 306; FW; MSW

Heilbrun, Carolyn Gold
See Heilbrun, Carolyn G.

Hein, Christoph 1944- .... **CLC 154**
See also CA 158; CANR 108, 210; CDWLB 2; CWW 2; DLB 124

Heine, Heinrich 1797-1856 ...... **NCLC 4, 54, 147, 249; PC 25**
See also CDWLB 2; DLB 90; EW 5; PFS 37; RGWL 2, 3; TWA

Heinemann, Larry 1944- .... **CLC 50**
See also CA 110; CAAS 21; CANR 31, 81, 156; DLBD 9; INT CANR-31

Heinemann, Larry Curtiss
See Heinemann, Larry

Heiney, Donald (William) 1921-1993 .. **CLC 9**
See also CA 1-4R; 142; CANR 3, 58; FANT

Heinlein, Robert A. 1907-1988 .... **CLC 1, 3, 8, 14, 26, 55; SSC 55**
See also AAYA 17; BPFB 2; BYA 4, 13; CA 1-4R; 125; CANR 1, 20, 53; CLR 75; CN 1, 2, 3, 4; CPW; DA3; DAM POP; DLB 8; EXPS; JRDA; LAIT 5; LMFS 2; MAICYA 1, 2; MTCW 1, 2; MTFW 2005; NFS 40; RGAL 4; SATA 9, 69; SATA-Obit 56; SCFW 1, 2; SFW 4; SSFS 7; YAW

Heinrich von dem Tuerlin
fl. c. 1230- .... **CMLC 133**
See also DLB 138

Hejinian, Lyn 1941- .... **PC 108**
See also CA 153; CANR 85, 214; CP 4, 5, 6, 7; CWP; DLB 165; PFS 27; RGAL 4

Held, Peter
See Vance, Jack

Heldris of Cornwall fl. 13th cent. ... **CMLC 97**

Helforth, John
See Doolittle, Hilda

Heliodorus fl. 3rd cent. .... **CMLC 52**
See also WLIT 8

Helisenne de Crenne
See Crenne, Helisenne de

Hellenhofferu, Vojtech Kapristian z
See Hasek, Jaroslav

Heller, Joseph 1923-1999 .... **CLC 1, 3, 5, 8, 11, 36, 63; TCLC 131, 151; WLC 3**
See also AAYA 24; AITN 1; AMWS 4; BPFB 2; BYA 1; CA 5-8R; 187; CABS 1; CANR 8, 42, 66, 126; CN 1, 2, 3, 4, 5, 6; CPW; DA; DA3; DAB; DAC; DAM MST, NOV, POP; DLB 2, 28, 227; DLBY 1980, 2002; EWL 3; EXPN; INT CANR-8; LAIT 4; MAL 5; MTCW 1, 2; MTFW 2005; NFS 1; RGAL 4; TUS; YAW

Heller, Peter 1959- .... **CLC 354**
See also CA 276; CANR 256

Hellman, Lillian 1905-1984 .... **CLC 2, 4, 8, 14, 18, 34, 44, 52; DC 1; TCLC 119**
See also AAYA 47; AITN 1, 2; AMWS 1; CA 13-16R; 112; CAD; CANR 33; CWD; DA3; DAM DRAM; DFS 1, 3, 14; DLB 7, 228; DLBY 1984; EWL 3; FL 1:6; FW; LAIT 3; MAL 5; MBL; MTCW 1, 2; MTFW 2005; RGAL 4; TUS

Hellman, Lillian Florence
See Hellman, Lillian

Heloise c. 1095-c. 1164 .... **CMLC 122**

Helprin, Mark 1947- .... **CLC 7, 10, 22, 32**
See also CA 81-84; CANR 47, 64, 124, 222; CDALBS; CN 7; CPW; DA3; DAM NOV, POP; DLB 335; DLBY 1985; FANT; MAL 5; MTCW 1, 2; MTFW 2005; SSFS 25; SUFW 2

Helvetius, Claude-Adrien 1715-1771 ... **LC 26**
See also DLB 313

Helyar, Jane Penelope Josephine
1933- .... **CLC 17**
See also CA 21-24R; CANR 10, 26; CWRI 5; SAAS 2; SATA 5; SATA-Essay 138

Hemans, Felicia 1793-1835 ..... **NCLC 29, 71**
See also DLB 96; RGEL 2

Hemingway, Ernest 1899-1961 .... **CLC 1, 3, 6, 8, 10, 13, 19, 30, 34, 39, 41, 44, 50, 61, 80; SSC 1, 25, 36, 40, 63, 117, 137, 168, 189, 190; TCLC 115, 203; WLC 3**
See also AAYA 19; AMW; AMWC 1; AMWR 1; BPFB 2; BYA 2, 3, 13, 15; CA 77-80; CANR 34; CDALB 1917-1929; CLR 168; DA; DA3; DAB; DAC; DAM MST, NOV; DLB 4, 9, 102, 210, 308, 316, 330; DLBD 1, 15, 16; DLBY 1981, 1987, 1996, 1998; EWL 3; EXPN; EXPS; LAIT 3, 4; LATS

1:1; MAL 5; MTCW 1, 2; MTFW 2005; NFS 1, 5, 6, 14; RGAL 4; RGSF 2; SSFS 17; TUS; WYA

Hemingway, Ernest Miller
See Hemingway, Ernest

Hempel, Amy 1951- .... **CLC 39**
See also AMWS 21; CA 118; 137; CANR 70, 166; DA3; DLB 218; EXPS; MTCW 2; MTFW 2005; SSFS 2

Henderson, Eleanor .... **CLC 334**
See also CA 324

Henderson, F. C.
See Mencken, H. L.

Henderson, Mary
See Mavor, Osborne Henry

Henderson, Sylvia
See Ashton-Warner, Sylvia (Constance)

Henderson, Zenna (Chlarson)
1917-1983 .... **SSC 29**
See also CA 1-4R; 133; CANR 1, 84; DLB 8; SATA 5; SFW 4

Henkin, Joshua 1964- .... **CLC 119**
See also CA 161; CANR 186; DLB 350

Henley, Beth 1952- .... **CLC 23, 255; DC 6, 14**
See also AAYA 70; CA 107; CABS 3; CAD; CANR 32, 73, 140; CD 5, 6; CSW; CWD; DA3; DAM DRAM, MST; DFS 2, 21, 26; DLBY 1986; FW; MTCW 1, 2; MTFW 2005

Henley, Elizabeth Becker
See Henley, Beth

Henley, William Ernest
1849-1903 .... **PC 127; TCLC 8**
See also CA 105; 234; DLB 19; PFS 43; RGEL 2

Hennissart, Martha 1929- .... **CLC 2**
See also BPFB 2; CA 85-88; CANR 64; CMW 4; DLB 306

Henry VIII 1491-1547 .... **LC 10**
See also DLB 132

Henry, O. 1862-1910 .... **SSC 5, 49, 117; TCLC 1, 19; WLC 3**
See also AAYA 41; AMWS 2; CA 104; 131; CDALB 1865-1917; DA; DA3; DAB; DAC; DAM MST; DLB 12, 78, 79; EXPS; MAL 5; MTCW 1, 2; MTFW 2005; RGAL 4; RGSF 2; SSFS 2, 18, 27, 31; TCWW 1, 2; TUS; YABC 2

Henry, Oliver
See Henry, O.

Henry, Patrick 1736-1799 .... **LC 25, 225**
See also LAIT 1

Henryson, Robert 1430(?)-1506(?) .... **LC 20, 110; PC 65**
See also BRWS 7; DLB 146; RGEL 2

Henschke, Alfred
See Klabund

Henson, Lance 1944- .... **NNAL**
See also CA 146; DLB 175

Hentoff, Nat(han Irving) 1925- ...... **CLC 26**
See also AAYA 4, 42; BYA 6; CA 1-4R; CAAS 6; CANR 5, 25, 77, 114; CLR 1, 52; DLB 345; INT CANR-25; JRDA; MAICYA 1, 2; SATA 42, 69, 133; SATA-Brief 27; WYA; YAW

Hentz, Caroline Lee 1800-1856 .... **NCLC 281**
See also DLB 3, 248

Heppenstall, (John) Rayner
1911-1981 .... **CLC 10**
See also CA 1-4R; 103; CANR 29; CN 1, 2; CP 1, 2, 3; EWL 3

Heraclitus c. 540B.C.-c. 450B.C. ... **CMLC 22**
See also DLB 176

Herbert, Edward 1583-1648 .... **LC 177**
See also DLB 121, 151, 252; RGEL 2

Herbert, Frank 1920-1986 .... **CLC 12, 23, 35, 44, 85**
See also AAYA 21; BPFB 2; BYA 4, 14; CA 53-56; 118; CANR 5, 43; CDALBS; CPW;

DAM POP; DLB 8; INT CANR-5; LAIT 5; MTCW 1, 2; MTFW 2005; NFS 17, 31; SATA 9, 37; SATA-Obit 47; SCFW 1, 2; SFW 4; YAW

Herbert, George 1593-1633 ...... **LC 24, 121; PC 4, 145**
See also BRW 2; BRWR 2; CDBLB Before 1660; DAB; DAM POET; DLB 126; EXPP; PFS 25, 43; RGEL 2; TEA; WP

Herbert, Zbigniew 1924-1998 .... **CLC 9, 43; PC 50; TCLC 168**
See also CA 89-92; 169; CANR 36, 74, 177; CDWLB 4; CWW 2; DAM POET; DLB 232; EWL 3; MTCW 1; PFS 22

Herbert of Cherbury, Lord
See Herbert, Edward

Herbst, Josephine (Frey)
1897-1969 .... **CLC 34; TCLC 243**
See also CA 5-8R; 25-28R; DLB 9

Herder, Johann Gottfried von
1744-1803 .... **NCLC 8, 186**
See also DLB 97; EW 4; TWA

Heredia, Jose Maria 1803-1839 ..... **HLCS 2; NCLC 209**
See also LAW

Hergesheimer, Joseph 1880-1954 ... **TCLC 11**
See also CA 109; 194; DLB 102, 9; RGAL 4

Herlihy, James Leo 1927-1993 .... **CLC 6**
See also CA 1-4R; 143; CAD; CANR 2; CN 1, 2, 3, 4, 5

Herman, William
See Bierce, Ambrose

Hermogenes fl. c. 175 .... **CMLC 6**

Hernandez, Felisberto 1902-1964 ... **SSC 152**
See also CA 213; EWL 3; LAWS 1

Hernandez, Jose 1834-1886 .... **NCLC 17, 269; PC 141**
See also LAW; RGWL 2, 3; WLIT 1

Herodotus c. 484B.C.-c. 420B.C. .. **CMLC 17**
See also AW 1; CDWLB 1; DLB 176; RGWL 2, 3; TWA; WLIT 8

Herr, Michael 1940(?)- .... **CLC 231**
See also CA 89-92; CANR 68, 142; DLB 185; MTCW 1

Herrick, Robert
1591-1674 .... **LC 13, 145; PC 9, 138**
See also BRW 2; BRWC 2; DA; DAB; DAC; DAM MST, POP; DLB 126; EXPP; PFS 13, 29, 39; RGAL 4; RGEL 2; TEA; WP

Herring, Guilles
See Somerville, Edith Oenone

Herriot, James 1916-1995 .... **CLC 12**
See also AAYA 1, 54; BPFB 2; CA 77-80; 148; CANR 40; CLR 80; CPW; DAM POP; LAIT 3; MAICYA 2; MAICYAS 1; MTCW 2; SATA 86, 135; SATA-Brief 44; TEA; YAW

Herris, Violet
See Hunt, Violet

Herrmann, Dorothy 1941- .... **CLC 44**
See also CA 107

Herrmann, Taffy
See Herrmann, Dorothy

Hersey, John 1914-1993 .... **CLC 1, 2, 7, 9, 40, 81, 97**
See also AAYA 29; BPFB 2; CA 17-20R; 140; CANR 33; CDALBS; CN 1, 2, 3, 4, 5; CPW; DAM POP; DLB 6, 185, 278, 299, 364; MAL 5; MTCW 1, 2; MTFW 2005; NFS 41; RGHL; SATA 25; SATA-Obit 76; TUS

Hersey, John Richard
See Hersey, John

Hervent, Maurice
See Grindel, Eugene

Herzen, Aleksandr Ivanovich
1812-1870 .... **NCLC 10, 61**
See also DLB 277

Herzen, Alexander
See Herzen, Aleksandr Ivanovich

Herzl, Theodor 1860-1904 .... **TCLC 36**
See also CA 168

Herzog, Werner 1942- .... **CLC 16, 236**
See also AAYA 85; CA 89-92; CANR 215

Hesiod fl. 8th cent. B.C. .... **CMLC 5, 102**
See also AW 1; DLB 176; RGWL 2, 3; WLIT 8

Hesse, Hermann 1877-1962 ..... **CLC 1, 2, 3, 6, 11, 17, 25, 69; SSC 9, 49; TCLC 148, 196; WLC 3**
See also AAYA 43; BPFB 2; CA 17-18; CAP 2; CDWLB 2; DA; DA3; DAB; DAC; DAM MST, NOV; DLB 66, 330; EW 9; EWL 3; EXPN; LAIT 1; MTCW 1, 2; MTFW 2005; NFS 6, 15, 24; RGWL 2, 3; SATA 50; TWA

Hewes, Cady
See De Voto, Bernard (Augustine)

Heyen, William 1940- .... **CLC 13, 18**
See also CA 33-36R; 220; CAAE 220; CAAS 9; CANR 98, 188; CP 3, 4, 5, 6, 7; DLB 5; RGHL

Heyerdahl, Thor 1914-2002 .... **CLC 26**
See also CA 5-8R; 207; CANR 5, 22, 66, 73; LAIT 4; MTCW 1, 2; MTFW 2005; SATA 2, 52

Heym, Georg (Theodor Franz Arthur)
1887-1912 .... **TCLC 9**
See also CA 106; 181

Heym, Stefan 1913-2001 .... **CLC 41**
See also CA 9-12R; 203; CANR 4; CWW 2; DLB 69; EWL 3

Heyse, Paul (Johann Ludwig von)
1830-1914 .... **TCLC 8**
See also CA 104; 209; DLB 129, 330

Heyward, (Edwin) DuBose 1885-1940 ... **HR 1:2; TCLC 59**
See also CA 108; 157; DLB 7, 9, 45, 249; MAL 5; SATA 21

Heywood, John 1497(?)-1580(?) .... **LC 65**
See also DLB 136; RGEL 2

Heywood, Thomas 1573(?)-1641 .... **DC 29; LC 111**
See also DAM DRAM; DLB 62; LMFS 1; RGEL 2; TEA

Hiaasen, Carl 1953- .... **CLC 238**
See also CA 105; CANR 22, 45, 65, 113, 133, 168; CMW 4; CPW; CSW; DA3; DLB 292; LNFS 2, 3; MTCW 2; MTFW 2005; SATA 208

Hibbert, Eleanor Alice Burford
1906-1993 .... **CLC 7**
See also BEST 90:4; BPFB 2; CA 17-20R; 140; CANR 9, 28, 59; CMW 4; CPW; DAM POP; MTCW 2; MTFW 2005; RHW; SATA 2; SATA-Obit 74

Hichens, Robert (Smythe)
1864-1950 .... **TCLC 64**
See also CA 162; DLB 153; HGG; RHW; SUFW

Higgins, Aidan 1927- .... **SSC 68**
See also CA 9-12R; CANR 70, 115, 148; CN 1, 2, 3, 4, 5, 6, 7; DLB 14

Higgins, George V(incent)
1939-1999 .... **CLC 4, 7, 10, 18**
See also BPFB 2; CA 77-80; 186; CAAS 5; CANR 17, 51, 89, 96; CMW 4; CN 2, 3, 4, 5, 6; DLB 2; DLBY 1981, 1998; INT CANR-17; MSW; MTCW 1

Higginson, Thomas Wentworth
1823-1911 .... **TCLC 36**
See also CA 162; DLB 1, 64, 243

Higgonet, Margaret .... **CLC 65**

Highet, Helen
See MacInnes, Helen (Clark)

Highsmith, Mary Patricia
See Highsmith, Patricia

Highsmith, Patricia 1921-1995 ..... **CLC 2, 4, 14, 42, 102**
See also AAYA 48; BRWS 5; CA 1-4R; 147; CANR 1, 20, 48, 62, 108; CMW 4; CN 1, 2, 3, 4, 5; CPW; DA3; DAM NOV, POP; DLB 306; GLL 1; MSW; MTCW 1, 2; MTFW 2005; NFS 27; SSFS 25

Highwater, Jamake (Mamake)
1942(?)-2001 .... **CLC 12**
See also AAYA 7, 69; BPFB 2; BYA 4; CA 65-68; 199; CAAS 7; CANR 10, 34, 84; CLR 17; CWRI 5; DLB 52; DLBY 1985; JRDA; MAICYA 1, 2; SATA 32, 69; SATA-Brief 30

Highway, Tomson 1951- .... **CLC 92, 333; DC 33; NNAL**
See also CA 151; CANR 75; CCA 1; CD 5, 6; CN 7; DAC; DAM MULT; DFS 2; DLB 334; MTCW 2

Hijuelos, Oscar 1951- .... **CLC 65; HLC 1**
See also AAYA 25; AMWS 8; BEST 90:1; CA 123; CANR 50, 75, 125, 205, 239; CPW; DA3; DAM MULT, POP; DLB 145; HW 1, 2; LLW; MAL 5; MTCW 2; MTFW 2005; NFS 17; RGAL 4; WLIT 1

Hikmet, Nazim 1902-1963 .... **CLC 40**
See also CA 141; 93-96; EWL 3; PFS 38, 41; WLIT 6

Hildegard von Bingen
1098-1179 .... **CMLC 20, 118**
See also DLB 148

Hildesheimer, Wolfgang
1916-1991 .... **CLC 49**
See also CA 101; 135; DLB 69, 124; EWL 3; RGHL

Hill, Aaron 1685-1750 .... **LC 148**
See also DLB 84; RGEL 2

Hill, Geoffrey 1932- .... **CLC 5, 8, 18, 45, 251; PC 125**
See also BRWR 3; BRWS 5; CA 81-84; CANR 21, 89; CDBLB 1960 to Present; CP 1, 2, 3, 4, 5, 6, 7; DAM POET; DLB 40; EWL 3; MTCW 1; RGEL 2; RGHL

Hill, George Roy 1921-2002 .... **CLC 26**
See also CA 110; 122; 213

Hill, John
See Koontz, Dean

Hill, Susan 1942- .... **CLC 4, 113**
See also BRWS 14; CA 33-36R; CANR 29, 69, 129, 172, 201; CN 2, 3, 4, 5, 6, 7; DAB; DAM MST, NOV; DLB 14, 139; HGG; MTCW 1; RHW; SATA 183

Hill, Susan Elizabeth
See Hill, Susan

Hillard, Asa G. III .... **CLC 70**

Hillerman, Anthony Grove
See Hillerman, Tony

Hillerman, Tony 1925-2008 ..... **CLC 62, 170**
See also AAYA 40; BEST 89:1; BPFB 2; CA 29-32R; 278; CANR 21, 42, 65, 97, 134; CMW 4; CPW; DA3; DAM POP; DLB 206, 306; MAL 5; MSW; MTCW 2; MTFW 2005; RGAL 4; SATA 6; SATA-Obit 198; TCWW 2; YAW

Hillesum, Etty 1914-1943 .... **TCLC 49**
See also CA 137; RGHL

Hilliard, Noel (Harvey) 1929-1996 ... **CLC 15**
See also CA 9-12R; CANR 7, 69; CN 1, 2, 3, 4, 5, 6

Hillis, Rick 1956- .... **CLC 66**
See also CA 134

Hilton, James 1900-1954 .... **TCLC 21**
See also AAYA 76; CA 108; 169; DLB 34, 77; FANT; SATA 34

Hilton, Walter 1343-1396(?) ... **CMLC 58, 141**
See also DLB 146; RGEL 2

Himes, Chester (Bomar)
1909-1984 .... **BLC 1:2; CLC 2, 4, 7, 18, 58, 108; TCLC 139**

See also AFAW 2; AMWS 16; BPFB 2; BW 2; CA 25-28R; 114; CANR 22, 89; CMW 4; CN 1, 2, 3; DAM MULT; DLB 2, 76, 143, 226; EWL 3; MAL 5; MSW; MTCW 1, 2; MTFW 2005; RGAL 4

Himmelfarb, Gertrude 1922- .... **CLC 202**
See also CA 49-52; CANR 28, 66, 102, 166

Hinde, Thomas 1926- .... **CLC 6, 11**
See also CA 5-8R; CN 1, 2, 3, 4, 5, 6; EWL 3

Hine, (William) Daryl 1936- .... **CLC 15**
See also CA 1-4R; CAAS 15; CANR 1, 20; CP 1, 2, 3, 4, 5, 6, 7; DLB 60

Hinkson, Katharine Tynan
See Tynan, Katharine

Hinojosa, Rolando 1929- .... **HLC 1**
See also CA 131; CAAS 16; CANR 62; DAM MULT; DLB 82; EWL 3; HW 1, 2; LLW; MTCW 2; MTFW 2005; RGAL 4

Hinton, S. E. 1950- .... **CLC 30, 111**
See also AAYA 2, 33; BPFB 2; BYA 2, 3; CA 81-84; CANR 32, 62, 92, 133; CDALBS; CLR 3, 23; CPW; DA; DA3; DAB; DAC; DAM MST, NOV; JRDA; LAIT 5; MAICYA 1, 2; MTCW 1, 2; MTFW 2005; NFS 5, 9, 15, 16, 35; SATA 19, 58, 115, 160; WYA; YAW

Hinton, Susan Eloise
See Hinton, S. E.

Hippius, Zinaida
See Gippius, Zinaida

Hiraoka, Kimitake 1925-1970 ...... **CLC 2, 4, 6, 9, 27; DC 1; SSC 4; TCLC 161; WLC 4**
See Mishima, Yukio
See also AAYA 50; BPFB 2; CA 97-100; 29-32R; DA3; DAM DRAM; DLB 182; EWL 3; GLL 1; MJW; MTCW 1, 2; RGSF 2; RGWL 2, 3; SSFS 5, 12

Hirsch, E.D., Jr. 1928- .... **CLC 79**
See also CA 25-28R; CANR 27, 51, 146, 181; DLB 67; INT CANR-27; MTCW 1

Hirsch, Edward 1950- .... **CLC 31, 50**
See also CA 104; CANR 20, 42, 102, 167, 229; CP 6, 7; DLB 120; PFS 22

Hirsch, Eric Donald, Jr.
See Hirsch, E.D., Jr.

Hitchcock, Alfred (Joseph)
1899-1980 .... **CLC 16**
See also AAYA 22; CA 159; 97-100; SATA 27; SATA-Obit 24

Hitchens, Christopher 1949-2011 ... **CLC 157**
See also CA 152; CANR 89, 155, 191

Hitchens, Christopher Eric
See Hitchens, Christopher

Hitler, Adolf 1889-1945 .... **TCLC 53**
See also CA 117; 147

Holderlin, (Johann Christian) Friedrich
1770-1843 ... **NCLC 16, 187, 263; PC 4**
See also CDWLB 2; DLB 90; EW 5; RGWL 2, 3

Hoagland, Edward (Morley)
1932- .... **CLC 28**
See also ANW; CA 1-4R; CANR 2, 31, 57, 107; CN 1, 2, 3, 4, 5, 6, 7; DLB 6; SATA 51; TCWW 2

Hoban, Russell 1925-2011 .... **CLC 7, 25**
See also BPFB 2; CA 5-8R; CANR 23, 37, 66, 114, 138, 218; CLR 3, 69, 139; CN 4, 5, 6, 7; CWRI 5; DAM NOV; DLB 52; FANT; MAICYA 1, 2; MTCW 1, 2; MTFW 2005; SATA 1, 40, 78, 136; SFW 4; SUFW 2; TCLE 1:1

Hoban, Russell Conwell
See Hoban, Russell

Hobbes, Thomas
1588-1679 .... **LC 36, 142, 199**
See also DLB 151, 252, 281; RGEL 2

Hobbs, Perry
See Blackmur, R(ichard) P(almer)

Hobson, Laura Z(ametkin)
1900-1986 .... **CLC 7, 25**
See also BPFB 2; CA 17-20R; 118; CANR 55; CN 1, 2, 3, 4; DLB 28; SATA 52

Hoccleve, Thomas c. 1368-c. 1437 ... **LC 75; PC 146**
See also DLB 146; RGEL 2

Hoch, Edward D. 1930-2008 .... **SSC 119**
See also CA 29-32R; CANR 11, 27, 51, 97; CMW 4; DLB 306; SFW 4

Hoch, Edward Dentinger
See Hoch, Edward D.

Hochhuth, Rolf 1931- .... **CLC 4, 11, 18**
See also CA 5-8R; CANR 33, 75, 136; CWW 2; DAM DRAM; DLB 124; EWL 3; MTCW 1, 2; MTFW 2005; RGHL

Hochman, Sandra 1936- .... **CLC 3, 8**
See also CA 5-8R; CP 1, 2, 3, 4, 5; DLB 5

Hochwaelder, Fritz
1911-1986 .... **CLC 36**
See also CA 29-32R; 120; CANR 42; DAM DRAM; EWL 3; MTCW 1; RGWL 2, 3

Hochwalder, Fritz
See Hochwaelder, Fritz

Hocking, Mary 1921- .... **CLC 13**
See also CA 101; CANR 18, 40

Hocking, Mary Eunice
See Hocking, Mary

Hodge, Merle 1944- .... **BLC 2:2**
See also EWL 3

Hodgins, Jack 1938- .... **CLC 23; SSC 132**
See also CA 93-96; CN 4, 5, 6, 7; DLB 60

Hodgson, William Hope
1877(?)-1918 .... **TCLC 13**
See also CA 111; 164; CMW 4; DLB 70, 153, 156, 178; HGG; MTCW 2; SFW 4; SUFW 1

Hoeg, Peter
See Hoeg, Peter

Hoffman, Alice 1952- .... **CLC 51**
See also AAYA 37; AMWS 10; CA 77-80; CANR 34, 66, 100, 138, 170, 237; CN 4, 5, 6, 7; CPW; DAM NOV; DLB 292; MAL 5; MTCW 1, 2; MTFW 2005; TCLE 1:1

Hoffman, Daniel (Gerard)
1923- .... **CLC 6, 13, 23**
See also CA 1-4R; CANR 4, 142; CP 1, 2, 3, 4, 5, 6, 7; DLB 5; TCLE 1:1

Hoffman, Eva 1945- .... **CLC 182**
See also AMWS 16; CA 132; CANR 146, 209

Hoffman, Stanley 1944- .... **CLC 5**
See also CA 77-80

Hoffman, William 1925-2009 .... **CLC 141**
See also AMWS 18; CA 21-24R; CANR 9, 103; CSW; DLB 234; TCLE 1:1

Hoffman, William M.
See Hoffman, William M(oses)

Hoffman, William M(oses) 1939- ... **CLC 40**
See also CA 57-60; CAD; CANR 11, 71; CD 5, 6

Hoffmann, E(rnst) T(heodor) A(madeus)
1776-1822 ... **NCLC 2, 183; SSC 13, 92**
See also CDWLB 2; CLR 133; DLB 90; EW 5; GL 2; RGSF 2; RGWL 2, 3; SATA 27; SUFW 1; WCH

Hofmann, Gert 1931-1993 .... **CLC 54**
See also CA 128; CANR 145; EWL 3; RGHL

Hofmannsthal, Hugo von
1874-1929 .... **DC 4; TCLC 11**
See also CA 106; 153; CDWLB 2; DAM DRAM; DFS 17; DLB 81, 118; EW 9; EWL 3; RGWL 2, 3

Hogan, Linda 1947- .... **CLC 73, 290; NNAL; PC 35**
See also AMWS 4; ANW; BYA 12; CA 120, 226; CAAE 226; CANR 45, 73, 129, 196; CWP; DAM MULT; DLB 175; SATA 132; TCWW 2

Hogarth, Charles
See Creasey, John

Hogarth, Emmett
See Polonsky, Abraham (Lincoln)

Hogarth, William 1697-1764 .... **LC 112**
See also AAYA 56

Hogg, James 1770-1835 .... **NCLC 4, 109, 260; SSC 130**
See also BRWS 10; DLB 93, 116, 159; GL 2; HGG; RGEL 2; SUFW 1

Holbach, Paul-Henri Thiry
1723-1789 .... **LC 14**
See also DLB 313

Holberg, Ludvig 1684-1754 .... **LC 6, 208**
See also DLB 300; RGWL 2, 3

Holbrook, John
See Vance, Jack

Holcroft, Thomas 1745-1809 .... **NCLC 85**
See also DLB 39, 89, 158; RGEL 2

Holden, Ursula 1921- .... **CLC 18**
See also CA 101; CAAS 8; CANR 22

Holdstock, Robert 1948-2009 .... **CLC 39**
See also CA 131; CANR 81, 207; DLB 261; FANT; HGG; SFW 4; SUFW 2

Holdstock, Robert P.
See Holdstock, Robert

Holinshed, Raphael fl. 1580 .... **LC 69, 217**
See also DLB 167; RGEL 2

Holland, Isabelle (Christian)
1920-2002 .... **CLC 21**
See also AAYA 11, 64; CA 21-24R; 205; CAAE 181; CANR 10, 25, 47; CLR 57; CWRI 5; JRDA; LAIT 4; MAICYA 1, 2; SATA 8, 70; SATA-Essay 103; SATA-Obit 132; WYA

Holland, Marcus
See Caldwell, (Janet Miriam) Taylor (Holland)

Hollander, John 1929- ...... **CLC 2, 5, 8, 14; PC 117**
See also CA 1-4R; CANR 1, 52, 136; CP 1, 2, 3, 4, 5, 6, 7; DLB 5; MAL 5; SATA 13

Hollander, Paul
See Silverberg, Robert

Holleran, Andrew 1943(?)- .... **CLC 38**
See also CA 144; CANR 89, 162; GLL 1

Holley, Marietta 1836(?)-1926 .... **TCLC 99**
See also CA 118; DLB 11; FL 1:3

Hollinghurst, Alan 1954- ... **CLC 55, 91, 329**
See also BRWS 10; CA 114; CN 5, 6, 7; DLB 207, 326; GLL 1

Hollis, Jim
See Summers, Hollis (Spurgeon, Jr.)

Holly, Buddy 1936-1959 .... **TCLC 65**
See also CA 213

Holmes, Gordon
See Shiel, M. P.

Holmes, John
See Souster, (Holmes) Raymond

Holmes, John Clellon 1926-1988 .... **CLC 56**
See also BG 1:2; CA 9-12R; 125; CANR 4; CN 1, 2, 3, 4; DLB 16, 237

Holmes, Oliver Wendell, Jr.
1841-1935 .... **TCLC 77**
See also CA 114; 186

Holmes, Oliver Wendell
1809-1894 .... **NCLC 14, 81; PC 71**
See also AMWS 1; CDALB 1640-1865; DLB 1, 189, 235; EXPP; PFS 24; RGAL 4; SATA 34

Holmes, Raymond
See Souster, (Holmes) Raymond

Holt, Samuel
See Westlake, Donald E.

Holt, Victoria
See Hibbert, Eleanor Alice Burford

312; INT CA-132; MAL 5; MTCW 2;
MTFW 2005; RGAL 4

Hyatt, Daniel
See James, Daniel (Lewis)

Hyde, Anthony 1946- .... **CLC 42**
See also CA 136; CCA 1

Hyde, Margaret O. 1917- .... **CLC 21**
See also CA 1-4R; CANR 1, 36, 137, 181;
CLR 23; JRDA; MAICYA 1, 2; SAAS 8;
SATA 1, 42, 76, 139

Hyde, Margaret Oldroyd
See Hyde, Margaret O.

Hynes, James 1956(?)- .... **CLC 65**
See also CA 164; CANR 105

Hypatia c. 370-415 .... **CMLC 35**

Ian, Janis 1951- .... **CLC 21**
See also CA 105; 187; CANR 206

Ibanez, Vicente Blasco
See Blasco Ibanez, Vicente

Ibarbourou, Juana de
1895(?)-1979 .... **HLCS 2**
See also DLB 290; HW 1; LAW

Ibarguengoitia, Jorge 1928-1983 ... **CLC 37;
TCLC 148**
See also CA 124; 113; EWL 3; HW 1

Ibn Arabi 1165-1240 .... **CMLC 105**

Ibn Battuta, Abu Abdalla
1304-1368(?) .... **CMLC 57**
See also WLIT 2

Ibn Hazm 994-1064 .... **CMLC 64**

Ibn Zaydun 1003-1070 .... **CMLC 89**

Ibsen, Henrik 1828-1906 .... **DC 2, 30;
TCLC 2, 8, 16, 37, 52; WLC 3**
See also AAYA 46; CA 104; 141; DA; DA3;
DAB; DAC; DAM DRAM, MST; DFS 1,
6, 8, 10, 11, 15, 16, 25; DLB 354; EW 7;
LAIT 2; LATS 1:1; MTFW 2005;
RGWL 2, 3

Ibsen, Henrik Johan
See Ibsen, Henrik

Ibuse, Masuji 1898-1993 .... **CLC 22**
See also CA 127; 141; CWW 2; DLB 180;
EWL 3; MJW; RGWL 3

Ibuse Masuji
See Ibuse, Masuji

Ichikawa, Kon 1915-2008 .... **CLC 20**
See also CA 121; 269

Ichiyo, Higuchi 1872-1896 .... **NCLC 49**
See also MJW

Idle, Eric 1943- .... **CLC 21**
See also CA 116; CANR 35, 91, 148;
DLB 352

Idris, Yusuf 1927-1991 .... **SSC 74;
TCLC 232**
See also AFW; DLB 346; EWL 3; RGSF 2,
3; RGWL 3; WLIT 2

Ignatieff, Michael 1947- .... **CLC 236**
See also CA 144; CANR 88, 156; CN 6, 7;
DLB 267

Ignatieff, Michael Grant
See Ignatieff, Michael

Ignatow, David 1914-1997 ..... **CLC 4, 7, 14,
40; PC 34**
See also CA 9-12R; 162; CAAS 3; CANR
31, 57, 96; CP 1, 2, 3, 4, 5, 6; DLB 5;
EWL 3; MAL 5

Ignotus
See Strachey, (Giles) Lytton

Ihimaera, Witi (Tame) 1944- .... **CLC 46, 329**
See also CA 77-80; CANR 130; CN 2, 3, 4,
5, 6, 7; RGSF 2; SATA 148

Il'f, Il'ia
See Fainzilberg, Ilya Arnoldovich

Ilf, Ilya
See Fainzilberg, Ilya Arnoldovich

Illyes, Gyula 1902-1983 .... **PC 16**
See also CA 114; 109; CDWLB 4; DLB 215;
EWL 3; RGWL 2, 3

Imalayen, Fatima-Zohra
See Djebar, Assia

Immermann, Karl (Lebrecht)
1796-1840 .... **NCLC 4, 49**
See also DLB 133

Ince, Thomas H. 1882-1924 .... **TCLC 89**
See also IDFW 3, 4

Inchbald, Elizabeth 1753-1821 .... **NCLC 62,
276**
See also BRWS 15; DLB 39, 89; RGEL 2

Inclan, Ramon del Valle
See Valle-Inclan, Ramon del

Incogniteau, Jean-Louis
See Kerouac, Jack

Infante, Guillermo Cabrera
See Cabrera Infante, G.

Ingalls, Rachel 1940- .... **CLC 42**
See also CA 123; 127; CANR 154

Ingalls, Rachel Holmes
See Ingalls, Rachel

Ingamells, Reginald Charles
See Ingamells, Rex

Ingamells, Rex 1913-1955 .... **TCLC 35**
See also CA 167; DLB 260

Inge, William (Motter) 1913-1973 ... **CLC 1,
8, 19; DC 37; TCLC 283**
See also CA 9-12R; CAD; CDALB 1941-
1968; DA3; DAM DRAM; DFS 1, 3, 5, 8;
DLB 7, 249; EWL 3; MAL 5; MTCW 1, 2;
MTFW 2005; RGAL 4; TUS

Ingelow, Jean 1820-1897 ...... **NCLC 39, 107;
PC 119**
See also DLB 35, 163; FANT; SATA 33

Ingram, Willis J.
See Harris, Mark

Innaurato, Albert (F.) 1948(?)- ... **CLC 21, 60**
See also CA 115; 122; CAD; CANR 78; CD
5, 6; INT CA-122

Innes, Michael
See Stewart, J(ohn) I(nnes) M(ackintosh)

Innis, Harold Adams 1894-1952 ... **TCLC 77**
See also CA 181; DLB 88

Insluis, Alanus de
See Alain de Lille

Iola
See Wells-Barnett, Ida B(ell)

Ionesco, Eugene 1909-1994 ..... **CLC 1, 4, 6,
9, 11, 15, 41, 86; DC 12; TCLC 232;
WLC 3**
See also CA 9-12R; 144; CANR 55, 132;
CWW 2; DA; DA3; DAB; DAC; DAM
DRAM, MST; DFS 4, 9, 25; DLB 321;
EW 13; EWL 3; GFL 1789 to the Present;
LMFS 2; MTCW 1, 2; MTFW 2005;
RGWL 2, 3; SATA 7; SATA-Obit 79; TWA

Iqbal, Muhammad 1877-1938 .... **TCLC 28**
See also CA 215; EWL 3

Ireland, Patrick
See O'Doherty, Brian

Irenaeus St. 130- .... **CMLC 42**

Irigaray, Luce 1930- .... **CLC 164, 326**
See also CA 154; CANR 121; FW

Irish, William
See Hopley-Woolrich, Cornell George

Irland, David
See Green, Julien

Iron, Ralph
See Schreiner, Olive

Irving, John 1942- .... **CLC 13, 23, 38,
112, 175**
See also AAYA 8, 62; AMWS 6; BEST 89:3;
BPFB 2; CA 25-28R; CANR 28, 73, 112,
133, 223; CN 3, 4, 5, 6, 7; CPW; DA3;
DAM NOV, POP; DLB 6, 278; DLBY
1982; EWL 3; MAL 5; MTCW 1, 2;
MTFW 2005; NFS 12, 14; RGAL 4; TUS

Irving, John Winslow
See Irving, John

Irving, Washington 1783-1859 .... **NCLC 2,
19, 95, 242; SSC 2, 37, 104; WLC 3**
See also AAYA 56; AMW; CDALB 1640-
1865; CLR 97; DA; DA3; DAB; DAC;
DAM MST; DLB 3, 11, 30, 59, 73, 74,
183, 186, 250, 254; EXPS; GL 2; LAIT 1;
RGAL 4; RGSF 2; SSFS 1, 8, 16; SUFW
1; TUS; WCH; YABC 2

Irwin, P. K.
See Page, P.K.

Isaacs, Jorge Ricardo 1837-1895 .. **NCLC 70**
See also LAW

Isaacs, Susan 1943- .... **CLC 32**
See also BEST 89:1; BPFB 2; CA 89-92;
CANR 20, 41, 65, 112, 134, 165, 226;
CPW; DA3; DAM POP; INT CANR-20;
MTCW 1, 2; MTFW 2005

Isherwood, Christopher
1904-1986 .... **CLC 1, 9, 11, 14, 44;
SSC 56; TCLC 227**
See also AMWS 14; BRW 7; CA 13-16R;
117; CANR 35, 97, 133; CN 1, 2, 3; DA3;
DAM DRAM, NOV; DLB 15, 195; DLBY
1986; EWL 3; IDTP; MTCW 1, 2; MTFW
2005; RGAL 4; RGEL 2; TUS; WLIT 4

Isherwood, Christopher William Bradshaw
See Isherwood, Christopher

Ishiguro, Kazuo 1954- .... **CLC 27, 56, 59,
110, 219**
See also AAYA 58; BEST 90:2; BPFB 2;
BRWR 3; BRWS 4; CA 120; CANR 49, 95,
133; CN 5, 6, 7; DA3; DAM NOV; DLB
194, 326; EWL 3; MTCW 1, 2; MTFW
2005; NFS 13, 35, 39; WLIT 4; WWE 1

Ishikawa, Hakuhin
See Ishikawa, Takuboku

Ishikawa, Takuboku 1886(?)-1912 .... **PC 10;
TCLC 15**
See Ishikawa Takuboku
See also CA 113; 153; DAM POET

Isidore of Seville c. 560-636 .... **CMLC 101**

Iskander, Fazil (Abdulovich) 1929- **CLC 47**
See also CA 102; DLB 302; EWL 3

Iskander, Fazil' Abdulevich
See Iskander, Fazil (Abdulovich)

Isler, Alan (David) 1934- .... **CLC 91**
See also CA 156; CANR 105

Ivan IV 1530-1584 .... **LC 17**

Ivanov, V.I.
See Ivanov, Vyacheslav

Ivanov, Vyacheslav 1866-1949 ...... **TCLC 33**
See also CA 122; EWL 3

Ivanov, Vyacheslav Ivanovich
See Ivanov, Vyacheslav

Ivask, Ivar Vidrik 1927-1992 .... **CLC 14**
See also CA 37-40R; 139; CANR 24

Ives, Morgan
See Bradley, Marion Zimmer

Ivo of Chartres c. 1040-1115 ..... **CMLC 116**

Izumi Shikibu c. 973-c. 1034 .... **CMLC 33**

J. R. S.
See Gogarty, Oliver St. John

Jabran, Kahlil
See Gibran, Kahlil

Jabran, Khalil
See Gibran, Kahlil

Jaccottet, Philippe 1925- .... **PC 98**
See also CA 116; 129; CWW 2; GFL 1789
to the Present

Jackson, Daniel
See Wingrove, David

Jackson, Helen Hunt
1830-1885 .... **NCLC 90, 256**
See also DLB 42, 47, 186, 189; RGAL 4

Jackson, Jesse 1908-1983 .... **CLC 12**
See also BW 1; CA 25-28R; 109; CANR 27;
CLR 28; CWRI 5; MAICYA 1, 2; SATA 2,
29; SATA-Obit 48

Jackson, Laura 1901-1991 .... **CLC 3, 7;**
PC 44; TCLC 240
See also CA 65-68; 135; CANR 28, 89; CP
1, 2, 3, 4, 5; DLB 48; RGAL 4

Jackson, Laura Riding
See Jackson, Laura

Jackson, Sam
See Trumbo, Dalton

Jackson, Sara
See Wingrove, David

Jackson, Shirley 1919-1965 ...... **CLC 11, 60,**
87; SSC 9, 39; TCLC 187; WLC 3
See also AAYA 9; AMWS 9; BPFB 2; CA 1-
4R; 25-28R; CANR 4, 52; CDALB 1941-
1968; DA; DA3; DAC; DAM MST; DLB
6, 234; EXPS; HGG; LAIT 4; MAL 5;
MTCW 2; MTFW 2005; NFS 37; RGAL
4; RGSF 2; SATA 2; SSFS 1, 27, 30, 37;
SUFW 1, 2

Jacob, (Cyprien-)Max 1876-1944 ... **TCLC 6**
See also CA 104; 193; DLB 258; EWL 3;
GFL 1789 to the Present; GLL 2; RGWL
2, 3

Jacobs, Harriet A.
1813(?)-1897 .... **NCLC 67, 162**
See also AFAW 1, 2; DLB 239; FL 1:3; FW;
LAIT 2; RGAL 4

Jacobs, Harriet Ann
See Jacobs, Harriet A.

Jacobs, Jim 1942- .... **CLC 12**
See also CA 97-100; INT CA-97-100

Jacobs, W(illiam) W(ymark)
1863-1943 .... **SSC 73; TCLC 22**
See also CA 121; 167; DLB 135; EXPS;
HGG; RGEL 2; RGSF 2; SSFS 2; SUFW 1

Jacobsen, Jens Peter
1847-1885 .... **NCLC 34, 237**

Jacobsen, Josephine (Winder)
1908-2003 .... **CLC 48, 102; PC 62**
See also CA 33-36R; 218; CAAS 18; CANR
23, 48; CCA 1; CP 2, 3, 4, 5, 6, 7; DLB
244; PFS 23; TCLE 1:1

Jacobson, Dan 1929- .... **CLC 4, 14; SSC 91**
See also AFW; CA 1-4R; CANR 2, 25, 66,
170; CN 1, 2, 3, 4, 5, 6, 7; DLB 14, 207,
225, 319; EWL 3; MTCW 1; RGSF 2

Jacopone da Todi 1236-1306 .... **CMLC 95**

Jacqueline
See Carpentier, Alejo

Jacques de Vitry
c. 1160-1240 .... **CMLC 63, 152**
See also DLB 208

Jagger, Michael Philip
See Jagger, Mick

Jagger, Mick 1943- .... **CLC 17**
See also CA 239

Jahiz, al- c. 780-c. 869 .... **CMLC 25**
See also DLB 311

Jakes, John 1932- .... **CLC 29**
See also AAYA 32; BEST 89:4; BPFB 2; CA
57-60, 214; CAAE 214; CANR 10, 43, 66,
111, 142, 171; CPW; CSW; DA3; DAM
NOV, POP; DLB 278; DLBY 1983; FANT;
INT CANR-10; MTCW 1, 2; MTFW
2005; RHW; SATA 62; SFW 4; TCWW
1, 2

Jakes, John William
See Jakes, John

James I 1394-1437 .... **LC 20**
See also RGEL 2

James, Alice 1848-1892 .... **NCLC 206**
See also DLB 221

James, Andrew
See Kirkup, James

James, C.L.R. 1901-1989 .... **BLCS; CLC 33**
See also AMWS 21; BW 2; CA 117; 125;
128; CANR 62; CN 1, 2, 3, 4; DLB 125;
MTCW 1

James, Daniel (Lewis) 1911-1988 ... **CLC 33**
See also CA 174; 125; DLB 122

James, Dynely
See Mayne, William

James, Henry Sr. 1811-1882 .... **NCLC 53**

James, Henry 1843-1916 .... **DC 41;**
SSC 8, 32, 47, 108, 150; TCLC 2, 11, 24,
40, 47, 64, 171; WLC 3
See also AAYA 84; AMW; AMWC 1;
AMWR 1; BPFB 2; BRW 6; CA 104;
132; CDALB 1865-1917; DA; DA3; DAB;
DAC; DAM MST, NOV; DLB 12, 71, 74,
189; DLBD 13; EWL 3; EXPS; GL 2;
HGG; LAIT 2; MAL 5; MTCW 1, 2;
MTFW 2005; NFS 12, 16, 19, 32, 37;
RGAL 4; RGEL 2; RGSF 2; SSFS 9;
SUFW 1; TUS

James, M. R.
See James, Montague

James, Mary
See Meaker, Marijane

James, Montague 1862-1936 ..... **SSC 16, 93;**
TCLC 6
See also CA 104; 203; DLB 156, 201; HGG;
RGEL 2; RGSF 2; SUFW 1

James, Montague Rhodes
See James, Montague

James, P. D. 1920- .... **CLC 18, 46, 122,**
226, 345
See also BEST 90:2; BPFB 2; BRWS 4; CA
21-24R; CANR 17, 43, 65, 112, 201, 231;
CDBLB 1960 to Present; CMW 4; CN 4,
5, 6, 7; CPW; DA3; DAM POP; DLB 87,
276; DLBD 17; MSW; MTCW 1, 2;
MTFW 2005; TEA

James, Philip
See Moorcock, Michael

James, Samuel
See Stephens, James

James, Seumas
See Stephens, James

James, Stephen
See Stephens, James

James, T. F.
See Fleming, Thomas

James, William 1842-1910 ...... **TCLC 15, 32**
See also CA 109; 193; DLB 270,
284; MAL 5; NCFS 5; RGAL 4

Jameson, Anna 1794-1860 .... **NCLC 43, 282**
See also DLB 99, 166

Jameson, Fredric 1934- .... **CLC 142**
See also CA 196; CANR 169; DLB 67;
LMFS 2

Jameson, Fredric R.
See Jameson, Fredric

James VI of Scotland 1566-1625 .... **LC 109**
See also DLB 151, 172

Jami, Nur al-Din 'Abd al-Rahman
1414-1492 .... **LC 9**

Jammes, Francis 1868-1938 .... **TCLC 75**
See also CA 198; EWL 3; GFL 1789 to the
Present

Jandl, Ernst 1925-2000 .... **CLC 34**
See also CA 200; EWL 3

Janowitz, Tama 1957- .... **CLC 43, 145**
See also CA 106; CANR 52, 89, 129; CN 5,
6, 7; CPW; DAM POP; DLB 292;
MTFW 2005

Jansson, Tove (Marika) 1914-2001 ... **SSC 96**
See also CA 17-20R; 196; CANR 38, 118;
CLR 2, 125; CWW 2; DLB 257; EWL 3;
MAICYA 1, 2; RGSF 2; SATA 3, 41

Japrisot, Sebastien 1931-
See Rossi, Jean-Baptiste

Jarrell, Randall 1914-1965 ...... **CLC 1, 2, 6,**
9, 13, 49; PC 41; TCLC 177
See also AMW; BYA 5; CA 5-8R; 25-28R;
CABS 2; CANR 6, 34; CDALB 1941-
1968; CLR 6, 111; CWRI 5; DAM POET;

DLB 48, 52; EWL 3; EXPP; MAICYA 1,
2; MAL 5; MTCW 1, 2; PAB; PFS 2, 31;
RGAL 4; SATA 7

Jarry, Alfred 1873-1907 ...... **DC 49; SSC 20;**
TCLC 2, 14, 147
See also CA 104; 153; DA3; DAM DRAM;
DFS 8; DLB 192, 258; EW 9; EWL 3;
GFL 1789 to the Present; RGWL 2, 3;
TWA

Jarvis, E.K.
See Ellison, Harlan; Silverberg, Robert

Jawien, Andrzej
See John Paul II, Pope

Jaynes, Roderick
See Coen, Ethan

Jeake, Samuel, Jr.
See Aiken, Conrad

Jean-Louis
See Kerouac, Jack

Jean Paul 1763-1825 .... **NCLC 7, 268**

Jefferies, (John) Richard
1848-1887 .... **NCLC 47**
See also BRWS 15; DLB 98, 141; RGEL 2;
SATA 16; SFW 4

Jefferies, William
See Deaver, Jeffery

Jeffers, John Robinson
See Jeffers, Robinson

Jeffers, Robinson 1887-1962 .... **CLC 2, 3,**
11, 15, 54; PC 17; WLC 3
See also AMWS 2; CA 85-88; CANR 35;
CDALB 1917-1929; DA; DAC; DAM
MST, POET; DLB 45, 212, 342; EWL
3; MAL 5; MTCW 1, 2; MTFW 2005;
PAB; PFS 3, 4; RGAL 4

Jefferson, Janet
See Mencken, H. L.

Jefferson, Thomas
1743-1826 .... **NCLC 11, 103**
See also AAYA 54; ANW; CDALB 1640-
1865; DA3; DLB 31, 183; LAIT 1; RGAL 4

Jeffrey, Francis 1773-1850 .... **NCLC 33**
See also DLB 107

Jelakowitch, Ivan
See Heijermans, Herman

Jelinek, Elfriede 1946- .... **CLC 169, 303**
See also AAYA 68; CA 154; CANR 169;
DLB 85, 330; FW

Jellicoe, (Patricia) Ann
1927- .... **CLC 27**
See also CA 85-88; CBD; CD 5, 6; CWD;
CWRI 5; DLB 13, 233; FW

Jelloun, Tahar ben
See Ben Jelloun, Tahar

Jemyma
See Holley, Marietta

Jen, Gish 1955- ..... **AAL; CLC 70, 198, 260**
See also AAYA 85; AMWC 2; CA 135;
CANR 89, 130, 231; CN 7; DLB 312;
NFS 30; SSFS 34

Jen, Lillian
See Jen, Gish

Jenkins, (John) Robin 1912- .... **CLC 52**
See also CA 1-4R; CANR 1, 135; CN 1, 2,
3, 4, 5, 6, 7; DLB 14, 271

Jennings, Elizabeth (Joan)
1926-2001 .... **CLC 5, 14, 131**
See also BRWS 5; CA 61-64; 200; CAAS 5;
CANR 8, 39, 66, 127; CP 1, 2, 3, 4, 5, 6,
7; CWP; DLB 27; EWL 3; MTCW 1;
SATA 66

Jennings, Waylon 1937-2002 .... **CLC 21**

Jensen, Johannes V(ilhelm)
1873-1950 .... **TCLC 41**
See also CA 170; DLB 214, 330; EWL 3;
RGWL 3

Jensen, Laura 1948- .... **CLC 37**
See also CA 103

Kane, Francis
See Robbins, Harold

Kane, Paul
See Simon, Paul

Kane, Sarah 1971-1999 .... **DC 31**
See also BRWS 8; CA 190; CD 5, 6; DLB 310

Kanin, Garson 1912-1999 .... **CLC 22**
See also AITN 1; CA 5-8R; 177; CAD; CANR 7, 78; DLB 7; IDFW 3, 4

Kaniuk, Yoram 1930- .... **CLC 19**
See also CA 134; DLB 299; RGHL

Kant, Immanuel 1724-1804 .... **NCLC 27, 67, 253**
See also DLB 94

Kant, Klerk
See Copeland, Stewart

Kantor, MacKinlay 1904-1977 .... **CLC 7**
See also CA 61-64; 73-76; CANR 60, 63; CN 1, 2; DLB 9, 102; MAL 5; MTCW 2; RHW; TCWW 1, 2

Kanze Motokiyo
See Zeami

Kaplan, David Michael 1946- .... **CLC 50**
See also CA 187

Kaplan, James 1951- .... **CLC 59**
See also CA 135; CANR 121, 228

Karadzic, Vuk Stefanovic
1787-1864 .... **NCLC 115**
See also CDWLB 4; DLB 147

Karageorge, Michael
See Anderson, Poul

Karamzin, Nikolai Mikhailovich
1766-1826 .... **NCLC 3, 173**
See also DLB 150; RGSF 2

Karapanou, Margarita 1946- .... **CLC 13**
See also CA 101

Karinthy, Frigyes 1887-1938 .... **TCLC 47**
See also CA 170; DLB 215; EWL 3

Karl, Frederick R(obert) 1927-2004 .. **CLC 34**
See also CA 5-8R; 226; CANR 3, 44, 143

Karr, Mary 1955- .... **CLC 188**
See also AMWS 11; CA 151; CANR 100, 191, 241; MTFW 2005; NCFS 5

Kastel, Warren
See Silverberg, Robert

Kataev, Evgeny Petrovich
1903-1942 .... **TCLC 21**
See also CA 120; DLB 272

Kataphusin
See Ruskin, John

Katz, Steve 1935- .... **CLC 47**
See also CA 25-28R; CAAS 14, 64; CANR 12; CN 4, 5, 6, 7; DLBY 1983

Kauffman, Janet 1945- .... **CLC 42**
See also CA 117; CANR 43, 84; DLB 218; DLBY 1986

Kaufman, Bob (Garnell)
1925-1986 .... **CLC 49; PC 74**
See also BG 1:3; BW 1; CA 41-44R; 118; CANR 22; CP 1; DLB 16, 41

Kaufman, George S. 1889-1961 .... **CLC 38; DC 17**
See also CA 108; 93-96; DAM DRAM; DFS 1, 10; DLB 7; INT CA-108; MTCW 2; MTFW 2005; RGAL 4; TUS

Kaufman, Moises 1963- .... **DC 26**
See also AAYA 85; CA 211; DFS 22; MTFW 2005

Kaufman, Sue
See Barondess, Sue K.

Kavafis, Konstantinos Petrov
See Cavafy, Constantine

Kavan, Anna 1901-1968 .... **CLC 5, 13, 82**
See also BRWS 7; CA 5-8R; CANR 6, 57; DLB 255; MTCW 1; RGEL 2; SFW 4

Kavanagh, Dan
See Barnes, Julian

Kavanagh, Julie 1952- .... **CLC 119**
See also CA 163; CANR 186

Kavanagh, Patrick (Joseph)
1904-1967 .... **CLC 22; PC 33, 105**
See also BRWS 7; CA 123; 25-28R; DLB 15, 20; EWL 3; MTCW 1; RGEL 2

Kawabata, Yasunari 1899-1972 ... **CLC 2, 5, 9, 18, 107; SSC 17**
See also CA 93-96; 33-36R; CANR 88; DAM MULT; DLB 180, 330; EWL 3; MJW; MTCW 2; MTFW 2005; NFS 42; RGSF 2; RGWL 2, 3; SSFS 29, 37

Kawabata Yasunari
See Kawabata, Yasunari

Kaye, Mary Margaret
See Kaye, M.M.

Kaye, M.M. 1908-2004 .... **CLC 28**
See also CA 89-92; 223; CANR 24, 60, 102, 142; MTCW 1, 2; MTFW 2005; RHW; SATA 62; SATA-Obit 152

Kaye, Mollie
See Kaye, M.M.

Kaye-Smith, Sheila 1887-1956 ...... **TCLC 20**
See also CA 118; 203; DLB 36

Kaymor, Patrice Maguilene
See Senghor, Leopold Sedar

Kazakov, Iurii Pavlovich
See Kazakov, Yuri Pavlovich

Kazakov, Yuri Pavlovich
1927-1982 .... **SSC 43**
See also CA 5-8R; CANR 36; DLB 302; EWL 3; MTCW 1; RGSF 2

Kazakov, Yury
See Kazakov, Yuri Pavlovich

Kazan, Elia 1909-2003 .... **CLC 6, 16, 63**
See also AAYA 83; CA 21-24R; 220; CANR 32, 78

Kazanjoglou, Elia
See Kazan, Elia

Kazantzakis, Nikos 1883(?)-1957 .... **PC 126; TCLC 2, 5, 33, 181**
See also AAYA 83; BPFB 2; CA 105; 132; DA3; EW 9; EWL 3; MTCW 1, 2; MTFW 2005; RGWL 2, 3

Kazin, Alfred 1915-1998 ... **CLC 34, 38, 119**
See also AMWS 8; CA 1-4R; CAAS 7; CANR 1, 45, 79; DLB 67; EWL 3

Koda Rohan
See Koda Shigeyuki

Keane, Mary Nesta 1904-1996 .... **CLC 31**
See also CA 108; 114; 151; CN 5, 6; INT CA-114; RHW; TCLE 1:1

Keane, Mary Nesta Skrine
See Keane, Mary Nesta

Keane, Molly
See Keane, Mary Nesta

Keates, Jonathan 1946(?)- .... **CLC 34**
See also CA 163; CANR 126

Keaton, Buster 1895-1966 .... **CLC 20**
See also AAYA 79; CA 194

Keats, John 1795-1821 .... **NCLC 8, 73, 121, 225; PC 1, 96; WLC 3**
See also AAYA 58; BRW 4; BRWR 1; CDBLB 1789-1832; DA; DA3; DAB; DAC; DAM MST, POET; DLB 96, 110; EXPP; LMFS 1; PAB; PFS 1, 2, 3, 9, 17, 32, 36; RGEL 2; TEA; WLIT 3; WP

Keble, John 1792-1866 .... **NCLC 87**
See also DLB 32, 55; RGEL 2

Keene, Donald 1922- .... **CLC 34**
See also CA 1-4R; CANR 5, 119, 190

Keillor, Garrison 1942- ... **CLC 40, 115, 222**
See also AAYA 2, 62; AMWS 16; BEST 89:3; BPFB 2; CA 111; 117; CANR 36, 59, 124, 180; CPW; DA3; DAM POP; DLBY 1987; EWL 3; MTCW 1, 2; MTFW 2005; SATA 58; TUS

Keillor, Gary Edward
See Keillor, Garrison

Keith, Carlos
See Lewton, Val

Keith, Michael
See Hubbard, L. Ron

Kell, Joseph
See Burgess, Anthony

Keller, Gottfried 1819-1890 ... **NCLC 2, 277; SSC 26, 107**
See also CDWLB 2; DLB 129; EW; RGSF 2; RGWL 2, 3

Keller, Nora Okja 1965- .... **CLC 109, 281**
See also CA 187

Kellerman, Jonathan 1949- .... **CLC 44**
See also AAYA 35; BEST 90:1; CA 106; CANR 29, 51, 150, 183, 236; CMW 4; CPW; DA3; DAM POP; INT CANR-29

Kelley, William Melvin 1937- .... **BLC 2:2; CLC 22**
See also BW 1; CA 77-80; CANR 27, 83; CN 1, 2, 3, 4, 5, 6, 7; DLB 33; EWL 3

Kellock, Archibald P.
See Mavor, Osborne Henry

Kellogg, Marjorie 1922-2005 .... **CLC 2**
See also CA 81-84; 246

Kellow, Kathleen
See Hibbert, Eleanor Alice Burford

Kelly, Lauren
See Oates, Joyce Carol

Kelly, M(ilton) T(errence) 1947- .... **CLC 55**
See also CA 97-100; CAAS 22; CANR 19, 43, 84; CN 6

Kelly, Robert 1935- .... **SSC 50**
See also CA 17-20R; CAAS 19; CANR 47; CP 1, 2, 3, 4, 5, 6, 7; DLB 5, 130, 165

Kelman, James 1946- .... **CLC 58, 86, 292**
See also BRWS 5; CA 148; CANR 85, 130, 199; CN 5, 6, 7; DLB 194, 319, 326; RGSF 2; WLIT 4

Kelton, Elmer 1926-2009 .... **CLC 299**
See also AAYA 78; AITN 1; BYA 9; CA 21-24R; 289; CANR 12, 36, 85, 149, 173, 209; DLB 256; TCWW 1, 2

Kelton, Elmer Stephen
See Kelton, Elmer

Kemal, Yasar
See Kemal, Yashar

Kemal, Yashar 1923(?)- ...., **CLC 14, 29**
See also CA 89-92; CANR 44; CWW 2; EWL 3; WLIT 6

Kemble, Fanny 1809-1893 .... **NCLC 18**
See also DLB 32

Kemelman, Harry 1908-1996 .... **CLC 2**
See also AITN 1; BPFB 2; CA 9-12R; 155; CANR 6, 71; CMW 4; DLB 28

Kempe, Margery
1373(?)-1440(?) .... **LC 6, 56, 224**
See also BRWS 12; DLB 146; FL 1:1; RGEL 2

Kempis, Thomas a 1380-1471 .... **LC 11**

Kenan, Randall (G.) 1963- .... **BLC 2:2**
See also BW 2, 3; CA 142; CANR 86; CN 7; CSW; DLB 292; GLL 1

Kendall, Henry 1839-1882 .... **NCLC 12**
See also DLB 230

Keneally, Thomas 1935- .... **CLC 5, 8, 10, 14, 19, 27, 43, 117, 279**
See also BRWS 4; CA 85-88; CANR 10, 50, 74, 130, 165, 198, 240; CN 1, 2, 3, 4, 5, 6, 7; CPW; DA3; DAM NOV; DLB 289, 299, 326; EWL 3; MTCW 1, 2; MTFW 2005; NFS 17, 38; RGEL 2; RGHL; RHW

Keneally, Thomas Michael
See Keneally, Thomas

Keneally, Tom
See Keneally, Thomas

Kingsley, Sidney 1906-1995 .... **CLC 44**
See also CA 85-88; 147; CAD; DFS 14, 19;
DLB 7; MAL 5; RGAL 4

Kingsolver, Barbara 1955- .... **CLC 55, 81,
130, 216, 269, 342**
See also AAYA 15; AMWS 7; CA 129; 134;
CANR 60, 96, 133, 179; CDALBS; CN 7;
CPW; CSW; DA3; DAM POP; DLB 206;
INT CA-134; LAIT 5; MTCW 2; MTFW
2005; NFS 5, 10, 12, 24; RGAL 4; TCLE 1:1

Kingston, Maxine Hong 1940- ... **AAL; CLC
12, 19, 58, 121, 271; SSC 136; WLCS**
See also AAYA 8, 55; AMWS 5; BPFB 2;
CA 69-72; CANR 13, 38, 74, 87, 128, 239;
CDALBS; CN 6, 7; DA3; DAM MULT,
NOV; DLB 173, 212, 312; DLBY 1980;
EWL 3; FL 1:6; FW; INT CANR-13;
LAIT 5; MAL 5; MBL; MTCW 1, 2;
MTFW 2005; NFS 6; RGAL 4; SATA
53; SSFS 3; TCWW 2

Kingston, Maxine Ting Ting Hong
See Kingston, Maxine Hong

Kinnell, Galway 1927- ... **CLC 1, 2, 3, 5, 13,
29, 129; PC 26**
See also AMWS 3; CA 9-12R; CANR 10,
34, 66, 116, 138, 175; CP 1, 2, 3, 4, 5, 6, 7;
DLB 5, 342; DLBY 1987; EWL 3; INT
CANR-34; MAL 5; MTCW 1, 2; MTFW
2005; PAB; PFS 9, 26, 35; RGAL 4; TCLE
1:1; WP

Kinsella, Thomas 1928- ..... **CLC 4, 19, 138,
274; PC 69**
See also BRWS 5; CA 17-20R; CANR 15,
122; CP 1, 2, 3, 4, 5, 6, 7; DLB 27; EWL 3;
MTCW 1, 2; MTFW 2005; RGEL 2; TEA

Kinsella, William Patrick
See Kinsella, W.P.

Kinsella, W.P. 1935- .... **CLC 27, 43, 166**
See also AAYA 7, 60; BPFB 2; CA 97-100,
222; CAAE 222; CAAS 7; CANR 21, 35,
66, 75, 129; CN 4, 5, 6, 7; CPW; DAC;
DAM NOV, POP; DLB 362; FANT; INT
CANR-21; LAIT 5; MTCW 1, 2; MTFW
2005; NFS 15; RGSF 2; SSFS 30

Kinsey, Alfred C(harles)
1894-1956 .... **TCLC 91**
See also CA 115; 170; MTCW 2

Kipling, Joseph Rudyard
See Kipling, Rudyard

Kipling, Rudyard 1865-1936 .... **PC 3, 91;
SSC 5, 54, 110; TCLC 8, 17, 167; WLC 3**
See also AAYA 32; BRW 6; BRWC 1, 2;
BRWR 3; BYA 4; CA 105; 120; CANR
33; CDBLB 1890-1914; CLR 39, 65;
CWRI 5; DA; DA3; DAB; DAC; DAM
MST, POET; DLB 19, 34, 141, 156, 330;
EWL 3; EXPS; FANT; LAIT 3; LMFS 1;
MAICYA 1, 2; MTCW 1, 2; MTFW 2005;
NFS 21; PFS 22; RGEL 2; RGSF 2; SATA
100; SFW 4; SSFS 8, 21, 22, 32, 42;
SUFW 1; TEA; WCH; WLIT 4; YABC 2

Kircher, Athanasius 1602-1680 .... **LC 121**
See also DLB 164

Kirk, Richard
See Holdstock, Robert

Kirk, Russell (Amos) 1918-1994 ... **TCLC 119**
See also AITN 1; CA 1-4R; 145; CAAS 9;
CANR 1, 20, 60; HGG; INT CANR-20;
MTCW 1, 2

Kirkham, Dinah
See Card, Orson Scott

Kirkland, Caroline M.
1801-1864 .... **NCLC 85**
See also DLB 3, 73, 74, 250, 254; DLBD 13

Kirkup, James 1918-2009 .... **CLC 1**
See also CA 1-4R; CAAS 4; CANR 2; CP 1,
2, 3, 4, 5, 6, 7; DLB 27; SATA 12

Kirkwood, James 1930(?)-1989 .... **CLC 9**
See also AITN 2; CA 1-4R; 128; CANR 6,
40; GLL 2

Kirsch, Sarah 1935- .... **CLC 176**
See also CA 178; CWW 2; DLB 75; EWL 3

Kirshner, Sidney
See Kingsley, Sidney

Kissinger, Henry A. 1923- .... **CLC 137**
See also CA 1-4R; CANR 2, 33, 66, 109;
MTCW 1

Kissinger, Henry Alfred
See Kissinger, Henry A.

Kittel, Frederick August
See Wilson, August

Kivi, Aleksis 1834-1872 .... **NCLC 30**

Kizer, Carolyn 1925- .. **CLC 15, 39, 80; PC 66**
See also CA 65-68; CAAS 5; CANR 24, 70,
134; CP 1, 2, 3, 4, 5, 6, 7; CWP; DAM
POET; DLB 5, 169; EWL 3; MAL 5;
MTCW 2; MTFW 2005; PFS 18; TCLE 1:1

Klabund 1890-1928 .... **TCLC 44**
See also CA 162; DLB 66

Klappert, Peter 1942- .... **CLC 57**
See also CA 33-36R; CSW; DLB 5

Klausner, Amos
See Oz, Amos

Klein, A. M. 1909-1972 .... **CLC 19**
See also CA 101; 37-40R; CP 1; DAB;
DAC; DAM MST; DLB 68; EWL 3;
RGEL 2; RGHL

Klein, Abraham Moses
See Klein, A. M.

Klein, Joe
See Klein, Joseph

Klein, Joseph 1946- .... **CLC 154**
See also CA 85-88; CANR 55, 164

Klein, Norma 1938-1989 .... **CLC 30**
See also AAYA 2, 35; BPFB 2; BYA 6, 7, 8;
CA 41-44R; 128; CANR 15, 37; CLR 2,
19, 162; INT CANR-15; JRDA; MAICYA
1, 2; SAAS 1; SATA 7, 57; WYA; YAW

Klein, T.E.D. 1947- .... **CLC 34**
See also CA 119; CANR 44, 75, 167; HGG

Klein, Theodore Eibon Donald
See Klein, T.E.D.

Kleinzahler, August 1949- .... **CLC 320**
See also CA 125; CANR 51, 101, 153, 210

Kleist, Heinrich von 1777-1811 .... **DC 29;
NCLC 2, 37, 222; SSC 22**
See also CDWLB 2; DAM DRAM; DLB 90;
EW 5; RGSF 2; RGWL 2, 3

Kalidasa fl. c. 400-455 .... **CMLC 9; PC 22**
See also RGWL 2, 3

Klima, Ivan 1931- .... **CLC 56, 172**
See also CA 25-28R; CANR 17, 50, 91;
CDWLB 4; CWW 2; DAM NOV; DLB
232; EWL 3; RGWL 3

Klimentev, Andrei Platonovich
See Klimentov, Andrei Platonovich

Klimentov, Andrei Platonovich
1899-1951 .... **SSC 42; TCLC 14**
See also CA 108; 232; DLB 272; EWL 3

Klinger, Friedrich Maximilian von
1752-1831 .... **NCLC 1**
See also DLB 94

Klingsor the Magician
See Hartmann, Sadakichi

Klopstock, Friedrich Gottlieb
1724-1803 .... **NCLC 11, 225**
See also DLB 97; EW 4; RGWL 2, 3

Kluge, Alexander 1932- .... **SSC 61**
See also CA 81-84; CANR 163; DLB 75

Knapp, Caroline 1959-2002 .... **CLC 99, 309**
See also CA 154; 207

Knebel, Fletcher 1911-1993 .... **CLC 14**
See also AITN 1; CA 1-4R; 140; CAAS 3;
CANR 1, 36; CN 1, 2, 3, 4, 5; SATA 36;
SATA-Obit 75

Kung, Hans 1928- .... **CLC 130**
See also CA 53-56; CANR 66, 134; MTCW
1, 2; MTFW 2005

Knickerbocker, Diedrich
See Irving, Washington

Knight, Etheridge 1931-1991 .... **BLC 1:2;
CLC 40; PC 14**
See also BW 1, 3; CA 21-24R; 133; CANR
23, 82; CP 1, 2, 3, 4, 5; DAM POET; DLB
41; MTCW 2; MTFW 2005; PFS 36;
RGAL 4; TCLE 1:1

Knight, Sarah Kemble 1666-1727 .... **LC 7**
See also DLB 24, 200

Knister, Raymond 1899-1932 .... **TCLC 56**
See also CA 186; DLB 68; RGEL 2

Knowles, John 1926-2001 .. **CLC 1, 4, 10, 26**
See also AAYA 10, 72; AMWS 12; BPFB 2;
BYA 3; CA 17-20R; 203; CANR 40, 74,
76, 132; CDALB 1968-1988; CLR 98; CN
1, 2, 3, 4, 5, 6, 7; DA; DAC; DAM MST,
NOV; DLB 6; EXPN; MTCW 1, 2; MTFW
2005; NFS 2; RGAL 4; SATA 8, 89;
SATA-Obit 134; YAW

Knox, Calvin M.
See Silverberg, Robert

Knox, John c. 1505-1572 .... **LC 37**
See also DLB 132

Knye, Cassandra
See Disch, Thomas M.

Koch, C(hristopher) J(ohn) 1932- ... **CLC 42**
See also CA 127; CANR 84; CN 3, 4, 5, 6,
7; DLB 289

Koch, Christopher
See Koch, C(hristopher) J(ohn)

Koch, Kenneth 1925-2002 ..... **CLC 5, 8, 44;
PC 80**
See also AMWS 15; CA 1-4R; 207; CAD;
CANR 6, 36, 57, 97, 131; CD 5, 6; CP 1,
2, 3, 4, 5, 6, 7; DAM POET; DLB 5; INT
CANR-36; MAL 5; MTCW 2; MTFW
2005; PFS 20; SATA 65; WP

Kochanowski, Jan 1530-1584 ..... **LC 10, 229**
See also RGWL 2, 3

Kock, Charles Paul de
1794-1871 .... **NCLC 16**

Koda Rohan
See Koda Shigeyuki

Koda Shigeyuki 1867-1947 .... **TCLC 22**
See also CA 121; 183; DLB 180

Koestler, Arthur 1905-1983 ..... **CLC 1, 3, 6,
8, 15, 33; TCLC 283**
See also BRWS 1; CA 1-4R; 109; CANR 1,
33; CDBLB 1945-1960; CN 1, 2, 3; DLBY
1983; EWL 3; MTCW 1, 2; MTFW 2005;
NFS 19; RGEL 2

Kogawa, Joy 1935- ... **CLC 78, 129, 262, 268**
See also AAYA 47; CA 101; CANR 19, 62,
126; CN 6, 7; CP 1; CWP; DAC; DAM
MST, MULT; DLB 334; FW; MTCW 2;
MTFW 2005; NFS 3; SATA 99

Kogawa, Joy Nozomi
See Kogawa, Joy

Kohout, Pavel 1928- .... **CLC 13**
See also CA 45-48; CANR 3

Koizumi, Yakumo
See Hearn, Lafcadio

Kolmar, Gertrud 1894-1943 .... **TCLC 40**
See also CA 167; EWL 3; RGHL

Komunyakaa, Yusef 1947- .... **BLC 2:2;
BLCS; CLC 86, 94, 207, 299; PC 51**
See also AFAW 2; AMWS 13; CA 147; CANR
83, 164, 211, 241; CP 6, 7; CSW; DLB 120;
EWL 3; PFS 5, 20, 30, 37; RGAL 4

Kong Shangren 1648-1718 .... **LC 210**

Konigsberg, Alan Stewart
See Allen, Woody

Konrad, George
See Konrad, Gyorgy

Konrad, George
See Konrad, Gyorgy

Author Index

Lieksman, Anders
See Haavikko, Paavo Juhani

Lifton, Robert Jay 1926- .... **CLC 67**
See also CA 17-20R; CANR 27, 78, 161, 239; INT CANR-27; SATA 66

Lightfoot, Gordon 1938- .... **CLC 26**
See also CA 109; 242

Lightfoot, Gordon Meredith
See Lightfoot, Gordon

Lightman, Alan P. 1948- .... **CLC 81**
See also CA 141; CANR 63, 105, 138, 178; MTFW 2005; NFS 29

Lightman, Alan Paige
See Lightman, Alan P.

Ligotti, Thomas 1953- .... **CLC 44; SSC 16**
See also CA 123; CANR 49, 135; HGG; SUFW 2

Ligotti, Thomas Robert
See Ligotti, Thomas

Li Ho 791-817 .... **PC 13**

Li Ju-chen c. 1763-c. 1830 .... **NCLC 137**

Liking, Werewere 1950- .... **BLC 2:2**
See also CA 293; DLB 360; EWL 3

Lilar, Francoise
See Mallet-Joris, Francoise

Liliencron, Detlev
See Liliencron, Detlev von

Liliencron, Detlev von 1844-1909 ... **TCLC 18**
See also CA 117

Liliencron, Friedrich Adolf Axel Detlev von
See Liliencron, Detlev von

Liliencron, Friedrich Detlev von
See Liliencron, Detlev von

Lille, Alain de
See Alain de Lille

Lillo, George 1691-1739 .... **LC 131**
See also DLB 84; RGEL 2

Lilly, William 1602-1681 .... **LC 27**

Lima, Jose Lezama
See Lezama Lima, Jose

Lima Barreto, Afonso Henrique de
1881-1922 .... **TCLC 23**
See also CA 117; 181; DLB 307; LAW

Lima Barreto, Afonso Henriques de
See Lima Barreto, Afonso Henrique de

Limonov, Eduard
See Limonov, Edward

Limonov, Edward 1944- .... **CLC 67**
See also CA 137; DLB 317

Lin, Frank
See Atherton, Gertrude (Franklin Horn)

Lin, Yutang 1895-1976 .... **TCLC 149**
See also CA 45-48; 65-68; CANR 2; RGAL 4

Lincoln, Abraham 1809-1865 ...... **NCLC 18, 201**
See also LAIT 2

Lincoln, Geoffrey
See Mortimer, John

Lind, Jakov
1927-2007 .... **CLC 1, 2, 4, 27, 82**
See also CA 9-12R; 257; CAAS 4; CANR 7; DLB 299; EWL 3; RGHL

Lindbergh, Anne Morrow
1906-2001 .... **CLC 82**
See also BPFB 2; CA 17-20R; 193; CANR 16, 73; DAM NOV; MTCW 1, 2; MTFW 2005; SATA 33; SATA-Obit 125; TUS

Lindbergh, Anne Spencer Morrow
See Lindbergh, Anne Morrow

Lindholm, Anna Margaret
See Haycraft, Anna

Lindsay, David 1878(?)-1945 .... **TCLC 15**
See also CA 113; 187; DLB 255; FANT; SFW 4; SUFW 1

Lindsay, Nicholas Vachel
See Lindsay, Vachel

Lindsay, Vachel 1879-1931 .... **PC 23, 139; TCLC 17; WLC 4**
See also AMWS 1; CA 114; 135; CANR 79; CDALB 1865-1917; DA; DA3; DAC; DAM MST, POET; DLB 54; EWL 3; EXPP; MAL 5; RGAL 4; SATA 40; WP

Linke-Poot
See Doblin, Alfred

Linney, Romulus 1930-2011 .... **CLC 51**
See also CA 1-4R; CAD; CANR 40, 44, 79; CD 5, 6; CSW; RGAL 4

Linton, Eliza Lynn 1822-1898 ...... **NCLC 41**
See also DLB 18

Li Po 701-763 .... **CMLC 2, 86; PC 29**
See also PFS 20, 40; WP

Lippard, George 1822-1854 .... **NCLC 198**
See also AMWS 23; DLB 202

Lipsius, Justus 1547-1606 .... **LC 16, 207**

Lipsyte, Robert 1938- .... **CLC 21**
See also AAYA 7, 45; CA 17-20R; CANR 8, 57, 146, 189; CLR 23, 76; DA; DAC; DAM MST, NOV; JRDA; LAIT 5; MAI-CYA 1, 2; NFS 35; SATA 5, 68, 113, 161, 198; WYA; YAW

Lipsyte, Robert Michael
See Lipsyte, Robert

Lish, Gordon 1934- .... **CLC 45; SSC 18**
See also CA 113; 117; CANR 79, 151; DLB 130; INT CA-117

Lish, Gordon Jay
See Lish, Gordon

Lispector, Clarice 1925(?)-1977 ..... **CLC 43; HLCS 2; SSC 34, 96**
See also CA 139; 116; CANR 71; CDWLB 3; DLB 113, 307; DNFS 1; EWL 3; FW; HW 2; LAW; RGSF 2; RGWL 2, 3; WLIT 1

Liszt, Franz 1811-1886 .... **NCLC 199**

Littell, Robert 1935(?)- .... **CLC 42**
See also CA 109; 112; CANR 64, 115, 162, 217; CMW 4

Little, Malcolm
See Malcolm X

Littlewit, Humphrey Gent.
See Lovecraft, H. P.

Litwos
See Sienkiewicz, Henryk (Adam Alexander Pius)

Llu, E. 1857-1909 .... **TCLC 15**
See also CA 115; 190; DLB 328

Lively, Penelope 1933- ...... **CLC 32, 50, 306**
See also BPFB 2; CA 41-44R; CANR 29, 67, 79, 131, 172, 222; CLR 7, 159; CN 5, 6, 7; CWRI 5; DAM NOV; DLB 14, 161, 207, 326; FANT; JRDA; MAICYA 1, 2; MTCW 1, 2; MTFW 2005; SATA 7, 60, 101, 164; TEA

Lively, Penelope Margaret
See Lively, Penelope

Livesay, Dorothy (Kathleen)
1909-1996 .... **CLC 4, 15, 79**
See also AITN 2; CA 25-28R; CAAS 8; CANR 36, 67; CP 1, 2, 3, 4, 5; DAC; DAM MST, POET; DLB 68; FW; MTCW 1; RGEL 2; TWA

Livius Andronicus
c. 284B.C.-c. 204B.C. .... **CMLC 102**

Livy c. 59B.C.-c. 12 .... **CMLC 11, 154**
See also AW 2; CDWLB 1; DLB 211; RGWL 2, 3; WLIT 8

Li Yaotang
See Jin, Ba

Li-Young, Lee
See Lee, Li-Young

Lizardi, Jose Joaquin Fernandez de
1776-1827 .... **NCLC 30**
See also LAW

Llewellyn, Richard
See Llewellyn Lloyd, Richard Dafydd Vivian

Llewellyn Lloyd, Richard Dafydd Vivian
1906-1983 .... **CLC 7, 80**
See also CA 53-56; 111; CANR 7, 71; DLB 15; NFS 30; SATA 11; SATA-Obit 37

Llosa, Jorge Mario Pedro Vargas
See Vargas Llosa, Mario

Llosa, Mario Vargas
See Vargas Llosa, Mario

Lloyd, Manda
See Mander, (Mary) Jane

Lloyd Webber, Andrew 1948- .... **CLC 21**
See also AAYA 1, 38; CA 116; 149; DAM DRAM; DFS 7; SATA 56

Llull, Ramon
c. 1235-c. 1316 .... **CMLC 12, 114**

Lonnbohm, Armas Eino Leopold
1878-1926 .... **TCLC 24**
See also CA 123; EWL 3

Lobb, Ebenezer
See Upward, Allen

Lochhead, Liz 1947- .... **CLC 286**
See also BRWS 17; CA 81-84; CANR 79; CBD; CD 5, 6; CP 2, 3, 4, 5, 6, 7; CWD; CWP; DLB 310

Lock, Anne c. 1530-c. 1595 .... **PC 135**

Locke, Alain Leroy 1885-1954 ... **BLCS; HR 1:3; TCLC 43**
See also AMWS 14; BW 1, 3; CA 106; 124; CANR 79; DLB 51; LMFS 2; MAL 5; RGAL 4

Locke, John 1632-1704 .... **LC 7, 35, 135**
See also DLB 31, 101, 213, 252; RGEL 2; WLIT 3

Locke-Elliott, Sumner
See Elliott, Sumner Locke

Lockhart, John Gibson 1794-1854 ... **NCLC 6**
See also DLB 110, 116, 144

Lockridge, Ross (Franklin), Jr.
1914-1948 .... **TCLC 111**
See also CA 108; 145; CANR 79; DLB 143; DLBY 1980; MAL 5; RGAL 4; RHW

Lockwood, Robert
See Johnson, Robert

Lodge, David 1935- .... **CLC 36, 141, 293**
See also BEST 90:1; BRWS 4; CA 17-20R; CANR 19, 53, 92, 139, 197, 243; CN 1, 2, 3, 4, 5, 6, 7; CPW; DAM POP; DLB 14, 194; EWL 3; INT CANR-19; MTCW 1, 2; MTFW 2005

Lodge, David John
See Lodge, David

Lodge, Thomas 1558-1625 .... **LC 41**
See also DLB 172; RGEL 2

Loewinsohn, Ron(ald William)
1937- .... **CLC 52**
See also CA 25-28R; CANR 71; CP 1, 2, 3, 4

Logan, Jake
See Smith, Martin Cruz

Logan, John (Burton) 1923-1987 ..... **CLC 5**
See also CA 77-80; 124; CANR 45; CP 1, 2, 3, 4; DLB 5

Lo-Johansson, (Karl) Ivar
1901-1990 .... **TCLC 216**
See also CA 102; 131; CANR 20, 79, 137; DLB 259; EWL 3; RGWL 2, 3

Lo Kuan-chung
See Luo Guanzhong

Lomax, Pearl
See Cleage, Pearl

Lomax, Pearl Cleage
See Cleage, Pearl

Lombard, Nap
See Johnson, Pamela Hansford

Lombard, Peter 1100(?)-1160(?) ... **CMLC 72**

Lombino, Salvatore
See Hunter, Evan

Luke, Peter (Ambrose Cyprian)
  1919-1995 .... **CLC 38**
  See also CA 81-84; 147; CANR 72; CBD;
  CD 5, 6; DLB 13

Lumet, Sidney 1924-2011 .... **CLC 341**

Lunar, Dennis
  See Mungo, Raymond

Luo Guanzhong 1315(?)-1385(?) .... **LC 12, 209**

Lurie, Alison 1926- ... **CLC 4, 5, 18, 39, 175**
  See also BPFB 1; CA 1-4R; CANR 2, 17,
  50, 88; CN 1, 2, 3, 4, 5, 6, 7; DLB 2, 350;
  MAL 5; MTCW 1; NFS 24; SATA 46,
  112; TCLE 1:1

Lustig, Arnost 1926-2011 .... **CLC 56**
  See also AAYA 3; CA 69-72; CANR 47,
  102; CWW 2; DLB 232, 299; EWL 3;
  RGHL; SATA 56

Luther, Martin 1483-1546 ..... **LC 9, 37, 150**
  See also CDWLB 2; DLB 179; EW 2;
  RGWL 2, 3

Luxemburg, Rosa 1870(?)-1919 .... **TCLC 63**
  See also CA 118

Lu Xun 1881-1936 ... **SSC 158; TCLC 3, 289**
  See also CA 243; DLB 328; RGSF 2;
  RGWL 2, 3

Luzi, Mario (Egidio Vincenzo)
  1914-2005 .... **CLC 13**
  See also CA 61-64; 236; CANR 9, 70;
  CWW 2; DLB 128; EWL 3

Levi-Strauss, Claude
  1908-2008 .... **CLC 38, 302**
  See also CA 1-4R; CANR 6, 32, 57; DLB
  242; EWL 3; GFL 1789 to the Present;
  MTCW 1, 2; TWA

L'vov, Arkady .... **CLC 59**

Lydgate, John c. 1370-1450(?) ... **LC 81, 175**
  See also BRW 1; DLB 146; RGEL 2

Lyly, John 1554(?)-1606 .... **DC 7; LC 41, 187**
  See also BRW 1; DAM DRAM; DLB 62,
  167; RGEL 2

L'Ymagier
  See Gourmont, Remy(-Marie-Charles) de

Lynch, B. Suarez
  See Borges, Jorge Luis

Lynch, David 1946- .... **CLC 66, 162**
  See also AAYA 55; CA 124; 129; CANR 111

Lynch, David Keith
  See Lynch, David

Lynch, James
  See Andreyev, Leonid

Lyndsay, Sir David 1485-1555 .... **LC 20**
  See also RGEL 2

Lynn, Kenneth S(chuyler) 1923-2001 .. **CLC 50**
  See also CA 1-4R; 196; CANR 3, 27, 65

Lynx
  See West, Rebecca

Lyons, Marcus
  See Blish, James

Lyotard, Jean-Francois 1924-1998 .. **TCLC 103**
  See also DLB 242; EWL 3

Lyre, Pinchbeck
  See Sassoon, Siegfried

Lytle, Andrew (Nelson) 1902-1995 .... **CLC 22**
  See also CA 9-12R; 150; CANR 70; CN 1,
  2, 3, 4, 5, 6; CSW; DLB 6; DLBY 1995;
  RGAL 4; RHW

Lyttelton, George 1709-1773 .... **LC 10**
  See also RGEL 2

Lytton, Edward G.E.L. Bulwer-Lytton Baron
  See Bulwer-Lytton, Edward

Lytton of Knebworth, Baron
  See Bulwer-Lytton, Edward

Maalouf, Amin 1949- .... **CLC 248**
  See also CA 212; CANR 194; DLB 346

Maas, Peter 1929-2001 .... **CLC 29**
  See also CA 93-96; 201; INT CA-93-96;
  MTCW 2; MTFW 2005

Mac A'Ghobhainn, Iain
  See Smith, Iain Crichton

Macaulay, Catharine 1731-1791 ... **LC 64, 227**
  See also BRWS 17; DLB 104, 336

Macaulay, (Emilie) Rose
  1881(?)-1958 .... **TCLC 7, 44**
  See also CA 104; DLB 36; EWL 3; RGEL 2;
  RHW

Macaulay, Thomas Babington
  1800-1859 .... **NCLC 42, 231**
  See also BRW 4; CDBLB 1832-1890; DLB
  32, 55; RGEL 2

MacBeth, George (Mann)
  1932-1992 .... **CLC 2, 5, 9**
  See also CA 25-28R; 136; CANR 61, 66; CP
  1, 2, 3, 4, 5; DLB 40; MTCW 1; PFS 8;
  SATA 4; SATA-Obit 70

MacCaig, Norman (Alexander)
  1910-1996 .... **CLC 36**
  See also BRWS 6; CA 9-12R; CANR 3, 34;
  CP 1, 2, 3, 4, 5, 6; DAB; DAM POET;
  DLB 27; EWL 3; RGEL 2

MacCarthy, Sir (Charles Otto) Desmond
  1877-1952 .... **TCLC 36**
  See also CA 167

MacDiarmid, Hugh
  See Grieve, C. M.

MacDonald, Anson
  See Heinlein, Robert A.

Macdonald, Cynthia 1928- .... **CLC 13, 19**
  See also CA 49-52; CANR 4, 44, 146;
  DLB 105

MacDonald, George 1824-1905 ..... **TCLC 9,
  113, 207**
  See also AAYA 57; BYA 5; CA 106; 137;
  CANR 80; CLR 67; DLB 18, 163, 178;
  FANT; MAICYA 1, 2; RGEL 2; SATA 33,
  100; SFW 4; SUFW; WCH

Macdonald, John
  See Millar, Kenneth

MacDonald, John D.
  1916-1986 .... **CLC 3, 27, 44**
  See also BPFB 2; CA 1-4R; 121; CANR 1,
  19, 60; CMW 4; CPW; DAM NOV, POP;
  DLB 8, 306; DLBY 1986; MSW; MTCW
  1, 2; MTFW 2005; SFW 4

Macdonald, John Ross
  See Millar, Kenneth

Macdonald, Ross
  See Millar, Kenneth

MacDonald Fraser, George
  See Fraser, George MacDonald

MacDougal, John
  See Blish, James

MacDowell, John
  See Parks, Tim

MacEwen, Gwendolyn (Margaret)
  1941-1987 .... **CLC 13, 55**
  See also CA 9-12R; 124; CANR 7, 22; CP 1,
  2, 3, 4; DLB 53, 251; SATA 50; SATA-
  Obit 55

MacGreevy, Thomas 1893-1967 .... **PC 82**
  See also CA 262

Macha, Karel Hynek 1810-1846 ... **NCLC 46**

Machado (y Ruiz), Antonio
  1875-1939 .... **TCLC 3**
  See also CA 104; 174; DLB 108; EW 9;
  EWL 3; HW 2; PFS 23; RGWL 2, 3

Machado de Assis, Joaquim Maria
  1839-1908 .... **BLC 1:2; HLCS 2;
  SSC 24, 118; TCLC 10, 269**
  See also CA 107; 153; CANR 91; DLB 307;
  LAW; RGSF 2; RGWL 2, 3; TWA; WLIT 1

Machaut, Guillaume de
  c. 1300-1377 .... **CMLC 64**
  See also DLB 208

Machen, Arthur
  See Jones, Arthur Llewellyn

Machen, Arthur Llewelyn Jones
  See Jones, Arthur Llewellyn

Machiavelli, Niccolo 1469-1527 .... **DC 16;
  LC 8, 36, 140; WLCS**
  See also AAYA 58; DA; DAB; DAC; DAM
  MST; EW 2; LAIT 1; LMFS 1; NFS 9;
  RGWL 2, 3; TWA; WLIT 7

MacInnes, Colin 1914-1976 .... **CLC 4, 23**
  See also CA 69-72; 65-68; CANR 21; CN 1,
  2; DLB 14; MTCW 1, 2; RGEL 2; RHW

MacInnes, Helen (Clark)
  1907-1985 .... **CLC 27, 39**
  See also BPFB 2; CA 1-4R; 117; CANR 1,
  28, 58; CMW 4; CN 1, 2; CPW; DAM
  POP; DLB 87; MSW; MTCW 1, 2; MTFW
  2005; SATA 22; SATA-Obit 44

Mackay, Mary 1855-1924 .... **TCLC 51**
  See also CA 118; 177; DLB 34, 156; FANT;
  RGEL 2; RHW; SUFW 1

Mackay, Shena 1944- .... **CLC 195**
  See also CA 104; CANR 88, 139, 207; DLB
  231, 319; MTFW 2005

Mackenzie, Compton (Edward Montague)
  1883-1972 .... **CLC 18; TCLC 116**
  See also CA 21-22; 37-40R; CAP 2; CN 1;
  DLB 34, 100; RGEL 2

Mackenzie, Henry 1745-1831 **NCLC 41, 284**
  See also DLB 39; RGEL 2

Mackey, Nathaniel 1947- ... **BLC 2:3; PC 49**
  See also CA 153; CANR 114; CP 6, 7;
  DLB 169

Mackey, Nathaniel Ernest
  See Mackey, Nathaniel

MacKinnon, Catharine
  See MacKinnon, Catharine A.

MacKinnon, Catharine A. 1946- ... **CLC 181**
  See also CA 128; 132; CANR 73, 140, 189;
  FW; MTCW 2; MTFW 2005

Mackintosh, Elizabeth 1896(?)-1952 .. **TCLC 14**
  See also CA 110; CMW 4; DLB 10, 77; MSW

Macklin, Charles 1699-1797 .... **LC 132**
  See also DLB 89; RGEL 2

MacLaren, James
  See Grieve, C. M.

MacLaverty, Bernard 1942- .... **CLC 31, 243**
  See also CA 116; 118; CANR 43, 88, 168; CN 5,
  6, 7; DLB 267; INT CA-118; RGSF 2

MacLean, Alistair 1922(?)-1987 .... **CLC 3,
  13, 50, 63**
  See also CA 57-60; 121; CANR 28, 61;
  CMW 4; CP 2, 3, 4, 5, 6, 7; CPW; DAM
  POP; DLB 276; MTCW 1; SATA 23;
  SATA-Obit 50; TCWW 2

MacLean, Alistair Stuart
  See MacLean, Alistair

Maclean, Norman (Fitzroy)
  1902-1990 .... **CLC 78; SSC 13, 136**
  See also AMWS 14; CA 102; 132; CANR
  49; CPW; DAM POP; DLB 206; TCWW 2

MacLeish, Archibald
  1892-1982 .... **CLC 3, 8, 14, 68;
  DC 43; PC 47; TCLC 276**
  See also AMW; CA 9-12R; 106; CAD;
  CANR 33, 63; CDALBS; CP 1, 2; DAM
  POET; DFS 15; DLB 4, 7, 45; DLBY 1982;
  EWL 3; EXPP; MAL 5; MTCW 1, 2;
  MTFW 2005; PAB; PFS 5; RGAL 4; TUS

MacLennan, (John) Hugh
  1907-1990 .... **CLC 2, 14, 92**
  See also CA 5-8R; 142; CANR 33; CN 1, 2,
  3, 4; DAC; DAM MST; DLB 68; EWL 3;
  MTCW 1, 2; MTFW 2005; RGEL 2; TWA

MacLeod, Alistair 1936- .... **CLC 56, 165;
  SSC 90**
  See also CA 123; CCA 1; DAC; DAM MST;
  DLB 60; MTCW 2; MTFW 2005; RGSF
  2; TCLE 1:2

Macleod, Fiona
  See Sharp, William

Marshallik
See Zangwill, Israel
Marsilius of Inghen
c. 1340-1396 .... **CMLC 106**
Marsten, Richard
See Hunter, Evan
Marston, John
1576-1634 .... **DC 37; LC 33, 172**
See also BRW 2; DAM DRAM; DLB 58, 172; RGEL 2
Marti, Jose 1853-1895 ... **HLC 2; NCLC 63; PC 76**
See also DAM MULT; DLB 290; HW 2; LAW; RGWL 2, 3; WLIT 1
Martel, Yann 1963- .... **CLC 192, 315**
See also AAYA 67; CA 146; CANR 114, 226; DLB 326, 334; LNFS 2; MTFW 2005; NFS 27
Martens, Adolphe-Adhemar
See Ghelderode, Michel de
Martha, Henry
See Harris, Mark
Martial c. 40-c. 104 .... **CMLC 35; PC 10**
See also AW 2; CDWLB 1; DLB 211; RGWL 2, 3
Martin, Ken
See Hubbard, L. Ron
Martin, Richard
See Creasey, John
Martin, Steve 1945- .... **CLC 30, 217**
See also AAYA 53; CA 97-100; CANR 30, 100, 140, 195, 227; DFS 19; MTCW 1; MTFW 2005
Martin, Valerie 1948- .... **CLC 89**
See also BEST 90:2; CA 85-88; CANR 49, 89, 165, 200
Martin, Violet Florence
1862-1915 .... **SSC 56; TCLC 51**
Martin, Webber
See Silverberg, Robert
Martindale, Patrick Victor
See White, Patrick
Martin du Gard, Roger
1881-1958 .... **TCLC 24**
See also CA 118; CANR 94; DLB 65, 331; EWL 3; GFL 1789 to the Present; RGWL 2, 3
Martineau, Harriet
1802-1876 .... **NCLC 26, 137**
See also BRWS 15; DLB 21, 55, 159, 163, 166, 190; FW; RGEL 2; YABC 2
Martines, Julia
See O'Faolain, Julia
Martinez, Enrique Gonzalez
See Gonzalez Martinez, Enrique
Martinez, Jacinto Benavente y
See Benavente, Jacinto
Martinez Ruiz, Jose 1873-1967 ...... **CLC 11**
See also CA 93-96; DLB 322; EW 3; EWL 3; HW 1
Martinez Sierra, Gregorio
1881-1947 .... **TCLC 6**
See also CA 115; EWL 3
Martinsen, Martin
See Follett, Ken
Martinson, Harry (Edmund)
1904-1978 .... **CLC 14**
See also CA 77-80; CANR 34, 130; DLB 259, 331; EWL 3
Martinez de la Rosa, Francisco de Paula
1787-1862 .... **NCLC 102**
See also TWA
Martinez Sierra, Gregorio
See Martinez Sierra, Maria
Martinez Sierra, Maria
1874-1974 .... **TCLC 6**
See also CA 250; 115; EWL 3

Martinez Sierra, Maria de la O'LeJarraga
See Martinez Sierra, Maria
Martyn, Edward 1859-1923 .... **TCLC 131**
See also CA 179; DLB 10; RGEL 2
Marti y Perez, Jose Julian
See Marti, Jose
Marut, Ret
See Traven, B.
Marut, Robert
See Traven, B.
Marvell, Andrew 1621-1678 .... **LC 4, 43, 179, 226; PC 10, 86, 144; WLC 4**
See also BRW 2; BRWR 2; CDBLB 1660-1789; DA; DAB; DAC; DAM MST, POET; DLB 131; EXPP; PFS 5; RGEL 2; TEA; WP
Marx, Karl 1818-1883 .... **NCLC 17, 114**
See also DLB 129; LATS 1:1; TWA
Marx, Karl Heinrich
See Marx, Karl
Masaoka, Shiki -1902
See Masaoka, Tsunenori
Masaoka, Tsunenori 1867-1902 .... **TCLC 18**
See also CA 117; 191; EWL 3; RGWL 3; TWA
Masaoka Shiki
See Masaoka, Tsunenori
Masefield, John (Edward)
1878-1967 .... **CLC 11, 47; PC 78**
See also CA 19-20; 25-28R; CANR 33; CAP 2; CDBLB 1890-1914; CLR 164; DAM POET; DLB 10, 19, 153, 160; EWL 3; EXPP; FANT; MTCW 1, 2; PFS 5; RGEL 2; SATA 19
Maso, Carole 1955(?)- .... **CLC 44**
See also CA 170; CANR 148; CN 7; GLL 2; RGAL 4
Mason, Bobbie Ann 1940- .... **CLC 28, 43, 82, 154, 303; SSC 4, 101, 193**
See also AAYA 5, 42; AMWS 8; BPFB 2; CA 53-56; CANR 11, 31, 58, 83, 125, 169, 235; CDALBS; CN 5, 6, 7; CSW; DA3; DLB 173; DLBY 1987; EWL 3; EXPS; INT CANR-31; MAL 5; MTCW 1, 2; MTFW 2005; NFS 4; RGAL 4; RGSF 2; SSFS 3, 8, 20; TCLE 1:2; YAW
Mason, Ernst
See Pohl, Frederik
Mason, Hunni B.
See Sternheim, (William Adolf) Carl
Mason, Lee W.
See Malzberg, Barry N(athaniel)
Mason, Nick 1945- .... **CLC 35**
Mason, Tally
See Derleth, August (William)
Mass, Anna .... **CLC 59**
Mass, William
See Gibson, William
Massinger, Philip 1583-1640 .... **DC 39; LC 70**
See also BRWS 11; DLB 58; RGEL 2
Master Lao
See Lao Tzu
Masters, Edgar Lee 1868-1950 ..... **PC 1, 36; TCLC 2, 25; WLCS**
See also AMWS 1; CA 104; 133; CDALB 1865-1917; DA; DAC; DAM MST, POET; DLB 54; EWL 3; EXPP; MAL 5; MTCW 1, 2; MTFW 2005; PFS 37; RGAL 4; TUS; WP
Masters, Hilary 1928- .... **CLC 48**
See also CA 25-28R; 217; CAAE 217; CANR 13, 47, 97, 171, 221; CN 6, 7; DLB 244
Masters, Hilary Thomas
See Masters, Hilary
Mastrosimone, William 1947- .... **CLC 36**
See also CA 186; CAD; CD 5, 6

Mathe, Albert
See Camus, Albert
Mather, Cotton 1663-1728 .... **LC 38**
See also AMWS 2; CDALB 1640-1865; DLB 24, 30, 140; RGAL 4; TUS
Mather, Increase 1639-1723 .... **LC 38, 161**
See also DLB 24
Mathers, Marshall
See Eminem
Mathers, Marshall Bruce
See Eminem
Matheson, Richard 1926- .... **CLC 37, 267**
See also AAYA 31; CA 97-100; CANR 88, 99, 236; DLB 8, 44; HGG; INT CA-97-100; SCFW 1, 2; SFW 4; SUFW 2
Matheson, Richard Burton
See Matheson, Richard
Mathews, Harry 1930- .... **CLC 6, 52**
See also CA 21-24R; CAAS 6; CANR 18, 40, 98, 160; CN 5, 6, 7
Mathews, John Joseph
1894-1979 .... **CLC 84; NNAL**
See also CA 19-20; 142; CANR 45; CAP 2; DAM MULT; DLB 175; TCWW 1, 2
Mathias, Roland 1915-2007 .... **CLC 45**
See also CA 97-100; 263; CANR 19, 41; CP 1, 2, 3, 4, 5, 6, 7; DLB 27
Mathias, Roland Glyn
See Mathias, Roland
Matshoba, Mtutuzeli 1950- .... **SSC 173**
See also CA 221
Matsuo Basho 1644(?)-1694 .... **LC 62; PC 3, 125**
See also DAM POET; PFS 2, 7, 18; RGWL 2, 3; WP
Mattheson, Rodney
See Creasey, John
Matthew, James
See Barrie, J. M.
Matthew of Vendome
c. 1130-c. 1200 .... **CMLC 99**
See also DLB 208
Matthew Paris
See Paris, Matthew
Matthews, (James) Brander
1852-1929 .... **TCLC 95**
See also CA 181; DLB 71, 78; DLBD 13
Matthews, Greg 1949- .... **CLC 45**
See also CA 135
Matthews, William (Procter III)
1942-1997 .... **CLC 40**
See also AMWS 9; CA 29-32R; 162; CAAS 18; CANR 12, 57; CP 2, 3, 4, 5, 6; DLB 5
Matthias, John (Edward) 1941- .... **CLC 9**
See also CA 33-36R; CANR 56; CP 4, 5, 6, 7
Matthiessen, F(rancis) O(tto)
1902-1950 .... **TCLC 100**
See also CA 185; DLB 63; MAL 5
Matthiessen, Francis Otto
See Matthiessen, F(rancis) O(tto)
Matthiessen, Peter 1927- .... **CLC 5, 7, 11, 32, 64, 245**
See also AAYA 6, 40; AMWS 5; ANW; BEST 90:4; BPFB 2; CA 9-12R; CANR 21, 50, 73, 100, 138; CN 1, 2, 3, 4, 5, 6, 7; DA3; DAM NOV; DLB 6, 173, 275; MAL 5; MTCW 1, 2; MTFW 2005; SATA 27
Maturin, Charles Robert
1780(?)-1824 .... **NCLC 6, 169**
See also BRWS 8; DLB 178; GL 3; HGG; LMFS 1; RGEL 2; SUFW
Matute (Ausejo), Ana Maria 1925- .. **CLC 11, 352**
See also CA 89-92; CANR 129; CWW 2; DLB 322; EWL 3; MTCW 1; RGSF 2
Maugham, W. S.
See Maugham, W. Somerset

Maugham, W. Somerset
1874-1965 .... **CLC 1, 11, 15, 67, 93; SSC 8, 94, 164; TCLC 208; WLC 4**
See also AAYA 55; BPFB 2; BRW 6; CA 5-8R; 25-28R; CANR 40, 127; CDBLB 1914-1945; CMW 4; DA; DA3; DAB; DAC; DAM DRAM, MST, NOV; DFS 22; DLB 10, 36, 77, 100, 162, 195; EWL 3; LAIT 3; MTCW 1, 2; MTFW 2005; NFS 23, 35; RGEL 2; RGSF 2; SATA 54; SSFS 17

Maugham, William S.
See Maugham, W. Somerset

Maugham, William Somerset
See Maugham, W. Somerset

Maupassant, Guy de 1850-1893 .... **NCLC 1, 42, 83, 234; SSC 1, 64, 132; WLC 4**
See also BYA 14; DA; DA3; DAB; DAC; DAM MST; DLB 123; EW 7; EXPS; GFL 1789 to the Present; LAIT 2; LMFS 1; RGSF 2; RGWL 2, 3; SSFS 4, 21, 28, 31; SUFW; TWA

Maupassant, Henri Rene Albert Guy de
See Maupassant, Guy de

Maupin, Armistead 1944- .... **CLC 95**
See also CA 125; 130; CANR 58, 101, 183; CPW; DA3; DAM POP; DLB 278; GLL 1; INT CA-130; MTCW 2; MTFW 2005

Maupin, Armistead Jones, Jr.
See Maupin, Armistead

Maurhut, Richard
See Traven, B.

Mauriac, Claude 1914-1996 .... **CLC 9**
See also CA 89-92; 152; CWW 2; DLB 83; EWL 3; GFL 1789 to the Present

Mauriac, Francois (Charles)
1885-1970 .... **CLC 4, 9, 56; SSC 24; TCLC 281**
See also CA 25-28; CAP 2; DLB 65, 331; EW 10; EWL 3; GFL 1789 to the Present; MTCW 1, 2; MTFW 2005; RGWL 2, 3; TWA

Mavor, Osborne Henry
1888-1951 .... **TCLC 3**
See also CA 104; DLB 10; EWL 3

Maxwell, Glyn 1962- .... **CLC 238**
See also CA 154; CANR 88, 183; CP 6, 7; PFS 23

Maxwell, William (Keepers, Jr.)
1908-2000 .... **CLC 19**
See also AMWS 8; CA 93-96; 189; CANR 54, 95; CN 1, 2, 3, 4, 5, 6, 7; DLB 218, 278; DLBY 1980; INT CA-93-96; MAL 5; SATA-Obit 128

May, Elaine 1932- .... **CLC 16**
See also CA 124; 142; CAD; CWD; DLB 44

Mayakovski, Vladimir
1893-1930 .... **TCLC 4, 18**
See also CA 104; 158; EW 11; EWL 3; IDTP; MTCW 2; MTFW 2005; RGWL 2, 3; SFW 4; TWA; WP

Mayakovski, Vladimir Vladimirovich
See Mayakovski, Vladimir

Mayakovsky, Vladimir
See Mayakovski, Vladimir

Mayhew, Henry
1812-1887 .... **NCLC 31**
See also BRWS 16; DLB 18, 55, 190

Mayle, Peter 1939(?)- .... **CLC 89**
See also CA 139; CANR 64, 109, 168, 218

Maynard, Joyce 1953- .... **CLC 23**
See also CA 111; 129; CANR 64, 169, 220

Mayne, William 1928-2010 .... **CLC 12**
See also AAYA 20; CA 9-12R; CANR 37, 80, 100; CLR 25, 123; FANT; JRDA; MAICYA 1, 2; MAICYAS 1; SAAS 11; SATA 6, 68, 122; SUFW 2; YAW

Mayne, William James Carter
See Mayne, William

Mayo, Jim
See L'Amour, Louis

Maysles, Albert 1926- .... **CLC 16**
See also CA 29-32R

Maysles, David 1932-1987 .... **CLC 16**
See also CA 191

Mazer, Norma Fox 1931-2009 .... **CLC 26**
See also AAYA 5, 36; BYA 1, 8; CA 69-72; 292; CANR 12, 32, 66, 129, 189; CLR 23; JRDA; MAICYA 1, 2; SAAS 1; SATA 24, 67, 105, 168, 198; WYA; YAW

Mažuranić, Ivan 1814-1890 .... **NCLC 259**
See also DLB 147

Mazzini, Guiseppe 1805-1872 .... **NCLC 34**

McAlmon, Robert (Menzies)
1895-1956 .... **TCLC 97**
See also CA 107; 168; DLB 4, 45; DLBD 15; GLL 1

McAuley, James Phillip
1917-1976 .... **CLC 45**
See also CA 97-100; CP 1, 2; DLB 260; RGEL 2

McBain, Ed
See Hunter, Evan

McBrien, William 1930- .... **CLC 44**
See also CA 107; CANR 90

McBrien, William Augustine
See McBrien, William

McCabe, Pat
See McCabe, Patrick

McCabe, Patrick 1955- .... **CLC 133**
See also BRWS 9; CA 130; CANR 50, 90, 168, 202; CN 6, 7; DLB 194

McCaffrey, Anne 1926-2011 .... **CLC 17**
See also AAYA 6, 34; AITN 2; BEST 89:2; BPFB 2; BYA 5; CA 25-28R, 227; CAAE 227; CANR 15, 35, 55, 96, 169, 234; CLR 49, 130; CPW; DA3; DAM NOV, POP; DLB 8; JRDA; MAICYA 1, 2; MTCW 1, 2; MTFW 2005; SAAS 11; SATA 8, 70, 116, 152; SATA-Essay 152; SFW 4; SUFW 2; WYA; YAW

McCaffrey, Anne Inez
See McCaffrey, Anne

McCall, Nathan 1955(?)- .... **CLC 86**
See also AAYA 59; BW 3; CA 146; CANR 88, 186

McCall Smith, Alexander
See Smith, Alexander McCall

McCann, Arthur
See Campbell, John W.

McCann, Colum 1965- ... **CLC 299; SSC 170**
See also CA 152; CANR 99, 149; DLB 267

McCann, Edson
See Pohl, Frederik

McCarthy, Charles
See McCarthy, Cormac

McCarthy, Charles, Jr.
See McCarthy, Cormac

McCarthy, Cormac 1933- .... **CLC 4, 57, 101, 204, 295, 310**
See also AAYA 41; AMWS 8; BPFB 2; CA 13-16R; CANR 10, 42, 69, 101, 161, 171; CN 6, 7; CPW; CSW; DA3; DAM POP; DLB 6, 143, 256; EWL 3; LATS 1:2; LNFS 3; MAL 5; MTCW 2; MTFW 2005; NFS 36, 40; TCLE 1:2; TCWW 2

McCarthy, Mary 1912-1989 .... **CLC 1, 3, 5, 14, 24, 39, 59; SSC 24**
See also AMW; BPFB 2; CA 5-8R; 129; CANR 16, 50, 64; CN 1, 2, 3, 4; DA3; DLB 2; DLBY 1981; EWL 3; FW; INT CANR-16; MAL 5; MBL; MTCW 1, 2; MTFW 2005; RGAL 4; TUS

McCarthy, Mary Therese
See McCarthy, Mary

McCartney, James Paul
See McCartney, Paul

McCartney, Paul 1942- .... **CLC 12, 35**
See also CA 146; CANR 111

McCauley, Stephen 1955- .... **CLC 50**
See also CA 141

McClaren, Peter .... **CLC 70**

McClure, Michael 1932- ... **CLC 6, 10; PC 136**
See also BG 1:3; CA 21-24R; CAD; CANR 17, 46, 77, 131, 231; CD 5, 6; CP 1, 2, 3, 4, 5, 6, 7; DLB 16; WP

McClure, Michael Thomas
See McClure, Michael

McCorkle, Jill 1958- .... **CLC 51**
See also CA 121; CANR 113, 218; CSW; DLB 234; DLBY 1987; SSFS 24

McCorkle, Jill Collins
See McCorkle, Jill

McCourt, Francis
See McCourt, Frank

McCourt, Frank 1930-2009 ... **CLC 109, 299**
See also AAYA 61; AMWS 12; CA 157; 288; CANR 97, 138; MTFW 2005; NCFS 1

McCourt, James 1941- .... **CLC 5**
See also CA 57-60; CANR 98, 152, 186

McCourt, Malachy 1931- .... **CLC 119**
See also SATA 126

McCoy, Edmund
See Gardner, John

McCoy, Horace (Stanley)
1897-1955 .... **TCLC 28**
See also AMWS 13; CA 108; 155; CMW 4; DLB 9

McCrae, John 1872-1918 .... **TCLC 12**
See also CA 109; DLB 92; PFS 5

McCreigh, James
See Pohl, Frederik

McCullers, Carson 1917-1967 ...... **CLC 1, 4, 10, 12, 48, 100; DC 35; SSC 9, 24, 99; TCLC 155; WLC 4**
See also AAYA 21; AMW; AMWC 2; BPFB 2; CA 5-8R; 25-28R; CABS 1, 3; CANR 18, 132; CDALB 1941-1968; DA; DA3; DAB; DAC; DAM MST, NOV; DFS 5, 18; DLB 2, 7, 173, 228; EWL 3; EXPS; FW; GLL 1; LAIT 3, 4; MAL 5; MBL; MTCW 1, 2; MTFW 2005; NFS 6, 13; RGAL 4; RGSF 2; SATA 27; SSFS 5, 32; TUS; YAW

McCullers, Lula Carson Smith
See McCullers, Carson

McCulloch, John Tyler
See Burroughs, Edgar Rice

McCullough, Colleen 1937- ..... **CLC 27, 107**
See also AAYA 36; BPFB 2; CA 81-84; CANR 17, 46, 67, 98, 139, 203; CPW; DA3; DAM NOV, POP; MTCW 1, 2; MTFW 2005; RHW

McCunn, Ruthanne Lum 1946- .... **AAL**
See also CA 119; CANR 43, 96; DLB 312; LAIT 2; SATA 63

McDermott, Alice 1953- .... **CLC 90**
See also AMWS 18; CA 109; CANR 40, 90, 126, 181; CN 7; DLB 292; MTFW 2005; NFS 23

McDonagh, Martin 1970(?)- .... **CLC 304**
See also AAYA 71; BRWS 12; CA 171; CANR 141; CD 6

McElroy, Joseph 1930- .... **CLC 5, 47**
See also CA 17-20R; CANR 149, 236; CN 3, 4, 5, 6, 7

McElroy, Joseph Prince
See McElroy, Joseph

McElroy, Lee
See Kelton, Elmer

McEwan, Ian 1948- .... **CLC 13, 66, 169, 269; SSC 106**
See also AAYA 84; BEST 90:4; BRWS 4; CA 61-64; CANR 14, 41, 69, 87, 132, 179, 232; CN 3, 4, 5, 6, 7; DAM NOV; DLB 14, 194, 319, 326; HGG; MTCW 1, 2; MTFW 2005; NFS 32; RGSF 2; SUFW 2; TEA

See also AAYA 25; AMW; AMWR 1; CDALB 1640-1865; DA; DA3; DAB; DAC; DAM MST, NOV; DLB 3, 74, 250, 254, 349, 366; EXPN; EXPS; GL 3; LAIT 1, 2; NFS 7, 9, 32, 41; RGAL 4; RGSF 2; SATA 59; SSFS 3; TUS

Members, Mark
See Powell, Anthony

Membreno, Alejandro .... **CLC 59**

Mena, Maria Cristina 1893-1965 ... **SSC 165**
See also DLB 209, 221

Menand, Louis 1952- .... **CLC 208**
See also CA 200

Menander c. 342B.C.-c. 293B.C. ... **CMLC 9, 51, 101; DC 3**
See also AW 1; CDWLB 1; DAM DRAM; DLB 176; LMFS 1; RGWL 2, 3

Menchu, Rigoberta 1959- ..... **CLC 160, 332; HLCS 2**
See also CA 175; CANR 135; DNFS 1; WLIT 1

Mencken, H. L. 1880-1956 ..... **TCLC 13, 18**
See also AAYA 85; AMW; CA 105; 125; CDALB 1917-1929; DLB 11, 29, 63, 137, 222; EWL 3; MAL 5; MTCW 1, 2; MTFW 2005; NCFS 4; RGAL 4; TUS

Mencken, Henry Louis
See Mencken, H. L.

Mendelsohn, Jane 1965- .... **CLC 99**
See also CA 154; CANR 94, 225

Mendelssohn, Moses 1729-1786 .... **LC 142**
See also DLB 97

Mendoza, Inigo Lopez de
See Santillana, Inigo Lopez de Mendoza, Marques de

Menken, Adah Isaacs 1835-1868 **NCLC 270**

Menton, Francisco de
See Chin, Frank

Mercer, David 1928-1980 .... **CLC 5**
See also CA 9-12R; 102; CANR 23; CBD; DAM DRAM; DLB 13, 310; MTCW 1; RGEL 2

Merchant, Paul
See Ellison, Harlan

Mercier, Louis-Sébastien 1740-1814 .... **NCLC 255**
See also DLB 314

Meredith, George 1828-1909 .... **PC 60; TCLC 17, 43**
See also CA 117; 153; CANR 80; CDBLB 1832-1890; DAM POET; DLB 18, 35, 57, 159; RGEL 2; TEA

Meredith, William 1919-2007 .... **CLC 4, 13, 22, 55; PC 28**
See also CA 9-12R; 260; CAAS 14; CANR 6, 40, 129; CP 1, 2, 3, 4, 5, 6, 7; DAM POET; DLB 5; MAL 5

Meredith, William Morris
See Meredith, William

Merezhkovsky, Dmitrii Sergeevich
See Merezhkovsky, Dmitry Sergeyevich

Merezhkovsky, Dmitry Sergeevich
See Merezhkovsky, Dmitry Sergeyevich

Merezhkovsky, Dmitry Sergeyevich 1865-1941 .... **TCLC 29**
See also CA 169; DLB 295; EWL 3

Merezhkovsky, Zinaida
See Gippius, Zinaida

Merkin, Daphne 1954- .... **CLC 44**
See also CA 123

Merleau-Ponty, Maurice 1908-1961 .... **TCLC 156**
See also CA 114; 89-92; DLB 296; GFL 1789 to the Present

Merlin, Arthur
See Blish, James

Mernissi, Fatima 1940- .... **CLC 171**
See also CA 152; DLB 346; FW

Merrill, James 1926-1995 .... **CLC 2, 3, 6, 8, 13, 18, 34, 91; PC 28; TCLC 173**
See also AMWS 3; CA 13-16R; 147; CANR 10, 49, 63, 108; CP 1, 2, 3, 4; DA3; DAM POET; DLB 5, 165; DLBY 1985; EWL 3; INT CANR-10; MAL 5; MTCW 1, 2; MTFW 2005; PAB; PFS 23; RGAL 4

Merrill, James Ingram
See Merrill, James

Merriman, Alex
See Silverberg, Robert

Merriman, Brian 1747-1805 .... **NCLC 70**

Merritt, E. B.
See Waddington, Miriam

Merton, Thomas 1915-1968 ... **CLC 1, 3, 11, 34, 83; PC 10**
See also AAYA 61; AMWS 8; CA 5-8R; 25-28R; CANR 22, 53, 111, 131; DA3; DLB 48; DLBY 1981; MAL 5; MTCW 1, 2; MTFW 2005

Merton, Thomas James
See Merton, Thomas

Merwin, W. S. 1927- .... **CLC 1, 2, 3, 5, 8, 13, 18, 45, 88; PC 45**
See also AMWS 3; CA 13-16R; CANR 15, 51, 112, 140, 209; CP 1, 2, 3, 4, 5, 6, 7; DA3; DAM POET; DLB 5, 169, 342; EWL 3; INT CANR-15; MAL 5; MTCW 1, 2; MTFW 2005; PAB; PFS 5, 15; RGAL 4

Merwin, William Stanley
See Merwin, W. S.

Metastasio, Pietro 1698-1782 .... **LC 115**
See also RGWL 2, 3

Metcalf, John 1938- .... **CLC 37; SSC 43**
See also CA 113; CN 4, 5, 6, 7; DLB 60; RGSF 2; TWA

Metcalf, Suzanne
See Baum, L. Frank

Mew, Charlotte (Mary) 1870-1928 .... **PC 107; TCLC 8**
See also CA 105; 189; DLB 19, 135; RGEL 2

Mewshaw, Michael 1943- .... **CLC 9**
See also CA 53-56; CANR 7, 47, 147, 213; DLBY 1980

Meyer, Conrad Ferdinand 1825-1898 .... **NCLC 81, 249; SSC 30**
See also DLB 129; EW; RGWL 2, 3

Meyer, Gustav 1868-1932 .... **TCLC 21**
See also CA 117; 190; DLB 81; EWL 3

Meyer, June
See Jordan, June

Meyer, Lynn
See Slavitt, David R.

Meyer, Stephenie 1973- .... **CLC 280**
See also AAYA 77; CA 253; CANR 192; CLR 142, 180; SATA 193

Meyer-Meyrink, Gustav
See Meyer, Gustav

Meyers, Jeffrey 1939- .... **CLC 39**
See also CA 73-76, 186; CAAE 186; CANR 54, 102, 159; DLB 111

Meynell, Alice (Christina Gertrude Thompson) 1847-1922 .... **PC 112; TCLC 6**
See also CA 104; 177; DLB 19, 98; RGEL 2

Meyrink, Gustav
See Meyer, Gustav

Mhlophe, Gcina 1960- .... **BLC 2:3**

Michaels, Leonard 1933-2003 .... **CLC 6, 25; SSC 16**
See also AMWS 16; CA 61-64; 216; CANR 21, 62, 119, 179; CN 3, 4, 5, 6, 7; DLB 130; MTCW 1; TCLE 1:2

Michaux, Henri 1899-1984 .... **CLC 8, 19**
See also CA 85-88; 114; DLB 258; EWL 3; GFL 1789 to the Present; RGWL 2, 3

Micheaux, Oscar (Devereaux) 1884-1951 .... **TCLC 76**
See also BW 3; CA 174; DLB 50; TCWW 2

Michelangelo 1475-1564 .... **LC 12**
See also AAYA 43

Michelet, Jules 1798-1874 .... **NCLC 31, 218**
See also EW 5; GFL 1789 to the Present

Michels, Robert 1876-1936 .... **TCLC 88**
See also CA 212

Michener, James A. 1907(?)-1997 ... **CLC 1, 5, 11, 29, 60, 109**
See also AAYA 27; AITN 1; BEST 90:1; BPFB 2; CA 5-8R; CANR 21, 45, 68; CN 1, 2, 3, 4, 5, 6; CPW; DA3; DAM NOV, POP; DLB 6; MAL 5; MTCW 1, 2; MTFW 2005; RHW; TCWW 1, 2

Michener, James Albert
See Michener, James A.

Mickiewicz, Adam 1798-1855 .... **NCLC 3, 101, 265; PC 38**
See also EW 5; RGWL 2, 3

Middleton, (John) Christopher 1926- .... **CLC 13**
See also CA 13-16R; CANR 29, 54, 117; CP 1, 2, 3, 4, 5, 6, 7; DLB 40

Middleton, Richard (Barham) 1882-1911 .... **TCLC 56**
See also CA 187; DLB 156; HGG

Middleton, Stanley 1919-2009 ..... **CLC 7, 38**
See also CA 25-28R; 288; CAAS 23; CANR 21, 46, 81, 157; CN 1, 2, 3, 4, 5, 6, 7; DLB 14, 326

Middleton, Thomas 1580-1627 .... **DC 5, 40; LC 33, 123**
See also BRW 2; DAM DRAM, MST; DFS 18, 22; DLB 58; RGEL 2

Migueis, Jose Rodrigues 1901-1980 .... **CLC 10**
See also DLB 287

Mihura, Miguel 1905-1977 .... **DC 34**
See also CA 214

Mikszath, Kalman 1847-1910 .... **TCLC 31**
See also CA 170

Miles, Jack .... **CLC 100**
See also CA 200

Miles, John Russiano
See Miles, Jack

Miles, Josephine (Louise) 1911-1985 .... **CLC 1, 2, 14, 34, 39**
See also CA 1-4R; 116; CANR 2, 55; CP 1, 2, 3, 4; DAM POET; DLB 48; MAL 5; TCLE 1:2

Militant
See Sandburg, Carl

Mill, Harriet (Hardy) Taylor 1807-1858 .... **NCLC 102**
See also FW

Mill, John Stuart 1806-1873 .... **NCLC 11, 58, 179, 223**
See also CDBLB 1832-1890; DLB 55, 190, 262, 366; FW 1; RGEL 2; TEA

Millar, Kenneth 1915-1983 ...... **CLC 1, 2, 3, 14, 34, 41**
See also AAYA 81; AMWS 4; BPFB 2; CA 9-12R; 110; CANR 16, 63, 107; CMW 4; CN 1, 2, 3; CPW; DA3; DAM POP; DLB 2, 226; DLBD 6; DLBY 1983; MAL 5; MSW; MTCW 1, 2; MTFW 2005; RGAL 4

Millay, E. Vincent
See Millay, Edna St. Vincent

Millay, Edna St. Vincent 1892-1950 ... **PC 6, 61; TCLC 4, 49, 169; WLCS**
See also AMW; CA 104; 130; CDALB 1917-1929; DA; DA3; DAB; DAC; DAM MST, POET; DFS 27; DLB 45, 249; EWL 3; EXPP; FL 1:6; GLL 1; MAL 5; MBL; MTCW 1, 2; MTFW 2005; PAB; PFS 3, 17, 31, 34, 41; RGAL 4; TUS; WP

Miller, Arthur 1915-2005 .... **CLC 1, 2, 6, 10, 15, 26, 47, 78, 179; DC 1, 31; WLC 4**

See also AAYA 15; AITN 1; AMW; AMWC 1; CA 1-4R; 236; CABS 3; CAD; CANR 2, 30, 54, 76, 132; CD 5, 6; CDALB 1941-1968; DA; DA3; DAB; DAC; DAM DRAM, MST; DFS 1, 3, 8, 27; DLB 7, 266; EWL 3; LAIT 1, 4; LATS 1:2; MAL 5; MTCW 1, 2; MTFW 2005; RGAL 4; RGHL; TUS; WYAS 1

Miller, Frank 1957- .... **CLC 278**
See also AAYA 45; CA 224

Miller, Henry (Valentine)
1891-1980 .... **CLC 1, 2, 4, 9, 14, 43, 84; TCLC 213; WLC 4**
See also AMW; BPFB 2; CA 9-12R; 97-100; CANR 33, 64; CDALB 1929-1941; CN 1, 2; DA; DA3; DAB; DAC; DAM MST, NOV; DLB 4, 9; DLBY 1980; EWL 3; MAL 5; MTCW 1, 2; MTFW 2005; RGAL 4; TUS

Miller, Hugh 1802-1856 .... **NCLC 143**
See also DLB 190

Miller, Jason 1939(?)-2001 .... **CLC 2**
See also AITN 1; CA 73-76; 197; CAD; CANR 130; DFS 12; DLB 7

Miller, Sue 1943- .... **CLC 44**
See also AMWS 12; BEST 90:3; CA 139; CANR 59, 91, 128, 194, 231; DA3; DAM POP; DLB 143

Miller, Walter M(ichael, Jr.)
1923-1996 .... **CLC 4, 30**
See also BPFB 2; CA 85-88; CANR 108; DLB 8; SCFW 1, 2; SFW 4

Millett, Kate 1934- .... **CLC 67**
See also AITN 1; CA 73-76; CANR 32, 53, 76, 110; DA3; DLB 246; FW; GLL 1; MTCW 1, 2; MTFW 2005

Millhauser, Steven 1943- .... **CLC 21, 54, 109, 300; SSC 57**
See also AAYA 76; CA 110; 111; CANR 63, 114, 133, 189; CN 6, 7; DA3; DLB 2, 350; FANT; INT CA-111; MAL 5; MTCW 2; MTFW 2005

Millhauser, Steven Lewis
See Millhauser, Steven

Millin, Sarah Gertrude
1889-1968 .... **CLC 49**
See also CA 102; 93-96; DLB 225; EWL 3

Milne, A. A. 1882-1956 .... **TCLC 6, 88**
See also BRWS 5; CA 104; 133; CLR 1, 26, 108; CMW 4; CWRI 5; DA3; DAB; DAC; DAM MST; DLB 10, 77, 100, 160, 352; FANT; MAICYA 1, 2; MTCW 1, 2; MTFW 2005; RGEL 2; SATA 100; WCH; YABC 1

Milne, Alan Alexander
See Milne, A. A.

Milner, Ron(ald) 1938-2004 .... **BLC 1:3; CLC 56**
See also AITN 1; BW 1; CA 73-76; 230; CAD; CANR 24, 81; CD 5, 6; DAM MULT; DLB 38; MAL 5; MTCW 1

Milnes, Richard Monckton
1809-1885 .... **NCLC 61**
See also DLB 32, 184

Milosz, Czeslaw 1911-2004 .... **CLC 5, 11, 22, 31, 56, 82, 253; PC 8, 136; WLCS**
See also AAYA 62; CA 81-84; 230; CANR 23, 51, 91, 126; CDWLB 4; CWW 2; DA3; DAM MST, POET; DLB 215, 331; EW 13; EWL 3; MTCW 1, 2; MTFW 2005; PFS 16, 29, 35; RGHL; RGWL 2, 3

Milton, John 1608-1674 .... **LC 9, 43, 92, 205, 225; PC 19, 29, 141; WLC 4**
See also AAYA 65; BRW 2; BRWR 2; CDBLB 1660-1789; DA; DA3; DAB; DAC; DAM MST, POET; DLB 131, 151, 281; EFS 1:1, 2:2; EXPP; LAIT 1; PAB; PFS 3, 17, 37, 44; RGEL 2; TEA; WLIT 3; WP

Min, Anchee 1957- .... **CLC 86, 291**
See also CA 146; CANR 94, 137, 222; MTFW 2005

Minehaha, Cornelius
See Wedekind, Frank

Miner, Valerie 1947- .... **CLC 40**
See also CA 97-100; CANR 59, 177; FW; GLL 2

Minimo, Duca
See D'Annunzio, Gabriele

Minot, Susan (Anderson)
1956- .... **CLC 44, 159**
See also AMWS 6; CA 134; CANR 118; CN 6, 7

Minus, Ed 1938- .... **CLC 39**
See also CA 185

Mirabai 1498(?)-1550(?) ...... **LC 143; PC 48**
See also PFS 24

Miranda, Javier
See Bioy Casares, Adolfo

Mirbeau, Octave 1848-1917 .... **TCLC 55**
See also CA 216; DLB 123, 192; GFL 1789 to the Present

Mirikitani, Janice 1942- .... **AAL**
See also CA 211; DLB 312; RGAL 4

Mirk, John (?)-c. 1414 .... **LC 105**
See also DLB 146

Miro (Ferrer), Gabriel (Francisco Victor)
1879-1930 .... **TCLC 5**
See also CA 104; 185; DLB 322; EWL 3

Misharin, Alexandr .... **CLC 59**

Mishima, Yukio
See Hiraoka, Kimitake
See also NFS 43

Mishima Yukio
See Hiraoka, Kimitake

Miss C. L. F.
See Grimke, Charlotte L. Forten

Mister X
See Hoch, Edward D.

Mistral, Frederic 1830-1914 .... **TCLC 51**
See also CA 122; 213; DLB 331; GFL 1789 to the Present

Mistral, Gabriela 1899-1957 .... **HLC 2; PC 32; TCLC 2, 277**
See also BW 2; CA 104; 131; CANR 81; DAM MULT; DLB 283, 331; DNFS; EWL 3; HW 1, 2; LAW; MTCW 1, 2; MTFW 2005; PFS 37, 42; RGWL 2, 3; WP

Mistry, Rohinton 1952- .... **CLC 71, 196, 281; SSC 73**
See also BRWS 10; CA 141; CANR 86, 114; CCA 1; CN 6, 7; DAC; DLB 334; NFS 43; SSFS 6

Mitchell, Clyde
See Ellison, Harlan; Silverberg, Robert

Mitchell, David 1969- .... **CLC 311**
See also BRWS 14; CA 210; CANR 159, 224

Mitchell, Emerson Blackhorse Barney
1945- .... **NNAL**
See also CA 45-48

Mitchell, James Leslie 1901-1935 ... **TCLC 4**
See also BRWS 14; CA 104; 188; DLB 15; RGEL 2

Mitchell, Joni 1943- .... **CLC 12**
See also CA 112; CCA 1

Mitchell, Joseph (Quincy)
1908-1996 .... **CLC 98**
See also CA 77-80; 152; CANR 69; CN 1, 2, 3, 4, 5, 6; CSW; DLB 185; DLBY 1996

Mitchell, Margaret
1900-1949 .... **TCLC 11, 170**
See also AAYA 23; BPFB 2; BYA 1; CA 109; 125; CANR 55, 94; CDALBS; DA3; DAM NOV, POP; DLB 9; LAIT 2; MAL 5; MTCW 1, 2; MTFW 2005; NFS 9, 38; RGAL 4; RHW; TUS; WYAS 1; YAW

Mitchell, Margaret Munnerlyn
See Mitchell, Margaret

Mitchell, Peggy
See Mitchell, Margaret

Mitchell, S(ilas) Weir 1829-1914 ... **TCLC 36**
See also CA 165; DLB 202; RGAL 4

Mitchell, W(illiam) O(rmond)
1914-1998 .... **CLC 25**
See also CA 77-80; 165; CANR 15, 43; CN 1, 2, 3, 4, 5, 6; DAC; DAM MST; DLB 88; TCLE 1:2

Mitchell, William (Lendrum)
1879-1936 .... **TCLC 81**
See also CA 213

Mitford, Mary Russell 1787-1855 ... **NCLC 4**
See also DLB 110, 116; RGEL 2

Mitford, Nancy 1904-1973 .... **CLC 44**
See also BRWS 10; CA 9-12R; CN 1; DLB 191; RGEL 2

Mieville, China 1972- .... **CLC 235**
See also AAYA 52; CA 196; CANR 138, 214, 239; MTFW 2005

Miyamoto, (Chujo) Yuriko
1899-1951 .... **TCLC 37**
See also CA 170, 174; DLB 180

Miyamoto Yuriko
See Miyamoto, (Chujo) Yuriko

Miyazawa, Kenji 1896-1933 .... **TCLC 76**
See also CA 157; EWL 3; RGWL 3

Miyazawa Kenji
See Miyazawa, Kenji

Mizoguchi, Kenji 1898-1956 .... **TCLC 72**
See also CA 167

Muller, Heiner 1929-1995 .... **DC 47**
See also CA 193; CWW 2; EWL 3

Muller, Herta 1953- .... **CLC 299**
See also CA 175; CANR 147, 210

Mo, Timothy (Peter) 1950- ...... **CLC 46, 134**
See also CA 117; CANR 128; CN 5, 6, 7; DLB 194; MTCW 1; WLIT 4; WWE 1

Mo, Yan
See Yan, Mo

Moberg, Carl Arthur
See Moberg, Vilhelm

Moberg, Vilhelm 1898-1973 .... **TCLC 224**
See also CA 97-100; 45-48; CANR 135; DLB 259; EW 11; EWL 3

Modarressi, Taghi (M.) 1931-1997 ... **CLC 44**
See also CA 121; 134; INT CA-134

Modiano, Patrick (Jean)
1945- .... **CLC 18, 218**
See also CA 85-88; CANR 17, 40, 115; CWW 2; DLB 83, 299; EWL 3; RGHL

Mofolo, Thomas 1875(?)-1948 .... **BLC 1:3; TCLC 22**
See also AFW; CA 121; 153; CANR 83; DAM MULT; DLB 225; EWL 3; MTCW 2; MTFW 2005; WLIT 2

Mofolo, Thomas Mokopu
See Mofolo, Thomas

Mohr, Nicholasa 1938- ...... **CLC 12; HLC 2**
See also AAYA 8, 46; CA 49-52; CANR 1, 32, 64; CLR 22; DAM MULT; DLB 145; HW 1, 2; JRDA; LAIT 5; LLW; MAICYA 2; MAICYAS 1; RGAL 4; SAAS 8; SATA 8, 97; SATA-Essay 113; WYA; YAW

Moi, Toril 1953- .... **CLC 172**
See also CA 154; CANR 102; FW

Mojtabai, A.G. 1938- .... **CLC 5, 9, 15, 29**
See also CA 85-88; CANR 88, 238

Mojtabai, Ann Grace
See Mojtabai, A.G.

Molin, Charles
See Mayne, William

Molina, Antonio Munoz 1956- ..... **CLC 289**
See also DLB 322

Mujica Lainez, Manuel 1910-1984 .. **CLC 31**
    See also CA 81-84; 112; CANR 32; EWL 3;
        HW 1
Mukherjee, Bharati 1940- ... **AAL; CLC 53,**
    115, 235; SSC 38, 173
        See also AAYA 46; BEST 89:2; CA 107,
        232; CAAE 232; CANR 45, 72, 128, 231;
        CN 5, 6, 7; DAM NOV; DLB 60, 218, 323;
        DNFS 1, 2; EWL 3; FW; MAL 5; MTCW
        1, 2; MTFW 2005; NFS 37; RGAL 4;
        RGSF 2; SSFS 7, 24, 32; TUS; WWE 1
Muldoon, Paul 1951- .... **CLC 32, 72, 166,**
    324; PC 143
        See also BRWS 4; CA 113; 129; CANR 52,
        91, 176; CP 2, 3, 4, 5, 6, 7; DAM
        POET; DLB 40; INT CA-129; PFS 7,
        22; TCLE 1:2
Mulisch, Harry 1927-2010 ...... **CLC 42, 270**
        See also CA 9-12R; CANR 6, 26, 56, 110;
        CWW 2; DLB 299; EWL 3
Mulisch, Harry Kurt Victor
        See Mulisch, Harry
Mull, Martin 1943- .... **CLC 17**
        See also CA 105
Mullen, Harryette 1953- .... **CLC 321**
        See also CA 218; CP 7
Mullen, Harryette Romell
        See Mullen, Harryette
Muller, Wilhelm .... **NCLC 73**
Mulock, Dinah Maria
        See Craik, Dinah Maria (Mulock)
Multatuli 1820-1881 .... **NCLC 165**
        See also RGWL 2, 3
Munday, Anthony 1560-1633 .... **LC 87**
        See also DLB 62, 172; RGEL 2
Munford, Robert 1737(?)-1783 .... **LC 5**
        See also DLB 31
Mungo, Raymond 1946- .... **CLC 72**
        See also CA 49-52; CANR 2
Munnings, Clare
        See Conway, Jill K.
Munro, Alice 1931- .... **CLC 6, 10, 19, 50,**
    95, 222; SSC 3, 95; WLCS
        See also AAYA 82; AITN 2; BPFB 2; CA 33-
        36R; CANR 33, 53, 75, 114, 177; CCA 1;
        CN 1, 2, 3, 4, 5, 6, 7; DA3; DAC; DAM
        MST, NOV; DLB 53; EWL 3; LNFS 3;
        MTCW 1, 2; MTFW 2005; NFS 27, RGEL
        2; RGSF 2; SATA 29; SSFS 5, 13, 19, 28;
        TCLE 1:2; WWE 1
Munro, Alice Anne
        See Munro, Alice
Munro, H. H.
        See Saki
Munro, Hector H.
        See Saki
Munro, Hector Hugh
        See Saki
Murakami, Haruki 1949- ...... **CLC 150, 274**
        See also CA 165; CANR 102, 146, 212;
        CWW 2; DLB 182; EWL 3; LNFS 2;
        MJW; RGWL 3; SFW 4; SSFS 23, 36
Murakami Haruki
        See Murakami, Haruki
Murasaki, Lady
        See Murasaki Shikibu
Murasaki Shikibu
    978(?)-1014(?) .... **CMLC 1, 79, 160**
        See also EFS 1:2, 2:2; LATS 1:1; RGWL 2, 3
Murdoch, Iris 1919-1999 ..... **CLC 1, 2, 3, 4,**
    6, 8, 11, 15, 22, 31, 51; TCLC 171
        See also BRWS 1; CA 13-16R; 179; CANR
        8, 43, 68, 103, 142; CBD; CDBLB 1960 to
        Present; CN 1, 2, 3, 4, 5, 6; CWD; DA3;
        DAB; DAC; DAM MST, NOV; DLB 14,
        194, 233, 326; EWL 3; INT CANR-8;
        MTCW 1, 2; MTFW 2005; NFS 18; RGEL
        2; TCLE 1:2; TEA; WLIT 4

Murdoch, Jean Iris
        See Murdoch, Iris
Murfree, Mary Noailles
    1850-1922 .... **SSC 22; TCLC 135**
        See also CA 122; 176; DLB 12, 74; RGAL 4
Murglie
        See Murnau, F.W.
Murnau, Friedrich Wilhelm
        See Murnau, F.W.
Murnau, F.W. 1888-1931 .... **TCLC 53**
        See also CA 112
Murphy, Arthur 1727-1805 .... **NCLC 229**
        See also DLB 89, 142; RGEL 2
Murphy, Richard 1927- .... **CLC 41**
        See also BRWS 5; CA 29-32R; CP 1, 2, 3, 4,
        5, 6, 7; DLB 40; EWL 3
Murphy, Sylvia 1937- .... **CLC 34**
        See also CA 121
Murphy, Thomas 1935- .... **CLC 51**
        See also CA 101; DLB 310
Murphy, Thomas Bernard
        See Murphy, Thomas
Murphy, Tom
        See Murphy, Thomas
Murray, Albert 1916- .... **BLC 2:3; CLC 73**
        See also BW 2; CA 49-52; CANR 26, 52, 78,
        160; CN 7; CSW; DLB 38; MTFW 2005
Murray, Albert L.
        See Murray, Albert
Murray, Diane Lain Johnson
        See Johnson, Diane
Murray, James Augustus Henry
    1837-1915 .... **TCLC 117**
Murray, Judith Sargent
    1751-1820 .... **NCLC 63, 243**
        See also DLB 37, 200
Murray, Les 1938- .... **CLC 40, 326**
        See also BRWS 7; CA 21-24R; CANR 11,
        27, 56, 103, 199, 236; CP 1, 2, 3, 4, 5, 6, 7;
        DAM POET; DLB 289; DLBY 2001;
        EWL 3; RGEL 2
Murray, Leslie Allan
        See Murray, Les
Murry, J. Middleton
        See Murry, John Middleton
Murry, John Middleton
    1889-1957 .... **TCLC 16**
        See also CA 118; 217; DLB 149
Musgrave, Susan 1951- .... **CLC 13, 54**
        See also CA 69-72; CANR 45, 84, 181;
        CCA 1; CP 2, 3, 4, 5, 6, 7; CWP
Musil, Robert (Edler von) 1880-1942 ... **SSC**
    18; TCLC 12, 68, 213, 291
        See also CA 109; CANR 55, 84; CDWLB 2;
        DLB 81, 124; EW 9; EWL 3; MTCW 2;
        RGSF 2; RGWL 2, 3
Muske, Carol
        See Muske-Dukes, Carol
Muske, Carol Anne
        See Muske-Dukes, Carol
Muske-Dukes, Carol 1945- .... **CLC 90**
        See also CA 65-68, 203; CAAE 203; CANR
        32, 70, 181; CWP; PFS 24
Muske-Dukes, Carol Ann
        See Muske-Dukes, Carol
Muske-Dukes, Carol Anne
        See Muske-Dukes, Carol
Musset, Alfred de 1810-1857 .... **DC 27;**
    NCLC 7, 150
        See also DLB 192, 217; EW 6; GFL 1789 to
        the Present; RGWL 2, 3; TWA
Musset, Louis Charles Alfred de
        See Musset, Alfred de
Mussolini, Benito (Amilcare Andrea)
    1883-1945 .... **TCLC 96**
        See also CA 116

Mutanabbi, Al-
        See al-Mutanabbi, Ahmad ibn al-Husayn
        Abu al-Tayyib al-Jufi al-Kindi
Mutis, Alvaro 1923- .... **CLC 283**
        See also CA 149; CANR 118; DLB 283;
        EWL 3; HW 1; LAWS 1
My Brother's Brother
        See Chekhov, Anton
Myers, L(eopold) H(amilton)
    1881-1944 .... **TCLC 59**
        See also CA 157; DLB 15; EWL 3; RGEL 2
Myers, Walter Dean 1937- .... **BLC 1:3, 2:3;**
    CLC 35
        See also AAYA 4, 23, 88; BW 2; BYA 6, 8,
        11; CA 33-36R; CANR 20, 42, 67, 108,
        184; CLR 4, 16, 35, 110; DAM MULT,
        NOV; DLB 33; INT CANR-20; JRDA;
        LAIT 5; LNFS 1; MAICYA 1, 2; MAICYAS
        1; MTCW 2; MTFW 2005; NFS 30, 33, 40;
        SAAS 2; SATA 41, 71, 109, 157, 193, 229;
        SATA-Brief 27; SSFS 31; WYA; YAW
Myers, Walter M.
        See Myers, Walter Dean
Myles, Symon
        See Follett, Ken
Nabokov, Vladimir 1899-1977 ..... **CLC 1, 2,**
    3, 6, 8, 11, 15, 23, 44, 46, 64; SSC 11, 86,
    163; TCLC 108, 189; WLC 4
        See also AAYA 45; AMW; AMWC 1;
        AMWR 1; BPFB 2; CA 5-8R; 69-72;
        CANR 20, 102; CDALB 1941-1968; CN
        1, 2; CP 2; DA; DA3; DAB; DAC; DAM
        MST, NOV; DLB 2, 244, 278, 317; DLBD
        3; DLBY 1980, 1991; EWL 3; EXPS;
        LATS 1:2; MAL 5; MTCW 1, 2; MTFW
        2005; NCFS 4; NFS 9; RGAL 4; RGSF 2;
        SSFS 6, 15; TUS
Nabokov, Vladimir Vladimirovich
        See Nabokov, Vladimir
Naevius c. 265B.C.-201B.C. .... **CMLC 37**
        See also DLB 211
Nafisi, Azar 1955- .... **CLC 313**
        See also CA 222; CANR 203; DLB 366;
        LNFS 2
Nagai, Kafu 1879-1959 .... **TCLC 51**
        See also CA 117; 276; DLB 180; EWL 3; MJW
Nagai, Sokichi
        See Nagai, Kafu
Nagai Kafu
        See Nagai, Kafu
na gCopaleen, Myles
        See O Nuallain, Brian
na Gopaleen, Myles
        See O Nuallain, Brian
Nagy, Laszlo 1925-1978 .... **CLC 7**
        See also CA 129; 112
Naidu, Sarojini 1879-1949 .... **TCLC 80**
        See also EWL 3; RGEL 2
Naipaul, Shiva 1945-1985 .... **CLC 32, 39;**
    TCLC 153
        See also CA 110; 112; 116; CANR 33; CN
        2, 3; DA3; DAM NOV; DLB 157; DLBY
        1985; EWL 3; MTCW 1, 2; MTFW 2005
Naipaul, Shivadhar Srinivasa
        See Naipaul, Shiva
Naipaul, Vidiahar Surajprasad
        See Naipaul, V. S.
Naipaul, V. S. 1932- .... **CLC 4, 7, 9, 13, 18,**
    37, 105, 199; SSC 38, 121
        See also BPFB 2; BRWS 1; CA 1-4R;
        CANR 1, 33, 51, 91, 126, 191; CDBLB
        1960 to Present; CDWLB 3; CN 1, 2, 3, 4,
        5, 6, 7; DA3; DAB; DAC; DAM MST,
        NOV; DLB 125, 204, 207, 326, 331; DLBY
        1985, 2001; EWL 3; LATS 1:2; MTCW 1,
        2; MTFW 2005; NFS 37; RGEL 2; RGSF
        2; SSFS 29; TWA; WLIT 4; WWE 1
Nair, Kamala
        See Das, Kamala

See also AITN 2; AMWS 10; BPFB 2; CA 13-16R; 69-72; CANR 22, 53; CN 1, 2; DAM NOV, POP; DLB 2, 4, 152; EWL 3; GLL 2; MAL 5; MBL; MTCW 1, 2; MTFW 2005; RGAL 4; RGSF 2

Nisbet, Robert A(lexander) 1913-1996 .... **TCLC 117**
See also CA 25-28R; 153; CANR 17; INT CANR-17

Nishida, Kitaro 1870-1945 .... **TCLC 83**

Nishiwaki, Junzaburo 1894-1982 .... **PC 15**
See also CA 194; 107; EWL 3; MJW; RGWL 3

Nissenson, Hugh 1933- .... **CLC 4, 9**
See also CA 17-20R; CANR 27, 108, 151; CN 5, 6; DLB 28, 335

Nister, Der
See Der Nister

Niven, Larry 1938- .... **CLC 8**
See also AAYA 27; BPFB 2; BYA 10; CA 21-24R, 207; CAAE 207; CAAS 12; CANR 14, 44, 66, 113, 155, 206; CPW; DAM POP; DLB 8; MTCW 1, 2; SATA 95, 171; SCFW 1, 2; SFW 4

Niven, Laurence Van Cott
See Niven, Larry

Niven, Laurence VanCott
See Niven, Larry

Nixon, Agnes Eckhardt 1927- .... **CLC 21**
See also CA 110

Nizan, Paul 1905-1940 .... **TCLC 40**
See also CA 161; DLB 72; EWL 3; GFL 1789 to the Present

Nkosi, Lewis 1936-2010 ... **BLC 1:3; CLC 45**
See also BW 1, 3; CA 65-68; CANR 27, 81; CBD; CD 5, 6; DAM MULT; DLB 157, 225; WWE 1

Nodier, (Jean) Charles (Emmanuel) 1780-1844 .... **NCLC 19**
See also DLB 119; GFL 1789 to the Present

Noguchi, Yone 1875-1947 .... **TCLC 80**

Nolan, Brian
See O Nuallain, Brian

Nolan, Christopher 1965-2009 .... **CLC 58**
See also CA 111; 283; CANR 88

Nolan, Christopher John
See Nolan, Christopher

Noon, Jeff 1957- .... **CLC 91**
See also CA 148; CANR 83; DLB 267; SFW 4

Nooteboom, Cees 1933- .... **CLC 323**
See also CA 124; 130; CANR 120, 177; EWL 3; RGWL 3

Nordan, Lewis 1939-2012 .... **CLC 304**
See also CA 117; CANR 40, 72, 121; CSW; DLB 234, 350

Norden, Charles
See Durrell, Lawrence

Nordhoff, Charles Bernard 1887-1947 .... **TCLC 23**
See also CA 108; 211; DLB 9; LAIT 1; RHW 1; SATA 23

Norfolk, Lawrence 1963- .... **CLC 76**
See also CA 144; CANR 85; CN 6, 7; DLB 267

Norman, Marsha (Williams) 1947- .... **CLC 28, 186; DC 8**
See also CA 105; CABS 3; CAD; CANR 41, 131; CD 5, 6; CSW; CWD; DAM DRAM; DFS 2; DLB 266; DLBY 1984; FW; MAL 5

Normyx
See Douglas, (George) Norman

Norris, Benjamin Franklin, Jr.
See Norris, Frank

Norris, Frank 1870-1902 .... **SSC 28; TCLC 24, 155, 211**
See also AAYA 57; AMW; AMWC 2; BPFB 2; CA 110; 160; CDALB 1865-1917; DLB

12, 71, 186; LMFS 2; MAL 5; NFS 12; RGAL 4; TCWW 1, 2; TUS

Norris, Kathleen 1947- .... **CLC 248**
See also CA 160; CANR 113, 199

Norris, Leslie 1921-2006 .... **CLC 14, 351**
See also CA 11-12; 251; CANR 14, 117; CAP 1; CP 1, 2, 3, 4, 5, 6, 7; DLB 27, 256

North, Andrew
See Norton, Andre

North, Anthony
See Koontz, Dean

North, Captain George
See Stevenson, Robert Louis

North, Captain George
See Stevenson, Robert Louis

North, Milou
See Erdrich, Louise

Northrup, B. A.
See Hubbard, L. Ron

North Staffs
See Hulme, T(homas) E(rnest)

Northup, Solomon 1808-1863 ..... **NCLC 105**

Norton, Alice Mary
See Norton, Andre

Norton, Andre 1912-2005 .... **CLC 12**
See also AAYA 83; BPFB 2; BYA 4, 10, 12; CA 1-4R; 237; CANR 2, 31, 68, 108, 149; CLR 50, 184; DLB 8, 52; JRDA; MAICYA 1, 2; MTCW 1; SATA 1, 43, 91; SUFW 1, 2; YAW

Norton, Caroline 1808-1877 .... **NCLC 47, 205**
See also DLB 21, 159, 199

Norway, Nevil Shute
See Shute, Nevil

Norwid, Cyprian Kamil 1821-1883 .... **NCLC 17**
See also RGWL 3

Nosille, Nabrah
See Ellison, Harlan

Nossack, Hans Erich 1901-1977 .... **CLC 6**
See also CA 93-96; 85-88; CANR 156; DLB 69; EWL 3

Nostradamus 1503-1566 .... **LC 27**

Nosu, Chuji
See Ozu, Yasujiro

Notenburg, Eleanora (Genrikhovna) von
See Guro, Elena (Genrikhovna)

Nothomb, Amélie 1967- .... **CLC 344**
See also CA 205; CANR 154, 205

Nova, Craig 1945- .... **CLC 7, 31**
See also CA 45-48; CANR 2, 53, 127, 223

Novak, Joseph
See Kosinski, Jerzy

Novalis 1772-1801 .... **NCLC 13, 178; PC 120**
See also CDWLB 2; DLB 90; EW 5; RGWL 2, 3

Novick, Peter 1934-2012 .... **CLC 164**
See also CA 188

Novis, Emile
See Weil, Simone

Nowlan, Alden (Albert) 1933-1983 .... **CLC 15**
See also CA 9-12R; CANR 5; CP 1, 2, 3; DAC; DAM MST; DLB 53; PFS 12

Noyes, Alfred 1880-1958 .... **PC 27; TCLC 7**
See also CA 104; 188; DLB 20; EXPP; FANT; PFS 4; RGEL 2

Nugent, Richard Bruce 1906(?)-1987 .... **HR 1:3**
See also BW 1; CA 125; CANR 198; DLB 51; GLL 2

Nunez, Elizabeth 1944- .... **BLC 2:3**
See also CA 223; CANR 220

Nunn, Kem .... **CLC 34**
See also CA 159; CANR 204

Nussbaum, Martha 1947- .... **CLC 203**
See also CA 134; CANR 102, 176, 213, 241

Nussbaum, Martha Craven
See Nussbaum, Martha

Nwapa, Flora (Nwanzuruaha) 1931-1993 .... **BLCS; CLC 133**
See also BW 2; CA 143; CANR 83; CDWLB 3; CLR 162; CWRI 5; DLB 125; EWL 3; WLIT 2

Nye, Robert 1939- .... **CLC 13, 42**
See also BRWS 10; CA 33-36R; CANR 29, 67, 107; CN 1, 2, 3, 4, 5, 6, 7; CP 1, 2, 3, 4, 5, 6, 7; CWRI 5; DAM NOV; DLB 14, 271; FANT; HGG; MTCW 1; RHW; SATA 6

Nyro, Laura 1947-1997 .... **CLC 17**
See also CA 194

O. Henry
See Henry, O.

Oates, Joyce Carol 1938- .... **CLC 1, 2, 3, 6, 9, 11, 15, 19, 33, 52, 108, 134, 228; SSC 6, 70, 121; WLC 4**
See also AAYA 15, 52; AITN 1; AMWS 2; BEST 89:2; BPFB 2; BYA 11; CA 5-8R; CANR 25, 45, 74, 113, 129, 165; CDALB 1968-1988; CN 1, 2, 3, 4, 5, 6, 7; CP 5, 6, 7; CPW; CWP; DA; DA3; DAB; DAC; DAM MST, NOV, POP; DLB 2, 5, 130; DLBY 1981; EWL 3; EXPS; FL 1:6; FW; GL 3; HGG; INT CANR-25; LAIT 4; MAL 5; MBL; MTCW 1, 2; MTFW 2005; NFS 8, 24; RGAL 4; RGSF 2; SATA 159; SSFS 1, 8, 17, 32; SUFW 2; TUS

Obradovic, Dositej 1740(?)-1811 .. **NCLC 254**
See also DLB 147

O'Brian, E.G.
See Clarke, Arthur C.

O'Brian, Patrick 1914-2000 .... **CLC 152**
See also AAYA 55; BRWS 12; CA 144; 187; CANR 74, 201; CPW; MTCW 2; MTFW 2005; RHW

O'Brien, Darcy 1939-1998 .... **CLC 11**
See also CA 21-24R; 167; CANR 8, 59

O'Brien, Edna 1930- .... **CLC 3, 5, 8, 13, 36, 65, 116, 237; SSC 10, 77, 192**
See also BRWS 5; CA 1-4R; CANR 6, 41, 65, 102, 169, 213; CDBLB 1960 to Present; CN 1, 2, 3, 4, 5, 6, 7; DA3; DAM NOV; DLB 14, 231, 319; EWL 3; FW; MTCW 1, 2; MTFW 2005; RGSF 2; WLIT 4

O'Brien, E.G.
See Clarke, Arthur C.

O'Brien, Fitz-James 1828-1862 .... **NCLC 21**
See also DLB 74; RGAL 4; SUFW

O'Brien, Flann
See O Nuallain, Brian

Ono no Komachi fl. c. 850- .... **CMLC 134**

O'Brien, Richard 1942- .... **CLC 17**
See also CA 124

O'Brien, Tim 1946- ...... **CLC 7, 19, 40, 103, 211, 305; SSC 74, 123**
See also AAYA 16; AMWS 5; CA 85-88; CANR 40, 58, 133; CDALBS; CN 5, 6, 7; CPW; DA3; DAM POP; DLB 152; DLBD 9; DLBY 1980; LATS 1:2; MAL 5; MTCW 2; MTFW 2005; NFS 37; RGAL 4; SSFS 5, 15, 29, 32; TCLE 1:2

O'Brien, William Timothy
See O'Brien, Tim

Obstfelder, Sigbjorn 1866-1900 .... **TCLC 23**
See also CA 123; DLB 354

Ocampo, Silvina 1906-1993 .... **SSC 175**
See also CA 131; CANR 87, CWW 2, HW 1, RGSF 2

O'Casey, Brenda
See Haycraft, Anna

O'Casey, Sean 1880-1964 .... **CLC 1, 5, 9, 11, 15, 88; DC 12; WLCS**
See also BRW 7; CA 89-92; CANR 62; CBD; CDBLB 1914-1945; DA3; DAB; DAC; DAM DRAM, MST; DFS 19; DLB

Opie, Amelia 1769-1853 .... **NCLC 65**
  See also DLB 116, 159; RGEL 2
Opitz, Martin 1597-1639 .... **LC 207**
  See also DLB 164
Oppen, George 1908-1984 ... **CLC 7, 13, 34;**
  PC 35; TCLC 107
  See also CA 13-16R; 113; CANR 8, 82; CP
  1, 2, 3; DLB 5, 165
Oppenheim, E(dward) Phillips
  1866-1946 .... **TCLC 45**
  See also CA 111; 202; CMW 4; DLB 70
Oppenheimer, Max
  See Ophuls, Max
Opuls, Max
  See Ophuls, Max
Ophuls, Max
  See Ophuls, Max
Orage, A(lfred) R(ichard)
  1873-1934 .... **TCLC 157**
  See also CA 122
Origen c. 185-c. 254 .... **CMLC 19**
Orlovitz, Gil 1918-1973 .... **CLC 22**
  See also CA 77-80; 45-48; CN 1; CP 1, 2;
  DLB 2, 5
Orosius c. 385-c. 420 .... **CMLC 100**
O'Rourke, P. J. 1947- .... **CLC 209**
  See also CA 77-80; CANR 13, 41, 67, 111,
  155, 217; CPW; DAM POP; DLB 185
O'Rourke, Patrick Jake
  See O'Rourke, P.J.
Orrery
  See Boyle, Roger
Orris
  See Ingelow, Jean
Ortega y Gasset, Jose 1883-1955 .... **HLC 2;**
  TCLC 9
  See also CA 106; 130; DAM MULT; EW 9;
  EWL 3; HW 1, 2; MTCW 1, 2; MTFW 2005
Ortese, Anna Maria 1914-1998 ...... **CLC 89**
  See also DLB 177; EWL 3
Ortiz, Simon
  See Ortiz, Simon J.
Ortiz, Simon J. 1941- .... **CLC 45, 208;**
  NNAL; PC 17
  See also AMWS 4; CA 134; CANR 69, 118,
  164; CP 3, 4, 5, 6, 7; DAM MULT, POET;
  DLB 120, 175, 256, 342; EXPP; MAL 5;
  PFS 4, 16; RGAL 4; SSFS 22; TCWW 2
Ortiz, Simon Joseph
  See Ortiz, Simon J.
Orton, Joe
  See Orton, John Kingsley
Orton, John Kingsley 1933-1967 ..... **CLC 4,**
  13, 43; DC 3; TCLC 157
  See also BRWS 5; CA 85-88; CANR 35, 66;
  CBD; CDBLB 1960 to Present; DAM
  DRAM; DFS 3, 6; DLB 13, 310; GLL
  1; MTCW 1, 2; MTFW 2005; RGEL 2;
  TEA; WLIT 4
Orwell, George 1903-1950 .... **SSC 68;**
  TCLC 2, 6, 15, 31, 51, 123, 128, 129,
  276; WLC 4
  See also BPFB 3; BRW 7; BYA 5; CA 104;
  132; CDBLB 1945-1960; CLR 68, 171; DA;
  DA3; DAB; DAC; DAM MST, NOV; DLB
  15, 98, 195, 255; EWL 3; EXPN; LAIT 4, 5;
  LATS 1:1; MTCW 1, 2; MTFW 2005; NFS
  3, 7; RGEL 2; SATA 29; SCFW 1, 2; SFW
  4; SSFS 4; TEA; WLIT 4; YAW X
Osborne, David
  See Silverberg, Robert
Osborne, Dorothy 1627-1695 .... **LC 141**
Osborne, George
  See Silverberg, Robert
Osborne, John 1929-1994 .... **CLC 1, 2, 5,**
  11, 45; DC 38; TCLC 153; WLC 4
  See also BRWS 1; CA 13-16R; 147; CANR
  21, 56; CBD; CDBLB 1945-1960; DA;

DAB; DAC; DAM DRAM, MST; DFS
4, 19, 24; DLB 13; EWL 3; MTCW 1,
2; MTFW 2005; RGEL 2
Osborne, Lawrence 1958- .... **CLC 50**
  See also CA 189; CANR 152
Osbourne, Lloyd 1868-1947 .... **TCLC 93**
Osceola
  See Blixen, Karen
Osgood, Frances Sargent
  1811-1850 .... **NCLC 141**
  See also DLB 250
Oshima, Nagisa 1932- .... **CLC 20**
  See also CA 116; 121; CANR 78
Oskison, John Milton 1874-1947 ...... **NNAL;**
  TCLC 35
  See also CA 144; CANR 84; DAM MULT;
  DLB 175
Osofisan, Femi 1946- .... **CLC 307**
  See also AFW; BW 2; CA 142; CANR 84;
  CD 5, 6; CDWLB 3; DLB 125; EWL 3
Ossian c. 3rd cent.
  See Macpherson, James
Ossoli, Sarah Margaret
  See Fuller, Margaret
Ossoli, Sarah Margaret Fuller
  See Fuller, Margaret
Ostriker, Alicia 1937- .... **CLC 132**
  See also CA 25-28R; CAAS 24; CANR 10,
  30, 62, 99, 167; CWP; DLB 120; EXPP;
  PFS 19, 26
Ostriker, Alicia Suskin
  See Ostriker, Alicia
Ostrovsky, Aleksandr Nikolaevich
  See Ostrovsky, Alexander
Ostrovsky, Alexander
  1823-1886 .... **NCLC 30, 57**
  See also DLB 277
Osundare, Niyi 1947- .... **BLC 2:3**
  See also AFW; BW 3; CA 176; CDWLB 3;
  CP 7; DLB 157
Oswald von Wolkenstein
  1377(?)-1455 .... **LC 208**
Otero, Blas de 1916-1979 .... **CLC 11**
  See also CA 89-92; DLB 134; EWL 3
O'Trigger, Sir Lucius
  See Horne, Richard Henry Hengist
Otto, Rudolf 1869-1937 .... **TCLC 85**
Otto, Whitney 1955- ,,,,,,,,,,,,,,,,,,,,,, **CLC 70**
  See also CA 140; CANR 120
Otway, Thomas 1652-1685 .... **DC 24;**
  LC 106, 170
  See also DAM DRAM; DLB 80; RGEL 2
Ouida
  See De La Ramee, Marie Louise
Ouologuem, Yambo 1940- ..... **CLC 146, 293**
  See also CA 111; 176
Ousmane, Sembene 1923-2007 ..... **BLC 1:3,**
  2:3; CLC 66
  See also AFW; BW 1, 3; CA 117; 125; 261;
  CANR 81; CWW 2; DLB 360; EWL 3;
  MTCW 1; WLIT 2
Ovid 43B.C.-17 .... **CMLC 7, 108; PC 2, 135**
  See also AW 2; CDWLB 1; DA3; DAM
  POET; DLB 211; PFS 22; RGWL 2, 3;
  WLIT 8; WP
Owen, Hugh
  See Faust, Frederick
Owen, Wilfred (Edward Salter)
  1893-1918 .... **PC 19, 102; TCLC 5,**
  27; WLC 4
  See also BRW 6; CA 104; 141; CDBLB 1914-
  1945; DA; DAB; DAC; DAM MST, POET;
  DLB 20; EWL 3; EXPP; MTCW 2; MTFW
  2005; PFS 10, 37; RGEL 2; WLIT 4
Owens, Louis (Dean)
  1948-2002 .... **CLC 321; NNAL**
  See also CA 137, 179; 207; CAAE 179;
  CAAS 24; CANR 71

Owens, Rochelle 1936- .... **CLC 8**
  See also CA 17-20R; CAAS 2; CAD; CANR
  39; CD 5, 6; CP 1, 2, 3, 4, 5, 6, 7; CWD;
  CWP
Owenson, Sydney
  See Morgan, Lady
Oz, Amos 1939- .... **CLC 5, 8, 11, 27, 33,**
  54; SSC 66
  See also AAYA 84; CA 53-56; CANR 27,
  47, 65, 113, 138, 175, 219; CWW 2; DAM
  NOV; EWL 3; MTCW 1, 2; MTFW 2005;
  RGHL; RGSF 2; RGWL 3; WLIT 6
Ozeki, Ruth L. 1956- .... **CLC 307**
  See also CA 181
Ozick, Cynthia 1928- .... **CLC 3, 7, 28, 62,**
  155, 262; SSC 15, 60, 123
  See also AMWS 5; BEST 90:1; CA 17-20R;
  CANR 23, 58, 116, 160, 187; CN 3, 4, 5,
  6, 7; CPW; DA3; DAM NOV, POP; DLB
  28, 152, 299; DLBY 1982; EWL 3; EXPS;
  INT CANR-23; MAL 5; MTCW 1, 2;
  MTFW 2005; RGAL 4; RGHL; RGSF
  2; SSFS 3, 12, 22
Ozu, Yasujiro 1903-1963 .... **CLC 16**
  See also CA 112
Pabst, G. W. 1885-1967 .... **TCLC 127**
Pacheco, C.
  See Pessoa, Fernando
Pacheco, Jose Emilio 1939- .... **HLC 2**
  See also CA 111; 131; CANR 65; CWW 2;
  DAM MULT; DLB 290; EWL 3; HW 1, 2;
  RGSF 2
Pa Chin
  See Jin, Ba
Pack, Robert 1929- .... **CLC 13**
  See also CA 1-4R; CANR 3, 44, 82; CP 1, 2,
  3, 4, 5, 6, 7; DLB 5; SATA 118
Packer, Vin
  See Meaker, Marijane
Padgett, Lewis
  See Kuttner, Henry
Padilla (Lorenzo), Heberto
  1932-2000 .... **CLC 38**
  See also AITN 1; CA 123; 131; 189; CWW
  2; EWL 3; HW 1
Paerdurabo, Frater
  See Crowley, Edward Alexander
Page, James Patrick 1944- .... **CLC 12**
  See also CA 204
Page, Jimmy 1944-
  See Page, James Patrick
Page, Louise 1955- .... **CLC 40**
  See also CA 140; CANR 76; CBD; CD 5, 6;
  CWD; DLB 233
Page, Patricia Kathleen
  See Page, P.K.
Page, P.K. 1916-2010 ..... **CLC 7, 18; PC 12**
  See also CA 53-56; CANR 4, 22, 65; CCA
  1; CP 1, 2, 3, 4, 5, 6, 7; DAC; DAM MST;
  DLB 68; MTCW 1; RGEL 2
Page, Stanton
  See Fuller, Henry Blake
Page, Thomas Nelson 1853-1922 ...... **SSC 23**
  See also CA 118; 177; DLB 12, 78; DLBD
  13; RGAL 4
Pagels, Elaine
  See Pagels, Elaine Hiesey
Pagels, Elaine Hiesey 1943- .... **CLC 104**
  See also CA 45-48; CANR 2, 24, 51, 151;
  FW; NCFS 4
Paget, Violet 1856-1935 .... **SSC 33, 98;**
  TCLC 5
  See also CA 104; 166; DLB 57, 153, 156,
  174, 178; GLL 1; HGG; SUFW 1
Paget-Lowe, Henry
  See Lovecraft, H. P.

Patmore, Coventry Kersey Dighton
1823-1896 .... **NCLC 9; PC 59**
See also DLB 35, 98; RGEL 2; TEA

Paton, Alan 1903-1988 .... **CLC 4, 10, 25, 55, 106; TCLC 165; WLC 4**
See also AAYA 26; AFW; BPFB 3; BRWS 2; BYA 1; CA 13-16; 125; CANR 22; CAP 1; CN 1, 2, 3, 4; DA; DA3; DAB; DAC; DAM MST, NOV; DLB 225; DLBD 17; EWL 3; EXPN; LAIT 4; MTCW 1, 2; MTFW 2005; NFS 3, 12; RGEL 2; SATA 11; SATA-Obit 56; SSFS 29; TWA; WLIT 2; WWE 1

Paton, Alan Stewart
See Paton, Alan

Paton Walsh, Gillian
See Paton Walsh, Jill

Paton Walsh, Jill 1937- .... **CLC 35**
See also AAYA 11, 47; BYA 1, 8; CA 262; CAAE 262; CANR 38, 83, 158, 229; CLR 2, 6, 128; DLB 161; JRDA; MAICYA 1, 2; SAAS 3; SATA 4, 72, 109, 190; SATA-Essay 190; WYA; YAW

Patsauq, Markoosie 1942- .... **NNAL**
See also CA 101; CLR 23; CWRI 5; DAM MULT

Patterson, (Horace) Orlando (Lloyd)
1940- .... **BLCS**
See also BW 1; CA 65-68; CANR 27, 84; CN 1, 2, 3, 4, 5, 6

Patton, George S(mith), Jr.
1885-1945 .... **TCLC 79**
See also CA 189

Paulding, James Kirke
1778-1860 .... **NCLC 2**
See also DLB 3, 59, 74, 250; RGAL 4

Paulin, Thomas Neilson
See Paulin, Tom

Paulin, Tom 1949- .... **CLC 37, 177**
See also CA 123; 128; CANR 98; CP 3, 4, 5, 6, 7; DLB 40

Paulinus of Nola 353?-431 .... **CMLC 156**

Pausanias c. 1st cent. .... **CMLC 36**

Paustovsky, Konstantin (Georgievich)
1892-1968 .... **CLC 40**
See also CA 93-96; 25-28R; DLB 272; EWL 3

Pavese, Cesare 1908-1950 .... **PC 13; SSC 19; TCLC 3, 240**
See also CA 104; 169; DLD 128, 177; EW 12; EWL 3; PFS 20; RGSF 2; RGWL 2, 3; TWA; WLIT 7

Pavic, Milorad 1929-2009 .... **CLC 60**
See also CA 136; CDWLB 4; CWW 2; DLB 181; EWL 3; RGWL 3

Pavlov, Ivan Petrovich
1849-1936 .... **TCLC 91**
See also CA 118; 180

Pavlova, Karolina Karlovna
1807-1893 .... **NCLC 138**
See also DLB 205

Payne, Alan
See Jakes, John

Payne, John Howard 1791-1852 ... **NCLC 241**
See also DLB 37; RGAL 4

Payne, Rachel Ann
See Jakes, John

Paz, Gil
See Lugones, Leopoldo

Paz, Octavio 1914-1998 ..... **CLC 3, 4, 6, 10, 19, 51, 65, 119; HLC 2; PC 1, 48; TCLC 211; WLC 4**
See also AAYA 50; CA 73-76; 165; CANR 32, 65, 104; CWW 2; DA; DA3; DAB; DAC; DAM MST, MULT, POET; DLB 290, 331; DLBY 1990, 1998; DNFS 1; EWL 3; HW 1, 2; LAW; LAWS 1; MTCW 1, 2; MTFW 2005; PFS 18, 30, 38; RGWL 2, 3; SSFS 13; TWA; WLIT 1

p'Bitek, Okot 1931-1982 .... **BLC 1:3; CLC 96; TCLC 149**
See also AFW; BW 2, 3; CA 124; 107; CANR 82; CP 1, 2, 3; DAM MULT; DLB 125; EWL 3; MTCW 1, 2; MTFW 2005; RGEL 2; WLIT 2

Peabody, Elizabeth Palmer
1804-1894 .... **NCLC 169**
See also DLB 1, 223

Peacham, Henry 1578-1644(?) .... **LC 119**
See also DLB 151

Peacock, Molly 1947- .... **CLC 60**
See also CA 103, 262; CAAE 262; CAAS 21; CANR 52, 84, 235; CP 5, 6, 7; DLB 120, 282

Peacock, Thomas Love
1785-1866 .... **NCLC 22; PC 87**
See also BRW 4; DLB 96, 116; RGEL 2; RGSF 2

Peake, Mervyn 1911-1968 .... **CLC 7, 54**
See also CA 5-8R; 25-28R; CANR 3; DLB 15, 160, 255; FANT; MTCW 1; RGEL 2; SATA 23; SFW 4

Pearce, Ann Philippa
See Pearce, Philippa

Pearce, Philippa 1920-2006 .... **CLC 21**
See also BRWS 19; BYA 5; CA 5-8R; 255; CANR 4, 109; CLR 9; CWRI 5; DLB 161; FANT; MAICYA 1; SATA 1, 67, 129; SATA-Obit 179

Pearl, Eric
See Elman, Richard (Martin)

Pearson, Jean Mary
See Gardam, Jane

Pearson, Thomas Reid
See Pearson, T.R.

Pearson, T.R. 1956- .... **CLC 39**
See also CA 120; 130; CANR 97, 147, 185; CSW; INT CA-130

Peck, Dale 1967- .... **CLC 81**
See also CA 146; CANR 72, 127, 180; GLL 2

Peck, John (Frederick) 1941- .... **CLC 3**
See also CA 49-52; CANR 3, 100; CP 4, 5, 6, 7

Peck, Richard 1934- .... **CLC 21**
See also AAYA 1, 24; BYA 1, 6, 8, 11; CA 85-88; CANR 19, 38, 129, 178; CLR 15, 142; INT CANR-19; JRDA; MAICYA 1, 2; SAAS 2; SATA 18, 55, 97, 110, 158, 190, 228; SATA-Essay 110; WYA; YAW

Peck, Richard Wayne
See Peck, Richard

Peck, Robert Newton 1928- .... **CLC 17**
See also AAYA 3, 43; BYA 1, 6; CA 81-84, 182; CAAE 182; CANR 31, 63, 127; CLR 45, 163; DA; DAC; DAM MST; JRDA; LAIT 3; MAICYA 1, 2; NFS 29; SAAS 1; SATA 21, 62, 111, 156; SATA-Essay 108; WYA; YAW

Peckinpah, David Samuel
See Peckinpah, Sam

Peckinpah, Sam 1925-1984 .... **CLC 20**
See also CA 109; 114; CANR 82

Pedersen, Knut 1859-1952 .... **TCLC 2, 14, 49, 151, 203**
See also AAYA 79; CA 104; 119; CANR 63; DLB 297, 330; EW 8; EWL 8; MTCW 1, 2; RGWL 2, 3

Peele, George 1556-1596 ..... **DC 27; LC 115**
See also BRW 1; DLB 62, 167; RGEL 2

Peeslake, Gaffer
See Durrell, Lawrence

Peirce, Charles Sanders
1839-1914 .... **TCLC 81**
See also CA 194; DLB 270

Pelagius c. 350-c. 418 .... **CMLC 118**

Pelecanos, George P. 1957- .... **CLC 236**
See also CA 138; CANR 122, 165, 194, 243; DLB 306

Pelevin, Victor 1962- .... **CLC 238**
See also CA 154; CANR 88, 159, 197; DLB 285

Pelevin, Viktor Olegovich
See Pelevin, Victor

Pellicer, Carlos 1897(?)-1977 .... **HLCS 2**
See also CA 153; 69-72; DLB 290; EWL 3; HW 1

Pena, Ramon del Valle y
See Valle-Inclan, Ramon del

Pendennis, Arthur Esquir
See Thackeray, William Makepeace

Penn, Arthur
See Matthews, (James) Brander

Penn, William 1644-1718 .... **LC 25**
See also DLB 24

Penny, Carolyn
See Chute, Carolyn

PEPECE
See Prado (Calvo), Pedro

Pepys, Samuel 1633-1703 .... **LC 11, 58; WLC 4**
See also BRW 2; CDBLB 1660-1789; DA; DA3; DAB; DAC; DAM MST; DLB 101, 213; NCFS 4; RGEL 2; TEA; WLIT 3

Percy, Thomas 1729-1811 .... **NCLC 95**
See also DLB 104

Percy, Walker 1916-1990 ..... **CLC 2, 3, 6, 8, 14, 18, 47, 65**
See also AMWS 3; BPFB 3; CA 1-4R; 131; CANR 1, 23, 64; CN 1, 2, 3, 4; CPW; CSW; DA3; DAM NOV, POP; DLB 2; DLBY 1980, 1990; EWL 3; MAL 5; MTCW 1, 2; MTFW 2005; RGAL 4; TUS

Percy, William Alexander
1885-1942 .... **TCLC 84**
See also CA 163; MTCW 2

Perdurabo, Frater
See Crowley, Edward Alexander

Pereda (y Sanchez de Porrua), Jose Maria de
1833-1906 .... **TCLC 16**
See also CA 117

Pereda y Porrua, Jose Maria de
See Pereda (y Sanchez de Porrua), Jose Maria de

Peregoy, George Weems
See Mencken, H. L.

Perelman, Bob 1947- .... **PC 132**
See also CA 154; CANR 85, 160; CP 5, 6, 7; DLB 193; RGAL 4

Perelman, Robert
See Perelman, Bob

Perelman, S(idney) J(oseph)
1904-1979 ...... **CLC 3, 5, 9, 15, 23, 44, 49; SSC 32**
See also AAYA 79; AITN 1, 2; BPFB 3; CA 73-76; 89-92; CANR 18; DAM DRAM; DLB 11, 44; MTCW 1, 2; MTFW 2005; RGAL 4

Perets, Yitskhok Leybush
See Peretz, Isaac Loeb

Peretz, Isaac Leib (?)-
See Peretz, Isaac Loeb

Peretz, Isaac Loeb 1851-1915 .... **SSC 26; TCLC 16**
See Peretz, Isaac Leib
See also CA 109; 201; DLB 333

Peretz, Yitzhok Leibush
See Peretz, Isaac Loeb

Peri Rossi, Cristina 1941- .... **CLC 156; HLCS 2**
See also CA 131; CANR 59, 81; CWW 2; DLB 145, 290; EWL 3; HW 1, 2

Perlata
See Peret, Benjamin

Perloff, Marjorie G(abrielle) 1931- ... **CLC 137**
See also CA 57-60; CANR 7, 22, 49, 104

Perrault, Charles 1628-1703 .... **LC 2, 56;**
SSC 144
 See also BYA 4; CLR 79, 134; DLB 268;
 GFL Beginnings to 1789; MAICYA 1, 2;
 RGWL 2, 3; SATA 25; WCH

Perrotta, Tom 1961- .... **CLC 266**
 See also CA 162; CANR 99, 155, 197

Perry, Anne 1938- .... **CLC 126**
 See also CA 101; CANR 22, 50, 84, 150, 177,
 238; CMW 4; CN 6, 7; CPW; DLB 276

Perry, Brighton
 See Sherwood, Robert E(mmet)

Perse, St.-John
 See Leger, Alexis Saint-Leger

Perse, Saint-John
 See Leger, Alexis Saint-Leger

Persius 34-62 .... **CMLC 74**
 See also AW 2; DLB 211; RGWL 2, 3

Perutz, Leo(pold) 1882-1957 .... **TCLC 60**
 See also CA 147; DLB 81

Peseenz, Tulio F.
 See Lopez y Fuentes, Gregorio

Pesetsky, Bette 1932- .... **CLC 28**
 See also CA 133; DLB 130

Peshkov, Alexei Maximovich
 See Gorky, Maxim

Pessoa, Fernando 1888-1935 .... **HLC 2;**
 PC 20; TCLC 27, 257
 See also CA 125; 183; CANR 182; DAM
 MULT; DLB 287; EW 10; EWL 3; RGWL
 2, 3; WP

Pessoa, Fernando Antonio Nogueira
 See Pessoa, Fernando

Peterkin, Julia Mood 1880-1961 .... **CLC 31**
 See also CA 102; DLB 9

Peter of Blois c. 1135-c. 1212 .... **CMLC 127**

Peters, Joan K(aren) 1945- .... **CLC 39**
 See also CA 158; CANR 109

Peters, Robert L(ouis) 1924- .... **CLC 7**
 See also CA 13-16R; CAAS 8; CP 1, 5, 6, 7;
 DLB 105

Peters, S. H.
 See Henry, O.

Petofi, Sandor 1823-1849 ...... **NCLC 21, 264**
 See also RGWL 2, 3

Petrakis, Harry Mark 1923- .... **CLC 3**
 See also CA 9-12R; CANR 4, 30, 85, 155;
 CN 1, 2, 3, 4, 5, 6, 7

Petrarch 1304-1374 .... **CMLC 20; PC 8**
 See also DA3; DAM POET; EW 2; LMFS 1;
 PFS 42; RGWL 2, 3; WLIT 7

Petrarch, Francesco
 See Petrarch

Petronius c. 20-66 .... **CMLC 34**
 See also AW 2; CDWLB 1; DLB 211;
 RGWL 2, 3; WLIT 8

Petrov, Eugene
 See Kataev, Evgeny Petrovich

Petrov, Evgenii
 See Kataev, Evgeny Petrovich

Petrov, Evgeny
 See Kataev, Evgeny Petrovich

Petrovsky, Boris
 See Mansfield, Katherine

Petry, Ann 1908-1997 .... **CLC 1, 7, 18;**
 SSC 161; TCLC 112
 See also AFAW 1, 2; BPFB 3; BW 1, 3;
 BYA 2; CA 5-8R; 157; CAAS 6; CANR 4,
 46; CLR 12; CN 1, 2, 3, 4, 5, 6; DLB 76;
 EWL 3; JRDA; LAIT 1; MAICYA 1, 2;
 MAICYAS 1; MTCW 1; NFS 33; RGAL
 4; SATA 5; SATA-Obit 94; TUS

Petry, Ann Lane
 See Petry, Ann

Petursson, Halligrimur 1614-1674 .... **LC 8**

Peychinovich
 See Vazov, Ivan (Minchov)

Peguy, Charles (Pierre)
 1873-1914 .... **TCLC 10**
 See also CA 107; 193; DLB 258; EWL 3;
 GFL 1789 to the Present

Phaedrus c. 15B.C.-c. 50 .... **CMLC 25**
 See also DLB 211

Phelge, Nanker
 See Richards, Keith

Phelps (Ward), Elizabeth Stuart
 See Phelps, Elizabeth Stuart

Phelps, Elizabeth Stuart
 1844-1911 .... **TCLC 113**
 See also CA 242; DLB 74; FW

Pheradausi
 See Ferdowsi, Abu'l Qasem

Philip, M(arlene) Nourbese 1947- .... **CLC 307**
 See also BW 3; CA 163; CWP; DLB 157,
 334

Philippe de Remi c. 1247-1296 ... **CMLC 102**

Philips, Katherine
 1632-1664 .... **LC 30, 145; PC 40**
 See also DLB 131; RGEL 2

Philipson, Ilene J. 1950- .... **CLC 65**
 See also CA 219

Philipson, Morris H. 1926-2011 ..... **CLC 53**
 See also CA 1-4R; CANR 4

Phillips, Caryl 1958- ... **BLCS; CLC 96, 224**
 See also BRWS 5; BW 2; CA 141; CANR
 63, 104, 140, 195; CBD; CD 5, 6; CN 5, 6,
 7; DA3; DAM MULT; DLB 157; EWL 3;
 MTCW 2; MTFW 2005; WLIT 4; WWE 1

Phillips, David Graham 1867-1911 **TCLC 44**
 See also CA 108; 176; DLB 9, 12, 303;
 RGAL 4

Phillips, Jack
 See Sandburg, Carl

Phillips, Jayne Anne 1952- ...... **CLC 15, 33,**
 139, 296; SSC 16
 See also AAYA 57; BPFB 3; CA 101;
 CANR 24, 50, 96, 200; CN 4, 5, 6, 7;
 CSW; DLBY 1980; INT CANR-24;
 MTCW 1, 2; MTFW 2005; RGAL 4;
 RGSF 2; SSFS 4

Phillips, Richard
 See Dick, Philip K.

Phillips, Robert (Schaeffer)
 1938- .... **CLC 28**
 See also CA 17-20R; CAAS 13; CANR 8;
 DLB 105

Phillips, Ward
 See Lovecraft, H. P.

Philo c. 20B.C.-c. 50 .... **CMLC 100**
 See also DLB 176

Philostratus, Flavius
 c. 179-c. 244 .... **CMLC 62**

Phiradausi
 See Ferdowsi, Abu'l Qasem

Piccolo, Lucio 1901-1969 .... **CLC 13**
 See also CA 97-100; DLB 114; EWL 3

Pickthall, Marjorie L(owry) C(hristie)
 1883-1922 .... **TCLC 21**
 See also CA 107; DLB 92

Pico della Mirandola, Giovanni
 1463-1494 .... **LC 15**
 See also LMFS 1

Piercy, Marge 1936- .... **CLC 3, 6, 14, 18,**
 27, 62, 128, 347; PC 29
 See also BPFB 3; CA 21-24R, 187; CAAE
 187; CAAS 1; CANR 13, 43, 66, 111; CN
 3, 4, 5, 6, 7; CP 1, 2, 3, 4, 5, 6, 7; CWP;
 DLB 120, 227; EXPP; FW; MAL 5; MTCW
 1, 2; MTFW 2005; PFS 9, 22, 32, 40;
 SFW 4

Pinero, Miguel (Antonio Gomez)
 1946-1988 .... **CLC 4, 55**
 See also CA 61-64; 125; CAD; CANR 29,
 90; DLB 266; HW 1; LLW

Piers, Robert
 See Anthony, Piers

Pieyre de Mandiargues, Andre
 1909-1991 .... **CLC 41**
 See also CA 103; 136; CANR 22, 82; DLB
 83; EWL 3; GFL 1789 to the Present

Pilkington, Laetitia 1709?-1750 .... **LC 211**

Pil'niak, Boris
 See Vogau, Boris Andreyevich

Pil'niak, Boris Andreevich
 See Vogau, Boris Andreyevich

Pilnyak, Boris 1894-1938
 See Vogau, Boris Andreyevich

Pinchback, Eugene
 See Toomer, Jean

Pincherle, Alberto 1907-1990 .... **CLC 2, 7,**
 11, 27, 46; SSC 26
 See also CA 25-28R; 132; CANR 33, 63,
 142; DAM NOV; DLB 127; EW 12; EWL
 3; MTCW 2; MTFW 2005; RGSF 2;
 RGWL 2, 3; WLIT 7

Pinckney, Darryl 1953- .... **CLC 76**
 See also BW 2, 3; CA 143; CANR 79

Pindar 518(?)B.C.-438(?)B.C. ...... **CMLC 12,**
 130; PC 19
 See also AW 1; CDWLB 1; DLB 176;
 RGWL 2

Pineda, Cecile 1942- .... **CLC 39**
 See also CA 118; DLB 209

Pinero, Arthur Wing 1855-1934 ... **TCLC 32**
 See also CA 110; 153; DAM DRAM; DLB
 10, 344; RGEL 2

Pinget, Robert 1919-1997 ..... **CLC 7, 13, 37**
 See also CA 85-88; 160; CWW 2; DLB 83;
 EWL 3; GFL 1789 to the Present

Pink Floyd
 See Barrett, Syd; Gilmour, David; Mason,
 Nick; Waters, Roger; Wright, Rick

Pinkney, Edward 1802-1828 .... **NCLC 31**
 See also DLB 248

Pinkwater, D. Manus
 See Pinkwater, Daniel

Pinkwater, Daniel 1941- .... **CLC 35**
 See also AAYA 1, 46; BYA 9; CA 29-32R;
 CANR 12, 38, 89, 143; CLR 4, 175; CSW;
 FANT; JRDA; MAICYA 1, 2; SAAS 3;
 SATA 8, 46, 76, 114, 158, 210, 243; SFW
 4; YAW

Pinkwater, Daniel M.
 See Pinkwater, Daniel

Pinkwater, Daniel Manus
 See Pinkwater, Daniel

Pinkwater, Manus
 See Pinkwater, Daniel

Pinsky, Robert 1940- ...... **CLC 9, 19, 38, 94,**
 121, 216; PC 27
 See also AMWS 6; CA 29-32R; CAAS 4;
 CANR 58, 97, 138, 177; CP 3, 4, 5, 6, 7;
 DA3; DAM POET; DLBY 1982, 1998;
 MAL 5; MTCW 2; MTFW 2005; PFS
 18, 44; RGAL 4; TCLE 1:2

Pinta, Harold
 See Pinter, Harold

Pinter, Harold 1930-2008 .... **CLC 1, 3, 6,**
 9, 11, 15, 27, 58, 73, 199; DC 15; WLC 4
 See also BRWR 1; BRWS 1; CA 5-8R; 280;
 CANR 33, 65, 112, 145; CBD; CD 5, 6;
 CDBLB 1960 to Present; CP 1; DA; DA3;
 DAB; DAC; DAM DRAM, MST; DFS
 5, 7, 14, 25; DLB 13, 310, 331; EWL 3;
 IDFW 3, 4; LMFS 2; MTCW 1, 2; MTFW
 2005; RGEL 2; RGHL; TEA

Piozzi, Hester Lynch (Thrale)
 1741-1821 .... **NCLC 57**
 See also DLB 104, 142

Pirandello, Luigi 1867-1936 .... **DC 5;**
 SSC 22, 148; TCLC 4, 29, 172; WLC 4
 See also CA 104; 153; CANR 103; DA;
 DA3; DAB; DAC; DAM DRAM, MST;

Rabelais, Francois 1494-1553 .... **LC 5, 60, 186; WLC 5**
See also DA; DAB; DAC; DAM MST; DLB 327; EW 2; GFL Beginnings to 1789; LMFS 1; RGWL 2, 3; TWA

Rabi`a al-`Adawiyya
c. 717-c. 801 .... **CMLC 83, 145**
See also DLB 311

Rabinovitch, Sholem
See Aleichem, Sholom

Rabinovitsh, Sholem Yankev
See Aleichem, Sholom

Rabinowitz, Sholem Yakov
See Rabinovitch, Sholem

Rabinyan, Dorit 1972- .... **CLC 119**
See also CA 170; CANR 147

Rachilde
See Vallette, Marguerite Eymery; Vallette, Marguerite Eymery

Racine, Jean 1639-1699 .... **DC 32; LC 28, 113**
See also DA3; DAB; DAM MST; DFS 28; DLB 268; EW 3; GFL Beginnings to 1789; LMFS 1; RGWL 2, 3; TWA

Radcliffe, Ann 1764-1823 .... **NCLC 6, 55, 106, 223**
See also BRWR 3; DLB 39, 178; GL 3; HGG; LMFS 1; RGEL 2; SUFW; WLIT 3

Radclyffe-Hall, Marguerite
See Hall, Radclyffe

Radiguet, Raymond 1903-1923 ..... **TCLC 29**
See also CA 162; DLB 65; EWL 3; GFL 1789 to the Present; RGWL 2, 3

Radishchev, Aleksandr Nikolaevich
1749-1802 .... **NCLC 190**
See also DLB 150

Radishchev, Alexander
See Radishchev, Aleksandr Nikolaevich

Radnoti, Miklos 1909-1944 .... **TCLC 16**
See also CA 118; 212; CDWLB 4; DLB 215; EWL 3; RGHL; RGWL 2, 3

Rado, James 1939- .... **CLC 17**
See also CA 105

Radvanyi, Netty 1900-1983 .... **CLC 7**
See also CA 85-88; 110; CANR 82; CDWLB 2; DLB 69; EWL 3

Rae, Ben
See Griffiths, Trevor

Raeburn, John (Hay) 1941- .... **CLC 34**
See also CA 57-60

Ragni, Gerome 1942-1991 .... **CLC 17**
See also CA 105; 134

Rahv, Philip
See Greenberg, Ivan

Rai, Navab
See Srivastava, Dhanpat Rai

Raimund, Ferdinand Jakob
1790-1836 .... **NCLC 69**
See also DLB 90

Raine, Craig 1944- .... **CLC 32, 103**
See also BRWS 13; CA 108; CANR 29, 51, 103, 171; CP 3, 4, 5, 6, 7; DLB 40; PFS 7

Raine, Craig Anthony
See Raine, Craig

Raine, Kathleen (Jessie)
1908-2003 .... **CLC 7, 45**
See also CA 85-88; 218; CANR 46, 109; CP 1, 2, 3, 4, 5, 6, 7; DLB 20; EWL 3; MTCW 1; RGEL 2

Rainis, Janis 1865-1929 .... **TCLC 29**
See also CA 170; CDWLB 4; DLB 220; EWL 3

Rakosi, Carl
See Rawley, Callman

Ralegh, Sir Walter
See Raleigh, Sir Walter

Raleigh, Richard
See Lovecraft, H. P.

Raleigh, Sir Walter 1554(?)-1618 ..... **LC 31, 39; PC 31**
See also BRW 1; CDBLB Before 1660; DLB 172; EXPP; PFS 14; RGEL 2; TEA; WP

Rallentando, H. P.
See Sayers, Dorothy L(eigh)

Ramal, Walter
See de la Mare, Walter (John)

Ramana Maharshi 1879-1950 .... **TCLC 84**

Ramon, Juan
See Jimenez, Juan Ramon

Ramoacn y Cajal, Santiago
1852-1934 .... **TCLC 93**

Ramos, Graciliano 1892-1953 .... **TCLC 32**
See also CA 167; DLB 307; EWL 3; HW 2; LAW; WLIT 1

Rampersad, Arnold 1941- .... **CLC 44**
See also BW 2, 3; CA 127; 133; CANR 81; DLB 111; INT CA-133

Rampling, Anne
See Rice, Anne

Ramsay, Allan 1686(?)-1758 .... **LC 29**
See also DLB 95; RGEL 2

Ramsay, Jay
See Campbell, Ramsey

Ramus, Peter
See La Ramee, Pierre de

Ramus, Petrus
See La Ramee, Pierre de

Ramuz, Charles-Ferdinand
1878-1947 .... **TCLC 33**
See also CA 165; EWL 3

Rand, Ayn 1905-1982 .... **CLC 3, 30, 44, 79; SSC 116; TCLC 261; WLC 5**
See also AAYA 10; AMWS 4; BPFB 3; BYA 12; CA 13-16R; 105; CANR 27, 73; CDALBS; CN 1, 2, 3; CPW; DA; DA3; DAC; DAM MST, NOV, POP; DLB 227, 279; MTCW 1, 2; MTFW 2005; NFS 10, 16, 29; RGAL 4; SFW 4; TUS; YAW

Randall, Dudley 1914-2000 .... **BLC 1:3; CLC 1, 135; PC 86**
See also BW 1, 3; CA 25-28R; 189; CANR 23, 82; CP 1, 2, 3, 4, 5; DAM MULT; DLB 41; PFS 5

Randall, Dudley Felker
See Randall, Dudley

Randall, Robert
See Silverberg, Robert

Randolph, Thomas 1605-1635 .... **LC 195**
See also DLB 58, 126; RGEL 2

Ranger, Ken
See Creasey, John

Rank, Otto 1884-1939 .... **TCLC 115**

Rankin, Ian 1960- .... **CLC 257**
See also BRWS 10; CA 148; CANR 81, 137, 171, 210; DLB 267; MTFW 2005

Rankin, Ian James
See Rankin, Ian

Ransom, John Crowe 1888-1974 ..... **CLC 2, 4, 5, 11, 24; PC 61**
See also AMW; CA 5-8R; 49-52; CANR 6, 34; CDALBS; CP 1, 2; DA3; DAM POET; DLB 45, 63; EWL 3; EXPP; MAL 5; MTCW 1, 2; MTFW 2005; RGAL 4; TUS

Rao, Raja 1908-2006 .... **CLC 25, 56, 255; SSC 99**
See also CA 73-76; 252; CANR 51; CN 1, 2, 3, 4, 5, 6; DAM NOV; DLB 323; EWL 3; MTCW 1, 2; MTFW 2005; RGEL 2; RGSF 2

Raphael, Frederic
1931- .... **CLC 2, 14**
See also CA 1-4R; CANR 1, 86, 223; CN 1, 2, 3, 4, 5, 6, 7; DLB 14, 319; TCLE 1:2

Raphael, Frederic Michael
See Raphael, Frederic

Raphael, Lev 1954- .... **CLC 232**
See also CA 134; CANR 72, 145, 217; GLL 1

Rastell, John c. 1475(?)-1536(?) .... **LC 183**
See also DLB 136, 170; RGEL 2

Ratcliffe, James P.
See Mencken, H. L.

Rathbone, Julian 1935-2008 .... **CLC 41**
See also CA 101; 269; CANR 34, 73, 152, 221

Rathbone, Julian Christopher
See Rathbone, Julian

Rattigan, Terence 1911-1977 .... **CLC 7; DC 18**
See also BRWS 7; CA 85-88; 73-76; CBD; CDBLB 1945-1960; DAM DRAM; DFS 8; DLB 13; IDFW 3, 4; MTCW 1, 2; MTFW 2005; RGEL 2

Rattigan, Terence Mervyn
See Rattigan, Terence

Ratushinskaya, Irina 1954- .... **CLC 54**
See also CA 129; CANR 68; CWW 2

Raven, Simon (Arthur Noel)
1927-2001 .... **CLC 14**
See also CA 81-84; 197; CANR 86; CN 1, 2, 3, 4, 5, 6; DLB 271

Ravenna, Michael
See Welty, Eudora

Rawley, Callman
1903-2004 .... **CLC 47; PC 126**
See also CA 21-24R; 228; CAAS 5; CANR 12, 32, 91; CP 1, 2, 3, 4, 5, 6, 7; DLB 193

Rawlings, Marjorie Kinnan
1896-1953 .... **TCLC 4, 248**
See also AAYA 20; AMWS 10; ANW; BPFB 3; BYA 3; CA 104; 137; CANR 74; CLR 63; DLB 9, 22, 102; DLBD 17; JRDA; MAICYA 1, 2; MAL 5; MTCW 2; MTFW 2005; RGAL 4; SATA 100; WCH; YABC 1; YAW

Raworth, Thomas Moore 1938- .... **PC 107**
See also CA 29-32R; CAAS 11; CANR 46; CP 1, 2, 3, 4, 5, 7; DLB 40

Raworth, Tom
See Raworth, Thomas Moore

Ray, Satyajit 1921-1992 .... **CLC 16, 76**
See also CA 114; 137; DAM MULT

Read, Herbert Edward 1893-1968 ... **CLC 4**
See also BRW 6; CA 85-88; 25-28R; DLB 20, 149; EWL 3; PAB; RGEL 2

Read, Piers Paul 1941- .... **CLC 4, 10, 25**
See also CA 21-24R; CANR 38, 86, 150; CN 2, 3, 4, 5, 6, 7; DLB 14; SATA 21

Reade, Charles 1814-1884 ... **NCLC 2, 74, 275**
See also DLB 21; RGEL 2

Reade, Hamish
See Gray, Simon

Reading, Peter 1946-2011 .... **CLC 47**
See also BRWS 8; CA 103; CANR 46, 96; CP 5, 6, 7; DLB 40

Reaney, James 1926-2008 .... **CLC 13**
See also CA 41-44R; CAAS 15; CANR 42; CD 5, 6; CP 1, 2, 3, 4, 5, 6, 7; DAC; DAM MST; DLB 68; RGEL 2; SATA 43

Reaney, James Crerar
See Reaney, James

Rebreanu, Liviu 1885-1944 .... **TCLC 28**
See also CA 165; DLB 220; EWL 3

Rechy, John 1934- .... **CLC 1, 7, 14, 18, 107; HLC 2**
See also CA 5-8R, 195; CAAE 195; CAAS 4; CANR 6, 32, 64, 152, 188; CN 1, 2, 3, 4, 5, 6, 7; DAM MULT; DLB 122, 278; DLBY 1982; HW 1, 2; INT CANR-6; LLW; MAL 5; RGAL 4

Rechy, John Francisco
See Rechy, John

Redcam, Tom 1870-1933 .... **TCLC 25**

Reddin, Keith 1956- .... **CLC 67**
See also CAD; CD 6

Redgrove, Peter (William)
1932-2003 .... **CLC 6, 41**
See also BRWS 6; CA 1-4R; 217; CANR 3, 39, 77; CP 1, 2, 3, 4, 5, 6, 7; DLB 40; TCLE 1:2

Redmon, Anne
See Nightingale, Anne Redmon

Reed, Eliot
See Ambler, Eric

Reed, Ishmael 1938- .... **BLC 1:3; CLC 2, 3, 5, 6, 13, 32, 60, 174; PC 68**
See also AFAW 1, 2; AMWS 10; BPFB 3; BW 2, 3; CA 21-24R; CANR 25, 48, 74, 128, 195; CN 1, 2, 3, 4, 5, 6, 7; CP 1, 2, 3, 4, 5, 6, 7; CSW; DA3; DAM MULT; DLB 2, 5, 33, 169, 227; DLBD 8; EWL 3; LMFS 2; MAL 5; MSW; MTCW 1, 2; MTFW 2005; PFS 6; RGAL 4; TCWW 2

Reed, Ishmael Scott
See Reed, Ishmael

Reed, John (Silas) 1887-1920 .... **TCLC 9**
See also CA 106; 195; MAL 5; TUS

Reed, Lou 1942- .... **CLC 21**
See also CA 117

Reese, Lizette Woodworth
1856-1935 .... **PC 29; TCLC 181**
See also CA 180; DLB 54

Reeve, Clara 1729-1807 .... **NCLC 19**
See also DLB 39; RGEL 2

Reich, Wilhelm 1897-1957 .... **TCLC 57**
See also CA 199

Reid, Christopher 1949- .... **CLC 33**
See also CA 140; CANR 89, 241; CP 4, 5, 6, 7; DLB 40; EWL 3

Reid, Christopher John
See Reid, Christopher

Reid, Desmond
See Moorcock, Michael

Reid, Thomas 1710-1796 .... **LC 201**
See also DLB 31, 252

Reid Banks, Lynne 1929- .... **CLC 23**
See also AAYA 6; BYA 7; CA 1-4R; CANR 6, 22, 38, 87; CLR 24, 86; CN 4, 5, 6; JRDA; MAICYA 1, 2; SATA 22, 75, 111, 165; YAW

Reilly, William K.
See Creasey, John

Reiner, Max
See Caldwell, (Janet Miriam) Taylor (Holland)

Reis, Ricardo
See Pessoa, Fernando

Reizenstein, Elmer Leopold
See Rice, Elmer (Leopold)

Remark, Erich Paul
See Remarque, Erich Maria

Remarque, Erich Maria
1898-1970 .... **CLC 21**
See also AAYA 27; BPFB 3; CA 77-80; 29-32R; CDWLB 2; CLR 159; DA; DA3; DAB; DAC; DAM MST, NOV; DLB 56; EWL 3; EXPN; LAIT 3; MTCW 1, 2; MTFW 2005; NFS 4, 36; RGHL; RGWL 2, 3

Remington, Frederic S(ackrider)
1861-1909 .... **TCLC 89**
See also CA 108; 169; DLB 12, 186, 188; SATA 41; TCWW 2

Remizov, A.
See Remizov, Aleksei (Mikhailovich)

Remizov, A. M.
See Remizov, Aleksei (Mikhailovich)

Remizov, Aleksei (Mikhailovich)
1877-1957 .... **TCLC 27**
See also CA 125; 133; DLB 295; EWL 3

Remizov, Alexey Mikhaylovich
See Remizov, Aleksei (Mikhailovich)

Renan, Joseph Ernest
1823-1892 .... **NCLC 26, 145**
See also GFL 1789 to the Present

Renard, Jules(-Pierre)
1864-1910 .... **TCLC 17**
See also CA 117; 202; GFL 1789 to the Present

Renart, Jean fl. 13th cent. .... **CMLC 83**

Renault, Mary 1905-1983 ..... **CLC 3, 11, 17**
See also BPFB 3; BYA 2; CA 81-84; 111; CANR 74; CN 1, 2, 3; DA3; DLBY 1983; EWL 3; GLL 1; LAIT 1; MTCW 2; MTFW 2005; RGEL 2; RHW; SATA 23; SATA-Obit 36; TEA

Rendell, Ruth
See Rendell, Ruth

Rendell, Ruth 1930- .... **CLC 28, 48, 50, 295**
See also BEST 90:4; BPFB 3; BRWS 9; CA 109; CANR 32, 52, 74, 127, 162, 190, 227; CN 5, 6, 7; CPW; DAM POP; DLB 87, 276; INT CANR-32; MSW; MTCW 1, 2; MTFW 2005

Rendell, Ruth Barbara
See Rendell, Ruth

Renoir, Jean 1894-1979 .... **CLC 20**
See also CA 129; 85-88

Rensie, Willis
See Eisner, Will

Resnais, Alain 1922- .... **CLC 16**

Restif de la Bretonne, Nicolas-Anne-Edme
1734-1806 .... **NCLC 257**
See also DLB 314; GFL Beginnings to 1789

Reuental, Niedhart von
See Neidhart von Ruental

Revard, Carter 1931- .... **NNAL**
See also CA 144; CANR 81, 153; PFS 5

Reverdy, Pierre
1889-1960 .... **CLC 53**
See also CA 97-100; 89-92; DLB 258; EWL 3; GFL 1789 to the Present

Reverend Mandju
See Su, Chien

Rexroth, Kenneth 1905-1982 .... **CLC 1, 2, 6, 11, 22, 49, 112; PC 20, 95**
See also BG 1:3; CA 5-8R; 107; CANR 14, 34, 63; CDALB 1941-1968; CP 1, 2, 3; DAM POET; DLB 16, 48, 165, 212; DLBY 1982; EWL 3; INT CANR-14; MAL 5; MTCW 1, 2; MTFW 2005; RGAL 4

Reyes, Alfonso 1889-1959 .... **HLCS 2; TCLC 33**
See also CA 131; EWL 3; HW 1; LAW

Reyes y Basoalto, Ricardo Eliecer Neftali
See Neruda, Pablo

Reymont, Wladyslaw (Stanislaw)
1868(?)-1925 .... **TCLC 5**
See also CA 104; DLB 332; EWL 3

Reynolds, John Hamilton
1794-1852 .... **NCLC 146**
See also DLB 96

Reynolds, Jonathan 1942- .... **CLC 6, 38**
See also CA 65-68; CANR 28, 176

Reynolds, Joshua 1723-1792 .... **LC 15**
See also DLB 104

Reynolds, Michael S(hane)
1937-2000 .... **CLC 44**
See also CA 65-68; 189; CANR 9, 89, 97

Reza, Yasmina 1959- .... **CLC 299; DC 34**
See also AAYA 69; CA 171; CANR 145; DFS 19; DLB 321

Reznikoff, Charles 1894-1976 .... **CLC 9; PC 124**
See also AMWS 14; CA 33-36; 61-64; CAP 2; CP 1, 2; DLB 28, 45; RGHL; WP

Rezzori, Gregor von
See Rezzori d'Arezzo, Gregor von

Rezzori d'Arezzo, Gregor von
1914-1998 .... **CLC 25**
See also CA 122; 136; 167

Rhine, Richard
See Silverstein, Alvin; Silverstein, Virginia B.

Rhodes, Eugene Manlove
1869-1934 .... **TCLC 53**
See also CA 198; DLB 256; TCWW 1, 2

R'hoone, Lord
See Balzac, Honore de

Rhys, Jean 1890-1979 .... **CLC 2, 4, 6, 14, 19, 51, 124; SSC 21, 76**
See also BRWS 2; CA 25-28R; 85-88; CANR 35, 62; CDBLB 1945-1960; CDWLB 3; CN 1, 2; DA3; DAM NOV; DLB 36, 117, 162; DNFS 2; EWL 3; LATS 1:1; MTCW 1, 2; MTFW 2005; NFS 19; RGEL 2; RGSF 2; RHW; TEA; WWE 1

Ribeiro, Darcy 1922-1997 .... **CLC 34**
See also CA 33-36R; 156; EWL 3

Ribeiro, Joao Ubaldo (Osorio Pimentel)
1941- .... **CLC 10, 67**
See also CA 81-84; CWW 2; EWL 3

Ribman, Ronald (Burt) 1932- .... **CLC 7**
See also CA 21-24R; CAD; CANR 46, 80; CD 5, 6

Ricci, Nino 1959- .... **CLC 70**
See also CA 137; CANR 130; CCA 1

Ricci, Nino Pio
See Ricci, Nino

Rice, Anne 1941- .... **CLC 41, 128, 349**
See also AAYA 9, 53; AMWS 7; BEST 89:2; BPFB 3; CA 65-68; CANR 12, 36, 53, 74, 100, 133, 190; CN 6, 7; CPW; CSW; DA3; DAM POP; DLB 292; GL 3; GLL 2; HGG; MTCW 2; MTFW 2005; SUFW 2; YAW

Rice, Elmer (Leopold) 1892-1967 .... **CLC 7, 49; DC 44; TCLC 221**
See also CA 21-22; 25-28R; CAP 2; DAM DRAM; DFS 12; DLB 4, 7; EWL 3; IDTP; MAL 5; MTCW 1, 2; RGAL 4

Rice, Tim 1944- .... **CLC 21**
See also CA 103; CANR 46; DFS 7

Rice, Timothy Miles Bindon
See Rice, Tim

Rich, Adrienne 1929-2012 .... **CLC 3, 6, 7, 11, 18, 36, 73, 76, 125, 328, 354; PC 5, 129**
See also AAYA 69; AMWR 2; AMWS 1; CA 9-12R; CANR 20, 53, 74, 128, 199, 233; CDALBS; CP 1, 2, 3, 4, 5, 6, 7; CSW; CWP; DA3; DAM POET; DLB 5, 67; EWL 3; EXPP; FL 1:6; FW; MAL 5; MBL; MTCW 1, 2; MTFW 2005; PAB; PFS 15, 29, 39; RGAL 4; RGHL; WP

Rich, Adrienne Cecile
See Rich, Adrienne

Rich, Barbara
See Graves, Robert

Rich, Robert
See Trumbo, Dalton

Richard, Keith
See Richards, Keith

Richards, David Adams 1950- .... **CLC 59**
See also CA 93-96; CANR 60, 110, 156; CN 7; DAC; DLB 53; TCLE 1:2

Richards, I(vor) A(rmstrong)
1893-1979 .... **CLC 14, 24**
See also BRWS 2; CA 41-44R; 89-92; CANR 34, 74; CP 1, 2; DLB 27; EWL 3; MTCW 2; RGEL 2

Richards, Keith 1943- .... **CLC 17**
See also CA 107; CANR 77

Richards, Scott
See Card, Orson Scott

Richardson, Anne
See Roiphe, Anne

Richardson, Dorothy Miller
1873-1957 .... **TCLC 3, 203**
See also BRWS 13; CA 104; 192; DLB 36; EWL 3; FW; RGEL 2

Richardson, Ethel Florence Lindesay
1870-1946 .... **TCLC 4**
See also CA 105; 190; DLB 197, 230; EWL 3; RGEL 2; RGSF 2; RHW

Richardson, Henrietta
See Richardson, Ethel Florence Lindesay
Richardson, Henry Handel
See Richardson, Ethel Florence Lindesay
Richardson, John 1796-1852 .... NCLC 55
See also CCA 1; DAC; DLB 99
Richardson, Samuel 1689-1761 ..... LC 1, 44,
138, 204; WLC 5
See also BRW 3; CDBLB 1660-1789; DA;
DAB; DAC; DAM MST, NOV; DLB 154;
RGEL 2; TEA; WLIT 3
Richardson, Willis
1889-1977 .... HR 1:3
See also BW 1; CA 124; DLB 51; SATA 60
Richardson Robertson, Ethel Florence
Lindesay
See Richardson, Ethel Florence Lindesay
Richler, Mordecai 1931-2001 .... CLC 3, 5,
9, 13, 18, 46, 70, 185, 271
See also AITN 1; CA 65-68; 201; CANR 31,
62, 111; CCA 1; CLR 17; CN 1, 2, 3, 4, 5,
7; CWRI 5; DAC; DAM MST, NOV; DLB
53; EWL 3; MAICYA 1, 2; MTCW 1, 2;
MTFW 2005; RGEL 2; RGHL; SATA 44,
98; SATA-Brief 27; TWA
Richter, Conrad (Michael)
1890-1968 .... CLC 30
See also AAYA 21; AMWS 18; BYA 2; CA
5-8R; 25-28R; CANR 23; DLB 9, 212;
LAIT 1; MAL 5; MTCW 1, 2; MTFW
2005; NFS 43; RGAL 4; SATA 3; TCWW
1, 2; TUS; YAW
Ricostranza, Tom
See Ellis, Trey
Riddell, Charlotte 1832-1906 .... TCLC 40
See also CA 165; DLB 156; HGG; SUFW
Riddell, Mrs. J. H.
See Riddell, Charlotte
Ridge, John Rollin 1827-1867 .... NCLC 82;
NNAL
See also CA 144; DAM MULT; DLB 175
Ridgeway, Jason
See Marlowe, Stephen
Ridgway, Keith 1965- .... CLC 119
See also CA 172; CANR 144
Riding, Laura
See Jackson, Laura
Riefenstahl, Berta Helene Amalia
See Riefenstahl, Leni
Riefenstahl, Leni
1902-2003 .... CLC 16, 190
See also CA 108; 220
Riefenstahl, Leni
See Riefenstahl, Berta Helene Amalia
Riera, Carme 1948- .... SSC 177
See also CA 254, DLB 322, EWL 3
Riffe, Ernest
See Bergman, Ingmar
Riffe, Ernest Ingmar
See Bergman, Ingmar
Riggs, (Rolla) Lynn 1899-1954 .... NNAL;
TCLC 56
See also CA 144; DAM MULT; DLB 175
Riis, Jacob A(ugust) 1849-1914 .... TCLC 80
See also CA 113; 168; DLB 23
Rikki
See Ducornet, Erica
Riley, James Whitcomb 1849-1916 ... PC 48;
TCLC 51
See also CA 118; 137; DAM POET; MAI-
CYA 1, 2; RGAL 4; SATA 17
Riley, Tex
See Creasey, John
Rilke, Rainer Maria 1875-1926 .. PC 2, 140;
TCLC 1, 6, 19, 195
See also CA 104; 132; CANR 62, 99;
CDWLB 2; DA3; DAM POET; DLB 81;

EW 9; EWL 3; MTCW 1, 2; MTFW 2005;
PFS 19, 27; RGWL 2, 3; TWA; WP
Rimbaud, Arthur 1854-1891 ... NCLC 4, 35,
82, 227; PC 3, 57; WLC 5
See also DA; DA3; DAB; DAC; DAM MST,
POET; DLB 217; EW 7; GFL 1789 to the
Present; LMFS 2; PFS 28; RGWL 2, 3;
TWA; WP
Rimbaud, Jean Nicholas Arthur
See Rimbaud, Arthur
Rinehart, Mary Roberts
1876-1958 .... TCLC 52
See also BPFB 3; CA 108; 166; RGAL 4;
RHW
Ringmaster, The
See Mencken, H. L.
Ringwood, Gwen(dolyn Margaret) Pharis
1910-1984 .... CLC 48
See also CA 148; 112; DLB 88
Rio, Michel 1945(?)- .... CLC 43
See also CA 201
Ritsos, Giannes
See Ritsos, Yannis
Ritsos, Yannis 1909-1990 ...... CLC 6, 13, 31
See also CA 77-80; 133; CANR 39, 61; EW
12; EWL 3; MTCW 1; RGWL 2, 3
Ritter, Erika 1948- .... CLC 52
See also CA 318; CD 5, 6; CWD; DLB 362
Rivera, Jose Eustasio 1889-1928 ... TCLC 35
See also CA 162; EWL 3; HW 1, 2; LAW
Rivera, Tomas 1935-1984 .... HLCS 2;
SSC 160
See also CA 49-52; CANR 32; DLB 82; HW
1; LLW; RGAL 4; SSFS 15; TCWW 2;
WLIT 1
Rivers, Conrad Kent 1933-1968 .... CLC 1
See also BW 1; CA 85-88; DLB 41
Rivers, Elfrida
See Bradley, Marion Zimmer
Riverside, John
See Heinlein, Robert A.
Rizal, Jose 1861-1896 .... NCLC 27
See also DLB 348
Rolaag, Ole Edvart
See Rolvaag, O.E.
Rolvaag, O.E.
See Rolvaag, O.E.
Rolvaag, O.E. 1876-1931 ...... TCLC 17, 207
See also AAYA 75; CA 117; 171; DLB 9,
212; MAL 5; NFS 5; RGAL 4; TCWW 1, 2
Roa Bastos, Augusto 1917-2005 .... CLC 45,
316, 355; HLC 2; SSC 174
See also CA 131; 238; CWW 2; DAM
MULT; DLB 113; EWL 3; HW 1; LAW;
RGSF 2; WLIT 1
Roa Bastos, Augusto Jose Antonio
See Roa Bastos, Augusto
Robbe-Grillet, Alain 1922-2008 .... CLC 1,
2, 4, 6, 8, 10, 14, 43, 128, 287
See also BPFB 3; CA 9-12R; 269; CANR
33, 65, 115; CWW 2; DLB 83; EW 13;
EWL 3; GFL 1789 to the Present; IDFW 3,
4; MTCW 1, 2; MTFW 2005; RGWL 2, 3;
SSFS 15
Robbins, Harold 1916-1997 .... CLC 5
See also BPFB 3; CA 73-76; 162; CANR
26, 54, 112, 156; DA3; DAM NOV;
MTCW 1, 2
Robbins, Thomas Eugene
See Robbins, Tom
Robbins, Tom 1936- .... CLC 9, 32, 64
See also AAYA 32; AMWS 10; BEST 90:3;
BPFB 3; CA 81-84; CANR 29, 59, 95,
139; CN 3, 4, 5, 6, 7; CPW; CSW; DA3;
DAM NOV, POP; DLBY 1980; MTCW 1,
2; MTFW 2005
Robbins, Trina 1938- .... CLC 21
See also AAYA 61; CA 128; CANR 152

Robert de Boron
fl. 12th cent. .... CMLC 94
Roberts, Charles G(eorge) D(ouglas)
1860-1943 .... SSC 91; TCLC 8
See also CA 105; 188; CLR 33; CWRI 5;
DLB 92; RGEL 2; RGSF 2; SATA 88;
SATA-Brief 29
Roberts, Elizabeth Madox
1886-1941 .... TCLC 68
See also CA 111; 166; CLR 100; CWRI 5;
DLB 9, 54, 102; RGAL 4; RHW; SATA
33; SATA-Brief 27; TCWW 2; WCH
Roberts, Kate 1891-1985 .... CLC 15
See also CA 107; 116; DLB 319
Roberts, Keith (John Kingston)
1935-2000 .... CLC 14
See also BRWS 10; CA 25-28R; CANR 46;
DLB 261; SFW 4
Roberts, Kenneth (Lewis)
1885-1957 .... TCLC 23
See also CA 109; 199; DLB 9; MAL 5;
RGAL 4; RHW
Roberts, Michele 1949- .... CLC 48, 178
See also BRWS 15; CA 115; CANR 58, 120,
164, 200; CN 6, 7; DLB 231; FW
Roberts, Michele Brigitte
See Roberts, Michele
Robertson, Ellis
See Ellison, Harlan; Silverberg, Robert
Robertson, Thomas William
1829-1871 .... NCLC 35
See also DAM DRAM; DLB 344; RGEL 2
Robertson, Tom
See Robertson, Thomas William
Robeson, Kenneth
See Dent, Lester
Robinson, Eden 1968- .... CLC 301
See also CA 171
Robinson, Edwin Arlington
1869-1935 .... PC 1, 35; TCLC 5, 101
See also AAYA 72; AMW; CA 104; 133;
CDALB 1865-1917; DA; DAC; DAM
MST, POET; DLB 54; EWL 3; EXPP;
MAL 5; MTCW 1, 2; MTFW 2005; PAB;
PFS 4, 35; RGAL 4; WP
Robinson, Henry Crabb
1775-1867 .... NCLC 15, 239
See also DLB 107
Robinson, Jill 1936- .... CLC 10
See also CA 102; CANR 120; INT CA-102
Robinson, Kim Stanley
1952- .... CLC 34, 248
See also AAYA 26; CA 126; CANR 113,
139, 173; CN 6, 7; MTFW 2005; SATA
109; SCFW 2; SFW 4
Robinson, Lloyd
See Silverberg, Robert
Robinson, Marilynne
1943- .... CLC 25, 180, 276
See also AAYA 69; AMWS 21; CA 116;
CANR 80, 140, 192, 240; CN 4, 5, 6, 7;
DLB 206, 350; MTFW 2005; NFS 24, 39
Robinson, Mary 1758-1800 .... NCLC 142
See also BRWS 13; DLB 158; FW
Robinson, Smokey 1940- .... CLC 21
See also CA 116
Robinson, William, Jr.
See Robinson, Smokey
Robison, Christopher
See Burroughs, Augusten
Robison, Mary 1949- .... CLC 42, 98
See also CA 113; 116; CANR 87, 206; CN
4, 5, 6, 7; DLB 130; INT CA-116; RGSF
2; SSFS 33
Rochester
See Wilmot, John

Rod, Edouard 1857-1910 .... **TCLC 52**

Rodo, Jose Enrique 1871(?)-1917 ... **HLCS 2**
See also CA 178; EWL 3; HW 2; LAW

Roddenberry, Eugene Wesley
See Roddenberry, Gene

Roddenberry, Gene 1921-1991 .... **CLC 17**
See also AAYA 5; CA 110; 135; CANR 37;
SATA 45; SATA-Obit 69

Rodgers, Mary 1931- .... **CLC 12**
See also BYA 5; CA 49-52; CANR 8, 55, 90;
CLR 20; CWRI 5; DFS 28; INT CANR-8;
JRDA; MAICYA 1, 2; SATA 8, 130

Rodgers, W(illiam) R(obert)
1909-1969 .... **CLC 7**
See also CA 85-88; DLB 20; RGEL 2

Rodman, Eric
See Silverberg, Robert

Rodman, Howard 1920(?)-1985 ...... **CLC 65**
See also CA 118

Rodman, Maia
See Wojciechowska, Maia (Teresa)

Rodolph, Utto
See Ouologuem, Yambo

Rodriguez, Claudio 1934-1999 .... **CLC 10**
See also CA 188; DLB 134

Rodriguez, Richard 1944- .... **CLC 155, 321;
HLC 2**
See also AMWS 14; CA 110; CANR 66,
116; DAM MULT; DLB 82, 256; HW 1, 2;
LAIT 5; LLW; MTFW 2005; NCFS 3;
WLIT 1

Roethke, Theodore 1908-1963 ..... **CLC 1, 3,
8, 11, 19, 46, 101; PC 15, 137**
See also AMW; CA 81-84; CABS 2;
CDALB 1941-1968; DA3; DAM POET;
DLB 5, 206; EWL 3; EXPP; MAL 5;
MTCW 1, 2; PAB; PFS 3, 34, 40; RGAL
4; WP

Roethke, Theodore Huebner
See Roethke, Theodore

Rogers, Carl R(ansom)
1902-1987 .... **TCLC 125**
See also CA 1-4R; 121; CANR 1, 18;
MTCW 1

Rogers, Samuel 1763-1855 .... **NCLC 69**
See also DLB 93; RGEL 2

Rogers, Thomas 1927-2007 .... **CLC 57**
See also CA 89-92; 259; CANR 163; INT
CA-89-92

Rogers, Thomas Hunton
See Rogers, Thomas

Rogers, Will(iam Penn Adair)
1879-1935 .... **NNAL; TCLC 8, 71**
See also CA 105; 144; DA3; DAM MULT;
DLB 11; MTCW 2

Rogin, Gilbert 1929- .... **CLC 18**
See also CA 65-68; CANR 15

Rohan, Koda
See Koda Shigeyuki

Rohlfs, Anna Katharine Green
See Green, Anna Katharine

Rohmer, Eric 1920-2010 .... **CLC 16**
See also CA 110

Rohmer, Sax
See Ward, Arthur Henry Sarsfield

Roiphe, Anne 1935- .... **CLC 3, 9**
See also CA 89-92; CANR 45, 73, 138, 170,
230; DLBY 1980; INT CA-89-92

Roiphe, Anne Richardson
See Roiphe, Anne

Rojas, Fernando de 1475-1541 ...... **HLCS 1,
2; LC 23, 169**
See also DLB 286; RGWL 2, 3

Rojas, Gonzalo 1917-2011 .... **HLCS 2**
See also CA 178; HW 2; LAWS 1

Rojas Zorrilla, Francisco de
1607-1648 .... **LC 204**

Roland (de la Platiere), Marie-Jeanne
1754-1793 .... **LC 98**
See also DLB 314

**Rolfe, Frederick (William Serafino Austin
Lewis Mary)** 1860-1913 .... **TCLC 12**
See also CA 107; 210; DLB 34, 156; GLL 1;
RGEL 2

Rolland, Romain 1866-1944 .... **TCLC 23**
See also CA 118; 197; DLB 65, 284,
332; EWL 3; GFL 1789 to the Present;
RGWL 2, 3

Rolle, Richard c. 1300-c. 1349 .... **CMLC 21**
See also DLB 146; LMFS 1; RGEL 2

Rolvaag, O.E.
See Rolvaag, O.E.

Romain Arnaud, Saint
See Aragon, Louis

Romains, Jules 1885-1972 .... **CLC 7**
See also CA 85-88; CANR 34; DLB 65, 321;
EWL 3; GFL 1789 to the Present; MTCW 1

Romero, Jose Ruben 1890-1952 ... **TCLC 14**
See also CA 114; 131; EWL 3; HW 1; LAW

Ronsard, Pierre de 1524-1585 ..... **LC 6, 54;
PC 11, 105**
See also DLB 327; EW 2; GFL Beginnings
to 1789; RGWL 2, 3; TWA

Rooke, Leon 1934- .... **CLC 25, 34**
See also CA 25-28R; CANR 23, 53; CCA 1;
CPW; DAM POP

Roosevelt, Franklin Delano
1882-1945 .... **TCLC 93**
See also CA 116; 173; LAIT 3

Roosevelt, Theodore 1858-1919 ... **TCLC 69**
See also CA 115; 170; DLB 47, 186, 275

Roper, Margaret c. 1505-1544 .... **LC 147**

Roper, William 1498-1578 .... **LC 10**

Roquelaure, A. N.
See Rice, Anne

Rios, Alberto 1952- .... **PC 57**
See also AAYA 66; AMWS 4; CA 113;
CANR 34, 79, 137; CP 6, 7; DLB 122;
HW 2; MTFW 2005; PFS 11

Rios, Alberto Alvaro
See Rios, Alberto

Rosa, Joao Guimaraes
See Guimaraes Rosa, Joao

Rose, Wendy 1948- .... **CLC 85; NNAL;
PC 13**
See also CA 53-56; CANR 5, 51; CWP;
DAM MULT; DLB 175; PFS 13; RGAL 4;
SATA 12

Rosen, R.D. 1949- .... **CLC 39**
See also CA 77-80; CANR 62, 120, 175;
CMW 4; INT CANR-30

Rosen, Richard
See Rosen, R.D.

Rosen, Richard Dean
See Rosen, R.D.

Rosenberg, Isaac 1890-1918 .... **PC 146;
TCLC 12**
See also BRW 6; CA 107; 188; DLB 20,
216; EWL 3; PAB; RGEL 2

Rosenblatt, Joe
See Rosenblatt, Joseph

Rosenblatt, Joseph 1933- .... **CLC 15**
See also CA 89-92; CP 3, 4, 5, 6, 7; INT
CA-89-92

Rosenfeld, Samuel
See Tzara, Tristan

Rosenstock, Sami
See Tzara, Tristan

Rosenstock, Samuel
See Tzara, Tristan

Rosenthal, M(acha) L(ouis)
1917-1996 .... **CLC 28**
See also CA 1-4R; 152; CAAS 6; CANR 4,
51; CP 1, 2, 3, 4, 5, 6; DLB 5; SATA 59

Ross, Barnaby
See Dannay, Frederic; Lee, Manfred B.

Ross, Bernard L.
See Follett, Ken

Ross, J. H.
See Lawrence, T. E.

Ross, John Hume
See Lawrence, T. E.

Ross, Martin 1862-1915
See Martin, Violet Florence
See also DLB 135; GLL 2; RGEL 2; RGSF 2

Ross, (James) Sinclair 1908-1996 ... **CLC 13;
SSC 24**
See also CA 73-76; CANR 81; CN 1, 2, 3, 4,
5, 6; DAC; DAM MST; DLB 88; RGEL 2;
RGSF 2; TCWW 1, 2

Rossetti, Christina 1830-1894 .... **NCLC 2,
50, 66, 186; PC 7, 119; WLC 5**
See also AAYA 51; BRW 5; BRWR 3; BYA
4; CLR 115; DA; DA3; DAB; DAC; DAM
MST, POET; DLB 35, 163, 240; EXPP; FL
1:3; LATS 1:1; MAICYA 1, 2; PFS 10, 14,
27, 34; RGEL 2; SATA 20; TEA; WCH

Rossetti, Christina Georgina
See Rossetti, Christina

Rossetti, Dante Gabriel
1828-1882 .... **NCLC 4, 77; PC 44;
WLC 5**
See also AAYA 51; BRW 5; CDBLB 1832-
1890; DA; DAB; DAC; DAM MST, POET;
DLB 35; EXPP; RGEL 2; TEA

Rossi, Cristina Peri
See Peri Rossi, Cristina

Rossi, Jean-Baptiste 1931-2003 .... **CLC 90**
See also CA 201; 215; CMW 4; NFS 18

Rossner, Judith 1935-2005 ..... **CLC 6, 9, 29**
See also AITN 2; BEST 90:3; BPFB 3; CA
17-20R; 242; CANR 18, 51, 73; CN 4, 5,
6, 7; DLB 6; INT CANR-18; MAL 5;
MTCW 1, 2; MTFW 2005

Rossner, Judith Perelman
See Rossner, Judith

Rostand, Edmond 1868-1918 .... **DC 10;
TCLC 6, 37**
See also CA 104; 126; DA; DA3; DAB;
DAC; DAM DRAM, MST; DFS 1; DLB
192; LAIT 1; MTCW 1; RGWL 2, 3; TWA

Rostand, Edmond Eugene Alexis
See Rostand, Edmond

Roth, Henry 1906-1995 .... **CLC 2, 6, 11,
104; SSC 134**
See also AMWS 9; CA 11-12; 149; CANR
38, 63; CAP 1; CN 1, 2, 3, 4, 5, 6; DA3;
DLB 28; EWL 3; MAL 5; MTCW 1, 2;
MTFW 2005; RGAL 4

Roth, (Moses) Joseph
1894-1939 .... **TCLC 33, 277**
See also CA 160; DLB 85; EWL 3; RGWL
2, 3

Roth, Philip 1933- ...... **CLC 1, 2, 3, 4, 6, 9,
15, 22, 31, 47, 66, 86, 119, 201, 336; SSC
26, 102, 176; WLC 5**
See also AAYA 67; AMWR 2; AMWS 3;
BEST 90:3; BPFB 3; CA 1-4R; CANR 1,
22, 36, 55, 89, 132, 170, 241; CDALB
1968-1988; CN 3, 4, 5, 6, 7; CPW 1; DA;
DA3; DAB; DAC; DAM MST, NOV, POP;
DLB 2, 28, 173; DLBY 1982; EWL 3;
MAL 5; MTCW 1, 2; MTFW 2005; NFS
25; RGAL 4; RGHL; RGSF 2; SSFS 12,
18; TUS

Roth, Philip Milton
See Roth, Philip

Rothenberg, Jerome 1931- .... **CLC 6, 57;
PC 129**
See also CA 45-48; CANR 1, 106; CP 1, 2,
3, 4, 5, 6, 7; DLB 5, 193

Sansom, William 1912-1976 .... CLC 2, 6;
SSC 21
See also CA 5-8R; 65-68; CANR 42; CN 1,
2; DAM NOV; DLB 139; EWL 3; MTCW
1; RGEL 2; RGSF 2

Santayana, George
1863-1952 .... TCLC 40
See also AMW; CA 115; 194; DLB 54, 71,
246, 270; DLBD 13; EWL 3; MAL 5;
RGAL 4; TUS

Santiago, Danny
See James, Daniel (Lewis)

Santillana, Inigo Lopez de Mendoza,
Marques de 1398-1458 .... LC 111
See also DLB 286

Santmyer, Helen Hooven
1895-1986 .... CLC 33; TCLC 133
See also CA 1-4R; 118; CANR 15, 33;
DLBY 1984; MTCW 1; RHW

Santoka, Taneda 1882-1940 .... TCLC 72

Santos, Bienvenido N(uqui)
1911-1996 .... AAL; CLC 22;
TCLC 156
See also CA 101; 151; CANR 19, 46; CP 1;
DAM MULT; DLB 312, 348; EWL;
RGAL 4; SSFS 19

Santos, Miguel
See Mihura, Miguel

Sapir, Edward 1884-1939 .... TCLC 108
See also CA 211; DLB 92

Sapper
See McNeile, Herman Cyril

Sapphire 1950- .... CLC 99
See also CA 262

Sapphire, Brenda
See Sapphire

Sappho c. 630 B.C.-c. 570 B.C. .... CMLC 3,
67, 160; PC 5, 117
See also CDWLB 1; DA3; DAM POET;
DLB 176; FL 1:1; PFS 20, 31, 38, 44;
RGWL 2, 3; WLIT 8; WP

Saramago, Jose 1922-2010 ... CLC 119, 275;
HLCS 1
See also CA 153; CANR 96, 164, 210, 242;
CWW 2; DLB 287, 332; EWL 3; LATS
1:2; NFS 27; SSFS 23

Sarduy, Severo 1937-1993 .... CLC 6, 97;
HLCS 2; TCLC 167
See also CA 89-92; 142; CANR 58, 81;
CWW 2; DLB 113; EWL 3; HW 1, 2;
LAW

Sargeson, Frank 1903-1982 .... CLC 31;
SSC 99
See also CA 25-28R; 106; CANR 38, 79;
CN 1, 2, 3; EWL 3; GLL 2; RGEL 2;
RGSF 2; SSFS 20

Sarmiento, Domingo Faustino
1811-1888 .... HLCS 2; NCLC 123
See also LAW; WLIT 1

Sarmiento, Felix Ruben Garcia
See Dario, Ruben

Saro-Wiwa, Ken(ule Beeson)
1941-1995 .... CLC 114; TCLC 200
See also BW 2; CA 142; 150; CANR 60;
DLB 157, 360

Saroyan, William 1908-1981 .... CLC 1, 8,
10, 29, 34, 56; DC 28; SSC 21; TCLC
137; WLC 5
See also AAYA 66; CA 5-8R; 103; CAD;
CANR 30; CDALBS; CN 1, 2; DA; DA3;
DAB; DAC; DAM DRAM, MST, NOV;
DFS 17; DLB 7, 9, 86; DLBY 1981; EWL
3; LAIT 4; MAL 5; MTCW 1, 2; MTFW
2005; NFS 39; RGAL 4; RGSF 2; SATA
23; SATA-Obit 24; SSFS 14; TUS

Sarraute, Nathalie 1900-1999 ...... CLC 1, 2,
4, 8, 10, 31, 80; TCLC 145
See also BPFB 3; CA 9-12R; 187; CANR
23, 66, 134; CWW 2; DLB 83, 321; EW

12; EWL 3; GFL 1789 to the Present;
MTCW 1, 2; MTFW 2005; RGWL 2, 3

Sarton, May 1912-1995 .... CLC 4, 14, 49,
91; PC 39; TCLC 120
See also AMWS 8; CA 1-4R; 149; CANR 1,
34, 55, 116; CN 1, 2, 3, 4, 5, 6; CP 1, 2, 3,
4, 5, 6; DAM POET; DLB 48; DLBY
1981; EWL 3; FW; INT CANR-34; MAL
5; MTCW 1, 2; MTFW 2005; RGAL 4;
SATA 36; SATA-Obit 86; TUS

Sartre, Jean-Paul 1905-1980 ... CLC 1, 4, 7,
9, 13, 18, 24, 44, 50, 52; DC 3; SSC 32;
WLC 5
See also AAYA 62; CA 9-12R; 97-100;
CANR 21; DA; DA3; DAB; DAC; DAM
DRAM, MST, NOV; DFS 5, 26; DLB 72,
296, 321, 332; EW 12; EWL 3; GFL 1789
to the Present; LMFS 2; MTCW 1, 2;
MTFW 2005; NFS 21; RGHL; RGSF 2;
RGWL 2, 3; SSFS 9; TWA

Sassoon, Siegfried 1886-1967 .... CLC 36,
130; PC 12
See also BRW 6; CA 104; 25-28R; CANR
36; DAB; DAM MST, NOV, POET; DLB
20, 191; DLBD 18; EWL 3; MTCW 1, 2;
MTFW 2005; PAB; PFS 28; RGEL 2; TEA

Sassoon, Siegfried Lorraine
See Sassoon, Siegfried

Satrapi, Marjane 1969- .... CLC 332
See also AAYA 55; CA 246

Satterfield, Charles
See Pohl, Frederik

Satyremont
See Peret, Benjamin

Saul, John 1942- .... CLC 46
See also AAYA 10, 62; BEST 90:4; CA 81-
84; CANR 16, 40, 81, 176, 221; CPW;
DAM NOV, POP; HGG; SATA 98

Saul, John W.
See Saul, John

Saul, John Woodruff III
See Saul, John

Saunders, Caleb
See Heinlein, Robert A.

Saunders, George 1958- .... CLC 325
See also CA 164; CANR 98, 157, 197; DLB
335

Saunders, George W.
See Saunders, George

Saura (Atares), Carlos 1932-1998 ... CLC 20
See also CA 114; 131; CANR 79; HW 1

Sauser, Frederic Louis
See Sauser-Hall, Frederic

Sauser-Hall, Frederic
1887-1961 .... CLC 18, 106
See also CA 102; 93-96; CANR 36, 62; DLB
258; EWL 3; GFL 1789 to the Present;
MTCW 1; WP

Saussure, Ferdinand de
1857-1913 .... TCLC 49
See also DLB 242

Savage, Catharine
See Brosman, Catharine Savage

Savage, Richard 1697(?)-1743 .... LC 96
See also DLB 95; RGEL 2

Savage, Thomas 1915-2003 .... CLC 40
See also CA 126; 132; 218; CAAS 15; CN 6,
7; INT CA-132; SATA-Obit 147; TCWW 2

Savan, Glenn 1953-2003 .... CLC 50
See also CA 225

Savonarola, Girolamo 1452-1498 .... LC 152
See also LMFS 1

Sax, Robert
See Johnson, Robert

Saxo Grammaticus
c. 1150-c. 1222 .... CMLC 58, 141

Saxton, Robert
See Johnson, Robert

Sayers, Dorothy L(eigh)
1893-1957 ... SSC 71; TCLC 2, 15, 237
See also BPFB 3; BRWS 3; CA 104; 119;
CANR 60; CDBLB 1914-1945; CMW 4;
DAM POP; DLB 10, 36, 77, 100; MSW;
MTCW 1, 2; MTFW 2005; RGEL 2; SSFS
12; TEA

Sayers, Valerie 1952- .... CLC 50, 122
See also CA 134; CANR 61; CSW

Sayles, John 1950- .... CLC 7, 10,
14, 198
See also CA 57-60; CANR 41, 84; DLB 44

Sayles, John Thomas
See Sayles, John

Scalapino, Leslie 1947-2010 .... PC 114
See also CA 123; CANR 67, 103; CP 5, 6, 7;
CWP; DLB 193

Scamander, Newt
See Rowling, J.K.

Scammell, Michael 1935- .... CLC 34
See also CA 156; CANR 222

Scannel, John Vernon
See Scannell, Vernon

Scannell, Vernon
1922-2007 .... CLC 49
See also CA 5-8R; 266; CANR 8, 24, 57,
143; CN 1, 2; CP 1, 2, 3, 4, 5, 6, 7; CWRI
5; DLB 27; SATA 59; SATA-Obit 188

Scarlett, Susan
See Streatfeild, Noel

Sa-Carneiro, Mario de
1890-1916 .... TCLC 83
See also DLB 287; EWL 3

Scarron 1847-1910
See Mikszath, Kalman

Scarron, Paul
1610-1660 .... LC 116
See also GFL Beginnings to 1789; RGWL 2, 3

Schaeffer, Susan Fromberg
1940-2011 .... CLC 6, 11, 22
See also CA 49-52; CANR 18, 65, 160; CN
4, 5, 6, 7; DLB 28, 299; MTCW 1, 2;
MTFW 2005; SATA 22

Schama, Simon 1945- .... CLC 150
See also BEST 89:4; CA 105; CANR 39, 91,
168, 207, 237

Schama, Simon Michael
See Schama, Simon

Schary, Jill
See Robinson, Jill

Schell, Jonathan 1943- .... CLC 35
See also CA 73-76; CANR 12, 117, 187

Schelling, Friedrich Wilhelm Joseph von
1775-1854 .... NCLC 30, 261
See also DLB 90, 366

Scherer, Jean-Marie Maurice
See Rohmer, Eric

Schevill, James (Erwin) 1920- .... CLC 7
See also CA 5-8R; CAAS 12; CAD; CD 5,
6; CP 1, 2, 3, 4, 5

Schiller, Friedrich von 1759-1805 .... DC 12;
NCLC 39, 69, 166
See also CDWLB 2; DAM DRAM; DLB 94;
EW 5; RGWL 2, 3; TWA

Schisgal, Murray (Joseph)
1926- .... CLC 6
See also CA 21-24R; CAD; CANR 48, 86;
CD 5, 6; MAL 5

Schlee, Ann 1934- .... CLC 35
See also CA 101; CANR 29, 88; SATA 44;
SATA-Brief 36

Schlegel, August Wilhelm von
1767-1845 .... NCLC 15, 142, 262
See also DLB 94; RGWL 2, 3

Schlegel, Friedrich
1772-1829 .... NCLC 45, 226
See also DLB 90; EW 5; RGWL 2, 3; TWA

Schlegel, Johann Elias (von) 1719
(?)-1749 .... **LC 5**

Schleiermacher, Friedrich
1768-1834 .... **NCLC 107**
See also DLB 90

Schlesinger, Arthur M., Jr.
1917-2007 .... **CLC 84**
See Schlesinger, Arthur Meier
See also AITN 1; CA 1 4R; 257; CANR 1,
28, 58, 105, 187; DLB 17; INT CANR-28;
MTCW 1, 2; SATA 61; SATA-Obit 181

Schlink, Bernhard 1944- .... **CLC 174, 347**
See also CA 163; CANR 116, 175, 217;
RGHL

Schmidt, Arno (Otto)
1914-1979 .... **CLC 56**
See also CA 128; 109; DLB 69; EWL 3

Schmitz, Aron Hector 1861-1928 ... **SSC 25;**
TCLC 2, 35, 244
See also CA 104; 122; DLB 264; EW 8;
EWL 3; MTCW 1; RGWL 2, 3; WLIT 7

Schnackenberg, Gjertrud 1953- .... **CLC 40;**
PC 45
See also AMWS 15; CA 116; CANR 100;
CP 5, 6, 7; CWP; DLB 120, 282; PFS 13,
25

Schnackenberg, Gjertrud Cecelia
See Schnackenberg, Gjertrud

Schneider, Leonard Alfred
See Bruce, Lenny

Schnitzler, Arthur 1862-1931 .... **DC 17;**
SSC 15, 61; TCLC 4, 275
See also CA 104; CDWLB 2; DLB 81, 118;
EW 8; EWL 3; RGSF 2; RGWL 2, 3

Schoenberg, Arnold Franz Walter
1874-1951 .... **TCLC 75**
See also CA 109; 188

Schonberg, Arnold
See Schoenberg, Arnold Franz Walter

Schopenhauer, Arthur
1788-1860 .... **NCLC 51, 157**
See also DLB 90; EW 5

Schor, Sandra (M.) 1932(?)-1990 ... **CLC 65**
See also CA 132

Schorer, Mark
1908-1977 .... **CLC 9**
See also CA 5-8R; 73-76; CANR 7; CN 1, 2;
DLB 103

Schrader, Paul (Joseph)
1946- .... **CLC 26, 212**
See also CA 37-40R; CANR 41; DLB 44

Schreber, Daniel 1842-1911 .... **TCLC 123**

Schreiner, Olive 1855-1920 ..... **TCLC 9, 235**
See also AFW; BRWS 2; CA 105; 154; DLB
18, 156, 190, 225; EWL 3; FW; RGEL 2;
TWA; WLIT 2; WWE 1

Schreiner, Olive Emilie Albertina
See Schreiner, Olive

Schulberg, Budd 1914-2009 .... **CLC 7, 48**
See also AMWS 18; BPFB 3; CA 25-28R;
289; CANR 19, 87, 178; CN 1, 2, 3, 4, 5,
6, 7; DLB 6, 26, 28; DLBY 1981, 2001;
MAL 5

Schulberg, Budd Wilson
See Schulberg, Budd

Schulberg, Seymour Wilson
See Schulberg, Budd

Schulman, Arnold
See Trumbo, Dalton

Schulz, Bruno
1892-1942 ... **SSC 13; TCLC 5, 51, 273**
See also CA 115; 123; CANR 86; CDWLB
4; DLB 215; EWL 3; MTCW 2; MTFW
2005; RGSF 2; RGWL 2, 3

Schulz, Charles M. 1922-2000 .... **CLC 12**
See also AAYA 39; CA 9-12R; 187; CANR
6, 132; CLR 188; INT CANR-6; MTFW
2005; SATA 10; SATA-Obit 118

Schulz, Charles Monroe
See Schulz, Charles M.

Schumacher, E(rnst) F(riedrich)
1911-1977 .... **CLC 80**
See also CA 81-84; 73-76; CANR 34, 85

Schumann, Robert 1810-1856 ..... **NCLC 143**

Schuyler, George Samuel 1895-1977 **HR 1:3**
See also BW 2; CA 81-84; 73-76; CANR 42;
DLB 29, 51

Schuyler, James Marcus
1923-1991 .... **CLC 5, 23; PC 88**
See also CA 101; 134; CP 1, 2, 3, 4, 5; DAM
POET; DLB 5, 169; EWL 3; INT CA-101;
MAL 5; WP

Schwartz, Delmore (David)
1913-1966 .... **CLC 2, 4, 10, 45, 87;**
PC 8; SSC 105
See also AMWS 2; CA 17-18; 25-28R;
CANR 35; CAP 2; DLB 28, 48; EWL
3; MAL 5; MTCW 1, 2; MTFW 2005;
PAB; RGAL 4; TUS

Schwartz, Ernst
See Ozu, Yasujiro

Schwartz, John Burnham 1965- ..... **CLC 59**
See also CA 132; CANR 116, 188

Schwartz, Lynne Sharon 1939- ...... **CLC 31**
See also CA 103; CANR 44, 89, 160, 214;
DLB 218; MTCW 2; MTFW 2005

Schwartz, Muriel A.
See Eliot, T. S.

Schwartzman, Adam 1973- .... **CLC 318**
See also CA 307

Schwarz-Bart, Andre 1928-2006 ... **CLC 2, 4**
See also CA 89-92; 253; CANR 109; DLB
299; RGHL

Schwarz-Bart, Simone 1938- .... **BLCS;**
CLC 7
See also BW 2; CA 97-100; CANR 117;
EWL 3

Schwerner, Armand 1927-1999 .... **PC 42**
See also CA 9-12R; 179; CANR 50, 85; CP
2, 3, 4, 5, 6; DLB 165

Schwitters, Kurt (Hermann Edward Karl
Julius) 1887-1948 .... **TCLC 95**
See also CA 158

Schwob, Marcel (Mayer Andre)
1867-1905 .... **TCLC 20**
See also CA 117; 168; DLB 123; GFL 1789
to the Present

Sciascia, Leonardo
1921-1989 .... **CLC 8, 9, 41**
See also CA 85-88; 130; CANR 35; DLB
177; EWL 3; MTCW 1; RGWL 2, 3

Scoppettone, Sandra 1936- .... **CLC 26**
See also AAYA 11, 65; BYA 8; CA 5-8R;
CANR 41, 73, 157; GLL 1; MAICYA 2;
MAICYAS 1; SATA 9, 92; WYA; YAW

Scorsese, Martin 1942- ..... **CLC 20, 89, 207**
See also AAYA 38; CA 110; 114; CANR
46, 85

Scotland, Jay
See Jakes, John

Scott, Duncan Campbell
1862-1947 .... **TCLC 6**
See also CA 104; 153; DAC; DLB 92;
RGEL 2

Scott, Evelyn 1893-1963 .... **CLC 43**
See also CA 104; 112; CANR 64; DLB 9,
48; RHW

Scott, F(rancis) R(eginald)
1899-1985 .... **CLC 22**
See also CA 101; 114; CANR 87; CP 1, 2, 3,
4; DLB 88; INT CA-101; RGEL 2

Scott, Frank
See Scott, F(rancis) R(eginald)

Scott, Joan
See Scott, Joan Wallach

Scott, Joan W.
See Scott, Joan Wallach

Scott, Joan Wallach 1941- .... **CLC 65**
See also CA 293

Scott, Joanna 1960- .... **CLC 50**
See also AMWS 17; CA 126; CANR 53,
92, 168, 219

Scott, Joanna Jeanne
See Scott, Joanna

Scott, Paul (Mark) 1920-1978 ..... **CLC 9, 60**
See also BRWS 1; CA 81-84; 77-80; CANR
33; CN 1, 2; DLB 14, 207, 326; EWL 3;
MTCW 1; RGEL 2; RHW; WWE 1

Scott, Ridley 1937- .... **CLC 183**
See also AAYA 13, 43

Scott, Sarah 1723-1795 .... **LC 44**
See also DLB 39

Scott, Sir Walter 1771-1832 .... **NCLC 15,**
69, 110, 209, 241, 270; PC 13; SSC 32;
WLC 5
See also AAYA 22; BRW 4; BYA 2; CDBLB
1789-1832; CLR 154; DA; DAB; DAC;
DAM MST, NOV, POET; DLB 93, 107,
116, 144, 159, 366; GL 3; HGG; LAIT 1;
NFS 31; RGEL 2; RGSF 2; SSFS 10;
SUFW 1; TEA; WLIT 3; YABC 2

Scotus, John Duns
1266(?)-1308 .... **CMLC 59, 138**
See also DLB 115

Scribe, Augustin Eugene
See Scribe, (Augustin) Eugene

Scribe, (Augustin) Eugene
1791-1861 .... **DC 5; NCLC 16**
See also DAM DRAM; DLB 192; GFL 1789
to the Present; RGWL 2, 3

Scrum, R.
See Crumb, R.

Scudery, Georges de 1601-1667 .... **LC 75**
See also GFL Beginnings to 1789

Scudery, Madeleine de 1607-1701 .. **LC 2, 58**
See also DLB 268; GFL Beginnings to 1789

Scum
See Crumb, R.

Scumbag, Little Bobby
See Crumb, R.

Sceve, Maurice c. 1500-c. 1564 ...... **LC 180;**
PC 111
See also DLB 327; GFL Beginnings to 1789

Soderberg, Hjalmar 1869-1941 ..... **TCLC 39**
See also DLB 259; EWL 3; RGSF 2

Sodergran, Edith 1892-1923 .... **TCLC 31**
See also CA 202; DLB 259; EW 11; EWL 3;
RGWL 2, 3

Seabrook, John
See Hubbard, L. Ron

Seacole, Mary Jane Grant
1805-1881 .... **NCLC 147**
See also DLB 166

Sealsfield, Charles 1793-1864 ..... **NCLC 233**
See also DLB 133, 186

Sealy, I(rwin) Allan 1951- .... **CLC 55**
See also CA 136; CN 6, 7

Search, Alexander
See Pessoa, Fernando

Seare, Nicholas
See Whitaker, Rod

Sears, Djanet 1959- .... **DC 46**
See also CA 259

Sears, Janet
See Sears, Djanet

Sebald, W(infried) G(eorg)
1944-2001 .... **CLC 194, 296**
See also BRWS 8; CA 159; 202; CANR 98;
MTFW 2005; RGHL

Sebastian, Lee
See Silverberg, Robert

Sebastian Owl
See Thompson, Hunter S.

Sebestyen, Igen
See Sebestyen, Ouida

74, 131, 208; CD 5, 6; CP 5, 6, 7; CWD;
CWP; DA3; DAM DRAM, MULT; DFS 2,
11; DLB 38, 249; FW; LAIT 4, 5; MAL 5;
MTCW 1, 2; MTFW 2005; NFS 11;
RGAL 4; SATA 157; YAW

Shanley, John Patrick 1950- .... **CLC 75**
See also AAYA 74; AMWS 14; CA 128; 133;
CAD; CANR 83, 154; CD 5, 6; DFS 23, 28

Shapcott, Thomas W(illiam) 1935- .... **CLC 38**
See also CA 69-72; CANR 49, 83, 103; CP
1, 2, 3, 4, 5, 6, 7; DLB 289

Shapiro, Jane 1942- .... **CLC 76**
See also CA 196

Shapiro, Karl 1913-2000 .... **CLC 4, 8, 15,
53; PC 25**
See also AMWS 2; CA 1-4R; 188; CAAS 6;
CANR 1, 36, 66; CP 1, 2, 3, 4, 5, 6; DLB
48; EWL 3; EXPP; MAL 5; MTCW 1, 2;
MTFW 2005; PFS 3; RGAL 4

Sharp, William 1855-1905 .... **TCLC 39**
See also CA 160; DLB 156; RGEL 2; SUFW

Sharpe, Thomas Ridley 1928- .... **CLC 36**
See also CA 114; 122; CANR 85; CN 4, 5,
6, 7; DLB 14, 231; INT CA-122

Sharpe, Tom
See Sharpe, Thomas Ridley

Shatrov, Mikhail .... **CLC 59**

Shaw, Bernard
See Shaw, George Bernard

Shaw, G. Bernard
See Shaw, George Bernard

Shaw, George Bernard 1856-1950 ... **DC 23;
TCLC 3, 9, 21, 45, 205, 293; WLC 5**
See also AAYA 61; BRW 6; BRWC 1;
BRWR 2; CA 104; 128; CDBLB 1914-
1945; DA; DA3; DAB; DAC; DAM
DRAM, MST; DFS 1, 3, 6, 11, 19, 22,
30; DLB 10, 57, 190, 332; EWL 3; LAIT
3; LATS 1:1; MTCW 1, 2; MTFW 2005;
RGEL 2; TEA; WLIT 4

Shaw, Henry Wheeler
1818-1885 .... **NCLC 15**
See also DLB 11; RGAL 4

Shaw, Irwin 1913-1984 .... **CLC 7, 23, 34**
See also AITN 1; BPFB 3; CA 13-16R; 112;
CANR 21; CDALB 1941-1968; CN 1, 2,
3; CPW; DAM DRAM, POP; DLB 6, 102;
DLBY 1984; MAL 5; MTCW 1, 21;
MTFW 2005

Shaw, Robert (Archibald) 1927-1978 ... **CLC 5**
See also AITN 1; CA 1-4R; 81-84; CANR 4;
CN 1, 2; DLB 13, 14

Shaw, T. E.
See Lawrence, T. E.

Shawn, Wallace 1943- .... **CLC 41**
See also CA 112; CAD; CANR 215; CD 5,
6; DLB 266

Shaykh, Hanan al- 1945- .... **CLC 218**
See also CA 135; CANR 111, 220; CWW 2;
DLB 346; EWL 3; WLIT 6

Shchedrin, N.
See Saltykov, Mikhail Evgrafovich

Shea, Lisa 1953- .... **CLC 86**
See also CA 147

Sheed, Wilfrid 1930-2011 .... **CLC 2, 4,
10, 53**
See also CA 65-68; CANR 30, 66, 181; CN
1, 2, 3, 4, 5, 6, 7; DLB 6; MAL 5; MTCW
1, 2; MTFW 2005

Sheed, Wilfrid John Joseph
See Sheed, Wilfrid

Sheehy, Gail 1937- .... **CLC 171**
See also CA 49-52; CANR 1, 33, 55, 92;
CPW; MTCW 1

Sheldon, Alice Hastings Bradley
1915(?)-1987 .... **CLC 48, 50**
See also CA 108; 122; CANR 34; DLB 8;
INT CA-108; MTCW 1; SCFW 1, 2; SFW 4

Sheldon, John
See Bloch, Robert (Albert)

Sheldon, Raccoona
See Sheldon, Alice Hastings Bradley

Shelley, Mary
See Shelley, Mary Wollstonecraft

Shelley, Mary Wollstonecraft
1797-1851 ...... **NCLC 14, 59, 103, 170;
SSC 92; WLC 5**
See also AAYA 20; BPFB 3; BRW 3; BRWC
2; BRWR 3; BRWS 3; BYA 5; CDBLB
1789-1832; CLR 133; DA; DA3; DAB;
DAC; DAM MST, NOV; DLB 110, 116,
159, 178; EXPN; FL 1:3; GL 3; HGG; LAIT
1; LMFS 1, 2; NFS 1, 37; RGEL 2; SATA
29; SCFW 1, 2; SFW 4; TEA; WLIT 3

Shelley, Percy Bysshe
1792-1822 ...... **NCLC 18, 93, 143, 175;
PC 14, 67; WLC 5**
See also AAYA 61; BRW 4; BRWR 1;
CDBLB 1789-1832; DA; DA3; DAB;
DAC; DAM MST, POET; DLB 96, 110,
158; EXPP; LMFS 1; PAB; PFS 2, 27, 32,
36; RGEL 2; TEA; WLIT 3; WP

Shepard, James R.
See Shepard, Jim

Shepard, Jim 1956- .... **CLC 36**
See also AAYA 73; CA 137; CANR 59, 104,
160, 199, 231; SATA 90, 164

Shepard, Lucius 1947- .... **CLC 34**
See also CA 128; 141; CANR 81, 124, 178;
HGG; SCFW 2; SFW 4; SUFW 2

Shepard, Sam 1943- .... **CLC 4, 6, 17, 34,
41, 44, 169; DC 5**
See also AAYA 1, 58; AMWS 3; CA 69-72;
CABS 3; CAD; CANR 22, 120, 140, 223;
CD 5, 6; DA3; DAM DRAM; DFS 3, 6, 7,
14; DLB 7, 212, 341; EWL 3; IDFW 3, 4;
MAL 5; MTCW 1, 2; MTFW 2005; RGAL
4

Shepherd, Jean (Parker)
1921-1999 .... **TCLC 177**
See also AAYA 69; AITN 2; CA 77-80; 187

Shepherd, Michael
See Ludlum, Robert

Sherburne, Zoa (Lillian Morin)
1912-1995 .... **CLC 30**
See also AAYA 13; CA 1-4R; 176; CANR 3,
37; MAICYA 1, 2; SAAS 18; SATA 3; YAW

Sheridan, Frances 1724-1766 .... **LC 7**
See also DLB 39, 84

Sheridan, Richard Brinsley
1751-1816 .... **DC 1; NCLC 5, 91;
WLC 5**
See also BRW 3; CDBLB 1660-1789; DA;
DAB; DAC; DAM DRAM, MST; DFS 15;
DLB 89; WLIT 3

Sherman, Jonathan Marc 1968- ..... **CLC 55**
See also CA 230

Sherman, Martin 1941(?)- .... **CLC 19**
See also CA 116; 123; CAD; CANR 86; CD
5, 6; DFS 20; DLB 228; GLL 1; IDTP;
RGHL

Sherwin, Judith Johnson
See Johnson, Judith

Sherwood, Frances 1940- .... **CLC 81**
See also CA 146, 220; CAAE 220;
CANR 158

Sherwood, Robert E(mmet)
1896-1955 .... **DC 36; TCLC 3**
See also CA 104; 153; CANR 86; DAM
DRAM; DFS 11, 15, 17; DLB 7, 26, 249;
IDFW 3, 4; MAL 5; RGAL 4

Shestov, Lev 1866-1938 .... **TCLC 56**

Shevchenko, Taras 1814-1861 .... **NCLC
54, 281**

Shiel, M. P. 1865-1947 .... **TCLC 8**
See also CA 106; 160; DLB 153; HGG;
MTCW 2; MTFW 2005; SCFW 1, 2; SFW
4; SUFW

Shiel, Matthew Phipps
See Shiel, M. P.

Shields, Carol 1935-2003 .... **CLC 91, 113,
193, 298; SSC 126**
See also AMWS 7; CA 81-84; 218; CANR
51, 74, 98, 133; CCA 1; CN 6, 7; CPW;
DA3; DAC; DLB 334, 350; MTCW 2;
MTFW 2005; NFS 23

Shields, David 1956- .... **CLC 97**
See also CA 124; CANR 48, 99, 112, 157

Shields, David Jonathan
See Shields, David

Shiga, Naoya 1883-1971 .... **CLC 33;
SSC 23; TCLC 172**
See also CA 101; 33-36R; DLB 180; EWL
3; MJW; RGWL 3

Shiga Naoya
See Shiga, Naoya

Shilts, Randy 1951-1994 .... **CLC 85**
See also AAYA 19; CA 115; 127; 144;
CANR 45; DA3; GLL 1; INT CA-127;
MTCW 2; MTFW 2005

Shimazaki, Haruki 1872-1943 .... **TCLC 5**
See also CA 105; 134; CANR 84; DLB 180;
EWL 3; MJW; RGWL 3

Shimazaki Toson
See Shimazaki, Haruki

Shi Mo
See Bei Dao

Shirley, James 1596-1666 ..... **DC 25; LC 96**
See also DLB 58; RGEL 2

Shamlu, Ahmad 1925-2000 .... **CLC 10**
See also CA 216; CWW 2

Sholokhov, Mikhail
1905-1984 .... **CLC 7, 15**
See also CA 101; 112; DLB 272, 332; EWL
3; MTCW 1, 2; MTFW 2005; RGWL 2, 3;
SATA-Obit 36

Sholokhov, Mikhail Aleksandrovich
See Sholokhov, Mikhail

Shone, Patric
See Hanley, James

Showalter, Elaine 1941- .... **CLC 169**
See also CA 57-60; CANR 58, 106, 208;
DLB 67; FW; GLL 2

Shreve, Susan
See Shreve, Susan Richards

Shreve, Susan Richards 1939- .... **CLC 23**
See also CA 49-52; CAAS 5; CANR 5, 38,
69, 100, 159, 199; MAICYA 1, 2; SATA
46, 95, 152; SATA-Brief 41

Shteyngart, Gary 1972- .... **CLC 319**
See also AAYA 68; CA 217; CANR 175

Shteyngart, Igor
See Shteyngart, Gary

Shue, Larry 1946-1985 .... **CLC 52**
See also CA 145; 117; DAM DRAM; DFS 7

Shu-Jen, Chou 1881-1936 .. **SSC 20; TCLC 3**
See also CA 104; EWL 3

Shulman, Alix Kates
1932- .... **CLC 2, 10**
See also CA 29-32R; CANR 43, 199; FW;
SATA 7

Shuster, Joe 1914-1992 .... **CLC 21**
See also AAYA 50

Shute, Nevil 1899-1960 .... **CLC 30**
See also BPFB 3; CA 102; 93-96; CANR 85;
DLB 255; MTCW 2; NFS 9, 38; RHW 4;
SFW 4

Shuttle, Penelope (Diane)
1947- .... **CLC 7**
See also CA 93-96; CANR 39, 84, 92, 108;
CP 3, 4, 5, 6, 7; CWP; DLB 14, 40

Sanchez, Luis Rafael 1936- .... **CLC 23**
    See also CA 128; DLB 305; EWL 3; HW 1;
    WLIT 1

Snodgrass, Quentin Curtius
    See Twain, Mark

Snodgrass, Thomas Jefferson
    See Twain, Mark

Snodgrass, W. D. 1926-2009 .... **CLC 2, 6,
    10, 18, 68; PC 74**
    See also AMWS 6; CA 1-4R; 282; CANR 6,
    36, 65, 85, 185; CP 1, 2, 3, 4, 5, 6, 7; DAM
    POET; DLB 5; MAL 5; MTCW 1, 2;
    MTFW 2005; PFS 29; RGAL 4; TCLE 1:2

Snodgrass, W. de Witt
    See Snodgrass, W. D.

Snodgrass, William de Witt
    See Snodgrass, W. D.

Snodgrass, William De Witt
    See Snodgrass, W. D.

Snorri Sturluson 1179-1241   **CMLC 56, 134**
    See also RGWL 2, 3

Snow, C(harles) P(ercy)
    1905-1980 .... **CLC 1, 4, 6, 9, 13, 19**
    See also BRW 7; CA 5-8R; 101; CANR 28;
    CDBLB 1945-1960; CN 1, 2; DAM NOV;
    DLB 15, 77; DLBD 17; EWL 3; MTCW 1,
    2; MTFW 2005; RGEL 2; TEA

Snow, Frances Compton
    See Adams, Henry

Snyder, Gary 1930- .... **CLC 1, 2, 5, 9,
    32, 120; PC 21**
    See also AAYA 72; AMWS 8; ANW; BG
    1:3; CA 17-20R; CANR 30, 60, 125; CP 1,
    2, 3, 4, 5, 6, 7; DA3; DAM POET; DLB 5,
    16, 165, 212, 237, 275, 342; EWL 3; MAL
    5; MTCW 2; MTFW 2005; PFS 9, 19;
    RGAL 4; WP

Snyder, Gary Sherman
    See Snyder, Gary

Snyder, Zilpha Keatley 1927- .... **CLC 17**
    See also AAYA 15; BYA 1; CA 9-12R, 252;
    CAAE 252; CANR 38, 202; CLR 31, 121;
    JRDA; MAICYA 1, 2; SAAS 2; SATA 1,
    28, 75, 110, 163, 226; SATA-Essay 112,
    163; YAW

Soares, Bernardo
    See Pessoa, Fernando

Sobh, A.
    See Shamlu, Ahmad

Sobh, Alef
    See Shamlu, Ahmad

Sobol, Joshua 1939- .... **CLC 60**
    See also CA 200; CWW 2; RGHL

Sobol, Yehoshua 1939-
    See Sobol, Joshua

Socrates 470B.C.-399B.C. .... **CMLC 27**

Soderbergh, Steven 1963- .... **CLC 154**
    See also AAYA 43; CA 243

Soderbergh, Steven Andrew
    See Soderbergh, Steven

Soedergran, Edith Irene
    See Sodergran, Edith

Softly, Edgar
    See Lovecraft, H. P.

Softly, Edward
    See Lovecraft, H. P.

Sokolov, Alexander V. 1943- .... **CLC 59**
    See also CA 73-76; CWW 2; DLB 285;
    EWL 3; RGWL 2, 3

Sokolov, Alexander Vsevolodovich
    See Sokolov, Alexander V.

Sokolov, Raymond 1941- .... **CLC 7**
    See also CA 85-88

Sokolov, Sasha
    See Sokolov, Alexander V.

Soli, Tatjana .... **CLC 318**
    See also CA 307

Solo, Jay
    See Ellison, Harlan

Sologub, Fedor
    See Teternikov, Fyodor Kuzmich

Sologub, Feodor
    See Teternikov, Fyodor Kuzmich

Sologub, Fyodor
    See Teternikov, Fyodor Kuzmich

Solomons, Ikey Esquir
    See Thackeray, William Makepeace

Solomos, Dionysios 1798-1857 ...... **NCLC 15**

Solwoska, Mara
    See French, Marilyn

Solzhenitsyn, Aleksandr 1918-2008 ... **CLC 1,
    2, 4, 7, 9, 10, 18, 26, 34, 78, 134, 235; SSC
    32, 105; WLC 5**
    See also AAYA 49; AITN 1; BPFB 3; CA
    69-72; CANR 40, 65, 116; CWW 2; DA;
    DA3; DAB; DAC; DAM MST, NOV; DLB
    302, 332; EW 13; EWL 3; EXPS; LAIT 4;
    MTCW 1, 2; MTFW 2005; NFS 6; PFS
    38; RGSF 2; RGWL 2, 3; SSFS 9; TWA

Solzhenitsyn, Aleksandr I.
    See Solzhenitsyn, Aleksandr

Solzhenitsyn, Aleksandr Isayevich
    See Solzhenitsyn, Aleksandr

Somers, Jane
    See Lessing, Doris

Somerville, Edith Oenone
    1858-1949 .... **SSC 56; TCLC 51**
    See also CA 196; DLB 135; RGEL 2; RGSF 2

Somerville & Ross
    See Martin, Violet Florence; Somerville,
    Edith Oenone

Sommer, Scott 1951- .... **CLC 25**
    See also CA 106

Sommers, Christina Hoff 1950- ... **CLC 197**
    See also CA 153; CANR 95

Sondheim, Stephen 1930- .... **CLC 30, 39,
    147; DC 22**
    See also AAYA 11, 66; CA 103; CANR 47,
    67, 125; DAM DRAM; DFS 25, 27, 28;
    LAIT 4

Sondheim, Stephen Joshua
    See Sondheim, Stephen

Sone, Monica 1919- .... **AAL**
    See also DLB 312

Song, Cathy 1955- .... **AAL; PC 21**
    See also CA 154; CANR 118; CWP; DLB
    169, 312; EXPP; FW; PFS 5, 43

Sontag, Susan 1933-2004 .... **CLC 1, 2,
    10, 13, 31, 105, 195, 277**
    See also AMWS 3; CA 17-20R; 234; CANR
    25, 51, 74, 97, 184; CN 1, 2, 3, 4, 5, 6, 7;
    CPW; DA3; DAM POP; DLB 2, 67; EWL
    3; MAL 5; MBL; MTCW 1, 2; MTFW
    2005; RGAL 4; RHW; SSFS 10

Sophocles 496(?)B.C.-406(?)B.C. ... **CMLC 2,
    47, 51, 86; DC 1; WLCS**
    See also AW 1; CDWLB 1; DA; DA3; DAB;
    DAC; DAM DRAM, MST; DFS 1, 4, 8,
    24; DLB 176; LAIT 1; LATS 1:1; LMFS 1;
    RGWL 2, 3; TWA; WLIT 8

Sordello 1189-1269 .... **CMLC 15**

Sorel, Georges 1847-1922 .... **TCLC 91**
    See also CA 118; 188

Sorel, Julia
    See Drexler, Rosalyn

Sorokin, Vladimir 1955- .... **CLC 59**
    See also CA 258; CANR 233; DLB 285

Sorokin, Vladimir Georgievich
    See Sorokin, Vladimir

Sorrentino, Gilbert 1929-2006 ..... **CLC 3, 7,
    14, 22, 40, 247**
    See also AMWS 21; CA 77-80; 250; CANR
    14, 33, 115, 157; CN 3, 4, 5, 6, 7; CP 1, 2,
    3, 4, 5, 6, 7; DLB 5, 173; DLBY 1980;
    INT CANR-14

Soto, Gary 1952- .... **CLC 32, 80; HLC 2;
    PC 28**
    See also AAYA 10, 37; BYA 11; CA 119;
    125; CANR 50, 74, 107, 157, 219; CLR
    38; CP 4, 5, 6, 7; DAM MULT; DFS 26;
    DLB 82; EWL 3; EXPP; HW 1, 2; INT
    CA-125; JRDA; LLW; MAICYA 2; MAI-
    CYAS 1; MAL 5; MTCW 2; MTFW 2005;
    PFS 7, 30; RGAL 4; SATA 80, 120, 174;
    SSFS 33; WYA; YAW

Soupault, Philippe 1897-1990 .... **CLC 68**
    See also CA 116; 147; 131; EWL 3; GFL
    1789 to the Present; LMFS 2

Souster, (Holmes) Raymond
    1921- .... **CLC 5, 14**
    See also CA 13-16R; CAAS 14; CANR 13,
    29, 53; CP 1, 2, 3, 4, 5, 6, 7; DA3; DAC;
    DAM POET; DLB 88; RGEL 2; SATA 63

Southern, Terry 1924(?)-1995 .... **CLC 7**
    See also AMWS 11; BPFB 3; CA 1-4R; 150;
    CANR 1, 55, 107; CN 1, 2, 3, 4, 5, 6; DLB
    2; IDFW 3, 4

Southerne, Thomas 1660-1746 .... **LC 99**
    See also DLB 80; RGEL 2

Southey, Robert 1774-1843 ..... **NCLC 8, 97;
    PC 111**
    See also BRW 4; DLB 93, 107, 142; RGEL
    2; SATA 54

Southwell, Robert 1561(?)-1595 .... **LC 108**
    See also DLB 167; RGEL 2; TEA

Southworth, Emma Dorothy Eliza Nevitte
    1819-1899 .... **NCLC 26**
    See also DLB 239

Souza, Ernest
    See Scott, Evelyn

Soyinka, Wole 1934- .... **BLC 1:3, 2:3;
    CLC 3, 5, 14, 36, 44, 179, 331; DC 2; PC
    118; WLC 5**
    See also AFW; BW 2, 3; CA 13-16R; CANR
    27, 39, 82, 136; CD 5, 6; CDWLB 3; CN
    6, 7; CP 1, 2, 3, 4, 5, 6 ,7; DA; DA3; DAB;
    DAC; DAM DRAM, MST, MULT; DFS
    10, 26; DLB 125, 332; EWL 3; MTCW 1,
    2; MTFW 2005; PFS 27, 40; RGEL 2;
    TWA; WLIT 2; WWE 1

Spackman, W(illiam) M(ode)
    1905-1990 .... **CLC 46**
    See also CA 81-84; 132

Spacks, Barry (Bernard) 1931- ...... **CLC 14**
    See also CA 154; CANR 33, 109; CP 3, 4, 5,
    6, 7; DLB 105

Spanidou, Irini 1946- .... **CLC 44**
    See also CA 185; CANR 179

Spark, Muriel 1918-2006 .... **CLC 2, 3, 5,
    8, 13, 18, 40, 94, 242; PC 72; SSC 10, 115**
    See also BRWS 1; CA 5-8R; 251; CANR 12,
    36, 76, 89, 131; CDBLB 1945-1960; CN 1,
    2, 3, 4, 5, 6, 7; CP 1, 2, 3, 4, 5, 6, 7; DA3;
    DAB; DAC; DAM MST, NOV; DLB 15,
    139; EWL 3; FW; INT CANR-12; LAIT 4;
    MTCW 1, 2; MTFW 2005; NFS 22; RGEL
    2; SSFS 28; TEA; WLIT 4; YAW

Spark, Muriel Sarah
    See Spark, Muriel

Spaulding, Douglas
    See Bradbury, Ray

Spaulding, Leonard
    See Bradbury, Ray

Speght, Rachel 1597-c. 1630 .... **LC 97**
    See also DLB 126

Spence, J. A. D.
    See Eliot, T. S.

Spencer, Anne 1882-1975 .... **HR 1:3; PC 77**
    See also BW 2; CA 161; DLB 51, 54

Spencer, Elizabeth 1921- .... **CLC 22;
    SSC 57**
    See also CA 13-16R; CANR 32, 65, 87; CN
    1, 2, 3, 4, 5, 6, 7; CSW; DLB 6, 218; EWL
    3; MTCW 1; RGAL 4; SATA 14

Spencer, Leonard G.
  See Silverberg, Robert
Spencer, Scott 1945- .... **CLC 30**
  See also CA 113; CANR 51, 148, 190;
  DLBY 1986
Spender, Stephen 1909-1995 .... **CLC 1, 2,**
  5, 10, 41, 91; PC 71
  See also BRWS 2; CA 9-12R; 149; CANR
  31, 54; CDBLB 1945-1960; CP 1, 2, 3, 4,
  5, 6; DA3; DAM POET; DLB 20; EWL 3;
  MTCW 1, 2; MTFW 2005; PAB; PFS 23,
  36; RGEL 2; TEA
Spender, Stephen Harold
  See Spender, Stephen
Spengler, Oswald (Arnold Gottfried)
  1880-1936 .... **TCLC 25**
  See also CA 118; 189
Spenser, Edmund 1552(?)-1599 .... **LC 5, 39,**
  117; PC 8, 42; WLC 5
  See also AAYA 60; BRW 1; CDBLB Before
  1660; DA; DA3; DAB; DAC; DAM MST,
  POET; DLB 167; EFS 1:2, 2:1; EXPP;
  PAB; PFS 32; RGEL 2; TEA; WLIT 3; WP
Spicer, Jack 1925-1965 .... **CLC 8, 18, 72**
  See also BG 1:3; CA 85-88; DAM POET;
  DLB 5, 16, 193; GLL 1; WP
Spiegelman, Art 1948- .... **CLC 76, 178**
  See also AAYA 10, 46; CA 125; CANR 41, 55,
  74, 124; DLB 299; MTCW 2; MTFW 2005;
  NFS 35; RGHL; SATA 109, 158; YAW
Spielberg, Peter 1929- .... **CLC 6**
  See also CA 5-8R; CANR 4, 48; DLBY 1981
Spielberg, Steven 1947- .... **CLC 20, 188**
  See also AAYA 8, 24; CA 77-80; CANR 32;
  SATA 32
Spillane, Frank Morrison
  See Spillane, Mickey
Spillane, Mickey 1918-2006 .... **CLC 3,**
  13, 241
  See also BPFB 3; CA 25-28R; 252; CANR
  28, 63, 125, 238; CMW 4; DA3; DLB 226;
  MSW; MTCW 1, 2; MTFW 2005; SATA
  66; SATA-Obit 176
Spinoza, Benedictus de
  1632-1677 .... **LC 9, 58, 177**
Spinrad, Norman (Richard)
  1940- .... **CLC 46**
  See also BPFB 3; CA 37-40R, 233; CAAE
  233; CAAS 19; CANR 20, 91; DLB 8;
  INT CANR-20; SFW 4
Spiotta, Dana 1966- .... **CLC 328**
  See also CA 246; CANR 238
Spitteler, Carl 1845-1924 .... **TCLC 12**
  See also CA 109; DLB 129, 332; EWL 3
Spitteler, Karl Friedrich Georg
  See Spitteler, Carl
Spivack, Kathleen (Romola Drucker)
  1938- .... **CLC 6**
  See also CA 49-52
Spivak, Gayatri Chakravorty
  1942- .... **CLC 233**
  See also CA 110; 154; CANR 91; FW;
  LMFS 2
Spofford, Harriet (Elizabeth) Prescott
  1835-1921 .... **SSC 87**
  See also CA 201; DLB 74, 221
Spoto, Donald 1941- .... **CLC 39**
  See also CA 65-68; CANR 11, 57, 93,
  173, 212
Springsteen, Bruce 1949- .... **CLC 17**
  See also CA 111
Springsteen, Bruce F.
  See Springsteen, Bruce
Spurling, Hilary 1940- .... **CLC 34**
  See also CA 104; CANR 25, 52, 94, 157, 224
Spurling, Susan Hilary
  See Spurling, Hilary
Spyker, John Howland
  See Elman, Richard (Martin)

Squared, A.
  See Abbott, Edwin A.
Squires, (James) Radcliffe
  1917-1993 .... **CLC 51**
  See also CA 1-4R; 140; CANR 6, 21; CP 1,
  2, 3, 4, 5
Surdas c. 1478-c. 1583 .... **LC 163**
  See also RGWL 2, 3
Srivastav, Dhanpat Ray
  See Srivastava, Dhanpat Rai
Srivastav, Dheanpatrai
  See Srivastava, Dhanpat Rai
Srivastava, Dhanpat Rai
  1880(?)-1936 .... **TCLC 21**
  See also CA 118; 197; EWL 3
Soseki Natsume 1867-1916 .... **TCLC 2,**
  10, 271
  See also CA 104; 195; DLB 180; EWL 3;
  MJW; RGWL 2, 3; TWA
Ssu-ma Ch'ien
  c. 145B.C.-c. 86B.C. .... **CMLC 96**
Ssu-ma T'an (?)-c. 110B.C. .... **CMLC 96**
Stacy, Donald
  See Pohl, Frederik
Stafford, Jean 1915-1979 .... **CLC 4, 7, 19,**
  68; SSC 26, 86
  See also CA 1-4R; 85-88; CANR 3, 65; CN 1,
  2; DLB 2, 173; MAL 5; MTCW 1, 2;
  MTFW 2005; RGAL 4; RGSF 2; SATA-
  Obit 22; SSFS 21; TCWW 1, 2; TUS
Stafford, William 1914-1993 .... **CLC 4, 7,**
  29; PC 71
  See also AMWS 11; CA 5-8R; 142; CAAS
  3; CANR 5, 22; CP 1, 2, 3, 4, 5;
  DAM POET; DLB 5, 206; EXPP; INT
  CANR-22; MAL 5; PFS 2, 8, 16; RGAL
  4; WP
Stafford, William Edgar
  See Stafford, William
Stagnelius, Eric Johan
  1793-1823 .... **NCLC 61**
Staines, Trevor
  See Brunner, John (Kilian Houston)
Stairs, Gordon
  See Austin, Mary Hunter
Stael
  See Stael-Holstein, Anne Louise Germaine
  Necker
Stael, Germaine de
  See Stael-Holstein, Anne Louise Germaine
  Necker
Stael-Holstein, Anne Louise Germaine Necker
  1766-1817 .... **NCLC 3, 91**
  See also DLB 119, 192; EW 5; FL 1:3; FW;
  GFL 1789 to the Present; RGWL 2, 3; TWA
Stalin, Joseph 1879-1953 .... **TCLC 92**
Stampa, Gaspara c. 1524-1554 .... **LC 114;**
  PC 43
  See also RGWL 2, 3; WLIT 7
Stampflinger, K.A.
  See Benjamin, Walter
Stancykowna
  See Szymborska, Wislawa
Standing Bear, Luther
  1868(?)-1939(?) .... **NNAL**
  See also CA 113; 144; DAM MULT
Stanislavsky, Constantin
  1863(?)-1938 .... **TCLC 167**
  See also CA 118
Stanislavsky, Konstantin
  See Stanislavsky, Constantin
Stanislavsky, Konstantin Sergeievich
  See Stanislavsky, Constantin
Stanislavsky, Konstantin Sergeivich
  See Stanislavsky, Constantin
Stanislavsky, Konstantin Sergeyevich
  See Stanislavsky, Constantin

Stannard, Martin 1947- .... **CLC 44**
  See also CA 142; CANR 229; DLB 155
Stanton, Elizabeth Cady
  1815-1902 .... **TCLC 73**
  See also CA 171; DLB 79; FL 1:3; FW
Stanton, Maura 1946- .... **CLC 9**
  See also CA 89-92; CANR 15, 123; DLB 120
Stanton, Schuyler
  See Baum, L. Frank
Stapledon, (William) Olaf
  1886-1950 .... **TCLC 22**
  See also CA 111; 162; DLB 15, 255; SCFW
  1, 2; SFW 4
Starbuck, George (Edwin)
  1931-1996 .... **CLC 53**
  See also CA 21-24R; 153; CANR 23; CP 1,
  2, 3, 4, 5, 6; DAM POET
Stark, Richard
  See Westlake, Donald E.
Statius c. 45-c. 96 .... **CMLC 91**
  See also AW 2; DLB 211
Staunton, Schuyler
  See Baum, L. Frank
Stead, Christina (Ellen)
  1902-1983 .... **CLC 2, 5, 8, 32, 80;**
  TCLC 244
  See also BRWS 4; CA 13-16R; 109; CANR
  33, 40; CN 1, 2, 3; DLB 260; EWL 3; FW;
  MTCW 1, 2; MTFW 2005; NFS 27; RGEL
  2; RGSF 2; WWE 1
Stead, Robert J(ames) C(ampbell)
  1880-1959 .... **TCLC 225**
  See also CA 186; DLB 92; TCWW 1, 2
Stead, William Thomas 1849-1912 .. **TCLC 48**
  See also BRWS 13; CA 167
Stebnitsky, M.
  See Leskov, Nikolai (Semyonovich)
Stedman, M. L. 19??- .... **CLC 354**
Steele, Richard 1672-1729 .... **LC 18,**
  156, 159
  See also BRW 3; CDBLB 1660-1789; DLB
  84, 101; RGEL 2; WLIT 3
Steele, Timothy (Reid)
  1948- .... **CLC 45**
  See also CA 93-96; CANR 16, 50, 92; CP 5,
  6, 7; DLB 120, 282
Steffens, (Joseph) Lincoln
  1866-1936 .... **TCLC 20**
  See also CA 117; 198; DLB 303; MAL 5
Stegner, Wallace 1909-1993 .... **CLC 9, 49,**
  81; SSC 27; TCLC 281
  See also AITN 1; AMWS 4; ANW; BEST
  90:3; BPFB 3; CA 1-4R; 141; CAAS 9;
  CANR 1, 21, 46; CN 1, 2, 3, 4, 5; DAM
  NOV; DLB 9, 206, 275; DLBY 1993;
  EWL 3; MAL 5; MTCW 1, 2; MTFW
  2005; RGAL 4; TCWW 1, 2; TUS
Stegner, Wallace Earle
  See Stegner, Wallace
Stein, Gertrude 1874-1946 ... **DC 19; PC 18;**
  SSC 42, 105; TCLC 1, 6, 28, 48, 276;
  WLC 5
  See also AAYA 64; AMW; AMWC 2; CA
  104; 132; CANR 108; CDALB 1917-1929;
  DA; DA3; DAB; DAC; DAM MST, NOV,
  POET; DLB 4, 54, 86, 228; DLBD 15;
  EWL 3; EXPS; FL 1:6; GLL 1; MAL 5;
  MBL; MTCW 1, 2; MTFW 2005; NCFS 4;
  NFS 27; PFS 38; RGAL 4; RGSF 2; SSFS
  5; TUS; WP
Steinbeck, John
  1902-1968 .... **CLC 1, 5, 9,**
  13, 21, 34, 45, 75, 124; DC 46; SSC 11,
  37, 77, 135; TCLC 135; WLC 5
  See also AAYA 12; AMW; BPFB 3; BYA 2,
  3, 13; CA 1-4R; 25-28R; CANR 1, 35;
  CDALB 1929-1941; CLR 172; DA; DA3;
  DAB; DAC; DAM DRAM, MST, NOV;
  DLB 7, 9, 212, 275, 309, 332, 364; DLBD

2; EWL 3; EXPS; LAIT 3; MAL 5;
MTCW 1, 2; MTFW 2005; NFS 1, 5, 7,
17, 19, 28, 34, 37, 39; RGAL 4; RGSF 2;
RHW; SATA 9; SSFS 3, 6, 22; TCWW 1,
2; TUS; WYA; YAW

Steinbeck, John Ernst
See Steinbeck, John

Steinem, Gloria 1934- .... **CLC 63**
See also CA 53-56; CANR 28, 51, 139; DLB
246; FL 1:1; FW; MTCW 1, 2; MTFW
2005

Steiner, George 1929- .... **CLC 24, 221**
See also CA 73-76; CANR 31, 67, 108, 212;
DAM NOV; DLB 67, 299; EWL 3; MTCW
1, 2; MTFW 2005; RGHL; SATA 62

Steiner, K. Leslie
See Delany, Samuel R., Jr.

Steiner, Rudolf 1861-1925 .... **TCLC 13**
See also CA 107

Stendhal 1783-1842 .... **NCLC 23, 46, 178;**
SSC 27; WLC 5
See also DA; DA3; DAB; DAC; DAM MST,
NOV; DLB 119; EW 5; GFL 1789 to the
Present; RGWL 2, 3; TWA

Stephen, Adeline Virginia
See Woolf, Virginia

Stephen, Sir Leslie 1832-1904 .... **TCLC 23**
See also BRW 5; CA 123; DLB 57, 144, 190

Stephen, Sir Leslie
See Stephen, Sir Leslie

Stephen, Virginia
See Woolf, Virginia

Stephens, James 1882(?)-1950 .... **SSC 50;**
TCLC 4
See also CA 104; 192; DLB 19, 153, 162;
EWL 3; FANT; RGEL 2; SUFW

Stephens, Reed
See Donaldson, Stephen R.

Stephenson, Neal 1959- .... **CLC 220**
See also AAYA 38; CA 122; CANR 88, 138,
195; CN 7; MTFW 2005; SFW 4

Steptoe, Lydia
See Barnes, Djuna

Sterchi, Beat 1949- .... **CLC 65**
See also CA 203

Sterling, Brett
See Bradbury, Ray; Hamilton, Edmond

Sterling, Bruce 1954- .... **CLC 72**
See also AAYA 78; CA 119; CANR 44, 135,
184; CN 7; MTFW 2005; SCFW 2; SFW 4

Sterling, George 1869-1926 .... **TCLC 20**
See also CA 117; 165; DLB 54

Stern, Gerald 1925- ... **CLC 40, 100; PC 115**
See also AMWS 9; CA 81-84; CANR 28,
94, 206; CP 3, 4, 5, 6, 7; DLB 105; PFS
26; RGAL 4

Stern, Richard (Gustave) 1928- ... **CLC 4, 39**
See also CA 1-4R; CANR 1, 25, 52, 120;
CN 1, 2, 3, 4, 5, 6, 7; DLB 218; DLBY
1987; INT CANR-25

Sternberg, Josef von 1894-1969 ..... **CLC 20**
See also CA 81-84

Sterne, Laurence 1713-1768 .... **LC 2, 48,**
156; WLC 5
See also BRW 3; BRWC 1; CDBLB 1660-
1789; DA; DAB; DAC; DAM MST, NOV;
DLB 39; RGEL 2; TEA

Sternheim, (William Adolf) Carl
1878-1942 .... **TCLC 8, 223**
See also CA 105; 193; DLB 56, 118; EWL
3; IDTP; RGWL 2, 3

Stetson, Charlotte Perkins
See Gilman, Charlotte Perkins

Stevens, Margaret Dean
See Aldrich, Bess Streeter

Stevens, Mark 1951- .... **CLC 34**
See also CA 122

Stevens, R. L.
See Hoch, Edward D.

Stevens, Wallace 1879-1955 .... **PC 6, 110;**
TCLC 3, 12, 45; WLC 5
See also AMW; AMWR 1; CA 104; 124;
CANR 181; CDALB 1929-1941; DA;
DA3; DAB; DAC; DAM MST, POET;
DLB 54, 342; EWL 3; EXPP; MAL 5;
MTCW 1, 2; PAB; PFS 13, 16, 35, 41;
RGAL 4; TUS; WP

Stevenson, Anne (Katharine)
1933- .... **CLC 7, 33**
See also BRWS 6; CA 17-20R; CAAS 9;
CANR 9, 33, 123; CP 3, 4, 5, 6, 7; CWP;
DLB 40; MTCW 1; RHW

Stevenson, Robert Louis 1850-1894 ... **NCLC 5,**
14, 63, 193, 274; PC 84; SSC 11, 51, 126;
WLC 5
See also AAYA 24; BPFB 3; BRW 5; BRWC
1; BRWR 1; BYA 1, 2, 4, 13; CDBLB
1890-1914; CLR 10, 11, 107, 180; DA;
DA3; DAB; DAC; DAM MST, NOV; DLB
18, 57, 141, 156, 174; DLBD 13; GL 3;
HGG; JRDA; LAIT 1, 3; MAICYA 1, 2;
NFS 11, 20, 33; RGEL 2; RGSF 2; SATA
100; SUFW; TEA; WCH; WLIT 4; WYA;
YABC 2; YAW

Stevenson, Robert Louis Balfour
See Stevenson, Robert Louis

Stewart, J(ohn) I(nnes) M(ackintosh) 1906-
1994 .... **CLC 7, 14, 32**
See also CA 85-88; 147; CAAS 3; CANR
47; CMW 4; CN 1, 2, 3, 4, 5; DLB 276;
MSW; MTCW 1, 2

Stewart, Mary (Florence Elinor)
1916- .... **CLC 7, 35, 117**
See also AAYA 29, 73; BPFB 3; CA 1-4R;
CANR 1, 59, 130; CMW 4; CPW; DAB;
FANT; RHW; SATA 12; YAW

Stewart, Mary Rainbow
See Stewart, Mary (Florence Elinor)

Stewart, Will
See Williamson, John Stewart

Stifle, June
See Campbell, Maria

Stifter, Adalbert 1805-1868 .... **NCLC 41,**
198; SSC 28
See also CDWLB 2; DLB 133; RGSF 2;
RGWL 2, 3

Still, James 1906-2001 .... **CLC 49**
See also CA 65-68; 195; CAAS 17; CANR
10, 26; CSW; DLB 9; DLBY 01; SATA 29;
SATA-Obit 127

Sting 1951- .... **CLC 26**
See also CA 167

Stirling, Arthur
See Sinclair, Upton

Stitt, Milan 1941-2009 .... **CLC 29**
See also CA 69-72; 284

Stitt, Milan William
See Stitt, Milan

Stockton, Francis Richard
1834-1902 .... **TCLC 47**
See also AAYA 68; BYA 4, 13; CA 108;
137; DLB 42, 74; DLBD 13; EXPS; MAI-
CYA 1, 2; SATA 44; SATA-Brief 32; SFW
4; SSFS 3; SUFW; WCH

Stockton, Frank R.
See Stockton, Francis Richard

Stoddard, Charles
See Kuttner, Henry

Stoker, Abraham
See Stoker, Bram

Stoker, Bram 1847-1912 .... **SSC 62;**
TCLC 8, 144; WLC 6
See also AAYA 23; BPFB 3; BRWS 3; BYA
5; CA 105; 150; CDBLB 1890-1914; CLR
178; DA; DA3; DAB; DAC; DAM MST,
NOV; DLB 304; GL 3; HGG; LATS 1:1;

MTFW 2005; NFS 18; RGEL 2; SATA 29;
SUFW; TEA; WLIT 4

Stolz, Mary 1920-2006 .... **CLC 12**
See also AAYA 8, 73; AITN 1; CA 5-8R;
255; CANR 13, 41, 112; JRDA; MAICYA
1, 2; SAAS 3; SATA 10, 71, 133; SATA-
Obit 180; YAW

Stolz, Mary Slattery
See Stolz, Mary

Stone, Irving 1903-1989 .... **CLC 7**
See also AITN 1; BPFB 3; CA 1-4R; 129;
CAAS 3; CANR 1, 23; CN 1, 2, 3, 4;
CPW; DA3; DAM POP; INT CANR-23;
MTCW 1, 2; MTFW 2005; RHW; SATA
3; SATA-Obit 64

Stone, Lucy 1818-1893 .... **NCLC 250**
See also DLB 79, 239

Stone, Oliver 1946- .... **CLC 73**
See also AAYA 15, 64; CA 110; CANR
55, 125

Stone, Oliver William
See Stone, Oliver

Stone, Robert 1937- .... **CLC 5, 23, 42,**
175, 331
See also AMWS 5; BPFB 3; CA 85-88;
CANR 23, 66, 95, 173; CN 4, 5, 6, 7;
DLB 152; EWL 3; INT CANR-23; MAL 5;
MTCW 1; MTFW 2005

Stone, Robert Anthony
See Stone, Robert

Stone, Ruth 1915-2011 .... **PC 53**
See also CA 45-48; CANR 2, 91, 209; CP 5,
6, 7; CSW; DLB 105; PFS 19, 40

Stone, Zachary
See Follett, Ken

Stoppard, Tom 1937- .... **CLC 1, 3, 4,**
5, 8, 15, 29, 34, 63, 91, 328; DC 6, 30;
WLC 6
See also AAYA 63; BRWC 1; BRWR 2;
BRWS 1; CA 81-84; CANR 39, 67, 125;
CBD; CD 5, 6; CDBLB 1960 to Present;
DA; DA3; DAB; DAC; DAM DRAM,
MST; DFS 2, 5, 8, 11, 13, 16; DLB 13,
233; DLBY 1985; EWL 3; LATS 1:2;
LNFS 3; MTCW 1, 2; MTFW 2005;
RGEL 2; TEA; WLIT 4

Storey, David (Malcolm) 1933- .... **CLC 2, 4,**
5, 8; DC 40
See also BRWS 1; CA 81-84; CANR 36;
CBD; CD 5, 6; CN 1, 2, 3, 4, 5, 6; DAM
DRAM; DLB 13, 14, 207, 245, 326; EWL
3; MTCW 1; RGEL 2

Storm, Hyemeyohsts 1935- ... **CLC 3; NNAL**
See also CA 81-84; CANR 45; DAM MULT

Storm, (Hans) Theodor (Woldsen)
1817-1888 .... **NCLC 1, 195;**
SSC 27, 106
See also CDWLB 2; DLB 129; EW; RGSF
2; RGWL 2, 3

Storni, Alfonsina 1892-1938 .... **HLC 2;**
PC 33; TCLC 5, 281
See also CA 104; 131; DAM MULT; DLB
283; HW 1; LAW

Stoughton, William 1631-1701 .... **LC 38**
See also DLB 24

Stout, Rex (Todhunter) 1886-1975 ... **CLC 3**
See also AAYA 79; AITN 2; BPFB 3; CA
61-64; CANR 71; CMW 4; CN 2; DLB
306; MSW; RGAL 4

Stow, John 1525-1605 .... **LC 186**
See also DLB 132; RGEL 2

Stow, (Julian) Randolph 1935- .... **CLC 23, 48**
See also CA 13-16R; CANR 33; CN 1, 2, 3,
4, 5, 6, 7; CP 1, 2, 3, 4; DLB 260; MTCW
1; RGEL 2

Stowe, Harriet Beecher 1811-1896 ... **NCLC 3,**
50, 133, 195; SSC 159; WLC 6
See also AAYA 53; AMWS 1; CDALB
1865-1917; CLR 131; DA; DA3; DAB;
DAC; DAM MST, NOV; DLB 1, 12, 42,

74, 189, 239, 243; EXPN; FL 1:3; JRDA; LAIT 2; MAICYA 1, 2; NFS 6; RGAL 4; TUS; YABC 1

Stowe, Harriet Elizabeth Beecher
See Stowe, Harriet Beecher

Strabo c. 63B.C.-c. 21 .... **CMLC 37, 121**
See also DLB 176

Strachey, (Giles) Lytton 1880-1932 .. **TCLC 12**
See also BRWS 2; CA 110; 178; DLB 149; DLBD 10; EWL 3; MTCW 2; NCFS 4

Stramm, August 1874-1915 .... **PC 50**
See also CA 195; EWL 3

Strand, Mark 1934- .... **CLC 6, 18, 41, 71; PC 63**
See also AMWS 4; CA 21-24R; CANR 40, 65, 100; CP 1, 2, 3, 4, 5, 6, 7; DAM POET; DLB 5; EWL 3; MAL 5; PAB; PFS 9, 18; RGAL 4; SATA 41; TCLE 1:2

Stratton-Porter, Gene 1863-1924 ... **TCLC 21**
See also AMWS 20; ANW; BPFB 3; CA 112; 137; CLR 87; CWRI 5; DLB 221; DLBD 14; MAICYA 1, 2; RHW; SATA 15

Stratton-Porter, Geneva Grace
See Stratton-Porter, Gene

Straub, Peter 1943- .... **CLC 28, 107**
See also AAYA 82; BEST 89:1; BPFB 3; CA 85-88; CANR 28, 65, 109; CPW; DAM POP; DLBY 1984; HGG; MTCW 1, 2; MTFW 2005; SUFW 2

Straub, Peter Francis
See Straub, Peter

Strauss, Botho 1944- .... **CLC 22**
See also CA 157; CWW 2; DLB 124

Strauss, Leo 1899-1973 .... **TCLC 141**
See also CA 101; 45-48; CANR 122

Streatfeild, Mary Noel
See Streatfeild, Noel

Streatfeild, Noel 1897(?)-1986 .... **CLC 21**
See also CA 81-84; 120; CANR 31; CLR 17, 83; CWRI 5; DLB 160; MAICYA 1, 2; SATA 20; SATA-Obit 48

Stribling, T(homas) S(igismund)
1881-1965 .... **CLC 23**
See also CA 189; 107; CMW 4; DLB 9; RGAL 4

Strindberg, August 1849-1912 .... **DC 18; TCLC 1, 8, 21, 47, 231; WLC 6**
See also CA 104; 135; DA; DA3; DAB; DAC; DAM DRAM, MST; DFS 4, 9, 29; DLB 259; EW 7; EWL 3; IDTP; LMFS 2; MTCW 2; MTFW 2005; RGWL 2, 3; TWA

Strindberg, Johan August
See Strindberg, August

Stringer, Arthur 1874-1950 .... **TCLC 37**
See also CA 161; DLB 92

Stringer, David
See Roberts, Keith (John Kingston)

Stroheim, Erich von 1885-1957 .... **TCLC 71**

Strout, Elizabeth 1956- .... **CLC 299**
See also AMWS 23; CA 178; CANR 154, 190; NFS 39

Strugatskii, Arkadii 1925-1991 .... **CLC 27**
See also CA 106; 135; DLB 302; SFW 4

Strugatskii, Arkadii Natanovich
See Strugatskii, Arkadii

Strugatskii, Boris 1933- .... **CLC 27**
See also CA 106; DLB 302; SFW 4

Strugatskii, Boris Natanovich
See Strugatskii, Boris

Strugatsky, Arkadii Natanovich
See Strugatskii, Arkadii

Strugatsky, Boris
See Strugatskii, Boris

Strugatsky, Boris Natanovich
See Strugatskii, Boris

Strummer, Joe 1952-2002 .... **CLC 30**

Strunk, William, Jr. 1869-1946 .... **TCLC 92**
See also CA 118; 164; NCFS 5

Stryk, Lucien 1924- .... **PC 27**
See also CA 13-16R; CANR 10, 28, 55, 110; CP 1, 2, 3, 4, 5, 6, 7

Stuart, Don A.
See Campbell, John W.

Stuart, Ian
See MacLean, Alistair

Stuart, Jesse (Hilton) 1906-1984 ..... **CLC 1, 8, 11, 14, 34; SSC 31**
See also CA 5-8R; 112; CANR 31; CN 1, 2, 3; DLB 9, 48, 102; DLBY 1984; SATA 2; SATA-Obit 36

Stubblefield, Sally
See Trumbo, Dalton

Sturgeon, Theodore (Hamilton)
1918-1985 .... **CLC 22, 39**
See also AAYA 51; BPFB 3; BYA 9, 10; CA 81-84; 116; CANR 32, 103; DLB 8; DLBY 1985; HGG; MTCW 1, 2; MTFW 2005; SCFW 2; SFW 4; SUFW

Sturges, Preston 1898-1959 .... **TCLC 48**
See also CA 114; 149; DLB 26

Styron, William 1925-2006 ...... **CLC 1, 3, 5, 11, 15, 60, 232, 244; SSC 25**
See also AMW; AMWC 2; BEST 90:4; BPFB 3; CA 5-8R; 255; CANR 6, 33, 74, 126, 191; CDALB 1968-1988; CN 1, 2, 3, 4, 5, 6, 7; CPW; CSW; DA3; DAM NOV, POP; DLB 2, 143, 299; DLBY 1980; EWL 3; INT CANR-6; LAIT 2; MAL 5; MTCW 1, 2; MTFW 2005; NCFS 1; NFS 22; RGAL 4; RGHL; RHW; TUS

Styron, William C.
See Styron, William

Styron, William Clark
See Styron, William

Su, Chien 1884-1918 .... **TCLC 24**
See also CA 123; EWL 3

Suarez Lynch, B.
See Bioy Casares, Adolfo; Borges, Jorge Luis

Suassuna, Ariano Vilar 1927- .... **HLCS 1**
See also CA 178; DLB 307; HW 2; LAW

Suckert, Kurt Erich
See Malaparte, Curzio

Suckling, Sir John 1609-1642 .... **LC 75; PC 30**
See also BRW 2; DAM POET; DLB 58, 126; EXPP; PAB; RGEL 2

Suckow, Ruth 1892-1960 .... **SSC 18; TCLC 257**
See also CA 193; 113; DLB 9, 102; RGAL 4; TCWW 2

Sudermann, Hermann 1857-1928 ... **TCLC 15**
See also CA 107; 201; DLB 118

Sue, Eugene 1804-1857 .... **NCLC 1**
See also DLB 119

Sueskind, Patrick
See Suskind, Patrick

Suetonius c. 70-c. 130 .... **CMLC 60**
See also AW 2; DLB 211; RGWL 2, 3; WLIT 8

Su Hsuan-ying
See Su, Chien

Su Hsuean-ying
See Su, Chien

Sui Sin Far
See Eaton, Edith Maude

Sukenick, Ronald 1932-2004 .... **CLC 3, 4, 6, 48**
See also CA 25-28R; 209; 229; CAAE 209; CAAS 8; CANR 32, 89; CN 3, 4, 5, 6, 7; DLB 173; DLBY 1981

Suknaski, Andrew 1942- .... **CLC 19**
See also CA 101; CP 3, 4, 5, 6, 7; DLB 53

Sullivan, Vernon
See Vian, Boris

Sully Prudhomme, Rene-Francois-Armand
1839-1907 .... **TCLC 31**

See also CA 170; DLB 332; GFL 1789 to the Present

Sulpicius Severus
c. 363-c. 425 .... **CMLC 120**

Su Man-shu
See Su, Chien

Sumarokov, Aleksandr Petrovich
1717-1777 .... **LC 104**
See also DLB 150

Summerforest, Ivy B.
See Kirkup, James

Summers, Andrew James
See Summers, Andy

Summers, Andy 1942- .... **CLC 26**
See also CA 255

Summers, Hollis (Spurgeon, Jr.)
1916- .... **CLC 10**
See also CA 5-8R; CANR 3; CN 1, 2, 3; CP 1, 2, 3, 4; DLB 6; TCLE 1:2

Summers, (Alphonsus Joseph-Mary Augustus) Montague
1880-1948 .... **TCLC 16**
See also CA 118; 163

Sumner, Gordon Matthew
See Sting

Sun Tzu c. 400B.C.-c. 320B.C. .... **CMLC 56**

Surayya, Kamala
See Das, Kamala

Surayya Kamala
See Das, Kamala

Surrey, Henry Howard
1517-1574 .... **LC 121; PC 59**
See also BRW 1; RGEL 2

Surtees, Robert Smith
1805-1864 .... **NCLC 14**
See also DLB 21; RGEL 2

Susann, Jacqueline 1921-1974 .... **CLC 3**
See also AITN 1; BPFB 3; CA 65-68; 53-56; MTCW 1, 2

Su Shi 1037-1101 .... **CMLC 15, 139**
See also RGWL 2, 3

Su Shih 1037-1101 .... **CMLC 15, 139**
See also RGWL 2, 3

Suskind, Patrick 1949- .... **CLC 44, 182, 339**
See also BPFB 3; CA 145; CWW 2

Suso, Heinrich c. 1295-1366 ... **CMLC 87, 150**

Sutcliff, Rosemary 1920-1992 .... **CLC 26**
See also AAYA 10; BRWS 16; BYA 1, 4; CA 5-8R; 139; CANR 37; CLR 1, 37, 138; CPW; DAB; DAC; DAM MST, POP; JRDA; LATS 1:1; MAICYA 1, 2; MAICYAS 1; RHW; SATA 6, 44, 78; SATA-Obit 73; WYA; YAW

Sutherland, Efua (Theodora Morgue)
1924-1996 .... **BLC 2:3**
See also AFW; BW 1; CA 105; CWD; DLB 117; EWL 3; IDTP; SATA 25

Sutro, Alfred 1863-1933 .... **TCLC 6**
See also CA 105; 185; DLB 10; RGEL 2

Sutton, Henry
See Slavitt, David R.

Su Yuan-ying
See Su, Chien

Su Yuean-ying
See Su, Chien

Suzuki, D. T.
See Suzuki, Daisetz Teitaro

Suzuki, Daisetz T.
See Suzuki, Daisetz Teitaro

Suzuki, Daisetz Teitaro
1870-1966 .... **TCLC 109**
See also CA 121; 111; MTCW 1, 2; MTFW 2005

Suzuki, Teitaro
See Suzuki, Daisetz Teitaro

Svareff, Count Vladimir
See Crowley, Edward Alexander

Tate, Nahum 1652(?)-1715 .... **LC 109**
See also DLB 80; RGEL 2

Tauler, Johannes c. 1300-1361 ..... **CMLC 37**
See also DLB 179; LMFS 1

Tavel, Ronald 1936-2009 .... **CLC 6**
See also CA 21-24R; 284; CAD; CANR 33;
CD 5, 6

Taviani, Paolo 1931- .... **CLC 70**
See also CA 153

Tawada, Yoko 1960- .... **CLC 310**
See also CA 296

Taylor, Bayard 1825-1878 .... **NCLC 89**
See also DLB 3, 189, 250, 254, 366; RGAL 4

Taylor, C(ecil) P(hilip) 1929-1981 .. **CLC 27**
See also CA 25-28R; 105; CANR 47; CBD

Taylor, Charles 1931- .... **CLC 317**
See also CA 13-16R; CANR 11, 27, 164, 200,
241

Taylor, Charles Margrave
See Taylor, Charles

Taylor, Edward 1642(?)-1729 ... **LC 11, 163;
PC 63**
See also AMW; DA; DAB; DAC; DAM
MST, POET; DLB 24; EXPP; PFS 31;
RGAL 4; TUS

Taylor, Eleanor Ross 1920-2011 .... **CLC 5**
See also CA 81-84; CANR 70

Taylor, Elizabeth
1912-1975 .... **CLC 2, 4, 29; SSC 100**
See also CA 13-16R; CANR 9, 70; CN 1, 2;
DLB 139; MTCW 1; RGEL 2; SATA 13

Taylor, Frederick Winslow
1856-1915 .... **TCLC 76**
See also CA 188

Taylor, Henry 1942- .... **CLC 44**
See also CA 33-36R; CAAS 7; CANR 31,
178; CP 6, 7; DLB 5; PFS 10

Taylor, Henry Splawn
See Taylor, Henry

Taylor, Jane 1783-1824 .... **NCLC 279**
See also DLB 163; SATA 35, 41

Taylor, Kamala
See Markandaya, Kamala

Taylor, Mildred D. 1943- .... **CLC 21**
See also AAYA 10, 47; BW 1; BYA 3, 8; CA
85-88; CANR 25, 115, 136; CLR 9, 59, 90,
144; CSW; DLB 52; JRDA; LAIT 3;
MAICYA 1, 2; MTFW 2005; SAAS 5;
SATA 135, WYA; YAW

Taylor, Peter (Hillsman)
1917-1994 .... **CLC 1, 4, 18, 37, 44,
50, 71; SSC 10, 84**
See also AMWS 5; BPFB 3; CA 13-16R;
147; CANR 9, 50; CN 1, 2, 3, 4, 5; CSW;
DLB 218, 278; DLBY 1981, 1994; EWL
3; EXPS; INT CANR-9; MAL 5; MTCW
1, 2; MTFW 2005; RGSF 2; SSFS 9; TUS

Taylor, Robert Lewis 1912-1998 .... **CLC 14**
See also CA 1-4R; 170; CANR 3, 64; CN 1,
2; SATA 10; TCWW 1, 2

Tchekhov, Anton
See Chekhov, Anton

Tchicaya, Gerald Felix
1931-1988 .... **CLC 101**
See also CA 129; 125; CANR 81; EWL 3

Tchicaya U Tam'si
See Tchicaya, Gerald Felix

Teasdale, Sara 1884-1933 ... **PC 31; TCLC 4**
See also CA 104; 163; DLB 45; GLL 1; PFS
14; RGAL 4; SATA 32; TUS

Tecumseh 1768-1813 .... **NNAL**
See also DAM MULT

Tegner, Esaias 1782-1846 .... **NCLC 2**

Teilhard de Chardin, (Marie Joseph) Pierre
1881-1955 .... **TCLC 9**
See also CA 105; 210; GFL 1789 to the Present

Temple, Ann
See Mortimer, Penelope (Ruth)

Tennant, Emma 1937- .... **CLC 13, 52**
See also BRWS 9; CA 65-68; CAAS 9;
CANR 10, 38, 59, 88, 177; CN 3, 4, 5,
6, 7; DLB 14; EWL 3; SFW 4

Tenneshaw, S.M.
See Silverberg, Robert

Tenney, Tabitha Gilman
1762-1837 .... **NCLC 122, 248**
See also DLB 37, 200

Tennyson, Alfred 1809-1892 .... **NCLC 30,
65, 115, 202; PC 6, 101; WLC 6**
See also AAYA 50; BRW 4; BRWR 3;
CDBLB 1832-1890; DA; DA3; DAB;
DAC; DAM MST, POET; DLB 32; EXPP;
PAB; PFS 1, 2, 4, 11, 15, 19, 44; RGEL 2;
TEA; WLIT 4; WP

Teran, Lisa St. Aubin de
See St. Aubin de Teran, Lisa

Terence c. 184B.C.-c. 159B.C. ..... **CMLC 14,
132; DC 7**
See also AW 1; CDWLB 1; DLB 211;
RGWL 2, 3; TWA; WLIT 8

Teresa de Jesus, St. 1515-1582 ... **LC 18, 149**

Teresa of Avila, St.
See Teresa de Jesus, St.

Terkel, Louis
See Terkel, Studs

Terkel, Studs 1912-2008 .... **CLC 38**
See also AAYA 32; AITN 1; CA 57-60; 278;
CANR 18, 45, 67, 132, 195; DA3; MTCW
1, 2; MTFW 2005; TUS

Terkel, Studs Louis
See Terkel, Studs

Terry, C. V.
See Slaughter, Frank G(ill)

Terry, Megan 1932- .... **CLC 19; DC 13**
See also CA 77-80; CABS 3; CAD; CANR
43; CD 5, 6; CWD; DFS 18; DLB 7, 249;
GLL 2

Tertullian c. 155-c. 245 .... **CMLC 29**

Tertz, Abram
See Sinyavsky, Andrei (Donatevich)

Tesich, Steve 1943(?)-1996 .... **CLC 40, 69**
See also CA 105; 152; CAD; DLBY 1983

Tesla, Nikola 1856-1943 .... **TCLC 88**
See also CA 157

Teternikov, Fyodor Kuzmich
1863-1927 .... **TCLC 9, 259**
See also CA 104; DLB 295; EWL 3

Tevis, Walter 1928-1984 .... **CLC 42**
See also CA 113; SFW 4

Tey, Josephine
See Mackintosh, Elizabeth

Thackeray, William Makepeace
1811-1863 .... **NCLC 5, 14, 22, 43,
169, 213; WLC 6**
See also BRW 5; BRWC 2; CDBLB 1832-
1890; DA; DA3; DAB; DAC; DAM MST,
NOV; DLB 21, 55, 159, 163; NFS 13;
RGEL 2; SATA 23; TEA; WLIT 3

Thakura, Ravindranatha
See Tagore, Rabindranath

Thames, C. H.
See Marlowe, Stephen

Tharoor, Shashi 1956- .... **CLC 70**
See also CA 141; CANR 91, 201; CN 6, 7

The Coen Brothers
See Coen, Ethan; Coen, Joel

Thelwall, John 1764-1834 .... **NCLC 162**
See also DLB 93, 158

Thelwell, Michael Miles 1939- .... **CLC 22**
See also BW 2; CA 101

Theo, Ion
See Arghezi, Tudor

Theobald, Lewis, Jr.
See Lovecraft, H. P.

Theocritus c. 310B.C. .... **CMLC 45**
See also AW 1; DLB 176; RGWL 2, 3

Theodorescu, Ion N.
See Arghezi, Tudor

Therion, Master
See Crowley, Edward Alexander

Theroux, Alexander 1939- .... **CLC 2, 25**
See also CA 85-88; CANR 20, 63, 190; CN
4, 5, 6, 7

Theroux, Alexander Louis
See Theroux, Alexander

Theroux, Paul 1941- .... **CLC 5, 8, 11, 15,
28, 46, 159, 303**
See also AAYA 28; AMWS 8; BEST 89:4;
BPFB 3; CA 33-36R; CANR 20, 45, 74,
133, 179, 233; CDALBS; CN 1, 2, 3, 4, 5, 6,
7; CP 1; CPW 1; DA3; DAM POP; DLB 2,
218; EWL 3; HGG; MAL 5; MTCW 1, 2;
MTFW 2005; RGAL 4; SATA 44, 109; TUS

Theroux, Paul Edward
See Theroux, Paul

Thesen, Sharon 1946- .... **CLC 56**
See also CA 163; CANR 125; CP 5, 6, 7;
CWP

Thespis fl. 6th cent. B.C. .... **CMLC 51**
See also LMFS 1

Thevenin, Denis
See Duhamel, Georges

Thibault, Jacques Anatole Francois
See France, Anatole

Thiele, Colin 1920-2006 .... **CLC 17**
See also CA 29-32R; CANR 12, 28, 53, 105;
CLR 27; CP 1, 2; DLB 289; MAICYA 1,
2; SAAS 2; SATA 14, 72, 125; YAW

Thiong'o, Ngugi Wa
See Ngugi wa Thiong'o

Thistlethwaite, Bel
See Wetherald, Agnes Ethelwyn

Thomas, Audrey (Callahan) 1935- ... **CLC 7,
13, 37, 107, 289; SSC 20**
See also AITN 2; CA 21-24R, 237; CAAE
237; CAAS 19; CANR 36, 58; CN 2, 3, 4,
5, 6, 7; DLB 60; MTCW 1; RGSF 2

Thomas, Augustus 1857-1934 .... **TCLC 97**
See also MAL 5

Thomas, D.M. 1935- ... **CLC 13, 22, 31, 132**
See also BPFB 3; BRWS 4; CA 61-64, 303;
CAAE 303; CAAS 11; CANR 17, 45, 75;
CDBLB 1960 to Present; CN 4, 5, 6, 7; CP
1, 2, 3, 4, 5, 6, 7; DA3; DLB 40, 207, 299;
HGG; INT CANR-17; MTCW 1, 2;
MTFW 2005; RGHL; SFW 4

Thomas, Donald Michael
See Thomas, D.M.

Thomas, Dylan 1914-1953 .... **PC 2, 52;
SSC 3, 44; TCLC 1, 8, 45, 105; WLC 6**
See also AAYA 45; BRWR 3; BRWS 1; CA
104; 120; CANR 65; CDBLB 1945-1960;
DA; DA3; DAB; DAC; DAM DRAM,
MST, POET; DLB 13, 20, 139; EWL 3;
EXPP; LAIT 3; MTCW 1, 2; MTFW 2005;
PAB; PFS 1, 3, 8; RGEL 2; RGSF 2; SATA
60; TEA; WLIT 4; WP

Thomas, Dylan Marlais
See Thomas, Dylan

Thomas, (Philip) Edward
1878-1917 .... **PC 53; TCLC 10**
See also BRW 6; BRWS 3; CA 106; 153;
DAM POET; DLB 19, 98, 156, 216; EWL
3; PAB; RGEL 2

Thomas, J. F.
See Fleming, Thomas

Thomas, Joyce Carol 1938- .... **CLC 35**
See also AAYA 12, 54; BW 2, 3; CA 113;
116; CANR 48, 114, 135, 206; CLR 19;
DLB 33; INT CA-116; JRDA; MAICYA 1,
2; MTCW 1, 2; MTFW 2005; SAAS 7;
SATA 40, 78, 123, 137, 210; SATA-Essay
137; WYA; YAW

Thomas, Lewis 1913-1993 .... **CLC 35**
See also ANW; CA 85-88; 143; CANR 38, 60; DLB 275; MTCW 1, 2

Thomas, M. Carey 1857-1935 ...... **TCLC 89**
See also FW

Thomas, Paul
See Mann, Thomas

Thomas, Piri 1928-2011 .. **CLC 17; HLCS 2**
See also CA 73-76; HW 1; LLW; SSFS 28

Thomas, R(onald) S(tuart)
1913-2000 .... **CLC 6, 13, 48; PC 99**
See also BRWS 12; CA 89-92; 189; CAAS 4; CANR 30; CDBLB 1960 to Present; CP 1, 2, 3, 4, 5, 6, 7; DAB; DAM POET; DLB 27; EWL 3; MTCW 1; RGEL 2

Thomas, Ross (Elmore) 1926-1995 ... **CLC 39**
See also CA 33-36R; 150; CANR 22, 63; CMW 4

Thompson, Francis (Joseph)
1859-1907 .... **TCLC 4**
See also BRW 5; CA 104; 189; CDBLB 1890-1914; DLB 19; RGEL 2; TEA

Thompson, Francis Clegg
See Mencken, H. L.

Thompson, Hunter S.
1937(?)-2005 ... **CLC 9, 17, 40, 104, 229**
See also AAYA 45; BEST 89:1; BPFB 3; CA 17-20R; 236; CANR 23, 46, 74, 77, 111, 133; CPW; CSW; DA3; DAM POP; DLB 185; MTCW 1, 2; MTFW 2005; TUS

Thompson, Hunter Stockton
See Thompson, Hunter S.

Thompson, James Myers
See Thompson, Jim

Thompson, Jim 1906-1977 .... **CLC 69**
See also BPFB 3; CA 140; CMW 4; CPW; DLB 226; MSW

Thompson, Judith (Clare Francesca)
1954- .... **CLC 39**
See also CA 143; CD 5, 6; CWD; DFS 22; DLB 334

Thomson, James 1700-1748 ... **LC 16, 29, 40**
See also BRWS 3; DAM POET; DLB 95; RGEL 2

Thomson, James 1834-1882 .... **NCLC 18**
See also DAM POET; DLB 35; RGEL 2

Thoreau, Henry David
1817-1862 .... **NCLC 7, 21, 61, 138, 207; PC 30; WLC 6**
See also AAYA 42; AMW; ANW; BYA 3; CDALB 1640-1865; DA; DA3; DAB; DAC; DAM MST; DLB 1, 183, 223, 270, 298, 366; LAIT 2; LMFS 1; NCFS 3; RGAL 4; TUS

Thorndike, E. L.
See Thorndike, Edward L(ee)

Thorndike, Edward L(ee)
1874-1949 .... **TCLC 107**
See also CA 121

Thornton, Hall
See Silverberg, Robert

Thorpe, Adam 1956- .... **CLC 176**
See also CA 129; CANR 92, 160; DLB 231

Thorpe, Thomas Bangs
1815-1878 .... **NCLC 183**
See also DLB 3, 11, 248; RGAL 4

Theriault, Yves 1915-1983 .... **CLC 79**
See also CA 102; CANR 150; CCA 1; DAC; DAM MST; DLB 88; EWL 3

Thubron, Colin 1939- .... **CLC 163**
See also CA 25-28R; CANR 12, 29, 59, 95, 171, 232; CN 5, 6, 7; DLB 204, 231

Thubron, Colin Gerald Dryden
See Thubron, Colin

Thucydides
c. 455B.C.-c. 399B.C. .... **CMLC 17, 117**
See also AW 1; DLB 176; RGWL 2, 3; WLIT 8

Thumboo, Edwin Nadason 1933- .... **PC 30**
See also CA 194; CP 1

Thurber, James 1894-1961 .... **CLC 5, 11, 25, 125; SSC 1, 47, 137**
See also AAYA 56; AMWS 1; BPFB 3; BYA 5; CA 73-76; CANR 17, 39; CDALB 1929-1941; CWRI 5; DA; DA3; DAB; DAC; DAM DRAM, MST, NOV; DLB 4, 11, 22, 102; EWL 3; EXPS; FANT; LAIT 3; MAICYA 1, 2; MAL 5; MTCW 1, 2; MTFW 2005; RGAL 4; RGSF 2; SATA 13; SSFS 1, 10, 19, 37; SUFW; TUS

Thurber, James Grover
See Thurber, James

Thurman, Wallace (Henry)
1902-1934 .... **BLC 1:3; HR 1:3; TCLC 6**
See also BW 1, 3; CA 104; 124; CANR 81; DAM MULT; DLB 51

Toibin, Colm 1955- .... **CLC 162, 285**
See also CA 142; CANR 81, 149, 213; CN 7; DLB 271

Tibullus c. 54B.C.-c. 18B.C. .... **CMLC 36**
See also AW 2; DLB 211; RGWL 2, 3; WLIT 8

Ticheburn, Cheviot
See Ainsworth, William Harrison

Ticknor, George
1791-1871 .... **NCLC 255**
See also DLB 1, 59, 140, 235

Tieck, (Johann) Ludwig
1773-1853 ... **NCLC 5, 46; SSC 31, 100**
See also CDWLB 2; DLB 90; EW 5; IDTP; RGSF 2; RGWL 2, 3; SUFW

Tiger, Derry
See Ellison, Harlan

Tilghman, Christopher 1946- .... **CLC 65**
See also CA 159; CANR 135, 151; CSW; DLB 244

Tillich, Paul (Johannes)
1886-1965 .... **CLC 131**
See also CA 5-8R; 25-28R; CANR 33; MTCW 1, 2

Tillinghast, Richard (Williford)
1940- .... **CLC 29**
See also CA 29-32R; CAAS 23; CANR 26, 51, 96; CP 2, 3, 4, 5, 6, 7; CSW

Tillman, Lynne (?)- .... **CLC 231, 312**
See also CA 173; CANR 144, 172, 238

Timrod, Henry 1828-1867 .... **NCLC 25**
See also DLB 3, 248; RGAL 4

Tindall, Gillian (Elizabeth) 1938- ..... **CLC 7**
See also CA 21-24R; CANR 11, 65, 107; CN 1, 2, 3, 4, 5, 6, 7

Ting Ling
See Chiang, Pin-chin

Tiptree, James, Jr.
See Sheldon, Alice Hastings Bradley

Tirone Smith, Mary-Ann 1944- ...... **CLC 39**
See also CA 118; 136; CANR 113, 210; SATA 143

Tirso de Molina 1580(?)-1648 .... **DC 13; HLCS 2; LC 73**
See also RGWL 2, 3

Titmarsh, Michael Angelo
See Thackeray, William Makepeace

Tocqueville, Alexis (Charles Henri Maurice Clerel Comte) de
1805-1859 .... **NCLC 7, 63, 267**
See also EW 6; GFL 1789 to the Present; TWA

Toe, Tucker
See Westlake, Donald E.

Toer, Pramoedya Ananta
1925-2006 .... **CLC 186**
See also CA 197; 251; CANR 170; DLB 348; RGWL 3

Toffler, Alvin 1928- .... **CLC 168**
See also CA 13-16R; CANR 15, 46, 67, 183; CPW; DAM POP; MTCW 1, 2

Tolkien, J. R. R. 1892-1973 .... **CLC 1, 2, 3, 8, 12, 38; SSC 156; TCLC 137; WLC 6**
See also AAYA 10; AITN 1; BPFB 3; BRWC 2; BRWS 2; CA 17-18; 45-48; CANR 36, 134; CAP 2; CDBLB 1914-1945; CLR 56, 152; CN 1; CPW 1; CWRI 5; DA; DA3; DAB; DAC; DAM MST, NOV, POP; DLB 15, 160, 255; EFS 1:2, 2:1; EWL 3; FANT; JRDA; LAIT 1; LATS 1:2; LMFS 2; MAICYA 1, 2; MTCW 1, 2; MTFW 2005; NFS 8, 26; RGEL 2; SATA 2, 32, 100; SATA-Obit 24; SFW 4; SUFW; TEA; WCH; WYA; YAW

Tolkien, John Ronald Reuel
See Tolkien, J. R. R.

Toller, Ernst 1893-1939 .... **TCLC 10, 235**
See also CA 107; 186; DLB 124; EWL 3; RGWL 2, 3

Tolson, M. B.
See Tolson, Melvin B(eaunorus)

Tolson, Melvin B(eaunorus)
1898(?)-1966 .... **BLC 1:3; CLC 36, 105; PC 88**
See also AFAW 1, 2; BW 1, 3; CA 124; 89-92; CANR 80; DAM MULT, POET; DLB 48, 76; MAL 5; RGAL 4

Tolstoi, Aleksei Nikolaevich
See Tolstoy, Alexey Nikolaevich

Tolstoi, Lev
See Tolstoy, Leo

Tolstoi, Aleksei Nikolaevich
See Tolstoy, Alexey Nikolaevich

Tolstoy, Alexey Nikolaevich
1882-1945 .... **TCLC 18**
See also CA 107; 158; DLB 272; EWL 3; SFW 4

Tolstoy, Leo 1828-1910 .... **SSC 9, 30, 45, 54, 131; TCLC 4, 11, 17, 28, 44, 79, 173, 260; WLC 6**
See also AAYA 56; CA 104; 123; DA; DA3; DAB; DAC; DAM MST, NOV; DLB 238; EFS 1:2, 2:2; EW 7; EXPS; IDTP; LAIT 2; LATS 1:1; LMFS 1; NFS 10, 28, 37; RGSF 2; RGWL 2, 3; SATA 26; SSFS 5, 28; TWA

Tolstoy, Count Leo
See Tolstoy, Leo

Tolstoy, Leo Nikolaevich
See Tolstoy, Leo

Tomalin, Claire 1933- .... **CLC 166**
See also CA 89-92; CANR 52, 88, 165; DLB 155

Tomasi di Lampedusa, Giuseppe
See Lampedusa, Giuseppe di

Tomlin, Lily 1939(?)- .... **CLC 17**
See also CA 117

Tomlin, Mary Jane
See Tomlin, Lily

Tomlin, Mary Jean
See Tomlin, Lily

Tomline, F. Latour
See Gilbert, W(illiam) S(chwenck)

Tomlinson, (Alfred) Charles
1927- .... **CLC 2, 4, 6, 13, 45; PC 17**
See also CA 5-8R; CANR 33; CP 1, 2, 3, 4, 5, 6, 7; DAM POET; DLB 40; TCLE 1:2

Tomlinson, H(enry) M(ajor)
1873-1958 .... **TCLC 71**
See also CA 118; 161; DLB 36, 100, 195

Tomlinson, Mary Jane
See Tomlin, Lily

Tomson, Graham R.
See Watson, Rosamund Marriott

Tonna, Charlotte Elizabeth
1790-1846 .... **NCLC 135**
See also DLB 163

Verga, Giovanni (Carmelo)
    1840-1922 ... SSC 21, 87; TCLC 3, 227
    See also CA 104; 123; CANR 101; EW 7;
    EWL 3; RGSF 2; RGWL 2, 3; WLIT 7
Vergil 70B.C.-19B.C. ...... CMLC 9, 40, 101;
    PC 12; WLCS
    See also AW 2; CDWLB 1; DA; DA3; DAB;
    DAC; DAM MST, POET; DLB 211; EFS
    1:1, 2:1; LAIT 1; LMFS 1; RGWL 2, 3;
    WLIT 8; WP
Vergil, Polydore c. 1470-1555 .... LC 108
    See also DLB 132
Verhaeren, Emile (Adolphe Gustave)
    1855-1916 .... TCLC 12
    See also CA 109; EWL 3; GFL 1789 to the
    Present
Verlaine, Paul 1844-1896 .... NCLC 2, 51,
    230; PC 2, 32
    See also DAM POET; DLB 217; EW 7; GFL
    1789 to the Present; LMFS 2; RGWL 2, 3;
    TWA
Verlaine, Paul Marie
    See Verlaine, Paul
Verne, Jules 1828-1905 ..... TCLC 6, 52, 245
    See also AAYA 16; BYA 4; CA 110; 131;
    CLR 88; DA3; DLB 123; GFL 1789 to the
    Present; JRDA; LAIT 2; LMFS 2; MAI-
    CYA 1, 2; MTFW 2005; NFS 30, 34;
    RGWL 2, 3; SATA 21; SCFW 1, 2; SFW
    4; TWA; WCH
Verne, Jules Gabriel
    See Verne, Jules
Verus, Marcus Annius
    See Aurelius, Marcus
Very, Jones 1813-1880 .... NCLC 9; PC 86
    See also DLB 1, 243; RGAL 4
Very, Rev. C.
    See Crowley, Edward Alexander
Vesaas, Tarjei 1897-1970 .... CLC 48
    See also CA 190; 29-32R; DLB 297; EW 11;
    EWL 3; RGWL 3
Vialis, Gaston
    See Simenon, Georges
Vian, Boris 1920-1959(?) .... TCLC 9, 283
    See also CA 106; 164; CANR 111; DLB 72,
    321; EWL 3; GFL 1789 to the Present;
    MTCW 2; RGWL 2, 3
Viator, Vacuus
    See Hughes, Thomas
Viaud, Julien 1850-1923 .... TCLC 11, 239
    See also CA 107; DLB 123; GFL 1789 to the
    Present
Viaud, Louis Marie Julien
    See Viaud, Julien
Vicar, Henry
    See Felsen, Henry Gregor
Vicente, Gil
    1465-c. 1536 .... LC 99
    See also DLB 318; IDTP; RGWL 2, 3
Vicker, Angus
    See Felsen, Henry Gregor
Vico, Giambattista
    See Vico, Giovanni Battista
Vico, Giovanni Battista 1668-1744 .. LC 138
    See also EW 3; WLIT 7
Vidal, Eugene Luther Gore
    See Vidal, Gore
Vidal, Gore 1925- .... CLC 2, 4, 6, 8, 10,
    22, 33, 72, 142, 289
    See also AAYA 64; AITN 1; AMWS 4;
    BEST 90:2; BPFB 3; CA 5-8R; CAD;
    CANR 13, 45, 65, 100, 132, 167; CD 5,
    6; CDALBS; CN 1, 2, 3, 4, 5, 6, 7; CPW;
    DA3; DAM NOV, POP; DFS 2; DLB 6,
    152; EWL 3; GLL 1; INT CANR-13;
    MAL 5; MTCW 1, 2; MTFW 2005; RGAL
    4; RHW; TUS

Viereck, Peter 1916-2006 ...... CLC 4; PC 27
    See also CA 1-4R; 250; CANR 1, 47; CP 1,
    2, 3, 4, 5, 6, 7; DLB 5; MAL 5; PFS 9, 14
Viereck, Peter Robert Edwin
    See Viereck, Peter
Vigny, Alfred de 1797-1863 .... NCLC 7,
    102, 278; PC 26
    See also DAM POET; DLB 119, 192, 217;
    EW 5; GFL 1789 to the Present; RGWL 2, 3
Vigny, Alfred Victor de
    See Vigny, Alfred de
Vilakazi, Benedict Wallet
    1906-1947 .... TCLC 37
    See also CA 168
Vile, Curt
    See Moore, Alan
Villa, Jose Garcia 1914-1997 .... AAL;
    PC 22; TCLC 176
    See also CA 25-28R; CANR 12, 118; CP 1,
    2, 3, 4; DLB 312; EWL 3; EXPP
Villard, Oswald Garrison
    1872-1949 .... TCLC 160
    See also CA 113; 162; DLB 25, 91
Villarreal, Jose Antonio 1924- .... HLC 2
    See also CA 133; CANR 93; DAM MULT;
    DLB 82; HW 1; LAIT 4; RGAL 4
Villaurrutia, Xavier 1903-1950 ..... TCLC 80
    See also CA 192; EWL 3; HW 1; LAW
Villaverde, Cirilo 1812-1894 .... NCLC 121
    See also LAW
Villehardouin, Geoffroi de
    1150(?)-1218(?) .... CMLC 38
Villiers, George 1628-1687 .... LC 107
    See also DLB 80; RGEL 2
Villiers de l'Isle Adam, Jean Marie Mathias
    Philippe Auguste
    1838-1889 .... NCLC 3, 237; SSC 14
    See also DLB 123, 192; GFL 1789 to the
    Present; RGSF 2
Villon, Francois 1431-1463(?) .... LC 62,
    166; PC 13
    See also DLB 208; EW 2; RGWL 2, 3; TWA
Vine, Barbara
    See Rendell, Ruth
Vinge, Joan (Carol) D(ennison)
    1948- .... CLC 30; SSC 24
    See also AAYA 32; BPFB 3; CA 93-96;
    CANR 72; SATA 36, 113; SFW 4; YAW
Viola, Herman J(oseph) 1938- .... CLC 70
    See also CA 61-64; CANR 8, 23, 48, 91;
    SATA 126
Violis, G.
    See Simenon, Georges
Viramontes, Helena Maria
    1954- .... HLCS 2; SSC 149
    See also CA 159; CANR 182; CLR 285;
    DLB 122, 350; HW 2; LLW
Virgil
    See Vergil
Visconti, Luchino 1906-1976 .... CLC 16
    See also CA 81-84; 65-68; CANR 39
Vitry, Jacques de
    See Jacques de Vitry
Vittorini, Elio 1908-1966 .... CLC 6, 9, 14
    See also CA 133; 25-28R; DLB 264; EW 12;
    EWL 3; RGWL 2, 3
Vivekananda, Swami 1863-1902 ... TCLC 88
Vives, Juan Luis 1493-1540 .... LC 170
    See also DLB 318
Vizenor, Gerald Robert 1934- ..... CLC 103,
    263; NNAL; SSC 179
    See also CA 13-16R, 205; CAAE 205;
    CAAS 22; CANR 5, 21, 44, 67, 233; DAM
    MULT; DLB 175, 227; MTCW 2; MTFW
    2005; TCWW 2
Vizinczey, Stephen 1933- .... CLC 40
    See also CA 128; CCA 1; INT CA-128

Vladislavic, Ivan 1957- .... SSC 178
    See also CA 259
Vliet, R(ussell) G(ordon)
    1929-1984 .... CLC 22
    See also CA 37-40R; 112; CANR 18; CP 2, 3
Vogau, Boris Andreevich
    See Vogau, Boris Andreyevich
Vogau, Boris Andreyevich 1894-1938 ... SSC
    48; TCLC 23
    See also CA 123; 218; DLB 272; EWL 3;
    RGSF 2; RGWL 2, 3
Vogel, Paula A. 1951- .... CLC 76, 290;
    DC 19
    See also CA 108; CAD; CANR 119, 140;
    CD 5, 6; CWD; DFS 14; DLB 341; MTFW
    2005; RGAL 4
Vogel, Paula Anne
    See Vogel, Paula A.
Vogelweide, Walther von der
    See Walther von der Vogelweide
Voigt, Cynthia 1942- .... CLC 30
    See also AAYA 3, 30; BYA 1, 3, 6, 7, 8; CA
    106; CANR 18, 37, 40, 94, 145; CLR 13,
    48, 141; INT CANR-18; JRDA; LAIT 5;
    MAICYA 1, 2; MAICYAS 1; MTFW
    2005; SATA 48, 79, 116, 160; SATA-Brief
    33; WYA; YAW
Voigt, Ellen Bryant 1943- .... CLC 54
    See also CA 69-72; CANR 11, 29, 55, 115,
    171; CP 5, 6, 7; CSW; CWP; DLB 120;
    PFS 23, 33
Voinovich, Vladimir 1932- .... CLC 10,
    49, 147
    See also CA 81-84; CAAS 12; CANR 33,
    67, 150; CWW 2; DLB 302; MTCW 1
Voinovich, Vladimir Nikolaevich
    See Voinovich, Vladimir
Vollmann, William T. 1959- .... CLC 89, 227
    See also AMWS 17; CA 134; CANR 67,
    116, 185; CN 7; CPW; DA3; DAM NOV,
    POP; DLB 350; MTCW 2; MTFW 2005
Voloshinov, V. N.
    See Bakhtin, Mikhail Mikhailovich
Voltaire 1694-1778 .... LC 14, 79, 110;
    SSC 12, 112, 167; WLC 6
    See also BYA 13; DA; DA3; DAB; DAC;
    DAM DRAM, MST; DLB 314; EW 4;
    GFL Beginnings to 1789; LATS 1:1;
    LMFS 1; NFS 7; RGWL 2, 3; TWA
von Aschendrof, Baron Ignatz
    See Ford, Ford Madox
von Chamisso, Adelbert
    See Chamisso, Adelbert von
von Daeniken, Erich 1935- .... CLC 30
    See also AITN 1; CA 37-40R; CANR 17, 44
von Daniken, Erich
    See von Daeniken, Erich
von dem Turlin, Heinrich
    See Heinrich von dem Tuerlin
von der Vogelweide, Walther
    See Walther von der Vogelweide
von Eschenbach, Wolfram
    c. 1170-c. 1220 ..... CMLC 5, 145, 153;
    PC 131
    See also CDWLB 2; DLB 138; EW 1;
    RGWL 2, 3
von Hartmann, Eduard
    1842-1906 .... TCLC 96
von Hayek, Friedrich August
    See Hayek, F(riedrich) A(ugust von)
von Heidenstam, (Carl Gustaf) Verner
    See Heidenstam, (Carl Gustaf) Verner von
von Heyse, Paul (Johann Ludwig)
    See Heyse, Paul (Johann Ludwig von)
von Hofmannsthal, Hugo
    See Hofmannsthal, Hugo von
von Horvath, Oedoen
    See Horvath, Odon von

von Horvath, Odon
See Horvath, Odon von

von Kleist, Heinrich
See Kleist, Heinrich von

von Reuental, Neidhart
See Neidhart von Reuental

Vonnegut, Kurt, Jr.
See Vonnegut, Kurt

Vonnegut, Kurt 1922-2007 ...... **CLC 1, 2, 3, 4, 5, 8, 12, 22, 40, 60, 111, 212, 254; SSC 8, 155; WLC 6**
See also AAYA 6, 44; AITN 1; AMWS 2; BEST 90:4; BPFB 3; BYA 3, 14; CA 1-4R; 259; CANR 1, 25, 49, 75, 92, 207; CDALB 1968-1988; CN 1, 2, 3, 4, 5, 6, 7; CPW 1; DA; DA3; DAB; DAC; DAM MST, NOV, POP; DLB 2, 8, 152; DLBD 3; DLBY 1980; EWL 3; EXPN; EXPS; LAIT 4; LMFS 2; MAL 5; MTCW 1, 2; MTFW 2005; NFS 3, 28; RGAL 4; SCFW; SFW 4; SSFS 5; TUS; YAW

Von Rachen, Kurt
See Hubbard, L. Ron

von Sternberg, Josef
See Sternberg, Josef von

Vorster, Gordon 1924- .... **CLC 34**
See also CA 133

Vosce, Trudie
See Ozick, Cynthia

Voznesensky, Andrei 1933-2010 .... **CLC 1, 15, 57**
See also CA 89-92; CANR 37; CWW 2; DAM POET; DLB 359; EWL 3; MTCW 1

Voznesensky, Andrei Andreievich
See Voznesensky, Andrei

Voznesensky, Andrey
See Voznesensky, Andrei

Wace, Robert c. 1100-c. 1175 ...... **CMLC 55**
See also DLB 146

Waddington, Miriam 1917-2004 ..... **CLC 28**
See also CA 21-24R; 225; CANR 12, 30; CCA 1; CP 1, 2, 3, 4, 5, 6, 7; DLB 68

Wade, Alan
See Vance, Jack

Wagman, Fredrica 1937- .... **CLC 7**
See also CA 97-100; CANR 166; INT CA-97-100

Wagner, Linda W.
See Wagner-Martin, Linda (C.)

Wagner, Linda Welshimer
See Wagner-Martin, Linda (C.)

Wagner, Richard 1813-1883 .... **NCLC 9, 119, 258**
See also DLB 129; EW 6

Wagner-Martin, Linda (C.) 1936- ... **CLC 50**
See also CA 159; CANR 135

Wagoner, David (Russell) 1926- ...... **CLC 3, 5, 15; PC 33**
See also AMWS 9; CA 1-4R; CAAS 3; CANR 2, 71; CN 1, 2, 3, 4, 5, 6, 7; CP 1, 2, 3, 4, 5, 6, 7; DLB 5, 256; SATA 14; TCWW 1, 2

Wah, Fred(erick James) 1939- .... **CLC 44, 338**
See also CA 107; 141; CP 1, 6, 7; DLB 60

Wahloo, Per 1926-1975 .... **CLC 7**
See also BPFB 3; CA 61-64; CANR 73; CMW 4; MSW

Wahloo, Peter
See Wahloo, Per

Wain, John 1925-1994 .... **CLC 2, 11, 15, 46**
See also BRWS 16; CA 5-8R; 145; CAAS 4; CANR 23, 54; CDBLB 1960 to Present; CN 1, 2, 3, 4, 5; CP 1, 2, 3, 4, 5; DLB 15, 27, 139, 155; EWL 3; MTCW 1, 2; MTFW 2005

Wajda, Andrzej 1926- .... **CLC 16, 219**
See also CA 102

Wakefield, Dan 1932- .... **CLC 7**
See also CA 21-24R, 211; CAAE 211; CAAS 7; CN 4, 5, 6, 7

Wakefield, Herbert Russell 1888-1965 .... **TCLC 120**
See also CA 5-8R; CANR 77; HGG; SUFW

Wakoski, Diane 1937- .... **CLC 2, 4, 7, 9, 11, 40; PC 15**
See also CA 13-16R, 216; CAAE 216; CAAS 1; CANR 9, 60, 106; CP 1, 2, 3, 4, 5, 6, 7; CWP; DAM POET; DLB 5; INT CANR-9; MAL 5; MTCW 2; MTFW 2005; PFS 43

Wakoski-Sherbell, Diane
See Wakoski, Diane

Walcott, Derek 1930- .... **BLC 1:3, 2:3; CLC 2, 4, 9, 14, 25, 42, 67, 76, 160, 282; DC 7; PC 46**
See also BW 2; CA 89-92; CANR 26, 47, 75, 80, 130, 230; CBD; CD 5, 6; CDWLB 3; CP 1, 2, 3, 4, 5, 6, 7; DA3; DAB; DAC; DAM MST, MULT, POET; DLB 117, 332; DLBY 1981; DNFS 1; EFS 1:1, 2:2; EWL 3; LMFS 2; MTCW 1, 2; MTFW 2005; PFS 6, 34, 39; RGEL 2; TWA; WWE 1

Walcott, Derek Alton
See Walcott, Derek

Waldman, Anne 1945- .... **CLC 7**
See also BG 1:3; CA 37-40R; CAAS 17; CANR 34, 69, 116, 219; CP 1, 2, 3, 4, 5, 6, 7; CWP; DLB 16

Waldman, Anne Lesley
See Waldman, Anne

Waldo, E. Hunter
See Sturgeon, Theodore (Hamilton)

Waldo, Edward Hamilton
See Sturgeon, Theodore (Hamilton)

Waldrop, Rosmarie 1935- .... **PC 109**
See also CA 101; CAAS 30; CANR 18, 39, 67; CP 6, 7; CWP; DLB 169

Walker, Alice 1944- ...... **BLC 1:3, 2:3; CLC 5, 6, 9, 19, 27, 46, 58, 103, 167, 319; PC 30; SSC 5; WLCS**
See also AAYA 3, 33; AFAW 1, 2; AMWS 3; BEST 89:4; BPFB 3; BW 2, 3; CA 37-40R; CANR 9, 27, 49, 66, 82, 131, 191, 238; CDALB 1968-1988; CN 4, 5, 6, 7; CPW; CSW; DA; DA3; DAB; DAC; DAM MST, MULT, NOV, POET, POP; DLB 6, 33, 143; EWL 3; EXPN; EXPS; FL 1:6; FW; INT CANR-27; LAIT 3; MAL 5; MBL; MTCW 1, 2; MTFW 2005; NFS 5; PFS 30, 34; RGAL 4; RGSF 2; SATA 31; SSFS 2, 11; TUS; YAW

Walker, Alice Malsenior
See Walker, Alice

Walker, David Harry 1911-1992 .... **CLC 14**
See also CA 1-4R; 137; CANR 1; CN 1, 2; CWRI 5; SATA 8; SATA-Obit 71

Walker, Edward Joseph 1934-2004 .... **CLC 13**
See also CA 21-24R; 226; CANR 12, 28, 53; CP 1, 2, 3, 4, 5, 6, 7; DLB 40

Walker, George F(rederick) 1947- .... **CLC 44, 61**
See also CA 103; CANR 21, 43, 59; CD 5, 6; DAB; DAC; DAM MST; DLB 60

Walker, Joseph A. 1935-2003 .... **CLC 19**
See also BW 1, 3; CA 89-92; CAD; CANR 26, 143; CD 5, 6; DAM DRAM, MST; DFS 12; DLB 38

Walker, Margaret 1915-1998 .... **BLC 1:3; CLC 1, 6; PC 20; TCLC 129**
See also AFAW 1, 2; BW 2, 3; CA 73-76; 172; CANR 26, 54, 76, 136; CN 1, 2, 3, 4, 5, 6; CP 1, 2, 3, 4, 5, 6; CSW; DAM MULT; DLB 76, 152; EXPP; FW; MAL 5; MTCW 1, 2; MTFW 2005; PFS 31; RGAL 4; RHW

Walker, Ted
See Walker, Edward Joseph

Wallace, David Foster 1962-2008 ... **CLC 50, 114, 271, 281; SSC 68**
See also AAYA 50; AMWS 10; CA 132; 277; CANR 59, 133, 190, 237; CN 7; DA3; DLB 350; MTCW 2; MTFW 2005

Wallace, Dexter
See Masters, Edgar Lee

Wallace, (Richard Horatio) Edgar 1875-1932 .... **TCLC 57**
See also CA 115; 218; CMW 4; DLB 70; MSW; RGEL 2

Wallace, Irving 1916-1990 .... **CLC 7, 13**
See also AITN 1; BPFB 3; CA 1-4R; 132; CAAS 1; CANR 1, 27; CPW; DAM NOV, POP; INT CANR-27; MTCW 1, 2

Wallant, Edward Lewis 1926-1962 .... **CLC 5, 10**
See also CA 1-4R; CANR 22; DLB 2, 28, 143, 299; EWL 3; MAL 5; MTCW 1, 2; RGAL 4; RGHL

Wallas, Graham 1858-1932 .... **TCLC 91**

Waller, Edmund 1606-1687 ... **LC 86; PC 72**
See also BRW 2; DAM POET; DLB 126; PAB; RGEL 2

Walley, Byron
See Card, Orson Scott

Walls, Jeannette 1960(?)- .... **CLC 299**
See also CA 242; CANR 220

Walpole, Horace 1717-1797 ... **LC 2, 49, 152**
See also BRW 3; DLB 39, 104, 213; GL 3; HGG; LMFS 1; RGEL 2; SUFW 1; TEA

Walpole, Hugh 1884-1941 .... **TCLC 5**
See also CA 104; 165; DLB 34; HGG; MTCW 2; RGEL 2; RHW

Walpole, Hugh Seymour
See Walpole, Hugh

Walrond, Eric (Derwent) 1898-1966 .... **HR 1:3**
See also BW 1; CA 125; DLB 51

Walser, Martin 1927- .... **CLC 27, 183**
See also CA 57-60; CANR 8, 46, 145; CWW 2; DLB 75, 124; EWL 3

Walser, Robert 1878-1956 .... **SSC 20; TCLC 18, 267**
See also CA 118; 165; CANR 100, 194; DLB 66; EWL 3

Walsh, Gillian Paton
See Paton Walsh, Jill

Walsh, Jill Paton
See Paton Walsh, Jill

Walter, Villiam Christian
See Andersen, Hans Christian

Walter of Chatillon c. 1135-c. 1202 .... **CMLC 111**

Walters, Anna L(ee) 1946- .... **NNAL**
See also CA 73-76

Walther von der Vogelweide c. 1170-1228 .... **CMLC 56**

Walther von der Vogelweide c. 1170-c. 1230 .... **CMLC 147**
See also DLB 138; EW 1; RGWL 2, 3

Walton, Izaak 1593-1683 .... **LC 72**
See also BRW 2; CDBLB Before 1660; DLB 151, 213; RGEL 2

Walzer, Michael 1935- .... **CLC 238**
See also CA 37-40R; CANR 15, 48, 127, 190

Walzer, Michael Laban
See Walzer, Michael

Wambaugh, Joseph, Jr. 1937- .... **CLC 3, 18**
See also AITN 1; BEST 89:3; BPFB 3; CA 33-36R; CANR 42, 65, 115, 167, 217; CMW 4; CPW 1; DA3; DAM NOV, POP; DLB 6; DLBY 1983; MSW; MTCW 1, 2

Wambaugh, Joseph Aloysius
See Wambaugh, Joseph, Jr.

1865-1917; CLR 136; DA; DA3; DAB; DAC; DAM MST, NOV; DLB 4, 9, 12, 78, 189; DLBD 13; EWL 3; EXPS; FL 1:6; GL 3; HGG; LAIT 2, 3; LATS 1:1; MAL 5; MBL; MTCW 1, 2; MTFW 2005; NFS 5, 11, 15, 20, 37; RGAL 4; RGSF 2; RHW; SSFS 6, 7; SUFW; TUS

Wharton, Edith Newbold Jones
See Wharton, Edith

Wharton, James
See Mencken, H. L.

Wharton, William 1925-2008 .... **CLC 18, 37**
See also CA 93-96; 278; CN 4, 5, 6, 7; DLBY 1980; INT CA-93-96

Wheatley, Phillis 1753(?)-1784 ...... **BLC 1:3; LC 3, 50, 183; PC 3, 142; WLC 6**
See also AFAW 1, 2; AMWS 20; CDALB 1640-1865; DA; DA3; DAC; DAM MST, MULT, POET; DLB 31, 50; EXPP; FL 1:1; PFS 13, 29, 36; RGAL 4

Wheatley Peters, Phillis
See Wheatley, Phillis

Wheelock, John Hall 1886-1978 ..... **CLC 14**
See also CA 13-16R; 77-80; CANR 14; CP 1, 2; DLB 45; MAL 5

Whim-Wham
See Curnow, (Thomas) Allen (Monro)

Whisp, Kennilworthy
See Rowling, J.K.

Whitaker, Rod 1931-2005 .... **CLC 29**
See also CA 29-32R; 246; CANR 45, 153; CMW 4

Whitaker, Rodney
See Whitaker, Rod

Whitaker, Rodney William
See Whitaker, Rod

White, Babington
See Braddon, Mary Elizabeth

White, E. B. 1899-1985 ...... **CLC 10, 34, 39**
See also AAYA 62; AITN 2; AMWS 1; CA 13-16R; 116; CANR 16, 37; CDALBS; CLR 1, 21, 107; CPW; DA3; DAM POP; DLB 11, 22; EWL 3; FANT; MAICYA 1, 2; MAL 5; MTCW 1, 2; MTFW 2005; NCFS 5; RGAL 4; SATA 2, 29, 100; SATA-Obit 44; TUS

White, Edmund 1940- .... **CLC 27, 110**
See also AAYA 7; CA 45-48; CANR 3, 19, 36, 62, 107, 133, 172, 212; CN 5, 6, 7; DA3; DAM POP; DLB 227; MTCW 1, 2; MTFW 2005

White, Edmund Valentine III
See White, Edmund

White, Elwyn Brooks
See White, E. B.

White, Hayden V. 1928- .... **CLC 148**
See also CA 128; CANR 135; DLB 246

White, Patrick 1912-1990 .... **CLC 3, 4, 5, 7, 9, 18, 65, 69; SSC 39; TCLC 176**
See also BRWS 1; CA 81-84; 132; CANR 43; CN 1, 2, 3, 4; DLB 260, 332; EWL 3; MTCW 1; RGEL 2; RGSF 2; RHW; TWA; WWE 1

White, Patrick Victor Martindale
See White, Patrick

White, Phyllis Dorothy James
See James, P. D.

White, T(erence) H(anbury)
1906-1964 .... **CLC 30**
See also AAYA 22; BPFB 3; BYA 4, 5; CA 73-76; CANR 37; CLR 139; DLB 160; FANT; JRDA; LAIT 1; MAICYA 1, 2; NFS 30; RGEL 2; SATA 12; SUFW 1; YAW

White, Terence de Vere 1912-1994 .... **CLC 49**
See also CA 49-52; 145; CANR 3

White, Walter
See White, Walter F(rancis)

White, Walter F(rancis)
1893-1955 .... **BLC 1:3; HR 1:3; TCLC 15**

See also BW 1; CA 115; 124; DAM MULT; DLB 51

White, William Hale 1831-1913 ... **TCLC 25**
See also CA 121; 189; DLB 18; RGEL 2

Whitehead, Alfred North
1861-1947 .... **TCLC 97**
See also CA 117; 165; DLB 100, 262

Whitehead, Colson
1969- .... **BLC 2:3; CLC 232, 348**
See also CA 202; CANR 162, 211

Whitehead, E(dward) A(nthony)
1933- .... **CLC 5**
See also CA 65-68; CANR 58, 118; CBD; CD 5, 6; DLB 310

Whitehead, Ted
See Whitehead, E(dward) A(nthony)

Whiteman, Roberta J. Hill 1947- ...... **NNAL**
See also CA 146

Whitemore, Hugh (John)
1936- .... **CLC 37**
See also CA 132; CANR 77; CBD; CD 5, 6; INT CA-132

Whitman, Sarah Helen (Power)
1803-1878 .... **NCLC 19**
See also DLB 1, 243

Whitman, Walt 1819-1892 .... **NCLC 4, 31, 81, 205, 268; PC 3, 91; WLC 6**
See also AAYA 42; AMW; AMWR 1; CDALB 1640-1865; DA; DA3; DAB; DAC; DAM MST, POET; DLB 3, 64, 224, 250; EXPP; LAIT 2; LMFS 1; PAB; PFS 2, 3, 13, 22, 31, 39; RGAL 4; SATA 20; TUS; WP; WYAS 1

Whitman, Walter
See Whitman, Walt

Whitney, Isabella
fl. 1565-fl. 1575 .... **LC 130; PC 116**
See also DLB 136

Whitney, Phyllis A. 1903-2008 .... **CLC 42**
See also AAYA 36; AITN 2; BEST 90:3; CA 1-4R; 269; CANR 3, 25, 38, 60; CLR 59; CMW 4; DA3; DAM POP; JRDA; MAICYA 1, 2; MTCW 2; RHW; SATA 1, 30; SATA-Obit 189; YAW

Whitney, Phyllis Ayame
See Whitney, Phyllis A.

Whittemore, Edward Reed
See Whittemore, Reed, Jr.

Whittemore, Reed, Jr.
1919-2012 .... **CLC 4**
See also CA 9-12R; 219; CAAE 219; CAAS 8; CANR 4, 119; CP 1, 2, 3, 4, 5, 6, 7; DLB 5; MAL 5

Whittier, John Greenleaf
1807-1892 .... **NCLC 8, 59; PC 93**
See also AMWS 1; DLB 1, 243; PFS 36; RGAL 4

Whittlebot, Hernia
See Coward, Noel

Wicker, Thomas Grey
See Wicker, Tom

Wicker, Tom 1926-2011 .... **CLC 7**
See also CA 65-68; CANR 21, 46, 141, 179

Wickham, Anna 1883-1947 .... **PC 110**
See also DLB 240

Wicomb, Zoe 1948- .... **BLC 2:3**
See also CA 127; CANR 106, 167; DLB 225

Wideman, John Edgar 1941- .... **BLC 1:3, 2:3; CLC 5, 34, 36, 67, 122, 316; SSC 62**
See also AFAW 1, 2; AMWS 10; BPFB 4; BW 2, 3; CA 85-88; CANR 14, 42, 67, 109, 140, 187; CN 4, 5, 6, 7; DAM MULT; DLB 33, 143; MAL 5; MTCW 2; MTFW 2005; RGAL 4; RGSF 2; SSFS 6, 12, 24; TCLE 1:2

Wiebe, Rudy 1934- .... **CLC 6, 11, 14, 138, 263**

See also CA 37-40R; CANR 42, 67, 123, 202; CN 1, 2, 3, 4, 5, 6, 7; DAC; DAM MST; DLB 60; RHW; SATA 156

Wiebe, Rudy Henry
See Wiebe, Rudy

Wieland, Christoph Martin
1733-1813 .... **NCLC 17, 177**
See also DLB 97; EW 4; LMFS 1; RGWL 2, 3

Wiene, Robert 1881-1938 .... **TCLC 56**

Wieners, John 1934- .... **CLC 7; PC 131**
See also BG 1:3; CA 13-16R; CP 1, 2, 3, 4, 5, 6, 7; DLB 16; WP

Wiesel, Elie 1928- .... **CLC 3, 5, 11, 37, 165; WLCS**
See also AAYA 7, 54; AITN 1; CA 5-8R; CAAS 4; CANR 8, 40, 65, 125, 207; CDALBS; CWW 2; DA; DA3; DAB; DAC; DAM MST, NOV; DLB 83, 299; DLBY 1987; EWL 3; INT CANR-8; LAIT 4; MTCW 1, 2; MTFW 2005; NCFS 4; NFS 4; RGHL; RGWL 3; SATA 56; YAW

Wiesel, Eliezer
See Wiesel, Elie

Wiggins, Marianne 1947- .... **CLC 57**
See also AAYA 70; BEST 89:3; CA 130; CANR 60, 139, 180; CN 7; DLB 335

Wigglesworth, Michael 1631-1705 ... **LC 106**
See also DLB 24; RGAL 4

Wiggs, Susan .... **CLC 70**
See also CA 201; CANR 173, 217

Wight, James Alfred
See Herriot, James

Wilbur, Richard 1921- .... **CLC 3, 6, 9, 14, 53, 110; PC 51**
See also AAYA 72; AMWS 3; CA 1-4R; CABS 2; CANR 2, 29, 76, 93, 139, 237; CDALBS; CP 1, 2, 3, 4, 5, 6, 7; DA; DAB; DAC; DAM MST, POET; DLB 5, 169; EWL 3; EXPP; INT CANR-29; MAL 5; MTCW 1, 2; MTFW 2005; PAB; PFS 11, 12, 16, 29; RGAL 4; SATA 9, 108; WP

Wilbur, Richard Purdy
See Wilbur, Richard

Wild, Peter 1940- .... **CLC 14**
See also CA 37-40R; CP 1, 2, 3, 4, 5, 6, 7; DLB 5

Wilde, Oscar 1854(?)-1900 .... **DC 17; PC 111; SSC 11, 77; TCLC 1, 8, 23, 41, 175, 272; WLC 6**
See also AAYA 49; BRW 5; BRWC 1, 2; BRWR 2; BYA 15; CA 104; 119; CANR 112; CDBLB 1890-1914; CLR 114; DA; DA3; DAB; DAC; DAM DRAM, MST, NOV; DFS 4, 8, 9, 21; DLB 10, 19, 34, 57, 141, 156, 190, 344; EXPS; FANT; GL 3; LATS 1:1; NFS 20; RGEL 2; RGSF 2; SATA 24; SSFS 7; SUFW; TEA; WCH; WLIT 4

Wilde, Oscar Fingal O'Flahertie Willis
See Wilde, Oscar

Wilder, Billy 1906-2002 .... **CLC 20**
See also AAYA 66; CA 89-92; 205; DLB 26

Wilder, Samuel
See Wilder, Billy

Wilder, Samuel 1906-2002 .... **CLC 20**
See also AAYA 66; CA 89-92; 205; DLB 26

Wilder, Stephen
See Marlowe, Stephen

Wilder, Thornton 1897-1975 ... **CLC 1, 5, 6, 10, 15, 35, 82; DC 1, 24; TCLC 284; WLC 6**
See also AAYA 29; AITN 2; AMW; CA 13-16R; 61-64; CAD; CANR 40, 132; CDALBS; CN 1, 2; DA; DA3; DAB; DAC; DAM DRAM, MST, NOV; DFS 1, 4, 16; DLB 4, 7, 9, 228; DLBY 1997; EWL 3; LAIT 3; MAL 5; MTCW 1, 2; MTFW 2005; NFS 24; RGAL 4; RHW; WYAS 1

Wilder, Thornton Niven
See Wilder, Thornton

Wilding, Michael 1942- .... **CLC 73; SSC 50**
See also CA 104; CANR 24, 49, 106; CN 4, 5, 6, 7; DLB 325; RGSF 2

Wiley, Richard 1944- .... **CLC 44**
See also CA 121; 129; CANR 71

Wilhelm, Kate
See Wilhelm, Katie

Wilhelm, Katie 1928- .... **CLC 7**
See also AAYA 83; BYA 16; CA 37-40R; CAAS 5; CANR 17, 36, 60, 94; DLB 8; INT CANR-17; MTCW 1; SCFW 2; SFW 4

Wilhelm, Katie Gertrude
See Wilhelm, Katie

Wilkins, Mary
See Freeman, Mary E(leanor) Wilkins

Willard, Nancy 1936- .... **CLC 7, 37**
See also BYA 5; CA 89-92; CANR 10, 39, 68, 107, 152, 186; CLR 5; CP 2, 3, 4, 5; CWP; CWRI 5; DLB 5, 52; FANT; MAI-CYA 1, 2; MTCW 1; SATA 37, 71, 127, 191; SATA-Brief 30; SUFW 2; TCLE 1:2

William of Malmesbury
c. 1090B.C.-c. 1140B.C. .. **CMLC 57, 140**

William of Moerbeke
c. 1215-c. 1286 .... **CMLC 91**

William of Ockham
1290-1349 .... **CMLC 32, 129**

Williams, Ben Ames 1889-1953 .... **TCLC 89**
See also CA 183; DLB 102

Williams, Charles
See Collier, James Lincoln

Williams, Charles 1886-1945 ... **TCLC 1, 11**
See also BRWS 9; CA 104; 163; DLB 100, 153, 255; FANT; RGEL 2; SUFW 1

Williams, Charles Walter Stansby
See Williams, Charles

Williams, C.K.
1936- .... **CLC 33, 56, 148, 306**
See also CA 37-40R; CAAS 26; CANR 57, 106, 225; CP 1, 2, 3, 4, 5, 6, 7; DAM POET; DLB 5; MAL 5

Williams, Ella Gwendolen Rees
See Rhys, Jean

Williams, Emlyn 1905-1987 .... **CLC 15**
See also CA 104, 123; CANR 36; DAM DRAM; DLB 10, 77; IDTP; MTCW 1

Williams, George Emlyn
See Williams, Emlyn

Williams, Hank 1923-1953 .... **TCLC 81**
See Williams, Hiram King
See also CA 188

Williams, Helen Maria
1761-1827 .... **NCLC 135**
See also DLB 158

Williams, Hiram King 1923-1953
See Williams, Hank

Williams, Hugo (Mordaunt)
1942- .... **CLC 42**
See also CA 17-20R; CANR 45, 119; CP 1, 2, 3, 4, 5, 6, 7; DLB 40

Williams, J. Walker
See Wodehouse, P. G.

Williams, John A(lfred) 1925- ...... **BLC 1:3; CLC 5, 13, 347**
See also AFAW 2; BW 2, 3; CA 53-56, 195; CAAE 195; CAAS 3; CANR 6, 26, 51, 118; CN 1, 2, 3, 4, 5, 6, 7; CSW; DAM MULT; DLB 2, 33; EWL 3; INT CANR-6; MAL 5; RGAL 4; SFW 4

Williams, Jonathan 1929-2008 .... **CLC 13**
See also CA 9-12R; 270; CAAS 12; CANR 8, 108; CP 1, 2, 3, 4, 5, 6, 7; DLB 5

Williams, Jonathan Chamberlain
See Williams, Jonathan

Williams, Joy 1944- .... **CLC 31**
See also CA 41-44R; CANR 22, 48, 97, 168; DLB 335; SSFS 25

Williams, Norman 1952- .... **CLC 39**
See also CA 118

Williams, Paulette Linda
See Shange, Ntozake

Williams, Roger 1603(?)-1683 .... **LC 129**
See also DLB 24

Williams, Sherley Anne
1944-1999 .... **BLC 1:3; CLC 89**
See also AFAW 2; BW 2, 3; CA 73-76; 185; CANR 25, 82; DAM MULT; POET; DLB 41; INT CANR-25; SATA 78; SATA-Obit 116

Williams, Shirley
See Williams, Sherley Anne

Williams, Tennessee 1911-1983 .... **CLC 1, 2, 5, 7, 8, 11, 15, 19, 30, 39, 45, 71, 111; DC 4; SSC 81; WLC 6**
See also AAYA 31; AITN 1, 2; AMW; AMWC 1; CA 5-8R; 108; CABS 3; CAD; CANR 31, 132, 174; CDALB 1941-1968; CN 1, 2, 3; DA; DA3; DAB; DAC; DAM DRAM, MST; DFS 17; DLB 7, 341; DLBD 4; DLBY 1983; EWL 3; GLL 1; LAIT 4; LATS 1:2; MAL 5; MTCW 1, 2; MTFW 2005; RGAL 4; TUS

Williams, Thomas (Alonzo)
1926-1990 .... **CLC 14**
See also CA 1-4R; 132; CANR 2

Williams, Thomas Lanier
See Williams, Tennessee

Williams, William C.
See Williams, William Carlos

Williams, William Carlos
1883-1963 .... **CLC 1, 2, 5, 9, 13, 22, 42, 67; PC 7, 109; SSC 31; TCLC 272; WLC 6**
See also AAYA 46; AMW; AMWR 1; CA 89-92; CANR 34; CDALB 1917-1929; DA; DA3; DAB; DAC; DAM MST, POET; DLB 4, 16, 54, 86; EWL 3; EXPP; MAL 5; MTCW 1, 2; MTFW 2005; NCFS 4; PAB; PFS 1, 6, 11, 34, 43; RGAL 4; RGSF 2; SSFS 27; TUS; WP

Williamson, David (Keith) 1942- ... **CLC 56; DC 47**
See also CA 103; CANR 41; CD 5, 6; DLB 289

Williamson, Jack
See Williamson, John Stewart

Williamson, John Stewart
1908-2006 .... **CLC 29**
See also AAYA 76; CA 17-20R; 255; CAAS 8; CANR 23, 70, 153; DLB 8; SCFW 1, 2; SFW 4

Willie, Frederick
See Lovecraft, H. P.

Willingham, Calder (Baynard, Jr.)
1922-1995 .... **CLC 5, 51**
See also CA 5-8R; 147; CANR 3; CN 1, 2, 3, 4, 5; CSW; DLB 2, 44; IDFW 3, 4; MTCW 1

Willis, Charles
See Clarke, Arthur C.

Willis, Nathaniel Parker
1806-1867 .... **NCLC 194**
See also DLB 3, 59, 73, 74, 183, 250; DLBD 13; RGAL 4

Willy
See Colette

Willy, Colette
See Colette

Wilmot, John 1647-1680 .... **LC 75; PC 66**
See also BRW 2; DLB 131; PAB; RGEL 2

Wilson, A. N. 1950- .... **CLC 33**
See also BRWS 6; CA 112; 122; CANR 156, 199; CN 4, 5, 6, 7; DLB 14, 155, 194; MTCW 2

Wilson, Andrew Norman
See Wilson, A. N.

Wilson, Angus 1913-1991 .... **CLC 2, 3, 5, 25, 34; SSC 21**
See also BRWS 1; CA 5-8R; 134; CANR 21; CN 1, 2, 3, 4; DLB 15, 139, 155; MTCW 1, 2; MTFW 2005; RGEL 2; RGSF 2

Wilson, Angus Frank Johnstone
See Wilson, Angus

Wilson, August 1945-2005 ..... **BLC 1:3, 2:3; CLC 39, 50, 63, 118, 222; DC 2, 31; WLCS**
See also AAYA 16; AFAW 2; AMWS 8; BW 2, 3; CA 115; 122; 244; CAD; CANR 42, 54, 76, 128; CD 5, 6; DA; DA3; DAB; DAC; DAM DRAM, MST, MULT; DFS 3, 7, 15, 17, 24, 30; DLB 228; EWL 3; LAIT 4; LATS 1:2; MAL 5; MTCW 1, 2; MTFW 2005; RGAL 4

Wilson, Brian 1942- .... **CLC 12**

Wilson, Colin 1931- .... **CLC 3, 14**
See also CA 1-4R; 315; CAAE 315; CAAS 5; CANR 1, 22, 33, 77; CMW 4; CN 1, 2, 3, 4, 5, 6; DLB 14, 194; HGG; MTCW 1; SFW 4

Wilson, Colin Henry
See Wilson, Colin

Wilson, Dirk
See Pohl, Frederik

Wilson, Edmund
1895-1972 .... **CLC 1, 2, 3, 8, 24**
See also AMW; CA 1-4R; 37-40R; CANR 1, 46, 110; CN 1; DLB 63; EWL 3; MAL 5; MTCW 1, 2; MTFW 2005; RGAL 4; TUS

Wilson, Ethel Davis (Bryant)
1888(?)-1980 .... **CLC 13**
See also CA 102; CN 1, 2; DAC; DAM POET; DLB 68; MTCW 1; RGEL 2

Wilson, G. Willow 1982- .... **CLC 354**
See also CA 302

Wilson, Harriet
See Wilson, Harriet E. Adams

Wilson, Harriet E.
See Wilson, Harriet E. Adams

Wilson, Harriet E. Adams
1827(?)-1863(?) .... **BLC 1:3; NCLC 78, 219**
See also DAM MULT; DLB 50, 239, 243

Wilson, John 1785-1854 .... **NCLC 5**
See also DLB 110

Wilson, John Anthony Burgess
See Burgess, Anthony

Wilson, John Burgess
See Burgess, Anthony

Wilson, Katharina .... **CLC 65**

Wilson, Kevin 1978- .... **CLC 334**
See also CA 295; CANR 236

Wilson, Lanford 1937-2011 .... **CLC 7, 14, 36, 197; DC 19**
See also CA 17-20R; CABS 3; CAD; CANR 45, 96; CD 5, 6; DAM DRAM; DFS 4, 9, 12, 16, 20; DLB 7, 341; EWL 3; MAL 5; TUS

Wilson, Robert M. 1941- .... **CLC 7, 9**
See also CA 49-52; CAD; CANR 2, 41; CD 5, 6; MTCW 1

Wilson, Robert McLiam 1964- .... **CLC 59**
See also CA 132; DLB 267

Wilson, Sloan 1920-2003 .... **CLC 32**
See also CA 1-4R; 216; CANR 1, 44; CN 1, 2, 3, 4, 5, 6

Wilson, Snoo 1948- .... **CLC 33**
See also CA 69-72; CBD; CD 5, 6

Wilson, Thomas 1523(?)-1581 .... **LC 184**
See also DLB 132, 236

Wilson, William S(mith) 1932- .... **CLC 49**
See also CA 81-84

Wilson, (Thomas) Woodrow
1856-1924 .... **TCLC 79**
See also CA 166; DLB 47

Wright, Charles
1932-2008 .... **BLC 1:3; CLC 49**
See also BW 1; CA 9-12R; 278; CANR 26;
CN 1, 2, 3, 4, 5, 6, 7; DAM MULT, POET;
DLB 33

Wright, Charles 1935- .... **CLC 6, 13, 28,**
119, 146; PC 142
See also AMWS 5; CA 29-32R; CAAS 7;
CANR 23, 36, 62, 88, 135, 180; CP 3, 4, 5,
6, 7; DLB 165; DLBY 1982; EWL 3;
MTCW 1, 2; MTFW 2005; PFS 10, 35

Wright, Charles Penzel, Jr.
See Wright, Charles

Wright, Charles Stevenson
See Wright, Charles

Wright, Frances 1795-1852 .... **NCLC 74**
See also DLB 73

Wright, Frank Lloyd
1867-1959 .... **TCLC 95**
See also AAYA 33; CA 174

Wright, Harold Bell 1872-1944 .. **TCLC 183**
See also BPFB 3; CA 110; DLB 9; TCWW 2

Wright, Jack R.
See Harris, Mark

Wright, James (Arlington)
1927-1980 ..... **CLC 3, 5, 10, 28; PC 36**
See also AITN 2; AMWS 3; CA 49-52; 97-
100; CANR 4, 34, 64; CDALBS; CP 1, 2;
DAM POET; DLB 5, 169, 342; EWL 3;
EXPP; MAL 5; MTCW 1, 2; MTFW 2005;
PFS 7, 8; RGAL 4; TUS; WP

Wright, Judith 1915-2000 .... **CLC 11, 53,**
327; PC 14
See also CA 13-16R; 188; CANR 31, 76, 93;
CP 1, 2, 3, 4, 5, 6, 7; CWP; DLB 260;
EWL 3; MTCW 1, 2; MTFW 2005; PFS 8;
RGEL 2; SATA 14; SATA-Obit 121

Wright, Judith Arundell
See Wright, Judith

Wright, L(aurali) R. 1939- .... **CLC 44**
See also CA 138; CMW 4

Wright, Richard 1908-1960 .... **BLC 1:3;**
CLC 1, 3, 4, 9, 14, 21, 48, 74; SSC 2,
109; TCLC 136, 180; WLC 6
See also AAYA 5, 42; AFAW 1, 2; AMW;
BPFB 3; BW 1; BYA 2; CA 108; CANR
64; CDALB 1929-1941; DA; DA3; DAB;
DAC; DAM MST, MULT, NOV; DLB 76,
102; DLBD 2; EWL 3; EXPN; LAIT 3, 4;
MAL 5; MTCW 1, 2; MTFW 2005; NCFS
1; NFS 1, 7; RGAL 4; RGSF 2; SSFS 3, 9,
15, 20; TUS; YAW

Wright, Richard B. 1937- .... **CLC 6**
See also CA 85-88; CANR 120; DLB 53

Wright, Richard Bruce
See Wright, Richard B.

Wright, Richard Nathaniel
See Wright, Richard

Wright, Rick 1945- .... **CLC 35**

Wright, Rowland
See Wells, Carolyn

Wright, Stephen 1946- .... **CLC 33**
See also CA 237; DLB 350

Wright, Willard Huntington
1888-1939 .... **TCLC 23**
See also CA 115; 189; CMW 4; DLB 306;
DLBD 16; MSW

Wright, William 1930- .... **CLC 44**
See also CA 53-56; CANR 7, 23, 154

Wroblewski, David 1959- .... **CLC 280**
See also CA 283

Wroth, Lady Mary 1587-1653(?) ..... **LC 30,**
139; PC 38
See also DLB 121

Wu Ch'eng-en 1500(?)-1582(?) .... **LC 7, 213**

Wu Ching-tzu 1701-1754 .... **LC 2**

Wulfstan c. 10th cent. -1023 ... **CMLC 59, 135**

Wurlitzer, Rudolph 1938(?)- .... **CLC 2, 4,**
15
See also CA 85-88; CN 4, 5, 6, 7; DLB 173

Wyatt, Sir Thomas c. 1503-1542 ...... **LC 70;**
PC 27
See also BRW 1; DLB 132; EXPP; PFS 25;
RGEL 2; TEA

Wycherley, William 1640-1716 .... **DC 41;**
LC 8, 21, 102, 136
See also BRW 2; CDBLB 1660-1789; DAM
DRAM; DLB 80; RGEL 2

Wyclif, John c. 1330-1384 ... **CMLC 70, 143**
See also DLB 146

Wyld, Evie 1980- .... **CLC 334**
See also CA 299

Wylie, Elinor (Morton Hoyt)
1885-1928 .... **PC 23; TCLC 8**
See also AMWS 1; CA 105; 162; DLB 9,
45; EXPP; MAL 5; RGAL 4

Wylie, Philip (Gordon)
1902-1971 .... **CLC 43**
See also CA 21-22; 33-36R; CAP 2; CN 1;
DLB 9; SFW 4

Wyndham, John
See Harris, John (Wyndham Parkes Lucas)
Beynon

Wyss, Johann David Von
1743-1818 .... **NCLC 10**
See also CLR 92; JRDA; MAICYA 1, 2;
SATA 29; SATA-Brief 27

X, Malcolm
See Malcolm X

Xenophon
c. 430B.C.-c. 354B.C. .... **CMLC 17, 137**
See also AW 1; DLB 176; RGWL 2, 3;
WLIT 8

Xingjian, Gao 1940- .... **CLC 167, 315**
See also CA 193; DFS 21; DLB 330; MTFW
2005; RGWL 3

Yakamochi 718-785 .... **CMLC 45; PC 48**

Yakumo Koizumi
See Hearn, Lafcadio

Yamada, Mitsuye (May) 1923- .... **PC 44**
See also CA 77-80

Yamamoto, Hisaye
1921-2011 ..... **AAL; CLC 343; SSC 34**
See also CA 214; DAM MULT; DLB 312;
LAIT 4; SSFS 14

Yamauchi, Wakako 1924- .... **AAL**
See also CA 214; DLB 312

Yan, Mo 1956(?)- .... **CLC 257, 354**
See also CA 201; CANR 192; EWL 3;
RGWL 3

Yanez, Jose Donoso
See Donoso, Jose

Yanovsky, Basile S.
See Yanovsky, V(assily) S(emenovich)

Yanovsky, V(assily) S(emenovich)
1906-1989 .... **CLC 2, 18**
See also CA 97-100; 129

Yates, Richard 1926-1992 .... **CLC 7, 8, 23**
See also AMWS 11; CA 5-8R; 139; CANR
10, 43; CN 1, 2, 3, 4, 5; DLB 2, 234; DLBY
1981, 1992; INT CANR-10; SSFS 24

Yau, John 1950- .... **PC 61**
See also CA 154; CANR 89; CP 4, 5, 6, 7;
DLB 234, 312; PFS 26

Yearsley, Ann
1753-1806 .... **NCLC 174; PC 149**
See also DLB 109

Yeats, W. B.
See Yeats, William Butler

Yeats, William Butler 1865-1939 ...... **DC 33;**
PC 20, 51, 129; TCLC 1, 11, 18, 31, 93,
116; WLC 6

See also AAYA 48; BRW 6; BRWR 1; CA
104; 127; CANR 45; CDBLB 1890-1914;
DA; DA3; DAB; DAC; DAM DRAM,
MST, POET; DLB 10, 19, 98, 156, 332;
EWL 3; EXPP; MTCW 1, 2; MTFW 2005;
NCFS 3; PAB; PFS 1, 2, 5, 7, 13, 15, 34,
42; RGEL 2; TEA; WLIT 4; WP

Yehoshua, A. B. 1936- ...... **CLC 13, 31, 243**
See also CA 33-36R; CANR 43, 90, 145,
202; CWW 2; EWL 3; RGHL; RGSF 2;
RGWL 3; WLIT 6

Yehoshua, Abraham B.
See Yehoshua, A. B.

Yellow Bird
See Ridge, John Rollin

Yep, Laurence 1948- .... **CLC 35**
See also AAYA 5, 31; BYA 7; CA 49-52;
CANR 1, 46, 92, 161; CLR 3, 17, 54, 132;
DLB 52; 312; FANT; JRDA; MAICYA 1,
2; MAICYAS 1; SATA 7, 69, 123, 176,
213, 242; WYA; YAW

Yep, Laurence Michael
See Yep, Laurence

Yerby, Frank G(arvin)
1916-1991 .... **BLC 1:3; CLC 1, 7, 22**
See also BPFB 3; BW 1, 3; CA 9-12R; 136;
CANR 16, 52; CN 1, 2, 3, 4, 5; DAM
MULT; DLB 76; INT CANR-16; MTCW
1; RGAL 4; RHW

Yesenin, Sergei Aleksandrovich
See Esenin, Sergei

Yevtushenko, Yevgeny Alexandrovich
See Yevtushenko, Yevgenyn

Yevtushenko, Yevgenyn 1933- ...... **CLC 1, 3,**
13, 26, 51, 126; PC 40
See also CA 81-84; CANR 33, 54; CWW 2;
DAM POET; DLB 359; EWL 3; MTCW 1;
PFS 29; RGHL; RGWL 2, 3

Yezierska, Anzia 1885(?)-1970 .... **CLC 46;**
SSC 144; TCLC 205
See also CA 126; 89-92; DLB 28, 221; FW;
MTCW 1; NFS 29; RGAL 4; SSFS 15

Yglesias, Helen 1915-2008 .... **CLC 7, 22**
See also CA 37-40R; 272; CAAS 20; CANR
15, 65, 95; CN 4, 5, 6, 7; INT CANR-15;
MTCW 1

Y.O.
See Russell, George William

Yokomitsu, Riichi 1898-1947 .... **TCLC 47**
See also CA 170; EWL 3

Yolen, Jane 1939- .... **CLC 256**
See also AAYA 4, 22, 85; BPFB 3; BYA 9,
10, 11, 14, 16; CA 13-16R; CANR 11, 29,
56, 91, 126, 185; CLR 4, 44, 149; CWRI 5;
DLB 52; FANT; INT CANR-29; JRDA;
MAICYA 1, 2; MTFW 2005; NFS 30;
SAAS 1; SATA 4, 40, 75, 112, 158,
194, 230; SATA-Essay 111; SFW 4; SSFS
29; SUFW 2; WYA; YAW

Yolen, Jane Hyatt
See Yolen, Jane

Yonge, Charlotte
1823-1901 .... **TCLC 48, 245**
See also BRWS 17; CA 109; 163; DLB 18,
163; RGEL 2; SATA 17; WCH

Yonge, Charlotte Mary
See Yonge, Charlotte

York, Jeremy
See Creasey, John

York, Simon
See Heinlein, Robert A.

Yorke, Henry Vincent
1905-1974 .... **CLC 2, 13, 97**
See also BRWS 2; CA 85-88; 175; 49-52;
DLB 15; EWL 3; RGEL 2

Yosano, Akiko 1878-1942 .... **PC 11;**
TCLC 59
See also CA 161; EWL 3; RGWL 3

Literary Criticism Series
Cumulative Topic Index

This index lists all topic entries in Gale's *Children's Literature Review* (CLR), *Classical and Medieval Literature Criticism* (CMLC), *Contemporary Literary Criticism* (CLC), *Drama Criticism* (DC), *Literature Criticism from 1400 to 1800* (LC), *Nineteenth-Century Literature Criticism* (NCLC), *Poetry Criticism* (PC), *Short Story Criticism* (SSC), and *Twentieth-Century Literary Criticism* (TCLC). The index also lists topic entries in the Gale Critical Companion Collection, which includes the following publications: *The Beat Generation* (BG), *Feminism in Literature* (FL), *Gothic Literature* (GL), and *Harlem Renaissance* (HR).

Topic Index

Topic Index

DC Cumulative Nationality Index

ALGERIAN

Camus, Albert **2**

AMERICAN

Albee, Edward **11**
Anderson, Maxwell **43**
Baldwin, James **1**
Baraka, Amiri **6**
Brown, William Wells **1**
Bullins, Ed **6**
Chase, Mary Coyle **1**
Childress, Alice **4**
Chin, Frank **7**
Cleage, Pearl **32**
Edson, Margaret **24**
Elder, Lonne III **8**
Eliot, T. S. **28**
Ensler, Eve **47**
Foote, Horton **42**
Fornés, Mariá Irene **10**
Fuller, Charles H., Jr. **1**
Gale, Zona **30**
Glaspell, Susan **10**
Gordone, Charles **8**
Green, Paul **37**
Gray, Spalding **7**
Gremké, Angelina Weld **38**
Guare, John **20**
Hansberry, Lorraine **2**
Hellman, Lillian **1**
Henley, Beth **6, 14**
Howard, Sidney **42**
Howe, Tina **43**
Hughes, Langston **3**
Hurston, Zora Neale **12**
Hwang, David Henry **4, 23**
Inge, William **37**
James, Henry **41**
Kaufman, George S. **17**
Kaufman, Moises **26**
Kennedy, Adrienne **5**
Kopit, Arthur **37**
Kramer, Larry **8**
Kushner, Tony **10, 50**
MacLeish, Archibald **43**
Mamet, David **4, 24**
Mann, Emily **7**
McCullers, Carson **35**
McNally, Terrence **27**
Miller, Arthur **1, 31**
Moraga, Cherríe **22**
Norman, Marsha **8**
Odets, Clifford **6**
O'Neill, Eugene **20**
Parker, Dorothy **40**
Parks, Suzan-Lori **23**
Rabe, David **16**
Rice, Elmer **44**
Saroyan, William **28**

Shange, Ntozake **3**
Shepard, Sam **5**
Sherwood, Robert E. **36**
Simon, Neil **14**
Sondheim, Stephen **22**
Stein, Gertrude **19**
Steinbeck, John **46**
Terry, Megan **13**
Uhry, Alfred **28**
Valdez, Luis **10**
Vogel, Paula **19**
Wasserstein, Wendy **4**
Wilder, Thornton **1, 24**
Williams, Tennessee **4**
Wilson, August **2, 31**
Wilson, Lanford **19**
Zindel, Paul **5**

AUSTRALIAN

Williamson, David (Keith) **47**

AUSTRIAN

Bernhard, Thomas **14**
Grillparzer, Franz **14**
Handke, Peter **17**
Hofmannsthal, Hugo von **4**
Nestroy, Johann **46**
Schnitzler, Arthur **17**
Turrini, Peter **49**

BARBADIAN

Kennedy, Adrienne **5**

BELGIAN

Ghelderode, Michel de **15**
Maeterlinck, Maurice **32**

CANADIAN

Highway, Tomson **33**
Pollock, Sharon **20**
Djanet, Sears **46**

CUBAN

Fornés, Mariá Irene **10**
Triana, José **39**

CZECH

Chapek, Karel **1**
Havel, Václav **6**

DUTCH

Bernhard, Thomas **14**

ENGLISH

Ayckbourn, Alan **13**
Beaumont, Francis **6**
Beddoes, Thomas Lovell **15**
Behn, Aphra **4**

Bond, Edward **45**
Brome, Richard **50**
Byron, Lord **24**
Centlivre, Susanna **25**
Chapman, George **19**
Christie, Agatha **39**
Churchill, Caryl **5**
Congreve, William **2**
Coward, Noël **45**
Davenant, William **48**
Dekker, Thomas **12**
Delaney, Shelagh **45**
Dryden, John **3**
Edgar, David **44**
Eliot, T. S. **28**
Etherege, George **23**
Farquhar, George **38**
Fletcher, John **6**
Ford, John **8**
Frayn, Michael **27**
Fry, Christopher **36**
Garrick, David **50**
Gay, John **39, 48**
Greene, Graham **41**
Hare, David **26**
Heywood, Thomas **29**
Jonson, Ben **4**
Kane, Sarah **31**
Kureishi, Hanif **26**
Kyd, Thomas **3**
Lawrence, D. H. **44**
Lyly, John **7**
Marlowe, Christopher **1**
Marston, John **37**
Massinger, Philip **39**
Middleton, Thomas **5, 40**
Orton, Joe **3**
Osborne, John **38**
Otway, Thomas **24**
Peele, George **27**
Pinter, Harold **15**
Rattigan, Terence **18**
Rowley, William **43**
Shaffer, Peter **7**
Shaw, George Bernard **23**
Sheridan, Richard Brinsley **1**
Shirley, James **25**
Stoppard, Tom **6, 30**
Storey, David **40**
Vanbrugh, John **40**
Webster, John **2**
Wilde, Oscar **17**
Wycherley, William **41**

FRENCH

Anouilh, Jean **8, 21**
Arrabal, Fernando **35**
Artaud, Antonin **14**
Beaumarchais, Pierre-Augustin Caron de **4**

491

DC Cumulative Title Index

Title Index

Title Index

Title Index

Title Index

Title Index

Title Index

Title Index

Title Index